HISTORY
OF THE WORLD
MAP BY MAP

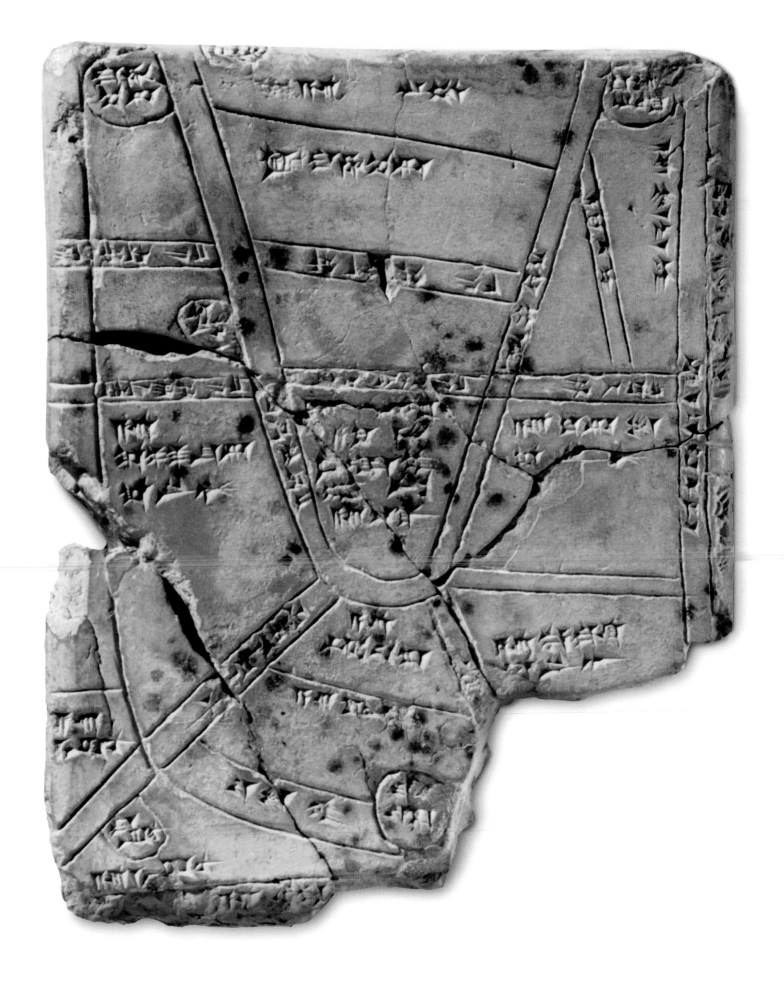

Smithsonian

HISTORY
OF THE WORLD
MAP BY MAP

FOREWORD BY
PETER SNOW

10

PREHISTORY   7 MYA–3000 BCE

28

THE ANCIENT WORLD   3000 BCE–500 CE

CONTENTS

 Penguin Random House

DK LONDON

Lead Senior Editor Rob Houston
Senior Editors Peter Frances, Janet Mohun
Editors Suhel Ahmed, Polly Boyd, Claire Gell,
Martyn Page, Tia Sarkar, Kaiya Shang, Kate Taylor
US Editors Kayla Dugger, Jennette ElNaggar
Project Management Briony Corbett
Managing Editor Angeles Gavira Guerrero
Associate Publisher Liz Wheeler
Publishing Director Jonathan Metcalf

Cartographers Simon Mumford, Ed Merritt,
Martin Darlison, Helen Stirling

Senior Art Editors Duncan Turner,
Ina Stradins
Project Art Editors Steve Woosnam-Savage,
Francis Wong
Designer Ala Uddin
Jacket Design Development Manager
Sophia MTT
Jacket Designer Surabhi Wadhwa
Producer (Pre-production)
Jacqueline Street-Elkayam
Producer Jude Crozier
Managing Art Editor Michael Duffy
Art Director Karen Self
Design Director Phil Ormerod

DK INDIA

Senior Editor Dharini Ganesh
Editor Priyanjali Narain
Assistant Editors Aashirwad Jain,
Shambhavi Thatte
Picture Researcher Deepak Negi
Picture Research Manager
Taiyaba Khatoon
Jackets Editorial Coordinator
Priyanka Sharma
Managing Editor Rohan Sinha
Managing Jackets Editor Saloni Singh
Pre-production Manager Balwant Singh
Senior Cartographer Subhashree Bharati
Cartographer Reetu Pandey
Cartography Manager Suresh Kumar

Senior Art Editor Vaibhav Rastogi
Project Art Editor Sanjay Chauhan,
Pooja Pipil
Art Editors Anjali Sachar, Sonali Sharma,
Sonakshi Singh
Assistant Art Editor Mridushmita Bose
Managing Art Editor Sudakshina Basu
Jacket Designer Suhita Dharamjit
Senior DTP Designers Harish Aggarwal,
Vishal Bhatia
DTP Designers Ashok Kumar, Nityanand Kumar
Production Manager Pankaj Sharma

COBALT ID

Designer Darren Bland
Art Director Paul Reid
Editorial Director Marek Walisiewicz

88

MIDDLE AGES 500–1450 CE

146

THE EARLY MODERN WORLD 1450–1700

First American Edition, 2018
Published in the United States by DK Publishing
1450 Broadway, Suite 801, New York, NY 10018

Copyright © 2018 Dorling Kindersley Limited
DK, a Division of Penguin Random House LLC
19 20 21 22 10 9 8 7 6 5 4
010–278615–Oct/2018

A catalog record for this book is available from the Library of Congress.
ISBN 978-1-4654-7585-5
Printed in Malaysia

A WORLD OF IDEAS:
SEE ALL THERE IS TO KNOW
www.dk.com

REVOLUTION AND INDUSTRY 1700–1850

PROGRESS AND EMPIRE 1850–1914

CONTRIBUTORS

PREHISTORY
David Summers, Derek Harvey

THE ANCIENT WORLD
Peter Chrisp, Jeremy Harwood, Phil Wilkinson

THE MIDDLE AGES, THE EARLY MODERN WORLD
Philip Parker

REVOLUTION AND INDUSTRY
Joel Levy

PROGRESS AND EMPIRE
Kay Celtel

THE MODERN WORLD
Simon Adams, R. G. Grant, Sally Regan

CONSULTANTS

PREHISTORY
Dr. Rebecca Wragg-Sykes Palaeolithic archaeologist and author, chercheur bénévole PACEA laboratory, Université de Bordeaux

THE ANCIENT WORLD
Prof. Neville Morley Professor of Classics and Ancient History, University of Exeter

Prof. Karen Radner Alexander von Humboldt Professor of the Ancient History of the Near and Middle East, University of Munich

THE MIDDLE AGES
Dr. Roger Collins Honorary Fellow in the School of History, Classics and Archaeology, University of Edinburgh

THE EARLY MODERN WORLD, REVOLUTION AND INDUSTRY
Dr. Glyn Redford FRHistS, Honorary Fellow, *The Historical Association*

PROGRESS AND EMPIRE, THE MODERN WORLD
Prof. Richard Overy FBA, FRHistS, Professor of History, University of Exeter

CHINA, KOREA, AND JAPAN
Jennifer Bond Researcher, SOAS, University of London

INDIA
Prof. David Arnold Professor of Asian and Global History, Warwick University

PRECOLUMBIAN AMERICAS
Dr. Elizabeth Baquedano Honorary Senior Lecturer, Institute of Archaeology, University College London

270

THE MODERN WORLD 1914–PRESENT

SMITHSONIAN

Established in 1846, the Smithsonian—the world's largest museum and research complex—includes 19 museums and galleries and the National Zoological Park. The total number of artifacts, works of art, and specimens in the Smithsonian's collections is estimated at 154 million, the bulk of which is contained in the National Museum of Natural History, which holds more than 126 million specimens and objects. The Smithsonian is a renowned research center, dedicated to public education, national service, and scholarship in the arts, sciences, and natural history.

FOREWORD

This book tells the story of life on Earth in more meticulous detail and with more arresting pictures than I've ever seen before. I believe that in this digital age, maps are more important than ever. People are losing sight of the need for them in a world where our knowledge is reduced to the distance between two zip codes. For me, a journey—certainly the contemplation of a journey—is a voyage across a map. But this beautiful book offers the added dimension of a state-of-the-art journey through time. These maps display the story of the world in delightfully accessible form. They demonstrate in a spectacular way how there is no substitute for the printed page, for the entrancing spread of color across paper that we can touch and

feel. The maps are large; the colors are bold. Text boxes spring out from places whose history matters. Clear and easily readable graphics reveal the ups and downs of empires, cultures, wars and other events both human and natural that have shaped our world from the beginning.

To me, history without maps would be unintelligible. A country's history is shaped by its geography—by its mountains and valleys, its rivers, its climate, its access to the sea, and its raw materials and harvests just as much as it is shaped by its population, its industry, its relations with its neighbors and its takeover by invaders from abroad. This book is more than a historical atlas: it describes the

geography of history but adds revealing pictures as well. For me, the history of World War I is admirably summed up by the map that describes the buildup to it on pages 268–269 and the following maps and accounts of the fighting, including the telling picture of the trenches.

I've been using maps to tell stories all my life as a television journalist and historian. The stories of the European Union and the collapse of communism were my constant companions when recounting the events of the last half century. That part of recent history only makes sense if it is also described by maps like those on pages 320–321 and 336–337. I have spent many hours as a journalist making maps with graphics artists at the BBC and ITN to illustrate the story of wars in the Middle East and Vietnam. Far better ones are now displayed for us in this book on pages 328–29 and 332–33. No historian can do justice to the story of the rise and fall of the great empires like that of the French Emperor Napoleon without maps like those on pages 208–211.

For its depth of learning and its variety of ways of giving us a picture of the history of our planet, this magnificent account—map by map—is second to none.

PETER SNOW British broadcaster and historian

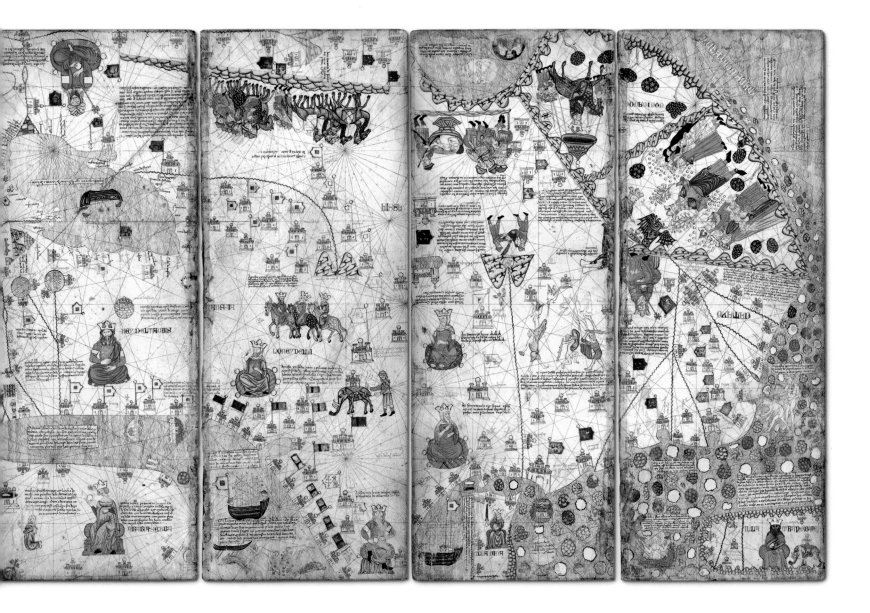

PREHISTORY

BEFORE WRITTEN RECORDS BEGAN AROUND 3000 BCE, THE STORY
OF HUMANS WAS RECORDED FOR MILLIONS OF YEARS BY THE FOSSILS
AND ARCHAEOLOGICAL TRACES OUR ANCESTORS LEFT BEHIND.

FROM APES TO FARMERS

The history of humankind is rooted in a part of the animal kingdom that includes monkeys, apes, and other primates. It took millions of years of evolution—over countless generations—for apelike ancestors to become modern *Homo sapiens*.

△ **Lucy**
Shown here are the fossilized remains of the apelike Lucy—a member of the genus *Australopithecus* from east Africa from over 3 MYA. The fossil is sufficiently complete to suggest that Lucy walked upright on two legs.

Scientific evidence links all humans to apes. Specifically, chimpanzees are our closest nonhuman relatives, and DNA—the ultimate bloodline indicator—suggests that we separated from a common ancestor some 6.5 million years ago (MYA). Indeed, humans are apes—albeit in an upright, naked form.

Monkeys, apes, and humans are primates that have a large brain, grasping digits, forward-facing eyes, and nails instead of claws. Fossilized remains of animals that lived in the distant past provide tantalizing evidence of just how apes became modern humans. Skeletons turn into fossils when they become mineralized into rock—a process that usually takes at least 10,000 years. Fossilized remains are usually fragmentary, but an expertise in anatomy helps scientists use the fossil record to reconstruct extinct species. Fossils can also be dated so scientists can build up a chronology of evolutionary change. For example, African fossils of a primate called *Proconsul*, dated to 21–14 MYA, resembled a monkey. But it lacked a tail—a feature more typical of apes—suggesting that *Proconsul* could have been the earliest known member of the ape family.

Hominids and hominins
Modern great apes (gorillas, orangutans, and chimpanzees), humans, and their prehistoric relatives are united in a biological family called hominids. As well

> *"We can see the focus, the center of evolution, for modern humans in Africa."*
>
> CHRIS STRINGER, BRITISH ANTHROPOLOGIST

as lacking a tail, they have bigger brains than their monkey ancestors. This meant that many prehistoric hominids doubtless used tools to forage for food—just as chimpanzees do today. Great apes also became bigger than monkeys, and many spent more time on the ground. One group evolved to walk on two legs, which freed grasping hands for other tasks. This group—called hominins—includes humans and their immediate ancestors and dates back at least 6.2–6.0 million years to the species *Orrorin tugenensis*—a very early bipedal hominin found in Kenya.

△ **Flint and stone**
For nearly 2 million years, human technology was represented by stone flake tools and hand axes. These were made by hitting flint or other workable rock with stone to produce sharp cutting edges.

The first humans
Not all hominins were direct ancestors of living people, but at least one branch of the genus *Australopithecus* might have been. Belonging to the genus *Homo*, the first humans were fully bipedal, with arched feet that no longer had opposable grasping toes and an S-shaped spine centered above a wide pelvis. Such adaptations helped them run quickly on open ground. The earliest species—*Homo habilis*, from 2.4 MYA—may have

THE RISE OF MODERN HUMANS

Even before the emergence of modern humans (*Homo sapiens*) almost 300,000 YA, hominins had developed the traits that would make them a dominating force on the planet. From just under 1 MYA, hominins were controlling fire—for cooking, and later to help with manufacturing processes. But with *Homo sapiens* came a more complex culture. Archaeological evidence indicates that these modern humans dispersed widely from their center of origin in Africa before 200,000 YA.

185,000 YA *Homo sapiens* migrates from Africa and into Asia 1.5 million years after the first hominins first left the African continent

135,000–100,000 YA Seashells perforated and used as ornamental beads in Middle East and North Africa are first jewelry—and earliest evidence of drilling

DISPERSAL

CULTURE

TECHNOLOGY

| 180,000 YA | 160,000 YA | 140,000 YA | 120,000 YA |

165,000 YA Earliest evidence of pigment use at Pinnacle Point, South Africa, for painting or as part of a tool handle

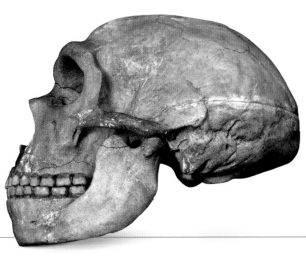

◁ **Close cousins**
Neanderthals—the closest extinct human species to modern humans, *Homo sapiens*—had larger skulls with more prominent eyebrows. *Homo sapiens* and Neanderthals were sufficiently similar to interbreed where they coexisted.

remained in Africa, but we know that later other *Homo* species dispersed widely across Eurasia.

The rise of *Homo sapiens*

Only one species of human—*Homo sapiens*—came to dominate the world after emerging from Africa about a quarter of a million years ago. Remarkably, brain capacity doubled between *Homo habilis* and *Homo sapiens*. Bigger brainpower meant that humans could skillfully manipulate the environment and resources around them—ultimately leading to the emergence of complex cultures and technologies.

For much of its time, *Homo sapiens* coexisted with other human species. In Ice-Age Eurasia, chunky-bodied Neanderthals (*Homo neanderthalensis*) successfully lived in a range of environmental conditions, developing their own advanced cultures. But the world's climate became especially unsuitable, and only *Homo sapiens* prevailed. They spread farther—reaching Australia by 65,000 YA and South America possibly by 18,500 YA. Evidently, *Homo sapiens* had the social structures to succeed in ways that their competitors could not. The first modern humans were efficient hunter-gatherers, inventing new technologies that helped them

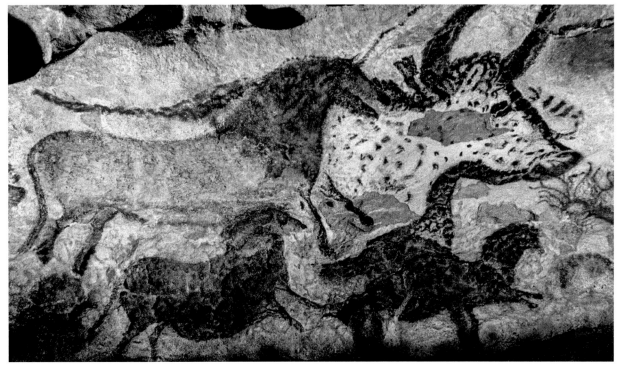

acquire more food and travel farther. This meant that they thrived in many different places, from the frozen Arctic to the hot tropics. Then, within the last 20,000 years, all around the world, modern humans began to abandon their nomadic ways in favor of fixed settlements, turning their skills to farming the land, supporting bigger societies, and—ultimately—planting the seeds of civilization itself.

△ **Early artists**
These depictions of Ice Age animals on the walls of the Lascaux Caves in southern France are about 17,000 years old. Similar paintings nearby show that prehistoric humans had developed a degree of creative expression as early as 30,000 years ago.

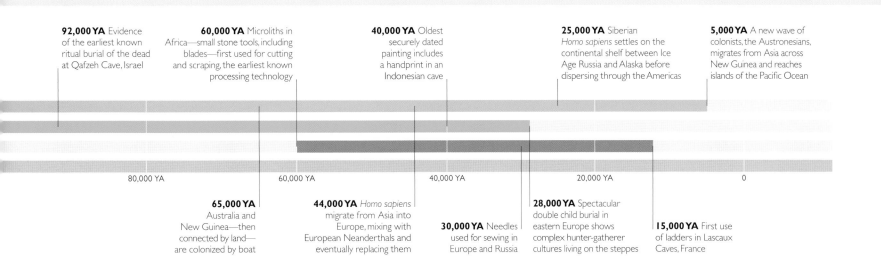

92,000 YA Evidence of the earliest known ritual burial of the dead at Qafzeh Cave, Israel

60,000 YA Microliths in Africa—small stone tools, including blades—first used for cutting and scraping, the earliest known processing technology

40,000 YA Oldest securely dated painting includes a handprint in an Indonesian cave

25,000 YA Siberian *Homo sapiens* settles on the continental shelf between Ice Age Russia and Alaska before dispersing through the Americas

5,000 YA A new wave of colonists, the Austronesians, migrates from Asia across New Guinea and reaches islands of the Pacific Ocean

80,000 YA   60,000 YA   40,000 YA   20,000 YA   0

65,000 YA Australia and New Guinea—then connected by land—are colonized by boat

44,000 YA *Homo sapiens* migrate from Asia into Europe, mixing with European Neanderthals and eventually replacing them

30,000 YA Needles used for sewing in Europe and Russia

28,000 YA Spectacular double child burial in eastern Europe shows complex hunter-gatherer cultures living on the steppes

15,000 YA First use of ladders in Lascaux Caves, France

THE FIRST HUMANS

The human story began in Africa 7 or 6 million years ago. Through the fossil record of this vast continent, we can draw a complex family tree of human relatives of which our species, *Homo sapiens*, is the last to survive.

We have fossil evidence for the existence of about 20 different species of African "hominin"—members of the human lineage that diverged from that of chimpanzees 7–10 million years ago. Each has been assigned to a biological group or "genus," but the relationships between the groups and species are still debated. Only certain hominins were the ancestors of modern humans; others, such as the *Paranthropus* species, may represent evolutionary dead ends.

Human evolution was not an inevitable, linear progression from apes. Some of our ancestors developed adaptations—in different combinations—that would ultimately mark out modern humans. Perhaps most notably, a larger brain enabled complex thought and behavior, including the development of stone-tool technologies, while walking on two legs became the main form of locomotion.

The earliest fossils assigned to our species—dated to around 300,000 years ago—were found in Morocco, but other early specimens have been found widely dispersed across Africa. This has led scientists to believe that the evolution of modern humans probably happened on a continental scale.

> *"I think Africa was the cradle, the crucible that created us as* Homo sapiens.*"*
>
> PALEOANTHROPOLOGIST DONALD JOHANSON, 2006

300,000 YA The earliest remains of *Homo sapiens* in the fossil record were unearthed here in Morocco

◁ **Turkana Boy**
The skull of a young male *Homo ergaster* was found along with his well-preserved, nearly complete skeleton near Lake Turkana, Kenya. Because his brain was about 60 percent the size of a modern human's, his skull narrows immediately behind the eye sockets.

THE FIRST HUMANLIKE APES 7–5.5 MYA

The sparse record of the earliest hominins— *Sahelanthropus* and *Orrorin*—shows that although they had shorter faces and smaller teeth, they had brains no larger than those of chimpanzees. The sole *Sahelanthropus* skull was discovered in Chad, far removed from other hominin sites in eastern and southern Africa. Fossils of both *Orrorin* and *Ardipithecus kadabba* are thought to exhibit features linked to developing two-legged locomotion.

Sahelanthropus **skull**

▲ *Sahelanthropus* ▼ *Orrorin* ■ *Ardipithecus*

EARLY HOMININ MIGRATION

Archaeological evidence from Asia and Europe suggests that by about 2 million years ago, hominins had begun to leave Africa for the first time—long before *Homo sapiens* began to disperse (see pp.16–17). Experts once assumed that the migration corresponded with the appearance of *Homo ergaster*, but older species might have been the pioneers—a 1.7-million-year-old fossil found in Dmanisi, Georgia, resembles the earlier *Homo habilis*. The earliest known hominin fossils from Southeast Asia are of *Homo erectus*—an Asian variant of *Homo ergaster*, found on the island of Java and dating to 1.8 million years ago. Stone tools from the Nihewan Basin, China, date to 1.6 million years ago. Two sites in Spain's Sierra de Atapuerca show that hominins had reached western Europe by 1.2 million years ago.

KEY

→ Likely route   ○ Sites of fossil finds

EUROPE

Swanscombe
Boxgrove
0.95–0.5 MYA
Happisburgh
Mauer
Steinheim
1.2 MYA
Atapuerca
Tautavel
Ceprano
Isernia la Pineta
Petralona
Kocabas
Ubeidiya
1.7 MYA
Dmanisi

ASIA

Nihewan
1.6–1.3 MYA
Zhoukoudian
Hexian
Lantian
Nanjing
Yunxian

AFRICA

MORE THAN 1.8 MYA
Buia
Daka
Bodo
Konso-Gardula
Lake Turkana
Koobi Fora
Olduvai Gorge
Olorgesailie

Narmada

1.8 MYA

Sangiran
Ngandong
Trinil
Mojokerto

ATLANTIC OCEAN

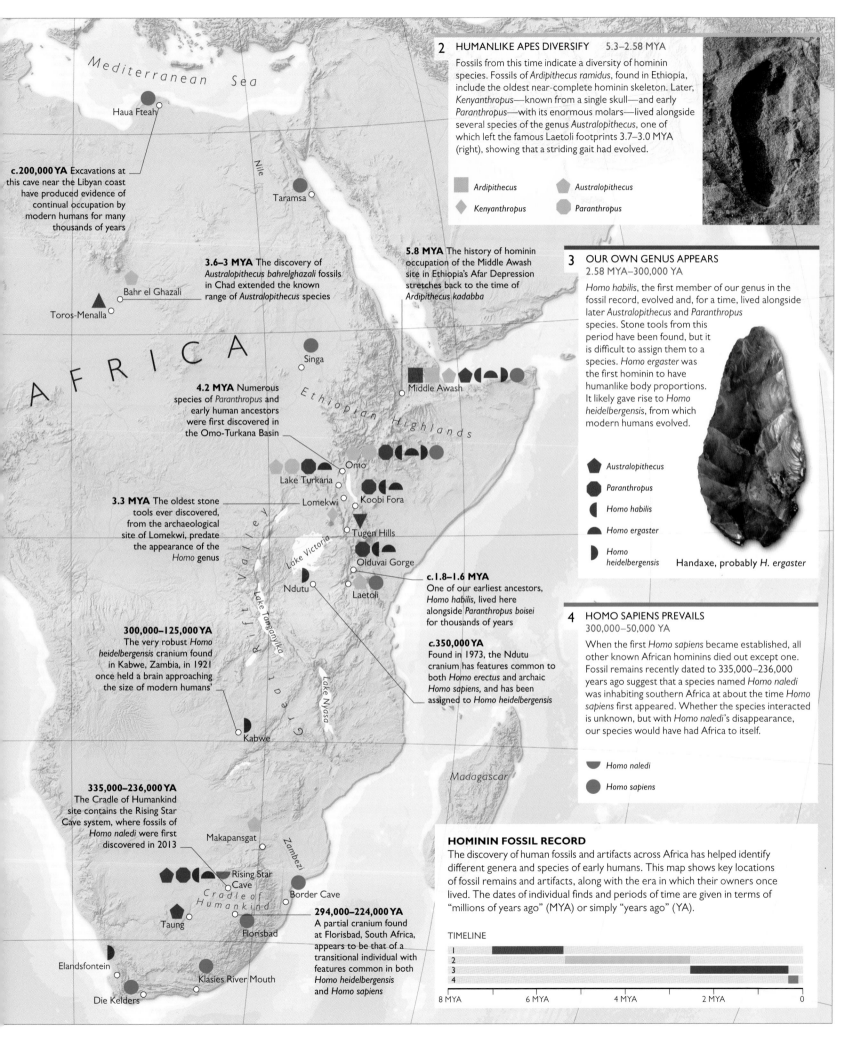

2 HUMANLIKE APES DIVERSIFY   5.3–2.58 MYA

Fossils from this time indicate a diversity of hominin species. Fossils of *Ardipithecus ramidus*, found in Ethiopia, include the oldest near-complete hominin skeleton. Later, *Kenyanthropus*—known from a single skull—and early *Paranthropus*—with its enormous molars—lived alongside several species of the genus *Australopithecus*, one of which left the famous Laetoli footprints 3.7–3.0 MYA (right), showing that a striding gait had evolved.

■ *Ardipithecus*   ⬠ *Australopithecus*

◆ *Kenyanthropus*   ⬡ *Paranthropus*

5.8 MYA The history of hominin occupation of the Middle Awash site in Ethiopia's Afar Depression stretches back to the time of *Ardipithecus kadabba*

c.200,000 YA Excavations at this cave near the Libyan coast have produced evidence of continual occupation by modern humans for many thousands of years

3.6–3 MYA The discovery of *Australopithecus bahrelghazali* fossils in Chad extended the known range of *Australopithecus* species

4.2 MYA Numerous species of *Paranthropus* and early human ancestors were first discovered in the Omo-Turkana Basin

3.3 MYA The oldest stone tools ever discovered, from the archaeological site of Lomekwi, predate the appearance of the *Homo* genus

300,000–125,000 YA The very robust *Homo heidelbergensis* cranium found in Kabwe, Zambia, in 1921 once held a brain approaching the size of modern humans'

335,000–236,000 YA The Cradle of Humankind site contains the Rising Star Cave system, where fossils of *Homo naledi* were first discovered in 2013

c.1.8–1.6 MYA One of our earliest ancestors, *Homo habilis*, lived here alongside *Paranthropus boisei* for thousands of years

c.350,000 YA Found in 1973, the Ndutu cranium has features common to both *Homo erectus* and archaic *Homo sapiens*, and has been assigned to *Homo heidelbergensis*

294,000–224,000 YA A partial cranium found at Florisbad, South Africa, appears to be that of a transitional individual with features common in both *Homo heidelbergensis* and *Homo sapiens*

3 OUR OWN GENUS APPEARS
2.58 MYA–300,000 YA

Homo habilis, the first member of our genus in the fossil record, evolved and, for a time, lived alongside later *Australopithecus* and *Paranthropus* species. Stone tools from this period have been found, but it is difficult to assign them to a species. *Homo ergaster* was the first hominin to have humanlike body proportions. It likely gave rise to *Homo heidelbergensis*, from which modern humans evolved.

⬠ *Australopithecus*

⬡ *Paranthropus*

◗ *Homo habilis*

◖ *Homo ergaster*

◗ *Homo heidelbergensis*

Handaxe, probably *H. ergaster*

4 HOMO SAPIENS PREVAILS
300,000–50,000 YA

When the first *Homo sapiens* became established, all other known African hominins died out except one. Fossil remains recently dated to 335,000–236,000 years ago suggest that a species named *Homo naledi* was inhabiting southern Africa at about the time *Homo sapiens* first appeared. Whether the species interacted is unknown, but with *Homo naledi*'s disappearance, our species would have had Africa to itself.

◗ *Homo naledi*

● *Homo sapiens*

HOMININ FOSSIL RECORD

The discovery of human fossils and artifacts across Africa has helped identify different genera and species of early humans. This map shows key locations of fossil remains and artifacts, along with the era in which their owners once lived. The dates of individual finds and periods of time are given in terms of "millions of years ago" (MYA) or simply "years ago" (YA).

TIMELINE

| 1 | 2 | 3 | 4 |

8 MYA   6 MYA   4 MYA   2 MYA   0

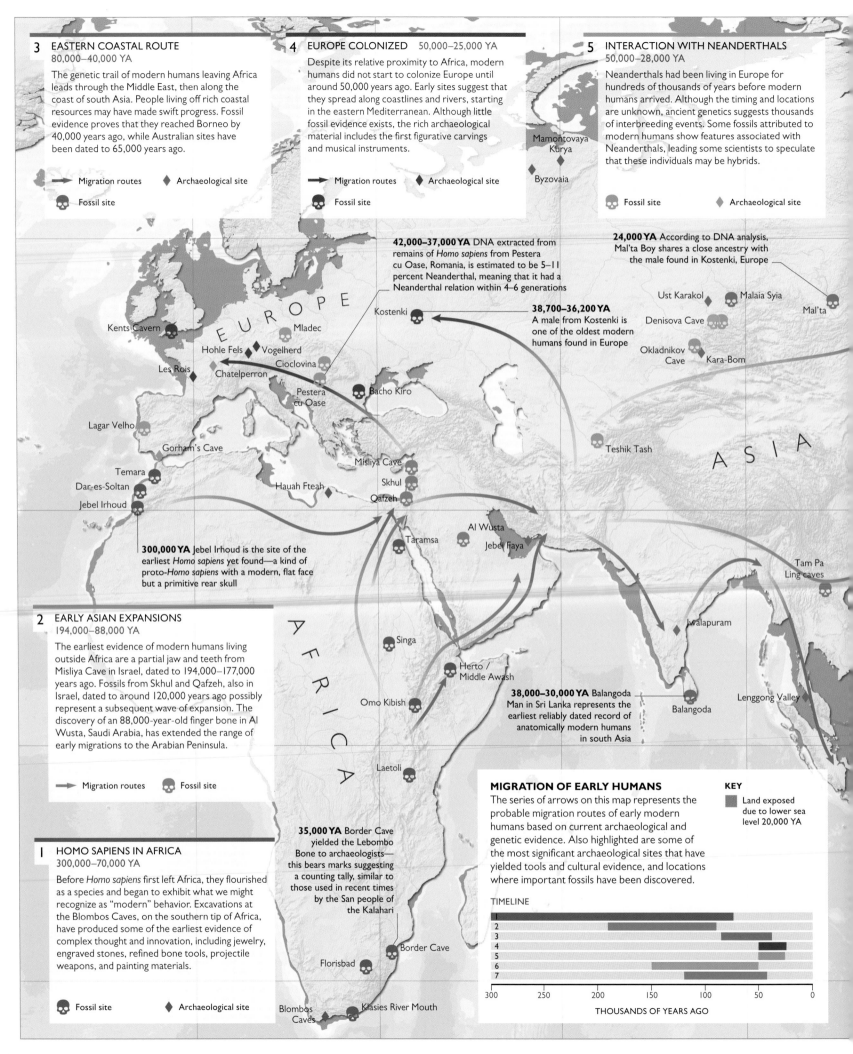

3 EASTERN COASTAL ROUTE
80,000–40,000 YA

The genetic trail of modern humans leaving Africa leads through the Middle East, then along the coast of south Asia. People living off rich coastal resources may have made swift progress. Fossil evidence proves that they reached Borneo by 40,000 years ago, while Australian sites have been dated to 65,000 years ago.

→ Migration routes   ◆ Archaeological site

💀 Fossil site

4 EUROPE COLONIZED   50,000–25,000 YA

Despite its relative proximity to Africa, modern humans did not start to colonize Europe until around 50,000 years ago. Early sites suggest that they spread along coastlines and rivers, starting in the eastern Mediterranean. Although little fossil evidence exists, the rich archaeological material includes the first figurative carvings and musical instruments.

→ Migration routes   ◆ Archaeological site

💀 Fossil site

5 INTERACTION WITH NEANDERTHALS
50,000–28,000 YA

Neanderthals had been living in Europe for hundreds of thousands of years before modern humans arrived. Although the timing and locations are unknown, ancient genetics suggests thousands of interbreeding events. Some fossils attributed to modern humans show features associated with Neanderthals, leading some scientists to speculate that these individuals may be hybrids.

💀 Fossil site   ◆ Archaeological site

42,000–37,000 YA DNA extracted from remains of *Homo sapiens* from Pestera cu Oase, Romania, is estimated to be 5–11 percent Neanderthal, meaning that it had a Neanderthal relation within 4–6 generations

38,700–36,200 YA A male from Kostenki is one of the oldest modern humans found in Europe

24,000 YA According to DNA analysis, Mal'ta Boy shares a close ancestry with the male found in Kostenki, Europe

300,000 YA Jebel Irhoud is the site of the earliest *Homo sapiens* yet found—a kind of proto-*Homo sapiens* with a modern, flat face but a primitive rear skull

2 EARLY ASIAN EXPANSIONS
194,000–88,000 YA

The earliest evidence of modern humans living outside Africa are a partial jaw and teeth from Misliya Cave in Israel, dated to 194,000–177,000 years ago. Fossils from Skhul and Qafzeh, also in Israel, dated to around 120,000 years ago possibly represent a subsequent wave of expansion. The discovery of an 88,000-year-old finger bone in Al Wusta, Saudi Arabia, has extended the range of early migrations to the Arabian Peninsula.

→ Migration routes   💀 Fossil site

1 HOMO SAPIENS IN AFRICA
300,000–70,000 YA

Before *Homo sapiens* first left Africa, they flourished as a species and began to exhibit what we might recognize as "modern" behavior. Excavations at the Blombos Caves, on the southern tip of Africa, have produced some of the earliest evidence of complex thought and innovation, including jewelry, engraved stones, refined bone tools, projectile weapons, and painting materials.

💀 Fossil site   ◆ Archaeological site

35,000 YA Border Cave yielded the Lebombo Bone to archaeologists— this bears marks suggesting a counting tally, similar to those used in recent times by the San people of the Kalahari

38,000–30,000 YA Balangoda Man in Sri Lanka represents the earliest reliably dated record of anatomically modern humans in south Asia

MIGRATION OF EARLY HUMANS

The series of arrows on this map represents the probable migration routes of early modern humans based on current archaeological and genetic evidence. Also highlighted are some of the most significant archaeological sites that have yielded tools and cultural evidence, and locations where important fossils have been discovered.

KEY

▉ Land exposed due to lower sea level 20,000 YA

TIMELINE

1					
2					
3					
4					
5					
6					
7					

300   250   200   150   100   50   0

THOUSANDS OF YEARS AGO

Map labels: Mamontovaya Kurya, Byzovaia, Kostenki, Mladec, Kents Cavern, Hohle Fels, Vogelherd, Cioclovina, Les Rois, Chatelperron, Pestera cu Oase, Bacho Kiro, Lagar Velho, Gorham's Cave, Temara, Dar-es-Soltan, Jebel Irhoud, Hauah Fteah, Misliya Cave, Skhul, Qafzeh, Al Wusta, Jebel Faya, Taramsa, Singa, Herto / Middle Awash, Omo Kibish, Laetoli, Border Cave, Florisbad, Blombos Caves, Klasies River Mouth, Teshik Tash, Ust Karakol, Malaia Syia, Denisova Cave, Okladnikov Cave, Kara-Bom, Mal'ta, Iwalapuram, Balangoda, Lenggong Valley, Tam Pa Ling caves

EUROPE   ASIA   AFRICA

6 MYSTERIOUS DENISOVANS
150,000–50,000 YA

DNA analysis of a finger bone and two teeth from Denisova Cave in Siberia has identified a previously unknown and distinct population, the Denisovans. Although their remains have only been found at one site, their genes indicate that they were widespread. Contemporaries of the Neanderthals, they also interbred with this species, as well as with *Homo sapiens*.

💀 Fossil site

Yana

45,000 YA Tools, along with mammoth and rhinoceros bones, show humans living above the Arctic Circle during the Ice Age

Ust-mil

Zhoukoudian

Tianyuan Cave

120,000–80,000 YA Human remains at Tianyuan cave are the oldest in east Asia

Yamashita-cho

40,000 YA Around 70 stone axes were found buried in dated volcanic sediment layers

△ **The emergence of art**
The Venus of Brassempouy (France), dating to about 25,000 years ago, features one of the earliest known representations of the human face.

Matenkupkum, Balof, and Panakiwuk

Huon Peninsula

Jerimalai

SAHUL

7 CENTRAL TO EAST ASIA
120,000–45,000 YA

Populations that spread to central and eastern Asia probably came from those that had originally colonized coastal southern Asia. The cold, bleak environments they encountered to the north would have demanded great adaptability. Those that reached the far northeast would give rise to the populations that went on to colonize the Americas.

→ Migration routes ◆ Archaeological site

💀 Fossil site

OUT OF AFRICA

The modern human, *Homo sapiens*, is a truly global species, inhabiting every continent. Our colonization of the planet started before 177,000 years ago, when groups began dispersing from their African homeland. By 40,000 years ago, our species lived in northern Europe and central and east Asia, and had crossed the sea to Australia.

Ancient hominins had moved from Africa into Asia and Europe well over a million years before our species first appeared (see p.14). But the details of how *Homo sapiens* relates to these earlier species are still emerging gradually with every fossil and archaeological discovery from the period. Genetic and archaeological evidence now overwhelmingly favors the Recent African Origin model, also known as the "Out-of-Africa" theory, which proposes that *Homo sapiens* evolved in Africa and later spread across the Old World, replacing all other hominin species.

Homo sapiens first left Africa some time after 200,000 years ago, and some groups appear to have reached east Asia by at least 80,000 years ago and perhaps as early as 120,000 years ago. Either via the Horn of Africa or the Sinai Peninsula, the first migrants traveled east along Asia's southern coastline and either north into China or eastward across Southeast Asia. Subsequent groups headed through central and eastern Asia and finally northwest into Europe.

As they moved into new territories, *Homo sapiens*' progress may have been hindered, particularly in Europe, by their encounters with other hominins, including Neanderthals and Denisovans. Little is yet known of the Denisovans, but the Neanderthal was the first fossil hominin discovered and is now known from thousands of specimens. Evidence of interaction with both species lives on in our genes.

"I, too, am convinced that our ancestors came from Africa."

KENYAN PALEOANTHROPOLOGIST RICHARD LEAKEY, 2005

THE STORY IN OUR GENES
EVIDENCE IN HUMAN DNA

By comparing the genetic makeup of living people from all over the world, scientists are able to analyze the evolutionary relationships between different populations. This has enabled them to confirm our African origins and describe how and when our species spread around the world. Genetic material (DNA) has also been extracted from the fossils of some extinct species. Analysis of the DNA of Neanderthals and Denisovans has revealed that they both interbred with *Homo sapiens* and contributed some of their genes to modern human populations.

The Vedda people of Sri Lanka
DNA analysis has been used to show that these are the earliest native inhabitants of Sri Lanka.

THE FIRST AUSTRALIANS

More than 60,000 years ago, hardy, resourceful people arrived in Australia after crossing the seas from Asia. They became Aboriginal Australians and went on to establish a unique way of life with a distinct culture.

During the last ice age, Australia, New Guinea, and Tasmania were joined in a single landmass (see p.17), which was colonized by a seafaring people who crossed the seas from Asia on bamboo vessels. These people were the first Australians. Their journey through the continent followed coastlines and river valleys. Archaeological evidence suggests that by 30,000 years ago, they had spread far and wide, from Tasmania in the south to the Swan River in the west and northward into New Guinea.

△ **Ancient art**
Discovered in western Australia in 1891, the ancient Bradshaw rock paintings show human figures engaged in display or hunting.

Indigenous Australians

Australia's indigenous peoples were seminomadic; instead of developing agricultural societies, they moved with the seasons. They lived in small family groups but were connected through extensive social networks. Already adept at hunting and gathering, they developed new technologies such as boomerangs, fish traps, and stone axes shaped by grinding.

Over time, the groups became culturally diverse. In the far north, people of the Torres Strait—between Australia and New Guinea—became distinct from the Australian Aborigines. Aboriginal life became centered on relationships between people and the natural world, or "Country," which included animals, plants, and rocks. These links, which have lasted into modern life, are formalized in the "Dreaming": oral histories of creation combined with moral codes, some of which are reflected in art.

THE COLONIZATION OF AUSTRALIA

The earliest known archaeological sites in Australia are 65,000 years old—a date that conforms with genetic evidence for the origins of indigenous Australians. Fossils of humans and their animal prey, as well as artifacts from the time, indicate that populations were centered around coastlines and the Murray–Darling river basins.

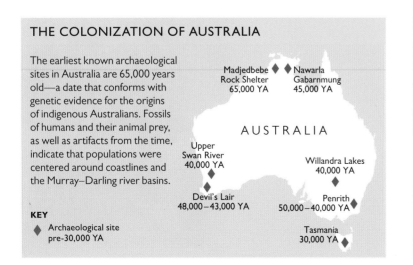

Madjedbebe ◆ ◆ Nawarla
Rock Shelter   Gabarnmung
65,000 YA   45,000 YA

AUSTRALIA

Upper
Swan River
40,000 YA

Willandra Lakes
40,000 YA

◆

Devil's Lair
48,000–43,000 YA

Penrith
50,000–40,000 YA ◆

Tasmania
30,000 YA ◆

KEY

◆ Archaeological site
pre-30,000 YA

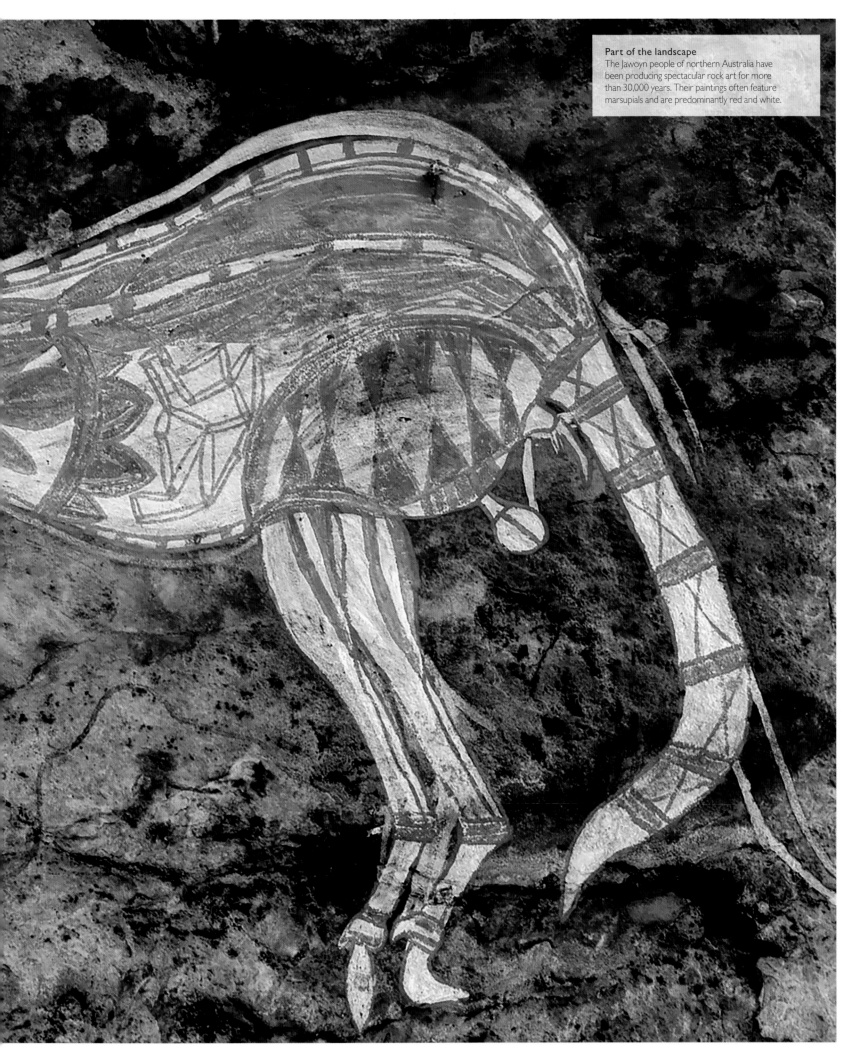

Part of the landscape
The Jawoyn people of northern Australia have been producing spectacular rock art for more than 30,000 years. Their paintings often feature marsupials and are predominantly red and white.

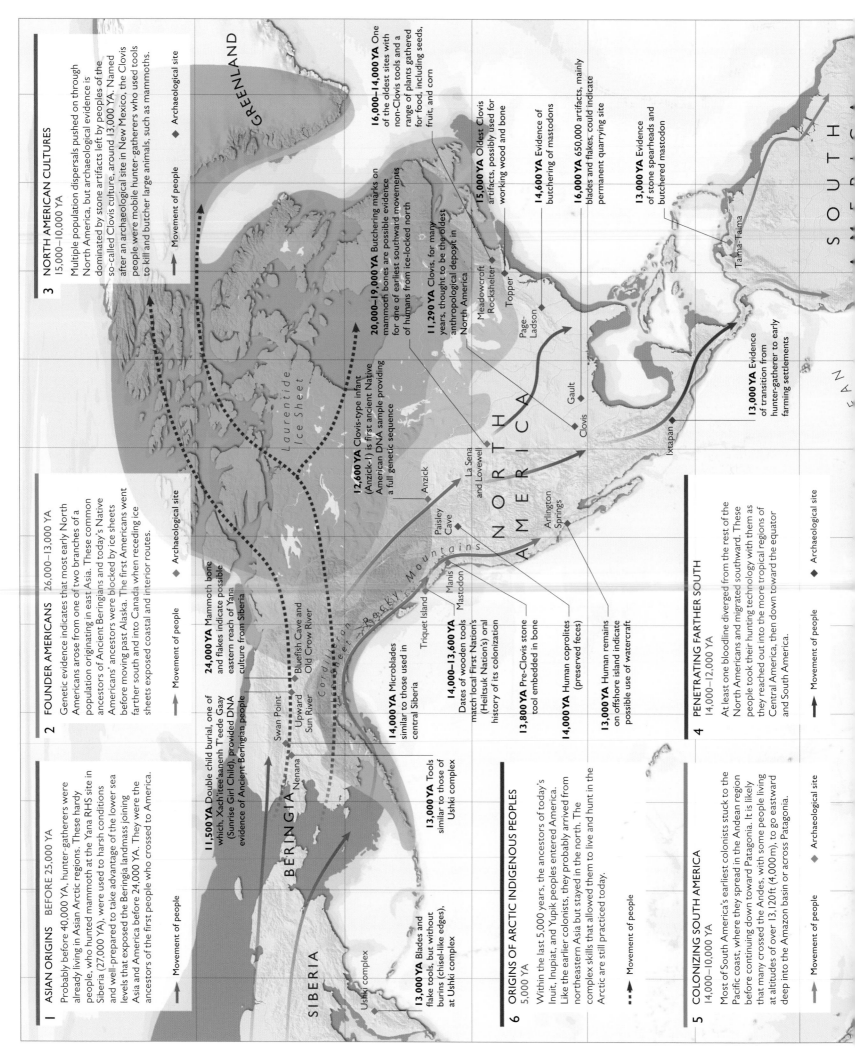

1 ASIAN ORIGINS BEFORE 25,000 YA

Probably before 40,000 YA, hunter-gatherers were already living in Asian Arctic regions. These hardy people, who hunted mammoth at the Yana RHS site in Siberia (27,000 YA), were used to harsh conditions and well-prepared to take advantage of the lower sea levels that exposed the Beringia landmass joining Asia and America before 24,000 YA. They were the ancestors of the first people who crossed to America.

→ Movement of people

11,500 YA Double child burial, one of which, Xach'itee'aanenh T'eede Gaay (Sunrise Girl Child), provided DNA evidence of Ancient Beringian people

24,000 YA Mammoth bone and flakes indicate possible eastern reach of Yana culture from Siberia

13,000 YA Blades and flake tools, but without burins (chisel-like edges), at Ushki complex

13,000 YA Tools similar to those of Ushki complex

2 FOUNDER AMERICANS 26,000–13,000 YA

Genetic evidence indicates that most early North Americans arose from one of two branches of a population originating in east Asia. These common ancestors of Ancient Beringians and today's Native Americans' ancestors were blocked by ice sheets before moving past Alaska. The first Americans went farther south and into Canada when receding ice sheets exposed coastal and interior routes.

→ Movement of people
◆ Archaeological site

3 NORTH AMERICAN CULTURES 15,000–10,000 YA

Multiple population dispersals pushed on through North America, but archaeological evidence is dominated by stone artifacts left by peoples of the so-called Clovis culture, around 13,000 YA. Named after an archaeological site in New Mexico, the Clovis people were mobile hunter-gatherers who used tools to kill and butcher large animals, such as mammoths.

→ Movement of people
◆ Archaeological site

16,000–14,000 YA One of the oldest sites with non-Clovis tools and a range of plants gathered for food, including seeds, fruit, and corn

15,000 YA Oldest Clovis artifacts, possibly used for working wood and bone

14,600 YA Evidence of butchering of mastodons

16,000 YA 650,000 artifacts, mainly blades and flakes, could indicate permanent quarrying site

13,000 YA Evidence of stone spearheads and butchered mastodon

20,000–19,000 YA Butchering marks on mammoth bones are possible evidence for one of earliest southward movements of humans from ice-locked north

11,290 YA Clovis, for many years, thought to be the oldest anthropological deposit in North America

12,600 YA Clovis-type infant (Anzick-1) is first ancient Native American DNA sample providing a full genetic sequence

14,000 YA Microblades similar to those used in central Siberia

14,000–13,600 YA Dates of wooden tools match local First Nation's (Heiltsuk Nation's) oral history of its colonization

13,800 YA Pre-Clovis stone tool embedded in bone

14,000 YA Human coprolites (preserved feces)

13,000 YA Human remains on offshore island indicate possible use of watercraft

6 ORIGINS OF ARCTIC INDIGENOUS PEOPLES 5,000 YA

Within the last 5,000 years, the ancestors of today's Inuit, Inupiat, and Yupik peoples entered America. Like the earlier colonists, they probably arrived from northeastern Asia but stayed in the north. The complex skills that allowed them to live and hunt in the Arctic are still practiced today.

⇢ Movement of people

4 PENETRATING FARTHER SOUTH 14,000–12,000 YA

At least one bloodline diverged from the rest of the North Americans and migrated southward. These people took their hunting technology with them as they reached out into the more tropical regions of Central America, then down toward the equator and South America.

→ Movement of people
◆ Archaeological site

13,000 YA Evidence of transition from hunter-gatherer to early farming settlements

5 COLONIZING SOUTH AMERICA 14,000–10,000 YA

Most of South America's earliest colonists stuck to the Pacific coast, where they spread in the Andean region before continuing down toward Patagonia. It is likely that many crossed the Andes, with some people living at altitudes of over 13,120ft (4,000m), to go eastward deep into the Amazon basin or across Patagonia.

→ Movement of people

Labels on map: GREENLAND, SIBERIA, BERINGIA, Laurentide Ice Sheet, Cordilleran Ice Sheet, Rocky Mountains, NORTH AMERICA, SOUTH AMERICA

Site labels: Ushki complex, Nenana, Swan Point, Upward Sun River, Bluefish Cave and Old Crow River, Anzick, La Sena and Lovewell, Paisley Cave, Manis Mastodon, Triquet Island, Arlington Springs, Meadowcroft Rockshelter, Topper, Page-Ladson, Gault, Clovis, Ixtapan, Taima-Taima

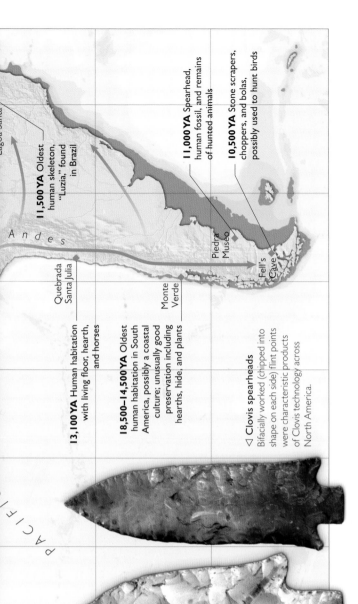

COLONIZING A NEW WORLD

Genetic studies and archaeological evidence from sites in Siberia, North America, and South America show that humans moved over a land bridge joining America to Asia at least 30,000–20,000 years ago (YA). As the land emerged from an ice age, these people then spread through the entire continent, possibly reaching along the coasts of southern South America by 18,000 YA.

11,500 YA Oldest human skeleton, "Luzia," found in Brazil

11,000 YA Spearhead, human fossil, and remains of hunted animals

10,500 YA Stone scrapers, choppers, and bolas, possibly used to hunt birds

13,100 YA Human habitation with living floor, hearth, and horses

18,500–14,500 YA Oldest human habitation in South America, possibly a coastal culture; unusually good preservation including hearths, hide, and plants

Quebrada Santa Julia

Piedra Museo

Monte Verde

Fell's Cave

Andes

PACIFI

Lagoa Santa

◁ **Clovis spearheads**
Bifacially worked (chipped into shape on each side) flint points were characteristic products of Clovis technology across North America.

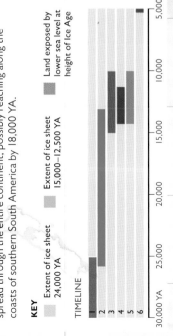

KEY

- Extent of ice sheet 24,000 YA
- Extent of ice sheet 15,000–12,500 YA
- Land exposed by lower sea level at height of Ice Age

TIMELINE

1
2
3
4
5
6

30,000 YA   25,000   20,000   15,000   10,000   5,000

PEOPLING THE AMERICAS

By the time Columbus set foot in the Americas in 1492, the continents had been peopled for thousands of years. The real discoverers of these new worlds had come from Siberia. They conquered ice and snow and trekked enormous distances to colonize a landmass of prairieland, desert, rainforest, and mountains.

Some 24,000 years ago, the world was locked in an ice age, when an Arctic ice sheet covered much of the northern world. With so much water frozen in glaciers, ocean levels were low enough to expose a connection of land, known as Beringia, between Asia and North America. This meant that people could walk across from one continent to the other, until their way became blocked as ice sheets closed in on them. There, America's founding peoples were isolated for thousands of years, until warmer times melted the ice and opened up corridors to the south, possibly as early as 20,000 YA.

DNA evidence from archaeological sites and the DNA of Native Americans alive today shows that two distinct populations split from the founding group that had entered the new lands across Beringia.

Only one of these went on to settle the Americas—the ancestors of Native Americans. The other population—known as the Ancient Beringians—may have been isolated on or outside Beringia until after the glacial melt, as evidence of their DNA is distinct from that of any past or present Native Americans. Genetics show that between 17,500 and 14,600 YA, the group that had entered America branched again into two new lineages, northern and southern. People who continued farther followed routes along the Pacific coast and far into the interior. Some became separated over vast distances but remained genetically similar, suggesting that they moved rapidly. Within a few thousand years, they had established themselves in Central America, and just centuries after that had entered Patagonia.

"They made prehistory, those latter-day Asians who, by jumping continents, became the first Americans. Theirs was a colonization the likes and scale of which … would never be repeated."

DAVID J. MELTZER, *FIRST PEOPLES IN A NEW WORLD: COLONIZING ICE AGE AMERICA*, 2009

THE CLOVIS
STONE AGE HUNTERS

The hunter-gatherer Clovis people were once viewed as the first Americans, but archaeological sites predating the Clovis period show this is not the case. However, the Clovis became a widespread influence. They used bifacial stone points and blades to hunt many of North America's large mammals, such as bison, mammoths, and sabertooth cats. In addition to the changing climate and habitats of these species, hunters were possibly one of the main factors that led to their extinction.

Extinct sabertooth cat

THE FIRST FARMERS

Working the land to grow food was an entirely new way of life for prehistoric humans. It turned them from nomads into farmers—and created settlements with permanent buildings, larger societies, and the potential to develop more elaborate technology and culture.

△ **Innovative tools**
Wooden tools called adzes had blades made from stone that were sufficiently strong to fell trees, open up land for pasture, or dig hard ground.

The earliest humans mostly lived in small nomadic bands and went wherever food was plentiful. They tracked the migrations of large animals as they hunted for meat, just as they followed the seasonal bounties of fruit and seeds. They built—and rebuilt—simple camps, carrying a few lightweight belongings with them.

This hunter-gatherer existence supported humans through the last ice age, but about 12,000 years ago, a rise in Earth's temperature opened up a world of alternative possibilities. One species of human—*Homo sapiens*—successfully emerged into this warmer world. By this time, these modern humans had spread far beyond their African ancestral home into Asia, Australasia, and America. And independently, all over the world, they had begun creating permanent farming settlements.

Settling down

Permanent camps with stronger houses made sense in places where the land was especially fertile—such as on floodplains of rivers. Settlers could support more hungry mouths by hunting, fishing, and gathering plant food around a local foraging ground that was rich in resources. This was just a small step from farming, as

▷ **Early farming villages**
This settlement at Mehrgarh in modern Pakistan dates from 7000 BCE. It had mud-brick houses and granaries to store surplus cultivated cereal grain.

it was more convenient to nurture or transplant food plants closer to home or plant their seeds and tubers (some recent evidence suggests people had started to do this as early as 23,000 years ago)—while the most amenable wild animals were confined to pens. These first farms produced more food to feed more people, so settlements could grow bigger and even produce a surplus to help with leaner times. Valuable food stores—defended from competing camps—became another reason to stay in one place.

Domestication

By about 10,000 BCE, agriculture had emerged in Eurasia, New Guinea, and America, with farmers relying on local plants and animals as favored sources of food. They learned that some species were more useful than others, and so these became staple parts of their diets.

In the fertile floodplains of Mesopotamia (modern Iraq), local wild wheat and barley became the cereal grains of choice, while goats and sheep provided meat. East Asia's main cereal grain was rice, and in Central America, farmers cultivated corn. In all cases, the first farmers selected the most manageable and high-yielding plants and animals. Over time and generations, their choices would change the traits of wild species, as crops and livestock passed on their characteristics to form the domesticated varieties we use today. With

SETTLED LIVING

As modern humans dispersed around the world, they relied on local plants and animals for sustenance. Nomadic societies gave way to settled communities as people planted the first crops or corralled the first livestock. Domestication of wild species began from about 12,000 years ago. The first farmers used the most edible species that were easiest to harvest, growing their food in abundance, providing enough to support larger populations, and ultimately outcompeting hunter-gatherers.

11,000–9000 BCE Wheat and barley are grown in southwest Asia to produce non-shattering seed heads that are easier to harvest—the first domesticated cereal grains

10,000 BCE Lentils, peas, and chickpeas in the Middle East provide an additional source of protein—improving the dietary balance along the Fertile Crescent

CROPS

ANIMALS

11,000 BCE   10,000 BCE   9000 BCE   8000 BCE

10,000 BCE In southwest Asia, local animals—including sheep, goats, pigs, and cattle—are domesticated and will become globally important livestock

10,000–5000 BCE Corn domesticated in Central America becomes the staple cereal grain in the Americas, while squash plants are selectively bred to reduce bitterness of their taste

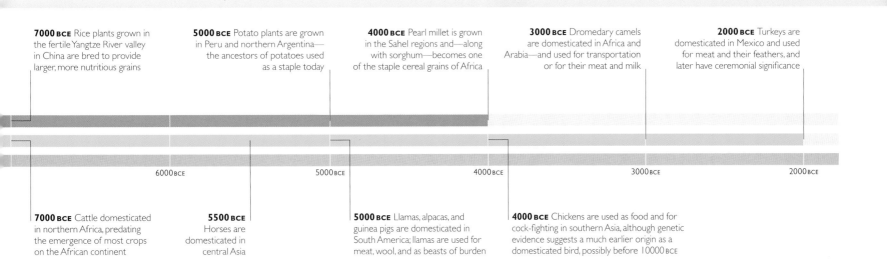

△ Working the land
A wooden model, from 2000 BCE, of a man plowing the land with oxen, depicts the earliest kind of scratch plow, which cut a furrow through hard ground ready for sowing seeds.

domestication, settlements became increasingly reliant on the limited kinds of plants and animals that provided the bulk of their food. As a result, although food was plentiful, it sometimes lacked dietary balance. More time was needed to work the land, and livestock could be lost during droughts. People's health was often poor, as crowded settlements encouraged the spread of infectious disease among humans, as well as their livestock.

Ultimately, agriculture's success, or otherwise, was a trade-off between these risks and benefits. In some parts of the world—such as the Australian interior—conditions favored more traditional nomadic lifestyles, and here humans largely remained hunter-gatherers. As farmers gained a better understanding of the needs of their crops and livestock, they developed ways of overcoming risks and increasing productivity. They learned how to use animal dung as fertilizer or to irrigate the land by diverting rivers—curtailing effects of seasonal drought. In Egypt, for example, the waters of the Nile were used for large-scale irrigation of farmland, helping to lengthen growing seasons.

Over time, food productivity became material wealth: more food not only fed more people but facilitated trade, too. At the same time, larger settlements could support people with different skills, such as craftsmen and merchants. It meant that the agricultural revolution would have far-reaching consequences for the history of humankind—including the emergence of industrial towns and cities.

> *"Farming was the precondition for the development of … civilizations in Egypt, Mesopotamia, the Indus Valley, China, the Americas, and Africa."*
>
> GRAEME BARKER, BRITISH ARCHAEOLOGIST, FROM *AGRICULTURAL REVOLUTION IN PREHISTORY*, 2006

△ Feral ancestor
The Armenian mouflon from south-western Asia is the possible ancestor of the domesticated sheep, which was one of the earliest animal species to be tamed, at around 10,000 BCE.

7000 BCE Rice plants grown in the fertile Yangtze River valley in China are bred to provide larger, more nutritious grains

5000 BCE Potato plants are grown in Peru and northern Argentina—the ancestors of potatoes used as a staple today

4000 BCE Pearl millet is grown in the Sahel regions and—along with sorghum—becomes one of the staple cereal grains of Africa

3000 BCE Dromedary camels are domesticated in Africa and Arabia—and used for transportation or for their meat and milk

2000 BCE Turkeys are domesticated in Mexico and used for meat and their feathers, and later have ceremonial significance

6000 BCE — 5000 BCE — 4000 BCE — 3000 BCE — 2000 BCE

7000 BCE Cattle domesticated in northern Africa, predating the emergence of most crops on the African continent

5500 BCE Horses are domesticated in central Asia

5000 BCE Llamas, alpacas, and guinea pigs are domesticated in South America; llamas are used for meat, wool, and as beasts of burden

4000 BCE Chickens are used as food and for cock-fighting in southern Asia, although genetic evidence suggests a much earlier origin as a domesticated bird, possibly before 10000 BCE

ORIGINS OF AGRICULTURE

When hunter-gatherers abandoned their nomadic life and became the first farmers, they were doing more than feeding their families. They were kick-starting an agricultural revolution that would have enormous implications for the future of humanity.

Evidence for agriculture's origins comes from archaeology and from DNA of crops or livestock and their wild counterparts. No one knows exactly why people started to work the land. Perhaps they transplanted wild crops closer to home for convenience or saw the potential of germinating seeds. Whatever happened, as climates warmed in the wake of the Ice Age and populations swelled, people around the world—entirely independently—became tied to farming. It brought a stable source of nourishment and sometimes, when yields were good, a surplus to sustain people through leaner times. Tending crops or corralling livestock demanded that communities stayed in one place long enough to reap the harvest. Other reasons for staying in one location would have been that the new farming tools were too heavy to carry from place to place and any food surplus had to be stored. While agrarian settlements grew to become the seeds of civilization, their communities spread, taking their skills, plants, and livestock with them.

"… Almost all of us are farmers or else are fed by farmers."

JARED DIAMOND, FROM *GUNS, GERMS, AND STEEL*, 1997

DOMESTICATION REVOLUTION
WILD SPECIES TO CROPS AND LIVESTOCK

The crops and livestock that humankind uses today descended from wild species that had rather different characteristics. Farmers chose to breed from individuals that served them best, such as by selecting ones that provided better yields or were more easily managed. This so-called artificial selection, applied over many generations and sometimes across centuries, gave rise to domesticated forms of plants and animals.

Teosinte (original wild plant)

Produce of artificial selection
Bigger cobs of domesticated corn (left) are descended from wild corn (right).

Modern corn cob

5 DIFFERENT KINDS OF CROPS AND LIVESTOCK: AMERICA 10,000–2000 BCE

Across the Old World, similar kinds of crops and livestock were being used in separate centers of agriculture. But the early colonizers of the Americas found entirely new plants, such as squashes and corn. The variety of these plants increased as people from different regions exchanged their produce. The only large animals suitable for domestication in the Americas, llamas and alpacas, were both found in the Andes.

- ◆ Archaeological site
- 🌾 Corn and millet
- 🥜 Peanut
- 🍎 Squash and sunflower
- 🍎 Squash and avocado
- 🥕 Potato
- 🦃 Turkey
- 🐂 Llama and alpaca

NORTH AMERICA

2000 BCE Corn cultivation spreads from Mesoamerica to North America

Mississippi Valley

5000 BCE Evidence of squash domestication

9000 BCE Rapid domestication of corn

Mesoamerica

2000 BCE Earliest domestication of turkeys by Mayans

Andes

6000 BCE Earliest domestication of llamas by Incas

SOUTH AMERICA

△ **Hungarian statuette**
Agriculture's significance to community life was frequently expressed in art, such as this 5th-millennium sickle-clasping idol from central Europe.

ADVENT OF AGRICULTURE

Agriculture arose independently in different parts of the world before diffusing into adjacent regions. Each area developed its own specific crops, dependent on the region's climate, and some produce went on to become globally important as communities expanded across the world.

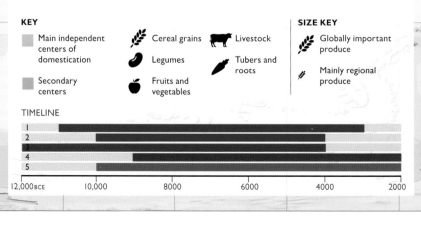

KEY
- ▬ Main independent centers of domestication
- ▬ Secondary centers
- 🌾 Cereal grains
- 🫘 Legumes
- 🍎 Fruits and vegetables
- 🐂 Livestock
- 🥕 Tubers and roots

SIZE KEY
- 🌾 Globally important produce
- 🌾 Mainly regional produce

TIMELINE

1					
2					
3					
4					
5					

12,000 BCE   10,000   8000   6000   4000   2000

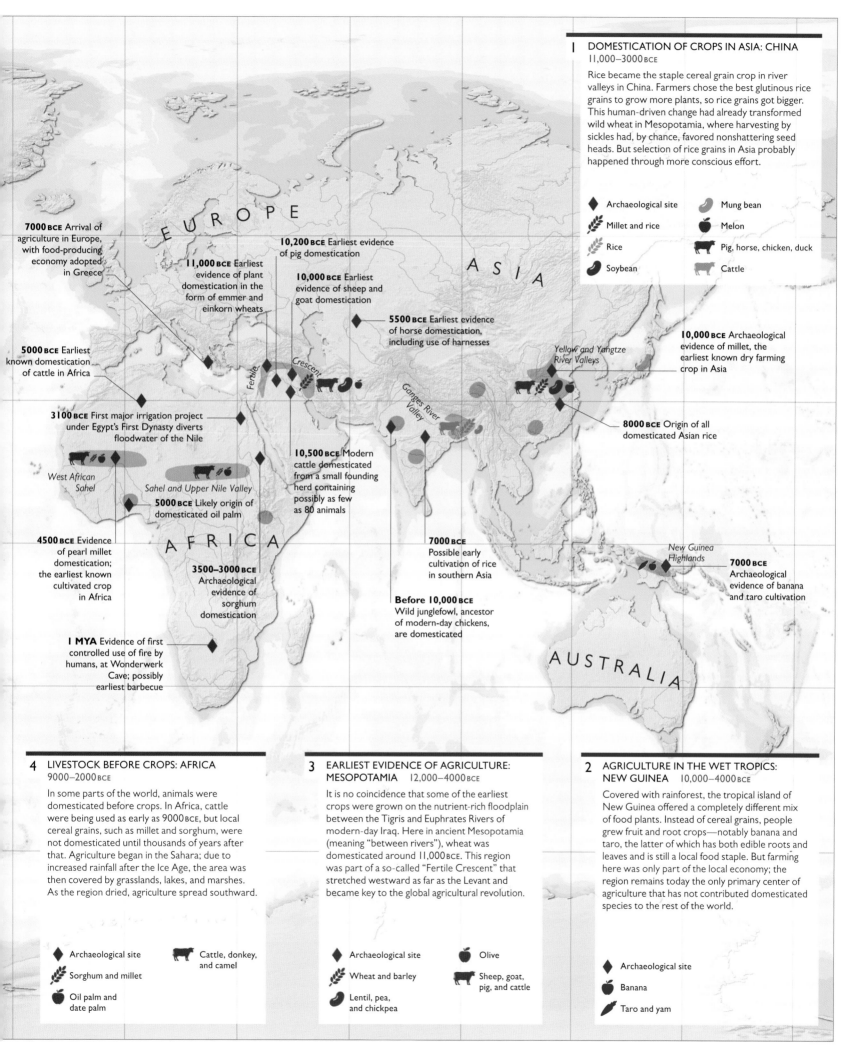

1 DOMESTICATION OF CROPS IN ASIA: CHINA
11,000–3000 BCE

Rice became the staple cereal grain crop in river valleys in China. Farmers chose the best glutinous rice grains to grow more plants, so rice grains got bigger. This human-driven change had already transformed wild wheat in Mesopotamia, where harvesting by sickles had, by chance, favored nonshattering seed heads. But selection of rice grains in Asia probably happened through more conscious effort.

◆ Archaeological site   Mung bean

Millet and rice   Melon

Rice   Pig, horse, chicken, duck

Soybean   Cattle

7000 BCE Arrival of agriculture in Europe, with food-producing economy adopted in Greece

11,000 BCE Earliest evidence of plant domestication in the form of emmer and einkorn wheats

10,200 BCE Earliest evidence of pig domestication

10,000 BCE Earliest evidence of sheep and goat domestication

5000 BCE Earliest known domestication of cattle in Africa

5500 BCE Earliest evidence of horse domestication, including use of harnesses

Yellow and Yangtze River Valleys

10,000 BCE Archaeological evidence of millet, the earliest known dry farming crop in Asia

3100 BCE First major irrigation project under Egypt's First Dynasty diverts floodwater of the Nile

Fertile Crescent

Ganges River Valley

8000 BCE Origin of all domesticated Asian rice

West African Sahel

Sahel and Upper Nile Valley

5000 BCE Likely origin of domesticated oil palm

10,500 BCE Modern cattle domesticated from a small founding herd containing possibly as few as 80 animals

4500 BCE Evidence of pearl millet domestication; the earliest known cultivated crop in Africa

3500–3000 BCE Archaeological evidence of sorghum domestication

7000 BCE Possible early cultivation of rice in southern Asia

New Guinea Highlands

7000 BCE Archaeological evidence of banana and taro cultivation

Before 10,000 BCE Wild junglefowl, ancestor of modern-day chickens, are domesticated

1 MYA Evidence of first controlled use of fire by humans, at Wonderwerk Cave; possibly earliest barbecue

4 LIVESTOCK BEFORE CROPS: AFRICA
9000–2000 BCE

In some parts of the world, animals were domesticated before crops. In Africa, cattle were being used as early as 9000 BCE, but local cereal grains, such as millet and sorghum, were not domesticated until thousands of years after that. Agriculture began in the Sahara; due to increased rainfall after the Ice Age, the area was then covered by grasslands, lakes, and marshes. As the region dried, agriculture spread southward.

◆ Archaeological site   Cattle, donkey, and camel

Sorghum and millet

Oil palm and date palm

3 EARLIEST EVIDENCE OF AGRICULTURE: MESOPOTAMIA   12,000–4000 BCE

It is no coincidence that some of the earliest crops were grown on the nutrient-rich floodplain between the Tigris and Euphrates Rivers of modern-day Iraq. Here in ancient Mesopotamia (meaning "between rivers"), wheat was domesticated around 11,000 BCE. This region was part of a so-called "Fertile Crescent" that stretched westward as far as the Levant and became key to the global agricultural revolution.

◆ Archaeological site   Olive

Wheat and barley   Sheep, goat, pig, and cattle

Lentil, pea, and chickpea

2 AGRICULTURE IN THE WET TROPICS: NEW GUINEA   10,000–4000 BCE

Covered with rainforest, the tropical island of New Guinea offered a completely different mix of food plants. Instead of cereal grains, people grew fruit and root crops—notably banana and taro, the latter of which has both edible roots and leaves and is still a local food staple. But farming here was only part of the local economy; the region remains today the only primary center of agriculture that has not contributed domesticated species to the rest of the world.

◆ Archaeological site

Banana

Taro and yam

VILLAGES TO TOWNS

As nomadic hunter-gatherers began farming, for the first time in history human populations became anchored to fixed points on a map of civilization. Settlements grew in size and complexity; the first villages became the first towns.

Just as agriculture turned humans into a more sedentary species, so the settlements they made drove the attributes of modern human society: material accumulation, industry, and trade. This happened in places around the world, but nowhere is the evidence for it clearer than in southwest Asia. Here, the first farmers produced enough food on fertile soils to support denser populations. Although life was labor-intensive, and there was a greater risk of disease from overcrowding and malnutrition, there were benefits of living together in one place over a long period. People could concentrate on producing a surplus and perfect skills to make their lives easier. Clay was baked into bricks for making stronger houses or fashioned into large storage vessels. As towns grew, they were sometimes fortified with surrounding walls. Shells from the Mediterranean showed wide trade links developing, while copper gradually supplanted flint for better tools. As society itself divided into craftspeople, merchants, and their leaders, these first local industries brought material wealth that formed the basis of the first exchange economies.

"… it made sense for men to band together … for … management of the environment."

J.M. ROBERTS, FROM *HISTORY OF THE WORLD*, 1990

POTTERY IN THE STONE AGE
HARNESSING THE POTENTIAL OF CLAY

Fired clay had been used to make figurines and pots before 20,000 YA. It later became important in constructing dwellings. Wet clay was used to reinforce brushwood walls. Solid bricks gave protection from the elements and enemies, while creative clay technology was used to fashion more decorative pots.

Halaf vase
Mesopotamian pottery was decorated with geometric designs as early as 6000 BCE.

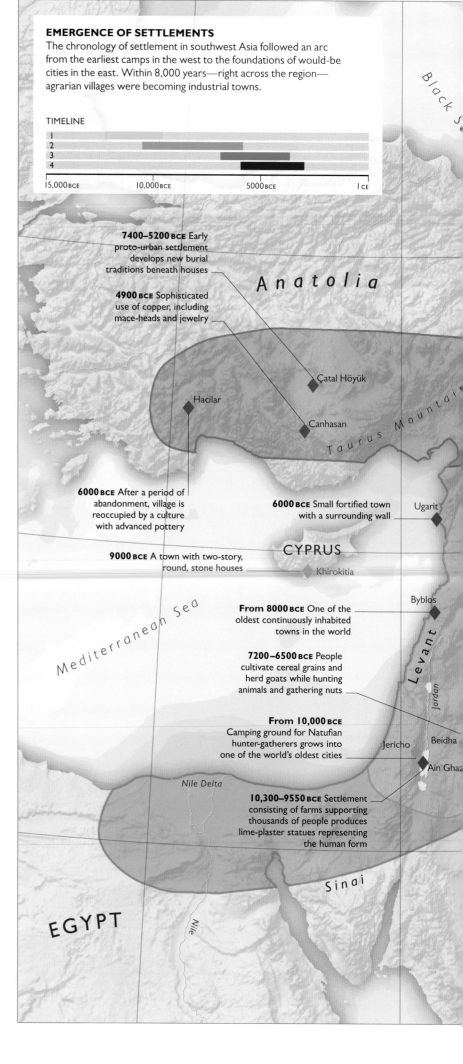

EMERGENCE OF SETTLEMENTS
The chronology of settlement in southwest Asia followed an arc from the earliest camps in the west to the foundations of would-be cities in the east. Within 8,000 years—right across the region—agrarian villages were becoming industrial towns.

TIMELINE
1
2
3
4
15,000 BCE   10,000 BCE   5000 BCE   1 CE

7400–5200 BCE Early proto-urban settlement develops new burial traditions beneath houses

4900 BCE Sophisticated use of copper, including mace-heads and jewelry

Anatolia

Çatal Höyük

Hacilar

Canhasan

Taurus Mountains

6000 BCE After a period of abandonment, village is reoccupied by a culture with advanced pottery

6000 BCE Small fortified town with a surrounding wall

Ugarit

9000 BCE A town with two-story, round, stone houses

CYPRUS

Khirokitia

Mediterranean Sea

From 8000 BCE One of the oldest continuously inhabited towns in the world

Byblos

7200–6500 BCE People cultivate cereal grains and herd goats while hunting animals and gathering nuts

Levant

Jordan

From 10,000 BCE Camping ground for Natufian hunter-gatherers grows into one of the world's oldest cities

Jericho

Beidha

Ain Ghazal

Nile Delta

10,300–9550 BCE Settlement consisting of farms supporting thousands of people produces lime-plaster statues representing the human form

Sinai

EGYPT

Nile

Black Sea

1 TRANSITION FROM NOMADS TO SETTLEMENTS 12,500–9000 BCE

The Natufian people, descended from nomads of the Levant and Sinai, made the earliest settlements in southwest Asia, from about 12,500 BCE. At first, these were probably nothing more than seasonal hunting camps, although evidence for these is scant because nomads had few material possessions. Their descendants stockpiled food that demanded permanent storage.

▨ Spread of settlements

◆ Archaeological site

2 FIRST AGRARIAN SETTLEMENTS 11,000–6000 BCE

Farmers emerged from early settlers who exploited wild cereal grains, such as rye, which was cultivated as early as 11,050 BCE. At first, settlers rallied together to protect wild food plants from grazing animals, but, over time, plants were moved or seeds sown closer to home. Houses became more permanent, as mud brick replaced perishable brushwood as building material.

▨ Spread of settlements

◆ Archaeological site

3 SPREAD OF MATERIAL CULTURE 7000–4000 BCE

More food supported bigger settlements as villages proliferated over a wider region, from Anatolia in the west to the Zagros Mountains in the east. Çatal Höyük, a rich archaeological site, might have supported up to 10,000 people. Although it lacked social hierarchy, it had a thriving industry in pottery and obsidian tools, and may have traded for seashells and flints from Syria.

▨ Spread of settlements

◆ Archaeological site

4 GROWTH OF URBAN LIFE 6000–3000 BCE

The Ubaid people were the first to colonize southeastern Mesopotamia as the Stone Age gave way to the Copper Age. They used copper to make tools, were led by hereditary chieftains, and may even have had a primitive democracy. Ubaid settlements merged to form bigger communities—notably Uruk, which would become one of the first true cities and a hub of major trade networks.

▨ Spread of settlements

◆ Archaeological site

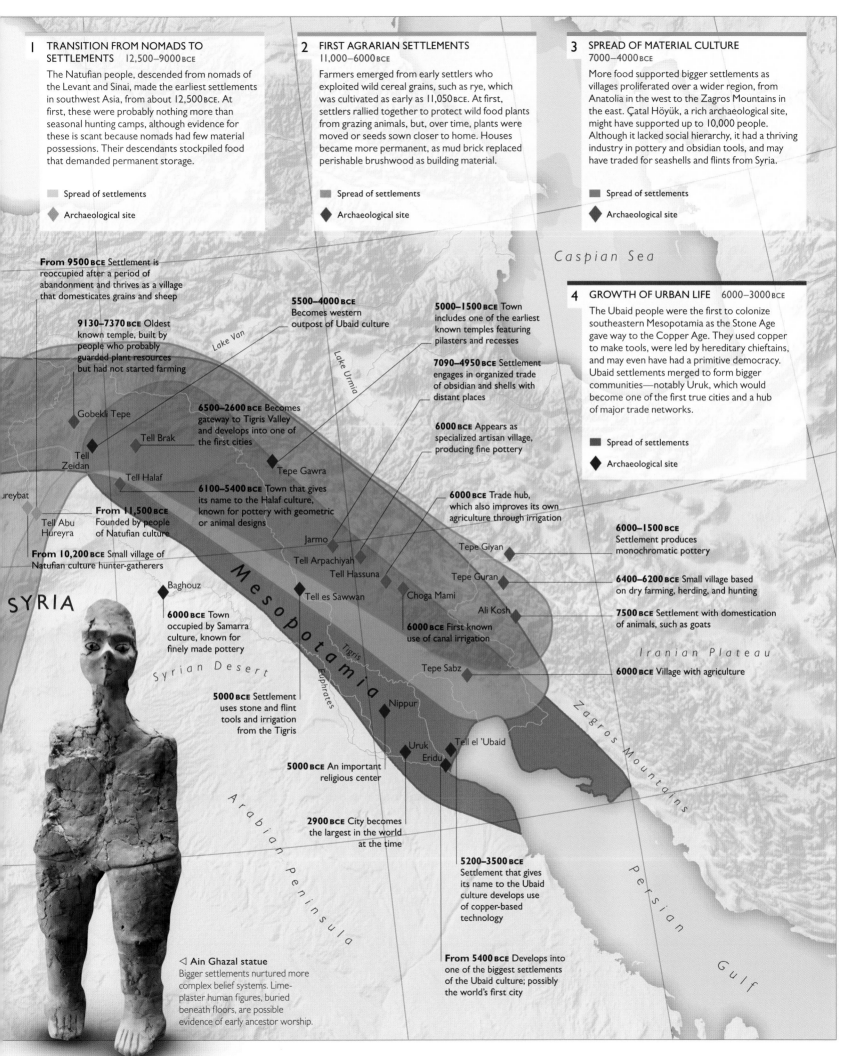

From 9500 BCE Settlement is reoccupied after a period of abandonment and thrives as a village that domesticates grains and sheep

9130–7370 BCE Oldest known temple, built by people who probably guarded plant resources but had not started farming

5500–4000 BCE Becomes western outpost of Ubaid culture

5000–1500 BCE Town includes one of the earliest known temples featuring pilasters and recesses

7090–4950 BCE Settlement engages in organized trade of obsidian and shells with distant places

6000 BCE Appears as specialized artisan village, producing fine pottery

6500–2600 BCE Becomes gateway to Tigris Valley and develops into one of the first cities

6100–5400 BCE Town that gives its name to the Halaf culture, known for pottery with geometric or animal designs

6000 BCE Trade hub, which also improves its own agriculture through irrigation

6000 BCE Settlement produces monochromatic pottery

From 11,500 BCE Founded by people of Natufian culture

From 10,200 BCE Small village of Natufian culture hunter-gatherers

6400–6200 BCE Small village based on dry farming, herding, and hunting

7500 BCE Settlement with domestication of animals, such as goats

6000 BCE Town occupied by Samarra culture, known for finely made pottery

6000 BCE First known use of canal irrigation

6000 BCE Village with agriculture

5000 BCE Settlement uses stone and flint tools and irrigation from the Tigris

5000 BCE An important religious center

2900 BCE City becomes the largest in the world at the time

5200–3500 BCE Settlement that gives its name to the Ubaid culture develops use of copper-based technology

From 5400 BCE Develops into one of the biggest settlements of the Ubaid culture; possibly the world's first city

Gobekli Tepe

Tell Brak

Tell Zeidan

Tell Halaf

Tepe Gawra

ureybat

Tell Abu Hureyra

Jarmo

Tell Arpachiyah

Tell Hassuna

Tepe Giyan

Tepe Guran

Ali Kosh

Baghouz

Tell es Sawwan

Choga Mami

SYRIA

Nippur

Uruk

Eridu

Tell el 'Ubaid

Tepe Sabz

Lake Van

Lake Urmia

Caspian Sea

Iranian Plateau

Zagros Mountains

Persian Gulf

Mesopotamia

Tigris

Euphrates

Syrian Desert

Arabian Peninsula

◁ **Ain Ghazal statue**
Bigger settlements nurtured more complex belief systems. Lime-plaster human figures, buried beneath floors, are possible evidence of early ancestor worship.

THE ANCIENT WORLD

ANCIENT HISTORY STRETCHES FROM WHEN THE FIRST CITIES
DEVELOPED AROUND 3000 BCE TO THE FALL OF POWERS SUCH AS
THE ROMAN EMPIRE AND HAN CHINA IN THE FIRST CENTURIES CE.

THE FIRST CIVILIZATIONS

Fertile soil, warm climate, and an ample supply of water, along with agriculture and a stone-working technology, allowed the first urban civilizations to develop. The earliest is thought to have flourished in Mesopotamia (modern-day Iraq) around 3500 BCE.

Of all the factors that helped civilizations grow, water was perhaps the most important. The earliest known civilization was born in Sumer, in southern Mesopotamia, in the fertile region between the rivers Tigris and Euphrates. The Sumerians were drawn to the area they settled in because of the abundance of fresh water the rivers provided.

A thriving trading center of the Sumerian civilization, Uruk is generally considered to be the world's first city. It boasted 6 miles of defensive walls and a population that numbered between 40,000 and 80,000 at the height of its glory in 2800 BCE. Other Sumerian city-states that contributed significantly to the civilization included Eridu, Ur, Nippur, Lagash, and Kish. Probably the most important Sumerian invention was the wheel, followed by the development of cuneiform writing.

△ **Architectural wonder**
Giza's pyramids were the tombs of three Old Kingdom pharaohs. From left to right, the three large pyramids seen here are the tombs of Menkaure, Khafre, and Khufu.

The first pyramids

Just as the Sumerians depended on the rivers Tigris and Euphrates, the Egyptian civilization could not have come into existence without the Nile. The water from the Nile flooded the plains for 6 months annually, leaving behind a nutrient-rich layer of thick, black silt. This meant that the early Egyptians could cultivate crops, including grains, and fruit and vegetables.

> *"This is the wall of Uruk, which no city on Earth can equal."*
>
> EPIC OF GILGAMESH, C. 2000 BCE

Around 3400 BCE, two Egyptian kingdoms flourished—Upper Egypt in the Nile Valley and Lower Egypt to the north. Some 300 years later, King Narmer unified the two kingdoms, establishing Memphis as the capital of united Egypt. It was near Memphis, at Saqqara, that the Egyptians built their first pyramid around 2611 BCE. The step pyramid was designed by Imhotep—one of King Djoser's most trusted advisors—as a tomb to house the corpse of his royal master. More than 130 pyramids followed. The most significant of these was the Great Pyramid, constructed at Giza for Khufu, who reigned from 2589 to 2566 BCE. Two more pyramids were erected on the same site for the pharaohs Khafre and Menkaure, Khufu's successors. Although completely unrelated, pyramid-shaped

△ **Ram in the thicket**
A fine example of Sumerian craftsmanship, this elaborately crafted statuette of a wild goat searching for food comes from the city-state of Ur in ancient Mesopotamia.

ANCIENT CIVILIZATIONS

City-based civilization is thought to have originated in Mesopotamia (the area between the rivers Euphrates and Tigris), followed by Egypt's Nile Valley. Civilizations grew independently in the fertile basins of the Yellow River in China and the Indus Valley in today's Pakistan and India. In each case, a great river created the conditions for intensive, efficient agriculture. Early cities also grew in Peru, for reasons not yet fully understood. In Europe, the Minoans built highly developed urban settlements centered on grand palaces.

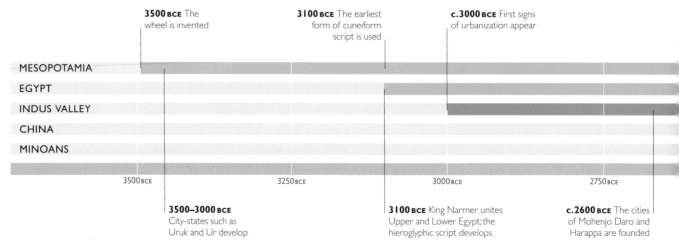

3500 BCE The wheel is invented

3100 BCE The earliest form of cuneiform script is used

c.3000 BCE First signs of urbanization appear

MESOPOTAMIA

EGYPT

INDUS VALLEY

CHINA

MINOANS

3500 BCE 3250 BCE 3000 BCE 2750 BCE

3500–3000 BCE
City-states such as Uruk and Ur develop

3100 BCE King Narmer unites Upper and Lower Egypt; the hieroglyphic script develops

c.2600 BCE The cities of Mohenjo Daro and Harappa are founded

▷ **Ritual vessel**
This Chinese bronze food bowl, or *gui*, was probably made between 1300 and 1050 BCE. It was used in Shang religious rituals.

structures were also constructed in what is now Peru by the Norte Chico civilization, builders of the first cities in Americas, sometime before 3000 BCE.

Civilizations of the east
Rivers played an equally important part in the development of civilizations in the Indus Valley (in the northwestern part of south Asia) and northern China. The Indus Valley people are known today as Harappans after Harappa—one of their greatest cities, along with Mohenjo Daro. The Harappans prospered from 3300 to 1900 BCE. Until recently, the Harappans were thought to have been overrun by Aryan invaders from the north, but a more modern theory suggests that tectonic shifts that affected the rivers on which they relied were the cause of the Indus Valley collapse. Yet another theory suggests that the drying up of local rivers led to the culture's decline.

A Chinese civilization flourished along the Huang He, or Yellow River, in the north. As with the Egyptian and Harappan civilizations, here, too, seasonal floods enriched the soil. This encouraged the development of farming, while the river itself provided a useful trade route. By 2000 BCE, bronze-working, silk-weaving, and pottery were being practiced.

The mysterious Minoans
Around the same time that the Chinese civilization was developing, another influential civilization was emerging on the Mediterranean island of Crete. Its people are known as the Minoans, so named by the British archaeologist Sir Arthur Evans to honor Minos, a legendary ruler who may or may not have existed. The Minoans were a great maritime trading power, exporting timber, pottery, and textiles. Trade brought wealth, and they built many palaces—Knossos being the most impressive. The Minoan civilization declined in the late 15th century BCE. Some historians attribute this to a volcanic explosion on the island of Thera (modern-day Santorini), while others argue that it was the result of an invasion by the Mycenaeans from mainland Greece.

▽ **Artistic expression**
This colorful fresco, depicting a Minoan funeral ritual honoring a dead nobleman, decorates a sarcophagus dating from the 14th century BCE.

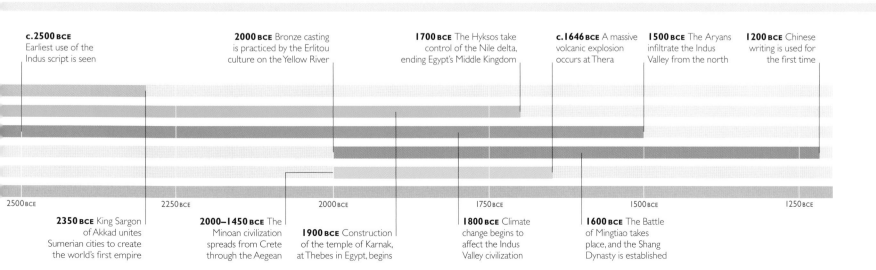

c.2500 BCE Earliest use of the Indus script is seen

2000 BCE Bronze casting is practiced by the Erlitou culture on the Yellow River

1700 BCE The Hyksos take control of the Nile delta, ending Egypt's Middle Kingdom

c.1646 BCE A massive volcanic explosion occurs at Thera

1500 BCE The Aryans infiltrate the Indus Valley from the north

1200 BCE Chinese writing is used for the first time

2500 BCE   2250 BCE   2000 BCE   1750 BCE   1500 BCE   1250 BCE

2350 BCE King Sargon of Akkad unites Sumerian cities to create the world's first empire

2000–1450 BCE The Minoan civilization spreads from Crete through the Aegean

1900 BCE Construction of the temple of Karnak, at Thebes in Egypt, begins

1800 BCE Climate change begins to affect the Indus Valley civilization

1600 BCE The Battle of Mingtiao takes place, and the Shang Dynasty is established

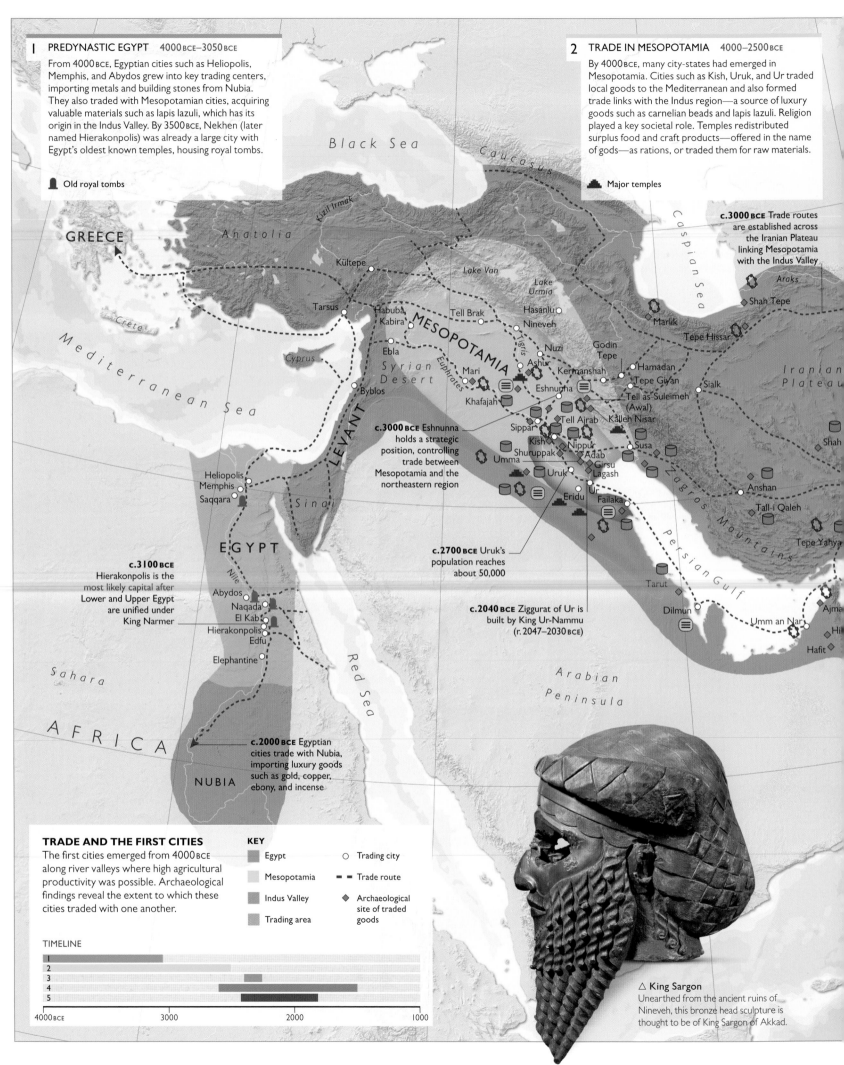

1 PREDYNASTIC EGYPT 4000 BCE–3050 BCE

From 4000 BCE, Egyptian cities such as Heliopolis, Memphis, and Abydos grew into key trading centers, importing metals and building stones from Nubia. They also traded with Mesopotamian cities, acquiring valuable materials such as lapis lazuli, which has its origin in the Indus Valley. By 3500 BCE, Nekhen (later named Hierakonpolis) was already a large city with Egypt's oldest known temples, housing royal tombs.

🛑 Old royal tombs

2 TRADE IN MESOPOTAMIA 4000–2500 BCE

By 4000 BCE, many city-states had emerged in Mesopotamia. Cities such as Kish, Uruk, and Ur traded local goods to the Mediterranean and also formed trade links with the Indus region—a source of luxury goods such as carnelian beads and lapis lazuli. Religion played a key societal role. Temples redistributed surplus food and craft products—offered in the name of gods—as rations, or traded them for raw materials.

🛕 Major temples

c.3000 BCE Trade routes are established across the Iranian Plateau linking Mesopotamia with the Indus Valley

c.3000 BCE Eshnunna holds a strategic position, controlling trade between Mesopotamia and the northeastern region

c.2700 BCE Uruk's population reaches about 50,000

c.3100 BCE Hierakonpolis is the most likely capital after Lower and Upper Egypt are unified under King Narmer

c.2040 BCE Ziggurat of Ur is built by King Ur-Nammu (r. 2047–2030 BCE)

c.2000 BCE Egyptian cities trade with Nubia, importing luxury goods such as gold, copper, ebony, and incense

TRADE AND THE FIRST CITIES

The first cities emerged from 4000 BCE along river valleys where high agricultural productivity was possible. Archaeological findings reveal the extent to which these cities traded with one another.

KEY

- Egypt
- Mesopotamia
- Indus Valley
- Trading area
- ○ Trading city
- ▬ ▬ Trade route
- ◆ Archaeological site of traded goods

TIMELINE

1
2
3
4
5

4000 BCE   3000   2000   1000

△ King Sargon
Unearthed from the ancient ruins of Nineveh, this bronze head sculpture is thought to be of King Sargon of Akkad.

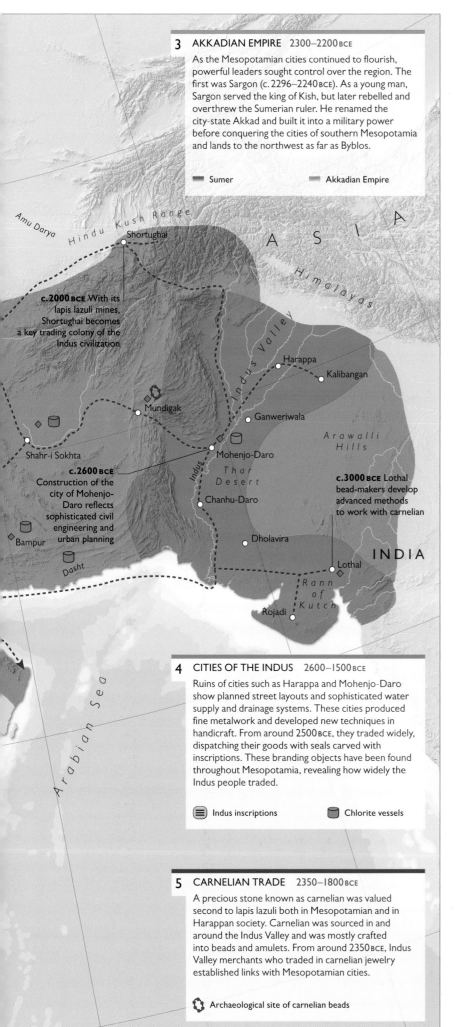

3 AKKADIAN EMPIRE 2300–2200 BCE

As the Mesopotamian cities continued to flourish, powerful leaders sought control over the region. The first was Sargon (c. 2296–2240 BCE). As a young man, Sargon served the king of Kish, but later rebelled and overthrew the Sumerian ruler. He renamed the city-state Akkad and built it into a military power before conquering the cities of southern Mesopotamia and lands to the northwest as far as Byblos.

■ Sumer   ■ Akkadian Empire

c.2000 BCE With its lapis lazuli mines, Shortughai becomes a key trading colony of the Indus civilization

c.2600 BCE Construction of the city of Mohenjo-Daro reflects sophisticated civil engineering and urban planning

c.3000 BCE Lothal bead-makers develop advanced methods to work with carnelian

4 CITIES OF THE INDUS 2600–1500 BCE

Ruins of cities such as Harappa and Mohenjo-Daro show planned street layouts and sophisticated water supply and drainage systems. These cities produced fine metalwork and developed new techniques in handicraft. From around 2500 BCE, they traded widely, dispatching their goods with seals carved with inscriptions. These branding objects have been found throughout Mesopotamia, revealing how widely the Indus people traded.

⊜ Indus inscriptions   ▢ Chlorite vessels

5 CARNELIAN TRADE 2350–1800 BCE

A precious stone known as carnelian was valued second to lapis lazuli both in Mesopotamian and in Harappan society. Carnelian was sourced in and around the Indus Valley and was mostly crafted into beads and amulets. From around 2350 BCE, Indus Valley merchants who traded in carnelian jewelry established links with Mesopotamian cities.

✿ Archaeological site of carnelian beads

THE FIRST CITIES

The first known cities developed along fertile river plains in Mesopotamia (modern Iraq), Egypt, and the Indus Valley. They became thriving trading centers with an organized social structure, and flourished in the fields of art, craft, and architecture.

By 3000 BCE, agricultural advances led to food surpluses in some parts of the world, namely the river valleys of the Nile in Egypt, the Indus, and the Tigris and Euphrates in Mesopotamia, allowing the communities living in these regions to branch out into a range of craftwork—from metalworking to masonry. This gave rise to the first markets, which channeled wealth into these sites, and in doing

"The Mesopotamians viewed their city-states as earthly copies of a divine model and order."

J. SPIELVOGEL, FROM *WESTERN CIVILIZATION* VOL. 1, 2014

so formed the nucleus of the world's first cities. These urban centers mostly grew on the riverbanks, in close proximity to fertile farmland and sources of clay for brick-making. The rivers served as vital routes for transporting raw material such as timber, precious stones, and metals into the cities. Trade goods also moved over land, in particular across the Levant and the Iranian Plateau, linking the cities of all three regions. Most notably, carnelian beads and seals (branding marks on documents accompanying goods) from the Indus Valley have been found widely in Mesopotamia. Many Mesopotamian cities grew into powerful city-states, some of which eventually became the capitals of some of the earliest known empires.

STANDARD OF UR
MESOPOTAMIAN ARTIFACT, 2600–2400 BCE

Excavated from the royal tombs of Ur in the 1920s, the Standard of Ur is a tapered box decorated with scenes. The original purpose of the artifact remains a mystery, but the images on the two side panels, dubbed the "War Side" and the "Peace Side," form a narrative that offers a vivid insight into the different aspects of life in the ancient city. The scenes also include the earliest known image of wheels used for transportation.

EGYPT OF THE PHARAOHS

Egypt was among the most enduring civilizations in the ancient world. With its succession of powerful rulers, unique religion and art, and trading networks, the culture exerted its influence in the Nile Valley and beyond for more than 3,000 years.

From c. 2700 to 1085 BCE, Egypt's kings, or pharaohs, ruled the Nile Valley for three long, separate periods, named by historians the Old, Middle, and New Kingdoms.

Egypt's ancient civilization grew along the banks of the River Nile, which was the main artery for travel and trade. The river was also rich in fish and flooded annually, covering the banks with fertile mud, making for a highly productive agricultural region. While Egypt's pharaohs ruled over this riverside zone, their influence spread much farther afield, mainly through land and sea trading expeditions, which became more widespread in the Middle and New Kingdom eras. The Egyptians developed their own system of writing, and the pharaohs bolstered their wealth by employing scribes to record goods traded and to ensure taxes were collected.

The Egyptian people worshipped multiple gods and also regarded the pharaohs as deities, which lent spiritual weight to the ruling power. The strength of the pharaohs' authority is evident in the impressive burial sites built during the ancient era, including the pyramids of the Old Kingdom and the colossal temples and tombs of the later kingdoms.

> "The All-Lord himself made me great. He gave to me the land while I was in the egg."
>
> RAMESSES II, PHARAOH OF THE NEW KINGDOM, 1279–1213 BCE

REGION UNDER EGYPTIAN CONTROL

The maps show the boundaries of the Old, Middle, and New Kingdoms of Ancient Egypt and include the trade routes that linked the sites of oases, cities, the great temples, forts, and pyramids.

KEY

🌴 Oasis

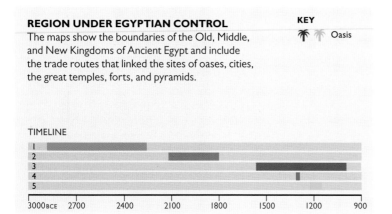

TIMELINE

	3000 BCE	2700	2400	2100	1800	1500	1200	900
1								
2								
3								
4								
5								

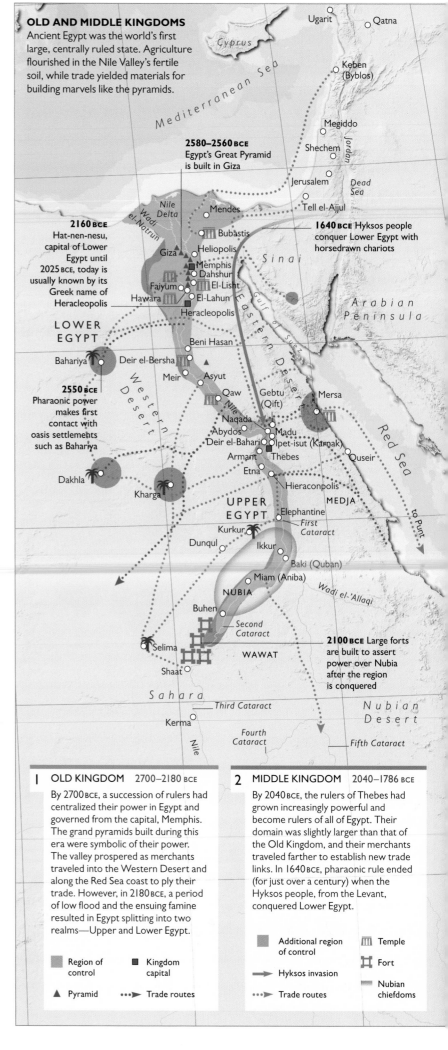

OLD AND MIDDLE KINGDOMS
Ancient Egypt was the world's first large, centrally ruled state. Agriculture flourished in the Nile Valley's fertile soil, while trade yielded materials for building marvels like the pyramids.

2580–2560 BCE Egypt's Great Pyramid is built in Giza

2160 BCE Hat-nen-nesu, capital of Lower Egypt until 2025 BCE, today is usually known by its Greek name of Heracleopolis

1640 BCE Hyksos people conquer Lower Egypt with horsedrawn chariots

2550 BCE Pharaonic power makes first contact with oasis settlements such as Bahariya

2100 BCE Large forts are built to assert power over Nubia after the region is conquered

Mediterranean Sea · Cyprus · Ugarit · Qatna · Keben (Byblos) · Megiddo · Shechem · Jordan · Jerusalem · Dead Sea · Tell el-Ajjul · Sinai · Arabian Peninsula · Red Sea · to Punt

Nile Delta · Wadi el-Natrun · Mendes · Bubastis · Heliopolis · Giza · Memphis · Dahshur · Faiyum · El-Lisht · Hawara · El-Lahun · Heracleopolis · Eastern Desert · Gulf of Suez

LOWER EGYPT · Bahariya · Deir el-Bersha · Meir · Beni Hasan · Asyut · Qaw · Gebtu (Qift) · Mersa · Naqada · Madu · Abydos · Ipet-isut (Karnak) · Deir el-Bahari · Armant · Thebes · Quseir · Etna · Hieraconpolis · Dakhla · Kharga · Western Desert · Nile

UPPER EGYPT · Elephantine · First Cataract · MEDJA · Kurkur · Dunqul · Ikkur · Baki (Quban) · Miam (Aniba) · NUBIA · Wadi el-'Allaqi · Buhen · Second Cataract ·
Selima · WAWAT · Shaat · Sahara · Third Cataract · Kerma · Fourth Cataract · Fifth Cataract · Nile · Nubian Desert

1 OLD KINGDOM 2700–2180 BCE

By 2700 BCE, a succession of rulers had centralized their power in Egypt and governed from the capital, Memphis. The grand pyramids built during this era were symbolic of their power. The valley prospered as merchants traveled into the Western Desert and along the Red Sea coast to ply their trade. However, in 2180 BCE, a period of low flood and the ensuing famine resulted in Egypt splitting into two realms—Upper and Lower Egypt.

■ Region of control
■ Kingdom capital
▲ Pyramid
••••► Trade routes

2 MIDDLE KINGDOM 2040–1786 BCE

By 2040 BCE, the rulers of Thebes had grown increasingly powerful and become rulers of all of Egypt. Their domain was slightly larger than that of the Old Kingdom, and their merchants traveled farther to establish new trade links. In 1640 BCE, pharaonic rule ended (for just over a century) when the Hyksos people, from the Levant, conquered Lower Egypt.

■ Additional region of control
→ Hyksos invasion
••••► Trade routes
▥ Temple
🏰 Fort
▬ Nubian chiefdoms

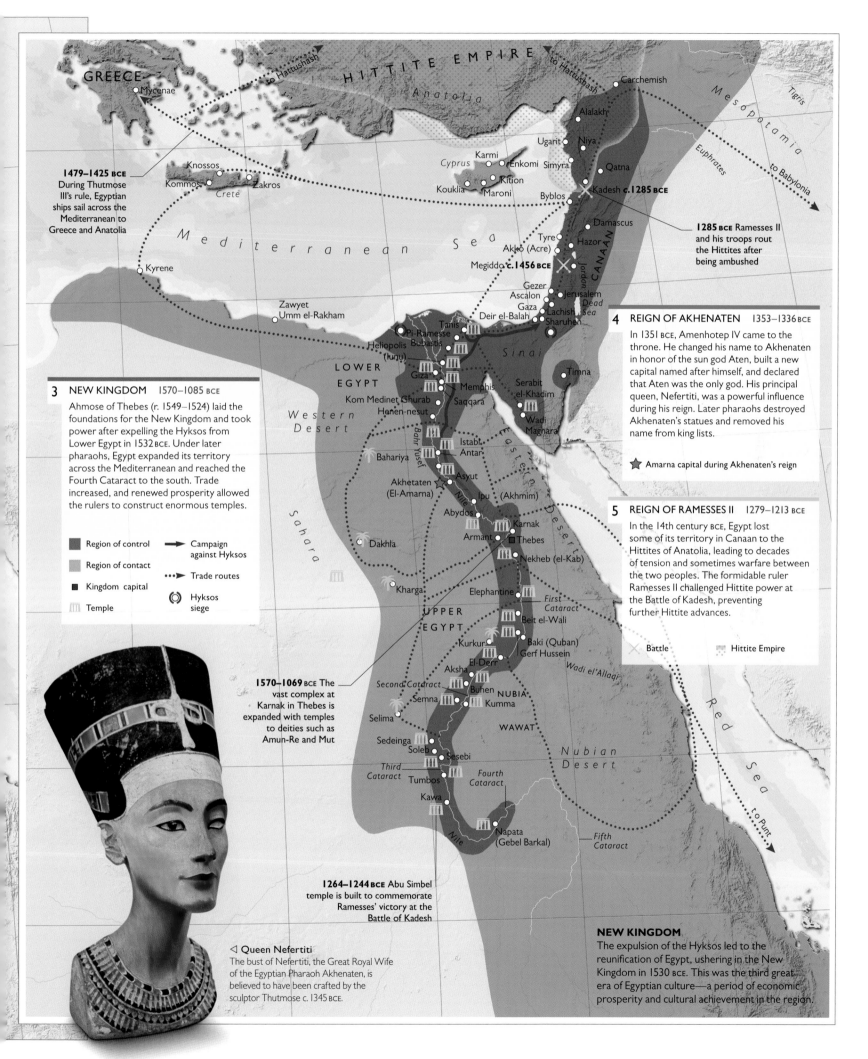

GREECE

Mycenae

1479–1425 BCE
During Thutmose III's rule, Egyptian ships sail across the Mediterranean to Greece and Anatolia

Knossos
Kommos
Zakros
Crete

Mediterranean Sea

Kyrene

H I T T I T E   E M P I R E
to Hattushash   to Hattushash
Anatolia
Carchemish
Alalakh
Ugarit   Niya
Karmi
Cyprus   Enkomi   Simyra
Kition
Kouklia   Maroni
Byblos   Kadesh **c.1285 BCE**
Mesopotamia
Tigris
Qatna
to Babylonia
Euphrates

Damascus
Tyre   Hazor
Akko (Acre)
Megiddo **c.1456 BCE**

C A N A A N

1285 BCE Ramesses II and his troops rout the Hittites after being ambushed

Zawyet
Umm el-Rakham

Gezer
Ascalon   Jerusalem
Gaza   *Dead*
Deir el-Balah   Lachish   *Sea*
Sharuhen

Tanis
Pi-Ramesse
Heliopolis   Bubastis
(Iunu)

S i n a i

4   REIGN OF AKHENATEN 1353–1336 BCE
In 1351 BCE, Amenhotep IV came to the throne. He changed his name to Akhenaten in honor of the sun god Aten, built a new capital named after himself, and declared that Aten was the only god. His principal queen, Nefertiti, was a powerful influence during his reign. Later pharaohs destroyed Akhenaten's statues and removed his name from king lists.

⭐ Amarna capital during Akhenaten's reign

3   NEW KINGDOM 1570–1085 BCE
Ahmose of Thebes (r. 1549–1524) laid the foundations for the New Kingdom and took power after expelling the Hyksos from Lower Egypt in 1532 BCE. Under later pharaohs, Egypt expanded its territory across the Mediterranean and reached the Fourth Cataract to the south. Trade increased, and renewed prosperity allowed the rulers to construct enormous temples.

LOWER
EGYPT

Giza
Memphis
Kom Medinet Ghurab
Hanen-nesut

Serabit
el-Khadim
Timna

Wadi
Maghara

*Western
Desert*

Istabl
Antar
Bahariya

Akhetaten
(El-Amarna)   Ipu   (Akhmim)
Abydos
Karnak

5   REIGN OF RAMESSES II 1279–1213 BCE
In the 14th century BCE, Egypt lost some of its territory in Canaan to the Hittites of Anatolia, leading to decades of tension and sometimes warfare between the two peoples. The formidable ruler Ramesses II challenged Hittite power at the Battle of Kadesh, preventing further Hittite advances.

Legend:
- Region of control
- Region of contact
- Kingdom capital
- Temple
- → Campaign against Hyksos
- ···▶ Trade routes
- ⊚ Hyksos siege

Sahara

Dakhla

Armant   Thebes
Nekheb (el-Kab)

Kharga

Elephantine
First Cataract
Beit el-Wali

UPPER
EGYPT

Kurkur   Baki (Quban)
Gerf Hussein
El-Derr
Aksha
Second Cataract   Buhen
Semna   Kumma

✕ Battle   Hittite Empire

1570–1069 BCE The vast complex at Karnak in Thebes is expanded with temples to deities such as Amun-Re and Mut

Selima

NUBIA

WAWAT

Sedeinga
Soleb
Sesebi
Third Cataract
Tumbos
Fourth Cataract
Kawa
Napata
(Gebel Barkal)
Fifth Cataract

Nubian Desert

Red Sea
to Punt

1264–1244 BCE Abu Simbel temple is built to commemorate Ramesses' victory at the Battle of Kadesh

◁ **Queen Nefertiti**
The bust of Nefertiti, the Great Royal Wife of the Egyptian Pharaoh Akhenaten, is believed to have been crafted by the sculptor Thutmose c. 1345 BCE.

NEW KINGDOM
The expulsion of the Hyksos led to the reunification of Egypt, ushering in the New Kingdom in 1530 BCE. This was the third great era of Egyptian culture—a period of economic prosperity and cultural achievement in the region.

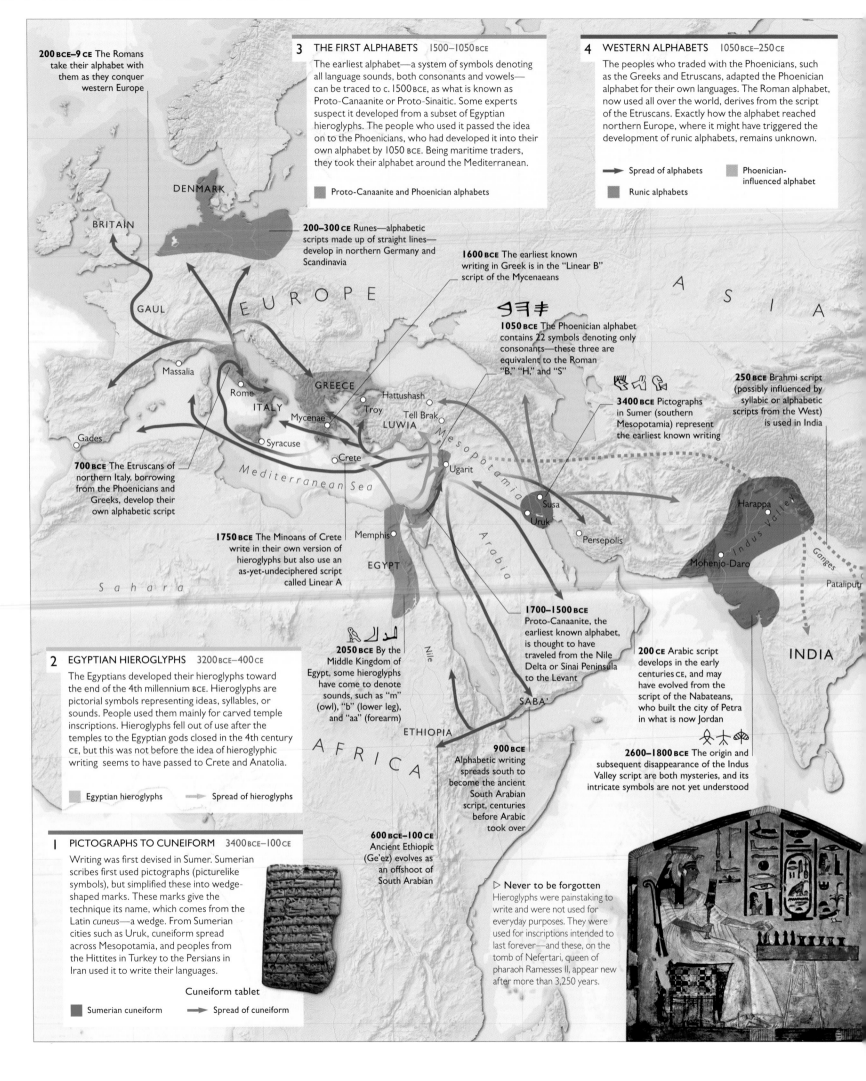

200 BCE–9 CE The Romans take their alphabet with them as they conquer western Europe

3 THE FIRST ALPHABETS 1500–1050 BCE

The earliest alphabet—a system of symbols denoting all language sounds, both consonants and vowels—can be traced to c. 1500 BCE, as what is known as Proto-Canaanite or Proto-Sinaitic. Some experts suspect it developed from a subset of Egyptian hieroglyphs. The people who used it passed the idea on to the Phoenicians, who had developed it into their own alphabet by 1050 BCE. Being maritime traders, they took their alphabet around the Mediterranean.

■ Proto-Canaanite and Phoenician alphabets

4 WESTERN ALPHABETS 1050 BCE–250 CE

The peoples who traded with the Phoenicians, such as the Greeks and Etruscans, adapted the Phoenician alphabet for their own languages. The Roman alphabet, now used all over the world, derives from the script of the Etruscans. Exactly how the alphabet reached northern Europe, where it might have triggered the development of runic alphabets, remains unknown.

➡ Spread of alphabets
■ Runic alphabets
■ Phoenician-influenced alphabet

200–300 CE Runes—alphabetic scripts made up of straight lines—develop in northern Germany and Scandinavia

1600 BCE The earliest known writing in Greek is in the "Linear B" script of the Mycenaeans

1050 BCE The Phoenician alphabet contains 22 symbols denoting only consonants—these three are equivalent to the Roman "B," "H," and "S"

3400 BCE Pictographs in Sumer (southern Mesopotamia) represent the earliest known writing

250 BCE Brahmi script (possibly influenced by syllabic or alphabetic scripts from the West) is used in India

700 BCE The Etruscans of northern Italy, borrowing from the Phoenicians and Greeks, develop their own alphabetic script

1750 BCE The Minoans of Crete write in their own version of hieroglyphs but also use an as-yet-undeciphered script called Linear A

1700–1500 BCE Proto-Canaanite, the earliest known alphabet, is thought to have traveled from the Nile Delta or Sinai Peninsula to the Levant

200 CE Arabic script develops in the early centuries CE, and may have evolved from the script of the Nabateans, who built the city of Petra in what is now Jordan

2050 BCE By the Middle Kingdom of Egypt, some hieroglyphs have come to denote sounds, such as "m" (owl), "b" (lower leg), and "aa" (forearm)

900 BCE Alphabetic writing spreads south to become the ancient South Arabian script, centuries before Arabic took over

2600–1800 BCE The origin and subsequent disappearance of the Indus Valley script are both mysteries, and its intricate symbols are not yet understood

2 EGYPTIAN HIEROGLYPHS 3200 BCE–400 CE

The Egyptians developed their hieroglyphs toward the end of the 4th millennium BCE. Hieroglyphs are pictorial symbols representing ideas, syllables, or sounds. People used them mainly for carved temple inscriptions. Hieroglyphs fell out of use after the temples to the Egyptian gods closed in the 4th century CE, but this was not before the idea of hieroglyphic writing seems to have passed to Crete and Anatolia.

■ Egyptian hieroglyphs ➡ Spread of hieroglyphs

600 BCE–100 CE Ancient Ethiopic (Ge'ez) evolves as an offshoot of South Arabian

1 PICTOGRAPHS TO CUNEIFORM 3400 BCE–100 CE

Writing was first devised in Sumer. Sumerian scribes first used pictographs (picturelike symbols), but simplified these into wedge-shaped marks. These marks give the technique its name, which comes from the Latin *cuneus*—a wedge. From Sumerian cities such as Uruk, cuneiform spread across Mesopotamia, and peoples from the Hittites in Turkey to the Persians in Iran used it to write their languages.

Cuneiform tablet

■ Sumerian cuneiform ➡ Spread of cuneiform

▷ **Never to be forgotten**
Hieroglyphs were painstaking to write and were not used for everyday purposes. They were used for inscriptions intended to last forever—and these, on the tomb of Nefertari, queen of pharaoh Ramesses II, appear new after more than 3,250 years.

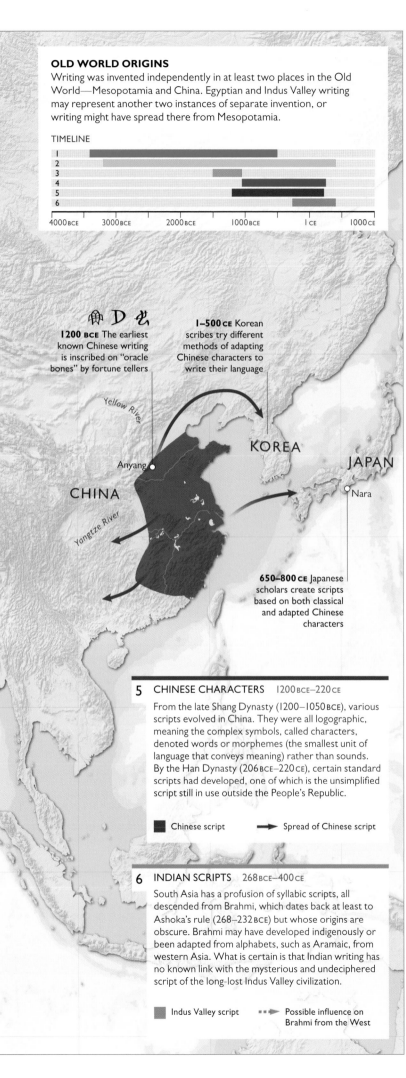

OLD WORLD ORIGINS

Writing was invented independently in at least two places in the Old World—Mesopotamia and China. Egyptian and Indus Valley writing may represent another two instances of separate invention, or writing might have spread there from Mesopotamia.

TIMELINE

	4000 BCE	3000 BCE	2000 BCE	1000 BCE	1 CE	1000 CE
1						
2						
3						
4						
5						
6						

1200 BCE The earliest known Chinese writing is inscribed on "oracle bones" by fortune tellers

1–500 CE Korean scribes try different methods of adapting Chinese characters to write their language

Yellow River

KOREA

Anyang

JAPAN

CHINA

Nara

Yangtze River

650–800 CE Japanese scholars create scripts based on both classical and adapted Chinese characters

5 CHINESE CHARACTERS 1200 BCE–220 CE

From the late Shang Dynasty (1200–1050 BCE), various scripts evolved in China. They were all logographic, meaning the complex symbols, called characters, denoted words or morphemes (the smallest unit of language that conveys meaning) rather than sounds. By the Han Dynasty (206 BCE–220 CE), certain standard scripts had developed, one of which is the unsimplified script still in use outside the People's Republic.

■ Chinese script   → Spread of Chinese script

6 INDIAN SCRIPTS 268 BCE–400 CE

South Asia has a profusion of syllabic scripts, all descended from Brahmi, which dates back at least to Ashoka's rule (268–232 BCE) but whose origins are obscure. Brahmi may have developed indigenously or been adapted from alphabets, such as Aramaic, from western Asia. What is certain is that Indian writing has no known link with the mysterious and undeciphered script of the long-lost Indus Valley civilization.

■ Indus Valley script   ▪▪▶ Possible influence on Brahmi from the West

THE FIRST WRITING

Writing developed first in c. 3400 BCE in western Asia, but also independently in China, Mesoamerica, and possibly the Indus Valley. From the start, symbols represented spoken language in different ways—either as words and ideas, the language's sounds, or a mixture of both.

By the 4th millennium BCE, cities had developed in Egypt, China, the Indus Valley, and Mesopotamia. The societies that built these cities traded on a large scale and had complex, organized religions. Both of these developments encouraged literacy—for writing accounts and goods traded or for recording calendars and sacred lore.

The earliest writing—in Mesopotamia—began as pictures scratched on damp clay tablets that were then baked in the sun to create a permanent document. Slowly, these evolved into "cuneiform" symbols made of wedges. Many surviving cuneiform tablets list goods or contain tax records, although there are also religious and literary works written with the technique. Around the same time, the Egyptians developed their hieroglyphs and later, the Chinese evolved their written characters, both of which were used for religious purposes initially. Alphabetic scripts, which originated in Sinai or the Levant, caught on widely as the Phoenicians disseminated their version. Alphabets needed only 20–30 symbols, as opposed to the hundreds used in syllabic scripts or the thousands in Chinese.

"Do not answer back against your father."

FROM THE SUMERIAN *INSTRUCTIONS OF SHURUPPAK*—PERHAPS THE WORLD'S EARLIEST SURVIVING LITERATURE, c. 2600 BCE

MESOAMERICAN SCRIPTS
WRITING OF THE OLMECS, ZAPOTECS, AND MAYA

Civilizations in Mesoamerica invented their own writing systems, but they did not spread beyond the region. Inscriptions date back to the mysterious Cascajal Block, possibly carved by Olmecs around 800 BCE. The Zapotecs used a pictographic script from at least 400 BCE and were followed by the Maya, whose intricate symbols, or glyphs (right), combined logograms (denoting ideas) and syllabic script. Maya glyphs came into use c. 300 BCE and remained current until the Spanish conquest (see pp.152–153).

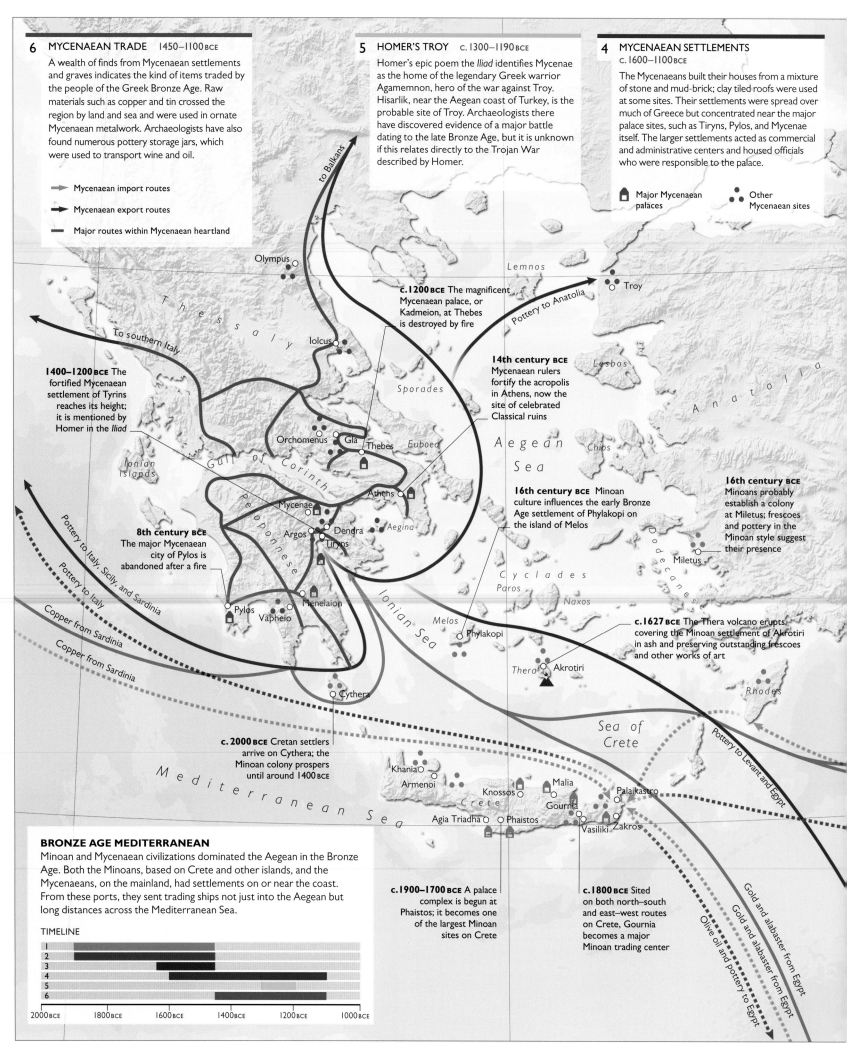

6 MYCENAEAN TRADE 1450–1100 BCE

A wealth of finds from Mycenaean settlements and graves indicates the kind of items traded by the people of the Greek Bronze Age. Raw materials such as copper and tin crossed the region by land and sea and were used in ornate Mycenaean metalwork. Archaeologists have also found numerous pottery storage jars, which were used to transport wine and oil.

→ Mycenaean import routes

→ Mycenaean export routes

— Major routes within Mycenaean heartland

5 HOMER'S TROY c.1300–1190 BCE

Homer's epic poem the *Iliad* identifies Mycenae as the home of the legendary Greek warrior Agamemnon, hero of the war against Troy. Hisarlik, near the Aegean coast of Turkey, is the probable site of Troy. Archaeologists there have discovered evidence of a major battle dating to the late Bronze Age, but it is unknown if this relates directly to the Trojan War described by Homer.

4 MYCENAEAN SETTLEMENTS c.1600–1100 BCE

The Mycenaeans built their houses from a mixture of stone and mud-brick; clay tiled roofs were used at some sites. Their settlements were spread over much of Greece but concentrated near the major palace sites, such as Tiryns, Pylos, and Mycenae itself. The larger settlements acted as commercial and administrative centers and housed officials who were responsible to the palace.

🏛 Major Mycenaean palaces

⋮ Other Mycenaean sites

c.1200 BCE The magnificent Mycenaean palace, or Kadmeion, at Thebes is destroyed by fire

14th century BCE Mycenaean rulers fortify the acropolis in Athens, now the site of celebrated Classical ruins

16th century BCE Minoan culture influences the early Bronze Age settlement of Phylakopi on the island of Melos

16th century BCE Minoans probably establish a colony at Miletus; frescoes and pottery in the Minoan style suggest their presence

1400–1200 BCE The fortified Mycenaean settlement of Tyrins reaches its height; it is mentioned by Homer in the *Iliad*

8th century BCE The major Mycenaean city of Pylos is abandoned after a fire

c.1627 BCE The Thera volcano erupts, covering the Minoan settlement of Akrotiri in ash and preserving outstanding frescoes and other works of art

c.2000 BCE Cretan settlers arrive on Cythera; the Minoan colony prospers until around 1400 BCE

To southern Italy

Pottery to Italy, Sicily, and Sardinia

Pottery to Italy

Copper from Sardinia

Copper from Sardinia

to Balkans

Pottery to Anatolia

Pottery to Levant and Egypt

Gold and alabaster from Egypt

Gold and alabaster from Egypt

Olive oil and pottery to Egypt

Olympus, Iolcus, Orchomenus, Gla, Thebes, Athens, Mycenae, Argos, Dendra, Tiryns, Pylos, Vapheio, Menelaion, Cythera, Melos, Phylakopi, Thera, Akrotiri, Khania, Armenoi, Knossos, Agia Triadha, Phaistos, Malia, Gournia, Vasiliki, Zakros, Palaikastro, Troy, Miletus

Thessaly, Sporades, Lemnos, Lesbos, Chios, Anatolia, Aegean Sea, Euboea, Aegina, Ionian Islands, Gulf of Corinth, Peloponnese, Ionian Sea, Cyclades, Paros, Naxos, Dodecanese, Rhodes, Sea of Crete, Mediterranean Sea, Crete

BRONZE AGE MEDITERRANEAN

Minoan and Mycenaean civilizations dominated the Aegean in the Bronze Age. Both the Minoans, based on Crete and other islands, and the Mycenaeans, on the mainland, had settlements on or near the coast. From these ports, they sent trading ships not just into the Aegean but long distances across the Mediterranean Sea.

c.1900–1700 BCE A palace complex is begun at Phaistos; it becomes one of the largest Minoan sites on Crete

c.1800 BCE Sited on both north–south and east–west routes on Crete, Gournia becomes a major Minoan trading center

TIMELINE

1	
2	
3	
4	
5	
6	

2000 BCE — 1800 BCE — 1600 BCE — 1400 BCE — 1200 BCE — 1000 BCE

*Black
Sea*

▷ **Bull's head vessel**
This ceremonial vessel from
c. 1400 BCE was found at the Palace
of Knossos. The Minoans venerated
the bull, considering it a symbol of man's
dominion over nature.

3 THE DECLINE OF MINOAN CIVILIZATION
c. 1640–1450 BCE

The reason for the decline of Minoan culture is unknown,
but it may be connected to the eruption of the volcano
on Thera in the middle of the 2nd millennium BCE. This
destroyed the Minoan settlement of Akrotiri and may have
disrupted the Minoan economy, allowing the Mycenaeans to
take Minoan trade routes and settlements, becoming the
dominant power in the area.

🌋 Volcanic eruption

2 MINOAN TRADE AND EXPANSION
c. 1900–1450 BCE

The Minoans traded widely, visiting other Greek islands
and settling on Rhodes, Thera (modern Santorini), Melos, and
Cythera. They traded with Cyprus, Egypt, and Syria (importing
metals such as copper, tin, and gold, as well as ivory), and
their influence spread as far as the Levant. The palace site
of Zakros was probably a center for trade.

▪▪▶ Minoan import   ▪▪▶ Minoan export
routes   routes

Ivory, tin from Syria

Copper to Crete

Copper to Mycenae

Cyprus

Olive oil and cloth to Tyre

1 MINOAN PALACES c. 1900–1450 BCE

These complex buildings, the largest of which was
at Knossos, seem to have combined the roles of palace,
administrative center, warehouse, and shrine. Constructed
of several stories supported by wooden tapering columns,
they were adorned with wall paintings. Some rooms,
decorated with bulls' horns and featuring altarlike
structures, almost certainly had some ceremonial use.

🏛 Minoan major palaces   ⦙ Other Minoan sites

MINOANS AND MYCENAEANS

During the Bronze Age, first the Minoan and then the
Mycenaean cultures dominated Greece and the Aegean.
These peoples developed a range of skills—such as
metalworking, architecture, and literacy—that laid the
foundations for the later Classical civilization of Greece.

The Minoan culture—considered by some to be the first European
civilization—flourished on Crete in the 2nd millennium BCE. Many
mysteries still surround the Minoans; scholars have been unable to
decipher their writing, so do not know their exact dates, or even
what they called themselves—the word "Minoan" is a modern term
of convenience. But they are known to have been highly influential
in trading across the Mediterranean, leaving inscriptions at several
places on the Greek mainland, as well as on some islands in the
Aegean. Minoan civilization was centered on several large, elegantly
decorated Cretan palaces that were not fortified, suggesting they were
a peaceful people.

From the mid-15th century BCE, the Mycenaeans—based on
mainland Greece—became the dominant power. They were a
trading people, exchanging goods with mainland Italy, Sicily, and
Sardinia. They also wielded military power, as seen by their fortified
palaces, and impressive weaponry and armor. Their script, known as
Linear B (probably derived from Cretan Linear A) has been
deciphered and was used to write an early form of Greek.

The Mycenaeans created several independent states in mainland
Greece with settlements on many of the islands. Each state centered
on a palace, and most were capable of major engineering projects,
such as stone fortifications, harbors, dams, and roads. Disputes
between the states may have contributed to the decline of the
Mycenaean civilization after about 1100 BCE.

KNOSSOS
EUROPE'S OLDEST CITY

At its height, Minoan Knossos was a
large city of 10,000–100,000 people.
At its heart was the palace complex,
which had 1,300 rooms covering some
6 acres (2.4 hectares). As well as large,
beautifully decorated residential or
ceremonial rooms, there were many
rooms set aside for storage. These
rooms contained hundreds of large
jars for oil, grain, or other foods.
Grain mills also formed part of the
palace complex.

Fresco fragment
The walls of the palace at Knossos were
decorated with images of animals,
mythological creatures, and people.

BRONZE AGE CHINA

Chinese culture began to take on its distinctive form in the Bronze Age, from about 1600 BCE onward, with the development of writing during the Shang Dynasty and its successor, the Zhou. Politically, China was still a collection of separate states, with one or more of the states taking a leading role at different times.

Most historians date the Bronze Age in China to c. 2000–c. 770 BCE, although the widespread use of bronze continued for centuries. The period coincides with the beginnings of literacy in China and with the rule of two influential dynasties, the Shang (c. 1600–1027 BCE) and the Zhou (1046–256 BCE).

The Shang controlled much of northern China, creating a feudal system with a core state and a number of vassal states. Its rulers cemented their power using rituals such as ancestor worship and divination using "oracle bones" (bones incised with written messages). The Shang moved their capital city several times, the last and largest being at Anyang, where archaeologists have uncovered a royal tomb containing bronze artifacts and oracle bones. They extended their influence through trade with northern and central Chinese neighbors, and with people of the steppes to the west.

Around the 11th century BCE, Ji Chang of the Zhou—a people from the Shang's western border—led a rebellion, and the Shang were conquered. The Zhou developed systems of coinage, and writing evolved into something closer to the modern Chinese script. Two of the most influential philosophers of all time, Confucius and Laozi, were active under the Zhou Dynasty.

SHANG CHINA

Before the Shang, the Yellow River valley was occupied by sophisticated cultures for centuries. The region became the Shang's heartland, where they made vassals of a number of local states.

KEY
● Shang city ••• Trade route ⇨ Main Shang campaign

TIMELINE

1						
2						
3						
4						

2200BCE   2000   1800   1600   1400   1200   1000

◁ **Shang bronze work**
This owl-shaped vessel exemplifies the exquisite patterns with which Shang metalworkers decorated their products; these included tableware, such as food and drinking vessels.

2nd millennium BCE
A western trade route links China with central Asia; it is a forerunner of the Silk Road between eastern and western Asia

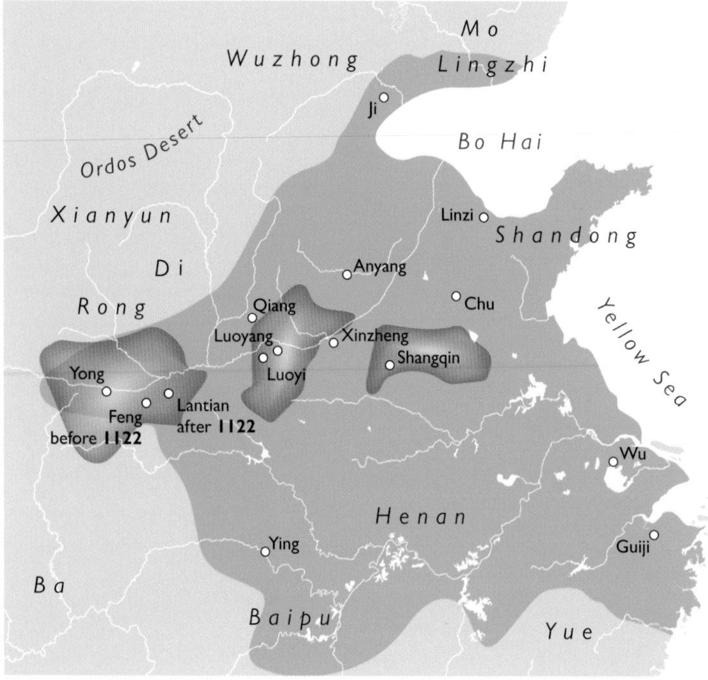

ZHOU CHINA

Zhou began as a vassal state in the far west of the Shang Empire. Toward the end of the Shang period, the Zhou challenged their overlords, moving eastward and establishing strongholds along the Yellow River before removing the Shang rulers by 1046 BCE. By 1000 BCE, their influence was felt across most of China, including the Shang's neighboring peoples, the Baipu, and encompassed the whole area to which urban civilization had spread.

KEY

▢ Distribution of urban civilization by c. 1000 BCE

▬ Zhou strongholds

○ Zhou capitals

BEFORE THE SHANG c. 2070–1600 BCE

A series of neolithic cultures predate the Shang in China—archaeologists have, for example, revealed the remains of the Longshan culture in the Yellow River valley and the Yueshi culture in the Shandong region. Other sites, such as Erlitou with its impressive buildings, tombs, and paved roads, point to more sophisticated cultures, such as the Xia Dynasty (who are thought to have existed from 2070 BCE).

★ Possible Xia capital

▬ Longshan culture, c. 3000–2000 BCE

▬ Yueshi culture, c. 1900–1500 BCE

Map labels: Wuzhong, Mo, Lingzhi, Ji, Bo Hai, Ordos Desert, Xianyun, Di, Rong, Linzi, Shandong, Anyang, Qiang, Chu, Luoyang, Xinzheng, Yong, Luoyi, Shangqin, Feng before 1122, Lantian after 1122, Yellow Sea, Wu, Henan, Ying, Guiji, Ba, Baipu, Yue, Yellow River

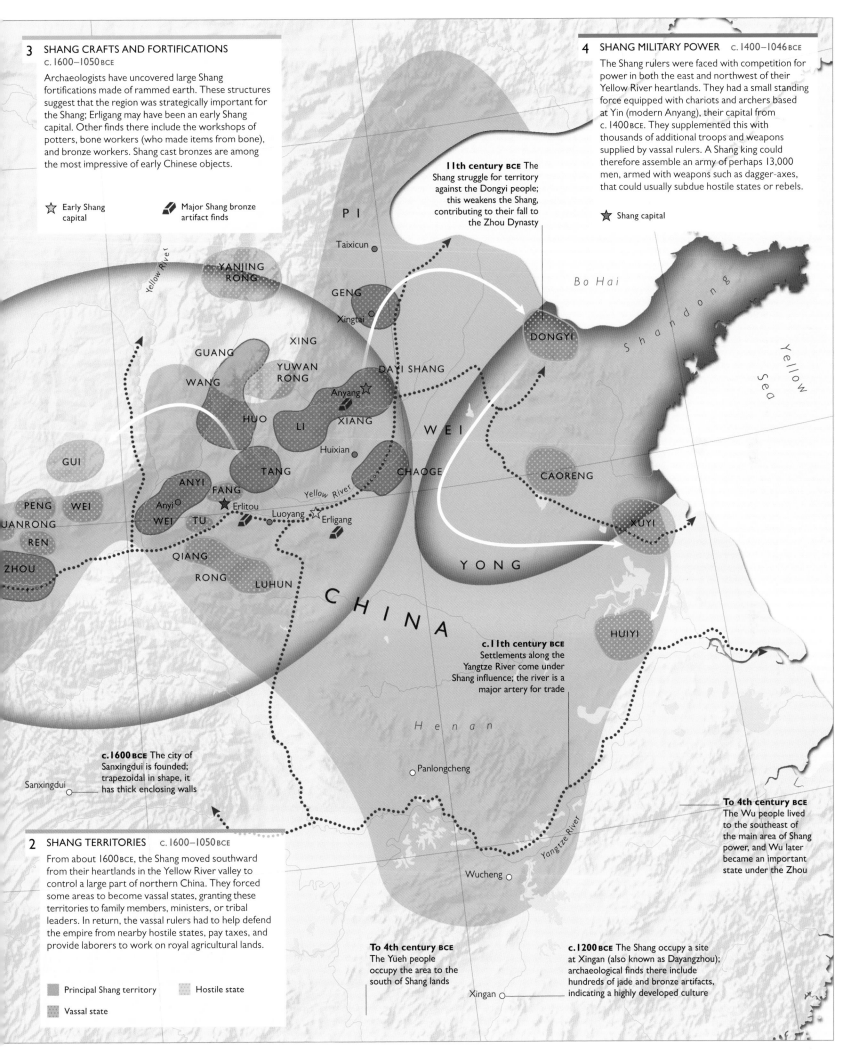

3 SHANG CRAFTS AND FORTIFICATIONS
c. 1600–1050 BCE

Archaeologists have uncovered large Shang fortifications made of rammed earth. These structures suggest that the region was strategically important for the Shang; Erligang may have been an early Shang capital. Other finds there include the workshops of potters, bone workers (who made items from bone), and bronze workers. Shang cast bronzes are among the most impressive of early Chinese objects.

☆ Early Shang capital

◢ Major Shang bronze artifact finds

4 SHANG MILITARY POWER c. 1400–1046 BCE

The Shang rulers were faced with competition for power in both the east and northwest of their Yellow River heartlands. They had a small standing force equipped with chariots and archers based at Yin (modern Anyang), their capital from c. 1400 BCE. They supplemented this with thousands of additional troops and weapons supplied by vassal rulers. A Shang king could therefore assemble an army of perhaps 13,000 men, armed with weapons such as dagger-axes, that could usually subdue hostile states or rebels.

★ Shang capital

11th century BCE The Shang struggle for territory against the Dongyi people; this weakens the Shang, contributing to their fall to the Zhou Dynasty

c. 11th century BCE Settlements along the Yangtze River come under Shang influence; the river is a major artery for trade

c. 1600 BCE The city of Sanxingdui is founded; trapezoidal in shape, it has thick enclosing walls

To 4th century BCE The Wu people lived to the southeast of the main area of Shang power, and Wu later became an important state under the Zhou

2 SHANG TERRITORIES c. 1600–1050 BCE

From about 1600 BCE, the Shang moved southward from their heartlands in the Yellow River valley to control a large part of northern China. They forced some areas to become vassal states, granting these territories to family members, ministers, or tribal leaders. In return, the vassal rulers had to help defend the empire from nearby hostile states, pay taxes, and provide laborers to work on royal agricultural lands.

▨ Principal Shang territory

▨ Vassal state

▨ Hostile state

To 4th century BCE The Yüeh people occupy the area to the south of Shang lands

c. 1200 BCE The Shang occupy a site at Xingan (also known as Dayangzhou); archaeological finds there include hundreds of jade and bronze artifacts, indicating a highly developed culture

Map labels: PI, Taixicun, YANJING RONG, GENG, Xingtai, XING, GUANG, WANG, YUWAN RONG, DAYI SHANG, Anyang, HUO, LI, XIANG, Huixian, GUI, TANG, CHAOGE, WEI, DONGYI, Bo Hai, Shandong, Yellow Sea, CAORENG, XUYI, YONG, HUIYI, ANYI, FANG, Anyi, WEI, TU, Erlitou, Luoyang, Erligang, QIANG, RONG, LUHUN, ZHOU, PENG, WEI, UANRONG, REN, CHINA, Henan, Panlongcheng, Wucheng, Xingan, Sanxingdui, Yangtze River, Yellow River

BRONZE AGE COLLAPSE

Between 1225 and 1175 BCE, several Bronze Age societies of the eastern Mediterranean collapsed. Citadels across the region were sacked by unknown enemies, and the Hittite Empire and Mycenaean kingdoms were destroyed.

△ **Last writing**
This fire-blackened tablet is one of the last documents of the Mycenaean civilization. It is written in an early Greek script called Linear B.

The first victim was the Hittite Empire, whose capital, Hattusa, was sacked around 1200 BCE. Meanwhile, in Greece, the Mycenaeans, fearing attack from the sea, were fortifying their palaces. Despite all preparations, the palaces were destroyed by fire. Egypt was also attacked, by a coalition from the Aegean they referred to as the "Sea Peoples." Pharaoh Ramesses III describes defeating the invaders in the 1170s. Driven out of Egypt, the Sea Peoples went on to conquer and settle the coast of the Levant.

The cause of the collapse remains unclear. It is unlikely that the Sea Peoples were solely responsible. There is evidence that climate change was the underlying cause of a cascade of disintegration. The period was exceptionally dry, and drought could have led to famine, weakening the palace economies and making them vulnerable to attack. Other factors that might have contributed to the collapse include earthquakes and internal rebellions. As cities fell, their populations were displaced and began to migrate, in turn unsettling other kingdoms. After the collapse, trade in bronze, which had previously been conducted on a large scale, was disrupted, and people turned increasingly to iron.

THE FALL OF BRONZE AGE CITIES

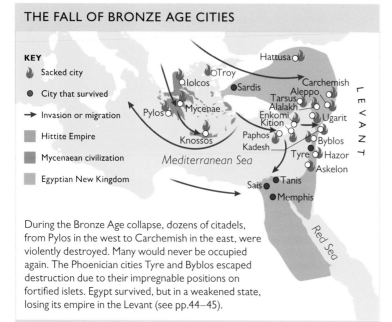

KEY
- Sacked city
- City that survived
- → Invasion or migration
- Hittite Empire
- Mycenaean civilization
- Egyptian New Kingdom

Hattusa · Troy · Iolcos · Sardis · Carchemish · Aleppo · Tarsus · Alalakh · Mycenae · Pylos · Enkomi · Kition · Ugarit · Knossos · Paphos · Byblos · Kadesh · Tyre · Hazor · Askelon · Sais · Tanis · Memphis · Mediterranean Sea · Red Sea · LEVANT

During the Bronze Age collapse, dozens of citadels, from Pylos in the west to Carchemish in the east, were violently destroyed. Many would never be occupied again. The Phoenician cities Tyre and Byblos escaped destruction due to their impregnable positions on fortified islets. Egypt survived, but in a weakened state, losing its empire in the Levant (see pp.44–45).

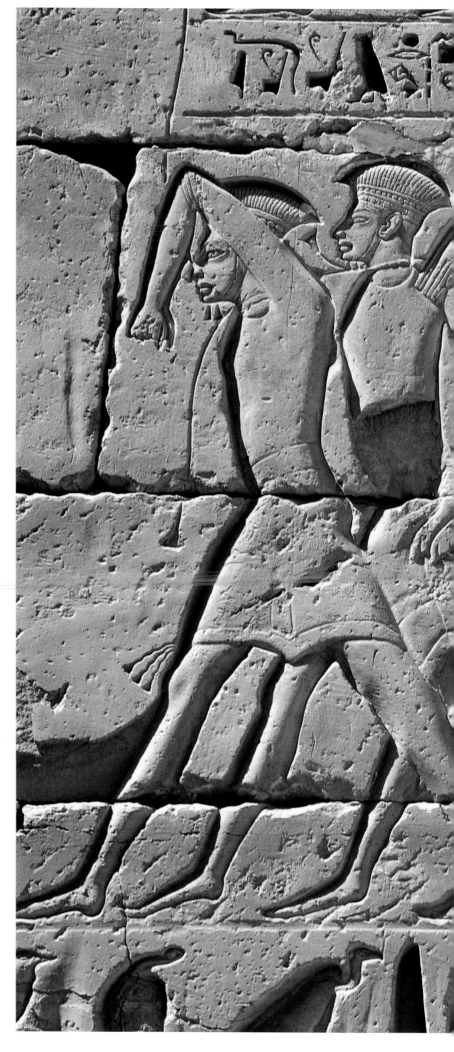

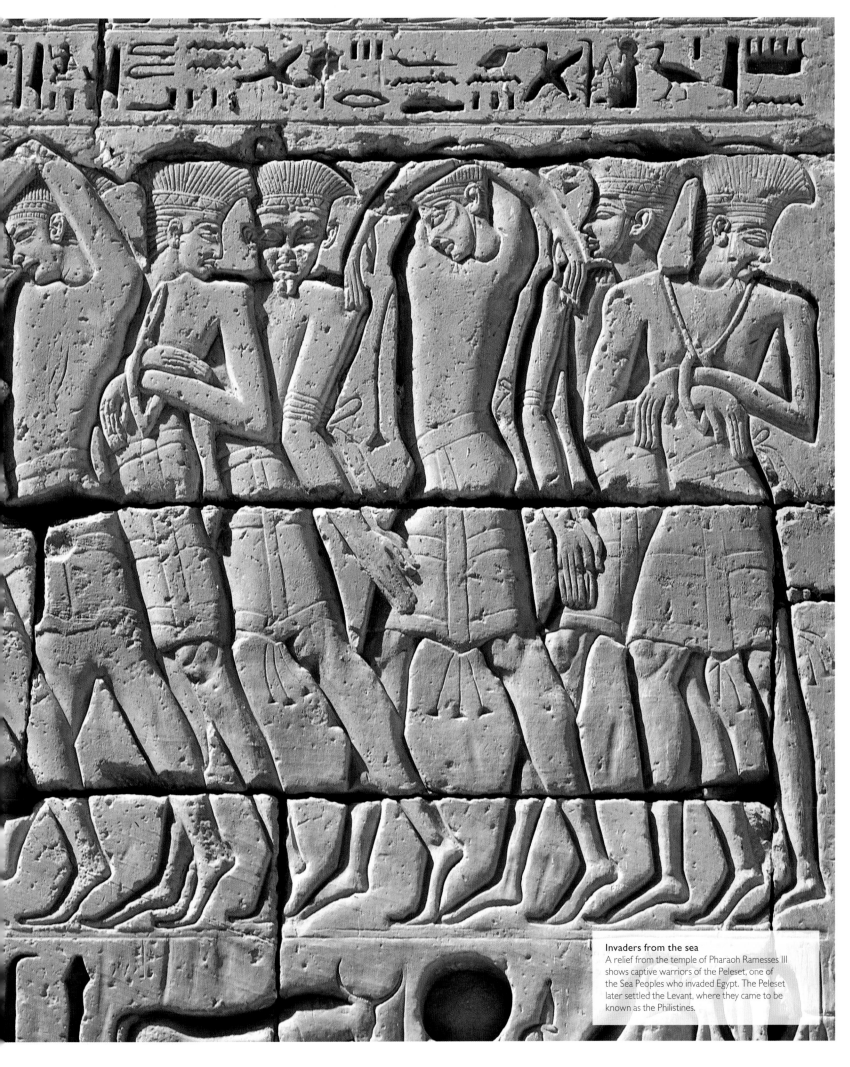

Invaders from the sea
A relief from the temple of Pharaoh Ramesses III shows captive warriors of the Peleset, one of the Sea Peoples who invaded Egypt. The Peleset later settled the Levant, where they came to be known as the Philistines.

THE ANCIENT LEVANT

The Levant is the fertile land to the east of the Mediterranean, called Canaan in the Hebrew Bible. It was dominated by powerful neighbors, but the resistance to Rome of one group of its people— the Jews—resulted in their expulsion, accelerating their diaspora across Asia and Europe.

The Levant was fought over by the great powers of the Bronze Age (see pp.42–43), including Egypt, the Hittites, and the old Assyrian state. It was full of rich and important cities such as Megiddo and Jericho when the biblical kingdom of Israel came into existence in around 1020 BCE. However, the region had been in decline for centuries, and its powerful neighbors were weak. On the coast, ports grew into city-states that became known as "Phoenician" in the Greek world (see pp.54–57). Phoenicians went on to form a network of trading colonies that eventually controlled most of the Mediterranean. Settlers on the coast to the south of the Phoenicians became known as Philistines. Meanwhile, Israel split into two kingdoms named Israel and Judah and spent centuries under the domination of first Assyria, then Babylon, then Persia.

By the time of the New Testament of the Bible, the former Hebrew kingdoms had become the Roman vassal state of Judea, and the teachings of Jesus Christ were spreading through the Roman Empire (see pp.86–87). Rebellions against Rome, including the Great Jewish Revolt (66–74 CE) and the Bar Kokhba Revolt (132–135 CE) then led to the destruction of Jerusalem, the dispersion of the Jewish people (now named Jews after Judah), and the merging of Judea with its neighbors to make a new Roman province called Syria Palaestina, after the Philistines.

MASADA
LAST BASTION OF JEWISH REVOLT

Herod the Great built a fortified palace at this spectacular mountaintop fortress in the desert, and it was here that the Zealots of the Great Jewish Revolt took their last stand against the Romans. After the Roman armies laid siege to Masada for 6 months, Jewish historians record that they built a siege ramp and set fire to the inner defensive walls. The 900 Jews inside reportedly killed themselves to avoid slavery.

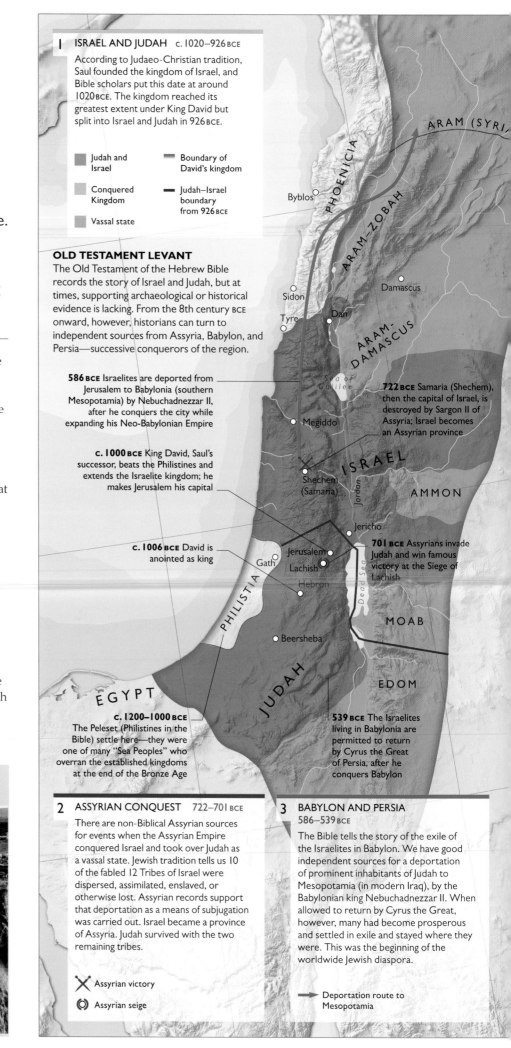

1 | ISRAEL AND JUDAH c. 1020–926 BCE

According to Judaeo-Christian tradition, Saul founded the kingdom of Israel, and Bible scholars put this date at around 1020 BCE. The kingdom reached its greatest extent under King David but split into Israel and Judah in 926 BCE.

- Judah and Israel
- Conquered Kingdom
- Vassal state
- Boundary of David's kingdom
- Judah–Israel boundary from 926 BCE

OLD TESTAMENT LEVANT

The Old Testament of the Hebrew Bible records the story of Israel and Judah, but at times, supporting archaeological or historical evidence is lacking. From the 8th century BCE onward, however, historians can turn to independent sources from Assyria, Babylon, and Persia—successive conquerors of the region.

586 BCE Israelites are deported from Jerusalem to Babylonia (southern Mesopotamia) by Nebuchadnezzar II, after he conquers the city while expanding his Neo-Babylonian Empire

c. 1000 BCE King David, Saul's successor, beats the Philistines and extends the Israelite kingdom; he makes Jerusalem his capital

c. 1006 BCE David is anointed as king

c. 1200–1000 BCE The Peleset (Philistines in the Bible) settle here—they were one of many "Sea Peoples" who overran the established kingdoms at the end of the Bronze Age

722 BCE Samaria (Shechem), then the capital of Israel, is destroyed by Sargon II of Assyria; Israel becomes an Assyrian province

701 BCE Assyrians invade Judah and win famous victory at the Siege of Lachish

539 BCE The Israelites living in Babylonia are permitted to return by Cyrus the Great of Persia, after he conquers Babylon

Map labels: ARAM (SYRIA), PHOENICIA, ARAM-ZOBAH, Byblos, Damascus, ARAM-DAMASCUS, Sidon, Tyre, Dan, Sea of Galilee, Megiddo, ISRAEL, Jordan, Shechem (Samaria), AMMON, Jericho, Gath, Jerusalem, Lachish, Hebron, Dead Sea, MOAB, PHILISTIA, Beersheba, JUDAH, EGYPT, EDOM

2 | ASSYRIAN CONQUEST 722–701 BCE

There are non-Biblical Assyrian sources for events when the Assyrian Empire conquered Israel and took over Judah as a vassal state. Jewish tradition tells us 10 of the fabled 12 Tribes of Israel were dispersed, assimilated, enslaved, or otherwise lost. Assyrian records support that deportation as a means of subjugation was carried out. Israel became a province of Assyria. Judah survived with the two remaining tribes.

- ✕ Assyrian victory
- ◎ Assyrian siege

3 | BABYLON AND PERSIA 586–539 BCE

The Bible tells the story of the exile of the Israelites in Babylon. We have good independent sources for a deportation of prominent inhabitants of Judah to Mesopotamia (in modern Iraq), by the Babylonian king Nebuchadnezzar II. When allowed to return by Cyrus the Great, however, many had become prosperous and settled in exile and stayed where they were. This was the beginning of the worldwide Jewish diaspora.

→ Deportation route to Mesopotamia

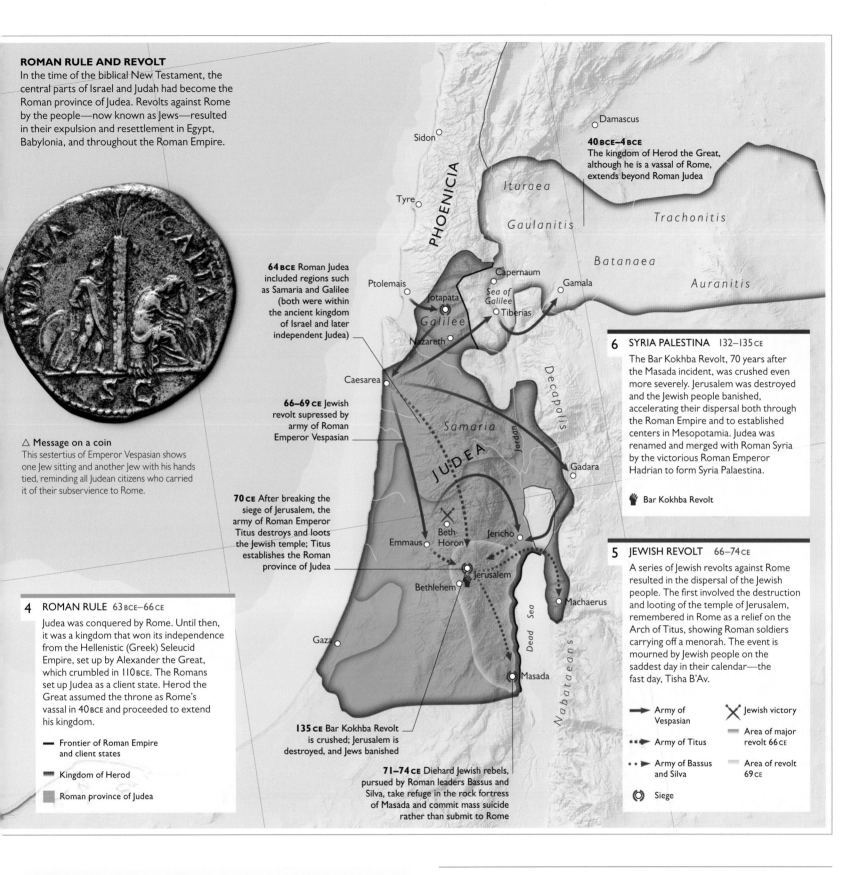

ROMAN RULE AND REVOLT
In the time of the biblical New Testament, the central parts of Israel and Judah had become the Roman province of Judea. Revolts against Rome by the people—now known as Jews—resulted in their expulsion and resettlement in Egypt, Babylonia, and throughout the Roman Empire.

△ **Message on a coin**
This sestertius of Emperor Vespasian shows one Jew sitting and another Jew with his hands tied, reminding all Judean citizens who carried it of their subservience to Rome.

64 BCE Roman Judea included regions such as Samaria and Galilee (both were within the ancient kingdom of Israel and later independent Judea)

66–69 CE Jewish revolt supressed by army of Roman Emperor Vespasian

70 CE After breaking the siege of Jerusalem, the army of Roman Emperor Titus destroys and loots the Jewish temple; Titus establishes the Roman province of Judea

4 ROMAN RULE 63 BCE–66 CE
Judea was conquered by Rome. Until then, it was a kingdom that won its independence from the Hellenistic (Greek) Seleucid Empire, set up by Alexander the Great, which crumbled in 110 BCE. The Romans set up Judea as a client state. Herod the Great assumed the throne as Rome's vassal in 40 BCE and proceeded to extend his kingdom.

— Frontier of Roman Empire and client states
▬ Kingdom of Herod
▬ Roman province of Judea

135 CE Bar Kokhba Revolt is crushed; Jerusalem is destroyed, and Jews banished

71–74 CE Diehard Jewish rebels, pursued by Roman leaders Bassus and Silva, take refuge in the rock fortress of Masada and commit mass suicide rather than submit to Rome

40 BCE–4 BCE The kingdom of Herod the Great, although he is a vassal of Rome, extends beyond Roman Judea

6 SYRIA PALESTINA 132–135 CE
The Bar Kokhba Revolt, 70 years after the Masada incident, was crushed even more severely. Jerusalem was destroyed and the Jewish people banished, accelerating their dispersal both through the Roman Empire and to established centers in Mesopotamia. Judea was renamed and merged with Roman Syria by the victorious Roman Emperor Hadrian to form Syria Palaestina.

✊ Bar Kokhba Revolt

5 JEWISH REVOLT 66–74 CE
A series of Jewish revolts against Rome resulted in the dispersal of the Jewish people. The first involved the destruction and looting of the temple of Jerusalem, remembered in Rome as a relief on the Arch of Titus, showing Roman soldiers carrying off a menorah. The event is mourned by Jewish people on the saddest day in their calendar—the fast day, Tisha B'Av.

➡ Army of Vespasian
✕ Jewish victory
▪▪▶ Army of Titus
▬ Area of major revolt 66 CE
• •▶ Army of Bassus and Silva
▬ Area of revolt 69 CE
◎ Siege

THE LEVANT
The narrow strip of land beside the eastern Mediterranean features in the Old Testament and the New Testament of the Hebrew Bible but also in the records of powerful neighbors, such as Egyptians, Assyrians, Persians, and Romans.

TIMELINE

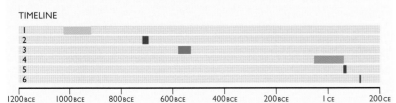

"I protest openly that I do not go over to the Romans as a deserter of the Jews, but as a minister from thee."

THE IRON AGE

When Bronze Age people learned how to smelt iron, they sparked off a technological revolution. Exactly where and why they first turned from bronze to iron is a mystery. The most likely explanation is that when supplies of tin and copper, the two constituents of bronze, ran short, necessity became the mother of invention.

▽ **Ruling the underworld**
A relief cut into the rocks of a temple in Hattusa—the ancient capital of the Hittites, in modern Turkey—depicts 12 deities of the underworld. The Hittites worshipped more than 1,000 deities.

Until recently, archaeological evidence suggested that ironworking first started in central Anatolia, Turkey, some time between 2000 and 1300 BCE, with the Hittites—an ancient Anatolian people—being credited with pioneering the new technology of iron smelting (heating iron ore to extract the metal). It was believed that the Hittites began to forge iron artifacts as early as the 18th century BCE and

▷ **Signs of iron in Europe**
Dating from 750–450 BCE, this iron dagger was found in one of the thousand graves discovered at Hallstatt (modern Austria), the hub of central Europe's first Iron Age culture.

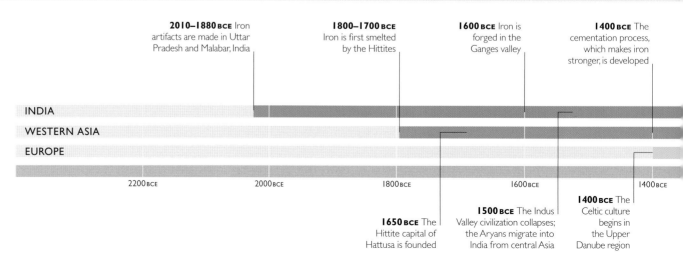

that their iron weapons—including swords, battleaxes, spear points, and arrowheads—gave them a massive military advantage over their neighbors. Following the collapse of their empire, their knowledge spread through the Middle East and from there to Greece and the Aegean region, eventually reaching central and western Europe. Modern archaeological research, however, has challenged this picture. It is now thought that Indian metalsmiths may have discovered how to forge iron at roughly the same time as the Hittites, or even earlier.

Early ironsmiths

Archaeological excavations of megalithic burial sites in Uttar Pradesh in northern India and Malabar in the south have uncovered iron artifacts dating from 2012 BCE and 1882 BCE. Other excavations in the Ganges valley have uncovered iron artifacts dating from around the same time that the Hittites were forging their first iron implements, while iron daggers found at sites in Hyderabad in southern India are thought to date from 2400–2000 BCE. In Europe, ironworking began with the Greeks, possibly as early as 1050 BCE. A few hundred years later, the Celts (the collective name for a variety of tribes in

THE BEGINNINGS OF THE IRON AGE

The Iron Age began almost 4,000 years ago, starting independently in central Anatolia (in modern Turkey) and India. Later, the knowledge of iron smelting and forging spread into central Europe via Greece and then through the rest of the continent. Iron, which was more widely available than the tin and copper needed to make bronze, replaced bronze for use in almost all utilitarian objects, from weapons to plows to utensils.

2010–1880 BCE Iron artifacts are made in Uttar Pradesh and Malabar, India

1800–1700 BCE Iron is first smelted by the Hittites

1600 BCE Iron is forged in the Ganges valley

1400 BCE The cementation process, which makes iron stronger, is developed

INDIA					
WESTERN ASIA					
EUROPE					
	2200 BCE	2000 BCE	1800 BCE	1600 BCE	1400 BCE

1650 BCE The Hittite capital of Hattusa is founded

1500 BCE The Indus Valley civilization collapses; the Aryans migrate into India from central Asia

1400 BCE The Celtic culture begins in the Upper Danube region

◁ **The versatile Celts**
The Celts were skilled at working various metals, not just iron. Discovered in a peat bog near Gundestrup, Denmark, in 1891, this cauldron was made from silver between the 2nd and 1st centuries BCE.

Europe) became masters of the craft.

The oldest archaeological evidence demonstrating their skill at forging iron and other metals comes from Hallstatt, near Salzburg in Austria. Tomb excavations there, which started as early as the mid-19th century, uncovered a rich treasury of grave goods, including iron swords dating from around 700 BCE. Why the culture centered around Hallstatt collapsed is uncertain.

The Hallstatt culture was replaced by the La Tène culture, which appeared in the mid-5th century BCE. Excavations have revealed more than 2,500 iron swords with decorated scabbards, as well as other metalwork items. The La Tène culture was artistically prolific. Its influence spread through much of western Europe as the Celtic tribes expanded out of their original homelands.

Worldwide usage
In Africa, knowledge of iron smelting seems to have developed at much the same time as it was spreading through western Europe. Some historians put this down to the Phoenicians, who carried their knowledge of iron

> *"[The Celts] are quick of mind and with good natural ability for learning."*
>
> DIDORUS SICULUS, GREEK HISTORIAN

smelting to their north African colonies, notably Carthage. The majority view now is that it was more likely a local development. Whatever the truth, there is no disputing the fact that African iron-making was extremely varied, with many distinct local technologies evolving over the centuries.

There is clear evidence of iron smelting in Ethiopia, the region of the Great Lakes, Tanzania, Ghana, Mali, and central Nigeria around the Niger and Benue Rivers, where the Nok culture emerged. In some respects, African metalsmiths were ahead of Europe. In east Africa, for instance, they were producing steel as early as 500 BCE.

From bronze to iron
Wherever and whenever the transition from the Bronze Age to the Iron Age happened, it brought with it significant changes to everyday life, from the way ancient peoples cultivated their crops to how they fought their wars. Some civilizations, however, missed out on the Iron Age altogether. In Central and South America, for example, various civilizations, most notably the Incas, were skillful metalworkers in gold, silver, copper, and bronze, but they simply never made the transition to iron.

▽ **Traditional metalworking**
Iron has been smelted and forged in Africa for three millennia. This 19th-century engraving shows small-scale ironworking near Lake Mobutu in east Africa.

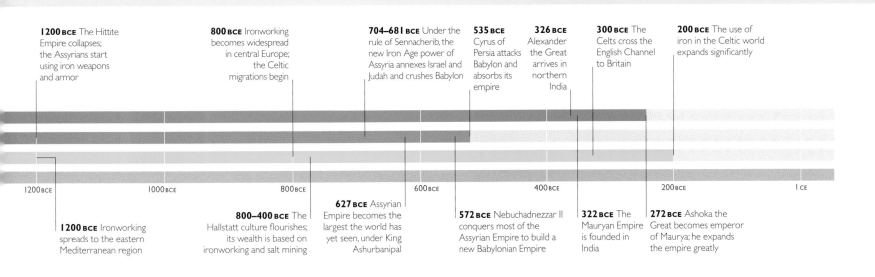

1200 BCE The Hittite Empire collapses; the Assyrians start using iron weapons and armor

800 BCE Ironworking becomes widespread in central Europe; the Celtic migrations begin

704–681 BCE Under the rule of Sennacherib, the new Iron Age power of Assyria annexes Israel and Judah and crushes Babylon

535 BCE Cyrus of Persia attacks Babylon and absorbs its empire

326 BCE Alexander the Great arrives in northern India

300 BCE The Celts cross the English Channel to Britain

200 BCE The use of iron in the Celtic world expands significantly

1200 BCE   1000 BCE   800 BCE   600 BCE   400 BCE   200 BCE   1 CE

1200 BCE Ironworking spreads to the eastern Mediterranean region

800–400 BCE The Hallstatt culture flourishes; its wealth is based on ironworking and salt mining

627 BCE Assyrian Empire becomes the largest the world has yet seen, under King Ashurbanipal

572 BCE Nebuchadnezzar II conquers most of the Assyrian Empire to build a new Babylonian Empire

322 BCE The Mauryan Empire is founded in India

272 BCE Ashoka the Great becomes emperor of Maurya; he expands the empire greatly

ASSYRIA AND BABYLONIA

The Iron Age in the Middle East was an age of empire. The Assyrians, based in what is now northern Iraq, created the blueprint for a new type of extensive state that employed direct and indirect rule to place a range of peoples and territories under the control of one sovereign.

After 1200 BCE, in the aftermath of the migrations at the end of the late Bronze Age (see pp.42–43), small-scale local states replaced large regional powers such as the Hittite state and the New Kingdom of Egypt. The kingdom of Assyria, protected by the Tigris River and the Taurus and Zagros Mountains, survived the upheaval despite losing peripheral territories to Aramaean clans. From 900 BCE, it started to grow again at the expense of these smaller neighbors.

Besides incorporating territories and putting them under eunuch governors loyal only to the king, the Assyrian Empire greatly favored indirect rule. From the eastern Mediterranean to what is now Iran, client rulers swore sacred oaths to accept the sovereignty of the god Ashur and his human representative, the Assyrian king, in return for local power. The empire was held together by these bonds of mutual obligation and by an innovative relay postal system—for the first time, information traveled much faster than if carried by a single messenger. The succeeding Babylonian Empire adopted much of this blueprint but replaced Ashur with its own god, Marduk, and dispensed with eunuch governors.

> *"The god Ashur is king, and Ashurbanipal is [his] representative, the creation of his hands."*
>
> CORONATION HYMN OF ASHURBANIPAL OF ASSYRIA

BABYLONIAN LAW
JUSTICE CARVED IN STONE

King Hammurabi of Babylon (r.1792–1750 BCE) compiled a set of 282 rulings, which were recorded on stone steles set up in temples across his realm. These laws were to "prevent the strong oppressing the weak" and specified fines and punishments to suit specific social contexts. More than 1,000 years later, in the days of the Assyrian and Babylonian Empires, Hammurabi was still revered as a model ruler.

Stele of Hammurabi
The king receives authority, symbolized by a measuring tape and a ruler, from the god Shamash, the patron of justice.

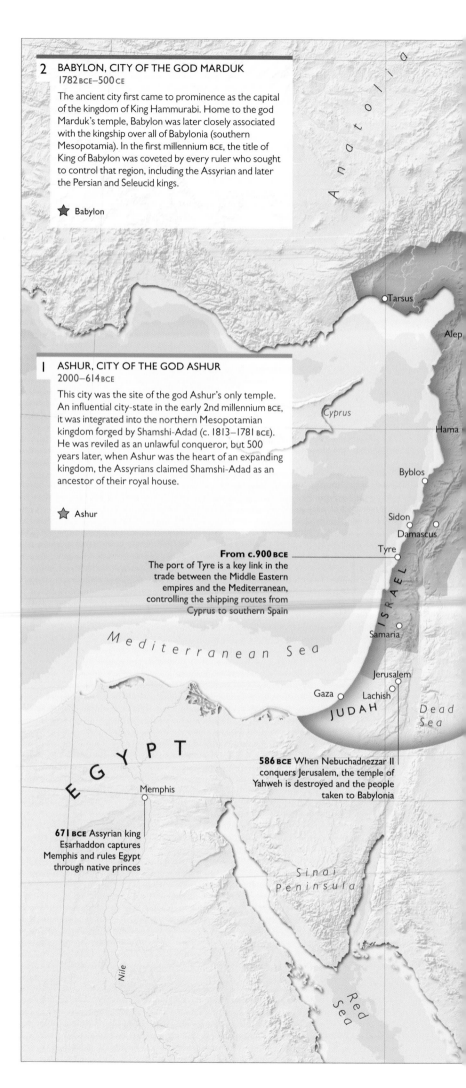

2 BABYLON, CITY OF THE GOD MARDUK
1782 BCE–500 CE

The ancient city first came to prominence as the capital of the kingdom of King Hammurabi. Home to the god Marduk's temple, Babylon was later closely associated with the kingship over all of Babylonia (southern Mesopotamia). In the first millennium BCE, the title of King of Babylon was coveted by every ruler who sought to control that region, including the Assyrian and later the Persian and Seleucid kings.

⭐ Babylon

1 ASHUR, CITY OF THE GOD ASHUR
2000–614 BCE

This city was the site of the god Ashur's only temple. An influential city-state in the early 2nd millennium BCE, it was integrated into the northern Mesopotamian kingdom forged by Shamshi-Adad (c. 1813–1781 BCE). He was reviled as an unlawful conqueror, but 500 years later, when Ashur was the heart of an expanding kingdom, the Assyrians claimed Shamshi-Adad as an ancestor of their royal house.

⭐ Ashur

From c.900 BCE
The port of Tyre is a key link in the trade between the Middle Eastern empires and the Mediterranean, controlling the shipping routes from Cyprus to southern Spain

586 BCE When Nebuchadnezzar II conquers Jerusalem, the temple of Yahweh is destroyed and the people taken to Babylonia

671 BCE Assyrian king Esarhaddon captures Memphis and rules Egypt through native princes

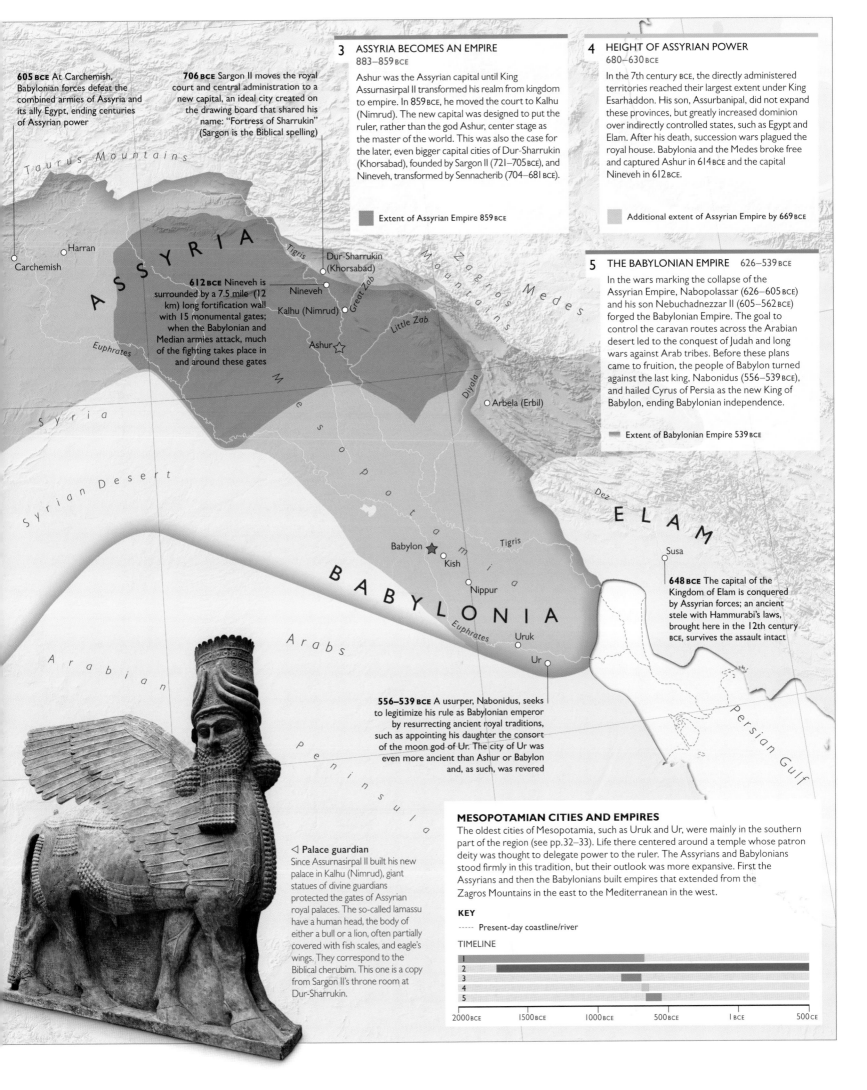

605 BCE At Carchemish, Babylonian forces defeat the combined armies of Assyria and its ally Egypt, ending centuries of Assyrian power

706 BCE Sargon II moves the royal court and central administration to a new capital, an ideal city created on the drawing board that shared his name: "Fortress of Sharrukin" (Sargon is the Biblical spelling)

3 ASSYRIA BECOMES AN EMPIRE
883–859 BCE

Ashur was the Assyrian capital until King Assurnasirpal II transformed his realm from kingdom to empire. In 859 BCE, he moved the court to Kalhu (Nimrud). The new capital was designed to put the ruler, rather than the god Ashur, center stage as the master of the world. This was also the case for the later, even bigger capital cities of Dur-Sharrukin (Khorsabad), founded by Sargon II (721–705 BCE), and Nineveh, transformed by Sennacherib (704–681 BCE).

■ Extent of Assyrian Empire 859 BCE

4 HEIGHT OF ASSYRIAN POWER
680–630 BCE

In the 7th century BCE, the directly administered territories reached their largest extent under King Esarhaddon. His son, Assurbanipal, did not expand these provinces, but greatly increased dominion over indirectly controlled states, such as Egypt and Elam. After his death, succession wars plagued the royal house. Babylonia and the Medes broke free and captured Ashur in 614 BCE and the capital Nineveh in 612 BCE.

■ Additional extent of Assyrian Empire by 669 BCE

5 THE BABYLONIAN EMPIRE 626–539 BCE

In the wars marking the collapse of the Assyrian Empire, Nabopolassar (626–605 BCE) and his son Nebuchadnezzar II (605–562 BCE) forged the Babylonian Empire. The goal to control the caravan routes across the Arabian desert led to the conquest of Judah and long wars against Arab tribes. Before these plans came to fruition, the people of Babylon turned against the last king, Nabonidus (556–539 BCE), and hailed Cyrus of Persia as the new King of Babylon, ending Babylonian independence.

■ Extent of Babylonian Empire 539 BCE

612 BCE Nineveh is surrounded by a 7.5 mile (12 km) long fortification wall with 15 monumental gates; when the Babylonian and Median armies attack, much of the fighting takes place in and around these gates

648 BCE The capital of the Kingdom of Elam is conquered by Assyrian forces; an ancient stele with Hammurabi's laws, brought here in the 12th century BCE, survives the assault intact

556–539 BCE A usurper, Nabonidus, seeks to legitimize his rule as Babylonian emperor by resurrecting ancient royal traditions, such as appointing his daughter the consort of the moon god of Ur. The city of Ur was even more ancient than Ashur or Babylon and, as such, was revered

◁ **Palace guardian**
Since Assurnasirpal II built his new palace in Kalhu (Nimrud), giant statues of divine guardians protected the gates of Assyrian royal palaces. The so-called lamassu have a human head, the body of either a bull or a lion, often partially covered with fish scales, and eagle's wings. They correspond to the Biblical cherubim. This one is a copy from Sargon II's throne room at Dur-Sharrukin.

MESOPOTAMIAN CITIES AND EMPIRES

The oldest cities of Mesopotamia, such as Uruk and Ur, were mainly in the southern part of the region (see pp.32–33). Life there centered around a temple whose patron deity was thought to delegate power to the ruler. The Assyrians and Babylonians stood firmly in this tradition, but their outlook was more expansive. First the Assyrians and then the Babylonians built empires that extended from the Zagros Mountains in the east to the Mediterranean in the west.

KEY

----- Present-day coastline/river

TIMELINE

1				
2				
3				
4				
5				

| 2000 BCE | 1500 BCE | 1000 BCE | 500 BCE | 1 BCE | 500 CE |

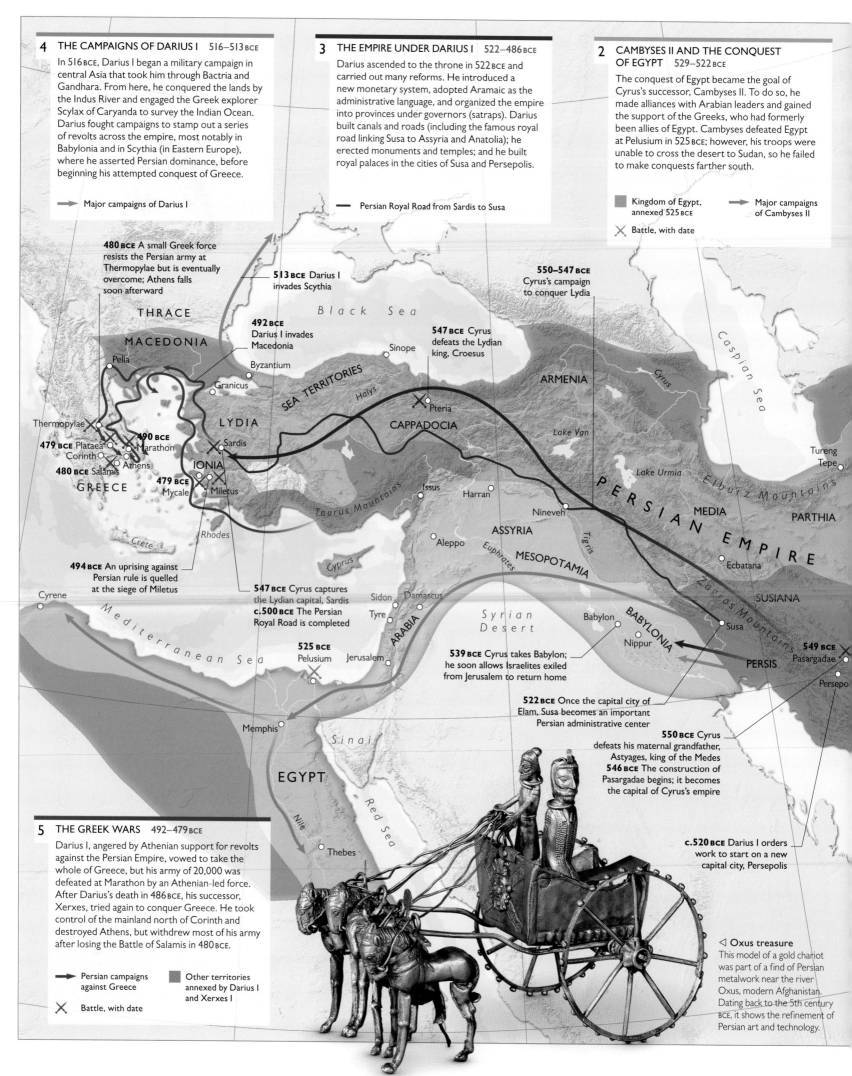

4 THE CAMPAIGNS OF DARIUS I 516–513 BCE

In 516 BCE, Darius I began a military campaign in central Asia that took him through Bactria and Gandhara. From here, he conquered the lands by the Indus River and engaged the Greek explorer Scylax of Caryanda to survey the Indian Ocean. Darius fought campaigns to stamp out a series of revolts across the empire, most notably in Babylonia and in Scythia (in Eastern Europe), where he asserted Persian dominance, before beginning his attempted conquest of Greece.

→ Major campaigns of Darius I

3 THE EMPIRE UNDER DARIUS I 522–486 BCE

Darius ascended to the throne in 522 BCE and carried out many reforms. He introduced a new monetary system, adopted Aramaic as the administrative language, and organized the empire into provinces under governors (satraps). Darius built canals and roads (including the famous royal road linking Susa to Assyria and Anatolia); he erected monuments and temples; and he built royal palaces in the cities of Susa and Persepolis.

— Persian Royal Road from Sardis to Susa

2 CAMBYSES II AND THE CONQUEST OF EGYPT 529–522 BCE

The conquest of Egypt became the goal of Cyrus's successor, Cambyses II. To do so, he made alliances with Arabian leaders and gained the support of the Greeks, who had formerly been allies of Egypt. Cambyses defeated Egypt at Pelusium in 525 BCE; however, his troops were unable to cross the desert to Sudan, so he failed to make conquests farther south.

▪ Kingdom of Egypt, annexed 525 BCE
→ Major campaigns of Cambyses II
✕ Battle, with date

480 BCE A small Greek force resists the Persian army at Thermopylae but is eventually overcome; Athens falls soon afterward

513 BCE Darius I invades Scythia

492 BCE Darius I invades Macedonia

550–547 BCE Cyrus's campaign to conquer Lydia

547 BCE Cyrus defeats the Lydian king, Croesus

490 BCE (Marathon)

479 BCE Plataea
479 BCE Mycale

480 BCE Salamis

494 BCE An uprising against Persian rule is quelled at the siege of Miletus

547 BCE Cyrus captures the Lydian capital, Sardis
c.500 BCE The Persian Royal Road is completed

525 BCE Pelusium

539 BCE Cyrus takes Babylon; he soon allows Israelites exiled from Jerusalem to return home

522 BCE Once the capital city of Elam, Susa becomes an important Persian administrative center

550 BCE Cyrus defeats his maternal grandfather, Astyages, king of the Medes
546 BCE The construction of Pasargadae begins; it becomes the capital of Cyrus's empire

549 BCE Pasargadae

c.520 BCE Darius I orders work to start on a new capital city, Persepolis

5 THE GREEK WARS 492–479 BCE

Darius I, angered by Athenian support for revolts against the Persian Empire, vowed to take the whole of Greece, but his army of 20,000 was defeated at Marathon by an Athenian-led force. After Darius's death in 486 BCE, his successor, Xerxes, tried again to conquer Greece. He took control of the mainland north of Corinth and destroyed Athens, but withdrew most of his army after losing the Battle of Salamis in 480 BCE.

→ Persian campaigns against Greece
✕ Battle, with date
▪ Other territories annexed by Darius I and Xerxes I

◁ **Oxus treasure**
This model of a gold chariot was part of a find of Persian metalwork near the river Oxus, modern Afghanistan. Dating back to the 5th century BCE, it shows the refinement of Persian art and technology.

Map labels: THRACE, MACEDONIA, Pella, Black Sea, Byzantium, Granicus, Sinope, SEA TERRITORIES, Halys, ARMENIA, Caspian Sea, Cyrus, Thermopylae, LYDIA, Sardis, Pteria, CAPPADOCIA, Lake Van, Tureng Tepe, IONIA, Corinth, Athens, Marathon, Miletus, Mycale, GREECE, Rhodes, Crete, Taurus Mountains, Issus, Harran, Lake Urmia, Nineveh, MEDIA, Elburz Mountains, PARTHIA, ASSYRIA, Aleppo, Euphrates, MESOPOTAMIA, Tigris, Ecbatana, Zagros Mountains, Cyprus, Cyrene, Mediterranean Sea, Sidon, Damascus, Tyre, ARABIA, Syrian Desert, Babylon, BABYLONIA, Nippur, Susa, SUSIANA, PERSIS, Persepolis, Pelusium, Jerusalem, Memphis, Sinai, Red Sea, EGYPT, Nile, Thebes, PERSIAN EMPIRE

THE EXPANSION OF PERSIAN TERRITORY

Cyrus conquered a huge swathe of western and central Asia, from Anatolia to what is now Afghanistan. His successors added gains in Egypt and Greece and ruled distant satrapies, such as Sogdiana, via governors known as satraps.

KEY

■ Persian Empire at greatest extent

TIMELINE

1
2
3
4
5

600 BCE   550   500   450   400

Oxus (Amu Darya)

c.530 BCE Cyrus is defeated against the Massagetae and killed

516 BCE Darius I reaches Gandhara at the northern reaches of the Indus River

HORASMIA

SOGDIANA

Balkh

Merv

545–540 BCE Cyrus pushes into central Asia

GANDHARA

BACTRIA

Herat

SATTAGYDIA

ARIA

Kandahar

INDIA

Iranian Plateau

Nad-i Ali

ARACHOSIA

Indus

515 BCE Darius I conquers the Indus Valley region

SAGARTIA

Bampur

GEDROSIA

Hormuz

MAKRAN

CYRUS THE GREAT AND HIS CONQUESTS
550–530 BCE

Born around 580 BCE, Cyrus II (known as Cyrus the Great) succeeded his father, Cambyses I, as king of Persia in 559 BCE. In a span of just 20 years, he cast off the yoke of the Median Empire, a victory that won him both territory and vassals. He then conquered Lydia and Babylonia, together with much of central Asia, to create a vast empire. Cyrus is thought to have died in battle around 530 BCE.

■ Persian homeland under Cyrus before 550 BCE	■ Kingdom of Lydia, annexed c. 547 BCE
■ Median Empire, annexed 550 BCE	■ Babylonian Empire, annexed 539 BCE
→ Major campaigns of Cyrus	✕ Battle, with date

RISE OF THE PERSIAN EMPIRE

The Persian Empire was enormous, stretching from Europe to India, and lasted from the military victories of its founder, Cyrus the Great, in the mid-6th century BCE until it was conquered by Alexander the Great some 200 years later.

In 612 BCE, the Assyrian city of Nineveh was destroyed by an alliance of the Assyrians' former subject peoples, including the Babylonians and Medes. The Medes and Persians were Indo-European peoples originally from central Asia, who occupied respectively the area southwest of the Caspian Sea and lands north of the Persian Gulf. To start, the Medes were the dominant power, but c. 550 BCE, the Persians—under a series of dynamic kings—began a series of conquests that created the largest empire the world had seen to date.

"Brevity is the soul of command. Too much talk suggests desperation on the part of the leader."

ATTRIBUTED TO CYRUS IN *CYROPEDIA*, c. 370 BCE

The Persians were tolerant conquerors—Cyrus the Great respected the beliefs and customs of the people he ruled and famously freed the Israelites who had been taken captive in Babylon. The Persians invested in organization, appointing local governors known as satraps to rule each province, and built roads and canals to enable troops and traders to move with ease. This organization, and their ability to deploy their armies quickly, enabled them to maintain their vast territories. The Persian Empire was still a major power when it was conquered by Alexander the Great in the 4th century BCE.

PASARGADAE
THE FIRST PERSIAN CAPITAL

Around 546 BCE, Cyrus the Great began to build the first Persian dynastic capital at Pasargadae, near the modern city of Shiraz. Its royal remains—which include the palace, audience hall, gatehouse, and the tomb of Cyrus himself—are some of the most impressive of the Persian Empire and show the influence of the peoples that Cyrus conquered. Later, Cambyses II founded another capital at Susa, and Darius built a third at Persepolis.

Protective winged spirit
This 5th-century BCE relief decorated a door in the ancient city of Pasargadae.

FIRST CITIES IN THE AMERICAS

The first city-based cultures in the Americas emerged from around 3500 BCE in coastal Peru, predating the first cities in southern Mexico and North America by about two millennia. All early American urban cultures built grand sites of worship and engaged extensively in trade.

CARAL
THE AMERICAS' FIRST URBAN CIVILIZATION

A substantial city by 2600 BCE, Caral was part of Peru's Norte Chico civilization. Other Norte Chico cities may be even older. Like many later pre-Columbian cities, Caral featured monumental architecture, such as platform mounds and plazas. These remains of a sunken plaza in Caral, 130 ft (40 m) across, were discovered in the late 1990s. The plaza is thought to have been used for communal acts of worship.

From around 5000 BCE, agricultural practices started replacing the hunter-gatherer lifestyle in the Americas, giving rise to the first settlements.

The Norte Chico culture in the Supe Valley region of coastal Peru emerged as the earliest known urban civilization on the continent, around 4000 BCE. The civilization included more than 30 large settlements, and it established its first major city around 3500 BCE. It thrived for more than 2,000 years. Early civilizations in other regions of the Americas include the Olmecs of southern Mexico and the Adena and Hopewell Mound Builder cultures of the upper Mississippi and Ohio valleys.

Unique cultures evolved in all these ancient communities, each defined by its arts, crafts, and religious practices, though they all built large-scale earthworks—platforms, pyramids, or mounds—mainly for ceremonial purposes. The towns and cities also traded, using rivers and other routes along coastal plains to transport goods.

EARLY CIVILIZATIONS IN AMERICA

From about 1500 BCE, farming cultures flourished in central America, and the Olmecs built their first cities. In North America, the Adena culture was among the first Mound Builders to emerge from about 1000 BCE, followed 800 years later by the Hopewells.

KEY

◆ Major urban centers

TIMELINE

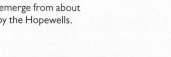

2000 BCE	1000 BCE	1 CE	1000 CE

MESOAMERICA'S ANCIENT CULTURES

By 1000 BCE, much of Mesoamerica was inhabited by farming communities, which grew into cities through trading in essential and exotic goods.

2 EARLY MAYA 1000 BCE–250 CE

From 1000 BCE, the Maya began forming complex urban settlements with an elite class and entrenched religious practices. These settlements also featured ceremonial sites in the form of plazas and earthen mounds. Maya artwork during this period drew influence from the Olmecs.

▬ Area of influence to 1000 BCE ◆ Preclassic sites

▬ Additional area of influence 800 BCE

1 OLMECS 1500 BCE–400 BCE

The Olmecs are known for their monumental earth platforms and mounds, fine jade artifacts, and giant head sculptures. Archaeological evidence suggests that the Olmecs created the first writing system and calendar in Mesoamerica. From their heartland in San Lorenzo, they traded widely into western Mexico and established trade relations with many Maya sites along the southern coast.

▬ Area of influence → Trade route

◆ Olmec sculpture site ◆ Olmec settlement

1000–700 BCE Ceramics produced in Tlatilco bear an Olmec influence

300 BCE Preclassic Maya construct among the earliest giant pyramid temples, bearing large stucco masks depicting the deities of Maya mythology

1200–900 BCE San Lorenzo is a major center for Olmec culture

300 BCE Monte Albán is among the fastest-growing cities in Mesoamerica, with a population of more than 5,000

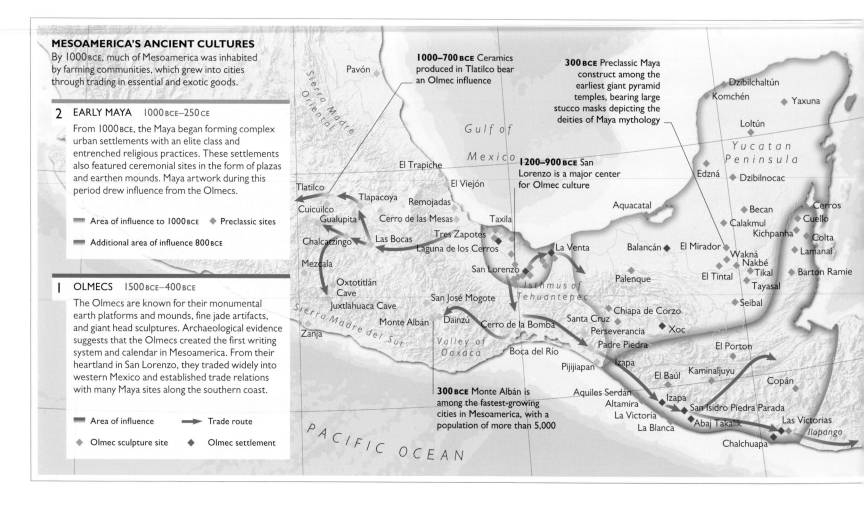

Gulf of Mexico
Yucatan Peninsula
Sierra Madre Oriental
Isthmus of Tehuantepec
Sierra Madre del Sur
Valley of Oaxaca
PACIFIC OCEAN

Pavón · Tlatilco · Tlapacoya · Remojadas · Cuicuilco · Gualupita · Cerro de las Mesas · Chalcatzingo · Las Bocas · Mezcala · El Trapiche · El Viejón · Tres Zapotes · Laguna de los Cerros · Taxila · La Venta · San Lorenzo · Oxtotitlán Cave · Juxtlahuaca Cave · San José Mogote · Monte Albán · Dainzú · Cerro de la Bomba · Zanja · Boca del Río · Santa Cruz · Perseverancia · Padre Piedra · Chiapa de Corzo · Xoc · Izapa · Pijijiapan · El Baúl · Kaminaljuyu · Aquiles Serdán · Altamira · Izapa · La Victoria · Abaj Takalik · La Blanca · San Isidro Piedra Parada · Las Victorias · Ilopango · Chalchuapa · Copán · El Porton · Aquacatal · Becan · Calakmul · Kichpanha · Cuello · Colta · Lamanaí · Balancán · El Mirador · Wakná · Nakbé · Tikal · Barton Ramie · Palenque · El Tintal · Tayasal · Seibal · Cerros · Dzibilchaltún · Komchén · Yaxuna · Loltún · Edzná · Dzibilnocac

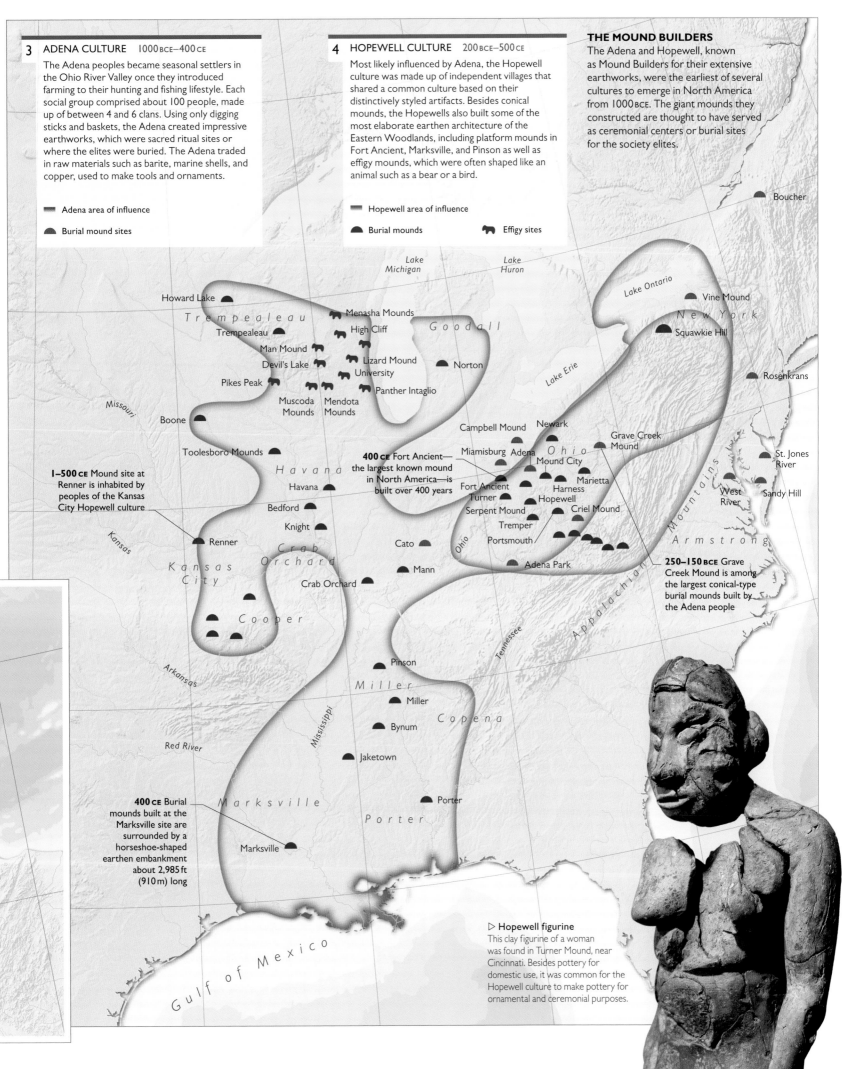

3 ADENA CULTURE 1000 BCE–400 CE

The Adena peoples became seasonal settlers in the Ohio River Valley once they introduced farming to their hunting and fishing lifestyle. Each social group comprised about 100 people, made up of between 4 and 6 clans. Using only digging sticks and baskets, the Adena created impressive earthworks, which were sacred ritual sites or where the elites were buried. The Adena traded in raw materials such as barite, marine shells, and copper, used to make tools and ornaments.

▬ Adena area of influence

◗ Burial mound sites

4 HOPEWELL CULTURE 200 BCE–500 CE

Most likely influenced by Adena, the Hopewell culture was made up of independent villages that shared a common culture based on their distinctively styled artifacts. Besides conical mounds, the Hopewells also built some of the most elaborate earthen architecture of the Eastern Woodlands, including platform mounds in Fort Ancient, Marksville, and Pinson as well as effigy mounds, which were often shaped like an animal such as a bear or a bird.

▬ Hopewell area of influence

◗ Burial mounds   🐾 Effigy sites

THE MOUND BUILDERS

The Adena and Hopewell, known as Mound Builders for their extensive earthworks, were the earliest of several cultures to emerge in North America from 1000 BCE. The giant mounds they constructed are thought to have served as ceremonial centers or burial sites for the society elites.

1–500 CE Mound site at Renner is inhabited by peoples of the Kansas City Hopewell culture

400 CE Fort Ancient—the largest known mound in North America—is built over 400 years

250–150 BCE Grave Creek Mound is among the largest conical-type burial mounds built by the Adena people

400 CE Burial mounds built at the Marksville site are surrounded by a horseshoe-shaped earthen embankment about 2,985 ft (910 m) long

Map labels

Lake Michigan · Lake Huron · Lake Ontario · Lake Erie
Missouri · Kansas · Arkansas · Red River · Mississippi · Tennessee · Ohio
Appalachian Mountains · Armstrong · Gulf of Mexico

Trempealeau · Goodall · New York · Havana · Ohio · Kansas City · Crab Orchard · Cooper · Miller · Copena · Marksville · Porter

Boucher · Vine Mound · Squawkie Hill · Rosenkrans · St. Jones River · Sandy Hill · West River · Grave Creek Mound · Newark · Campbell Mound · Marietta · Harness · Hopewell · Criel Mound · Adena · Mound City · Miamisburg · Fort Ancient · Turner · Serpent Mound · Tremper · Portsmouth · Adena Park · Norton

Howard Lake · Menasha Mounds · High Cliff · Trempealeau · Man Mound · Lizard Mound · University · Devil's Lake · Pikes Peak · Muscoda Mounds · Mendota Mounds · Panther Intaglio · Boone · Toolesboro Mounds · Havana · Bedford · Knight · Renner · Cato · Mann · Crab Orchard · Pinson · Miller · Bynum · Jaketown · Porter · Marksville

▷ Hopewell figurine

This clay figurine of a woman was found in Turner Mound, near Cincinnati. Besides pottery for domestic use, it was common for the Hopewell culture to make pottery for ornamental and ceremonial purposes.

THE PHOENICIANS

In the 1st millennium BCE, the Phoenicians were the leading seafaring merchants of the Mediterranean. Expert craftworkers, they specialized in luxury goods, including carved ivory, metalwork, and textiles.

△ **Phoenician warship**
This Phoenician warship is a bireme, propelled by two rows of oars. Although the bireme was later improved by the ancient Greeks, it may have been invented by the Phoenicians. A row of shields protects the upper deck.

The Phoenicians lived in port cities in what is now Lebanon. Among these, the most significant were Byblos, Tyre, and Sidon, each ruled by a king. It was the Greeks who named these people "Phoenicians" after their most expensive product, a nonfading purple (*phoinix* in Greek) dye derived from the murex sea snail.

The mountains of Lebanon were covered in cedar forests, which supplied the Phoenicians with long, straight timber. They used the cedar to build their ships and also exported it to Egypt, Greece, and Mesopotamia, which were all short on good timber. Their cities were also centers of craft production, producing purple textiles, glassware, engraved bronze bowls, and wooden furniture decorated with ivory panels. The craftworkers were influenced by Egyptian art, which the Phoenicians spread across the eastern Mediterranean and Mesopotamia. Alongside their own products, they traded in tin and silver from Spain, copper from Cyprus, Arabian incense, African ivory, Egyptian papyrus, Indian spices, and silk from Persian merchants.

Colonies and exploration

From the 10th century BCE, the Phoenicians founded colonies, as trading stations, across the Mediterranean. One such colony, Carthage (in North Africa), later became the center of a great empire. Searching for new markets, the Phoenicians became the greatest navigators of the ancient world. Beyond the Mediterranean, they explored the Atlantic coast of Europe and, around 600 BCE, circumnavigated the whole of Africa. Their lasting legacy is their alphabet, which had just 22 letters. Adapted by the Greeks, the Phoenician alphabet formed the basis of all western writing systems.

▷ **Cultural influences**
This Phoenician ivory carving shows a human-headed winged animal, Mesopotamian in origin, wearing an Egyptian royal headdress.

Cedar for the royalty
Assyrian kings imported cedar from Lebanon to build their palaces. A frieze from the palace of King Sargon II (722–705 BCE) shows Phoenicians bringing cedar logs, towing them alongside their ships.

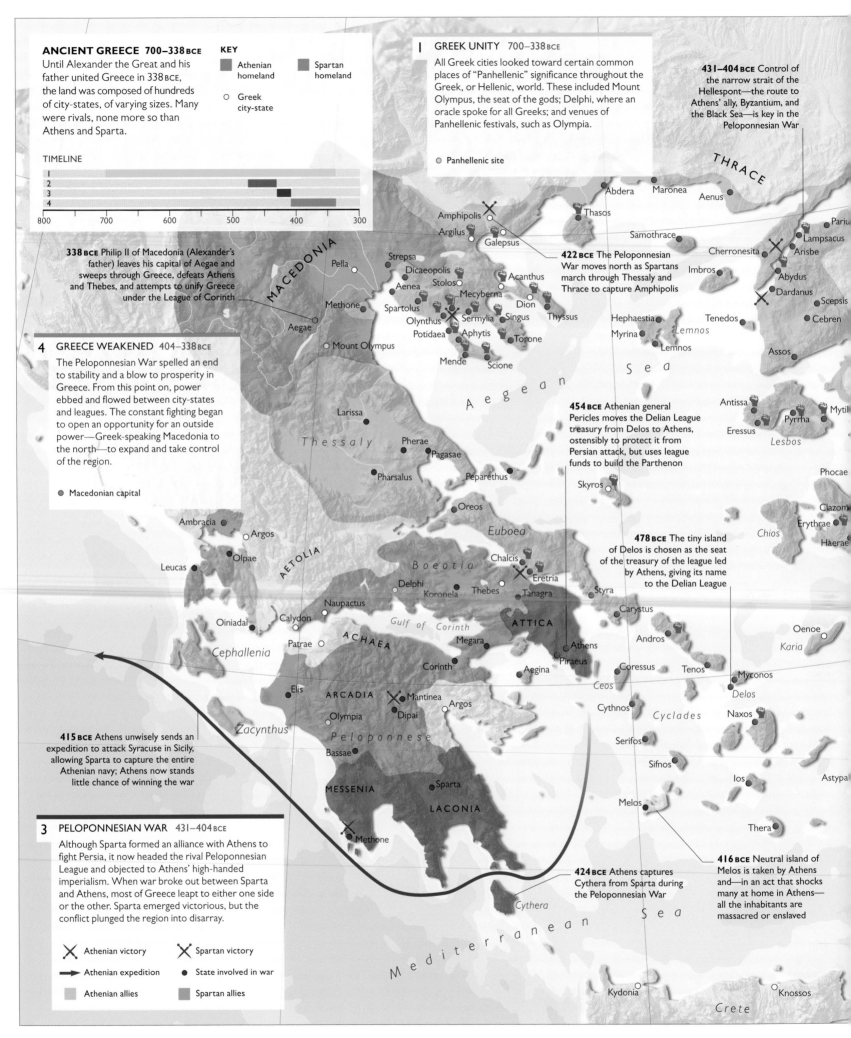

ANCIENT GREECE 700–338 BCE

Until Alexander the Great and his father united Greece in 338 BCE, the land was composed of hundreds of city-states, of varying sizes. Many were rivals, none more so than Athens and Sparta.

KEY

▢ Athenian homeland
▢ Spartan homeland

○ Greek city-state

TIMELINE

1		
2		
3		
4		

800   700   600   500   400   300

338 BCE Philip II of Macedonia (Alexander's father) leaves his capital of Aegae and sweeps through Greece, defeats Athens and Thebes, and attempts to unify Greece under the League of Corinth

4 GREECE WEAKENED 404–338 BCE

The Peloponnesian War spelled an end to stability and a blow to prosperity in Greece. From this point on, power ebbed and flowed between city-states and leagues. The constant fighting began to open an opportunity for an outside power—Greek-speaking Macedonia to the north—to expand and take control of the region.

● Macedonian capital

1 GREEK UNITY 700–338 BCE

All Greek cities looked toward certain common places of "Panhellenic" significance throughout the Greek, or Hellenic, world. These included Mount Olympus, the seat of the gods; Delphi, where an oracle spoke for all Greeks; and venues of Panhellenic festivals, such as Olympia.

◉ Panhellenic site

431–404 BCE Control of the narrow strait of the Hellespont—the route to Athens' ally, Byzantium, and the Black Sea—is key in the Peloponnesian War

422 BCE The Peloponnesian War moves north as Spartans march through Thessaly and Thrace to capture Amphipolis

454 BCE Athenian general Pericles moves the Delian League treasury from Delos to Athens, ostensibly to protect it from Persian attack, but uses league funds to build the Parthenon

478 BCE The tiny island of Delos is chosen as the seat of the treasury of the league led by Athens, giving its name to the Delian League

415 BCE Athens unwisely sends an expedition to attack Syracuse in Sicily, allowing Sparta to capture the entire Athenian navy; Athens now stands little chance of winning the war

3 PELOPONNESIAN WAR 431–404 BCE

Although Sparta formed an alliance with Athens to fight Persia, it now headed the rival Peloponnesian League and objected to Athens' high-handed imperialism. When war broke out between Sparta and Athens, most of Greece leapt to either one side or the other. Sparta emerged victorious, but the conflict plunged the region into disarray.

424 BCE Athens captures Cythera from Sparta during the Peloponnesian War

416 BCE Neutral island of Melos is taken by Athens and—in an act that shocks many at home in Athens—all the inhabitants are massacred or enslaved

✕ Athenian victory
✕ Spartan victory
→ Athenian expedition
● State involved in war
▢ Athenian allies
▢ Spartan allies

Labels on map: THRACE, Abdera, Maronea, Aenus, Thasos, Samothrace, Parium, Lampsacus, Cherronesita, Arisbe, Imbros, Abydus, Dardanus, Scepsis, Cebren, Amphipolis, Argilus, Galepsus, Strepsa, Dicaeopolis, Stolos, Acanthus, Aenea, MACEDONIA, Pella, Methone, Spartolus, Mecyberna, Dion, Olynthus, Sermylia, Singus, Thyssus, Potidaea, Aphytis, Torone, Hephaestia, Myrina, Lemnos, Mende, Scione, Tenedos, Assos, Aegae, Mount Olympus, Lemnos, Aegean Sea, Antissa, Mytilene, Larissa, Pyrrha, Thessaly, Eressus, Lesbos, Pherae, Pagasae, Peparethus, Pharsalus, Skyros, Phocae, Oreos, Euboea, Clazomenae, Erythrae, Chios, Haerae, Ambracia, Argos, Olpae, Chalcis, Eretria, Leucas, AETOLIA, Boeotia, Styra, Delphi, Koronela, Thebes, Tanagra, Carystus, Naupactus, Oenoe, Oiniadai, Calydon, Gulf of Corinth, ATTICA, Andros, Karia, Patrae, ACHAEA, Megara, Athens, Coressus, Tenos, Myconos, Cephallenia, Corinth, Piraeus, Delos, Aegina, Ceos, Cythnos, Cyclades, Naxos, Elis, ARCADIA, Mantinea, Argos, Serifos, Olympia, Dipai, Sifnos, Zacynthus, Peloponnese, Bassae, Ios, Astypalaia, Melos, MESSENIA, Sparta, Thera, LACONIA, Methone, Cythera, Mediterranean Sea, Kydonia, Knossos, Crete

THE GREEK CITY-STATES

In a seminal period for Western civilization, the Greek people spread through the Mediterranean, exporting their culture as they went. But they were never unified politically. Leagues of independent city-states became close-knit only when faced with a common threat.

The cornerstone of Greek civilization was the *polis*, or city-state. These self-governing communities, frequently isolated by Greece's rugged terrain, were based on walled cities with outlying villages and farmland. Despite being fiercely independent, these hundreds of city-states, scattered around the Mediterranean, had language, religion, and many cultural practices in common. Even remote colonies strove to express their identity with the building of temples and theaters and the

output of fine ceramics. The Greek world was also more or less united at times in loose confederations, never more so than when the need arose to repulse the invading Persian Empire (see pp.58–59). The major alliance that arose in the aftermath of the Persian Wars, the Delian League, became dominated by Athens—to the annoyance not only of many other league members but also of other leagues—principally that headed by Sparta. Athens' ruthless leadership of what had effectively become its empire sucked it into conflict with Sparta at a time when they were both great nations. By the end of the war, they were weakened and depleted, leaving a power vacuum for others to fill.

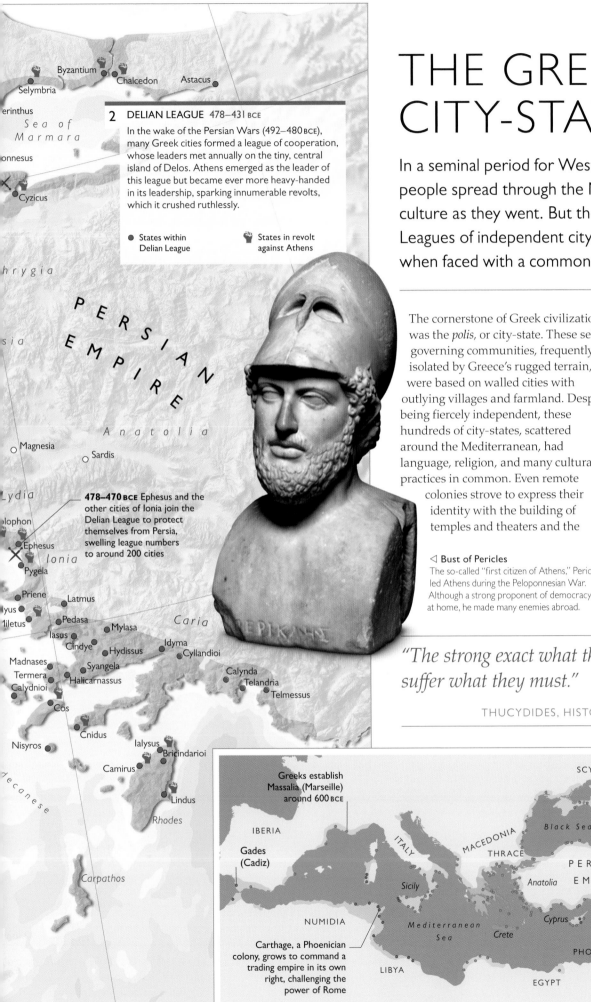

◁ **Bust of Pericles**
The so-called "first citizen of Athens," Pericles led Athens during the Peloponnesian War. Although a strong proponent of democracy at home, he made many enemies abroad.

2 DELIAN LEAGUE 478–431 BCE
In the wake of the Persian Wars (492–480 BCE), many Greek cities formed a league of cooperation, whose leaders met annually on the tiny, central island of Delos. Athens emerged as the leader of this league but became ever more heavy-handed in its leadership, sparking innumerable revolts, which it crushed ruthlessly.

● States within Delian League
✊ States in revolt against Athens

478–470 BCE Ephesus and the other cities of Ionia join the Delian League to protect themselves from Persia, swelling league numbers to around 200 cities

"The strong exact what they can, and the weak suffer what they must."

THUCYDIDES, HISTORY OF THE PELOPONNESIAN WAR, 400 BCE

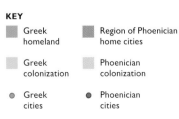

MEDITERRANEAN COLONISTS
In 800–300 BCE, two cultures spread across the Mediterranean. Greek colonists looked for fertile land, since their homeland had little, first in western Anatolia then the Black Sea shores, Sicily, Italy, and France. The Phoenicians went in search of metals and trade; they began colonizing copper-rich Cyprus, and reached as far as Gades and its silver mines.

Greeks establish Massalia (Marseille) around 600 BCE

Carthage, a Phoenician colony, grows to command a trading empire in its own right, challenging the power of Rome

GREEK AND PHOENICIAN INFLUENCE BY 338 BCE

KEY
■ Greek homeland
■ Region of Phoenician home cities
■ Greek colonization
■ Phoenician colonization
● Greek cities
● Phoenician cities

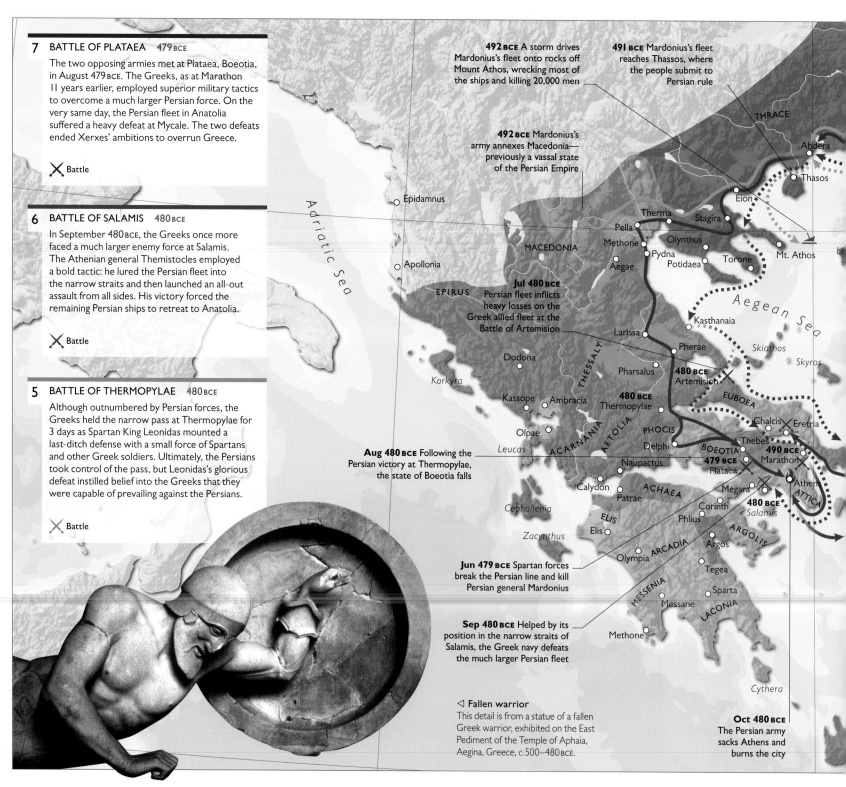

7 BATTLE OF PLATAEA 479 BCE

The two opposing armies met at Plataea, Boeotia, in August 479 BCE. The Greeks, as at Marathon 11 years earlier, employed superior military tactics to overcome a much larger Persian force. On the very same day, the Persian fleet in Anatolia suffered a heavy defeat at Mycale. The two defeats ended Xerxes' ambitions to overrun Greece.

✕ Battle

6 BATTLE OF SALAMIS 480 BCE

In September 480 BCE, the Greeks once more faced a much larger enemy force at Salamis. The Athenian general Themistocles employed a bold tactic: he lured the Persian fleet into the narrow straits and then launched an all-out assault from all sides. His victory forced the remaining Persian ships to retreat to Anatolia.

✕ Battle

5 BATTLE OF THERMOPYLAE 480 BCE

Although outnumbered by Persian forces, the Greeks held the narrow pass at Thermopylae for 3 days as Spartan King Leonidas mounted a last-ditch defense with a small force of Spartans and other Greek soldiers. Ultimately, the Persians took control of the pass, but Leonidas's glorious defeat instilled belief into the Greeks that they were capable of prevailing against the Persians.

✕ Battle

492 BCE A storm drives Mardonius's fleet onto rocks off Mount Athos, wrecking most of the ships and killing 20,000 men

491 BCE Mardonius's fleet reaches Thassos, where the people submit to Persian rule

492 BCE Mardonius's army annexes Macedonia—previously a vassal state of the Persian Empire

Jul 480 BCE Persian fleet inflicts heavy losses on the Greek allied fleet at the Battle of Artemision

Aug 480 BCE Following the Persian victory at Thermopylae, the state of Boeotia falls

Jun 479 BCE Spartan forces break the Persian line and kill Persian general Mardonius

Sep 480 BCE Helped by its position in the narrow straits of Salamis, the Greek navy defeats the much larger Persian fleet

◁ **Fallen warrior**
This detail is from a statue of a fallen Greek warrior, exhibited on the East Pediment of the Temple of Aphaia, Aegina, Greece, c. 500–480 BCE.

Oct 480 BCE The Persian army sacks Athens and burns the city

GREECE AND PERSIA AT WAR

Following a series of revolts in its western provinces, the vast Persian Empire pushed westward in 492 BCE in an attempt to conquer the Greek city-states and colonies around the Aegean Sea. This led to a destructive series of wars in which their superior military tactics and some timely good fortune helped the Greeks halt the much larger Persian forces.

By about 550 BCE, the Persian Empire had expanded westward, moving into Anatolia, where its armies had defeated the powerful king of Lydia, Croesus, and conquered numerous Ionian cities, which until then had been colonies of Greece. In 499 BCE, however, the Ionian Greeks in the city of Miletus rebelled against Persian rule, triggering uprisings not only in Ionia but also in cities across the Persian western frontier.

The Persian military response precipitated the first wave of hostilities, in which the Persian forces took 5 years to crush the Ionian rebellion, finally recapturing Miletus in 494 BCE. Then, in retaliation for the support the Greek city-states of Athens and Eretria had given to the Ionian cities during their revolt, Persia's King Darius (r. 522–486 BCE) launched a military invasion of Greece in 492 BCE. The attack was two-pronged: a land and naval campaign directed at Thrace and Macedonia, headed by the Persian general Mardonius,

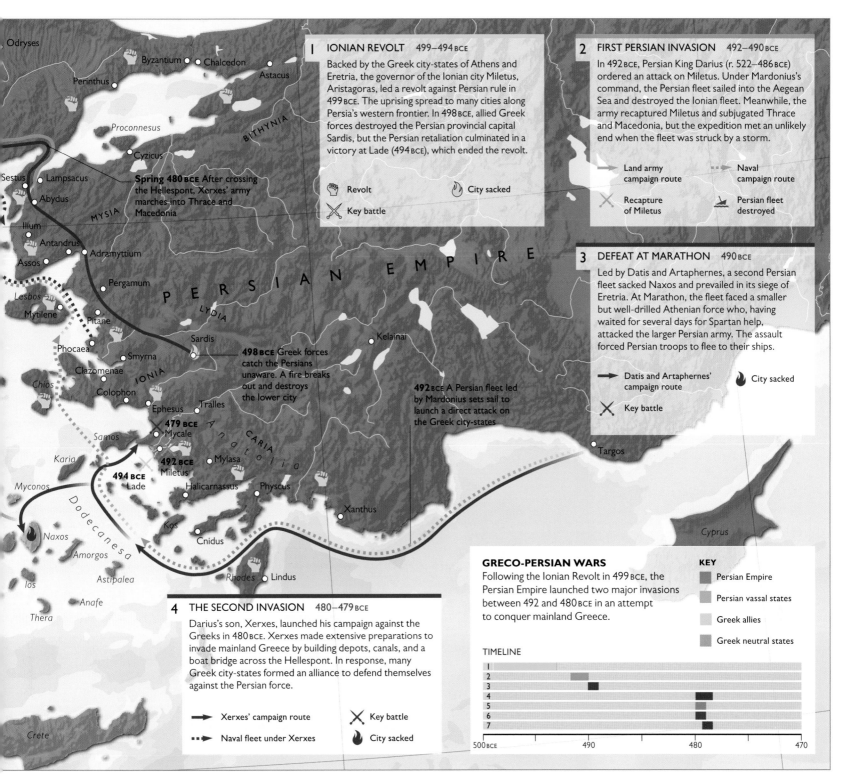

Odryses

Byzantium ○ ○ Chalcedon

Perinthus

Astacus

BITHYNIA

Proconnesus

Cyzicus

Sestus ○
Lampsacus
Abydus

MYSIA

Ilium
Antandrus
Assos

Adramyttium

Pergamum

Lesbos
Mytilene
Pitane

LYDIA

Phocaea
Smyrna
Clazomenae

Chios

IONIA

Colophon

Ephesus
Tralles

479 BCE Mycale

Samos

492 BCE Mylasa
Miletus

Karia

494 BCE Lade

CARIA

Anatolia

Myconos

Dodecanesa

Halicarnassus
Physcus

Naxos

Kos

Cnidus

Amorgos

Ios

Astipalea

Rhodes ○ Lindus

Anafe

Thera

Crete

Sardis

Kelainai

Xanthus

Targos

Cyprus

P E R S I A N   E M P I R E

Spring 480 BCE After crossing the Hellespont, Xerxes' army marches into Thrace and Macedonia

498 BCE Greek forces catch the Persians unaware. A fire breaks out and destroys the lower city

492 BCE A Persian fleet led by Mardonius sets sail to launch a direct attack on the Greek city-states

1 IONIAN REVOLT 499–494 BCE

Backed by the Greek city-states of Athens and Eretria, the governor of the Ionian city Miletus, Aristagoras, led a revolt against Persian rule in 499 BCE. The uprising spread to many cities along Persia's western frontier. In 498 BCE, allied Greek forces destroyed the Persian provincial capital Sardis, but the Persian retaliation culminated in a victory at Lade (494 BCE), which ended the revolt.

✊ Revolt   🔥 City sacked

✗ Key battle

2 FIRST PERSIAN INVASION 492–490 BCE

In 492 BCE, Persian King Darius (r. 522–486 BCE) ordered an attack on Miletus. Under Mardonius's command, the Persian fleet sailed into the Aegean Sea and destroyed the Ionian fleet. Meanwhile, the army recaptured Miletus and subjugated Thrace and Macedonia, but the expedition met an unlikely end when the fleet was struck by a storm.

→ Land army campaign route   ┄► Naval campaign route

✗ Recapture of Miletus   ⚓ Persian fleet destroyed

3 DEFEAT AT MARATHON 490 BCE

Led by Datis and Artaphernes, a second Persian fleet sacked Naxos and prevailed in its siege of Eretria. At Marathon, the fleet faced a smaller but well-drilled Athenian force who, having waited for several days for Spartan help, attacked the larger Persian army. The assault forced Persian troops to flee to their ships.

➡ Datis and Artaphernes' campaign route   🔥 City sacked

✗ Key battle

4 THE SECOND INVASION 480–479 BCE

Darius's son, Xerxes, launched his campaign against the Greeks in 480 BCE. Xerxes made extensive preparations to invade mainland Greece by building depots, canals, and a boat bridge across the Hellespont. In response, many Greek city-states formed an alliance to defend themselves against the Persian force.

➡ Xerxes' campaign route   ✗ Key battle

┅► Naval fleet under Xerxes   🔥 City sacked

GRECO-PERSIAN WARS

Following the Ionian Revolt in 499 BCE, the Persian Empire launched two major invasions between 492 and 480 BCE in an attempt to conquer mainland Greece.

KEY

▪ Persian Empire

▪ Persian vassal states

▪ Greek allies

▪ Greek neutral states

TIMELINE

	500 BCE	490	480	470
1				
2				
3				
4				
5				
6				
7				

and a second led by Datis and Artaphernes. The missions brought many Greek cities under Persian control and also turned Macedonia into a client kingdom. But, the Persian armies were eventually forced to withdraw, as a storm wrecked Mardonius's fleet off the coast of Mount Athos. The second Persian army suffered a loss against the smaller but more tactically astute Athenian army at the Battle of Marathon in 490 BCE.

Ten years later, Xerxes I (r. 486–465 BCE), Darius's son and successor, restarted hostilities against Athens, having spent several years planning his campaign. Once more, the Persian forces outnumbered their Greek counterparts, in part because Athens could not always persuade other Greek states (in particular, the militaristic city of Sparta) to join them in battle. Nevertheless, the Persians were unable to exploit this advantage, and the Greek city-states ensured their independence with victories at Salamis and Plataea.

DARIUS I
550–486 BCE

Darius I was the third Persian king of the Achaemenid Empire, during whose reign the empire reached its peak. His administrative skill combined with his strong and intelligent leadership earned him the title of Darius the Great. He also built the magnificent city of Persepolis and left behind inscriptions telling the story of his successes.

Great King Darius
The king sits on his throne in a bas-relief exhibited in Persepolis, c. 500 BCE.

ALEXANDER THE GREAT

The young king of Macedonia, Alexander III, ascended to the throne in 336 BCE following his father's death, inheriting a highly efficient army. Within 10 years, he conquered the vast Persian Empire, creating a realm that stretched from Greece to the River Indus. Although the empire fell soon after his death, it left a lasting cultural mark throughout the region.

On his succession to the Macedonian throne in 359 BCE, King Philip II (r. 359–336 BCE) transformed his army into the world's most effective fighting machine—based on the heavy infantry phalanx armed with long pikes. During his reign, his armies mounted efficient sieges to gain control of Thessaly, Illyria, and Thrace, and asserted control over the Greek mainland despite Greek hostility. However, just as Philip was preparing to invade Persia in 336 BCE, he was assassinated by one of his bodyguards.

Alexander becomes king

Philip's 21-year-old son, Alexander III, immediately claimed the throne and wielded his military force to suppress the revolts that had erupted in Greece and the Balkans following Philip's death. Thereafter, Alexander set out to realize his late father's ambitions, leading an army of 30,000 soldiers and a 5,000-strong cavalry on a masterfully drilled military campaign to conquer the Persian Empire. Alexander swept through the Persian territories of Anatolia, Syria, and Egypt without losing a single battle. He then marched east to the Persian homeland, waging a tireless campaign, and by 327 BCE

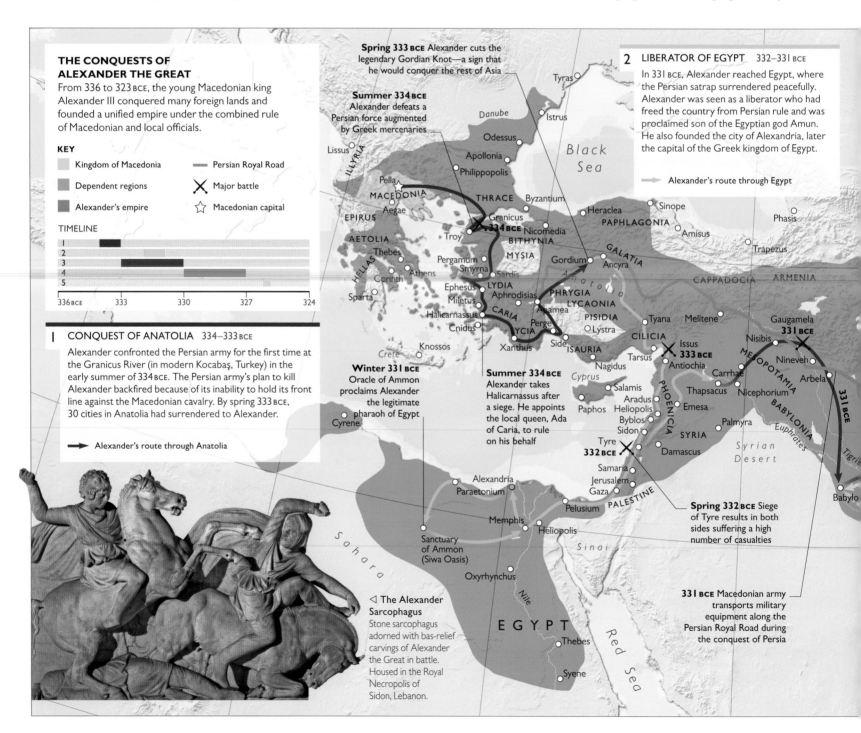

THE CONQUESTS OF ALEXANDER THE GREAT
From 336 to 323 BCE, the young Macedonian king Alexander III conquered many foreign lands and founded a unified empire under the combined rule of Macedonian and local officials.

KEY

- Kingdom of Macedonia
- Dependent regions
- Alexander's empire
- ▬ Persian Royal Road
- ✕ Major battle
- ☆ Macedonian capital

TIMELINE

1	2	3	4	5

336 BCE | 333 | 330 | 327 | 324

1 CONQUEST OF ANATOLIA 334–333 BCE
Alexander confronted the Persian army for the first time at the Granicus River (in modern Kocabaş, Turkey) in the early summer of 334 BCE. The Persian army's plan to kill Alexander backfired because of its inability to hold its front line against the Macedonian cavalry. By spring 333 BCE, 30 cities in Anatolia had surrendered to Alexander.

➡ Alexander's route through Anatolia

Spring 333 BCE Alexander cuts the legendary Gordian Knot—a sign that he would conquer the rest of Asia

Summer 334 BCE Alexander defeats a Persian force augmented by Greek mercenaries

2 LIBERATOR OF EGYPT 332–331 BCE
In 331 BCE, Alexander reached Egypt, where the Persian satrap surrendered peacefully. Alexander was seen as a liberator who had freed the country from Persian rule and was proclaimed son of the Egyptian god Amun. He also founded the city of Alexandria, later the capital of the Greek kingdom of Egypt.

➡ Alexander's route through Egypt

Winter 331 BCE Oracle of Ammon proclaims Alexander the legitimate pharaoh of Egypt

Summer 334 BCE Alexander takes Halicarnassus after a siege. He appoints the local queen, Ada of Caria, to rule on his behalf

Spring 332 BCE Siege of Tyre results in both sides suffering a high number of casualties

331 BCE Macedonian army transports military equipment along the Persian Royal Road during the conquest of Persia

◁ **The Alexander Sarcophagus** Stone sarcophagus adorned with bas-relief carvings of Alexander the Great in battle. Housed in the Royal Necropolis of Sidon, Lebanon.

Black Sea

Mediterranean Sea

Tyras, Istrus, Odessus, Apollonia, Philippopolis, Lissus, Pella, MACEDONIA, Aegae, EPIRUS, AETOLIA, HELLAS, Thebes, Athens, Corinth, Sparta, Crete, Knossos, THRACE, Byzantium, Troy, Pergamum, Smyrna, Ephesus, Miletus, Halicarnassus, Cnidus, Xanthus, Granicus 334 BCE, Nicomedia, BITHYNIA, MYSIA, Sardis, LYDIA, Aphrodisias, CARIA, LYCIA, Perge, Side, Heraclea, PAPHLAGONIA, Gordium, Ancyra, GALATIA, Anatolia, PHRYGIA, LYCAONIA, Apamea, PISIDIA, Lystra, ISAURIA, Nagidus, CILICIA, Tarsus, Issus 333 BCE, Antiochia, Sinope, Amisus, Phasis, Trapezus, CAPPADOCIA, ARMENIA, Tyana, Melitene, Gaugamela 331 BCE, Nisibis, Nineveh, Arbela, MESOPOTAMIA, Carrhae, Thapsacus, Nicephorium, BABYLONIA, Babylo[n], Euphrates, Tigris, Cyprus, Salamis, Aradus, Paphos, Heliopolis, Byblos, Sidon, Tyre 332 BCE, Emesa, Palmyra, PHOENICIA, SYRIA, Damascus, Syrian Desert, Samaria, Jerusalem, Gaza, PALESTINE, Pelusium, Alexandria, Paraetonium, Cyrene, Sahara, Sanctuary of Ammon (Siwa Oasis), Memphis, Heliopolis, Sinai, Oxyrhynchus, EGYPT, Thebes, Syene, Nile, Red Sea, ILLYRIA, Danube

crushed the Achaemenid Dynasty—rulers of the first Persian Empire. Alexander forged an empire that stretched from Greece to the River Indus and introduced Greek culture to the vast realm. In addition, he was an astute diplomat and encouraged the mixing of cultures, adopting Persian customs in an attempt to unify his empire and establish trade routes between Asia and Europe.

Alexander set his sights on invading India next, but his weary troops refused to fight on, forcing their king to lead them home. Alexander survived a perilous journey across the Makran desert, but in 323 BCE—at the age of 32—he died in Babylon of a fever, exhaustion, or possibly from being poisoned. A tussle for power ensued after his death and led to the breakup of his vast empire.

> *"... the end and object of conquest is to avoid doing the same thing as the conquered."*
>
> ALEXANDER III, FROM *LIVES* BY PLUTARCH, c. 100 CE

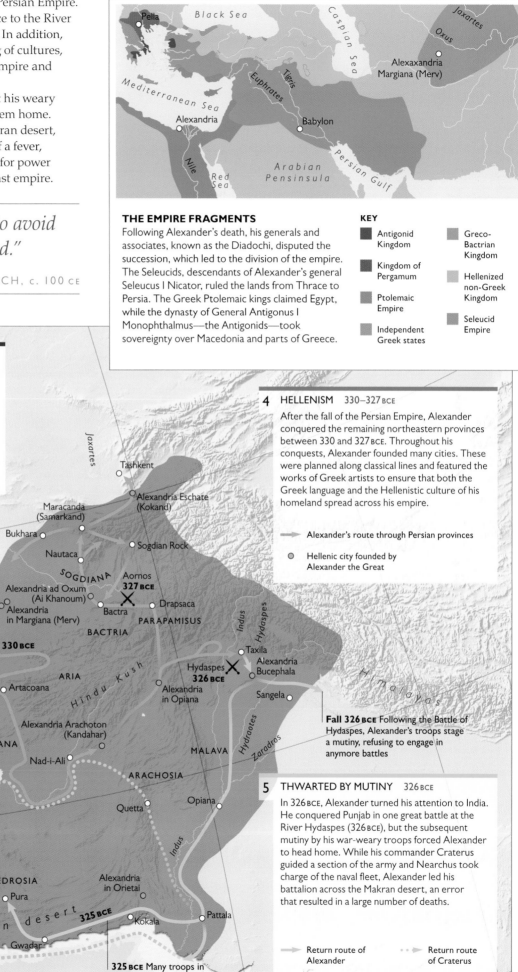

THE EMPIRE FRAGMENTS

Following Alexander's death, his generals and associates, known as the Diadochi, disputed the succession, which led to the division of the empire. The Seleucids, descendants of Alexander's general Seleucus I Nicator, ruled the lands from Thrace to Persia. The Greek Ptolemaic kings claimed Egypt, while the dynasty of General Antigonus I Monophthalmus—the Antigonids—took sovereignty over Macedonia and parts of Greece.

KEY

- Antigonid Kingdom
- Kingdom of Pergamum
- Ptolemaic Empire
- Independent Greek states
- Greco-Bactrian Kingdom
- Hellenized non-Greek Kingdom
- Seleucid Empire

---

3 FIGHT AGAINST PERSIA 333–330 BCE

Alexander's first direct engagement with Persian king Darius III had occurred at the Battle of Issus (333 BCE), where he emerged victorious and forced Darius to flee the battlefield. Alexander went on to capture Persepolis—the Persian ceremonial capital. A weak Persian Empire was all but wiped out when King Darius was killed by his satrap, Bessos, who then met his own fate at the hands of Alexander.

➤ Alexander's route through Persia

4 HELLENISM 330–327 BCE

After the fall of the Persian Empire, Alexander conquered the remaining northeastern provinces between 330 and 327 BCE. Throughout his conquests, Alexander founded many cities. These were planned along classical lines and featured the works of Greek artists to ensure that both the Greek language and the Hellenistic culture of his homeland spread across his empire.

➤ Alexander's route through Persian provinces

⊙ Hellenic city founded by Alexander the Great

Fall 326 BCE Following the Battle of Hydaspes, Alexander's troops stage a mutiny, refusing to engage in anymore battles

5 THWARTED BY MUTINY 326 BCE

In 326 BCE, Alexander turned his attention to India. He conquered Punjab in one great battle at the River Hydaspes (326 BCE), but the subsequent mutiny by his war-weary troops forced Alexander to head home. While his commander Craterus guided a section of the army and Nearchus took charge of the naval fleet, Alexander led his battalion across the Makran desert, an error that resulted in a large number of deaths.

→ Return route of Alexander

···→ Return route of Craterus

⇥ Route of Nearchus

325 BCE Under Nearchus's command, Alexander's fleet sails back up the Persian Gulf

325 BCE Many troops in Alexander's battalion perish in the heat of the Makran desert

△ **Iconic design**
This bronze helmet from the 6th century BCE was first worn by soldiers of the city-state Corinth but later gained popularity throughout Greece.

THE CLASSICAL AGE

Conventionally, the term "classical civilization" has been used to define the two different but related cultures that developed in the Mediterranean world from about 800 BCE to 400 CE. The first of these emerged in and around Greece, and the second rose in Rome, from where it spread across the entire European world.

The immense contribution of Greece to western civilization is universally recognized. Although Athens has traditionally been given the greatest credit for this advance, modern historians believe that there is far more to the story.

Rise of the city-states

It was during the Archaic Period (800–479 BCE) of Greek history that the seeds of Greek civilization were sown. It was an age of experimentation and intellectual ferment. City-states such as Athens, Sparta, Corinth, Argos, Eleusis, Thebes, Miletus, and Syracuse emerged. The population expanded, and by classical times, it is estimated that there were more than 1,000 communities scattered across the Greek world.

Art and architecture flourished, and cities along the coast of Anatolia (modern-day Turkey) became important centers of early philosophical and other intellectual developments. The great plays of Sophocles, Euripides, Aeschylus, and Aristophanes were first staged at the Theater of Dionysus Eleutherus on the southern slopes of Athens' Acropolis. Herodotus and Thucydides were the first great historians. Socrates, Plato, and Aristotle revolutionized philosophy, all three founding their own philosophical schools. Other notable figures of the time included the statesmen Solon and Pericles, the generals

Alcibiades and Themistocles, the poets Pindar and Sappho, the sculptor Phidias, and the physician Hippocrates—the father of modern medicine.

Success in war cemented these achievements. The defeat of the invading Persians at the town of Marathon in 490 BCE and at the island of Salamis 10 years later are regarded as pivotal moments in world history. Had the Persians emerged victorious, it is likely that the Greek achievements, which form the building blocks on which modern Western civilization is founded, would have been stifled at birth.

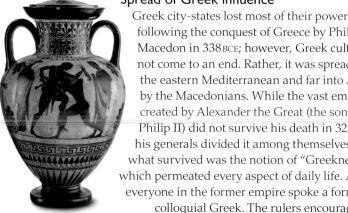

△ **Greek art**
The Greeks used vases for storage and at occasions such as weddings. The painting on this vase, which dates from 530 BCE, depicts the hero Hercules.

Spread of Greek influence

Greek city-states lost most of their power following the conquest of Greece by Philip II of Macedon in 338 BCE; however, Greek culture did not come to an end. Rather, it was spread across the eastern Mediterranean and far into Asia by the Macedonians. While the vast empire created by Alexander the Great (the son of Philip II) did not survive his death in 323 BCE—his generals divided it among themselves—what survived was the notion of "Greekness," which permeated every aspect of daily life. Almost everyone in the former empire spoke a form of colloquial Greek. The rulers encouraged the growth of learning in the empire. In Egypt, under the Macedonian general Ptolemy I, the university at Alexandria became home to the mathematicians Euclid, Eratosthenes,

POWERFUL CIVILIZATIONS

Various civilizations rose and fell in the Mediterranean region during the so-called Classical period of world history. However, the Greek and Roman civilizations emerged as the most dynamic during this era. The Etruscan civilization is also included in this timeline because of its close links with the early days of Rome. The city of Rome itself has a long history but played a relatively minor part until the Romans expanded their influence in the 3rd century BCE.

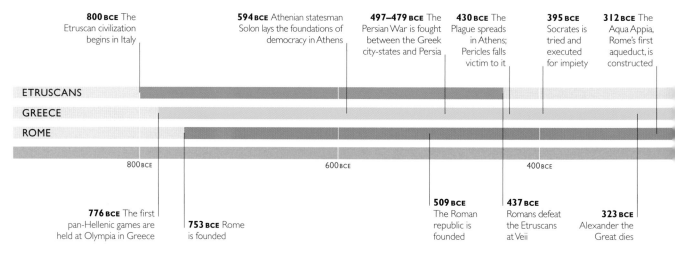

800 BCE The Etruscan civilization begins in Italy

594 BCE Athenian statesman Solon lays the foundations of democracy in Athens

497–479 BCE The Persian War is fought between the Greek city-states and Persia

430 BCE The Plague spreads in Athens; Pericles falls victim to it

395 BCE Socrates is tried and executed for impiety

312 BCE The Aqua Appia, Rome's first aqueduct, is constructed

ETRUSCANS

GREECE

ROME

800 BCE

600 BCE

400 BCE

776 BCE The first pan-Hellenic games are held at Olympia in Greece

753 BCE Rome is founded

509 BCE The Roman republic is founded

437 BCE Romans defeat the Etruscans at Veii

323 BCE Alexander the Great dies

◁ **Public works**
The Aqua Appia was the first aqueduct built to supply Rome with drinking water. It dropped only 33 ft (10m) in height along its length of 10 miles (16km). Commissioned in 312 BCE, it was an early sign of the skill and ambition of Roman infrastructure projects.

and Archimedes, along with the inventors Heron and Ktesibios. The great library there came to be a wonder of the ancient Mediterranean world.

Rise and fall of Rome

Rome arose from a small trading settlement on the banks of the River Tiber. Initially, it came under the influence of the powerful Etruscan civilization to its north. The last Etruscan king, Lucius Tarquinius Superbus, was driven out by the Romans in 509 BCE, after which Rome became a republic, ruled by a senate and two consuls, elected annually.

It was war that made the republic great. Its increasing dominance in Italy brought it into conflict with its Mediterranean rival city Carthage. The defeat of the Carthaginians ensured Roman dominance of the western Mediterranean. The successful wars that the Romans fought against the Macedonians and others in the east gave Rome control over the entire Mediterranean region.

In the 1st century BCE, Rome was still a republic, with powerful senators such as Julius Caesar. Whether he would have made himself emperor had he not been assassinated must remain speculation. It was Octavian, his adopted great-nephew, who, after a bitter civil war, became Rome's first emperor in 31 BCE, taking the title Imperator Caesar Augustus.

In the 3rd century CE, the empire went through a period of crisis due to pressure on its frontiers and as a result of political instability, and it was divided into a western and an eastern half. Emperor Diocletian restored stability, partly by appointing colleagues to share his authority. Some later emperors, notably Constantine, ruled alone. It was he who legalized Christianity and founded Constantinople to rival Rome as the imperial capital. Following him, the eastern and western halves of the empire increasingly went their separate ways.

"Freedom is the sure possession of those alone who have the courage to defend it."

PERICLES, ATHENIAN STATESMAN, 495–429 BCE

◁ **Romanized Greek art**
Roman artists were influenced by their Greek counterparts. This marble statue of a discus-thrower is a Roman version of a Greek original that was lost. The Greek statue was cast in bronze in the 5th century BCE by the sculptor Myron.

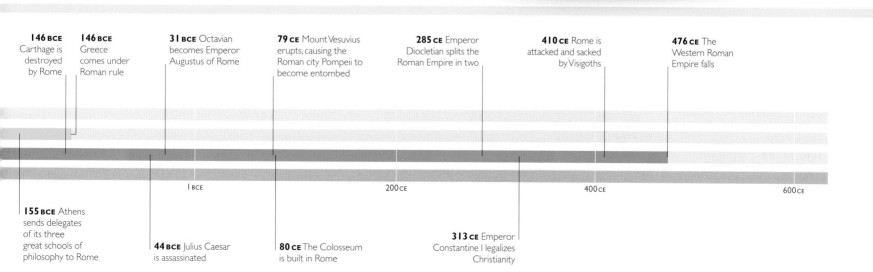

146 BCE Carthage is destroyed by Rome

146 BCE Greece comes under Roman rule

31 BCE Octavian becomes Emperor Augustus of Rome

79 CE Mount Vesuvius erupts, causing the Roman city Pompeii to become entombed

285 CE Emperor Diocletian splits the Roman Empire in two

410 CE Rome is attacked and sacked by Visigoths

476 CE The Western Roman Empire falls

155 BCE Athens sends delegates of its three great schools of philosophy to Rome

1 BCE

200 CE

400 CE

600 CE

44 BCE Julius Caesar is assassinated

80 CE The Colosseum is built in Rome

313 CE Emperor Constantine I legalizes Christianity

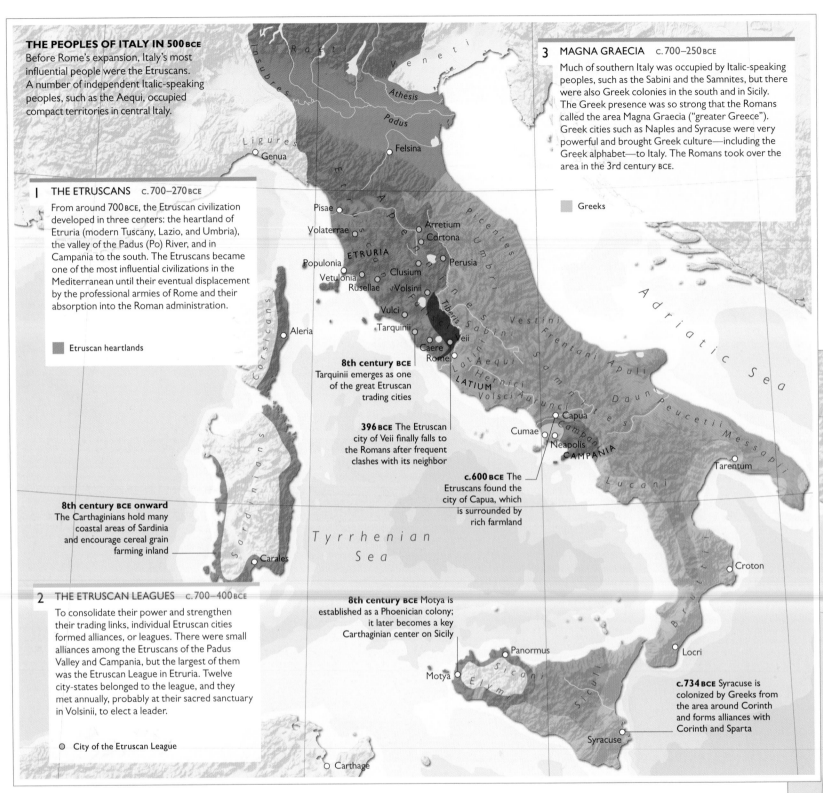

THE PEOPLES OF ITALY IN 500 BCE
Before Rome's expansion, Italy's most influential people were the Etruscans. A number of independent Italic-speaking peoples, such as the Aequi, occupied compact territories in central Italy.

3 MAGNA GRAECIA c. 700–250 BCE
Much of southern Italy was occupied by Italic-speaking peoples, such as the Sabini and the Samnites, but there were also Greek colonies in the south and in Sicily. The Greek presence was so strong that the Romans called the area Magna Graecia ("greater Greece"). Greek cities such as Naples and Syracuse were very powerful and brought Greek culture—including the Greek alphabet—to Italy. The Romans took over the area in the 3rd century BCE.

☐ Greeks

1 THE ETRUSCANS c. 700–270 BCE
From around 700 BCE, the Etruscan civilization developed in three centers: the heartland of Etruria (modern Tuscany, Lazio, and Umbria), the valley of the Padus (Po) River, and in Campania to the south. The Etruscans became one of the most influential civilizations in the Mediterranean until their eventual displacement by the professional armies of Rome and their absorption into the Roman administration.

■ Etruscan heartlands

8th century BCE
Tarquinii emerges as one of the great Etruscan trading cities

396 BCE The Etruscan city of Veii finally falls to the Romans after frequent clashes with its neighbor

c. 600 BCE The Etruscans found the city of Capua, which is surrounded by rich farmland

8th century BCE onward
The Carthaginians hold many coastal areas of Sardinia and encourage cereal grain farming inland

8th century BCE Motya is established as a Phoenician colony; it later becomes a key Carthaginian center on Sicily

2 THE ETRUSCAN LEAGUES c. 700–400 BCE
To consolidate their power and strengthen their trading links, individual Etruscan cities formed alliances, or leagues. There were small alliances among the Etruscans of the Padus Valley and Campania, but the largest of them was the Etruscan League in Etruria. Twelve city-states belonged to the league, and they met annually, probably at their sacred sanctuary in Volsinii, to elect a leader.

○ City of the Etruscan League

c. 734 BCE Syracuse is colonized by Greeks from the area around Corinth and forms alliances with Corinth and Sparta

ETRUSCAN ART
TOMB DECORATIONS

The Etruscans developed art in various forms, including realist figurative sculpture in bronze and terracotta, engraved gems, vase paintings, and frescoes (right). Much of this art was strongly influenced by the Greeks. Most of the best surviving examples of frescoes and terracotta sculptures are from tombs, especially those found in Tarquinia, Italy.

SHIFTING POWER IN ITALY, 500–200 BCE
In 500 BCE, the Italian peninsula was home to many different tribes, as well as colonies founded by the Carthaginians of north Africa and the Greeks. By the end of the 2nd century BCE, Rome was the dominant presence in Italy and was continuing to expand.

KEY
■ Italic-speaking peoples
■ Italic-speaking peoples and Etruscans
■ Carthaginians

TIMELINE

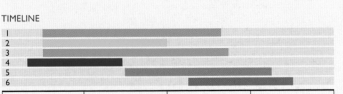

ETRUSCANS AND THE RISE OF ROME

By about 800 BCE, the dominant people in northern Italy were the Etruscans—people who lived in city-states and spoke a unique, non-Indo-European language. One of the cities they ruled was Rome, which began to grow into a major power from 500 BCE, annexing its neighbors and founding colonies throughout Italy.

The Etruscan civilization most probably grew out of an interaction between migrants from the eastern Mediterranean and the Villanovans, iron-age people who lived between the Padus (Po) River valley and the site of Rome.

The Etruscans flourished in this part of northern Italy, which they called Etruria, and in the area of Campania, around modern Naples. They built cities, developed distinctive styles of art—especially mural painting and sculpture—and formed trading alliances.

Rome was originally a settlement in Latium. Central Italy was home to a number of Italic peoples—the Umbri, Sabini, and others—who spoke Indo-European languages. Up until 509 BCE, Rome was ruled by kings of Etruscan origin. Rome then became a republic, governed by two annually elected magistrates, known as consuls. The Roman Republic expanded its territory, first into Latium, then into Etruria and the south. It did this through military victories over the Sabini and Aequi peoples of central Italy and by defeating Veii, an Etruscan city northwest of Rome. The Romans consolidated their position by founding colonies that gave them dominance over much of Italy. By the early 3rd century BCE, Rome had nearly 300,000 citizens, distributed across the Italian peninsula. Roman culture was influenced by its contact with both the Etruscans and the Greeks.

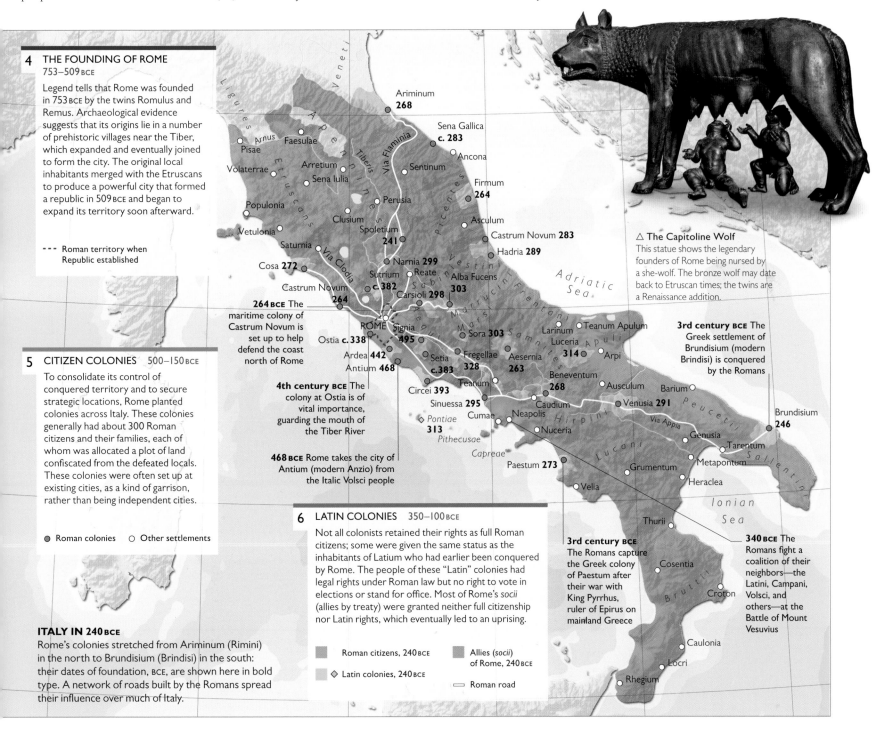

4 THE FOUNDING OF ROME 753–509 BCE

Legend tells that Rome was founded in 753 BCE by the twins Romulus and Remus. Archaeological evidence suggests that its origins lie in a number of prehistoric villages near the Tiber, which expanded and eventually joined to form the city. The original local inhabitants merged with the Etruscans to produce a powerful city that formed a republic in 509 BCE and began to expand its territory soon afterward.

- - - Roman territory when Republic established

△ **The Capitoline Wolf**
This statue shows the legendary founders of Rome being nursed by a she-wolf. The bronze wolf may date back to Etruscan times; the twins are a Renaissance addition.

264 BCE The maritime colony of Castrum Novum is set up to help defend the coast north of Rome

3rd century BCE The Greek settlement of Brundisium (modern Brindisi) is conquered by the Romans

5 CITIZEN COLONIES 500–150 BCE

To consolidate its control of conquered territory and to secure strategic locations, Rome planted colonies across Italy. These colonies generally had about 300 Roman citizens and their families, each of whom was allocated a plot of land confiscated from the defeated locals. These colonies were often set up at existing cities, as a kind of garrison, rather than being independent cities.

4th century BCE The colony at Ostia is of vital importance, guarding the mouth of the Tiber River

468 BCE Rome takes the city of Antium (modern Anzio) from the Italic Volsci people

- ● Roman colonies ○ Other settlements

6 LATIN COLONIES 350–100 BCE

Not all colonists retained their rights as full Roman citizens; some were given the same status as the inhabitants of Latium who had earlier been conquered by Rome. The people of these "Latin" colonies had legal rights under Roman law but no right to vote in elections or stand for office. Most of Rome's *socii* (allies by treaty) were granted neither full citizenship nor Latin rights, which eventually led to an uprising.

3rd century BCE The Romans capture the Greek colony of Paestum after their war with King Pyrrhus, ruler of Epirus on mainland Greece

340 BCE The Romans fight a coalition of their neighbors—the Latini, Campani, Volsci, and others—at the Battle of Mount Vesuvius

ITALY IN 240 BCE
Rome's colonies stretched from Ariminum (Rimini) in the north to Brundisium (Brindisi) in the south: their dates of foundation, BCE, are shown here in bold type. A network of roads built by the Romans spread their influence over much of Italy.

- Roman citizens, 240 BCE
- ◇ Latin colonies, 240 BCE
- Allies (*socii*) of Rome, 240 BCE
- ══ Roman road

ROME BUILDS ITS POWER BASE

As the Roman Republic expanded in the 3rd century BCE, it came into conflict with the well-established Carthaginian civilization. Rome's victory in the three ensuing Punic Wars gave it hegemony over the western Mediterranean, and further Roman victories in Greece pushed Roman power eastward as well.

In the early 3rd century BCE, Rome's power was confined mainly to its colonies in Italy. In 264 BCE, it began to expand its influence, first and foremost by fighting a series of wars with Carthage, then the most powerful city in the western Mediterranean.

Carthage had been founded by the seafaring Phoenician civilization (*Punicus* in Latin, hence Punic Wars), which had thrived in the eastern Mediterranean from around 1500 BCE. Carthage was not a formal empire but the preeminent city in a league of cities that defended one another and maintained trading networks. Located on the coast of what is modern Tunisia,

it built up formidable sea power, with a fleet of around 350 ships by the year 256 BCE. To defeat Carthage and its allies, Rome not only had to fight skilled Carthaginian generals in land battles but had to build and equip its own navy. Roman victories against Carthage brought it many provinces: Sicilia (Sicily), Corsica, and Sardinia after the first Punic War (264–241 BCE); two Spanish provinces after the second (218–201 BCE); and the province of Africa (northern Tunisia), on the site of Carthage itself, in the third (149–146 BCE). Further victories in Greece gave Rome the dominant position in the Mediterranean that it would hold until the 5th century CE.

> *"I have come not to make war on the Italians, but to aid the Italians against Rome."*
>
> HANNIBAL AT THE BATTLE OF LACUS TRASIMENUS, 217 BCE

THE ROMANS IN GREECE

Greece was disrupted by political tensions because the most powerful cities, such as Corinth and Athens, wanted independence from the main powers in the region—the Macedonians and the Seleucid Empire of Persia. This gave Rome the chance to move into the area. After a number of military victories, beginning with the Battle of Corinth in 146 BCE, Rome was to gain many Greek cities and later set up provinces, which they called Macedonia, Achaia, and Epirus.

ROMAN PROVINCES IN GREECE c. 100 BCE

CARTHAGE AND ITS TERRITORIES
814–146 BCE

From its origins as a trading post set up by the Phoenicians in 814 BCE, Carthage grew into a major power with outposts that extended along the North African coast into southern Spain and to parts of islands such as Corsica, Sardinia, and Sicily. The city's formidable naval power made it seem strong against Rome, which in the early 3rd century BCE had no navy.

209 BCE The Romans surround and defeat the Carthaginian base of Carthago Nova, forcing the Carthaginians to leave the eastern coast of Spain.

◁ **War elephants**
The army that Hannibal took across the Alps reportedly included 37 war elephants, an innovation that came to the Mediterranean from India and that is depicted on this 3rd-century BCE Italian dish.

THE PUNIC WARS

This series of three wars took place over more than a century and involved the Carthaginians in long, grueling marches through difficult territory. Both sides lost many soldiers, but Carthage was eventually weakened by the power of Rome.

KEY

- Carthaginian territory 264 BCE
- Carthaginian territory 200 BCE
- Roman territory 264 BCE
- Roman gains by 241 BCE
- Roman gains by 202 BCE

TIMELINE

1
2
3
4
5

1000 BCE | 800 BCE | 600 BCE | 400 BCE | 200 BCE | 1 CE

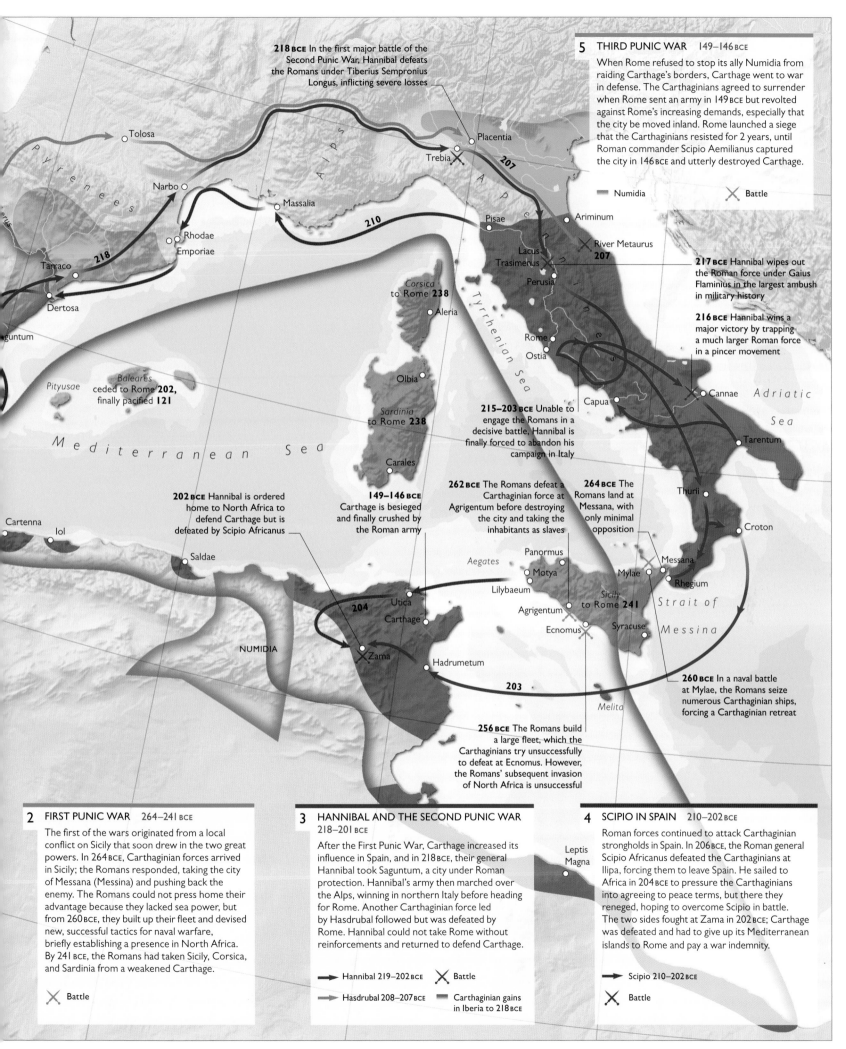

218 BCE In the first major battle of the Second Punic War, Hannibal defeats the Romans under Tiberius Sempronius Longus, inflicting severe losses

5 THIRD PUNIC WAR 149–146 BCE

When Rome refused to stop its ally Numidia from raiding Carthage's borders, Carthage went to war in defense. The Carthaginians agreed to surrender when Rome sent an army in 149 BCE but revolted against Rome's increasing demands, especially that the city be moved inland. Rome launched a siege that the Carthaginians resisted for 2 years, until Roman commander Scipio Aemilianus captured the city in 146 BCE and utterly destroyed Carthage.

— Numidia ✕ Battle

217 BCE Hannibal wipes out the Roman force under Gaius Flaminius in the largest ambush in military history

216 BCE Hannibal wins a major victory by trapping a much larger Roman force in a pincer movement

215–203 BCE Unable to engage the Romans in a decisive battle, Hannibal is finally forced to abandon his campaign in Italy

262 BCE The Romans defeat a Carthaginian force at Agrigentum before destroying the city and taking the inhabitants as slaves

264 BCE The Romans land at Messana, with only minimal opposition

202 BCE Hannibal is ordered home to North Africa to defend Carthage but is defeated by Scipio Africanus

149–146 BCE Carthage is besieged and finally crushed by the Roman army

260 BCE In a naval battle at Mylae, the Romans seize numerous Carthaginian ships, forcing a Carthaginian retreat

256 BCE The Romans build a large fleet, which the Carthaginians try unsuccessfully to defeat at Ecnomus. However, the Romans' subsequent invasion of North Africa is unsuccessful

Corsica to Rome **238**

Sardinia to Rome **238**

Balears ceded to Rome **202**, finally pacified **121**

Sicily to Rome **241**

2 FIRST PUNIC WAR 264–241 BCE

The first of the wars originated from a local conflict on Sicily that soon drew in the two great powers. In 264 BCE, Carthaginian forces arrived in Sicily; the Romans responded, taking the city of Messana (Messina) and pushing back the enemy. The Romans could not press home their advantage because they lacked sea power, but from 260 BCE, they built up their fleet and devised new, successful tactics for naval warfare, briefly establishing a presence in North Africa. By 241 BCE, the Romans had taken Sicily, Corsica, and Sardinia from a weakened Carthage.

✕ Battle

3 HANNIBAL AND THE SECOND PUNIC WAR 218–201 BCE

After the First Punic War, Carthage increased its influence in Spain, and in 218 BCE, their general Hannibal took Saguntum, a city under Roman protection. Hannibal's army then marched over the Alps, winning in northern Italy before heading for Rome. Another Carthaginian force led by Hasdrubal followed but was defeated by Rome. Hannibal could not take Rome without reinforcements and returned to defend Carthage.

→ Hannibal 219–202 BCE ✕ Battle

→ Hasdrubal 208–207 BCE ▪ Carthaginian gains in Iberia to 218 BCE

4 SCIPIO IN SPAIN 210–202 BCE

Roman forces continued to attack Carthaginian strongholds in Spain. In 206 BCE, the Roman general Scipio Africanus defeated the Carthaginians at Ilipa, forcing them to leave Spain. He sailed to Africa in 204 BCE to pressure the Carthaginians into agreeing to peace terms, but there they reneged, hoping to overcome Scipio in battle. The two sides fought at Zama in 202 BCE; Carthage was defeated and had to give up its Mediterranean islands to Rome and pay a war indemnity.

→ Scipio 210–202 BCE

✕ Battle

c.142 CE The Romans extend the northern frontier to the Antonine Wall before withdrawing later back to Hadrian's Wall

Antonine Wall
c.145 CE

Hadrian's Wall
c.125 CE

9 CE Rome loses territory south of the Elbe after a defeat by Germanic tribes

3 THE CONQUEST OF BRITAIN 55 BCE–c. 50 CE

Julius Caesar unsuccessfully attempted to invade Britain in the 50s BCE, but the country was conquered from 43 CE onward under the emperor Claudius. The Romans took the southeast easily after a major battle but encountered resistance elsewhere, especially in Wales and the north, so the country took decades to bring under imperial control. During the 2nd century, the Romans established a northern border by building Hadrian's Wall.

Roman Britain

121 BCE Gallia Narbonensis (Languedoc and Provence) becomes the first Roman colony in France

58 BCE Julius Caesar reaches the River Rhine; the river becomes the Roman Empire's northern frontier

1st and 2nd centuries CE The Romans gradually absorb Spain into the empire, assimilating local tribes and putting down rebellions

2 NORTH AFRICA 33 BCE–44 CE

In 33 BCE, the Berber kingdom of Mauretania became a Roman client kingdom. It was later annexed by Rome, and from 44 CE, was ruled directly as the provinces of Mauretania Caesariensis and Mauretania Tingitana. Farther east, Octavian defeated his rival Mark Antony and his lover Queen Cleopatra VII of Egypt, creating the province of Aegyptus in 30 BCE. North Africa became a valued supplier of corn, marble, slaves, and other goods to Rome.

Roman provinces in North Africa

49–44 BCE The city of Carthage, destroyed during the Punic Wars, is rebuilt by the Romans: it becomes an important "granary" of the empire

31 BCE Octavian defeats Mark Antony and Cleopatra at the Battle of Actium, giving Rome control of Egypt

27 BCE The ancient Greek city of Ephesus is made capital of the province of Asia by Augustus

80 BCE The city of Alexandria formally passes into Roman hands; it remains an important center for shipping grain across the Mediterranean

1 THE CONQUEST OF GAUL 58–50 BCE

The Romans had annexed the southern parts of Gallia (Gaul) in 121 BCE, but the whole territory (the extent of modern France and Belgium) was conquered between 58 and 50 BCE by Julius Caesar. As well as opening up sources of raw materials, including lead and silver, this conquest allowed Rome to take advantage of the River Rhine as a line of communication. It also won Julius Caesar popularity and his army's loyalty.

Roman Gaul

◁ **The Arch of Trajan**
This relief shows the Emperor Trajan being greeted by Roman citizens. It is part of the decorative scheme on an arch built in his honor in 114–117 CE in Benevento, southern Italy.

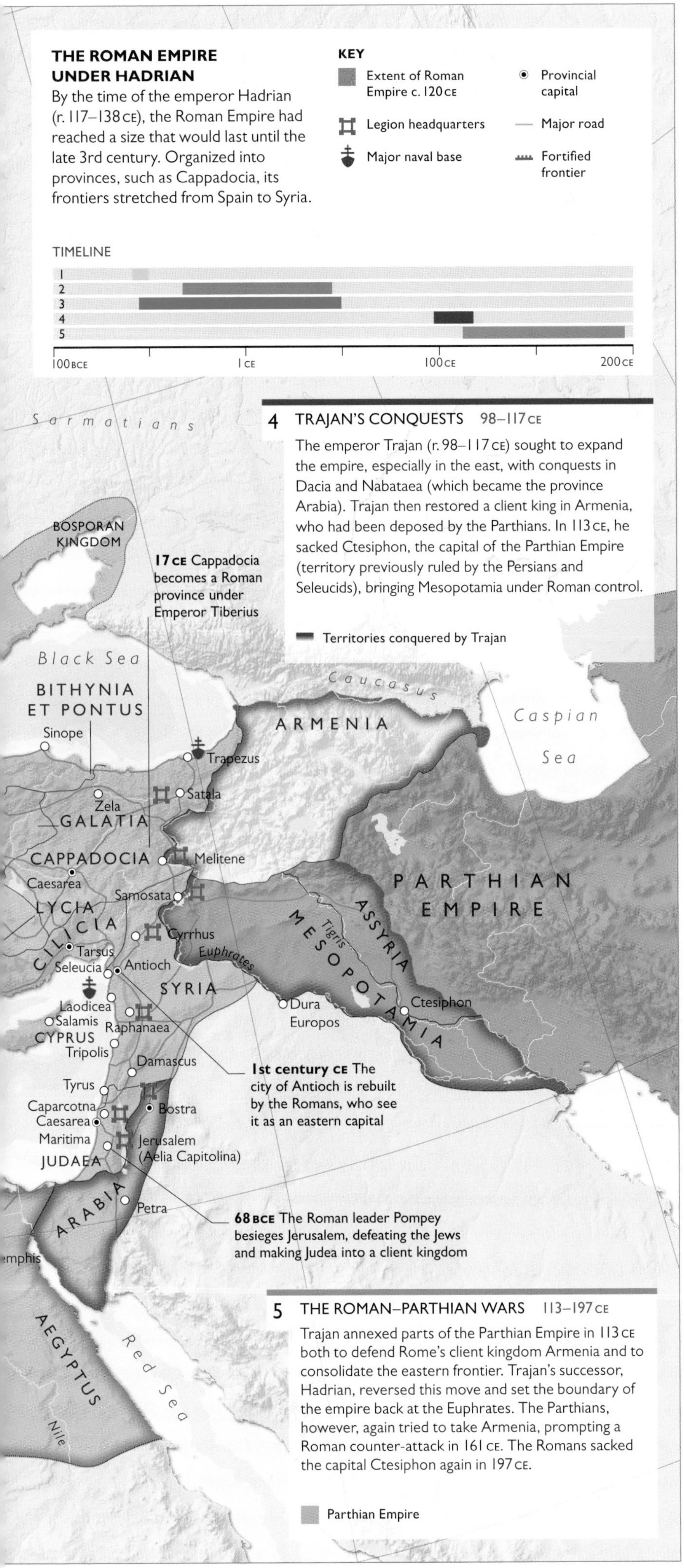
KEY
Extent of Roman Empire c. 120 CE
Provincial capital
Legion headquarters
Major road
Major naval base
Fortified frontier
TIMELINE
1
2
3
4
5
100 BCE
1 CE
100 CE
200 CE
Sarmatians
BOSPORAN KINGDOM
17 CE Cappadocia becomes a Roman province under Emperor Tiberius
Territories conquered by Trajan
Black Sea
BITHYNIA ET PONTUS
Sinope
Caucasus
ARMENIA
Caspian Sea
Trapezus
Satala
Zela
GALATIA
CAPPADOCIA
Melitene
Caesarea
LYCIA
Samosata
CILICIA
Tarsus
Cyrrhus
Seleucia
Antioch
Euphrates
SYRIA
PARTHIAN EMPIRE
ASSYRIA
MESOPOTAMIA
Tigris
Dura Europos
Ctesiphon
Laodicea
Salamis
CYPRUS
Raphanaea
Tripolis
Damascus
1st century CE The city of Antioch is rebuilt by the Romans, who see it as an eastern capital
Tyrus
Caparcotna
Caesarea Maritima
Bostra
Jerusalem (Aelia Capitolina)
JUDAEA
ARABIA
Petra
68 BCE The Roman leader Pompey besieges Jerusalem, defeating the Jews and making Judea into a client kingdom
Memphis
AEGYPTUS
Nile
Red Sea
Parthian Empire

THE ROMAN EMPIRE UNDER HADRIAN
By the time of the emperor Hadrian (r. 117–138 CE), the Roman Empire had reached a size that would last until the late 3rd century. Organized into provinces, such as Cappadocia, its frontiers stretched from Spain to Syria.

4 TRAJAN'S CONQUESTS 98–117 CE
The emperor Trajan (r. 98–117 CE) sought to expand the empire, especially in the east, with conquests in Dacia and Nabataea (which became the province Arabia). Trajan then restored a client king in Armenia, who had been deposed by the Parthians. In 113 CE, he sacked Ctesiphon, the capital of the Parthian Empire (territory previously ruled by the Persians and Seleucids), bringing Mesopotamia under Roman control.

5 THE ROMAN–PARTHIAN WARS 113–197 CE
Trajan annexed parts of the Parthian Empire in 113 CE both to defend Rome's client kingdom Armenia and to consolidate the eastern frontier. Trajan's successor, Hadrian, reversed this move and set the boundary of the empire back at the Euphrates. The Parthians, however, again tried to take Armenia, prompting a Roman counter-attack in 161 CE. The Romans sacked the capital Ctesiphon again in 197 CE.

ROMAN EMPIRE AT ITS HEIGHT

Rome's territories expanded steadily during the period of the Republic. By the time of the accession of the first emperor, Augustus, in 27 BCE, Rome controlled all of the Mediterranean. By 120 CE, the empire's borders were settled, and it entered the period of its greatest stability.

The Roman Republic grew by military conquest and by establishing client kingdoms that accepted Roman domination in return for stability and good trading relations. The first emperor, Augustus, adopted a policy of not expanding Roman boundaries, which was followed by many later emperors, with exceptions such as Trajan, who added substantial but short-lived provinces in the east.

Guarding this huge empire was the job of an army of some 300,000 men, mostly based in camps along the empire's boundaries. The Roman navy protected shipping on the Mediterranean that carried the trade on which the city depended—everything from raw materials and slaves to foods such as grain and olive oil. Relations with the provinces were usually harmonious: the Roman way of life proved very attractive, helped to stimulate further trade, and encouraged people of conquered territories to become "Romanized" and accept imperial rule. The resulting balance of military power and economic prosperity kept the area relatively stable and peaceful in the first 200 years of the empire.

"You cheer my heart, who build as if Rome would be eternal."

AUGUSTUS CAESAR

FROM REPUBLIC TO EMPIRE
POWER STRUGGLES IN ROME

When Julius Caesar seized power as a dictator in 49 BCE, it set Rome on a path from republic to empire. After Julius Caesar's assassination in 44 BCE, Mark Antony, Lepidus, and Octavian ruled the Republic as a triumvirate, but they vied for power, and a series of disputes and civil wars ensued. Octavian ousted Lepidus in a political maneuver and then defeated Antony in battle, becoming the first emperor, under the name Augustus Caesar, in 27 BCE.

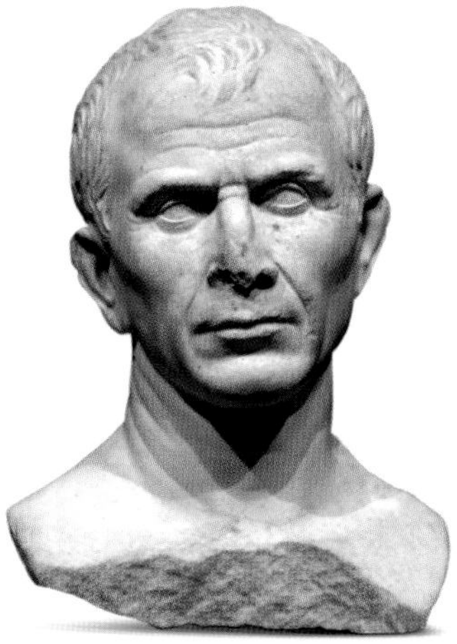

Bust of Julius Caesar
Julius Caesar was a powerful military leader and politician. His actions helped bring about the end of the Republic.

THE ROOTS OF INDIAN HISTORY

In the 2nd millennium BCE, after the decline of the Indus Valley civilization, a people calling themselves *Arya* (noble ones) migrated from the Iranian plateau into northwest India. They spoke Sanskrit, an Indo-European language.

What is known of this time in the Indian subcontinent comes mostly from the Indo-Aryans' sacred texts—the four *Vedas* (from the Sanskrit word for knowledge)—composed and passed on orally. Mostly liturgical texts, used while offering sacrifices to deities such as Indra, the god of war, the Vedas also provide evidence of social structures.

△ **Delicate pottery**
From 1000 to 600 BCE, distinctive painted grayware pottery, decorated with simple lines or geometric designs, spread across northern India. It was so thin and delicate that it must have been a luxury or ritual item.

This period is called the Vedic Age. The early *Rig Veda*, composed from 1500 BCE onward, shows the Indo-Aryans as nomadic pastoralists—chariot-riding tribal warriors raiding each other for cattle. From around 1100 BCE, they moved east to the Ganges plain, where they became settled farmers.

Many villages appeared, where people grew rice, wheat, and barley. Later, several large towns, fortified with ditches and embankments, developed. Marking the beginning of India's caste system, social classes appeared: the priestly *brahmins*, who composed and memorized the *Vedas*; the *kshatriyas*, or noble warriors; the *vaishyas*, or traders; and the *shudras*, or servants. The society changed from a tribal system, where assemblies of chieftains chose a king, or *raja*, to hereditary kingship. New kings received their legitimacy from sacrificial rituals overseen by the *brahmins*, which imbued each new king with divine power.

THE FIRST INDIAN KINGDOMS

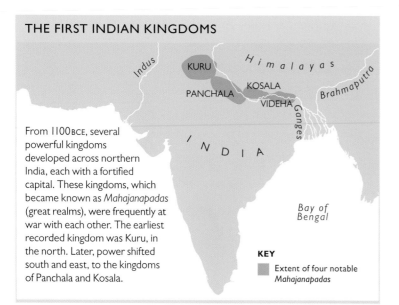

From 1100 BCE, several powerful kingdoms developed across northern India, each with a fortified capital. These kingdoms, which became known as *Mahajanapadas* (great realms), were frequently at war with each other. The earliest recorded kingdom was Kuru, in the north. Later, power shifted south and east, to the kingdoms of Panchala and Kosala.

KEY

▮ Extent of four notable *Mahajanapadas*

Epic war
A war for the throne of Kuru is the subject of the later Hindu epic, the *Mahabharata*. This scene shows the warrior Karna (center) using a magical weapon to kill Ghatotkacha, who is half-human and half-demon.

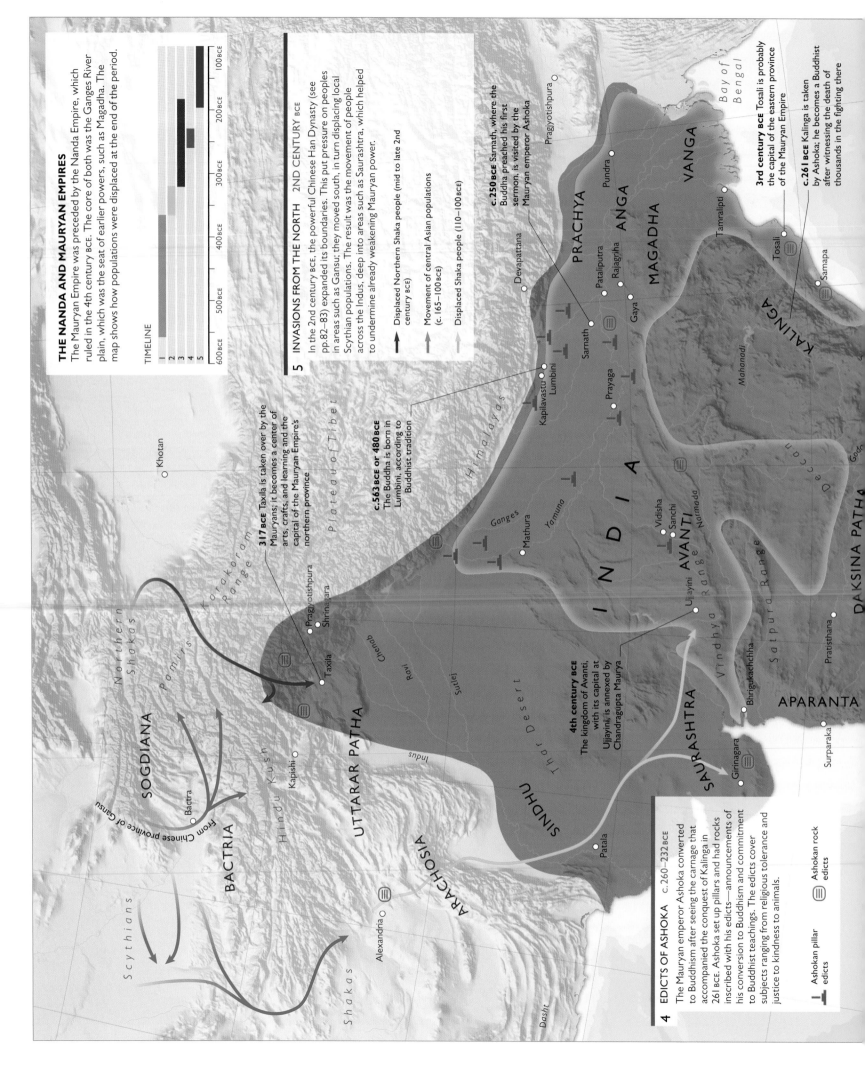

THE NANDA AND MAURYAN EMPIRES

The Mauryan Empire was preceded by the Nanda Empire, which ruled in the 4th century BCE. The core of both was the Ganges River plain, which was the seat of earlier powers, such as Magadha. The map shows how populations were displaced at the end of the period.

TIMELINE

600 BCE   500 BCE   400 BCE   300 BCE   200 BCE   100 BCE

1
2
3
4
5

5 INVASIONS FROM THE NORTH 2ND CENTURY BCE

In the 2nd century BCE, the powerful Chinese Han Dynasty (see pp.82–83) expanded its boundaries. This put pressure on peoples in areas such as Gansu; they moved south, in turn displacing local Scythian populations. The result was the movement of people across the Indus, deep into areas such as Saurashtra, which helped to undermine already weakening Mauryan power.

➤ Displaced Northern Shaka people (mid to late 2nd century BCE)

➤ Movement of central Asian populations (c. 165–100 BCE)

➤ Displaced Shaka people (110–100 BCE)

317 BCE Taxila is taken over by the Mauryans; it becomes a center of arts, crafts, and learning and the capital of the Mauryan Empire's northern province

c.563 BCE or 480 BCE The Buddha is born in Lumbini, according to Buddhist tradition

c.250 BCE Sarnath, where the Buddha preached his first sermon, is visited by the Mauryan emperor Ashoka

3rd century BCE Tosali is probably the capital of the eastern province of the Mauryan Empire

c.261 BCE Kalinga is taken by Ashoka; he becomes a Buddhist after witnessing the death of thousands in the fighting there

4th century BCE The kingdom of Avanti, with its capital at Ujjayini, is annexed by Chandragupta Maurya

4 EDICTS OF ASHOKA c. 260–232 BCE

The Mauryan emperor Ashoka converted to Buddhism after seeing the carnage that accompanied the conquest of Kalinga in 261 BCE. Ashoka set up pillars and had rocks inscribed with his edicts—announcements of his conversion to Buddhism and commitment to Buddhist teachings. The edicts cover subjects ranging from religious tolerance and justice to kindness to animals.

⌶ Ashokan pillar edicts

▥ Ashokan rock edicts

Khotan

Plateau of Tibet

Karakoram Range

Pamirs

Northern Shakas

SOGDIANA

Bactra

From Chinese province of Gansu

BACTRIA

Hindu Kush

Kapishi

Scythians

Shakas

Dasht

Alexandria

ARACHOSIA

Patala

SINDHU

Thar Desert

Indus

UTTARAR PATHA

Taxila

Shrinagara

Pragjyotishpura

Chenab

Ravi

Sutlej

SAURASHTRA

Girinagara

Bhrigukachchha

APARANTA

Surparaka

AVANTI

Ujjayini

Vindhya Range

Satpura Range

Narmada

Pratisthana

DAKSINA PATHA

Godā

Mathura

Yamuna

Ganges

Vidisha

Sanchi

Prayaga

Kapilavastu

Lumbini

Sarnath

Devapattana

Pataliputra

Rajagriha

Gaya

PRACHYA

MAGADHA

ANGA

Pundra

VANGA

Tamralipti

Tosali

Samapa

KALINGA

Mahanadi

Deccan

Himalayas

INDIA

Bay of Bengal

Pragjyotishpura

MAURYAN INDIA

India's largest ancient empire was founded by Chandragupta Maurya in c. 321 BCE. The Mauryan emperors—particularly the great Ashoka—worked to unite India for the first time, to increase prosperity through agriculture and trade, and to promote nonviolence through Jainism and, especially, through the Buddhist faith.

India was a patchwork of independent states until the 6th century BCE, when one state, Magadha, began to take over its neighbors, creating an empire on the plain of the Ganges River. Magadha formed the basis of a larger empire that emerged under the Nanda Dynasty in the mid-4th century. However, India's great Mauryan Empire came into being when Chandragupta Maurya filled a vacuum in the northwest caused by the death of Alexander the Great. He formed an army, marched on Magadha, defeated its king, and was made emperor. At the end of his life, he converted to Jainism, encouraging social awareness and nonviolence.

The Mauryans came to rule all of India except the far southern tip. They maintained power using a system of provincial governors and a well-organized civil service. Traders were taxed, and the government collected tolls from roads and river crossings.

Ashoka, who ruled as emperor c. 268–232 BCE, eventually renounced war and became a committed Buddhist, building and repairing stupas, sponsoring Buddhist missionaries, and passing laws in line with the compassionate tenets of the faith. Mauryan rule lasted until the 180s BCE, when the last emperor was assassinated.

ASHOKA PILLARS
ANNOUNCEMENTS OF BUDDHIST FAITH

Twenty pillars inscribed with Ashoka's edicts still survive, including one (below) at Sarnath near Varanasi. Most of the inscriptions are written in the Brahmi script, a form of writing that became widespread during the Mauryan period and was used throughout India. Dozens of later south Asian scripts derive from Brahmi, including Devanagari, often used to write the Sanskrit language.

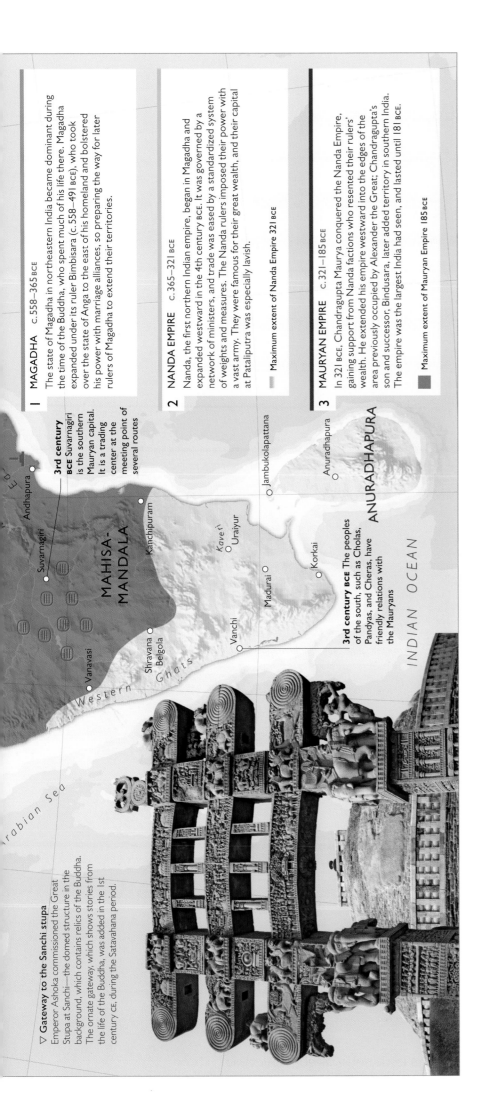

1 MAGADHA   c. 558–365 BCE

The state of Magadha in northeastern India became dominant during the time of the Buddha, who spent much of his life there. Magadha expanded under its ruler Bimbisara (c. 558–491 BCE), who took over the state of Anga to the east of his homeland and bolstered his power with marriage alliances, so preparing the way for later rulers of Magadha to extend their territories.

2 NANDA EMPIRE   c. 365–321 BCE

Nanda, the first northern Indian empire, began in Magadha and expanded westward in the 4th century BCE. It was governed by a network of ministers, and trade was eased by a standardized system of weights and measures. The Nanda rulers imposed their power with a vast army. They were famous for their great wealth, and their capital at Pataliputra was especially lavish.

■ Maximum extent of Nanda Empire 321 BCE

3 MAURYAN EMPIRE   c. 321–185 BCE

In 321 BCE, Chandragupta Maurya conquered the Nanda Empire, gaining support from Nanda factions who resented their rulers' wealth. He extended his empire westward into the edges of the area previously occupied by Alexander the Great; Chandragupta's son and successor, Bindusara, later added territory in southern India. The empire was the largest India had seen, and lasted until 181 BCE.

■ Maximum extent of Mauryan Empire 185 BCE

3rd century BCE Suvarnagiri is the southern Mauryan capital. It is a trading center at the meeting point of several routes.

3rd century BCE The peoples of the south, such as Cholas, Pandyas, and Cheras, have friendly relations with the Mauryans

▽ **Gateway to the Sanchi stupa**
Emperor Ashoka commissioned the Great Stupa at Sanchi—the domed structure in the background, which contains relics of the Buddha. The ornate gateway, which shows stories from the life of the Buddha, was added in the 1st century CE, during the Satavahana period.

Andhapura
Suvarnagiri
Vanavasi
Shravana Belgola
MAHISA-MANDALA
Kanchipuram
Kaveri
Uraiyur
Madurai
Vanchi
Korkai
Jambukolapattana
Anuradhapura
ANURADHAPURA
Western Ghats
Arabian Sea
INDIAN OCEAN

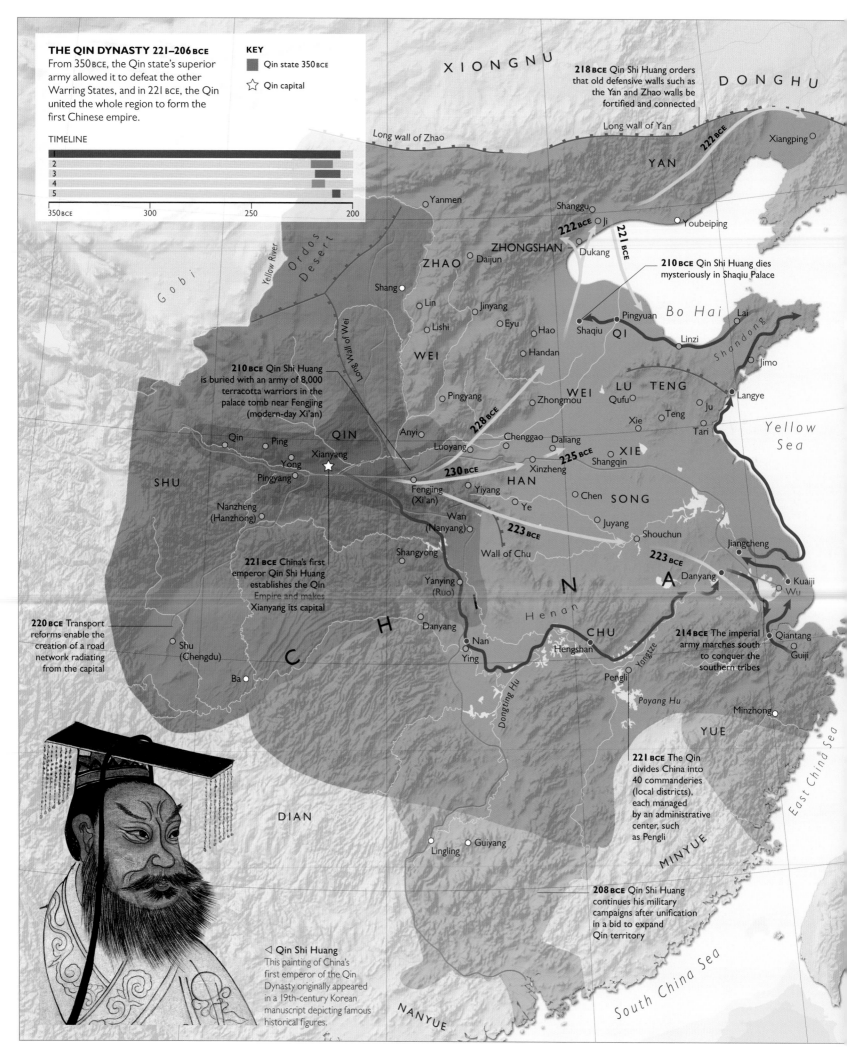

THE QIN DYNASTY 221–206 BCE
From 350 BCE, the Qin state's superior army allowed it to defeat the other Warring States, and in 221 BCE, the Qin united the whole region to form the first Chinese empire.

KEY
Qin state 350 BCE
☆ Qin capital

TIMELINE

1
2
3
4
5

350 BCE   300   250   200

218 BCE Qin Shi Huang orders that old defensive walls such as the Yan and Zhao walls be fortified and connected

210 BCE Qin Shi Huang dies mysteriously in Shaqiu Palace

210 BCE Qin Shi Huang is buried with an army of 8,000 terracotta warriors in the palace tomb near Fengjing (modern-day Xi'an)

221 BCE China's first emperor Qin Shi Huang establishes the Qin Empire and makes Xianyang its capital

220 BCE Transport reforms enable the creation of a road network radiating from the capital

214 BCE The imperial army marches south to conquer the southern tribes

221 BCE The Qin divides China into 40 commanderies (local districts), each managed by an administrative center, such as Pengli

208 BCE Qin Shi Huang continues his military campaigns after unification in a bid to expand Qin territory

◁ **Qin Shi Huang**
This painting of China's first emperor of the Qin Dynasty originally appeared in a 19th-century Korean manuscript depicting famous historical figures.

XIONGNU

DONGHU

Long wall of Zhao

Long wall of Yan

YAN

Xiangping

222 BCE

Yanmen

Shanggu

Youbeiping

222 BCE Ji

221 BCE

ZHONGSHAN

Dukang

Daijun

ZHAO

Shang

Lin

Jinyang

Lishi

Eyu

Hao

WEI

Handan

Pingyuan

Shaqiu

QI

Bo Hai

Lai

Linzi

Jimo

Shandong

Pingyang

WEI

LU

TENG

Zhongmou

Qufu

Ju

Langye

Yellow Sea

Qin

Ping

QIN

Anyi

Xie

Teng

Yong

Xianyang

Luoyang

Chenggao

Daliang

Tari

Pingyang

230 BCE

225 BCE

XIE

228 BCE

Xinzheng

Shangqin

SHU

Fengjing (Xi'an)

Yiyang

HAN

Chen

SONG

Nanzheng (Hanzhong)

Wan (Nanyang)

Ye

Juyang

Shouchun

223 BCE

Jiangcheng

Shangyong

Wall of Chu

223 BCE

Danyang

Kuaiji

Yanying (Ruo)

C

H

Danyang

I

N

A

Wu

Qiantang

Shu (Chengdu)

Henan

CHU

Guiji

Ba

Nan

Hengshan

Ying

Yangtze

Dongting Hu

Pengli

Poyang Hu

Minzhong

YUE

DIAN

Lingling

Guiyang

East China Sea

MINYUE

NANYUE

South China Sea

1 QIN EXPANSIONISM 350–206 BCE

Originally a small state on the western borders, Qin defeated neighboring states during the Warring States period and took control of a large swathe of western and southern China. Victory over the Han state in 230 BCE gave Qin the impetus to conquer the remaining states within a decade. In 221 BCE, Qin leader Ying Zheng took the title of Qin Shi Huang (The First Emperor) and ruled from Xianyang.

→ Route of Qin campaign

■ Qin conquests by unification 221 BCE

■ Qin expansion by 288 BCE

■ Qin conquests to 206 BCE

2 REIGN OF QIN SHI HUANG 221–210 BCE

Qin Shi Huang introduced a series of reforms to strengthen the unity of China. These included the abolition of feudalism (to eliminate the traditional local and family loyalties that could threaten central power) and the establishment of a new system of administrative districts. He unified China economically by standardizing weights and measures across the realm.

⊙ Administrative center

3 FORTIFYING DEFENSIVE WALLS 218–206 BCE

Faced with the threat of attacks from nomadic people in the north and west, Qin Shi Huang mobilized a labor force numbering thousands to construct a unified fortification out of the defensive walls, built by several Chinese rulers during the Warring States period. The Great Wall would become the Qin Dynasty's most famous legacy.

⊔⊔ Early sections of the Great Wall

4 QIN TRANSPORT NETWORKS 220–214 BCE

Another major construction to begin during Qin Shi Huang's reign was a complex road system to allow easier travel between cities and encourage trade nationwide. The emperor also ordered the construction of a major canal linking the Xiang and the Li Jiang Rivers to ferry supplies to the army.

— Imperial roads

5 THE FALL OF QIN 210–206 BCE

In 210 BCE, Qin Shi Huang died while on a tour of eastern China. The people were told that he was making the trip to inspect the empire, but it was in fact a quest to find an elixir of immortality. Civil disorder erupted following the emperor's death and ended with the Qin Dynasty collapsing in 206 BCE.

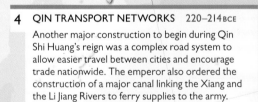

→ Qin Shi Huang's tour   ● Town visited during Qin Shi Huang's tour

CHINA'S FIRST EMPEROR

After a period in which numerous Chinese states fought for supremacy, it was the Qin state that eventually triumphed and unified China in 221 BCE. The Qin emperor, Qin Shi Huang, established a strict and highly centralized form of rule—a system that would become the model for China's future governance.

Between the 11th and 8th centuries BCE, China was made up of a mosaic of city-states loyal to the Zhou Dynasty, which employed a form of feudalism to rule the land. However, following the Warring States period (475–221 BCE), in which the Qin state triumphed over the Zhou Dynasty and six other rival states, the Qin leader, Ying Zheng, unified China under his leadership.

As the Qin's first emperor, Ying Zheng took the name Qin Shi Huang and replaced the old kinship-based government with an efficient bureaucratic system. He proved a formidable ruler with a clear vision for the realm, establishing a ruthless penal code to enforce his despotic rule. He actively suppressed philosophies—by the burning of books—that he felt either criticized or challenged his authority. His untimely death in 210 BCE, however, preceded the swift decline and end of his dynasty in 206 BCE. Although the Qin Empire lasted only 15 years, it had set up institutions that paved the way for Liu Bang to form the more enduring Han Dynasty (see pp.82–83).

"I am Emperor, my descendants will be numerous ... my line will not end."

EMPEROR QIN SHI HUANG

THE WARRING STATES PERIOD

China was a patchwork of states, each ruled by high-ranking nobles who swore allegiance to the Zhou kings. But as the Zhou's authority waned, the stronger states saw their opportunity and fought one another to gain control of China. In what historians call the Warring States period (475–221 BCE), six major states—Chu, Han, Yan, Qi, Qin, and Zhao—fought one another for dominance over the region.

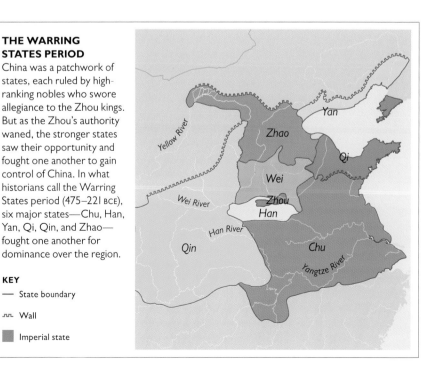

KEY

— State boundary

⊓⊓ Wall

■ Imperial state

TERRACOTTA ARMY

In 1974, farmers digging wells in Xi'an, China, unearthed the first of four vast pits containing an army of terracotta figures. About 7,000 life-size warriors, 150 cavalry horses, 130 chariots, and 520 chariot horses were found.

△ Warrior's face
The warriors' heads were made in molds, with features such as facial hair added by hand modeling. No two faces are the same.

The army had been buried in 210 BCE to protect Qin Shi Huang, the First Emperor of China (see pp.74–75), who lies in his tomb under a vast artificial mountain. According to Sima Qian, a historian from the early Han Dynasty (see pp.82–83), the tomb was built by 700,000 men and held a model of China, with its palaces. The tomb has still not been excavated, partly because of the archaeological challenge it presents but also because of the awe in which the First Emperor is still held by the Chinese.

Ruling from the afterlife

The First Emperor had planned to continue ruling from his tomb for eternity, so he was buried with everything he might need. He was accompanied by terracotta civil servants and entertainers—acrobats, wrestlers, and musicians. The army was there to protect him in the afterlife from the vengeful ghosts of all the men he had killed while on Earth. Nearby pits held suits of armor made of stone plates, as well as 40,000 bronze weapons whose blades remained razor sharp. They had been plated with chromium oxide to protect them from corrosion, a technique only reinvented in the 20th century.

Before the First Emperor, there had been no tradition of life-size, realistic statues in China. A theory suggests a Greek inspiration, but the style of the terracotta army remained distinctively Chinese.

▽ Eternal transportation
This half life-size scale model of a chariot pulled by horses is made of bronze. It provided the emperor transportation for tours of his kingdom in the afterlife.

Standing guard
For more than 2,000 years, the terracotta warriors have been standing at attention in massed ranks. They face east, with the tomb they are protecting directly behind them.

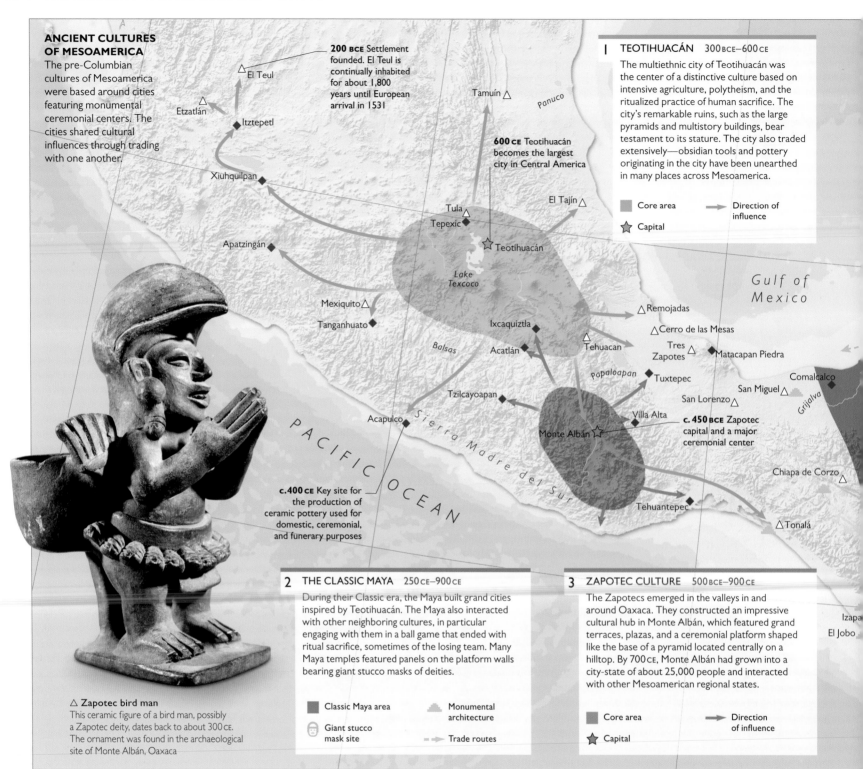

ANCIENT CULTURES OF MESOAMERICA
The pre-Columbian cultures of Mesoamerica were based around cities featuring monumental ceremonial centers. The cities shared cultural influences through trading with one another.

200 BCE Settlement founded. El Teul is continually inhabited for about 1,800 years until European arrival in 1531

600 CE Teotihuacán becomes the largest city in Central America

c.400 CE Key site for the production of ceramic pottery used for domestic, ceremonial, and funerary purposes

c.450 BCE Zapotec capital and a major ceremonial center

El Teul · Etzatlán · Itztepetl · Tamuín · Panuco · Xiuhquilpan · Tula · Tepexic · El Tajín · Teotihuacán · Apatzingán · Lake Texcoco · Gulf of Mexico · Mexiquito · Tanganhuato · Ixcaquiztla · Remojadas · Cerro de las Mesas · Tehuacan · Tres Zapotes · Matacapan Piedra · Balsas · Acatlán · Popaloapan · Tuxtepec · Comalcalco · Tzilcayoapan · San Miguel · San Lorenzo · Grijalva · Acapulco · Villa Alta · Monte Albán · Chiapa de Corzo · PACIFIC OCEAN · Sierra Madre del Sur · Tehuantepec · Tonalá · Izapa · El Jobo

1 TEOTIHUACÁN 300 BCE–600 CE
The multiethnic city of Teotihuacán was the center of a distinctive culture based on intensive agriculture, polytheism, and the ritualized practice of human sacrifice. The city's remarkable ruins, such as the large pyramids and multistory buildings, bear testament to its stature. The city also traded extensively—obsidian tools and pottery originating in the city have been unearthed in many places across Mesoamerica.

- Core area
- Direction of influence
- Capital

2 THE CLASSIC MAYA 250 CE–900 CE
During their Classic era, the Maya built grand cities inspired by Teotihuacán. The Maya also interacted with other neighboring cultures, in particular engaging with them in a ball game that ended with ritual sacrifice, sometimes of the losing team. Many Maya temples featured panels on the platform walls bearing giant stucco masks of deities.

- Classic Maya area
- Giant stucco mask site
- Monumental architecture
- Trade routes

3 ZAPOTEC CULTURE 500 BCE–900 CE
The Zapotecs emerged in the valleys in and around Oaxaca. They constructed an impressive cultural hub in Monte Albán, which featured grand terraces, plazas, and a ceremonial platform shaped like the base of a pyramid located centrally on a hilltop. By 700 CE, Monte Albán had grown into a city-state of about 25,000 people and interacted with other Mesoamerican regional states.

- Core area
- Direction of influence
- Capital

△ **Zapotec bird man**
This ceramic figure of a bird man, possibly a Zapotec deity, dates back to about 300 CE. The ornament was found in the archaeological site of Monte Albán, Oaxaca

ANCIENT AMERICAN CIVILIZATIONS

In the period 250–900 CE, increased agricultural productivity in Mesoamerica, led to the rise of the great cities of Teotihuacán and Monte Albán. The cities influenced the Maya city-states to the east, ushering in a time of prosperity known as the Classic Maya period. Meanwhile, the mastery of irrigation techniques allowed a succession of empires to rule the Andean region of South America.

Teotihuacán and Monte Albán (the Zapotec capital) were Mesoamerica's two most powerful trading centers in the early Classic era. Teotihuacán traded with the first Classic Maya cities to form in the highlands, and its influence reached other similar independent Maya states that were emerging in the Yucatan Peninsula at this time. The Maya culture would reach its high point during the Classic period, evident in the architecture, the widespread use of written inscriptions, and the complex Maya calendar.

All three cultures based their cities around ceremonial zones, often with pyramidal temples that served as sites of rituals, including human sacrifice. They also built recreational ball courts and sculpted stelae to glorify their rulers.

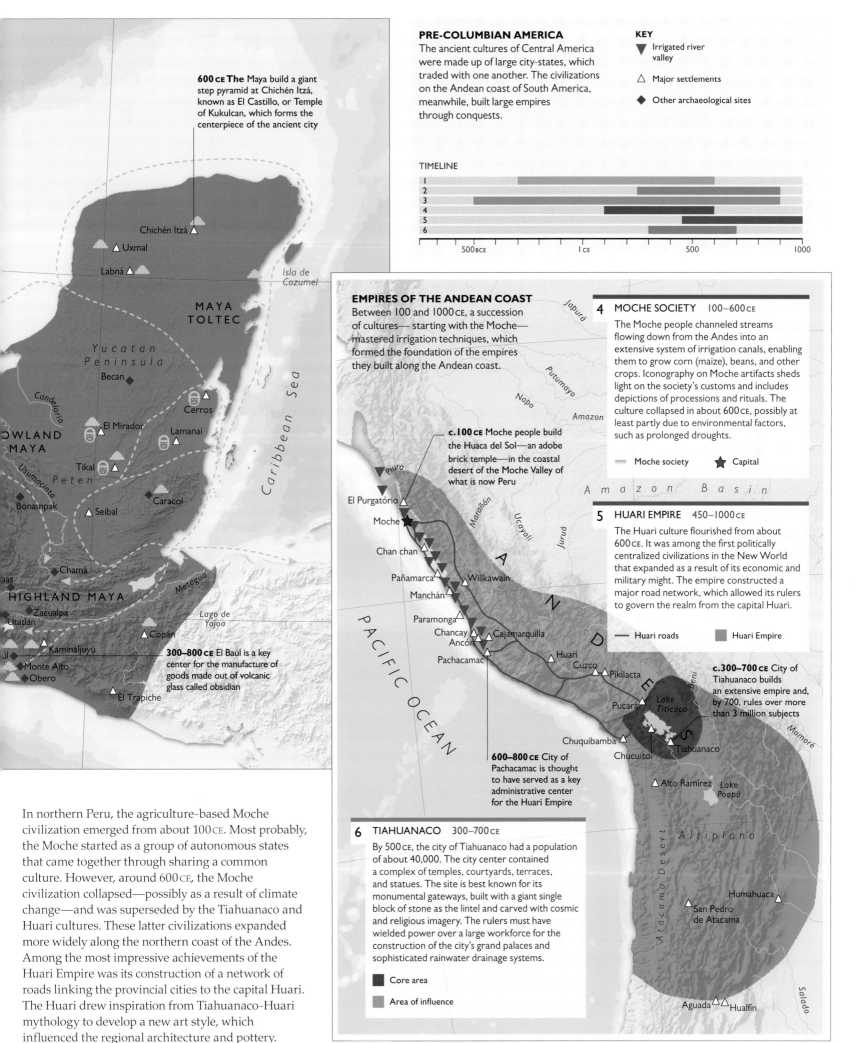

600 CE The Maya build a giant step pyramid at Chichén Itzá, known as El Castillo, or Temple of Kukulcan, which forms the centerpiece of the ancient city

PRE-COLUMBIAN AMERICA
The ancient cultures of Central America were made up of large city-states, which traded with one another. The civilizations on the Andean coast of South America, meanwhile, built large empires through conquests.

KEY

▼ Irrigated river valley

△ Major settlements

◆ Other archaeological sites

TIMELINE

1	
2	
3	
4	
5	
6	

500 BCE   1 CE   500   1000

EMPIRES OF THE ANDEAN COAST
Between 100 and 1000 CE, a succession of cultures— starting with the Moche— mastered irrigation techniques, which formed the foundation of the empires they built along the Andean coast.

c.100 CE Moche people build the Huaca del Sol—an adobe brick temple—in the coastal desert of the Moche Valley of what is now Peru

4 MOCHE SOCIETY 100–600 CE

The Moche people channeled streams flowing down from the Andes into an extensive system of irrigation canals, enabling them to grow corn (maize), beans, and other crops. Iconography on Moche artifacts sheds light on the society's customs and includes depictions of processions and rituals. The culture collapsed in about 600 CE, possibly at least partly due to environmental factors, such as prolonged droughts.

— Moche society ★ Capital

5 HUARI EMPIRE 450–1000 CE

The Huari culture flourished from about 600 CE. It was among the first politically centralized civilizations in the New World that expanded as a result of its economic and military might. The empire constructed a major road network, which allowed its rulers to govern the realm from the capital Huari.

— Huari roads ▨ Huari Empire

c.300–700 CE City of Tiahuanaco builds an extensive empire and, by 700, rules over more than 3 million subjects

300–800 CE El Baúl is a key center for the manufacture of goods made out of volcanic glass called obsidian

600–800 CE City of Pachacamac is thought to have served as a key administrative center for the Huari Empire

6 TIAHUANACO 300–700 CE

By 500 CE, the city of Tiahuanaco had a population of about 40,000. The city center contained a complex of temples, courtyards, terraces, and statues. The site is best known for its monumental gateways, built with a giant single block of stone as the lintel and carved with cosmic and religious imagery. The rulers must have wielded power over a large workforce for the construction of the city's grand palaces and sophisticated rainwater drainage systems.

■ Core area

■ Area of influence

In northern Peru, the agriculture-based Moche civilization emerged from about 100 CE. Most probably, the Moche started as a group of autonomous states that came together through sharing a common culture. However, around 600 CE, the Moche civilization collapsed—possibly as a result of climate change—and was superseded by the Tiahuanaco and Huari cultures. These latter civilizations expanded more widely along the northern coast of the Andes. Among the most impressive achievements of the Huari Empire was its construction of a network of roads linking the provincial cities to the capital Huari. The Huari drew inspiration from Tiahuanaco-Huari mythology to develop a new art style, which influenced the regional architecture and pottery.

c.400 As the Picts move south, Irish Celts settle in the northern parts of the British Isles and become Scots

c.441 Germanic peoples from northern Europe begin to settle in Britain
c.457 Britons flee Kent after an Anglo-Saxon victory at Aylesford

456 The Visigoths begin to expand their kingdom in southern Gaul. They conquer most of Iberia by c. 500

414 Athaulf, leader of the Visigoths, marries Galla Placidia, daughter of the late Roman Emperor Theodosius, at Narbo

428–429 The Vandals cross the Strait of Gibraltar into North Africa; the kingdom they establish lasts until the 6th century

430 The Vandals take the city of Hippo; St. Augustine, church father and bishop of the city, dies during the siege

---

1 VISIGOTHS 378–418 CE

The Visigoths (western Goths) defeated the Romans at Adrianopolis (Edirne) in 378 before moving west. Led by their king Alaric, they reached Rome in 410 and sacked the city. By 418, they had settled in southern Gaul, allowed to stay by Rome in return for service as mercenaries. This agreement did not last, and the Visigoths established their own capital at Tolosa (Toulouse).

⇨ Visigoths   ••▸ Goths

2 THE HUNS 370–440 CE

The Huns arrived in what is now southern Russia from central Asia in the 370s. From here, they moved west, conquering the territory of the Alans and overwhelming the eastern Goths. Under their powerful leader Attila, they established a large eastern European empire, centered on what is now Hungary, near the borders of both the eastern and western Roman Empires.

⟶ Hun migration to Hungary

453 Attila dies, and the Huns' empire disintegrates

376 Thousands of Goths move into Roman territory in Dacia and Lower Moesia

452 The Huns sack Aquileia, opening a way into northern Italy for Attila

492–493 The Visigoths under Theoderic besiege Ravenna, the western Roman capital

410 The Visigoth king Alaric dies; the Visigoths abandon their plan to invade Africa

396–397 Athens and Corinth are among the cities ravaged by the Visigoths

378 A force of Goths, Alans, and others defeats the army of the Eastern Roman Empire

KINGDOM OF THE VISIGOTHS

ATLANTIC OCEAN

SCOTLAND · Scots · Picts

Irish Celts

IRELAND

BRITAIN · Thames · Londinium · 457

North Sea

Angles · Saxons · Franks · Rhine pre-357

Baltic Sea

GERMANY

Vistula

Sueves pre-406

Vandals pre-406

Carpathian Mountains

EMPIRE OF THE HUNS c.420

DACIA

Goths pre-376

420

Visigoths from 382

LOWER MOESIA

441

Danube

Scheldt · 486 · Meuse

Seine · Lutetia · Borbetomagus · 451

GAUL

451 Catalaunian Fields ✕

443

Saône

Alps

Mediolanum · Verona · Ticinum · Patavium · Po · Genua · Ravenna

Aquileia · 453

PANNONIA

Ostrogoths from 450

Tisza

Narbo · 409 · 414 · 418 · c.418

Alans, Vandals, Sueves

Tolosa

456

Sueves

Alans

Douro · Tagus

Toletum

Corduba (Córdoba)

IBERIA

Tarraco

WESTERN ROMAN EMPIRE (From 395)

Corsica

Balearic Islands

Sardinia

Rome · 455 · 410 · 489

Neapolis

Adriatic Sea

ITALY

THRACE · Adrianopolis · 378 ✕

Philippopolis

Constantinople

395

EASTERN

Thermopylae

Corinth · Athens · Ephesus

GREECE

Crete

Strait of Gibraltar

Malaca · Carthago Nova

429

429

Vandals · 439

Atlas Mountains

MAURETANIA

NUMIDIA

Hippo · Carthage · 430

Panormus · Sicily

Mediterranean Sea

AFRICA

Leptis Magna · c.456

406–407 Alans

---

7 FRANKISH EXPANSION 357–550 CE

The Frankish tribes who lived along the empire's border on the Rhine sometimes cooperated with their Roman neighbors and sometimes raided their lands. In 357, their large domain was recognized by the empire, and when Roman power collapsed in the 5th century, the Franks, united under the Merovingian Dynasty, conquered most of Gaul.

⟶ Franks

6 OSTROGOTHS 453–493 CE

The Ostrogoths (eastern Goths) were one of the peoples subjugated by the Huns in the 4th century. They settled in the Roman province of Pannonia, and after the death of Attila in 453, moved westward and then to northern Italy. From there, under their great leader Theoderic, they extended their power across Italy in the 480s and 490s.

⟶ Ostrogoths

5 THE CAMPAIGNS OF ATTILA 440–453 CE

Led by Attila, the Huns devastated the Balkans and Thrace, attacked Greece, and extracted tribute from the Eastern Roman emperor. They then invaded Gaul, where they were defeated by the Romans at the Battle of the Catalaunian Fields in 451. The Huns moved into Italy, sacking numerous cities, before the Roman Empire sued for peace and Attila finally left Italy.

⟶ Campaigns of Attila

3 THE GREAT MIGRATION 406 CE

In the winter of 406, a vast group of nomadic peoples—Alans, Vandals, and Sueves—migrated westward and crossed the Rhine into Roman territory. From here, they moved through Gaul and into the Iberian Peninsula, where the Alans and Sueves settled. The Vandals moved on farther, crossing the Strait of Gibraltar into North Africa in 429.

- - - ▶ Alans, Vandals, and Sueves ⟶ Alans

c.370 The Huns make their first appearance in the west, having arrived from central Asia

370 After reaching the Volga across the steppes, the Huns start their rapid movement westward

▷ **Visigothic brooch**
This bronze and garnet brooch, found in southwest Spain, dates from the 6th century. The eagle shape was adapted by the Visigoths from the Roman imperial insignia.

Huns pre-**376**

Alans pre-**376**

Black Sea

OMAN EMPIRE
(From 395)

ASIA MINOR
○ Antioch

SYRIA

Cyprus

4 MIGRATIONS TO BRITAIN c.400–460 CE

By the early 5th century, Rome had withdrawn its troops from Britain in order to fight invaders elsewhere. In 410, Emperor Honorius instructed the cities of Britain to "look to your own defenses," marking the end of Roman rule in the province. Abandoned by Rome, Britain was invaded and settled by Picts, Irish Celts, and Angles and Saxons from northern Europe.

⟶ Irish ⟶ Picts ⟶ Angles and Saxons

MIGRATIONS OF PEOPLES 300–500 CE

The 4th and 5th centuries saw long-distance population movements across western Asia and Europe. These changes weakened the power of the Roman Empire, destroyed major cities such as Rome, and paved the way for the western empire's disintegration at the end of the 5th century.

KEY

■ Extent of Roman Empire c.390 ✗ Major battle

TIMELINE

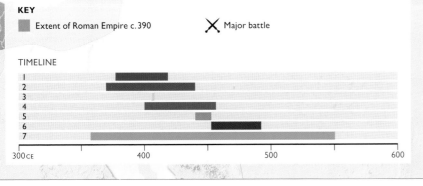

300 CE 400 500 600

AGE OF MIGRATIONS

The decline of the Roman Empire was accelerated in the 4th and 5th centuries by invasions of nomadic peoples from the east. This caused a cascade of movement, with new peoples settling in Europe and North Africa and changing the balance of power.

From the late 4th century onward, a series of peoples moved into lands previously governed by the Romans. Many of these newcomers, such as the Alans and the Huns, originated in central Asia, but others, such as the Franks, were people from near the empire's borders. The invaders came for different reasons. The nomadic Huns came to plunder, moving quickly across the landscape and taking whatever they could. Others, facing problems such as famine or displacement due to invasion at home, were desperate to find somewhere new to settle. For example, the Visigoths (western Goths), who had previously been settled in the Danubian Plain near the Black Sea, made agreements with Rome, gaining land in return for supplying mercenaries to the empire's armies.

By the time the invasions began, Roman power was already in decline. There were many reasons for this—famine, unemployment, inflation, and corruption all played their part. So did the empire's size, which made it hard to govern and led to its division into eastern and western halves in 285 CE. The invasions weakened it further, and the leaders of the mercenary forces were well placed to take over parts of the empire in the 5th century after Rome itself fell.

> *"Attila was a man born into the world to shake the nations, the scourge of all lands."*
>
> JORDANES, GOTHIC HISTORIAN, c.551

THE DIVIDED EMPIRE
EASTERN AND WESTERN REALMS

Troubled by enemies to the north and east, and riven by internal strife, Diocletian decided that the empire was too large to rule as one realm. He split it in two in 285, ruling the eastern part himself, with the west governed by Maximian. There were subsequent periods of unification, but the east–west administration system survived for centuries, until the western empire was dissolved in 480.

3rd-century bust of Emperor Diocletian

HAN DYNASTY

Rebel leader Liu Bang reunified China in 206 BCE and founded the Han Empire. He instated a highly effective centralized government based on the system introduced by Qin Shi Huang's former Qin Empire. At the height of the Han's 400-year rule, China was the dominant cultural, political, and economic force in Asia.

The Han era (206 BCE–220 CE) is considered a golden age in Chinese history, during which the realm flourished in the areas of commerce, technology, arts, and politics. Through its conquests, the dynasty also brought a huge swathe of central Asia under its rule, creating an empire that at its height was comparable in size and wealth to its Roman counterpart. To consolidate its power, the Han fortified the Great Wall and set up military garrisons to protect its outposts. These measures allowed the empire to open the Silk Road—a major trade artery—in 130 BCE (see pp.102–103) and establish lucrative commercial links with the wider world, exporting luxury goods such as silk and lacquerwork. Under the Han, technology advanced, the coinage was standardized, Chinese calligraphy evolved into an art, and technological innovations culminated in the invention of cast iron tools, silk-weaving looms, and paper. However, despite the Han's military achievements, the steppe peoples, in particular the Xiongnu, remained a constant threat. In tandem with peasant rebellions in the 2nd century, they played a pivotal role in eroding the empire's authority and bringing about its eventual downfall.

> *"Where will I find brave men to guard the four corners of my land?"*
>
> EMPEROR GAOZU, FROM *SONG OF THE GREAT WIND*, 195 BCE

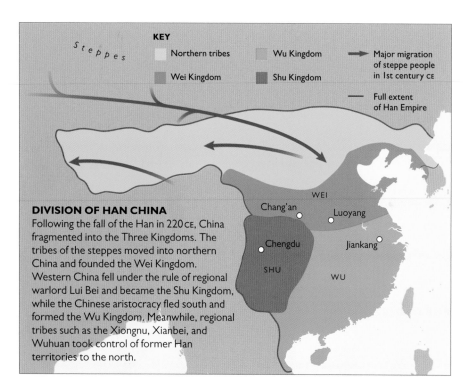

KEY

- ☐ Northern tribes
- ☐ Wei Kingdom
- ☐ Wu Kingdom
- ☐ Shu Kingdom
- → Major migration of steppe people in 1st century CE
- — Full extent of Han Empire

DIVISION OF HAN CHINA
Following the fall of the Han in 220 CE, China fragmented into the Three Kingdoms. The tribes of the steppes moved into northern China and founded the Wei Kingdom. Western China fell under the rule of regional warlord Lui Bei and became the Shu Kingdom, while the Chinese aristocracy fled south and formed the Wu Kingdom. Meanwhile, regional tribes such as the Xiongnu, Xianbei, and Wuhuan took control of former Han territories to the north.

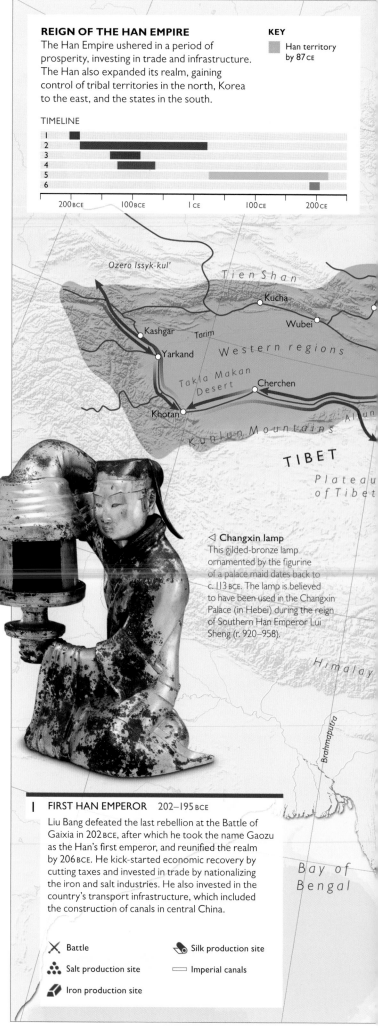

REIGN OF THE HAN EMPIRE
The Han Empire ushered in a period of prosperity, investing in trade and infrastructure. The Han also expanded its realm, gaining control of tribal territories in the north, Korea to the east, and the states in the south.

KEY

☐ Han territory by 87 CE

TIMELINE

1 2 3 4 5 6

200 BCE   100 BCE   1 CE   100 CE   200 CE

◁ **Changxin lamp**
This gilded-bronze lamp, ornamented by the figurine of a palace maid, dates back to c. 113 BCE. The lamp is believed to have been used in the Changxin Palace (in Hebei) during the reign of Southern Han Emperor Lui Sheng (r. 920–958).

FIRST HAN EMPEROR 202–195 BCE

Liu Bang defeated the last rebellion at the Battle of Gaixia in 202 BCE, after which he took the name Gaozu as the Han's first emperor, and reunified the realm by 206 BCE. He kick-started economic recovery by cutting taxes and invested in trade by nationalizing the iron and salt industries. He also invested in the country's transport infrastructure, which included the construction of canals in central China.

- ✕ Battle
- ⁘ Salt production site
- ◿ Iron production site
- ⬙ Silk production site
- ▭ Imperial canals

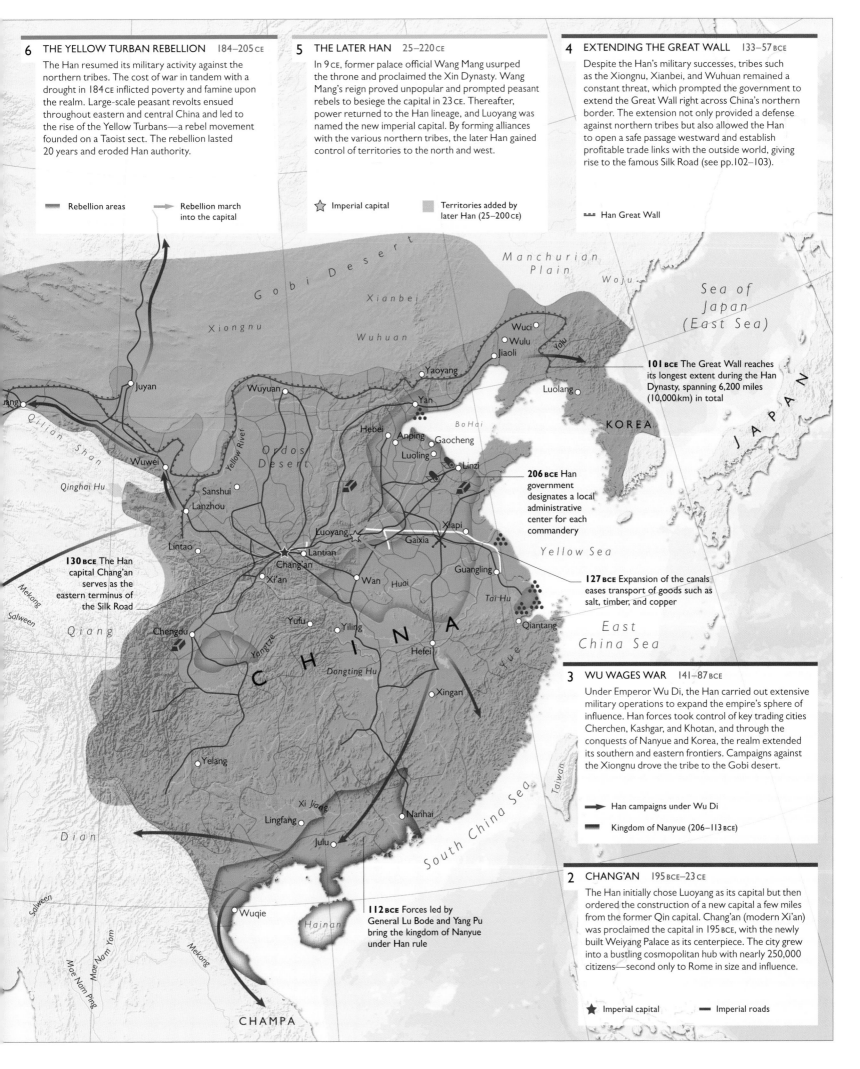

6 THE YELLOW TURBAN REBELLION 184–205 CE

The Han resumed its military activity against the northern tribes. The cost of war in tandem with a drought in 184 CE inflicted poverty and famine upon the realm. Large-scale peasant revolts ensued throughout eastern and central China and led to the rise of the Yellow Turbans—a rebel movement founded on a Taoist sect. The rebellion lasted 20 years and eroded Han authority.

— Rebellion areas   → Rebellion march into the capital

5 THE LATER HAN 25–220 CE

In 9 CE, former palace official Wang Mang usurped the throne and proclaimed the Xin Dynasty. Wang Mang's reign proved unpopular and prompted peasant rebels to besiege the capital in 23 CE. Thereafter, power returned to the Han lineage, and Luoyang was named the new imperial capital. By forming alliances with the various northern tribes, the later Han gained control of territories to the north and west.

☆ Imperial capital   ▨ Territories added by later Han (25–200 CE)

4 EXTENDING THE GREAT WALL 133–57 BCE

Despite the Han's military successes, tribes such as the Xiongnu, Xianbei, and Wuhuan remained a constant threat, which prompted the government to extend the Great Wall right across China's northern border. The extension not only provided a defense against northern tribes but also allowed the Han to open a safe passage westward and establish profitable trade links with the outside world, giving rise to the famous Silk Road (see pp.102–103).

▰▰▰ Han Great Wall

101 BCE The Great Wall reaches its longest extent during the Han Dynasty, spanning 6,200 miles (10,000 km) in total

206 BCE Han government designates a local administrative center for each commandery

130 BCE The Han capital Chang'an serves as the eastern terminus of the Silk Road

127 BCE Expansion of the canals eases transport of goods such as salt, timber, and copper

3 WU WAGES WAR 141–87 BCE

Under Emperor Wu Di, the Han carried out extensive military operations to expand the empire's sphere of influence. Han forces took control of key trading cities Cherchen, Kashgar, and Khotan, and through the conquests of Nanyue and Korea, the realm extended its southern and eastern frontiers. Campaigns against the Xiongnu drove the tribe to the Gobi desert.

→ Han campaigns under Wu Di

— Kingdom of Nanyue (206–113 BCE)

112 BCE Forces led by General Lu Bode and Yang Pu bring the kingdom of Nanyue under Han rule

2 CHANG'AN 195 BCE–23 CE

The Han initially chose Luoyang as its capital but then ordered the construction of a new capital a few miles from the former Qin capital. Chang'an (modern Xi'an) was proclaimed the capital in 195 BCE, with the newly built Weiyang Palace as its centerpiece. The city grew into a bustling cosmopolitan hub with nearly 250,000 citizens—second only to Rome in size and influence.

★ Imperial capital   — Imperial roads

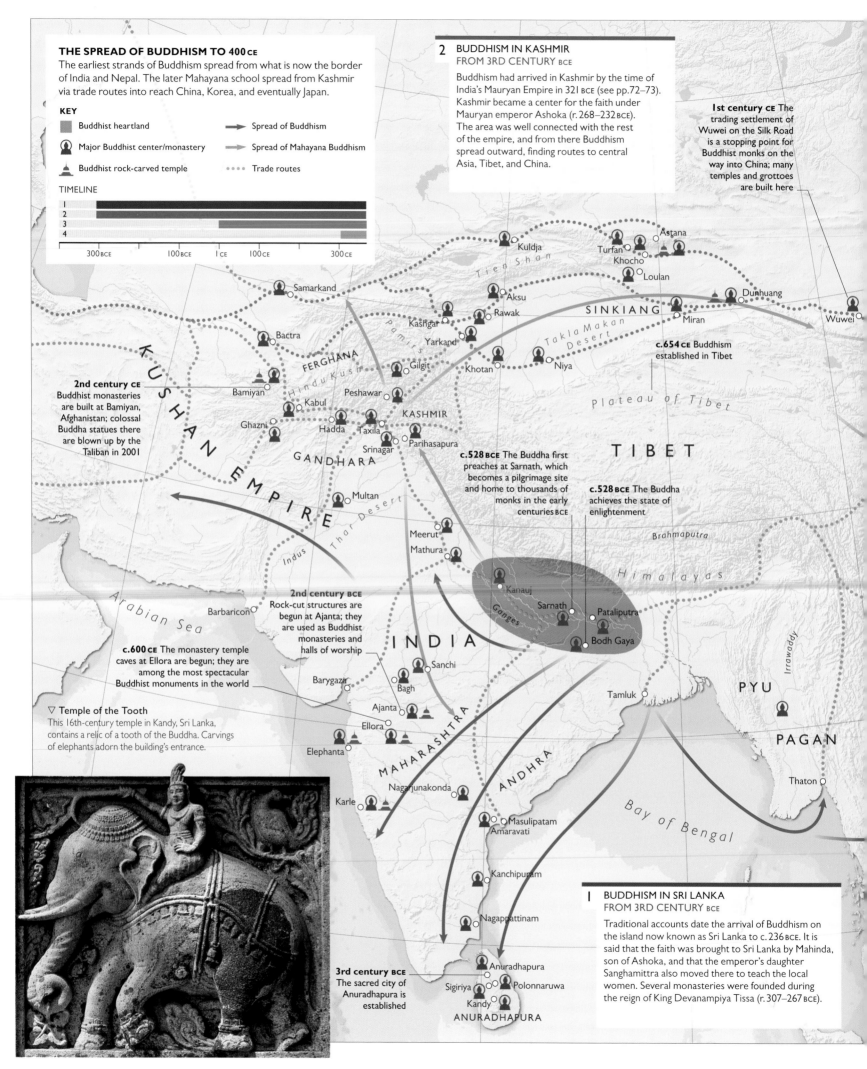

THE SPREAD OF BUDDHISM TO 400 CE

The earliest strands of Buddhism spread from what is now the border of India and Nepal. The later Mahayana school spread from Kashmir via trade routes into reach China, Korea, and eventually Japan.

KEY

- ▬ Buddhist heartland
- 👤 Major Buddhist center/monastery
- 🛕 Buddhist rock-carved temple
- ➡ Spread of Buddhism
- ➡ Spread of Mahayana Buddhism
- ⋯ Trade routes

TIMELINE

1					
2					
3					
4					
300 BCE	100 BCE	1 CE	100 CE	300 CE

2 BUDDHISM IN KASHMIR
FROM 3RD CENTURY BCE

Buddhism had arrived in Kashmir by the time of India's Mauryan Empire in 321 BCE (see pp.72–73). Kashmir became a center for the faith under Mauryan emperor Ashoka (r. 268–232 BCE). The area was well connected with the rest of the empire, and from there Buddhism spread outward, finding routes to central Asia, Tibet, and China.

1st century CE The trading settlement of Wuwei on the Silk Road is a stopping point for Buddhist monks on the way into China; many temples and grottoes are built here

2nd century CE Buddhist monasteries are built at Bamiyan, Afghanistan; colossal Buddha statues there are blown up by the Taliban in 2001

c.654 CE Buddhism established in Tibet

c.528 BCE The Buddha first preaches at Sarnath, which becomes a pilgrimage site and home to thousands of monks in the early centuries BCE

c.528 BCE The Buddha achieves the state of enlightenment

2nd century BCE Rock-cut structures are begun at Ajanta; they are used as Buddhist monasteries and halls of worship

c.600 CE The monastery temple caves at Ellora are begun; they are among the most spectacular Buddhist monuments in the world

▽ **Temple of the Tooth**
This 16th-century temple in Kandy, Sri Lanka, contains a relic of a tooth of the Buddha. Carvings of elephants adorn the building's entrance.

3rd century BCE The sacred city of Anuradhapura is established

1 BUDDHISM IN SRI LANKA
FROM 3RD CENTURY BCE

Traditional accounts date the arrival of Buddhism on the island now known as Sri Lanka to c. 236 BCE. It is said that the faith was brought to Sri Lanka by Mahinda, son of Ashoka, and that the emperor's daughter Sanghamittra also moved there to teach the local women. Several monasteries were founded during the reign of King Devanampiya Tissa (r. 307–267 BCE).

Map labels: Kuldja, Turfan, Astana, Khocho, Loulan, Samarkand, Aksu, Dunhuang, Wuwei, Bactra, Kashgar, Rawak, Miran, SINKIANG, Pamirs, Yarkand, Khotan, Niya, Takla Makan Desert, FERGHANA, Gilgit, c.654 CE Buddhism established in Tibet, Bamiyan, Hindu Kush, Peshawar, Plateau of Tibet, Kabul, KUSHAN EMPIRE, Ghazni, Hadda, Taxila, Srinagar, Parihasapura, KASHMIR, TIBET, GANDHARA, Multan, Brahmaputra, Indus, Thar Desert, Meerut, Mathura, Himalayas, Arabian Sea, Barbaricon, Kanauj, Sarnath, Pataliputra, Ganges, Bodh Gaya, INDIA, Sanchi, Barygaza, Bagh, Ajanta, Ellora, Tamluk, PYU, Irrawaddy, Elephanta, MAHARASHTRA, PAGAN, Nagarjunakonda, ANDHRA, Karle, Thaton, Masulipatam, Amaravati, Bay of Bengal, Kanchipuram, Nagappattinam, Anuradhapura, Sigiriya, Polonnaruwa, Kandy, ANURADHAPURA

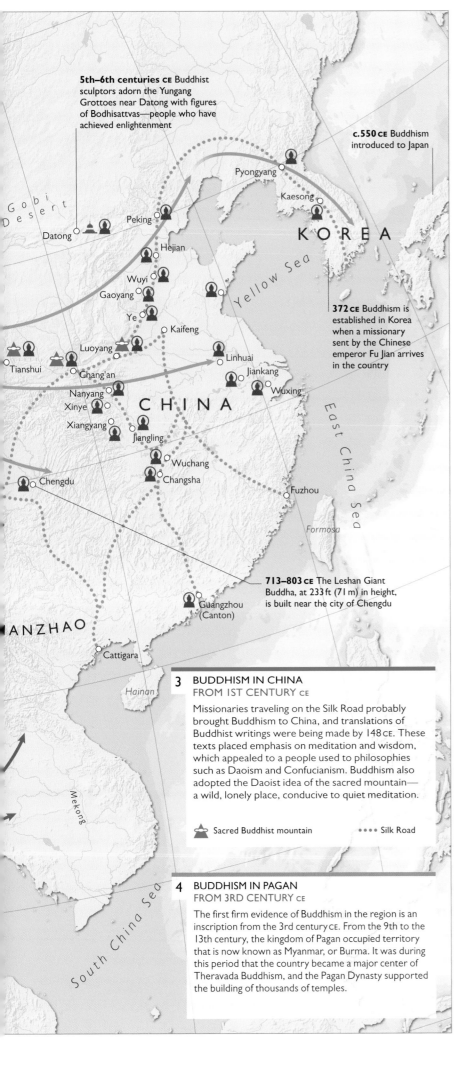

5th–6th centuries CE Buddhist sculptors adorn the Yungang Grottoes near Datong with figures of Bodhisattvas—people who have achieved enlightenment

c.550 CE Buddhism introduced to Japan

372 CE Buddhism is established in Korea when a missionary sent by the Chinese emperor Fu Jian arrives in the country

713–803 CE The Leshan Giant Buddha, at 233 ft (71 m) in height, is built near the city of Chengdu

3 BUDDHISM IN CHINA
FROM 1ST CENTURY CE

Missionaries traveling on the Silk Road probably brought Buddhism to China, and translations of Buddhist writings were being made by 148 CE. These texts placed emphasis on meditation and wisdom, which appealed to a people used to philosophies such as Daoism and Confucianism. Buddhism also adopted the Daoist idea of the sacred mountain—a wild, lonely place, conducive to quiet meditation.

🏔 Sacred Buddhist mountain ••••• Silk Road

4 BUDDHISM IN PAGAN
FROM 3RD CENTURY CE

The first firm evidence of Buddhism in the region is an inscription from the 3rd century CE. From the 9th to the 13th century, the kingdom of Pagan occupied territory that is now known as Myanmar, or Burma. It was during this period that the country became a major center of Theravada Buddhism, and the Pagan Dynasty supported the building of thousands of temples.

THE SPREAD OF BUDDHISM

From its origins in northern India and Nepal, Buddhism spread through Asia from the 5th century BCE to the 3rd century CE. It won the support of powerful figures, such as the Mauryan emperor Ashoka, which ensured that it took root across the continent.

Buddhism is based on the teachings of Siddhartha Gautama, known as the Buddha (the enlightened one). The Buddha is said to have been born in Lumbini, but his life dates are widely disputed (he may have died in 420–380 BCE). He did not write his teachings down, so initially his ideas were spread by word of mouth, and there were disagreements between his disciples over the exact meaning of his teachings. This led to a number of different early "schools" of Buddhism that spread around India, and across the sea to Sri Lanka and Myanmar, in the centuries after the Buddha died.

One of the earliest schools, which still survives today, is Theravada Buddhism, which emphasizes the individual route to enlightenment. It developed in Sri Lanka, where its sacred writings, the Pali Canon, were compiled in the 1st century BCE. From here, Theravada spread to what is now Myanmar, Cambodia, Laos, and Thailand. The other major branch of Buddhism, Mahayana Buddhism, stressed the importance of helping others to reach enlightenment. It became especially strong in Kashmir and spread across India in the 3rd century BCE. By the 1st century CE, the faith had been adopted by the Kushan emperor Kanishka in central Asia and was being carried along the Silk Road to China.

THE ORIGINS OF BUDDHISM
The Buddha traveled mainly in the plain of the Ganges River. He preached to all classes of society that, while life involves suffering, this suffering can be overcome by following the path he described.

KEY
◆ Places visited by the Buddha
••••• Major routes

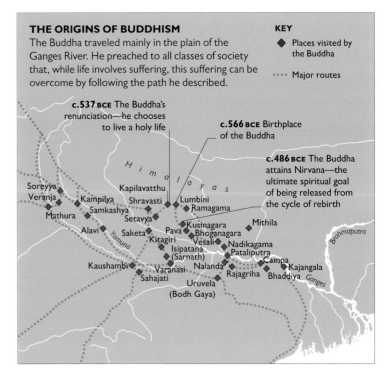

c.537 BCE The Buddha's renunciation—he chooses to live a holy life

c.566 BCE Birthplace of the Buddha

c.486 BCE The Buddha attains Nirvana—the ultimate spiritual goal of being released from the cycle of rebirth

THE RISE OF CHRISTIANITY

Christianity spread across the Roman Empire and some neighboring areas in the first centuries CE. Its adherents were persecuted until the early 4th century, when the religion gained official recognition, having gradually found more favor among the elite.

Most notable among the missionaries who spread the Christian message in the 1st century CE were Peter, who according to tradition founded the church at Rome, and Paul, a Jewish convert who made a series of missionary journeys in Asia Minor, Greece, the Aegean, and Italy. They initially addressed Jewish communities but soon won a wider audience. Christian ideas appealed to the poor, but also shared concerns with classical philosophy. Some pagan scholars attacked it, but others recognized its moral value, and by the 2nd century CE, Christian writers were offering a robust intellectual defense.

The excellent communications and administrative framework of the empire gave the Christian faith arteries along which it spread and a template for church organization. By the end of the 1st century, there were churches all over the eastern Mediterranean and in Rome, and the following century saw churches founded across the whole Mediterranean and beyond. Some emperors saw Christianity as a threat and persecuted believers, but Constantine gave the religion official approval in 313 CE, rooting it strongly in the empire.

> *"We multiply whenever we are mown down by you; the blood of Christians is seed."*
>
> TERTULLIAN (THEOLOGIAN) FROM *APOLOGETICUS*, 197 CE

THE EARLY CHURCH IN ROME
WORSHIP IN THE SEAT OF EMPIRE

The Saints Paul and Peter probably arrived in Rome around 50 CE and were martyred, most likely under the emperor Nero, in c. 64 CE. There were bishops in Rome by the late 1st century but, at that time, a church was often a room in a private home, since Christians were widely persecuted. By the early 4th century, their faith was more widely accepted, and more churches were built.

Catacombs of Rome
Christians favored burial over cremation. They decorated the city catacombs where they placed their dead with frescoes.

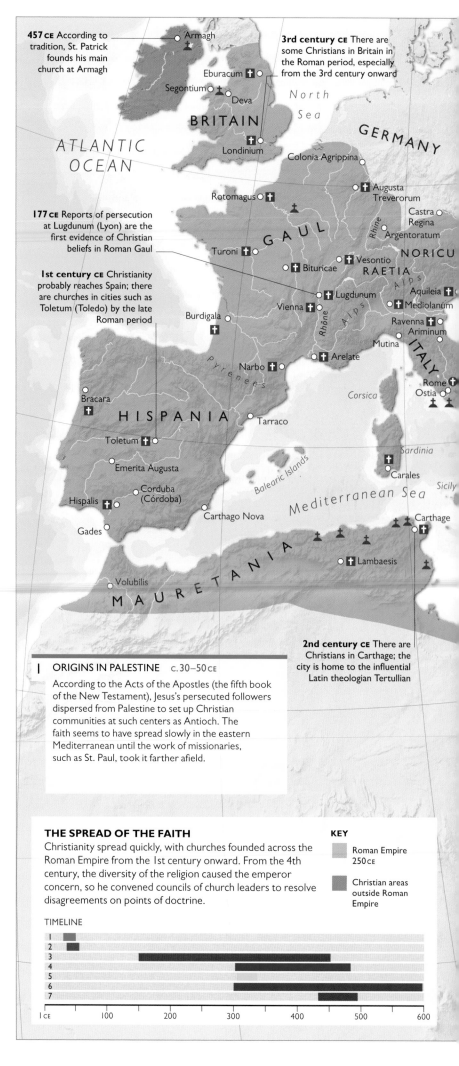

457 CE According to tradition, St. Patrick founds his main church at Armagh

3rd century CE There are some Christians in Britain in the Roman period, especially from the 3rd century onward

177 CE Reports of persecution at Lugdunum (Lyon) are the first evidence of Christian beliefs in Roman Gaul

1st century CE Christianity probably reaches Spain; there are churches in cities such as Toletum (Toledo) by the late Roman period

2nd century CE There are Christians in Carthage; the city is home to the influential Latin theologian Tertullian

ORIGINS IN PALESTINE c. 30–50 CE

According to the Acts of the Apostles (the fifth book of the New Testament), Jesus's persecuted followers dispersed from Palestine to set up Christian communities at such centers as Antioch. The faith seems to have spread slowly in the eastern Mediterranean until the work of missionaries, such as St. Paul, took it farther afield.

THE SPREAD OF THE FAITH

Christianity spread quickly, with churches founded across the Roman Empire from the 1st century onward. From the 4th century, the diversity of the religion caused the emperor concern, so he convened councils of church leaders to resolve disagreements on points of doctrine.

KEY

■ Roman Empire 250 CE

■ Christian areas outside Roman Empire

TIMELINE

1
2
3
4
5
6
7

1 CE   100   200   300   400   500   600

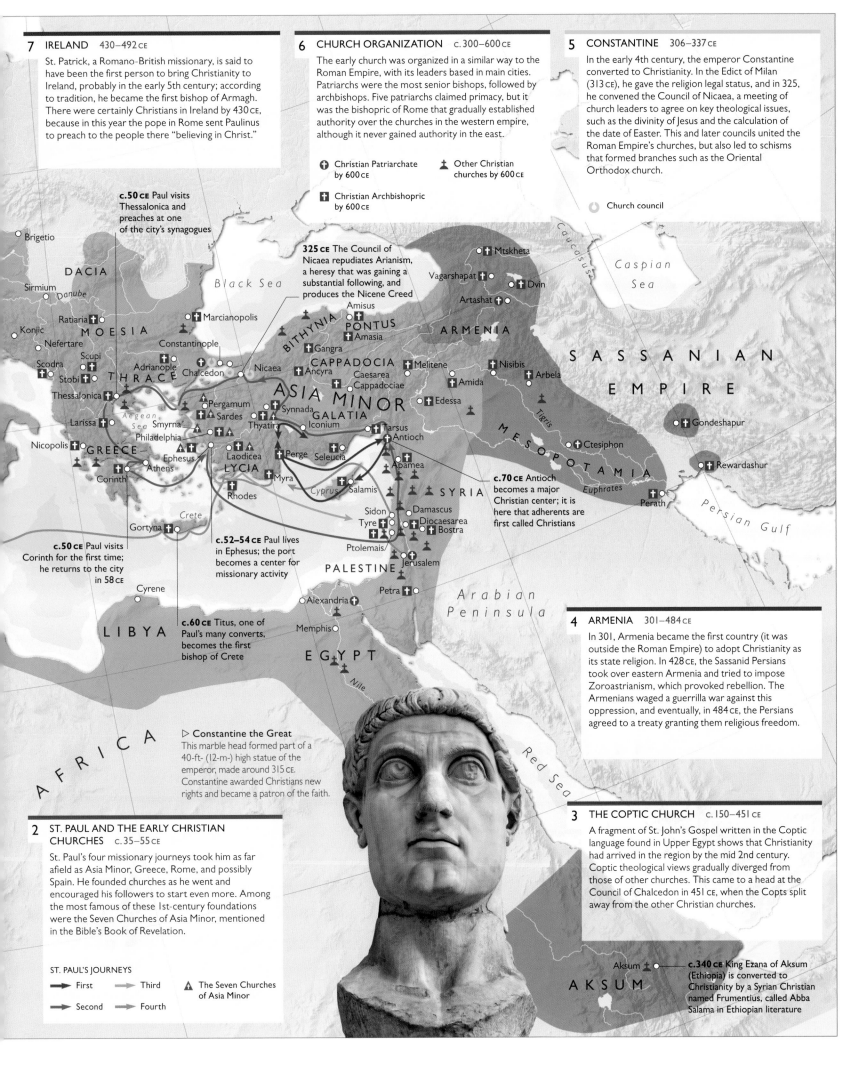

7 IRELAND 430–492 CE

St. Patrick, a Romano-British missionary, is said to have been the first person to bring Christianity to Ireland, probably in the early 5th century; according to tradition, he became the first bishop of Armagh. There were certainly Christians in Ireland by 430 CE, because in this year the pope in Rome sent Paulinus to preach to the people there "believing in Christ."

6 CHURCH ORGANIZATION c.300–600 CE

The early church was organized in a similar way to the Roman Empire, with its leaders based in main cities. Patriarchs were the most senior bishops, followed by archbishops. Five patriarchs claimed primacy, but it was the bishopric of Rome that gradually established authority over the churches in the western empire, although it never gained authority in the east.

✠ Christian Patriarchate by 600 CE

✠ Christian Archbishopric by 600 CE

✠ Other Christian churches by 600 CE

5 CONSTANTINE 306–337 CE

In the early 4th century, the emperor Constantine converted to Christianity. In the Edict of Milan (313 CE), he gave the religion legal status, and in 325, he convened the Council of Nicaea, a meeting of church leaders to agree on key theological issues, such as the divinity of Jesus and the calculation of the date of Easter. This and later councils united the Roman Empire's churches, but also led to schisms that formed branches such as the Oriental Orthodox church.

◯ Church council

c.50 CE Paul visits Thessalonica and preaches at one of the city's synagogues

325 CE The Council of Nicaea repudiates Arianism, a heresy that was gaining a substantial following, and produces the Nicene Creed

c.70 CE Antioch becomes a major Christian center; it is here that adherents are first called Christians

c.50 CE Paul visits Corinth for the first time; he returns to the city in 58 CE

c.52–54 CE Paul lives in Ephesus; the port becomes a center for missionary activity

c.60 CE Titus, one of Paul's many converts, becomes the first bishop of Crete

▷ **Constantine the Great**
This marble head formed part of a 40-ft- (12-m-) high statue of the emperor, made around 315 CE. Constantine awarded Christians new rights and became a patron of the faith.

4 ARMENIA 301–484 CE

In 301, Armenia became the first country (it was outside the Roman Empire) to adopt Christianity as its state religion. In 428 CE, the Sassanid Persians took over eastern Armenia and tried to impose Zoroastrianism, which provoked rebellion. The Armenians waged a guerrilla war against this oppression, and eventually, in 484 CE, the Persians agreed to a treaty granting them religious freedom.

3 THE COPTIC CHURCH c.150–451 CE

A fragment of St. John's Gospel written in the Coptic language found in Upper Egypt shows that Christianity had arrived in the region by the mid 2nd century. Coptic theological views gradually diverged from those of other churches. This came to a head at the Council of Chalcedon in 451 CE, when the Copts split away from the other Christian churches.

2 ST. PAUL AND THE EARLY CHRISTIAN CHURCHES c.35–55 CE

St. Paul's four missionary journeys took him as far afield as Asia Minor, Greece, Rome, and possibly Spain. He founded churches as he went and encouraged his followers to start even more. Among the most famous of these 1st-century foundations were the Seven Churches of Asia Minor, mentioned in the Bible's Book of Revelation.

c.340 CE King Ezana of Aksum (Ethiopia) is converted to Christianity by a Syrian Christian named Frumentius, called Abba Salama in Ethiopian literature

ST. PAUL'S JOURNEYS

→ First → Third → The Seven Churches of Asia Minor
→ Second → Fourth

MIDDLE AGES

IN MEDIEVAL TIMES, 500–1450 CE, THE CHRISTIAN CHURCH KEPT THE
STATUS QUO IN EUROPE, WHILE PARTS OF ASIA AND THE AMERICAS
REACHED NEW CULTURAL AND TECHNOLOGICAL HEIGHTS.

THE MIDDLE AGES

The Roman Empire's collapse by the 5th century was followed by a millennium in which Europe became an economic and political backwater, eclipsed by a technologically advanced China and by a powerful Islamic empire.

△ **Golden mask**
This "Mask of the Winged Eyes" from the Sicán culture, at its height in coastal northern Peru around 900–1100, demonstrates pre-Inca mastery of gold working.

By the 6th century, large empires that had dominated the classical world fell to attacks by neighboring peoples. In western Europe, the invaders had begun to build their own states, which retained elements of Roman law and administration but with the infusion of a Christian culture. A form of government known as vassalage developed, in which nobles held lands from their sovereigns in exchange for military service, while the lower orders held theirs in return for their labor, a system known as feudalism. None of the Germanic successors to Rome succeeded in uniting its former territories. The empire of the Carolingian ruler Charlemagne (r. 768–814) came closest, but it fell apart after his death. Islamic armies from North Africa overwhelmed Visigothic Spain in 711.

In Central America, the Maya city-states had collapsed by 900. In the same region, the Aztec Empire emerged in the 14th century, paralleled in South America with the rapid growth of the Inca state in the mid-15th century. In India, Hun invaders had destroyed the Gupta Empire by 606. Stability was only partially restored in the early 13th century by a sultanate based in Delhi.

Islam and the Crusades

Islam first appeared in Arabia in the early 7th century and spread rapidly, creating a vast empire that extended from Spain to central Asia. Its rulers—the Umayyad and, later, the Abbasid caliphs—presided over a prosperous and culturally vibrant realm, but the difficulties of ruling such a vast area proved impossible to overcome. By the 10th century, it had begun to break apart into competing emirates and rival caliphates. Into this fragmented sphere arrived the first European military expedition outside the continent for centuries.

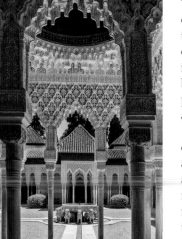

△ **Moorish marvel**
The ornate Court of the Lions, built c. 1370 by the Nasrid Sultan Muhammad V at the Alhambra palace in Granada, is typical of the sophistication of late Islamic Spain.

Europe in the Middle Ages

The Crusades were campaigns to gain control of the holy city of Jerusalem from the Muslims. The Crusaders succeeded in establishing Christian-controlled states in Palestine between 1096 and 1291, but fell to a series of resurgent Islamic powers, including the Mamluks in Egypt and the Seljuk Turks.

The Papacy, which had inspired the crusaders, remained a potent political as well as spiritual force in Europe, and engaged in a long struggle for recognition of its primacy over secular rulers. This led it into a conflict with the Holy Roman Emperors—the German-based rivals to their claim (see pp.116–119).

Europe had been buffeted by further invasions: by the Vikings, who preyed on northwestern Europe's coastlines for two centuries from around 800; by the

TURBULENT TIMES

The early Middle Ages—from the 6th to the 10th centuries—was a time of turbulence, as the collapse of the major civilizations of the classical world was followed by the emergence of new powers, such as the Franks in western Europe, the Islamic empire in the Middle East, and the Tang Dynasty in China. The 13th and 14th centuries saw renewed instability, as the Mongols created a vast Eurasian empire and a plague pandemic killed an estimated 25 million people in Europe.

	533–535 Byzantine emperor Justinian launches a war to reconquer North Africa and Italy from Germanic kings	**618** The Tang Dynasty reunifies China after four centuries of disunity	**622** The Hegira—the flight of the Prophet Muhammad and his followers from Mecca to Medina—starts the Islamic era	**750** The Abbasids start a new caliphate in Baghdad
RUSSIA AND THE BYZANTINE EMPIRE				
INDIA AND EAST ASIA				
THE ISLAMIC WORLD				
WESTERN EUROPE				
THE AMERICAS				
	500	600	700	800

606 India's Gupta Empire finally collapses

711 The Visigothic kingdom of Spain is overthrown by a Muslim army invading from North Africa

800 The Frankish ruler Charlemagne is crowned emperor

◁ **The dance of death**
The 15th-century frieze *Danse Macabre* by German artist Bernt Notke shows the heightened European preoccupation with mortality at the time of the Black Death, when death seemed to strike the rich and poor indiscriminately.

Magyars, who established themselves on the Hungarian plain around 900; and by the Mongols, able horseback archers, who descended on eastern Europe in the 1240s.

Rise of the Mongols

The Mongols also conquered China, which had been united by the Sui Dynasty in 589 and then prospered under the Tang Dynasty from 618 and the Song Dynasty from 960.

At the eastern end of the Silk Road, which transmitted wealth and new ideas between east Asia and the Middle East, China pioneered the use of gunpowder, printing, and the marine compass but never succeeded in taming the Mongols, who also attacked Southeast Asia, destroying the kingdom of Pagan in modern Myanmar and threatening the Cambodian state of Angkor. Their armies tried to invade Japan, too, but were twice driven back by storms. Japan continued to be ruled by the shoguns—dynasties of military strongmen backed by clans of samurai warriors whose military ethos dominated the state.

European revival

Despite a global pandemic of plague and Mongol intrusion on its eastern fringe, Europe survived and prospered. The plague, or Black Death, killed more than one-third of the continent's population. However, it also improved the lot of the peasantry, whose labor was now a scarcer commodity, thus undermining the roots of feudalism.

New ideas now began to emerge in Europe. In Italy, a revived interest in classical art and ideas gave birth to the rich cultural movement of the Renaissance (see pp.160–161).

Italian merchants pioneered methods of banking, and the maritime empires of Venice and Genoa spread across the eastern Mediterranean. By 1450, Europe's ambitions and horizons were beginning to expand again.

▽ **Mongols defeated**
This 19th-century engraving by Japanese artist Kuniyoshi Utagawa shows the Japanese monk Nichiren summoning storms that destroyed Mongol fleets in 1274 and 1281.

"And believing it to be the end of the world, no one wept for the dead, for all expected to die."

CHRONICLER AGNOLO DI TURA ON THE BLACK DEATH IN ITALY, 1348

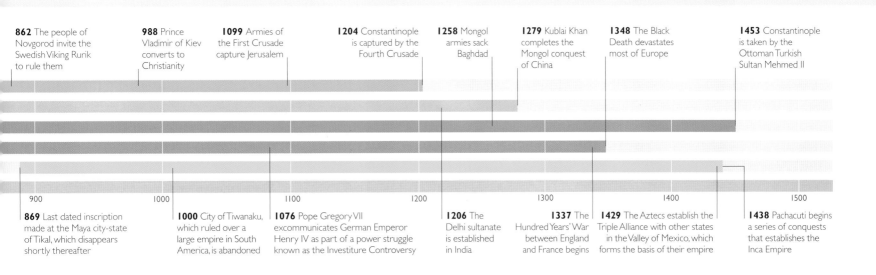

862 The people of Novgorod invite the Swedish Viking Rurik to rule them

988 Prince Vladimir of Kiev converts to Christianity

1099 Armies of the First Crusade capture Jerusalem

1204 Constantinople is captured by the Fourth Crusade

1258 Mongol armies sack Baghdad

1279 Kublai Khan completes the Mongol conquest of China

1348 The Black Death devastates most of Europe

1453 Constantinople is taken by the Ottoman Turkish Sultan Mehmed II

869 Last dated inscription made at the Maya city-state of Tikal, which disappears shortly thereafter

1000 City of Tiwanaku, which ruled over a large empire in South America, is abandoned

1076 Pope Gregory VII excommunicates German Emperor Henry IV as part of a power struggle known as the Investiture Controversy

1206 The Delhi sultanate is established in India

1337 The Hundred Years' War between England and France begins

1429 The Aztecs establish the Triple Alliance with other states in the Valley of Mexico, which forms the basis of their empire

1438 Pachacuti begins a series of conquests that establishes the Inca Empire

THE BYZANTINE EMPIRE

In 330, Roman Emperor Constantine moved the capital from Rome to the former Greek colony of Byzantium, which later became Constantinople. In 395, the Empire split in two, and in 476 the western half collapsed. The Eastern Roman Empire, however, endured for another 1,000 years, helped by the might of Constantinople.

After the last western Roman emperor was deposed in 476, the Eastern Roman Empire (called Byzantine by historians) continued as the sole entity of Roman sovereignty—though predominantly Greek-speaking (unlike its fallen Latin-speaking western counterpart).

By 554, Emperor Justinian I (r. 527–565) had reconquered large parts of the western Mediterranean coast, including Rome itself, which the empire held for two more centuries. To mark his achievements, Justinian ordered the construction of the church of Hagia Sophia, which would later become the center of the Eastern Orthodox Church while also inspiring a new wave of architecture, in particular across the Islamic world. However, in the 7th century, Byzantium lost North Africa and its Middle Eastern territories to the rising power of Islam, and much of the Balkans fell to invaders led by the Slavs. Although the Byzantine Empire rallied under the Macedonian Dynasty (867–1056), regaining lost territory, its split from the Church of Rome (1054) and the resulting threat it posed to the Pope's authority led the Venetians to divert the army of the Fourth Crusade to the sacking of the Byzantine capital instead, permanently weakening the empire.

Nevertheless. throughout much of its 1,000-year existence, the Byzantine Empire buffered Europe from newly emerging forces to the east, and its thriving capital exerted great influence upon the fields of art, literature, science, and philosophy—both as an intellectual hub and as custodian of Ancient Greek texts, thereby helping to shape modern European civilization.

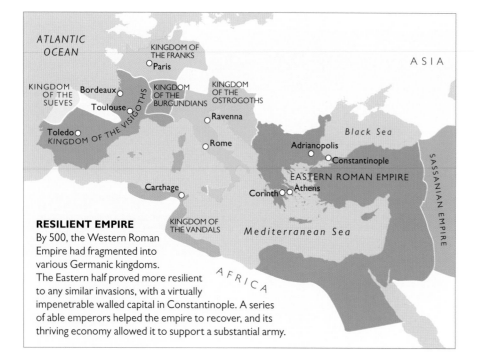

RESILIENT EMPIRE
By 500, the Western Roman Empire had fragmented into various Germanic kingdoms. The Eastern half proved more resilient to any similar invasions, with a virtually impenetrable walled capital in Constantinople. A series of able emperors helped the empire to recover, and its thriving economy allowed it to support a substantial army.

JUSTINIAN'S RECONQUESTS 527–565

In 533, under Justinian, the Byzantine Empire launched an invasion of North Africa and conquered it from the Vandals. In 535, Justinian sent an army to fight the Ostrogoths in Italy, seeking the reconquest of the old imperial capital, Rome. The war lasted 18 years, and Byzantine victory eventually came at a huge financial cost. Rome, however, was relinquished to the Lombards two centuries later.

■ Justinian's reconquests   ☆ Byzantine capital
✕ Byzantine victory

507–711 Toledo is the Visigothic capital until the Arab conquest of the region

6 THE FOURTH CRUSADE 1202–1204

When the Fourth Crusade hit difficulties raising money, the Venetians offered their financial backing, but as a condition, they diverted the Crusaders into a conquest of Constantinople. The Crusaders looted, terrorized, and vandalized the city. In the aftermath, the empire was divided between Venetians and Crusader lords, while a few Greek areas remained independent, notably the Byzantine state of Nicaea. The sacking reduced the empire to a city-state.

➡ Fourth crusade attack route   ◉ Key siege

RISE AND FALL OF BYZANTIUM

Under Justinian, Byzantium reclaimed Roman provinces for the empire. From the mid-6th century, however, defensive warfare became endemic, as the empire fought invasions from different groups at different times.

KEY
■ Lands lost 565–1025
■ Lands lost 1025–1360
■ Empire in 1360

TIMELINE

500	700	900	1100	1300	

2 DEFENDING AGAINST PERSIA 610–641

Byzantine emperor Heraclius (r. 610–641) came to power in the midst of an invasion of the empire by the Sassanid Persians. The Sassanids had already seized control of Egypt and the Levant and attempted a siege of Constantinople. In 627, Heraclius launched a counterattack into the Persian capital, Ctesiphon, and surrounded the city, eventually forcing a peace deal that subdued the Sassanid threat.

→ Persian invasions   ⇢ Heraclius's counterinvasion

★ Persian capital

3 NOMADIC RAIDS 600–1200

In the 10th century, seminomadic peoples, such as the Slavs, Avars, and Bulgars, invaded the Balkans—the region between the Greek Peloponnese and the Danube River. In 1014, Byzantine emperor Basil II (r. 976–1025) destroyed the Bulgarian Kingdom and annexed the territory—a feat for which he earned the nickname "Bulgar-Slayer." However, revolts against Byzantine rule in 1185 led to a loss of the Balkans and undermined the Byzantine Empire.

→ Nomadic raids   ⚔ Byzantine victory

4 ISLAMIC INVASION 629–1180

Under the leadership of the first caliphs, Arab Muslim armies invaded both Sassanid Persia and the Byzantine Empire. At the Battle of Yarmuk in 636, the Byzantine army suffered a huge loss. In the aftermath, first Syria and Palestine and then Egypt were conquered by Arab armies and fell under the influence of Islam. Under the rule of the Macedonian Dynasty (867–1056), the Byzantine Empire managed to recapture territories lost to Muslim conquests in the 7th century.

→ Muslim invasions   ⚔ Byzantine defeat

1202 Army of the Fourth Crusade pillages the port of Zara

1014 Basil II defeats Bulgars and annexes Bulgarian Kingdom

1091 Byzantine Empire loses most of Anatolia to Seljuk Turk invasion

552–553 Battle of Mons Lactarius

533 Battle of Ad Decimum. Byzantine victory in Carthage leads to the collapse of the Vandal Kingdom

1071 Manzikert

627 Byzantine troops march into the Persian capital to counter the Sassanid invasion

636 Battle of Yarmuk

5 BYZANTINE–SELJUK WARS 1048–1071

The Seljuk Turks, a group of warriors on horseback from central Asia, invaded the Byzantine Empire in the 11th century. During the Battle of Manzikert (1071), the Byzantine Emperor Romanus Diogenes was taken prisoner. The Seljuk threat to Constantinople forced Byzantium to send a distress call to Rome, which triggered the First Crusade (see pp. 106–107).

⚔ Byzantine defeat

→ Seljuk Turks invasion

Seljuk cavalry armed for battle

▷ **Emperor Justinian**
This mosaic depicting Byzantine emperor Justinian is on the wall of the Basilica of San Vitale in Ravenna. It was completed in 547 after Justinian had reconquered the old imperial capital.

THE ASCENT OF ISLAM

Beginning with a series of revelations received by the prophet Muhammad around 610 CE, the new faith of Islam rapidly gained followers in Arabia. Within a century, armies fighting under its banner had conquered a vast swathe of territory from Persia to Spain.

Muhammad was born around 570 into an influential merchant family in Mecca. From the age of 40, he experienced a series of divine revelations, and from around 613, he began to preach that there was only one God, Allah. His condemnation of polytheism and idol worship was unpopular, and he was forced to flee to the town of Yathrib (Medina). His message of monotheism began to attract followers, and he soon built up an army that captured Mecca.

Under Muhammad's successors, known as caliphs, Muslim forces defeated the Byzantine and Persian Empires, which had been severely weakened by a war between them that lasted from 602 to 628. The Byzantine Empire lost Syria, Palestine (including the holy city of Jerusalem), and Egypt to the Muslims, but the Sassanian Persian Empire was conquered in its entirety, bringing the fledgling Islamic state new provinces from Iraq to the borders of India.

The Umayyad caliphs, a dynasty that ruled the Islamic empire from 661 from their capital at Damascus, established a complex administration that made use of the experience of Greek-speaking officials in the former Byzantine provinces. They encouraged the integration into the empire of peoples beyond Arabia; and as ever more people converted to the faith, Islamic armies pushed westward, conquering the remainder of North Africa and much of Spain by 711. Briefly, in the mid-8th century, all this territory was united under the authority of a single ruler, guided by a faith whose tenets had by now found written form in a sacred book, the Qur'an.

THE DIVISION OF ISLAM 634–661 CE
SUNNI AND SHIA

The question of who should hold political and religious authority within Islam after the death of Muhammad proved incredibly divisive. Many felt the succession should pass through the family of Ali, the son-in-law of Muhammad, and these formed the Shia (the party of Ali), while others, who rejected this view and adhered to the Umayyads in Damascus and their successors, became the Sunni. This division in Islam has persisted until the present day.

Calligraphic succession
In this 18th-century Turkish artwork, the red writing indicates Allah; the central name in blue is Ali, first Imam of the Shia; the green writing gives the name of the prophet Muhammad.

THE GROWTH OF THE ISLAMIC WORLD 610–750
Muslim armies occupied much of the Middle East and North Africa within a decade of their emergence from Arabia, and over the next century advanced to northern Spain and the edge of central Asia. The map shows the date each city was captured or surrendered.

KEY
- → Muslim raid, with date
- ★ New city founded by Muslims
- ⊞ Muslim fortress
- ▬ Byzantine Empire c.610
- Sassanian Empire c.610
- Muslim lands by 632
- Muslim lands by 656
- Muslim lands by 756

TIMELINE

1 | 2 | 3 | 4
600 — 650 — 700 — 750

732 The Frankish army under Charles Martel halts the Arab advance

718 Covadonga

714 Saragossa

721

720 Narbonne

720

712 Toledo

711 Lisbon

711 Cordova

711 Berber general Tariq leads troops into Spain and conquers the Visigothic kingdom

698 Muslim armies capture Carthage

720

647 Tripoli

KINGDOM OF ASTURIAS
Oviedo
Mérida
Rio Barbate
Strait of Gibraltar
Fez
Rabat
Tahert
Douro
Ebro
Iberian Peninsula
KINGDOM OF THE VISIGOTHS
Maghreb
Atlas Mountains

ATLANTIC OCEAN
Rhine
E U R O P
FRANKISH EMPIRE
AVAR KINGDOM
Loire
Poitiers
Toulouse
Pyrenees
Garonne
Rhône
Alps
LOMBARD KINGDOM
Rome
Corsica
Sardinia
Balearic Islands
Sicily
Carthage
Tunis
Sousse
Kairouan
Monastir
Mahdia
TRIPOLI
A F R I C A
Sahar

▽ The Dome of the Rock
This Islamic shrine—a landmark in the city of Jerusalem—was built under the fifth Umayyad caliph, Abd al-Malik. Completed in 691, parts (including the dome) have been rebuilt since.

1 MUHAMMAD, THE HEGIRA, AND THE CONQUEST OF ARABIA   610–632

Many of Muhammad's clan, the Quraysh, saw his rejection of the traditional Arab worship of many gods as a threat to their authority. In 622, he had to flee to Medina—an exodus known as the Hegira, which marks the traditional beginning of the Muslim era. A military as well as a religious leader, Muhammad made alliances and raised an army that took Mecca in 630. By the time of his death in 632 CE, he had conquered most of Arabia.

✗ Battle or capture

751 The Abbasid Caliphate (succeeding the Umayyads) defeats the Tang Chinese at the Talas River, consolidating their hold on Transoxiana for the next 400 years

FERGHANA Tang protectorate

642 Yazdegerd III is defeated at Nehavend, leading to the rapid Muslim conquest of the rest of Persia

636 At Yarmuk, Khalid ibn al-Walid destroys the main Byzantine field army, leaving the rest of Syria and Palestine open to Muslim conquest

636 Muslim victory against the Persians leads to the conquest of Mesopotamia

661 Ali is assassinated while at prayer, leading to a schism between Sunni and Shia Muslims; Muawiya becomes the first Umayyad caliph, ruling from Damascus

642 'Amr ibn al-As captures Alexandria, the last Byzantine stronghold in Egypt

624 The Muslim army defeats Meccan forces, beginning the process by which Muhammad conquers the whole of Arabia

622 Muhammad and his principal followers are forced to flee to the oasis town of Yathrib (later known as Medina)

630 Muhammad conquers Mecca

610 Muhammad receives revelations from the archangel Gabriel in a cave in the hills outside Mecca

2 UMAR AND THE CONQUEST OF SYRIA AND EGYPT   634–644

Under the second caliph, Umar (who had been a companion of Muhammad), Muslim armies achieved astonishing successes against the Byzantine army, which had been weakened by its long war with Persia. First Damascus, the chief city of Syria, fell to the Muslims, and then they seized Jerusalem. They went on to subdue the Byzantine province of Egypt, where religious divisions among the Christian population undermined opposition to the Muslims.

✗ Battle or capture

3 THE CONQUEST OF PERSIA AND KHURASAN 636–656

The Sassanian rulers of Persia had almost captured the Byzantine capital of Constantinople by 626, but the effort exhausted their resources. After a Muslim army defeated them in Mesopotamia in 636, the Persians lost their western provinces. The Persian shah Yazdegerd III became a fugitive, and his domains were absorbed into the growing Islamic empire. Within 5 years, much of Khurasan (Khorasan), in central Asia, had been added to the empire, too.

✗ Battle or capture

4 LATE UMAYYAD CONQUESTS   670–750

The Muslims' expansion west of Egypt was slow until they built a base at Kairouan (in modern Tunisia) in 670. From this stronghold, they captured the remainder of the Byzantine Empire in north Africa, taking its capital Carthage in 698. In 711, an Arab–Berber army crossed into the Christian Visigothic kingdom of Spain and, within 20 years, had conquered almost all of it. In central Asia, Muslim armies won Transoxiana. In 750, the Umayyads were overthrown by the Abbasid Dynasty, who took control of the caliphate.

✗ Battle or capture

THE RULE OF THE CALIPHS

The Umayyads, who had ruled over the Islamic world from 661, fell in 749–750. Their empire was inherited by a new dynasty, the Abbasids, but its integrity was soon challenged as local rulers broke away, leaving the Abbasids with control over little more than Baghdad.

The Umayyad Caliphate (see pp.94–95) collapsed after a brief civil war in 749–750, which was partly caused by their discrimination against non-Arab Muslims. The Abbasids, a dynasty descended from the uncle of Muhammad, rose to power and—from its base in Baghdad—was able to restore stability. However, controlling the vast Muslim empire eventually proved an impossible task. A series of civil wars between 809 and 833 weakened the caliphate, and numerous local dynasties broke away: Spain had already been lost to a branch of the Umayyads in 756 and Ifriqiya (the area around Tunisia) became independent under the Aghlabids from 800. In Egypt, the Tulunids threw off central control in 868, and the Fatimids later grew strong there. The Buwayhids firmly established themselves in Iran from 926, and the Ghaznavids occupied eastern territories from about 977.

As the new dynasties emerged, Abbasid rule withered away until the caliph was a mere cypher, ruling a small sliver of land in Mesopotamia. Even this was swept away by a Mongol invasion in 1258, which sacked Baghdad and put an end to the caliphate.

> *"Don't be satisfied with stories. How things have gone with others. Unfold your own myth."*
>
> RUMI, 13TH-CENTURY ISLAMIC SCHOLAR AND POET

THE GOLDEN AGE OF ISLAM
SCIENCE AND CULTURE UNDER THE ABBASIDS

Scholars of all types congregated in the Abbasid capital of Baghdad. Accessible from both Europe and Asia, the city became a place to exchange ideas, many of which had reemerged from the translation of classical works by Arab scholars. Abbasid caliphs, including Harun al-Rashid and his son al-Ma'mun, directly encouraged learning and scholarship in Baghdad by establishing a House of Wisdom.

Games of the Golden Age
Having reached Baghdad from India via Persia, chess became popular in the Muslim world, as shown in this 9th-century illustration.

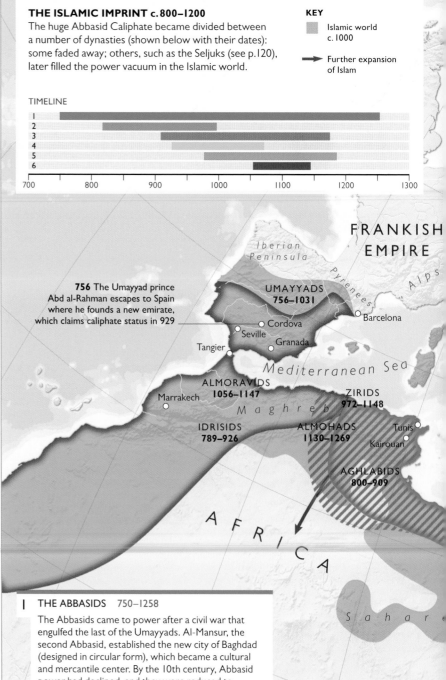

THE ISLAMIC IMPRINT c.800–1200
The huge Abbasid Caliphate became divided between a number of dynasties (shown below with their dates): some faded away; others, such as the Seljuks (see p.120), later filled the power vacuum in the Islamic world.

KEY
- Islamic world c.1000
- → Further expansion of Islam

TIMELINE
1 2 3 4 5 6
700 800 900 1000 1100 1200 1300

756 The Umayyad prince Abd al-Rahman escapes to Spain where he founds a new emirate, which claims caliphate status in 929

FRANKISH EMPIRE
Iberian Peninsula
Pyrenees
Alps
UMAYYADS 756–1031
Cordova
Barcelona
Seville
Granada
Tangier
Mediterranean Sea
ALMORAVIDS 1056–1147
Marrakech
ZIRIDS 972–1148
Maghreb
IDRISIDS 789–926
ALMOHADS 1130–1269
Tunis
Kairouan
AGHLABIDS 800–909
AFRICA
Sahara

1 THE ABBASIDS 750–1258
The Abbasids came to power after a civil war that engulfed the last of the Umayyads. Al-Mansur, the second Abbasid, established the new city of Baghdad (designed in circular form), which became a cultural and mercantile center. By the 10th century, Abbasid power had declined, and they were reduced to seeking the protection of other groups, such as the Buwayhids and Hamdanids, to ensure their survival. The last caliph, al-Musta'sim, was killed when the Mongols sacked Baghdad in 1258.

▬ Extent of Abbasid Caliphate c.800

2 THE SAMANIDS 819–999
The Samanids were former Abbasid governors in eastern Iran, who gradually asserted their independence and in 900 captured Bukhara in Khorasan, which became their capital. Their empire prospered economically and culturally, with its artistic production including fine pottery and the *Shahnameh*, the Persian national epic, written by the poet Ferdowsi around 977. Pressure on their eastern borders undermined the Samanids, and in 999 the Turkic Qarakhanids took Bukhara, bringing their empire to an end.

▦ Extent of Samanid Empire c.900

6 THE ALMORAVIDS 1056–1147

A confederation of Berber tribes, the Almoravids were at the center of an 11th-century religious revival aimed at purifying Islam. They combined religious fervor with conquest, taking Morocco and founding the city of Marrakein in 1062. Asked by the Islamic kingdoms in Spain to help them resist Christian reconquest (see pp.122–123), the Almoravids crossed into Iberia, where they came to dominate in the south under their leader Yusuf Ibn Tashfin. By 1145, however, they were being forced out of Spain and challenged in north Africa by another revivalist movement, the Almohads, who captured Marrakech in 1147.

▬ Almoravid territory c.1100

5 THE GHAZNAVIDS 977–1186

The Ghaznavids, a dynasty of Turkic origin, established themselves in Ghazni, in Khorasan, from 977, and gradually expanded until they took over the western portion of the former Samanid Empire by 1005. They then conquered the eastern portion of the Buwayhid Empire before a disastrous defeat by the Seljuks at Dandanaqan in 1040 reduced them to a small area of eastern Khorasan, where they ruled until 1186.

▬ Ghaznavid territory c.1028

✕ Battle

△ **11th-century Fatimid pendant**
The Fatimids controlled gold mines in Nubia (present-day Sudan) and crafted the metal into jewelry with fine filigree work.

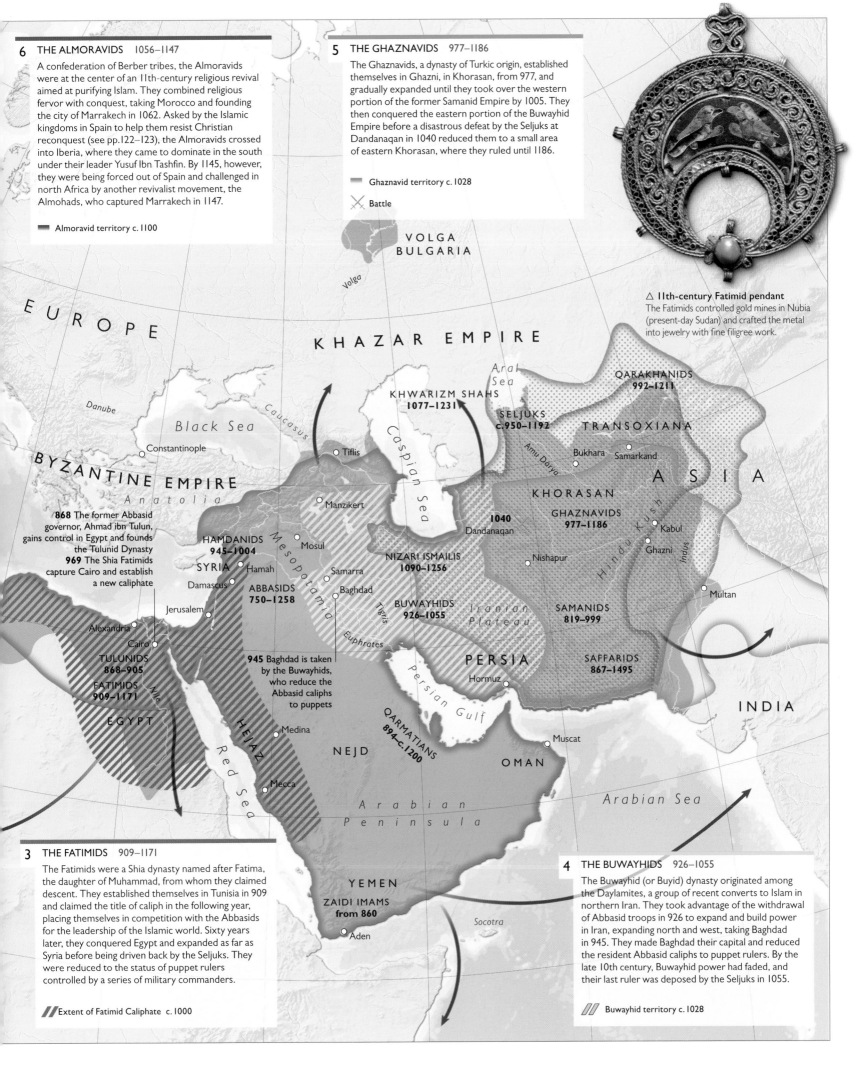

3 THE FATIMIDS 909–1171

The Fatimids were a Shia dynasty named after Fatima, the daughter of Muhammad, from whom they claimed descent. They established themselves in Tunisia in 909 and claimed the title of caliph in the following year, placing themselves in competition with the Abbasids for the leadership of the Islamic world. Sixty years later, they conquered Egypt and expanded as far as Syria before being driven back by the Seljuks. They were reduced to the status of puppet rulers controlled by a series of military commanders.

╱╱ Extent of Fatimid Caliphate c.1000

4 THE BUWAYHIDS 926–1055

The Buwayhid (or Buyid) dynasty originated among the Daylamites, a group of recent converts to Islam in northern Iran. They took advantage of the withdrawal of Abbasid troops in 926 to expand and build power in Iran, expanding north and west, taking Baghdad in 945. They made Baghdad their capital and reduced the resident Abbasid caliphs to puppet rulers. By the late 10th century, Buwayhid power had faded, and their last ruler was deposed by the Seljuks in 1055.

╱╱╱ Buwayhid territory c.1028

THE VIKINGS

At the end of the 8th century CE, the Vikings, a warrior-people from Scandinavia, burst forth from their homelands and for the next two centuries spread across Europe and the Atlantic as raiders, traders, and settlers.

Scandinavia in the 8th century was divided into small territories ruled by warlords. Instability grew as these chiefs fought to unite regions and a growing population put pressure on resources. Attracted by the wealth of trading centers and monasteries in northwest Europe, young men took up raiding and became known as Vikings. What followed was an amazing expansion enabled by fast and maneuverable Viking longships, used for raiding, and sturdier ocean-going knorrs, used for longer trading voyages. Vikings from Norway and Denmark exploited

> *"They overran the entire kingdom and destroyed all the monasteries to which they came."*
>
> ANGLO-SAXON CHRONICLE, 869

weaknesses in France, Britain, and Ireland to strike their victims unaware, seizing plunder and exacting tribute. In the 9th century, the Vikings in these areas turned from raids to conquest, carving out territories that in some cases they ruled for centuries. Their search for land also took them across unexplored waters to Iceland, Greenland, and finally the coast of North America around 1000.

In the East, Swedish Vikings, in the role of traders, penetrated the navigable rivers of what is now Russia and Ukraine to dominate trade with Constantinople and the Arabs and to exact tribute from Slavic tribes. These Varangians (as the eastern Vikings were called) founded Kievan Rus', the first Russian state.

LEIF ERIKSON
VIKING EXPLORER

Son of Erik the Red—founder of Viking Greenland—Leif Erikson is the star of sagas telling of the exploration of the lands we now know as North America. Other than the archaeological site of L'Anse aux Meadows in Newfoundland, it is difficult to know exactly where Vikings such as Erikson and his crew went, but they must have reached forested lands south of the tundra-clad Labrador Coast (which they knew as Markland) since they were desperate for timber.

Commemoration
A modern monument in Iceland recognizes Erikson, the first European known to have reached the Americas.

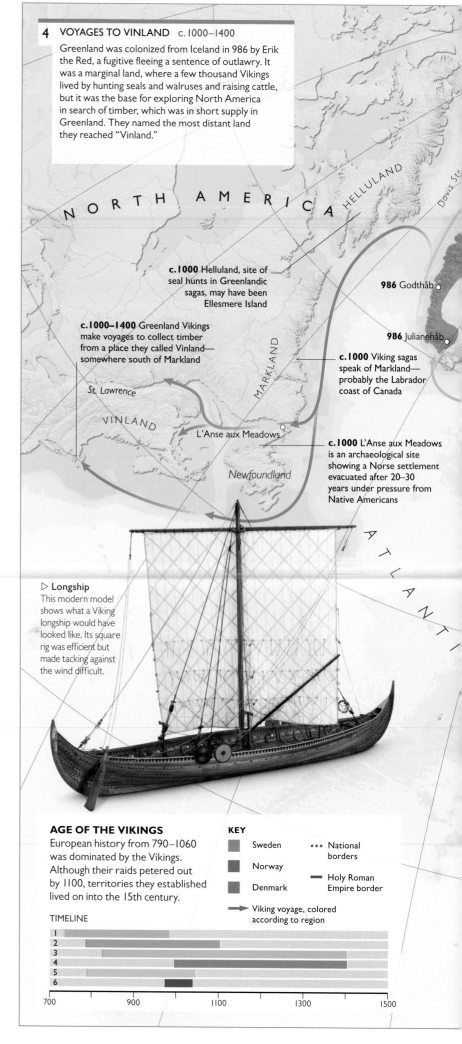

4 VOYAGES TO VINLAND c. 1000–1400
Greenland was colonized from Iceland in 986 by Erik the Red, a fugitive fleeing a sentence of outlawry. It was a marginal land, where a few thousand Vikings lived by hunting seals and walruses and raising cattle, but it was the base for exploring North America in search of timber, which was in short supply in Greenland. They named the most distant land they reached "Vinland."

c. 1000 Helluland, site of seal hunts in Greenlandic sagas, may have been Ellesmere Island

986 Godthåb

c. 1000–1400 Greenland Vikings make voyages to collect timber from a place they called Vinland—somewhere south of Markland

986 Julianehåb

c. 1000 Viking sagas speak of Markland—probably the Labrador coast of Canada

c. 1000 L'Anse aux Meadows is an archaeological site showing a Norse settlement evacuated after 20–30 years under pressure from Native Americans

NORTH AMERICA
HELLULAND
MARKLAND
VINLAND
St. Lawrence
L'Anse aux Meadows
Newfoundland
ATLANTIC
Davis Str.

▷ **Longship**
This modern model shows what a Viking longship would have looked like. Its square rig was efficient but made tacking against the wind difficult.

AGE OF THE VIKINGS
European history from 790–1060 was dominated by the Vikings. Although their raids petered out by 1100, territories they established lived on into the 15th century.

KEY

▮ Sweden	•••	National borders
▮ Norway	—	Holy Roman Empire border
▮ Denmark		
→ Viking voyage, colored according to region		

TIMELINE

	700	900	1100	1300	1500
1					
2					
3					
4					
5					
6					

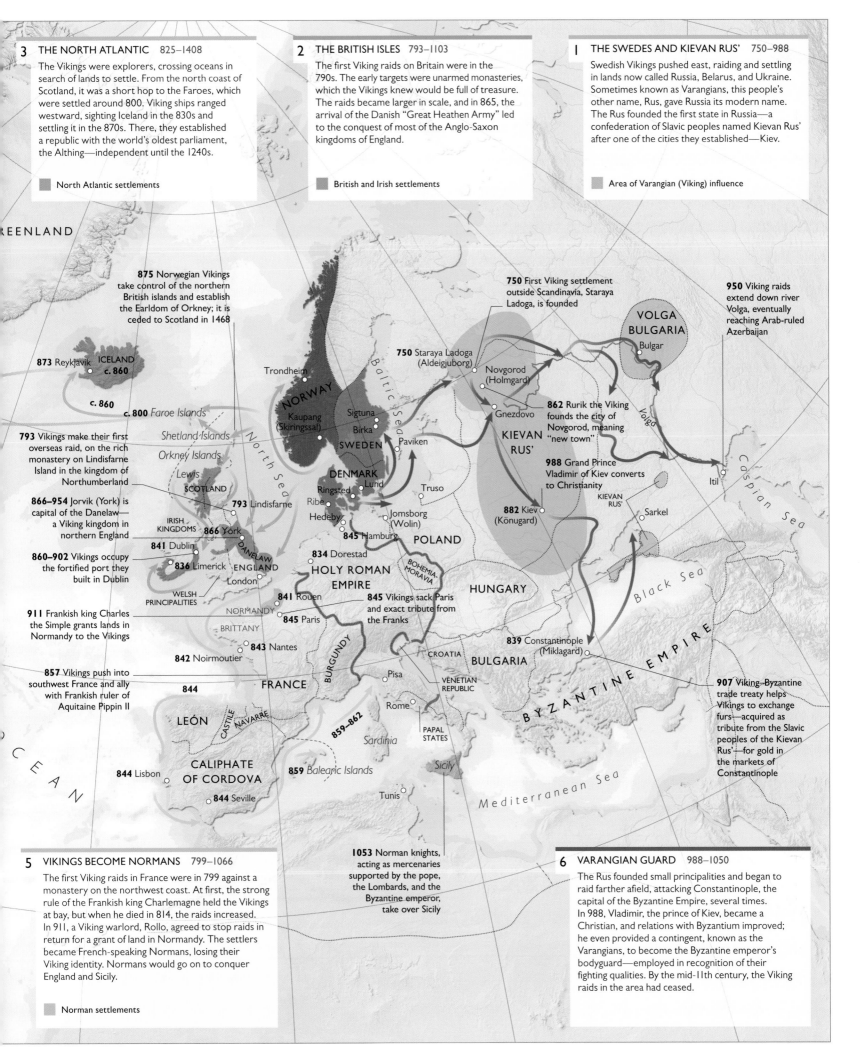

3 THE NORTH ATLANTIC 825–1408

The Vikings were explorers, crossing oceans in search of lands to settle. From the north coast of Scotland, it was a short hop to the Faroes, which were settled around 800. Viking ships ranged westward, sighting Iceland in the 830s and settling it in the 870s. There, they established a republic with the world's oldest parliament, the Althing—independent until the 1240s.

- ◼ North Atlantic settlements

2 THE BRITISH ISLES 793–1103

The first Viking raids on Britain were in the 790s. The early targets were unarmed monasteries, which the Vikings knew would be full of treasure. The raids became larger in scale, and in 865, the arrival of the Danish "Great Heathen Army" led to the conquest of most of the Anglo-Saxon kingdoms of England.

- ◼ British and Irish settlements

1 THE SWEDES AND KIEVAN RUS' 750–988

Swedish Vikings pushed east, raiding and settling in lands now called Russia, Belarus, and Ukraine. Sometimes known as Varangians, this people's other name, Rus, gave Russia its modern name. The Rus founded the first state in Russia—a confederation of Slavic peoples named Kievan Rus' after one of the cities they established—Kiev.

- ◼ Area of Varangian (Viking) influence

875 Norwegian Vikings take control of the northern British islands and establish the Earldom of Orkney; it is ceded to Scotland in 1468

750 First Viking settlement outside Scandinavia, Staraya Ladoga, is founded

950 Viking raids extend down river Volga, eventually reaching Arab-ruled Azerbaijan

873 Reykjavik

750 Staraya Ladoga (Aldeigjuborg)

862 Rurik the Viking founds the city of Novgorod, meaning "new town"

793 Vikings make their first overseas raid, on the rich monastery on Lindisfarne Island in the kingdom of Northumberland

988 Grand Prince Vladimir of Kiev converts to Christianity

866–954 Jorvik (York) is capital of the Danelaw—a Viking kingdom in northern England

882 Kiev (Könugard)

793 Lindisfarne

866 York

841 Dublin

860–902 Vikings occupy the fortified port they built in Dublin

836 Limerick

845 Hamburg

834 Dorestad

911 Frankish king Charles the Simple grants lands in Normandy to the Vikings

841 Rouen

845 Vikings sack Paris and exact tribute from the Franks

845 Paris

843 Nantes

842 Noirmoutier

857 Vikings push into southwest France and ally with Frankish ruler of Aquitaine Pippin II

844

839 Constantinople (Miklagard)

907 Viking–Byzantine trade treaty helps Vikings to exchange furs—acquired as tribute from the Slavic peoples of the Kievan Rus'—for gold in the markets of Constantinople

859–862

844 Lisbon

859 Balearic Islands

844 Seville

1053 Norman knights, acting as mercenaries supported by the pope, the Lombards, and the Byzantine emperor, take over Sicily

5 VIKINGS BECOME NORMANS 799–1066

The first Viking raids in France were in 799 against a monastery on the northwest coast. At first, the strong rule of the Frankish king Charlemagne held the Vikings at bay, but when he died in 814, the raids increased. In 911, a Viking warlord, Rollo, agreed to stop raids in return for a grant of land in Normandy. The settlers became French-speaking Normans, losing their Viking identity. Normans would go on to conquer England and Sicily.

- ◼ Norman settlements

6 VARANGIAN GUARD 988–1050

The Rus founded small principalities and began to raid farther afield, attacking Constantinople, the capital of the Byzantine Empire, several times. In 988, Vladimir, the prince of Kiev, became a Christian, and relations with Byzantium improved; he even provided a contingent, known as the Varangians, to become the Byzantine emperor's bodyguard—employed in recognition of their fighting qualities. By the mid-11th century, the Viking raids in the area had ceased.

THE NORMANS

Originally a band of Viking raiders, the Normans acquired land in northern France, where they established a duchy. They then spread more widely, and by the mid-11th century had conquered England, Sicily, and much of southern Italy.

Norman abbey
With its arcaded Romanesque nave, the Saint-Etienne Abbey in Caen, France, is a fine example of Norman architecture.

In 911, as marauding Viking armies overwhelmed northern France, the Frankish king Charles the Simple made a pact with a group of Norwegian Vikings led by Rollo. In exchange for land, Rollo agreed to keep other Vikings away. He only partly held to his agreement, slowly expanding his holdings in what became known as Normandy (the land of the Northmen). By the time he bequeathed Normandy to his son William Longsword in 927, a mixed culture had emerged: part-French, part-Scandinavian, and increasingly Christianized. In 1066, William the Conqueror, the great-great-great grandson of Rollo, invaded England to assert a claim to its throne. His success marked the beginning of an Anglo-Norman Dynasty whose descendants still rule.

Setting down roots

Elsewhere, ambitious Normans took military service with feuding local autocratic rulers in southern Italy from the early 11th century. Later, led by ruthless warriors such as the de Haubevilles and Robert and Roger Guiscard, they carved out their own fiefdom in southern Italy. In 1060, Roger Guiscard invaded Sicily, conquering much of it within a decade and establishing a kingdom where a hybrid Arab-Norman culture flourished until its conquest by the German Hohenstaufens in 1194.

THE NORMAN CONQUEST

After William the Conqueror won at Hastings in 1066, he consolidated his rule over England, awarding land to his followers. Upon his death, Normandy and England were divided between his sons Robert Curthose and William Rufus. After Robert's defeat by William's successor, Henry I of England, at Tinchebrai in 1106, England and Normandy were reunified.

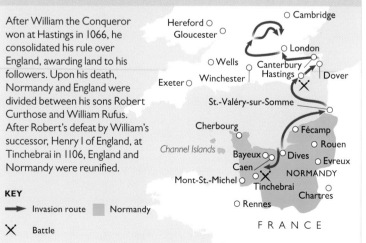

Hereford
Gloucester
Cambridge
Wells
London
Exeter
Winchester
Canterbury
Hastings
Dover
St.-Valéry-sur-Somme
Cherbourg
Fécamp
Rouen
Channel Islands
Bayeux
Dives
Evreux
Caen
NORMANDY
Mont-St.-Michel
Tinchebrai
Chartres
Rennes
FRANCE

KEY
→ Invasion route   ▢ Normandy
✕ Battle

Tapestry of war
In this scene from the Bayeux Tapestry, woven to commemorate the Norman victory over the English at Hastings in 1066, William the Conqueror (right) removes his helmet to show his followers that the rumor that he had been killed was false.

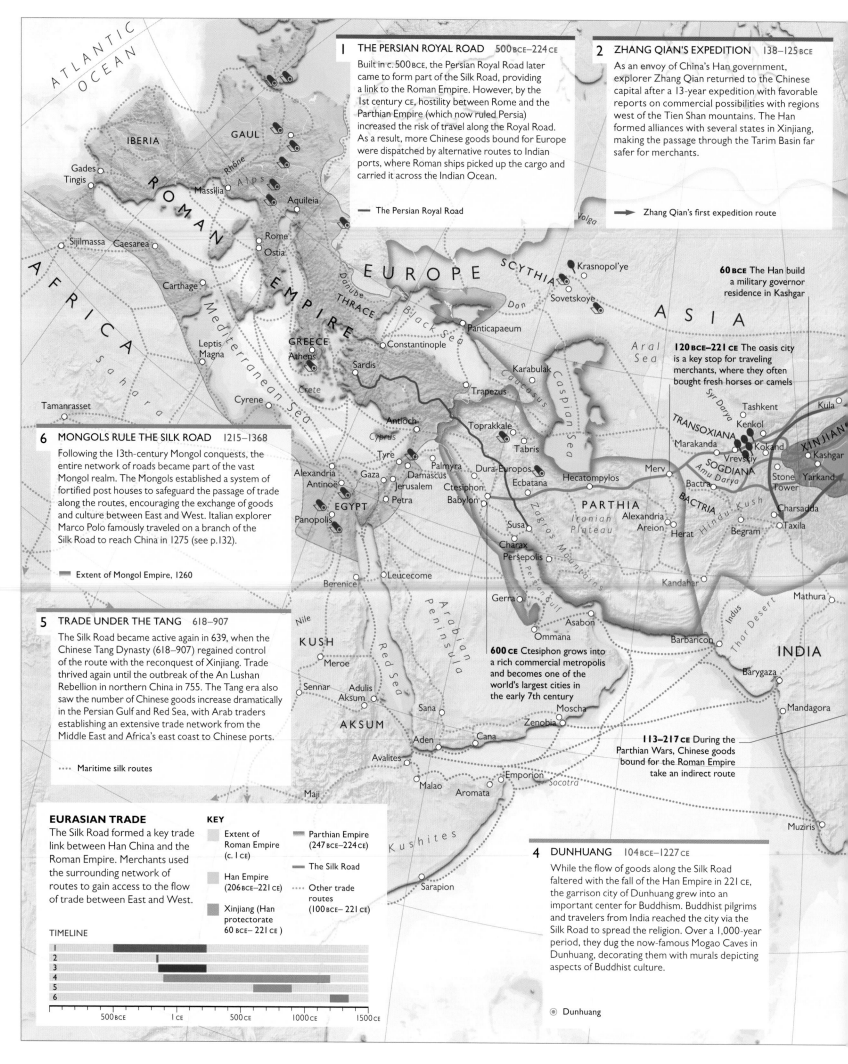

1 THE PERSIAN ROYAL ROAD 500 BCE–224 CE

Built in c. 500 BCE, the Persian Royal Road later came to form part of the Silk Road, providing a link to the Roman Empire. However, by the 1st century CE, hostility between Rome and the Parthian Empire (which now ruled Persia) increased the risk of travel along the Royal Road. As a result, more Chinese goods bound for Europe were dispatched by alternative routes to Indian ports, where Roman ships picked up the cargo and carried it across the Indian Ocean.

— The Persian Royal Road

2 ZHANG QIAN'S EXPEDITION 138–125 BCE

As an envoy of China's Han government, explorer Zhang Qian returned to the Chinese capital after a 13-year expedition with favorable reports on commercial possibilities with regions west of the Tien Shan mountains. The Han formed alliances with several states in Xinjiang, making the passage through the Tarim Basin far safer for merchants.

→ Zhang Qian's first expedition route

60 BCE The Han build a military governor residence in Kashgar

120 BCE–221 CE The oasis city is a key stop for traveling merchants, where they often bought fresh horses or camels

6 MONGOLS RULE THE SILK ROAD 1215–1368

Following the 13th-century Mongol conquests, the entire network of roads became part of the vast Mongol realm. The Mongols established a system of fortified post houses to safeguard the passage of trade along the routes, encouraging the exchange of goods and culture between East and West. Italian explorer Marco Polo famously traveled on a branch of the Silk Road to reach China in 1275 (see p.132).

■ Extent of Mongol Empire, 1260

5 TRADE UNDER THE TANG 618–907

The Silk Road became active again in 639, when the Chinese Tang Dynasty (618–907) regained control of the route with the reconquest of Xinjiang. Trade thrived again until the outbreak of the An Lushan Rebellion in northern China in 755. The Tang era also saw the number of Chinese goods increase dramatically in the Persian Gulf and Red Sea, with Arab traders establishing an extensive trade network from the Middle East and Africa's east coast to Chinese ports.

⋯⋯ Maritime silk routes

600 CE Ctesiphon grows into a rich commercial metropolis and becomes one of the world's largest cities in the early 7th century

113–217 CE During the Parthian Wars, Chinese goods bound for the Roman Empire take an indirect route

EURASIAN TRADE

The Silk Road formed a key trade link between Han China and the Roman Empire. Merchants used the surrounding network of routes to gain access to the flow of trade between East and West.

KEY

▨ Extent of Roman Empire (c. 1 CE)

▨ Han Empire (206 BCE–221 CE)

▨ Xinjiang (Han protectorate 60 BCE– 221 CE)

▨ Parthian Empire (247 BCE–224 CE)

— The Silk Road

⋯⋯ Other trade routes (100 BCE– 221 CE)

4 DUNHUANG 104 BCE–1227 CE

While the flow of goods along the Silk Road faltered with the fall of the Han Empire in 221 CE, the garrison city of Dunhuang grew into an important center for Buddhism. Buddhist pilgrims and travelers from India reached the city via the Silk Road to spread the religion. Over a 1,000-year period, they dug the now-famous Mogao Caves in Dunhuang, decorating them with murals depicting aspects of Buddhist culture.

◉ Dunhuang

TIMELINE

500 BCE   1 CE   500 CE   1000 CE   1500 CE

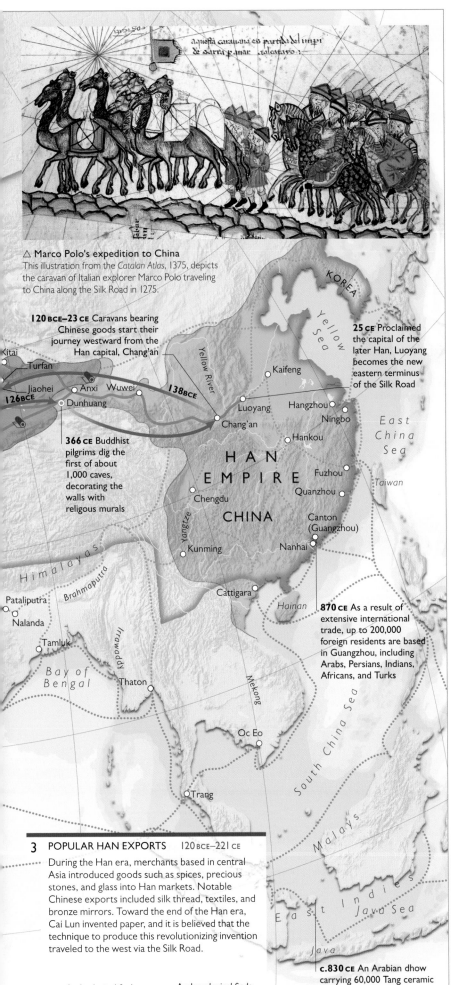

△ Marco Polo's expedition to China
This illustration from the *Catalan Atlas*, 1375, depicts the caravan of Italian explorer Marco Polo traveling to China along the Silk Road in 1275.

120 BCE–23 CE Caravans bearing Chinese goods start their journey westward from the Han capital, Chang'an

25 CE Proclaimed the capital of the later Han, Luoyang becomes the new eastern terminus of the Silk Road

366 CE Buddhist pilgrims dig the first of about 1,000 caves, decorating the walls with religous murals

870 CE As a result of extensive international trade, up to 200,000 foreign residents are based in Guangzhou, including Arabs, Persians, Indians, Africans, and Turks

3 POPULAR HAN EXPORTS 120 BCE–221 CE

During the Han era, merchants based in central Asia introduced goods such as spices, precious stones, and glass into Han markets. Notable Chinese exports included silk thread, textiles, and bronze mirrors. Toward the end of the Han era, Cai Lun invented paper, and it is believed that the technique to produce this revolutionizing invention traveled to the west via the Silk Road.

Archaelogical finds of Han mirrors

Archaeological finds of Chinese silk

c.830 CE An Arabian dhow carrying 60,000 Tang ceramic pieces bound for the Middle East capsizes. The wreck is discovered in 1998

THE SILK ROAD

The extension of Han control in China in the 2nd century BCE made communication with the rest of the world easier and safer. The network of roads linking East and West operated for 1,500 years and became famous for the luxurious Chinese silk that traveled along them.

The origin of the Silk Road can be traced back to the Han Empire's conquest of the Tarim Basin around 120 BCE, when its armies banished various tribal groups from the region. This allowed the empire to open a safe passage for trade that stretched from the Chinese capital Chang'an (Xi'an) to a wealth of cities in central Asia and beyond.

The Han engaged in vibrant trading with India, Persia, and the Roman Empire, where Chinese silk was highly coveted by the ruling class. Besides the luxury goods that traveled along the route, including silk, spices, precious stones, and ornaments, the Silk Road was also a conduit for the dissemination of religion, philosophy, technology, language, science, and even disease.

Trade along the route faltered following the collapse of the Han in 221 CE but revived in the Tang era (618–907) when China partially recovered its central Asian provinces. Trade fell again in the 8th century after the Tibetans and Uighurs took control of Xinjiang, but 500 years later the route experienced a major resurgence following the Mongol conquests (see pp.130–131). The importance of the Silk Road fell again after the Mongol Empire's decline in the 14th century, and in the 16th century it was replaced by maritime trading routes.

> *"The Seres (Chinese) are famous for the woollen substance obtained from their forests."*
>
> PLINY THE ELDER, FROM *NATURALIS HISTORIA*, 79 CE

CHINESE SILK
UNIQUE CHINESE EXPORT

Once China introduced silk to the West in the 1st century BCE, the material became popular among elites in the Roman Empire. The silk-making process was unknown in the West until around 550 CE, when Byzantine Emperor Justinian I persuaded two monks to smuggle silkworms from China inside their bamboo canes.

Silk-making in China
This is a section of a larger 12th-century silk painting that depicts court ladies preparing silk.

12TH-CENTURY RENAISSANCE IN EUROPE

The 12th century saw the establishment of universities and of new monastic orders and the translation of important scientific manuscripts from Arabic into European languages.

KEY

— Frontiers 1200

TIMELINE

| | | | | | | |
|1|2|3|4|5|
700 800 900 1000 1100 1200 1300 1400

1 CHARLEMAGNE'S RENAISSANCE 800–814

The crowning of Charlemagne as "Emperor of the Romans" in 800 brought about a sense that the Roman Empire had been revived in western Europe. Literature, arts, writing, architecture, and scriptural studies flourished under his rule. The cultural gains of Charlemagne's court dissipated soon after his death in 814 and the passage of the imperial title to a series of German nobles.

— Extent of Charlemagne's empire, 814

2 THE CISTERCIANS AND THE NEW MONASTICISM 1098–1153

The Cistercians emerged as the old monastic orders came to be seen as wealthy, self-serving, and distant from their original spiritual missions. Founded in 1098, the Cistercians spread under the influence of St. Bernard of Clairvaux and had over 300 monasteries throughout Europe by his death in 1153. With a rigorous observance of the Rule of St. Benedict, the Cistercians became noted for their piety and offered "the surest road to heaven."

⚜ Major Cistercian house with date of foundation

1078 Anselm is elected as Abbot of Bec, which becomes an important theological school

1160s Student numbers at Oxford University grow; it gains a royal charter in 1248

1209 Students fleeing unrest in Oxford help to establish Cambridge University

1130s A school of translators established by Archbishop Raymond translates many Arabic and Hebrew works

1088 Bologna, an important center for legal studies, becomes the first university in Europe

10th century onward The medical school at Salerno acts as conduit for Arabic medical works

NORWAY
SWEDEN
North Sea
DENMARK
Baltic Sea
SCOTLAND
IRELAND
1140 Newbattle
1142 Melrose
1142 Mellifont
1150 Jervaulx
1132 Rievaulx
1132 Fountains
1147 Kirkstall
WALES ENGLAND
Oxford
early 12th century
1128 Waverley
London
Canterbury
c.1209 Cambridge
1143 Alvastra
Lubeck
Elbe
1143 Wagrowiec
POLAND
1132 Camp
Cologne
Rhine
Worms
1348 Prague
Bec
Rheims
Chartres
c.1200
Paris
c.1236 Orléans
Meung
Tours
KINGDOM OF GERMANY
c.1250 Angers
1114 Pontigny
1115 Clairvaux
1115 Morimond
1124 Lützel
1135 Eberbach
1127 Ebrach
1098 Cîteaux
1112 La Ferté
1137 Heiligenkreuz
FRANCE
Alps
1332 Cahors
1229 Toulouse
1339 Grenoble
Milan
1303 Avignon
1204 Vicenza
1222 Padua (law)
1248 Piacenza
Genoa
Venice
VENETIAN REPUBLIC
1142 Czikador
LEÓN
León
1132 Moreruela
NAVARRE
Pamplona
1308 Coimbra
PORTUGAL
1148 Alcobaça
1218 Salamanca
Segovia
CASTILE
Tarazona
1300 Lérida
ARAGON
Béziers
Narbonne
Montpellier (medicine)
Marseille
Barcelona
12th century
KINGDOM OF ITALY
1088 Bologna (law)
Pisa
1215 Arezzo
1246 Siena
1308 Perugia
PAPAL STATES
Rome
c.1140
1245
1224 Naples
SERBIA
1290 Lisbon
Toledo
1254 Seville
Cordova
ALMOHAD EMPIRE
ATLANTIC OCEAN
Balearic Islands
Corsica
Sardinia
Mediterranean Sea
Salerno (medicine)
since 9th century
KINGDOM OF SICILY
Palermo
Sicily
Pyrenees

△ **Students attending their lessons**
This carving of students at the University of Bologna dates from around 1412 and adorns the tomb of the great teacher and legal thinker Bartolomeo da Saliceto.

5 DEVELOPMENTS IN LITERATURE AND SONG 1100–1200

The 12th century saw an upsurge in literature in the vernacular (local languages), many of them epic poems such as the German sagas the *Nibelungenlied* and Wolfram von Eschenbach's *Parzival*. In southern France troubadours, traveling performer-poets, spread *chansons de geste* ("songs of deeds," tales of romance, heroic deeds, and courtly love), such as the *Chanson de Roland*, which recounted episodes from Charlemagne's campaigns against the Muslims in northern Spain in the 770s.

4 INFLUENCE OF ARAB SCHOLARSHIP 1085–1300

Many scientific and philosophical works by Greek scholars had survived only in the Islamic world, often translated into Arabic and added to by Muslim writers. In the 12th century, these filtered into Europe, through areas such as Sicily and parts of Spain such as Toledo that had recently been conquered from Muslim powers. Manuscripts of many works by Aristotle, Ptolemy, and Euclid were then translated into Latin and helped fuel the 12th-century revival in scholarship.

🕌 Center of contact with Arab scholarship

⬛ Muslim lands reconquered by Christians 1030–1200

⬛ Muslim lands reconquered by Christians 1200–1300

3 THE NEW UNIVERSITIES 1088–1348

In the 12th century, scholars such as Abelard (at Paris) and Anselm of Aosta (at Bec) taught classes in theology and logic that attracted large numbers of students. Their schools developed into *studia generalia*, or universities, which offered a wider range of courses. Bologna University was among the first of these institutions.

🏛 University with date of foundation

🏛 Other important theological school

MEDIEVAL RENAISSANCE

The 12th century saw the intellectual, spiritual, and cultural life of Europe undergo a renewal. This encompassed the revival of monasteries, the foundation of schools and universities, the development of new architectural forms, and the acquisition of knowledge through translations from Greek and Arabic manuscripts.

After the fall of the Roman Empire in the West in the 5th century, much classical knowledge was lost, and most remaining manuscripts were confined to monasteries. Although there were local cultural revivals in France under Charlemagne (r. 768–814), in England under Alfred the Great (r. 871–899), and in Germany under Otto I (r. 962–973), they did not long survive the deaths of their royal patrons. However, in the late 11th century, a new movement began, in part stimulated by a desire for a return to purer forms of religious observance and in part by the needs of increasingly complex royal bureaucracies. New monastic movements, such as the Cistercians, gave impetus to a revival of spirituality, and schools grew up around cathedrals and abbeys that welcomed lay students and clergy alike. They taught a curriculum that focused on logic, grammar, and rhetoric but also encouraged debate and academic disputation. The largest centers, such as Paris and Bologna, attracted students from all over western Europe and developed into universities. Scholars there enjoyed access to works that had been unknown in Europe since the fall of Rome, as well as original Arabic works and translations of classical authors that came via the former Islamic territories in Sicily and Spain.

> *"By doubting we come to examine, and by examining we reach the truth."*
>
> PETER ABELARD, FRENCH THEOLOGIAN, 1079–1142

GOTHIC ARCHITECTURE
A NEW LANGUAGE OF CONSTRUCTION

In the early 12th century, a new architectural style replaced the solid masses and round arches typical of the previous Romanesque tradition. Known as Gothic, its pointed arches, ribbed buttresses, and soaring vaults allowed for higher ceilings and the penetration of more light into buildings (with windows often glazed in decorative stained glass). The style became the predominant one for large churches and cathedrals in western Europe for the next 300 years.

Wells Cathedral
This 12th-century English cathedral is one of the earliest examples of architecture that is wholly Gothic in style.

49
drzejów

RUSSIAN PRINCIPALITIES

HUNGARY

Danube

BULGARIA

BYZANTINE EMPIRE

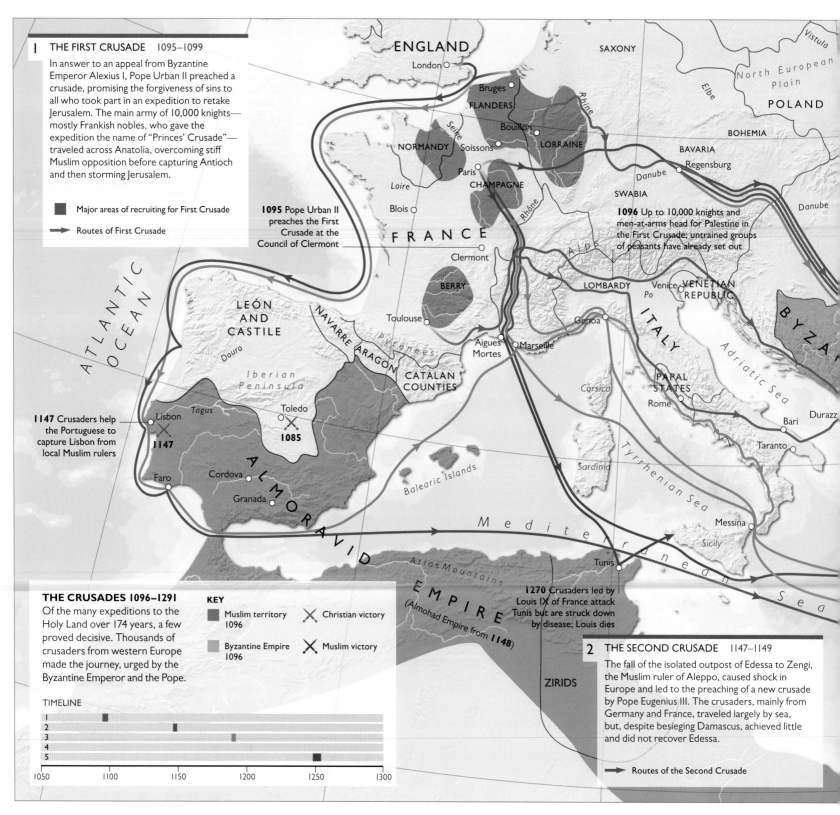

THE FIRST CRUSADE 1095–1099

In answer to an appeal from Byzantine Emperor Alexius I, Pope Urban II preached a crusade, promising the forgiveness of sins to all who took part in an expedition to retake Jerusalem. The main army of 10,000 knights—mostly Frankish nobles, who gave the expedition the name of "Princes' Crusade"—traveled across Anatolia, overcoming stiff Muslim opposition before capturing Antioch and then storming Jerusalem.

■ Major areas of recruiting for First Crusade

➤ Routes of First Crusade

1095 Pope Urban II preaches the First Crusade at the Council of Clermont

1096 Up to 10,000 knights and men-at-arms head for Palestine in the First Crusade; untrained groups of peasants have already set out

1147 Crusaders help the Portuguese to capture Lisbon from local Muslim rulers

1270 Crusaders led by Louis IX of France attack Tunis but are struck down by disease; Louis dies

THE CRUSADES 1096–1291

Of the many expeditions to the Holy Land over 174 years, a few proved decisive. Thousands of crusaders from western Europe made the journey, urged by the Byzantine Emperor and the Pope.

KEY

■ Muslim territory 1096
✕ Christian victory
■ Byzantine Empire 1096
✕ Muslim victory

TIMELINE

1050	1100	1150	1200	1250	1300
1					
2					
3					
4					
5					

2 THE SECOND CRUSADE 1147–1149

The fall of the isolated outpost of Edessa to Zengi, the Muslim ruler of Aleppo, caused shock in Europe and led to the preaching of a new crusade by Pope Eugenius III. The crusaders, mainly from Germany and France, traveled largely by sea, but, despite besieging Damascus, achieved little and did not recover Edessa.

➤ Routes of the Second Crusade

THE CRUSADES

Beginning in 1095, a series of military expeditions set out from Christian Europe to capture Jerusalem and the Holy Land, which had been part of the Islamic Caliphate since the mid-7th century. These Crusades established states in the area, but once Muslim rulers had overcome their previous disunity, they expelled the crusaders, capturing their last important stronghold in 1291.

Jerusalem fell into Muslim hands in 639, when the Caliphate took the provinces of the Byzantine Empire in Palestine and Syria. In the 11th century, a new Muslim group—the Seljuk Turks—gained more Byzantine territory and threatened the rights of Christian pilgrims to visit Jerusalem. In response to an appeal from the Byzantine emperor, the Pope called for a crusade—an armed expedition—to liberate the Holy City. Thousands of knights responded and marched to Palestine, where they captured many Muslim-controlled cities, including Jerusalem itself. The crusaders established states in Palestine, but their numbers were few, and Muslim counterattacks resulted in the fall of Edessa in 1144, a disaster that sparked the Second Crusade. The Third Crusade was inspired by the loss of

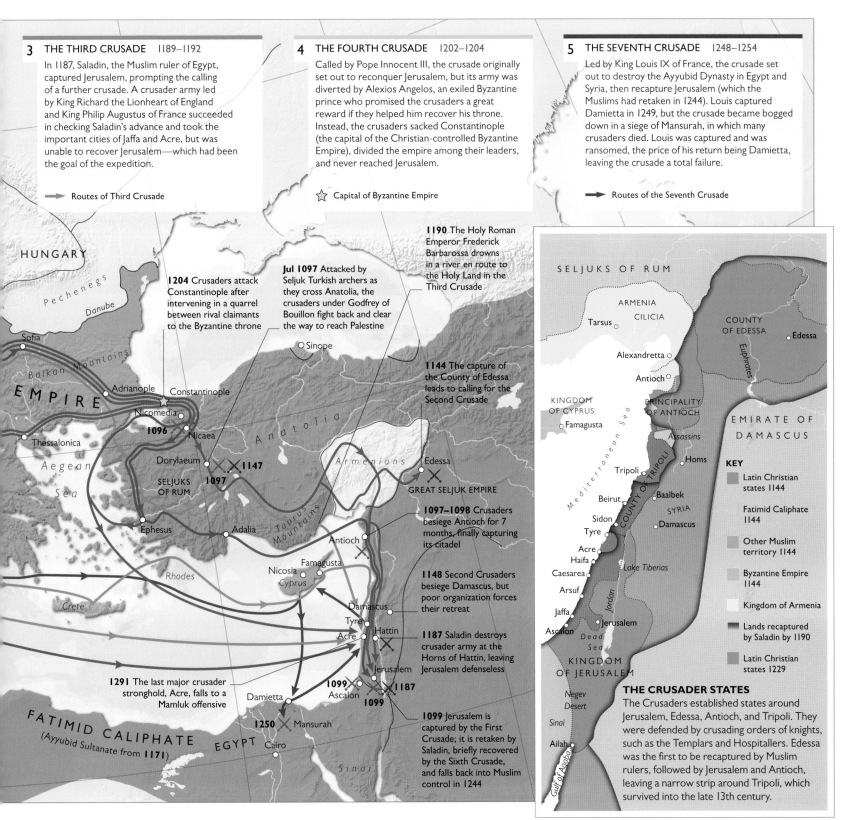

In 1187, Saladin, the Muslim ruler of Egypt, captured Jerusalem, prompting the calling of a further crusade. A crusader army led by King Richard the Lionheart of England and King Philip Augustus of France succeeded in checking Saladin's advance and took the important cities of Jaffa and Acre, but was unable to recover Jerusalem—which had been the goal of the expedition.

➡ Routes of Third Crusade

Called by Pope Innocent III, the crusade originally set out to reconquer Jerusalem, but its army was diverted by Alexios Angelos, an exiled Byzantine prince who promised the crusaders a great reward if they helped him recover his throne. Instead, the crusaders sacked Constantinople (the capital of the Christian-controlled Byzantine Empire), divided the empire among their leaders, and never reached Jerusalem.

☆ Capital of Byzantine Empire

Led by King Louis IX of France, the crusade set out to destroy the Ayyubid Dynasty in Egypt and Syria, then recapture Jerusalem (which the Muslims had retaken in 1244). Louis captured Damietta in 1249, but the crusade became bogged down in a siege of Mansurah, in which many crusaders died. Louis was captured and was ransomed, the price of his return being Damietta, leaving the crusade a total failure.

➡ Routes of the Seventh Crusade

1190 The Holy Roman Emperor Frederick Barbarossa drowns in a river en route to the Holy Land in the Third Crusade

Jul 1097 Attacked by Seljuk Turkish archers as they cross Anatolia, the crusaders under Godfrey of Bouillon fight back and clear the way to reach Palestine

1204 Crusaders attack Constantinople after intervening in a quarrel between rival claimants to the Byzantine throne

1144 The capture of the County of Edessa leads to calling for the Second Crusade

1097–1098 Crusaders besiege Antioch for 7 months, finally capturing its citadel

1148 Second Crusaders besiege Damascus, but poor organization forces their retreat

1187 Saladin destroys crusader army at the Horns of Hattin, leaving Jerusalem defenseless

1291 The last major crusader stronghold, Acre, falls to a Mamluk offensive

1250

1099 Jerusalem is captured by the First Crusade; it is retaken by Saladin, briefly recovered by the Sixth Crusade, and falls back into Muslim control in 1244

THE CRUSADER STATES

The Crusaders established states around Jerusalem, Edessa, Antioch, and Tripoli. They were defended by crusading orders of knights, such as the Templars and Hospitallers. Edessa was the first to be recaptured by Muslim rulers, followed by Jerusalem and Antioch, leaving a narrow strip around Tripoli, which survived into the late 13th century.

KEY
- Latin Christian states 1144
- Fatimid Caliphate 1144
- Other Muslim territory 1144
- Byzantine Empire 1144
- Kingdom of Armenia
- Lands recaptured by Saladin by 1190
- Latin Christian states 1229

Jerusalem to Saladin in 1187; while it halted the Muslim advance, it did not recover the Holy City. With no coherent strategy to secure the crusader states, several subsequent crusades were launched to address immediate crises. Jerusalem was eventually recovered in 1229 in the Sixth Crusade, but later expeditions were largely ineffective and aimed at Muslim-controlled regions outside Palestine, such as Egypt in 1249 and Tunis in 1270. The area under crusader control gradually shrank until campaigns by the Ayyubids and Mamluks retook the last of the Crusader castles, ending with the fall of Acre.

▷ **The departure for the Second Crusade**
This 12th-century fresco from a Templar chapel in southwest France shows knights leaving for the Holy Land. Most would be away for years in Palestine, and some would settle there.

THE INHERITORS OF ROME

The Western Roman Empire's fall was followed by the rise of several kingdoms of Germanic invaders in former Roman provinces. While the level of continuity with Roman life varied, within 200 years, some of their systems harked back, at least in part, to Rome.

△ **Roman elite**
This late 4th-century ivory diptych portrays the Roman general Stilicho and his wife and son. Regent for Emperor Honorius, the part-Vandal Stilicho was one of the Western Empire's most powerful men.

Pressure grew on the Roman frontiers along the Rhine and the Danube Rivers from the 3rd century, as Germanic invaders migrated westward. In 406, helped partly by problems within the empire, large numbers of Vandals, Alans, and Sueves flooded across the Rhine and fanned out through Gaul and Spain. As the empire's grip on these provinces contracted, its ability to raise taxes to support the army diminished, accelerating the process by which the newcomers had to be accommodated rather than expelled. Other encroachments followed. After some reshaping of the invading ethnic groups, the Western Roman Empire was left with a presence of Visigoths, Ostrogoths, Burgundians, and Franks. The Roman hold on the western provinces had slipped away, not as a result of a single defeat, but through simple lack of resources to defend them.

New kingdoms

By 418, a Visigothic kingdom had been established at Toulouse, which expanded to include much of southwestern France and Spain. This displaced the Vandals, who, in

▷ **Fortune for the church**
This jeweled cross is part of a cache of votive objects donated by the Visigothic kings of Spain to a church in the 7th century. After the conversion of King Reccared to Catholicism in 589, the Church became a key player in the consolidation of royal power in Spain.

429, crossed over into North Africa, where they founded their own kingdom (see pp.92–93). Northern France fell out of imperial control in the mid-5th century, as Frankish tribes pushed westward, and finally, in 476, Italy succumbed to an advance led by Odovacer, who was, in turn, supplanted by Ostrogoths under Theoderic the Great in 493. The Roman province of Britain, which had broken away from the empire in 411, suffered complete political collapse as Angles and Saxons mounted invasions across the North Sea.

Europe after Rome

The disappearance of the security that the Roman Empire had guaranteed had profound consequences. Trade declined, the economy collapsed in many areas, and long-distance communication became more difficult. Urban settlements contracted, disappearing almost entirely in England. Even Rome, which once had a population of more than half a million, shrank to only around 30,000 inhabitants by the 7th century. The new rulers adopted some elements of Roman life. As chieftains of war-bands, they were ill-equipped to rule large, static populations and, in Italy in particular, many of the former senatorial elite took service with their new masters. Statesmen such as Cassiodorus served under Theoderic and attempted to reconcile Ostrogoths and Romans. Gaul retained a centralized administration with tax-levying powers,

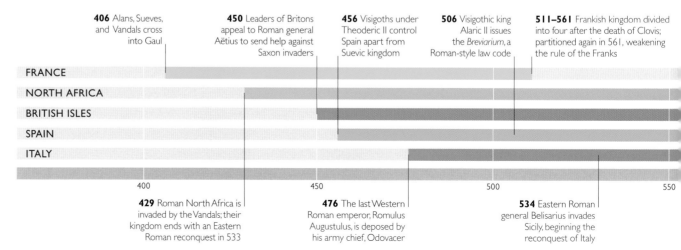

THE NEW ORDER

The early 5th century saw Germanic invaders breach the Rhine frontier of the Roman Empire. This was followed by a rapid collapse of imperial control over its western provinces. The Franks established a kingdom in northern France and expanded through the south and east, while the Visigoths overran Spain and the Vandals occupied Roman North Africa. In these areas, the new Germanic rulers gradually established administrations. England, however, remained divided among smaller kingdoms.

406 Alans, Sueves, and Vandals cross into Gaul

450 Leaders of Britons appeal to Roman general Aëtius to send help against Saxon invaders

456 Visigoths under Theoderic II control Spain apart from Suevic kingdom

506 Visigothic king Alaric II issues the *Breviarium*, a Roman-style law code

511–561 Frankish kingdom divided into four after the death of Clovis; partitioned again in 561, weakening the rule of the Franks

FRANCE
NORTH AFRICA
BRITISH ISLES
SPAIN
ITALY

400   450   500   550

429 Roman North Africa is invaded by the Vandals; their kingdom ends with an Eastern Roman reconquest in 533

476 The last Western Roman emperor, Romulus Augustulus, is deposed by his army chief, Odovacer

534 Eastern Roman general Belisarius invades Sicily, beginning the reconquest of Italy

◁ **Holy ruins**
These are the remains of the 12th-century Benedictine priory on Lindisfarne Island, off the northeast coast of Northumbria, England. It was built on the site of an earlier abbey destroyed by the first Viking raid on England in 793.

▷ **Anglo-Saxon helmet**
This reconstruction of a helmet found in an early 7th-century ship burial at Sutton Hoo, East Anglia, England, shows the great skill of Anglo-Saxon metalworkers.

while in Spain, the Visigoths combined the interests of Romans and Goths, issuing law codes that legislated differently for the two groups. In Britain, however, the prolonged military struggle between the invading Anglo-Saxons and indigenous Britons meant that not even fragments of the old Roman administration survived.

In 533–534, the emperor of the surviving Eastern Roman (Byzantine) Empire, Justinian, launched a military campaign to recover Rome's western provinces and destroyed the Vandal kingdom of North Africa. His campaign in Italy led to a 20-year war that ended with the fall of the Ostrogothic kingdom in 553. It also left the peninsula ravaged, unable to yield any taxes and ripe for a new invasion by the Lombards, who conquered much of the peninsula in 568–572, confining the Byzantines to a series of scattered enclaves.

Recovery and consolidation

Elsewhere, however, despite several civil wars, the 7th century saw a process of consolidation. In England, larger kingdoms emerged, most notably Northumbria in the north, Mercia and East Anglia in central England, and Wessex and Kent in the south. All of these converted to Christianity in the century following a mission in 597 sent by Pope Gregory I and led by one of his monks, Augustine. Lombard Italy stabilized after the invasion period, when Lombard king Agilulf (r. 590–616) made peace with the Franks following a series of invasions. In 643, King Rothari issued a law code setting down the customary law of the Lombards in written form for the first time.

By 700, Visigothic Spain, Frankish Gaul, and Lombard Italy had achieved relative stability. There, and in still-fragmented Anglo-Saxon England, the persistence of Latin as a means of formal written communication and the spread of the Christian Church provided living reminders of continuity with the late Roman world. If the invaders who settled in the Roman Empire discarded some of what they found there, they also inherited much from their Roman predecessors.

"This King Rothari collected ... the laws of the Lombards ... and he directed this code to be called the Edict."

PAUL THE DEACON, FROM *HISTORY OF THE LOMBARDS*, c. 790

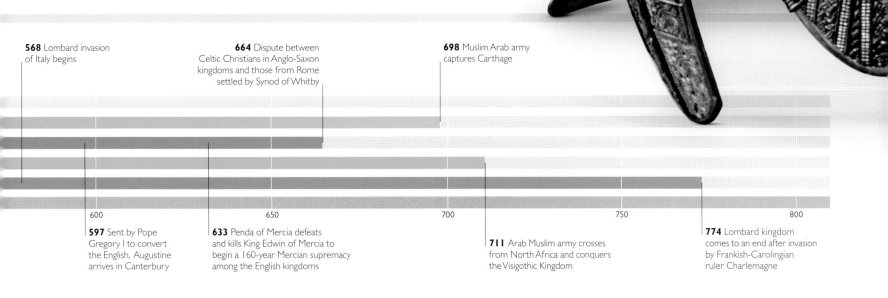

568 Lombard invasion of Italy begins

664 Dispute between Celtic Christians in Anglo-Saxon kingdoms and those from Rome settled by Synod of Whitby

698 Muslim Arab army captures Carthage

600

650

700

750

800

597 Sent by Pope Gregory I to convert the English, Augustine arrives in Canterbury

633 Penda of Mercia defeats and kills King Edwin of Mercia to begin a 160-year Mercian supremacy among the English kingdoms

711 Arab Muslim army crosses from North Africa and conquers the Visigothic Kingdom

774 Lombard kingdom comes to an end after invasion by Frankish-Carolingian ruler Charlemagne

THE HUNDRED YEARS' WAR

A conflict between the kings of England and of France over the English rulers' claim to the French throne began in 1337 and lasted for 116 years. While at times the English managed to conquer large parts of France, by the end of the conflict in 1453, they retained only the port town of Calais.

Edward III of England had a claim to the French throne through his mother, the sister of Charles IV of France. When Charles died without an heir, Edward laid claim to the French throne against his rival, Philip. This, combined with Edward's earlier refusal to pay homage to the French monarch for land he held, led to war. The conflict fell into three phases. In the initial phase (1337–1360) under Edward III, the English won significant victories. This phase came to an end with the Treaty of Brétigny, which left England with enlarged holdings in France. In the second phase

(1369–1389), the English initially made large gains but were pushed back. This phase ended in a truce, with England retaining only Calais and small areas around Brest, Bordeaux, and Bayonne. In the early 1400s, France was in a state of virtual civil war between supporters of the Duke of Burgundy and the Armagnacs. Taking advantage of this disruption, Henry V of England resumed war with France in 1415. At first, English forces took huge areas. However, inspired by Joan of Arc, the French fought back, and by the end of the war, England held only Calais.

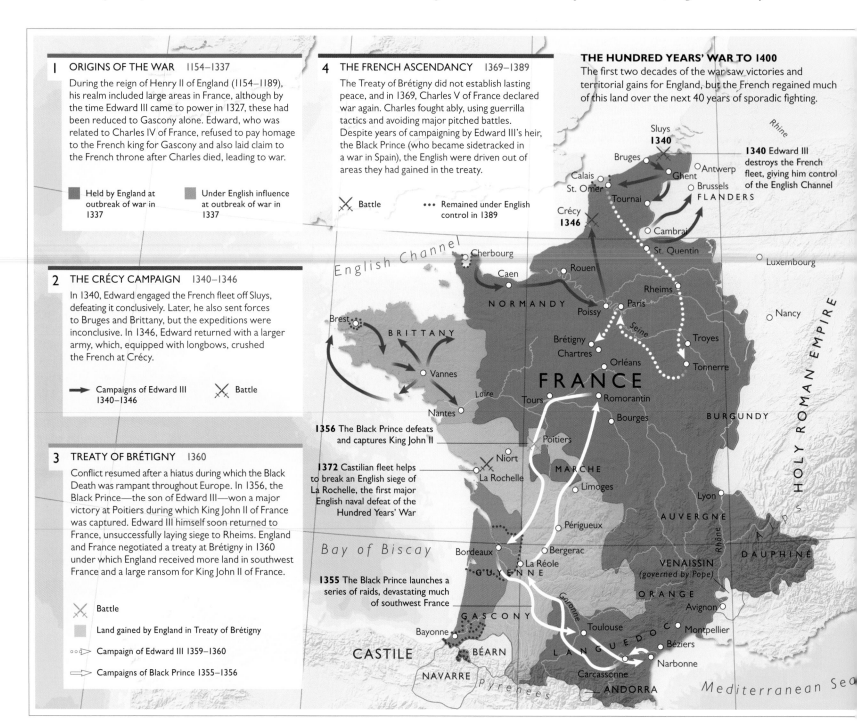

1 ORIGINS OF THE WAR   1154–1337

During the reign of Henry II of England (1154–1189), his realm included large areas in France, although by the time Edward III came to power in 1327, these had been reduced to Gascony alone. Edward, who was related to Charles IV of France, refused to pay homage to the French king for Gascony and also laid claim to the French throne after Charles died, leading to war.

- ■ Held by England at outbreak of war in 1337
- ■ Under English influence at outbreak of war in 1337

2 THE CRÉCY CAMPAIGN   1340–1346

In 1340, Edward engaged the French fleet off Sluys, defeating it conclusively. Later, he also sent forces to Bruges and Brittany, but the expeditions were inconclusive. In 1346, Edward returned with a larger army, which, equipped with longbows, crushed the French at Crécy.

- → Campaigns of Edward III 1340–1346
- ✕ Battle

3 TREATY OF BRÉTIGNY   1360

Conflict resumed after a hiatus during which the Black Death was rampant throughout Europe. In 1356, the Black Prince—the son of Edward III—won a major victory at Poitiers during which King John II of France was captured. Edward III himself soon returned to France, unsuccessfully laying siege to Rheims. England and France negotiated a treaty at Brétigny in 1360 under which England received more land in southwest France and a large ransom for King John II of France.

- ✕ Battle
- ■ Land gained by England in Treaty of Brétigny
- ∘∘∘ Campaign of Edward III 1359–1360
- ⇒ Campaigns of Black Prince 1355–1356

4 THE FRENCH ASCENDANCY   1369–1389

The Treaty of Brétigny did not establish lasting peace, and in 1369, Charles V of France declared war again. Charles fought ably, using guerrilla tactics and avoiding major pitched battles. Despite years of campaigning by Edward III's heir, the Black Prince (who became sidetracked in a war in Spain), the English were driven out of areas they had gained in the treaty.

- ✕ Battle
- ••• Remained under English control in 1389

THE HUNDRED YEARS' WAR TO 1400
The first two decades of the war saw victories and territorial gains for England, but the French regained much of this land over the next 40 years of sporadic fighting.

1340 Edward III destroys the French fleet, giving him control of the English Channel

1356 The Black Prince defeats and captures King John II

1372 Castilian fleet helps to break an English siege of La Rochelle, the first major English naval defeat of the Hundred Years' War

1355 The Black Prince launches a series of raids, devastating much of southwest France

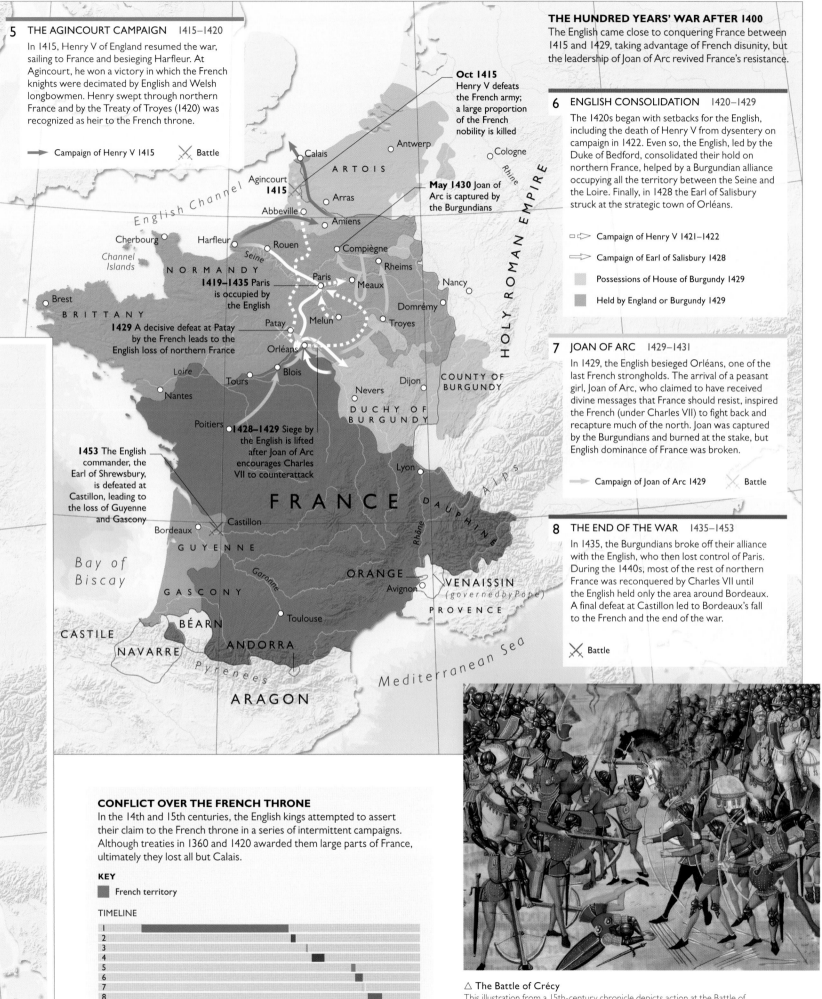

5 THE AGINCOURT CAMPAIGN 1415–1420

In 1415, Henry V of England resumed the war, sailing to France and besieging Harfleur. At Agincourt, he won a victory in which the French knights were decimated by English and Welsh longbowmen. Henry swept through northern France and by the Treaty of Troyes (1420) was recognized as heir to the French throne.

→ Campaign of Henry V 1415   ✕ Battle

Oct 1415 Henry V defeats the French army; a large proportion of the French nobility is killed

May 1430 Joan of Arc is captured by the Burgundians

1419–1435 Paris is occupied by the English

1429 A decisive defeat at Patay by the French leads to the English loss of northern France

1453 The English commander, the Earl of Shrewsbury, is defeated at Castillon, leading to the loss of Guyenne and Gascony

1428–1429 Siege by the English is lifted after Joan of Arc encourages Charles VII to counterattack

THE HUNDRED YEARS' WAR AFTER 1400

The English came close to conquering France between 1415 and 1429, taking advantage of French disunity, but the leadership of Joan of Arc revived France's resistance.

6 ENGLISH CONSOLIDATION 1420–1429

The 1420s began with setbacks for the English, including the death of Henry V from dysentery on campaign in 1422. Even so, the English, led by the Duke of Bedford, consolidated their hold on northern France, helped by a Burgundian alliance occupying all the territory between the Seine and the Loire. Finally, in 1428 the Earl of Salisbury struck at the strategic town of Orléans.

▭▭▷ Campaign of Henry V 1421–1422

▭▷ Campaign of Earl of Salisbury 1428

▢ Possessions of House of Burgundy 1429

▢ Held by England or Burgundy 1429

7 JOAN OF ARC 1429–1431

In 1429, the English besieged Orléans, one of the last French strongholds. The arrival of a peasant girl, Joan of Arc, who claimed to have received divine messages that France should resist, inspired the French (under Charles VII) to fight back and recapture much of the north. Joan was captured by the Burgundians and burned at the stake, but English dominance of France was broken.

→ Campaign of Joan of Arc 1429   ✕ Battle

8 THE END OF THE WAR 1435–1453

In 1435, the Burgundians broke off their alliance with the English, who then lost control of Paris. During the 1440s, most of the rest of northern France was reconquered by Charles VII until the English held only the area around Bordeaux. A final defeat at Castillon led to Bordeaux's fall to the French and the end of the war.

✕ Battle

CONFLICT OVER THE FRENCH THRONE

In the 14th and 15th centuries, the English kings attempted to assert their claim to the French throne in a series of intermittent campaigns. Although treaties in 1360 and 1420 awarded them large parts of France, ultimately they lost all but Calais.

KEY

▬ French territory

TIMELINE

1 2 3 4 5 6 7 8

1100 1200 1300 1400 1500

△ **The Battle of Crécy**
This illustration from a 15th-century chronicle depicts action at the Battle of Crécy, in which the English longbow proved its superiority over the crossbow, which was slower to load and had a shorter range.

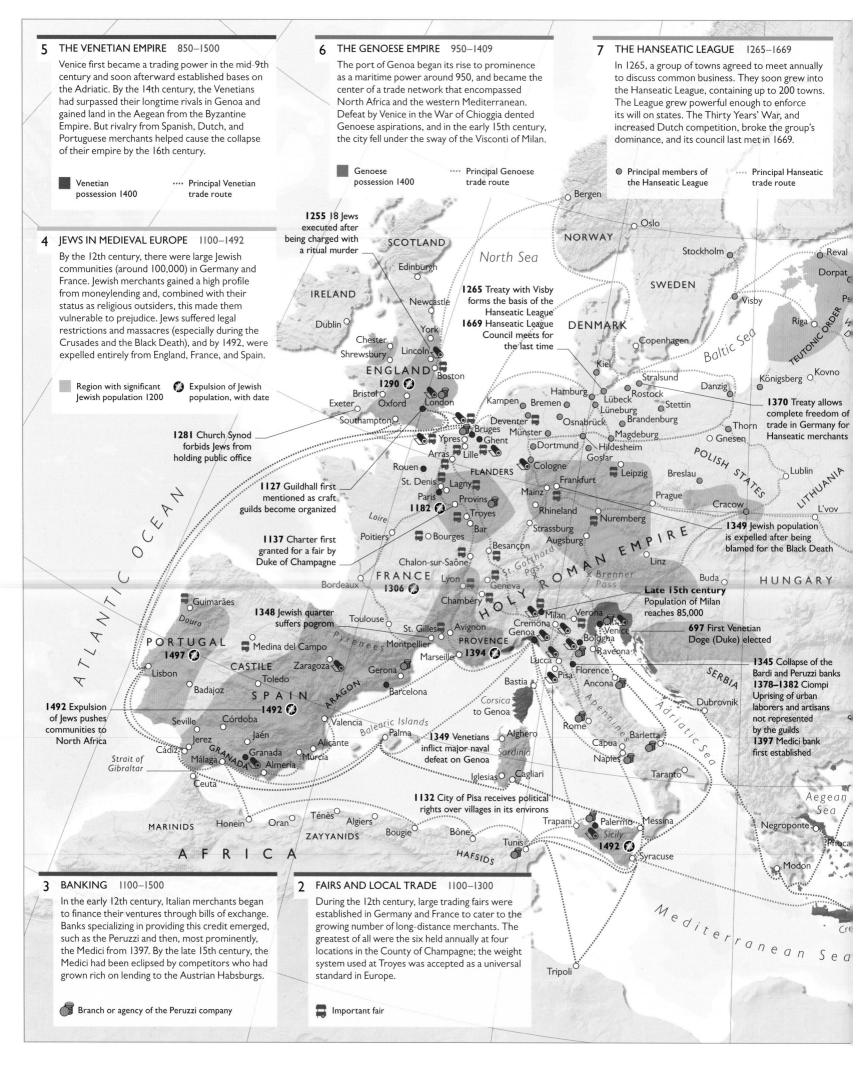

5 THE VENETIAN EMPIRE 850–1500

Venice first became a trading power in the mid-9th century and soon afterward established bases on the Adriatic. By the 14th century, the Venetians had surpassed their longtime rivals in Genoa and gained land in the Aegean from the Byzantine Empire. But rivalry from Spanish, Dutch, and Portuguese merchants helped cause the collapse of their empire by the 16th century.

- ■ Venetian possession 1400
- ⋯ Principal Venetian trade route

6 THE GENOESE EMPIRE 950–1409

The port of Genoa began its rise to prominence as a maritime power around 950, and became the center of a trade network that encompassed North Africa and the western Mediterranean. Defeat by Venice in the War of Chioggia dented Genoese aspirations, and in the early 15th century, the city fell under the sway of the Visconti of Milan.

- ■ Genoese possession 1400
- ⋯ Principal Genoese trade route

7 THE HANSEATIC LEAGUE 1265–1669

In 1265, a group of towns agreed to meet annually to discuss common business. They soon grew into the Hanseatic League, containing up to 200 towns. The League grew powerful enough to enforce its will on states. The Thirty Years' War, and increased Dutch competition, broke the group's dominance, and its council last met in 1669.

- ● Principal members of the Hanseatic League
- ⋯ Principal Hanseatic trade route

4 JEWS IN MEDIEVAL EUROPE 1100–1492

By the 12th century, there were large Jewish communities (around 100,000) in Germany and France. Jewish merchants gained a high profile from moneylending and, combined with their status as religious outsiders, this made them vulnerable to prejudice. Jews suffered legal restrictions and massacres (especially during the Crusades and the Black Death), and by 1492, were expelled entirely from England, France, and Spain.

- ▨ Region with significant Jewish population 1200
- ⊕ Expulsion of Jewish population, with date

1255 18 Jews executed after being charged with a ritual murder

1265 Treaty with Visby forms the basis of the Hanseatic League
1669 Hanseatic League Council meets for the last time

1370 Treaty allows complete freedom of trade in Germany for Hanseatic merchants

1281 Church Synod forbids Jews from holding public office

1127 Guildhall first mentioned as craft guilds become organized

1137 Charter first granted for a fair by Duke of Champagne

1182 ⊕

1306 ⊕ FRANCE

1349 Jewish population is expelled after being blamed for the Black Death

Late 15th century Population of Milan reaches 85,000

697 First Venetian Doge (Duke) elected

1348 Jewish quarter suffers pogrom

1345 Collapse of the Bardi and Peruzzi banks
1378–1382 Ciompi Uprising of urban laborers and artisans not represented by the guilds
1397 Medici bank first established

1497 ⊕ PORTUGAL

1492 ⊕ SPAIN

1492 Expulsion of Jews pushes communities to North Africa

1394 ⊕

1349 Venetians inflict major naval defeat on Genoa

1132 City of Pisa receives political rights over villages in its environs

1492 ⊕ Sicily

Bergen · Oslo · Stockholm · Reval · Dorpat · NORWAY · SCOTLAND · North Sea · SWEDEN · Edinburgh · IRELAND · Newcastle · Visby · Riga · TEUTONIC ORDER · Dublin · York · DENMARK · Copenhagen · Baltic Sea · Chester · Lincoln · Kiel · Königsberg · Kovno · Shrewsbury · ENGLAND · Boston · Hamburg · Lübeck · Stralsund · Rostock · Danzig · Stettin · Thorn · Gnesen · Bristol · Oxford · London · Kampen · Bremen · Lüneburg · Brandenburg · Magdeburg · POLISH STATES · Lublin · Exeter · Ypres · Bruges · Deventer · Münster · Osnabrück · Dortmund · Hildesheim · Goslar · Breslau · LITHUANIA · Southampton · Arras · Lille · Ghent · FLANDERS · Cologne · Frankfurt · Leipzig · Prague · Cracow · L'vov · Rouen · St. Denis · Lagny · Mainz · Rhineland · Nuremberg · Paris · Provins · Troyes · Strassburg · Augsburg · Linz · Loire · Bar · Besançon · HUNGARY · Poitiers · Bourges · Chalon-sur-Saône · St. Gotthard Pass · Brenner Pass · Buda · Bordeaux · Lyon · Geneva · HOLY ROMAN EMPIRE · Chambéry · Milan · Verona · Guimarães · Toulouse · St. Gilles · Avignon · PROVENCE · Cremona · Genoa · Bologna · Venice · SERBIA · Douro · Medina del Campo · Montpellier · Marseille · Lucca · Ravenna · Dubrovnik · PORTUGAL · Lisbon · CASTILE · Zaragoza · Gerona · Pisa · Florence · Ancona · Adriatic Sea · Badajoz · Toledo · SPAIN · Barcelona · Bastia · Rome · Barletta · Jerez · Córdoba · Jaén · Valencia · Corsica to Genoa · Capua · Naples · Seville · GRANADA · Granada · Murcia · Alicante · Palma · Alghero · Taranto · Cádiz · Málaga · Almería · Balearic Islands · Sardinia · Aegean Sea · Ceuta · Iglesias · Cagliari · MARINIDS · Honein · Oran · Ténès · Algiers · Bougie · Bône · Trapani · Palermo · Messina · Negroponte · ZAYYANIDS · AFRICA · Tunis · HAFSIDS · Sicily · Syracuse · Modon · Tripoli · Mediterranean Sea · ATLANTIC OCEAN · Pyrenees · ARAGON · Strait of Gibraltar · Apennines

3 BANKING 1100–1500

In the early 12th century, Italian merchants began to finance their ventures through bills of exchange. Banks specializing in providing this credit emerged, such as the Peruzzi and then, most prominently, the Medici from 1397. By the late 15th century, the Medici had been eclipsed by competitors who had grown rich on lending to the Austrian Habsburgs.

- 🏛 Branch or agency of the Peruzzi company

2 FAIRS AND LOCAL TRADE 1100–1300

During the 12th century, large trading fairs were established in Germany and France to cater to the growing number of long-distance merchants. The greatest of all were the six held annually at four locations in the County of Champagne; the weight system used at Troyes was accepted as a universal standard in Europe.

- 🚚 Important fair

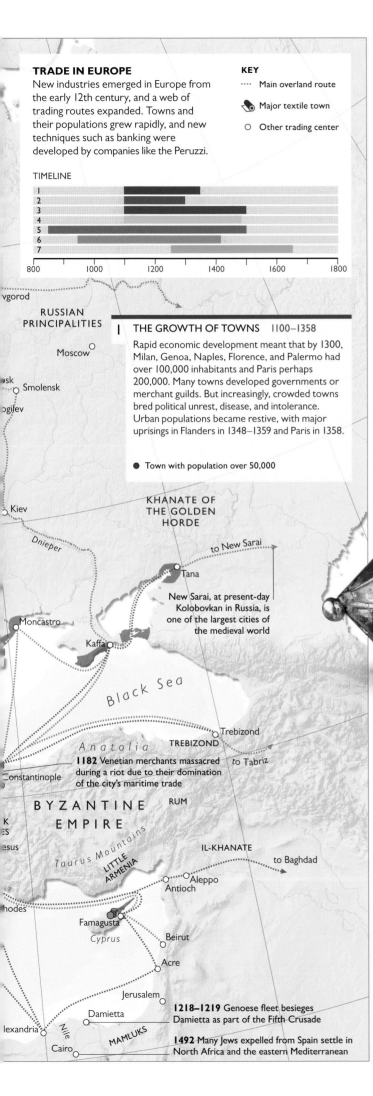

TRADE IN EUROPE

New industries emerged in Europe from the early 12th century, and a web of trading routes expanded. Towns and their populations grew rapidly, and new techniques such as banking were developed by companies like the Peruzzi.

KEY

···· Main overland route

🧵 Major textile town

○ Other trading center

TIMELINE

	800	1000	1200	1400	1600	1800
1						
2						
3						
4						
5						
6						
7						

vgorod

RUSSIAN PRINCIPALITIES

Moscow ○

sk

○ Smolensk

ogilev

THE GROWTH OF TOWNS 1100–1358

Rapid economic development meant that by 1300, Milan, Genoa, Naples, Florence, and Palermo had over 100,000 inhabitants and Paris perhaps 200,000. Many towns developed governments or merchant guilds. But increasingly, crowded towns bred political unrest, disease, and intolerance. Urban populations became restive, with major uprisings in Flanders in 1348–1359 and Paris in 1358.

● Town with population over 50,000

○ Kiev

KHANATE OF THE GOLDEN HORDE

Dnieper

to New Sarai

○ Tana

New Sarai, at present-day Kolobovkan in Russia, is one of the largest cities of the medieval world

○ Moncastro

Kaffa ○

Black Sea

○ Trebizond

Anatolia TREBIZOND

to Tabriz

1182 Venetian merchants massacred during a riot due to their domination of the city's maritime trade

Constantinople

BYZANTINE EMPIRE RUM

K
ES
esus

Taurus Mountains

LITTLE ARMENIA

IL-KHANATE

to Baghdad

○ Aleppo
Antioch

hodes

Famagusta ○

○ Beirut

Cyprus

○ Acre

Jerusalem ○

1218–1219 Genoese fleet besieges Damietta as part of the Fifth Crusade

○ Damietta

1492 Many Jews expelled from Spain settle in North Africa and the eastern Mediterranean

lexandria

Nile

Cairo ○

MAMLUKS

MEDIEVAL EUROPEAN TRADE

From the 12th century, Europe experienced a period of economic and population growth. Guilds and town councils threatened royal monopolies of power, and merchants pioneered new methods of banking. Yet not all shared the fruits of this prosperity, and Jewish communities suffered increasing persecutions.

Europe saw a renewed flourishing of urban life in the 12th century. New towns were built under royal patronage in England and France, and others expanded significantly in size. Fairs sprang up, where merchants traveled from across the continent to acquire goods and hawk their wares. Cities became more important, too, as many places acquired

△ **Jewish wedding ring**
This ornate ring comes from Colmar, in northeastern France, which had a thriving Jewish community by the 13th century.

their own councils that were not always amenable to royal persuasion, while in Italy a network of independent city-states developed. The area became a fertile ground for innovation in finance, including the establishment of the first investment banks. The wealth generated by their merchants enabled Genoa and Venice to establish maritime empires in the Mediterranean and become international powers in their own right. Similarly, in northern Europe, the Hanseatic League—a federation of trading cities—developed after 1265 and dominated trade in the Baltic and North Seas for two centuries. Jewish communities, however, were expelled from much of western and southern Europe. They had previously played a central role in providing moneylending services, but by 1500, main centers of Jewish life on the continent had shifted to eastern Europe, Italy, and the lands under Muslim control.

CLOTH TRADE
THE FIRST GREAT EUROPEAN INDUSTRY

Cloth was the first commodity in medieval Europe whose production grew into a great industry. The main centers were in Flanders, England, and Italy, which all had access to important sources of wool. The spinning, weaving, fulling (cleansing the cloth and making it thicker), and dyeing processes provided employment to large numbers of artisans and incomes for merchants. Guilds, associations of artisans and merchants, were established in major cities, and merchants used their wealth to endow lavish cloth halls—where cloth was sold.

Textile workers dyeing cloth

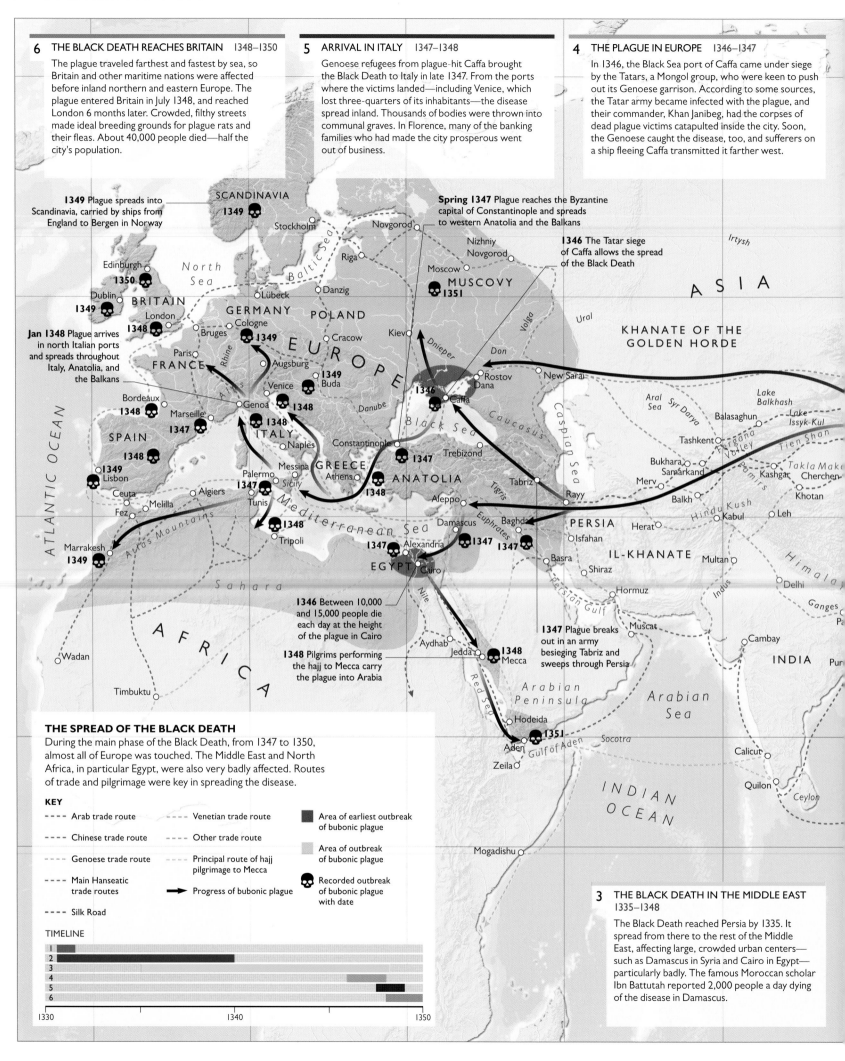

6 THE BLACK DEATH REACHES BRITAIN 1348–1350

The plague traveled farthest and fastest by sea, so Britain and other maritime nations were affected before inland northern and eastern Europe. The plague entered Britain in July 1348, and reached London 6 months later. Crowded, filthy streets made ideal breeding grounds for plague rats and their fleas. About 40,000 people died—half the city's population.

5 ARRIVAL IN ITALY 1347–1348

Genoese refugees from plague-hit Caffa brought the Black Death to Italy in late 1347. From the ports where the victims landed—including Venice, which lost three-quarters of its inhabitants—the disease spread inland. Thousands of bodies were thrown into communal graves. In Florence, many of the banking families who had made the city prosperous went out of business.

4 THE PLAGUE IN EUROPE 1346–1347

In 1346, the Black Sea port of Caffa came under siege by the Tatars, a Mongol group, who were keen to push out its Genoese garrison. According to some sources, the Tatar army became infected with the plague, and their commander, Khan Janibeg, had the corpses of dead plague victims catapulted inside the city. Soon, the Genoese caught the disease, too, and sufferers on a ship fleeing Caffa transmitted it farther west.

1349 Plague spreads into Scandinavia, carried by ships from England to Bergen in Norway

Spring 1347 Plague reaches the Byzantine capital of Constantinople and spreads to western Anatolia and the Balkans

1346 The Tatar siege of Caffa allows the spread of the Black Death

Jan 1348 Plague arrives in north Italian ports and spreads throughout Italy, Anatolia, and the Balkans

1346 Between 10,000 and 15,000 people die each day at the height of the plague in Cairo

1348 Pilgrims performing the hajj to Mecca carry the plague into Arabia

1347 Plague breaks out in an army besieging Tabriz and sweeps through Persia

THE SPREAD OF THE BLACK DEATH

During the main phase of the Black Death, from 1347 to 1350, almost all of Europe was touched. The Middle East and North Africa, in particular Egypt, were also very badly affected. Routes of trade and pilgrimage were key in spreading the disease.

KEY

- - - Arab trade route
- - - Chinese trade route
- - - Genoese trade route
- - - Main Hanseatic trade routes
- - - Silk Road
- - - Venetian trade route
- - - Other trade route
- - - Principal route of hajj pilgrimage to Mecca
→ Progress of bubonic plague

■ Area of earliest outbreak of bubonic plague
■ Area of outbreak of bubonic plague
☠ Recorded outbreak of bubonic plague with date

TIMELINE

1330   1340   1350

3 THE BLACK DEATH IN THE MIDDLE EAST 1335–1348

The Black Death reached Persia by 1335. It spread from there to the rest of the Middle East, affecting large, crowded urban centers—such as Damascus in Syria and Cairo in Egypt—particularly badly. The famous Moroccan scholar Ibn Battutah reported 2,000 people a day dying of the disease in Damascus.

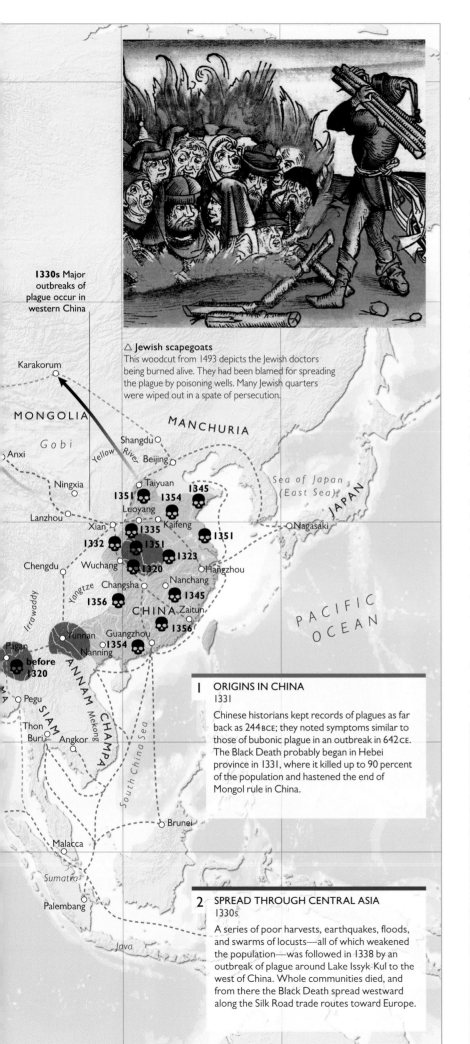

1330s Major outbreaks of plague occur in western China

△ **Jewish scapegoats**
This woodcut from 1493 depicts the Jewish doctors being burned alive. They had been blamed for spreading the plague by poisoning wells. Many Jewish quarters were wiped out in a spate of persecution.

THE BLACK DEATH

In 1347, a new disease entered Europe from China and central Asia. The bubonic plague, or Black Death (after the black spots it caused on the skin), spread rapidly, and, with no cure available, killed around 150 million people—roughly one-third of the world's population.

The Black Death was transmitted through the bite of infected rat fleas, so it spread quickly in the crowded, unsanitary conditions of medieval towns. It moved along trade routes once it reached Italy in 1347, and over time developed into more virulent forms. Doctors prescribed sweet-smelling posies, complex brews of herbs and spices, and the fumigation of rooms, only the last of which—by killing the fleas—had the slightest effect in stopping the epidemic's course. Those who tried to flee simply spread the disease to new areas.

The disease caused terror and an outpouring of mysticism, and also had profound social consequences. There was a huge rise in crime—the murder rate in England doubled—as people broke faith with traditional values. Peasants, now scarce in number, could demand better conditions and pay from their feudal masters.

By the end of 1350, the Black Death had mainly run its course, but there were many recurrences; even today, there are occasional cases all over the world.

"They sickened by the thousands daily, and died unattended and without help."

GIOVANNI BOCACCIO, FROM THE *DECAMERON*, 1348–1353

1 ORIGINS IN CHINA
1331

Chinese historians kept records of plagues as far back as 244 BCE; they noted symptoms similar to those of bubonic plague in an outbreak in 642 CE. The Black Death probably began in Hebei province in 1331, where it killed up to 90 percent of the population and hastened the end of Mongol rule in China.

2 SPREAD THROUGH CENTRAL ASIA
1330s

A series of poor harvests, earthquakes, floods, and swarms of locusts—all of which weakened the population—was followed in 1338 by an outbreak of plague around Lake Issyk-Kul to the west of China. Whole communities died, and from there the Black Death spread westward along the Silk Road trade routes toward Europe.

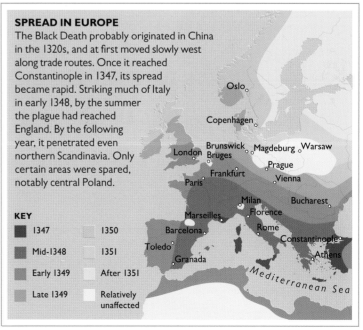

SPREAD IN EUROPE
The Black Death probably originated in China in the 1320s, and at first moved slowly west along trade routes. Once it reached Constantinople in 1347, its spread became rapid. Striking much of Italy in early 1348, by the summer the plague had reached England. By the following year, it penetrated even northern Scandinavia. Only certain areas were spared, notably central Poland.

KEY

■ 1347	■ 1350		
■ Mid-1348	■ 1351		
■ Early 1349	□ After 1351		
■ Late 1349	□ Relatively unaffected		

Coronation and excommunication
This painting shows Pope Innocent III both conferring the imperial crown on Frederick II (on the right) and removing it from Otto IV (on the left). It demonstrates the power of a pope to make and unmake emperors.

THE EMPEROR AND THE POPE

During the 11th and 12th centuries, relations between popes and rulers of the Holy Roman Empire were fraught with tensions, as both laid claim to supreme authority within the empire. It was only when imperial authority declined within Germany that the struggle between them finally subsided.

From the 10th century—with the empire extending across what is now Germany, the Czech Republic, and parts of France—there was a tussle for power between popes and emperors. While popes maintained that ultimate authority should rest with them as heads of the Church, emperors vigorously defended their position as supreme secular rulers. The struggle, known as the Investiture Controversy, focused on the monarch's right to invest bishops, who in turn had to pay homage to the emperor for their lands. Pope Gregory VII refused to accept this, and excommunicated Emperor Henry IV twice, first in 1076 and again in 1080. The Investiture Controversy was resolved in 1122 through a compromise whereby bishops in the empire could have a dual investiture, once by the Emperor for their lands and once by the Pope for their spiritual position.

△ **Crowning glory**
The ornamental crown seen here was used for the coronation of Holy Roman Emperors from the late 10th century.

Shift in the seat of power

Popes continued to interfere in imperial succession until 1356, when a document known as the Golden Bull decreed that emperors would be chosen by a college of electors—three bishops and four (later six) German princes. This gave German princes more power in their territories. Also, the shift of the power base of the Habsburg emperors toward Austria and Spain in the 15th and 16th centuries, the rise of specifically German imperial institutions such as the Imperial Diet, and the weakening of the Catholic Church in Germany after the Reformation (see pp.166–167) meant that by the 17th century, the Papal–Imperial rivalry had become largely irrelevant.

◁ **Divine coronation**
This 11th-century miniature depicts Christ crowning Emperor Henry II. The idea that an emperor's power was bestowed by God undermined claims of papal authority.

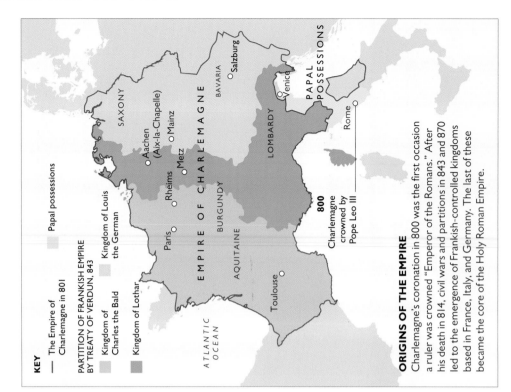

THE HOLY ROMAN EMPIRE

The crowning of the Frankish ruler Charlemagne as emperor in 800 marked the birth of an institution that came to be called the Holy Roman Empire. Although it survived for over a millennium, the empire's territorial core contracted until it became largely German and a sometimes chaotic mosaic of multiple and overlapping jurisdictions.

When Pope Leo III offered a new imperial title to Charlemagne, the ruler of the Franks, it was partly through nostalgia for the lost stability of the Roman Empire and a desire for protection. Having conquered much of northwest Europe since his accession in 768, he seemed an appropriate successor to the Caesars of old. However, the disintegration of the Frankish Empire into civil war after Charlemagne's death in 814 meant that imperial power was often short-lived. Sometimes there was no recognized emperor, until the Ottonian family acquired the title "Emperor of the Romans" in 962—an event most now regard as the true beginning of the empire. Thereafter, the empire became mainly a German affair, passing through the hands of successive dynasties: the Ottonians, Salians, Hohenstaufen, Luxembourg, and Habsburgs. Imperial lands were ceded to local princes and towns while the emperor was in Italy or on crusade

or when he was preoccupied with campaigning. This caused a general weakening of imperial control. Stronger emperors, such as Henry IV, tried to assert imperial authority, clashing with the Papacy over the right to appoint bishops. But his humiliation in being excommunicated and forced to make penance in 1077 demonstrated the limit of the imperial writ.

The empire briefly reached a new apogee under Frederick II in the early 13th century, when Sicily came into the imperial orbit. But a long domination by the Habsburgs from 1438, who also had lands outside the Holy Roman Empire to rule, contributed to a further withering of imperial power. The settlement at the end of the Thirty Years' War (see pp.168–169) in 1648 gave the German states almost complete independence, and the forced abdication of the last emperor, the Habsburg Francis II, in 1806 ended a defunct institution.

ORIGINS OF THE EMPIRE

Charlemagne's coronation in 800 was the first occasion a ruler was crowned "Emperor of the Romans." After his death in 814, civil wars and partitions in 843 and 870 led to the emergence of Frankish-controlled kingdoms based in France, Italy, and Germany. The last of these became the core of the Holy Roman Empire.

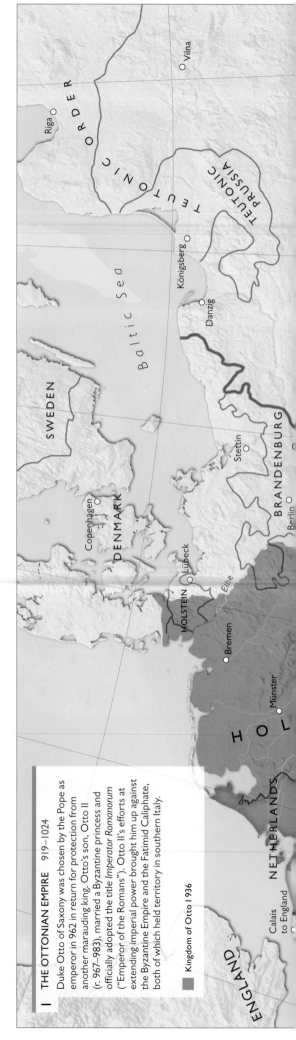

THE OTTONIAN EMPIRE 919–1024

Duke Otto of Saxony was chosen by the Pope as emperor in 962 in return for protection from another marauding king. Otto's son, Otto II (r. 967–983), married a Byzantine princess and officially adopted the title *Imperator Romanorum* ("Emperor of the Romans"). Otto II's efforts at extending imperial power brought him up against the Byzantine Empire and the Fatimid Caliphate, both of which held territory in southern Italy.

■ Kingdom of Otto I 936

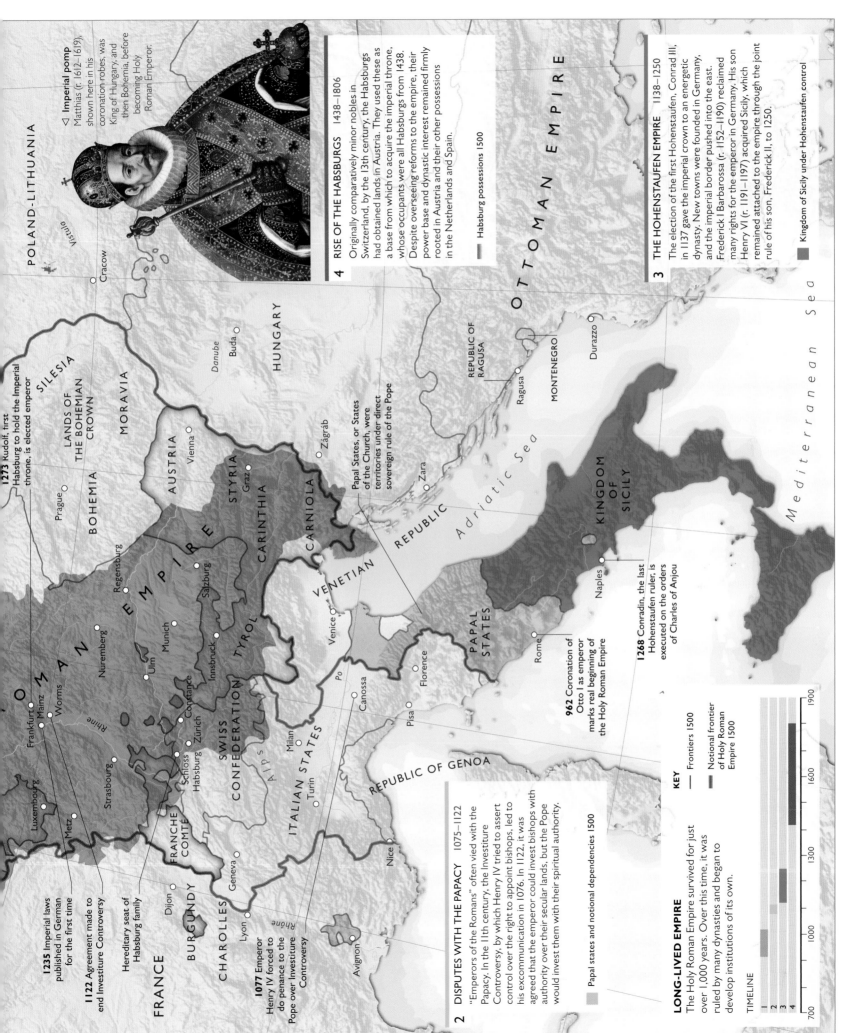

△ **Imperial pomp**
Matthias (r. 1612–1619), shown here in his coronation robes, was King of Hungary, and then Bohemia, before becoming Holy Roman Emperor.

4 RISE OF THE HABSBURGS 1438–1806

Originally comparatively minor nobles in Switzerland, by the 13th century, the Habsburgs had obtained lands in Austria. They used these as a base from which to acquire the imperial throne, whose occupants were all Habsburgs from 1438. Despite overseeing reforms to the empire, their power base and dynastic interest remained firmly rooted in Austria and their other possessions in the Netherlands and Spain.

▬ Habsburg possessions 1500

3 THE HOHENSTAUFEN EMPIRE 1138–1250

The election of the first Hohenstaufen, Conrad III, in 1137 gave the imperial crown to an energetic dynasty. New towns were founded in Germany, and the imperial border pushed into the east. Frederick I Barbarossa (r. 1152–1190) reclaimed many rights for the emperor in Germany. His son Henry VI (r. 1191–1197) acquired Sicily, which remained attached to the empire through the joint rule of his son, Frederick II, to 1250.

▬ Kingdom of Sicily under Hohenstaufen control

POLAND-LITHUANIA

Vistula

Cracow

OTTOMAN EMPIRE

REPUBLIC OF RAGUSA

Durazzo

MONTENEGRO

Ragusa

Zara

Adriatic Sea

SILESIA

LANDS OF THE BOHEMIAN CROWN

MORAVIA

Danube

Buda

HUNGARY

Prague

BOHEMIA

AUSTRIA

Vienna

STYRIA

Graz

Zágráb

CARINTHIA

CARNIOLA

Papal States, or States of the Church, were territories under direct sovereign rule of the Pope

VENETIAN REPUBLIC

Venice

Mediterranean Sea

1273 Rudolf, first Habsburg to hold the Imperial throne, is elected emperor

ROMAN EMPIRE

Regensburg

Nuremberg

Munich

Ulm

Salzburg

Innsbruck

TYROL

Milan

Po

Florence

PAPAL STATES

Rome

KINGDOM OF SICILY

Naples

1268 Conradin, the last Hohenstaufen ruler, is executed on the orders of Charles of Anjou

962 Coronation of Otto I as emperor marks real beginning of the Holy Roman Empire

Frankfurt

Mainz

Worms

Rhine

Schloss Habsburg

Zürich

Constance

SWISS CONFEDERATION

Canossa

Pisa

Luxembourg

Metz

Strasbourg

FRANCHE COMTÉ

Dijon

BURGUNDY

CHAROLLES

Geneva

Lyon

Rhône

Avignon

Nice

ITALIAN STATES

Turin

Alps

REPUBLIC OF GENOA

FRANCE

1235 Imperial laws published in German for the first time

1122 Agreement made to end Investiture Controversy

Hereditary seat of Habsburg family

1077 Emperor Henry IV forced to do penance to the Pope over Investiture Controversy

2 DISPUTES WITH THE PAPACY 1075–1122

"Emperors of the Romans" often vied with the Papacy. In the 11th century, the Investiture Controversy, by which Henry IV tried to assert control over the right to appoint bishops, led to his excommunication in 1076. In 1122, it was agreed that the emperor could invest bishops with authority over their secular lands, but the Pope would invest them with their spiritual authority.

▬ Papal states and notional dependencies 1500

LONG-LIVED EMPIRE

The Holy Roman Empire survived for just over 1,000 years. Over this time, it was ruled by many dynasties and began to develop institutions of its own.

KEY

— Frontiers 1500

▬ Notional frontier of Holy Roman Empire 1500

▬ Papal states and notional dependencies 1500

TIMELINE

1 2 3 4

700 1000 1300 1600 1900

RISE OF THE OTTOMANS

In the late 13th century, the Ottoman Turks were one of several emirates fighting on the borders of the Byzantine Empire. By 1500, they had conquered much of Anatolia and parts of the Balkans and had taken Constantinople. Their sultanate stretched from Hungary to Mesopotamia.

As the Byzantine Empire weakened in the 11th century, new Muslim groups surged into Anatolia, principal among them the Seljuk Turks. Within a century, they, too, had fragmented, leaving a large number of small, competing Islamic states. In the 1290s, one of them—the Ottomans—took advantage of their position right against the Byzantine border to expand and attract warriors eager for glory.

By the 1350s, Ottoman armies had crossed into Europe; they soon occupied most of what was left of Byzantine territory, defeating Serbia, Bulgaria, and Hungary, the main Christian principalities of the Balkans. In 1402, the Ottomans suffered a defeat by the Mongols, but they soon recovered and, in 1453, Sultan Mehmed II seized the prize of Constantinople, the Byzantine capital. From there, the Ottoman sultans ruled and, over the next two centuries, continued to expand their domain into a huge multinational empire. Eventually, however, the Ottoman expansion was brought to an end by the Safavids in Persia and the Habsburgs in Europe (see pp.172–173).

RISE OF THE OTTOMAN EMPIRE

From their origins as a small emirate in northwest Anatolia around 1300, the Ottomans rose rapidly, conquering most of the Byzantine Empire's possessions in Asia by 1400. Within 60 years, they had captured Constantinople and overrun most of the Balkans.

KEY

- ▬ Holy Roman Empire c. 1480
- ┄┄ Frontiers in 1481
- ◎ Siege, with date

TIMELINE

	1200	1300	1400	1500
1				
2				
3				
4				
5				
6				

◁ **Mehmed II**
This Turkish miniature from around 1585 shows the great sultan, who conquered Constantinople and extended the Ottoman Empire.

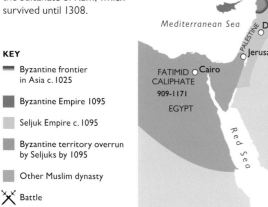

THE SELJUKS

Even before the Ottoman expansion, Byzantine control over Anatolia had been weakened by the Seljuks, a Turkic people who had migrated west from central Asia. They defeated the Byzantines at Manzikert in 1071, after which they overran most of Anatolia and established the Sultanate of Rum, which survived until 1308.

KEY

- ▬ Byzantine frontier in Asia c. 1025
- Byzantine Empire 1095
- Seljuk Empire c. 1095
- Byzantine territory overrun by Seljuks by 1095
- Other Muslim dynasty
- ✕✕ Battle

3 OTTOMANS IN THE BALKANS 1354–1389

In 1354, the Ottomans crossed over to Gallipoli, establishing a foothold in Europe. Under Murad I, they occupied much of Thrace, making Edirne (Adrianople) their new capital. The defeat of Serbia at the Battle of Kosovo (1389) marked the beginning of Ottoman supremacy in the Balkans.

- Conquests of Murad I 1362–1389
- ● Ottomans enter Europe 1354
- ✕ Battle
- ★ Ottoman capital 1369

2 THE CONQUEST OF ANATOLIA 1326–1402

Under Orhan, the Ottomans conquered most of the remaining Byzantine cities in northwest Anatolia, leaving only isolated outposts. Anatolia was later unified under Ottoman control by Orhan's grandson (the son of Murad I), Bayezid I, who conquered the beyliks in the southwest soon after he became sultan in 1389.

- Conquests of Orhan 1326–1362
- Conquests of Bayezid I 1389–1402

4 MONGOL THREAT 1400–1405

In 1400–1401, the Mongol prince Timur, angered by Bayezid I's demands for tribute from one of his vassals, invaded the Ottoman Empire. At Ankara in 1402, Timur crushed the Ottomans, causing many of the former beyliks of Anatolia to break away from Ottoman rule. Only Timur's death in 1405 saved the Ottomans from further losses.

⋀⋀ Ottoman eastern frontier following Timur's invasion 1402

⚔ Battle

5 THE SIEGE OF CONSTANTINOPLE 1451–1453

By the time Mehmed II became Ottoman sultan in 1451, the Byzantine Empire consisted of little more than the city of Constantinople. Mehmed throttled the city's supply lines and laid siege to it in April 1453. The Byzantine emperor Constantine XI resisted for nearly 8 weeks before the Ottomans finally took the city. The Byzantine Empire was at an end, and the Ottoman Empire had a new capital.

⭐ Ottoman capital 1453

6 CONQUESTS OF MEHMED II 1460–1481

Having captured Constantinople, Mehmed II dealt with the remaining fragments of the Byzantine Empire, capturing Morea in 1460 and the breakaway Empire of Trebizond in 1461. The defeat of Bosnia in 1463 and the reduction of Wallachia and Moldavia to vassal status meant that resistance to Ottoman rule in the Balkans was confined to a few scattered fortresses and the Venetian possessions in Greece and along the Adriatic coast.

▮ Vassal of Ottoman Empire by 1481

▮ Further Ottoman conquest by 1481

▮ Under Venetian control c. 1460

Map labels

POLAND

HUNGARY

Buda

LITHUANIA

Dniester

Don

Dnieper

Sea of Azov

MOLDAVIA

KHANATE OF THE CRIMEA

1389 Ottoman victory at Kosovo leads to the conquest of Serbia

1456 The failure of a siege by Mehmed II puts an end to Ottoman advance into Hungary

TRANSYLVANIA

Belgrade

Argesh

Bükres (Bucharest)

Kefe (Kaffa)

WALLACHIA

1444 An attempted crusade to prevent Ottoman expansion is defeated

Danube

RZEGOVINA

SERBIA

Kosovo

Nicopolis

Balkan Mountains

Varna

Black Sea

1453 The capture of Constantinople after a siege marks the end of the Byzantine Empire

1402 Bayezid defeated by Timur

1461 Ottomans conquer Empire of Trebizond, a breakaway Byzantine region

Sofia (Sofya)

BULGARIA

arazzo

1430 Salonica is captured by the Ottomans

Edirne (Adrianople)

1326 Bursa becomes the first Ottoman capital

Trebizond

ALBANIA

Selânik (Salonica)

THRACE

Istanbul (Constantinople)

Iznik (Nicaea)

Erzurum

Gallipoli

Bursa

Söğüt

Ankara

OTTOMANS

KARASI

Anatolia

Aegean Sea

Izmir (Smyrna)

SARUHAN

GERMIYAN

Athens

AYDIN

HAMID

MOREA

MENTEŞE

KARAMAN

Duchy of Naxos

TEKE

Monemvasia

Rhodes

1 THE ORIGINS OF THE OTTOMAN EMPIRE 1280–1326

After the collapse of the Seljuk Empire, western Anatolia was divided into a number of competing states, known as beyliks. One of them, based around the small town of Söğüt, began to expand in the 1280s under Osman. His son, Orhan, captured the important Byzantine town of Bursa in 1326 and made it his capital. From here, he conquered much of the rest of Anatolia and sent the first Ottoman army into Europe.

▮ Ottoman territory 1326

☐ Anatolian beyliks c. 1300

☆ Ottoman capital 1326

Crete

Cyprus

Mediterranean Sea

THE RECONQUISTA

Islamic armies overran the Iberian peninsula in the early 8th century. Christian rulers slowly reversed this process in the Reconquista ("reconquest"), which culminated with the fall of Granada in 1492 and the expulsion of most of Spain's Muslim population.

The Visigothic kingdom of Spain rapidly fell to an Islamic army that crossed from Muslim-held North Africa in 711, and by 718, only a small area in the remote Asturian mountains remained unconquered. The subsequent reconquest of the Muslim-ruled parts of Spain and Portugal (al-Andalus) by Christian states took nearly eight centuries. First, the far northeast was recaptured by the armies of the Frankish ruler Charlemagne, rather than by the comparatively weak Spanish Christian kingdoms. Gradually, though, Castile and Leon in the west and Navarre and Aragon in the east gathered strength and pushed southward.

The emergence of crusading ideology from the late 11th century accelerated the Reconquista, as Christian armies were now infused with the sense of fighting a religiously justified war. The political fragmentation of the Umayyad Caliphate also weakened the Muslim hold on central Spain, leading to the loss of the strategic city of Toledo in 1085. An influx of new groups from North Africa—first the Almoravids and then the Almohads—reunited al-Andalus, but a crushing defeat by Alfonso VIII of Castile in 1212 reduced the Muslim-held area to Granada. By then, a much shorter process of reconquest had taken place in Portugal.

Granada survived as an Islamic emirate until 1492, when Ferdinand II of Aragon and Isabella of Castille sent an army to besiege the town. Its fall, after a brief resistance, marked the end of Islamic Spain and the completion of the Reconquista.

THE INQUISITION
THE FIGHT AGAINST HERESY IN SPAIN

For centuries, Muslims, Jews, and Christians coexisted in Spain, but by the late 14th century, a desire for religious unity grew in the country. Jews and Muslims were forcibly converted to Christianity, and the converts became targets for persecution. In 1478, Pope Sixtus IV authorized the establishment of the Inquisition, which led to public tests of faith and execution of "heretics." The accused were dressed up and paraded in an Auto da fe ceremony (right) while their guilt and punishment were decided.

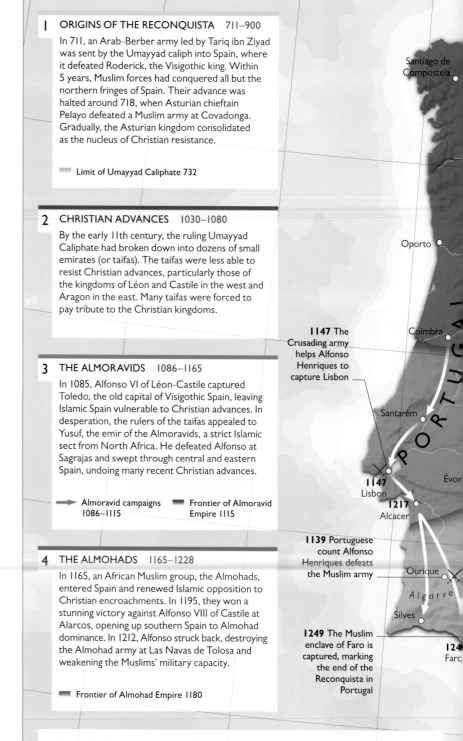

1 ORIGINS OF THE RECONQUISTA   711–900
In 711, an Arab-Berber army led by Tariq ibn Ziyad was sent by the Umayyad caliph into Spain, where it defeated Roderick, the Visigothic king. Within 5 years, Muslim forces had conquered all but the northern fringes of Spain. Their advance was halted around 718, when Asturian chieftain Pelayo defeated a Muslim army at Covadonga. Gradually, the Asturian kingdom consolidated as the nucleus of Christian resistance.

▭ Limit of Umayyad Caliphate 732

2 CHRISTIAN ADVANCES   1030–1080
By the early 11th century, the ruling Umayyad Caliphate had broken down into dozens of small emirates (or taifas). The taifas were less able to resist Christian advances, particularly those of the kingdoms of Léon and Castile in the west and Aragon in the east. Many taifas were forced to pay tribute to the Christian kingdoms.

3 THE ALMORAVIDS   1086–1165
In 1085, Alfonso VI of Léon-Castile captured Toledo, the old capital of Visigothic Spain, leaving Islamic Spain vulnerable to Christian advances. In desperation, the rulers of the taifas appealed to Yusuf, the emir of the Almoravids, a strict Islamic sect from North Africa. He defeated Alfonso at Sagrajas and swept through central and eastern Spain, undoing many recent Christian advances.

→ Almoravid campaigns 1086–1115   ▭ Frontier of Almoravid Empire 1115

4 THE ALMOHADS   1165–1228
In 1165, an African Muslim group, the Almohads, entered Spain and renewed Islamic opposition to Christian encroachments. In 1195, they won a stunning victory against Alfonso VIII of Castile at Alarcos, opening up southern Spain to Almohad dominance. In 1212, Alfonso struck back, destroying the Almohad army at Las Navas de Tolosa and weakening the Muslims' military capacity.

▭ Frontier of Almohad Empire 1180

Santiago de Compostela

Oporto

Coimbra

1147 The Crusading army helps Alfonso Henriques to capture Lisbon

Santarém

PORTUGAL

1147 Lisbon

1217 Alcacer

Évora

1139 Portuguese count Alfonso Henriques defeats the Muslim army

1249 The Muslim enclave of Faro is captured, marking the end of the Reconquista in Portugal

Ourique

Algarve

Silves

Faro

THE RECONQUEST OF SPAIN
The Reconquista, by which the Christian kingdoms of Spain reconquered the Iberian Peninsula, took over 700 years to complete. Progress was slowest when the Muslims united around movements such as the Almoravids and Almohads.

KEY

✕ Muslim victory with date
✕ Christian victory with date

EXTENSION OF CHRISTIAN CONTROL

▮ By 1030   ▮ By 1280
▮ By 1115   ▯ By 1492
▮ By 1180   — Frontiers 1493

TIMELINE

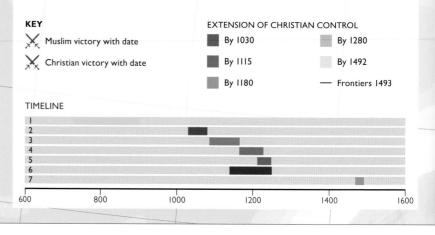

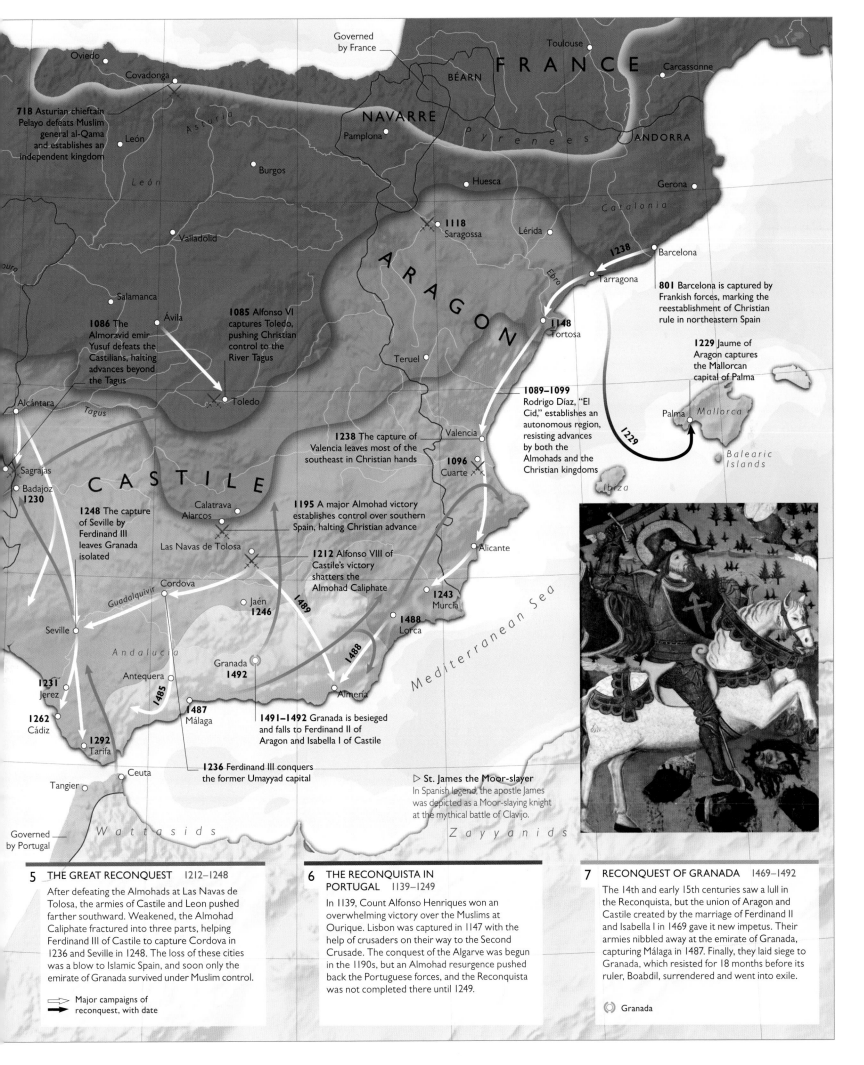

718 Asturian chieftain Pelayo defeats Muslim general al-Qama and establishes an independent kingdom

Governed by France

801 Barcelona is captured by Frankish forces, marking the reestablishment of Christian rule in northeastern Spain

1229 Jaume of Aragon captures the Mallorcan capital of Palma

1118 Saragossa

1238 Barcelona

1148 Tortosa

1086 The Almoravid emir Yusuf defeats the Castilians, halting advances beyond the Tagus

1085 Alfonso VI captures Toledo, pushing Christian control to the River Tagus

1089–1099 Rodrigo Díaz, "El Cid," establishes an autonomous region, resisting advances by both the Almohads and the Christian kingdoms

1238 The capture of Valencia leaves most of the southeast in Christian hands

1096 Cuarte

1195 A major Almohad victory establishes control over southern Spain, halting Christian advance

1248 The capture of Seville by Ferdinand III leaves Granada isolated

1212 Alfonso VIII of Castile's victory shatters the Almohad Caliphate

1243 Murcia

1488 Lorca

1246 Jaén

1488 Almería

1485

1489

1231 Jerez

1262 Cádiz

1292 Tarifa

1487 Málaga

1491–1492 Granada is besieged and falls to Ferdinand II of Aragon and Isabella I of Castile

1236 Ferdinand III conquers the former Umayyad capital

1230 Badajoz

Granada **1492**

Antequera

Mediterranean Sea

Balearic Islands

Palma *Mallorca*

Ibiza

Governed by Portugal

Wattasids   *Zayyanids*

▷ **St. James the Moor-slayer**
In Spanish legend, the apostle James was depicted as a Moor-slaying knight at the mythical battle of Clavijo.

FRANCE
BÉARN
NAVARRE
Pyrenees
ANDORRA
Catalonia
ARAGON
CASTILE
Andalucía

Toulouse, Carcassonne, Oviedo, Covadonga, Pamplona, León, Burgos, Huesca, Gerona, Lérida, Valladolid, Tarragona, Ebro, Ávila, Teruel, Valencia, Alcántara, Toledo, Tagus, Sagrajas, Calatrava, Alarcos, Las Navas de Tolosa, Cordova, Alicante, Seville, Guadalquivir, Granada, Almería, Ceuta, Tangier, Douro, Asturias, Salamanca

5 THE GREAT RECONQUEST 1212–1248

After defeating the Almohads at Las Navas de Tolosa, the armies of Castile and Leon pushed farther southward. Weakened, the Almohad Caliphate fractured into three parts, helping Ferdinand III of Castile to capture Cordova in 1236 and Seville in 1248. The loss of these cities was a blow to Islamic Spain, and soon only the emirate of Granada survived under Muslim control.

⇨ Major campaigns of reconquest, with date

6 THE RECONQUISTA IN PORTUGAL 1139–1249

In 1139, Count Alfonso Henriques won an overwhelming victory over the Muslims at Ourique. Lisbon was captured in 1147 with the help of crusaders on their way to the Second Crusade. The conquest of the Algarve was begun in the 1190s, but an Almohad resurgence pushed back the Portuguese forces, and the Reconquista was not completed there until 1249.

7 RECONQUEST OF GRANADA 1469–1492

The 14th and early 15th centuries saw a lull in the Reconquista, but the union of Aragon and Castile created by the marriage of Ferdinand II and Isabella I in 1469 gave it new impetus. Their armies nibbled away at the emirate of Granada, capturing Málaga in 1487. Finally, they laid siege to Granada, which resisted for 18 months before its ruler, Boabdil, surrendered and went into exile.

◎ Granada

MEDIEVAL EAST ASIA

China was the dominant power in east Asia in the 6th–15th centuries. Its form of government was imitated widely in the region, from Japan to Korea and Vietnam. However, just like the other states of the period, China, too, suffered long periods of disunity and conquest by foreign powers.

In China, the division that followed the collapse of the Han Dynasty in 220 ended only when the Sui Dynasty captured Nanjing, the capital of six successive Southern dynasties, in 589. The Sui, and their successors the Tang, intervened repeatedly in neighboring states, and Chinese rule expanded deep into central Asia. Although economically strong, Tang rule was undermined by fighting among factions, a defeat at the hands of an Arab army in 751, and a major revolt 4 years later. A weakened Tang Dynasty limped on until 907, when China fell apart again, to be restored in 960 by the Song, whose rule saw a period of economic and technological progress. However, by 1127, the Jurchen, a nomadic group from the north, had reduced the Song to a southern kingdom based in Nanjing. This in turn fell in 1251–1279 to the Mongols, whose leader

▷ **Symbol of peace**
This 11th-century wooden statue from Japan shows a seated Buddha. The hand gesture symbolizes peace and the protection of believers from fear. Buddhism was the state religion during the Nara period.

Genghis Khan established the Yuan, the first non-Chinese dynasty to rule China. In time, Mongol rule weakened, and in 1368, the rebel general Zhu Yuanzhang captured Beijing, declaring himself the first emperor of the Ming Dynasty.

Japan and Korea

A centralized Japanese state emerged during the Nara period (710–794), with a Chinese-style bureaucracy, a system of provinces, and the dominance of Buddhism. In 794, the imperial court moved to Heian (modern-day Kyoto) to reduce the influence of Buddhist monks, but over time, powerful aristocratic families such as the Minamoto and Taira took real power away from the emperor. Rivalry between them led to the Genpei War in 1180–1185, ending with the defeat of the Taira and the establishment of a Minamoto military government, or shogunate, at Kamakura. The emperors became symbolic leaders—although Emperor Go-Daigo did spark a revolt in 1331, in an attempt to assert imperial power. The shoguns, first the Kamakura and then the Muromachi, became the real rulers. By the mid-15th century, however, the shogunate in turn lost power to the daimyo, local warlords, as Japan fragmented into a series of warring statelets.

◁ **Off to work**
A merchant rides a camel in this Tang-era terracotta figurine. Bactrian camels—hardy species capable of carrying heavy loads—were ideal for the Silk Road trade through central Asia.

POWER SHIFTS IN EAST ASIA

The medieval period saw the process of state formation in Southeast Asia and Japan, both of which were strongly influenced by Chinese models of government and by Buddhism. In China itself, a period of disunity was followed by the reestablishment of strong central control under the Tang and Song Dynasties. India, in contrast, fragmented after the collapse of the Gupta Empire in the 6th century, and many separate dynasties ruled the north and south of the subcontinent.

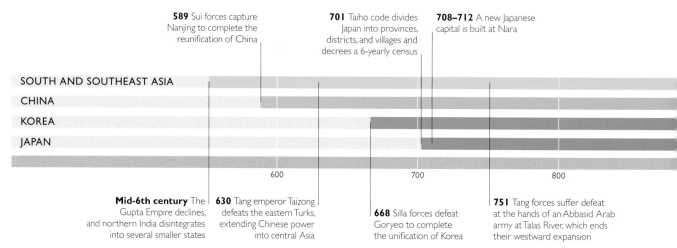

589 Sui forces capture Nanjing to complete the reunification of China

701 Taiho code divides Japan into provinces, districts, and villages and decrees a 6-yearly census

708–712 A new Japanese capital is built at Nara

SOUTH AND SOUTHEAST ASIA
CHINA
KOREA
JAPAN

600   700   800

Mid-6th century The Gupta Empire declines, and northern India disintegrates into several smaller states

630 Tang emperor Taizong defeats the eastern Turks, extending Chinese power into central Asia

668 Silla forces defeat Goryeo to complete the unification of Korea

751 Tang forces suffer defeat at the hands of an Abbasid Arab army at Talas River, which ends their westward expansion

◁ **Heavenly dancers**
This intricate carving from the 12th-century
Angkor Wat temple complex in Cambodia
depicts four *apsaras*, or heavenly dancers,
who provided entertainment to gods and
granted favors to humans in the heaven of
the Hindu god Indra.

After the departure of Chinese administrators in 313, the Korean peninsula was divided between three warring states: Goryeo, Silla, and Paekche. China tried to reconquer Korea, but Silla exploited Chinese attacks on the other two states to reunite Korea under its rule in 668. Unified Silla installed a Chinese-style bureaucracy but collapsed amid a wave of revolts around 900. In 935, Wang Kon founded the Goryeo Dynasty, reuniting Korea, but Mongol invasions from 1231 reduced Korea to a vassal (subordinate) state, until King Kongmin reasserted its independence in 1356. Chinese pressure continued until, in 1388, Yi Song-gye defeated the Ming and established the Choson Dynasty, which ruled Korea until 1910.

Kingdoms of Southeast Asia

The period from the 9th to the 11th centuries saw a series of strong territorial states being established in Southeast Asia. The Pagan kingdom under Anawrahta united most of what is now Myanmar, while the Angkor kingdom (in today's Cambodia) under Suryavarman II reached the height of its power. In 1181, the Angkor Empire under Jayavarman VII defeated the Champa Empire, which had ruled southern

Cambodia since the 7th century and had also sacked Angkor in 1177. However, the Southeast Asian kingdoms suffered under Mongol attacks, which weakened Pagan and nearly defeated the Vietnamese kingdom of Dai Viet. By the late 15th century, the great medieval kingdoms were crumbling: the Champa capital Vijaya was captured by Dai Viet, and Angkor was sacked by the Thai kingdom of Ayutthaya.

Smaller states had risen in northern India after the fall of the Gupta Empire in the mid-6th century. These were united by Harsha Vardhen of the Pushyabhuti Dynasty, but his kingdom fell apart after his murder in 647. It was only after the invasion of Muhammad of Ghur in 1192 and the founding of the Delhi Sultanate in 1206 that northern India was reunited once more. The south of India developed separately; the Chola Empire expanded in the 10th–11th centuries, occupying northern Sri Lanka and ports along the Malay peninsula, but it collapsed in the 12th century. The kingdom of Vijayanagara, founded in 1336, dominated southern India until its conquest by the Mughals in the 17th century.

> "*Baekje [Paekche] is at full moon, Silla is at half moon.*"
>

▽ **Divine architecture**
The 10th-century Mukteshwar Temple
in Odisha, southern India, forms part
of a larger complex of temples there.
Dedicated to the Hindu god Shiva, it
was built under the Somavanshi Dynasty,
which ruled parts of southeastern India
between the 9th and 12th centuries.

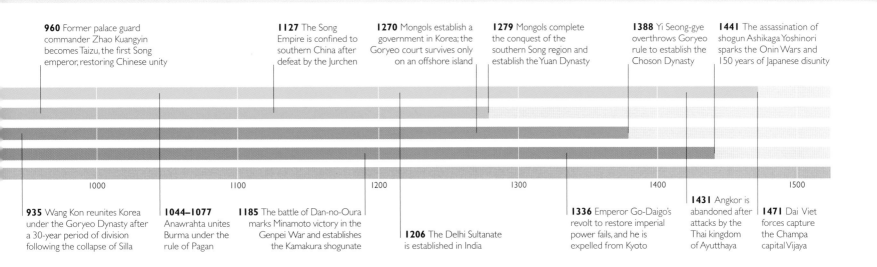

960 Former palace guard commander Zhao Kuangyin becomes Taizu, the first Song emperor, restoring Chinese unity

1127 The Song Empire is confined to southern China after defeat by the Jurchen

1270 Mongols establish a government in Korea; the Goryeo court survives only on an offshore island

1279 Mongols complete the conquest of the southern Song region and establish the Yuan Dynasty

1388 Yi Seong-gye overthrows Goryeo rule to establish the Choson Dynasty

1441 The assassination of shogun Ashikaga Yoshinori sparks the Onin Wars and 150 years of Japanese disunity

1000   1100   1200   1300   1400   1500

935 Wang Kon reunites Korea under the Goryeo Dynasty after a 30-year period of division following the collapse of Silla

1044–1077 Anawrahta unites Burma under the rule of Pagan

1185 The battle of Dan-no-Oura marks Minamoto victory in the Genpei War and establishes the Kamakura shogunate

1206 The Delhi Sultanate is established in India

1336 Emperor Go-Daigo's revolt to restore imperial power fails, and he is expelled from Kyoto

1431 Angkor is abandoned after attacks by the Thai kingdom of Ayutthaya

1471 Dai Viet forces capture the Champa capital Vijaya

TANG AND SONG CHINA

After a long period of disunity following the fall of the Han Dynasty, China was reunited under the Sui and then the Tang and Song Dynasties. China prospered, and Chinese power prevailed across central Asia before the Song were finally conquered by the Mongols.

Following the end of the Han Dynasty in 220 CE, China broke apart. The Sui Dynasty (581–618) reunified China, but after a rebellion in 618, Li Yuan took the throne. He and his son, Li Shimin, established the Tang Dynasty, enacting reforms that brought order to the provinces of China. In 639, Li Shimin (by now Emperor Taizong) sent armies into Turkestan, establishing Tang control over a string of strategic trading settlements, such as Dunhuang.

In 755, the dynasty was weakened by a revolt led by general An Lushan; although imperial forces regained control, a series of weak rulers later led to the Tang's collapse in 907. A dozen rival kingdoms vied for power until the Song Dynasty subdued the others and established rule over the whole country by 960. In this resurgent China, trade guilds emerged, paper money was adopted on a large scale, and inventions such as gunpowder and the magnetic compass came into widespread use. By the early 12th century, the dynasty had begun to weaken; nomadic Jurchen tribes conquered the north of China, confining the Song to the south of their former territory.

TANG CHINA

After unifying China, the Tang defeated the Eastern and Western Turks. From the 750s, rebellions and weakened government led to a decline in Tang influence.

751 Tang forces are defeated by Arabs at the Talas River

657 The Tang defeat the Western Turks and control the area until a rebellion in 665

Aral Sea

KHWARIZM

TRANSOXIANA

WESTERN TURKESTAN

Lake Balkhash

Bactra

Talas River

Tien Shan

Kashgar

Aksu

Ta

Khotan

UNIFICATION AND FRAGMENTATION

The Tang Dynasty expanded to its furthest extent by 742. The influence of Chinese culture also spread during this time, assisted by the imperial highways, which centered on the capital Chang'an. When China fragmented once again, the Song Dynasty arose in northern China.

KEY

- Area of Chinese cultural influence
- ● Metropolitan prefecture
- ● City of over 300,000 population
- ○ Other major city
- 🐉 Under China's influence
- Great Wall
- Imperial highway

TIMELINE

| 1 | 2 | 3 | 4 | 5 | 6 |

500 600 700 800 900 1000 1100 1200 1300

SONG CHINA

The Song Dynasty was founded in 960 by Zhao Kuangyin (later Emperor Taizu), a general under one of the "Five Dynasties" that ruled northern China after the Tang. The dynasty is usually divided into two distinct periods, Northern and Southern. The Song suffered constant pressure from the Khitan Liao and the Jurchen in the north, finally losing the whole of the north of China to the Jurchen in 1126.

Gobi

LIAO EMPIRE

Yellow River

Bo Hai

GAOLI

○ Xijinfu

Zhending

Xingqingfu

Taiyuan

Daming

Henan

Danzhou

Jingzhou

Yingtian

Kaifeng

Yangzhou

Xingyuan Xiangyang

Kuizhou

Chengdu

Hangzhou

SONG CHINA

NANZHAO

Longxing

Yangtze

Fuzhou

BURMA

Xi Jiang

Qingzhou

Taiwan

ANNAM

Guangzhou

Yamen

South China Sea

Hainan

1279 Mongols defeat the Song fleet; the last Song emperor, 7-year-old Zhao Bing, drowns

5 THE NORTHERN SONG DYNASTY
960–1126

From 960, Emperor Taizu conquered and reunited much of the land that had once belonged to the Han and Tang Empires. He imposed high taxes on the peasantry, and when Jurchen nomads invaded the north, they faced little resistance. In 1126, the Jurchen took the Song capital, Kaifeng, and the Song court fled to southern China.

- Under Northern Song rule

6 THE SOUTHERN SONG DYNASTY   1127–1279

From 1127, the surviving Song governed from Hangzhou in southern China, while the Jurchen (as the Jin Dynasty) ruled the north. In 1233, the Southern Song allied with the Mongols to attack the Jurchen. But, after destroying the Jurchen, the Mongols then invaded the south, in 1268. They took Hangzhou in 1276, and 3 years later defeated the last Southern Song forces.

- Under Southern Song rule
- → Mongol attacks from 1268

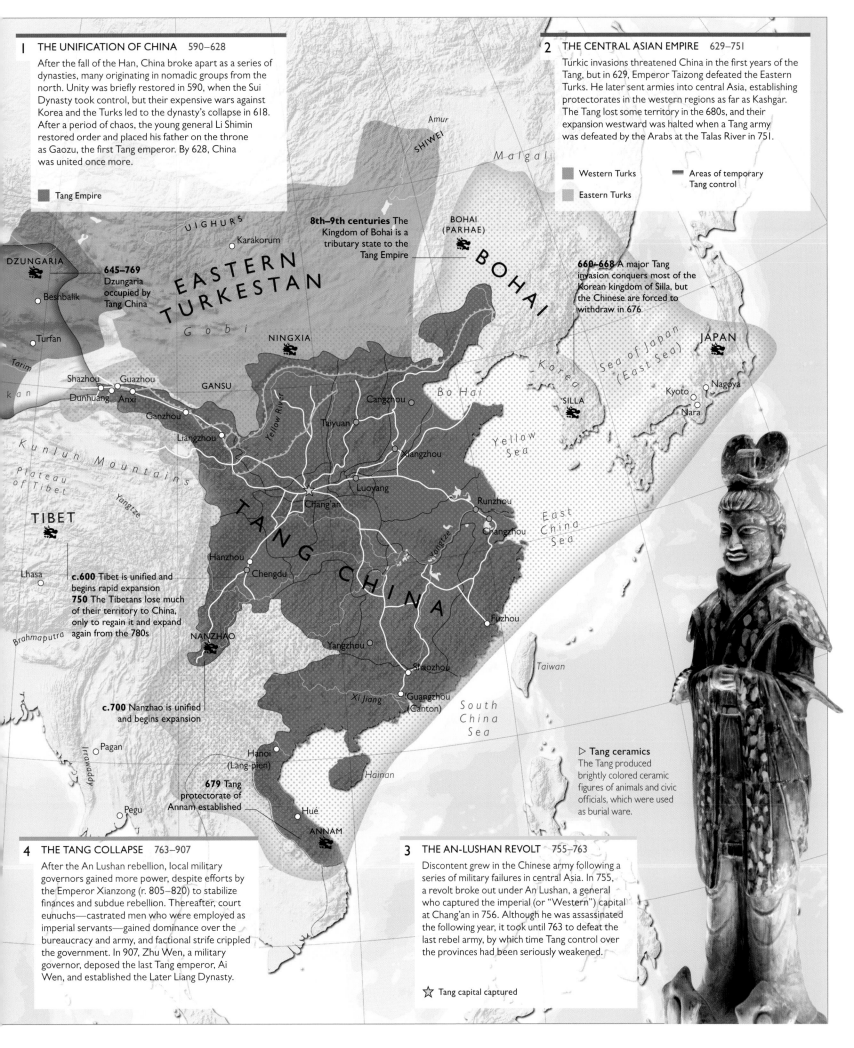

1 THE UNIFICATION OF CHINA 590–628

After the fall of the Han, China broke apart as a series of dynasties, many originating in nomadic groups from the north. Unity was briefly restored in 590, when the Sui Dynasty took control, but their expensive wars against Korea and the Turks led to the dynasty's collapse in 618. After a period of chaos, the young general Li Shimin restored order and placed his father on the throne as Gaozu, the first Tang emperor. By 628, China was united once more.

☐ Tang Empire

2 THE CENTRAL ASIAN EMPIRE 629–751

Turkic invasions threatened China in the first years of the Tang, but in 629, Emperor Taizong defeated the Eastern Turks. He later sent armies into central Asia, establishing protectorates in the western regions as far as Kashgar. The Tang lost some territory in the 680s, and their expansion westward was halted when a Tang army was defeated by the Arabs at the Talas River in 751.

☐ Western Turks   — Areas of temporary Tang control
☐ Eastern Turks

8th–9th centuries The Kingdom of Bohai is a tributary state to the Tang Empire

645–769 Dzungaria occupied by Tang China

660–668 A major Tang invasion conquers most of the Korean kingdom of Silla, but the Chinese are forced to withdraw in 676

c.600 Tibet is unified and begins rapid expansion
750 The Tibetans lose much of their territory to China, only to regain it and expand again from the 780s

c.700 Nanzhao is unified and begins expansion

679 Tang protectorate of Annam established

▷ **Tang ceramics**
The Tang produced brightly colored ceramic figures of animals and civic officials, which were used as burial ware.

4 THE TANG COLLAPSE 763–907

After the An Lushan rebellion, local military governors gained more power, despite efforts by the Emperor Xianzong (r. 805–820) to stabilize finances and subdue rebellion. Thereafter, court eunuchs—castrated men who were employed as imperial servants—gained dominance over the bureaucracy and army, and factional strife crippled the government. In 907, Zhu Wen, a military governor, deposed the last Tang emperor, Ai Wen, and established the Later Liang Dynasty.

3 THE AN-LUSHAN REVOLT 755–763

Discontent grew in the Chinese army following a series of military failures in central Asia. In 755, a revolt broke out under An Lushan, a general who captured the imperial (or "Western") capital at Chang'an in 756. Although he was assassinated the following year, it took until 763 to defeat the last rebel army, by which time Tang control over the provinces had been seriously weakened.

☆ Tang capital captured

MEDIEVAL KOREA AND JAPAN

Korea and Japan both began developing a centralized bureaucratic monarchy in the 8th century, drawing strong influence from the Tang Dynasty of neighboring China. In addition, the cultural landscapes of both states were largely shaped by the arrival of Buddhism from China in the 4th century.

In the mid-7th century, the Korean state of Silla enlisted the military support of Tang China to defeat the rival kingdom of Koguryo and Paekche to unify the country under its leadership. After ruling for almost three centuries, Silla disintegrated in the ensuing chaos following the fall of China's Tang Dynasty in 906. Thereafter, the Goryeo state (founded in 901 by former Koguryo leaders) reunified Korea in 936 and presided over a period of economic and cultural prosperity. However, a series of Mongol attacks from 1231 eventually resulted in Goryeo's fall and, from 1270, it became a vassal state of the Mongol Yuan Empire for the next 80 years.

In Japan, the introduction of Buddhism in 538 coincided with the fall of Yamato rule, as powerful clans and regional kingdoms fought for power. The Taiku Reforms of 646 paved the way for Japan to unify under a centralized government based on the Chinese model.

The emperors of the Nara period slowly lost power, first to the Fujiwara family in the 10th and 11th centuries, and then to the samurai, who supported a military dictatorship called the shogun. The powerful Kamakura shogunate thwarted two Mongol invasions, but it was eventually toppled by a rival clan, and thereafter power ebbed to the local daimyo, or domain lords, leading to a century-long civil war (see pp.180–181).

" … my armor and helmet were my pillow; my bow and arrows were my trade … "

YOSHITSUNE MINAMOTO, MINAMOTO GENERAL, c.1189

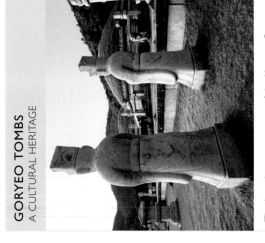

GORYEO TOMBS
A CULTURAL HERITAGE

The best-known remains of the Korean Goryeo kingdom are the tombs of its society's elites. Built of stone and covered by stone or earthen mounds, these tombs are customarily adorned with wall paintings. In the complex of tombs around Gaegyeong (modern Kaesong), the Goryeo capital, among the most famous is the Hyonjongrung Royal Tomb of King Kongmin. The twin mounds contain the remains of the monarch and his wife—the Mongolian princess Noguk.

STATE CREATION IN KOREA AND JAPAN

Regional wars between the 4th and 7th centuries led to the unification of the Korean peninsula under first the Silla and then the Goryeo kingdom. Meanwhile, in Japan, a succession of powerful clans brought the country's mosaic of chiefdoms under a single rule.

TIMELINE

1
2
3
4
5
6
7

500   1000   1500   2000

7   THE KAMAKURA SHOGUNATE
1192–1333

Minamoto Yoritomo founded the Kamakura shogunate in 1221. The shogunate reestablished contact with China, which resulted in Japan absorbing new sects of Buddhism, in particular Zen Buddhism. The shogunate appointed its own military governors, or shugo, as heads of each province and named stewards to supervise the individual estates into which the provinces had been divided, thereby establishing an effective national network to maintain stability.

✿ Buddhist temple c.1200

6   RISE OF THE SAMURAI   900–1868

From the early 900s, weak Heian rule caused dissatisfaction to spread across the provinces. Nobles began hiring warriors to safeguard their own interests, giving rise to the early samurai. By the 1100s, provincial lords were fighting one another for supremacy, which culminated in the Minamoto clan seizing power after defeating the Taira clan in the Genpei War (1156–1185).

→ Minamoto campaign
⚔ Minamoto victory
⚔ Minamoto defeat

AREAS OF CONTROL, 1180
Fujiwara   Minamoto   Taira

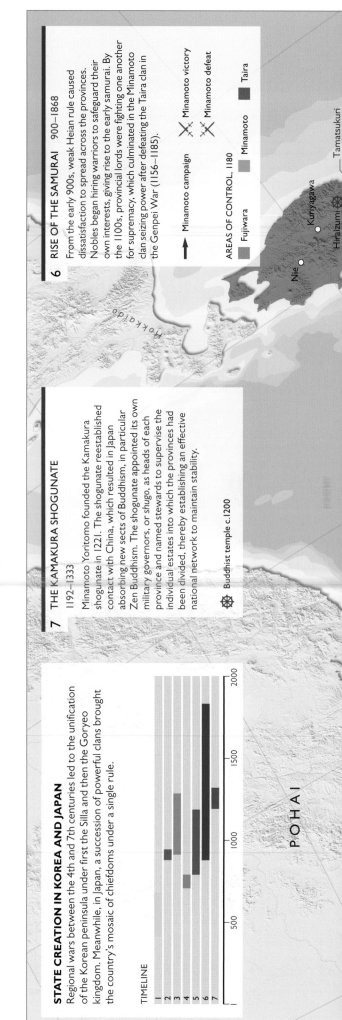

Hokkaido

Nie
Kuriyagawa
Hiraizumi
Tamatsukuri

POHAI

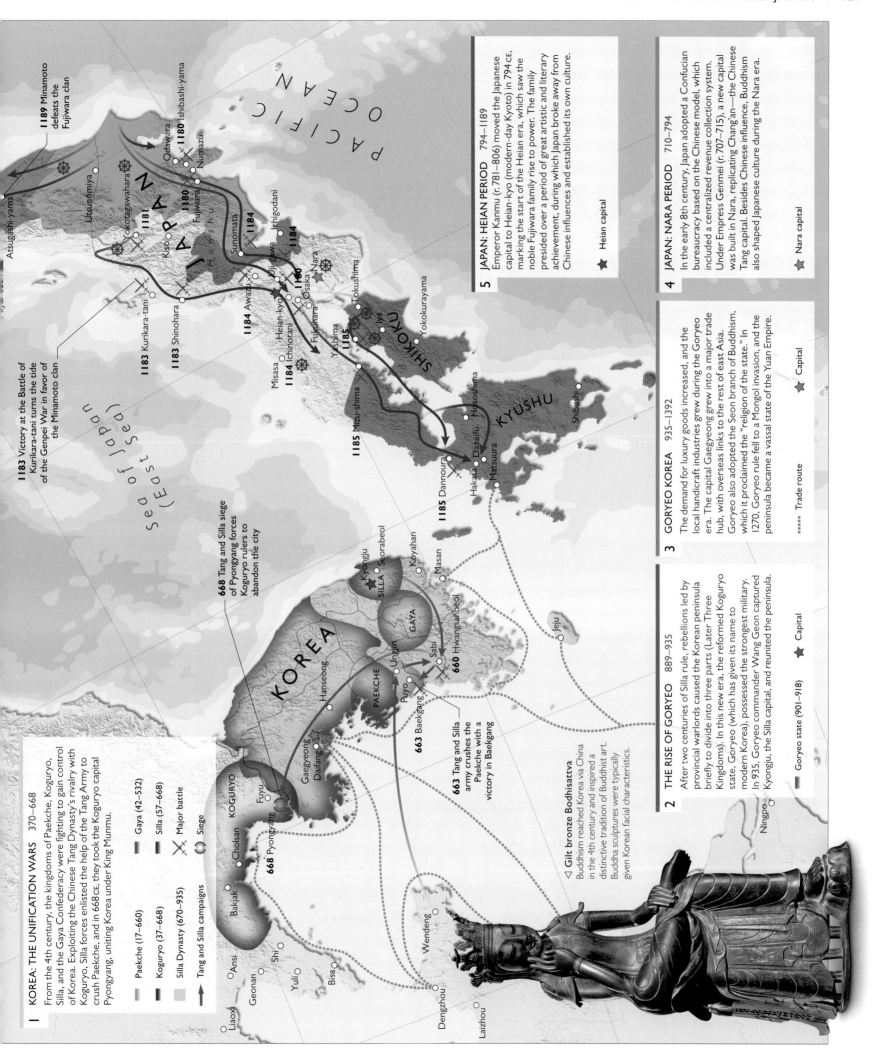

1 KOREA: THE UNIFICATION WARS 370–668

From the 4th century, the kingdoms of Paekche, Koguryo, Silla, and the Gaya Confederacy were fighting to gain control of Korea. Exploiting the Chinese Tang Dynasty's rivalry with Koguryo, Silla forces enlisted the help of the Tang Army to crush Paekche, and in 668 CE, they took the Koguryo capital Pyongyang, uniting Korea under King Munmu.

■ Paekche (17–660)
■ Koguryo (37–668)
■ Silla Dynasty (670–935)
➤ Tang and Silla campaigns
■ Gaya (42–532)
■ Silla (57–668)
✕ Major battle
◎ Siege

▽ **Gilt bronze Bodhisattva**
Buddhism reached Korea via China in the 4th century and inspired a distinctive tradition of Buddhist art. Buddha sculptures were typically given Korean facial characteristics.

2 THE RISE OF GORYEO 889–935

After two centuries of Silla rule, rebellions led by provincial warlords caused the Korean peninsula briefly to divide into three parts (Later Three Kingdoms). In this new era, the reformed Koguryo state, Goryeo (which has given its name to modern Korea), possessed the strongest military. In 935, Goryeo commander Wang Geon captured Kyongju, the Silla capital, and reunited the peninsula.

▬ Goryeo state (901–918)   ★ Capital

3 GORYEO KOREA 935–1392

The demand for luxury goods increased, and the local handicraft industries grew during the Goryeo era. The capital Gaegyeong grew into a major trade hub, with overseas links to the rest of east Asia. Goryeo also adopted the Seon branch of Buddhism, which it proclaimed the "religion of the state." In 1270, Goryeo rule fell to a Mongol invasion, and the peninsula became a vassal state of the Yuan Empire.

┅┅ Trade route   ★ Capital

4 JAPAN: NARA PERIOD 710–794

In the early 8th century, Japan adopted a Confucian bureaucracy based on the Chinese model, which included a centralized revenue collection system. Under Empress Genmei (r. 707–715), a new capital was built in Nara, replicating Chang'an—the Chinese Tang capital. Besides Chinese influence, Buddhism also shaped Japanese culture during the Nara era.

★ Nara capital

5 JAPAN: HEIAN PERIOD 794–1189

Emperor Kanmu (r. 781–806) moved the Japanese capital to Heian-kyo (modern-day Kyoto) in 794 CE, marking the start of the Heian era, which saw the noble Fujiwara family rise to power. The family presided over a period of great artistic and literary achievement, during which Japan broke away from Chinese influences and established its own culture.

★ Heian capital

1189 Minamoto defeats the Fujiwara clan

1183 Victory at the Battle of Kurikara-tani turns the tide of the Genpei War in favor of the Minamoto clan

1183 Kurikara-tani
1183 Shinohara
1184 Awazu
1184 Ichinotani
1184 Misasa
1181
1180 Odawara
1180 Ishibashi-yama
1180
1184
1184
1185 Mizu-shima
1185
1185 Dannoura

668 Tang and Silla siege of Pyongyang forces Koguryo rulers to abandon the city

668 Pyongyang

663 Baekgang

663 Tang and Silla army crushes the Paekche with a victory in Baekgang

660 Hwangsanbeol

PACIFIC OCEAN

Sea of Japan (East Sea)

JAPAN

HONSHU

SHIKOKU

KYUSHU

KOREA

KOGURYO

PAEKCHE

SILLA

GAYA

Atsugashi-yama
Utsunomiya
Yokotagawahara
Kiso
Sunomata
Ichigodani
Numazu
Fujiwara
Nara
Osaka
Heian-kyo
Fukuhara
Uji-gawa
Yashima
Iya
Tokushima
Yokokurayama
Hososhima
Dazaifu
Matsuura
Hakata
Shibushi
Jeju
Koyahan
Masan
Kyongju
Seorabeol
Sabi
Ungjin
Puyo
Baekgang
Hanseong
Gaegyeong
Daifang
Fuyu
Pyongyang
Cholsan
Baljak
Ansi
Geonan
Shi
Yulli
Bisa
Dengzhou
Laizhou
Wendeng
Ningbo

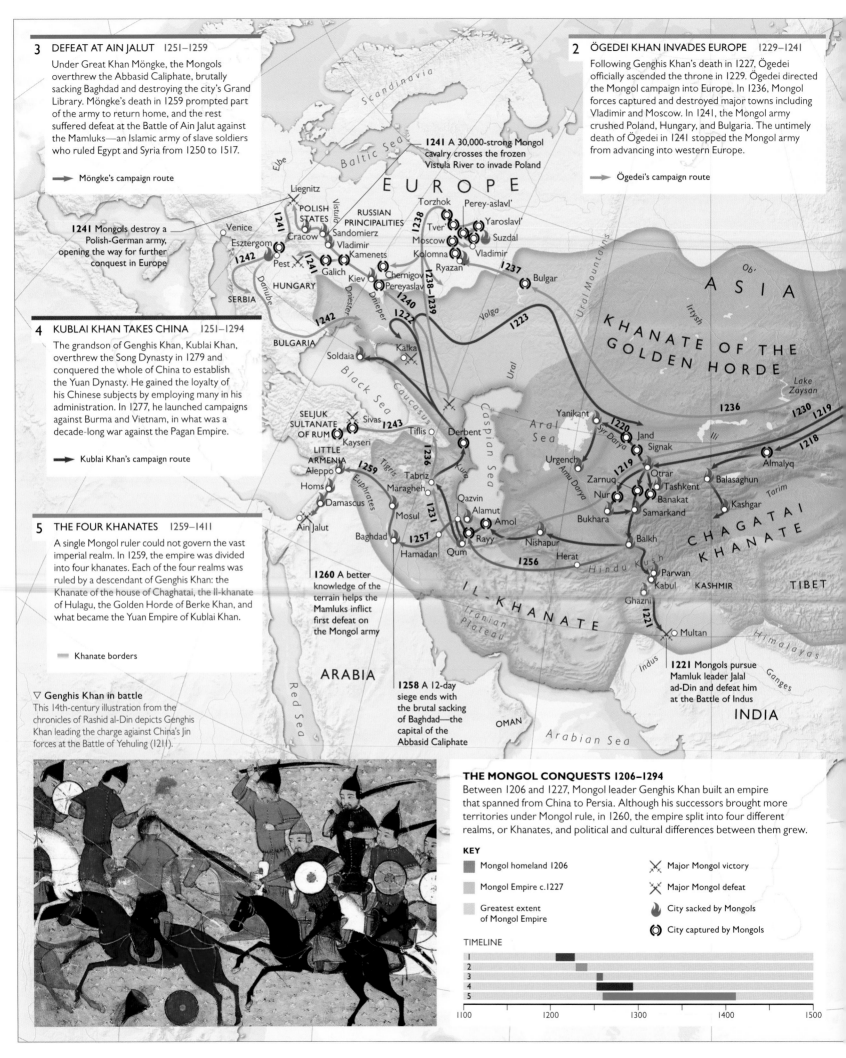

3 DEFEAT AT AIN JALUT 1251–1259

Under Great Khan Möngke, the Mongols overthrew the Abbasid Caliphate, brutally sacking Baghdad and destroying the city's Grand Library. Möngke's death in 1259 prompted part of the army to return home, and the rest suffered defeat at the Battle of Ain Jalut against the Mamluks—an Islamic army of slave soldiers who ruled Egypt and Syria from 1250 to 1517.

→ Möngke's campaign route

2 ÖGEDEI KHAN INVADES EUROPE 1229–1241

Following Genghis Khan's death in 1227, Ögedei officially ascended the throne in 1229. Ögedei directed the Mongol campaign into Europe. In 1236, Mongol forces captured and destroyed major towns including Vladimir and Moscow. In 1241, the Mongol army crushed Poland, Hungary, and Bulgaria. The untimely death of Ögedei in 1241 stopped the Mongol army from advancing into western Europe.

→ Ögedei's campaign route

1241 A 30,000-strong Mongol cavalry crosses the frozen Vistula River to invade Poland

1241 Mongols destroy a Polish-German army, opening the way for further conquest in Europe

4 KUBLAI KHAN TAKES CHINA 1251–1294

The grandson of Genghis Khan, Kublai Khan, overthrew the Song Dynasty in 1279 and conquered the whole of China to establish the Yuan Dynasty. He gained the loyalty of his Chinese subjects by employing many in his administration. In 1277, he launched campaigns against Burma and Vietnam, in what was a decade-long war against the Pagan Empire.

→ Kublai Khan's campaign route

5 THE FOUR KHANATES 1259–1411

A single Mongol ruler could not govern the vast imperial realm. In 1259, the empire was divided into four khanates. Each of the four realms was ruled by a descendant of Genghis Khan: the Khanate of the house of Chaghatai, the Il-khanate of Hulagu, the Golden Horde of Berke Khan, and what became the Yuan Empire of Kublai Khan.

▬ Khanate borders

1260 A better knowledge of the terrain helps the Mamluks inflict first defeat on the Mongol army

1258 A 12-day siege ends with the brutal sacking of Baghdad—the capital of the Abbasid Caliphate

1221 Mongols pursue Mamluk leader Jalal ad-Din and defeat him at the Battle of Indus

▽ **Genghis Khan in battle**
This 14th-century illustration from the chronicles of Rashid al-Din depicts Genghis Khan leading the charge against China's Jin forces at the Battle of Yehuling (1211).

THE MONGOL CONQUESTS 1206–1294

Between 1206 and 1227, Mongol leader Genghis Khan built an empire that spanned from China to Persia. Although his successors brought more territories under Mongol rule, in 1260, the empire split into four different realms, or Khanates, and political and cultural differences between them grew.

KEY

▬ Mongol homeland 1206

▬ Mongol Empire c.1227

▬ Greatest extent of Mongol Empire

✕ Major Mongol victory

✖ Major Mongol defeat

♨ City sacked by Mongols

◉ City captured by Mongols

TIMELINE

| 1 | 2 | 3 | 4 | 5 |

1100   1200   1300   1400   1500

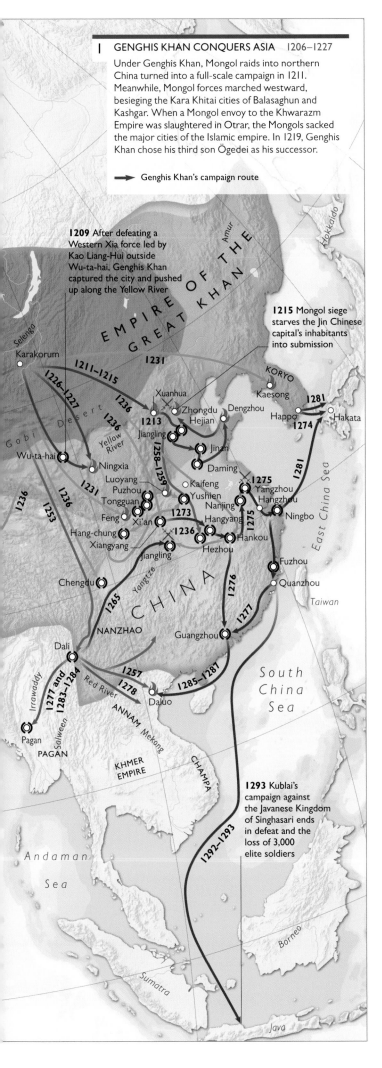

GENGHIS KHAN CONQUERS ASIA 1206–1227

Under Genghis Khan, Mongol raids into northern China turned into a full-scale campaign in 1211. Meanwhile, Mongol forces marched westward, besieging the Kara Khitai cities of Balasaghun and Kashgar. When a Mongol envoy to the Khwarazm Empire was slaughtered in Otrar, the Mongols sacked the major cities of the Islamic empire. In 1219, Genghis Khan chose his third son Ögedei as his successor.

➤ Genghis Khan's campaign route

1209 After defeating a Western Xia force led by Kao Liang-Hui outside Wu-ta-hai, Genghis Khan captured the city and pushed up along the Yellow River

1215 Mongol siege starves the Jin Chinese capital's inhabitants into submission

1293 Kublai's campaign against the Javanese Kingdom of Singhasari ends in defeat and the loss of 3,000 elite soldiers

THE MONGOL CONQUESTS

The Mongols were a mix of Mongolian and Turkic-speaking tribes who united under the leadership of Temujin in the early 13th century. From their homeland in modern-day Mongolia, the fierce Mongol warriors then swept across Asia and Europe, creating the largest land empire in history.

Chosen as the Mongol leader at a tribal meeting in 1206, Temujin took the name Genghis Khan (meaning universal ruler) and united all the tribes under his leadership. In command of a formidable army of warriors on horseback, Genghis Khan organized his army and embarked on a conquest that lasted more than 20 years and resulted in the majority of Asia falling under his rule.

In 1211, Mongol armies invaded northern China, raiding and sacking many Chinese cities. In a long and hard-fought battle, the Mongols took the Chinese capital, Zhongdu, and forced the Jin emperor to flee south.

In 1218, Genghis Khan defeated the Kara Khitai Empire in central Asia after besieging the capital Balasaghun. He then redirected his army against the Islamic world and overwhelmed the lands of the Khwarazm Shah, wreaking great destruction upon the cities of Bukhara and Samarkand. The Mongol army's expertise at traversing long distances and fighting on horseback, combined with its brutal reputation, struck terror into most adversaries. Although Genghis Khan died in 1227, while on a campaign in China, the empire continued to grow under his son Ögedei, who eliminated the Jin Empire in China in 1234 and also fought campaigns in Russia and eastern Europe. The expansion of the empire slowed after Ögedei died in 1241 and ended in 1260 following the Mongols' first major defeat by the army of the Mamluk Sultanate (1250–1517) at Ain Jalut in Palestine. Soon afterward, the empire fragmented, with separate khans ruling China, Persia, central Asia, and the Russian Principalities.

A century later, a last Mongol resurgence took place under Timur—ruler of a Mongol principality in Transoxiana (a remnant of the Chagatai Khanate). He briefly conquered a vast territory across central Asia but was unable to consolidate the empire.

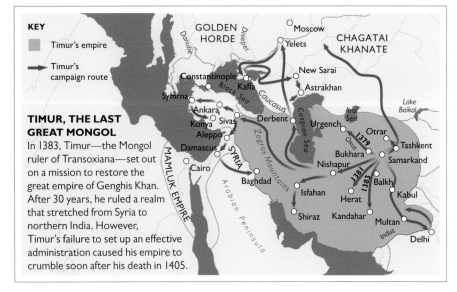

KEY

▨ Timur's empire

➤ Timur's campaign route

TIMUR, THE LAST GREAT MONGOL
In 1383, Timur—the Mongol ruler of Transoxiana—set out on a mission to restore the great empire of Genghis Khan. After 30 years, he ruled a realm that stretched from Syria to northern India. However, Timur's failure to set up an effective administration caused his empire to crumble soon after his death in 1405.

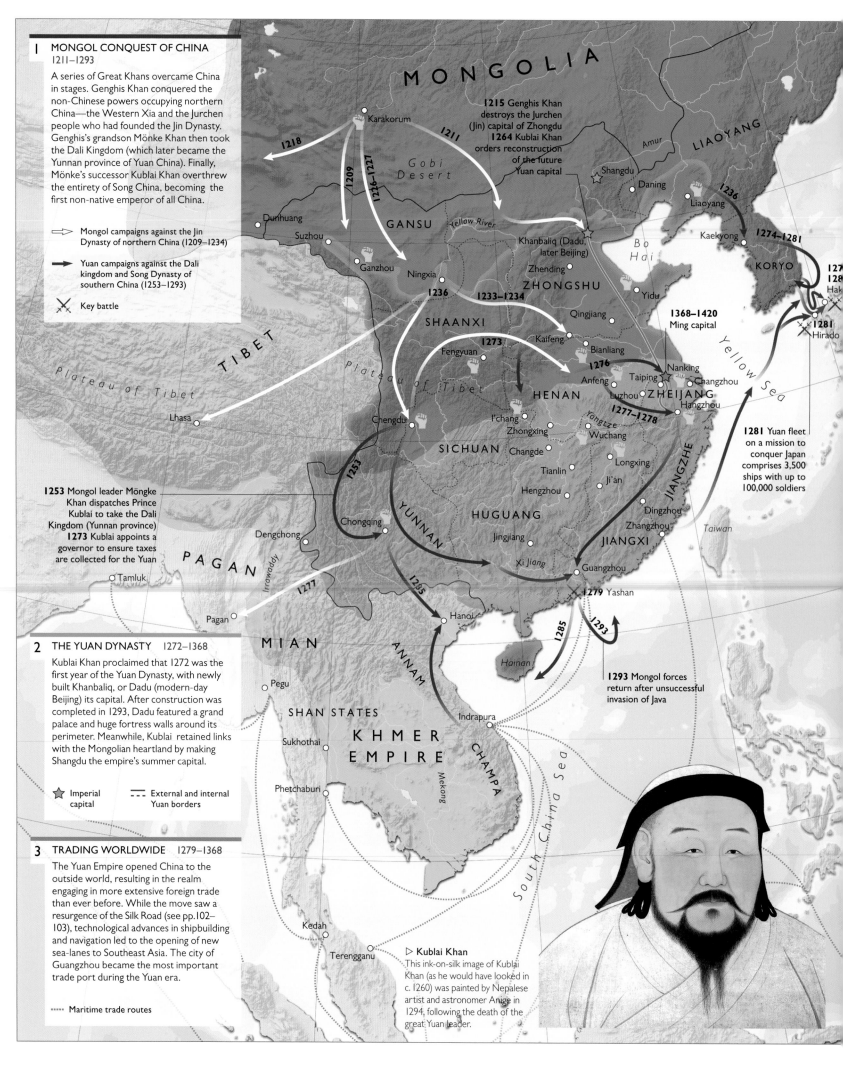

1 MONGOL CONQUEST OF CHINA
1211–1293

A series of Great Khans overcame China in stages. Genghis Khan conquered the non-Chinese powers occupying northern China—the Western Xia and the Jurchen people who had founded the Jin Dynasty. Genghis's grandson Mönke Khan then took the Dali Kingdom (which later became the Yunnan province of Yuan China). Finally, Mönke's successor Kublai Khan overthrew the entirety of Song China, becoming the first non-native emperor of all China.

⇨ Mongol campaigns against the Jin Dynasty of northern China (1209–1234)

➡ Yuan campaigns against the Dali kingdom and Song Dynasty of southern China (1253–1293)

✕ Key battle

1253 Mongol leader Mönke Khan dispatches Prince Kublai to take the Dali Kingdom (Yunnan province)
1273 Kublai appoints a governor to ensure taxes are collected for the Yuan

2 THE YUAN DYNASTY 1272–1368

Kublai Khan proclaimed that 1272 was the first year of the Yuan Dynasty, with newly built Khanbaliq, or Dadu (modern-day Beijing) its capital. After construction was completed in 1293, Dadu featured a grand palace and huge fortress walls around its perimeter. Meanwhile, Kublai retained links with the Mongolian heartland by making Shangdu the empire's summer capital.

⭐ Imperial capital

┅ External and internal Yuan borders

3 TRADING WORLDWIDE 1279–1368

The Yuan Empire opened China to the outside world, resulting in the realm engaging in more extensive foreign trade than ever before. While the move saw a resurgence of the Silk Road (see pp.102–103), technological advances in shipbuilding and navigation led to the opening of new sea-lanes to Southeast Asia. The city of Guangzhou became the most important trade port during the Yuan era.

┅┅┅ Maritime trade routes

1215 Genghis Khan destroys the Jurchen (Jin) capital of Zhongdu
1264 Kublai Khan orders reconstruction of the future Yuan capital

1368–1420 Ming capital

1281 Yuan fleet on a mission to conquer Japan comprises 3,500 ships with up to 100,000 soldiers

1293 Mongol forces return after unsuccessful invasion of Java

▷ **Kublai Khan**
This ink-on-silk image of Kublai Khan (as he would have looked in c. 1260) was painted by Nepalese artist and astronomer Anige in 1294, following the death of the great Yuan leader.

MONGOLIA

Karakorum

1218 · 1211 · 1209 · 1226–1227

Gobi Desert

GANSU

Yellow River

Amur

LIAOYANG

Shangdu

Daning

Liaoyang 1236

Dunhuang

Suzhou

Ganzhou

Ningxia

1236

Khanbaliq (Dadu, later Beijing)

Zhending

Kaekyong

KORYO 1274–1281

Bo Hai

TIBET

Plateau of Tibet

Lhasa

1233–1234

ZHONGSHU

Qingjiang

Yidu

Yellow Sea

1281 Hirado

SHAANXI

Fengyuan

1273

Kaifeng

Bianliang

1276

Anfeng Taiping Nanking

Changzhou

ZHEIJANG

Hangzhou

HENAN

Luzhou

1277–1278

Plateau of Tibet

Chengdu

I'chang

Zhongxing

Wuchang

Yangtze

JIANGZHE

SICHUAN

Changde

Tianlin

Longxing

1253

Chongqing

YUNNAN

Jingjiang

HUGUANG

Ji'an

Hengzhou

Dingzhou

Zhangzhou

Taiwan

Dengchong

JIANGXI

Xi Jiang

Guangzhou

Irrawaddy

1277

PAGAN

Tamluk

Pagan

1285

1279 Yashan

1285 · 1293

Hainan

Hanoi

MIAN

Pegu

ANNAM

CHAMPA

SHAN STATES

Indrapura

Sukhothai

KHMER EMPIRE

Mekong

Phetchaburi

South China Sea

Kedah

Terengganu

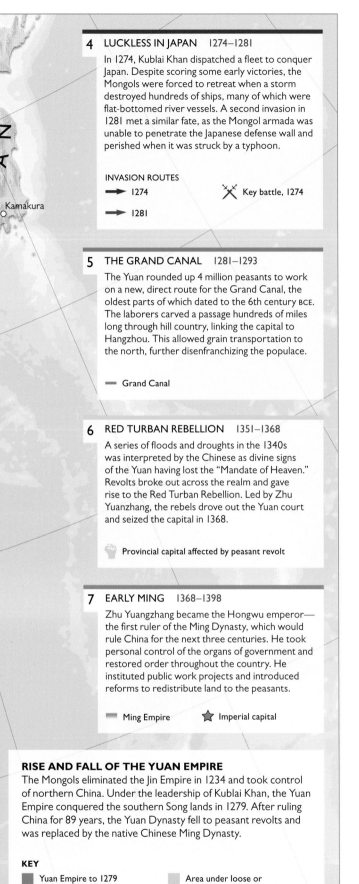

4 LUCKLESS IN JAPAN 1274–1281

In 1274, Kublai Khan dispatched a fleet to conquer Japan. Despite scoring some early victories, the Mongols were forced to retreat when a storm destroyed hundreds of ships, many of which were flat-bottomed river vessels. A second invasion in 1281 met a similar fate, as the Mongol armada was unable to penetrate the Japanese defense wall and perished when it was struck by a typhoon.

INVASION ROUTES

➡ 1274

✕✕ Key battle, 1274

➡ 1281

5 THE GRAND CANAL 1281–1293

The Yuan rounded up 4 million peasants to work on a new, direct route for the Grand Canal, the oldest parts of which dated to the 6th century BCE. The laborers carved a passage hundreds of miles long through hill country, linking the capital to Hangzhou. This allowed grain transportation to the north, further disenfranchizing the populace.

— Grand Canal

6 RED TURBAN REBELLION 1351–1368

A series of floods and droughts in the 1340s was interpreted by the Chinese as divine signs of the Yuan having lost the "Mandate of Heaven." Revolts broke out across the realm and gave rise to the Red Turban Rebellion. Led by Zhu Yuanzhang, the rebels drove out the Yuan court and seized the capital in 1368.

✊ Provincial capital affected by peasant revolt

7 EARLY MING 1368–1398

Zhu Yuanzhang became the Hongwu emperor— the first ruler of the Ming Dynasty, which would rule China for the next three centuries. He took personal control of the organs of government and restored order throughout the country. He instituted public work projects and introduced reforms to redistribute land to the peasants.

▭ Ming Empire   ★ Imperial capital

RISE AND FALL OF THE YUAN EMPIRE

The Mongols eliminated the Jin Empire in 1234 and took control of northern China. Under the leadership of Kublai Khan, the Yuan Empire conquered the southern Song lands in 1279. After ruling China for 89 years, the Yuan Dynasty fell to peasant revolts and was replaced by the native Chinese Ming Dynasty.

KEY

▪ Yuan Empire to 1279

▪ Yuan expansion 1280–1368

▪ Area under loose or temporary Yuan control

TIMELINE

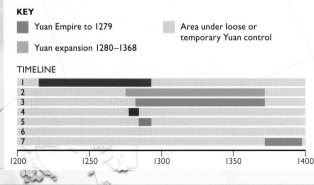

YUAN CHINA TO THE EARLY MING

In 1272, Genghis Khan's grandson, Kublai Khan, founded China's first foreign-led empire, the Yuan, and 9 years later, he wrested control of the whole realm. However, a system of rule that repressed the Chinese eventually gave rise to widespread rebellion that led to the empire's downfall 89 years later.

Kublai Khan ruled China as an independent realm of the Mongol Empire. He enforced a rigid racial hierarchy, placing the Mongols at the top while denying the Chinese any roles in the government or the military.

Kublai made Dadu (Beijing) the Yuan capital, encouraged trade links with the outside world, and brought paper money into common circulation. Kublai's successors, however, faced a populace that was increasingly aggrieved over rising inflation and the oppressive taxes borne out of the dynasty's discriminatory social policies. Moreover, the arrival of the Black Death in the 1330s (see pp.114–115), along with a spate of natural disasters, wrought great hardship upon the poorer classes. From the 1340s, revolts broke out in every province, giving rise to a movement known as the Red Turban Rebellion, led by Zhu Yuanzhang.

In 1368, Zhu seized Dadu and expelled the Mongol rulers. He founded the Ming Dynasty and introduced reforms that improved the prospects of the peasant classes.

"… one can conquer the empire on horseback, but one cannot govern it on horseback."

KUBLAI KHAN, YUAN DYNASTY EMPEROR, 1271–1294

MARCO POLO TRAVELS TO CHINA

Mongol control of Eurasia ushered in a period of peace and stability, known as "Pax Mongolica," which allowed Italian merchant and explorer Marco Polo to embark along the Silk Road on a trade mission to China. According to his travel writings, Marco Polo spent 17 years in China serving emperor Kublai Khan as a government official.

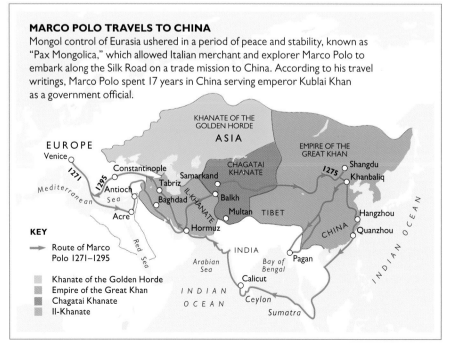

TEMPLE STATES OF SOUTHEAST ASIA

The kingdoms that emerged in Southeast Asia from the start of the 1st millennium CE were strongly influenced by their powerful neighbors. Forms of government and religious ideas were imported via trade routes from India, while China's diplomatic and commercial strength shaped the formation of states in the east.

Organized states appeared in Southeast Asia around the 2nd century CE, with the Indian-influenced kingdom of Funan in Cambodia's Mekong Delta among the earliest. They imported key ideas from India, most notably in art, government, and religion. Buddhism reached the Mon kingdom of Burma (modern-day Myanmar) by the late 3rd century and Funan by 375. Hinduism, too, spread rapidly, reaching Borneo by 400 and becoming the favored religion of the Angkor kingdom (in modern-day Cambodia). Rulers took on the characteristics of god-kings (sometimes using the title *cakravartin*, or universal ruler, borrowed from India) and built lavish capitals adorned with Buddhist and Hindu temples. While Indian cultural influence predominated in the west, direct Chinese political influence touched the eastern states. These sent diplomatic missions to Tang China and, in the case of Vietnam,

suffered direct military interventions. By the 9th century, a constellation of large states had emerged from Pagan in Myanmar, to Champa and Angkor in Cambodia, and Dai Viet in modern Vietnam. The Sailendra Empire of Srivijaya, based on Sumatra, dominated the Indonesian archipelago.

In 1287, the Mongols invaded (see pp.130–131) and captured Pagan. Invasion and growth of new competitors, notably the Dvaravati kingdoms of Thailand, shook the stability of the temple kingdoms. By the late 15th century, Angkor, Pagan, Champa, and Srivijaya had all collapsed, leaving a fractured system of regional states by the time Europeans reached the region a century later.

▷ **Pyramid temple**
The Bayon temple at Angkor was built c. 1200 for Jayavarman VII, one of the empire's kings. Some of its towers feature carvings of Jayavarman's face, while others have faces of Buddhist gods.

HINDUISM
RELIGIOUS INFLUENCE ACROSS SOUTHEAST ASIA

Hinduism developed in the 2nd millennium BCE, when its most ancient texts, the *Rig-Veda* hymns, were composed. The worship of many gods—all aspects of a single divine truth—within a temple-based system produced an extremely diverse religion. By the time of the Gupta Empire in the 3rd century CE, the principal forms of Hinduism were Vaishnavism (focused on the worship of Vishnu) and Sivaism (worship of Shiva, the god of creation and destruction), both of which spread widely in Southeast Asia.

Hindu carvings
This 10th-century temple shows the influence of Sivaism in Angkor.

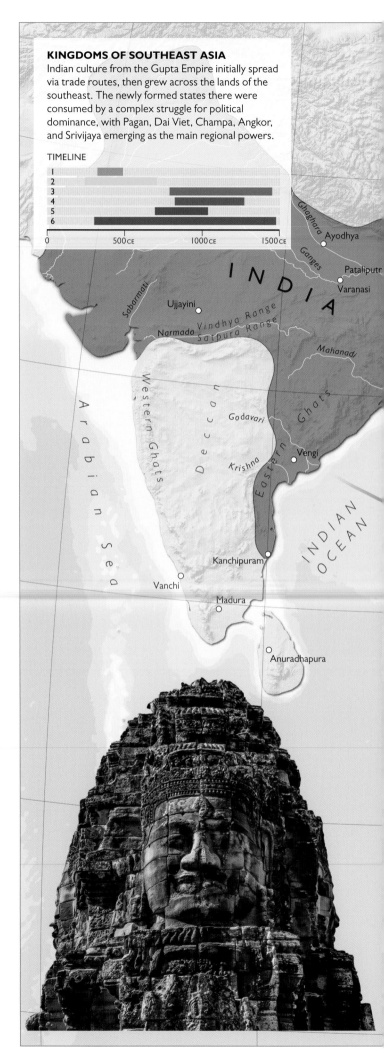

KINGDOMS OF SOUTHEAST ASIA
Indian culture from the Gupta Empire initially spread via trade routes, then grew across the lands of the southeast. The newly formed states there were consumed by a complex struggle for political dominance, with Pagan, Dai Viet, Champa, Angkor, and Srivijaya emerging as the main regional powers.

TIMELINE

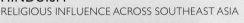

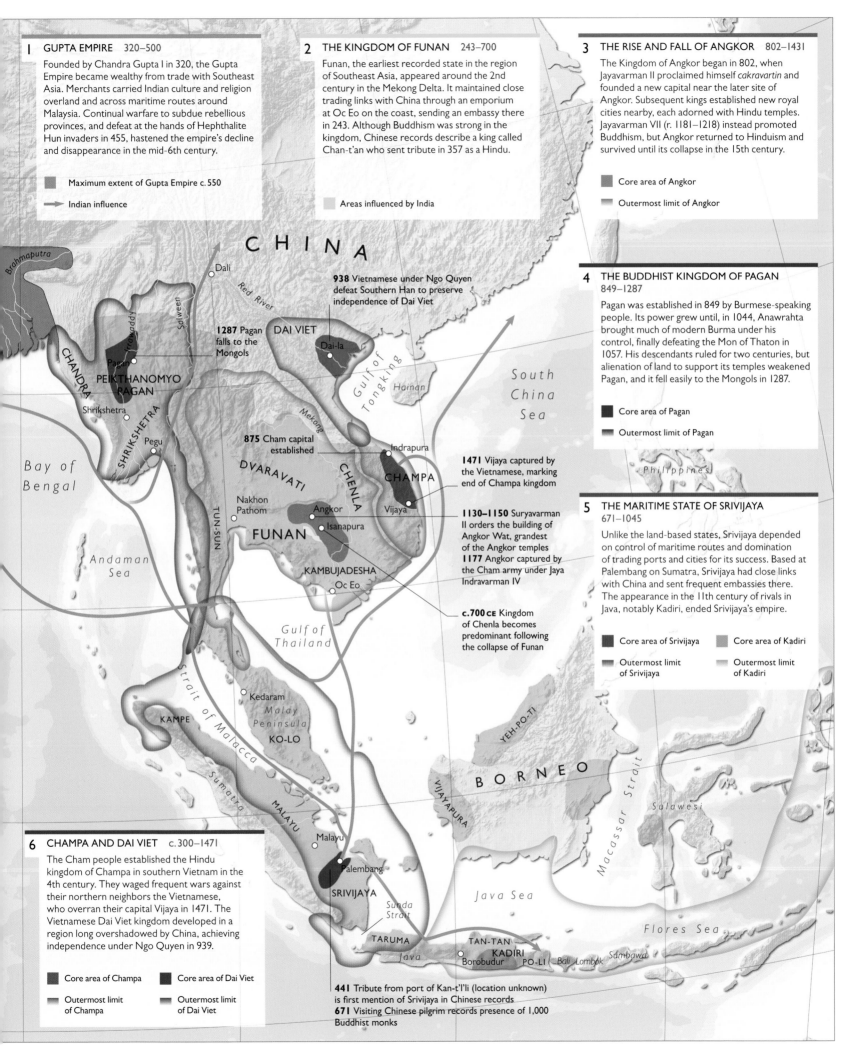

1 GUPTA EMPIRE 320–500

Founded by Chandra Gupta I in 320, the Gupta Empire became wealthy from trade with Southeast Asia. Merchants carried Indian culture and religion overland and across maritime routes around Malaysia. Continual warfare to subdue rebellious provinces, and defeat at the hands of Hephthalite Hun invaders in 455, hastened the empire's decline and disappearance in the mid-6th century.

▪ Maximum extent of Gupta Empire c. 550

→ Indian influence

2 THE KINGDOM OF FUNAN 243–700

Funan, the earliest recorded state in the region of Southeast Asia, appeared around the 2nd century in the Mekong Delta. It maintained close trading links with China through an emporium at Oc Eo on the coast, sending an embassy there in 243. Although Buddhism was strong in the kingdom, Chinese records describe a king called Chan-t'an who sent tribute in 357 as a Hindu.

▪ Areas influenced by India

3 THE RISE AND FALL OF ANGKOR 802–1431

The Kingdom of Angkor began in 802, when Jayavarman II proclaimed himself *cakravartin* and founded a new capital near the later site of Angkor. Subsequent kings established new royal cities nearby, each adorned with Hindu temples. Jayavarman VII (r. 1181–1218) instead promoted Buddhism, but Angkor returned to Hinduism and survived until its collapse in the 15th century.

▪ Core area of Angkor

▪ Outermost limit of Angkor

4 THE BUDDHIST KINGDOM OF PAGAN 849–1287

Pagan was established in 849 by Burmese-speaking people. Its power grew until, in 1044, Anawrahta brought much of modern Burma under his control, finally defeating the Mon of Thaton in 1057. His descendants ruled for two centuries, but alienation of land to support its temples weakened Pagan, and it fell easily to the Mongols in 1287.

▪ Core area of Pagan

▪ Outermost limit of Pagan

5 THE MARITIME STATE OF SRIVIJAYA 671–1045

Unlike the land-based states, Srivijaya depended on control of maritime routes and domination of trading ports and cities for its success. Based at Palembang on Sumatra, Srivijaya had close links with China and sent frequent embassies there. The appearance in the 11th century of rivals in Java, notably Kadiri, ended Srivijaya's empire.

▪ Core area of Srivijaya   ▪ Core area of Kadiri

▪ Outermost limit of Srivijaya   ▪ Outermost limit of Kadiri

6 CHAMPA AND DAI VIET c. 300–1471

The Cham people established the Hindu kingdom of Champa in southern Vietnam in the 4th century. They waged frequent wars against their northern neighbors the Vietnamese, who overran their capital Vijaya in 1471. The Vietnamese Dai Viet kingdom developed in a region long overshadowed by China, achieving independence under Ngo Quyen in 939.

▪ Core area of Champa   ▪ Core area of Dai Viet

▪ Outermost limit of Champa   ▪ Outermost limit of Dai Viet

Map labels and annotations:

938 Vietnamese under Ngo Quyen defeat Southern Han to preserve independence of Dai Viet

1287 Pagan falls to the Mongols

875 Cham capital established

1471 Vijaya captured by the Vietnamese, marking end of Champa kingdom

1130–1150 Suryavarman II orders the building of Angkor Wat, grandest of the Angkor temples

1177 Angkor captured by the Cham army under Jaya Indravarman IV

c. 700 CE Kingdom of Chenla becomes predominant following the collapse of Funan

441 Tribute from port of Kan-t'l'li (location unknown) is first mention of Srivijaya in Chinese records

671 Visiting Chinese pilgrim records presence of 1,000 Buddhist monks

CHINA

Brahmaputra · Dali · Red River · Salween · Irrawaddy · CHANDRA · Pagan · PEIKTHANOMYO PAGAN · Shrikshetra · SHRIKSHETRA · Pegu · DAI VIET · Dai-la · Gulf of Tongking · Hainan · South China Sea · Philippines · Bay of Bengal · DVARAVATI · Nakhon Pathom · Mekong · CHENLA · Indrapura · CHAMPA · Angkor · Isanapura · Vijaya · FUNAN · TUN-SUN · KAMBUJADESHA · Oc Eo · Andaman Sea · Gulf of Thailand · Kedaram · Malay Peninsula · KAMPE · KO-LO · Strait of Malacca · Sumatra · MALAYU · Malayu · VIJAYAPURA · BORNEO · Macassar Strait · Sulawesi · YEH-PO-TI · Palembang · SRIVIJAYA · Java Sea · Sunda Strait · TARUMA · Java · TAN-TAN · KADIRI · Borobudur · PO-LI · Bali · Lombok · Sumbawa · Flores Sea

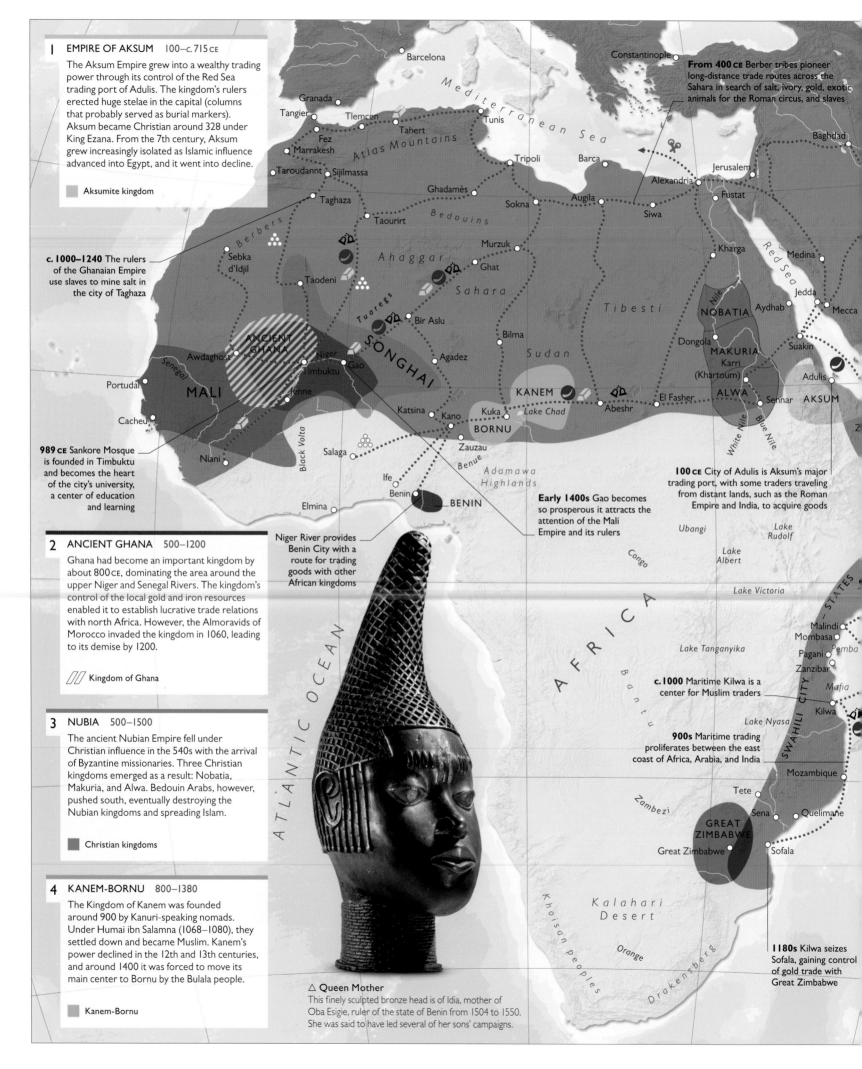

1 EMPIRE OF AKSUM 100–c. 715 CE

The Aksum Empire grew into a wealthy trading power through its control of the Red Sea trading port of Adulis. The kingdom's rulers erected huge stelae in the capital (columns that probably served as burial markers). Aksum became Christian around 328 under King Ezana. From the 7th century, Aksum grew increasingly isolated as Islamic influence advanced into Egypt, and it went into decline.

■ Aksumite kingdom

c. 1000–1240 The rulers of the Ghanaian Empire use slaves to mine salt in the city of Taghaza

989 CE Sankore Mosque is founded in Timbuktu and becomes the heart of the city's university, a center of education and learning

2 ANCIENT GHANA 500–1200

Ghana had become an important kingdom by about 800 CE, dominating the area around the upper Niger and Senegal Rivers. The kingdom's control of the local gold and iron resources enabled it to establish lucrative trade relations with north Africa. However, the Almoravids of Morocco invaded the kingdom in 1060, leading to its demise by 1200.

▨ Kingdom of Ghana

3 NUBIA 500–1500

The ancient Nubian Empire fell under Christian influence in the 540s with the arrival of Byzantine missionaries. Three Christian kingdoms emerged as a result: Nobatia, Makuria, and Alwa. Bedouin Arabs, however, pushed south, eventually destroying the Nubian kingdoms and spreading Islam.

■ Christian kingdoms

4 KANEM-BORNU 800–1380

The Kingdom of Kanem was founded around 900 by Kanuri-speaking nomads. Under Humai ibn Salamna (1068–1080), they settled down and became Muslim. Kanem's power declined in the 12th and 13th centuries, and around 1400 it was forced to move its main center to Bornu by the Bulala people.

■ Kanem-Bornu

From 400 CE Berber tribes pioneer long-distance trade routes across the Sahara in search of salt, ivory, gold, exotic animals for the Roman circus, and slaves

100 CE City of Adulis is Aksum's major trading port, with some traders traveling from distant lands, such as the Roman Empire and India, to acquire goods

Early 1400s Gao becomes so prosperous it attracts the attention of the Mali Empire and its rulers

Niger River provides Benin City with a route for trading goods with other African kingdoms

c. 1000 Maritime Kilwa is a center for Muslim traders

900s Maritime trading proliferates between the east coast of Africa, Arabia, and India

1180s Kilwa seizes Sofala, gaining control of gold trade with Great Zimbabwe

△ **Queen Mother**
This finely sculpted bronze head is of Idia, mother of Oba Esigie, ruler of the state of Benin from 1504 to 1550. She was said to have led several of her sons' campaigns.

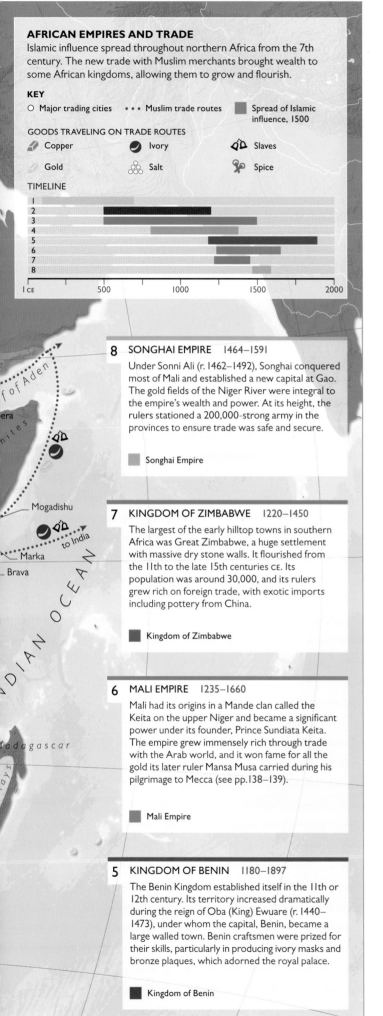

AFRICAN EMPIRES AND TRADE

Islamic influence spread throughout northern Africa from the 7th century. The new trade with Muslim merchants brought wealth to some African kingdoms, allowing them to grow and flourish.

KEY

○ Major trading cities   ••• Muslim trade routes   ■ Spread of Islamic influence, 1500

GOODS TRAVELING ON TRADE ROUTES

Copper   Ivory   Slaves

Gold   Salt   Spice

TIMELINE

8 SONGHAI EMPIRE   1464–1591

Under Sonni Ali (r. 1462–1492), Songhai conquered most of Mali and established a new capital at Gao. The gold fields of the Niger River were integral to the empire's wealth and power. At its height, the rulers stationed a 200,000-strong army in the provinces to ensure trade was safe and secure.

■ Songhai Empire

7 KINGDOM OF ZIMBABWE   1220–1450

The largest of the early hilltop towns in southern Africa was Great Zimbabwe, a huge settlement with massive dry stone walls. It flourished from the 11th to the late 15th centuries CE. Its population was around 30,000, and its rulers grew rich on foreign trade, with exotic imports including pottery from China.

■ Kingdom of Zimbabwe

6 MALI EMPIRE   1235–1660

Mali had its origins in a Mande clan called the Keita on the upper Niger and became a significant power under its founder, Prince Sundiata Keita. The empire grew immensely rich through trade with the Arab world, and it won fame for all the gold its later ruler Mansa Musa carried during his pilgrimage to Mecca (see pp.138–139).

■ Mali Empire

5 KINGDOM OF BENIN   1180–1897

The Benin Kingdom established itself in the 11th or 12th century. Its territory increased dramatically during the reign of Oba (King) Ewuare (r. 1440–1473), under whom the capital, Benin, became a large walled town. Benin craftsmen were prized for their skills, particularly in producing ivory masks and bronze plaques, which adorned the royal palace.

■ Kingdom of Benin

AFRICAN PEOPLES AND EMPIRES

By 1000 CE, Africa's great range of environments and differing access to natural resources had led to a huge diversity of societies. State formation accelerated in the Middle Ages, a process in part provoked by the spread of Islam into the continent.

Africa's cultures ranged from the Islamic caliphates in the north to hunter-gatherer bands in the southern Kalahari Desert, with chiefdoms and complex trading states in between. Islam spread into east Africa and was carried by Muslim merchants into west Africa. States that already existed there, such as Ghana, became rich, and their rulers were able to extend their sway across the Sahel belt, south of the Sahara. Increased wealth also sparked competition for resources. Ghana suffered attacks from the Almoravids of Morocco in the mid-11th century and was finally snuffed out by the rival Sahel state of Mali, which was in turn supplanted by Songhai in the mid-14th century. By this time, a new Islamic sultanate had arisen at Borno, in modern Chad, sustained by its control of salt mines in the desert basins.

Not all state formations were the result of Islamic influence, however. In the northeast, a variety of Christian kingdoms formed in the aftermath of the breakup of Aksum in the late first millennium CE. The kingdom of Zimbabwe, and the iron-working kingdom of Benin in west Africa, which flourished from the 14th century, both imported artifacts and raw materials from abroad but were not subject to direct Islamic influence.

"They exchanged gold until they depressed its value in Egypt and caused its price to fall."

MANSA MUSA DESCRIBED BY ARAB HISTORIAN AL-UMARI, C. 1350

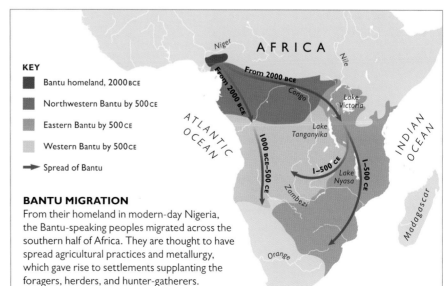

KEY

■ Bantu homeland, 2000 BCE

■ Northwestern Bantu by 500 CE

■ Eastern Bantu by 500 CE

■ Western Bantu by 500 CE

→ Spread of Bantu

BANTU MIGRATION

From their homeland in modern-day Nigeria, the Bantu-speaking peoples migrated across the southern half of Africa. They are thought to have spread agricultural practices and metallurgy, which gave rise to settlements supplanting the foragers, herders, and hunter-gatherers.

On his way
This 17th-century print gives an impression of the sheer scale of Mansa Musa's caravan. He was said to have brought 60,000 followers—including 12,000 slaves—and 80 camels to carry the vast quantity of gold needed to fund his expedition.

MANSA MUSA

In 1324, Mansa Musa, the ruler of Mali, made a pilgrimage to Mecca that became famous for its lavishness. The vast quantities of gold the king brought with him were a sign of the prosperity of Islamic west Africa.

Islam was brought to central Africa by merchants and by the 11th century had reached west Africa, where a series of kingdoms grew rich on trade in gold and slaves. By the early 14th century, the Sundjata Kingdom of Mali, ruled by Mansa Musa (r. 1312–1337), had become the most powerful kingdom in west Africa. Musa extended its boundaries farther, reaching as far as northern Nigeria and Timbuktu.

△ **Great mosque**
One of Africa's greatest Islamic monuments, the Djingareyber Mosque was built in 1327 by Abu Ishaq al-Sahili, an architect Musa met in Mecca.

The famous pilgrim

As a show of his power, in 1324, Musa set off to perform his duty as a devout Muslim by undertaking the *hajj*, or pilgrimage to Mecca, taking with him thousands of followers and chests full of gold. His spending was so extravagant that it caused a sudden inflation of prices in Cairo, and when he paid back his debts on his return, the price of gold plummeted. He brought Islamic scholars and architects back with him, founding dozens of Quranic schools and encouraging the growth of a university at Timbuktu, which had more than 1,000 students. The fame of his pilgrimage caused Mali to become known even in Europe. However, after his death, the Sundjata Kingdom went into decline, collapsing in 1433 after Timbuktu fell to the Songhai Empire of Gao (see pp.136–137).

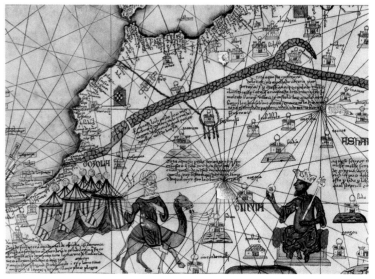

△ **Wealth and fame**
Mansa Musa, holding a golden scepter and a gold nugget, is prominent in west Africa in this atlas compiled in Spain in 1325. News of his lavish spending, which included a gift of 50,000 dinars to Egypt's sultan, spread far beyond the Islamic world.

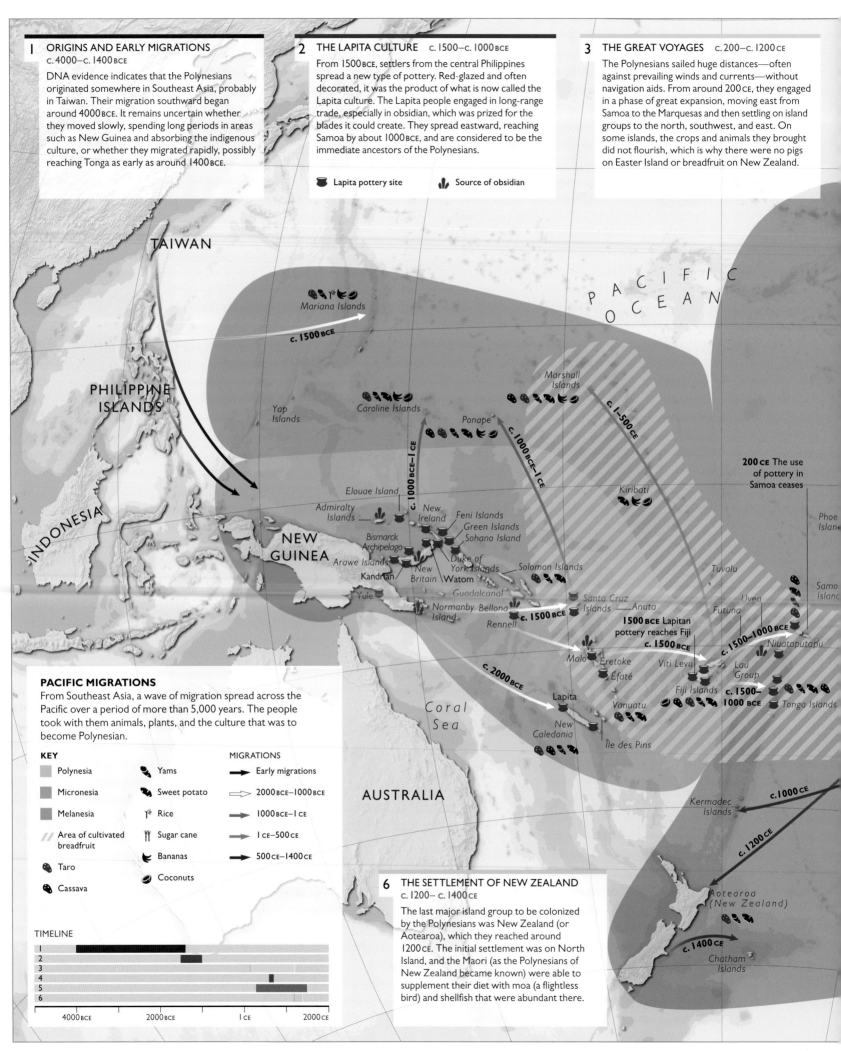

1 ORIGINS AND EARLY MIGRATIONS
c. 4000–c. 1400 BCE

DNA evidence indicates that the Polynesians originated somewhere in Southeast Asia, probably in Taiwan. Their migration southward began around 4000 BCE. It remains uncertain whether they moved slowly, spending long periods in areas such as New Guinea and absorbing the indigenous culture, or whether they migrated rapidly, possibly reaching Tonga as early as around 1400 BCE.

2 THE LAPITA CULTURE c. 1500–c. 1000 BCE

From 1500 BCE, settlers from the central Philippines spread a new type of pottery. Red-glazed and often decorated, it was the product of what is now called the Lapita culture. The Lapita people engaged in long-range trade, especially in obsidian, which was prized for the blades it could create. They spread eastward, reaching Samoa by about 1000 BCE, and are considered to be the immediate ancestors of the Polynesians.

🏺 Lapita pottery site   🔱 Source of obsidian

3 THE GREAT VOYAGES c. 200–c. 1200 CE

The Polynesians sailed huge distances—often against prevailing winds and currents—without navigation aids. From around 200 CE, they engaged in a phase of great expansion, moving east from Samoa to the Marquesas and then settling on island groups to the north, southwest, and east. On some islands, the crops and animals they brought did not flourish, which is why there were no pigs on Easter Island or breadfruit on New Zealand.

PACIFIC MIGRATIONS

From Southeast Asia, a wave of migration spread across the Pacific over a period of more than 5,000 years. The people took with them animals, plants, and the culture that was to become Polynesian.

KEY

▨ Polynesia	🦶 Yams
▨ Micronesia	🦶 Sweet potato
▨ Melanesia	🌾 Rice
⁄⁄ Area of cultivated breadfruit	🍴 Sugar cane
🥔 Taro	🍌 Bananas
🥔 Cassava	🥥 Coconuts

MIGRATIONS

➡ Early migrations
⇨ 2000 BCE–1000 BCE
➡ 1000 BCE–1 CE
➡ 1 CE–500 CE
➡ 500 CE–1400 CE

6 THE SETTLEMENT OF NEW ZEALAND
c. 1200–c. 1400 CE

The last major island group to be colonized by the Polynesians was New Zealand (or Aotearoa), which they reached around 1200 CE. The initial settlement was on North Island, and the Maori (as the Polynesians of New Zealand became known) were able to supplement their diet with moa (a flightless bird) and shellfish that were abundant there.

TIMELINE

4000 BCE   2000 BCE   1 CE   2000 CE

Map labels:
TAIWAN
PHILIPPINE ISLANDS
INDONESIA
NEW GUINEA
AUSTRALIA
PACIFIC OCEAN
Coral Sea
Mariana Islands
Yap Islands
Caroline Islands
Ponape
Marshall Islands
Kiribati
Elouae Island
Admiralty Islands
New Ireland
Feni Islands
Green Islands
Sohano Island
Bismarck Archipelago
Arawe Islands
New Britain
Duke of York Islands
Watom
Kandrian
Yule
Normanby Island
Bellona
Rennell
Guadalcanal
Solomon Islands
Santa Cruz Islands
Anuta
Tuvalu
Uvea
Futuna
Niuatoputapu
Malo
Eretoke
Éfaté
Viti Levu
Fiji Islands
Lau Group
Vanuatu
New Caledonia
Île des Pins
Lapita
Tonga Islands
Phoenix Islands
Samoa Islands
Kermadec Islands
Aotearoa (New Zealand)
Chatham Islands

Migration dates on map:
c. 1500 BCE
c. 1000 BCE–1 CE
c. 1–500 CE
200 CE The use of pottery in Samoa ceases
1500 BCE Lapita pottery reaches Fiji
c. 1500 BCE
c. 1500–1000 BCE
c. 2000 BCE
c. 1000 CE
c. 1200 CE
c. 1400 CE

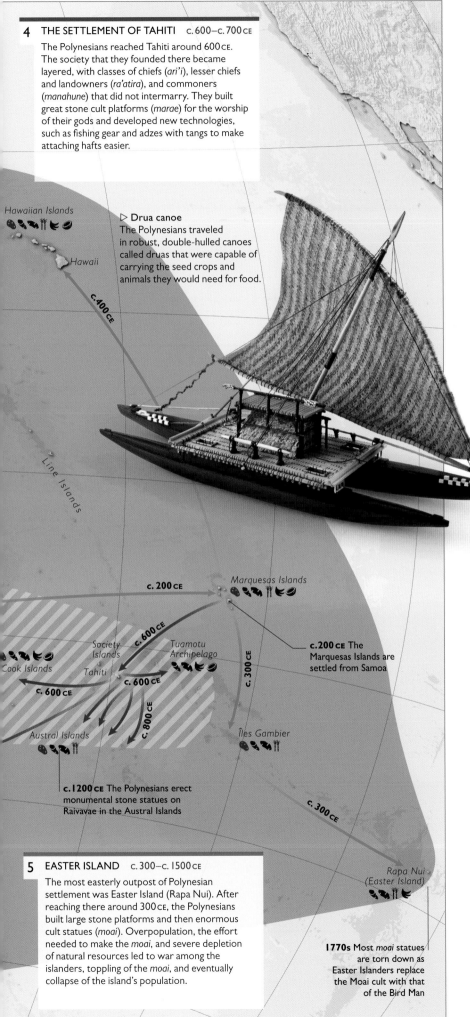

4 THE SETTLEMENT OF TAHITI c.600–c.700 CE

The Polynesians reached Tahiti around 600 CE. The society that they founded there became layered, with classes of chiefs (ari'i), lesser chiefs and landowners (ra'atira), and commoners (manahune) that did not intermarry. They built great stone cult platforms (marae) for the worship of their gods and developed new technologies, such as fishing gear and adzes with tangs to make attaching hafts easier.

Hawaiian Islands

Hawaii

▷ **Drua canoe**
The Polynesians traveled in robust, double-hulled canoes called druas that were capable of carrying the seed crops and animals they would need for food.

c.400 CE

Line Islands

c.200 CE

Marquesas Islands

c.200 CE The Marquesas Islands are settled from Samoa

Society Islands

c.600 CE

Tuamotu Archipelago

c.300 CE

Cook Islands

Tahiti

c.600 CE

c.600 CE

Íles Gambier

c.800 CE

Austral Islands

c.1200 CE The Polynesians erect monumental stone statues on Raivavae in the Austral Islands

c.300 CE

Rapa Nui (Easter Island)

5 EASTER ISLAND c.300–c.1500 CE

The most easterly outpost of Polynesian settlement was Easter Island (Rapa Nui). After reaching there around 300 CE, the Polynesians built large stone platforms and then enormous cult statues (moai). Overpopulation, the effort needed to make the moai, and severe depletion of natural resources led to war among the islanders, toppling of the moai, and eventually collapse of the island's population.

1770s Most moai statues are torn down as Easter Islanders replace the Moai cult with that of the Bird Man

THE POLYNESIANS

An island people of the central Pacific, the Polynesians originated in Southeast Asia. By around 1000 BCE, they had reached Tonga and Samoa. They then embarked on a great migration to reach previously unpopulated islands as distant as Easter Island and New Zealand.

The Polynesians' original ancestors probably came from Taiwan, and they spoke Austronesian languages similar to those heard in present-day Indonesia and the Philippines. From about 4000 BCE, they spread southward and eastward, passing through the Philippines and areas settled more than 20,000 years earlier by Melanesians (an ethnic group related to modern Australian aboriginals). The eastward spread of their early culture (called Lapita) to Tonga and Samoa can be traced through the remains of its distinctive red-glazed pottery.

The Polynesians developed double-hulled voyaging canoes with balancing outriggers that allowed them to reach distant island groups, including the Cook and Marquesas islands, Hawaii, and New Zealand. They took with them taro, yams, sweet potatoes, breadfruit, and bananas that they would cultivate on the islands, and chickens and pigs they would raise for meat. The far-flung nature of their island settlement meant that their societies diverged significantly from one another, with less stratified societies to the west and more complex ones to the east, especially in Hawaii, where a monarchy and centralized government emerged.

EASTER ISLAND *MOAI*
STATUES OF THE SPIRITS

The *moai*, monumental stone statues up to 33 ft (10 m) high, were erected on Easter Island between 1200 and 1600. They are thought to represent protective ancestral spirits. More than 900 *moai* were erected, but the effort required to quarry and haul 88-ton (80-tonne) blocks from the interior of the island and to set them up on *ahau* (platforms) facing out to sea was a major drain on the Easter Islanders' resources. By 1700, the island was almost completely deforested, and its inhabitants could not even build new canoes to fish. In the second half of the 18th century, the Moai cult was superseded by the Bird Man cult, and the *moai* statues were pulled down.

NORTH AMERICAN CULTURES

From 500 to 1500, many diverse cultures flourished in North America, including complex chiefdoms. Various nomadic groups turned to farming, including the Puebloan cultures in the southwest, evolving into large communities that traded extensively. Meanwhile, a new wave of Mound Builder cultures emerged to the east.

The ancient cultures of North America were shaped largely by the environment and available food resources.

In the southwest, the adoption of corn followed by the development of irrigation practices—as conditions became drier around 1000 BCE—forced previously nomadic groups to adopt complex social structures to ensure their survival, giving rise to the early Puebloan settlements. By 400 CE, these settlements had developed into complexes of cliff-dwellings or small towns, which clustered around a large centre featuring low platform mounds and ceremonial ball courts (which hint at Mesoamerican influences). These communities made pottery and basketware, and also mined turquoise, which they traded with the great Mesoamerican cities to the south. Several distinct cultures emerged, and each dominated at different times and in different regions of the southwest.

Elsewhere, the introduction of corn, later supplemented by beans, led to the birth of the Mississippian Mound Builder cultures, following the decline of the Adena and Hopewell (see pp. 52–53). The various Mississippian subgroups flourished between 800 and 1500, each ruled by chiefs residing in fortified centers featuring mounds that served as foundations for temples. Some Mississippian centers grew into towns, the largest of which, Cahokia, thrived from 1050 to 1250. With up to 20,000 inhabitants, these settlements each had a palisaded center, ringed by large earthen platform mounds.

> *"… a group of mounds… at a distance resembling enormous haystacks scattered through a meadow"*
>
> WRITER HENRY MARIE BRACKENRIDGE ON SEEING CAHOKIA, 1811

MESA VERDE
GREAT ANCIENT PUEBLOAN SETTLEMENT

From about 700 CE, many of the Ancient Puebloans of the southwest began constructing settlements high in the cliffs, which offered protection. The largest of these was Mesa Verde, comprising 4,500 residential sites, of which 600 were cliff dwellings: villages built into the giant alcoves of the mesa walls. By about 1200, the population of Mesa Verde proper reached about 30,000 people, most of whom lived in dense settlements at the heads of the area's canyons.

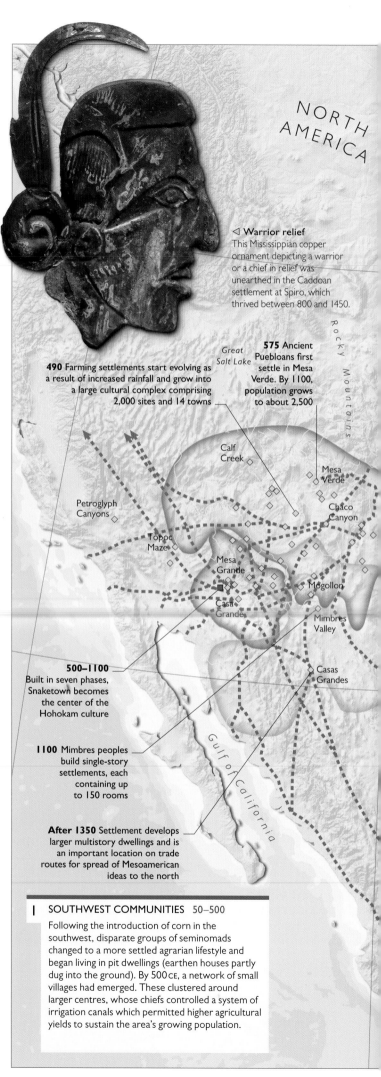

◁ **Warrior relief**
This Mississippian copper ornament depicting a warrior or a chief in relief was unearthed in the Caddoan settlement at Spiro, which thrived between 800 and 1450.

490 Farming settlements start evolving as a result of increased rainfall and grow into a large cultural complex comprising 2,000 sites and 14 towns

575 Ancient Puebloans first settle in Mesa Verde. By 1100, population grows to about 2,500

Great Salt Lake

Rocky Mountains

Calf Creek

Mesa Verde

Petroglyph Canyons

Chaco Canyon

Topoc Maze

Mesa Grande

Mogollon

Casa Grande

Mimbres Valley

Casas Grandes

500–1100
Built in seven phases, Snaketown becomes the center of the Hohokam culture

Gulf of California

1100 Mimbres peoples build single-story settlements, each containing up to 150 rooms

After 1350 Settlement develops larger multistory dwellings and is an important location on trade routes for spread of Mesoamerican ideas to the north

SOUTHWEST COMMUNITIES 50–500

Following the introduction of corn in the southwest, disparate groups of seminomads changed to a more settled agrarian lifestyle and began living in pit dwellings (earthen houses partly dug into the ground). By 500 CE, a network of small villages had emerged. These clustered around larger centres, whose chiefs controlled a system of irrigation canals which permitted higher agricultural yields to sustain the area's growing population.

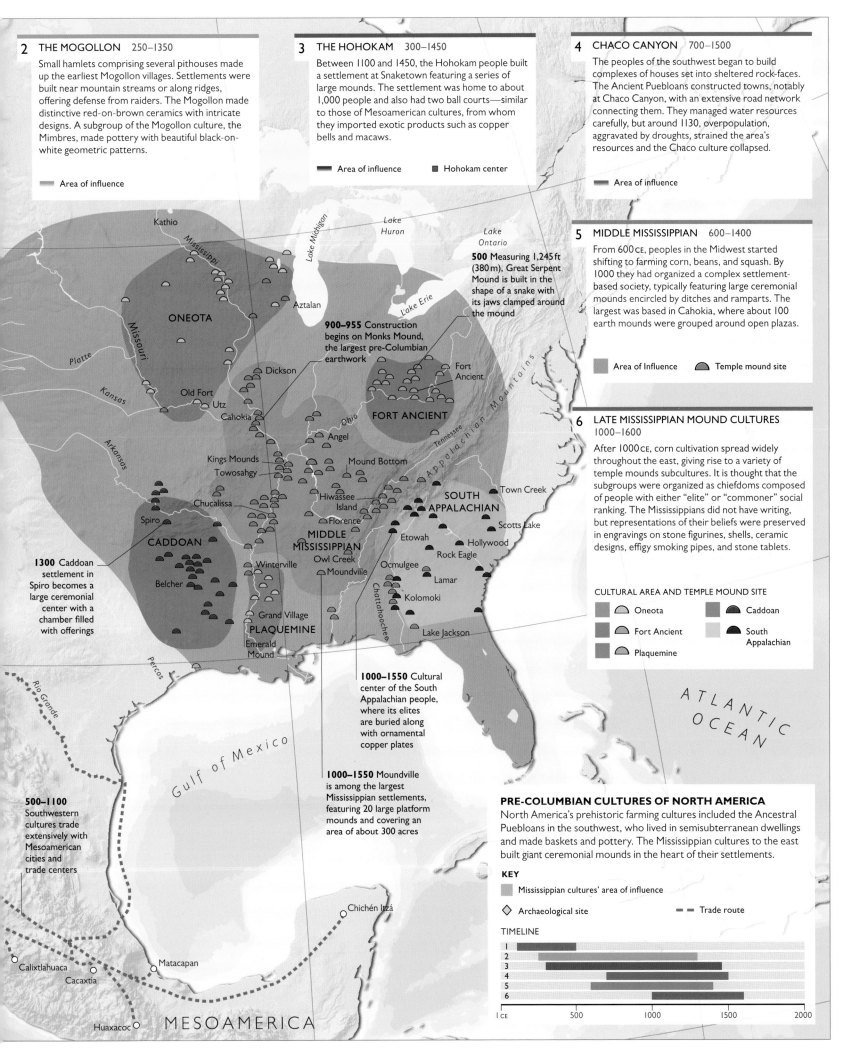

2 THE MOGOLLON 250–1350

Small hamlets comprising several pithouses made up the earliest Mogollon villages. Settlements were built near mountain streams or along ridges, offering defense from raiders. The Mogollon made distinctive red-on-brown ceramics with intricate designs. A subgroup of the Mogollon culture, the Mimbres, made pottery with beautiful black-on-white geometric patterns.

▬ Area of influence

3 THE HOHOKAM 300–1450

Between 1100 and 1450, the Hohokam people built a settlement at Snaketown featuring a series of large mounds. The settlement was home to about 1,000 people and also had two ball courts—similar to those of Mesoamerican cultures, from whom they imported exotic products such as copper bells and macaws.

▬ Area of influence   ■ Hohokam center

4 CHACO CANYON 700–1500

The peoples of the southwest began to build complexes of houses set into sheltered rock-faces. The Ancient Puebloans constructed towns, notably at Chaco Canyon, with an extensive road network connecting them. They managed water resources carefully, but around 1130, overpopulation, aggravated by droughts, strained the area's resources and the Chaco culture collapsed.

▬ Area of influence

5 MIDDLE MISSISSIPPIAN 600–1400

From 600 CE, peoples in the Midwest started shifting to farming corn, beans, and squash. By 1000 they had organized a complex settlement-based society, typically featuring large ceremonial mounds encircled by ditches and ramparts. The largest was based in Cahokia, where about 100 earth mounds were grouped around open plazas.

▬ Area of Influence   ⌓ Temple mound site

6 LATE MISSISSIPPIAN MOUND CULTURES 1000–1600

After 1000 CE, corn cultivation spread widely throughout the east, giving rise to a variety of temple mounds subcultures. It is thought that the subgroups were organized as chiefdoms composed of people with either "elite" or "commoner" social ranking. The Mississippians did not have writing, but representations of their beliefs were preserved in engravings on stone figurines, shells, ceramic designs, effigy smoking pipes, and stone tablets.

CULTURAL AREA AND TEMPLE MOUND SITE

⌓ Oneota   ◖ Caddoan
⌓ Fort Ancient   ◕ South Appalachian
⌓ Plaquemine

500 Measuring 1,245 ft (380 m), Great Serpent Mound is built in the shape of a snake with its jaws clamped around the mound

900–955 Construction begins on Monks Mound, the largest pre-Columbian earthwork

1300 Caddoan settlement in Spiro becomes a large ceremonial center with a chamber filled with offerings

1000–1550 Cultural center of the South Appalachian people, where its elites are buried along with ornamental copper plates

1000–1550 Moundville is among the largest Mississippian settlements, featuring 20 large platform mounds and covering an area of about 300 acres

500–1100 Southwestern cultures trade extensively with Mesoamerican cities and trade centers

PRE-COLUMBIAN CULTURES OF NORTH AMERICA

North America's prehistoric farming cultures included the Ancestral Puebloans in the southwest, who lived in semisubterranean dwellings and made baskets and pottery. The Mississippian cultures to the east built giant ceremonial mounds in the heart of their settlements.

KEY

▮ Mississippian cultures' area of influence

◇ Archaeological site   ▬ ▬ Trade route

TIMELINE

	1 CE	500	1000	1500	2000
1					
2					
3					
4					
5					
6					

AZTEC AND INCA EMPIRES

Two large empires emerged in the Americas in the 14th century. In Mesoamerica, the Aztec culture grew into a major civilization, famous for its tribute system, warfare, art, and architecture. Meanwhile, starting in Peru's Cuzco valley, the Inca people created a vast realm along the Andes and asserted their rule using a sophisticated bureaucracy and a sprawling network of roads.

The Aztecs originally settled on an island in Lake Texcoco and founded the city of Tenochtitlan in 1325. The culture privileged the training of a warrior elite, and within half a century amassed a formidable army. Following the Triple Alliance—a partnership the Aztecs formed with the cities of Texcoco and Tlacopan—the Aztecs engaged in a phase of conquests. Their army invaded neighboring communities, overthrew the local chieftains, and turned these territories into vassals. Aztec officials were then appointed to ensure that tributes—the main source of revenue for the empire—as well as captives for human sacrifice were sent to the capital, where the rulers pooled the resources into building monuments and artworks.

The Incas emerged as the predominant group in Peru's Cuzco valley after settling in the region in about 1250, developing techniques to farm on mountain terraces. The Incas began a phase of conquests in 1438; by the early 1500s, they had overthrown powerful neighbors the Chimú and the Chancas and extended their rule to Quito in the north and the Araucanian desert of Chile to the south. The Incas instituted a strong administrative structure and built a complex road network to help them govern the vast empire.

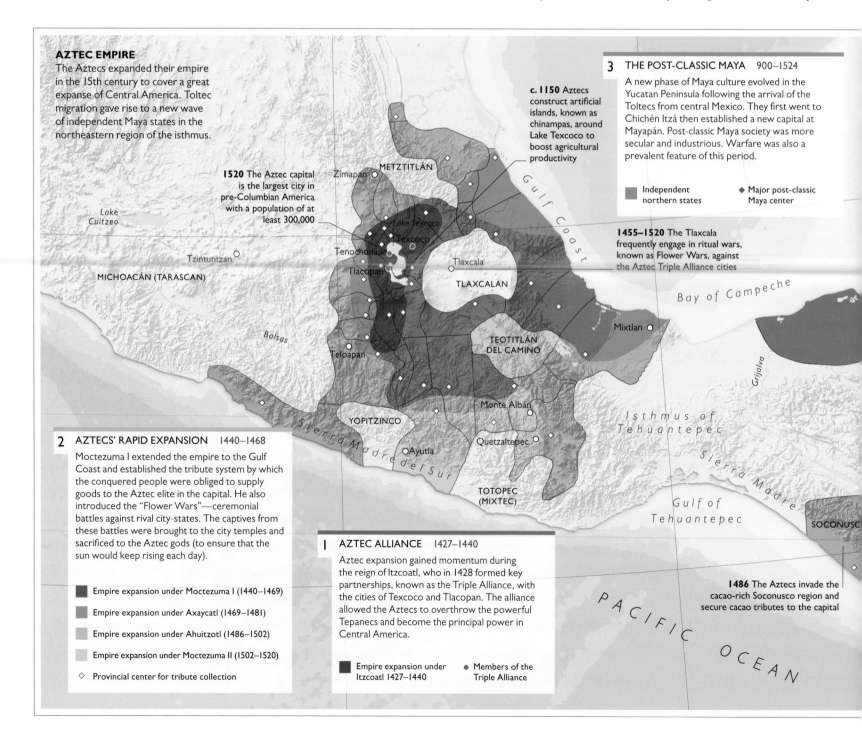

AZTEC EMPIRE
The Aztecs expanded their empire in the 15th century to cover a great expanse of Central America. Toltec migration gave rise to a new wave of independent Maya states in the northeastern region of the isthmus.

1520 The Aztec capital is the largest city in pre-Columbian America with a population of at least 300,000

c. 1150 Aztecs construct artificial islands, known as chinampas, around Lake Texcoco to boost agricultural productivity

3 THE POST-CLASSIC MAYA 900–1524
A new phase of Maya culture evolved in the Yucatan Peninsula following the arrival of the Toltecs from central Mexico. They first went to Chichén Itzá then established a new capital at Mayapán. Post-classic Maya society was more secular and industrious. Warfare was also a prevalent feature of this period.

- ◼ Independent northern states
- ◆ Major post-classic Maya center

1455–1520 The Tlaxcala frequently engage in ritual wars, known as Flower Wars, against the Aztec Triple Alliance cities

Lake Cuitzeo

METZTITLÁN

Zimapan

Lake Texcoco
Texcoco
Tenochtitlan
Tlacopan
Tlaxcala

TLAXCALAN

Bay of Campeche

Tzintuntzan

MICHOACÁN (TARASCAN)

Balsas

Teloapan

TEOTITLÁN DEL CAMINO

Mixtlan

Gulf Coast

Grijalva

2 AZTECS' RAPID EXPANSION 1440–1468
Moctezuma I extended the empire to the Gulf Coast and established the tribute system by which the conquered people were obliged to supply goods to the Aztec elite in the capital. He also introduced the "Flower Wars"—ceremonial battles against rival city-states. The captives from these battles were brought to the city temples and sacrificed to the Aztec gods (to ensure that the sun would keep rising each day).

- ◼ Empire expansion under Moctezuma I (1440–1469)
- ◼ Empire expansion under Axaycatl (1469–1481)
- ◻ Empire expansion under Ahuitzotl (1486–1502)
- ◻ Empire expansion under Moctezuma II (1502–1520)
- ◇ Provincial center for tribute collection

YOPITZINCO

Monte Albán

Quetzaltepec

Ayutla

TOTOPEC (MIXTEC)

Sierra Madre del Sur

Sierra Madre

Gulf of Tehuantepec

Isthmus of Tehuantepec

SOCONUSCO

1 AZTEC ALLIANCE 1427–1440
Aztec expansion gained momentum during the reign of Itzcoatl, who in 1428 formed key partnerships, known as the Triple Alliance, with the cities of Texcoco and Tlacopan. The alliance allowed the Aztecs to overthrow the powerful Tepanecs and become the principal power in Central America.

- ◼ Empire expansion under Itzcoatl 1427–1440
- ● Members of the Triple Alliance

1486 The Aztecs invade the cacao-rich Soconusco region and secure cacao tributes to the capital

PACIFIC OCEAN

AZTEC AND INCA CONQUESTS

The Aztec and Inca Empires, as well as the independent post-classic Maya states, were the largest urban civilizations in Central and South America before the Europeans' arrival in the 16th century. In particular, the Aztecs and Incas were territorial and embarked on a phase of conquests to absorb other societies and extend their rule over a larger area.

KEY

○ Major urban centers

TIMELINE

1		
2		
3		
4		
5		
6		

800 950 1100 1250 1400 1550

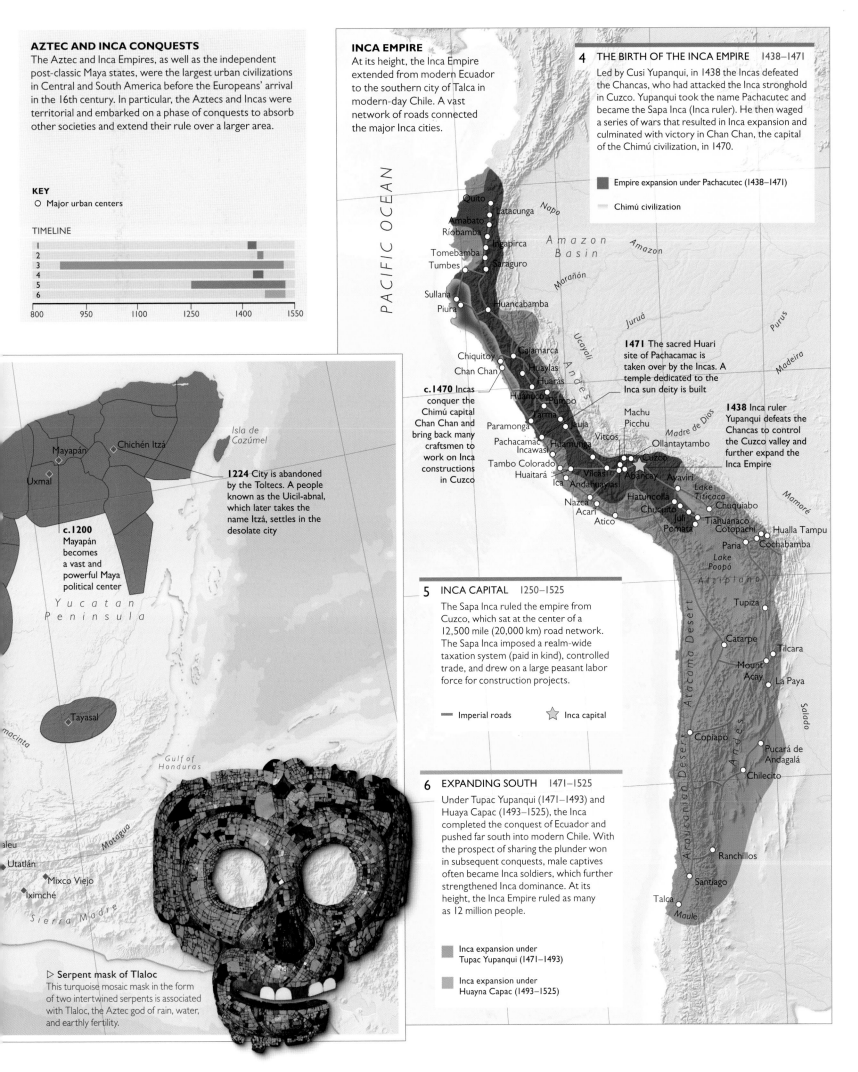

INCA EMPIRE

At its height, the Inca Empire extended from modern Ecuador to the southern city of Talca in modern-day Chile. A vast network of roads connected the major Inca cities.

4 THE BIRTH OF THE INCA EMPIRE 1438–1471

Led by Cusi Yupanqui, in 1438 the Incas defeated the Chancas, who had attacked the Inca stronghold in Cuzco. Yupanqui took the name Pachacutec and became the Sapa Inca (Inca ruler). He then waged a series of wars that resulted in Inca expansion and culminated with victory in Chan Chan, the capital of the Chimú civilization, in 1470.

■ Empire expansion under Pachacutec (1438–1471)

▬ Chimú civilization

1471 The sacred Huari site of Pachacamac is taken over by the Incas. A temple dedicated to the Inca sun deity is built

c.1470 Incas conquer the Chimú capital Chan Chan and bring back many craftsmen to work on Inca constructions in Cuzco

1438 Inca ruler Yupanqui defeats the Chancas to control the Cuzco valley and further expand the Inca Empire

5 INCA CAPITAL 1250–1525

The Sapa Inca ruled the empire from Cuzco, which sat at the center of a 12,500 mile (20,000 km) road network. The Sapa Inca imposed a realm-wide taxation system (paid in kind), controlled trade, and drew on a large peasant labor force for construction projects.

▬ Imperial roads   ☆ Inca capital

6 EXPANDING SOUTH 1471–1525

Under Tupac Yupanqui (1471–1493) and Huaya Capac (1493–1525), the Inca completed the conquest of Ecuador and pushed far south into modern Chile. With the prospect of sharing the plunder won in subsequent conquests, male captives often became Inca soldiers, which further strengthened Inca dominance. At its height, the Inca Empire ruled as many as 12 million people.

■ Inca expansion under Tupac Yupanqui (1471–1493)

■ Inca expansion under Huayna Capac (1493–1525)

1224 City is abandoned by the Toltecs. A people known as the Uicil-abnal, which later takes the name Itzá, settles in the desolate city

c.1200 Mayapán becomes a vast and powerful Maya political center

▷ **Serpent mask of Tlaloc**
This turquoise mosaic mask in the form of two intertwined serpents is associated with Tlaloc, the Aztec god of rain, water, and earthly fertility.

THE EARLY MODERN WORLD

AS HORIZONS WIDENED IN 1450–1700, CONTACT BETWEEN EAST
AND WEST MADE TRADE AND CULTURAL EXCHANGE GLOBAL
AND THE WORLD RECOGNIZABLY MODERN.

THE EARLY MODERN WORLD

Between 1450 and 1700, European explorers reached the Americas and began to explore maritime routes around Africa into Asia. Military and scientific revolutions in Europe also enabled its leading powers to encroach on non-European territories.

△ **Competing for souls**
This 1614 painting by the Dutch artist Adriaen van de Venne is symbolic of the religious rivalry that divided Europe. Here, the "catch" of the Protestants (to the left) is depicted as greater than that of their Catholic rivals.

In 1450, a politically fragmented Europe exerted little influence outside its borders—France and England were still at war, Spain was divided, and the trading city-states of Italy seemed to be the continent's most dynamic powers. It was the impulse to trade that eventually revolutionized Europe's position in the world.

Discovering new worlds

Portuguese mariners inched around the African coastline in search of new routes to the lucrative spice markets of Asia—succeeding in 1498, when Vasco da Gama's fleet reached the Indian port of Calicut (now Kozhikode). By then, however, an even more astonishing discovery had been made—Christopher Columbus had stumbled upon a Caribbean island in 1492. This had opened up the Americas, which had been isolated from the rest of the world for millennia.

Spanish adventurers poured across the Atlantic into the Americas, toppling the native Aztec and Inca Empires with surprising ease. They established the first European colonial empire and sent back treasures and silver, which contributed to inflation in Spain but also boosted the country's Habsburg rulers' ability to fight continental wars. This was an invaluable asset at a volatile time; the

religious unity of western Europe had broken down after the German priest Martin Luther had made protests in 1517 against corruption in the Roman Catholic Church. This had prompted a series of reformers to establish alternative Protestant churches, which in turn provoked a spasm of religious warfare. Matters came to a head with the outbreak of the Thirty Years' War in 1618, which pitched German Catholic and Protestant princes against each other and brought in armies from France, the Habsburg Empire, and Sweden that criss-crossed the continent and left it utterly devastated.

Wars in Europe

The arrival of gunpowder warfare heralded the beginnings of European standing armies, trained in the use of firearms and operating in units far larger than ever before. This military revolution in the 16th century immeasurably enhanced the powers of European monarchs but raised the risks of warfare. England suffered the consequences of civil war when tension between an autocratic monarch and a resentful parliament burst into conflict—resulting in the execution of King Charles I in 1649

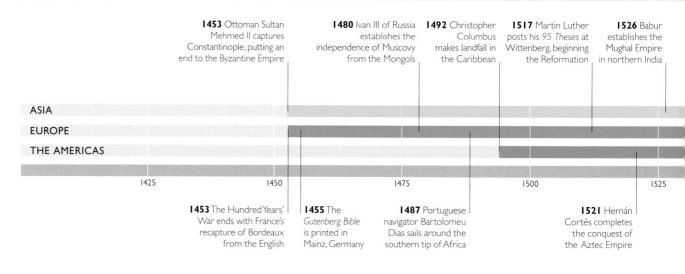

◁ **Art flourishes in India**
This beautiful edition of the *Divan*, the collected works of the popular 14th-century Persian poet Hafiz, was compiled in Mughal India—a rich period for both visual art and literature.

EXPLORATION AND SCHISM

The Early Modern period was one of profound transformation. European explorers reached the New World in 1492, precipitating the collapse of previously dominant societies. Although European traders also reached the spice-producing areas of Asia by rounding Africa, the footholds they established there were much more modest. Europe itself was racked by religious conflicts marred by violence that only ended after a century of warfare.

1453 Ottoman Sultan Mehmed II captures Constantinople, putting an end to the Byzantine Empire

1480 Ivan III of Russia establishes the independence of Muscovy from the Mongols

1492 Christopher Columbus makes landfall in the Caribbean

1517 Martin Luther posts his *95 Theses* at Wittenberg, beginning the Reformation

1526 Babur establishes the Mughal Empire in northern India

ASIA							
EUROPE							
THE AMERICAS							
	1425	1450		1475		1500	1525

1453 The Hundred Years' War ends with France's recapture of Bordeaux from the English

1455 The *Gutenberg Bible* is printed in Mainz, Germany

1487 Portuguese navigator Bartolomeu Dias sails around the southern tip of Africa

1521 Hernán Cortés completes the conquest of the Aztec Empire

◁ **Way of the warrior**
During Japan's Edo, or Tokugawa, period, samurai warriors had gained a high ranking in a rigidly followed caste system. This military armor of a samurai warrior dates from the 19th century.

and the establishment of a republic for 12 years, the only one in Britain's history. By the time monarchy was restored in 1660, Britain faced new rivals: a resurgent France under Louis XIV, and the infant Dutch Republic, whose traders displaced the Portuguese and the Spanish in parts of Asia.

Further expansion

France and Britain extended their competition to the Americas, where they ate away at the Portuguese and Spanish duopoly. They also began to encroach upon Asia, but here they faced strong rivals.

The Ottoman Empire had expanded to occupy the whole of Turkey and much of the Middle East and North Africa. The Safavid Empire brought a golden age to Persia (modern Iran), while the Mughals seized Delhi in 1526 and had conquered most of the Indian subcontinent by 1700. In China, the Ming and Qing Dynasties, both socially

> *"The church needs a reformation ... it is the work of God alone ..."*
>
> MARTIN LUTHER, GERMAN THEOLOGIAN

▷ **Celestial model**
With the Sun at its center, this model, called an armillary sphere, was used to represent the positions of celestial objects.

and diplomatically conservative, regarded the foreigners—who came in increasing numbers—as little more than irritants. In Japan, however, the shogun Tokugawa, who had reunited the country in 1600 after a long civil war, foresaw the dangers posed by foreign powers and gradually excluded them, allowing only the Dutch to persist in a tiny trading enclave off Nagasaki. The Japanese were thus protected from the European tide that began to wash against other Asian powers. They were also insulated from the scientific revolution that began in Europe, which overturned centuries-old orthodoxies and paved the way for new theories, such as Copernicus's Sun-centered Universe and Isaac Newton's work on gravity. As Europe's military power grew, its economic reach widened and its scientific resourcefulness burgeoned. By 1700, European powers stood on the brink of pulling definitively ahead of their Asian rivals.

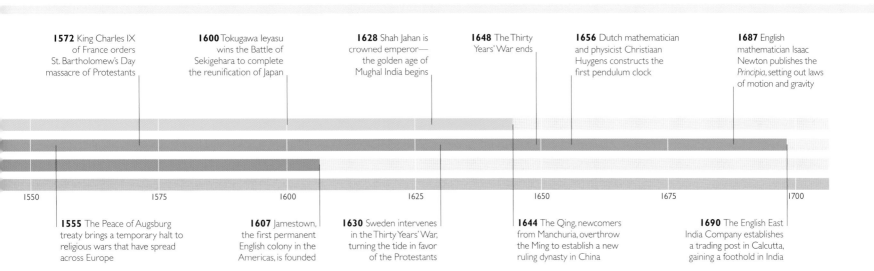

1572 King Charles IX of France orders St. Bartholomew's Day massacre of Protestants

1600 Tokugawa Ieyasu wins the Battle of Sekigehara to complete the reunification of Japan

1628 Shah Jahan is crowned emperor— the golden age of Mughal India begins

1648 The Thirty Years' War ends

1656 Dutch mathematician and physicist Christiaan Huygens constructs the first pendulum clock

1687 English mathematician Isaac Newton publishes the *Principia*, setting out laws of motion and gravity

1550   1575   1600   1625   1650   1675   1700

1555 The Peace of Augsburg treaty brings a temporary halt to religious wars that have spread across Europe

1607 Jamestown, the first permanent English colony in the Americas, is founded

1630 Sweden intervenes in the Thirty Years' War, turning the tide in favor of the Protestants

1644 The Qing, newcomers from Manchuria, overthrow the Ming to establish a new ruling dynasty in China

1690 The English East India Company establishes a trading post in Calcutta, gaining a foothold in India

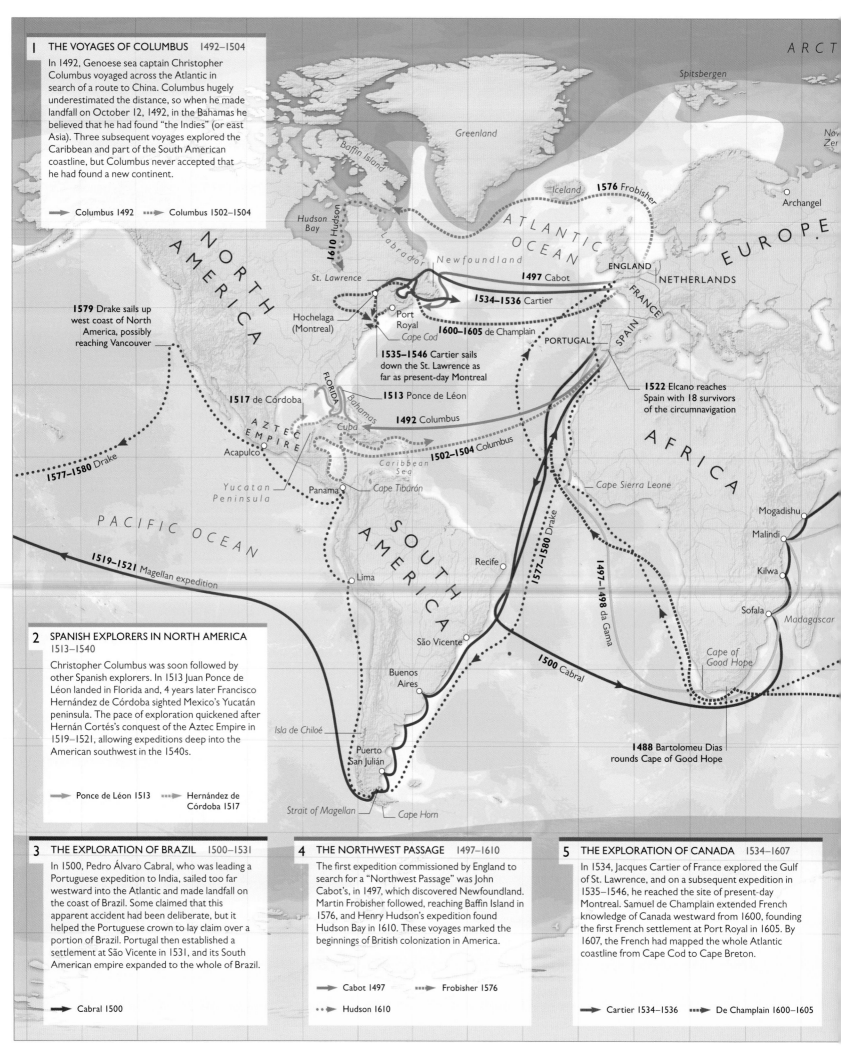

1 THE VOYAGES OF COLUMBUS 1492–1504

In 1492, Genoese sea captain Christopher Columbus voyaged across the Atlantic in search of a route to China. Columbus hugely underestimated the distance, so when he made landfall on October 12, 1492, in the Bahamas he believed that he had found "the Indies" (or east Asia). Three subsequent voyages explored the Caribbean and part of the South American coastline, but Columbus never accepted that he had found a new continent.

→ Columbus 1492   ⇢ Columbus 1502–1504

1579 Drake sails up west coast of North America, possibly reaching Vancouver

1517 de Córdoba

1535–1546 Cartier sails down the St. Lawrence as far as present-day Montreal

1513 Ponce de Léon

1492 Columbus

1502–1504 Columbus

1577–1580 Drake

1519–1521 Magellan expedition

1522 Elcano reaches Spain with 18 survivors of the circumnavigation

1497 Cabot

1534–1536 Cartier

1600–1605 de Champlain

1610 Hudson

1576 Frobisher

1577–1580 Drake

1497–1498 da Gama

1500 Cabral

1488 Bartolomeu Dias rounds Cape of Good Hope

2 SPANISH EXPLORERS IN NORTH AMERICA 1513–1540

Christopher Columbus was soon followed by other Spanish explorers. In 1513 Juan Ponce de Léon landed in Florida and, 4 years later Francisco Hernández de Córdoba sighted Mexico's Yucatán peninsula. The pace of exploration quickened after Hernán Cortés's conquest of the Aztec Empire in 1519–1521, allowing expeditions deep into the American southwest in the 1540s.

→ Ponce de Léon 1513   ⇢ Hernández de Córdoba 1517

3 THE EXPLORATION OF BRAZIL 1500–1531

In 1500, Pedro Álvaro Cabral, who was leading a Portuguese expedition to India, sailed too far westward into the Atlantic and made landfall on the coast of Brazil. Some claimed that this apparent accident had been deliberate, but it helped the Portuguese crown to lay claim over a portion of Brazil. Portugal then established a settlement at São Vicente in 1531, and its South American empire expanded to the whole of Brazil.

→ Cabral 1500

4 THE NORTHWEST PASSAGE 1497–1610

The first expedition commissioned by England to search for a "Northwest Passage" was John Cabot's, in 1497, which discovered Newfoundland. Martin Frobisher followed, reaching Baffin Island in 1576, and Henry Hudson's expedition found Hudson Bay in 1610. These voyages marked the beginnings of British colonization in America.

→ Cabot 1497   ⇢ Frobisher 1576
⇢ Hudson 1610

5 THE EXPLORATION OF CANADA 1534–1607

In 1534, Jacques Cartier of France explored the Gulf of St. Lawrence, and on a subsequent expedition in 1535–1546, he reached the site of present-day Montreal. Samuel de Champlain extended French knowledge of Canada westward from 1600, founding the first French settlement at Port Royal in 1605. By 1607, the French had mapped the whole Atlantic coastline from Cape Cod to Cape Breton.

→ Cartier 1534–1536   ⇢ De Champlain 1600–1605

Map labels: ARCT, Spitsbergen, Greenland, Nov Zer, Baffin Island, Iceland, Archangel, ATLANTIC OCEAN, Hudson Bay, Labrador, Newfoundland, St. Lawrence, ENGLAND, NETHERLANDS, EUROPE, FRANCE, PORTUGAL, SPAIN, Hochelaga (Montreal), Port Royal, Cape Cod, NORTH AMERICA, FLORIDA, Bahamas, Cuba, AZTEC EMPIRE, Acapulco, Yucatan Peninsula, Panama, Cape Tiburón, Caribbean Sea, AFRICA, Cape Sierra Leone, Mogadishu, Malindi, Kilwa, Sofala, Madagascar, PACIFIC OCEAN, SOUTH AMERICA, Recife, Lima, São Vicente, Buenos Aires, Isla de Chiloé, Puerto San Julián, Cape of Good Hope, Strait of Magellan, Cape Horn

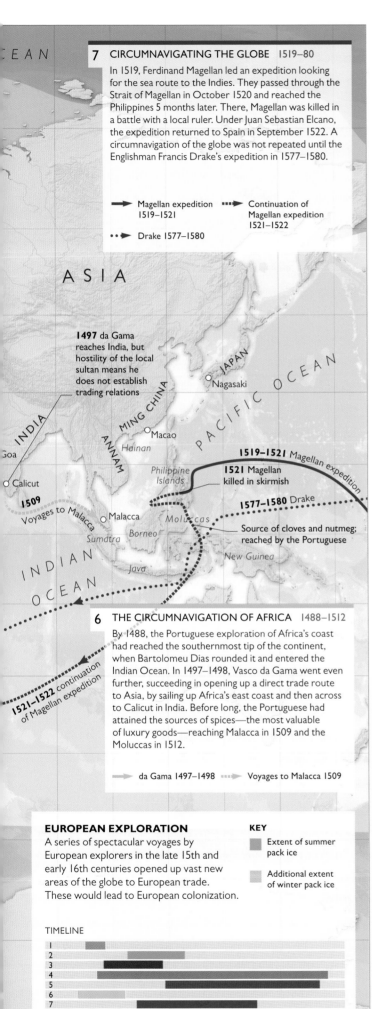

7 CIRCUMNAVIGATING THE GLOBE 1519–80

In 1519, Ferdinand Magellan led an expedition looking for the sea route to the Indies. They passed through the Strait of Magellan in October 1520 and reached the Philippines 5 months later. There, Magellan was killed in a battle with a local ruler. Under Juan Sebastian Elcano, the expedition returned to Spain in September 1522. A circumnavigation of the globe was not repeated until the Englishman Francis Drake's expedition in 1577–1580.

→ Magellan expedition 1519–1521
┈► Continuation of Magellan expedition 1521–1522
••► Drake 1577–1580

ASIA

1497 da Gama reaches India, but hostility of the local sultan means he does not establish trading relations

JAPAN

Nagasaki

PACIFIC OCEAN

MING CHINA

Macao

Hainan

ANNAM

INDIA

Goa

Calicut

1509 Voyages to Malacca

Philippine Islands

1519–1521 Magellan expedition

1521 Magellan killed in skirmish

1577–1580 Drake

Malacca

Moluccas

Borneo

Sumatra

Source of cloves and nutmeg; reached by the Portuguese

New Guinea

Java

INDIAN OCEAN

1521–1522 continuation of Magellan expedition

6 THE CIRCUMNAVIGATION OF AFRICA 1488–1512

By 1488, the Portuguese exploration of Africa's coast had reached the southernmost tip of the continent, when Bartolomeu Dias rounded it and entered the Indian Ocean. In 1497–1498, Vasco da Gama went even further, succeeding in opening up a direct trade route to Asia, by sailing up Africa's east coast and then across to Calicut in India. Before long, the Portuguese had attained the sources of spices—the most valuable of luxury goods—reaching Malacca in 1509 and the Moluccas in 1512.

→ da Gama 1497–1498   ┈► Voyages to Malacca 1509

EUROPEAN EXPLORATION

A series of spectacular voyages by European explorers in the late 15th and early 16th centuries opened up vast new areas of the globe to European trade. These would lead to European colonization.

KEY

▮ Extent of summer pack ice

▮ Additional extent of winter pack ice

TIMELINE

1 2 3 4 5 6 7

1470   1520   1570   1620

VOYAGES OF EXPLORATION

The 15th and 16th centuries saw a massive increase in the reach of European nations. Voyages set out in search of new routes to exploit the trade in luxury goods. Portuguese explorers pushed eastward, their Spanish counterparts voyaged west, and soon the English, French, and Dutch joined the scramble to find new lands.

The breakup of the Mongol Empire in the 14th century and expansion of the Ottoman Turks in the eastern Mediterranean blocked the Silk Road, which had been the traditional conduit for trade from Europe to east Asia. Maritime nations on Europe's western coasts began to explore alternative routes by which to access the rich east Asian trade in luxuries and, in particular, spices. From the mid-1420s Portuguese-sponsored voyages edged around the west coast of Africa. It took until 1497, however, for the Portuguese captain Vasco da Gama to circumnavigate Africa and reach the markets of India. By then, the Spanish-sponsored voyage of Christopher Columbus had encountered the coastline of the Americas. The Portuguese established a toehold in Brazil by 1500, and British and French expeditions tried to locate the "Northwest Passage" to access Asia by sailing north around North America.

More ambitious voyages yet circumnavigated the globe, beginning with that led by the Portuguese explorer Ferdinand Magellan in 1519. The consequences of these voyages were profound. Parts of the world that had had little or no communication with each other were now linked by trading routes and by networks of trading outposts. These were either directly state-controlled or governed by great trading corporations such as the British and Dutch East India Companies (founded in 1600 and 1602). Soldiers and settlers soon followed since what had originally been an effort to secure trading routes became the precursor to the establishment of global European empires.

△ A new world
This late-17th-century engraving by the Flemish-German publisher Theodor de Bry depicts Christopher Columbus arriving in the Americas and is part of a series that portrayed famous explorers surrounded by allegorical scenes.

SPANISH CONQUESTS IN THE AMERICAS

In the first half of the 16th century, the Spanish established a vast empire in the Americas. Their conquest of the rich native cultures of Mexico and Peru between 1519 and 1533 encouraged Spanish explorers to seize further large tracts of territory. They established an empire that remained in Spanish hands until a series of nationalist revolts in the 1800s.

Following Columbus's discovery of the Americas in 1492, initial Spanish efforts were focused on the Caribbean. However, there were few resources to exploit, and the collapse of the native population pushed Spanish adventurers onto the mainland. The conquest of the Aztec Empire by Hernán Cortés from 1519–1521 and of the Inca Empire of Peru by Francisco Pizarro from 1531–1533 (see pp.154–155) transformed the prospects for the Spanish possessions in the Americas. Christian missionaries soon followed in the wake of the conquistadors and made large numbers of converts among the Aztecs and Inca, whose central religious hierarchy had been swept away. These rich, centralized territories fell rapidly into the hands of the conquistadors and formed the nucleus from which

further Spanish expeditions fanned out across the continent—penetrating into Colombia and Venezuela in 1537–1543 and northward into Florida and the southwest of the modern United States in the 1540s.

The Spanish brought new diseases to the Americas (such as smallpox), and the native population had declined to around one-tenth its former level by 1600. However, throughout the 16th century there was also an influx of around 100,000 European settlers, the importation of African slaves to work plantations, and the discovery of rich silver deposits (in Peru in 1545 and in Mexico in 1546). The Spanish empire thrived and developed a distinctive colonial society that lasted until Spanish rule was overthrown by revolutionary nationalists in the early 19th century.

"I and my companions suffer from a disease of the heart, which can only be cured with gold."

HERNÁN CORTÉS, CONQUEROR OF MEXICO, c.1520

Spain and Portugal were very confident in their future pursuits of new lands. In 1493, the Spanish persuaded Pope Alexander VI to issue an edict, or decree, that set a dividing line to avoid disputes over any new territories either country might discover. After Portuguese lobbying, the Treaty of Tordesillas (1494) pushed the line westward, which placed Brazil within their sector. The Treaty of Zaragoza (1529) established an antimeridian demarcating Spanish and Portuguese territory in east Asia.

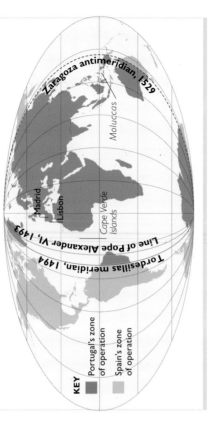

Zaragoza antimeridian, 1529
Moluccas
Madrid
Lisbon
Cape Verde Islands
Line of Pope Alexander VI, 1493
Tordesillas meridian, 1494

KEY
- Portugal's zone of operation
- Spain's zone of operation

1 CORTÉS AND MEXICO 1519–1524

The expedition of Hernán Cortés to Mexico in 1519 overwhelmed the rich Aztec Empire within 3 years. The centralized nature of the empire meant that the Spanish acquired all of its resources and tribute-bearing provinces, providing them with a base from which to move southward into the Yucatán Peninsula by 1524.

2 THE CONQUEST OF THE MAYA 1527–1697

The Maya of the Yucatán Peninsula were politically fragmented, and so the Spanish conquistadors had to reduce each Maya city-state individually. Francisco de Montejo began the process in 1527, but the only made significant progress in the 1540s. The last Maya city, Tayasal, finally fell to the Spanish in 1697.

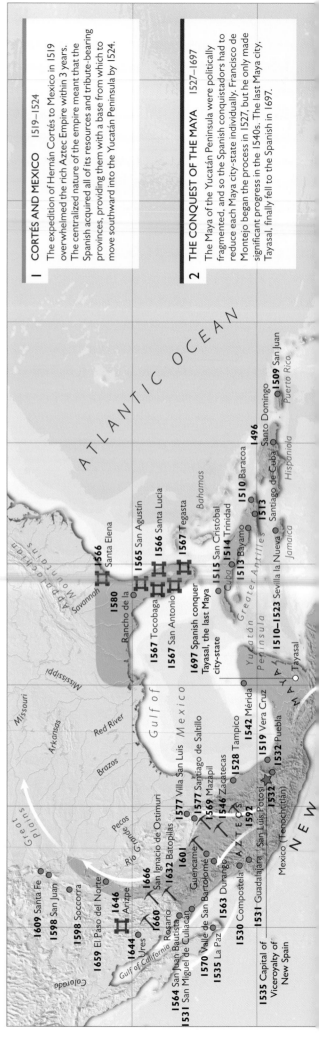

ATLANTIC OCEAN

1509 San Juan
Puerto Rico
Santo Domingo
Hispaniola
1496
1510 Baracoa
1513
Santiago de Cuba
1513 Bayamo
Jamaica
Greater Antilles
Cuba
1514 Trinidad
1515 San Cristóbal
Bahamas
1567 Tegasta
1566 Santa Lucía
1566 Tocobaga
1565 San Agustín
1567 San Antonio
1580
Rancho de la
Santa Elena
Savannah
Mississippi
Madre Mountains
Colorado
Missouri
Arkansas
Red River
Brazos
Pecos
Río Grande
Great Plains
Gulf of California
Gulf of Mexico
Mexico
Yucatán Peninsula
M A Y A
Tayasal
1697 Spanish conquer Tayasal, the last Maya city-state
1510–1523 Sevilla la Nueva
1542 Mérida
1519 Vera Cruz
1532 Puebla
1528 Tampico
1546 Zacatecas
1569 Mazapil
1577 Santiago de Saltillo
1601
1632 Batopilas
1666
San Ignacio de Ostimuri
Guencame
1592
A Z T E C S
Mexico (Tenochtitlán)
1531 Guadalajara
San Luis Potosí
1532
1535 Capital of Viceroyalty of New Spain
1530 Compostela
1563 Durango
1570 Valle de San Bartolomé
1535 La Paz
1531 San Miguel de Culiacán
1564 San Juan Bautista
Rosario
1660
1644
Ures
1646
Arizpe
1659 El Paso del Norte
1598 Soccorra
1598 San Juan
1609 Santa Fe
N E W

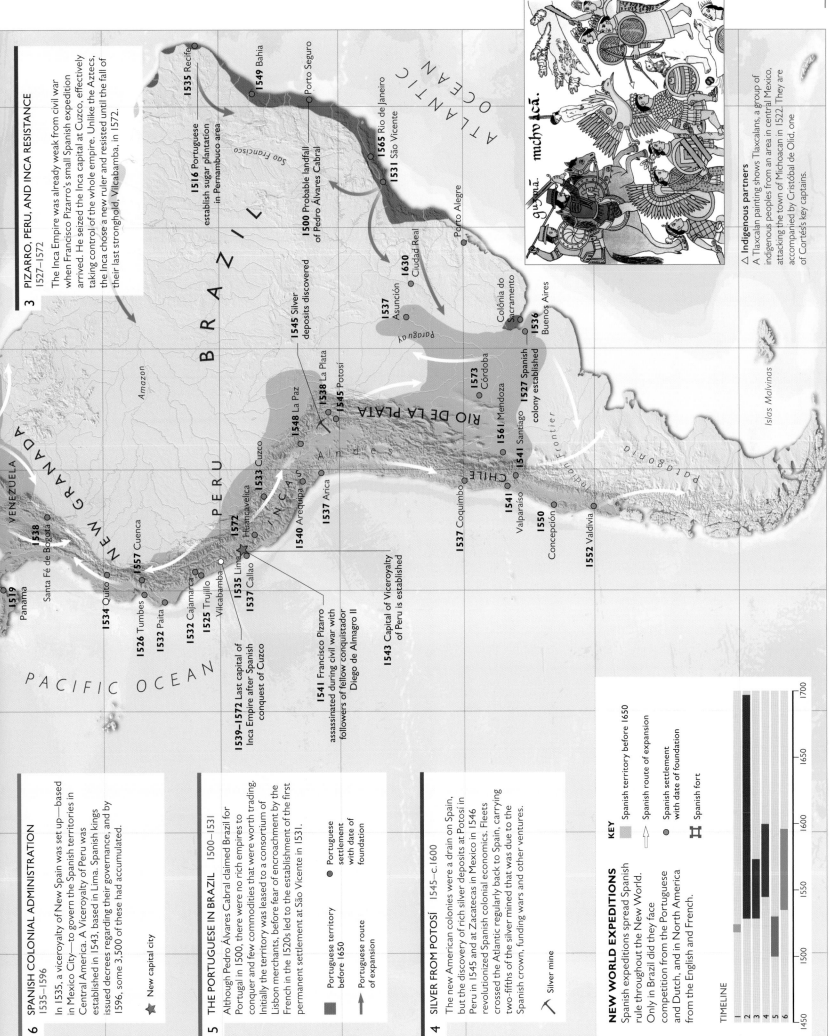

6 SPANISH COLONIAL ADMINISTRATION
1535–1596

In 1535, a viceroyalty of New Spain was set up—based in Mexico City—to govern the Spanish territories in Central America. A Viceroyalty of Peru was established in 1543, based in Lima. Spanish kings issued decrees regarding their governance, and by 1596, some 3,500 of these had accumulated.

★ New capital city

5 THE PORTUGUESE IN BRAZIL 1500–1531

Although Pedro Álvares Cabral claimed Brazil for Portugal in 1500, there were no rich empires to conquer and few commodities that were worth trading. Initially the territory was leased to a consortium of Lisbon merchants, before fear of encroachment by the French in the 1520s led to the establishment of the first permanent settlement at São Vicente in 1531.

■ Portuguese territory before 1650

● Portuguese settlement with date of foundation

➡ Portuguese route of expansion

4 SILVER FROM POTOSÍ 1545–c.1600

The new American colonies were a drain on Spain, but the discovery of rich silver deposits at Potosí in Peru in 1545 and at Zacatecas in Mexico in 1546 revolutionized Spanish colonial economics. Fleets crossed the Atlantic regularly back to Spain, carrying two-fifths of the silver that was due to the Spanish crown, funding wars and other ventures.

⚒ Silver mine

NEW WORLD EXPEDITIONS

Spanish expeditions spread Spanish rule throughout the New World. Only in Brazil did they face competition from the Portuguese and Dutch, and in North America from the English and French.

KEY

■ Spanish territory before 1650

⇨ Spanish route of expansion

● Spanish settlement with date of foundation

⊓ Spanish fort

TIMELINE

1450 1500 1550 1600 1650 1700

1
2
3
4
5
6

3 PIZARRO, PERU, AND INCA RESISTANCE
1527–1572

The Inca Empire was already weak from civil war when Francisco Pizarro's small Spanish expedition arrived. He seized the Inca capital at Cuzco, effectively taking control of the whole empire. Unlike the Aztecs, the Inca chose a new ruler and resisted until the fall of their last stronghold, Vilcabamba, in 1572.

1539–1572 Last capital of Inca Empire after Spanish conquest of Cuzco

1541 Francisco Pizarro assassinated during civil war with followers of fellow conquistador Diego de Almagro II

1543 Capital of Viceroyalty of Peru is established

1516 Portuguese establish sugar plantation in Pernambuco area

1500 Probable landfall of Pedro Álvares Cabral

1545 Silver deposits discovered

Map labels

PACIFIC OCEAN

ATLANTIC OCEAN

BRAZIL

PERU

NEW GRANADA

VENEZUELA

INCA

RIO DE LA PLATA

CHILE

Andes

Amazon

São Francisco

Paraguay

Patagonia

Indian Frontier

Islas Malvinas

1519 Panamá
Santa Fé de Bogotá
1538
1557 Cuenca
1534 Quito
1526 Tumbes
1532 Paita
1532 Cajamarca
1525 Trujillo
Vilcabamba
1572
1535 Lima
1537 Callao
Huancavelica
1533 Cuzco
1540 Arequipa
1537 Arica
1548 La Paz
1538 La Plata
1545 Potosí
1537 Coquimbo
1541 Valparaíso
1550 Concepción
1552 Valdivia
1541 Santiago
1561 Mendoza
1573 Córdoba
1527 Spanish colony established
1536 Buenos Aires
Colônia do Sacramento
1537 Asunción
1630 Ciudad Real
Porto Alegre
1531 São Vicente
1565 Rio de Janeiro
Porto Seguro
1549 Bahia
1535 Recife

△ **Indigenous partners**
A Tlaxcalan painting shows Tlaxcalans, a group of indigenous peoples from an area in central Mexico, attacking the town of Michoacan in 1522. They are accompanied by Cristóbal de Olid, one of Cortés's key captains.

guāmā. mchoícā.

THE SPANISH IN AMERICA

Within 25 years of their arrival, the Spanish ruled a vast colonial empire in the Americas. Their astonishing success was enabled by exploitation of the political weakness of indigenous empires, superior weaponry, and the diseases that came in their wake.

△ **Soldier-explorer**
Hernán Cortés had a reputation for ruthlessness. After founding the city of Vera Cruz, he burned his ships to prevent his forces from turning back.

The principal indigenous empires of the Americas, the Aztec of Mexico and the Inca of Peru (see pp.144–145), were highly centralized and dependent on rigid hierarchies and a deeply ingrained respect for their rulers—the Aztec *Tlatoani* in the capital Tenochtitlan and the Sapa Inca in Cuzco. These empires expanded rapidly by conquest in the 14th and 15th centuries, and their hold on recently conquered or peripheral peoples was fragile. When the Spanish arrived in Mexico in 1519 and in Peru in 1531, the Aztec and Inca leaders underestimated the threat they posed.

In Mexico, the Spanish formed alliances with dissenting groups, and in Peru, rapid and ruthless action led to the capture of the Sapa Inca, Atahualpa. Leaderless, the indigenous empires rapidly collapsed—a process accelerated by epidemics of diseases brought by the Spanish, to which native Americans had no resistance. Once embedded, the invaders—known as conquistadors—proved impossible to remove. A constant supply of ambitious yet landless men with military training from the Iberian Peninsula allowed the Spanish to absorb the Maya of Central America in the 1540s–1550s, push into southern North America, and extend into Amazonian South America. Financed by silver, which was discovered in Peru in 1545, and ruled through viceroys, the Spanish empire in South America would last for over 250 years (see pp.152–153).

CORTÉS'S CAMPAIGNS

Nov 1519 Cortés first enters Tenochtitlan

Dec 1520–Aug 1521 Cortés returns to Tenochtitlan and finally completes recapture

Spanish conquistador Hernán Cortés and his force of 600 men entered the Aztec capital Tenochtitlan in November 1519 and took the *Tlatoani* Montezuma captive. Although the Spanish were expelled with heavy losses in June 1520, they returned and took the city after an 8-month siege, putting an end to the Aztec Empire.

May 1520 Cortés defeats fellow conquistador Panfilo de Narvaez

Mar 1519 Cempoala

Yucatán

Feb 1519 Leaves Cuba

Tenochtitlán

Vera Cruz Tabasco

AZTEC MAYA

KEY
→ Cortés's route

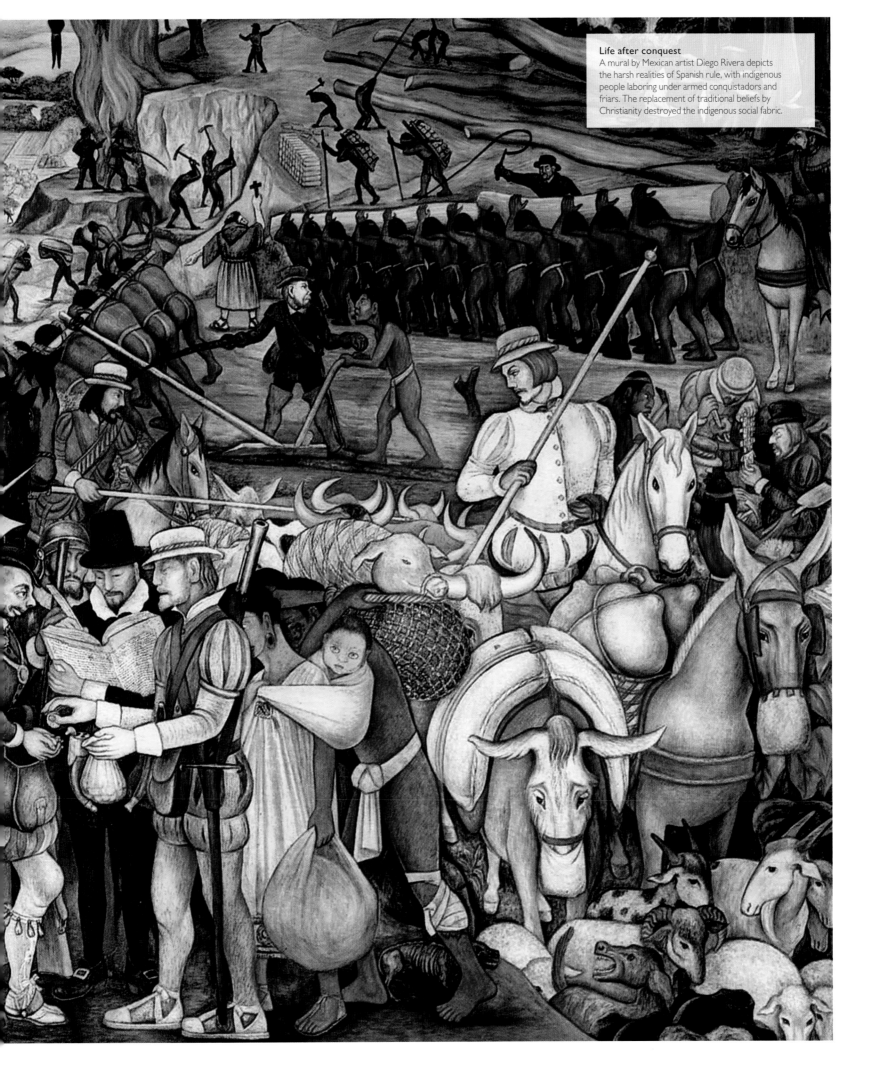

Life after conquest
A mural by Mexican artist Diego Rivera depicts the harsh realities of Spanish rule, with indigenous people laboring under armed conquistadors and friars. The replacement of traditional beliefs by Christianity destroyed the indigenous social fabric.

THE COLONIZATION OF NORTH AMERICA

The Europeans first successfully colonized North America in the early 17th century. While the French and Spanish colonies depended on their crowns for orders, the English colonies—founded by a mix of religious dissidents, merchant companies, and royal initiatives—operated at arm's length, gaining an advantage over their rivals.

In 1585, Sir Walter Raleigh attempted to found Roanoke as the first English colony of the New World, but the colony failed. The first successful English colony was Jamestown, founded in 1607. A century later, around 200,000 British migrants had arrived, and the number of British colonies in America had grown to 13. European slave traders also brought close to 175,000 African slaves to America to work on the plantations.

French settlers laid down roots in Quebec, Canada, in 1608, and started populating the St. Lawrence River basin and the accessible inland areas. They established forts as far south as New

Orleans, stoking a rivalry with the British that erupted in war in 1689. Meanwhile, the Spanish were unable to develop their fledgling colony in Florida or to capitalize on their explorations of the American Southwest, which had begun in the 1520s. Growing European presence disturbed local power structures, and Native American groups eventually fought to reclaim their lost land, beginning a phase of conflict that would last for almost three centuries. By the mid-1700s, tension was also increasing between the colonists themselves and their overseas rulers in Britain.

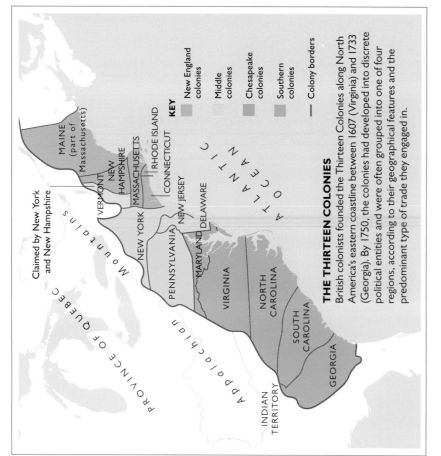

THE THIRTEEN COLONIES

British colonists founded the Thirteen Colonies along North America's eastern coastline between 1607 and 1733 (Georgia). By 1750, the colonies had developed into discrete political entities and were often grouped into one of four regions, according to their geographical features and the predominant type of trade they engaged in.

NORTH AMERICA COLONIZED, 1750

By 1750, the French and Spanish empires in North America were territorially larger than that of the British but were thinly populated, with a limited economic presence. In contrast, migrants were pouring into the British colonies, drawn by their rapidly growing economies.

KEY
- English, Scottish, or British territory, settlement
- Spanish territory, settlement
- French territory, settlement

TIMELINE

1 THE SPANISH IN FLORIDA 1565–1718

Spain was first to establish a European settlement in North America—St. Augustine, Florida, in 1565. Its initial colonial efforts had been focused on Mexico and Peru, where there was gold to acquire and empires to conquer. The Spanish were penned into Florida by the growth of English colonies to the north and the arrival of the French in New Orleans to the west in 1718.

→ Spanish migration route

2 NEW FRANCE 1605–1718

The French established a settlement at Port Royal in 1605 and then at Quebec (within the Canada colony—territory along the St. Lawrence River) in 1608. When Quebec fell to the English in 1629–1632, Scots founded the colony of Nova Scotia. The French had also claimed land along the Mississippi and named it Louisiana. France's North American colonies were known as New France.

→ French migration route

3 THE ARRIVAL OF THE ENGLISH 1620

In December 1620, nearly 100 English settlers, aboard the *Mayflower*, reached American shores seeking religious freedom and founded a settlement in Plymouth. Many perished during a difficult first winter, but the settlement survived with help from the Mashpee Wampanoag tribe. Over subsequent decades, more migrants arrived from Britain to colonize the eastern seaboard.

⇨ English or British migration route

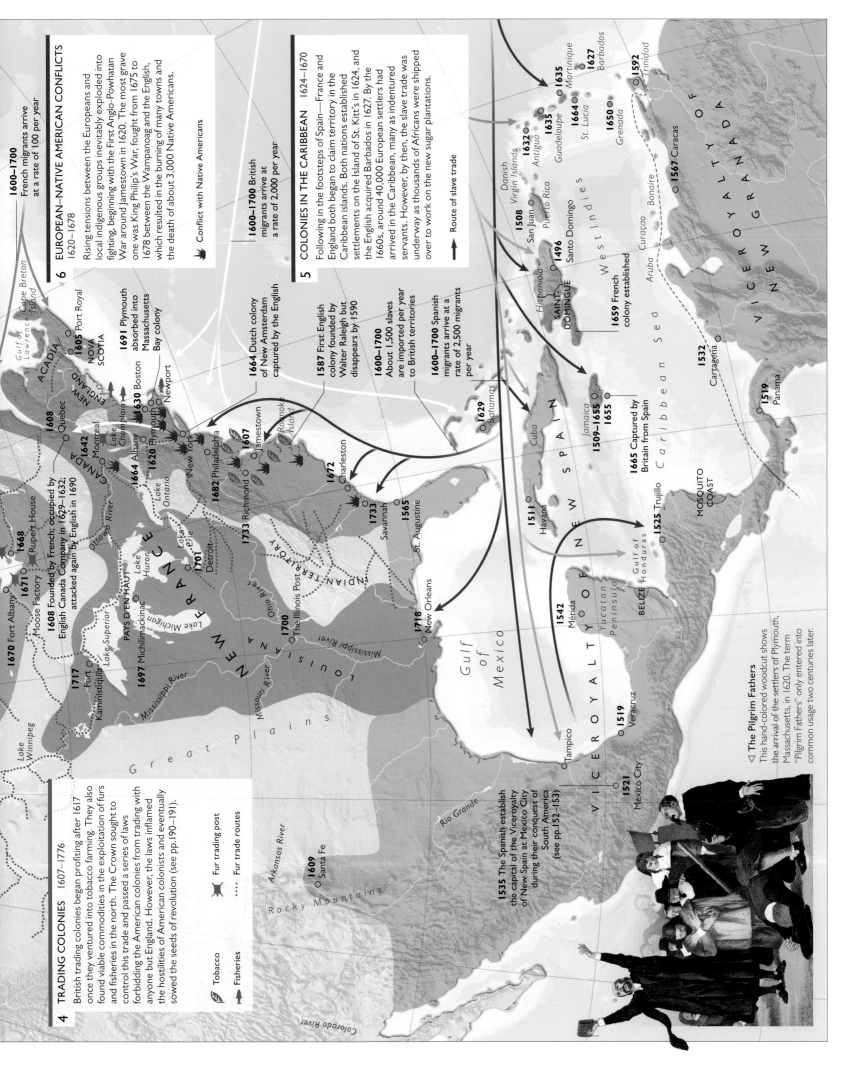

4 TRADING COLONIES 1607–1776

British trading colonies began profiting after 1617 once they ventured into tobacco farming. They also found viable commodities in the exploitation of furs and fisheries in the north. The Crown sought to control this trade and passed a series of laws forbidding the American colonies from trading with anyone but England. However, the laws inflamed the hostilities of American colonists and eventually sowed the seeds of revolution (see pp.190–191).

- 🌿 Tobacco
- Fisheries
- 🦫 Fur trading post
- ···· Fur trade routes

6 EUROPEAN–NATIVE AMERICAN CONFLICTS 1620–1678

Rising tensions between the Europeans and local indigenous groups inevitably exploded into fighting, beginning with the First Anglo-Powhatan War around Jamestown in 1620. The most grave one was King Philip's War, fought from 1675 to 1678 between the Wampanoag and the English, which resulted in the burning of many towns and the death of about 3,000 Native Americans.

- Conflict with Native Americans

5 COLONIES IN THE CARIBBEAN 1624–1670

Following in the footsteps of Spain—France and England both began to claim territory in the Caribbean islands. Both nations established settlements on the Island of St. Kitt's in 1624, and the English acquired Barbados in 1627. By the 1660s, around 40,000 European settlers had arrived in the Caribbean, many as indentured servants. However, by then, the slave trade was underway as thousands of Africans were shipped over to work on the new sugar plantations.

- → Route of slave trade

1600–1700 French migrants arrive at a rate of 100 per year

1600–1700 British migrants arrive at a rate of 2,000 per year

1664 Dutch colony of New Amsterdam captured by the English

1587 First English colony founded by Walter Raleigh but disappears by 1590

1691 Plymouth absorbed into Massachusetts Bay colony

1600–1700 About 1,500 slaves are imported per year to British territories

1600–1700 Spanish migrants arrive at a rate of 2,500 migrants per year

1659 French colony established

1535 The Spanish establish the capital of the Viceroyalty of New Spain at Mexico City during their conquest of South America (see pp.152–153)

◁ **The Pilgrim Fathers**
This hand-colored woodcut shows the arrival of the settlers at Plymouth, Massachusetts, in 1620. The term "Pilgrim Fathers" only entered into common usage two centuries later.

THE AGE OF EXCHANGE

Human migration across the world and the resulting exchange of food crops and animals started in Neolithic times, but it was not until 1492, when European explorers reached the New World (the Americas), that a biological exchange had such dramatic effects.

The domestication of crops occurred independently in various areas around the world between 11,000 BCE and 6000 BCE. Among the "founder crops" that formed the cornerstone of early agriculture, wheat was the first to be cultivated on a large scale in western Asia in about 9500 BCE, and rice emerged as a staple crop in east Asia 1,500 years later. Farming communities in the Americas, meanwhile, domesticated an entirely different set of crops owing to their complete isolation from the Old World (Africa, Asia, and Europe).

When European explorers reached the Americas in the late 15th century (see pp.150–151), the Old and New Worlds began to embark on an unprecedented level of biological exchange, in what would become known as the Columbian Exchange. Old World staples such as wheat, rice, pigs, cattle, and horses were introduced to the Americas, while New World foods such as tomatoes, corn, potatoes, and cassava were exported to the rest of the world. Tobacco and the furs of animals native to the Americas became highly profitable commodities that allowed settlers to finance their new colonies. However, not all aspects of the Columbian Exchange were positive. Disease traveled between the two worlds, with syphilis crossing into Europe and Old World diseases such as smallpox, measles, and influenza spreading to the Americas, decimating the native population. Consequently, European plantation owners replaced their depleted Native American workforce with slaves procured from Africa—leading to the displacement and deaths of tens of millions.

THE HORSE
THE IMPACT OF THE HORSE ON NATIVE AMERICAN TRIBES

Horses were reintroduced to the Americas in the late 15th century, when Christopher Columbus brought a herd of 25 animals with him on his second voyage to the continent. By 1750, the animal had dispersed into an area of 10 states known as the Great Plains and revolutionized the lives of the people living there. Almost overnight, Plains Indians found a superior animal with which to hunt their main food staple, buffalo.

Native American painting

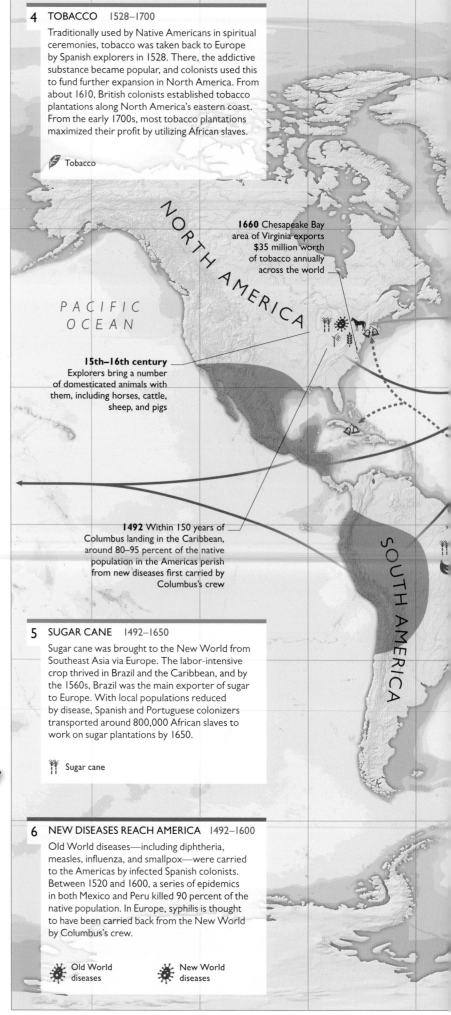

4 TOBACCO 1528–1700

Traditionally used by Native Americans in spiritual ceremonies, tobacco was taken back to Europe by Spanish explorers in 1528. There, the addictive substance became popular, and colonists used this to fund further expansion in North America. From about 1610, British colonists established tobacco plantations along North America's eastern coast. From the early 1700s, most tobacco plantations maximized their profit by utilizing African slaves.

🪶 Tobacco

1660 Chesapeake Bay area of Virginia exports $35 million worth of tobacco annually across the world

PACIFIC OCEAN

NORTH AMERICA

15th–16th century Explorers bring a number of domesticated animals with them, including horses, cattle, sheep, and pigs

1492 Within 150 years of Columbus landing in the Caribbean, around 80–95 percent of the native population in the Americas perish from new diseases first carried by Columbus's crew

SOUTH AMERICA

5 SUGAR CANE 1492–1650

Sugar cane was brought to the New World from Southeast Asia via Europe. The labor-intensive crop thrived in Brazil and the Caribbean, and by the 1560s, Brazil was the main exporter of sugar to Europe. With local populations reduced by disease, Spanish and Portuguese colonizers transported around 800,000 African slaves to work on sugar plantations by 1650.

🎋 Sugar cane

6 NEW DISEASES REACH AMERICA 1492–1600

Old World diseases—including diphtheria, measles, influenza, and smallpox—were carried to the Americas by infected Spanish colonists. Between 1520 and 1600, a series of epidemics in both Mexico and Peru killed 90 percent of the native population. In Europe, syphilis is thought to have been carried back from the New World by Columbus's crew.

☀ Old World diseases   ☀ New World diseases

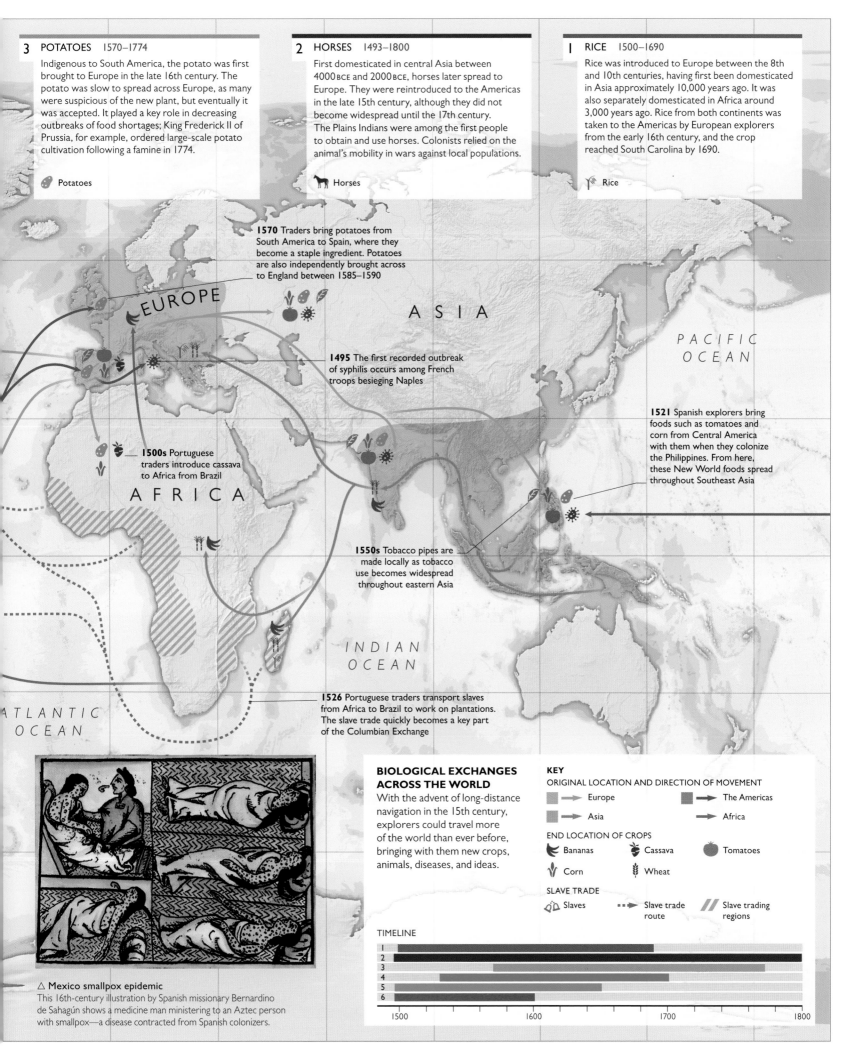

3 POTATOES 1570–1774

Indigenous to South America, the potato was first brought to Europe in the late 16th century. The potato was slow to spread across Europe, as many were suspicious of the new plant, but eventually it was accepted. It played a key role in decreasing outbreaks of food shortages; King Frederick II of Prussia, for example, ordered large-scale potato cultivation following a famine in 1774.

🥔 Potatoes

2 HORSES 1493–1800

First domesticated in central Asia between 4000 BCE and 2000 BCE, horses later spread to Europe. They were reintroduced to the Americas in the late 15th century, although they did not become widespread until the 17th century. The Plains Indians were among the first people to obtain and use horses. Colonists relied on the animal's mobility in wars against local populations.

🐎 Horses

1 RICE 1500–1690

Rice was introduced to Europe between the 8th and 10th centuries, having first been domesticated in Asia approximately 10,000 years ago. It was also separately domesticated in Africa around 3,000 years ago. Rice from both continents was taken to the Americas by European explorers from the early 16th century, and the crop reached South Carolina by 1690.

🌾 Rice

1570 Traders bring potatoes from South America to Spain, where they become a staple ingredient. Potatoes are also independently brought across to England between 1585–1590

EUROPE

ASIA

1495 The first recorded outbreak of syphilis occurs among French troops besieging Naples

PACIFIC OCEAN

1521 Spanish explorers bring foods such as tomatoes and corn from Central America with them when they colonize the Philippines. From here, these New World foods spread throughout Southeast Asia

1500s Portuguese traders introduce cassava to Africa from Brazil

AFRICA

1550s Tobacco pipes are made locally as tobacco use becomes widespread throughout eastern Asia

INDIAN OCEAN

1526 Portuguese traders transport slaves from Africa to Brazil to work on plantations. The slave trade quickly becomes a key part of the Columbian Exchange

ATLANTIC OCEAN

△ **Mexico smallpox epidemic**
This 16th-century illustration by Spanish missionary Bernardino de Sahagún shows a medicine man ministering to an Aztec person with smallpox—a disease contracted from Spanish colonizers.

BIOLOGICAL EXCHANGES ACROSS THE WORLD

With the advent of long-distance navigation in the 15th century, explorers could travel more of the world than ever before, bringing with them new crops, animals, diseases, and ideas.

KEY

ORIGINAL LOCATION AND DIRECTION OF MOVEMENT

- → Europe
- → Asia
- → The Americas
- → Africa

END LOCATION OF CROPS

- 🍌 Bananas
- 🌽 Corn
- 🥔 Cassava
- 🌾 Wheat
- 🍅 Tomatoes

SLAVE TRADE

- 👥 Slaves
- ∙∙∙→ Slave trade route
- ⫽ Slave trading regions

TIMELINE

	1500	1600	1700	1800
1				
2				
3				
4				
5				
6				

THE RENAISSANCE

In 15th-century Italy, a revival of interest in classical learning and secular studies, along with a flowering of artistic production, gave rise to the Renaissance (meaning "rebirth"). The movement soon spread to northern Europe, reshaping the continent's cultural landscape.

△ **Daring satire**
Written in 1509 by Desiderius Erasmus, *In Praise of Folly* pokes fun at some of the excesses of the contemporary Catholic Church and ends with a call for a return to a purer sense of Christian morality.

Knowledge of classical authors had declined in Europe after the fall of the Roman Empire in the 5th century, although Latin and Greek texts, particularly those dealing with law and the philosophy of Aristotle, had been rediscovered in the 11th and 12th centuries. This renewal, however, was based within the church and focused on a narrow curriculum designed for the education of clerics. Fourteenth-century Italy was made up of dozens of independent city-states. Most of these, such as Florence and Venice, were republics governed by their more prosperous citizens, made wealthy by the late medieval growth in trade and industry. The growth in secular wealth, uncontrolled by monarchs or the Catholic Church, slowly created a class of patrons whose interests inclined more toward the promotion of their own cities than praise for the Church.

Rediscovering the past

An awareness of past glories led to a thirst to recover the knowledge that had made the Roman Empire great. Scholars such as Poggio Bracciolini scoured the archives of monasteries looking for new texts—a search that yielded eight new speeches by the orator Cicero and a manuscript of the *Ten Books on Architecture* by Marcus Vitruvius Pollio. Although he served as papal secretary, Bracciolini formed part of a new humanist movement, which placed human nature—and not just God—at the center of its studies, encouraging a wider approach to education.

Artistic renaissance

Accompanying humanism was a new interest in the production of literature in vernacular languages, rather than Latin, which had been the medium of almost all

▷ **Patronage in art**
Florentine artist Sandro Botticelli painted *Primavera* (meaning "Spring") for a member of Florence's ruling Medici family. With its portrayal of Venus, the Three Graces, and Mercury, the painting is typical of the works of art commissioned by rich Italian patrons during the Renaissance.

EUROPE'S REBIRTH

Although there had been periods of cultural renewal in the 9th and 12th centuries, the Renaissance—which began in Italy in the 15th century—was remarkable in the breadth of artistic, literary, educational, and political endeavors it touched. Its first stirrings occurred in the 14th century, with paintings by artists such as Titian and Giotto di Bondone, and it continued to exert influence well into the 17th century. However, the key events of this movement took place in the 125 years from around 1400.

1345 Italian writer Francesco Petrarca (or Petrarch) rediscovers some letters written by the Roman politician and writer Cicero; their publication is credited with helping to initiate the Renaissance

1401 Florentine artist Lorenzo Ghiberti is commissioned to cast new doors for Florence cathedral's baptistry

LITERATURE

ARCHITECTURE

EDUCATION

PAINTING AND SCULPTURE

1360   1380   1400

1348–1353 Giovanni Bocaccio writes *The Decameron*, one of the best early works of Italian prose

1417 Bracciolini unearths a manuscript of *De Rerum Natura* ("Of the Nature of Things") by ancient Roman philosopher Lucretius

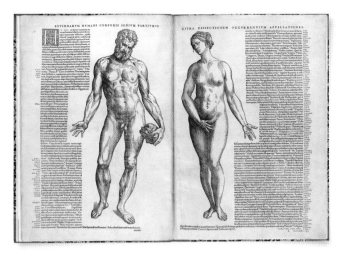

◁ **A revolution in anatomy**
The central illustration of Flemish anatomist Andreas Vesalius's *Epitome*, which was published in 1543, shows human anatomy in great detail. Vesalius revolutionized the study of the human body.

"The first thing I shall do as soon as the money arrives … buy some Greek authors; after that, I shall buy clothes."

DESIDERIUS ERASMUS, DUTCH SCHOLAR, 1498

scholarship for centuries. The Florentine poet Dante Alighieri was a pioneer in this; his *Divine Comedy* (1320) virtually invented the Italian literary language. By the 16th century, vernacular literatures had been firmly established in many countries, producing works as vibrant as the plays of William Shakespeare in England and the philosophy of Michel de Montaigne in France. The Dutch scholar Desiderius Erasmus pioneered a critical approach to historical analysis and penned *In Praise of Folly*, a satirical attack on religious superstition. An increase in literacy among the affluent and the invention of printing in the 1450s all helped loosen the hold of the Church—whose near-monopoly on the dissemination of manuscripts and on education provided in Europe's universities and theological schools had done much to stifle dissent. This in turn paved the way for the Reformation—a movement that questioned the excesses of the Church, as well as Catholic doctrine. By the 15th century, the wealthy patrons of the Italian city-states had begun to enrich their home towns with tangible signs of the new learning.

Italian artists had been experimenting since the early 14th century with new techniques, seeking to endow their work with a fresher and more realistic approach. Florentine artists such as Masaccio, who developed expertise in portraying nature and a depth in landscapes, were followed by generations of painters such as Sandro Botticelli, Leonardo da Vinci, and Raphael, whose works are considered among the greatest masterpieces in artistic history. Sculptors produced pieces of public art, such as the statue of David created by Michelangelo, which was placed outside the seat of Florence's city government. Architects, too, advanced their crafts, most notably Filippo Brunelleschi, who designed the *Duomo* at Florence, the largest masonry dome ever constructed.

Culmination of the movement

The movement spread rapidly, as Flemish masters such as Jan van Eyck and German scholars like Rudolph Agricola produced works inspired by advances in Italy. Its influence also extended to political thought, as Florentine historian Niccolò Machiavelli wrote a series of works examining how rulers should best govern. By the latter part of the 16th century, Italy's wealth and power had declined in comparison to other rising states such as France, England, and the Dutch Republic, and as its status as a cultural powerhouse waned, the Renaissance drew to a close.

▽ **Architectural feat**
Florence's cathedral, the *Duomo*, started in 1296, was still incomplete in 1418 when Filippo Brunelleschi won the competition to design its dome. He used innovative techniques to spread the dome's weight across the vast span.

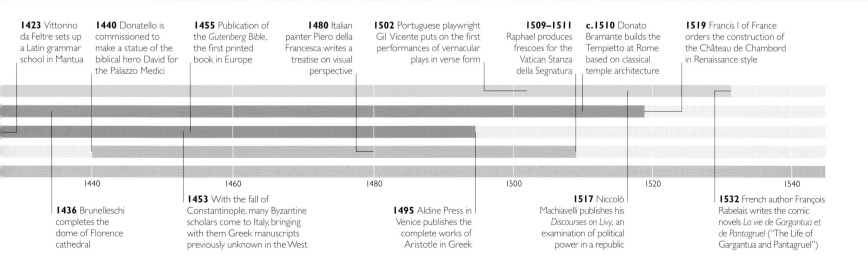

1423 Vittorino da Feltre sets up a Latin grammar school in Mantua

1440 Donatello is commissioned to make a statue of the biblical hero David for the Palazzo Medici

1455 Publication of the *Gutenberg Bible*, the first printed book in Europe

1480 Italian painter Piero della Francesca writes a treatise on visual perspective

1502 Portuguese playwright Gil Vicente puts on the first performances of vernacular plays in verse form

1509–1511 Raphael produces frescoes for the Vatican Stanza della Segnatura

c.1510 Donato Bramante builds the Tempietto at Rome based on classical temple architecture

1519 Francis I of France orders the construction of the Château de Chambord in Renaissance style

1440

1460

1480

1500

1520

1540

1436 Brunelleschi completes the dome of Florence cathedral

1453 With the fall of Constantinople, many Byzantine scholars come to Italy, bringing with them Greek manuscripts previously unknown in the West

1495 Aldine Press in Venice publishes the complete works of Aristotle in Greek

1517 Niccolò Machiavelli publishes his *Discourses on Livy*, an examination of political power in a republic

1532 French author François Rabelais writes the comic novels *La vie de Gargantua et de Pantagruel* ("The Life of Gargantua and Pantagruel")

THE COLONIAL SPICE TRADE

The discovery of a sea route from Europe to India in the late 15th century resulted in several European countries swiftly establishing fortified trading posts along the coast of sub-Saharan Africa and in south Asia. In doing so, these countries gained access to sources of spices—a product highly prized in European markets.

During medieval times, Asian spices such as nutmeg, cloves, and pepper reached Europe via overland routes and in doing so passed through the hands of many traders, which accounted for their high price. The aim of European exploration around the coastline of Africa was to find a route that would bypass Muslim-controlled areas of Asia and secure direct access to the sources of these spices.

Vasco Da Gama's pioneering voyage around Africa in 1497–1498 led to Portuguese fleets establishing posts in Mozambique (1505), Goa (1510), Hormuz (1515), and Malacca (1511). Spain, by contrast, largely confined itself to outposts in the Philippines (1565). Under Afonso de Albuquerque's governorship (1509–1515), Portugal took control of trade in the Indian Ocean but was superseded in 1609 by the Dutch, who established posts in the Moluccas (later known as the Spice Islands).

Britain, too, was attracted by the lucrative returns promised by the spice trade but, unable to break the Dutch monopoly in the Moluccas, turned its attention to India. From 1613, Britain's commercial arm, the British East India Company, set up a series of trading posts and factories in India and gained a foothold that would form the nucleus of its empire in the 18th century.

> "Nutmeges be good for them which have cold in their head and doth comforte the syght and the brain."
>
> ANDREW BORDE, FROM *DYETARY OF HELTH*, 1452

AMBOINA MASSACRE 1623
DUTCH MEASURES TO PROTECT THE SPICE TRADE

By 1621, the Dutch East India Company (VOC) fully controlled the islands in the Moluccas, gaining a monopoly on spices, such as nutmeg, mace, cloves, and pepper, that were cultivated exclusively in the region. In February 1623, the Dutch company allegedly foiled a terrorist plot by British merchants to infiltrate Amboina Island (now Ambon) and sieze the fort. The Dutch proceeded to arrest the guilty party (which also included Japanese and Portuguese personnel employed by the VOC), of which 20 were subsequently tortured and executed for acts against Dutch sovereignty.

1 EUROPEAN COLONIES IN AFRICA 1482–1721

Permanent European presence in sub-Saharan Africa began in 1482 with the Portuguese erecting the Elmina Castle (later a British possession) in modern Ghana, initially for trading gold. Further outposts were added at Kilwa, Mozambique, and Luanda, Angola. As focus shifted to the slave trade, the British, French, and Dutch began setting up posts along the African coastline. The Dutch took control of the Portuguese slave trading port at Delagoa Bay from 1721–1730.

▨ Area of European influence

1482 Portuga establishes fo taken over by Dutch in 163

1641–1648 Dutch occupy the island befo it returns to t Portuguese

1448 Explorer Diogo Cão claims Angola for the Portuguese

7 DUTCH VOC EXERT CONTROL 1602–1796

Founded in 1602, the Dutch East India Company, or VOC (*Verenigde Oost-Indische Compagnie*), financed trading operations throughout Southeast Asia. The VOC reached the Spice Islands in 1602 and dominated the spice trade for the next two centuries, stamping out periodic threats posed by the Portuguese, British, and native Bandanese. The company was nationalized in 1796.

- - ▶ Dutch trade routes   ○ Main base of VOC

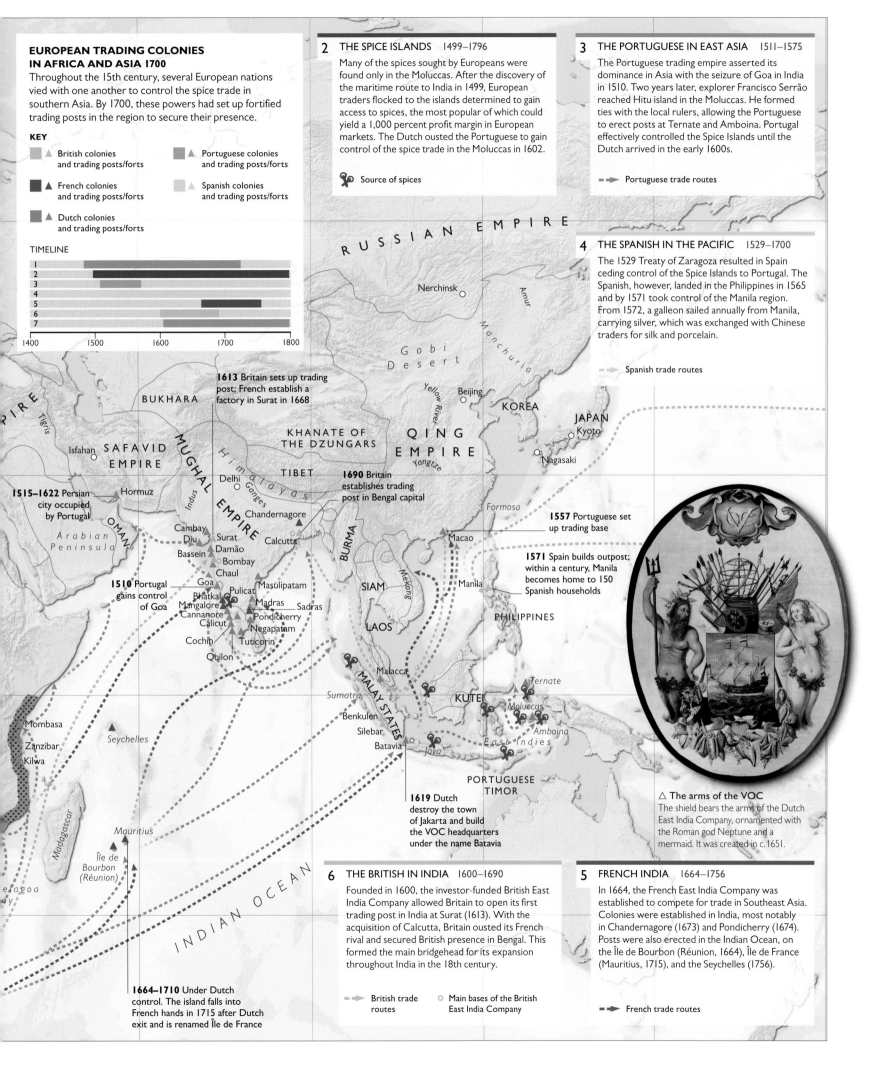

EUROPEAN TRADING COLONIES IN AFRICA AND ASIA 1700

Throughout the 15th century, several European nations vied with one another to control the spice trade in southern Asia. By 1700, these powers had set up fortified trading posts in the region to secure their presence.

KEY

▲ British colonies and trading posts/forts

▲ Portuguese colonies and trading posts/forts

▲ French colonies and trading posts/forts

▲ Spanish colonies and trading posts/forts

▲ Dutch colonies and trading posts/forts

TIMELINE

| | 1 | 2 | 3 | 4 | 5 | 6 | 7 |

1400 1500 1600 1700 1800

2 THE SPICE ISLANDS   1499–1796

Many of the spices sought by Europeans were found only in the Moluccas. After the discovery of the maritime route to India in 1499, European traders flocked to the islands determined to gain access to spices, the most popular of which could yield a 1,000 percent profit margin in European markets. The Dutch ousted the Portuguese to gain control of the spice trade in the Moluccas in 1602.

⚓ Source of spices

3 THE PORTUGUESE IN EAST ASIA   1511–1575

The Portuguese trading empire asserted its dominance in Asia with the seizure of Goa in India in 1510. Two years later, explorer Francisco Serrão reached Hitu island in the Moluccas. He formed ties with the local rulers, allowing the Portuguese to erect posts at Ternate and Amboina. Portugal effectively controlled the Spice Islands until the Dutch arrived in the early 1600s.

- - ▶ Portuguese trade routes

4 THE SPANISH IN THE PACIFIC   1529–1700

The 1529 Treaty of Zaragoza resulted in Spain ceding control of the Spice Islands to Portugal. The Spanish, however, landed in the Philippines in 1565 and by 1571 took control of the Manila region. From 1572, a galleon sailed annually from Manila, carrying silver, which was exchanged with Chinese traders for silk and porcelain.

- - ▶ Spanish trade routes

1613 Britain sets up trading post; French establish a factory in Surat in 1668

1515–1622 Persian city occupied by Portugal

1510 Portugal gains control of Goa

1690 Britain establishes trading post in Bengal capital

1557 Portuguese set up trading base

1571 Spain builds outpost; within a century, Manila becomes home to 150 Spanish households

1619 Dutch destroy the town of Jakarta and build the VOC headquarters under the name Batavia

△ **The arms of the VOC**
The shield bears the arms of the Dutch East India Company, ornamented with the Roman god Neptune and a mermaid. It was created in c.1651.

1664–1710 Under Dutch control. The island falls into French hands in 1715 after Dutch exit and is renamed Île de France

6 THE BRITISH IN INDIA 1600–1690

Founded in 1600, the investor-funded British East India Company allowed Britain to open its first trading post in India at Surat (1613). With the acquisition of Calcutta, Britain ousted its French rival and secured British presence in Bengal. This formed the main bridgehead for its expansion throughout India in the 18th century.

- - ▶ British trade routes

○ Main bases of the British East India Company

5 FRENCH INDIA 1664–1756

In 1664, the French East India Company was established to compete for trade in Southeast Asia. Colonies were established in India, most notably in Chandernagore (1673) and Pondicherry (1674). Posts were also erected in the Indian Ocean, on the Île de Bourbon (Réunion, 1664), Île de France (Mauritius, 1715), and the Seychelles (1756).

- - ▶ French trade routes

PRINTING

The invention of the printing press revolutionized the spread of knowledge. Books that previously had to be laboriously copied by hand could now be printed in the hundreds or thousands for a wider market.

△ **Antique print**
This is a page from the *Diamond Sutra*, the world's oldest dated printed book. It was produced in 868 CE using wood-block printing techniques, and rediscovered in western China in 1907.

Printing was not a new technology. Engraved wooden blocks had been used for printing in east Asia since the 2nd century CE. In 1041, Chinese inventor Bi Sheng came up with movable type, which meant new pages could be composed rapidly without having to engrave a new block each time. However, the key innovation in printing came in 1439 with German printer Johannes Gutenberg's printing press. By using a long lever and a screw to press down on paper laid over a wooden tray in which inked type was arrayed, it could accurately create printed sheets at a rate of more than 200 per hour.

Reaching a wider audience

Gutenberg set up his printing press in Mainz, Germany, in the early 1440s, and by 1455, he had produced his *Forty-two-line Bible*, one of the most famous works ever printed. From here, the technique spread quickly, and by 1500, around 60 German towns had printing presses. Printing reached Italy in 1465, France in 1470, and England by 1476. It made larger editions of books practical, helping the new humanist ideas that were emerging as part of the Renaissance (see pp.104–105) to spread more rapidly. Cheaper in the long run to produce than handwritten manuscripts, these editions were affordable to wider social groups and helped advance literacy. Although Gutenberg could not have known it, he had unleashed a knowledge revolution.

◁ **World's first newspaper**
Relation Aller Fürnemmen und Gedenckwürdigen Historien (Collection of all Distinguished and Commemorable News), probably the world's first newspaper, was printed by German publisher Johann Carolus at Strasbourg in 1605.

"The present book of the Psalms … has been fashioned by an ingenious invention of printing …"

FROM THE PSALMS PRINTED BY FUST AND SCHOEFFER, 1457

THE REFORMATION

Long-standing dissatisfaction at the conduct of the Roman Catholic Church led to a schism in 1517, causing Reformed (or Protestant) churches to spring up throughout Europe. A period of hostility followed as Catholic states tried to reassert papal authority.

In 1517, Martin Luther, a German Augustinian friar, composed his *Ninety-five Theses*—a tract condemning many of the practices of the Roman Catholic Church. The Church's hostile reaction forced Luther to reject the Catholic hierarchy and adopt a new theological position. He attracted large numbers of supporters, who formed the nucleus of the Reformed churches which proliferated throughout the German states. Once German princes began supporting this movement, a series of religious wars broke out. Amid the hostilities, more radical Protestant reformers appeared, such as Calvin in Switzerland, while

> *"A simple layman armed with Scripture is greater than the mightiest pope without it."*
>
> MARTIN LUTHER, 1519

the English and Swedish kings either rejected papal authority or even adopted Protestantism, increasing the geographical spread of Reformed churches. In 1542, the Catholic church council at Trent strengthened the education of the clergy and clamped down on its more dubious practices, and in 1555, a peace agreement was brokered at Augsburg, granting limited religious tolerance to Protestants. The peace, however, was brittle at best, and renewed religious conflict broke out in France in the 1560s and simmered elsewhere, too, before exploding anew in 1618 in the Thirty Years' War (see pp.168–169).

ST. BARTHOLOMEW'S DAY MASSACRE
A BLOODY EPISODE IN FRENCH HISTORY

On August 24, 1572, on the instruction of the Queen Mother, King Charles IX of France ordered the assassination of Huguenot Protestant leaders in Paris. Among those marked for death was the Huguenot leader, Admiral Gaspard de Coligny, who was brutally beaten and thrown out of his bedroom window just before dawn. The act set off a wave of mass fanaticism as Catholic mobs took to the streets and massacred 10,000–20,000 Protestants throughout the country.

RELIGIOUS MAP OF EUROPE

A powerful force of revivalism swept across Europe following Martin Luther's attack on the Roman Catholic Church in 1517. Secular rulers in Germany and Scandinavia established Protestantism along Lutheran lines. Calvinism became dominant in the Netherlands, Scotland, and Eastern Europe, while Anglicanism emerged in England.

KEY

■ Catholic majority areas 1555

▬ Frontier of the Roman Holy Empire c. 1570

■ Protestant majority areas 1555

TIMELINE

	1500	1520	1540	1560	1580	1600
1						
2						
3						
4						
5						
6						
7						

1 THE *NINETY-FIVE THESES*   1517–1521

Martin Luther pinned his *Ninety-five Theses*, to the door of Wittenberg Castle Church in October 1517. The document listed 95 complaints against the Church and adopted new theological positions on topics such as salvation and the interpretation of communion. The tract caused a huge stir throughout Europe, and led to his excommunication by the Catholic Church in 1521.

◆ Birthplace of Lutheranism   ➡ Spread of Lutheranism

▬ Lutheran areas

2 CATHOLIC-PROTESTANT CONFLICT   1530–1555

In 1530, the Holy Roman Emperor Charles V ordered all Protestant churches to abandon their reforms, sparking a series of wars in the 1540s and 1550s. Eventually, peace was brokered in 1555 at Augsburg, Germany, with the Catholic Church agreeing to accept Protestantism but only in those German states that had already adopted the religion.

🤝 Site of Augsburg Agreement

3 RELIGIOUS CONFLICT IN FRANCE   1534–1598

Religious wars initially broke out in 1534 after King Francis I (r. 1515–1537) tried to repress Protestantism on French soil. On St. Bartholomew's Day in 1572, thousands of Protestants, known as Huguenots, were massacred in Paris. In 1598, Henri IV (r. 1589–1610), a former Huguenot, issued the Edict of Nantes, which tolerated Protestantism in France. Protestants also faced persecution in London and Rome.

✝ Site of persecution   🤝 Edict of Nantes

● Huguenot centers

4 CALVINISM   1540–1600

The French theologian John Calvin established a Protestant community in Geneva in the 1540s. His movement advanced a theology more radical than that of Luther, emphasizing God's sovereignty and the doctrine of predestination. Calvinism spread rapidly in France, the German states, the Netherlands, Scotland, and many parts of central Europe.

▬ Calvinism   ➡ Spread of Calvinism

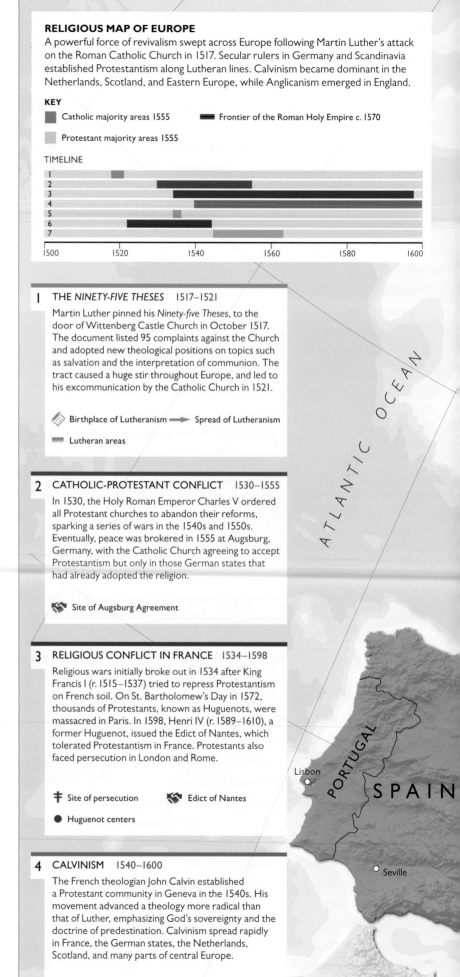

5 THE CHURCH OF ENGLAND 1531–1534

The Reformation made little headway in England until King Henry VIII (r. 1509–1547) quarreled with the Papacy over his decision to divorce (an act forbidden by Catholic canon law) his wife, Catherine of Aragon. He rejected papal supremacy and established in 1534, through the Act of Supremacy, the Church of England and introduced Protestantism to England.

▬ Church of England

6 THE REFORMATION IN SWEDEN 1523–1544

As Lutheran ideas spread across Sweden, King Gustavus Vasa (r. 1523–1560) sought to establish a national church, still in communion with the papacy. However, following an assembly led by reformer Olavus Petri at Västeras in 1527, Catholic Church property was seized. In 1544, Sweden was officially declared a Protestant nation.

✷ Site of Västeras assembly

7 THE COUNTER-REFORMATION 1545–1563

The three sessions held by the General Council of Trent between 1545 and 1563 was the high point of the Catholic Reformation. The Church hierarchy upheld papal supremacy and core Catholic doctrines, but reformed education of the clergy and banned abuses such as the sale of Indulgences—where a penitent was able to gain absolution for a monetary contribution.

✷ Site of Council of Trent

SCOTLAND

1559 Calvinist reformer John Knox returns to Scotland, beginning the Reformation there

Edinburgh

ELAND

Dublin

York

North Sea

1521 Imperial Diet orders Luther to recant; Luther's refusal forces him to go into hiding

ENGLAND

London ✝

1572 St. Bartholomew's Day Massacre of Protestants aggravates religious civil war in France

NETHERLANDS

Rouen ✝

Meaux ✝✝

Paris ✝

Nantes

Orléans ✝

Troyes

Bourges ✝

FRANCE

Cognac ✝

Bordeaux ✝

1536 Protestant reformer John Calvin publishes his *Institutes of the Christian Religion*

Barcelona

Saragossa

Balearic Islands

1555 Peace of Augsburg determines that religion in German states be determined by their ruling power

SARDINIA

Mediterranean Sea

DENMARK-NORWAY

1527 Church synod disendows monasteries, weakening the Catholic Church

SWEDEN

Västeras

Stockholm

Uppsala

Copenhagen

1593 Swedish Church becomes Lutheran and adopts the Augsburg Confession of Faith

Hamburg

Berlin

SMALL GERMAN STATES

Wittenberg

Worms

Prague

AUSTRIA

Augsburg

FRANCHE COMTÉ

Zürich

SWISS CONFEDERATION

Lyon

Geneva

SAVOY

Milan

Trent

Venice

Genoa

Florence

Papal States

Adriatic Sea

Rome ✝

Naples

RUSSIA

Riga

PRUSSIA

POLAND-LITHUANIA

Cracow

1545 First session of Catholic Church Council opens the Counter-Reformation

HUNGARY

Buda

Debrecen

MOLDAVIA

TRANSYLVANIA

WALLACHIA

Belgrade

OTTOMAN EMPIRE

Toulouse ✝

Avignon

Aix ✝

▷ **Martin Luther**
German theologian Martin Luther forever changed Christianity when he began the Protestant Reformation in 16th-century Europe.

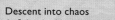

Descent into chaos
As Sebastien Vrancx records in his 1620 painting, widespread looting and plundering by soldiers was rife during the Thirty Years' War—by both sides—and there are numerous first-hand accounts of the atrocities committed.

THE THIRTY YEARS' WAR

When war broke out in 1618, it concerned the rights of Protestant minorities in Bohemia. But the fighting spread, pitting the Catholic rulers of Austria, Bavaria, and the Holy Roman Empire against German Protestant princes and, eventually, several foreign powers.

The Peace of Augsburg in 1555 (see pp.166–167) led to an agreement that each ruler in the Holy Roman Empire should be able to choose between Catholicism or Protestantism as their realm's religion, but a simmering tension still existed between Catholics and Protestants.

The pressure finally boiled over in 1617, when Catholic zealot Ferdinand, Archduke of Styria, was named as King of Bohemia, a primarily Protestant realm. Bohemian Protestants feared for their religious freedom and revolted in May 1618. The conflict that then erupted spread across Greater Bohemia. Imperial forces, supported by Spain, eventually crushed the rebellion at the Battle of White Mountain (1620) and enforced Catholicism as the Bohemian state religion.

Over several years, resentment of the Catholic regime grew and set the stage for neighboring Protestant states to wage war against the empire, starting with Denmark (1625–1629), followed by Sweden (1630–1635), and finally France (1635–1648), which, though Catholic, fought on the Protestant side.

The Thirty Years' War was one of the most intensely fought and devastating wars in European history and reduced the empire's population of 20–25 million by one-third. Peace would finally be brokered in 1648, bringing about an end to widespread Protestant discrimination and the European Wars of Religion.

▷ **King of Sweden (r. 1611–1632)**
Gustavus led his country to military supremacy during the Thirty Years' War, smashing the Imperial army at Breitenfeld in 1631 (right) and overrunning much of Germany and Bohemia. His death during Sweden's victory at the Battle of Lützen in 1632 slowed Sweden's progress.

"All the things that happened in this robber-war can barely be described."

PETER THIELE, EYEWITNESS ACCOUNT

BRITISH CIVIL WARS

In the 1640s and early 1650s, the British Isles were engulfed in a series of intertwined wars, as a king with tendencies to be an absolute monarch tried to take on Parliament. What resulted was a short-lived republican revolution, during which radical political groups pushed for radical social and political reforms.

By the 16th century, it had become customary that English monarchs had to seek parliamentary approval for most taxation. Charles I had to pay for wars against France and Spain in 1636–1637 and Scotland in 1639–1640, but until 1640, he resorted to expedients that did not need parliamentary approval, such as Ship Money, an antiquated naval tax. He avoided summoning Parliament from 1629 to 1640, which led to suspicions that he wanted to dispense with it. Meanwhile, a tide of Puritanism, a radical religious strain that opposed the traditional hierarchy of the Church of England, was rising. Parliament

insisted on stronger powers, which complicated negotiations with the king, and in 1642, war broke out between royalists and parliamentarians.

In the First Civil War, parliamentary armies under the guidance of Oliver Cromwell left the royalist side utterly defeated. The king turned to the Scots during the Second Civil War, but a Scottish-backed invasion failed. Charles was tried and executed, then his son, Charles II, was defeated in the Third Civil War. Political radicals then installed an English Republic which, slightly moderated under the rule of Oliver Cromwell as Lord Protector, lasted until 1660.

OLIVER CROMWELL
1599–1658

Oliver Cromwell was a Puritan who became a member of parliament (MP) in 1628. He rose to prominence in Britain during the Civil Wars. In 1645, Cromwell became second in command of the New Model Army. This radically new army thrived on its focus on a person's ability, rather than social standing. It was based on light armed cavalry, which greatly increased its speed of attack. Cromwell rose to commander of the parliamentary army in 1650. During the English Republic, he was appointed Lord Protector, a role with quasi-monarchical powers, to stem a rising tide of radicalism. He occupied this position until his death.

"I shall go from a corruptible to an incorruptible Crown, where no disturbance can be."

CHARLES I'S LAST WORDS BEFORE HIS EXECUTION. 1649

PARLIAMENTARY UPRISING

Struggles between king and Parliament led to three Civil Wars, which involved England, Scotland, Wales, and Ireland and ended with a short-lived English Republic. The king gradually lost land to Parliament, leaving him with only isolated strongholds.

TIMELINE

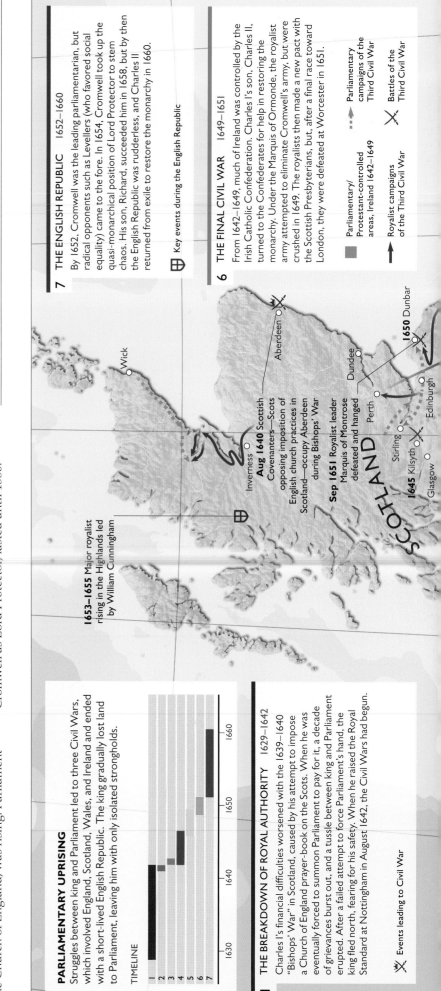

7 THE ENGLISH REPUBLIC 1652–1660

By 1652, Cromwell was the leading parliamentarian, but radical opponents such as Levellers (who favored social equality) came to the fore. In 1654, Cromwell took up the quasi-monarchical position of Lord Protector to stem chaos. His son, Richard, succeeded him in 1658, but by then the English Republic was rudderless, and Charles II returned from exile to restore the monarchy in 1660.

✠ Key events during the English Republic

6 THE FINAL CIVIL WAR 1649–1651

From 1642–1649, much of Ireland was controlled by the Irish Catholic Confederation. Charles I's son, Charles II, turned to the Confederates for help in restoring the monarchy. Under the Marquis of Ormonde, the royalist army attempted to eliminate Cromwell's army, but were crushed in 1649. The royalists then made a new pact with the Scottish Presbyterians, but, after a final race toward London, they were defeated at Worcester in 1651.

◼ Parliamentary/
Protestant-controlled
areas, Ireland 1642–1649

⇢ Parliamentary
campaigns of the
Third Civil War

➤ Royalist campaigns
of the Third Civil War

✗ Battles of the
Third Civil War

1 THE BREAKDOWN OF ROYAL AUTHORITY 1629–1642

Charles I's financial difficulties worsened with the 1639–1640 "Bishops' War" in Scotland, caused by his attempt to impose a Church of England prayer-book on the Scots. When he was eventually forced to summon Parliament to pay for it, a decade of grievances burst out, and a tussle between king and Parliament erupted. After a failed attempt to force Parliament's hand, the king fled north, fearing for his safety. When he raised the Royal Standard at Nottingham in August 1642, the Civil Wars had begun.

✗ Events leading to Civil War

1653–1655 Major royalist rising in the Highlands led by William Cunningham

Wick

Aberdeen

Aug 1640 Scottish Covenanters—Scots opposing imposition of English church practices in Scotland—occupy Aberdeen during Bishops' War

Inverness

1650 Dunbar

Dundee

Sep 1651 Royalist leader Marquis of Montrose defeated and hanged

Perth

Stirling

1645 Kilsyth

SCOTLAND

Glasgow
Edinburgh

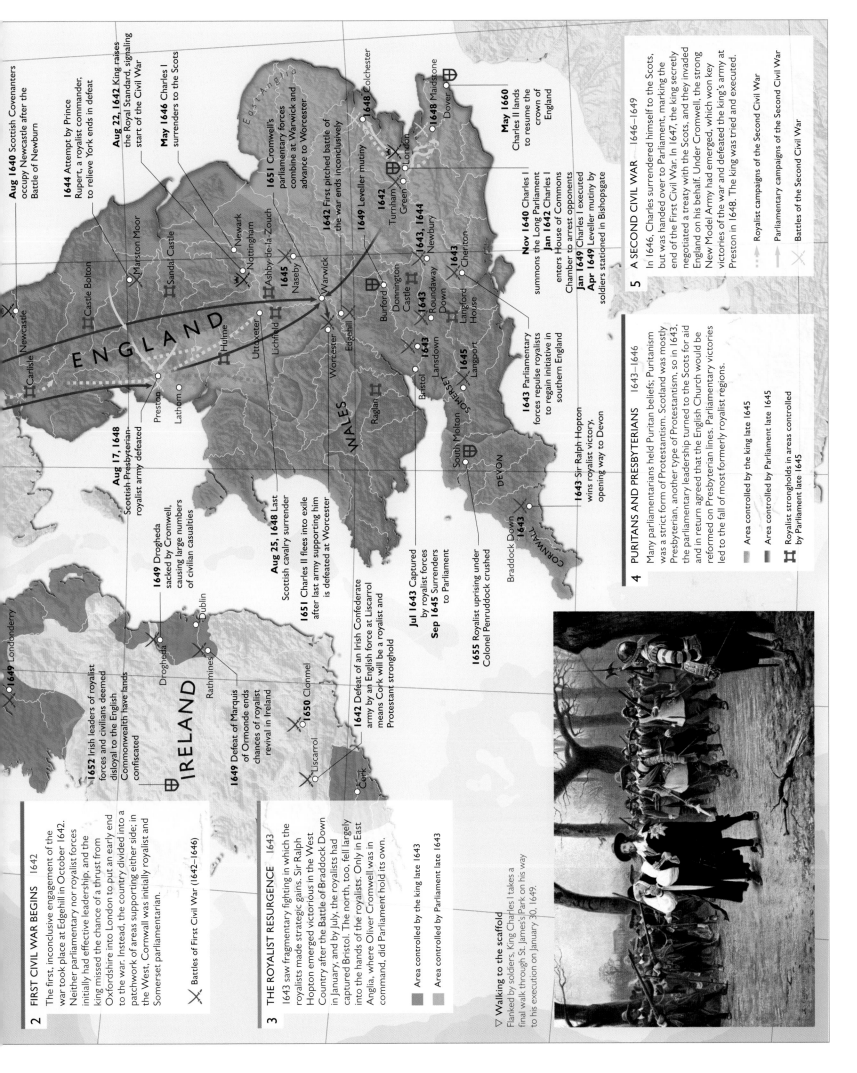

2 FIRST CIVIL WAR BEGINS 1642

The first, inconclusive engagement of the war took place at Edgehill in October 1642. Neither parliamentary nor royalist forces initially had effective leadership, and the king missed the chance of a thrust from Oxfordshire into London to put an early end to the war. Instead, the country divided into a patchwork of areas supporting either side; in the West, Cornwall was initially royalist and Somerset parliamentarian.

✕ Battles of First Civil War (1642–1646)

- Area controlled by the king late 1643
- Area controlled by Parliament late 1643

3 THE ROYALIST RESURGENCE 1643

1643 saw fragmentary fighting in which the royalists made strategic gains. Sir Ralph Hopton emerged victorious in the West Country after the Battle of Braddock Down in January, and by July, the royalists had captured Bristol. The north, too, fell largely into the hands of the royalists. Only in East Anglia, where Oliver Cromwell was in command, did Parliament hold its own.

▽ **Walking to the scaffold**
Flanked by soldiers, King Charles I takes a final walk through St. James's Park on his way to his execution on January 30, 1649.

4 PURITANS AND PRESBYTERIANS 1643–1646

Many parliamentarians held Puritan beliefs; Puritanism was a strict form of Protestantism. Scotland was mostly Presbyterian, another type of Protestantism, so in 1643, the parliamentary leadership turned to the Scots for aid and in return agreed that the English Church would be reformed on Presbyterian lines. Parliamentary victories led to the fall of most formerly royalist regions.

- Area controlled by the king late 1645
- Area controlled by Parliament late 1645
- ⌗ Royalist strongholds in areas controlled by Parliament late 1645

5 A SECOND CIVIL WAR 1646–1649

In 1646, Charles surrendered himself to the Scots, but was handed over to Parliament, marking the end of the First Civil War. In 1647, the king secretly negotiated a treaty with the Scots, and they invaded England on his behalf. Under Cromwell, the strong New Model Army had emerged, which won key victories of the war and defeated the king's army at Preston in 1648. The king was tried and executed.

- → Royalist campaigns of the Second Civil War
- ⇢ Parliamentary campaigns of the Second Civil War
- ✕ Battles of the Second Civil War

Map labels and annotations

Aug 1640 Scottish Covenanters occupy Newcastle after the Battle of Newburn

1644 Attempt by Prince Rupert, a royalist commander, to relieve York ends in defeat

Aug 22, 1642 King raises the Royal Standard, signaling start of the Civil War

May 1646 Charles I surrenders to the Scots

1651 Cromwell's parliamentary forces combine at Warwick and advance to Worcester

1642 First pitched battle of the war ends inconclusively

1649 Leveller mutiny

1648 Colchester

1648 Maidstone

1648 Charles I lands to resume the crown of England

May 1660 Charles II lands to resume the crown of England

1642 Turnham Green

London

1643, 1644 Newbury

1643 Cheriton

Nov 1640 Charles I summons the Long Parliament

Jan 1642 Charles I enters House of Commons Chamber to arrest opponents

Jan 1649 Charles I executed

Apr 1649 Leveller mutiny by soldiers stationed in Bishopsgate

1643 Parliamentary forces repulse royalists to regain initiative in southern England

1643 Sir Ralph Hopton wins royalist victory, opening way to Devon

Newcastle
Carlisle
Castle Bolton
Marston Moor
Sandal Castle
Newark
Nottingham
Ashby-de-la-Zouch
Holme
Uttoxeter
Lichfield
1645 Naseby
Warwick
Edgehill
Worcester
Burford
Donnington Castle
1643 Roundaway Down
1643 Langford House
Lansdown
Bristol
1645 Langport
Raglan
South Molton
Braddock Down **1643**
CORNWALL
DEVON
SOMERSET
WALES
ENGLAND
East Anglia
Dover

Aug 17, 1648 Scottish-Presbyterian-royalist army defeated

1649 Drogheda sacked by Cromwell, causing large numbers of civilian casualties

Aug 25, 1648 Last Scottish cavalry surrender

1651 Charles II flees into exile after last army supporting him is defeated at Worcester

Jul 1643 Captured by royalist forces
Sep 1645 Surrenders to Parliament

1655 Royalist uprising under Colonel Penruddock crushed

1649 Londonderry

1652 Irish leaders of royalist forces and civilians deemed disloyal to the English Commonwealth have lands confiscated

1649 Defeat of Marquis of Ormonde ends chances of royalist revival in Ireland

1642 Defeat of an Irish Confederate army by an English force at Liscarrol means Cork will be a royalist and Protestant stronghold

Dublin
Drogheda
Rathmines
1650 Clonmel
1649 Liscarrol
Cork
IRELAND

Prestor
Lathom

Carlisle

Castle Bolton

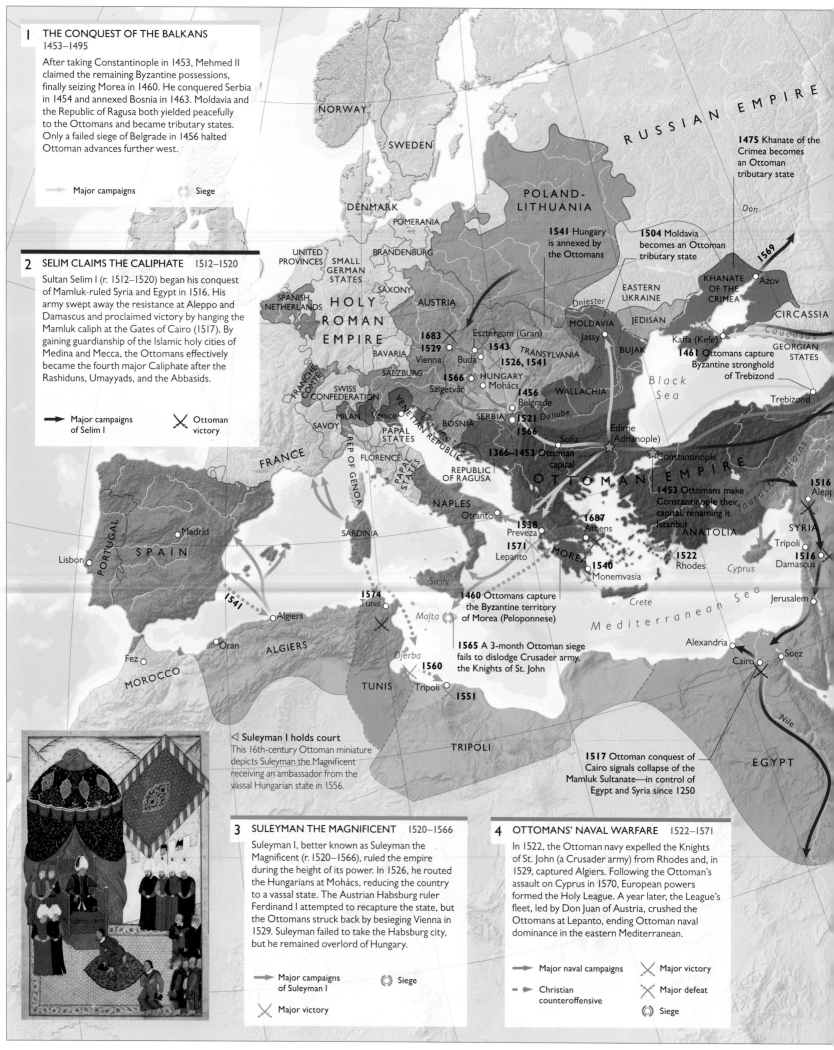

1 THE CONQUEST OF THE BALKANS
1453–1495

After taking Constantinople in 1453, Mehmed II claimed the remaining Byzantine possessions, finally seizing Morea in 1460. He conquered Serbia in 1454 and annexed Bosnia in 1463. Moldavia and the Republic of Ragusa both yielded peacefully to the Ottomans and became tributary states. Only a failed siege of Belgrade in 1456 halted Ottoman advances further west.

→ Major campaigns   ◯ Siege

2 SELIM CLAIMS THE CALIPHATE   1512–1520

Sultan Selim I (r. 1512–1520) began his conquest of Mamluk-ruled Syria and Egypt in 1516. His army swept away the resistance at Aleppo and Damascus and proclaimed victory by hanging the Mamluk caliph at the Gates of Cairo (1517). By gaining guardianship of the Islamic holy cities of Medina and Mecca, the Ottomans effectively became the fourth major Caliphate after the Rashiduns, Umayyads, and the Abbasids.

→ Major campaigns of Selim I   ⚔ Ottoman victory

1475 Khanate of the Crimea becomes an Ottoman tributary state

1541 Hungary is annexed by the Ottomans

1504 Moldavia becomes an Ottoman tributary state

1461 Ottomans capture Byzantine stronghold of Trebizond

1683
1529
Vienna

1543
Esztergom (Gran)
Buda

1526, 1541

1566
Szigetvár

1456
Belgrade

1521
1566

1538
Preveza

1687
Athens

1571
Lepanto

1540
Monemvasia

1522
Rhodes

1453 Ottomans make Constantinople their capital, renaming it Istanbul

1366–1453 Ottoman capital

1460 Ottomans capture the Byzantine territory of Morea (Peloponnese)

1565 A 3-month Ottoman siege fails to dislodge Crusader army, the Knights of St. John

1574
Tunis

1560

1551

1541

1517 Ottoman conquest of Cairo signals collapse of the Mamluk Sultanate—in control of Egypt and Syria since 1250

1516 Aleppo

1516 Damascus

1569

⊲ **Suleyman I holds court**
This 16th-century Ottoman miniature depicts Suleyman the Magnificent receiving an ambassador from the vassal Hungarian state in 1556.

3 SULEYMAN THE MAGNIFICENT   1520–1566

Suleyman I, better known as Suleyman the Magnificent (r. 1520–1566), ruled the empire during the height of its power. In 1526, he routed the Hungarians at Mohács, reducing the country to a vassal state. The Austrian Habsburg ruler Ferdinand I attempted to recapture the state, but the Ottomans struck back by besieging Vienna in 1529. Suleyman failed to take the Habsburg city, but he remained overlord of Hungary.

→ Major campaigns of Suleyman I   ◯ Siege   ⚔ Major victory

4 OTTOMANS' NAVAL WARFARE   1522–1571

In 1522, the Ottoman navy expelled the Knights of St. John (a Crusader army) from Rhodes and, in 1529, captured Algiers. Following the Ottoman's assault on Cyprus in 1570, European powers formed the Holy League. A year later, the League's fleet, led by Don Juan of Austria, crushed the Ottomans at Lepanto, ending Ottoman naval dominance in the eastern Mediterranean.

→ Major naval campaigns   ⚔ Major victory
-- Christian counteroffensive   ⚔ Major defeat
◯ Siege

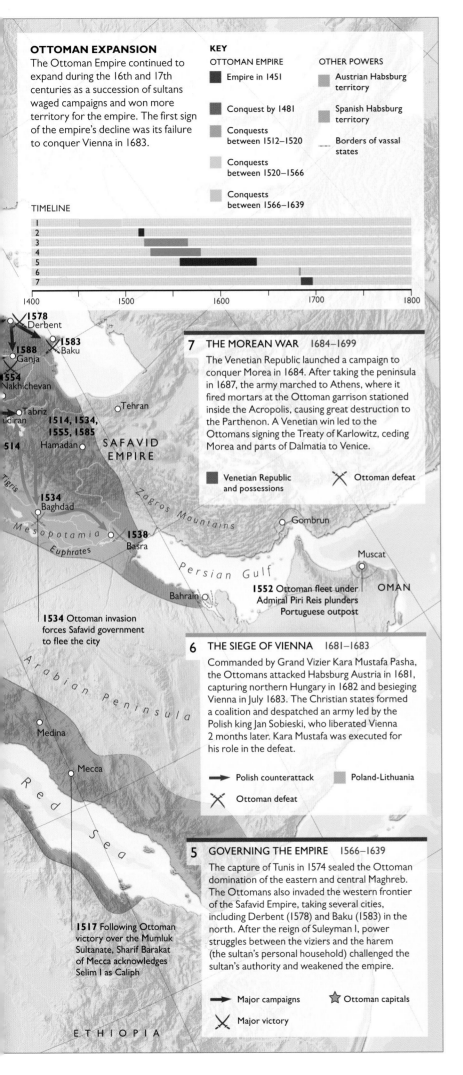

OTTOMAN EXPANSION

The Ottoman Empire continued to expand during the 16th and 17th centuries as a succession of sultans waged campaigns and won more territory for the empire. The first sign of the empire's decline was its failure to conquer Vienna in 1683.

KEY

OTTOMAN EMPIRE
- Empire in 1451
- Conquest by 1481
- Conquests between 1512–1520
- Conquests between 1520–1566
- Conquests between 1566–1639

OTHER POWERS
- Austrian Habsburg territory
- Spanish Habsburg territory
- Borders of vassal states

TIMELINE

1400 1500 1600 1700 1800

1578 Derbent
1583 Baku
1588 Ganja
1554 Nakhichevan
1514, 1534, 1555, 1585 Tabriz / Čaldiran
514 Hamadan
Tehran

SAFAVID EMPIRE

1534 Baghdad

Mesopotamia
Euphrates
Tigris
Zagros Mountains

1538 Basra

Gombrun

1534 Ottoman invasion forces Safavid government to flee the city

Muscat

1552 Ottoman fleet under Admiral Piri Reis plunders Portuguese outpost

Bahrain

Persian Gulf

OMAN

Arabian Peninsula

Medina

Mecca

Red Sea

1517 Following Ottoman victory over the Mumluk Sultanate, Sharif Barakat of Mecca acknowledges Selim I as Caliph

ETHIOPIA

7 THE MOREAN WAR 1684–1699

The Venetian Republic launched a campaign to conquer Morea in 1684. After taking the peninsula in 1687, the army marched to Athens, where it fired mortars at the Ottoman garrison stationed inside the Acropolis, causing great destruction to the Parthenon. A Venetian win led to the Ottomans signing the Treaty of Karlowitz, ceding Morea and parts of Dalmatia to Venice.

- Venetian Republic and possessions
- Ottoman defeat

6 THE SIEGE OF VIENNA 1681–1683

Commanded by Grand Vizier Kara Mustafa Pasha, the Ottomans attacked Habsburg Austria in 1681, capturing northern Hungary in 1682 and besieging Vienna in July 1683. The Christian states formed a coalition and despatched an army led by the Polish king Jan Sobieski, who liberated Vienna 2 months later. Kara Mustafa was executed for his role in the defeat.

- Polish counterattack
- Poland-Lithuania
- Ottoman defeat

5 GOVERNING THE EMPIRE 1566–1639

The capture of Tunis in 1574 sealed the Ottoman domination of the eastern and central Maghreb. The Ottomans also invaded the western frontier of the Safavid Empire, taking several cities, including Derbent (1578) and Baku (1583) in the north. After the reign of Suleyman I, power struggles between the viziers and the harem (the sultan's personal household) challenged the sultan's authority and weakened the empire.

- Major campaigns
- Ottoman capitals
- Major victory

REIGN OF THE OTTOMANS

The 15th century heralded an era of expansion for the Ottoman Empire, in which it extended its domain in the Balkans, Syria, and Egypt. At the pinnacle of its power, the empire posed a challenge to western Europe, forcing Christian states to form alliances to protect their lands.

With the capture of the Byzantine capital, Constantinople, in 1453, the Ottoman Empire consolidated its position as the principal Islamic power of the modern era. Sultan Mehmed II (r. 1444–1446 and 1451–1481) proceeded to annex the remnants of Byzantium, lands in the northern Balkans and eastern Anatolia, and bolstered the sultanate's power by earning revenues from these new conquests. In 1481, the Ottomans sent shock waves across western Europe by launching an attack on Otranto in southern Italy, but Mehmed's untimely death a year later put a stop to the campaign.

Successor Bayezid II (r. 1481–1512) made further gains in the Balkans, and Selim I's (r. 1512–1520) conquest of Egypt and the Holy Lands allowed him to lay claim to the caliphate and claim preeminence among Muslim rulers. Suleyman the Magnificent (r. 1520–1566) ruled an empire at the height of its power, notably invading Hungary in 1526. The Habsburg rulers proved an obdurate foe, but still most of the country was lost to the Ottomans.

From the mid-16th century, the authority of the sultanate began to diminish as internal power wranglings led to military officials taking greater regional control while government ministers, notably the grand vizier, rose to power. Although Murad IV (r. 1623–1640) and Mehmed IV (r. 1648–1687) made fitful attempts at reform, their efforts proved largely ineffectual. The Ottoman Empire's increasingly dysfunctional leadership was evident in its failed siege of Vienna in 1683, and defeat marked the start of its decline.

OTTOMAN ARCHITECTURE
BYZANTINE INSPIRATION

After the conquest of Constantinople, Sultan Mehmed II headed to the Hagia Sophia church—the centrepiece of the former Byzantine capital—and converted it to a mosque. The majesty of the building inspired great Ottoman architects such as Sinan, who went on to design mosques with soaring domes, vast open interiors, and multiple minarets, such as the Sülemaniye mosque (1558) in Istanbul.

Hagia Sophia
This 16th-century painting shows the church of Hagia (Saint) Sophia transformed into a mosque.

EAST MEETS WEST

The arrival of Europeans in the Indian Ocean in the 15th century began a 200-year-long period in which western travelers, goods, and ideas reached Asia in increasing numbers. In turn, information about the continent and its powerful indigenous empires filtered back to Europe.

△ Trading hub
This 1665 painting shows the Dutch flag flying over the trading station of the Dutch East India Company at Hooghly in Bengal, India. Dutch ships can be seen navigating the Ganges.

Before the late 15th century, European knowledge of Asia had been minimal, derived mainly from the observations of the Venetian merchant Marco Polo about the Mongol Empire. It was the desire to acquire spices such as nutmeg, pepper, cinnamon, and cloves—prized for their culinary and medicinal uses—that drew Europeans to Asia once more. Spices were expensive and could only be sourced along overland routes controlled by the Chinese, Mughal, and Ottoman Empires.

To Asia by sea

The Italian explorer Christopher Columbus sailed westward across the Atlantic in 1492 in an attempt to reach India and China. However, it was the Portuguese captain Vasco da Gama who finally reached Calicut (modern-day Kozhikode) on India's Malabar Coast in 1498 by sailing around Africa and then eastward into the Indian Ocean. Thereafter, the Portuguese returned in greater force and established a series of trading posts across southern Asia: at Goa, India, in 1510; in Malacca on the Malay peninsula in 1511; and in the Moluccas, in modern-day Indonesia, in 1512.

The Portuguese soon lost ground to other European rivals—notably the Dutch, who began to encroach on the Moluccas in 1599, and the English, who established a trading post at Surat in India in 1612. By then, however, Portugal had acquired a trading post at Macao, China, from where European missionaries and merchants traveled into China and Japan. In China, Jesuit missionaries (members of the Catholic order of the Society of Jesus) under the leadership of Matteo Ricci adopted many Chinese customs, including their dress, and established a presence at the Ming court in Beijing. Although they made few converts and only secured formal toleration of Christianity in 1692, the missionaries introduced China to European astronomical, medical, and mathematical ideas. In turn, knowledge of China was transmitted back to the West,

◁ Adopting local customs
An illustration from Jesuit Athanasius Kirchner's *China Illustrata* shows Matteo Ricci (left) and another Christian missionary dressed in Chinese-style robes that made their acceptance at the imperial court easier.

MISSIONARIES AND MERCHANTS

The arrival of Vasco da Gama in India was followed by the setting up of Portuguese forts in south and Southeast Asia. From these, traders and missionaries traveled into Asia, particularly India, Japan, and China. By the mid-17th century, the Portuguese had largely been supplanted by the Dutch and the British. Although their missionary effort was less notable than that of the Portuguese, their merchants helped to spread European ideas into Asia and transmit knowledge about Asia to the West.

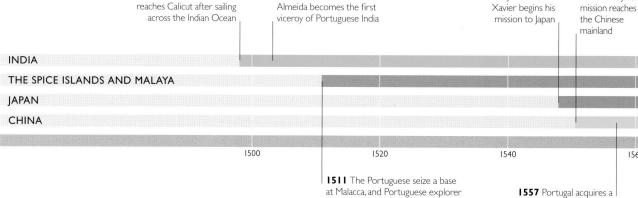

1498 Vasco da Gama reaches Calicut after sailing across the Indian Ocean

1505 Francisco de Almeida becomes the first viceroy of Portuguese India

1549 Jesuit Francis Xavier begins his mission to Japan

1555 First Jesuit mission reaches the Chinese mainland

INDIA

THE SPICE ISLANDS AND MALAYA

JAPAN

CHINA

1500   1520   1540   1560

1511 The Portuguese seize a base at Malacca, and Portuguese explorer Antonio de Abreu reaches the Banda Islands, a part of the Spice Islands

1557 Portugal acquires a base at Macao, but trade is strictly controlled

◁ **Painting foreigners**
This painting from the 16th–17th century showing a Portuguese expedition arriving in Japan is in the Nanban style, a Japanese school of art that specialized in the depiction of foreigners and foreign themes.

in works such as the *China Illustrata* (1667), compiled by the Jesuit Athanasius Kirchner, which reproduced Chinese texts for a European audience for the first time.

Japan in the 16th century was mired in internal wars. The shipwreck of two Portuguese sailors in 1543 introduced modern firearms into Japan, increasing the bloodiness of the civil wars. The Jesuit Francis Xavier established a mission in 1549, and its converts included the daimyo lord Omura Sumitada, who gave the Portuguese the site of Nagasaki in 1571, from where they operated a growing trading network.

Although European goods were valued, and the Portuguese introduced copper-plate engraving and painting in oils and watercolors to the Japanese, the increasing number of Christian converts worried the Tokugawa shoguns who ruled Japan after 1600. The Shimabara Revolt of 1637, an uprising that included many Japanese Roman Catholics, proved to be the final straw. Christianity was savagely repressed and the Portuguese expelled; henceforth, the only contact allowed with Europeans was through a trading enclave off Nagasaki run by the Dutch.

Trade and diplomacy in India

In India, rather than winning converts, the English sought to expand their trade by gaining access to the principal centers of power, which in the north meant the court of the Mughals. Although the English East India Company acquired Fort St. George (modern-day Chennai) in 1641 and Fort William (modern-day Kolkata) in 1690, they avoided large-scale political commitments that would exhaust their resources.

Trade, though, required knowledge, and the English diplomat Sir Thomas Roe's embassy to the Mughal court from 1615–1618 was one of many that reported back on the topography, customs, and politics of India. Indians traveling to the west were limited to servants and *lascars* (seamen of Indian origin) aboard company vessels, though a few high-status Indians also traveled.

By then, the terms of engagement between Asia and Europe were changing. Within a century, the British would directly occupy much of India, the Ottoman Empire would begin to fragment, the Qing Empire would become dependent on trade with Europeans, and Japan would cut itself off from the outside world. East and West, though, would be inextricably intertwined in an increasingly globalized world.

▷ **Camouflaged piety**
This Japanese ivory figurine depicts the Virgin Mary as Kannon, the Buddhist goddess of mercy, a pretense made necessary by the outlawing of Christianity in Japan from 1614.

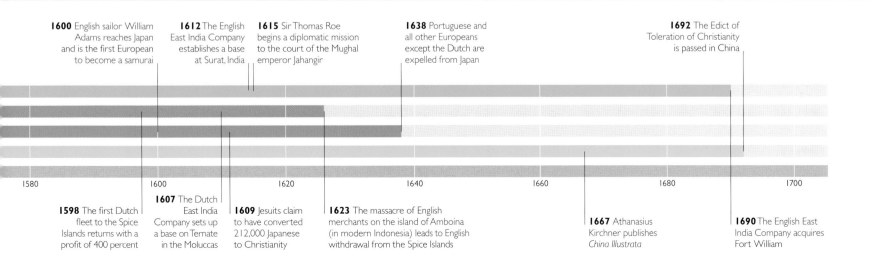

1600 English sailor William Adams reaches Japan and is the first European to become a samurai

1612 The English East India Company establishes a base at Surat, India

1615 Sir Thomas Roe begins a diplomatic mission to the court of the Mughal emperor Jahangir

1638 Portuguese and all other Europeans except the Dutch are expelled from Japan

1692 The Edict of Toleration of Christianity is passed in China

1580   1600   1620   1640   1660   1680   1700

1598 The first Dutch fleet to the Spice Islands returns with a profit of 400 percent

1607 The Dutch East India Company sets up a base on Ternate in the Moluccas

1609 Jesuits claim to have converted 212,000 Japanese to Christianity

1623 The massacre of English merchants on the island of Amboina (in modern Indonesia) leads to English withdrawal from the Spice Islands

1667 Athanasius Kirchner publishes *China Illustrata*

1690 The English East India Company acquires Fort William

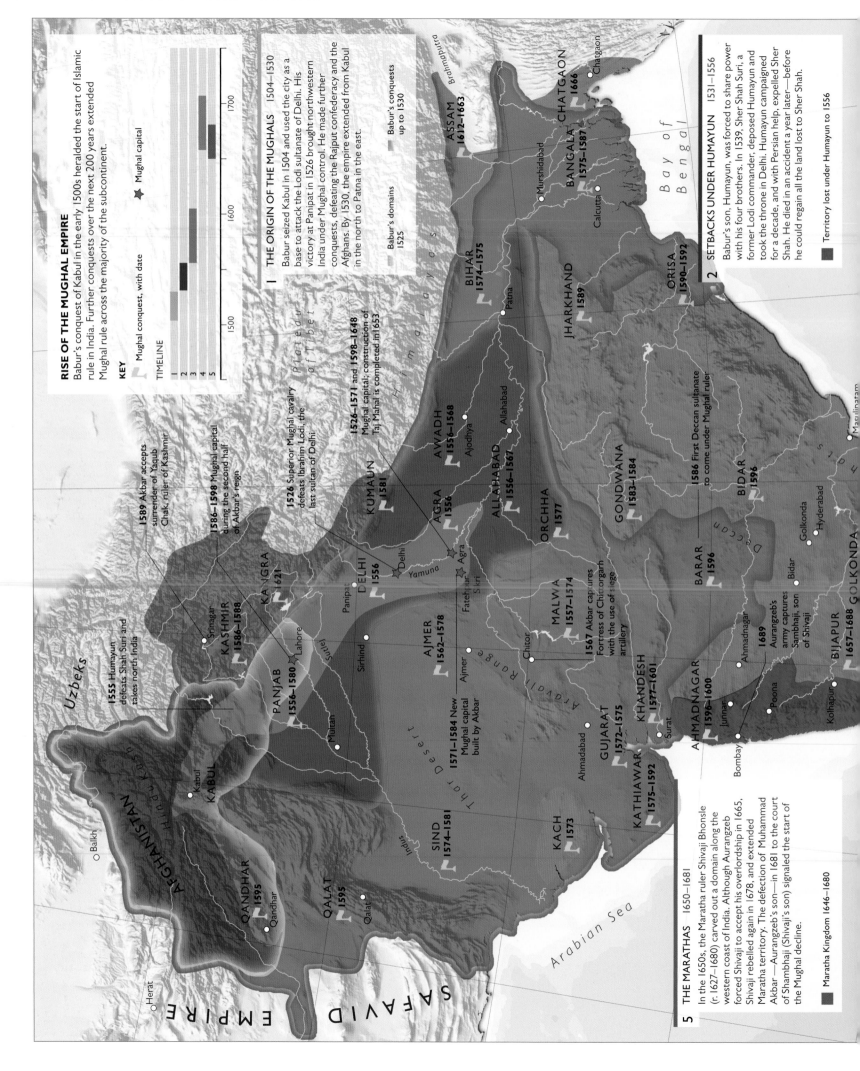

RISE OF THE MUGHAL EMPIRE

Babur's conquest of Kabul in the early 1500s heralded the start of Islamic rule in India. Further conquests over the next 200 years extended Mughal rule across the majority of the subcontinent.

KEY

⭐ Mughal capital

TIMELINE

1500   1600   1700

1
2
3
4
5

🏳 Mughal conquest, with date

1 THE ORIGIN OF THE MUGHALS 1504–1530

Babur seized Kabul in 1504 and used the city as a base to attack the Lodi sultanate of Delhi. His victory at Panipat in 1526 brought northwestern India under Mughal control. He made further conquests, defeating the Rajput confederacy and the Afghans. By 1530, the empire extended from Kabul in the north to Patna in the east.

Babur's domains
1525

Babur's conquests
up to 1530

2 SETBACKS UNDER HUMAYUN 1531–1556

Babur's son, Humayun, was forced to share power with his four brothers. In 1539, Sher Shah Suri, a former Lodi commander, deposed Humayun and took the throne in Delhi. Humayun campaigned for a decade, and with Persian help, expelled Sher Shah. He died in an accident a year later—before he could regain all the land lost to Sher Shah.

Territory lost under Humayun to 1556

5 THE MARATHAS 1650–1681

In the 1650s, the Maratha ruler Shivaji Bhonsle (r. 1627–1680) carved out a domain along the western coast of India. Although Aurangzeb forced Shivaji to accept his overlordship in 1665, Shivaji rebelled again in 1678, and extended Maratha territory. The defection of Muhammad Akbar—Aurangzeb's son—in 1681 to the court of Shambhaji (Shivaji's son) signaled the start of the Mughal decline.

Maratha Kingdom 1646–1680

1589 Akbar accepts surrender of Yaqub Chak, ruler of Kashmir

1586–1598 Mughal capital during the second half of Akbar's reign

1526 Superior Mughal cavalry defeats Ibrahim Lodi, the last sultan of Delhi

1526–1571 and 1598–1648 Mughal capital: construction of Taj Mahal is completed in 1653

1555 Humayun defeats Shah Suri and takes north India

1571–1584 New Mughal capital built by Akbar

1567 Akbar captures Fortress of Chittorgarh with the use of siege artillery

1586 First Deccan sultanate to come under Mughal ruler

1689 Aurangzeb's army captures Sambhaji, son of Shivaji

Uzbeks

Plateau of Tibet

Himalayas

Hindu Kush

AFGHANISTAN

SAFAVID EMPIRE

Balkh ○
○ *Herat*

○ *Qandhar*
QANDHAR 1595

QALAT 1595
○ *Qalat*

Kabul ○
KABUL

KASHMIR 1586–1588
Srinagar ○

KANGRA 1621

PANJAB 1556–1580
Lahore ⭐

Sutlej
Multan ○

SIND 1574–1581

Indus

Thar Desert

KATHIAWAR 1575–1592

KACH 1573

GUJARAT 1572–1575
Ahmadabad ○

Aravalli Range

AJMER 1562–1578
Ajmer ○

Sirhind ○

DELHI 1556
Delhi ⭐
Panipat ○
Yamuna

KUMAUN 1581

AGRA 1556
Agra ⭐
Fatehpur Sikri ⭐

AWADH 1556–1568
Ajodhya ○

ALLAHABAD 1556–1561
Allahabad ○

ORCHHA 1577

MALWA 1557–1574
Chitor ○

KHANDESH 1577–1601

AHMADNAGAR 1596–1600
Ahmadnagar ○

Bombay ○

Junnar ○

Poona ○

Surat ○

BARAR 1596

GONDWANA 1583–1584

JHARKHAND 1589

BIHAR 1574–1575
Patna ○

BANGALA 1575–1587
Murshidabad ○
Calcutta ○

ASSAM 1612–1663

Brahmaputra

CHATGAON 1666
Chatgaon ○

ORISA 1590–1592

Deccan

BIDAR 1596
Bidar ○

GOLKONDA 1657–1688
Golkonda ○
Hyderabad ○

BIJAPUR
Kolhapur ○

Masulipatam

Bay of Bengal

Arabian Sea

3 THE EMPIRE UNDER AKBAR 1556–1605

Seventeen-year-old Akbar came to power after the death of his father, Humayun. Akbar not only restored the Mughal Empire's old boundaries but also expanded the empire through conquests, annexing Afghanistan, Kashmir, Sind, Gujarat, and Bengal, and pushed south into the Deccan. By abolishing the "jizya" tax on non-Muslims, he won the acceptance of the Hindu territories.

Akbar's domains 1556
Akbar's gains 1605

4 AURANGZEB'S REIGN 1658–1707

Aurangzeb seized the throne after a long civil war against his brothers. He reasserted Mughal power in many of the empire's territories, including Bengal, and also muted a Rajput revolt in 1680. He then annexed Koch Bihar, reclaimed the Deccan, and pushed the imperial boundary as far south as Tanjore. His promotion of Islam and restoration of the jizya tax alienated many Hindus.

Areas brought under Mughal rule 1658–1707

SHAH JAHAN AND MUMTAZ
AN EMPEROR'S UNDYING LOVE

This miniature painting depicts the Mughal emperor Shah Jahan embracing his wife, Mumtaz Mahal, who he cherished over his two other wives. In 1631, Shah Jahan was left heartbroken after Mumtaz died during childbirth. The following year, he ordered the construction of the Taj Mahal in Agra—a white marble mausoleum, inlaid with gemstones—as a tribute to his beloved.

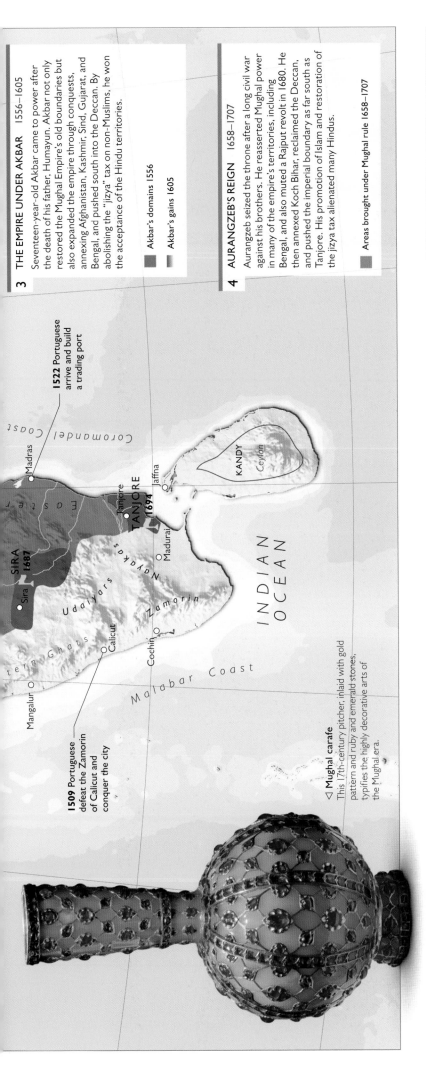

1509 Portuguese defeat the Zamorin of Calicut and conquer the city

1522 Portuguese arrive and build a trading port

▽ **Mughal carafe**
This 17th-century pitcher, inlaid with gold pattern and ruby and emerald stones, typifies the highly decorative arts of the Mughal era.

MUGHAL INDIA

In the 1520s, the Mughals, a Muslim group from central Asia, founded an empire in northern India that expanded over the next 150 years to cover most of the subcontinent. A succession of Mughal rulers presided over a culture whose rich legacy includes grand architectural pieces such as the Taj Mahal and the Red Fort in Delhi.

In 1526, Babur, a descendant of the Mongol warlord Timur, defeated the Lodi sultan of Delhi, conquered a swathe of northern India, and founded the Mughal dynasty. During his reign, he doubled the size of the empire through further conquests. Babur's son and successor, Humayun, however, lost Mughal territories to rival Sher Shah Suri— and lived in exile for 15 years before enlisting the help of Safavid Persia to regain the throne shortly before his death in 1556. It was Humayun's son, Akbar (r. 1556–1605), who secured the empire's future, extending its boundaries to the south and east,

establishing a well-organized and secular government that brought unity to the realm. The next two Mughal rulers, Jahangir (r. 1605–1627) and Shah Jahan (r. 1628–1658), presided over brilliant courts and marked the empire's golden age. Shah Jahan's passion for grand architecture led to the building of the Taj Mahal in Agra and the grand mosque, Jama Masjid, in Delhi, but his overzealous military campaigns also drained the empire's wealth. Under Aurangzeb (r. 1658–1707), the empire extended deep into southern India, but his harsher religious policies alienated many Hindu rulers, giving rise to local revolts, such as that of the Marathas, causing imperial borders to start fraying. The encroaching European powers took advantage of the instability and further eroded Mughal power, and by the early 1800s, Mughal rule extended scarcely beyond the suburbs of Delhi.

"Miracles occur in the temples of every creed."

AKBAR THE GREAT, FROM AKBARNAMA, c. 1603

CHINA FROM THE MING TO THE QING

The Ming Dynasty (1368–1644) encouraged industry and foreign trade, heralding a renaissance in China's economy and technological development. However, from 1506, a succession of feckless rulers eroded Ming authority. When civil rebellion broke out across the land following a famine in the 1620s, the non-Han Chinese Jurchen (later known as Manchus) took their opportunity and ousted the beleaguered Ming to become China's new rulers.

The Ming governed the realm according to systems set up long ago by the Qin (see pp. 74–75). China's manufacturing blossomed under the Ming, encouraged by foreign trade. Under Emperor Yongle (r. 1403–1424), the Forbidden City was built in the new capital Beijing (which replaced Nanjing as the main seat of imperial residence). He also increased China's trade influence across Asia and Africa.

The later emperors lacked the same vision, which led to a gradual waning of Ming power. Emperor Xuande (r. 1425–1435) established a Grand Secretariat to streamline legislation and, in doing so, reduced the burden on his rule. The Ming suffered a blow in 1449 when the

young Emperor Zhengtong (r. 1435–1449 and 1457–1464) was taken prisoner by Mongol tribes while leading a battle against them. The second half of the Ming era saw court officials displace the traditional bureaucracy, leading to factionalism and poor governance. The empire's fall was presaged in the 1620s by a severe famine, which triggered lawlessness and peasant rebellions across the realm.

In 1644, the Manchus seized Beijing. Initially, the Chinese ruling classes were excluded from government positions, leading to revolts, but reforms thereafter created stability for Qing rule under Emperors Shunzhi (r. 1644–1661) and Kangxi (r. 1661–1722).

ADMIRAL ZHENG HE
THE MING TREASURE VOYAGES

Between 1405 and 1433, Admiral Zheng He led seven state-sponsored naval missions, known as the "Ming Treasure Voyages," across the Indian Ocean. With a fleet comprising more than 200 ships and 27,800 crewmen, Zheng He sailed as far as Arabia and the east coast of Africa, establishing new trade links and extending China's commercial influence.

◁ **Chinese porcelain**
During the Ming era, expert potters used local clay and imported Persian cobalt to create beautifully decorated porcelain products. Manufactured only in China, porcelain goods became as highly prized as silk in European and Middle Eastern markets.

1 GOLDEN AGE OF THE MING 1368–1435

The Ming engaged extensively in domestic and foreign trade, establishing major commercial centers predominantly along China's eastern coast. The country exported manufactured goods such as porcelain, silk cloth, and paper. During this period, the growth in international trade encouraged many Chinese people to settle in cities throughout Southeast Asia.

▲ Major trading center

2 FROM EMPEROR TO PRISONER 1449–1457

In 1449, Emperor Zhengtong was captured after leading an ill-advised war against the Mongols. He was released after a year but spent several years battling to return to the throne. Throughout Ming rule, measures were taken to reinforce the northern frontier against any Mongol invasion: the Great Wall was extended and then fortified with a series of garrisons and 1,200 watchtowers.

▲ Great Wall garrison

3 THE MING IN DECLINE 1506–1620

Emperor Zhengde (r. 1506–1521) adopted Confucianism—a system of ethics based on mutual responsibility. His successor Jianjing (r. 1521–1567), however, favored the more carefree, nature-based teachings of Daoism. In reaction, he left the problem of governing to court officials and ignored the problem of Japanese pirate raids, devoting himself to sporting pastimes and hosting lavish Daoist ceremonies. Ming authority became even more ineffectual under Emperor Wanli (r. 1573–1620).

■ Japanese pirate raids

↑ Area affected by the pirate raids

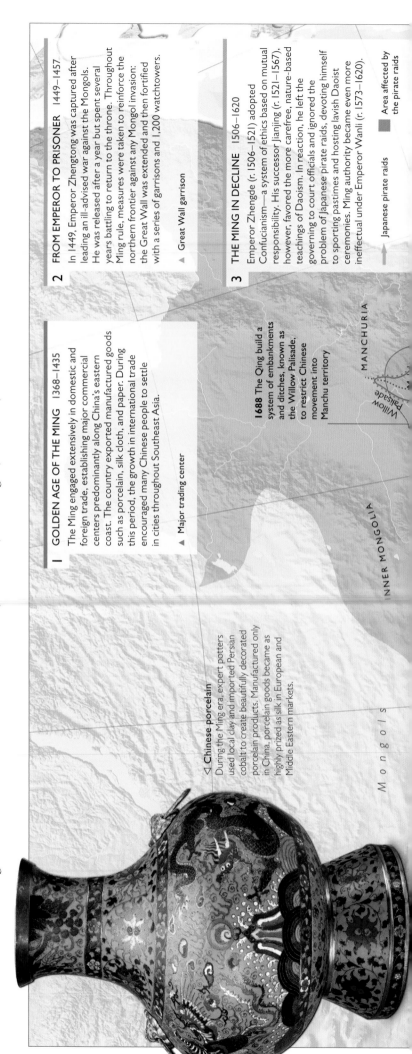

1688 The Qing build a system of embankments and ditches, known as the Willow Palisade, to restrict Chinese movement into Manchu territory

Willow Palisade

MANCHURIA

INNER MONGOLIA

Mongols

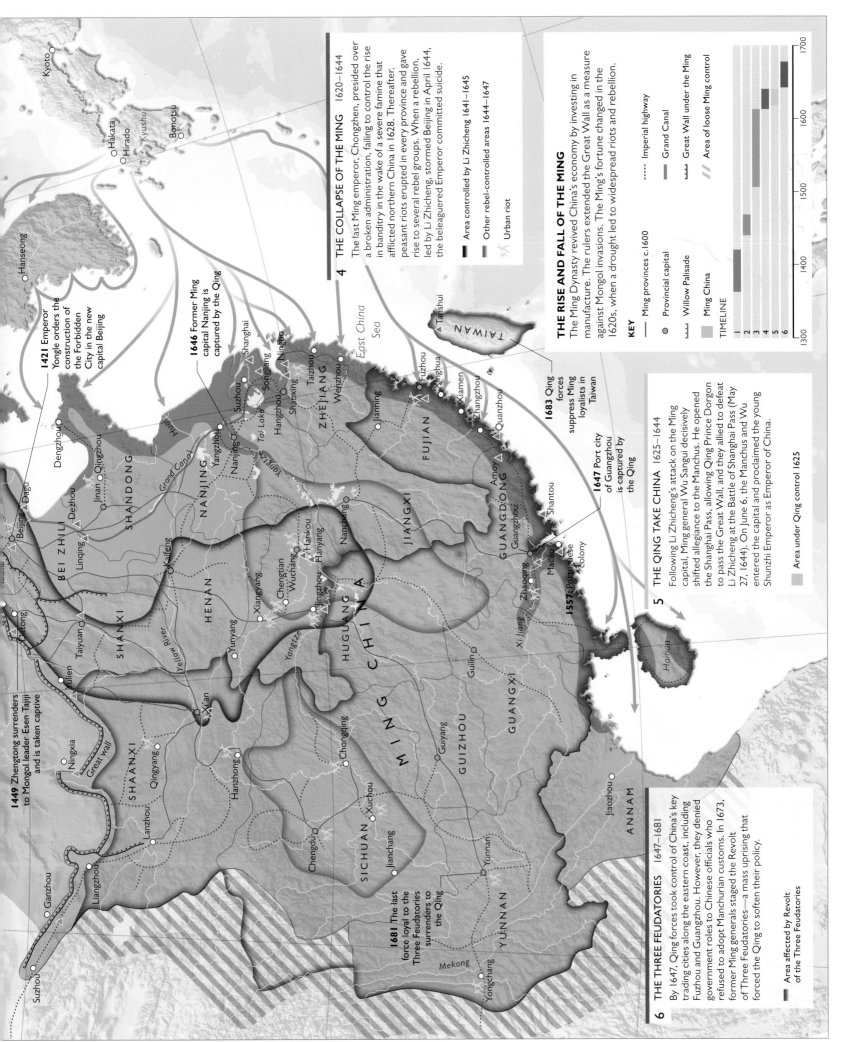

1421 Emperor Yongle orders the construction of the Forbidden City in the new capital Beijing

1646 Former Ming capital Nanjing is captured by the Qing

1449 Zhengtong surrenders to Mongol leader Esen Taijii and is taken captive

1681 The last force loyal to the Three Feudatories surrenders to the Qing

1683 Qing forces suppress Ming loyalists in Taiwan

1647 Port city of Guangzhou is captured by the Qing

1557 Portuguese colony

4 THE COLLAPSE OF THE MING 1620–1644

The last Ming emperor, Chongzhen, presided over a broken administration, failing to control the rise in banditry in the wake of a severe famine that afflicted northern China in 1628. Thereafter, peasant riots erupted in every province and gave rise to several rebel groups. When a rebellion, led by Li Zhicheng, stormed Beijing in April 1644, the beleaguered Emperor committed suicide.

▬ Area controlled by Li Zhicheng 1641–1645
▨ Other rebel-controlled areas 1644–1647
⚔ Urban riot

THE RISE AND FALL OF THE MING

The Ming Dynasty revived China's economy by investing in manufacture. The rulers extended the Great Wall as a measure against Mongol invasions. The Ming's fortune changed in the 1620s, when a drought led to widespread riots and rebellion.

KEY

— Ming provinces c.1600
⦿ Provincial capital
⋯⋯ Willow Palisade
▦ Ming China
⋯⋯⋯ Imperial highway
— Grand Canal
▬ Great Wall under the Ming
╱╱ Area of loose Ming control

TIMELINE

	1300	1400	1500	1600	1700
1					
2					
3					
4					
5					
6					

5 THE QING TAKE CHINA 1625–1644

Following Li Zhicheng's attack on the Ming capital, Ming general Wu Sangui decisively shifted allegiance to the Manchus. He opened the Shanhai Pass, allowing Qing Prince Dorgon to pass the Great Wall, and they allied to defeat Li Zhicheng at the Battle of Shanhai Pass (May 27, 1644). On June 6, the Manchus and Wu entered the capital and proclaimed the young Shunzhi Emperor as Emperor of China.

▦ Area under Qing control 1625

6 THE THREE FEUDATORIES 1647–1681

By 1647, Qing forces took control of China's key trading cities along the eastern coast, including Fuzhou and Guangzhou. However, they denied government roles to Chinese officials who refused to adopt Manchurian customs. In 1673, former Ming generals staged the Revolt of Three Feudatories—a mass uprising that forced the Qing to soften their policy.

▬ Area affected by Revolt of the Three Feudatories

TOKUGAWA IEYASU
1543—1616

JAPAN UNIFIES UNDER THE TOKUGAWA

Following the Onin War (1467—1477) involving Japan's two most powerful families, the daimyos (provincial warlords) fought for supremacy, keeping the country in a state of civil unrest for almost a century. Peace came in stages as a succession of men assumed control, but it was Tokugawa Ieyasu who finally restored long-term stability, establishing a tightly controlled regime that would endure for 265 years.

A dispute between Japan's powerful Hosakawa and Yamana clans in 1467 erupted into a violent conflict over who should succeed Ashikaga Yoshimata as *shogun* (Japan's military commander). The resulting Onin War raged on for a decade, destroying the capital, Kyoto, and ended with the Yamana yielding.

With the two families left markedly weakened by the ravages of war, the daimyos saw their opportunity to sieze power. Japan was thus thrown into further turmoil as rival daimyo lords battled one

"The strong manly ones in life are those who understand the meaning of the word patience."

TOKUGAWA IEYASU, FIRST TOKUGAWA SHOGUN, 1616

another for supremacy. Daimyo Oda Nobunaga emerged victorious almost a century later, forming alliances to defeat his rivals in a campaign spanning 15 years. On the cusp of becoming Japan's new leader, however, Nobunaga was forced into committing suicide in June 1582, at the hands of his samurai general.

Nobunaga's former ally, Toyotomi Hideyoshi, fought for the next 8 years to defeat daimyos from the Katsuie, Shimazu, and Hojo clans to reunify Japan. His death from ill health in 1598 led to another series of battles, in which Tokugawa Ieyasu (r. 1603—1605) scored a decisive victory at Sekigahara (1600) and earned the title of shogun.

Ieyasu introduced strict reforms, which were also enforced by his Tokugawa successors, to curb the powers of the daimyo lords. He also removed the growing threat of Christian wars on Japanese soil by limiting European presence in the port cities of Kyushu, thereby ensuring stability under Tokugawa rule.

Inheritor of the minor Okazaki domain in eastern Mikawa Province (modern-day Aichi Prefecture), Tokugawa Ieyasu began his military training with the Imagawa family. He allied himself with the powerful forces of Oda Nobunaga first and then Toyotomi Hideyoshi and expanded his land holdings by defeating the neighboring Hojo family to the east. After Hideyoshi's death in 1603, Ieyasu became shogun to Japan's imperial court and founded the Tokugawa shogunate.

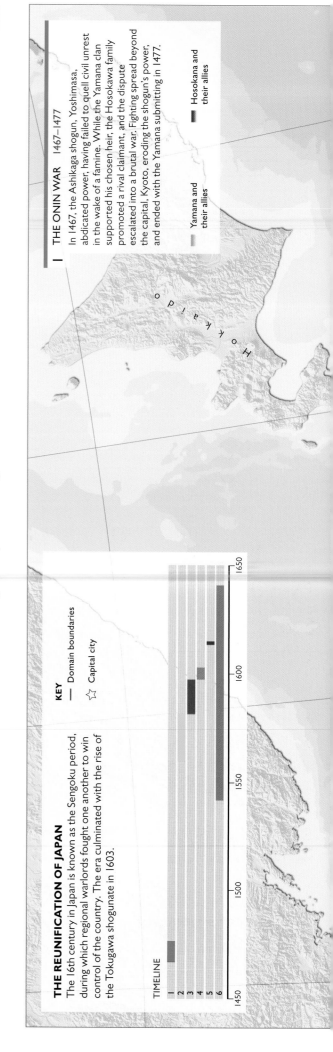

THE REUNIFICATION OF JAPAN

The 16th century in Japan is known as the Sengoku period, during which regional warlords fought one another to win control of the country. The era culminated with the rise of the Tokugawa shogunate in 1603.

KEY

— Domain boundaries

☆ Capital city

TIMELINE

1450	1500	1550	1600	1650	

THE ONIN WAR 1467—1477

In 1467, the Ashikaga shogun, Yoshimasa, abdicated power, having failed to quell civil unrest in the wake of a famine. While the Yamana clan supported his chosen heir, the Hosokawa family promoted a rival claimant, and the dispute escalated into a brutal war. Fighting spread beyond the capital, Kyoto, eroding the shogun's power, and ended with the Yamana submitting in 1477.

■ Yamana and their allies

■ Hosokana and their allies

Hokkaido

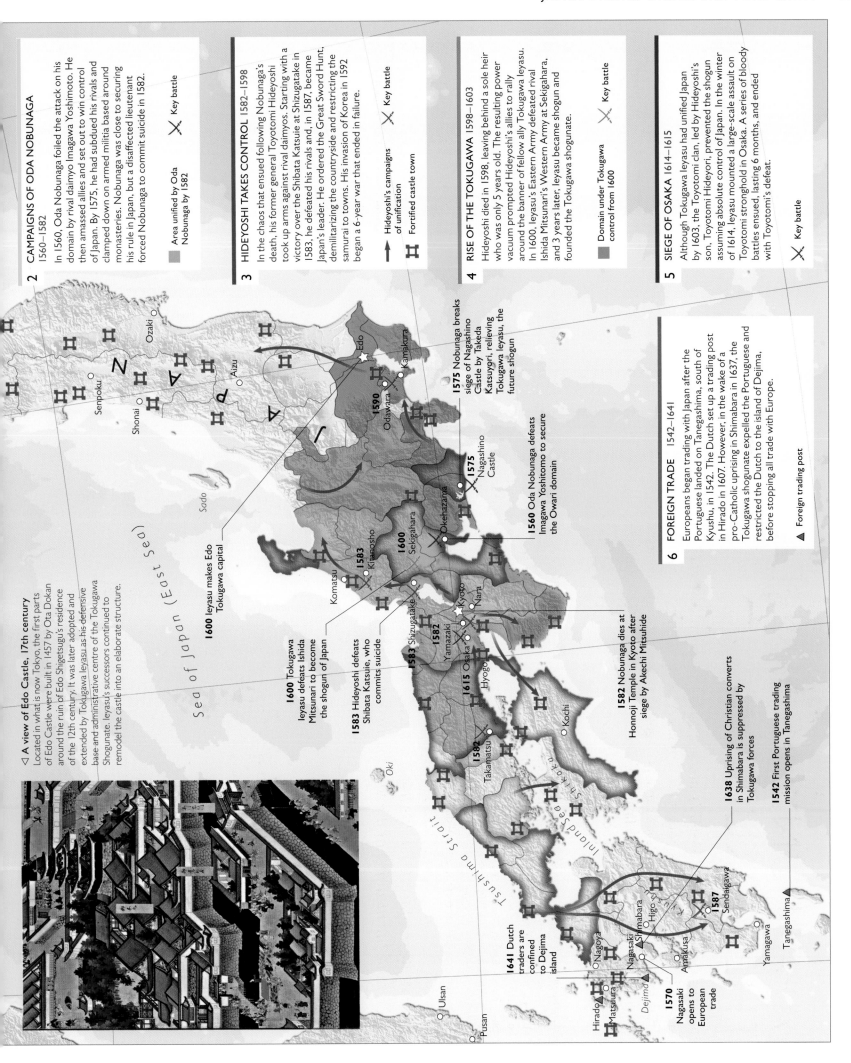

2 CAMPAIGNS OF ODA NOBUNAGA
1560–1582

In 1560, Oda Nobunaga foiled the attack on his domain by rival daimyo Imagawa Yoshimoto. He then amassed allies and set out to win control of Japan. By 1575, he had subdued his rivals and clamped down on armed militia based around monasteries. Nobunaga was close to securing his rule in Japan, but a disaffected lieutenant forced Nobunaga to commit suicide in 1582.

☐ Area unified by Oda Nobunaga by 1582   ✕ Key battle

3 HIDEYOSHI TAKES CONTROL 1582–1598

In the chaos that ensued following Nobunaga's death, his former general Toyotomi Hideyoshi took up arms against rival daimyos. Starting with a victory over the Shibata Katsuie at Shizugatake in 1583, he defeated his rivals and, in 1587, became Japan's leader. He ordered the Great Sword Hunt, demilitarizing the countryside and restricting the samurai to towns. His invasion of Korea in 1592 began a 6-year war that ended in failure.

→ Hideyoshi's campaigns of unification   ✕ Key battle

☐ Fortified castle town

4 RISE OF THE TOKUGAWA 1598–1603

Hideyoshi died in 1598, leaving behind a sole heir who was only 5 years old. The resulting power vacuum prompted Hideyoshi's allies to rally around the banner of fellow ally Tokugawa Ieyasu. In 1600, Ieyasu's Eastern Army defeated rival Ishida Mitsunari's Western Army at Sekigahara, and 3 years later, Ieyasu became shogun and founded the Tokugawa shogunate.

☐ Domain under Tokugawa control from 1600   ✕ Key battle

5 SIEGE OF OSAKA 1614–1615

Although Tokugawa Ieyasu had unified Japan by 1603, the Toyotomi clan, led by Hideyoshi's son, Toyotomi Hideyori, prevented the shogun assuming absolute control of Japan. In the winter of 1614, Ieyasu mounted a large-scale assault on Toyotomi stronghold in Osaka. A series of bloody battles ensued, lasting 6 months, and ended with Toyotomi's defeat.

✕ Key battle

6 FOREIGN TRADE 1542–1641

Europeans began trading with Japan after the Portuguese landed on Tanegashima, south of Kyushu, in 1542. The Dutch set up a trading post in Hirado in 1607. However, in the wake of a pro-Catholic uprising in Shimabara in 1637, the Tokugawa shogunate expelled the Portuguese and restricted the Dutch to the island of Dejima, before stopping all trade with Europe.

▲ Foreign trading post

△ **A view of Edo Castle, 17th century**
Located in what is now Tokyo, the first parts of Edo Castle were built in 1457 by Ota Dokan around the ruin of Edo Shigetsugu's residence of the 12th century. It was later adopted and extended by Tokugawa Ieyasu as his defensive base and administrative centre of the Tokugawa Shogunate. Ieyasu's successors continued to remodel the castle into an elaborate structure.

Sea of Japan (East Sea)

Sado

Ozaki
Senpoku
Shonai
Aizu
Edo
Kamakura
1590 Odawara
1575 Nobunaga breaks siege of Nagashino Castle by Takeda Katsuyori, relieving Tokugawa Ieyasu, the future shogun
1575 Nagashino Castle
1560 Oda Nobunaga defeats Imagawa Yoshitomo to secure the Owari domain
Okehazama

1600 Ieyasu makes Edo Tokugawa capital
1600 Tokugawa Ieyasu defeats Ishida Mitsunari to become the shogun of Japan
1583 Hideyoshi defeats Shibata Katsuie, who commits suicide
1583 Shizugatake
Komatsu
1583 Kitanosho
1600 Sekigahara
Kyoto
Nara
1582 Yamazaki
1615 Osaka
Hyogo
1582 Nobunaga dies at Honnoji Temple in Kyoto after siege by Akechi Mitsuhide
Kochi

Oki

Shikoku

Inland Sea

1582 Takamatsu

1638 Uprising of Christian converts in Shimabara is suppressed by Tokugawa forces
1542 First Portuguese trading mission opens in Tanegashima
1587 Sendaigawa
Tanegashima
Yamagawa
Anrakusa
Higo
Shimabara
Nagoya
Nagasaki
Dejima
Hirado
Matsuura
1641 Dutch traders are confined to Dejima island
1570 Nagasaki opens to European trade
Tsushima Strait
Pusan
Ulsan

N

Master and disciple
This 1892 painting by Italian painter Tito Lessi shows
Galileo Galilei (right), who became blind toward the end
of his life. Galileo is accompanied by his assistant Vincenzo
Viviani, who calculated the speed of sound in 1660 by
observing the sound and light flash from a cannon.

THE SCIENTIFIC REVOLUTION

In the mid-16th to late 17th centuries, scientists such as Nicolaus Copernicus, Galileo Galilei, and Isaac Newton inspired a revolution that overturned traditional views of the workings of nature and the Universe.

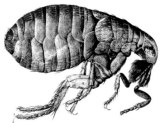

△ **Microscopic observation**
The English naturalist Robert Hooke produced this drawing of a flea in 1665 using the recently invented microscope—another instrument that helped advance scientific observation.

Before 1500, scholars had largely confined themselves to commentaries on the works of ancient writers such as Ptolemy, whose astronomical work in the 2nd century CE described an Earth-centric solar system. In 1543, dissatisfaction with Ptolemy's theory led Polish astronomer Nicolaus Copernicus to propose an alternative— he observed that Earth orbits the Sun. German astronomer Johannes Kepler refined the Copernican system and, in 1619, discovered that planetary orbits are elliptical and not circular. Copernicus's work encouraged others to base their theories on observation rather than orthodoxy. In 1609–1610, Italian astronomer Galileo Galilei discovered the four moons of Jupiter using the newly invented telescope. He also made huge advances in dynamics, establishing laws for the acceleration of falling bodies.

Far-ranging efforts

In the field of medicine, the direct observation of patients and dissection of corpses yielded new insights, such as the discovery of blood circulation in the human body by English physician William Harvey in 1628. The culmination of the scientific revolution came in the late 17th century with English mathematician Isaac Newton's three Laws of Motion and Theory of Gravity, which provided a mathematical explanation of planetary orbits. By then, the view that the Universe could be described in mechanical terms, by mathematical formulae rather than theological dogma, had been firmly established.

MAPPING THE WORLD

The voyages of European explorers in the 15th and 16th centuries inspired a revolution in mapping. The Netherlands became a center of expertise, where, in 1569, the Flemish cartographer Gerardus Mercator produced a world map using a new projection. This became the standard for maps for centuries to come.

THE DUTCH GOLDEN AGE

The Netherlands began to assert its independence from Spain in 1568; a golden age for the new country followed. Abroad, the Dutch East India Company out-competed other European nations in the Spice Islands (see pp.162–163) and constructed a maritime empire.

The revolt of the Netherlands against Spanish rule in 1568 initially devastated the main rebel areas in the north. On winning their independence, these areas became known as the Dutch Republic or United Provinces. After the country had recovered from the war, economic prosperity returned, and a "Regent" class emerged. Though wealthy, this class privileged the virtues of self-reliance and hard work, an ethic that their religious leaders applauded. Yet they also provided a pool of patrons in the fields of arts and sciences that made the first century of Dutch independence a golden era.

Together with early forms of maritime insurance, state banks, and stock exchanges, the Dutch Republic pioneered the joint stock company, in which investors pooled their risks (and shared equally in the profits). The most important, the Verenigde Oost-Indische Compagnie (the VOC, or Dutch East India Company), founded in 1602, exploited a favorable investment climate in the spice markets, which included a lack of state interference. The VOC captured Ambon in 1605, at the center of the spice production region of the Moluccas—also known as the Spice Islands—and it became the VOC headquarters from 1610–1619. The VOC expanded its network of forts and outposts until, by the 1660s, the Dutch had built an empire that stretched from Surinam in South America to Cape Town, Ceylon (modern Sri Lanka), and large parts of the Indonesian archipelago.

DUTCH GOLDEN AGE PAINTING
ART AFTER INDEPENDENCE

The growing wealth of the Dutch Republic meant that there were many rich mercantile families who could act as patrons, encouraging the flourishing artistic scene. Their lack of interest in religious subjects meant that the Netherlands' leading artists were masters in history paintings (Rembrandt van Rijn, 1606–1669), genre scenes (Johannes Vermeer, 1632–1675), landscapes (Jacob van Ruisdael, 1629–1682), and portraits (Frans Hals, 1582–1666).

Domestic art
Vermeer's *The Milkmaid* (c.1666) is typical of scenes of domestic tranquility favored by many Dutch patrons.

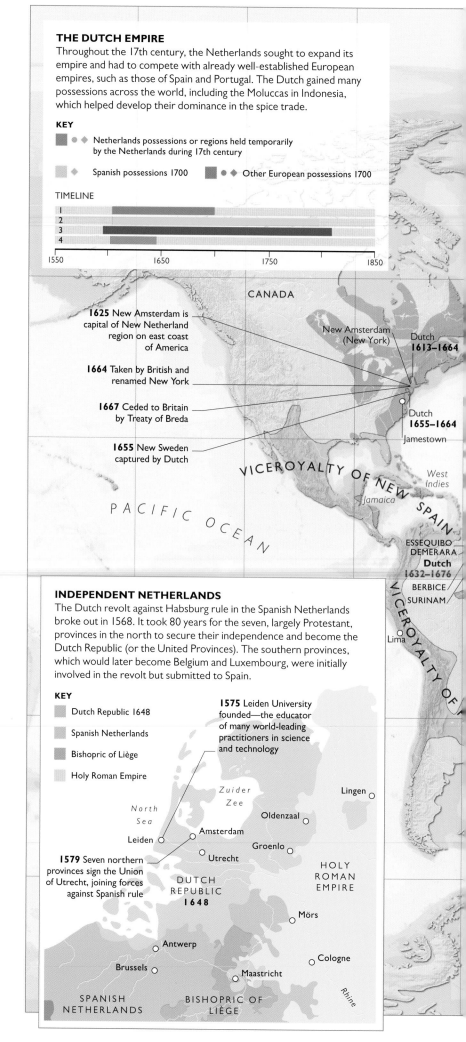

THE DUTCH EMPIRE
Throughout the 17th century, the Netherlands sought to expand its empire and had to compete with already well-established European empires, such as those of Spain and Portugal. The Dutch gained many possessions across the world, including the Moluccas in Indonesia, which helped develop their dominance in the spice trade.

KEY

- Netherlands possessions or regions held temporarily by the Netherlands during 17th century
- Spanish possessions 1700
- Other European possessions 1700

TIMELINE

1
2
3
4

1550 1650 1750 1850

1625 New Amsterdam is capital of New Netherland region on east coast of America

New Amsterdam (New York)

Dutch **1613–1664**

1664 Taken by British and renamed New York

1667 Ceded to Britain by Treaty of Breda

Dutch **1655–1664**

Jamestown

1655 New Sweden captured by Dutch

CANADA

VICEROYALTY OF NEW SPAIN

PACIFIC OCEAN

West Indies

Jamaica

ESSEQUIBO DEMERARA
Dutch **1632–1676**

BERBICE
SURINAM

Lima

VICEROYALTY OF

INDEPENDENT NETHERLANDS
The Dutch revolt against Habsburg rule in the Spanish Netherlands broke out in 1568. It took 80 years for the seven, largely Protestant, provinces in the north to secure their independence and become the Dutch Republic (or the United Provinces). The southern provinces, which would later become Belgium and Luxembourg, were initially involved in the revolt but submitted to Spain.

KEY

- Dutch Republic 1648
- Spanish Netherlands
- Bishopric of Liège
- Holy Roman Empire

1575 Leiden University founded—the educator of many world-leading practitioners in science and technology

1579 Seven northern provinces sign the Union of Utrecht, joining forces against Spanish rule

North Sea
Zuider Zee
Lingen
Oldenzaal
Amsterdam
Groenlo
Leiden
Utrecht
DUTCH REPUBLIC 1648
HOLY ROMAN EMPIRE
Mörs
Antwerp
Cologne
Brussels
Maastricht
SPANISH NETHERLANDS
BISHOPRIC OF LIÈGE
Rhine

1 THE DUTCH ECONOMY AND POLITICS
1602–1700

The need to finance foreign trading expeditions led to the foundation of the Amsterdam stock exchange in 1602 and of the Bank of Amsterdam in 1609. Both were able to provide investment funds and loans at much lower interest rates than foreign competitors. Statesmen such as Johan van Oldenbarnevelt (1547–1619) and Johan de Witt (1625–1672) provided the able leadership and political stability for the new United Provinces.

2 THE DUTCH EAST INDIA COMPANY
1602–1799

The VOC was established in 1602, financed by 6.5 million florins put in by investors and governed by a board of 17 directors in Amsterdam. The establishment of a base on Java in 1619 and the forceful direction of the VOC's Governor-General in the East Indies enabled it to marginalize the Portuguese in the Spice Islands and dominate the Indonesian archipelago until its dissolution in 1799.

☆ VOC Headquarters

3 THE DUTCH IN AFRICA   1592–1814

Dutch voyages to West Africa began around 1592. Unsuccessful attempts to seize Elmina, which they finally took in 1637, led to the establishment of Fort Nassau in 1612—and served as the capital of the Dutch Gold Coast. By the 1640s, the Dutch were threatening the Portuguese base in Angola, and in 1652, an outpost was set up at Cape Town, at the southern tip of Africa. Cape Town received significant numbers of Dutch settlers and remained in Dutch hands until 1814.

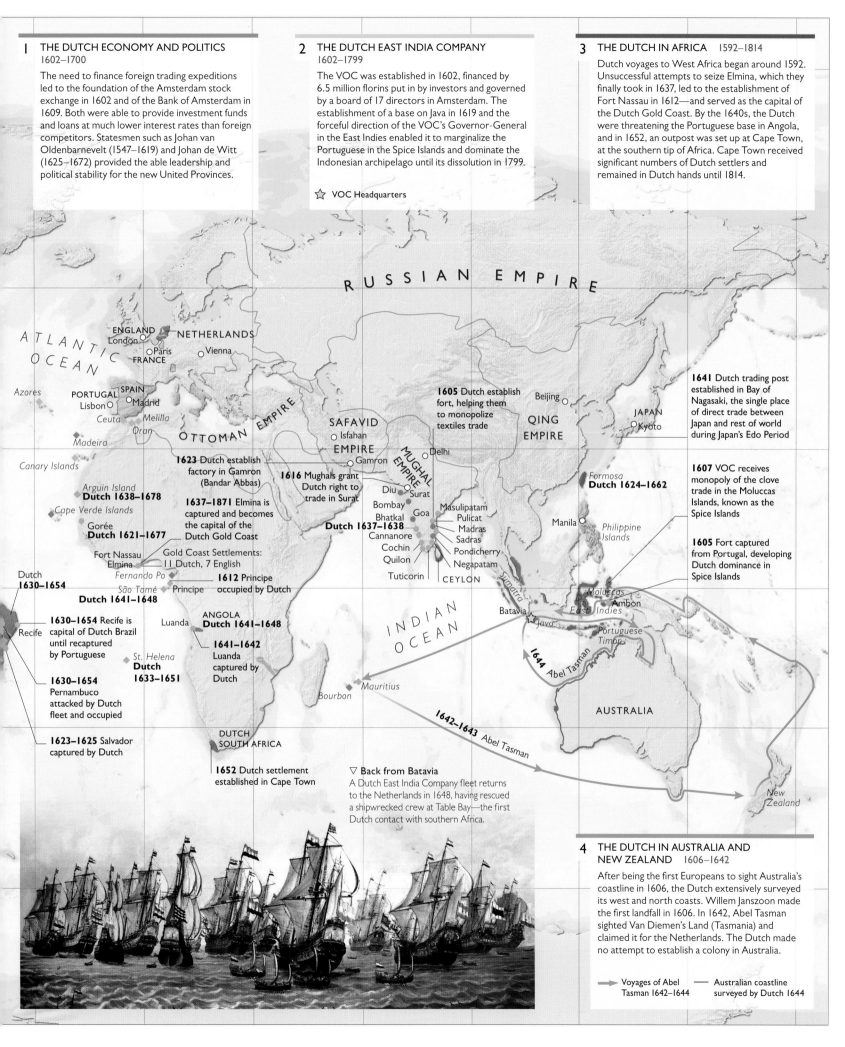

1605 Dutch establish fort, helping them to monopolize textiles trade

1641 Dutch trading post established in Bay of Nagasaki, the single place of direct trade between Japan and rest of world during Japan's Edo Period

1623 Dutch establish factory in Gamron (Bandar Abbas)

1616 Mughals grant Dutch right to trade in Surat

Arguin Island
Dutch 1638–1678

Gorée
Dutch 1621–1677

1637–1871 Elmina is captured and becomes the capital of the Dutch Gold Coast

Dutch 1637–1638

Fort Nassau
Elmina

Gold Coast Settlements:
11 Dutch, 7 English

Fernando Po

São Tomé

1612 Principe occupied by Dutch

Dutch
1630–1654

Dutch 1641–1648

1630–1654 Recife is capital of Dutch Brazil until recaptured by Portuguese

Recife

Luanda

ANGOLA
Dutch 1641–1648

St. Helena
Dutch 1633–1651

1641–1642 Luanda captured by Dutch

1607 VOC receives monopoly of the clove trade in the Moluccas Islands, known as the Spice Islands

1605 Fort captured from Portugal, developing Dutch dominance in Spice Islands

Formosa
Dutch 1624–1662

1630–1654 Pernambuco attacked by Dutch fleet and occupied

1623–1625 Salvador captured by Dutch

DUTCH SOUTH AFRICA

1652 Dutch settlement established in Cape Town

▽ **Back from Batavia**
A Dutch East India Company fleet returns to the Netherlands in 1648, having rescued a shipwrecked crew at Table Bay—the first Dutch contact with southern Africa.

4 THE DUTCH IN AUSTRALIA AND NEW ZEALAND   1606–1642

After being the first Europeans to sight Australia's coastline in 1606, the Dutch extensively surveyed its west and north coasts. Willem Janszoon made the first landfall in 1606. In 1642, Abel Tasman sighted Van Diemen's Land (Tasmania) and claimed it for the Netherlands. The Dutch made no attempt to establish a colony in Australia.

→ Voyages of Abel Tasman 1642–1644   — Australian coastline surveyed by Dutch 1644

REVOLUTION AND INDUSTRY

IN 1700–1850, MUCH OF THE WORLD WAS REVOLUTIONIZED BY NEW SCIENTIFIC AND POLITICAL IDEAS. PERHAPS THE MOST FAR-REACHING CHANGE, HOWEVER, WAS THE INDUSTRIAL REVOLUTION.

THE AGE OF REVOLUTION

The era from 1700 to 1850 could be called by many names—the age of empire, of industry, of nation-states, of Enlightenment, or of Romanticism and Nationalism. It was all these and more—it was the Age of Revolution, which formed the modern world.

The overriding and underlying force of this period in world history was growth. An explosion in world population went hand in hand with innovations that, in turn, resulted in a growth in productivity, trade, economies, urbanization, agriculture and industry, literacy and education, and media and technology, among others. The end result was the expansion of some empires and the toppling of others, as different political entities and systems tried—and sometimes failed—to cope with the sudden growth. Some nations thrived, often with brutal economic and human ramifications, as with the British exploitation of global resources, which was underpinned by the slave trade, or with the expansion of the US farther into the North American continent (see pp.260–261). Others, from east Asia to western Europe, failed to cope with the pressure, unleashing revolutions with long-term effects.

△ **Fight to the finish**
In one of the decisive naval battles of the Seven Years' War, the British took control of the French fortress of Louisbourg (in modern Canada) in July 1758. The victory enabled the British to take over the French North American capital of Quebec the next year.

△ **Party in Boston**
Of all the tea chests thrown into the harbor at the Boston Tea Party in 1773 by Americans protesting against British rule, this is the only chest to have survived.

Reshaping the world

The early 18th century saw change on several fronts. Innovations in agriculture, industry, and other kinds of technology prompted colonization by European settlers in America, Asia, Australia, and New Zealand. The consequences for indigenous populations were horrific—for example, the expansion of the US into Native American territory, or the genocide of Aboriginal peoples in Australia. Advances in technology meant that the scale and lethality of conflicts grew exponentially, whether in Europe where

GROWING CONNECTIONS

As the connections between different parts of the world increased, populations grew, and travel and communication became easier. The consequences were seen in the movement of people, a change in the scale of world economies, and political developments within and between nations, including global conflicts. It was a period that saw immense strides in the development of human understanding of nature and the subsequent ability to control and exploit it.

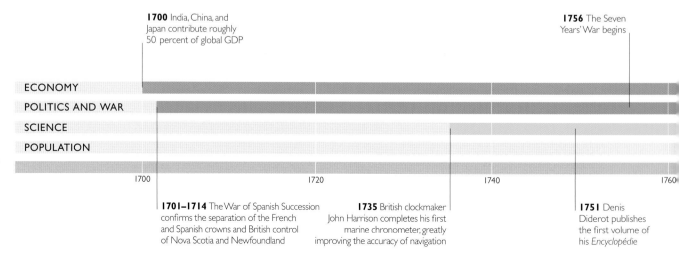

1700 India, China, and Japan contribute roughly 50 percent of global GDP

1756 The Seven Years' War begins

ECONOMY			
POLITICS AND WAR			
SCIENCE			
POPULATION			

| 1700 | 1720 | 1740 | 1760 |

1701–1714 The War of Spanish Succession confirms the separation of the French and Spanish crowns and British control of Nova Scotia and Newfoundland

1735 British clockmaker John Harrison completes his first marine chronometer, greatly improving the accuracy of navigation

1751 Denis Diderot publishes the first volume of his *Encyclopédie*

◁ **Heads up**
An 18th-century etching depicts French revolutionaries displaying the heads of the guards killed during the storming of the Bastille on July 14, 1789—one of the great symbolic acts of the French Revolution.

the Napoleonic Wars (see pp.208–211) saw the mobilization of huge armies; in New Zealand, where muskets transformed traditional Maori warfare; in India where small European forces were able to defeat larger local forces; or in Africa, where slaving empires flourished due to new weapons.

Global impacts

The 18th century saw the world's first global war, when the Seven Years' War (see pp.192–193), fought between European powers, spread to theaters around the world—from North America to Southeast Asia. As networks of trade and finance reached into every corner of the world, the consequences could be felt everywhere: on the plains of the American Midwest, where coast-to-coast railroads led to economic growth but also wiped out buffalo herds that sustained indigenous ways of life; across Africa, where the slave trade resulted in massive depopulation; and in south Asia, where British imperialism eventually resulted in the thorough dislocation of local economies and trade. In China, problems with currency and trade in commodities led to the Opium Wars; while in Australasia, colonial land grabs resulted in the depletion of indigenous populations.

Such immense transformations inevitably had profound political consequences. In Europe and the Americas, growing middle and artisan classes pushed for change, by revolution if necessary, so that the period 1700–1850 saw a slew of revolutionary conflicts, with the American and French revolutions of the 18th century and the nationalist and

political revolutions of the early 19th century in South America. The greatest upheavals came in China, where the 19th century saw near-constant unrest as the country failed to cope with economic, technological, and political changes in the world.

By 1850, the world was vastly richer overall but with greater inequality than ever before. Despite celebrated advances in politics, society, and culture, with revolutionary, liberation, and emancipation movements, the Englightenment, and the Scientific Revolution, it was the global sum of human misery that had grown most of all. Achievements in industry, trade, technology, and culture had been built on foundations of exploitation, slavery, genocide, and injustice.

▷ **Map of the future**
This map was drawn during the Lewis and Clark Expedition (1804–1806), which helped open North America to settlement and accelerated the expansion of the US.

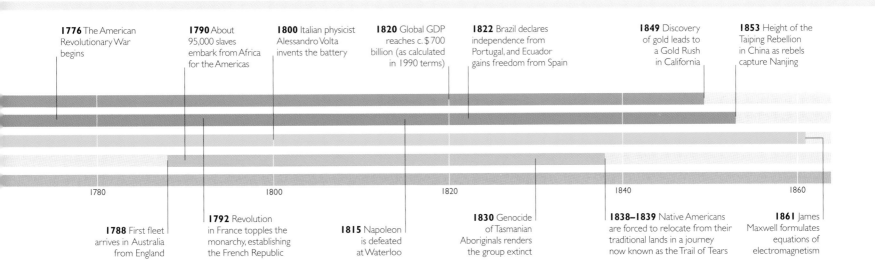

1776 The American Revolutionary War begins

1790 About 95,000 slaves embark from Africa for the Americas

1800 Italian physicist Alessandro Volta invents the battery

1820 Global GDP reaches c. $700 billion (as calculated in 1990 terms)

1822 Brazil declares independence from Portugal, and Ecuador gains freedom from Spain

1849 Discovery of gold leads to a Gold Rush in California

1853 Height of the Taiping Rebellion in China as rebels capture Nanjing

1780   1800   1820   1840   1860

1788 First fleet arrives in Australia from England

1792 Revolution in France topples the monarchy, establishing the French Republic

1815 Napoleon is defeated at Waterloo

1830 Genocide of Tasmanian Aboriginals renders the group extinct

1838–1839 Native Americans are forced to relocate from their traditional lands in a journey now known as the Trail of Tears

1861 James Maxwell formulates equations of electromagnetism

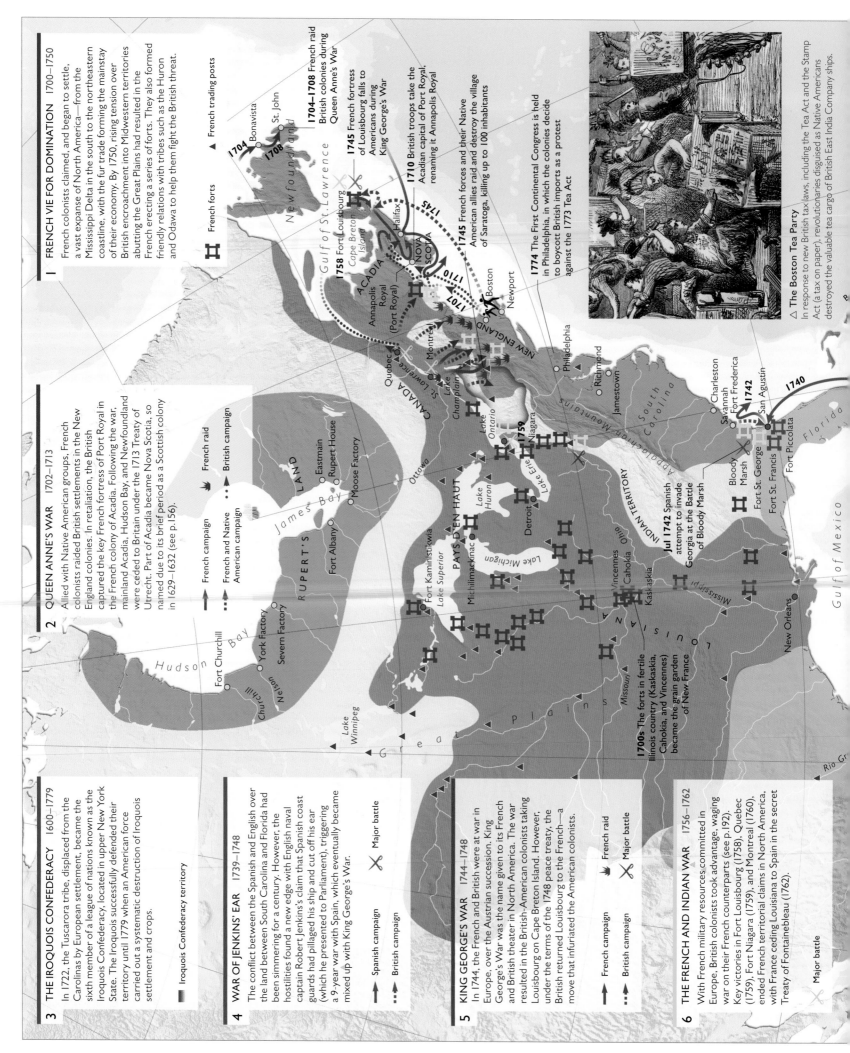

1 FRENCH VIE FOR DOMINATION 1700–1750

French colonists claimed, and began to settle, a vast expanse of North America—from the Mississippi Delta in the south to the northeastern coastline, with the fur trade forming the mainstay of their economy. By 1750, rising tension over British encroachment into Midwestern territories abutting the Great Plains had resulted in the French erecting a series of forts. They also formed friendly relations with tribes such as the Huron and Odawa to help them fight the British threat.

⌗ French forts ▲ French trading posts

1704 Bonavista
1708 St. John

1704–1708 French raid British colonies during Queen Anne's War

1745 French fortress of Louisbourg falls to Americans during King George's War

1710 British troops take the Acadian capital of Port Royal, renaming it Annapolis Royal

1758 Fort Louisbourg

1745 French forces and their Native American allies raid and destroy the village of Saratoga, killing up to 100 inhabitants

1774 The First Continental Congress is held in Philadelphia, in which the colonies decide to boycott British imports as a protest against the 1773 Tea Act

△ The Boston Tea Party
In response to new British tax laws, including the Tea Act and the Stamp Act (a tax on paper), revolutionaries disguised as Native Americans destroyed the valuable tea cargo of British East India Company ships.

2 QUEEN ANNE'S WAR 1702–1713

Allied with Native American groups, French colonists raided British settlements in the New England colonies. In retaliation, the British captured the key French fortress of Port Royal in the French colony of Acadia. Following the war, mainland Acadia, Hudson Bay, and Newfoundland were ceded to Britain under the 1713 Treaty of Utrecht. Part of Acadia became Nova Scotia, so named due to its brief period as a Scottish colony in 1629–1632 (see p.156).

→ French campaign → French raid
⋯ French and Native ⋯ British campaign
   American campaign

3 THE IROQUOIS CONFEDERACY 1600–1779

In 1722, the Tuscarora tribe, displaced from the Carolinas by European settlement, became the sixth member of a league of nations known as the Iroquois Confederacy, located in upper New York State. The Iroquois successfully defended their territory until 1779 when an American force carried out a systematic destruction of Iroquois settlement and crops.

▬ Iroquois Confederacy territory

4 WAR OF JENKINS' EAR 1739–1748

The conflict between the Spanish and English over the land between South Carolina and Florida had been simmering for a century. However, the hostilities found a new edge with English naval captain Robert Jenkins's claim that Spanish coast guards had pillaged his ship and cut off his ear (which he presented to Parliament), triggering a 9-year war with Spain, which eventually became mixed up with King George's War.

→ Spanish campaign → Major battle
⋯ British campaign

5 KING GEORGE'S WAR 1744–1748

In 1744, the French and British were at war in Europe, over the Austrian succession. King George's War was the name given to its French and British theater in North America. The war resulted in the British-American colonists taking Louisbourg on Cape Breton Island. However, under the terms of the 1748 peace treaty, the British returned Louisbourg to the French—a move that infuriated the American colonists.

→ French campaign → French raid
⋯ British campaign ✕ Major battle

Jul 1742 Spanish attempt to invade Georgia at the Battle of Bloody Marsh

1742 Fort Frederica
1740 San Agustín

1700s The forts in fertile Illinois country (Kaskaskia, Cahokia, and Vincennes) became the grain garden of New France

6 THE FRENCH AND INDIAN WAR 1756–1762

With French military resources committed in Europe, British colonists took advantage, waging war on their French counterparts (see p.192). Key victories in Fort Louisbourg (1758), Quebec (1759), Fort Niagara (1759), and Montreal (1760), ended French territorial claims in North America, with France ceding Louisiana to Spain in the secret Treaty of Fontainebleau (1762).

✕ Major battle

Gulf of St. Lawrence
Cape Breton Island
Halifax
Newfoundland
ACADIA
Annapolis Royal (Port Royal)
NOVA SCOTIA
CANADA
Quebec
St. Lawrence
Montreal
Lake Champlain
NEW ENGLAND
Boston
Newport
Philadelphia
Richmond
Jamestown
South Carolina
Appalachian Mountains
Charleston
Savannah
Fort Frederica
San Agustín
Fort St. George
Fort St. Francis
Fort Piccolata
Florida
Gulf of Mexico

Lake Ontario
Niagara **1759**
Lake Erie
Detroit
INDIAN TERRITORY
Ohio
Vincennes
Cahokia
Kaskaskia
PAYS D'EN HAUT
Lake Huron
Lake Michigan
Michilimackinac
Fort Kaministikwia
Lake Superior
RUPERT'S LAND
James Bay
Eastmain
Rupert House
Moose Factory
Fort Albany
Ottawa
Hudson Bay
Fort Churchill
York Factory
Severn Factory
Nelson
Churchill
Lake Winnipeg
Great Plains
LOUISIANA
Mississippi
Missouri
New Orleans
Rio Grande
Bloody Marsh

NORTH AMERICA, 1763
The map of North America changed dramatically following British victory in the French and Indian War (1754–1760) as Britain wrested all lands east of the Mississippi from the French. Meanwhile, Spain gained nominal control over Louisiana and ceded Florida to the British. To appease Native American groups, the British government drew up the Proclamation Line of 1763, which forbade colonial settlement beyond the line of the Appalachian Mountains.

KEY

British territory

Spanish territory

French territory

Proclamation Line

COLONIAL CONFLICTS IN NORTH AMERICA
From 1700, the rapidly growing population of the British Atlantic colonies posed a threat to French-controlled territories. French attempts to assert its own presence led to a series of conflicts that ended in a British victory in 1763.

KEY

British territory or colony, 1750

French territory or colony, 1750

Spanish territory or colony, 1750

British fort

Spanish fort

TIMELINE

7 TAXATION TYRANNY 1763–1773
In the years following the French and Indian War, Britain passed a series of taxation laws—not only to earn its share of profits from colonial trade in America but also to recoup the cost of the war. When Britain attempted to gain a monopoly on the lucrative tea trade by enforcing the Tea Act (1773), a group of colonists boarded British tea ships in Boston and dumped 342 chests of tea into the harbor—an act now known as the Boston Tea Party.

Boston Tea Party

1740 During the War of Jenkins' Ear, a British-colonial raid on Cartagena results in the death of the majority of the raiding army

8 THE FIRST CONTINENTAL CONGRESS 1774
In 1774, delegates from 12 of the 13 colonies (Georgia did not send a representative) convened in Philadelphia for the First Continental Congress. The delegates agreed that colonists were entitled to the rights of "life, liberty, and property," and called on the colonies to stop imports from Britain. As the stance hardened on both sides, the relationship between Britain and the American colonists became irreparable.

First Continental Congress

BATTLE FOR NORTH AMERICA

In the first half of the 18th century, North America became another theater for the expression of the imperial rivalries between France, Britain, and Spain. Britain would eventually triumph, but the cost of victory would sow the seeds of revolutionary sentiment into the hearts of the American colonists.

The population of Britain's North American colonies had reached 1.2 million by 1750—far outnumbering the 65,000 French and 20,000 or so Spanish colonists on the continent.

In contrast, the native population was in rapid decline, ravaged by displacement, massacres, and diseases borne from the Old World. For example, Native American numbers east of the Appalachians had dwindled from about 120,000 at the start of European colonization to just 20,000 in 1750. Moreover, the Native American groups struggled to find unity among themselves to help them withstand the tide of incomers. The French sought to contain the burgeoning British Atlantic colonies by strategically locating their own settlements

and forming alliances with Native Americans. The tactic gave rise to skirmishes but could not prevent the British colonies from extending their territory, displacing French colonists in the northeast, and destroying Spanish outposts that threatened to curtail their expansion to the south. The conflicts culminated in the French and Indian War (part of the Seven Years' War; see pp.192–193)—a bloody and costly campaign that earned the British a sweeping victory, and which all but ended French territorial claims on the continent. However, in the war's aftermath, the British government imposed laws and taxes to recoup the cost of the war, stoking resentment among colonists about being ruled from afar.

THE SEVEN YEARS' WAR

The outbreak of a conflict between Britain and France for colonial domination drew in allies on both sides. With hostilities extending from North America to India and from the Caribbean to Russia, this was the first war on a truly global scale.

The Seven Years' War pitted the alliance of Britain, Prussia, and Hanover against the alliance of France, Austria, Sweden, Saxony, Russia, and Spain. The war was driven by commercial and imperial rivalry, and by the antagonism between Prussia and Austria. In Europe, Prussia made a preemptive strike on Saxony in August 1756 after finding itself surrounded by enemies, once France had ended its ancient rivalry with Habsburg Austria and, along with Russia, formed a grand alliance. Britain aligned itself with Prussia, partly so that the British king could protect his German possession, Hanover, from the threat of a French takeover. However, Britain's main aim was to destroy France as a commercial rival, and its attack focused on the French navy and French colonies overseas, particularly in North America. Heavily committed to the European cause, France had few resources to spare for its colonies and consequently suffered substantial losses in North America, the Caribbean, west Africa, and also India (see pp.224–225). Fought simultaneously on five continents, the Seven Years' War culminated in 1763 with Britain emerging as the world's largest colonial power.

> *"While we had France for an enemy, Germany was the scene to employ and baffle her arms."*
>
> WILLIAM PITT, BRITISH PRIME MINISTER, 1762

COLONIAL DOMINATION

The Seven Years' War tested the military might of European powers—France, Britain, and Spain—in North America as they fought for colonial supremacy. Fighting battles on two fronts, in Europe and in the colonies, strained both resources and colonists' loyalties.

TIMELINE

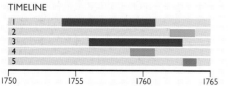

1750   1755   1760   1765

KEY

- ⚔ British fort
- ⚔ French fort
- ⚔ Spanish fort
- ⚓ British naval base
- ⚓ French naval base
- ⚓ Spanish naval base
- British possessions
- French possessions
- Spanish possessions

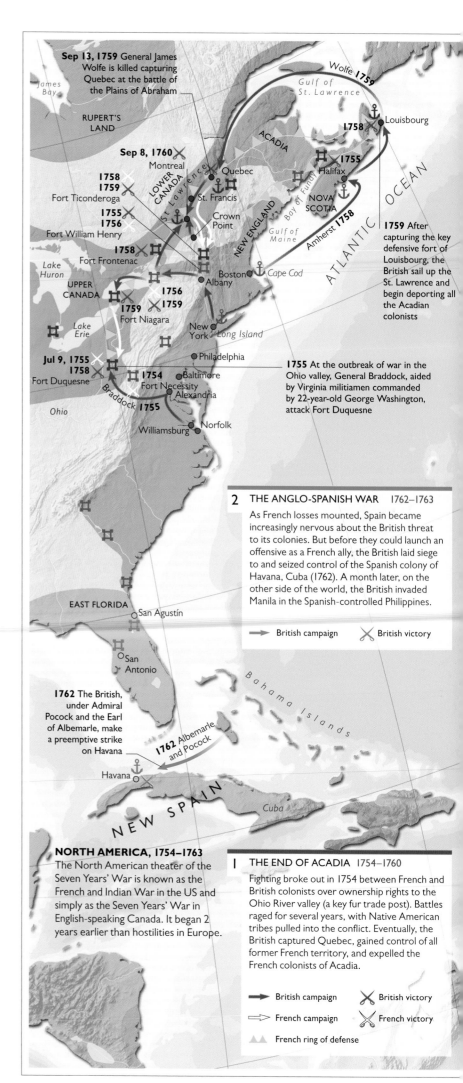

Sep 13, 1759 General James Wolfe is killed capturing Quebec at the battle of the Plains of Abraham

Sep 8, 1760 Montreal

1758
1759
Fort Ticonderoga

1755
1756
Fort William Henry

1758
Fort Frontenac

1756
1759   1759
Fort Niagara

Jul 9, 1755
1758
Fort Duquesne

1754
Fort Necessity

Braddock 1755

Wolfe 1759

1758   Louisbourg

1755
Halifax

Amherst 1758

1759 After capturing the key defensive fort of Louisbourg, the British sail up the St. Lawrence and begin deporting all the Acadian colonists

1755 At the outbreak of war in the Ohio valley, General Braddock, aided by Virginia militiamen commanded by 22-year-old George Washington, attack Fort Duquesne

2 THE ANGLO-SPANISH WAR 1762–1763

As French losses mounted, Spain became increasingly nervous about the British threat to its colonies. But before they could launch an offensive as a French ally, the British laid siege to and seized control of the Spanish colony of Havana, Cuba (1762). A month later, on the other side of the world, the British invaded Manila in the Spanish-controlled Philippines.

→ British campaign   ✗ British victory

1762 The British, under Admiral Pocock and the Earl of Albemarle, make a preemptive strike on Havana

1762 Albemarle and Pocock

NORTH AMERICA, 1754–1763

The North American theater of the Seven Years' War is known as the French and Indian War in the US and simply as the Seven Years' War in English-speaking Canada. It began 2 years earlier than hostilities in Europe.

1 THE END OF ACADIA 1754–1760

Fighting broke out in 1754 between French and British colonists over ownership rights to the Ohio River valley (a key fur trade post). Battles raged for several years, with Native American tribes pulled into the conflict. Eventually, the British captured Quebec, gained control of all former French territory, and expelled the French colonists of Acadia.

→ British campaign   ✗ British victory
⇨ French campaign   ✗ French victory
▲▲▲ French ring of defense

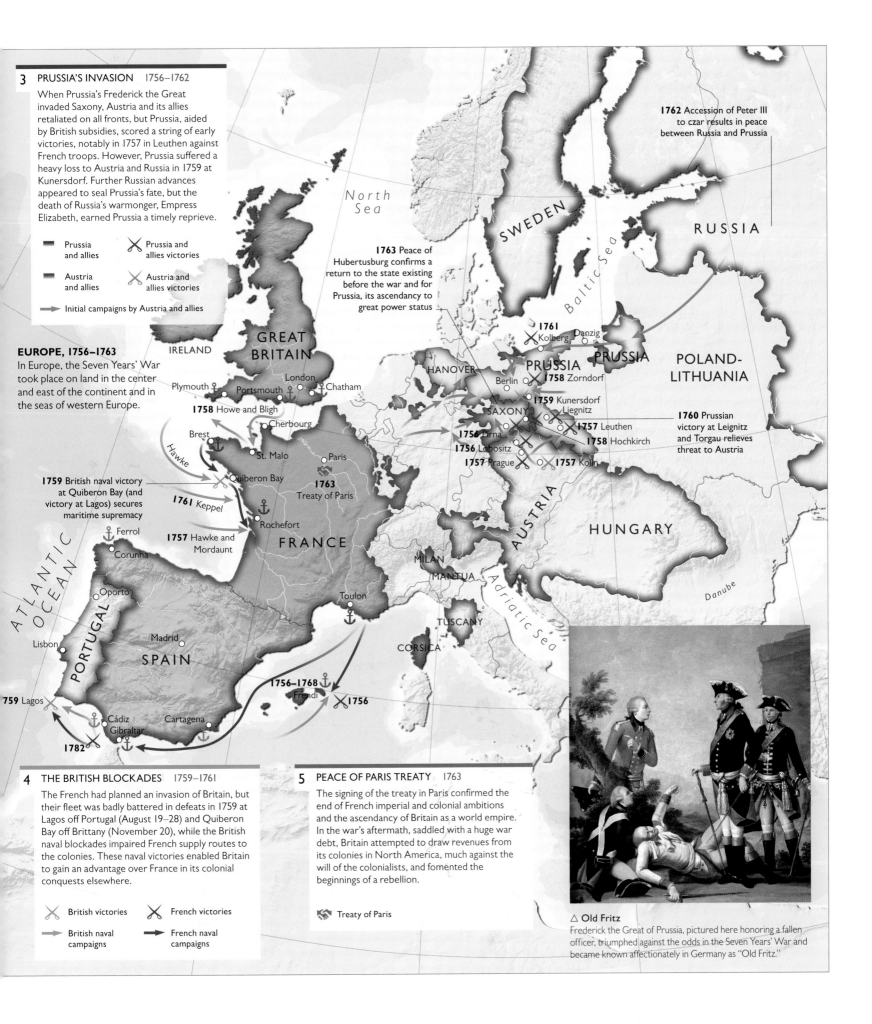

3 PRUSSIA'S INVASION 1756–1762

When Prussia's Frederick the Great invaded Saxony, Austria and its allies retaliated on all fronts, but Prussia, aided by British subsidies, scored a string of early victories, notably in 1757 in Leuthen against French troops. However, Prussia suffered a heavy loss to Austria and Russia in 1759 at Kunersdorf. Further Russian advances appeared to seal Prussia's fate, but the death of Russia's warmonger, Empress Elizabeth, earned Prussia a timely reprieve.

▬ Prussia and allies
✕ Prussia and allies victories

▬ Austria and allies
✕ Austria and allies victories

→ Initial campaigns by Austria and allies

EUROPE, 1756–1763

In Europe, the Seven Years' War took place on land in the center and east of the continent and in the seas of western Europe.

1759 British naval victory at Quiberon Bay (and victory at Lagos) secures maritime supremacy

1761 Keppel

1757 Hawke and Mordaunt

1758 Howe and Bligh

North Sea

SWEDEN

RUSSIA

1762 Accession of Peter III to czar results in peace between Russia and Prussia

Baltic Sea

1763 Peace of Hubertusburg confirms a return to the state existing before the war and for Prussia, its ascendancy to great power status

1761 Kolberg Danzig
Kolberg

POLAND-LITHUANIA

HANOVER PRUSSIA PRUSSIA

Berlin **1758** Zorndorf
1759 Kunersdorf
Liegnitz
SAXONY **1757** Leuthen **1760** Prussian victory at Leignitz and Torgau relieves threat to Austria
1756 Pirna **1758** Hochkirch
1756 Lobositz
1757 Prague **1757** Kolin

AUSTRIA

HUNGARY

IRELAND

GREAT BRITAIN

London
Plymouth Chatham
Portsmouth

Brest
Cherbourg
St. Malo
Paris
1763 Treaty of Paris

Hawke

Quiberon Bay

Rochefort

FRANCE

Ferrol
Corunha

ATLANTIC OCEAN

Oporto

Lisbon
PORTUGAL Madrid
SPAIN

759 Lagos

1782 Cádiz
Gibraltar Cartagena

MILAN
MANTUA
Toulon

TUSCANY

Adriatic Sea

CORSICA

Danube

1756–1768 Frendi ✕**1756**

4 THE BRITISH BLOCKADES 1759–1761

The French had planned an invasion of Britain, but their fleet was badly battered in defeats in 1759 at Lagos off Portugal (August 19–28) and Quiberon Bay off Brittany (November 20), while the British naval blockades impaired French supply routes to the colonies. These naval victories enabled Britain to gain an advantage over France in its colonial conquests elsewhere.

✕ British victories
✕ French victories
→ British naval campaigns
→ French naval campaigns

5 PEACE OF PARIS TREATY 1763

The signing of the treaty in Paris confirmed the end of French imperial and colonial ambitions and the ascendancy of Britain as a world empire. In the war's aftermath, saddled with a huge war debt, Britain attempted to draw revenues from its colonies in North America, much against the will of the colonialists, and fomented the beginnings of a rebellion.

🤝 Treaty of Paris

△ **Old Fritz**
Frederick the Great of Prussia, pictured here honoring a fallen officer, triumphed against the odds in the Seven Years' War and became known affectionately in Germany as "Old Fritz."

THE AGRICULTURAL REVOLUTION

The term "Agricultural Revolution" is traditionally associated with the rapid increase in agricultural productivity from the early 18th to the mid-19th centuries. It began mainly in Britain and later spread throughout Europe, the US, and beyond.

△ **New land from the sea**
This illustration from 1705 is one of the most dramatic portrayals of the impact of land reclamation—the Dutch literally enlarged their nation by using dams and dikes to drain land that had previously been below sea level.

Beginning in the early 18th century, innovative British farmers adopted and adapted techniques, crops, and technologies from other parts of the world, particularly the Low Countries (modern-day Belgium and Holland), to achieve a dramatic increase in agricultural productivity. Between 1750 and 1850, grain productivity in Britain tripled, supporting a similar expansion of the population far beyond historically sustainable levels. Many of the practices and ideas involved may have been drawn from continental Europe, but by 1815, British agricultural productivity far outstripped that of any other European country. In the 19th century, these innovations spread across the developed world. The four pillars of this revolution in agriculture were: agricultural technology, such as seed drills and mechanization; crop rotation; selective breeding to improve livestock yields; and enclosure, reclamation, and other changes in land-use practices.

Innovation and mechanization

In 1701, English farmer and agronomist Jethro Tull developed an improved seed drill—a device that planted seeds in rows, making it easier to weed and tend the crop, and thus increasing labor efficiency. Although initially slow to catch on, the seed drill was emblematic of the potential of technology to greatly improve the productivity of both land and labor. In the US, Cyrus McCormick developed a machine called the reaper; in 1840, he was able to cut 12½ times more wheat with it in a day than was possible with a scythe.

Another source of increasing yields was the use of new crop types, such as high-yielding wheat and barley—which replaced low-yielding rye—and turnips, root vegetables that could be grown without impeding weed clearance. However, perhaps the greatest boost came by overcoming the factor that was primarily limiting yields: the level of biologically available nitrogen in the soil. Although they did not yet understand the underlying biology, farmers in the Low Countries had discovered that crops such as legumes and clover could improve soil fertility and reduce the need for land to be left fallow. This is because bacterial root nodules on such crops can fix, or assimilate, atmospheric nitrogen, fertilizing the soil even as they produce useful food and

▷ **Seed drill**
This relatively simple device greatly improved agricultural productivity by planting seeds with consistent depth, spacing, and alignment.

DRIVING THE REVOLUTION

The introduction of high-yielding crop varieties, crop rotation, and the economic impact of nonfood cash crops were some of the primary drivers of the Agricultural Revolution. Other milestones included new livestock breeds and how they were brought to market. New areas of land were tilled in the New World even as land use was transformed in the Old World. Shifts in urban and rural demographics changed the labor force, while new technologies boosted productivity.

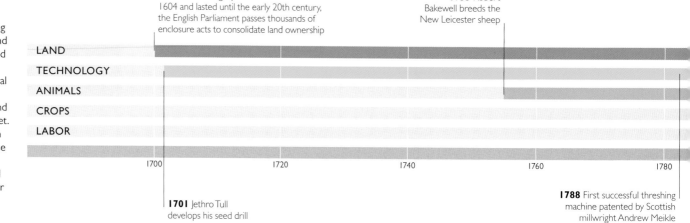

1700 Continuing a process that started in 1604 and lasted until the early 20th century, the English Parliament passes thousands of enclosure acts to consolidate land ownership

1755 Robert Bakewell breeds the New Leicester sheep

LAND
TECHNOLOGY
ANIMALS
CROPS
LABOR

1700　　1720　　1740　　1760　　1780

1701 Jethro Tull develops his seed drill

1788 First successful threshing machine patented by Scottish millwright Andrew Meikle

◁ **Bakewell's Leicester ram**
This engraving shows a Dishley or New Leicester ram, one of the products of Robert Bakewell's extensive program of selective breeding to create more productive livestock.

fodder crops. In Norfolk, for example, between 1700 and 1850, a switch to clover and the doubling of the cultivation area of legumes tripled the rate of nitrogen fixation.

Changing practices

Meanwhile, changes in the way livestock were reared (stall rearing instead of pasturing, for example) made it possible to collect manure to use as fertilizer. Together, such innovations increased wheat yields by about one-quarter between 1700 and 1800, and then by about half between 1800 and 1850. Eventually, scientific knowledge caught up with empirical wisdom to reveal nitrogen as the key element in fertilizers, and from the mid-19th century imported sources such as guano became important.

Better yields and cultivation of fodder plants resulted in an increase in livestock rearing, and selective breeding led to higher-yielding breeds. Breeds such as the Merino sheep, famous for its wool, radicalized Australian agriculture from 1807; by the 1850s, there were 39 sheep for every Australian.

> *"Agriculture not only gives riches to a nation, but the only riches she can call her own."*
>
> SAMUEL JOHNSON, ENGLISH ESSAYIST (1709–1784)

In Britain, enclosures—the fencing in of wasteland or common land to make it private property—increased the land available for intensive farming, as did the clearing of woodland, the reclamation of upland pastures, and the reclamation of fenland. From the mid-17th to the mid-19th centuries, nearly one-third of England's agricultural land was affected. Land that had previously been pasture became arable, as pasture was replaced by fodder crops, especially those produced in the crop rotation system. Crop rotation, especially when crops were planted in rows, meant that fields need not be left fallow to allow weeding.

The Agricultural Revolution laid the foundations for the Industrial Revolution (see pp.212–213). It sustained high levels of population growth and increased the productivity of land and workers, freeing up labor from agriculture and the countryside and driving the growth of cities and industrial workforces.

△ **Muck spreading**
This pleasant country scene somewhat obscures the true nature of the product being advertised—guano, or fertilizer made from bird droppings.

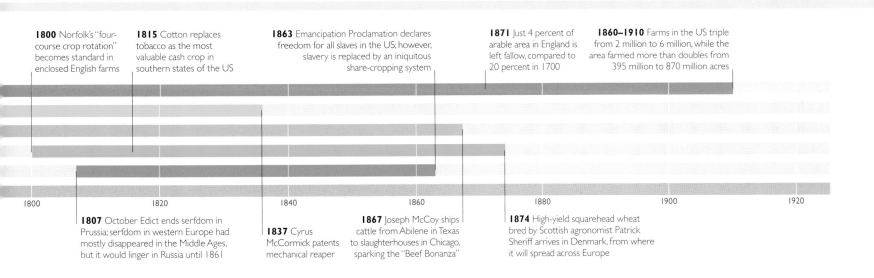

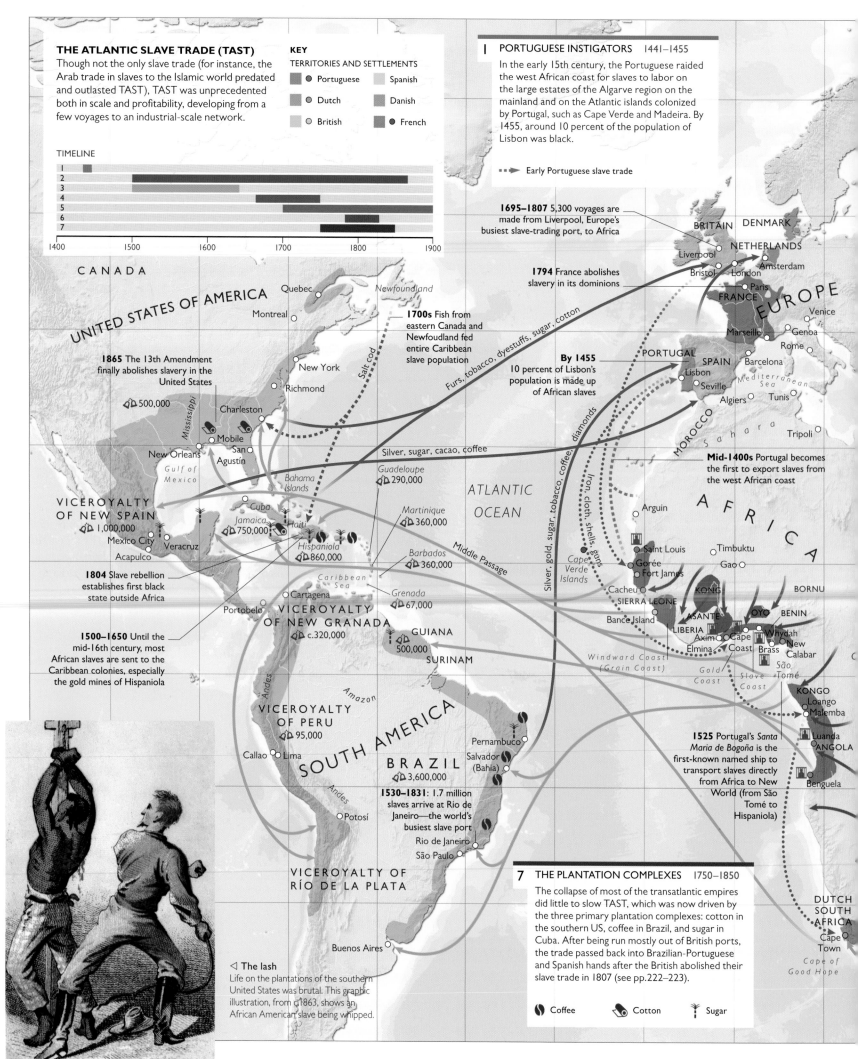

THE ATLANTIC SLAVE TRADE (TAST)

Though not the only slave trade (for instance, the Arab trade in slaves to the Islamic world predated and outlasted TAST), TAST was unprecedented both in scale and profitability, developing from a few voyages to an industrial-scale network.

KEY

TERRITORIES AND SETTLEMENTS

- Portuguese
- Dutch
- British
- Spanish
- Danish
- French

TIMELINE

```
1
2
3
4
5
6
7
1400   1500   1600   1700   1800   1900
```

I PORTUGUESE INSTIGATORS 1441–1455

In the early 15th century, the Portuguese raided the west African coast for slaves to labor on the large estates of the Algarve region on the mainland and on the Atlantic islands colonized by Portugal, such as Cape Verde and Madeira. By 1455, around 10 percent of the population of Lisbon was black.

---▶ Early Portuguese slave trade

1695–1807 5,300 voyages are made from Liverpool, Europe's busiest slave-trading port, to Africa

1794 France abolishes slavery in its dominions

1700s Fish from eastern Canada and Newfoudland fed entire Caribbean slave population

By 1455 10 percent of Lisbon's population is made up of African slaves

Mid-1400s Portugal becomes the first to export slaves from the west African coast

1865 The 13th Amendment finally abolishes slavery in the United States
🏴 500,000

1804 Slave rebellion establishes first black state outside Africa

1500–1650 Until the mid-16th century, most African slaves are sent to the Caribbean colonies, especially the gold mines of Hispaniola

VICEROYALTY OF NEW SPAIN
🏴 1,000,000

Guadeloupe 🏴 290,000

Martinique 🏴 360,000

Barbados 🏴 360,000

Cuba
Jamaica 🏴 750,000
Haiti
Hispaniola 🏴 860,000

Grenada 🏴 67,000

VICEROYALTY OF NEW GRANADA
🏴 c.320,000

GUIANA 🏴 500,000

SURINAM

VICEROYALTY OF PERU
🏴 95,000

BRAZIL
🏴 3,600,000

1530–1831: 1.7 million slaves arrive at Rio de Janeiro—the world's busiest slave port

VICEROYALTY OF RÍO DE LA PLATA

Furs, tobacco, dyestuffs, sugar, cotton

Silver, sugar, cacao, coffee

Silver, gold, sugar, tobacco, coffee, diamonds

Iron, cloth, shells, guns

Middle Passage

ATLANTIC OCEAN

A F R I C A

Arguin

Saint Louis
Gorée
Fort James
Cacheu
SIERRA LEONE
Bance Island
LIBERIA
Axim
Elmina
Cape Coast
ASANTE
KONG
OYO BENIN
Whydah
New Calabar
Brass
São Tomé

Timbuktu
Gao

BORNU

Windward Coast (Grain Coast)
Gold Coast
Slave Coast

Cape Verde Islands

KONGO
Loango
Malemba
Luanda
ANGOLA

1525 Portugal's *Santa Maria de Bogoña* is the first-known named ship to transport slaves directly from Africa to New World (from São Tomé to Hispaniola)

Benguela

DUTCH SOUTH AFRICA
Cape Town
Cape of Good Hope

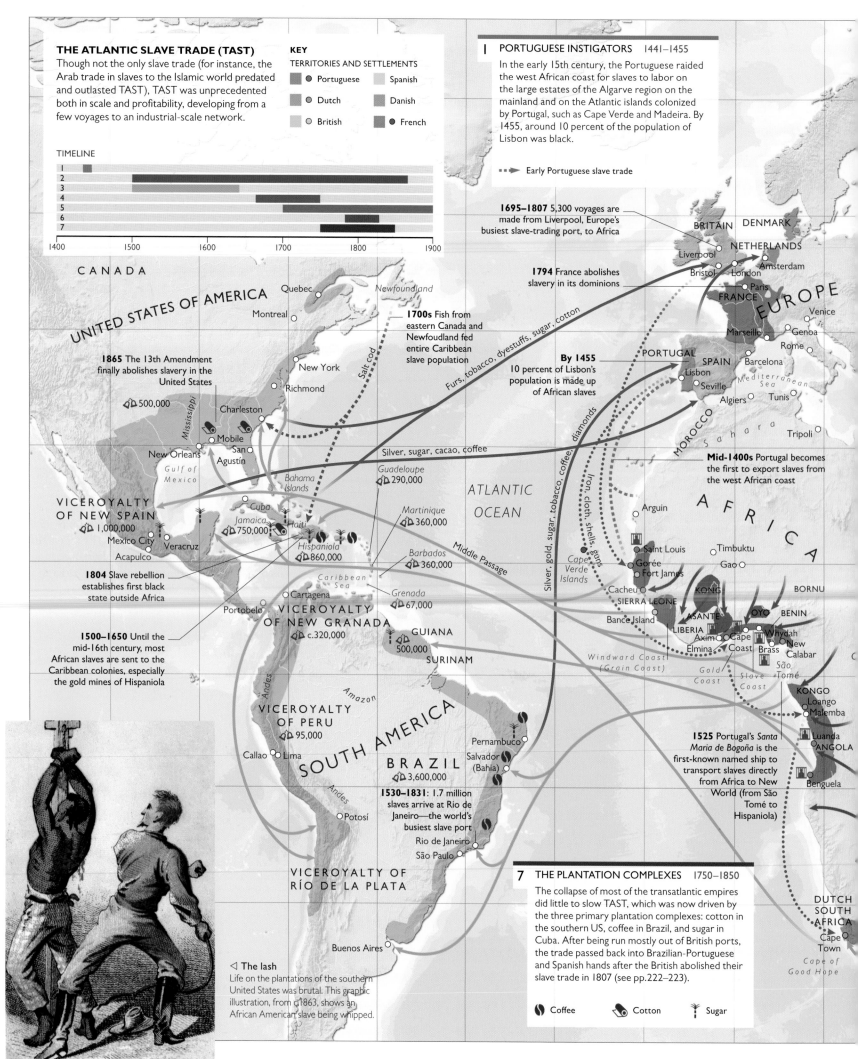

◁ **The lash**
Life on the plantations of the southern United States was brutal. This graphic illustration, from c.1863, shows an African American slave being whipped.

7 THE PLANTATION COMPLEXES 1750–1850

The collapse of most of the transatlantic empires did little to slow TAST, which was now driven by the three primary plantation complexes: cotton in the southern US, coffee in Brazil, and sugar in Cuba. After being run mostly out of British ports, the trade passed back into Brazilian-Portuguese and Spanish hands after the British abolished their slave trade in 1807 (see pp.222–223).

🐚 Coffee   🔫 Cotton   🌾 Sugar

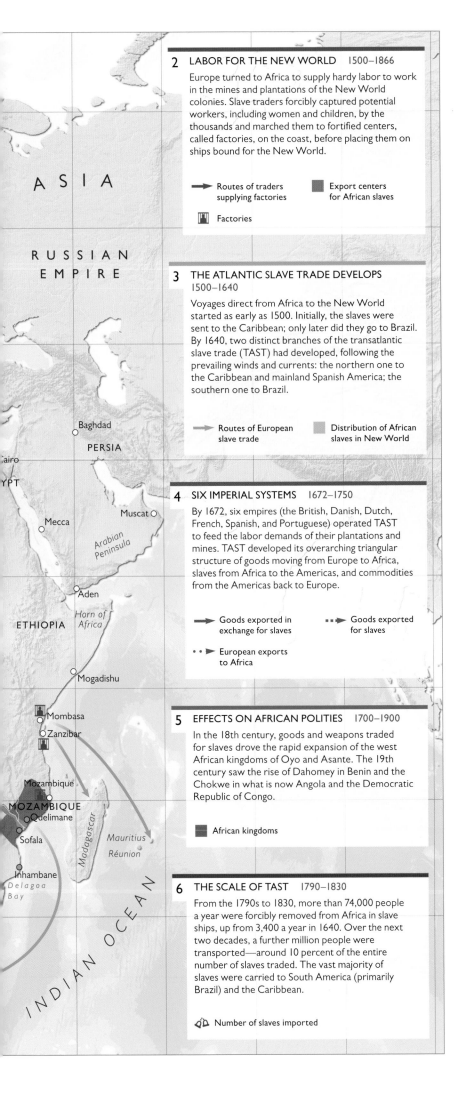

2 LABOR FOR THE NEW WORLD   1500–1866

Europe turned to Africa to supply hardy labor to work in the mines and plantations of the New World colonies. Slave traders forcibly captured potential workers, including women and children, by the thousands and marched them to fortified centers, called factories, on the coast, before placing them on ships bound for the New World.

→ Routes of traders supplying factories

▪ Export centers for African slaves

▯ Factories

3 THE ATLANTIC SLAVE TRADE DEVELOPS 1500–1640

Voyages direct from Africa to the New World started as early as 1500. Initially, the slaves were sent to the Caribbean; only later did they go to Brazil. By 1640, two distinct branches of the transatlantic slave trade (TAST) had developed, following the prevailing winds and currents: the northern one to the Caribbean and mainland Spanish America; the southern one to Brazil.

→ Routes of European slave trade

▪ Distribution of African slaves in New World

4 SIX IMPERIAL SYSTEMS   1672–1750

By 1672, six empires (the British, Danish, Dutch, French, Spanish, and Portuguese) operated TAST to feed the labor demands of their plantations and mines. TAST developed its overarching triangular structure of goods moving from Europe to Africa, slaves from Africa to the Americas, and commodities from the Americas back to Europe.

→ Goods exported in exchange for slaves

▪▪▶ Goods exported for slaves

• •▶ European exports to Africa

5 EFFECTS ON AFRICAN POLITIES   1700–1900

In the 18th century, goods and weapons traded for slaves drove the rapid expansion of the west African kingdoms of Oyo and Asante. The 19th century saw the rise of Dahomey in Benin and the Chokwe in what is now Angola and the Democratic Republic of Congo.

▪ African kingdoms

6 THE SCALE OF TAST   1790–1830

From the 1790s to 1830, more than 74,000 people a year were forcibly removed from Africa in slave ships, up from 3,400 a year in 1640. Over the next two decades, a further million people were transported—around 10 percent of the entire number of slaves traded. The vast majority of slaves were carried to South America (primarily Brazil) and the Caribbean.

⚓ Number of slaves imported

THE ATLANTIC SLAVE TRADE

The Atlantic slave trade was an international system of commerce and human misery that saw around 12.5 million people forcibly transported to the New World, and about 2 million killed in the process. The trade transformed the world economy and the nations involved.

Slavery was still a major feature of 15th-century life, especially in Iberia and Italy, with slaves coming from eastern Europe as well as Africa. Though slaves were often domestic servants, this provided a model when the colonization and exploitation of the New World got under way, as the intense demand for labor drove the development of one of the first global systems of large-scale commerce: a triangular system in which manufactured goods from Europe were traded for slaves in Africa, who were then transported to the New World and forced to produce raw materials to be shipped back to Europe.

Slave trading was immensely profitable, so much so that it may have underwritten the entire edifice of Western capitalism. Even as some of the nations that had profited the most sought to stamp out the trade, it continued at high volumes into the early part of the 19th century. The trade had profound effects on the populations and subsequent development of both exporting and importing regions and constituted one of the greatest forced migration events in history. It was an atrocity on an immense scale, the ramifications of which are still barely acknowledged today.

"The shrieks and groans rendered the whole scene of horror almost unimaginable."

FORMER SLAVE OLAUDAH EQUIANO, 1789

THE MIDDLE PASSAGE
THE JOURNEY AND THE DESTINATION

The journey across the Atlantic was the "middle" leg of the triangular trade and so was known as the Middle Passage. Slaves, most of whom had never before seen the sea, were shackled and tightly packed together, confined in horrific conditions for 6–8 weeks, or sometimes up to 13 weeks with adverse weather. Disease, murder, and suicide were rampant and 10–20 percent of slaves died on the voyage.

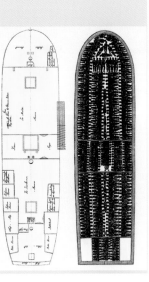

Packed together
This harrowing deck plan shows the unimaginable way in which slaves were packed together in the hold of a slave ship.

THE AMERICAN REVOLUTION

Also known as the American War of Independence, the American Revolution was the culmination of increasing tensions between Britain and its colonies in the Americas. The war pitted Patriots (who wanted independence) against Loyalists (who were loyal to the Crown) in a conflict that would forge a new nation in America.

Seeking to defray the costs of war debt, as well as the many expenses of securing the western frontier and protecting colonists from Native Americans, Britain looked to impose more taxation on its 13 colonies. The colonies, however, resented this repressive taxation, since they did not receive any direct representation in British Parliament in return. Fired by Enlightenment ideals of liberty and justice, many colonists resisted the acts of a distant Parliament, staging rebellious stunts such as the Boston Tea Party in 1773 and summoning a Continental Congress in 1774 to press for autonomous rights and liberties.

Growing tension between Patriots and foreign troops spilled over into war when the first shots were fired at Lexington, Massachusetts, in April 1775. The war was as much a civil conflict as a revolution; many colonists remained loyal to the Crown, and

Loyalist militia composed a significant portion of British forces. British efforts to crush George Washington's Patriot army in the north ended in a stalemate, yet the Patriots won key symbolic victories, such as their defeat of a column marched from Canada, which convinced the French to enter the war on the Patriots' side. When the British began to attack from the south, and after a crushing British victory at Charleston, the Revolution looked to be in danger, but slowly things changed in the Patriots' favor, and the British began to feel the strain of fighting a war from such a distance—orders, troops, and supplies could take months to cross the Atlantic. When the French fleet chased off British naval relief in 1781, Washington and his French allies were able to trap the British commander Charles Cornwallis in Yorktown, Virginia, and force the British to agree to a peace treaty.

THOMAS JEFFERSON
1743–1826

A lawyer and plantation owner from Virginia, Thomas Jefferson emerged as one of the prime intellectual powerhouses of the Patriot cause with his 1774 defense of American independence, *A Summary View of the Rights of British America*. He was asked to help write the Declaration of Independence, and his draft was adopted in 1776, with only minor changes. He went on to found the Democratic Party, serve as third president of the US, and oversee major expansion of US territory.

Declaring independence
Thomas Jefferson presents the Declaration of Independence to Congress.

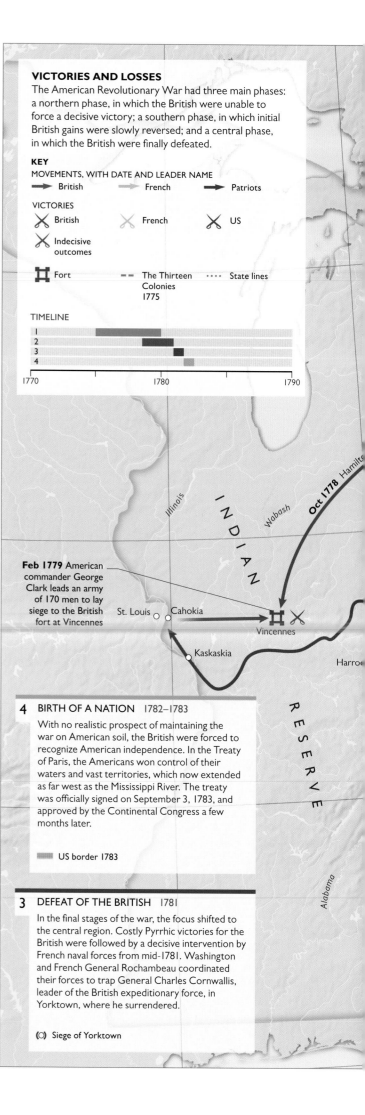

VICTORIES AND LOSSES
The American Revolutionary War had three main phases: a northern phase, in which the British were unable to force a decisive victory; a southern phase, in which initial British gains were slowly reversed; and a central phase, in which the British were finally defeated.

KEY
MOVEMENTS, WITH DATE AND LEADER NAME
→ British → French → Patriots

VICTORIES
✕ British ✕ French ✕ US
✕ Indecisive outcomes

⊞ Fort – – The Thirteen Colonies 1775 ···· State lines

TIMELINE
1 2 3 4
1770 1780 1790

Feb 1779 American commander George Clark leads an army of 170 men to lay siege to the British fort at Vincennes

Oct 1778 Hamilton

Illinois
Wabash
INDIAN
St. Louis Cahokia
Vincennes
Kaskaskia
Harro
RESERVE
Alabama

4 BIRTH OF A NATION 1782–1783

With no realistic prospect of maintaining the war on American soil, the British were forced to recognize American independence. In the Treaty of Paris, the Americans won control of their waters and vast territories, which now extended as far west as the Mississippi River. The treaty was officially signed on September 3, 1783, and approved by the Continental Congress a few months later.

▥ US border 1783

3 DEFEAT OF THE BRITISH 1781

In the final stages of the war, the focus shifted to the central region. Costly Pyrrhic victories for the British were followed by a decisive intervention by French naval forces from mid-1781. Washington and French General Rochambeau coordinated their forces to trap General Charles Cornwallis, leader of the British expeditionary force, in Yorktown, where he surrendered.

(○) Siege of Yorktown

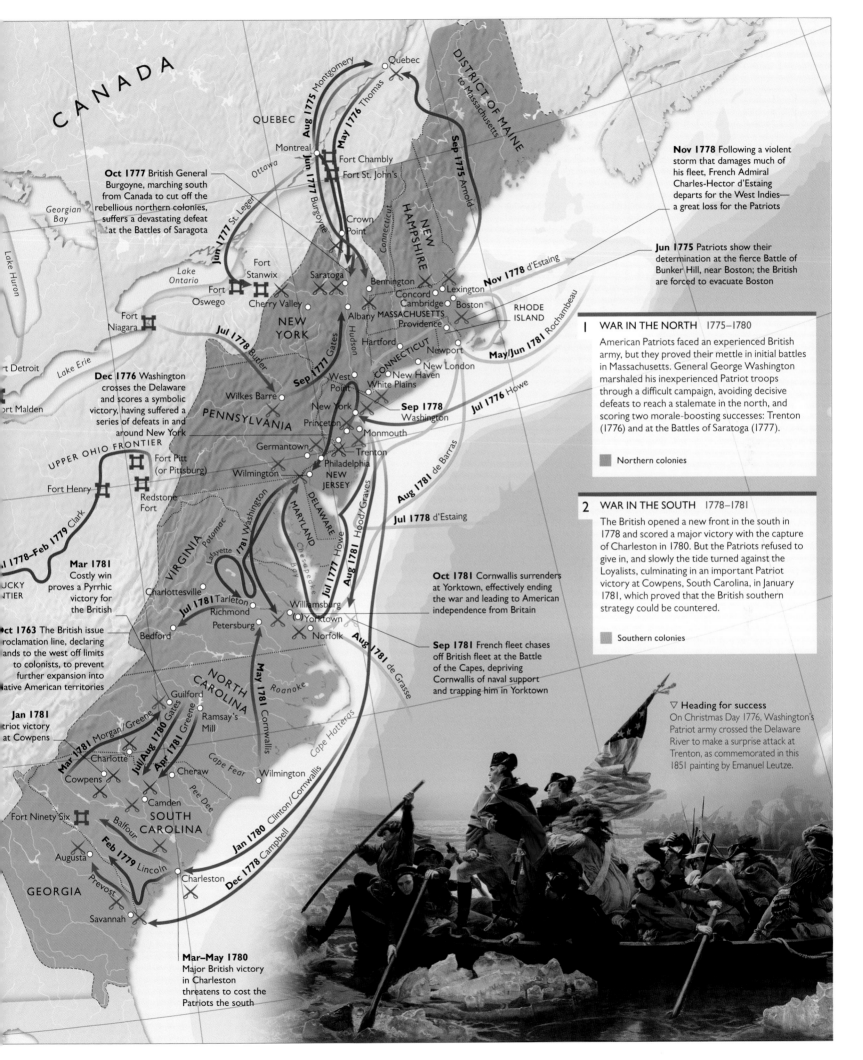

CANADA

QUEBEC

Aug 1775 Montgomery

May 1776 Thomas

Quebec

DISTRICT OF MAINE
to Massachusetts

Montreal

Fort Chambly

Jun 1777

Fort St. John's

Ottawa

Sep 1775 Arnold

Oct 1777 British General
Burgoyne, marching south
from Canada to cut off the
rebellious northern colonies,
suffers a devastating defeat
at the Battles of Saragota

Jun 1777 St. Leger

Aug 1777 Burgoyne

*Georgian
Bay*

Crown
Point

*Lake
Ontario*

Fort
Stanwix

Saratoga

Bennington

**NEW
HAMPSHIRE**

Nov 1778 Following a violent
storm that damages much of
his fleet, French Admiral
Charles-Hector d'Estaing
departs for the West Indies—
a great loss for the Patriots

Connecticut

Concord
Cambridge

Lexington

Boston

Nov 1778 d'Estaing

Jun 1775 Patriots show their
determination at the fierce Battle of
Bunker Hill, near Boston; the British
are forced to evacuate Boston

Fort
Oswego

Cherry Valley

Albany **MASSACHUSETTS**
Providence

**RHODE
ISLAND**

Lake Huron

Fort
Niagara

**NEW
YORK**

Hartford

CONNECTICUT

Newport

May/Jun 1781 Rochambeau

1 WAR IN THE NORTH 1775–1780

Jul 1778 Butler

New London

New Haven

Hudson

Sep 1777 Gates

West
Point

White Plains

Lake Erie

rt Detroit

Dec 1776 Washington
crosses the Delaware
and scores a symbolic
victory, having suffered a
series of defeats in and
around New York

Wilkes Barre

New York

Sep 1778
Washington

Jul 1776 Howe

American Patriots faced an experienced British
army, but they proved their mettle in initial battles
in Massachusetts. General George Washington
marshaled his inexperienced Patriot troops
through a difficult campaign, avoiding decisive
defeats to reach a stalemate in the north, and
scoring two morale-boosting successes: Trenton
(1776) and at the Battles of Saratoga (1777).

ort Malden

PENNSYLVANIA

Princeton

Monmouth

Northern colonies

Germantown

Trenton

UPPER OHIO FRONTIER

Fort Pitt
(or Pittsburg)

Philadelphia
**NEW
JERSEY**

Aug 1781 de Barras

Wilmington

Fort Henry

Redstone
Fort

Jul 1778–Feb 1779 Clark

MARYLAND

DELAWARE

Jul 1777 Howe

Hood/Graves

Aug 1781 de Grasse

Jul 1778 d'Estaing

2 WAR IN THE SOUTH 1778–1781

Mar 1781
Costly win
proves a Pyrrhic
victory for
the British

UCKY
TIER

Lafayette 1781 Washington

Potomac

VIRGINIA

Charlottesville

Oct 1781 Cornwallis surrenders
at Yorktown, effectively ending
the war and leading to American
independence from Britain

The British opened a new front in the south in
1778 and scored a major victory with the capture
of Charleston in 1780. But the Patriots refused to
give in, and slowly the tide turned against the
Loyalists, culminating in an important Patriot
victory at Cowpens, South Carolina, in January
1781, which proved that the British southern
strategy could be countered.

Jul 1781 Tarleton

Richmond

Aug 1781 Howe

Chesapeake Bay

Williamsburg

Yorktown

Oct 1763 The British issue
roclamation line, declaring
ands to the west off limits
to colonists, to prevent
further expansion into
ative American territories

Petersburg

Bedford

Norfolk

Aug 1781 Cornwallis

Southern colonies

Jan 1781
triot victory
at Cowpens

**NORTH
CAROLINA**

May 1781 Cornwallis

Guilford

Gates

Roanoke

Sep 1781 French fleet chases
off British fleet at the Battle
of the Capes, depriving
Cornwallis of naval support
and trapping him in Yorktown

Mar 1781 Morgan/Greene

Ramsay's
Mill

Apr 1781 Greene

Jul/Aug 1780 Gates

▽ **Heading for success**
On Christmas Day 1776, Washington's
Patriot army crossed the Delaware
River to make a surprise attack at
Trenton, as commemorated in this
1851 painting by Emanuel Leutze.

Charlotte

Cheraw

Cape Fear

Wilmington

Cowpens

Pee Dee

Cape Hatteras

Camden

Fort Ninety Six

**SOUTH
CAROLINA**

Balfour

Jan 1780 Clinton/Cornwallis

Feb 1779 Lincoln

Augusta

Prevost

Dec 1778 Campbell

Charleston

GEORGIA

Savannah

Mar–May 1780 Major British victory
in Charleston
threatens to cost the
Patriots the south

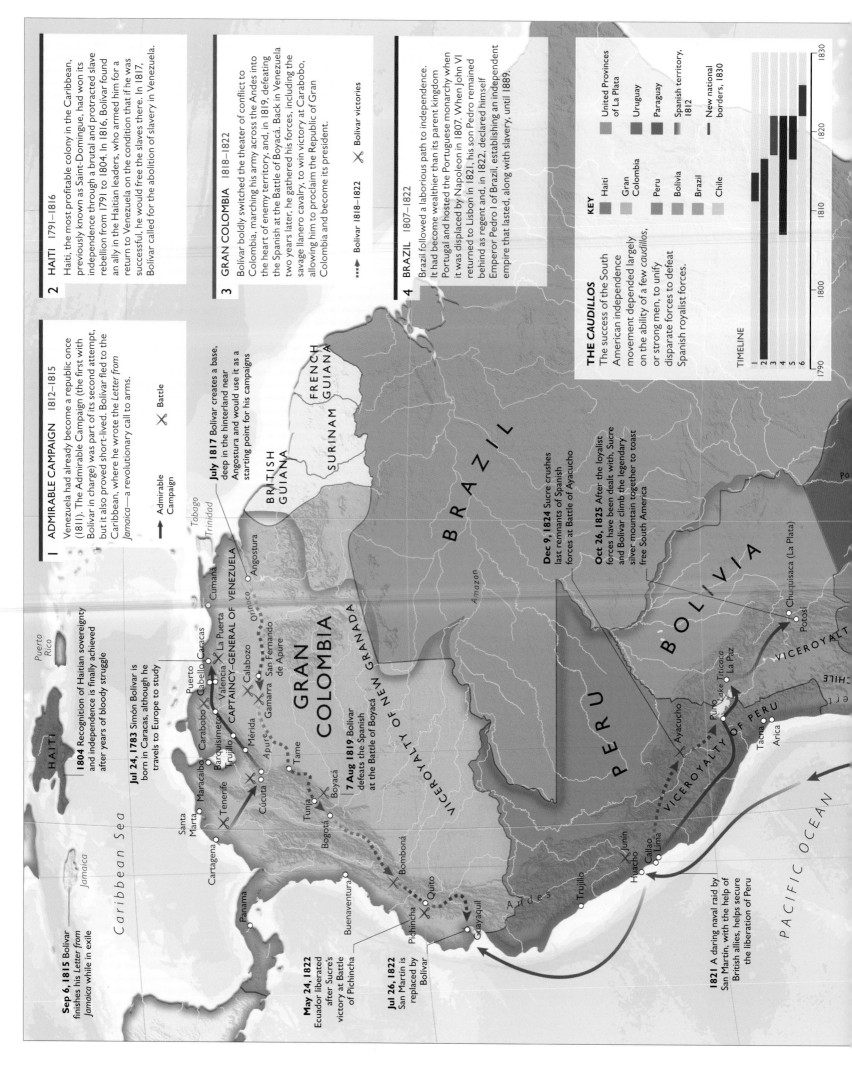

1 | ADMIRABLE CAMPAIGN 1812–1815

Venezuela had already become a republic once (1811). The Admirable Campaign (with Bolívar in charge) was part of its second attempt, but it also proved short-lived. Bolívar fled to the Caribbean, where he wrote the *Letter from Jamaica*—a revolutionary call to arms.

→ Admirable Campaign   ✕ Battle

Sep 6, 1815 Bolívar finishes his *Letter from Jamaica* while in exile

1804 Recognition of Haitian sovereignty and independence is finally achieved after years of bloody struggle

Jul 24, 1783 Simón Bolívar is born in Caracas, although he travels to Europe to study

May 24, 1822 Ecuador liberated after Sucre's victory at Battle of Pichincha

Jul 26, 1822 San Martín is replaced by Bolívar

2 | HAITI 1791–1816

Haiti, the most profitable colony in the Caribbean, previously known as Saint-Domingue, had won its independence through a brutal and protracted slave rebellion from 1791 to 1804. In 1816, Bolívar found an ally in the Haitian leaders, who armed him for a return to Venezuela on the condition that if he was successful, he would free the slaves there. In 1817, Bolívar called for the abolition of slavery in Venezuela.

3 | GRAN COLOMBIA 1818–1822

Bolívar boldly switched the theater of conflict to Colombia, marching his army across the Andes into the heart of enemy territory, and, in 1819, defeating the Spanish at the Battle of Boyacá. Back in Venezuela two years later, he gathered his forces, including the savage llanero cavalry, to win victory at Carabobo, allowing him to proclaim the Republic of Gran Colombia and become its president.

July 1817 Bolívar creates a base, deep in the hinterland near Angostura and would use it as a starting point for his campaigns

- - - → Bolívar 1818–1822   ✕ Bolívar victories

4 | BRAZIL 1807–1822

Brazil followed a laborious path to independence. It had become wealthier than its parent kingdom Portugal and hosted the Portuguese monarchy when it was displaced by Napoleon in 1807. When John VI returned to Lisbon in 1821, his son Pedro remained behind as regent and, in 1822, declared himself Emperor Pedro I of Brazil, establishing an independent empire that lasted, along with slavery, until 1889.

Dec 9, 1824 Sucre crushes last remnants of Spanish forces at Battle of Ayacucho

Oct 26, 1825 After the loyalist forces have been dealt with, Sucre and Bolívar climb the legendary silver mountain together to toast free South America

7 Aug 1819 Bolívar defeats the Spanish at the Battle of Boyacá

1821 A daring naval raid by San Martín, with the help of British allies, helps secure the liberation of Peru

THE CAUDILLOS

The success of the South American independence movement depended largely on the ability of a few *caudillos*, or strong men, to unify disparate forces to defeat Spanish royalist forces.

KEY

- Haiti
- Gran Colombia
- Peru
- Bolivia
- Brazil
- Chile
- United Provinces of La Plata
- Uruguay
- Paraguay
- Spanish territory, 1812
- New national borders, 1830

TIMELINE

1790   1800   1810   1820   1830

1 2 3 4 5 6

Puerto Rico

Jamaica

Caribbean Sea

HAITI

Tobago
Trinidad

Santa Marta

Cartagena

Panama

Maracaibo

Puerto Cabello

Valencia
Caracas
Carabobo
La Puerta
Barquisimeto
Trujillo
Mérida
Tenerife
Cúcuta

Calabozo
San Fernando de Apure
Apure
Gamarra

Cumaná

Angostura

Orinoco

CAPTAINCY-GENERAL OF VENEZUELA

GRAN COLOMBIA

Tame

Tunja

Bogotá

Boyacá

Buenaventura

Bomboná

Pichincha
Quito

Guayaquil

BRITISH GUIANA

FRENCH GUIANA

SURINAM (SURINAME)

B R A Z I L

VICEROYALTY OF NEW GRANADA

Amazon

Andes

Trujillo

Huacho
Lima
Callao

Junín

P E R U

VICEROYALTY OF PERU

Ayacucho

Puno
Lake Titicaca
La Paz

Tacna
Arica

B O L I V I A

Chuquisaca (La Plata)

Potosí

VICEROYALTY

CHILE

PACIFIC OCEAN

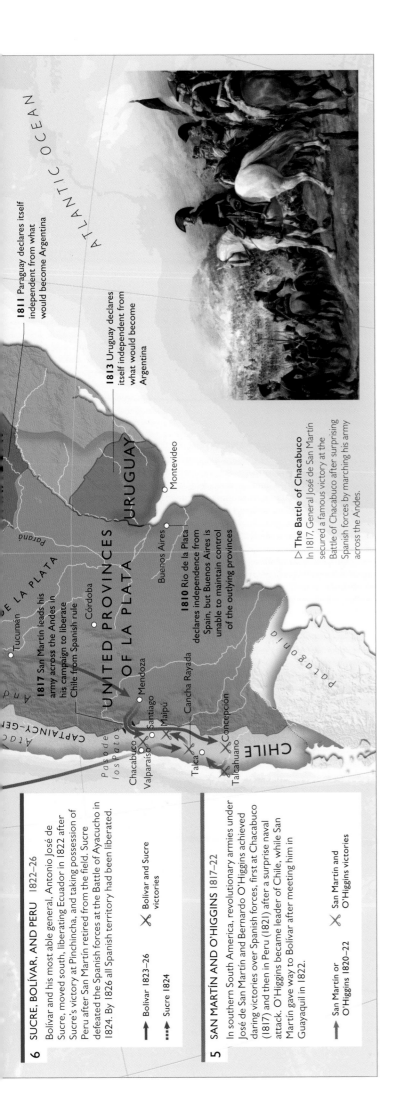

1811 Paraguay declares itself independent from what would become Argentina

1813 Uruguay declares itself independent from what would become Argentina

1810 Río de la Plata declares independence from Spain, but Buenos Aires is unable to maintain control of the outlying provinces

1817 San Martín leads his army across the Andes in his campaign to liberate Chile from Spanish rule

△ **The Battle of Chacabuco**
In 1817, General José de San Martín secured a famous victory at the Battle of Chacabuco after surprising Spanish forces by marching his army across the Andes.

6 SUCRE, BOLÍVAR, AND PERU 1822–26

Bolívar and his most able general, Antonio José de Sucre, moved south, liberating Ecuador in 1822 after Sucre's victory at Pinchincha, and taking possession of Peru after San Martín retired from the field. Sucre defeated the Spanish forces at the Battle of Ayacucho in 1824. By 1826 all Spanish territory had been liberated.

→ Bolívar 1823–26
╳ Bolívar and Sucre victories
···▶ Sucre 1824

5 SAN MARTÍN AND O'HIGGINS 1817–22

In southern South America, revolutionary armies under José de San Martín and Bernardo O'Higgins achieved daring victories over Spanish forces, first at Chacabuco (1817) and then in Peru (1821) after a surprise naval attack. O'Higgins became leader of Chile, while San Martín gave way to Bolívar after meeting him in Guayaquil in 1822.

→ San Martín or O'Higgins 1820–22
╳ San Martín and O'Higgins victories

SIMÓN BOLÍVAR
1783–1830

The greatest hero of the South American liberation movement, Bolívar was born to a wealthy family in Caracas (in what is now Venezuela). He spent time in Europe, where he absorbed liberal ideas, and returned to South America fired with revolutionary zeal. A brilliant military strategist, he won a string of key victories against royalist forces but post-independence was unable to realize his dream of pan-Latin American unification.

SOUTH AMERICAN INDEPENDENCE

South American desire for independence from distant Iberian overlords was driven mainly by the creole (American-born) elite and put into action by a handful of charismatic and dynamic revolutionary generals. In the Spanish colonies, after a rocky start in the north, liberation from Spanish rule swept across the continent from south and north, while Brazil forged its own path to independence.

At the start of the 19th century, South America was simmering with political, economic, and racial tension. Creoles—those born in the Americas, often with mixed heritage—controlled most of the wealth and the plantations that produced it. Overall political power, however, came from the Iberian Peninsula, representing distant imperial authority that restricted trade and industry. The creoles resented this imposition but feared the consequences that revolution might bring; their fears were heightened by the example of Haiti, a former French colony in which slaves had staged the only successful slave uprising in the New World.

The tension between patriots and out-of-touch European rulers and those loyal to them resembled that in prerevolutionary North America, and it would be stoked by men like Simón Bolívar—leading creoles who were steeped in the the liberal nationalism emerging in Europe.

When Napoleon invaded Spain and Portugal in 1808 and 1809 and toppled or exiled the royal families of those countries, contact between Spain and Portugal and their colonies was cut. All the ingredients for revolution were present.

Initial attempts to proclaim republican independence were thwarted by the defeat of Napoleon and the restoration of the Spanish crown, which triggered aggressive action to reclaim the colonies. In 1815, the Spanish restored royal control in Venezuela and New Granada. Bolívar went into exile in Jamaica and Haiti, but the impetus of independence would not be checked. In the south, San Martín liberated Chile and Peru, while in the north Bolívar and his lieutenant Sucre liberated Colombia and Ecuador, finally chasing Spanish royalist forces out of South America for good in December 1824.

THE ENLIGHTENMENT

Spanning the mid-17th to early 19th centuries, the Enlightenment was a period in which thinkers championed reason over superstition and made significant advances in the sciences, arts, politics, economics, and religion.

△ **Enlightened empress**
As well as modernizing and expanding the Russian Empire during her 34-year rule, Empress Catherine the Great championed Enlightenment ideas and advanced state education for women.

Also known as the Age of Reason, the Enlightenment blossomed in pockets across the Western world, advocating rationalism and religious tolerance over superstition and sectarianism.

In Germany, it took the shape of a philosophical and literary movement, known as the *Aufklärung*, which helped invigorate literature and philosophy in eastern Europe. In France, the movement was associated with *philosophes*—men of letters, science, and philosophy—starting with René Descartes and including Voltaire and Jean-Jacques Rousseau, among others. Their ideas combined rationalism with a desire to bring about social change and overcome inequality and injustice. Their belief in the supremacy of reason, religious tolerance, and constitutional governments formed a critique of a dogmatic church and absolute monarchy in France. Their writings provided an intellectual basis for the French Revolution. The US Founding Fathers drew inspiration from them when framing the constitution of their new nation.

In England, the Enlightenment included thinkers such as John Locke and Thomas Paine, who in turn influenced poets, as well as writers such as Mary Wollstonecraft. In Scotland, the movement flourished in and around Edinburgh between 1750 and 1800 thanks to writers such as David Hume and Adam Smith. This Age of Reason encouraged not only literary realism and the growth of the novel, but also created a cultural reaction in the form of Romanticism—an artistic and literary movement in the late 18th century (see pp.216–217).

THE EXPANSION OF RATIONAL THOUGHT

"Rationalist hotspots" in Europe ranged from Stockholm to Lisbon and from Dublin to St. Petersburg. In the United States, they included Boston and Philadelphia. The increasing communication between these centers allowed rapid exchange of ideas, mirroring the development of international trade.

Edinburgh
Stockholm
Dublin
St Petersburg
London
Copenhagen
Amsterdam
Paris
Berlin
Vienna
Lisbon

KEY
● Main centers of the Enlightenment

Learning from Voltaire
The guests at this Paris salon in 1755 include Denis Diderot and Jean Le Rond d'Alembert. The *philosophes* are gathered around a bust of Voltaire to hear a reading of one of his plays, in which blind force and barbarism are defeated by genius and reason.

THE FATE OF NATIVE AMERICANS

Native American societies across North America were transforming even before direct contact with the United States, but the young nation's increasing belief that westward expansion was its destiny would bring drastic change—two centuries of brutal conflict and near-eradication of America's native peoples.

In 1783, the United States became a sovereign nation, no longer bound by the limitations on settlement imposed by Britain. This newfound freedom inspired in the American settlers a belief that they were the natural inheritors of the continent, giving birth to the empowering phrase "manifest destiny" (see below), which drove their expansion westward.

By 1790, about 500,000 settlers had laid down roots west of the original Thirteen States (see pp.156–157). The expansion gained momentum during the next 50 years as explorers ventured westward in wagon trains or sailed to the Pacific Coast to join the Gold Rush. Pioneers paved the way for migrants to settle on the western coast, especially

after railroads replaced the wagon trails. By 1860, approximately 16 million colonists had migrated and settled west of the Appalachians, their arrival displacing and disenfranchising the 250,000 or so Native Americans in the Great Plains and the West.

Many indigenous groups fought for their lands and mounted some notable defenses, but it was only a matter of time before their resistance was crushed by the might and momentum of this Euro-American expansion. By 1890, the remaining Native Americans who had survived the wars were forced out of their homes and herded into specially designated sites called reservations, which amounted to a little more than 2 percent of the area of the United States.

> *"Kill them all, big and little: nits make lice."*
>
> JOHN CHIVINGTON, US COLONEL, 1864

MANIFEST DESTINY
THE RIGHT TO COLONIZE

Coined in 1845, the term "manifest destiny" encompassed the belief in American settlers of their divine right to inhabit and "civilize" the whole expanse of the continent. Although the hunger for land and opportunities in the west had long been features of American colonization, after independence, it evolved into a sense of continental entitlement that drove mass migration westward. In his painting *American Progress* (1872), John Gast depicts Columbia—a personification of the US—leading settlers westward. The figure strings a telegraph wire, implying that the settlers are bringing "light" to the west.

Great Plains

Olympia — 1866 Seattle
1856 Cascades — 1858 Walla Walla
Portland
Salem
1858 Steptoe Butte
1877 Clear Water
Helena
1873 Yellow
1856 Birch Creek
1841 First wagons along the Oregon Trail
1876 Little Bighorn
1877 Big Hole — Virginia City
1877
1878 Whitebird Creek
1873 Fetterman's Defeat
1855 Grave Creek
Steen Mountains — Boise
1856 Big Meadows
1866 Owyhee Forks
UNITED
1867 Pit River
1863 Bear River
1860 Pyramid Lake
1860 Truckee
Salt Lake City
Che
Sacramento
Carson City
1847 Mormons arrive and settle in Salt Lake City
San Francisco
1879 Meeker Agency
Monterey
Rocky Mount
Colorado
Santa Barbara
1864 Canyon de Chelly
Santa F
Los Angeles
1824 More tha 2,000 settler read Texas via th Santa Fe Tra
San Diego
Phoenix
1872 Skull Cave
PACIFIC OCEAN
Tucson
El Paso

US EXPANSIONISM 1783–1890
US land claims in Native American territories began in earnest after the Revolutionary War (1775–1783), leading to 200 years of brutal conflict. The wars decimated the indigenous population to about 300,000 and, by 1890, the majority were corralled into reservations.

KEY
- Native American territory 1850
- Native American territory 1880
- Reservation 1890

TIMELINE
1 2 3 4 5 6 7

1750   1800   1850   1900

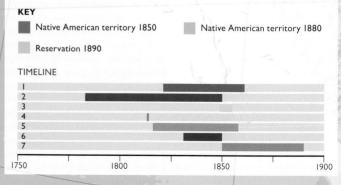

2 CLAIMING THE OLD NORTHWEST
1783–1850

Following independence, the legal boundary drawn by the British no longer applied, allowing Euro-American settlers to move into the western regions beyond the Appalachians. The settlers dealt with Native American resistance by inflicting a crushing defeat at the Battle of Fallen Timbers in 1794. The last of the resistance in the region fell at the Battle of Tippecanoe in 1811, with some settlers' sights already set farther west.

✕ Local wars

3 THE GOLD RUSH 1849–1855

The discovery of gold in California set off a frenzied Gold Rush in 1849, as hopeful prospectors poured into the region to profit from this new find, leading to a genocide of the Native American population. Between 1850 and 1860, war, disease, and starvation reduced Native American numbers in California from 150,000 to 35,000. The pattern was repeated when gold was discovered in other parts of North America.

◢ Major gold sites

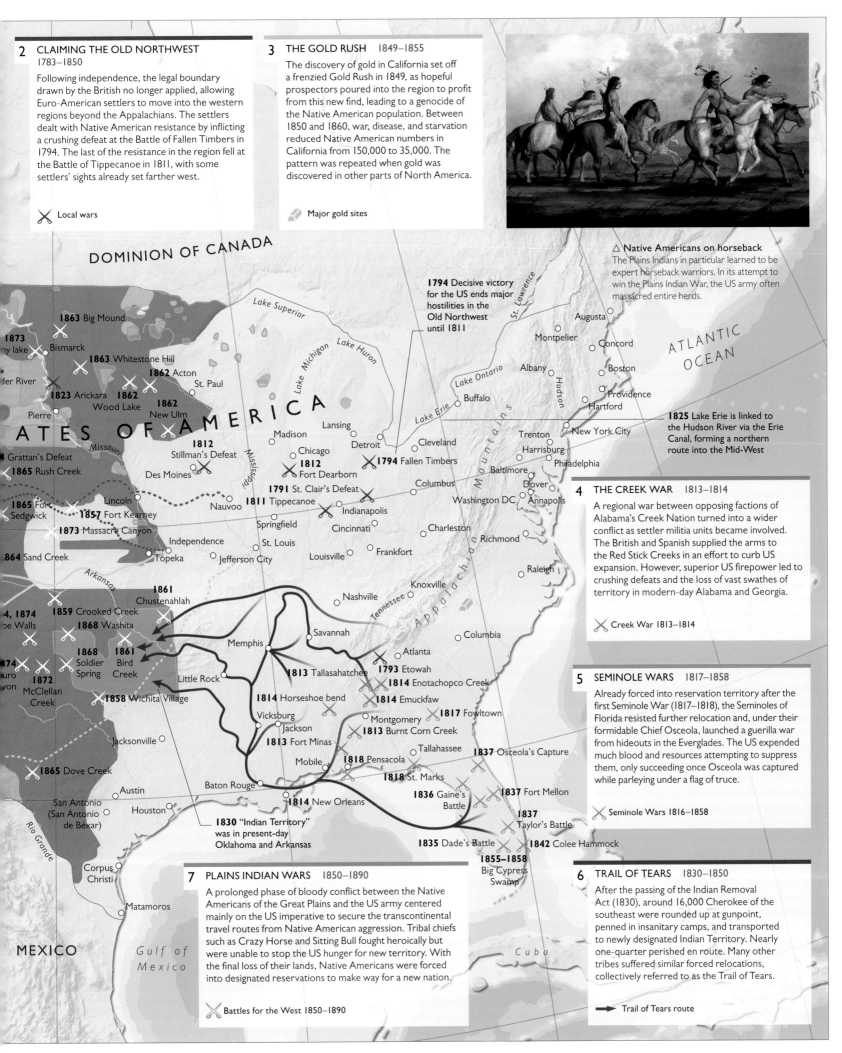

△ **Native Americans on horseback**
The Plains Indians in particular learned to be expert horseback warriors. In its attempt to win the Plains Indian War, the US army often massacred entire herds.

DOMINION OF CANADA

1794 Decisive victory for the US ends major hostilities in the Old Northwest until 1811

1825 Lake Erie is linked to the Hudson River via the Erie Canal, forming a northern route into the Mid-West

Lake Superior

St. Lawrence

1863 Big Mound
1873 ny lake
Bismarck
1863 Whitestone Hill
1862 Acton
St. Paul
1823 Arickara 1862 Wood Lake
1862 New Ulm
Pierre

Lake Michigan
Lake Huron
Lake Ontario
Lake Erie

Augusta
Montpelier
Concord
Albany
Boston
Buffalo
Providence
Hartford

ATES OF AMERICA

Madison
Lansing
Detroit
Cleveland
Trenton
New York City
1812 Stillman's Defeat
Chicago
Harrisburg
Philadelphia
1812 Fort Dearborn
1794 Fallen Timbers
Baltimore
Des Moines
Columbus
Dover
Annapolis
1791 St. Clair's Defeat
Washington DC
Indianapolis
1811 Tippecanoe
Springfield
Cincinnati
Grattan's Defeat
1865 Rush Creek
Lincoln
Nauvoo
1857 Fort Kearney
1865 Fort Sedgwick
1873 Massacre Canyon
Independence
St. Louis
Louisville
Frankfort
Charleston
Richmond
Topeka
Jefferson City
864 Sand Creek
Raleigh
Arkansas
1861 Chustenahlah
Nashville
Knoxville
4, 1874 1859 Crooked Creek
oe Walls 1868 Washita
1868 1861
874 Soldier Bird
Spring Creek
1872 McClellan Creek
1858 Wichita Village
Little Rock
Memphis
Savannah
Columbia
Atlanta
1813 Tallasahatchee
1793 Etowah
1814 Enotachopco Creek
1814 Horseshoe bend
1814 Emuckfaw
Vicksburg
1817 Fowltown
Jackson
Montgomery
1813 Burnt Corn Creek
1813 Fort Minas
Tallahassee
1837 Osceola's Capture
Jacksonville
Mobile
1818 Pensacola
1818 St. Marks
1865 Dove Creek
Baton Rouge
1814 New Orleans
1836 Gaine's Battle
1837 Fort Mellon
Austin
San Antonio (San Antonio de Béxar)
Houston
1837 Taylor's Battle
1830 "Indian Territory" was in present-day Oklahoma and Arkansas
1835 Dade's Battle
1842 Colee Hammock
1855–1858 Big Cypress Swamp
Rio Grande
Corpus Christi
Matamoros

MEXICO
Gulf of Mexico
Cuba

Missouri
Mississippi
Tennessee
Appalachian Mountains
Hudson

4 THE CREEK WAR 1813–1814

A regional war between opposing factions of Alabama's Creek Nation turned into a wider conflict as settler militia units became involved. The British and Spanish supplied the arms to the Red Stick Creeks in an effort to curb US expansion. However, superior US firepower led to crushing defeats and the loss of vast swathes of territory in modern-day Alabama and Georgia.

✕ Creek War 1813–1814

5 SEMINOLE WARS 1817–1858

Already forced into reservation territory after the first Seminole War (1817–1818), the Seminoles of Florida resisted further relocation and, under their formidable Chief Osceola, launched a guerilla war from hideouts in the Everglades. The US expended much blood and resources attempting to suppress them, only succeeding once Osceola was captured while parleying under a flag of truce.

✕ Seminole Wars 1816–1858

7 PLAINS INDIAN WARS 1850–1890

A prolonged phase of bloody conflict between the Native Americans of the Great Plains and the US army centered mainly on the US imperative to secure the transcontinental travel routes from Native American aggression. Tribal chiefs such as Crazy Horse and Sitting Bull fought heroically but were unable to stop the US hunger for new territory. With the final loss of their lands, Native Americans were forced into designated reservations to make way for a new nation.

⚔ Battles for the West 1850–1890

6 TRAIL OF TEARS 1830–1850

After the passing of the Indian Removal Act (1830), around 16,000 Cherokee of the southeast were rounded up at gunpoint, penned in insanitary camps, and transported to newly designated Indian Territory. Nearly one-quarter perished en route. Many other tribes suffered similar forced relocations, collectively referred to as the Trail of Tears.

➤ Trail of Tears route

THE FRENCH REVOLUTION

The French Revolution was actually a series of revolutions accompanied by pan-continental war. Three revolutionary forces converged to drive the transformation of the French state: a liberal aristocratic and bourgeois movement that brought about constitutional change; a popular revolutionary mob in the streets of Paris; and an agrarian revolt by peasants across the country.

In 1789, Louis XVI convoked the Estates-General (for the first time in 175 years) as he sought financial reforms to alleviate France's huge debt. The Estates-General was the Ancien Régime's representative assembly, made up of three estates: clergy (First Estate); nobility (Second Estate); and commoners (Third Estate). In May 1789, the majority Third Estate insisted on greater voting rights. When they were refused, they broke away to form the National Assembly. This triggered a period of great change: a constitutional monarchy was created; and the Declaration of the Rights of Man was drafted, defining a single set of individual and collective rights for all men.

The Assembly, formed out of the National Assembly, pushed through a new constitution and other major reforms, such as the end of feudalism. Factional struggles between the Girondists on the one hand and the Jacobins, headed by Robespierre,

Marat, and Danton, on the other, dominated the Assembly.

The threat posed to France's neighbors by a revolutionary state exporting its ideals prompted a reactionary coalition against France. With enemy armies pressing on all sides and domestic counterrevolutionary uprisings, the revolutionaries panicked. The Revolution descended into a second, extremist phase known as the Reign of Terror. In July 1794, the Jacobins were overthrown in the Thermidor coup, and this instituted the third phase of the Revolution, with the more moderate Directory taking power in October 1795 and attempting to restore the liberal, constitutional values of the first phase. By November 1799, however, enemy armies once more threatened the survival of the Republic, and a coup engineered by Bonaparte to make himself First Consul is traditionally held to mark the end of the Revolution and the start of the Napoleonic era.

DECLARATION OF THE RIGHTS OF MAN
PRINCIPLES OF THE REVOLUTION

The Declaration of the Rights of Man and Citizen was a statement of the principles of the Revolution, establishing the sovereignty of the people and the principle of "liberty, equality, and fraternity." Louis XVI was forced to accept it in the 1791 constitution. The painting shows an officer of the National Guard swearing an oath of allegiance before the Altar of the Convention.

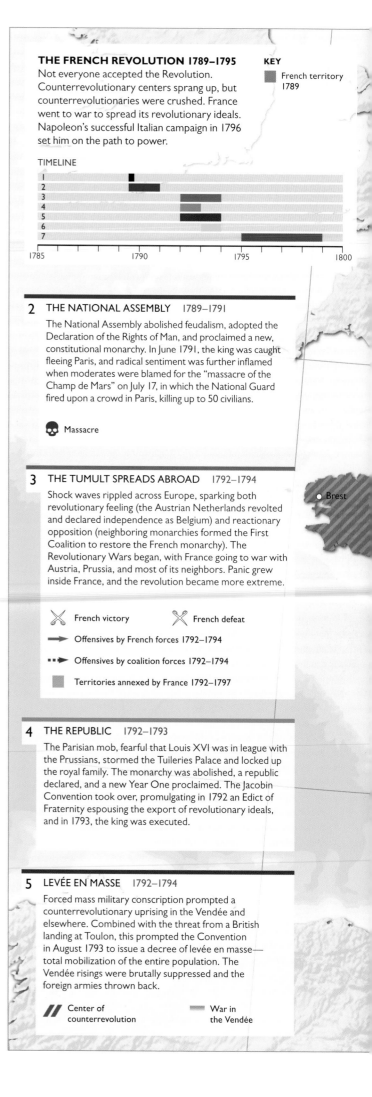

THE FRENCH REVOLUTION 1789–1795

KEY

■ French territory 1789

Not everyone accepted the Revolution. Counterrevolutionary centers sprang up, but counterrevolutionaries were crushed. France went to war to spread its revolutionary ideals. Napoleon's successful Italian campaign in 1796 set him on the path to power.

TIMELINE

1785   1790   1795   1800

2 THE NATIONAL ASSEMBLY 1789–1791

The National Assembly abolished feudalism, adopted the Declaration of the Rights of Man, and proclaimed a new, constitutional monarchy. In June 1791, the king was caught fleeing Paris, and radical sentiment was further inflamed when moderates were blamed for the "massacre of the Champ de Mars" on July 17, in which the National Guard fired upon a crowd in Paris, killing up to 50 civilians.

☠ Massacre

3 THE TUMULT SPREADS ABROAD 1792–1794

Shock waves rippled across Europe, sparking both revolutionary feeling (the Austrian Netherlands revolted and declared independence as Belgium) and reactionary opposition (neighboring monarchies formed the First Coalition to restore the French monarchy). The Revolutionary Wars began, with France going to war with Austria, Prussia, and most of its neighbors. Panic grew inside France, and the revolution became more extreme.

⚔ French victory   ⚔ French defeat

➡ Offensives by French forces 1792–1794

▪▪➤ Offensives by coalition forces 1792–1794

■ Territories annexed by France 1792–1797

○ Brest

4 THE REPUBLIC 1792–1793

The Parisian mob, fearful that Louis XVI was in league with the Prussians, stormed the Tuileries Palace and locked up the royal family. The monarchy was abolished, a republic declared, and a new Year One proclaimed. The Jacobin Convention took over, promulgating in 1792 an Edict of Fraternity espousing the export of revolutionary ideals, and in 1793, the king was executed.

5 LEVÉE EN MASSE 1792–1794

Forced mass military conscription prompted a counterrevolutionary uprising in the Vendée and elsewhere. Combined with the threat from a British landing at Toulon, this prompted the Convention in August 1793 to issue a decree of levée en masse— total mobilization of the entire population. The Vendée risings were brutally suppressed and the foreign armies thrown back.

/// Center of counterrevolution   War in the Vendée

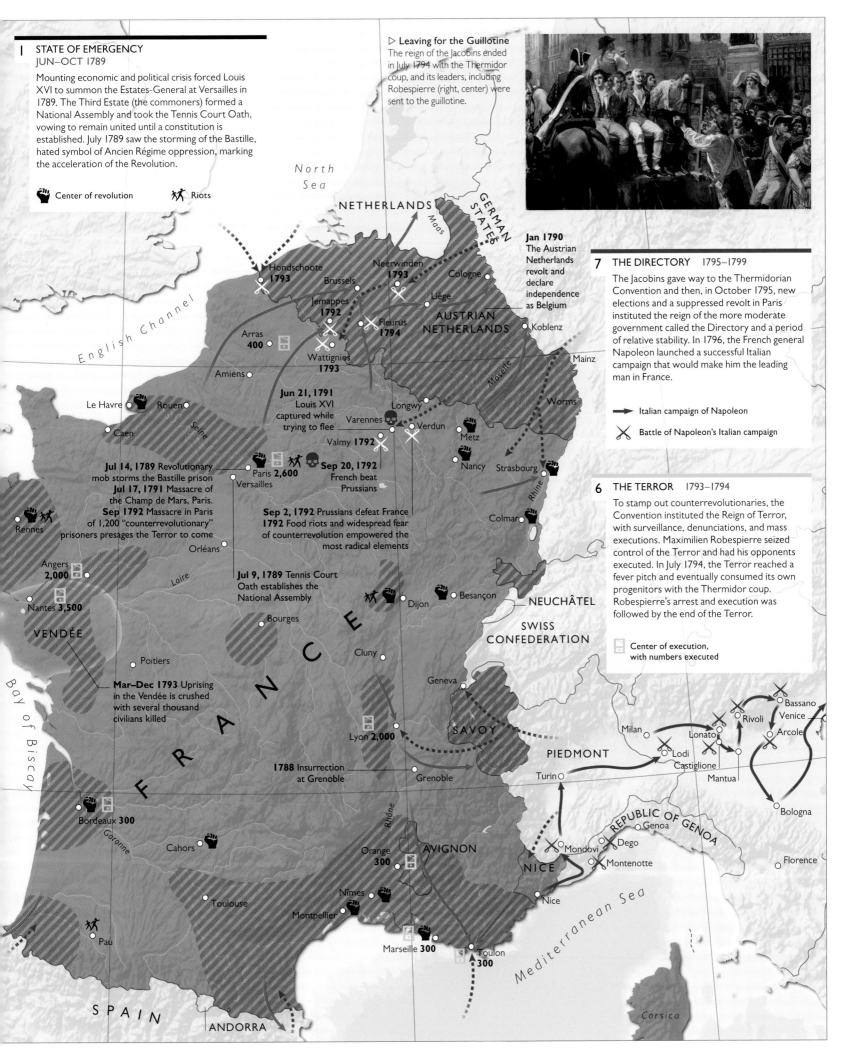

1 STATE OF EMERGENCY
JUN–OCT 1789

Mounting economic and political crisis forced Louis XVI to summon the Estates-General at Versailles in 1789. The Third Estate (the commoners) formed a National Assembly and took the Tennis Court Oath, vowing to remain united until a constitution is established. July 1789 saw the storming of the Bastille, hated symbol of Ancien Régime oppression, marking the acceleration of the Revolution.

✊ Center of revolution   🏃 Riots

▷ **Leaving for the Guillotine**
The reign of the Jacobins ended in July 1794 with the Thermidor coup, and its leaders, including Robespierre (right, center) were sent to the guillotine.

Jan 1790
The Austrian Netherlands revolt and declare independence as Belgium

7 THE DIRECTORY 1795–1799

The Jacobins gave way to the Thermidorian Convention and then, in October 1795, new elections and a suppressed revolt in Paris instituted the reign of the more moderate government called the Directory and a period of relative stability. In 1796, the French general Napoleon launched a successful Italian campaign that would make him the leading man in France.

➡ Italian campaign of Napoleon

✂ Battle of Napoleon's Italian campaign

6 THE TERROR 1793–1794

To stamp out counterrevolutionaries, the Convention instituted the Reign of Terror, with surveillance, denunciations, and mass executions. Maximilien Robespierre seized control of the Terror and had his opponents executed. In July 1794, the Terror reached a fever pitch and eventually consumed its own progenitors with the Thermidor coup. Robespierre's arrest and execution was followed by the end of the Terror.

🗄 Center of execution, with numbers executed

Jun 21, 1791
Louis XVI captured while trying to flee

Jul 14, 1789 Revolutionary mob storms the Bastille prison
Jul 17, 1791 Massacre of the Champ de Mars, Paris.
Sep 1792 Massacre in Paris of 1,200 "counterrevolutionary" prisoners presages the Terror to come

Sep 20, 1792 French beat Prussians

Sep 2, 1792 Prussians defeat France
1792 Food riots and widespread fear of counterrevolution empowered the most radical elements

Jul 9, 1789 Tennis Court Oath establishes the National Assembly

Mar–Dec 1793 Uprising in the Vendée is crushed with several thousand civilians killed

1788 Insurrection at Grenoble

Map labels

North Sea

NETHERLANDS

GERMAN STATES

Maas

Hondschoote **1793**
Neerwinden **1793**
Cologne
Brussels
Jemappes **1792**
Liège
Fleurus **1794**
AUSTRIAN NETHERLANDS
Koblenz
Arras **400**
Wattignies **1793**
Amiens
Mainz
Moselle
Le Havre
Rouen
Longwy
Worms
Caen
Varennes
Verdun
Metz
Seine
Valmy **1792**
Nancy
Paris **2,600**
Versailles
Strasbourg
Rhine
Rennes
Colmar
Orléans
Loire
Angers **2,000**
Besançon
Nantes **3,500**
Dijon
Bourges
NEUCHÂTEL
VENDÉE
SWISS CONFEDERATION
Poitiers
Cluny
Geneva
Bordeaux **300**
Lyon **2,000**
SAVOY
Garonne
Grenoble
PIEDMONT
Bassano
Rivoli
Venice
Milan
Lonato
Arcole
Cahors
Lodi
Castiglione
Turin
Mantua
Bologna
Orange **300**
AVIGNON
Rhône
Bay of Biscay
English Channel
Toulouse
NICE
REPUBLIC OF GENOA
Genoa
Nîmes
Dego
Montpellier
Mondovi
Florence
Marseille **300**
Montenotte
Toulon **300**
Nice
FRANCE
Pau
Mediterranean Sea
SPAIN
ANDORRA
Corsica

1 THE WAR AT SEA 1794–1805

Since the French Revolutionary Wars (see pp.206–207), British command of the seas had been a constant thorn in Napoleon's side. British operations as far-flung as the Caribbean and Denmark assured their naval superiority, even before the decisive Battle of Trafalgar ended French ambitions to rule the seas.

→ French forces
✕ French victories
⤍ British forces
✕ British victories

Jul 1805 British commander Horatio Nelson defeats the French under Villeneuve, having outmaneuvered them in the Caribbean

Jun 1, 1794 British victory over a French fleet (which was protecting a grain convoy from the US) on the so-called "Glorious First of June" allows the British to blockade the French navy in port for years

Sep 1805 Nelson sails on to intercept a Franco-Spanish fleet at Trafalgar

1797 Spanish fleet intercepted off Cape St. Vincent by the British before it can join the French in an invasion of Britain

Oct 21,1805 British Navy scores a decisive victory over a French fleet allied with the Spanish; British hero Admiral Nelson is fatally wounded

1798 French attempt to stir up Irish rebellion against the British, but fail to land

1801, 1807 British twice bombard Copenhagen to prevent the Danish navy becoming a powerful ally of Napoleon

1807 Prussians forced to sign a humiliating treaty at Tilsit after Fourth-Coalition defeat at Friedland

Aug 1805 Napoleon abandons plans to invade Britain from Boulogne and marches his Grande Armée to confront the Austrians at Ulm

Oct 14, 1806 Jena-Auerstädt

Oct 1806 Nap— occupies Berlin beating the Prus— at Jena-Auerstäd—

1801 Austria forced to make peace after French victories at Zurich and Hohenlinden

Dec 1799 Napoleon takes his army through St. Bernard Pass in the Alps in midwinter to surprise the Austrians, who are besieging Genoa

Jun 14, 1800 Marengo

1800 Hohenlinden

1799 Zurich

Dec 2, 1805 Austria makes peac— after French victor— at Austerlitz

Jun 12, 1798

NAPOLEON'S SUCCESSES

The period 1794–1809 saw a string of successes for Napoleon as he rose to lead France and expand its influence, briefly, over all of Europe. In 1802, France had not advanced far beyond its historical borders, but it would soon become an empire.

KEY

■ France in 1802
— National borders in 1802
■ Border of Holy Roman Empire

TIMELINE

1
2
3
4

1790 1795 1800 1805 1810 1815

2 THE EGYPTIAN CAMPAIGN 1798–1801

Napoleon set off to control Egypt (and therefore probably to threaten British interests beyond—in India). He evaded Nelson's fleet and landed in Egypt. He won the Battle of the Pyramids against the Mamluks (who ruled Egypt under the Ottoman sultan) and occupied Cairo.

→ French forces
⤍ British forces
✕ French victories
✕ British victories

3 WAR OF THE SECOND COALITION 1799–1802

In 1799, a coalition of nations attacked French interests while Napoleon was in Egypt. Russians beat the French in Italy, and Austrians drove them back over the Rhine. Napoleon returned from Egypt and staged a military coup, becoming "First Consul," before addressing the crisis in northern Italy.

→ French forces
✕ French victories

NAPOLEON'S EMPIRE, 1812
At its greatest extent in 1812, Napoleon's domain included most of Europe. Only Britain consistently opposed him.

KEY
- French Empire
- French client states
- Independent allies
- Countries at war with Napoleon

4 WARS OF THE THIRD AND FOURTH COALITIONS
1805–1807

Austria joined a British-financed anti-French coalition that already included Russia, Sweden, and the Kingdom of Naples. After heavy defeats, Austria agreed on peace terms with France and Russia and retreated to Poland. France created the Confederation of the Rhine, as a client state, in the ashes of the Holy Roman Empire. Prussia was threatened by this and made war with France, which ended in Prussian defeat and the creation of another client, the Duchy of Warsaw (Poland), from former Austrian and Prussian lands.

→ French forces
✕ French victories

1798 Ottoman sultan declares jihad on Napoleon in response to his invasion of Egypt

Mar 1799 Undeterred by losing his fleet, Napoleon presses on and besieges the Ottomans at Acre, who resist him with the help of British guns

Aug 1798 In the Battle of the Nile, Nelson destroys the French fleet, crippling Napoleon's Egyptian campaign

Apr 1799 Napoleon wins a battle on his retreat to Egypt

I 21, 1798 Napoleon defeats the Mamluk rulers of Egypt and captures Cairo

MOLDAVIA
WALLACHIA
Bucharest
Varna
OTTOMAN EMPIRE
Constantinople
Smyrna
Crete
Cyprus
Beirut
Damascus
Acre
Jaffa
Gaza
Jerusalem
Alexandria
EGYPT
Cairo
to Aswan

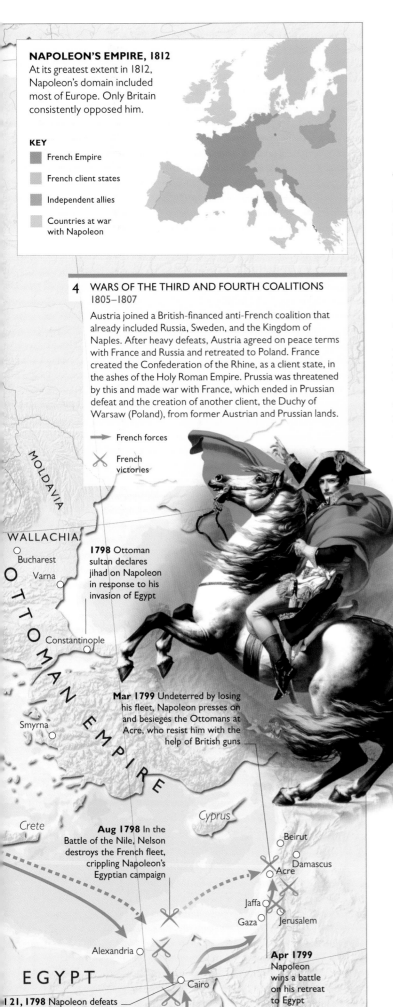

NAPOLEON ADVANCES

Napoleon established his reputation as leader of the French Revolutionary Army with his bold, unexpected maneuvers against Austria in Italy (1796–1797). By 1804, 10 years after France's republican revolution, he had crowned himself emperor. By 1809, he had complete control of central Europe.

From the maelstrom of the French Revolutionary Wars, Napoleon Bonaparte emerged as a young, ambitious general. Among his early remarkable successes, he pushed the armies of Austria and the kingdom of Sardinia out of northern Italy (1796–1797). Austrian forces retreated all the way back to Vienna, leaving northern Italy in the hands of the French. By 1809, Napoleon had absorbed the southern Netherlands (Batavia), the west bank of the Rhine, and a large part of Italy into French territory. He

had created client states under French control (for example, the Confederation of the Rhine). He had placed family members on thrones all over Europe, married Marie Louise of Austria, and made Prussia and Austria reluctant allies.

Throughout, Britain remained at war with Napoleon. The British established naval superiority, and it was naval power that thwarted Napoleon's ambitions in Egypt and the Middle East. Napoleon retaliated by isolating Britain with a trade blockade called the Continental System. Its aim of destroying British commerce failed, however, as it was impossible to enforce compliance throughout Europe, from Portugal to Russia.

◁ **The man and the myth**
Jacques-Louis David's equestrian portrait (1800–1801), which pictured Napoleon crossing the Alps, fed into the leader's desired image of a classical hero.

"In war there is but one favorable moment; the great art is to seize it!"

NAPOLEON BONAPARTE, 1804

NAPOLEON BONAPARTE
1769–1821

Napoleon rose to prominence during the French Revolution and led several successful campaigns during the French Revolutionary Wars. As Napoleon I, he was endorsed by the Pope as Emperor of the French 1804–1814, and again in 1815 (see pp.210–211). Napoleon dominated European and global affairs for more than a decade while leading France against a series of coalitions in the Napoleonic Wars. He won most of these wars and the vast majority of his battles, building an empire that ruled over continental Europe before its final collapse in 1815.

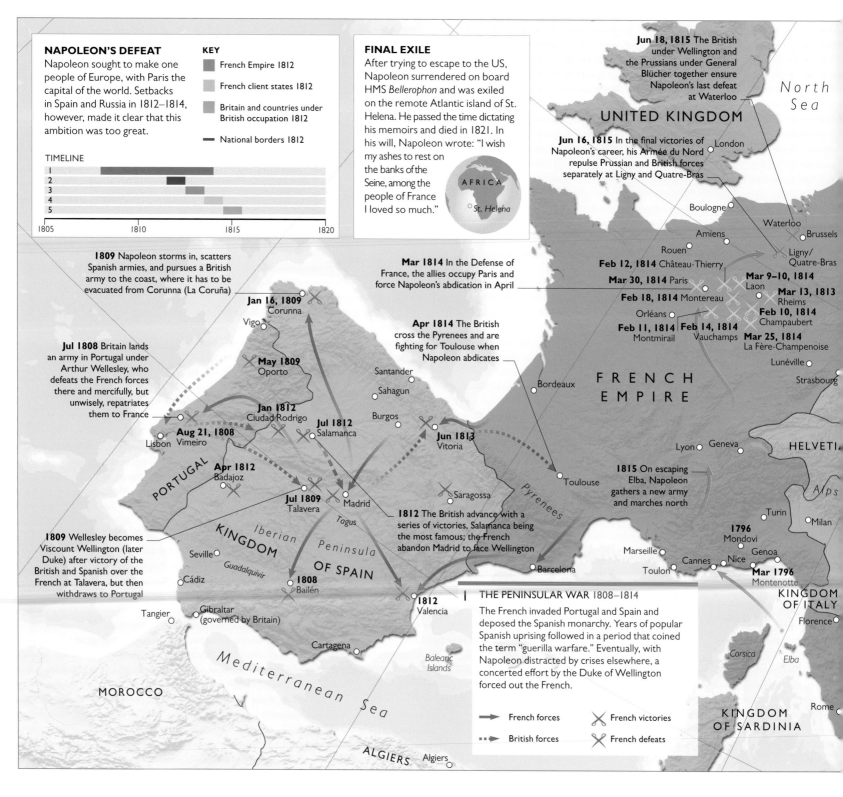

NAPOLEON'S DEFEAT
Napoleon sought to make one people of Europe, with Paris the capital of the world. Setbacks in Spain and Russia in 1812–1814, however, made it clear that this ambition was too great.

KEY
French Empire 1812
French client states 1812
Britain and countries under British occupation 1812
National borders 1812

TIMELINE
1
2
3
4
5
1805 1810 1815 1820

FINAL EXILE
After trying to escape to the US, Napoleon surrendered on board HMS *Bellerophon* and was exiled on the remote Atlantic island of St. Helena. He passed the time dictating his memoirs and died in 1821. In his will, Napoleon wrote: "I wish my ashes to rest on the banks of the Seine, among the people of France I loved so much."

AFRICA
St. Helena

Jun 18, 1815 The British under Wellington and the Prussians under General Blücher together ensure Napoleon's last defeat at Waterloo

North Sea

UNITED KINGDOM

Jun 16, 1815 In the final victories of Napoleon's career, his Armée du Nord repulse Prussian and British forces separately at Ligny and Quatre-Bras

London

1809 Napoleon storms in, scatters Spanish armies, and pursues a British army to the coast, where it has to be evacuated from Corunna (La Coruña)

Jan 16, 1809 Corunna

Vigo

Mar 1814 In the Defense of France, the allies occupy Paris and force Napoleon's abdication in April

Apr 1814 The British cross the Pyrenees and are fighting for Toulouse when Napoleon abdicates

Jul 1808 Britain lands an army in Portugal under Arthur Wellesley, who defeats the French forces there and mercifully, but unwisely, repatriates them to France

May 1809 Oporto

Santander
Sahagun

Boulogne
Waterloo
Brussels
Amiens
Ligny/Quatre-Bras
Rouen
Feb 12, 1814 Château-Thierry
Mar 30, 1814 Paris
Feb 18, 1814 Montereau
Orléans
Feb 11, 1814 Montmirail
Feb 14, 1814 Vauchamps
Mar 9–10, 1814 Laon
Mar 13, 1813 Rheims
Feb 10, 1814 Champaubert
Mar 25, 1814 La Fère-Champenoise
Lunéville

Jan 1812 Ciudad Rodrigo

Jul 1812 Salamanca

Burgos

Bordeaux

F R E N C H
E M P I R E

Strasbourg

Aug 21, 1808 Vimeiro
Lisbon

Apr 1812 Badajoz

Jun 1813 Vitoria

1815 On escaping Elba, Napoleon gathers a new army and marches north

Lyon
Geneva
HELVETI

1809 Wellesley becomes Viscount Wellington (later Duke) after victory of the British and Spanish over the French at Talavera, but then withdraws to Portugal

Jul 1809 Talavera
Madrid

PORTUGAL

Iberian
KINGDOM
Peninsula
OF SPAIN

Tagus
Saragossa
Toulouse

1812 The British advance with a series of victories, Salamanca being the most famous; the French abandon Madrid to face Wellington

Marseille
Cannes
Toulon

1796 Mondovi
Turin
Milan

Alps

Seville
Guadalquivir
Cádiz

1808 Bailén

Barcelona

Nice
Genoa
Mar 1796 Montenotte

KINGDOM
OF ITALY

Tangier
Gibraltar (governed by Britain)

1812 Valencia

THE PENINSULAR WAR 1808–1814
The French invaded Portugal and Spain and deposed the Spanish monarchy. Years of popular Spanish uprising followed in a period that coined the term "guerilla warfare." Eventually, with Napoleon distracted by crises elsewhere, a concerted effort by the Duke of Wellington forced out the French.

Corsica
Elba

Florence

Cartagena

Balearic Islands

Mediterranean Sea

MOROCCO

French forces French victories
British forces French defeats

KINGDOM
OF SARDINIA

Rome

ALGIERS Algiers

NAPOLEON'S DOWNFALL

Napoleon's efforts to dominate Europe took him to the far eastern and western ends of the continent. After failing to control Spain, Portugal, and Russia, he was met and defeated by a coalition of nations in central Europe. He was exiled first to Elba, then to far-off St. Helena.

Napoleon's 1809 defeat of Prussia and the Fourth Coalition (see pp.208–209) seemed to consolidate his hold over Europe, but Britain had not made peace, and he would not rest. His strategy to defeat Britain—a trade blockade called the Continental System—needed the cooperation of Spain, Portugal, and Russia. The Spanish monarchy was sympathetic, but a French army invaded Portugal in 1807 to force the Portuguese hand, and soon also replaced the Spanish king to assert direct control in Spain as well.

In May 1809, a popular revolt in Madrid spread across Spain and began a guerilla war that Napoleon came to know as his "Spanish ulcer." Although the French leader took matters into his own hands early on and chased the British out of Spain, he was distracted by a new declaration of war by Austria in 1809. He beat the Austrians at Wagram, but with huge losses—the cost of controlling Europe was beginning to mount. Napoleon's plans unraveled more profoundly

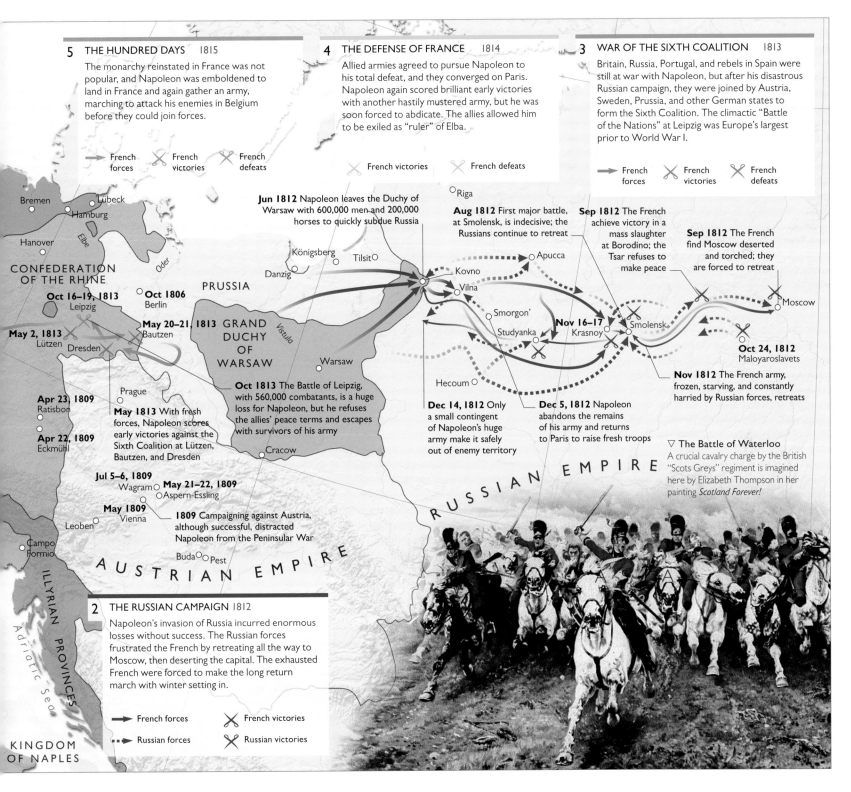

5 THE HUNDRED DAYS 1815

The monarchy reinstated in France was not popular, and Napoleon was emboldened to land in France and again gather an army, marching to attack his enemies in Belgium before they could join forces.

→ French forces ✕ French victories ✕ French defeats

4 THE DEFENSE OF FRANCE 1814

Allied armies agreed to pursue Napoleon to his total defeat, and they converged on Paris. Napoleon again scored brilliant early victories with another hastily mustered army, but he was soon forced to abdicate. The allies allowed him to be exiled as "ruler" of Elba.

✕ French victories ✕ French defeats

3 WAR OF THE SIXTH COALITION 1813

Britain, Russia, Portugal, and rebels in Spain were still at war with Napoleon, but after his disastrous Russian campaign, they were joined by Austria, Sweden, Prussia, and other German states to form the Sixth Coalition. The climactic "Battle of the Nations" at Leipzig was Europe's largest prior to World War I.

→ French forces ✕ French victories ✕ French defeats

Jun 1812 Napoleon leaves the Duchy of Warsaw with 600,000 men and 200,000 horses to quickly subdue Russia

Aug 1812 First major battle, at Smolensk, is indecisive; the Russians continue to retreat

Sep 1812 The French achieve victory in a mass slaughter at Borodino; the Tsar refuses to make peace

Sep 1812 The French find Moscow deserted and torched; they are forced to retreat

Oct 1813 The Battle of Leipzig, with 560,000 combatants, is a huge loss for Napoleon, but he refuses the allies' peace terms and escapes with survivors of his army

May 1813 With fresh forces, Napoleon scores early victories against the Sixth Coalition at Lützen, Bautzen, and Dresden

1809 Campaigning against Austria, although successful, distracted Napoleon from the Peninsular War

Dec 14, 1812 Only a small contingent of Napoleon's huge army make it safely out of enemy territory

Dec 5, 1812 Napoleon abandons the remains of his army and returns to Paris to raise fresh troops

Nov 1812 The French army, frozen, starving, and constantly harried by Russian forces, retreats

Oct 24, 1812 Maloyaroslavets

▽ **The Battle of Waterloo**
A crucial cavalry charge by the British "Scots Greys" regiment is imagined here by Elizabeth Thompson in her painting *Scotland Forever!*

2 THE RUSSIAN CAMPAIGN 1812

Napoleon's invasion of Russia incurred enormous losses without success. The Russian forces frustrated the French by retreating all the way to Moscow, then deserting the capital. The exhausted French were forced to make the long return march with winter setting in.

→ French forces ✕ French victories
--▶ Russian forces ✕ Russian victories

when he attempted to force the cooperation of Russia, which had been persuaded by Britain to renounce the Continental System. In 1812, he invaded Russia with a vast army but retreated with a few ragged, emaciated survivors. The other European powers saw their chance and assembled the largest anti-French coalition yet, which pursued him eventually to Paris and forced him into exile. Although Napoleon escaped for a final flourish at Waterloo, his time was over.

"I used to say of him [Napoleon] that his presence on the field made the difference of 40,000 men."

ARTHUR WELLESLEY, DUKE OF WELLINGTON, 1831

DUKE OF WELLINGTON
1769–1852

Irish-born Arthur Wellesley, later the Duke of Wellington, first distinguished himself fighting the Kingdom of Mysore and the Marathas (people from Maharashtra state) in India. His success in the Peninsular War made him a British national hero, a status enhanced by his leading role in the defeat of Napoleon at Waterloo in 1815. Usually a cautious general, he was also capable of bold attacking strokes, as at Salamanca in 1812. He was never careless of his men's lives and took only necessary risks.

THE INDUSTRIAL REVOLUTION

Industrialization is probably the single greatest event in world economic history, at least since the advent of agriculture several millennia earlier. The process, which began in the late 18th century, had far-reaching consequences that would reshape the world.

△ Slave to the machine
This engraving celebrating American inventor Eli Whitney's cotton gin also reveals the human suffering and exploitation that helped to make the Industrial Revolution possible.

Before the late 18th century, the Western world's economy was largely static. Although it periodically expanded as populations grew, this population growth tended to outstrip the carrying capacity of the economy, leading to famine, disease, or war and resulting in population crashes followed by economic contraction.

However, from the late 18th century, economic growth broke free of this trap and began to rise continually. What changed was that the efficiency of the economy began to increase relentlessly. Known as the Industrial Revolution, this transformation began in Britain and then spread to the rest of the world.

The Industrial Revolution was not a single event but a series of changes that took place in a piecemeal fashion in different places and different parts of the economy at different times. Some of these changes had already begun well before the 18th century. For example, a miniature revolution in the manufacture of woolen textiles, thanks to water-mill technology, can be traced to the 13th century.

Labor, materials, and technology

Industrialization was underpinned by population growth and enabled by the Agricultural Revolution (see pp.194–195), which had dramatically increased agricultural efficiency and output. Another contributor was slavery. The abuse and exploitation of slave labor in the New World drove an explosive growth in the production of raw cotton to fuel the dynamic textile industries of the era. Slavery also enabled large-scale production of sugar, tobacco, and other raw materials. The profits from the trade contributed to the growing financial might of Europe, and later the US, underwriting the injections of capital that helped transform cottage industries into global ones.

The Industrial Revolution was also powered by changes in technology. The invention of the steam engine provided the power for the textile mills and other factory machinery. The need to fuel these engines created an increased demand for coal that could be met because of improved mining and better distribution, first by canal and later by rail. In the later part of the revolution, improvements in steel-making provided an impetus to change as stronger, more versatile kinds of steel began to replace iron.

A global phenomenon

Although the revolution began in Britain, it was not long before it spread throughout Europe and to America. Industrialization was readily adopted in countries with enthusiastic entrepreneurs and governments open to change. In the US, iron production and shipbuilding

▽ Flying shuttles
Patented by John Kay in England in 1733, these shuttles drew threads back and forth on mechanical looms, halving the labor force required to produce cloth.

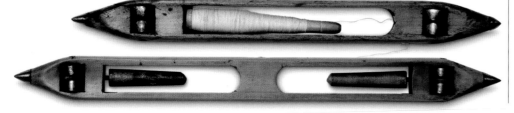

SEEDING INDUSTRIALIZATION

The Industrial Revolution involved a complex set of factors. Demographics—the growth and distribution of population—influenced the supply of raw materials and demand for products. This in turn drove developments in finance, which provided the capital needed by industries. Innovations in communication, power, and transportation—inspired by new materials and the rising social and economic demand—led to a dramatic boost in productivity.

1694 The Bank of England is established, setting the model for most subsequent central banks

1750 Global population of about 715 million, mostly concentrated in south and east Asia, will almost double over the next century with the most growth in Europe and the Americas

FINANCE

DEMOGRAPHICS

INNOVATION

TRADE

TRANSPORTATION

1690   1710   1730   1750

1720 The South Sea Bubble, rampant speculation in a British Company granted a monopoly to trade with South America, causes a financial crisis

◁ **The Barton Aqueduct**
Part of a coal-shipping canal network that made
Francis Egerton, the Duke of Bridgewater, a
fortune when completed in 1761, this aqueduct
helped to transport raw material from the duke's
mines to market at a vastly reduced cost.

were the first industries to undergo transformation. In
Europe, Belgium and Prussia led the way as the French
Revolution initially stalled development in France. A fresh
wave of industrialization followed German unification
in the 1870s, and by 1900, industrial output in Germany
and the US had overtaken that in Britain.

The consequences of industrialization

With better transportation, it was no longer necessary to
build factories close to the sources of raw materials.
Industries were built in cities, and urban populations grew
rapidly. In 1800, there were 28 cities in Europe with
populations over 100,000; by 1848, there were 45 such cities.
However, conditions for urban workers were harsh. Wages
were low, living standards were poor, and inequality grew,
especially during the early part of the revolution.

As the revolution progressed, new patterns of trade
emerged. Improvements in transportation, combined with
the invention of communication technologies such as the
telegraph, led to a rise in global trade. In turn, trade fueled

further growth as raw materials could be sourced more
cheaply and markets for finished products expanded. The
Industrial Revolution has many echoes in the present—not
least, the changes in climate we are now experiencing,
the onset of which can be traced to the increased use of fossil
fuels such as coal in the very first wave of industrialization.

▽ **Bessemer converters**
The Bessemer process, which used
vast furnaces such as those installed
at the Krupp Steel Works at Essen
in Germany, transformed industrial
output in Europe.

*"The process of industrialization is
necessarily painful."*

E. P. THOMPSON, BRITISH HISTORIAN, FROM *THE
MAKING OF THE ENGLISH WORKING CLASS*, 1963

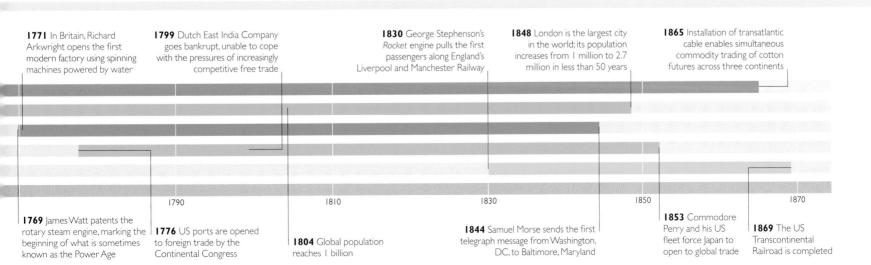

1771 In Britain, Richard
Arkwright opens the first
modern factory using spinning
machines powered by water

1799 Dutch East India Company
goes bankrupt, unable to cope
with the pressures of increasingly
competitive free trade

1830 George Stephenson's
Rocket engine pulls the first
passengers along England's
Liverpool and Manchester Railway

1848 London is the largest city
in the world; its population
increases from 1 million to 2.7
million in less than 50 years

1865 Installation of transatlantic
cable enables simultaneous
commodity trading of cotton
futures across three continents

1790   1810   1830   1850   1870

1769 James Watt patents the
rotary steam engine, marking the
beginning of what is sometimes
known as the Power Age

1776 US ports are opened
to foreign trade by the
Continental Congress

1804 Global population
reaches 1 billion

1844 Samuel Morse sends the first
telegraph message from Washington,
DC, to Baltimore, Maryland

1853 Commodore
Perry and his US
fleet force Japan to
open to global trade

1869 The US
Transcontinental
Railroad is completed

JAMES WATT
1736–1819

Born in Greenock, Scotland, in 1736, inventor and engineer James Watt is chiefly remembered for his improvements to steam engine technology. Watt worked to make Thomas Newcomen's 1712 steam engine more efficient by creating a separate condensing chamber to prevent loss of steam. Watt patented his invention in 1769.

INDUSTRIAL BRITAIN

The Industrial Revolution, which began in Britain in the late 18th century, was a period of rapid development in industry that led to changes in politics, society, and the economy. It was in Britain that many of the technological advances occurred that would drive mechanization, urbanization, and capitalism, and lead to the growth of industries such as cotton, coal, and iron.

Many factors contributed to the start of the Industrial Revolution in Britain, as well as to its rapid progression. One significant cause was the Agricultural Revolution (see pp.194–195), which saw improvements to the farming process. Agricultural production became more efficient, and Britain was able to sustain a larger workforce. Fewer agricultural workers were needed to work on the land, and many were now able to move to urban areas to find work in the new factories. The political system in Britain was also conducive to rapid industrialization. As a nation now dependent on trading across the globe, the British government took steps to encourage commercial innovation, such as introducing laws

to protect intellectual property rights. The geographical location of Britain was a key factor, allowing it to communicate and trade with the rest of the world. Britain also had an abundance of natural resources, such as water to power mills and factories, coal to burn for energy, and ores to smelt for metals, which proved invaluable.

Combined with these factors, a series of important technological innovations in the 18th and early 19th century, funded by an increasingly wealthy middle class, revolutionized many industrial processes. By the end of the 19th century, Britain was transformed from a predominantly rural society into an urban one, and almost every aspect of daily life had been altered.

1 COTTON TEXTILE INDUSTRY 1700–1790

Britain's expansion across the globe, and slave labor in its colonies, created a boom in cotton production. It provided the raw material for a new mass-market product—cotton textiles. Richard Arkwright's combination of innovations created the first modern factories, which wove cloth at ever greater levels of productivity, especially with the adoption of steam power. Cotton was seen as a threat to the wool trade, which was slower to mechanize.

🐑 Textile mills 1870   → Cotton imports from North America and India

🐖 Wool production 1870

2 STEAM POWER 1712–1802

Steam power was the defining technology of the Industrial Revolution, as it provided the energy needed to drive highly productive factories. English engineer Thomas Newcomen's crude steam engines had powered some mines, but improvements by James Watt in the 1770s heralded a new age of steam power. Using Watt's engine, coal could be extracted from deeper levels, making available the fuel source that would power factories, steamships, and railways.

⚙ Significant steam engine developments

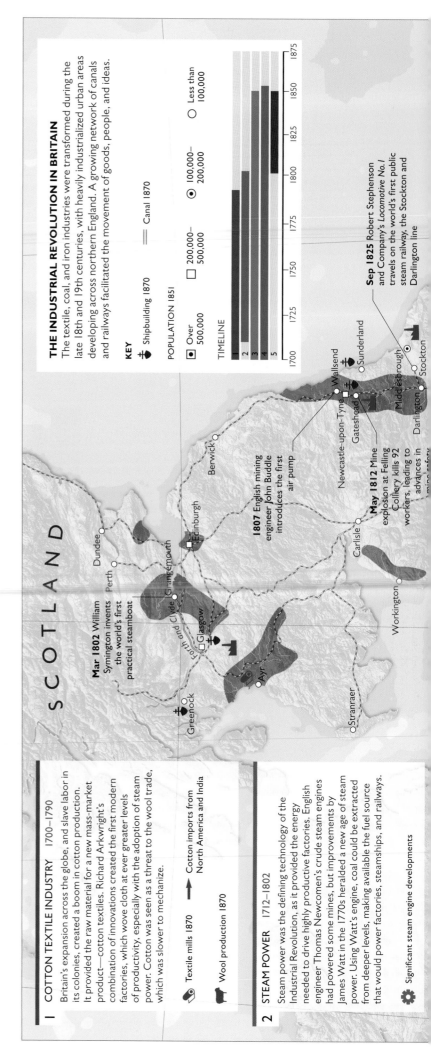

THE INDUSTRIAL REVOLUTION IN BRITAIN
The textile, coal, and iron industries were transformed during the late 18th and 19th centuries, with heavily industrialized urban areas developing across northern England. A growing network of canals and railways facilitated the movement of goods, people, and ideas.

KEY

⚓ Shipbuilding 1870   ═ Canal 1870

POPULATION 1851

◉ Over 500,000   ☐ 200,000– 500,000   ◉ 100,000– 200,000   ○ Less than 100,000

TIMELINE

1700 · 1725 · 1750 · 1775 · 1800 · 1825 · 1850 · 1875

SCOTLAND

Mar 1802 William Symington invents the world's first practical steamboat

1807 English mining engineer John Buddle introduces the first air pump

May 1812 Mine explosion at Felling Colliery kills 92 workers, leading to advances in mine safety

Sep 1825 Robert Stephenson and Company's *Locomotive No.1* travels on the world's first public steam railway, the Stockton and Darlington line

Dundee
Perth
Edinburgh
Glasgow
Forth and Clyde
Ayr
Stranraer
Greenock
Berwick
Workington
Carlisle
Newcastle-upon-Tyne
Wallsend
Gateshead
Sunderland
Middlesbrough
Darlington
Stockton

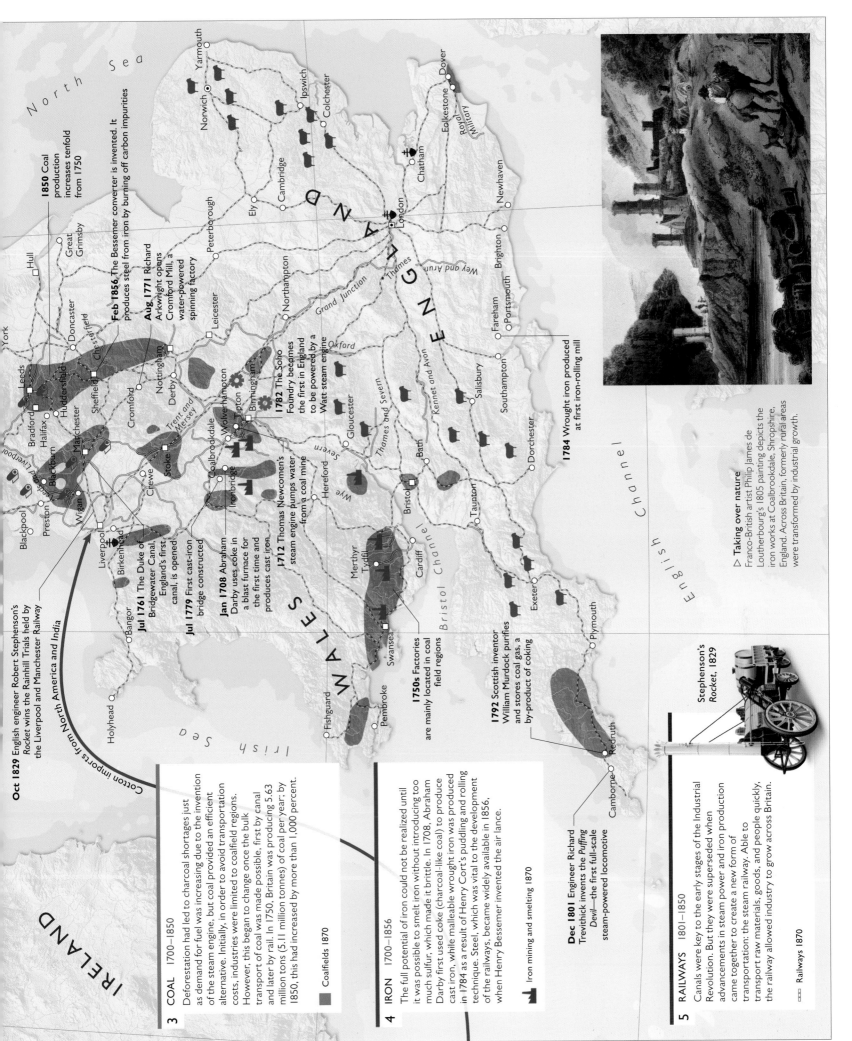

North Sea

Yarmouth

Norwich

Ipswich
Colchester

1850 Coal production increases tenfold from 1750

Feb 1856 The Bessemer converter is invented. It produces steel from iron by burning off carbon impurities

Aug. 1771 Richard Arkwright opens Cromford Mill, a water-powered spinning factory

Hull

Great Grimsby

Doncaster

York

Leeds
Bradford
Huddersfield
Halifax

Chesterfield
Sheffield

Cambridge

Ely

Peterborough

Leicester

Northampton

Oxford

E N G L A N D

Dover
Folkestone
Royal Military

Chatham

London

Thames

Wey and Arun

Newhaven

Brighton

Fareham
Portsmouth

Southampton

Salisbury

Dorchester

Bath

Grand Junction

Thames and Severn

Kennet and Avon

1784 Wrought iron produced at first iron-rolling mill

Oct 1829 English engineer Robert Stephenson's *Rocket* wins the Rainhill Trials held by the Liverpool and Manchester Railway

Cotton imports from North America and India

Jul 1761 The Duke of Bridgewater Canal, England's first canal, is opened

Jul 1779 First cast-iron bridge constructed

Jan 1708 Abraham Darby uses coke in a blast furnace for the first time and produces cast iron.

1712 Thomas Newcomen's steam engine pumps water from a coal mine

1782 The Soho Foundry becomes the first in England to be powered by a Watt steam engine

Nottingham
Cromford
Derby
Stoke
Crewe
Trent and Mersey

Wolverhampton
Tipton
Birmingham
Coalbrookdale
Ironbridge

Gloucester

Hereford
Wye
Severn

Bristol

Taunton

Exeter

Plymouth

Merthyr Tydfil
Cardiff
Swansea

Pembroke
Fishguard

W A L E S

Bristol Channel

English Channel

1750s Factories are mainly located in coal field regions

1792 Scottish inventor William Murdock purifies and stores coal gas, a by-product of coking

Redruth
Camborne

Irish Sea

Holyhead
Bangor

Liverpool
Birkenhead
Preston
Blackpool
Blackburn
Wigan
Manchester
Leeds and Liverpool

△ **Taking over nature**
Franco-British artist Philip James de Loutherbourg's 1805 painting depicts the iron works at Coalbrookdale, Shropshire, England. Across Britain, formerly rural areas were transformed by industrial growth.

Stephenson's *Rocket*, 1829

I R E L A N D

3 COAL 1700–1850

Deforestation had led to charcoal shortages just as demand for fuel was increasing due to the invention of the steam engine, but coal provided an efficient alternative. Initially, in order to avoid transportation costs, industries were limited to coalfield regions. However, this began to change once the bulk transport of coal was made possible, first by canal and later by rail. In 1750, Britain was producing 5.63 million tons (5.11 million tonnes) of coal per year; by 1850, this had increased by more than 1,000 percent.

▪ Coalfields 1870

4 IRON 1700–1856

The full potential of iron could not be realized until it was possible to smelt iron without introducing too much sulfur, which made it brittle. In 1708, Abraham Darby first used coke (charcoal-like coal) to produce cast iron, while malleable wrought iron was produced in 1784 as a result of Henry Cort's puddling and rolling technique. Steel, which was vital to the development of the railways, became widely available in 1856, when Henry Bessemer invented the air lance.

⬛ Iron mining and smelting 1870

Dec 1801 Engineer Richard Trevithick invents the *Puffing Devil*—the first full-scale steam-powered locomotive

5 RAILWAYS 1801–1850

Canals were key to the early stages of the Industrial Revolution. But they were superseded when advancements in steam power and iron production came together to create a new form of transportation: the steam railway. Able to transport raw materials, goods, and people quickly, the railway allowed industry to grow across Britain.

▭ Railways 1870

ROMANTICISM AND NATIONALISM

Romanticism and Nationalism were intertwined cultural and political movements that spread across the Western world from the late 18th to the early 20th centuries, emphasizing emotion and patriotism over reason and cosmopolitanism.

△ **Early Romantic poetry**
The title page of the 1794 poem *Songs of Experience* was written, illustrated, and hand-printed by William Blake—a key early proponent of both Romanticism and Nationalism.

Romanticism was a cultural movement that began in the late 18th century and affected art, literature, music, theater, and politics. It was a reaction against the rationalism of the Enlightenment (see pp.202–203) and insisted on the primacy of imagination and emotion. The Romantics were fascinated with nature and its relationship with the human psyche. This led to the belief that a land and its people shared a special bond, hence the Romantic enthusiasm for folk culture and legends.

Romanticism became a driving force for the emerging Nationalist movement, which declared the nation state to be the defining unit in politics, culture, language, and history. Aspirations for nationhood, as opposed to sprawling dynasties such as the Austro-Hungarian Empire, became bound up with liberal aspirations for greater rights for citizens.

Romantic Nationalism and culture

Culture was to be at the forefront of Romantic Nationalism, celebrating the unifying legends and arts of traditional culture and creating new ones. Writers collected folk tales and made up their own in literature, drama, and national epics. Painters sought to capture characteristic scenes or create nationalist allegories. Composers incorporated folk songs and country dances into their music, produced stirring new anthems, and, at their most ambitious, sought to create what German composer Richard Wagner called a *Gesamtkunstwerk*, or "total work of art"—a synthesis of arts in the service of the soul of the nation.

Romantic Nationalism shaped the world order in the early 20th century. It can be credited with the creation of independent states in Europe and the birth of populist movements that resulted in claims of supremacy based on ethnic identities. For example, in Germany, the notion of racial superiority of Germans over other peoples contributed to the rise of Nazism.

◁ **Influential composer**
Richard Wagner's *Ring Cycle* of operas was based on Germanic legends and is seen as the high point of Romanticism. It was embraced by German Nationalists as a potential foundational myth.

Revolutionary sentiments
French artist Eugène Delacroix's painting *Liberty Leading The People* (1830), based on an uprising he witnessed, is a classic example of Romantic Nationalist art, symbolizing the revolutionary power of liberal, nationalist aspiration.

THE REVOLUTIONS OF 1848

Frustration was growing at the failure of the European ruling classes to modernize or to answer the aspirations of a wealthier population for greater liberties and rights to nationhood. Tension boiled over in 1848 as a string of revolts and rebellions flared up across the continent, prompting a bloody, reactionary backlash.

The Congress of Vienna in 1815, after the Napoleonic Wars (see pp.208–211), was supposed to create a lasting European settlement. Statesmen from the powers that had brought down Napoleonic France gathered at Vienna to decide how to redraw the borders of Europe. The resulting agreement was essentially conservative: an attempt to stamp out nationalism, a movement centerd on the concept of the nation as a legitimate and necessary political and cultural unit, the rise of which, in France, had shattered the old order of Europe. And, for 30 years, it succeeded.

However, major change in the years following the congress continued and even accelerated. The population of Europe had increased by 50 percent since 1800, and it had urbanized rapidly, with the number of cities having populations over 100,000 increasing from 28 in 1800 to 45 in 1848. In the political arena, the preservation of the Holy Alliance empires—Prussia, Russia, and, especially, Austria—had come at the cost of suppressing and frustrating awakening nationalist sentiment, particularly in Germany, Poland, and Italy.

Social and economic changes had led to the rapid growth of the middle classes. Such growth fostered liberal sentiments that fueled an appetite for change, with demands for greater representation and freedoms—including the freedom for nations to self-determine.

On Europe's borders, the crumbling of the Ottoman Empire lent impetus to Balkan drives for self-determination, with the Serbs gaining autonomy in 1817 and the Greeks in 1821 (see pp.266–267). Revolutionary sentiment that had convulsed Europe in the Napoleonic era stirred once more, and the growing demand for a more liberal political order meant that many parts of Europe were like a tinderbox, waiting for a spark.

SOWING SEEDS FOR THE FUTURE
THE SIGNIFICANCE OF THE 1848 REVOLUTIONS

The 1848 Revolutions ended in failure, harsh repression, and disillusionment among liberals, but they did leave crucial legacies. They led to the formation of different political groups; accelerated the abolition of serfdom and feudal systems; and stimulated political awareness among the masses. Widespread dreams of nationalism may have been stifled momentarily, but they had not been quashed entirely: both Italy and Germany were unified by 1871 (see pp.264–265). The nationalist mood can be seen in this painting from 1860: Germania is seen holding a shield and sword, defending the Rhine River.

△ **Down with the monarchy**
This 19th-century illustration shows people burning the French throne in the Place de la Bastille during the 1848 Revolution in France.

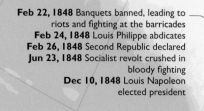

Feb 22, 1848 Banquets banned, leading to riots and fighting at the barricades
Feb 24, 1848 Louis Philippe abdicates
Feb 26, 1848 Second Republic declared
Jun 23, 1848 Socialist revolt crushed in bloody fighting
Dec 10, 1848 Louis Napoleon elected president

EUROPE AFTER THE CONGRESS OF VIENNA

Exhausted by decades of revolutionary turmoil, the great powers of Europe had agreed at the Congress of Vienna a geopolitical dispensation that often cut across linguistic and nationalistic lines, brewing trouble for the future.

KEY

- German Confederation
- Prussia
- Small German states
- Other countries subject to 1848 revolts
- — Frontiers 1848

TIMELINE

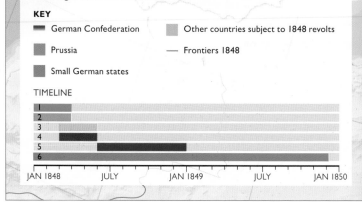

| JAN 1848 | JULY | JAN 1849 | JULY | JAN 1850 |

1 OUTBREAK OF REVOLUTION IN FRANCE AND SICILY JAN–MAR 1848

In Palermo, Sicily, a revolt broke out against the Spanish Borbón king Ferdinand II, and it soon spread to Naples. In France, King Louis-Philippe suppressed public meetings, triggering riots in Paris. The mob was fired upon, Louis-Philippe fled, and the Second Republic was declared. Unrest erupted across France as workers took to the streets.

🚩 Nationalist revolution   ✊ Republican revolution

👑 Abdication of monarch

2 THE FIRE CATCHES JAN–MAR 1848

Revolutionary sentiment spread across Italy. The Milanese rose up and drove the Austrian soldiers, under Marshal Radetzky, out of the city, appealing to the Piedmontese King, Charles Albert, to take them under his protection. Venice declared itself a Republic and had the support of a number of surrounding cities, including Treviso and Udine, while Parma revolted. Charles Albert declared war on Austria but lacked allies to win.

🚩 Nationalist revolution   ✊ Republican revolution

3 A UNITED GERMAN NATION MAR–MAY 1848

The death of King Christian VIII of Denmark in January ignited the Schleswig-Holstein question (see pp.264–265) and prompted an outpouring of pan-German nationalism, with demands for unification under a liberal constitution. Nationalist assemblies in Berlin and Frankfurt called on the Prussian king to unite Germany, and revolts flared up across the German Confederation.

🚩 Nationalist revolution   👑 Abdication of monarch

4 THE ESTABLISHMENT HANGS IN THE BALANCE MAR–MAY 1848

The fate of the establishment hung in the balance as the forces of reaction fought to cling on. Revolution in Vienna forced foreign minister Metternich to resign and the Emperor to flee; a liberal constitution was granted. Imperial forces crushed a pan-Slav conference in Prague but failed to prevent nationalist uprisings in Hungary.

🚩 Nationalist revolution   👑 Establishment victory

👑 Abdication of monarch

5 REACTION ASCENDANT JUN–DEC 1848

Reactionary forces turned the tide. In France, the newly elected Assembly proved to be reactionary, resulting in riots in Limoges and elsewhere and a bloodily suppressed socialist uprising in Paris. Imperial forces subdued Vienna in June but failed to crush the Hungarian uprising. In Italy, Austrian forces crushed the Piedmontese at Custoza in July.

👑 Establishment victory

6 REPUBLICANISM DEFEATED 1848–1849

Republican risings in the Rhineland and southern Germany were put down after the Prussian king refused to unite Germany under his aegis. Rome, where Garibaldi had proclaimed a republic, held out for a month but was defeated by an army sent from France, where Louis Napoleon had been elected president. Republican outposts in Venice and Tuscany were also crushed, as was the Hungarian uprising.

👑 Establishment victory   ✊ Republican revolution

Jan 1848 King Christian VIII of Denmark dies

Jun 1848 Bloody repression by Habsburg troops ends efforts for constitutional reform

Mar 20, 1848 Uprising in Poland
May Uprising suppressed by Prussian troops

Mar 12, 1848 Metternich resigns

Mar 15, 1848 Outbreak of revolution; Hungary granted independence
Oct 1949 Hungarians defeated

May–June 1848 Revolution suppressed

Mar 23, 1848 King Charles Albert declares war on Austria
Aug 6, 1848 Austrian forces retake Milan

Mar 23, 1848 Republic declared
Aug 28, 1849 Retaken by Austria

Jul 24–25, 1848 Austrian forces defeat Piedmontese revolt

Nov 1848 Pope flees
Feb 1849 Garibaldi declares Republic
Jul 1849 Republic defeated

Jan 12, 1848 Revolution breaks out
Mar 25, 1848 Sicilian parliament declares independence
May 15, 1848 Bourbon troops retake Sicily

North Sea
Baltic Sea
Black Sea
Mediterranean Sea

SWEDEN
DENMARK
SCHLESWIG-HOLSTEIN
Copenhagen
Bornholm
Hamburg
Amsterdam
THE NETHERLANDS
HANOVER
BRUSSELS
BELGIUM
PRUSSIA
Berlin
Danzig
EAST PRUSSIA
RUSSIA
St. Petersburg
Warsaw
POLAND
Frankfurt
SAXONY
Prague
BOHEMIA
Cracow
GALICIA
Paris
FRANCE
BAVARIA
WÜRTTEMBERG
Stuttgart
BADEN
Munich
BAVARIA
SWITZERLAND
Geneva
Vienna
AUSTRIA
Buda
Pest
HUNGARY
TRANSYLVANIA
MOLDAVIA
Milan
Custoza
Venice
PIEDMONT
MODENA
SAN MARINO
PARMA
MONACO
LUCCA
TUSCANY
PAPAL STATES
Corsica
Rome
Sardinia
Naples
THE TWO SICILIES
MONTENEGRO
BOSNIA
Belgrade
SERBIA
WALLACHIA
Bucharest
Sebastopol
OTTOMAN EMPIRE
MACEDONIA
Salonica
Corfu
GREECE
Athens
Ionian Islands
Palermo
Sicily
Malta
TUNISIA
KINGDOM
Bornholm

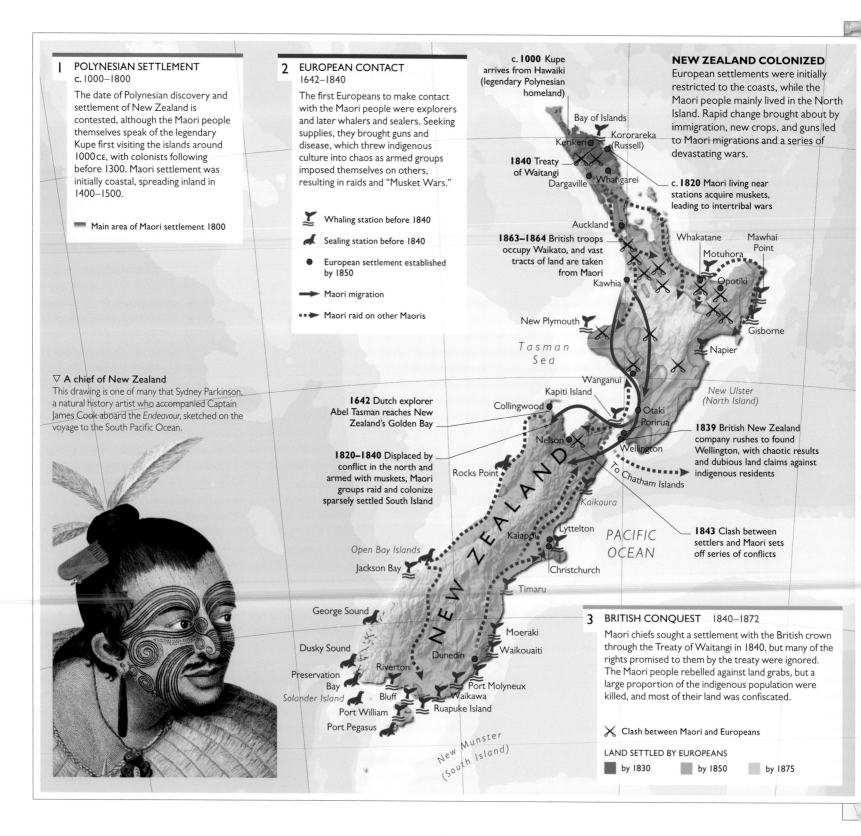

1 POLYNESIAN SETTLEMENT c.1000–1800

The date of Polynesian discovery and settlement of New Zealand is contested, although the Maori people themselves speak of the legendary Kupe first visiting the islands around 1000 CE, with colonists following before 1300. Maori settlement was initially coastal, spreading inland in 1400–1500.

■ Main area of Maori settlement 1800

2 EUROPEAN CONTACT 1642–1840

The first Europeans to make contact with the Maori people were explorers and later whalers and sealers. Seeking supplies, they brought guns and disease, which threw indigenous culture into chaos as armed groups imposed themselves on others, resulting in raids and "Musket Wars."

🐋 Whaling station before 1840

🦭 Sealing station before 1840

● European settlement established by 1850

➡ Maori migration

╌➤ Maori raid on other Maoris

▽ **A chief of New Zealand**
This drawing is one of many that Sydney Parkinson, a natural history artist who accompanied Captain James Cook aboard the *Endeavour*, sketched on the voyage to the South Pacific Ocean.

c.1000 Kupe arrives from Hawaiki (legendary Polynesian homeland)

NEW ZEALAND COLONIZED
European settlements were initially restricted to the coasts, while the Maori people mainly lived in the North Island. Rapid change brought about by immigration, new crops, and guns led to Maori migrations and a series of devastating wars.

Bay of Islands
Kororareka (Russell)
Kerikeri
1840 Treaty of Waitangi
Dargaville Whangarei

c.1820 Maori living near stations acquire muskets, leading to intertribal wars

Auckland

1863–1864 British troops occupy Waikato, and vast tracts of land are taken from Maori
Kawhia

Whakatane Mawhai Point
Motuhora
Opotiki

New Plymouth

Tasman Sea

Gisborne

Napier

Wanganui

Kapiti Island

Collingwood

New Ulster (North Island)

1642 Dutch explorer Abel Tasman reaches New Zealand's Golden Bay

1820–1840 Displaced by conflict in the north and armed with muskets, Maori groups raid and colonize sparsely settled South Island

Nelson

Otaki
Porirua
Wellington

To Chatham Islands

1839 British New Zealand company rushes to found Wellington, with chaotic results and dubious land claims against indigenous residents

Rocks Point

Kaikoura

Open Bay Islands

Kaiapoi
Lyttelton
PACIFIC OCEAN

1843 Clash between settlers and Maori sets off series of conflicts

N E W   Z E A L A N D

Christchurch

Jackson Bay

Timaru

George Sound

Moeraki
Waikouaiti

Dusky Sound

Dunedin

Riverton

Preservation Bay
Solander Island
Bluff
Port William
Port Pegasus
Waikawa
Ruapuke Island
Port Molyneux

New Munster (South Island)

3 BRITISH CONQUEST 1840–1872

Maori chiefs sought a settlement with the British crown through the Treaty of Waitangi in 1840, but many of the rights promised to them by the treaty were ignored. The Maori people rebelled against land grabs, but a large proportion of the indigenous population were killed, and most of their land was confiscated.

✕ Clash between Maori and Europeans

LAND SETTLED BY EUROPEANS
■ by 1830   ■ by 1850   ▫ by 1875

NEW ZEALAND AND AUSTRALIA

Motives ranging from whaling to exiling criminals drove European colonization of New Zealand and Australia. This had shocking and often tragic consequences for the indigenous peoples, including warfare and genocide.

Settlement of the land now known as Australia dates back to the earliest days of modern humanity (see pp.18–19). After that, remoteness led to relative cultural isolation for both Australia and for its southern neighbor New Zealand—probably the last habitable place on Earth to be settled by humans.

This would change with the increasing technological reach and territorial appetite of European powers, particularly Britain, in the 18th and 19th centuries. To these powers, the unknown lands of the Antipodes appeared as a blank canvas upon which all manner of colonial and imperial fantasies could be projected. In fact, they were home to a diverse range of cultures and

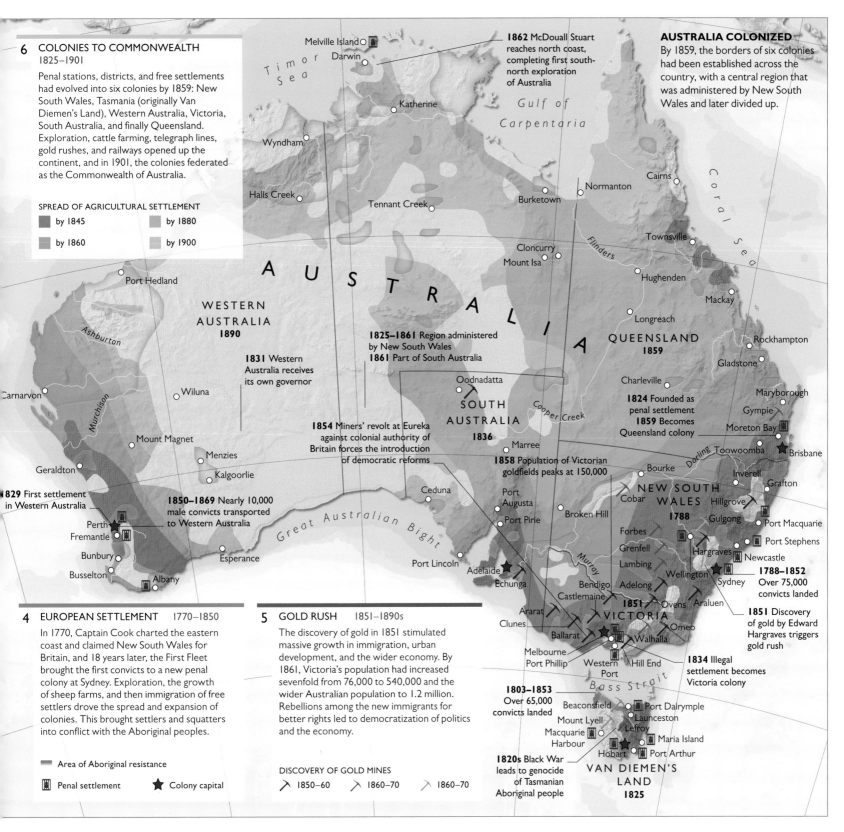

6 COLONIES TO COMMONWEALTH
1825–1901

Penal stations, districts, and free settlements had evolved into six colonies by 1859: New South Wales, Tasmania (originally Van Diemen's Land), Western Australia, Victoria, South Australia, and finally Queensland. Exploration, cattle farming, telegraph lines, gold rushes, and railways opened up the continent, and in 1901, the colonies federated as the Commonwealth of Australia.

SPREAD OF AGRICULTURAL SETTLEMENT
- by 1845
- by 1860
- by 1880
- by 1900

1862 McDouall Stuart reaches north coast, completing first south-north exploration of Australia

AUSTRALIA COLONIZED
By 1859, the borders of six colonies had been established across the country, with a central region that was administered by New South Wales and later divided up.

1825–1861 Region administered by New South Wales
1861 Part of South Australia

WESTERN AUSTRALIA 1890

1831 Western Australia receives its own governor

SOUTH AUSTRALIA 1836

QUEENSLAND 1859

1824 Founded as penal settlement
1859 Becomes Queensland colony

1854 Miners' revolt at Eureka against colonial authority of Britain forces the introduction of democratic reforms

1858 Population of Victorian goldfields peaks at 150,000

NEW SOUTH WALES 1788

1829 First settlement in Western Australia

1850–1869 Nearly 10,000 male convicts transported to Western Australia

1788–1852 Over 75,000 convicts landed

1851 Discovery of gold by Edward Hargraves triggers gold rush

VICTORIA 1851

1834 Illegal settlement becomes Victoria colony

4 EUROPEAN SETTLEMENT 1770–1850

In 1770, Captain Cook charted the eastern coast and claimed New South Wales for Britain, and 18 years later, the First Fleet brought the first convicts to a new penal colony at Sydney. Exploration, the growth of sheep farms, and then immigration of free settlers drove the spread and expansion of colonies. This brought settlers and squatters into conflict with the Aboriginal peoples.

- Area of Aboriginal resistance
- Penal settlement
- Colony capital

5 GOLD RUSH 1851–1890s

The discovery of gold in 1851 stimulated massive growth in immigration, urban development, and the wider economy. By 1861, Victoria's population had increased sevenfold from 76,000 to 540,000 and the wider Australian population to 1.2 million. Rebellions among the new immigrants for better rights led to democratization of politics and the economy.

DISCOVERY OF GOLD MINES
- 1850–60
- 1860–70
- 1860–70

1803–1853 Over 65,000 convicts landed

1820s Black War leads to genocide of Tasmanian Aboriginal people

VAN DIEMEN'S LAND 1825

---

societies. European arrivals in New Zealand began with sealing and whaling stations, where foreign ships could harvest resources, make repairs, and resupply. In Australia, the new arrivals began with the transportation of convicts from Britain and Ireland to penal colonies. The British soon took advantage in regions where the climate was familiar and introduced crops and livestock from home to drive a rapid colonial expansion. Growing numbers of new settlers increased the demand for land and also introduced firearms and unfamiliar diseases to the native peoples. These factors contributed to the severe decline of the populations of both the Maori people in New Zealand and the Aboriginal peoples in Australia.

EUROPEAN COLONIZATION

European settlement of New Zealand and Australia began slowly in the late 18th and early 19th centuries, but accelerated rapidly in the mid-19th century, with consequences for indigenous peoples inhabiting the land that settlers appropriated for farming.

TIMELINE

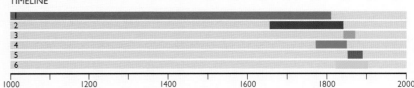

THE ABOLITION OF SLAVERY

The explosive economic growth that brought European powers to global ascendancy was driven in large part by slavery. However, from the 18th century, a long process to abolish the global slave trade was set in motion.

△ **Anti-slavery crusaders**
The British Anti-slavery Society, whose emblem is seen here, was a major force in the battle over abolition.

The abolition movement, or abolitionism, was a moral, social, and political campaign to ban the slave trade. It was distinct from, but related to, the movement to emancipate slaves. Abolitionism first took shape among the Quakers, a Protestant Christian group, who in 1787 in Britain set up the Committee for the Abolition of the Slave Trade.

The cause's success was checked when the movement associated itself with radical sentiments following the French Revolution in 1789. Public fears about reprisals that might follow abolition were also stoked by a revolt among Haitian slaves in 1791–1804. Nonetheless, skillful use of propaganda, and alliances with evangelical Christians and women's groups helped abolitionism gain ground. Although the slave trade was abolished by a Bill of Parliament in Britain in 1807, followed by other European nations such as France, Spain, and Portugal, the practice of slavery continued in many colonies.

The enactment of anti-slavery legislation in Europe boosted the cause of emancipation in America's northern states, fed by a religious revival known as the Second Great Awakening and by voters' resentment of "fugitive slave" laws. Increasing radical responses by both pro- and anti-abolitionists that ensued in the US helped tip the dispute over slavery into civil war (see pp.170–171).

THE ABOLITION OF SLAVERY AROUND THE WORLD

KEY
DATE OF ABOLITION

- 1775–1799
- 1800–1629
- 1830–1859
- 1860–1889
- 1890–1919
- 1920–1969
- 1970–present
- No data/no modern slavery

Massachusetts and Connecticut in the US were among the earliest places to abolish slavery. Although European nations tended not to practice slavery in their own territories, they were responsible for the trans-Atlantic slave trade. Despite being illegal, slavery is still practiced in many parts of the world.

The ceremony of Bois-Caiman
A legendary voodoo ceremony that has become part of the foundation myth of Haiti is depicted here by Haitian painter Andre Normil. The island nation was the site of perhaps the only successful slave rebellion in history.

RISE OF BRITISH POWER IN INDIA

From initial footholds in the southeast and Bengal, the power of the British East India Company, a corporate concern with imperial pretensions, spread across all of India, conquering territory and winning fealty through guile, brutality, and arrogance. Eventually, almost the entire subcontinent came under Company control.

European nations had been trading extensively with India since the 16th century, and by the late 17th century, five European powers had trading ports in the subcontinent. Among them was the British East India Company, a commercial organization first chartered in 1600 to profit from trade with the Moluccas (or Spice Islands) in Southeast Asia. Rebuffed by the Dutch, the British East India Company focused instead on trade in textiles and spices with south India, where it had won trading concessions with the Mughal Empire.

Under the Mughals (see pp.176–177), India was a developed, sophisticated polity, with a strong military and wealth and population outstripping that of Europe. However, the collapse of Mughal rule in the 18th century led to the rise of a mosaic of princely states, confederations, and small kingdoms. With no major, unifying power in India, imperialistic and mercantile European powers had the opportunity to exploit the subcontinent, and it would be the British that took it. Faced with foreign competitors and sometimes hostile hosts, the East India Company developed its own military force to strengthen and protect its interests. Over about the next 100 years, the Company first overcame its competitors and then widened its control of territory, trade, and power in India, using a combination of diplomacy, bribery, and force.

In consolidating its power, the Company faced formidable opponents, including the French, the sultans of Mysore, the Maratha Confederacy, the Sikh kingdom, and the Afghans. The Company was not always victorious, but it was relentless, and it eventually controlled all of India. However, in the wake of a bloody revolt (see pp.244–245), the Company was effectively abolished in 1858. Its possessions and forces were taken over by the British government, and direct colonial rule began.

SIR ROBERT CLIVE
1725–1774

Commonly known as Clive of India, Robert Clive played a key role in establishing the power of the British East India Company in the subcontinent, gaining honors and wealth in the process. After leading several successful military actions—notably defeat of a French and Mughal force at Plassey in 1757—he twice served as Governor of Bengal (1758–1760, 1765–1767). He returned to England in 1767 and died—possibly by suicide—7 years later in London.

A meeting of allies
Robert Clive meeting Mir Jafar after the Battle of Plassey. Mir Jafar supported Clive in the battle and was made Nawab of Bengal in return for his support.

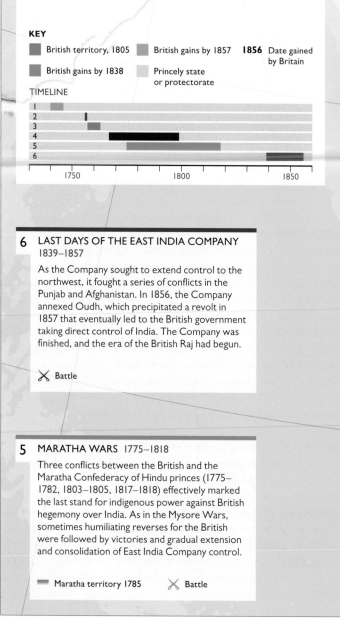

1 THE FRENCH THREATEN BRITISH POWER
1740–1746

The Dutch and French had their own India companies, which initially vied with the British for supremacy. Dutch ambitions were ended after defeat by forces of the state of Travancore at Colachel in 1741, but in 1746, the French took Madras from the British and then defeated an Indian army, establishing European military supremacy in the subcontinent.

✕ Battle   ● French colony

GROWTH OF BRITISH TERRITORY

From its early 19th-century strongholds in the southeast and northeast, Britain gained increasing territorial control through piecemeal acquisition of lands in central and western India and by means of a network of protectorates and vassal states.

KEY

■ British territory, 1805	■ British gains by 1857
■ British gains by 1838	British gains by 1857 **1856** Date gained by Britain
	Princely state or protectorate

TIMELINE
1 2 3 4 5 6
1750   1800   1850

6 LAST DAYS OF THE EAST INDIA COMPANY
1839–1857

As the Company sought to extend control to the northwest, it fought a series of conflicts in the Punjab and Afghanistan. In 1856, the Company annexed Oudh, which precipitated a revolt in 1857 that eventually led to the British government taking direct control of India. The Company was finished, and the era of the British Raj had begun.

✕ Battle

5 MARATHA WARS 1775–1818

Three conflicts between the British and the Maratha Confederacy of Hindu princes (1775–1782, 1803–1805, 1817–1818) effectively marked the last stand for indigenous power against British hegemony over India. As in the Mysore Wars, sometimes humiliating reverses for the British were followed by victories and gradual extension and consolidation of East India Company control.

▬ Maratha territory 1785   ✕ Battle

AFGHANISTAN

1876
BALUCHISTAN

Karach

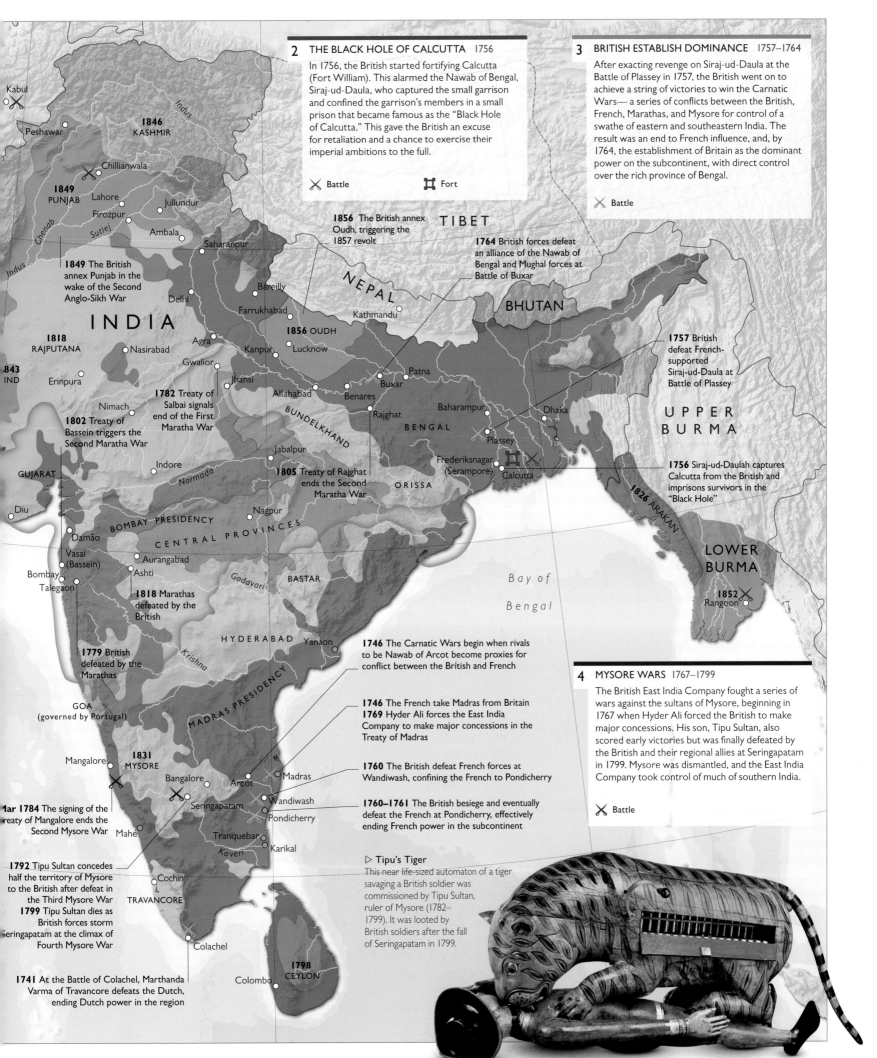

2 THE BLACK HOLE OF CALCUTTA 1756

In 1756, the British started fortifying Calcutta (Fort William). This alarmed the Nawab of Bengal, Siraj-ud-Daula, who captured the small garrison and confined the garrison's members in a small prison that became famous as the "Black Hole of Calcutta." This gave the British an excuse for retaliation and a chance to exercise their imperial ambitions to the full.

✕ Battle ⊞ Fort

3 BRITISH ESTABLISH DOMINANCE 1757–1764

After exacting revenge on Siraj-ud-Daula at the Battle of Plassey in 1757, the British went on to achieve a string of victories to win the Carnatic Wars— a series of conflicts between the British, French, Marathas, and Mysore for control of a swathe of eastern and southeastern India. The result was an end to French influence, and, by 1764, the establishment of Britain as the dominant power on the subcontinent, with direct control over the rich province of Bengal.

✕ Battle

Kabul ✕

1846 KASHMIR

Peshawar

Chillianwala ✕

1849 PUNJAB Lahore Jullundur

Firozpur

Ambala

Saharanpur

1849 The British annex Punjab in the wake of the Second Anglo-Sikh War

INDIA

Delhi

Bareilly

1856 The British annex Oudh, triggering the 1857 revolt

TIBET

NEPAL Kathmandu

BHUTAN

1764 British forces defeat an alliance of the Nawab of Bengal and Mughal forces at Battle of Buxar

1757 British defeat French-supported Siraj-ud-Daula at Battle of Plassey

1818 RAJPUTANA Nasirabad

Farrukhabad

Agra

1856 OUDH

Lucknow

Kanpur

843 IND Erinpura

Gwalior

Jhansi

1782 Treaty of Salbai signals end of the First Maratha War

Allahabad Benares

Buxar

Patna

Baharampur

Dhaka

UPPER BURMA

Nimach

1802 Treaty of Bassein triggers the Second Maratha War

BUNDELKHAND

Rajghat

1805 Treaty of Rajghat ends the Second Maratha War

BENGAL

Frederiksnagar (Serampore)

Plassey ⊞ ✕

Calcutta

1756 Siraj-ud-Daulah captures Calcutta from the British and imprisons survivors in the "Black Hole"

GUJARAT

Indore

Jabalpur

Narmada

ORISSA

1826 ARAKAN

Diu

Nagpur

BOMBAY PRESIDENCY

CENTRAL PROVINCES

Damão

Vasai (Bassein)

Aurangabad

Ashti

LOWER BURMA

Bombay Talegaon

Godavari

BASTAR

1818 Marathas defeated by the British

Bay of Bengal

1852 ✕ Rangoon

1779 British defeated by the Marathas

Krishna

HYDERABAD Yanaon

1746 The Carnatic Wars begin when rivals to be Nawab of Arcot become proxies for conflict between the British and French

GOA (governed by Portugal)

MADRAS PRESIDENCY

4 MYSORE WARS 1767–1799

The British East India Company fought a series of wars against the sultans of Mysore, beginning in 1767 when Hyder Ali forced the British to make major concessions. His son, Tipu Sultan, also scored early victories but was finally defeated by the British and their regional allies at Seringapatam in 1799. Mysore was dismantled, and the East India Company took control of much of southern India.

✕ Battle

1746 The French take Madras from Britain
1769 Hyder Ali forces the East India Company to make major concessions in the Treaty of Madras

Mangalore

1831 MYSORE

Bangalore

Arcot

Madras

1760 The British defeat French forces at Wandiwash, confining the French to Pondicherry

Mar 1784 The signing of the Treaty of Mangalore ends the Second Mysore War

Seringapatam

Wandiwash

Pondicherry

Mahé

1760–1761 The British besiege and eventually defeat the French at Pondicherry, effectively ending French power in the subcontinent

1792 Tipu Sultan concedes half the territory of Mysore to the British after defeat in the Third Mysore War
1799 Tipu Sultan dies as British forces storm Seringapatam at the climax of Fourth Mysore War

Tranquebar

Kaveri Karikal

▷ Tipu's Tiger
This near life-sized automaton of a tiger savaging a British soldier was commissioned by Tipu Sultan, ruler of Mysore (1782–1799). It was looted by British soldiers after the fall of Seringapatam in 1799.

Cochin

TRAVANCORE

Colachel

1798 CEYLON

Colombo

1741 At the Battle of Colachel, Marthanda Varma of Travancore defeats the Dutch, ending Dutch power in the region

THE OPIUM WARS

In the early 1800s, opium was being illegally imported into China (mainly by Britain), which eventually sparked confrontations over foreign trade. China's rulers, the Qing Dynasty, badly misjudged their strength in relation to Britain, which used "gunboat diplomacy" to force China to open to international trade.

The Chinese imperial court viewed trade as a favor bestowed on foreign tributaries; the British, in contrast, viewed it as the lifeblood of international relations and a way to exploit their colonies. Specifically, the British were seeking to monetize their colonization of India, and they saw opium as the key. India produced high-grade cash crop opium, which could be sold in China for silver, which was promptly swapped for tea—a valuable commodity for the domestic British market. The only problem with the arrangement was that it was illegal to sell opium to China. The trade fed massive corruption and a huge black economy, at the same time as contributing to monetary problems that the Qing were suffering

linked to inflation. Tension inevitably flared, boiling over into confrontations between the Chinese and the British, which the latter were happy to exploit.

The "gunboat diplomacy" that followed saw China lose a series of battles across two wars, with the Qing forced to make severe concessions in what became known as the "unequal treaties." These stoked resentment in China and inflicted lasting humiliation that even today affects Chinese relations with Western powers. The damage to the prestige of the Qing Dynasty undermined their mandate to rule, instigating the series of colossal rebellions that would convulse and eventually destroy imperial China (see pp.252–253).

THE OPIUM TRADE
CHINA'S ADDICTION, BRITAIN'S FINANCIAL GAIN

Poppy plants were grown and the seeds dried (see below) in factories in India. Produced and processed by the quasi-governmental British East India Company, the opium was then imported to China by private merchants, allowing the British to wash their hands of the trade's illegality. Chests of opium were unloaded onto floating warehouses off the coast of Guangzhou, where Chinese smugglers bought it with silver and shipped it upriver, paying bribes and spreading corruption to get around official prohibitions.

GUNBOAT DIPLOMACY

In the First Opium War, British forces attacked China, and in the Second Opium War, they were supported by France. The Western powers were victorious and forced China to open a string of ports to foreign trade.

- ⬛ Chinese defensive bases
- ⬛ Qing Empire

TIMELINE

May 1858 English-French force attacked the Taku Forts
Jun 1858 Qing Army reoccupy the Taku Forts
Jun 1859 English-French forces attack the forts for a second time

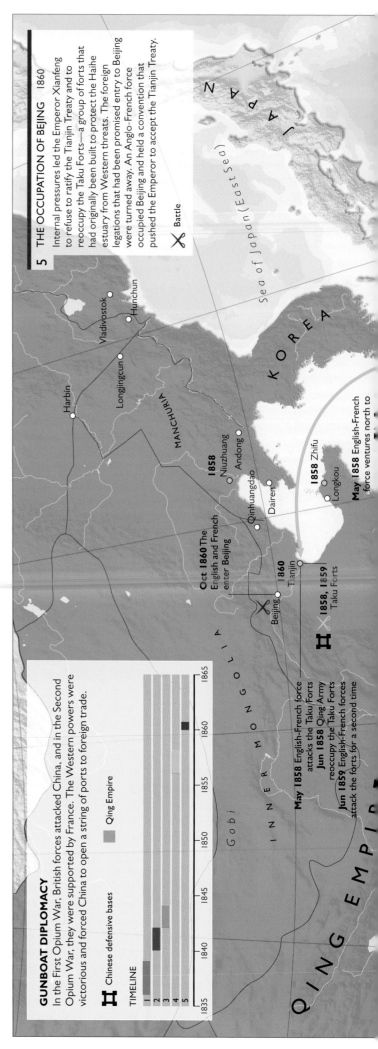

5 THE OCCUPATION OF BEIJING 1860

Internal pressures led the Emperor Xianfeng to refuse to ratify the Tianjin Treaty and to reoccupy the Taku Forts—a group of forts that had originally been built to protect the Haihe estuary from Western threats. The foreign legations that had been promised entry to Beijing were turned away. An Anglo-French force occupied Beijing and held a convention that pushed the Emperor to accept the Tianjin Treaty.

✗ Battle

1858
1858 Niuzhuang
Andong
1858 Zhifu
May 1858 English-French force ventures north to
1860 Tianjin
Oct 1860 The English and French enter Beijing
Beijing
1858, 1859 Taku Forts

Qinhuangdao
Dairen
Longkou

Harbin
Longjingcun
Hunchun
Vladivostok

MANCHURIA
KOREA
JAPAN
Sea of Japan (East Sea)

Gobi
INNER MONGOLIA
QING EMPIRE

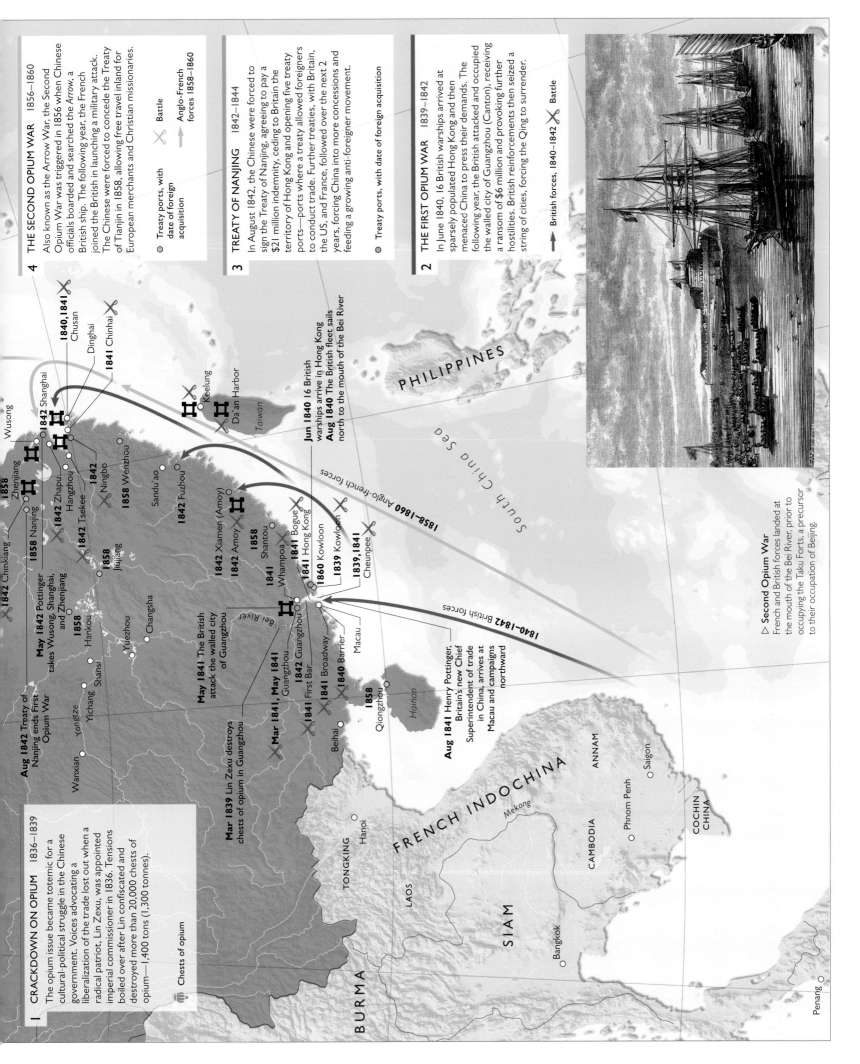

1 CRACKDOWN ON OPIUM 1836–1839

The opium issue became totemic for a cultural-political struggle in the Chinese government. Voices advocating a liberalization of the trade lost out when a radical patriot, Lin Zexu, was appointed imperial commissioner in 1836. Tensions boiled over after Lin confiscated and destroyed more than 20,000 chests of opium—1,400 tons (1,300 tonnes).

◉ Chests of opium

2 THE FIRST OPIUM WAR 1839–1842

In June 1840, 16 British warships arrived at sparsely populated Hong Kong and then menaced China to press their demands. The following year, the British attacked and occupied the walled city of Guangzhou (Canton), receiving a ransom of $6 million and provoking further hostilities. British reinforcements then seized a string of cities, forcing the Qing to surrender.

➡ British forces, 1840–1842

3 TREATY OF NANJING 1842–1844

In August 1842, the Chinese were forced to sign the Treaty of Nanjing, agreeing to pay a $21 million indemnity, ceding to Britain the territory of Hong Kong and opening five treaty ports—ports where a treaty allowed foreigners to conduct trade. Further treaties, with Britain, the US, and France, followed over the next 2 years, forcing China into more concessions and feeding a growing anti-foreigner movement.

◉ Treaty ports, with date of foreign acquisition

4 THE SECOND OPIUM WAR 1856–1860

Also known as the Arrow War, the Second Opium War was triggered in 1856 when Chinese officials boarded and searched the Arrow, a British ship. The following year, the French joined the British in launching a military attack. The Chinese were forced to concede the Treaty of Tianjin in 1858, allowing free travel inland for European merchants and Christian missionaries.

◉ Treaty ports, with date of foreign acquisition

✗ Battle

⬆ Anglo-French forces 1858–1860

△ **Second Opium War**
French and British forces landed at the mouth of the Bei River, prior to occupying the Taku Forts, a precursor to their occupation of Beijing.

PHILIPPINES

South China Sea

1858–1860 Anglo-French forces

1840–1842 British forces

Jun 1840 16 British warships arrive in Hong Kong
Aug 1840 The British fleet sails north to the mouth of the Bei River

1840, 1841 Chusan
Dinghai
1841 Chinhai
1842 Shanghai
Wusong
Keelung
Da'an Harbor
Taiwan
1858
Zhenjiang
1842 Zhapu
Hangzhou
1842 Tsekee
Ningbo
1842
1858 Wenzhou
Sandu ao
1842 Chinkiang
1858 Nanjing
May 1842 Pottinger takes Wusong, Shanghai, and Zhenjiang
Aug 1842 Treaty of Nanjing ends First Opium War
Hankou
1858
Jiujiang
1858
Fuzhou
1842
1842 Xiamen (Amoy)
1842 Amoy
1858
Shantou
1858
Yuezhou
Changsha
Tuezhou
Shansi
Yichang
Wanxian
Yangtze
1858 Hankou

Mar 1839 Lin Zexu destroys chests of opium in Guangzhou
May 1841 The British attack the walled city of Guangzhou
Mar 1841, May 1841 Guangzhou
1842 Guangzhou
1841 First Bar
1841 Broadway
1840 Barrier
Macau
Bei River
1841 Whampoa
1841 Bogue
1841 Hong Kong
1860 Kowloon
1839, 1841 Cheunpee
1858 Qiongzhou
Beihai
Hainan
Aug 1841 Henry Pottinger, Britain's new Chief Superintendent of trade in China, arrives at Macau and campaigns northward

BURMA
SIAM
FRENCH INDOCHINA
TONGKING
LAOS
Hanoi
Mekong
CAMBODIA
Phnom Penh
ANNAM
Saigon
COCHIN CHINA
Bangkok
Penang

PROGRESS
AND EMPIRE

THE HIGH POINT OF IMPERIALISM WAS REACHED IN THE
PERIOD 1850–1914, BUT THE WORLD'S GREAT POWERS WERE
ON AN INEXORABLE PATH TOWARD GLOBAL CONFLICT.

CITIES AND INDUSTRY

Industrialization shaped every aspect of life in the 19th century. It not only affected where and how people lived, and how they traveled and communicated with each other, but also helped shape public health, politics, and people's attitudes.

△ **Unequal world**
Poverty was rife in many cities, as this photograph of a child in Paris from 1900 illustrates.

Industrialization became a global phenomenon in the second half of the 19th century. Where the industrial advances at the end of the 18th and beginning of the 19th centuries had predominantly benefited Britain (see pp.212–215), the development of heavy industry based on coal, iron, and steel, and the transport revolution of the mid-19th century, reshaped the world.

As western Europe, Japan, Russia, and the US all began to industrialize rapidly from 1870, they experienced huge social, cultural, and population changes. The world's population grew as land reform and modern farming methods—the utilization of chemical fertilizers, steel tools, and steam-powered machinery—helped sustain more people. Millions moved from the countryside into the cities seeking employment and opportunities. In 1800, 5 percent of the world's population lived in urban areas; by 1925, that figure had reached 20 percent, and in the industrialized regions of Europe and the US, 71.2 percent of the population lived in cities. Millions took advantage of the improved transportation offered by oceangoing steamships to migrate overseas (see pp.238–239). The immigrants who traveled

to find gold in the US, Canada, South Africa, and Australia contributed to the creation of a world in which all but a few currencies were convertible to gold. The gold standard—a monetary system that backed paper money with gold—in turn facilitated international trade, stimulating new markets for industrial products and creating a period of great financial stability. The people made rich by industrialization sought new avenues for investment, feeding a wave of imperial activity that saw Africa carved up by the European nations, the ancient Chinese Empire come under threat, and Latin America brought within the spheres of influence of Britain and the US.

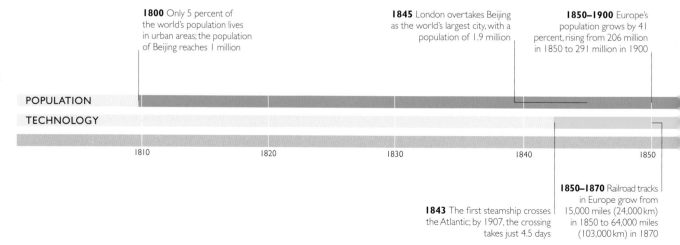

△ **New horizons**
In this photograph from 1906, immigrants crowd the decks of an Atlantic liner as it approaches Ellis Island—the gateway to a new, better life in the US. Third-class passengers would remain at Ellis Island until they passed health and legal checks.

The modern city

Society developed in multifarious ways in the 19th century—industrialization fueled the gap between the rich and the poor but also created a middle class comprising lawyers, doctors, businessmen, merchants, civil servants, shopkeepers, and clerks. While a generation of tycoons became wealthy on the back of industry and investment, in the cities where their workers lived, poverty, pollution, and diseases—such as dysentery, tuberculosis, rickets, and cholera—were rife. Work itself involved long hours in hazardous conditions, and many

CITIES OF THE INDUSTRIAL AGE

The technological developments of the 19th century brought with them profound changes in the size and distribution of the world's population. There was a shift away from rural to city life in the industrialized West. Europe outdid Asia for the first time in terms of the number and size of its cities. The population grew rapidly, particularly in Europe. Modern transportation meant that the overspill from Europe's cities could move easily to the high-rise cities in the US.

1800 Only 5 percent of the world's population lives in urban areas; the population of Beijing reaches 1 million

1845 London overtakes Beijing as the world's largest city, with a population of 1.9 million

1850–1900 Europe's population grows by 41 percent, rising from 206 million in 1850 to 291 million in 1900

POPULATION

TECHNOLOGY

1810　　1820　　1830　　1840　　1850

1843 The first steamship crosses the Atlantic; by 1907, the crossing takes just 4.5 days

1850–1870 Railroad tracks in Europe grow from 15,000 miles (24,000 km) in 1850 to 64,000 miles (103,000 km) in 1870

◁ **Cleaning up**
British engineer Sir Joseph William Bazalgette (top right) surveys work on London's sewers. His sanitation systems transformed public health in cities around the world.

children had to work. Yet the cities also provided the means to combat this inequality and solve some of the ills of industrialized society. Migrants from rural areas and other countries arrived into a melting pot of social classes and ethnic backgrounds. Social and religious taboos broke down, and the exchange of ideas gave rise to movements for social change. Various workers' unions came into existence campaigning for better pay and improved working conditions. The demands for suffrage for both men and women also began to increase. Charitable organizations proliferated as both wealthy philanthropists and Christian societies such as the Salvation Army sought to meet the city populations' physical and spiritual needs. A deeper understanding of poverty combined with political activism ensured that by the 20th century, Germany and Britain—the most industrialized nations— had in place the beginnings of a welfare system that would care for the elderly and the sick.

By then, industry and the wealth it generated had also begun to solve some of the practical problems of city life. Steel construction made high-rise living and working a reality; steel-framed buildings provided a way for offices and accommodations to be erected swiftly and made the best use of limited space by reaching upward. The development of modern sanitation—the use of iron tanks and steam-powered pumping stations—saved city dwellers from the horrors of diseases such as cholera. Underground transportation meant that workers could move swiftly around the city, and connections with the railroads meant they could escape the city for the suburbs. The speed and breadth of technological change in the 19th century was unprecedented, and even the telecommunication revolution of the 20th century could not match the impact of industrialization on modern society.

> "It is from the midst of this putrid sewer that the greatest river of human industry springs up ..."
>
> ALEXIS DE TOCQUEVILLE, FRENCH HISTORIAN, FROM *VOYAGES EN ANGLETERRE ET IRLANDE* (JOURNEYS TO ENGLAND AND IRELAND), 1835

△ **Gold rush**
A presidential election poster from 1900 shows US President William McKinley held aloft on a gold coin, celebrating the prosperity of the Gold Standard era.

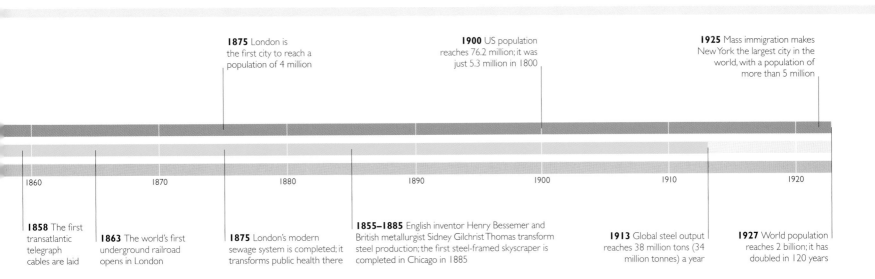

1875 London is the first city to reach a population of 4 million

1900 US population reaches 76.2 million; it was just 5.3 million in 1800

1925 Mass immigration makes New York the largest city in the world, with a population of more than 5 million

1860   1870   1880   1890   1900   1910   1920

1858 The first transatlantic telegraph cables are laid

1863 The world's first underground railroad opens in London

1875 London's modern sewage system is completed; it transforms public health there

1855–1885 English inventor Henry Bessemer and British metallurgist Sidney Gilchrist Thomas transform steel production; the first steel-framed skyscraper is completed in Chicago in 1885

1913 Global steel output reaches 38 million tons (34 million tonnes) a year

1927 World population reaches 2 billion; it has doubled in 120 years

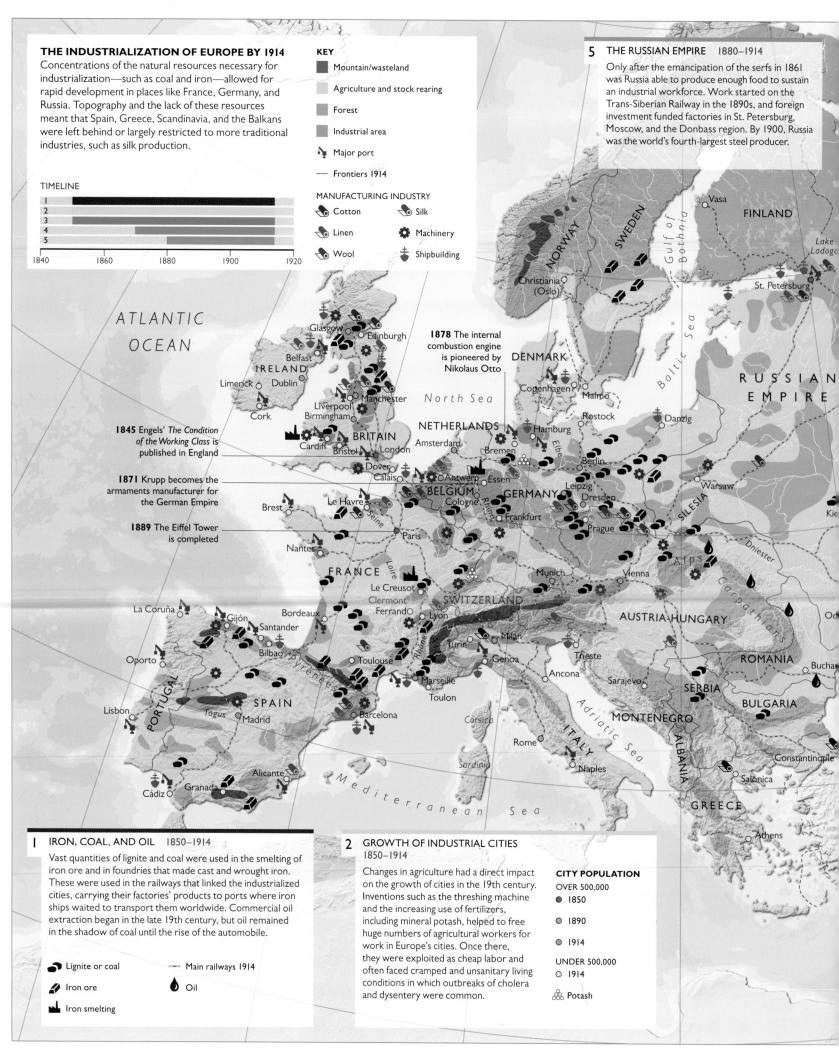

THE INDUSTRIALIZATION OF EUROPE BY 1914

Concentrations of the natural resources necessary for industrialization—such as coal and iron—allowed for rapid development in places like France, Germany, and Russia. Topography and the lack of these resources meant that Spain, Greece, Scandinavia, and the Balkans were left behind or largely restricted to more traditional industries, such as silk production.

KEY

- Mountain/wasteland
- Agriculture and stock rearing
- Forest
- Industrial area
- Major port
- Frontiers 1914

MANUFACTURING INDUSTRY

- Cotton
- Linen
- Wool
- Silk
- Machinery
- Shipbuilding

TIMELINE

1 2 3 4 5

1840 1860 1880 1900 1920

5 THE RUSSIAN EMPIRE 1880–1914

Only after the emancipation of the serfs in 1861 was Russia able to produce enough food to sustain an industrial workforce. Work started on the Trans-Siberian Railway in the 1890s, and foreign investment funded factories in St. Petersburg, Moscow, and the Donbass region. By 1900, Russia was the world's fourth-largest steel producer.

1845 Engels' *The Condition of the Working Class* is published in England

1871 Krupp becomes the armaments manufacturer for the German Empire

1889 The Eiffel Tower is completed

1878 The internal combustion engine is pioneered by Nikolaus Otto

1 IRON, COAL, AND OIL 1850–1914

Vast quantities of lignite and coal were used in the smelting of iron ore and in foundries that made cast and wrought iron. These were used in the railways that linked the industrialized cities, carrying their factories' products to ports where iron ships waited to transport them worldwide. Commercial oil extraction began in the late 19th century, but oil remained in the shadow of coal until the rise of the automobile.

- Lignite or coal
- Iron ore
- Iron smelting
- Main railways 1914
- Oil

2 GROWTH OF INDUSTRIAL CITIES 1850–1914

Changes in agriculture had a direct impact on the growth of cities in the 19th century. Inventions such as the threshing machine and the increasing use of fertilizers, including mineral potash, helped to free huge numbers of agricultural workers for work in Europe's cities. Once there, they were exploited as cheap labor and often faced cramped and unsanitary living conditions in which outbreaks of cholera and dysentery were common.

CITY POPULATION

OVER 500,000
- 1850
- 1890
- 1914

UNDER 500,000
- 1914
- Potash

INDUSTRIALIZED EUROPE

From 1850, Britain's position as the unchallenged leader of industrialization was threatened as other countries, notably the US and Germany, began to modernize. The industrializing nations of this second revolution pioneered technologies that helped change the world.

In 1851, Great Britain held the Great Exhibition, a showcase of the achievements of British industry, at the Crystal Palace in London's Hyde Park. It marked the pinnacle of Britain's industrial dominance. Britain's success had been built on the mechanization of the textile industry and leadership in the iron industry. But, by 1850, much of northern Europe was catching up, building factories and developing their own exploitation of mineral resources, such as coal and iron. In the second half of the 19th century, social and political changes in Germany, the United States, Russia, and Japan sparked a new wave of industrialization, and the industrial balance shifted in their favor. World industrial output from 1870 to 1914 increased at an extraordinary rate: coal production rose by 650 percent; steel by 2,500 percent; and steam engine capacity by over 350 percent.

This second industrial revolution brought significant innovations in engineering and science: the internal combustion engine, petroleum, communication technologies, armaments, and chemicals all played a part. It also brought new opportunities for the wealthy nations of the West to extend their influence through investment and control of industrial knowledge. However, the developed nations of the late 19th century also had to contend with an increasingly educated and informed urban working class, ready to fight for their rights to better living and working conditions.

EMPIRE AND INDUSTRIALIZATION

The pace of industrialization was, in many countries, determined by the interests of colonial powers. In South America, European investment helped to build railways and shipyards to facilitate exports of coffee and meat. In India—which was both a source of raw materials and a market for Britain's industrial goods—the British saw little to be gained from industrialization.

KEY

▮ Major industrial regions c. 1914

✿ Heavy machinery

⚒ Iron and steel

🧵 Textile production

4 THE RISE OF GERMANY 1870–1914
Germany made rapid progress following unification in 1871. Chancellor Bismarck's economic policies created a secure environment for investment, and the country benefited from the settlement from France after the Franco-Prussian War (1870–1871). Plentiful coal from the Ruhr Valley helped to fuel the developing steel, chemical, and electrical industries.

Jan 1905 Moscow is crippled by strikers protesting the working and living conditions and the lack of political reform in Russia

○ Solikamsk
Perm' ○
Ekaterinburg ○

Volga

Moscow

1869 Donetsk company is founded by British businessman John Hughes, who builds steelworks and several collieries in the region

Donetsk

DONBASS

EXPOSITION UNIVERSELLE DE 1900
Cⁱᵉ INTERNATIONALE DES WAGONS-LITS
PANORAMA MOUVANT Voyage de MOSCOU à PÉKIN
au TROCADÉRO
TRANSSIBÉRIEN
THÉÂTRE CHINOIS
RESTAURANTS RUSSE & CHINOIS
pour les Gares de MOSCOU & de PÉKIN

△ **World's Fair**
This poster for the 1900 World's Fair in Paris, France, trumpets the achievements of the industrialized world, such as the Trans-Siberian Railway.

Caucasus

Caspian Sea

Baku

AZERBAIJAN

Black Sea

1890s Branobel, set up in Azerbaijan, becomes one of the largest oil producers in the world

PERSIA

OTTOMAN EMPIRE

3 SOUTHERN EUROPE LEFT BEHIND 1850–1914
Politics, geology, and poverty conspired against southern Europe in the 19th century. In Spain, progress in the mining and steel industries was hampered by the country's dependence on subsistence farming and cultural pressures against entrepreneurship. A lack of iron and coal made industrialization hard in Italy. Only the advent of hydroelectric power late in the century brought much progress, and then only in the north.

NEW ZEALAND
Sydney
Melbourne
Adelaide
AUSTRALIA
Perth

PACIFIC OCEAN

UNITED STATES OF AMERICA
San Francisco
MEXICO
Mexico City
New Orleans
CANADA
Cuba
Montreal
UNITED KINGDOM
New York
PANAMA
Valparaíso
CHILE
ARGENTINA
Buenos Aires
BRAZIL
Montevideo
URUGUAY
Rio de Janeiro
ATLANTIC OCEAN

Tokyo
Manila
Shanghai
Beijing
Hong Kong
Singapore
CHINA
BURMA
RUSSIAN EMPIRE
Delhi
INDIA
Moscow
Bombay
Berlin
London
Paris
Constantinople
FRANCE
SPAIN
Rome
Aden
ITALY
EGYPT
INDIAN OCEAN
Madagascar
LIBERIA
NIGERIA
AFRICA
Johannesburg
CAPE COLONY
NATAL
Cape Town

SOCIALISM AND ANARCHISM

Socialist ideas of common ownership of resources and production had a long history. However, socialism developed as a political theory in the 1840s; it spread across the world in several forms, including a variant taken up by anarchists.

△ **Fathers of socialism**
A statue of Karl Marx (left) and Friedrich Engels stands in the Marx-Engels Forum, a public park in Berlin, Germany.

In 1848, German thinkers Karl Marx and Friedrich Engels published *The Communist Manifesto*, suggesting that workers would inevitably revolt against capitalists and move toward communism—public ownership and control of production and resources.

The ideas quickly spread. At a meeting in London in 1864, an influential federation of labor groups called the First International was founded. In 1871, the Paris Commune created the world's first, albeit short-lived, socialist government. By 1872, socialists were divided over how to achieve their aims. While moderates developed political parties to work within the parliamentary system, radicals turned to anarchism—a philosophy that deems all governments unnecessary. Anarchism took many forms; some were peaceful, but others came to be associated with terrorism. By the early 1900s, anarchists had bombed several western cities and assassinated King Umberto I of Italy and US President William McKinley.

A revolutionary direction

Socialism took another path in Russia when Vladimir Lenin proposed that workers needed a Revolutionary Party to lead them to communism. In 1922, Russia formed the Union of Soviet Socialist Republics (USSR)—a socialist state that finally collapsed in 1991.

△ **Violent display of anarchy**
A contemporary illustration shows the anarchist Leon Czolgosz shooting US President William McKinley while the president greets visitors at the Pan-American Exposition in Buffalo, New York, on September 6, 1901. The president died 8 days later.

Paris's Bloody Week
This print shows Paris burning after the French National Guard set fire to the Paris Commune's headquarters on May 24, 1871. More than 20,000 supporters of the Commune were killed in the "Bloody Week."

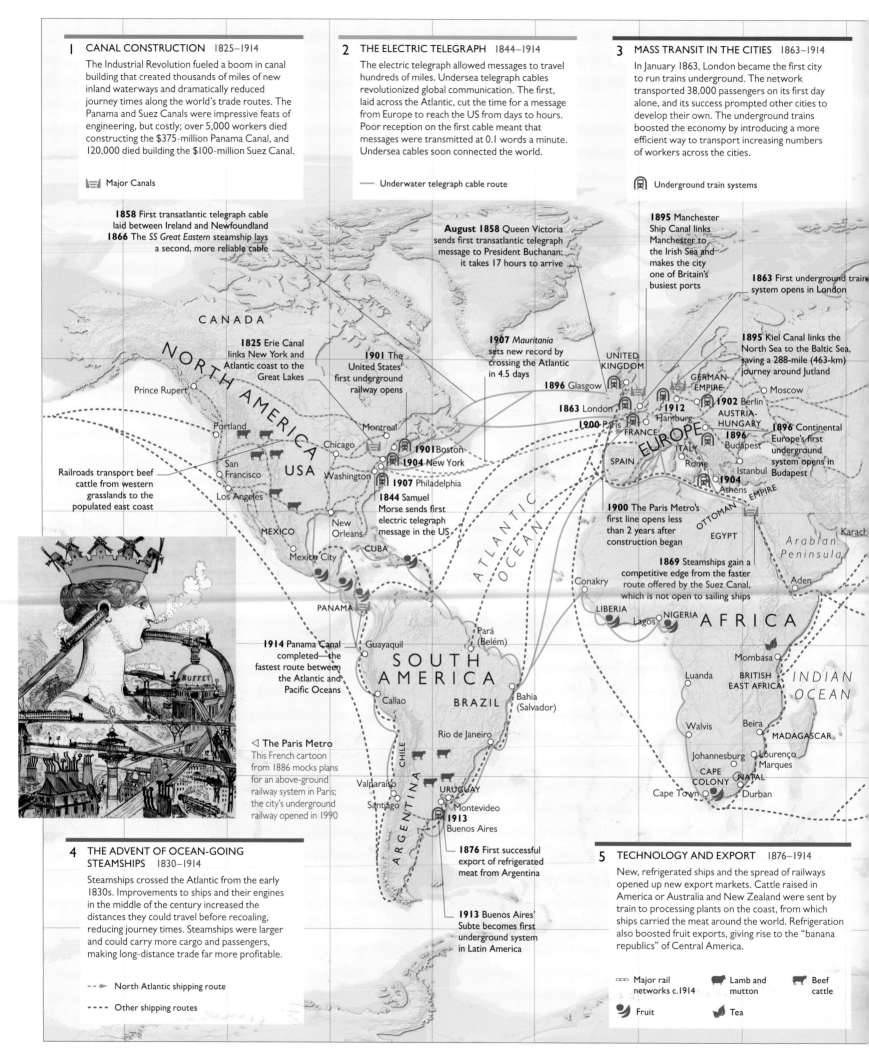

1 CANAL CONSTRUCTION 1825–1914

The Industrial Revolution fueled a boom in canal building that created thousands of miles of new inland waterways and dramatically reduced journey times along the world's trade routes. The Panama and Suez Canals were impressive feats of engineering, but costly; over 5,000 workers died constructing the $375-million Panama Canal, and 120,000 died building the $100-million Suez Canal.

🚢 Major Canals

2 THE ELECTRIC TELEGRAPH 1844–1914

The electric telegraph allowed messages to travel hundreds of miles. Undersea telegraph cables revolutionized global communication. The first, laid across the Atlantic, cut the time for a message from Europe to reach the US from days to hours. Poor reception on the first cable meant that messages were transmitted at 0.1 words a minute. Undersea cables soon connected the world.

— Underwater telegraph cable route

3 MASS TRANSIT IN THE CITIES 1863–1914

In January 1863, London became the first city to run trains underground. The network transported 38,000 passengers on its first day alone, and its success prompted other cities to develop their own. The underground trains boosted the economy by introducing a more efficient way to transport increasing numbers of workers across the cities.

🚇 Underground train systems

1858 First transatlantic telegraph cable laid between Ireland and Newfoundland
1866 The *SS Great Eastern* steamship lays a second, more reliable cable

August 1858 Queen Victoria sends first transatlantic telegraph message to President Buchanan; it takes 17 hours to arrive

1895 Manchester Ship Canal links Manchester to the Irish Sea and makes the city one of Britain's busiest ports

1863 First underground train system opens in London

1825 Erie Canal links New York and Atlantic coast to the Great Lakes

1901 The United States' first underground railway opens

1907 *Mauritania* sets new record by crossing the Atlantic in 4.5 days

1895 Kiel Canal links the North Sea to the Baltic Sea, saving a 288-mile (463-km) journey around Jutland

CANADA

NORTH AMERICA

Prince Rupert

1896 Glasgow
1863 London
1912 Hamburg
1900 Paris
1902 Berlin
1896 Budapest

UNITED KINGDOM
GERMAN EMPIRE
FRANCE
EUROPE
AUSTRIA-HUNGARY
ITALY
Rome
SPAIN
Moscow
Istanbul
1904 Athens

1896 Continental Europe's first underground system opens in Budapest

Portland
Chicago
Montreal

1901 Boston
1904 New York
1907 Philadelphia

San Francisco
USA
Washington

1844 Samuel Morse sends first electric telegraph message in the US

Railroads transport beef cattle from western grasslands to the populated east coast

Los Angeles

MEXICO

New Orleans

Mexico City
CUBA

1900 The Paris Metro's first line opens less than 2 years after construction began

1869 Steamships gain a competitive edge from the faster route offered by the Suez Canal, which is not open to sailing ships

OTTOMAN EMPIRE
EGYPT
Arabian Peninsula
Karach
Aden

PANAMA

Conakry
LIBERIA
Lagos NIGERIA
AFRICA

ATLANTIC OCEAN

Pará (Belém)
Guayaquil

1914 Panama Canal completed—the fastest route between the Atlantic and Pacific Oceans

SOUTH AMERICA

Callao

BRAZIL

Bahia (Salvador)

Rio de Janeiro

Mombasa
Luanda
BRITISH EAST AFRICA
INDIAN OCEAN

Walvis
Beira
MADAGASCAR

Johannesburg
Lourenço Marques
CAPE COLONY
NATAL
Cape Town
Durban

◁ **The Paris Metro**
This French cartoon from 1886 mocks plans for an above-ground railway system in Paris; the city's underground railway opened in 1990.

Valparaíso
Santiago
CHILE
ARGENTINA
URUGUAY
Montevideo
1913 Buenos Aires

1876 First successful export of refrigerated meat from Argentina

1913 Buenos Aires' Subte becomes first underground system in Latin America

4 THE ADVENT OF OCEAN-GOING STEAMSHIPS 1830–1914

Steamships crossed the Atlantic from the early 1830s. Improvements to ships and their engines in the middle of the century increased the distances they could travel before recoaling, reducing journey times. Steamships were larger and could carry more cargo and passengers, making long-distance trade far more profitable.

- - - North Atlantic shipping route
- - - - Other shipping routes

5 TECHNOLOGY AND EXPORT 1876–1914

New, refrigerated ships and the spread of railways opened up new export markets. Cattle raised in America or Australia and New Zealand were sent by train to processing plants on the coast, from which ships carried the meat around the world. Refrigeration also boosted fruit exports, giving rise to the "banana republics" of Central America.

🚃 Major rail networks c.1914
🐑 Lamb and mutton
🐄 Beef cattle
🍃 Fruit
🌱 Tea

THE IMPACT OF ADVANCES
Technological advances in shipbuilding, electric telegraphy, mass transit, canal construction, the railways, and refrigeration contributed to the economic revolution in the 19th century, helping create a worldwide trading system.

TIMELINE

1866 The steamship *Agamemnon* successfully sails from London to China with only one stop, substantially outpacing sailing ships on the route

1870 Cables between Singapore and Darwin in north Australia complete a telegraphic link between Britain and its farthest dominions

1880 Refrigerated beef and mutton is successfully shipped 15,000 miles (24,000 km) from Australia to London

1879 The *Dunedin* successfully transports the first full cargo of refrigerated meat from New Zealand to London

TRANSPORT AND COMMUNICATIONS

In the 19th century, transport and communications were transformed. In turn, they transformed the world's economy by improving productivity in the cities, speeding up intercontinental communication, and increasing trade profits. Developments in refrigeration and the railways created new export opportunities.

Advances in technology made the world a much smaller place. The sailing ships that had, for centuries, plied the long-distance routes around the globe gave way to steamships capable of carrying more cargo more quickly and profitably. In the 1830s, steamer journeys across the Atlantic took 17 days. Continued steam engine improvements made the ships even faster and by 1910, transatlantic journey times had been reduced to just 5 days. The shortcuts provided by the great Canals built during the 19th and early 20th centuries allowed ships to bypass notoriously dangerous passages like those around the Cape of Africa and the

tip of South America. And as journeys became less risky, insurance costs came down and profits increased further. By the end of the 19th century, even the farthest-flung corners of the world were participating in the global economy. Once refrigeration had been mastered, frozen beef, lamb, and mutton from as far afield as New Zealand and the tip of South America, along with fruit from South Africa and Central America, were crossing the oceans to feed the hungry workforces of Europe's and North America's industrial cities. Electric telegraphy and mass transportation systems ensured that the wheels of commerce in the cities turned smoothly.

"Cunard's liners and the electric telegraph, are ... signs that ... there is a mighty spirit working among us."

CHARLES KINGSLEY, FROM HIS NOVEL *YEAST* (1851)

SAMUEL MORSE
1791–1872

A successful artist born in Massachusetts in 1791, Samuel Morse began working on improving electric telegraphy in the 1830s after hearing about the newly invented electromagnet on a ship home from Europe. Morse's design used a single telegraph wire to send messages. He created a system for encoding messages, known as Morse Code, using short and long electrical signals to represent letters. These signals were then sent along the wire to a stylus operated by an electromagnet that embossed the code onto a moving paper tape. He completed America's first electric telegraph line in 1844.

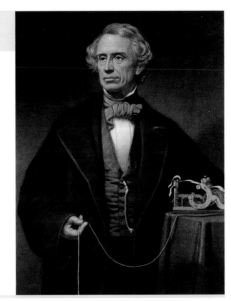

MASS MIGRATIONS

In the 19th century, millions left their home countries in search of stability, freedom, and employment. As they left the Old World behind, flowing out from Russia, Europe, China, and India, the younger countries of the Americas and Australasia saw their populations boom.

The political, social, and economic changes wrought by the Industrial Revolution, coupled with new forms of mass transportation, caused a huge surge in migration in the 19th century. Newly mechanized industries demanded a concentration of labor on a scale never seen before. A ready supply of migrant labor was to be found among those fleeing economic hardship in Europe, India, and China. And with political upheaval and anti-Semitism in central Europe and the Russian Empire swelling the ranks of those seeking a new life, more than 80 million people left their country of origin in the 19th and early 20th centuries.

Many headed for the rapidly industrializing coastal regions of the United States, due to the end of the Civil War and the opening up of Native American land to new settlers. The emerging economies of South America drew millions from southern Europe, and hundreds of thousands were attracted by the promise of riches in the gold rush towns of Australia, Canada, and South Africa. That so many could travel so far was a result of the advances brought by the Industrial Revolution: the railroads, faster and safer ships, and new routes through the Panama and Suez Canals.

▷ *The Last of England*, 1855
This painting by the English artist Ford Madox Brown shows the apprehension on the faces of emigrants bound for an uncertain future in the gold fields of Australia.

I **THE AMERICAN DREAM** 1800–1914
Over 50 million migrants traveled to North America in the 19th century, the majority of them to the United States, as wave after wave left their homes for the economic opportunities and political and religious freedom offered by the "land of the free." They initially came from northern Europe—Germany, Scandinavia, Britain, and Ireland—but from 1880, migrants from southern Europe, particularly Italy, began to arrive in large numbers.

1882 The US passes the Chinese Exclusion Act, stopping labor immigration from China

1860–1920 More than 5 million European migrants travel to Canada

1850–1880 Tens of thousands of Chinese laborers come to work in Peru's guano, sugar, and cotton industries

1888 Slavery is abolished in Brazil, triggering a large influx of immigrants

JEWISH MIGRATION (1880–1914)
The 19th century brought persecution to the world's largest Jewish population, in Russia. When the assassination of Alexander II in 1881 prompted years of government-sanctioned pogroms, the Jews flooded out of Russia, heading for the Holy Land. Some Jews moved toward western Europe and were soon joined by those fleeing anti-Semitism in the Ottoman Empire.

KEY

- Major concentration of Jews in the Russian Empire
- Region with emigrating Jewish population
- Region with substantial Jewish immigration
- ● Gateway city
- → Jewish migrations
- ● Number of Jewish immigrants 1880–1914

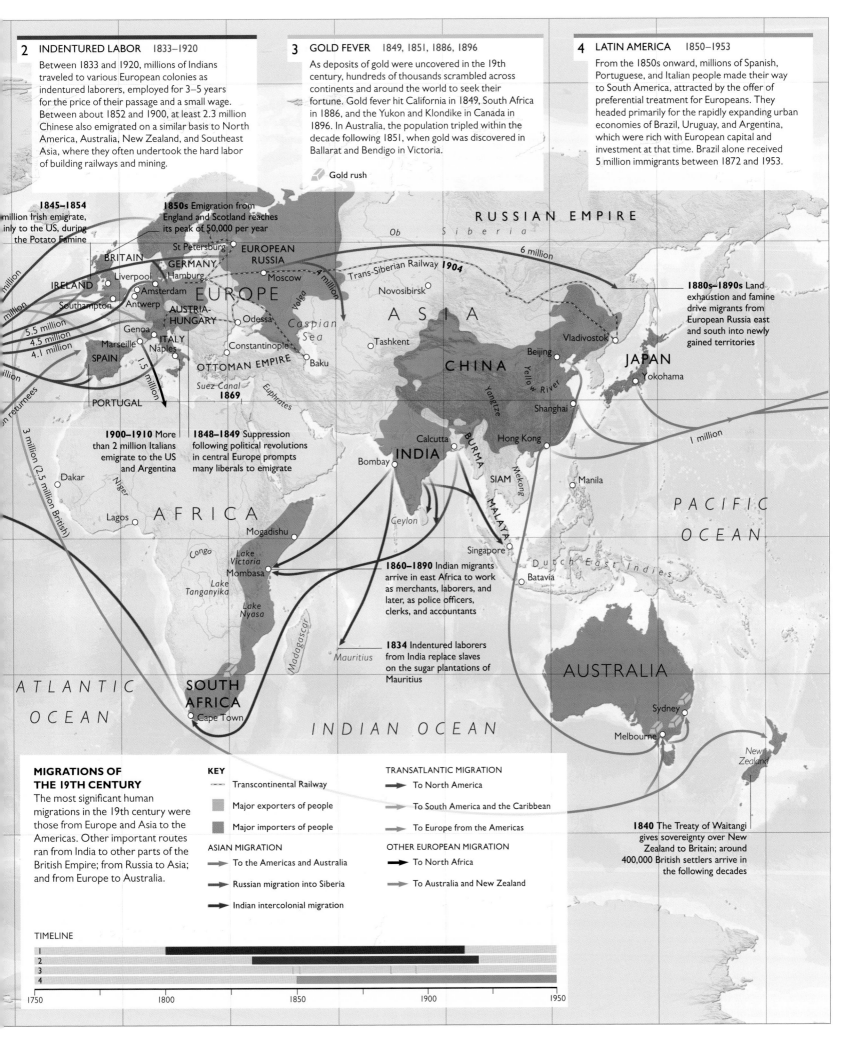

2 INDENTURED LABOR 1833–1920

Between 1833 and 1920, millions of Indians traveled to various European colonies as indentured laborers, employed for 3–5 years for the price of their passage and a small wage. Between about 1852 and 1900, at least 2.3 million Chinese also emigrated on a similar basis to North America, Australia, New Zealand, and Southeast Asia, where they often undertook the hard labor of building railways and mining.

3 GOLD FEVER 1849, 1851, 1886, 1896

As deposits of gold were uncovered in the 19th century, hundreds of thousands scrambled across continents and around the world to seek their fortune. Gold fever hit California in 1849, South Africa in 1886, and the Yukon and Klondike in Canada in 1896. In Australia, the population tripled within the decade following 1851, when gold was discovered in Ballarat and Bendigo in Victoria.

◈ Gold rush

4 LATIN AMERICA 1850–1953

From the 1850s onward, millions of Spanish, Portuguese, and Italian people made their way to South America, attracted by the offer of preferential treatment for Europeans. They headed primarily for the rapidly expanding urban economies of Brazil, Uruguay, and Argentina, which were rich with European capital and investment at that time. Brazil alone received 5 million immigrants between 1872 and 1953.

1845–1854 ...million Irish emigrate, ...inly to the US, during the Potato Famine

1850s Emigration from England and Scotland reaches its peak of 50,000 per year

1880s–1890s Land exhaustion and famine drive migrants from European Russia east and south into newly gained territories

6 million

Trans-Siberian Railway **1904**

4 million

RUSSIAN EMPIRE

Ob   Siberia

St Petersburg   EUROPEAN RUSSIA

BRITAIN   GERMANY   Moscow

Liverpool   Hamburg

IRELAND   Amsterdam   EUROPE   Novosibirsk

Southampton   Antwerp   AUSTRIA-HUNGARY   Odessa   Caspian Sea   Volga   ASIA

5.5 million   Genoa   ITALY   Constantinople   Tashkent   Vladivostok   JAPAN

4.5 million   Marseille   Naples   OTTOMAN EMPIRE   Baku   CHINA   Yokohama

4.1 million   SPAIN   1.5 million   Suez Canal **1869**   Euphrates   Beijing   Yellow River

PORTUGAL   Shanghai

1900–1910 More than 2 million Italians emigrate to the US and Argentina

1848–1849 Suppression following political revolutions in central Europe prompts many liberals to emigrate

3 million (2.5 million British)

Dakar   Niger   Lagos   AFRICA   Mogadishu

Congo   Lake Victoria   Mombasa

Lake Tanganyika

Lake Nyasa

Madagascar   Mauritius

SOUTH AFRICA   Cape Town

Calcutta   BURMA   Hong Kong   1 million

Bombay   INDIA   SIAM   Manila   PACIFIC OCEAN

Ceylon   MALAYA

Singapore   Dutch East Indies

Batavia

1860–1890 Indian migrants arrive in east Africa to work as merchants, laborers, and later, as police officers, clerks, and accountants

1834 Indentured laborers from India replace slaves on the sugar plantations of Mauritius

AUSTRALIA

ATLANTIC OCEAN

INDIAN OCEAN

Sydney

Melbourne

New Zealand

MIGRATIONS OF THE 19TH CENTURY

The most significant human migrations in the 19th century were those from Europe and Asia to the Americas. Other important routes ran from India to other parts of the British Empire; from Russia to Asia; and from Europe to Australia.

KEY

- ⌁ Transcontinental Railway
- ▨ Major exporters of people
- ▨ Major importers of people

ASIAN MIGRATION
- → To the Americas and Australia
- → Russian migration into Siberia
- → Indian intercolonial migration

TRANSATLANTIC MIGRATION
- → To North America
- → To South America and the Caribbean
- → To Europe from the Americas

OTHER EUROPEAN MIGRATION
- → To North Africa
- → To Australia and New Zealand

1840 The Treaty of Waitangi gives sovereignty over New Zealand to Britain; around 400,000 British settlers arrive in the following decades

TIMELINE

	1750	1800	1850	1900	1950
1					
2					
3					
4					

THE AGE OF IMPERIALISM

In the 19th century, forces of imperialism reshaped the world, as nations sought to gain control of overseas territories that would provide valuable resources, space for growing populations, and power in a competitive world.

△ **Ravaging their colonies**
Contemporary cartoons frequently satirized the plundering nature of imperialism. In this American cartoon from 1885, Germany, England, and Russia grab pieces of Africa and Asia.

The middle of the 19th century witnessed a dramatic shift in European overseas expansion. For centuries, European activities overseas had been dominated by trade and the creation of a chain of staging posts, by which the riches of the East could be brought to Europe. However, this changed in the 1870s. Countries everywhere scrambled to annex new territories and strengthen their control over existing colonies, and new nations competed with the old colonial powers. By 1900, the world was largely imperial, setting the stage for World War I.

Reasons for imperialism

The shift from colonialism to imperialism was largely driven and facilitated by industrialization (see pp.232–233), which required vast amounts of raw materials. Imperialism gave nations control over raw materials, access to labor and huge new markets, and plenty of investment opportunities.

The colonies offered ample chances for those hoping to make their fortune, and some countries—mainly Britain and France—needed space for their growing populations. The desire to become a "Great Power" also nudged many countries to expand. European countries were keen to reassert themselves or carve out new identities. Britain hoped to recover its stature after losing its American colonies, France wanted to rebuild its power, and Russia continued its push eastward into the weakening Qing Empire in China. From the 1860s, the young nations of Germany, Italy, and the US sought to become world powers. Emerging from centuries of

isolation, Japan, too, was keen to gain access to the resources it lacked and living space for its people, while being painfully aware that it was itself vulnerable to imperialism.

In addition to the economic and political benefits of imperialism, there was also a belief in the superiority of the white man. As scientists sought to apply Charles Darwin's theory of evolution to humankind, the perceived "advanced" state of Western society was used to justify imperialism. Many Westerners felt that they had a moral duty to Christianize "native" cultures. It was an attitude neatly summed up in Kipling's 1899 poem "The White Man's Burden," which exhorted Americans to colonize the Philippines. It spoke of a white man's moral obligation to rule the nonwhite peoples, or the "other," and encourage their economic, cultural, and social progress.

Building empires

The huge empires built in the 19th century were largely made possible by the advances brought about by industrialization. Modern medicine, such as the discovery of quinine as a treatment for malaria, meant that Europeans could push farther than ever before into lands rife with tropical disease. Modern communications, such as railways and telegraph lines, allowed large areas to be easily

◁ **Resisting imperialism**
Zulu chief Cetshwayo kaMpande led his warriors against the British in 1879. His defeat removed a major threat to British colonial interests in South Africa.

THE IMPERIAL WORLD

Patterns of imperial activity varied around the world. While the colonization of Africa was marked by a scramble in which almost all major European countries took part, India and Southeast Asia were mainly dominated by the British and French, respectively. The decaying Qing Empire provided easy pickings for Japan and Russia. While Britain and the US sought to bring Latin America within their spheres of influence, Latin American countries also embarked on their own expansionist ventures.

1857–1858 The Indian Mutiny against the British results in the tightening of British control and the declaration of the "Raj"

1864–1870 Argentina, Brazil, and Uruguay attempt to carve up Paraguay between them in the Paraguayan War, or the War of the Triple Alliance

ASIA					
LATIN AMERICA					
AFRICA					
1850	1855	1860	1865	1870

1849–1852 The British annex Punjab and occupy Lower Burma; Upper Burma is annexed in 1886

1859–1867 France extends control in Southeast Asia, capturing Saigon and establishing protectorates in Cambodia and Cochin China

◁ **Soft imperialism**
Built with British expertise, using British materials, the Retiro Railway Station in Buenos Aires is an example of how imperial influence extended beyond official colonies through cultural, financial, and industrial means.

controlled. New mechanized weaponry made it possible to suppress local resistance; this also meant that brutality was a frequent companion of imperialism.

Even countries that were not directly colonized came under the influence of imperialist nations. For example, in Latin America, political and economic intervention helped secure American and British influence in the region. Cultural influence helped the imperialist nations to embed their lifestyles and aspirations both in their colonies and beyond.

"I am an anti-imperialist. I am opposed to having the eagle put its talons on any other land."

MARK TWAIN, WRITER,
NEW YORK HERALD, 1900

▽ **Military might**
Japan destroyed Russia's Baltic Fleet at the Battle of Tsushima in 1905 during the Russo-Japanese War. Japan's victory was proof of her increasing military and imperial power and of Russia's growing weakness.

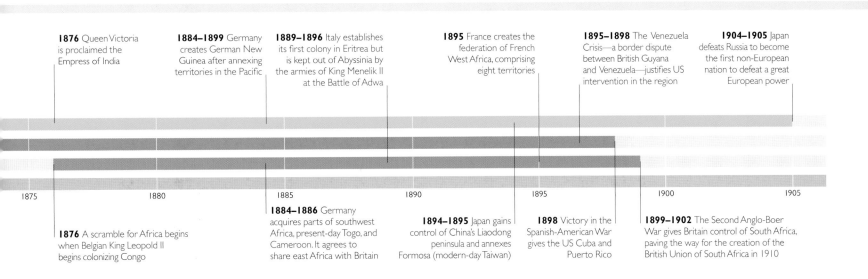

1876 Queen Victoria is proclaimed the Empress of India

1884–1899 Germany creates German New Guinea after annexing territories in the Pacific

1889–1896 Italy establishes its first colony in Eritrea but is kept out of Abyssinia by the armies of King Menelik II at the Battle of Adwa

1895 France creates the federation of French West Africa, comprising eight territories

1895–1898 The Venezuela Crisis—a border dispute between British Guyana and Venezuela—justifies US intervention in the region

1904–1905 Japan defeats Russia to become the first non-European nation to defeat a great European power

1875   1880   1885   1890   1895   1900   1905

1876 A scramble for Africa begins when Belgian King Leopold II begins colonizing Congo

1884–1886 Germany acquires parts of southwest Africa, present-day Togo, and Cameroon. It agrees to share east Africa with Britain

1894–1895 Japan gains control of China's Liaodong peninsula and annexes Formosa (modern-day Taiwan)

1898 Victory in the Spanish-American War gives the US Cuba and Puerto Rico

1899–1902 The Second Anglo-Boer War gives Britain control of South Africa, paving the way for the creation of the British Union of South Africa in 1910

THE NEW IMPERIALISM

The 19th century saw a remarkable wave of imperial activity as freedom from war, the second wave of the Industrial Revolution, and the emergence of new countries fueled the land grab of most of Africa, the Pacific, and southern Asia among European powers.

In 1830, the European colonies were in retreat. The French, British, and Spanish had been swept out of the Americas in a wave of revolution. Only Russia, with its vast empire in north and central Asia, and Britain, holding Canada, Australia, and India, retained significant territory. However, conditions were ripe for the emergence of renewed imperial activity and new forms of imperialism.

Britain made a cautious start. Many of its acquisitions—Singapore (1819), Malacca (1824), Hong Kong (1842), Natal (1843), and Lower Burma (1852)—were driven by a desire to secure the trade routes to the East Indies and protect its position in India. France acquired Algeria (1830s) and Tahiti and the Marquesas in the South Pacific (1840s), then gained a foothold in Indochina (1858–1859).

By 1870, Europeans had not yet penetrated Africa's interior, and much of Indochina and China remained untouched, but this was not to last far beyond 1880, when the Second Industrial Revolution created a strong demand for raw materials and markets. By then, the unified countries of Germany and Italy—along with the US and Japan—were eager to challenge the older colonial powers. In the last 20 years of the century, the European nations carved up almost all of Africa, while in Asia, the weakness of the Qing Dynasty allowed the French, British, Russians, and Japanese to extend their influence deep into China. Between 1880 and 1914, Europe added 8.5 million square miles (20.7 million sq km) to its overseas possessions, and Britain and France ruled more than 500 million people between them.

OVERCOMING RESISTANCE
FORCE AND TRICKERY IN THE COLONIES

Colonists faced almost constant pressure from local uprisings. In Indochina, for example, the French were engaged in a guerilla war from 1883–1913. Brute force was the usual response—the Herero rising against the Germans in Southwest Africa in 1904 ended in genocide—but trickery played a part, too, as Cecil Rhodes showed when in 1888, he deceived King Lobengula into signing away mining rights for his territory in Matabeleland.

Cecil Rhodes with the Matabeles
Rhodes, prime minister of Britain's Cape Colony, confronts the Matabele in this contemporary illustration.

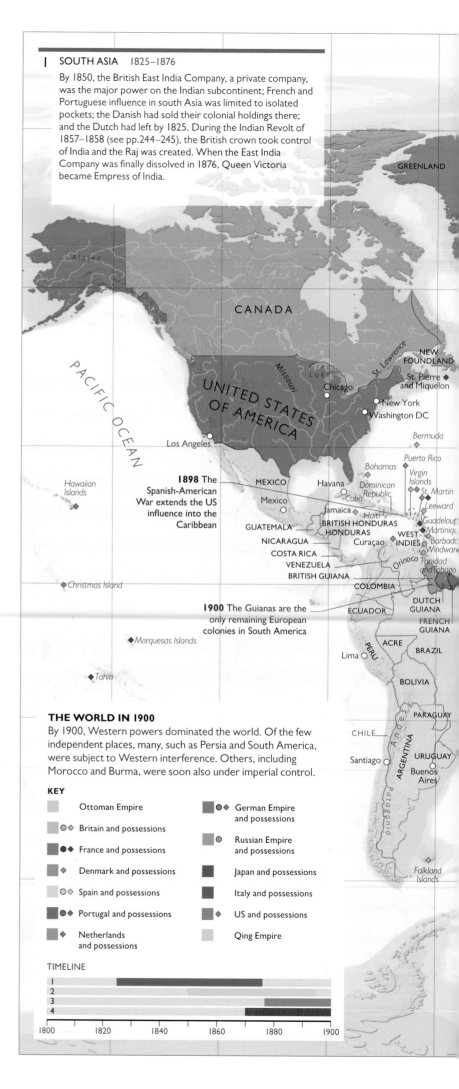

SOUTH ASIA 1825–1876
By 1850, the British East India Company, a private company, was the major power on the Indian subcontinent; French and Portuguese influence in south Asia was limited to isolated pockets; the Danish had sold their colonial holdings there; and the Dutch had left by 1825. During the Indian Revolt of 1857–1858 (see pp.244–245), the British crown took control of India and the Raj was created. When the East India Company was finally dissolved in 1876, Queen Victoria became Empress of India.

1898 The Spanish-American War extends the US influence into the Caribbean

1900 The Guianas are the only remaining European colonies in South America

THE WORLD IN 1900
By 1900, Western powers dominated the world. Of the few independent places, many, such as Persia and South America, were subject to Western interference. Others, including Morocco and Burma, were soon also under imperial control.

KEY

Ottoman Empire		German Empire and possessions	
Britain and possessions		Russian Empire and possessions	
France and possessions		Japan and possessions	
Denmark and possessions		Italy and possessions	
Spain and possessions		US and possessions	
Portugal and possessions		Qing Empire	
Netherlands and possessions			

TIMELINE

1800   1820   1840   1860   1880   1900

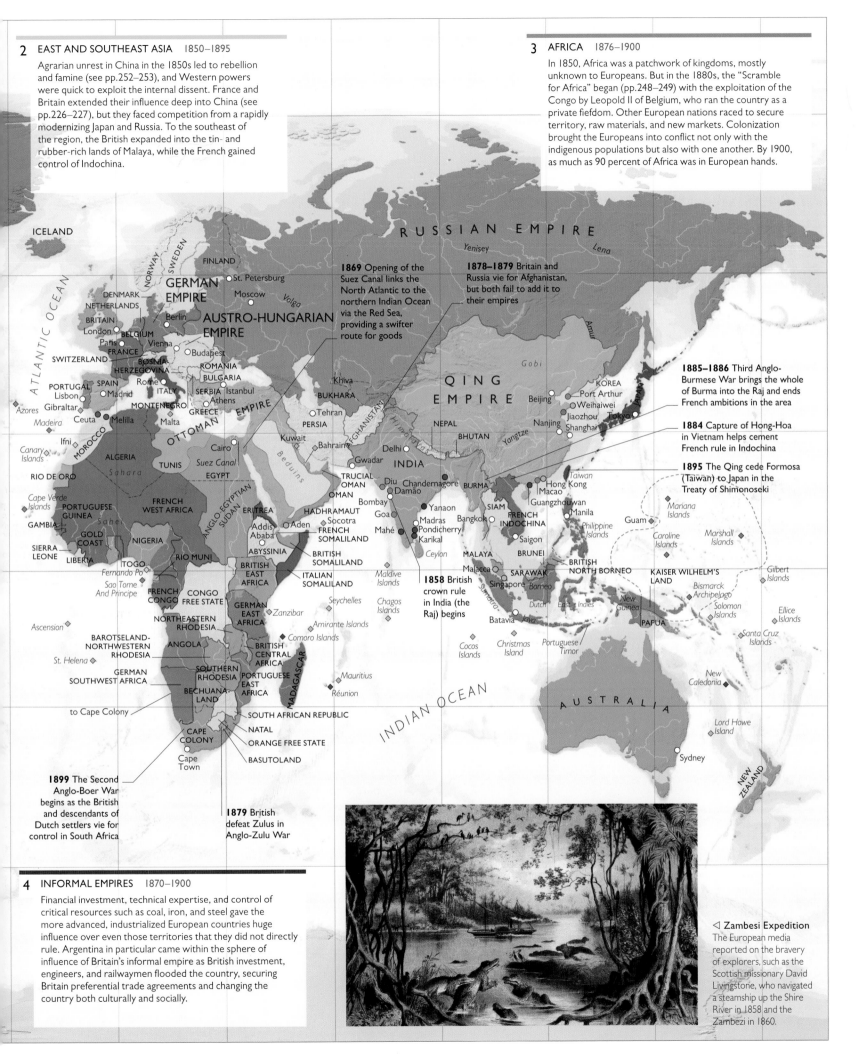

2 EAST AND SOUTHEAST ASIA 1850–1895

Agrarian unrest in China in the 1850s led to rebellion and famine (see pp.252–253), and Western powers were quick to exploit the internal dissent. France and Britain extended their influence deep into China (see pp.226–227), but they faced competition from a rapidly modernizing Japan and Russia. To the southeast of the region, the British expanded into the tin- and rubber-rich lands of Malaya, while the French gained control of Indochina.

3 AFRICA 1876–1900

In 1850, Africa was a patchwork of kingdoms, mostly unknown to Europeans. But in the 1880s, the "Scramble for Africa" began (pp.248–249) with the exploitation of the Congo by Leopold II of Belgium, who ran the country as a private fiefdom. Other European nations raced to secure territory, raw materials, and new markets. Colonization brought the Europeans into conflict not only with the indigenous populations but also with one another. By 1900, as much as 90 percent of Africa was in European hands.

1869 Opening of the Suez Canal links the North Atlantic to the northern Indian Ocean via the Red Sea, providing a swifter route for goods

1878–1879 Britain and Russia vie for Afghanistan, but both fail to add it to their empires

1885–1886 Third Anglo-Burmese War brings the whole of Burma into the Raj and ends French ambitions in the area

1884 Capture of Hong-Hoa in Vietnam helps cement French rule in Indochina

1895 The Qing cede Formosa (Taiwan) to Japan in the Treaty of Shimonoseki

1858 British crown rule in India (the Raj) begins

1899 The Second Anglo-Boer War begins as the British and descendants of Dutch settlers vie for control in South Africa

1879 British defeat Zulus in Anglo-Zulu War

4 INFORMAL EMPIRES 1870–1900

Financial investment, technical expertise, and control of critical resources such as coal, iron, and steel gave the more advanced, industrialized European countries huge influence over even those territories that they did not directly rule. Argentina in particular came within the sphere of influence of Britain's informal empire as British investment, engineers, and railwaymen flooded the country, securing Britain preferential trade agreements and changing the country both culturally and socially.

◁ **Zambesi Expedition**
The European media reported on the bravery of explorers, such as the Scottish missionary David Livingstone, who navigated a steamship up the Shire River in 1858 and the Zambezi in 1860.

RESISTANCE AND THE RAJ

In 1857–1858, a revolt by Indian soldiers threatened to force the British out of India. Instead, the British increased their control, creating the Raj under the direct rule of Queen Victoria.

Unrest was growing in India in the 1850s. Indians were worried about British expansionism and feared forced conversion to Christianity, suspecting that the British were trying to undermine traditional culture.

In 1857, a rumor spread among the sepoys (native soldiers) employed by the British. They came to believe that cartridges for the new Enfield rifles, which had to be opened with the teeth, were greased with cow or pig fat. This caused offense to both Hindus, who believed cows were sacred, and Muslims, who thought pigs were unclean. In spite of British reassurances that the cartridges were free from animal fat, the sepoys on parade at Meerut on May 10, 1857, refused to use them and mutinied.

△ **Enfield rifle cartridges**
Rumors about the fat used to grease the new Enfield rifle cartridges sparked a mutiny among India's sepoys, which developed into a wide-reaching Indian Revolt.

The mutiny quickly developed into a general revolt, spreading through Bengal, Oudh, and the Northwest Provinces as local princes, such as Nana Sahib and Lakshmi Bai, the Rani of Jhansi, tried to drive out the British. After atrocities on both sides, the British succeeded in quelling the rebellion by the end of 1858. Their position in India was totally changed. The East India Company was abolished, and the last ruler of the Mughal line, Bahadur Shah Zafar, was tried for treason and exiled, opening the way for direct rule by the British over India. The British Raj had been born.

THE REVOLT OF 1857–1858

From Meerut, the mutiny soon spread to other sepoy regiments around India and to the general populace. Some princely states remained neutral or loyal to the British, while others seized the chance to rebel. The revolt remained largely centered in northern India.

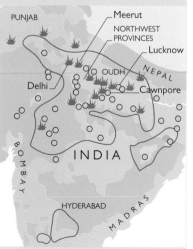

KEY

▨ British India	◦ Posts at which Indian troops mutinied
▨ Princely states	
— Areas affected by the revolt	⚝ Main centers of rebellion

The Siege of Lucknow
Part of the British administrative headquarters, or Residency, in Lucknow, the Chattar Manzil palace was besieged by rebel forces for several months. The siege was eventually broken by the British in March 1858.

1808 The Treaty of Tilsit between Russia and France allows Russia to move against their common enemy—Sweden—and annex Finland

SWEDEN

FINLAND

Severnaya Zemlya

Barents Sea

Baltic Sea

Novaya Zemlya

St. Petersburg

POLISH-LITHUANIAN COMMONWEALTH

1709 Swedish defeat in the Battle of Poltava marks beginning of Russian supremacy in eastern Europe

Moscow

Ural Mountains

Ob'

Yenisey

TOBOL'SK

YENISEYSK

RUSSIA

S

Poltava

Ural'sk

Kazan

Perm

1594 Surgut

CRIMEAN KHANATE

Samara

Yekaterinburg

1587 Tobol'sk

Sevastopol

Volga

19th century Russia conquers the Caucasus from the Persian Empire

1743 Orenburg

1619 Yeniseysk

1854–1855 The Siege of Sevastopol ends Russia's attempt to expand its territories in the Black Sea region

Black Sea

Astrakhan

1730

1716 Omsk

1604 Tomsk

1628 Krasnoyarsk

URAL'SK

1731

1734

TOMSK

Caucasus

1824

TURGAY

AKMOLINSK

Irtysh

1718 Semipalatinsk

Baku

Caspian Sea

Aral Sea

1824

SEMIPALATINSK **1864**

Altai Mountains

1912–21 URYANKHAI

1 THE CONQUEST OF SIBERIA 1600–1812

Russia first tried to find a sea passage from the Arctic to the Pacific Ocean. When this failed, it turned to conquering Siberia in order to gain access to the Pacific coast and to win control over its land, minerals, and fur trade. Military forays and massacres, as well as diseases brought in by Russian trappers and traders, subdued the indigenous peoples. By 1650, Russia had colonized the whole of north Asia. Russia then reached North America, where it founded colonies in Alaska (1784) and California (1812).

1873 KHIVA

1873

Syr Darya

1854

Lake Balkhash

TRANSCASPIAN

Khiva

Amu Darya

SYR DARYA

1864 SEMIRECH'YE **1871**

Ashkhabad

Tashkent

Tehran

Bukhara

1868–1870 SAMARKAND

Tien Shan

1871–1881 ILI

Sep 1895 The Pamir Boundary Commission protocols define the border between Afghanistan and the Russian Empire

MONG

2 EXPANSION TO THE WEST 1768–1815

For centuries, the Swedish Empire and the Polish-Lithuanian Commonwealth had limited Russia's western territory. However, the military reforms of two czars, Ivan V and Peter the Great, helped to bring much of Poland and Lithuania into the empire by 1795. Success against Sweden in the Finnish War (1808–1809) gave Russia the Grand Duchy of Finland. A final shuffle of Polish territories after the Napoleonic Wars (1803–1815) defined the western limits of the Russian Empire.

Samarkand

1868 BUKHARA

TURKESTAN FERGHANA

Pamirs

1895

AFGHANISTAN

Takla Makan Desert

PERSIA

Kabul

Hindu Kush

Himalayas

XINJIANG

INDIA

TIBET

QING EMPIRE

3 THE BLACK SEA AND CRIMEA 1768–1856

Under Empress Catherine the Great, Russia moved toward the Black Sea, securing the independence of the Crimean Khanate from the Ottoman Empire in the Russo-Turkish War (1768–1774) and then annexing it in 1783. By 1815, Russia had gained control of the entire northern shore of the Black Sea, and finally it had a warm-water port. Russia's attempt to occupy the Balkans, however, was swiftly suppressed in the Crimean War (1853–1856).

⚓ New Russian port

4 CENTRAL ASIA AND "THE GREAT GAME" 1830–1895

As Russia moved south and Britain moved north from its power base in India, a series of political and diplomatic confrontations known as "The Great Game" played out, as each side tried to expand its influence in Afghanistan and its surrounding countries. Ultimately, Afghanistan became a buffer zone, but Russia was able to annex the valuable lands of Bukhara, Khiva, and Samarkand.

🚩 Acquired by Russia during "The Great Game"

▮ Afghanistan

5 RUSSIA AND MANCHURIA 1858–1914

From 1858, a weakening Qing Empire ceded Outer Manchuria to Russia—an area from which it had previously been excluded by the Treaty of Nerchinsk (1689). Russia founded Vladivostok, a relatively ice-free port and, in 1898, leased the Liaodong Peninsula from China, gaining the warm-water port of Port Arthur. Alarmed by Japan's growing interest in China, Russia occupied southern Manchuria but was defeated in the Russo-Japanese War (1904–1905) and abandoned its imperial ambitions in the area.

⚓ New Russian port

△ **The *Petropavlovsk* sinks**
Russia clashed with Japan over rival imperial ambitions in Manchuria and Korea. The battleship *Petropavlovsk*, shown in this illustration, was a casualty of the Russo-Japanese War in 1904.

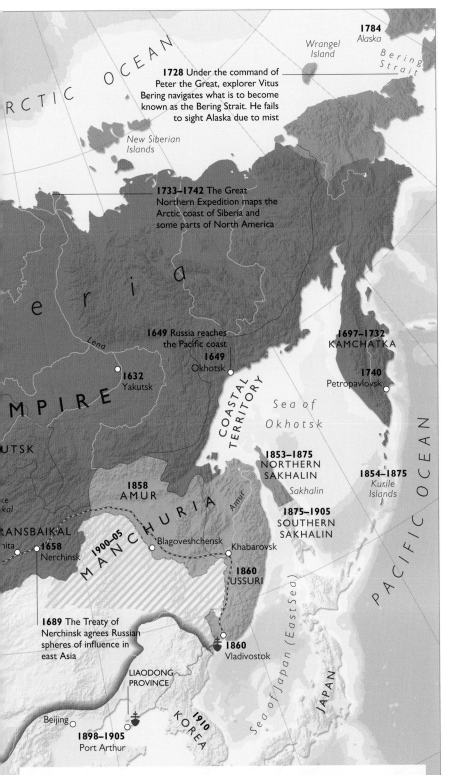

1784 Alaska

Wrangel Island

Bering Strait

1728 Under the command of Peter the Great, explorer Vitus Bering navigates what is to become known as the Bering Strait. He fails to sight Alaska due to mist

New Siberian Islands

1733–1742 The Great Northern Expedition maps the Arctic coast of Siberia and some parts of North America

1649 Russia reaches the Pacific coast

1649 Okhotsk

1632 Yakutsk

1697–1732 KAMCHATKA

1740 Petropavlovsk

Sea of Okhotsk

COASTAL TERRITORY

1853–1875 NORTHERN SAKHALIN

Sakhalin

1854–1875 Kurile Islands

1858 AMUR

1875–1905 SOUTHERN SAKHALIN

Amur

MANCHURIA

1900–05

Blagoveshchensk

Khabarovsk

1860 USSURI

RANSBAIKAL

1658 Nerchinsk

1689 The Treaty of Nerchinsk agrees Russian spheres of influence in east Asia

1860 Vladivostok

LIAODONG PROVINCE

Beijing

KOREA

1910

1898–1905 Port Arthur

Sea of Japan (East Sea)

JAPAN

PACIFIC OCEAN

ARCTIC OCEAN

Lena

RUSSIAN EXPANSION IN ASIA, 1600–1914
Russia gained territory in stages (dates of acquisition in bold). It spread across north Asia, then into Poland, the Baltic region, and south into central Asia. It then gained parts of China and reached Afghanistan and Persia's borders.

KEY

- Russian Empire, c.1600
- Acquisitions, 1600–1725
- Acquisitions, 1726–1855
- Acquisitions, 1856–1876
- Acquisitions, 1877–1914
- Temporary acquisitions, with dates
- Russian sphere of influence, 1914
- Trans-Siberian Railway, built 1891–1917
- Borders, 1914

TIMELINE

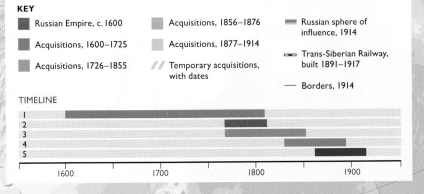

RUSSIAN EMPIRE EXPANDS

From 1600, Russia set out on a mission to expand its territory. It conquered Siberia, reached North America, drove deep into central Asia, and gained a foothold in the Black Sea region. By the 19th century, Russia's sizeable empire had begun to alarm Europe.

In 1600, the Czardom of Russia spread from the Ural Mountains in the east to the edge of the great Polish-Lithuanian Commonwealth in the west. It was, however, effectively landlocked; the Arctic Ocean was often frozen, and the Baltic Sea was controlled by Russia's enemy, Sweden. Consequently, Russia's expansion over the next 400 years was driven, to a great extent, by the search for a warm-water port that would allow it to house a fleet to rival the French and British navies and that would provide access to international trade.

Russia seized Siberia by conquest, but the growth of the empire was largely achieved by a process of accretion. Territories occupied by Russian migrants were slowly incorporated into the empire, and as the older powers—such as the Polish-Lithuanian Commonwealth, the Ottoman Empire in central Asia, and the Qing Empire in China—weakened, Russia simply took over. Russia's attempts at more aggressive expansion in the Balkans, Manchuria, and to the north of Afghanistan met with varying degrees of success, and, in the end, the limits of Russia's empire were defined by other imperial powers.

"Russia has only two allies: her army and her fleet."

ALEXANDER III, EMPEROR OF RUSSIA, c.1890

IVAN IV VASILYEVICH
1530–1584

The Grand Prince of Moscow from 1533–1547, Ivan IV Vasilyevich (also known as "the Terrible") became the first czar of Russia in 1547. A brutal autocrat, his rule is considered to mark the beginning of the Russian Empire, as he set about bringing Russia's aristocracy under his autocratic rule and uniting their lands under a central administration. By the time of his death in 1584, Ivan had not only united Russia's princedoms but also conquered Kazan, Astrakhan, and parts of Siberia, setting the foundation for a vast empire that would span much of Europe and Asia.

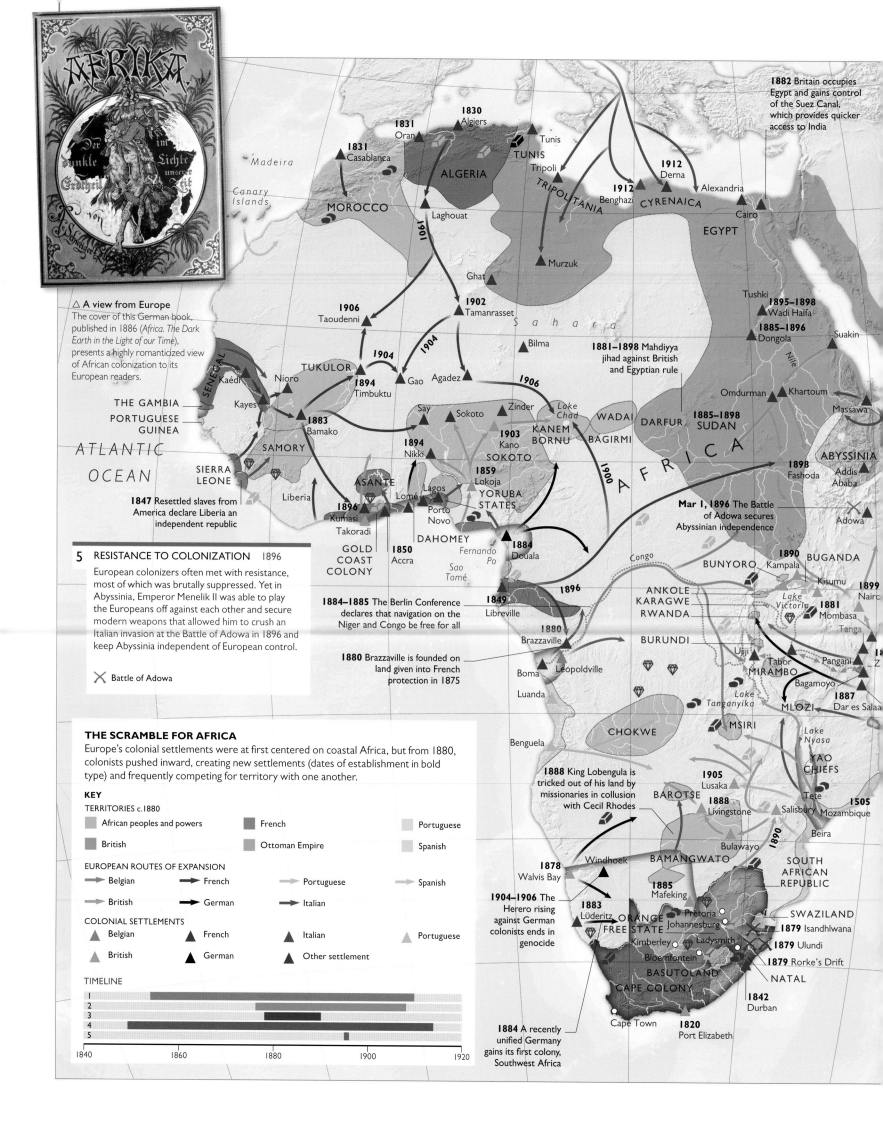

1882 Britain occupies Egypt and gains control of the Suez Canal, which provides quicker access to India

1830 Algiers

1831 Oran

1831 Casablanca

TUNIS

Tripoli

Tunis

TRIPOLITANIA

1912 Derna

1912 Benghazi

CYRENAICA

Alexandria

Cairo

EGYPT

ALGERIA

MOROCCO

Laghouat

Madeira

Canary Islands

Ghat

Murzuk

Sahara

Tushki

1895–1898 Wadi Halfa

1885–1896 Dongola

Suakin

1906 Taoudenni

1902 Tamanrasset

Bilma

1881–1898 Mahdiyya jihad against British and Egyptian rule

Omdurman

Khartoum

Massawa

1904

1904

1906

△ A view from Europe
The cover of this German book, published in 1886 (*Africa. The Dark Earth in the Light of our Time*), presents a highly romanticized view of African colonization to its European readers.

SENEGAL

Kaédi

Nioro

TUKULOR

1894 Timbuktu

Gao

Agadez

Say

Sokoto

Zinder

Lake Chad

WADAI

DARFUR

1885–1898 SUDAN

ABYSSINIA

1898 Fashoda

Addis Ababa

Kayes

THE GAMBIA

PORTUGUESE GUINEA

ATLANTIC OCEAN

SIERRA LEONE

SAMORY

1883 Bamako

1894 Nikki

1903 Kano

SOKOTO

KANEM BORNU

BAGIRMI

1900

A F R I C A

Adowa

Mar 1, 1896 The Battle of Adowa secures Abyssinian independence

1847 Resettled slaves from America declare Liberia an independent republic

Liberia

ASANTE

1896 Kumasi

Takoradi

GOLD COAST COLONY

1850 Accra

Lomé

Lagos

Porto Novo

DAHOMEY

Fernando Po

Sao Tomé

1859 Lokoja

YORUBA STATES

1884 Douala

1890

BUNYORO

Kampala

BUGANDA

Kisumu

1899 Nair...

Lake Victoria

1881 Mombasa

Tanga

5 RESISTANCE TO COLONIZATION 1896
European colonizers often met with resistance, most of which was brutally suppressed. Yet in Abyssinia, Emperor Menelik II was able to play the Europeans off against each other and secure modern weapons that allowed him to crush an Italian invasion at the Battle of Adowa in 1896 and keep Abyssinia independent of European control.

✕ Battle of Adowa

1884–1885 The Berlin Conference declares that navigation on the Niger and Congo be free for all

1849 Libreville

1896

Congo

ANKOLE KARAGWE RWANDA

BURUNDI

1880 Brazzaville is founded on land given into French protection in 1875

1880 Brazzaville

Boma

Leopoldville

Luanda

1887 Dar es Sala...

Ujiji

Tabor

MIRAMBO

Bagamoyo

Lake Tanganyika

MLOZI

MSIRI

Lake Nyasa

THE SCRAMBLE FOR AFRICA
Europe's colonial settlements were at first centered on coastal Africa, but from 1880, colonists pushed inward, creating new settlements (dates of establishment in bold type) and frequently competing for territory with one another.

CHOKWE

Benguela

YAO CHIEFS

Tete

1505

1888 King Lobengula is tricked out of his land by missionaries in collusion with Cecil Rhodes

1905 Lusaka

BAROTSE

1888 Livingstone

Salisbury

Mozambique

Beira

KEY
TERRITORIES c.1880

▧ African peoples and powers	▧ French	▧ Portuguese
▧ British	▧ Ottoman Empire	▧ Spanish

EUROPEAN ROUTES OF EXPANSION

→ Belgian	→ French	→ Portuguese	→ Spanish
→ British	→ German	→ Italian	

COLONIAL SETTLEMENTS

▲ Belgian	▲ French	▲ Italian	▲ Portuguese
▲ British	▲ German	▲ Other settlement	

1878 Walvis Bay

Windhoek

BAMANGWATO

Bulawayo

1890

SOUTH AFRICAN REPUBLIC

1904–1906 The Herero rising against German colonists ends in genocide

1885 Mafeking

1883 Lüderitz

ORANGE FREE STATE

Pretoria

Johannesburg

SWAZILAND

1879 Isandhlwana

1884 A recently unified Germany gains its first colony, Southwest Africa

Kimberley

Ladysmith

1879 Ulundi

1879 Rorke's Drift

Bloemfontein

NATAL

BASUTOLAND

CAPE COLONY

Cape Town

1820 Port Elizabeth

1842 Durban

TIMELINE

1
2
3
4
5

1840   1860   1880   1900   1920

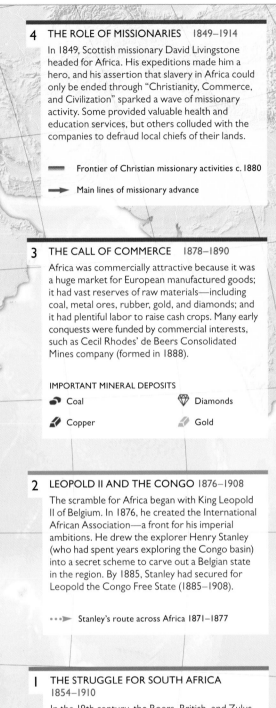

4 THE ROLE OF MISSIONARIES 1849–1914

In 1849, Scottish missionary David Livingstone headed for Africa. His expeditions made him a hero, and his assertion that slavery in Africa could only be ended through "Christianity, Commerce, and Civilization" sparked a wave of missionary activity. Some provided valuable health and education services, but others colluded with the companies to defraud local chiefs of their lands.

▬ Frontier of Christian missionary activities c.1880

➤ Main lines of missionary advance

3 THE CALL OF COMMERCE 1878–1890

Africa was commercially attractive because it was a huge market for European manufactured goods; it had vast reserves of raw materials—including coal, metal ores, rubber, gold, and diamonds; and it had plentiful labor to raise cash crops. Many early conquests were funded by commercial interests, such as Cecil Rhodes' de Beers Consolidated Mines company (formed in 1888).

IMPORTANT MINERAL DEPOSITS

🝆 Coal   ◈ Diamonds

⬧ Copper   ▭ Gold

2 LEOPOLD II AND THE CONGO 1876–1908

The scramble for Africa began with King Leopold II of Belgium. In 1876, he created the International African Association—a front for his imperial ambitions. He drew the explorer Henry Stanley (who had spent years exploring the Congo basin) into a secret scheme to carve out a Belgian state in the region. By 1885, Stanley had secured for Leopold the Congo Free State (1885–1908).

•••➤ Stanley's route across Africa 1871–1877

1 THE STRUGGLE FOR SOUTH AFRICA 1854–1910

In the 19th century, the Boers, British, and Zulus fought for control of South Africa. Since 1852, the Boers (descendants of the first European settlers) had lived independently in the Orange Free State and Transvaal, while British power was concentrated in Cape Colony and Natal. In 1877, the British annexed Transvaal after gold was found there. At the same time, they decisively crushed the Zulu kingdom. In 1910, after two Anglo-Boer wars (1880–1881, 1899–1902), Transvaal (by then, the South African Republic), the Orange Free State, and the Zulu lands were subsumed by a new British dominion—the Union of South Africa.

■ Cape Colony and Natal 1854

■ Territory under British control 1895

■ South African Republic 1895

■ Orange Free State 1895

✕ Battle in Zulu wars

▬ Union of South Africa boundary 1910

AFRICA COLONIZED

In 1880, only a few European colonies dotted the African coastline. Much of the north was formally part of the Ottoman Empire, but most of Africa was free of direct control from outside. By 1914, nine-tenths of the continent had been divided between seven nations, each hungry for resources and keen to build their empires.

The shifting balance of power in Europe in the 19th century was to have lasting consequences for Africa, as nationalist, liberal, and commercial interests converged in an orgy of colonization. Having lost their American colonies, Spain and Portugal also lost influence in Africa, but Britain and France were ready to build their empires after the Napoleonic wars, and the newly unified nations of Italy and Germany sought to bolster their international standing. Tales from African explorers about diamonds, gold, copper, and coal stirred Europe's commercial interest, so when news reached Europe in the 1880s that the Belgian king, Leopold II, had made a grab for the Congo, the race to conquer Africa's interior began.

Competition between the colonizers nearly resulted in conflict, so the Berlin Conference (1884–1885) was called to settle claims and set rules for partition. Missionaries, companies, and military forces all played a part in the colonization process, but it was also made possible by technological and scientific advances that came out of the Industrial Revolution. Steamships—and the discovery of effective antimalarial treatments—allowed Europeans to navigate deep into the continent's interior. The weapons of local peoples were no match for the breech-loading rifle, and within 20 years, Africa had been carved up by European powers with little regard for the traditions of the indigenous peoples.

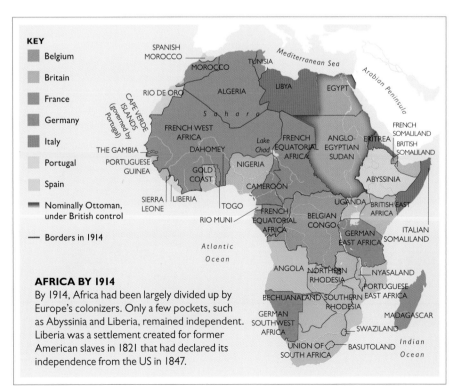

KEY

■ Belgium
■ Britain
■ France
■ Germany
■ Italy
■ Portugal
■ Spain
▬ Nominally Ottoman, under British control
— Borders in 1914

AFRICA BY 1914

By 1914, Africa had been largely divided up by Europe's colonizers. Only a few pockets, such as Abyssinia and Liberia, remained independent. Liberia was a settlement created for former American slaves in 1821 that had declared its independence from the US in 1847.

FOREIGN POWERS IN CHINA

By the mid-19th century, the Qing Empire in China was facing internal strife, as well as pressure from foreign powers. Anger against growing foreign dominance erupted in the Boxer Rebellion, but it was swiftly repressed by a coalition of foreign forces. The subsequent war reparations crippled the empire.

Two hundred years of Qing rule had created a vast empire that flourished economically. Foreign traders were granted access to only one port, Canton (modern Guangzhou), but requests for further concessions were rebuffed.

Western merchants began to bribe officials and pay for goods with opium, which damaged the Chinese economy and led to a rise in opium addiction. The First Opium War (see pp.226–227) resulted in the transfer of Hong Kong and other ports to Britain, and over the next decades, parts of the empire fell under the influence of Britain, France, Russia, Germany, Japan, and the US.

△ **Assassination of Baron Ketteler**
In revenge for his having beaten and shot a boy suspected of being a Boxer, German diplomat Baron Clemens von Ketteler was murdered in Beijing on June 20, 1900. His assassin was later beheaded.

The Boxer Rebellion

By 1900, anger at foreign control of trade and at Christian missionary activity made many Chinese join a secret group known as the Society of Righteous and Harmonious Fists. Popularly called "Boxers," its members began attacking Westerners and Chinese Christians.

In June 1900, Qing forces and the Boxers besieged the foreign legations in Peking (Beijing). Soldiers from an eight-nation alliance lifted the siege 55 days later, and then demanded war reparations. Damaged by its failure to expel the foreigners and by internal rebellions, the Qing Dynasty could not prevent further losses to foreign powers or stop the spread of revolutionary ideas. In 1912, the last emperor abdicated and China became a republic.

△ **The Peking Protocol**
Having defeated the Boxers, the foreign powers demanded in the Peking Protocol (1901) that China punish the government officials involved in the uprising, pay reparations equivalent to $330 million, and allow foreign troops to be stationed there.

Storming the Imperial Palace
On August 14, 1900, a multinational force, including British, American, and Japanese soldiers, broke the siege of the Imperial Palace in Peking (modern Beijing) by Qing forces and Boxer rebels.

DECLINE OF QING CHINA

The richest and most populous state in the world, Qing China should have been a major presence on the world stage competing with Western powers. Instead, however, it underwent a long decline from the mid-1800s, racked with rebellions and civil wars and repeatedly carved up by foreign military adventures.

The Qing Dynasty was founded by a clan of Manchurians who had seized the Chinese empire and, under a series of forceful emperors (see pp.178–179), enlarged it with conquests in central Asia. But their failure to modernize had exacerbated a series of problems that afflicted China in the 19th century, including population growth and the constant threat of famine; problems with the money supply; failure to open the economy to foreign trade; and failure to keep pace with the technology and military power of foreign states that wanted to impose trade liberalization, and possibly even carve up China between themselves (see pp.250–251).

The humiliations inflicted as a result of the Opium Wars (see pp.226–227) had severely damaged the authority of the Qing and centralized government. In the resulting power vacuum, there flourished corruption, smuggling, and "secret societies"—networks of local leaders and low-ranking nobility with diverse cultural, political, and economic agendas. The threat of rebellion was relentless, and the ground was fertile for mass movements to galvanize resistance to the Qing. This feverish atmosphere would spark the greatest civil war in history and eventually bring to an end the Qing Dynasty and millennia of imperial rule.

"Heaven sees as the people see; Heaven hears as the people hear … China is weak, the only thing we can depend on is the hearts of the people."

DOWAGER EMPRESS CIXI DURING THE BOXER REBELLION, 1899–1901

PUYI
1906–1967

The turbulent life of the last Emperor of China traced the history of 20th-century China. Puyi became emperor in 1908, aged only 2, but was forced to abdicate in 1912 as a result of the Xinhai revolution. He was briefly restored as puppet emperor by a warlord in 1917 and again by the Japanese in 1934. Later, he was captured by the Soviets, then handed over to the Chinese Communists after World War II and reeducated to be a common citizen. He died in Beijing in 1967.

Emperor Puyi as a child
Puyi (seen here aged 3) was proclaimed the Xuantong Emperor by his great-aunt, the Dowager Empress Cixi.

△ **Imperial troops march against the Taiping**
A contemporary image of imperial troops marching to battle against the Taiping rebels. The civil war set off by the rebellion was one of the largest conflicts the world had ever seen.

QINGHAI

1 | OUTBREAK OF THE TAIPING REBELLION
1844–1853

Hong Xiuquan was a quasi-Christian visionary around whom a cult grew in Guangxi province in the 1840s. In 1851, Hong proclaimed a new dynasty, the Taiping Tianguo ("Heavenly Kingdom of Great Peace"), and assumed the title of Tianwang, or "Heavenly King." Shrugging off imperial assaults, his rebellion gathered strength and made Nanjing its capital.

⟹ Hong's march to Nanjing 1850–1853

2 | THE TAIPING EMPIRE 1853–1860

The Taiping Empire presented a challenge to the Qing, but infighting and failed military expeditions checked its momentum. In 1856, feuding between the Taiping's top military leaders saw two of them murdered and a third flee with many men. An 1860 attempt to take Shanghai was stopped by the "Ever-Victorious Army," Western-trained and led troops fighting for the Qing.

▪ Area controlled by rebels c.1861
➡ Unsuccessful northern campaign 1853–1855

THE END OF IMPERIAL RULE

The power of the Qing Dynasty started to decline significantly from the 1840s, and a series of uprisings finally ended their rule in 1911–1912.

KEY
▪ Qing Empire 1850

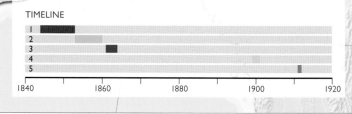

TIMELINE

| 1840 | 1860 | 1880 | 1900 | 1920 |

3 FALL OF THE TAIPING 1861–1864

With the capture of Anqing in October 1861 by the Hunan Army (a local militia force fighting for the Qing), the revolutionary cause was doomed. In 1862, Imperial General Zeng Guofan surrounded Nanjing, and in July 1864, the city fell, ending the Taiping Heavenly Kingdom. Including those lost through famine, the greatest civil war in history had cost 25–30 million lives.

→ Advance of Western troops
•••► Advance of Qing troops

4 BOXER REBELLION 1899–1901

Economic woes, natural disasters, and growing anti-foreign sentiment sparked an uprising called the Militia in Righteousness (known as the "Boxers" in English). The Boxers killed foreigners and destroyed foreign property. The Qing supported the anti-foreign crusade, but some regional warlords cooperated with foreign powers to crush the uprising, which was ended when an eight-nation military alliance occupied Beijing.

Area of Boxer uprising 1900–1901

5 XINHAI REVOLUTION 1911–1912

In 1908, the Dowager Empress Cixi died, leaving the infant Puyi as emperor. Reformist and revolutionary movements then sought to harness domestic discontent. In 1911, the discovery of an anti-imperialist plot in Wuchang triggered open revolt, leading to the formation of a republican government under revolutionary leader Sun Yixian (Sun Yat-sen) in Nanjing and the end of imperial rule.

Revolution 1911–1912

Sep 1901 International forces defeat the Boxers in Beijing. China agrees to pay swingeing reparations, but US determination to protect its trade interests prevents other Western powers from partitioning China

May 1853 The Taipings send an expedition to northern China. It reaches the neighborhood of Tianjin, but finally collapses in early 1855

Jul 1864 The Taipings are finally defeated by Qing troops under General Zeng Guofan. Hong, the Taiping's leader, had committed suicide in June
Dec 1911 A provisional republican government is set up in Nanjing, with Sun Yixian (Sun Yat-sen) as premier

Oct 1911 An anti-imperialist plot is uncovered among army officers in Wuchang, triggering them into an open revolt that quickly spreads, marking the start of the Xinhai revolution

Sep 1851 The Taiping rebels establish a base in Yongan, where they are besieged by the imperial army but emerge victorious

1860 An attempt by the Taipings to regain strength by taking Shanghai is stopped by the Western-trained "Ever-Victorious Army" commanded by the American adventurer Frederick Townsend Ward

Oct 1861 Anqing, the capital of Anhui, is captured by the Hunan Army, severely damaging the Taiping revolutionary cause

Gobi

INNER MONGOLIA

Yellow River

ZHILI
Beijing
Tianjin

SHANXI
Oct 29
Nov 7

Nov 13
Nov 10

SHANDONG
Nov 3

Mar 11, 1912
Lanzhou

GANSU
Oct 22

SHAANXI

Kaifeng
HENAN
Dec 22

JIANGSU
Nov 5

Nanjing
Nov 8
Nov 3
Shanghai

HUBEI
Hankou
Wuchang
Oct 10
Yuezhou
Yangtze

ANHUI
Oct 23
Anqing

Nov 4
Hangzhou

SICHUAN
Nov 22

JIANGXI
Jiujiang
Nanchang
Oct 23

ZHEJIANG

HUNAN
22 Oct

Oct 31

FUJIAN
Nov 9

GUIZHOU
Nov 4

Oct 30
Kunming
UNNAN

Nov 6
Guilin
Yongan

Jintian
GUANGXI

GUANGDONG
Nov 9
Canton
Hong Kong
Macau

HAINAN

Sea of Japan (East Sea)

KOREA

Yellow Sea

East China Sea

PACIFIC OCEAN

South China Sea

JAPAN TRANSFORMED

The restoration of the Meiji ("enlightened rule") emperor in 1868 kick-started a process of modernization that would see Japan transformed from an isolationist, feudal country to an outward-looking industrial nation with an educated population and an army and navy ready to defend and strengthen its position in the world.

By 1850, Japan had endured 200 years of isolation under the Tokugawa shogunate (see pp.180–181). The country was weak compared to foreign powers and was forced to accept unfavorable treaties that undermined its sovereignty.

An alliance of samurai from Japan's western domains began to coalesce around the imperial court in Kyoto, and by 1868 sought to restore imperial power and to modernize Japan. The shogun, Tokugawa Yoshinobu, resigned in an attempt to maintain peace but could not prevent the clash between imperial and government forces in the Boshin War of 1868–1869. The imperial faction won the conflict, securing the emperor's position, although not his personal power. A group of ambitious young samurai took control of the country and soon began to implement profound reform. They asked the feudal lords to give up their domains in favor of a centralized state, placed the nation's defense in the hands of a new imperial army and navy, and promoted rapid industrialization to transform Japan's economic base.

It was little wonder that many of the older samurai from the most powerful clans balked at the changes and rebelled in 1877. The rebellion (known after its origin in Satsuma Domain) failed, but it forced a reassessment of reform, ensuring that Japanese values were not lost in the race to modernize.

MODERNIZATION OF JAPAN

The modernization of Japan progressed swiftly between 1868 and 1918, as the new government swept away feudal structures and established power bases during the Boshin War and Satsuma Rebellion, paving the way for rapidly developing industrial areas and increasing urbanization.

TIMELINE

2 BOSHIN WAR 1868–1869

Civil war broke out between imperial forces and troops loyal to the ex-shogun, Tokugawa Yoshinobu, when Yoshinobu was stripped of all titles and land. The imperial troops won the war's first battle, at Fushimi on January 27, 1868. They then moved east to secure Edo's surrender, before heading north to Hokkaido to defeat the remaining government supporters at Hakodate in June 1869.

→ Route of imperial army   ✕ Battle, with date

■ Imperial alliance

1 MODERNIZATION OF THE ARMY AND NAVY 1868–1890

The Meiji government's determination to modernize the military cut across the privileges of Japan's warrior class, the samurai. In 1869, their fleets were subsumed by the new Imperial Japanese Navy, and in 1873, their exclusive right to bear arms was broken by the introduction of conscription. Many samurai became officers in the new regime, where their discipline helped to create the most powerful military force in Asia by the 1890s.

EMERGENCE AS AN INTERNATIONAL POWER

From the 1870s, the Japanese empire sought to expand its territory and influence. While the Imperial Navy swept out to incorporate the islands south of Japan, the successful deployment of both the army and navy in the Sino-Japanese (1894–1895) and Russo-Japanese (1904–1905) wars gave Japan a substantial foothold on mainland east Asia, Korea, Formosa (Taiwan), and southern Manchuria. By the time the Meiji Emperor died in 1912, it was clear Japan was an international power.

KEY

■ Japan in 1868

◇ Gains by 1894

■ Gains by 1910

■ Spheres of influence by 1918

● Treaty ports allowing Japan–China trade

Feb 1877 Satsuma forces are blocked at Kumamoto and pushed back to Kagoshima

Sep 1877 The last stand of the Satsuma rebels in Kagoshima ends in Saigo's suicide

3 INDUSTRIALIZATION 1871–1918

The abolition of feudalism in Japan freed millions of people to choose their occupation and move around the country. The government encouraged industrialization, building railway and shipping lines and telegraph and telephone systems, as well as opening mines; shipyards; and munitions, glass, textile, and chemical factories. Many of these were privatized when a European-style banking system was introduced in 1882, leaving the government free to invest in education and the armed forces.

MODERNIZATION UNDER THE MEIJI

▧ Main industrial areas by 1918

▭▭▭ Railways built 1868–1918

TRADITIONAL INDUSTRIES

🏺 Ceramics   🧵 Textiles   🐛 Silk

INDUSTRIES DEVELOPED AFTER 1868

🏭 Manufacturing   ⚓ Shipbuilding

⚙ Machine-building   ⚗ Chemicals

4 URBAN GROWTH 1871–1918

By 1871, all of Japan's ancient feudal domains, loyal to the local lord, had been reorganized into prefectures, each with a chief executive answerable to the central government. Initially, Japan's urban prefectures—Tokyo, Osaka, and Kyoto—lost population as people adjusted to the new regime and migrated to other areas. However, by 1883, the work offered through industrialization was driving population growth in the urban prefectures and in emerging cities such as Kobe, Yokohama, Nagasaki, and Hiroshima.

◇ City of over 500,000 in 1918   ○ Other major city

▢ City of over 100,000 in 1918

✕ **Jun 27, 1869**
◇ Hakodate

Oct 1868–May 1869
Hakodate is besieged by imperial forces in the final stage of the Boshin War

1871 Akita is one of the prefectures—the divisions of the new centralized state created when the feudal domains are abolished

5 SATSUMA REBELLION 1877

Some samurai felt that the spirit of Japan was being destroyed by rapid reforms. In February 1877, Saigo Takamori, a key figure in the restoration who disliked the changes that were being pressed on the emperor, marched from his base in Satsuma (now part of Kagoshima prefecture) with an army of samurai. They were heading for Tokyo, but their advance was blocked by the Imperial Army at Kumamoto. Forced back to Kagoshima, the rebels were finally defeated in September.

✕ Battle

Jan 1868 Meiji Restoration begins at the imperial court in Kyoto

Jan 27, 1868

Jan 1868 The city of Edo is renamed Tokyo

1868 The port of Yokohama is developed for the export of silk, predominantly to Britain

1871 Japan's first domestically produced warship, *Seiki*, is completed at Yokosuka Shipyards

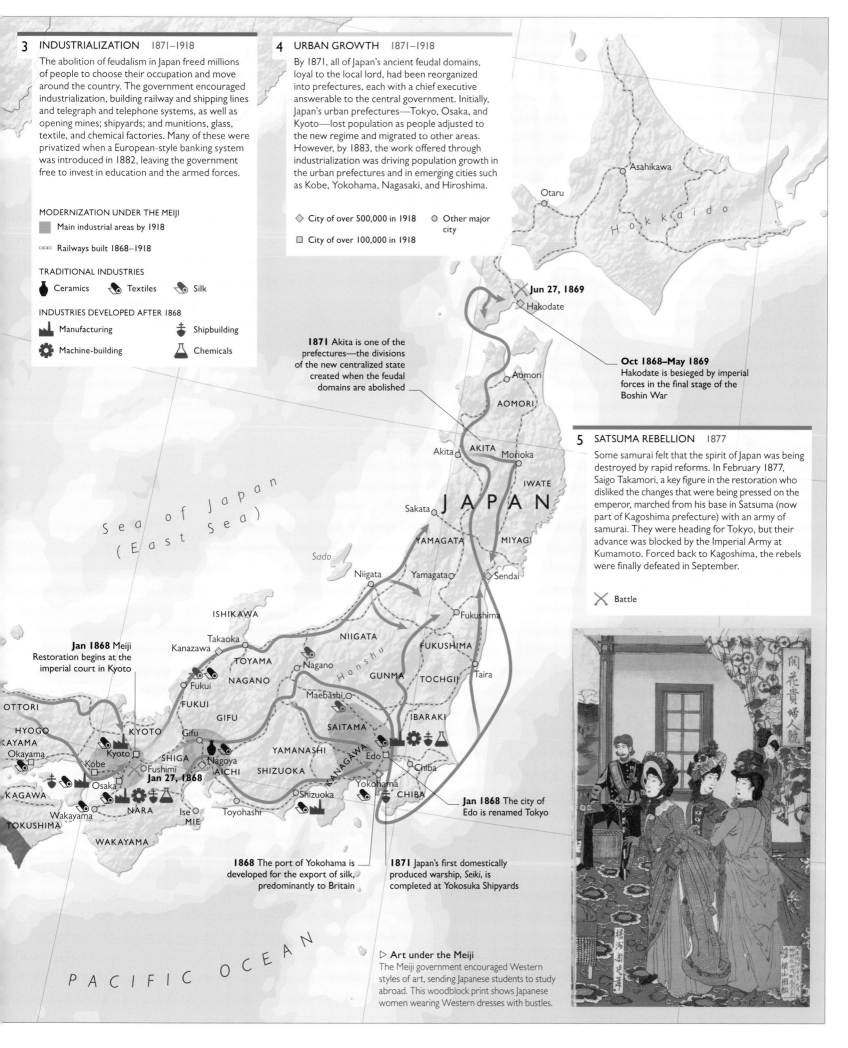

▷ **Art under the Meiji**
The Meiji government encouraged Western styles of art, sending Japanese students to study abroad. This woodblock print shows Japanese women wearing Western dresses with bustles.

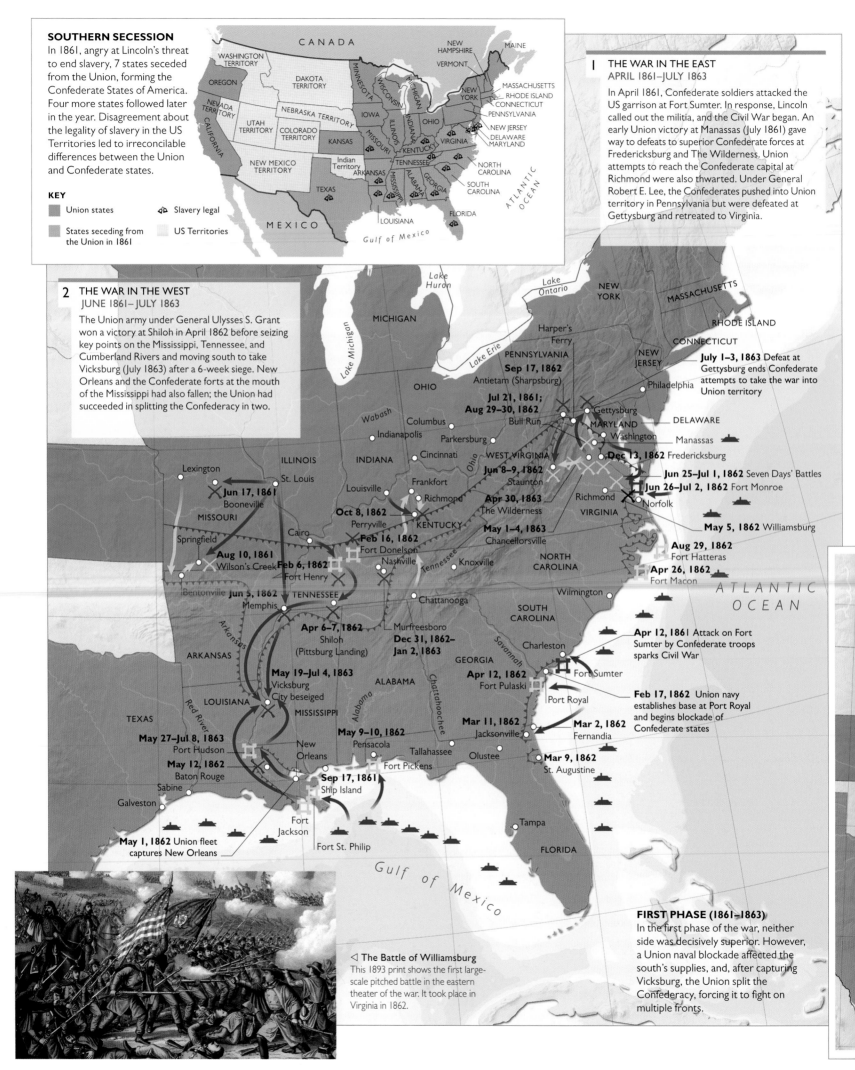

SOUTHERN SECESSION

In 1861, angry at Lincoln's threat to end slavery, 7 states seceded from the Union, forming the Confederate States of America. Four more states followed later in the year. Disagreement about the legality of slavery in the US Territories led to irreconcilable differences between the Union and Confederate states.

KEY

- Union states
- States seceding from the Union in 1861
- Slavery legal
- US Territories

I THE WAR IN THE EAST
APRIL 1861–JULY 1863

In April 1861, Confederate soldiers attacked the US garrison at Fort Sumter. In response, Lincoln called out the militia, and the Civil War began. An early Union victory at Manassas (July 1861) gave way to defeats to superior Confederate forces at Fredericksburg and The Wilderness. Union attempts to reach the Confederate capital at Richmond were also thwarted. Under General Robert E. Lee, the Confederates pushed into Union territory in Pennsylvania but were defeated at Gettysburg and retreated to Virginia.

2 THE WAR IN THE WEST
JUNE 1861–JULY 1863

The Union army under General Ulysses S. Grant won a victory at Shiloh in April 1862 before seizing key points on the Mississippi, Tennessee, and Cumberland Rivers and moving south to take Vicksburg (July 1863) after a 6-week siege. New Orleans and the Confederate forts at the mouth of the Mississippi had also fallen; the Union had succeeded in splitting the Confederacy in two.

Jul 1–3, 1863 Defeat at Gettysburg ends Confederate attempts to take the war into Union territory

Sep 17, 1862 Antietam (Sharpsburg)

Jul 21, 1861; Aug 29–30, 1862 Bull Run

Dec 13, 1862 Fredericksburg

Jun 25–Jul 1, 1862 Seven Days' Battles

Jun 26–Jul 2, 1862 Fort Monroe

Jun 8–9, 1862 Staunton

Apr 30, 1863 The Wilderness

May 1–4, 1863 Chancellorsville

May 5, 1862 Williamsburg

Aug 29, 1862 Fort Hatteras

Apr 26, 1862 Fort Macon

Jun 17, 1861 Booneville

Aug 10, 1861 Wilson's Creek

Jun 5, 1862 Bentonville

Feb 16, 1862 Fort Donelson

Feb 6, 1862 Fort Henry

Oct 8, 1862 Perryville

Apr 6–7, 1862 Shiloh (Pittsburg Landing)

Dec 31, 1862–Jan 2, 1863 Murfreesboro

May 19–Jul 4, 1863 Vicksburg City besieged

May 27–Jul 8, 1863 Port Hudson

May 12, 1862 Baton Rouge

May 9–10, 1862 Pensacola

May 1, 1862 Union fleet captures New Orleans

Sep 17, 1861 Ship Island

Apr 12, 1861 Attack on Fort Sumter by Confederate troops sparks Civil War

Apr 12, 1862 Fort Pulaski

Feb 17, 1862 Union navy establishes base at Port Royal and begins blockade of Confederate states

Mar 2, 1862 Fernandia

Mar 11, 1862 Jacksonville

Mar 9, 1862 St. Augustine

◁ The Battle of Williamsburg

This 1893 print shows the first large-scale pitched battle in the eastern theater of the war. It took place in Virginia in 1862.

FIRST PHASE (1861–1863)

In the first phase of the war, neither side was decisively superior. However, a Union naval blockade affected the south's supplies, and, after capturing Vicksburg, the Union split the Confederacy, forcing it to fight on multiple fronts.

NORTH VERSUS SOUTH

In two phases, 1861–1863 and 1864–1865, the north's Union forces moved on several fronts into the Confederate states. Although isolated by the north's naval blockade and often outnumbered, the Confederates won several victories but were ultimately beaten by the Union's superior power.

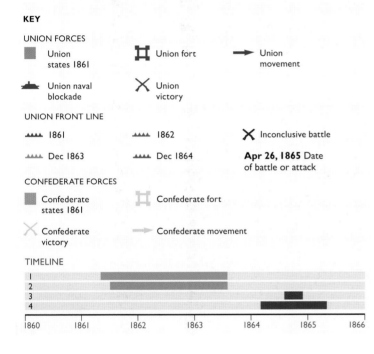

KEY

UNION FORCES

- ■ Union states 1861
- ⊟ Union fort
- → Union movement
- ◣ Union naval blockade
- ✕ Union victory

UNION FRONT LINE

- ▲▲▲ 1861
- ▲▲▲ 1862
- ✕ Inconclusive battle
- ▲▲▲ Dec 1863
- ▲▲▲ Dec 1864
- **Apr 26, 1865** Date of battle or attack

CONFEDERATE FORCES

- ■ Confederate states 1861
- ⊟ Confederate fort
- ✕ Confederate victory
- ➡ Confederate movement

TIMELINE

1
2
3
4

1860 1861 1862 1863 1864 1865 1866

THE CIVIL WAR

The American Revolution created the United States, but it was the Civil War of 1861–1865 that decided its future, forging a nation under one government and ensuring that freedom and equality remained its guiding principles, albeit at a terrible human cost.

After independence in 1783, the US developed into two regions. The rich, libertarian north was dominated by industry and finance, while the south relied on farming driven by slave labor and was anxious about the north's desire to restrict slave ownership. By 1860, the US—composed of 18 "free" states and 15 "slave" states—was just about held together by the Democratic Party, but after the party split in 1859, and Abraham Lincoln was elected president in 1860 on an antislavery platform, the Union collapsed. Several southern states seceded to form the Confederate States of America, and civil war followed. The Confederate armies put up fierce resistance, and it was 4 years before the north's forces finally prevailed. By the time the war ended in April 1865, about 650,000 men had died. Yet America's slaves had also been emancipated, and the states reunited under a supreme federal government.

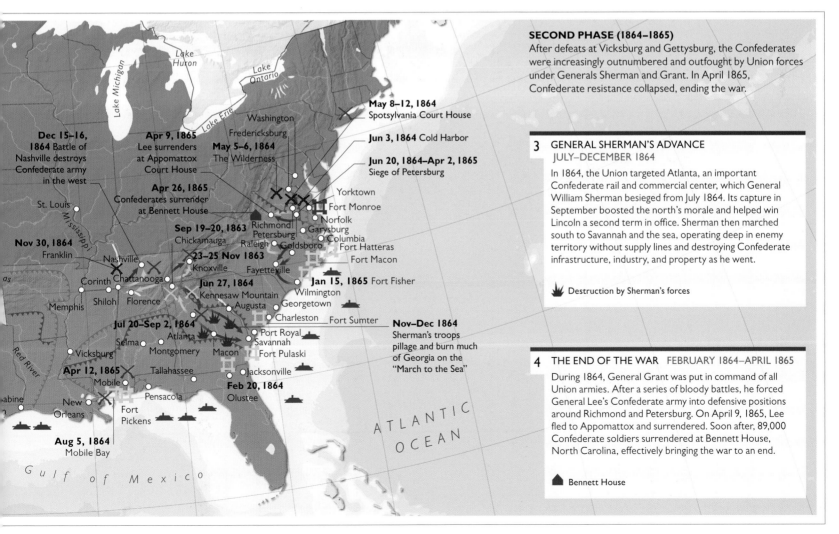

SECOND PHASE (1864–1865)
After defeats at Vicksburg and Gettysburg, the Confederates were increasingly outnumbered and outfought by Union forces under Generals Sherman and Grant. In April 1865, Confederate resistance collapsed, ending the war.

3 GENERAL SHERMAN'S ADVANCE
JULY–DECEMBER 1864

In 1864, the Union targeted Atlanta, an important Confederate rail and commercial center, which General William Sherman besieged from July 1864. Its capture in September boosted the north's morale and helped win Lincoln a second term in office. Sherman then marched south to Savannah and the sea, operating deep in enemy territory without supply lines and destroying Confederate infrastructure, industry, and property as he went.

🌿 Destruction by Sherman's forces

4 THE END OF THE WAR FEBRUARY 1864–APRIL 1865

During 1864, General Grant was put in command of all Union armies. After a series of bloody battles, he forced General Lee's Confederate army into defensive positions around Richmond and Petersburg. On April 9, 1865, Lee fled to Appomattox and surrendered. Soon after, 89,000 Confederate soldiers surrendered at Bennett House, North Carolina, effectively bringing the war to an end.

⛊ Bennett House

May 8–12, 1864 Spotsylvania Court House

Jun 3, 1864 Cold Harbor

Jun 20, 1864–Apr 2, 1865 Siege of Petersburg

Dec 15–16, 1864 Battle of Nashville destroys Confederate army in the west

Apr 9, 1865 Lee surrenders at Appomattox Court House

May 5–6, 1864 The Wilderness

Apr 26, 1865 Confederates surrender at Bennett House

Nov 30, 1864 Franklin

Sep 19–20, 1863 Chickamauga

23–25 Nov 1863

Jun 27, 1864 Kennesaw Mountain

Jan 15, 1865 Fort Fisher

Jul 20–Sep 2, 1864 Atlanta

Nov–Dec 1864 Sherman's troops pillage and burn much of Georgia on the "March to the Sea"

Apr 12, 1865 Mobile

Feb 20, 1864 Olustee

Aug 5, 1864 Mobile Bay

Lake Huron · Lake Ontario · Lake Erie · Lake Michigan · Lake Superior

Washington · Fredericksburg · Yorktown · Fort Monroe · Norfolk · Richmond · Petersburg · Garysburg · Columbia · Raleigh · Goldsboro · Fort Hatteras · Fort Macon · Knoxville · Fayetteville · Wilmington · Georgetown · Charleston · Fort Sumter · Port Royal · Savannah · Fort Pulaski · Jacksonville

St. Louis · Nashville · Corinth · Chattanooga · Shiloh · Florence · Memphis · Vicksburg · Selma · Montgomery · Macon · Augusta · Tallahassee · Mobile · Pensacola · New Orleans · Fort Pickens · Fort

Mississippi · Red River · Sabine

ATLANTIC OCEAN

Gulf of Mexico

At home in her laboratory
French-Polish physicist Marie Curie received
two Nobel Prizes for her work on radioactivity.
Renowned for her efforts at the front during World
War I and for her research into cancer treatments,
her contribution to medical science is invaluable.

SCIENCE AND INNOVATION

In the 19th century, new techniques and improvements in laboratory equipment enabled scientists to make important advances that changed our understanding of the world and revolutionized public health.

△ **Founder of microbiology**
In the 1860s, French biologist Louis Pasteur proved that decay and disease were caused by microbes, or germs; this knowledge changed the course of medicine.

The roots of many of the things that define modern life—such as plastics, fiber optics, and radar—can be traced back to the 19th century. Yet, perhaps the most important discoveries of the time were in the field of medicine. In 1869, Russian chemist Dmitri Mendeleev developed the periodic table, a framework for understanding chemical elements and their reactions. Knowledge of chemistry quickly advanced, creating a new a pharmaceutical industry, and soon the use of synthetic drugs, such as aspirin and barbiturates, became commonplace.

Medical breakthroughs

The discovery of X-rays (1895), radiation (1896), and the radioactive elements polonium and radium (1898) revolutionized medical treatment. Radiography made diagnoses more accurate, and radiation therapies were developed for cancer. Combined with the discovery of the electron (1897) and of the source of radioactivity (1901), these findings also paved the way for nuclear power. Louis Pasteur's theory that microorganisms were the transmitters of disease radicalized approaches to disease control. Vaccines for cholera, anthrax, rabies, diphtheria, and typhoid soon followed. Deaths from infection were much reduced by the introduction of carbolic to disinfect both operation theaters and surgeons. Together, these advances contributed to a population explosion in the early 20th century.

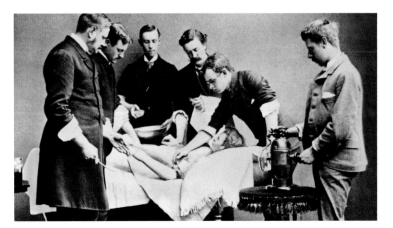

Safer surgery
Building on Pasteur's work, English surgeon Joseph Lister introduced carbolic acid (phenol) to clean wounds and sterilize surgical equipment. His promotion of antiseptic surgery dramatically reduced postoperative infections.

EXPANSION OF THE US

US territory grew in the 19th century through the agencies of war, political agreement, and annexation. Settlement by migrants helped bring new areas into cultivation, while rapid industrialization from the 1870s fueled urbanization and population growth.

In 1800, the borders of the United States reached only to the Mississippi River, but the next 100 years saw a swift westward expansion as Britain withdrew its claim on Oregon Country and the US annexed Texas and defeated Mexico in the war of 1846–1848. By 1900, the country stretched from the Atlantic to the Pacific and covered an area of almost 3 million sq miles (7.8 million sq km).

The promise of cheap land attracted immigrants from abroad who settled alongside American frontiersmen and women. In 1890, the US Census declared the frontier closed—there were no longer any continuous unsettled areas in the west. By then, America's cattle barons were driving their herds to railheads that supplied growing cities in the east, where industrialization was taking hold. By 1900, the US was producing more steel than Britain and Germany combined. Cities such as Chicago—just a small town in 1837—had grown into metropolises of more than 1 million people. New York's Ellis Island had become a key entry point for millions of migrants to America's vast cities. The industrial boom of the late 19th century made millions of dollars for a few, but it was punctuated by periods of depression that boded ill for America's rapidly growing population.

IMMIGRATION AND TRADE IN THE US 1860–1920
Cattle, oil, industrialization, and immigration drove the development of the largest American cities in the 19th century, creating heavily urbanized areas in the Midwest and on the Pacific coast.

KEY
— US state boundaries c. 1920

TIMELINE

	1850	1870	1890	1910	1930
1					
2					
3					
4					

1867 US purchases Alaska from Russia for $7.2 millio[n]

△ Railroad construction crew
This image from 1886 documents one of the many crews employed on the US rail network. The first transcontinental railroad, covering nearly 2,000 miles (3,200 km), was built by three private companies in 1869.

FROM CHINA

1882 Chinese immigration into the US is banned after anti-Chinese sentiment spreads from San Francisco during the economic depression of 1877

TERRITORIAL EXPANSION

The United States grew from just 13 colonies in 1776 to a nation of 48 states in 1912. Territory was acquired through a series of purchases and treaties: France sold a vast swathe of land to the US in the Louisiana Purchase; and the British gave up the northwest territories in the Oregon Treaty. Some regions—including Texas—were annexed, while much of the west was won in the war with Mexico (1846–1848) or through subsequent land purchases from the cash-hungry Mexican regime.

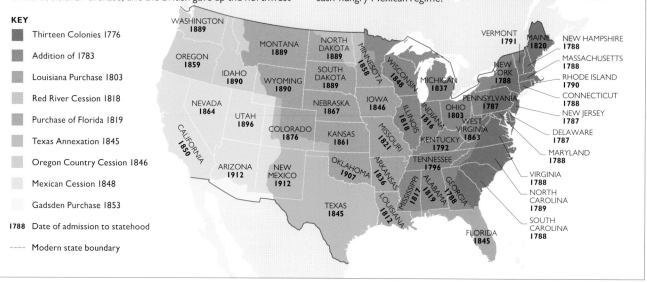

KEY

- Thirteen Colonies 1776
- Addition of 1783
- Louisiana Purchase 1803
- Red River Cession 1818
- Purchase of Florida 1819
- Texas Annexation 1845
- Oregon Country Cession 1846
- Mexican Cession 1848
- Gadsden Purchase 1853
- **1788** Date of admission to statehood
- ········· Modern state boundary

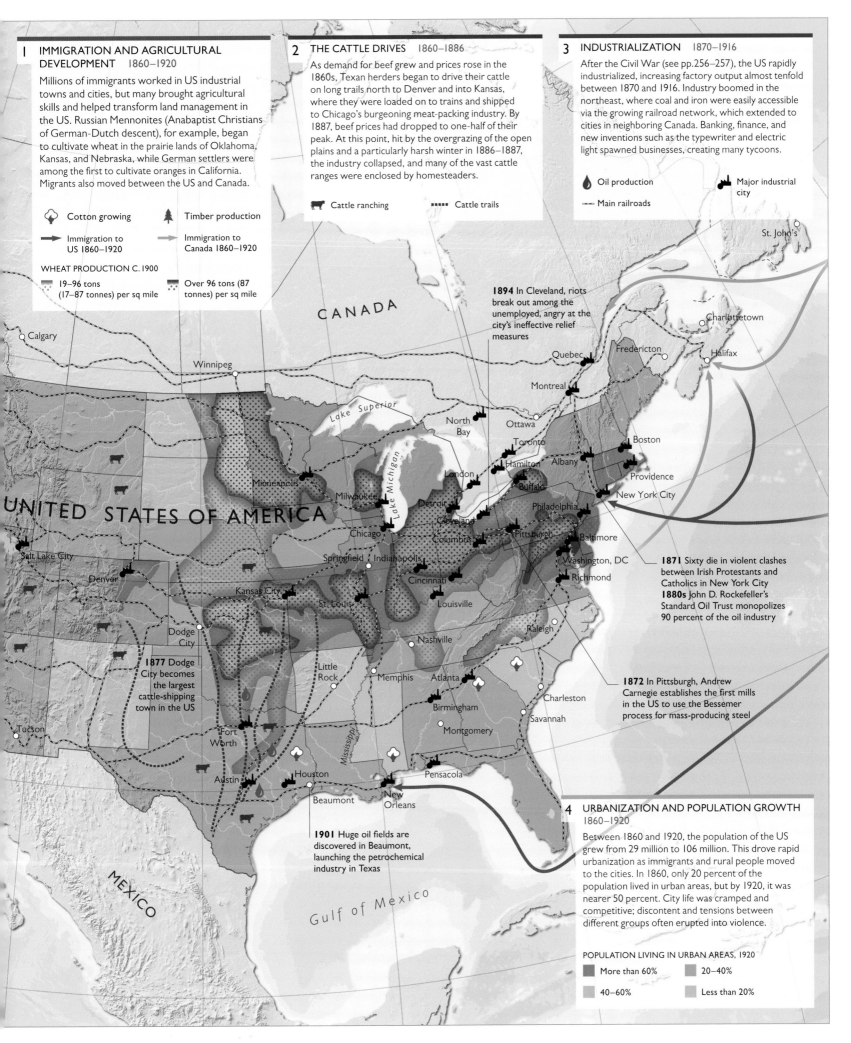

1 IMMIGRATION AND AGRICULTURAL DEVELOPMENT 1860–1920

Millions of immigrants worked in US industrial towns and cities, but many brought agricultural skills and helped transform land management in the US. Russian Mennonites (Anabaptist Christians of German-Dutch descent), for example, began to cultivate wheat in the prairie lands of Oklahoma, Kansas, and Nebraska, while German settlers were among the first to cultivate oranges in California. Migrants also moved between the US and Canada.

⬡ Cotton growing

🌲 Timber production

→ Immigration to US 1860–1920

→ Immigration to Canada 1860–1920

WHEAT PRODUCTION C. 1900

▦ 19–96 tons (17–87 tonnes) per sq mile

▦ Over 96 tons (87 tonnes) per sq mile

2 THE CATTLE DRIVES 1860–1886

As demand for beef grew and prices rose in the 1860s, Texan herders began to drive their cattle on long trails north to Denver and into Kansas, where they were loaded on to trains and shipped to Chicago's burgeoning meat-packing industry. By 1887, beef prices had dropped to one-half of their peak. At this point, hit by the overgrazing of the open plains and a particularly harsh winter in 1886–1887, the industry collapsed, and many of the vast cattle ranges were enclosed by homesteaders.

🐄 Cattle ranching

┅┅ Cattle trails

3 INDUSTRIALIZATION 1870–1916

After the Civil War (see pp.256–257), the US rapidly industrialized, increasing factory output almost tenfold between 1870 and 1916. Industry boomed in the northeast, where coal and iron were easily accessible via the growing railroad network, which extended to cities in neighboring Canada. Banking, finance, and new inventions such as the typewriter and electric light spawned businesses, creating many tycoons.

🛢 Oil production

🏭 Major industrial city

┅ Main railroads

1894 In Cleveland, riots break out among the unemployed, angry at the city's ineffective relief measures

1871 Sixty die in violent clashes between Irish Protestants and Catholics in New York City

1880s John D. Rockefeller's Standard Oil Trust monopolizes 90 percent of the oil industry

1872 In Pittsburgh, Andrew Carnegie establishes the first mills in the US to use the Bessemer process for mass-producing steel

1877 Dodge City becomes the largest cattle-shipping town in the US

1901 Huge oil fields are discovered in Beaumont, launching the petrochemical industry in Texas

4 URBANIZATION AND POPULATION GROWTH 1860–1920

Between 1860 and 1920, the population of the US grew from 29 million to 106 million. This drove rapid urbanization as immigrants and rural people moved to the cities. In 1860, only 20 percent of the population lived in urban areas, but by 1920, it was nearer 50 percent. City life was cramped and competitive; discontent and tensions between different groups often erupted into violence.

POPULATION LIVING IN URBAN AREAS, 1920

■ More than 60%

■ 20–40%

■ 40–60%

■ Less than 20%

A charismatic but brutal military dictator, Juan Manuel de Rosas was the archetypal *caudillo*. As governor of Buenos Aires province, Rosas controlled all of Argentina for 17 years and extended the country's territories deep into Patagonia through a violent campaign against the indigenous people there. Ousted from power by a rival general in 1852, he fled to England and died there in 1877.

INDEPENDENT LATIN AMERICA

The decades following liberation in Latin America were marked by the appearance of successive military dictators, civil wars, and battles between states over resources and territories. The shadow of imperialism continued to hang over the region, too, as financial investment and military intervention secured American and British influence.

In the aftermath of liberation, many countries in South America saw power seized by *caudillos*, military dictators such as José Antonio Páez in Venezuela and Juan Manuel de Rosas in Argentina. Civil wars were common as new dictators fought for leadership, as happened in Mexico in 1910. Border disputes were also common as the young states sought to extend their territory or gain control of valuable natural resources. Bolivia and Peru both lost lands to Chile

in the War of the Pacific, fought over the Atacama Desert's nitrates, which were used in fertilizers and explosives. Brazil, Bolivia, and Argentina took almost half of Paraguay's territory in Latin America's bloodiest war. The region's economies depended on the export of raw materials and food to feed Europe's burgeoning industries and consumer markets: coffee and rubber from Brazil; copper and tin from Chile and Peru; and salted and frozen meat from Argentina. Access to the Atlantic trade routes gave Argentina in particular an advantage, and the country developed rapidly. Yet foreign power lingered in the region. It was evident in the United States' interference in Central America and the Caribbean—where it annexed Puerto Rico and occupied or made Protectorates of many other countries—and in the large profits made by British and American firms investing in the region's railways and mines.

"I'd rather die on my feet, than live on my knees."

ATTRIBUTED TO EMILIANO ZAPATA, 1913

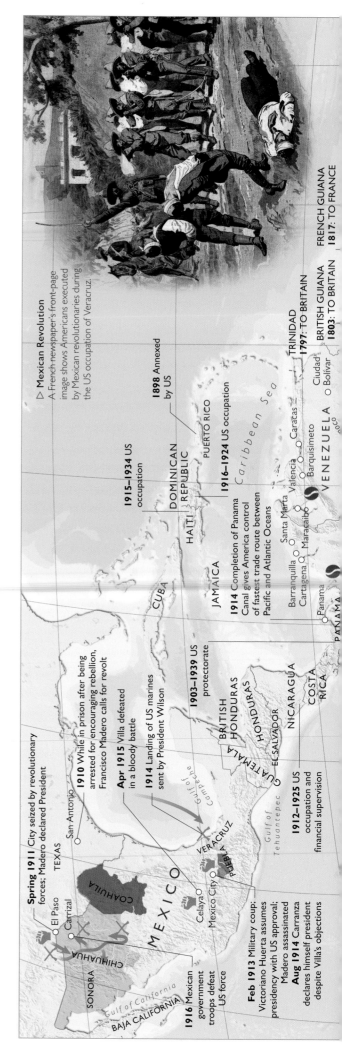

△ **Mexican Revolution**
A French newspaper's front-page image shows Americans executed by Mexican revolutionaries during the US occupation of Veracruz.

Map labels

BRAZIL

Planalto do Mato Grosso

Xingu

Tapajós

Solimões

Madeira

Amazon

Rio Negro

Putumayo

COLOMBIA

ECUADOR

PERU

Andes

BOLIVIA

ACRE

PARAGUAY

CHILE

ARGENTINA

URUGUAY

Patagonia

Tierra del Fuego

PACIFIC OCEAN

Place names:

Maceió · São Luiz do Maranhão · Pará (Belém) · Santarém · Manáos · Santa Cruz · Bahia (Salvador) · Minas Novas · Diamantina · Goyaz · Pirapora · Belo Horizonte · Ouro Prêto · Victoria · Rio de Janeiro · São Paulo · Porto Alegre · Rio Grande · Montevideo · Colonia · La Plata · Buenos Aires · Rosario · Corrientes · Corumbá · Santa Cruz · Asunción · Paraguay · Paraná · Uruguay · Mar del Plata · Bahia Blanca · Neuquén · Río Negro · Punta Arenas · Puerto Montt · Valdivia · Concepción · Talca · Santiago · Valparaíso · Viña del Mar · Mendoza · Córdoba · Tucumán · Catamarca · Salta · Jujuy · La Serena · Caldera · Copiapó · Antofagasta · Punta de Angamos · Tocopilla · Iquique · Arica · Tacna · Mollendo · Pisco · Islas de Chincha · Callao · Lima · Yungay · Trujillo · Tumbes · Cuenca · Guayaquil · Quito · Iquitos · Cuzco · Potosí · La Paz · Lake Titicaca · Lake Poopó · ATACAMA · TARAPACÁ · Nova Coimbra · BUENOS AIRES

Timeline annotations

Dec 27, 1865 Paraguayans invade Brazil and attack the Brazilian garrison at Nova Coimbra fort

Dec 21–22, 1868 Battle of Lomas Valentinas

1870–1914 Brazil's economy becomes heavily dependent on coffee exports

Apr 1866 Argentina's President Mitre invades southwest Paraguay

Jun 11, 1865 Brazilian navy defeats Paraguayan flotilla in Battle of Riachuelo on the Paraná River near Corrientes

1884 Work begins on development of Buenos Aires port, funded by the British Barings Bank

1850–1914 Argentina's largely British-built railways make large-scale beef exports possible

1870–1914 Tin becomes Bolivia's main export

1890–1920 Manáos flourishes as center of rubber boom in Amazon region

1890–1920

1881–1884 Lima and Callao occupied by Chilean forces

1884 Tacna and Arica conquered by Chile

1929 Tacna area awarded to Peru, Arica area to Chile

Oct 20, 1883 Peru and Chile sign Treaty of Ancón; Tarapacá area ceded to Chile

Oct 8, 1879 Sinking of a Peruvian ironclad, the *Huáscar*, gives Chile control of the sea

Feb 14, 1879 Chilean armed forces occupy Antofagasta

1878 Bolivia demands more taxes from the Chilean Antofagasta Nitrate Company working in the Atacama

Side panels

4 EXPORT AND INVESTMENT 1850–1920

As the world entered a second phase of industrialization at the end of the 19th century, South America experienced a series of export booms in nitrates, rubber, copper, and tin. South America also became a major coffee producer, and British investment in the region's railways and ports made wheat and beef viable export products.

- Major ports
- Tin
- Beef
- Nitrates
- Rubber
- Coffee

3 THE MEXICAN REVOLUTION 1910–1917

In 1910, Francisco Madero challenged Mexico's dictator for the presidency and called for revolution. Armies under Pascual Orozco, Pancho Villa, and Emiliano Zapata all attacked government positions. Successive presidents failed to pacify the country, and the US intervened militarily. A new constitution was agreed on in 1917, and Venustiano Carranza became President.

AREA OF LEADERSHIP
- Venustiano Carranza
- Pancho Villa
- Emiliano Zapata
- Francisco Madero

- US/Mexican clash
- Major incident in revolution
- Route of US expedition

2 WAR OF THE PACIFIC 1879–1883

In 1879, Bolivia, Chile, and Peru went to war over control of the Atacama Desert's nitrate deposits. Chile landed an army at Antofagasta, taking the Bolivian coastline and the southern provinces of Peru. Chilean troops then sailed to attack Lima, and the city was occupied by a Chilean force between 1881 and 1884.

- Chile before 1874
- Gained from Bolivia
- Gained from Peru
- Conquered by Chile
- Battle

1 THE PARAGUAYAN WAR 1864–1870

In 1864, Paraguay was pitted against an alliance of Argentina, Brazil, and Uruguay set on conquest. Outnumbered 10 to 1, Paraguay's army was destroyed at the Battle of Lomas Valentinas in 1868. Guerrilla war rumbled on until 1870, but ultimately Paraguay lost around 54,000 square miles (140,000 square km) of territory and around half its population in the conflict.

- Battle
- Former Paraguay

Key panel

AFTER INDEPENDENCE

Latin America was marked by civil war, competition for resources, and interference from outside, all of which determined its future development.

TIMELINE

1840 · 1860 · 1880 · 1900 · 1920

1 · 2 · 3 · 4 · 5

KEY
- 1930 international borders
- Railways

▷ **Battling hussars**
A painting by German artist Christian Sell the Elder shows a clash between French and German cavalry in the Franco-Prussian War.

UNIFICATION OF ITALY AND GERMANY

After 1835, powerful German and Italian leaders emerged who contested Austrian power and—in a rapid succession of political and military campaigns from 1850 to 1870—created the unified nations of Italy and Germany.

TIMELINE

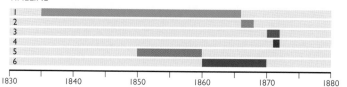

1830   1840   1850   1860   1870   1880

1 AUSTRIA CHALLENGED 1835–1866

In 1863, Bismarck engineered an alliance with Austria to claim the provinces of Schleswig and Holstein from Denmark. By October 1864, Schleswig belonged to Prussia and Holstein to Austria. The arrangement was unworkable because Holstein was isolated and hemmed in by Prussia. When Austria sought a resolution to the issue, Prussia used it as a pretext for conflict, beginning the Seven Weeks' War (1866).

    Boundary of German Confederation of 1815

→ Austro-Prussian forces in Denmark 1864

    Prussia in 1815

GERMANY UNIFIED

German unification was achieved in several stages that saw Prussia free the north German states from Austrian authority and then defeat Austria and France to create a new empire in 1871.

Sep 1, 1870
Prussia captures Napoleon III at the Battle of Sedan

1871 Prussians march through France to besiege and occupy Paris

May 1871 The French cede Alsace-Lorraine to Germany in the Treaty of Frankfurt

Jul 3, 1866 The Battle of Sadowa gives Prussia a decisive victory over Austria in the Seven Weeks' War

2 THE NORTH GERMAN CONFEDERATION 1866–1867

Prussia defeated Austria in the Seven Weeks' War. Prussia kept the territories it had won in the conflict and formed a North German Confederation, in which each state kept its own laws and sent an elected representative to a federal parliament.

→ Prussian armies in Seven Weeks' War 1866

✕ Battle

    Prussian gains by 1866

    Other states in North German Confederation 1867

    Other German states 1866–1867

    Austro-Hungarian Empire 1867

4 UNIFICATION AND EMPIRE 1871

As a result of the war, France lost the region of Alsace-Lorraine to Germany and was forced to pay compensation. The now unified German states adopted a new imperial constitution, with William I as kaiser (emperor). The empire, with Prussia firmly in control, comprised 26 states.

    Boundary of German Empire 1871

3 FRANCO-PRUSSIAN WAR 1870–1871

Another great power, France, viewed Prussia's growing status with concern. Bismarck engineered a political situation that provoked the French emperor, Napoleon III, into declaring war. This prompted the southern German states to ally with the Northern Confederation. The Germans crushed their French enemies, captured Napoleon III, and took Paris in 1871.

→ Prussian invasion of France 1870–1871

✕ Battle

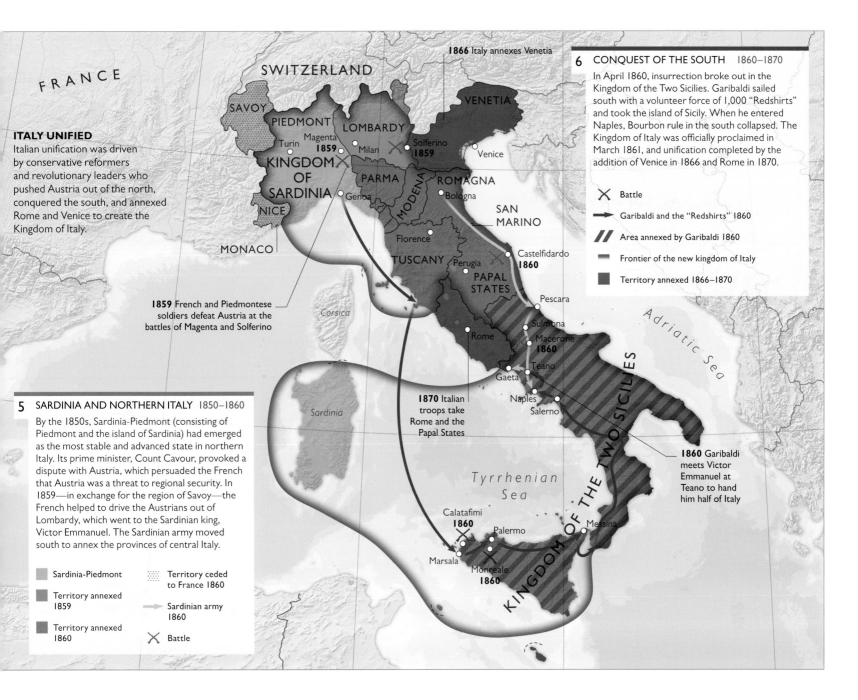

ITALY UNIFIED

Italian unification was driven by conservative reformers and revolutionary leaders who pushed Austria out of the north, conquered the south, and annexed Rome and Venice to create the Kingdom of Italy.

1866 Italy annexes Venetia

6 CONQUEST OF THE SOUTH 1860–1870

In April 1860, insurrection broke out in the Kingdom of the Two Sicilies. Garibaldi sailed south with a volunteer force of 1,000 "Redshirts" and took the island of Sicily. When he entered Naples, Bourbon rule in the south collapsed. The Kingdom of Italy was officially proclaimed in March 1861, and unification completed by the addition of Venice in 1866 and Rome in 1870.

✕ Battle

→ Garibaldi and the "Redshirts" 1860

// Area annexed by Garibaldi 1860

– Frontier of the new kingdom of Italy

■ Territory annexed 1866–1870

1859 French and Piedmontese soldiers defeat Austria at the battles of Magenta and Solferino

1870 Italian troops take Rome and the Papal States

1860 Garibaldi meets Victor Emmanuel at Teano to hand him half of Italy

5 SARDINIA AND NORTHERN ITALY 1850–1860

By the 1850s, Sardinia-Piedmont (consisting of Piedmont and the island of Sardinia) had emerged as the most stable and advanced state in northern Italy. Its prime minister, Count Cavour, provoked a dispute with Austria, which persuaded the French that Austria was a threat to regional security. In 1859—in exchange for the region of Savoy—the French helped to drive the Austrians out of Lombardy, which went to the Sardinian king, Victor Emmanuel. The Sardinian army moved south to annex the provinces of central Italy.

▨ Sardinia-Piedmont	▦ Territory ceded to France 1860
■ Territory annexed 1859	→ Sardinian army 1860
■ Territory annexed 1860	✕ Battle

GERMANY AND ITALY UNIFIED

In 1850, Germany and Italy were fragmented. Germany was a loose confederation of states dominated by Austria, while Italy was a mixture of duchies and kingdoms with little direction. By 1870, through war, diplomacy, and a certain amount of political machination, both had been unified into new nations.

A wave of popular nationalism followed the Napoleonic Wars (see pp.208–211). In 1848–1849, this erupted in a series of republican revolutions (see pp.218–219), which began in Sicily and extended across much of Europe. These revolts were repressed by armies loyal to their respective goverments; and popular fervor had largely dissipated by the 1850s, leaving the German and Italian states as fragmented as ever.

The yoke of unification was, however, taken up by conservative reformers in both Italy and Germany in the 1860s. Afraid of revolution from below, they took control of reform from above, seeing in unification a chance to curb Austro-Hungarian power and carve out strong new kingdoms.

After the Napoleonic Wars, Prussia was one of a confederation of 39 states under the leadership of Austria. It was the only one of these states powerful enough to compete with Austria-Hungary for control of the fiercely independent German principalities, so it took the lead on unification. In 1864, Prussia, led by its formidable prime minister, Otto von Bismarck, made its move against Austria. Within 7 years, through a combination of war, political maneuvering, and luck, the threat to unification posed by both Austria and France had been neutralized, and Bismarck had forged a unified German empire. Bismark became the first chancellor of the Empire in 1871.

In Italy, following the failure of Giuseppe Mazzini's nationalist revolution in 1848, the prime minister of Sardinia-Piedmont, Count Cavour, steered the process of unification. By allying with France against the Austrians in northern Italy and harnessing the talents of the great nationalist revolutionary Giuseppe Garibaldi to secure the south, Cavour was able to create a unified kingdom by 1860.

5 THE SECOND BALKAN WAR 1913

In June 1913, tension over the division of Macedonia turned to war when the Bulgarians attacked Greek and Serbian positions in the region. When Romanian and Ottoman forces invaded Bulgaria, looking for gains of their own, Bulgaria soon sued for peace, and Macedonia was largely divided between Greece and Serbia.

- Serbian gain 1913
- Greek gain 1913
- Romanian gain 1913
- Bulgarian gain 1913
- Montenegrin gain 1913
- ✗ Battles

Mar 1821 Greek revolutionaries in Moldavia occupy Jassy and call on all Greeks and Christians to rise up against the Ottomans

1878 Treaty of Berlin puts Bosnia-Herzegovina under Austria-Hungary's control, although it remains an Ottoman possession

Oct 7, 1908 Serbia mobilizes its troops and demands Novi Pazar region as compensation

1878 Enlarged by the treaty of San Stefano, Serbia becomes independent

1878 Romania becomes independent and gains Dobruja

Sep 30, 1913 Treaty of Bucharest ends Second Balkan War

Oct 6, 1908 Austria-Hungary annexes Bosnia-Herzegovina

Dec 1877 Ottoman garrison at Pleven submits after being besieged by Russian and Romanian force for 5 months

Jul 10, 1913 Romanians occupy Varna

1878 Montenegro doubles its territory and gains independence

Oct 5, 1908 Prince Ferdinand of Bulgaria declares Bulgaria's independence

1878–1885 Treaty of Berlin returns Eastern Rumelia to Ottoman Empire, but Bulgaria reclaims it in 1885

Oct 23–24, 1912 Serbian army defeats Ottomans at Battle of Kumanovo and joins forces with Montenegrins to enter Skopje

Jun 30–Jul 8, 1913 Bulgarian army defeated by Serbs at Battle of Bregalnica

Oct 19–20, 1912 Greek army defeats Ottomans and captures Yanitza

May 21, 1864 Britain transfers the Ionian islands to Greece as a gesture of support for King George I

Jul 19–21, 1913 Greek victory against the Bulgarians at the Battle of Kilkis

Oct 21, 1912 The Bulgarians defeat the main Ottoman forces in Thrace and reach Constantinople

Jan 1878 Russians take Edirne, then known as Adrianople

Mar 26, 1913 Edirne falls to the Bulgarians

Jul 23, 1913 Ottomans force Bulgarians out of Edirne

Mar 1878 Treaty of San Stefano ends Russo-Turkish War

Jul 1881 Ottoman Empire cedes Thessaly to Greece following the Russo-Turkish War

Mar 6, 1913 Janina falls to the Greeks

Jul 1908 Young Turks establish a constitutional government in Constantinople and begin program of reform

4 THE FIRST BALKAN WAR 1912–1913

In 1912, Russia encouraged Serbia, Bulgaria, Greece, and Montenegro to band together and take Macedonia from Turkey. Montenegro declared war on Turkey and was joined by the other league nations. By May 1913, the war was over and the Ottoman Empire had lost most of its remaining European territories, including Albania.

- ✗ Significant Ottoman defeats
- Albania 1913

Aug 1826 Ottoman forces capture Athens

Jan 1822 Greek National Assembly declares Greece a free and independent state

3 BOSNIA CRISIS 1908

Fearing that the Young Turks in Constantinople might reinvigorate Turkey, Austria-Hungary decided to annex Bosnia and Herzegovina. When Serbia demanded that they receive compensation for the annexation, Russia supported their claim. But when Austria—backed by Germany—threatened to invade Serbia, Russia was forced to back down and accept the annexation.

- ✗ The Bosnia Crisis
- Annexation border

Oct 20, 1827 British, French, and Russian naval fleets destroy the Egyptian fleet supporting the Ottomans

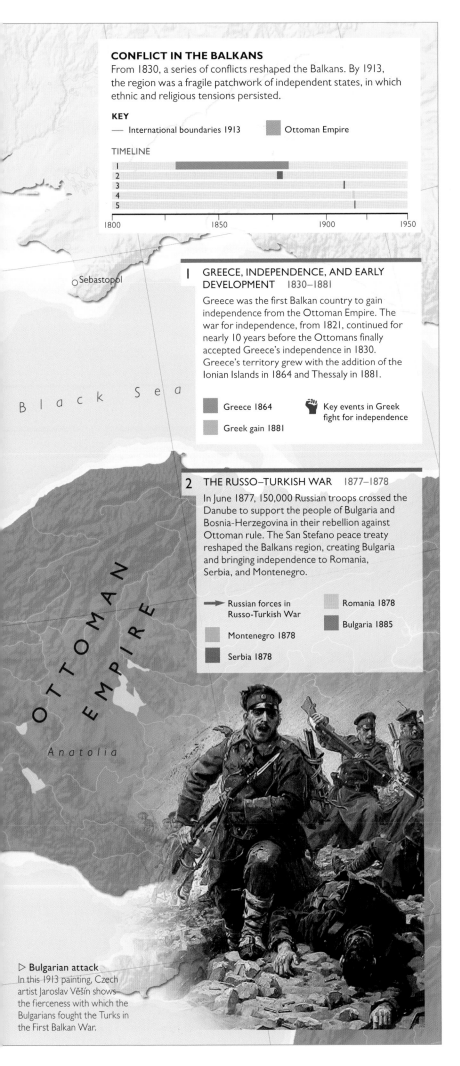

CONFLICT IN THE BALKANS

From 1830, a series of conflicts reshaped the Balkans. By 1913, the region was a fragile patchwork of independent states, in which ethnic and religious tensions persisted.

KEY

— International boundaries 1913   ▦ Ottoman Empire

TIMELINE

1
2
3
4
5

1800   1850   1900   1950

○ Sebastopol

B l a c k   S e a

1   GREECE, INDEPENDENCE, AND EARLY DEVELOPMENT   1830–1881

Greece was the first Balkan country to gain independence from the Ottoman Empire. The war for independence, from 1821, continued for nearly 10 years before the Ottomans finally accepted Greece's independence in 1830. Greece's territory grew with the addition of the Ionian Islands in 1864 and Thessaly in 1881.

■ Greece 1864

■ Greek gain 1881

✊ Key events in Greek fight for independence

2   THE RUSSO–TURKISH WAR   1877–1878

In June 1877, 150,000 Russian troops crossed the Danube to support the people of Bulgaria and Bosnia-Herzegovina in their rebellion against Ottoman rule. The San Stefano peace treaty reshaped the Balkans region, creating Bulgaria and bringing independence to Romania, Serbia, and Montenegro.

→ Russian forces in Russo-Turkish War

■ Montenegro 1878

■ Serbia 1878

■ Romania 1878

■ Bulgaria 1885

O T T O M A N   E M P I R E

A n a t o l i a

▷ **Bulgarian attack**
In this 1913 painting, Czech artist Jaroslav Věšín shows the fierceness with which the Bulgarians fought the Turks in the First Balkan War.

BALKAN WARS

A wave of nationalism swept through the Balkans in the 19th century. As the Balkan countries coalesced and gained independence—often under the influence of the Great Powers—ethnic and religious diversity created conflict, feeding the instability in the region.

The Balkans in the 19th and early 20th centuries endured a series of conflicts as Ottoman power receded and the peoples of the region fought for independence. In 1830, Greece broke away from the Ottoman Empire. There were further conflicts, at the expense of the Ottomans, over the next 80 years. The Great Powers of Russia, Britain, and Austria-Hungary all played a part in these conflicts and regarded the region with an uneasy mix of ambition and anxiety. Russia supported Slavic nationalism, hoping that the Bulgarians, Montenegrins, Bosnians, and Serbs would provide it with allies. Austria-Hungary watched the emergence of Serbia with concern, aware that its own population of Serbs might make a claim for independence. And Britain, wary of Russian influence in the region, sought to bolster the Greeks. But for all their involvement in peace treaties and territory division, the Great Powers could not solve the problem at the heart of the Balkans: the region's ethnic groups would not be separated neatly into nations. By 1914, Turkey may have lost all but a small part of its European possessions, but few were happy with the outcome of 70 years of struggle. The two Balkan Wars alone resulted in more than half a million casualties, and the conflicts pushed the Great Powers closer to a European war.

"A ... peninsula filled with sprightly people ... who had a splendid talent for starting wars."

C.L. SULZBERGER, FROM *A LONG ROW OF CANDLES*, 1969

EDIRNE
THE IMPORTANCE OF ADRIANOPLE

The city of Edirne (formerly known as Adrianople) was one of the largest in the Ottoman Empire. It guarded the route to Constantinople, the capital of the Ottoman Empire, so was of vital strategic importance to the Ottomans. Heavily fortified with a network of trenches, fences, and 20 massive concrete forts, the fortress at Edirne was believed to be unassailable; its capture by the Bulgarians in 1913 was a huge blow to Ottoman confidence.

Flight from Edirne, 1913
A stream of foreigners flees the Bulgarian attack on Edirne.

1 GERMANY, AUSTRIA-HUNGARY, AND RUSSIA 1871–1918

Germany negotiated alliances with Austria-Hungary and Russia to limit or prevent war. The defensive Austro-German alliance, later joined by Italy (creating the Triple Alliance), prevented Austria siding with Russia in any attack on Germany; Romania secretly joined in 1883. The Three Emperors' Alliance helped to ease the tension between Russia and Austria over the Balkans and isolated France.

● Austro-German alliance 1879–1918

◆ Three Emperors' Alliance 1881–1887

⬟ Triple Alliance 1882–1915

2 THE DEVELOPMENT OF THE TRIPLE ENTENTE 1894–1907

After the Three Emperors' Alliance collapsed, Bismarck arranged the Reinsurance Treaty between Germany and Russia. In 1890, Kaiser Wilhelm II refused to renew this treaty, leaving Russia free to ally with France. The Franco-Russian alliance provided reassurances of mutual military support. Britain sought to limit threats to her Empire, and in 1904 allied with France, and then in 1907 with Russia, creating what was called the Triple Entente.

■ Franco-Russian alliance 1894–1917

▲ Anglo-Russian Entente 1907

★ Entente Cordiale 1904

1887–1890 Germany agrees to Reinsurance Treaty with Russia, guaranteeing neutrality in any war with a third power, excluding France and Austria

1909–1910 Tsar Nicholas II commits around 1 million rubles to construction of a military air force

1907 Construction begins on Rosyth naval dockyard

1907 Britain reorganizes its army to create Expeditionary Force of 160,000 troops and a volunteer, part-time force of 300,000 Territorials

1903 Krupp's dockyard in Kiel completes the first fully functioning U-boat

1910 First aviation school opens in Gatchina

Feb 1906 Launch of HMS *Dreadnought*, the first "all-big-gun" battleship, fuels naval race

Mar 1908 Germany launches its first "all-big-gun" dreadnought battleship, SMS *Nassau*

1898–1912 German naval laws signal Germany's ambition to build a navy to rival Britain's

1883–1916 Romania secretly joins the Triple Alliance with Germany, Austria-Hungary, and Italy

1839 Treaty of London guarantees Belgian neutrality and commits Austria, Belgium, France, the German Confederation, the Netherlands, Russia, and Britain to military intervention if neutrality is breached

1908 Austria-Hungary annexes Bosnia, driving Serbia closer to Russia

1906 Britain supports France over Morocco at the Algeciras Conference, and the two countries begin talks on a military alliance

1882 Italy joins the Austro-German alliance to create the Triple Alliance

1905–1906 Germany tests the strength of the Anglo-French Entente by recognizing Morocco as independent

1881–1895 Serbia associates with the Triple Alliance through the Austro-Serb alliance

NORWAY

SWEDEN

St. Petersburg

DENMARK

North Sea

NETHERLANDS

BELGIUM

BRITAIN

London

Chatham

Brussels

Portsmouth

Plymouth

ATLANTIC OCEAN

Brest

Paris

FRANCE

Munich

Rosyth

Kiel

Wilhelmshaven

Berlin

GERMANY

Warsaw

RUSSIAN EMPIRE

Baltic Sea

AUSTRIA-HUNGARY

Trieste

Genoa

SWITZERLAND

ITALY

Toulon

Taranto

Belgrade

SERBIA

ROMANIA

BULGARIA

MONTENEGRO

ALBANIA

Sarajevo

Constantinople

GREECE

OTTOMAN EMPIRE

SPAIN

PORTUGAL

Algeciras

Tangier

MOROCCO to France

ALGERIA to France

TUNISIA to France

LIBYA to Italy

EGYPT

Mediterranean Sea

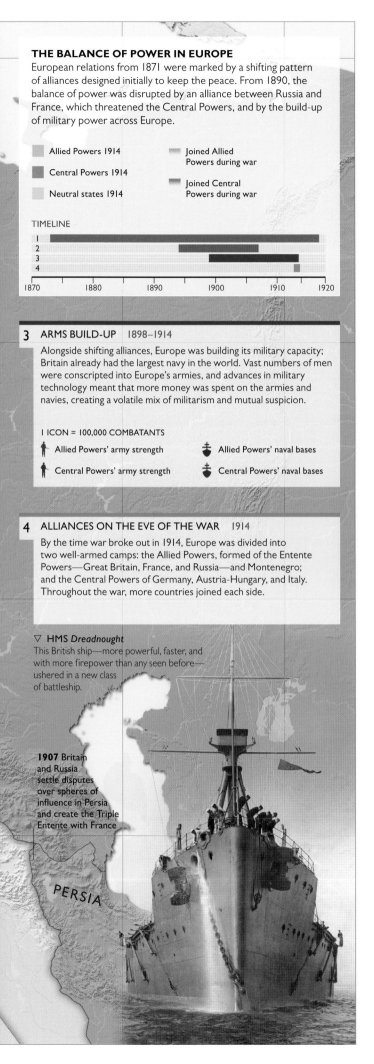

THE BALANCE OF POWER IN EUROPE

European relations from 1871 were marked by a shifting pattern of alliances designed initially to keep the peace. From 1890, the balance of power was disrupted by an alliance between Russia and France, which threatened the Central Powers, and by the build-up of military power across Europe.

- Allied Powers 1914
- Central Powers 1914
- Neutral states 1914
- Joined Allied Powers during war
- Joined Central Powers during war

TIMELINE

1
2
3
4

1870 1880 1890 1900 1910 1920

---

3 ARMS BUILD-UP 1898–1914

Alongside shifting alliances, Europe was building its military capacity; Britain already had the largest navy in the world. Vast numbers of men were conscripted into Europe's armies, and advances in military technology meant that more money was spent on the armies and navies, creating a volatile mix of militarism and mutual suspicion.

1 ICON = 100,000 COMBATANTS

- Allied Powers' army strength
- Central Powers' army strength
- Allied Powers' naval bases
- Central Powers' naval bases

---

4 ALLIANCES ON THE EVE OF THE WAR 1914

By the time war broke out in 1914, Europe was divided into two well-armed camps: the Allied Powers, formed of the Entente Powers—Great Britain, France, and Russia—and Montenegro; and the Central Powers of Germany, Austria-Hungary, and Italy. Throughout the war, more countries joined each side.

▽ HMS *Dreadnought*
This British ship—more powerful, faster, and with more firepower than any seen before—ushered in a new class of battleship.

1907 Britain and Russia settle disputes over spheres of influence in Persia and create the Triple Entente with France

PERSIA

THE EVE OF WORLD WAR

War between the Great Powers—Austria-Hungary, Britain, France, Germany, Italy, and Russia—was prevented throughout the late 19th century by a series of defensive alliances. However, those alliances were eroded by the crises in the Balkans in the early 20th century and by the rise of militarism.

Since the end of the Napoleonic War in 1815, Europe had maintained a delicate balance of power. The creation of Germany in 1871 (see pp.264–265) brought a powerful new force into play. Yet instead of breaking the balance of power, Germany was instrumental in maintaining it for many years. Under the leadership of Otto von Bismarck, Germany set about allying with the more conservative powers in Europe—Austria-Hungary and Russia. This ensured that the other two would remain neutral if any one of them took military action against any nonallied country, and if Russia attacked Austria, it would have to face Germany as well.

As tensions in the Balkans increased (see pp.266–267), so did the tensions between the Great Powers. Russia moved to ally with France, and Austria's annexation of Bosnia in 1908 humiliated Russia and pushed it closer to Austria's nemesis, Serbia. By then, an arms race had begun that saw millions of marks, pounds, rubles, and francs poured into military reorganization and new technology. In 1913 alone, Germany spent $140 million on its military and Britain spent $106 million. By 1914, the bond that prevented a major war had been broken, and Europe was divided into two heavily armed blocs, primed for war.

"England, France, and Russia have conspired … to wage a war of annihilation against us."

KAISER WILHELM II, MEMORANDUM WRITTEN JULY 30, 1914

OTTO VON BISMARCK
(1815–1898)

Architect of the unification of Germany and its rise as a major power, Otto von Bismarck guided Germany's fate, first as chief minister of Prussia (1862–1890) and then as chancellor of the German Empire (1871–1890). His skilled diplomacy ensured that there was no major European conflict in the late 19th century; he created an alliance with Austria-Hungary and also kept friendly relations with Russia. However, Kaiser Wilhelm II came to the throne in 1888 with a more aggressive desire to lead the German Empire toward global power, and in 1890, he forced von Bismarck's resignation. Without his hand to steady international relations, Europe moved inexorably toward war.

THE MODERN WORLD

WORLD WARS, UNPRECEDENTED TECHNOLOGICAL AND ECONOMIC
DEVELOPMENT, AND EXPLOSIVE POPULATION GROWTH HAVE MADE
THE 20TH AND 21ST CENTURIES THE MOST EVENTFUL IN HISTORY.

THE MODERN WORLD

The early 20th century was dominated by extraordinary developments in technology, economics, and new ideologies that transformed societies. However, demands for national independence and a better way of life destroyed old structures, leading to unprecedented violence and turbulence before a new world order was formed.

△ **The face of nationalism**
A Bosnian nationalist, Gavrilo Princip shot Austrian Archduke Franz Ferdinand on June 28, 1914. The event catapulted the Great Powers into World War I, a century-defining conflict that caused the downfall of empires.

By the dawn of the 20th century, the old had begun giving way to the new. Although new empires were still being formed in South Africa, Korea, and elsewhere, some established empires were in turmoil as people demanded emancipation from oppression and political exclusion. In Russia, thousands marched against Czar Nicholas II, demanding reform, while the czar's forces were being routed by the Japanese in the Russo-Japanese War. Around the same time, imperial China was crumbling under the pressure of European imperialism and internal strife. By 1912, China had done away with the Qing Dynasty and become a republic.

In 1908, the vast Ottoman Empire was shaken when the Young Turks (a Turkish nationalist party) revolted and brought in a constitution and multiparty politics. Taking advantage of these unsettled affairs, a league of Balkan states—Serbia, Bulgaria, Greece, and Montenegro—went to war with Turkey and then squabbled over the spoils, leading to yet another war.

Constant turmoil

The assassination of the Austrian Archduke Franz Ferdinand by a radical nationalist, Gavrilo Princip, in Sarajevo, Bosnia, set off World War I (see pp. 274–275). Lasting 4 long years, the war became a stalemate at an incalculable cost—a generation of young men was mown down as deadly technological advances saw aircraft, poison gas, tanks, and submarines deployed on a mass scale. By the third year of World

◁ **The cost of war**
Passchendaele (the Third Battle of Ypres) was fought in 1917. It cost the Allies 300,000 lives and brought them a gain of a meager 5 miles (8 km). It became a byword for the utter futility of war.

TROUBLED TIMES

The early part of the 20th century was dominated by conflict; the timeline shown here ends with the ominous build-up to yet another world war. Unlike Europe and east Asia, North America avoided major turbulence until its involvement in World War I. However, its stock market collapse in 1929 was one of the most damaging events in its, and the world's, history. Despite the convulsions of the period, this era was also one of great technological innovation and productivity.

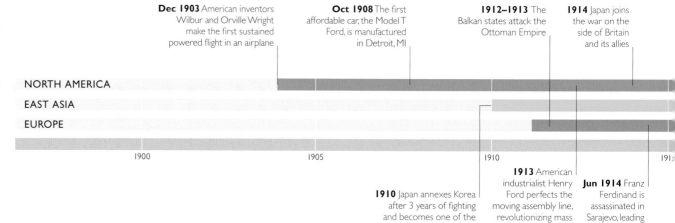

Dec 1903 American inventors Wilbur and Orville Wright make the first sustained powered flight in an airplane

Oct 1908 The first affordable car, the Model T Ford, is manufactured in Detroit, MI

1912–1913 The Balkan states attack the Ottoman Empire

1914 Japan joins the war on the side of Britain and its allies

NORTH AMERICA

EAST ASIA

EUROPE

1900   1905   1910   191

1910 Japan annexes Korea after 3 years of fighting and becomes one of the world's leading powers

1913 American industrialist Henry Ford perfects the moving assembly line, revolutionizing mass production

Jun 1914 Franz Ferdinand is assassinated in Sarajevo, leading to World War I

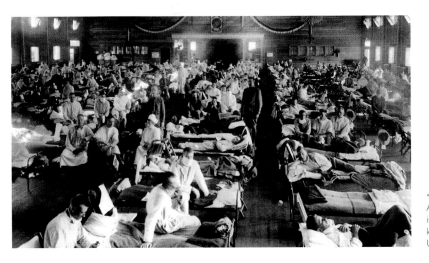

◁ **Worldwide epidemic**
An outbreak of Spanish flu in 1918–19 infected around 500 million people and killed up to 50 million. Starting in the US, it became a global catastrophe.

War I, Russia was in tatters. Into this chaos stepped revolutionary Vladimir Lenin, who saw his Bolshevik Party to power. By 1919, the Russian, Austrian, and German empires had collapsed. The Ottoman Empire was the last great casualty of the war—the Treaty of Sèvres was signed in 1920, and the empire was dismantled.

Meanwhile, around Easter 1916, an armed uprising in Dublin set southern Ireland on a path to independence from British rule, and the Irish Free State was founded in 1922.

Global repercussions

The US had followed an isolationist policy at the start of the war but was drawn into the conflict by German submarine attacks on their commercial ships. During and after the war, Americans embraced and invested heavily in technology, pioneering methods of assembly-line production. Women, who had contributed so much to the war effort, had been granted the right to vote in 1918 in the UK, Austria, Germany, and Canada. Most American women were given the same right in 1920. However, the good times came to a grinding halt with the Stock Market Crash of 1929.

The Great Depression that followed (see pp.286–287) led to mass unemployment and strikes. It became a global crisis, leading to poverty on an unprecedented scale. The 1930s were haunted by violent political extremism. China, in turmoil due to a civil war, was also under attack from Japan. In Germany, more than 40 percent of industrial workers were unemployed. Already hit severely by the collapse of world trade, a starving Germany suffered, and the time was ripe for an ambitious

Adolf Hitler to form the Nationalist Socialist (Nazi) Party. With his promise to restore Germany's status as a great power, he was poised to assume total control.

Totalitarianism and the seeds of war

Other European nations, too, became seduced by right-wing politics and propaganda. While Germany had *der Führer* (Adolf Hitler), Italy had *il Duce* (Benito Mussolini) and fascist-leaning Spaniards had *el Caudillo* (Francisco Franco). In July 1936, Franco's forces fought the forces of the Spanish Left in a brutal civil war. Aided by Hitler and Mussolini, Franco was victorious in this precursor to the next global war. World War I—called the Great War—was supposed to have been the conflict to end all conflicts. Instead, the peace treaty that followed in 1919—the Treaty of Versailles—redrew the map of Europe, breeding discontent and resentment. Together with the Great Depression, it paved the way for the world's bloodiest conflict yet—World War II (see pp.294–295).

△ **Germany on fire**
The mysterious fire of the German parliament building on February 27, 1933, was a key moment in Nazi history, acting as a stepping-stone to the total dictatorship of Adolf Hitler.

◁ **Man of the masses**
A founding member of the Chinese Communist Party, Mao Zedong went on to become the leader of the People's Republic of China and one of the most influential figures of the 20th century.

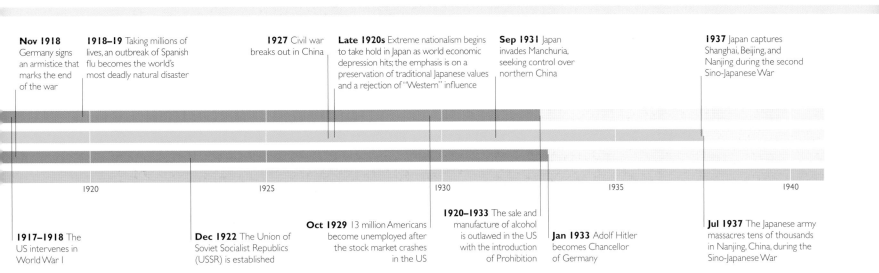

Nov 1918 Germany signs an armistice that marks the end of the war

1918–19 Taking millions of lives, an outbreak of Spanish flu becomes the world's most deadly natural disaster

1927 Civil war breaks out in China

Late 1920s Extreme nationalism begins to take hold in Japan as world economic depression hits; the emphasis is on a preservation of traditional Japanese values and a rejection of "Western" influence

Sep 1931 Japan invades Manchuria, seeking control over northern China

1937 Japan captures Shanghai, Beijing, and Nanjing during the second Sino-Japanese War

1920   1925   1930   1935   1940

1917–1918 The US intervenes in World War I

Dec 1922 The Union of Soviet Socialist Republics (USSR) is established

Oct 1929 13 million Americans become unemployed after the stock market crashes in the US

1920–1933 The sale and manufacture of alcohol is outlawed in the US with the introduction of Prohibition

Jan 1933 Adolf Hitler becomes Chancellor of Germany

Jul 1937 The Japanese army massacres tens of thousands in Nanjing, China, during the Sino-Japanese War

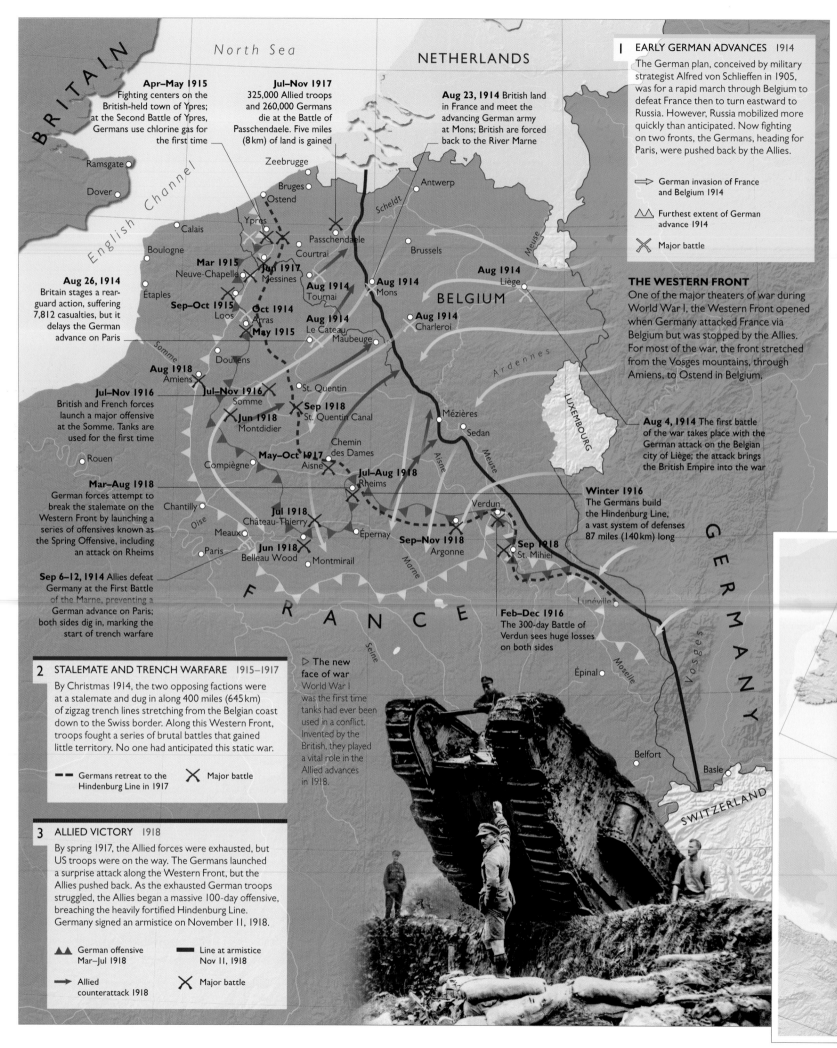

Apr–May 1915 Fighting centers on the British-held town of Ypres; at the Second Battle of Ypres, Germans use chlorine gas for the first time

Jul–Nov 1917 325,000 Allied troops and 260,000 Germans die at the Battle of Passchendaele. Five miles (8km) of land is gained

Aug 23, 1914 British land in France and meet the advancing German army at Mons; British are forced back to the River Marne

Aug 26, 1914 Britain stages a rear-guard action, suffering 7,812 casualties, but it delays the German advance on Paris

Mar 1915 Neuve-Chapelle

Jun 1917 Messines

Aug 1914 Tournai

Aug 1914 Mons

Aug 1914 Charleroi

Aug 1914 Liège

Sep–Oct 1915 Loos

Oct 1914 Arras **May 1915**

Aug 1914 Le Cateau

Aug 1918 Amiens

Jul–Nov 1916 Somme

Jul–Nov 1916 British and French forces launch a major offensive at the Somme. Tanks are used for the first time

Sep 1918 St. Quentin Canal

Jun 1918 Montdidier

May–Oct 1917 Aisne

Chemin des Dames

Jul–Aug 1918 Rheims

Mar–Aug 1918 German forces attempt to break the stalemate on the Western Front by launching a series of offensives known as the Spring Offensive, including an attack on Rheims

Winter 1916 The Germans build the Hindenburg Line, a vast system of defenses 87 miles (140km) long

Jul 1918 Château-Thierry

Sep–Nov 1918 Argonne

Sep 1918 St. Mihiel

Jun 1918 Belleau Wood

Sep 6–12, 1914 Allies defeat Germany at the First Battle of the Marne, preventing a German advance on Paris; both sides dig in, marking the start of trench warfare

Feb–Dec 1916 The 300-day Battle of Verdun sees huge losses on both sides

1 EARLY GERMAN ADVANCES 1914

The German plan, conceived by military strategist Alfred von Schlieffen in 1905, was for a rapid march through Belgium to defeat France then to turn eastward to Russia. However, Russia mobilized more quickly than anticipated. Now fighting on two fronts, the Germans, heading for Paris, were pushed back by the Allies.

⇨ German invasion of France and Belgium 1914

△△ Furthest extent of German advance 1914

✕ Major battle

THE WESTERN FRONT

One of the major theaters of war during World War I, the Western Front opened when Germany attacked France via Belgium but was stopped by the Allies. For most of the war, the front stretched from the Vosges mountains, through Amiens, to Ostend in Belgium.

Aug 4, 1914 The first battle of the war takes place with the German attack on the Belgian city of Liège; the attack brings the British Empire into the war

▷ **The new face of war** World War I was the first time tanks had ever been used in a conflict. Invented by the British, they played a vital role in the Allied advances in 1918.

2 STALEMATE AND TRENCH WARFARE 1915–1917

By Christmas 1914, the two opposing factions were at a stalemate and dug in along 400 miles (645km) of zigzag trench lines stretching from the Belgian coast down to the Swiss border. Along this Western Front, troops fought a series of brutal battles that gained little territory. No one had anticipated this static war.

--- Germans retreat to the Hindenburg Line in 1917

✕ Major battle

3 ALLIED VICTORY 1918

By spring 1917, the Allied forces were exhausted, but US troops were on the way. The Germans launched a surprise attack along the Western Front, but the Allies pushed back. As the exhausted German troops struggled, the Allies began a massive 100-day offensive, breaching the heavily fortified Hindenburg Line. Germany signed an armistice on November 11, 1918.

△△ German offensive Mar–Jul 1918

▬ Line at armistice Nov 11, 1918

➡ Allied counterattack 1918

✕ Major battle

WORLD WAR I

World War I was one of the defining events of the 20th century. Bound by the chains of interlocking alliances and provoked by the massive buildup of battleships and weaponry, governments sent their armies off to face a new kind of warfare.

On June 28, 1914, Archduke Franz Ferdinand, heir to the Austrian throne, was assassinated in Sarajevo, Bosnia. Blaming their bitter rival, Austria-Hungary declared war on Serbia. Events quickly escalated, and the wider system of alliances (see pp.268–269) got drawn into the war. Russia hurried to the aid of Serbia, while Germany, coming to the support of Austria-Hungary, declared war on both Russia and France. When Germany, on its way to France, invaded neutral Belgium on August 4, 1914, Britain declared war on Germany. Stalemate quickly followed. The Germans, British, and French dug a network of trenches stretching from the Swiss border to the North Sea, and with modern weaponry, the Western Front became a killing field. On the more fluid Eastern Front, the better-equipped German army defeated the Russians, and in December 1917 Russia signed an armistice. The arrival of the US into the war in April 1917 turned the tide in the Allies' favor, and following a series of brutal battles, an armistice was agreed on November 11, 1918. At the start of the war, both the Central Powers and the Allies had been convinced it would be short and decisive; neither was prepared for this long war of attrition.

WAR ON TWO FRONTS

World War I was fought largely on the Western Front (in western Europe) and the Eastern Front (in eastern Europe), although countries from around the world were gradually pulled into the conflict. There were two opposing alliances: the Central Powers (Germany and Austria-Hungary) and the Allies (Russia, France, and Britain). Despite early German successes, the Allies achieved victory in November 1918.

KEY

- Central Powers
- Allies
- Russian Empire

TIMELINE

1914 1915 1916 1917 1918 1919

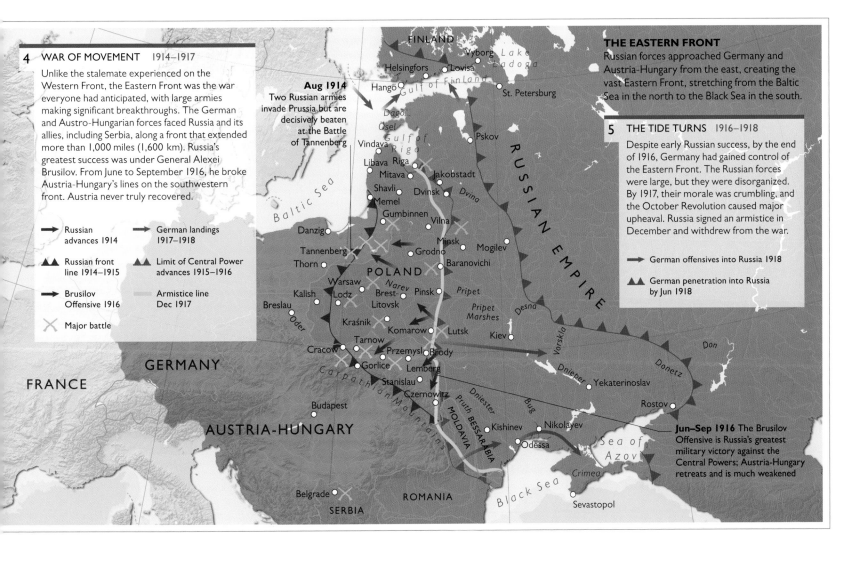

- → Russian advances 1914
- → German landings 1917–1918
- ▲▲ Russian front line 1914–1915
- ▲▲ Limit of Central Power advances 1915–1916
- → Brusilov Offensive 1916
- ▬ Armistice line Dec 1917
- ✕ Major battle

THE EASTERN FRONT

Russian forces approached Germany and Austria-Hungary from the east, creating the vast Eastern Front, stretching from the Baltic Sea in the north to the Black Sea in the south.

5 THE TIDE TURNS 1916–1918

Despite early Russian success, by the end of 1916, Germany had gained control of the Eastern Front. The Russian forces were large, but they were disorganized. By 1917, their morale was crumbling, and the October Revolution caused major upheaval. Russia signed an armistice in December and withdrew from the war.

- → German offensives into Russia 1918
- ▲▲ German penetration into Russia by Jun 1918

Aug 1914 Two Russian armies invade Prussia, but are decisively beaten at the Battle of Tannenberg

Jun–Sep 1916 The Brusilov Offensive is Russia's greatest military victory against the Central Powers; Austria-Hungary retreats and is much weakened

THE TRENCHES

Much of the fighting in World War I was characterized by the mud and blood of the trenches. The prolonged stalemate between trench-bound enemies was marked by mass killings over just a few yards of land.

△ **Lines of communication**
Telephones were used extensively to give orders directly to front-line troops. A web of telephone and telegraph wires crisscrossed the battlefields.

The German advance across France was halted in the early fall of 1914. Confronted with deadly machine guns, mortars, and howitzers, both sides reached for their spades to dig rudimentary trenches, from where they could both defend and attack. The era of modern trench warfare had begun.

By mid-October 1914, two lines of trenches faced each other in a meandering line that ran from the Swiss border in the south to the North Sea. It became known as the Western Front. The early Allied trenches were crude and shallow. The German trenches, on the other hand, were more solidly built and on higher ground. Some even had electricity and toilets. Sandbags, wire mesh, and wooden frames were brought in to reinforce the walls.

The human cost

Life in the trenches was appalling. They were filled with rats, flies, and lice and prone to flooding. Frightened young men stood in knee-deep mud waiting for the call to go "over the top." Casualty rates were high, not only from major battles such as Passchendaele (July–November 1917), but also from the ever-present threats of sniper fire, random shells, and poison gas. Diseases, such as typhoid and trench foot, put many out of action. The constant bombardment and sound of enemy fire led to the diagnosis of a new condition called "shell shock," which prompted a range of disabling psychosomatic conditions.

For soldiers trapped in the trenches, there was no way out. Deserters were shot and malingerers penalized. Trench warfare in World War I resulted in a 4-year-long impasse, with soldiers dying from not just new weaponry but horrific living conditions.

△ **Crossing the trenches**
German troops clamber over the top of their trenches and advance across no-man's-land—the area that separated the enemy trenches—toward British lines. Soldiers marched into the guns and were mown down in droves.

Battle of the Somme
While a soldier from the 11th Cheshire Regiment keeps watch during the Battle of the Somme (July–November 1916), his comrades catch what sleep they can amid the rubble of their trench.

THE WIDER WAR

Although the main theater of battle during World War I (1914–1918) was in Europe, the conflict extended across the globe. It was shaped by the major European powers, spreading through a series of alliances, as well as through their empires and colonies.

World War I originated in central Europe. However, since many of the European belligerents were colonial powers, they had valuable assets and troops stationed all over the globe. Millions of soldiers were recruited from colonized countries and brought in to fight on the front lines. As the war spread, new fronts opened up in the Balkans, Mesopotamia, Anatolia (modern Turkey), East Africa, and Salonika. Italy joined the war on the side of the Allies in May 1915, and a series of brutal battles were fought along its border with Austria-Hungary.

In the Balkans, already a volatile region, loyalties were divided. In September 1918, Allied forces attacked from northern Greece, eventually liberating Serbia. The entry of the Turkish Ottoman Empire as an ally of Germany in fall 1914 had brought the Middle East into the conflict. The Turks had initial successes against the British, but struggled against Russia in the Caucasus. In 1916, a widespread Arab uprising against Ottoman rule helped the British cause by tying up Ottoman forces. By the time Turkey sued for an armistice in October 1918, the centuries-old empire had collapsed.

"We were casting them by thousands into the fire to the worst of deaths."

T. E. LAWRENCE, BRITISH MILITARY OFFICER

T. E. LAWRENCE
1888–1935

One of the most iconic figures of World War I, Thomas Edward Lawrence—popularly known by his nickname, Lawrence of Arabia—was an Arabic-speaking British archaeologist who traveled and worked in the Middle East. During World War I, he joined the British army and became an intelligence officer in Cairo, Egypt. His daring raids made him an international legend. Lawrence developed a deep sympathy for the Arabs living under Turkish rule and worked for their emancipation. He died in England in a motorcycle accident in 1935.

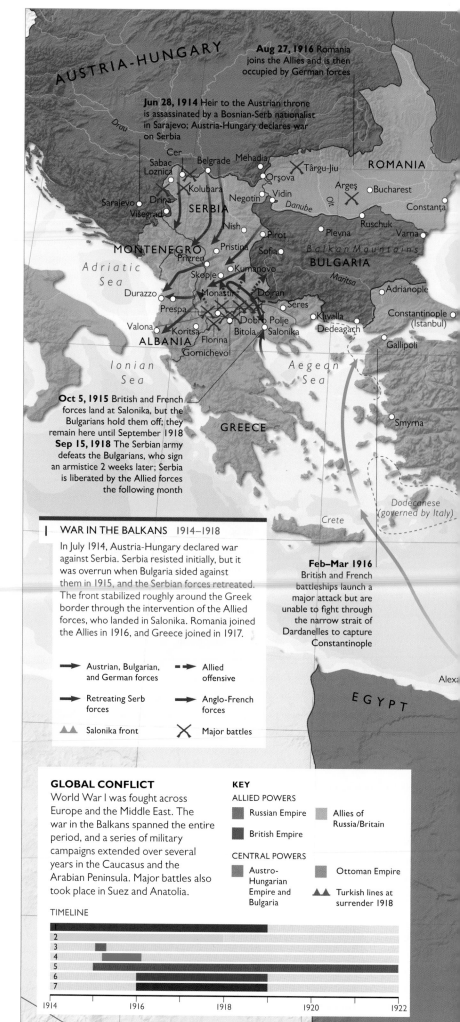

Aug 27, 1916 Romania joins the Allies and is then occupied by German forces

Jun 28, 1914 Heir to the Austrian throne is assassinated by a Bosnian-Serb nationalist in Sarajevo; Austria-Hungary declares war on Serbia

Oct 5, 1915 British and French forces land at Salonika, but the Bulgarians hold them off; they remain here until September 1918
Sep 15, 1918 The Serbian army defeats the Bulgarians, who sign an armistice 2 weeks later; Serbia is liberated by the Allied forces the following month

Feb–Mar 1916 British and French battleships launch a major attack but are unable to fight through the narrow strait of Dardanelles to capture Constantinople

WAR IN THE BALKANS 1914–1918

In July 1914, Austria-Hungary declared war against Serbia. Serbia resisted initially, but it was overrun when Bulgaria sided against them in 1915, and the Serbian forces retreated. The front stabilized roughly around the Greek border through the intervention of the Allied forces, who landed in Salonika. Romania joined the Allies in 1916, and Greece joined in 1917.

→ Austrian, Bulgarian, and German forces
⇢ Allied offensive
→ Retreating Serb forces
→ Anglo-French forces
▲▲ Salonika front
✕ Major battles

GLOBAL CONFLICT

World War I was fought across Europe and the Middle East. The war in the Balkans spanned the entire period, and a series of military campaigns extended over several years in the Caucasus and the Arabian Peninsula. Major battles also took place in Suez and Anatolia.

KEY
ALLIED POWERS
■ Russian Empire
■ British Empire
■ Allies of Russia/Britain

CENTRAL POWERS
■ Austro-Hungarian Empire and Bulgaria
■ Ottoman Empire
▲▲ Turkish lines at surrender 1918

TIMELINE

1914   1916   1918   1920   1922

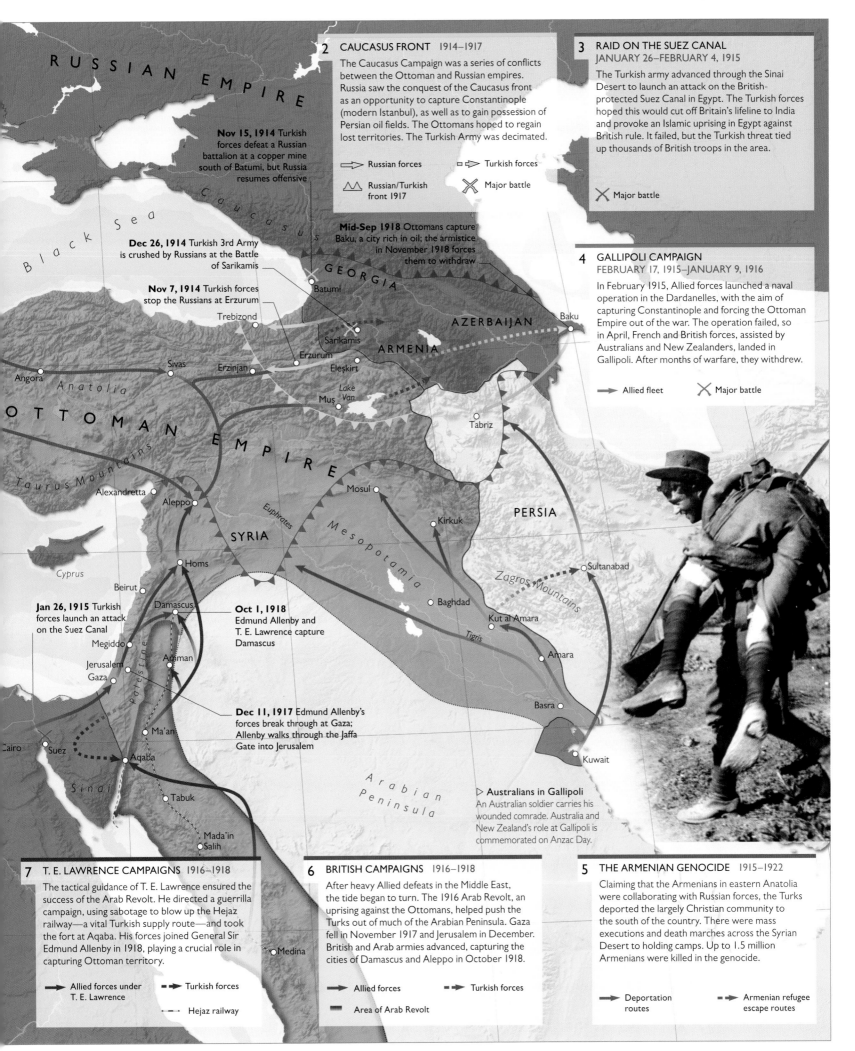

2 CAUCASUS FRONT 1914–1917

The Caucasus Campaign was a series of conflicts between the Ottoman and Russian empires. Russia saw the conquest of the Caucasus front as an opportunity to capture Constantinople (modern Istanbul), as well as to gain possession of Persian oil fields. The Ottomans hoped to regain lost territories. The Turkish Army was decimated.

→ Russian forces   ▭⇨ Turkish forces
⋀⋀ Russian/Turkish front 1917   ✕ Major battle

3 RAID ON THE SUEZ CANAL
JANUARY 26–FEBRUARY 4, 1915

The Turkish army advanced through the Sinai Desert to launch an attack on the British-protected Suez Canal in Egypt. The Turkish forces hoped this would cut off Britain's lifeline to India and provoke an Islamic uprising in Egypt against British rule. It failed, but the Turkish threat tied up thousands of British troops in the area.

✕ Major battle

4 GALLIPOLI CAMPAIGN
FEBRUARY 17, 1915–JANUARY 9, 1916

In February 1915, Allied forces launched a naval operation in the Dardanelles, with the aim of capturing Constantinople and forcing the Ottoman Empire out of the war. The operation failed, so in April, French and British forces, assisted by Australians and New Zealanders, landed in Gallipoli. After months of warfare, they withdrew.

→ Allied fleet   ✕ Major battle

Nov 15, 1914 Turkish forces defeat a Russian battalion at a copper mine south of Batumi, but Russia resumes offensive

Dec 26, 1914 Turkish 3rd Army is crushed by Russians at the Battle of Sarikamis

Nov 7, 1914 Turkish forces stop the Russians at Erzurum

Mid-Sep 1918 Ottomans capture Baku, a city rich in oil; the armistice in November 1918 forces them to withdraw

Jan 26, 1915 Turkish forces launch an attack on the Suez Canal

Oct 1, 1918 Edmund Allenby and T. E. Lawrence capture Damascus

Dec 11, 1917 Edmund Allenby's forces break through at Gaza; Allenby walks through the Jaffa Gate into Jerusalem

▷ **Australians in Gallipoli**
An Australian soldier carries his wounded comrade. Australia and New Zealand's role at Gallipoli is commemorated on Anzac Day.

7 T. E. LAWRENCE CAMPAIGNS 1916–1918

The tactical guidance of T. E. Lawrence ensured the success of the Arab Revolt. He directed a guerrilla campaign, using sabotage to blow up the Hejaz railway—a vital Turkish supply route—and took the fort at Aqaba. His forces joined General Sir Edmund Allenby in 1918, playing a crucial role in capturing Ottoman territory.

→ Allied forces under T. E. Lawrence   ⇢ Turkish forces
⋯→ Hejaz railway

6 BRITISH CAMPAIGNS 1916–1918

After heavy Allied defeats in the Middle East, the tide began to turn. The 1916 Arab Revolt, an uprising against the Ottomans, helped push the Turks out of much of the Arabian Peninsula. Gaza fell in November 1917 and Jerusalem in December. British and Arab armies advanced, capturing the cities of Damascus and Aleppo in October 1918.

→ Allied forces   ⇢ Turkish forces
▬ Area of Arab Revolt

5 THE ARMENIAN GENOCIDE 1915–1922

Claiming that the Armenians in eastern Anatolia were collaborating with Russian forces, the Turks deported the largely Christian community to the south of the country. There were mass executions and death marches across the Syrian Desert to holding camps. Up to 1.5 million Armenians were killed in the genocide.

→ Deportation routes   ⇢ Armenian refugee escape routes

4 CIVIL WAR BREAKS OUT 1917–1922

Although the Bolsheviks had gained power, they were a minority in Russia. Lenin started the "Red Terror"— a campaign of intimidation against anyone thought to be a threat to the regime—which was carried out by the new Bolshevik secret police, the Cheka. Meanwhile, a violent civil war broke out between the Bolsheviks (the "Reds") and anti-Bolshevik forces, including the White Army, formed of Tsarist supporters and military officers. Russia's former allies—Britain, France, and the US—supported the Whites, fearing the spread of communism.

3 RUSSIA PULLS OUT OF WORLD WAR I 1917–1918

The new Bolshevik government, led by Lenin, signed an armistice with the Central Powers (see p.275) in December 1917. The terms, which were harsh on Russia, were formalized in the Treaty of Brest-Litovsk in March 1918. Russia relinquished control of the Baltic States and Ukraine and was forced to pay 6 billion German marks in reparations. Anger at these losses fueled opposition to the Bolsheviks.

2 INDEPENDENT REPUBLICS 1917–1921

The Russian Empire was ethnically diverse, and calls for self-determination had been growing among non-Russian nationalities. After the revolution, Finland, Estonia, Poland, Latvia, Lithuania, and Ukraine declared independence, while Armenia, Azerbaijan, and Georgia formed a short-lived republic. Faced with financial crisis and militarily weak, Ukraine and the Caucasus states were later reabsorbed into the USSR.

> ▆ Countries declaring independence from Russia 1917–1918

> ⬛ Russian boundary after Treaty of Brest-Litovsk 1918

> 🏴 Temporarily independent from Russia 1917–1921

Feb 1919–Oct 1920 With growing Bolshevik success in the civil war, Lenin seeks to gain back lost territory in Poland. After initial success, the Bolsheviks are defeated at the Battle of Warsaw

Dec 18, 1918 France, an ally of the Whites, enters the civil war by sending troops to Odessa

Apr 8, 1919 Allied forces lose Odessa to the Red Army

Nov 7–17, 1920 The Siege of Perekop leads to another Red victory, and the Red Army occupy the Crimea

Apr 10–13, 1918 At the Battle of Yekaterinodar, the first major battle between the two armies, the commander of the White Army is killed in combat

Mar 1918 Russia moves the state capital to Moscow (from Petrograd), after German soldiers march through Russia virtually unopposed

Jul 16–17, 1918 Tsar Nicholas II is shot by the Bolsheviks, along with his wife, five children, and four royal staff members

Aug 1918 Allied forces offer support to the leader of the White Army, Admiral Alexander Kolchak, who sets up his government in Omsk

Sep 5–10, 1918 The White Army, allied with the Czechs, suffer a defeat at the Battle of Kazan

5 COSSACK ATTACK 1917–1920

The Cossacks, a group who formed self-governing communities, rose to fight against the Bolsheviks, and many anti-Bolsheviks fled to join them in southern Russia. United with the Whites, the Cossacks put the Bolsheviks on the defensive along the Southern Front, wrecking their lines of communication, laying siege to the port city of Tsaritsyn from 1918–1920, and briefly occupying the city of Voronezh in September 1919.

> ⬛ Don Cossacks   ▆ Kuban Cossacks

6 BOLSHEVIK ADVANCES 1917–1922

Although the Whites had the support of many countries outside of Russia, the Bolsheviks had a brilliant tactical leader in Leon Trotsky and were better organized. Crucially, they had control of the industrial cities of Moscow and Petrograd, which included much of Russia's railroad network. When the civil war ended in October 1922, the Bolsheviks had total control of Russia.

> ✕ Bolshevik battles   ▬ Bolshevik territories 1919

7 USSR FOUNDED DECEMBER 1922

After the civil war, the country was in tatters. Around 6 million peasants had died from famine between 1921 and 1922, and there was rioting in many cities. Lenin suffered a stroke in May 1922. In December 1922, the Union of Soviet Socialist Republics (USSR) was established, based on one-party rule. Lenin died in 1924, worried about political infighting in his party. His legacy, however, was the world's first socialist state.

> ⬛ USSR 1922

OCTOBER REVOLUTION OCTOBER 1917

When Lenin returned to Russia in fall 1917, having been in hiding in Finland, he urged immediate action. The Red Guards seized control of Petrograd, and on October 26, 1917, guards at the Winter Palace—the seat of the Provisional Government—willingly surrendered. Power passed to the Bolsheviks, with Lenin establishing a Marxist one-party state after closing down the Russian Constituent Assembly in January 1918.

● Towns where Bolsheviks gained control

Bering Sea

R

Lena

Sea of Okhotsk

May 1918
Allied forces guard the Trans-Siberian Railway to protect their war supplies from Bolshevik attacks and to keep the railway running

Khabarovsk

Blagoveshchensk

Chita

Bator

I A

Jan 1919
Troops from Allied nations are sent to fight with the Whites, largely in Siberia, through the city of Vladivostok

Vladivostok

KOREA

△ **Lenin returns**
A statue of Lenin at Finland Station, in St. Petersburg, marks his return from exile and the start of the revolution.

COUNTRY IN TURMOIL

Russia experienced extreme turbulence from February 1917 to the founding of the USSR in 1922. In a country battered by World War I, the end of the monarchy, revolution, civil war, and famine, Lenin emerged as virtual dictator.

KEY

→ Bolshevik forces

➡ Allied forces

⇨ White Army forces

▪▬▪ Railway

TIMELINE

1
2
3
4
5
6
7

1917   1919   1921   1923   1925

THE RUSSIAN REVOLUTION

For centuries, the Russian Empire was ruled by absolute monarchs, or Tsars. However, in one tumultuous year, the people of Russia rose up to topple Tsarist rule. Vladimir Lenin's communist party, the Bolsheviks, took control and set the stage for the creation of the USSR.

The outbreak of World War I in 1914 briefly united a discontented Russia, but the war did not go well. Huge military losses and food shortages led to increasing resentment against Tsar Nicholas II. On February 23, 1917, a riot broke out in Petrograd, led by women who had waited hours for bread. The riot grew into a general strike. The Tsar was forced to abdicate in March 1917, and a provisional government was put in charge, but it was weak. Meanwhile, the Petrograd Soviet of Workers' and Soldiers' Deputies, a council pushing for change, grew in popularity. Lenin, the leader of the Bolshevik faction of the Russian Social Democratic Party, who was in exile for Marxist activities, returned to Russia, convinced it was the time to implement his ideas. However, the Provisional Government leader, Alexander Kerensky, banned the Bolsheviks and ordered the arrest of Lenin, who fled to Finland. By August 1917, the Bolsheviks had taken control of the Petrograd Soviet. Sensing victory, Lenin returned home in the fall, certain that the Bolsheviks could seize power.

"History will not forgive us if we do not assume power now."

VLADIMIR LENIN, REVOLUTIONARY, SEPTEMBER 1917

LEON TROTSKY
1879–1940

Originally a member of the Mensheviks—a faction of the Russian socialist movement in opposition to the Bolsheviks—Leon Trotsky was in exile in the US for anti-war activities when the Tsar was overthrown in March 1917. He returned to Russia and joined the Bolshevik Party. Trotsky helped to organize the October Revolution and form the Red Army, which he then commanded in the Russian Civil War (1917–1922). After Lenin's death in 1924, he clashed with Joseph Stalin. Trotsky was exiled again in 1929 and found asylum in Mexico. In 1940, he was fatally stabbed by a Stalinist assassin.

POLITICAL EXTREMISM

World War I left a poisonous legacy. Several nations—
including Germany, Italy, and Spain—looked for solutions
to their problems in political extremism.

△ **The birth of fascism**
Charismatic Italian dictator Benito
Mussolini inspired thousands at
mass rallies. His stiff-armed salute
became a symbol of fascism.

After World War I, Europe saw
a rise in communism, triggering
the emergence of extreme right-
wing groups. People turned to
leaders willing to assume political
authority, and Benito Mussolini,
who coined the term "fascism" to
describe his right-wing movement,
became Italy's military dictator
in 1922.
Mussolini's mass rallies and use
of propaganda influenced Adolf
Hitler, the rising star of Germany's Right
and leader of the National Socialist
German Workers (Nazi) Party, which
was openly racist, anti-Semitic, and anti-
communist. The 1930s became a period
of extreme turbulence. The Great Depression (see pp.286–287) led to a
global economic crisis. Both communism and fascism offered answers
to hungry, unemployed people. Authoritarian governments came to
power in central and eastern Europe, and democracy was in decline.

Crisis and conflict

In Germany, as Nazi groups battled communists and against
a backdrop of economic crisis, Hitler assumed power in 1933.
The Spanish Civil War (see pp.292–293) epitomized the antipathy
between fascists and the left. Italy and Germany supported
fascist General Francisco Franco and used the war to test new
weapons and strategies against the Republican government,
which was supported with supplies and advisers by the
USSR. Europe
was once again
choosing sides and
forming alliances.

▷ **Bombing Guernica**
The bombing of the Basque
town of Guernica, Spain, on
April 26, 1937 during the
Spanish Civil War was carried
out by the Nazis in support
of General Francisco Franco.

"The truth is that men are tired of liberty."

BENITO MUSSOLINI, ITALIAN DICTATOR, 1934

The rise of the Nazis
Nazi leader Adolf Hitler addresses a rally
of paramilitary SA (*Sturmabteilung*) troops
in Germany in 1933. Such larger-than-life
displays built up support for the Nazi
Party to fever pitch.

6 IRELAND 1916–1922

The outbreak of World War I interrupted a political crisis in Britain over Ireland's future. The failure to resolve this crisis first caused a wartime insurrection (the Easter Rising, 1916), then a War of Independence (1919–1921), when Irish separatists fought to establish an independent Irish Republic. The partition of Ireland in 1922 into Northern Ireland and the Irish Free State led to further unrest.

■ Irish Free State 1922

1922 Ireland is divided into two parts: the six mainly Protestant counties of Ulster become Northern Ireland and are subordinate to London

7 GERMAN LOSSES 1918–1919

The terms set out against Germany by the 1919 Treaty of Versailles were punitive. One-eighth of its prewar territory was lost, including land in Poland, Denmark, Belgium, and France. It was stripped of its colonial possessions, its armed forces were reduced, and its merchant fleet confiscated. Germany was made to pay war reparations, provoking bitter, long-lasting resentment.

— German border 1918

1920 Russia recognizes Fin independence the Treaty of

1920 Estonia is liberated from Russia following the Estonian War of Independence

1921 Under the Treaty of Riga, Russia pledges to respect Latvia's independence

1923 The borders of Poland are finally settled

1920 A peace treaty is signed between Lithuania and Soviet Russia after the Lithuanian War of Independence

1918 The region of Bessarabia is added to Romani

5 COLLAPSE AND DIVISION OF AUSTRIA-HUNGARY 1918–1923

After the Habsburg regime collapsed in 1918, new national states were created in Austria, Hungary, and Czechoslovakia. Habsburg territories were also absorbed by the new states of Poland and Yugoslavia. The Austrian army was restricted and reparations imposed, and Hungary lost two-thirds of its old land, principally to Yugoslavia and Romania.

— Austria-Hungary border 1914

1919 Treaty of St.-Germain sets the borders for the new state of Austria

4 PALESTINE 1922–1947

In 1922, the British were formally given the mandate to govern the region, having pledged to establish a home for Jews in Palestine. The Arabs rose up against the British, and many were killed in the Arab Revolt (1936–1939). The influx of Jewish refugees from Nazi-occupied territories, and the suggestion from the United Nations that Palestine be divided into Arab and Jewish states, exacerbated tensions. Civil war broke out in 1947 (see pp.332–333).

■ Mandatory Palestine 1922

1918 The Kingdom of the Serbs, Croats, and Slovenes is formed from parts of the old Austro-Hungarian Empire and Serbia. It is renamed Yugoslavia in 1929

1919 Greece occupies Smyrna, leading to war between Greece and Turkey

3 TURKEY 1922–1923

The Turkish War of Independence (1919–1922) saw Atatürk and a rebel army fight against the Ottoman sultan and the proxies of the Allied forces. Following the nationalists' victory, a new government was set up in Ankara, and the Treaty of Sèvres was abandoned. The Treaty of Lausanne (1923) legitimized the newly independent Turkish Republic and marked the end of the Ottoman Empire.

■ Turkey after Treaty of Sèvres 1920
■ Restored to Turkey after Treaty of Lausanne 1923
■ Annexed by Turkey 1921

2 BRITISH AND FRENCH MANDATES 1920–1946

The Treaty of Sèvres, signed in August 1920, divided parts of the defeated Ottoman Empire into British and French control. The Ottoman government accepted the treaty. However, it was rejected by Turkish nationalists, led by Mustafa Kemal Atatürk, who were determined to drive out foreign armies. In Egypt (a British protectorate), the diminishing British military presence after the war allowed the nationalist Wafd Party to launch a revolution. Limited independence was gained in February 1922.

■ French mandate
■ British mandate
■ British protectorate

1922 The growing popular support of the nationalistic Wafd Party prompts Britain to grant Egypt limited independence

AFTER WORLD WAR I

The postwar period saw territorial winners and losers. Russia lost the most, with Germany close behind. Many of the old empires had fallen, except for Britain and France, which retained influence and colonies worldwide.

KEY

■ New states

— National borders 1923

TIMELINE

```
1
2
3
4
5
6
7
1910    1920    1930    1940    1950
```

△ **The Wafd Party**
Members of the Egyptian nationalist party, the Wafd Party, gather in 1936. The party was instrumental in gaining independence.

RUSSIAN LOSSES 1918–1922

The Bolshevik regime could not hold on to its new empire. In the 1918 Treaty of Brest-Litovsk, Russia recognized the independence of the Baltic States, Ukraine, Georgia, and Finland. Ukraine and Georgia both joined the USSR in 1922, and the Baltic States did not achieve true independence until the 1920s.

— Russian border 1918

Black Sea

TURKEY

TURKISH ARMENIA

Lake Van

TURKISH KURDISTAN

Anatolia

Adana

Cyprus

SYRIA

Baghdad

PERSIA

LEBANON

IRAQ

PALESTINE

NEJD

Jerusalem

TRANSJORDAN

KUWAIT
to Britain

Persian Gulf

1915–1922 Over 1.5 million Armenians living in Turkey are killed by Turkish nationalists; in September 1922, the Turkish Army enters Smyrna, setting fires and massacring many Armenians, and forcing others to leave the city

1920 The Transjordan region is made into a League of Nations mandate to be administered by Britain

1920 An uprising against the British briefly unites Sunni and Shia Muslims; more than 100,000 British and Indian troops are deployed to quell the revolt, and thousands of Arabs are killed

1920s Anti-Jewish riots in 1920, 1921, and 1929 reveal the failure of British security forces to maintain order

AFTERMATH OF THE GREAT WAR

By the end of World War I, the political landscape of Europe and the Middle East had changed forever. Centuries-old empires and dynasties had collapsed, borders were redrawn, new nation-states were created, and the seeds of future conflict were sown.

World War I had a profound effect on global politics, bringing to an end three powerful monarchies—Germany, Russia, and Austria-Hungary. The victorious Allies assembled at the 1919 Paris Peace Conference to draw up a settlement. The main result was the Treaty of Versailles, which punished Germany harshly. Austria-Hungary, Turkey, and Bulgaria also suffered losses, while Italy, which had entered the war in 1915, was given former Habsburg lands in northern Italy. Also to gain were nine new nation-states created in Europe. The Middle East was also hugely impacted by the war. In 1916, the Sykes-Picot Agreement set out the intention to divide the Ottoman Empire's Middle Eastern territory between British and French zones of control. In many areas, the act of being placed under British or French control in 1920 fueled nationalist sentiments.

The victors of World War I hoped to build a lasting peace, but disputes rumbled on across the globe, and mass unemployment, bitter ideological divisions, fanatical nationalism, and the threat of communism created escalating international tension.

"This [the Treaty of Versailles] is not peace. It is an armistice for 20 years."

FERDINAND FOCH, FRENCH GENERAL, JUNE 28, 1919

THE LEAGUE OF NATIONS
1920–1946

Proposed by US President Woodrow Wilson, the League of Nations was an international organization set up in Geneva in 1920 to preserve peace. Conflict was to be settled by negotiation; diplomacy; and, if necessary, sanctions. The league relied on international goodwill, but Germany and Russia were excluded, and the US Senate refused to ratify US membership. In 1946, the league was replaced by the United Nations.

President Wilson arrives in Italy to discuss founding the League of Nations.

THE GREAT DEPRESSION

The US stock market crash in October 1929 was part of a worldwide economic recession that crippled the future of an entire generation. As people lost faith in democracy, new extremist politics gained popularity, setting the stage for the horrors of World War II.

The US recovered quickly after World War I. Factories used in the war effort switched to making consumer goods, and industrial growth doubled in the 1920s. Thousands of Americans invested in the stock market, often using borrowed money. A boom time, it became known as the "Roaring Twenties." However, by mid-1929, there were signs of trouble. Unemployment was rising, and car sales had dipped. The crisis broke on October 24, when the stock market dropped by 11 percent. Panic set in, and over the next 6 days, the market crashed. One-quarter of the US working population became unemployed. In mid-1932, Franklin Roosevelt replaced Herbert Hoover as president and pledged a "New Deal" of social and economic reforms.

The Great Depression spread around the globe, leading to massive poverty. The only country not adversely affected was the USSR. In Germany, the US's demand for outstanding loans to be repaid further impoverished the country, fueling the popularity of Adolf Hitler's National Socialist (Nazi) Party.

> *"There may be a recession in stock prices, but not anything in the nature of a crash."*
>
> IRVING FISHER, US ECONOMIST, SEPTEMBER 5, 1929

THE DUST BOWL

In 1932, severe droughts hit the US from Texas to the Dakotas. Exposed topsoil turned to dust, and without windbreaks such as trees, high winds churned the dust into huge storms. Settlers and livestock choked on the dirt. Farmers, already hit by the Great Depression, were forced to migrate west to California, where regular harvests meant more jobs. Many rode along Route 66, which became known as the "road to opportunity."

KEY

- Area of severe damage
- Other areas damaged by dust storms
- → Migration route

1 STOCK MARKET CRASH AND STRIKES 1929–1934

Approximately $25 billion was lost in the 1929 crash. People became bankrupt, factories closed, trade collapsed, wages fell, and homelessness soared. There were strikes and riots across the country as workers sought protection offered by the unions, as well as greater involvement of the US government in the economy.

Strikes

May–Jul 1934 Dock workers go on strike at ports in San Francisco, as well as all other West Coast ports, shutting down about 2,000 miles (3,200 km) of coastline

Oct 1929 The financial bubble bursts, and panic hits Wall Street in New York; banks close, bankrupting millions overnight

1931–1932 Miners strike in Harlan County, Kentucky; like many strikes at the time, it turns violent

Jul–Aug 1934 Textile workers strike in Huntsville, Alabama; the strike spreads from the south of the country to the north, becoming one of the biggest industrial strikes in US history

2 LATIN AMERICA 1929–1933

After the crash, some of Latin America saw a drop of over 70 percent in exports to the US. In Colombia, this hit its coffee, banana, and oil markets. Brazil's coffee economy also suffered. In Cuba, reliant on its sugar exports, the impact was devastating. Chile, which exported nitrate and copper, was one of the worst-hit countries. Argentina and Venezuela, however, recovered relatively quickly.

1931–1932 In Chile, copper exports collapse, and the value of sodium nitrate exports to the US drops from $21 million to $1.4 million

1929–1930 In Argentina, exports of wheat and beef drop by more than two-thirds, and inflation increases; subsequent political instability leads to a military dictatorship

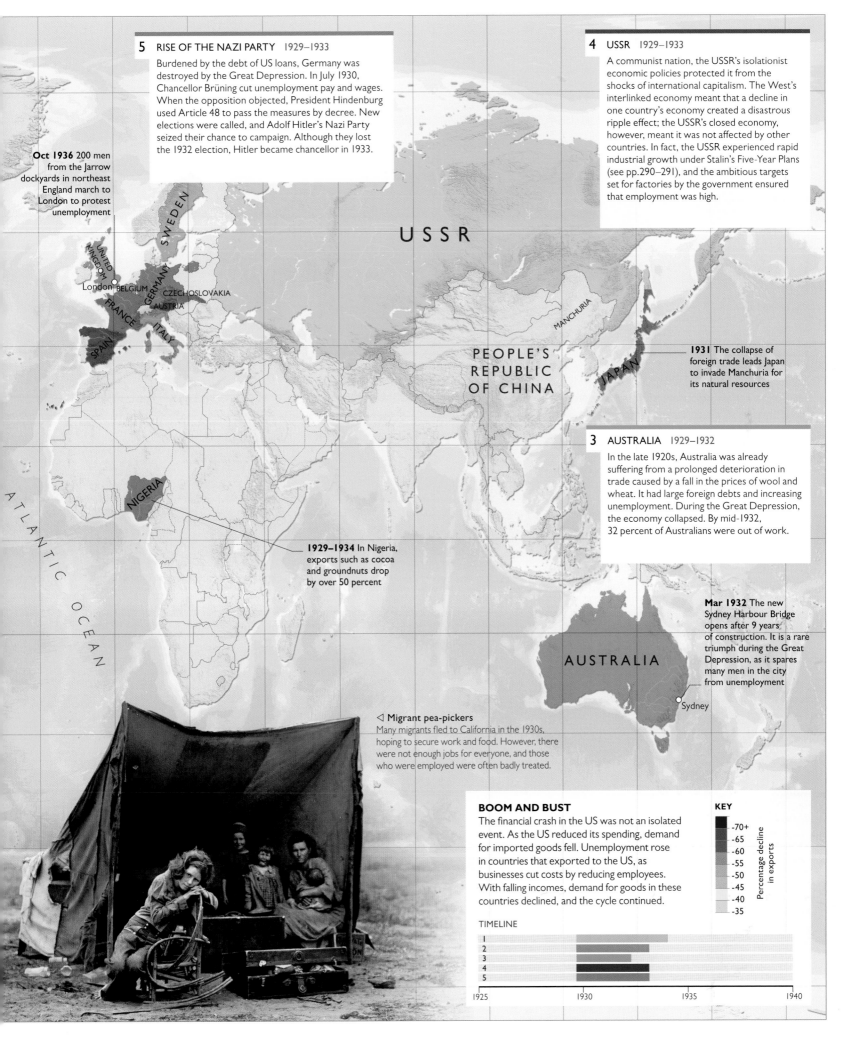

5 RISE OF THE NAZI PARTY 1929–1933

Burdened by the debt of US loans, Germany was destroyed by the Great Depression. In July 1930, Chancellor Brüning cut unemployment pay and wages. When the opposition objected, President Hindenburg used Article 48 to pass the measures by decree. New elections were called, and Adolf Hitler's Nazi Party seized their chance to campaign. Although they lost the 1932 election, Hitler became chancellor in 1933.

Oct 1936 200 men from the Jarrow dockyards in northeast England march to London to protest unemployment

4 USSR 1929–1933

A communist nation, the USSR's isolationist economic policies protected it from the shocks of international capitalism. The West's interlinked economy meant that a decline in one country's economy created a disastrous ripple effect; the USSR's closed economy, however, meant it was not affected by other countries. In fact, the USSR experienced rapid industrial growth under Stalin's Five-Year Plans (see pp.290–291), and the ambitious targets set for factories by the government ensured that employment was high.

USSR

SWEDEN

UNITED KINGDOM

London BELGIUM GERMANY CZECHOSLOVAKIA

FRANCE AUSTRIA

SPAIN ITALY

MANCHURIA

PEOPLE'S REPUBLIC OF CHINA

JAPAN

1931 The collapse of foreign trade leads Japan to invade Manchuria for its natural resources

ATLANTIC OCEAN

NIGERIA

1929–1934 In Nigeria, exports such as cocoa and groundnuts drop by over 50 percent

3 AUSTRALIA 1929–1932

In the late 1920s, Australia was already suffering from a prolonged deterioration in trade caused by a fall in the prices of wool and wheat. It had large foreign debts and increasing unemployment. During the Great Depression, the economy collapsed. By mid-1932, 32 percent of Australians were out of work.

Mar 1932 The new Sydney Harbour Bridge opens after 9 years of construction. It is a rare triumph during the Great Depression, as it spares many men in the city from unemployment

AUSTRALIA

Sydney

◁ **Migrant pea-pickers**
Many migrants fled to California in the 1930s, hoping to secure work and food. However, there were not enough jobs for everyone, and those who were employed were often badly treated.

BOOM AND BUST

The financial crash in the US was not an isolated event. As the US reduced its spending, demand for imported goods fell. Unemployment rose in countries that exported to the US, as businesses cut costs by reducing employees. With falling incomes, demand for goods in these countries declined, and the cycle continued.

KEY

Percentage decline in exports

-70+
-65
-60
-55
-50
-45
-40
-35

TIMELINE

1
2
3
4
5

1925   1930   1935   1940

2 BREAKDOWN OF THE ALLIANCE 1927–1936

In the early 1920s, the USSR supported the KMT, seeing it as part of an anti-imperialist revolution. In 1923, they ordered the CCP to join the KMT, but a bitter rivalry between the parties remained. After a temporary alliance, in 1927, Chiang dismissed his Soviet advisors and then turned against the CCP in a savage attack in Shanghai. It marked the beginning of years of violence between the parties.

✊ Clashes between the CCP and KMT, with date

3 CHINESE REUNIFICATION 1928

During the second stage of the Northern Expedition, some warlords allied themselves with the KMT. This new support allowed the KMT to capture the city of Beijing. The Kuomintang became the single most powerful force in China, and Chiang Kai-shek was made president of the Republic of China in 1928.

▨ Kuomintang control by 1928

➡ Warlords joining the Northern Expedition

1 THE NORTHERN EXPEDITION 1926–1928

Outside the few KMT-controlled provinces, China was ruled by regional warlords. Led by Chiang Kai-shek and supported by communist USSR, the KMT and CCP combined forces and advanced northward from Guangzhou to unify China in a campaign known as the Northern Expedition. During the first phase, they seized wealthy and heavily populated southern, central, and eastern areas.

➡ Northern Expedition 1926–1928

NATIONALIST CHINA, 1926–1937
The Kuomintang (KMT) seized vast amounts of territory from 1926, but their control was challenged by both domestic and international forces eager to seize land.

1912–1945 Chiang is unable to capture Shanxi, which is in the hands of the warlord Yan Xishan; however, in 1927, Yan briefly forms an alliance with Chiang

Jun 8, 1928 Beijing falls, an important victory that brings the far north under KMT control

Mar 1927 Captured by Chiang's forces, Nanjing is made the new capital of the Republic of China

Apr 20, 1929 Wuhan, which was set up as a capital by rival left-wing elements of the KMT, is captured by Chiang's troops

Apr 12, 1927 Shanghai ✊

Aug 1, 1927 Nanchang ✊

Sep 13, 1927 Changsa ✊

9 Dec, 1927 ✊ Canton (Guangzhou)

Dec 9, 1927 A violent communist uprising occurs after the KMT severs its alliance with the CCP

▽ **Chiang Kai-shek**
Following the death of its founder, Sun Yat-sen, Chiang Kai-shek became the leader of the KMT in 1926. He attempted to modernize China, but struggled to do so in a country beset by internal strife and constant threat from Japan.

4 INCOMPLETE UNIFICATION 1931–1937

Despite the success of the Northern Expedition, China was only partly unified. Chiang was unable to defeat all the warlords, especially in the north. Faced with the Japanese invasion of Manchuria in September 1931, he became determined to eliminate domestic conflict. From 1935–1937, Chiang brought more provinces under the influence of the Republic of China.

▨ Japanese control by 1936

▨ Kuomintang control by 1937

CHINA AND NATIONALISM

When its last emperor abdicated in 1912 (see pp.252–253), China was torn apart as warlords and China's Nationalist Party rushed to fill the void. After Japan was given territory in China in 1919, political unrest grew, leading to the emergence of the Communist Party. Years of fighting between the two parties and Japan followed, which carried on during the wider conflict of World War II.

The years following the fall of the Qing Dynasty were tumultuous. Regional warlords fought among themselves for territory, and the Nationalist Party, the Kuomintang (KMT) (Guomindang in modern Pinyin)—which had helped to overthrow the Qing Dynasty—battled them for control. After Japan was given land in China following the Paris Peace Conference (1919), a radical group known as the May Fourth Movement demanded change, and the Chinese Communist Party (CCP) emerged.

In 1924, the KMT set up a government in Guangzhou and built up an army. In 1926, the new leader, Chiang Kai-shek, then began a military campaign to crush the warlords and unite China. The CCP initially helped, but in 1927, fearing a power struggle, Chiang turned against them, massacring communists in Shanghai. This outburst led to years of civil war (see pp.310–311). The KMT and the CCP came to an uneasy truce in 1937, when Japan invaded the country and began seizing territory.

CHINA

During the first half of the 20th century, China experienced constant turbulence, with battles fought against regional warlords in attempts to unify the vast nation, frequent struggles between the nationalist and communist parties, and the ever-present threat of Japanese invasion.

TIMELINE

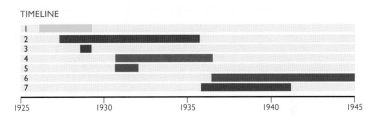

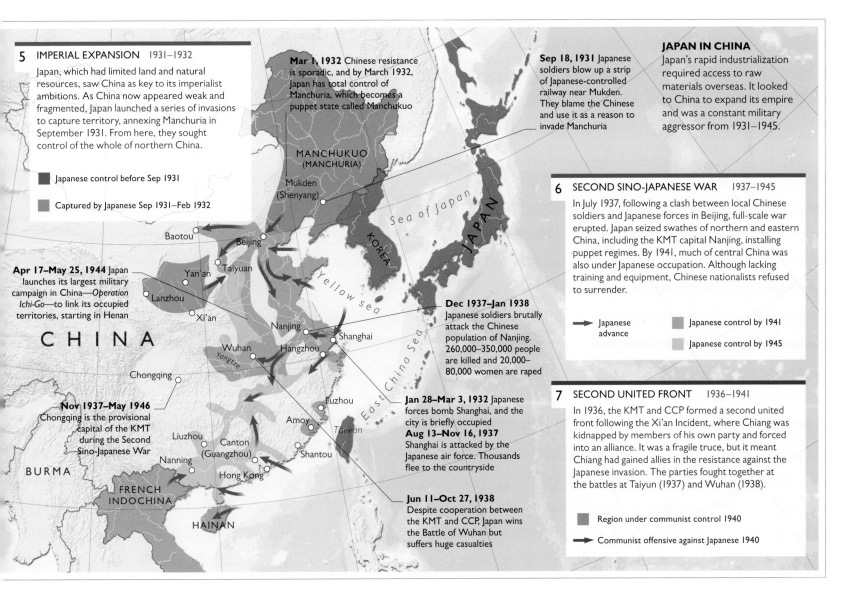

5 IMPERIAL EXPANSION 1931–1932

Japan, which had limited land and natural resources, saw China as key to its imperialist ambitions. As China now appeared weak and fragmented, Japan launched a series of invasions to capture territory, annexing Manchuria in September 1931. From here, they sought control of the whole of northern China.

▪ Japanese control before Sep 1931

▪ Captured by Japanese Sep 1931–Feb 1932

Mar 1, 1932 Chinese resistance is sporadic, and by March 1932, Japan has total control of Manchuria, which becomes a puppet state called Manchukuo

Apr 17–May 25, 1944 Japan launches its largest military campaign in China—*Operation Ichi-Go*—to link its occupied territories, starting in Henan

Nov 1937–May 1946 Chongqing is the provisional capital of the KMT during the Second Sino-Japanese War

Dec 1937–Jan 1938 Japanese soldiers brutally attack the Chinese population of Nanjing. 260,000–350,000 people are killed and 20,000–80,000 women are raped

Jan 28–Mar 3, 1932 Japanese forces bomb Shanghai, and the city is briefly occupied

Aug 13–Nov 16, 1937 Shanghai is attacked by the Japanese air force. Thousands flee to the countryside

Jun 11–Oct 27, 1938 Despite cooperation between the KMT and CCP, Japan wins the Battle of Wuhan but suffers huge casualties

Sep 18, 1931 Japanese soldiers blow up a strip of Japanese-controlled railway near Mukden. They blame the Chinese and use it as a reason to invade Manchuria

JAPAN IN CHINA

Japan's rapid industrialization required access to raw materials overseas. It looked to China to expand its empire and was a constant military aggressor from 1931–1945.

6 SECOND SINO-JAPANESE WAR 1937–1945

In July 1937, following a clash between local Chinese soldiers and Japanese forces in Beijing, full-scale war erupted. Japan seized swathes of northern and eastern China, including the KMT capital Nanjing, installing puppet regimes. By 1941, much of central China was also under Japanese occupation. Although lacking training and equipment, Chinese nationalists refused to surrender.

→ Japanese advance

▪ Japanese control by 1941

▪ Japanese control by 1945

7 SECOND UNITED FRONT 1936–1941

In 1936, the KMT and CCP formed a second united front following the Xi'an Incident, where Chiang was kidnapped by members of his own party and forced into an alliance. It was a fragile truce, but it meant Chiang had gained allies in the resistance against the Japanese invasion. The parties fought together at the battles at Taiyun (1937) and Wuhan (1938).

▪ Region under communist control 1940

➤ Communist offensive against Japanese 1940

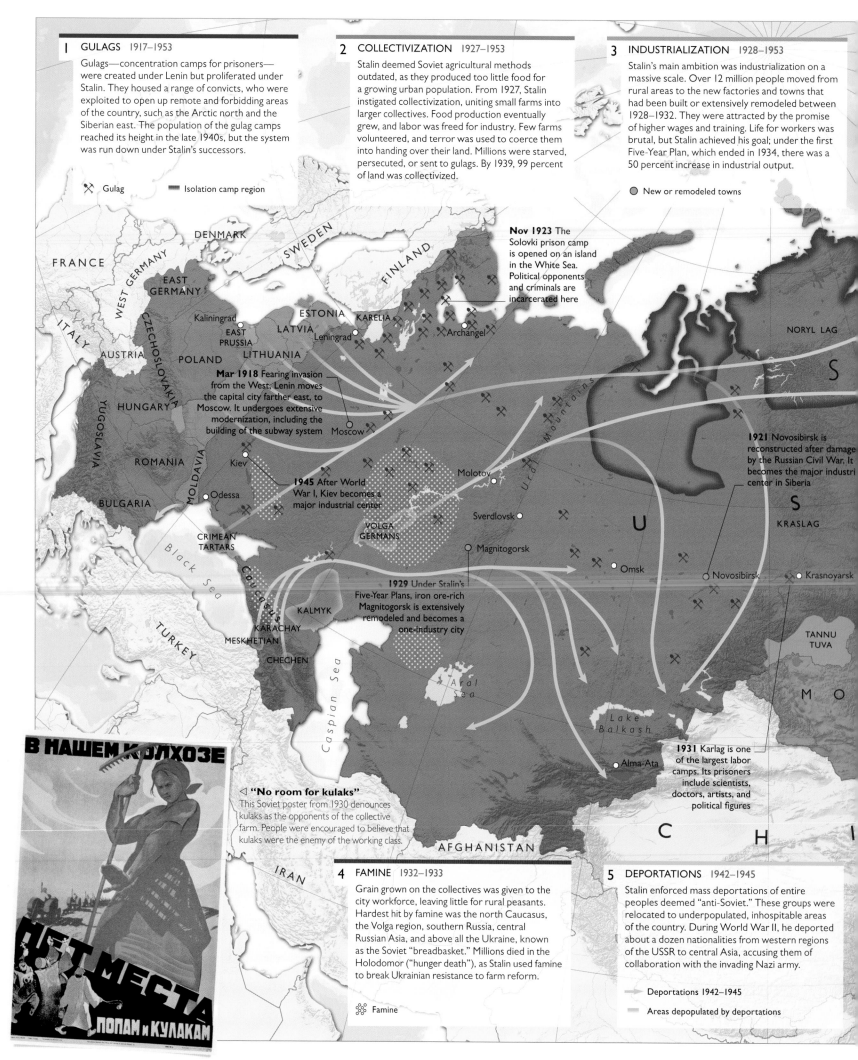

1 GULAGS 1917–1953

Gulags—concentration camps for prisoners—were created under Lenin but proliferated under Stalin. They housed a range of convicts, who were exploited to open up remote and forbidding areas of the country, such as the Arctic north and the Siberian east. The population of the gulag camps reached its height in the late 1940s, but the system was run down under Stalin's successors.

⚒ Gulag   ▬ Isolation camp region

2 COLLECTIVIZATION 1927–1953

Stalin deemed Soviet agricultural methods outdated, as they produced too little food for a growing urban population. From 1927, Stalin instigated collectivization, uniting small farms into larger collectives. Food production eventually grew, and labor was freed for industry. Few farms volunteered, and terror was used to coerce them into handing over their land. Millions were starved, persecuted, or sent to gulags. By 1939, 99 percent of land was collectivized.

3 INDUSTRIALIZATION 1928–1953

Stalin's main ambition was industrialization on a massive scale. Over 12 million people moved from rural areas to the new factories and towns that had been built or extensively remodeled between 1928–1932. They were attracted by the promise of higher wages and training. Life for workers was brutal, but Stalin achieved his goal; under the first Five-Year Plan, which ended in 1934, there was a 50 percent increase in industrial output.

◉ New or remodeled towns

Nov 1923 The Solovki prison camp is opened on an island in the White Sea. Political opponents and criminals are incarcerated here

Mar 1918 Fearing invasion from the West, Lenin moves the capital city farther east, to Moscow. It undergoes extensive modernization, including the building of the subway system

1945 After World War I, Kiev becomes a major industrial center

1921 Novosibirsk is reconstructed after damage by the Russian Civil War. It becomes the major industri center in Siberia

1929 Under Stalin's Five-Year Plans, iron ore-rich Magnitogorsk is extensively remodeled and becomes a one-industry city

1931 Karlag is one of the largest labor camps. Its prisoners include scientists, doctors, artists, and political figures

◁ **"No room for kulaks"**
This Soviet poster from 1930 denounces kulaks as the opponents of the collective farm. People were encouraged to believe that kulaks were the enemy of the working class.

4 FAMINE 1932–1933

Grain grown on the collectives was given to the city workforce, leaving little for rural peasants. Hardest hit by famine was the north Caucasus, the Volga region, southern Russia, central Russian Asia, and above all the Ukraine, known as the Soviet "breadbasket." Millions died in the Holodomor ("hunger death"), as Stalin used famine to break Ukrainian resistance to farm reform.

⬡ Famine

5 DEPORTATIONS 1942–1945

Stalin enforced mass deportations of entire peoples deemed "anti-Soviet." These groups were relocated to underpopulated, inhospitable areas of the country. During World War II, he deported about a dozen nationalities from western regions of the USSR to central Asia, accusing them of collaboration with the invading Nazi army.

→ Deportations 1942–1945

▬ Areas depopulated by deportations

1922 A series of gulags is set up in the Kolyma region, an area rich in gold and tin

ARCTIC OCEAN

KOLYMA

Yakutsk

Siberia

USSR

SAKHALIN

BURLAG

Lake Baikal

KHSIBLAG

MANCHURIA

Vladivostok

MONGOLIA

JAPAN

NORTH KOREA

Dairen

SOUTH KOREA

CHINA

THE SOVIET UNION UNDER STALIN

Under Stalin's rule, Russia was transformed. Entire peoples were relocated, land was taken from eastern Europe, and industrialized areas grew across the country.

KEY

- ◼ Pre-World War II Soviet territory
- ◼ Pre-World War II satellite states
- ◼ Territory annexed to USSR 1939–1940
- ◼ Territory annexed to USSR 1944–1945
- ◼ Post-World War II satellite states

TIMELINE

	1915	1925	1935	1945	1955
1					
2					
3					
4					
5					

SOVIET UNION UNDER STALIN

With civil war at an end by 1922, Joseph Stalin had ambitions to transform the newly formed Soviet Union into an industrialized, modern society. He achieved extraordinary economic growth for Russia but became one of the most brutal tyrants of the 20th century.

After the death of Vladimir Lenin in 1924, Stalin manipulated his way to becoming leader of the USSR. Stalin wanted to transform the country into an international power, but this required rapid industrial growth. To achieve this, he launched a series of Five-Year Plans, starting in 1928. He began by taking farms from wealthy peasant landowners (kulaks), combining them into vast farms to be run collectively, providing more crops for the population. When these measures were resisted, he unleashed a wave of terror across the countryside. Millions of kulaks were deported, sent to labor camps, or deliberately starved when their grain was seized.

Ever fearful of dissent, Stalin launched a campaign of terror from 1936–1938 to wipe out anyone who might oppose him. During this "Great Terror," the gulag concentration camp system was expanded, with hundreds of thousands executed after a brief trial. Meanwhile, Stalin promoted himself as the "Father of the People." He rallied his troops against a German invasion in World War II (see pp.296–297), and after the war, he expanded communism beyond the USSR. By the 1950s, a modern Russia had emerged, but at a terrible cost.

"The death of one man is a tragedy. The death of a million is a statistic."

JOSEPH STALIN, LEADER OF THE USSR

JOSEPH STALIN
1878–1953

Joseph Stalin began his rise to power in 1905, when he befriended Vladimir Lenin. His political career was quite unpredictable; in 1917, he had been a minor figure in the Bolshevik Revolution, but when he was made General Secretary of the Party in 1922, he used this role to expand his power. Once leader, he set about making the USSR a great industrial power. He used propaganda to build a cult of personality, which reached its peak during World War II, when he led the USSR to victory over Germany. After the war, Stalin led the USSR into a Cold War with its former allies.

THE SPANISH CIVIL WAR

The Spanish Civil War (1936–1939) epitomized the struggle between the old and new political orders. A prequel to World War II, it ushered in a new and horrific form of warfare that would come to define future conflicts in the 20th century.

Spain in the 1930s was a divided country, split between Church and State, rich and poor, town and countryside. Politics was also polarized. On one side was the left-wing Popular Front (Republicans), made up of socialists, communists, liberals, and anarchists. On the other side was the right-wing National Front (Nationalists), supported by the Falange (a Spanish fascist party), monarchists, and some Catholics.

On February 16, 1936, the Republicans narrowly won a general election. Fearing a communist revolution, General Francisco Franco, a career army officer and one of the Nationalist leaders, launched a military uprising in Spanish Morocco and across southwestern Spain. Pro-government groups rallied against the Nationalist rebels, but Franco received significant help from Nazi Germany and Fascist Italy, both keen to stop the spread of communism in Europe. By November 1936, Franco's troops had made it to the outskirts of Madrid, where support for the Republicans was strong. Unable to capture the city, the Nationalists laid siege to Madrid for two and a half years.

The Republicans continued to control eastern Spain and much of the southeast. However, Franco's forces were better coordinated, and areas under Republican control gradually shrank. The Nationalist victory at the Battle of Teruel (December 1937–February 1938) was a turning point in the war, and at the Battle of the Ebro (July–November 1938), the Republican troops were all but wiped out. By spring 1939, the bitter conflict was over, and Franco's government was recognized by most of Europe.

> *"Better to die on one's feet than to live on one's knees."*
>
> DOLORES IBARRURI, REPUBLICAN, JULY 18, 1936

GENERAL FRANCO
1892–1975

Born into a military family, General Francisco Franco became the youngest general in the Spanish Army in 1926. Franco led the Nationalist forces to victory in the Spanish Civil War, and then became the head of state in Spain from 1939 until his death in 1975. Although he sympathized with the Axis powers, Franco kept Spain out of World War II, and under his rule, the country became more industrialized and prosperous. However, he was a ruthless military dictator who presided over a totalitarian regime.

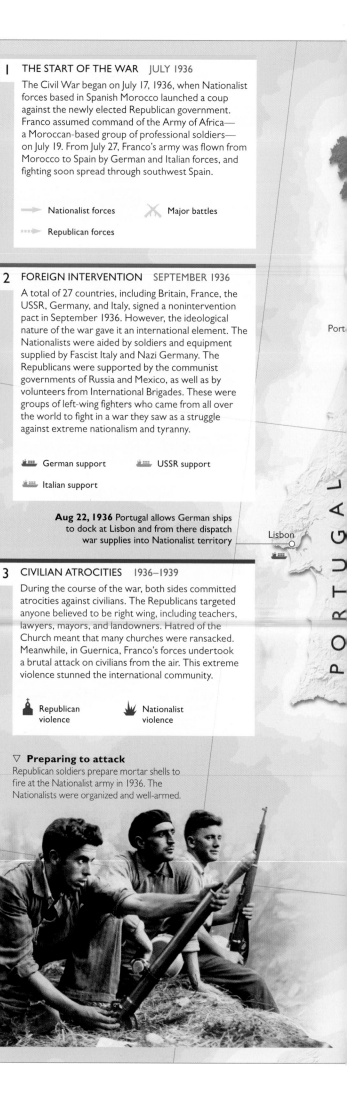

1 THE START OF THE WAR   JULY 1936

The Civil War began on July 17, 1936, when Nationalist forces based in Spanish Morocco launched a coup against the newly elected Republican government. Franco assumed command of the Army of Africa—a Moroccan-based group of professional soldiers—on July 19. From July 27, Franco's army was flown from Morocco to Spain by German and Italian forces, and fighting soon spread through southwest Spain.

→ Nationalist forces   ✕ Major battles

···▶ Republican forces

2 FOREIGN INTERVENTION   SEPTEMBER 1936

A total of 27 countries, including Britain, France, the USSR, Germany, and Italy, signed a nonintervention pact in September 1936. However, the ideological nature of the war gave it an international element. The Nationalists were aided by soldiers and equipment supplied by Fascist Italy and Nazi Germany. The Republicans were supported by the communist governments of Russia and Mexico, as well as by volunteers from International Brigades. These were groups of left-wing fighters who came from all over the world to fight in a war they saw as a struggle against extreme nationalism and tyranny.

🚢 German support   🚢 USSR support

🚢 Italian support

Aug 22, 1936 Portugal allows German ships to dock at Lisbon and from there dispatch war supplies into Nationalist territory

3 CIVILIAN ATROCITIES   1936–1939

During the course of the war, both sides committed atrocities against civilians. The Republicans targeted anyone believed to be right wing, including teachers, lawyers, mayors, and landowners. Hatred of the Church meant that many churches were ransacked. Meanwhile, in Guernica, Franco's forces undertook a brutal attack on civilians from the air. This extreme violence stunned the international community.

🛐 Republican violence   🌿 Nationalist violence

▽ **Preparing to attack**
Republican soldiers prepare mortar shells to fire at the Nationalist army in 1936. The Nationalists were organized and well-armed.

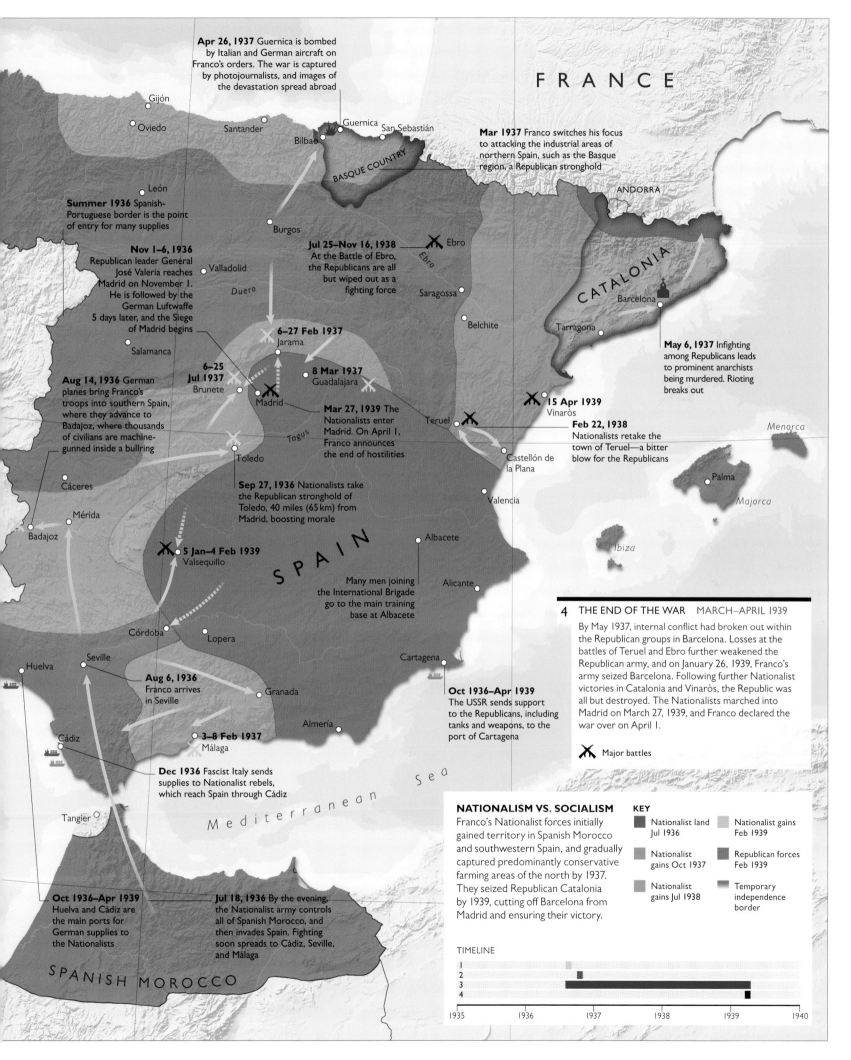

F R A N C E

Apr 26, 1937 Guernica is bombed by Italian and German aircraft on Franco's orders. The war is captured by photojournalists, and images of the devastation spread abroad

Mar 1937 Franco switches his focus to attacking the industrial areas of northern Spain, such as the Basque region, a Republican stronghold

Gijón

Oviedo

Santander

Guernica San Sebastián

Bilbao

BASQUE COUNTRY

ANDORRA

León

Summer 1936 Spanish-Portuguese border is the point of entry for many supplies

Burgos

Jul 25–Nov 16, 1938 At the Battle of Ebro, the Republicans are all but wiped out as a fighting force

Ebro

CATALONIA

Nov 1–6, 1936 Republican leader General José Valeria reaches Madrid on November 1. He is followed by the German Luftwaffe 5 days later, and the Siege of Madrid begins

Valladolid

Duero

Ebro

Saragossa

Barcelona

Belchite

Tarragona

May 6, 1937 Infighting among Republicans leads to prominent anarchists being murdered. Rioting breaks out

Salamanca

6–27 Feb 1937
Jarama

6–25 Jul 1937
Brunete

8 Mar 1937
Guadalajara

15 Apr 1939
Vinaròs

Aug 14, 1936 German planes bring Franco's troops into southern Spain, where they advance to Badajoz, where thousands of civilians are machine-gunned inside a bullring

Madrid

Mar 27, 1939 The Nationalists enter Madrid. On April 1, Franco announces the end of hostilities

Teruel

Feb 22, 1938 Nationalists retake the town of Teruel—a bitter blow for the Republicans

Menorca

Tagus

Toledo

Castellón de la Plana

Cáceres

Sep 27, 1936 Nationalists take the Republican stronghold of Toledo, 40 miles (65 km) from Madrid, boosting morale

Valencia

Palma

Majorca

Mérida

S P A I N

Albacete

Ibiza

Badajoz

5 Jan–4 Feb 1939
Valsequillo

Many men joining the International Brigade go to the main training base at Albacete

Alicante

THE END OF THE WAR MARCH–APRIL 1939

By May 1937, internal conflict had broken out within the Republican groups in Barcelona. Losses at the battles of Teruel and Ebro further weakened the Republican army, and on January 26, 1939, Franco's army seized Barcelona. Following further Nationalist victories in Catalonia and Vinaròs, the Republic was all but destroyed. The Nationalists marched into Madrid on March 27, 1939, and Franco declared the war over on April 1.

Córdoba

Lopera

Cartagena

Oct 1936–Apr 1939 The USSR sends support to the Republicans, including tanks and weapons, to the port of Cartagena

Huelva

Seville

Aug 6, 1936 Franco arrives in Seville

Granada

Almería

Major battles

Cádiz

3–8 Feb 1937
Málaga

M e d i t e r r a n e a n   S e a

Dec 1936 Fascist Italy sends supplies to Nationalist rebels, which reach Spain through Cádiz

Tangier

NATIONALISM VS. SOCIALISM

Franco's Nationalist forces initially gained territory in Spanish Morocco and southwestern Spain, and gradually captured predominantly conservative farming areas of the north by 1937. They seized Republican Catalonia by 1939, cutting off Barcelona from Madrid and ensuring their victory.

KEY

Nationalist land Jul 1936

Nationalist gains Feb 1939

Nationalist gains Oct 1937

Republican forces Feb 1939

Nationalist gains Jul 1938

Temporary independence border

Oct 1936–Apr 1939 Huelva and Cádiz are the main ports for German supplies to the Nationalists

Jul 18, 1936 By the evening, the Nationalist army controls all of Spanish Morocco, and then invades Spain. Fighting soon spreads to Cádiz, Seville, and Málaga

S P A N I S H   M O R O C C O

TIMELINE

1
2
3
4

1935   1936   1937   1938   1939   1940

WORLD WAR II

A European and Asian conflict that became a global war, World War II (1939–1945) was the most brutal conflict in history, engulfing the world in a struggle over ideology and national sovereignty. It was also the costliest war in terms of human life—at least 55 million people were killed in battle, in concentration camps, and in bombed-out cities. The war marked a watershed in world history.

▽ **Paris under siege**
Seen here in front of the iconic Eiffel Tower, Adolf Hitler, flanked by German officials, takes a tour of conquered Paris in June 1940, marking the end of the French Campaign.

The treaties meant to bring peace after World War I (see pp. 274–275) sowed the seeds for future conflict. Germany was made to pay substantial war reparations. In 1923, the currency collapsed, impoverishing millions, and in 1929–1932, the Great Depression (see pp.286–287) plunged Germany into severe recession. Here, and elsewhere in Europe, people were disenchanted with liberal politics and weak governments that polarized political opinion into the Right and Left. Right-wing politics prevailed in Italy, Germany, and Japan—known collectively as the Axis powers, although each had its own ambitions for territorial expansion.

The Axis aggression

Japan invaded Manchuria then attacked the rest of China; Italy overran Abyssinia (modern Ethiopia); and in Germany, Adolf Hitler pursued his plans to unite all German-speaking people in one country. In March 1938, Germany annexed Austria. The German-speaking districts of Czechoslovakia— the Sudetenland—were occupied next. In September 1939, Hitler invaded Poland, convinced that Britain and France would do nothing. To his surprise, both countries declared war.

The invasion of Poland lasted just over a month. Hitler put aside his hatred of communists to work in cooperation with the Soviets, who attacked Poland from the east. The world watched in shock as Germany attacked Denmark and Norway then France, Belgium, and the Netherlands. Within 6 weeks, France had fallen. Hitler then turned his sights on Britain. His plans to invade were abandoned, however, after the *Luftwaffe*—the German air force—failed to win the Battle of Britain (1940).

Total war

The European War became a world war. In June 1940, Italy declared war on Britain and France. "Total War" was brought to civilians when bombing raids pulverized European cities. With men joining the army, women were recruited to work on farms and in factories. Europe experienced food shortages, which led to food rationing. Despite having signed strategic pacts with the USSR in the past, Germany invaded Russia in June 1941, and Britain gained a new ally.

As German troops swept into the USSR, they inflicted a campaign of extermination against communists. Then, in December 1941, the US entered the war after its naval

△ **Japanese ambitions**
Determined to become a major colonial power, Japan built up the largest navy in the Pacific Ocean. This recruitment poster seeks pilots for its aircraft carriers.

THEATERS OF CONFLICT

World War II became a global war but had two main theaters— Europe and the Pacific. In Europe, the war started with the Western Front as the German "blitzkrieg" swept through Western Europe into France. The Eastern Front opened when Germany turned on the USSR. The Pacific theater, fought over by the Allies and Japan, stretched throughout eastern China and Southeast Asia, including the Pacific Ocean and its islands. The role of the US in this arena was pivotal.

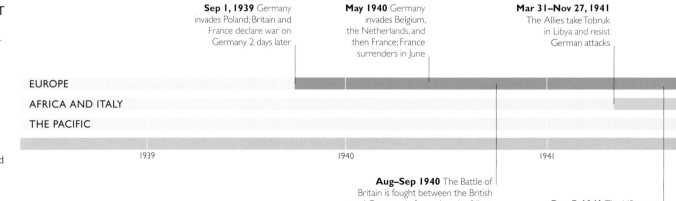

Sep 1, 1939 Germany invades Poland; Britain and France declare war on Germany 2 days later

May 1940 Germany invades Belgium, the Netherlands, and then France; France surrenders in June

Mar 31–Nov 27, 1941 The Allies take Tobruk in Libya and resist German attacks

EUROPE

AFRICA AND ITALY

THE PACIFIC

1939   1940   1941

Aug–Sep 1940 The Battle of Britain is fought between the British and German air forces, but the failure to defeat the British compels Hitler to abandon plans to invade England

Dec 7, 1941 The US enters the war as Japan attacks Pearl Harbor, Hawaii

◁ **Gateway of death**
Millions of unsuspecting Jews arrived by train at the infamous death camp, Auschwitz-Birkenau, where they were gassed. It became a memorial site after the war.

base at Pearl Harbor in the Hawaiian Islands was attacked by Japan. Japan won quick victories in the Pacific and dominated the region. In North Africa, British troops struggled against German and Italian forces. By the summer of 1942, Hitler was at the height of his power, but in November, the German General Erwin Rommel was stopped at El Alamein in Egypt. Soviet victories at Stalingrad and Kursk in 1943 destroyed the German sixth army, which was forced to surrender. This defeat marked the beginning of a retreat that was to end in Berlin.

The tide turns

A strategy was devised by the Allies—Britain, France, the US, and the USSR—in 1943 to free Europe. While the USSR drove the Germans back in the east, and the British and Americans advanced through Italy, a huge Allied force landed in Normandy in June 1944. Almost a year later, it reached the River Elbe in northern Germany. As Soviet troops took Berlin, Hitler committed suicide on April 30, 1945. Germany surrendered a week later. The war was over in Europe but not in the Pacific, where Americans fought island by island. Japan finally surrendered soon after Hiroshima and Nagasaki were destroyed by American atomic bombs in August 1945 (see pp.306–307).

World War II changed the world forever. New military technology had shown the capacity for massive destruction, with U-boats, jet aircraft, and, ultimately, nuclear bombs. Germany's Nazis displayed new, efficient, and horrific methods of mass killing in their genocide of almost 6 million Jews. Countries went bankrupt, major cities were destroyed, and the great European empires were on their last legs. Representatives of 50 nations met in 1945 to form the United Nations in the hope that out of this devastation, a new era of international understanding could begin.

▽ **Bombed city**
Ferocious bombing raids on major cities defined WWII. This 1945 photograph shows the German city of Dresden, which was among the last to be destroyed in the war.

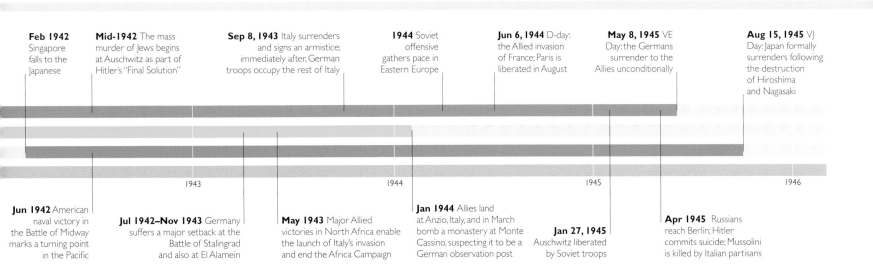

Feb 1942 Singapore falls to the Japanese

Mid-1942 The mass murder of Jews begins at Auschwitz as part of Hitler's "Final Solution"

Sep 8, 1943 Italy surrenders and signs an armistice; immediately after, German troops occupy the rest of Italy

1944 Soviet offensive gathers pace in Eastern Europe

Jun 6, 1944 D-day: the Allied invasion of France; Paris is liberated in August

May 8, 1945 VE Day: the Germans surrender to the Allies unconditionally

Aug 15, 1945 VJ Day: Japan formally surrenders following the destruction of Hiroshima and Nagasaki

1943   1944   1945   1946

Jun 1942 American naval victory in the Battle of Midway marks a turning point in the Pacific

Jul 1942–Nov 1943 Germany suffers a major setback at the Battle of Stalingrad and also at El Alamein

May 1943 Major Allied victories in North Africa enable the launch of Italy's invasion and end the Africa Campaign

Jan 1944 Allies land at Anzio, Italy, and in March bomb a monastery at Monte Cassino, suspecting it to be a German observation post

Jan 27, 1945 Auschwitz liberated by Soviet troops

Apr 1945 Russians reach Berlin; Hitler commits suicide; Mussolini is killed by Italian partisans

8 THE BATTLE OF STALINGRAD
AUGUST 1942–FEBRUARY 1943

A new Axis offensive in 1942 brought them to the industrial city of Stalingrad. In one of the largest and bloodiest battles of the war, almost 800,000 civilians and soldiers were killed. It ended with a humiliating German surrender, and this marked a turning point in WWII.

◎ Siege

7 INVASION OF THE SOVIET UNION
JUNE–DECEMBER 1941

Germany, along with its Axis allies, attacked the Soviet Union with 4 million troops, on a front of almost 1,000 miles. In 3 months, the invaders had almost reached Moscow and Leningrad, but here they failed to win complete victories. The advance was halted in December 1941.

◎ Siege

6 BRITAIN UNDER ATTACK
JULY 1940–MAY 1941

Hitler's plans to invade Britain were scuppered when Germany failed to beat Britain in the skies in 1940. Hitler switched to bombing Britain's cities, but he abandoned the campaign in May 1941 in favor of invading the Soviet Union.

✸ German bombing raids

5 ITALY'S CAMPAIGNS
JUNE 1940–FEBRUARY 1942

Italy invaded southern France in June 1940, keen to profit from German successes and to give Italy a place at any later peace conference. To gain control of the Mediterranean, Mussolini then attacked British and British Empire forces in north Africa and attempted to invade Greece. The Italians were repelled in both Egypt and Greece, and Hitler had to divert German troops in support of his ally.

➡ Italian advance ┅➤ Allied offensive

AXIS CONQUESTS 1939–1943

Germany launched offensives in both eastern and western Europe, while Italy advanced in the Mediterranean. German forces used armor and aircraft to great effect.

KEY

■ Axis powers	■ Axis conquests 1941
■ Axis satellites	■ Allied powers
■ Axis conquests 1939	→ German advance
■ Axis conquests 1940	▽ Airborne attacks

TIMELINE

1 2 3 4 5 6 7 8

1939   1940   1941   1942   1943   1944

Map labels and annotations:

ICELAND

Apr 1940 German forces enter Norwegian waters, starting a two-month conflict that ends in defeat for the Allies

Apr 9, 1940 German paratroopers land in Norway. It is the first airborne attack in history

Petsamo

Narvik

Sep 1941–Jan 1944 The 900-day Siege of Leningrad by German forces results in over 1 million civilian deaths

Suomussalm

Faeroe Islands

Åndalsnes

NORWAY

SWEDEN

FINLAND

Shetland Islands

Sep 7, 1940–May 16, 1941 Hitler bombs Britain's cities, in an offensive known as The Blitz

Oslo

Stavanger

Helsinki

Lening

North Sea

ESTONIA

Glasgow

Belfast

IRELAND

BRITAIN

Liverpool

Manchester Hull

Birmingham

Bristol

Plymouth Coventry

Southampton London

Dunkirk

DENMARK

Copenhagen

Baltic Sea

LATVIA

LITHUANIA

Königsberg

Danzig EAST PRUSSIA Wilno

Sep 1–27, 1939 Polish forces atte to defend Warsaw but are outgunne

Jul 10–Sep 6, 1940 During the Battle of Britain, the Luftwaffe (German airforce) target airfields and ports along the English Channel

NETHER-LANDS

Hamburg

Berlin

May–Jun 1940 335,000 British and French soldiers are evacuated from Dunkirk

Rotterdam

Essen

BELGIUM GERMANY

Warsaw

Sep 17, 1939 Soviet forces attack Poland from the east

Jun 14, 1940 German forces occupy Paris

Paris Sedan

LUXEMBOURG

POLAND

Orléans

Prague

BOHEMIA AND MORAVIA

Cracow

Lwów

UKRAINE

Kie

FRANCE

Munich Linz

Vienna

SLOVAKIA

Vichy SWITZERLAND

AUSTRIA (OSTMARK)

Bratislava

Lyon

Budapest

1940 To Hungary

VICHY FRANCE

Alps

Milan

HUNGARY

ROMANIA

Madrid

Marseille

Pyrenees

Zagreb

CROATIA

Belgrade

Ploeşti

Bucharest

SPAIN

Corsica

Balearic Islands

Rome

Sardinia

ITALY

Sarajevo

YUGOSLAVIA

1940 To Bulga

BULGARIA

Istanbul

Tirana

ALBANIA

GREECE

Apr 6, 1941 Germany invades Yugoslavia, allowing it to attack, and ultimately seize, Greece

Aegean Sea

Atlas Mountains

SPANISH NORTH AFRICA

MOROCCO ALGERIA

Tunis

TUNISIA

Sicily

Malta

Athens

Oct 1940 Italy attacks Greece via Albania, which it had annexed in 1939, but the invasion fails

Crete

Mediterranean Sea

Tripoli

LIBYA

Benghazi

El Agheila

Tobruk Sidi Barrani Alexandr

EGYPT

Jan 1941 Allied forces seize the key port of Tobruk from Italian forces

Sep 13, 1940 A second Italian offensive into British-occupied Egypt is a failure

1 INVASION OF POLAND   SEPTEMBER 1939

Germany invaded Poland from the west on September 1, 1939, and besieged Warsaw with heavy aerial and artillery bombardment. The Soviet Union then attacked from the east. With the fall of Warsaw on September 27, Polish independence was over, and the country was divided between the two aggressors. At least 70,000 Poles lost their lives in 30 days.

✺ Bombing of Warsaw

2 SOVIET CONQUESTS
NOVEMBER 1939–JUNE 1940

After Poland, Stalin invaded Finland. The Finns held out for some time but by March 1940 were made to give up strategically important territories, leaving them bitter for revenge. In June 1940, Stalin annexed Estonia, Latvia, and Lithuania, countries that Hitler also wanted for Germany.

— Soviet conquests 1939–1940

Oct 2, 1941–Jan 7, 1942 Soviet counteroffensives drive Axis armies back from Moscow

Jun 28, 1942– Feb 2, 1943 Soviet forces successfully defend Stalingrad city. Axis forces are left exhausted

△ Messerschmitt Bf 109
One of the most advanced aircraft in 1939, this fighter plane was key to Germany's early successes. It provided air support for the armored vehicles that spearheaded Germany's "blitzkrieg," or high-speed, attacks.

3 INVASION OF SCANDINAVIA AND THE LOW COUNTRIES   APRIL–JUNE 1940

In the spring of 1940, an emboldened Germany successfully invaded Denmark and attacked Norway with its navy and pioneering paratroop operations. In May, more than 2 million German troops on land and in the air invaded Belgium, Luxembourg, and the Netherlands.

4 THE FALL OF FRANCE   MAY–JUNE 1940

France had fortified part of its border with the Maginot Line and sent its best armies into Belgium and the Netherlands to defend against a German attack. German armored forces cut them off by an advance through the Ardennes Forest behind them and defeated the Allies at Sedan. It was a disaster. France, under a new leader, Marshal Philippe Pétain, sued for an armistice on June 17.

Jun 1941 British forces invade Vichy France-held Lebanon and Syria to prevent Axis forces using them as bases from which to attack Egypt

— Maginot Line

AXIS POWERS ADVANCE

Between 1939 and 1942, the armies of Nazi Germany and its Axis allies conquered most of mainland Europe in a series of lightning campaigns. Germany was denied total victory by the stubborn resistance of Britain and the Soviet Union.

An agreement between two dictators, Germany's Adolf Hitler and Soviet ruler Joseph Stalin, to divide Poland between them was a prelude to World War II in Europe. When the Germans invaded Poland, Britain and France declared war on Germany but made no practical effort to aid the Poles. The initiative stayed with Hitler, who again took the offensive in spring 1940. Outclassed by the aggression and professionalism of German forces, the Allied armies were defeated on the Western Front. France surrendered, but Britain fought on under a new prime minister, Winston Churchill, surviving air attack and blockade by German submarines.

Italian dictator Benito Mussolini belatedly entered the war in June 1940, once it seemed clear Germany was winning, but his forces were of lamentably poor quality. Hitler was drawn into fighting in the Mediterranean zone to save his ally from humiliating defeat by the British.

Hitler's long-term goal, however, had always been to establish the Germans as a master race controlling the Slav lands to the east, so in June 1941, he ordered the invasion of the Soviet Union. He was joined by his allies: Italy, the second Axis power; Finland, which had recently lost land to the Soviets in their conflict of 1939–1940; and Hungary, Romania, and Slovakia, whose right-wing governments became allied to the Axis powers and were pressured into joining the Soviet invasion. Despite further victories that saw his armies occupy vast tracts of Soviet territory, by the end of 1942, it seemed that Hitler had overreached himself. The era of German triumphs came to an end at the Battle of Stalingrad in 1943.

ADOLF HITLER
1889–1945

Hitler was born in Austria, the son of a minor official. He fought in the German army in World War I and after the war became leader of the small National Socialist (Nazi) Party. The party came to prominence after Hitler attempted a coup in 1923; the coup failed, but the Nazis went on to attract mass support during the Great Depression. Appointed Chancellor of Germany in 1933, Hitler soon assumed dictatorial powers. He re-armed Germany in defiance of the Treaty of Versailles and set out to dominate Europe, but his aggressive policies led to a war that ultimately brought disaster to Germany. He died at his bunker in Berlin in April 1945.

1 GHETTOS 1939–1942

Under Nazi occupation, Jewish people living in small towns and villages were transferred to ghettos set up within the cities. The Nazis established more than 1,000 ghettos in Poland and the Soviet Union alone. Starvation and disease were rife due to food shortages and poor sanitation. In 1942, after the Nazis decided to kill the Jews, the Germans destroyed many of the ghettos and deported the Jews to death camps.

✡ Ghettos

2 POLITICAL CONTROL 1939–1945

Nazi Germany persuaded Hungary, Romania, and Bulgaria to accede to the Tripartite Pact as Axis allies. In Slovakia, Norway, and Croatia, puppet regimes were installed—these countries had their own government but with restricted autonomy and Nazi commissioners in residence. In unoccupied France, the Vichy regime was forced to accept the terms of a German-imposed armistice.

🏛 Puppet regimes

3 LABOR CONSCRIPTION 1940–1945

In all the countries occupied, Germany controlled labor and industry for its war effort; the free deployment of labor was prohibited. Laborers were issued with workbooks and either worked in plants in the occupied countries or were sent to Germany. By the end of 1944, about 8.2 million foreign civilians and prisoners of war, as well as 700,000 concentration camp prisoners, were workers in the German Reich.

✗ Forced labor conscription

7 EXTERMINATION CAMPS
1942–1945

Dedicated death camps did not come into operation until 1942, when the Nazis implemented a policy to exterminate the Jews of Europe. Most victims were killed immediately upon their arrival, in the gas chambers, but a minority were kept as slave labor. Roma people, communists, homosexuals, and other "undesirables" were included in the mass murder.

⚒ Extermination camps

6 MASS KILLINGS 1941–1943

During the invasion of the Soviet Union, the Nazis deliberately slaughtered large groups of Jews. Einsatzgruppen (mobile killing units) followed the German army as it advanced; they went directly to the home communities of Jews and massacred them. Other massacres, such as Kragujevac in Serbia and Lidice in Bohemia-Moravia, were carried out as reprisals for the killing of Nazi officials by local resistance fighters.

☠ Site and date of massacre

5 CONCENTRATION CAMPS
1933–1945

The Nazis established concentration camps in Germany on coming to power in 1933. Designed for the imprisonment of enemies of the state, concentration camps were not initially set up to kill, but victims died by starvation and physical exhaustion. Some of these camps were later converted into extermination camps, such as Majdanek in Poland, which was originally built for Soviet prisoners of war.

⚒ Concentration camps

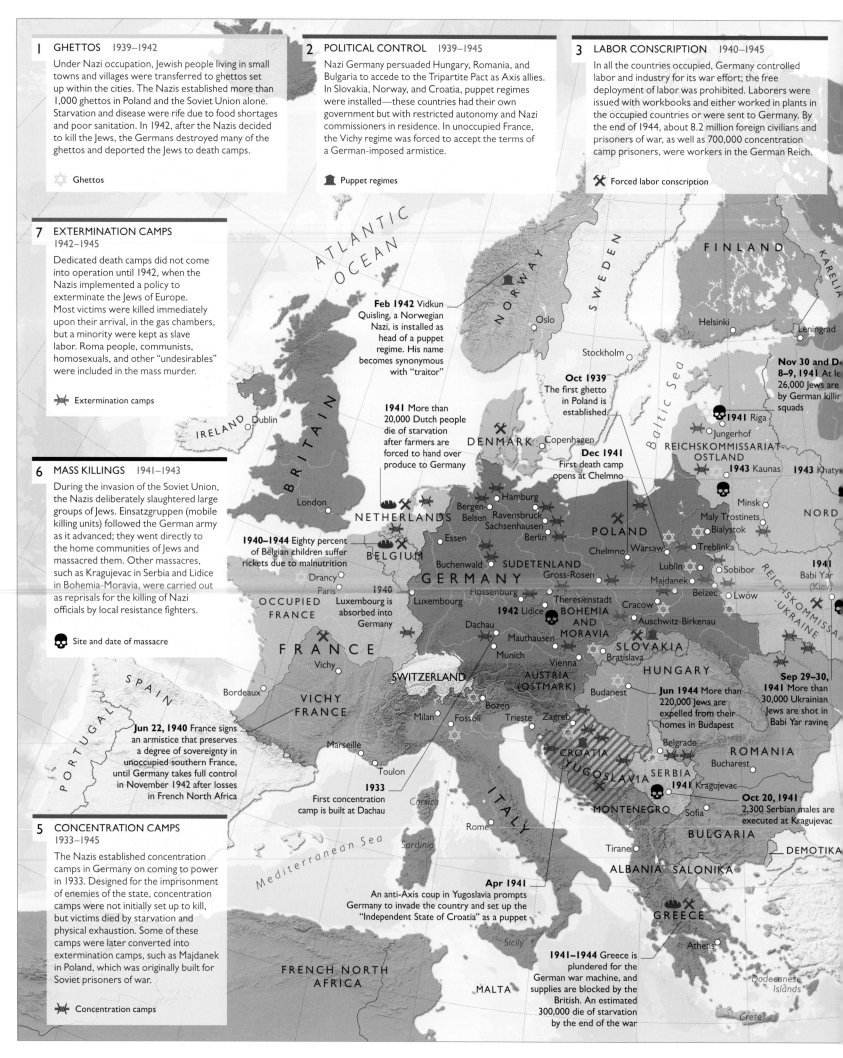

Feb 1942 Vidkun Quisling, a Norwegian Nazi, is installed as head of a puppet regime. His name becomes synonymous with "traitor"

Oct 1939 The first ghetto in Poland is established

Dec 1941 First death camp opens at Chelmno

1941 More than 20,000 Dutch people die of starvation after farmers are forced to hand over produce to Germany

Nov 30 and D 8–9, 1941 At le 26,000 Jews are by German killir squads

1941 Riga

1943 Kaunas

1943 Khaty

1940–1944 Eighty percent of Belgian children suffer rickets due to malnutrition

1940 Luxembourg is absorbed into Germany

1942 Lidice

1941 Babi Yar (Kiev)

Jun 1944 More than 220,000 Jews are expelled from their homes in Budapest

Sep 29–30, 1941 More than 30,000 Ukrainian Jews are shot in Babi Yar ravine

Jun 22, 1940 France signs an armistice that preserves a degree of sovereignty in unoccupied southern France, until Germany takes full control in November 1942 after losses in French North Africa

1933 First concentration camp is built at Dachau

Apr 1941 An anti-Axis coup in Yugoslavia prompts Germany to invade the country and set up the "Independent State of Croatia" as a puppet

1941 Kragujevac

Oct 20, 1941 2,300 Serbian males are executed at Kragujevac

1941–1944 Greece is plundered for the German war machine, and supplies are blocked by the British. An estimated 300,000 die of starvation by the end of the war

THE GREATER GERMAN REICH

By 1942, the Axis powers and their satellites dominated Europe. Germany and Italy placed some regions under military occupation, while others were absorbed to create the "Greater German Reich."

KEY

- Greater German Reich 1942
- Areas occupied by Germany and Finland
- Italy and areas occupied by Italy
- Axis satellites
- Temporary Axis satellite
- Allied territories

TIMELINE

1 2 3 4 5 6 7

1932 1934 1936 1938 1940 1942 1944 1946

△ **Holocaust survivors**
The Soviet army discovered the Nazi death camps as they advanced through eastern Europe in 1944–1945, including Auschwitz-Birkenau in southern Poland, where the children in this photo were found.

1941–1944 Approximately 2.6 million Soviet prisoners die of starvation and disease in German captivity. The people of occupied USSR are forced to eat dogs and rats and cook their food in paraffin

Moscow

Kharkov

Stalingrad

SÜD

Black Sea

Caucasus

URKEY

SYRIA

4 THE BATTLE FOR FOOD 1940–1945

At least 20 million people died of starvation during World War II. Hitler sought to create a Reich that was self-sufficient and independent of world trade. He regarded the whole of Eastern Europe as an industrial site and a food source and was prepared to let its people starve in his pursuit of Lebensraum (living space) for German-speaking peoples. In other parts of Europe, Jews and non-Germans were starved, either by deliberate German policy or by Allied blockades.

Major food shortages

OCCUPIED EUROPE

The Axis occupation of a large area of Europe in World War II brought hardship or death to many millions of the continent's inhabitants. The brutal experience of Nazi rule, and resistance to it, had profound effects on European politics and society.

The German victories early in the war were met with a mixed response in the defeated nations. In all countries, there were both anti-Nazi resistance fighters and also collaborators—those who accepted defeat and sought a role in the new German-dominated Europe. In some places, such as Croatia, Lithuania, and Ukraine, the Nazis were initially welcomed as liberators. The French government, based at Vichy, was a willing collaborator for the Germans.

Some German officials dreamed of a New Order in which all of Europe would flourish under German leadership, but Nazi leader Adolf Hitler was interested only in domination and exploitation. In practice, the Nazis simply plundered the conquered countries for their resources of food and labor, treating collaborators with contempt and suppressing opposition with terror. The worst suffering was in eastern Europe, where Hitler planned to reduce the Slavic peoples to servile status and colonize the land with German settlers in order to achieve his ultimate goal of gaining more Lebensraum (living space) for German-speaking peoples. Germany's borders were expanded and redrawn to create the Greater German Reich (realm). One-fifth of Poland's people were killed during the war, including most of its Jewish population. The only check to the Nazis' extermination of the Jews of Europe was their need to keep Jewish prisoners alive for use as slave labor.

ARMED RESISTANCE
1940 ONWARD

The hardships of life under Nazi rule inspired armed resistance movements, backed by the Allies. The largest of these forces fought in Poland, Yugoslavia, the western Soviet Union, and northern Italy after German occupation in 1943. Communists played a leading role, and in some places, notably Yugoslavia, there was bitter conflict between communist and noncommunist resistance fighters. Armed resistance in France was limited in scale but essential to French pride.

Russian resistance
Women and girls in the occupied western Soviet Union practice shooting guns in a trench in order to defend themselves.

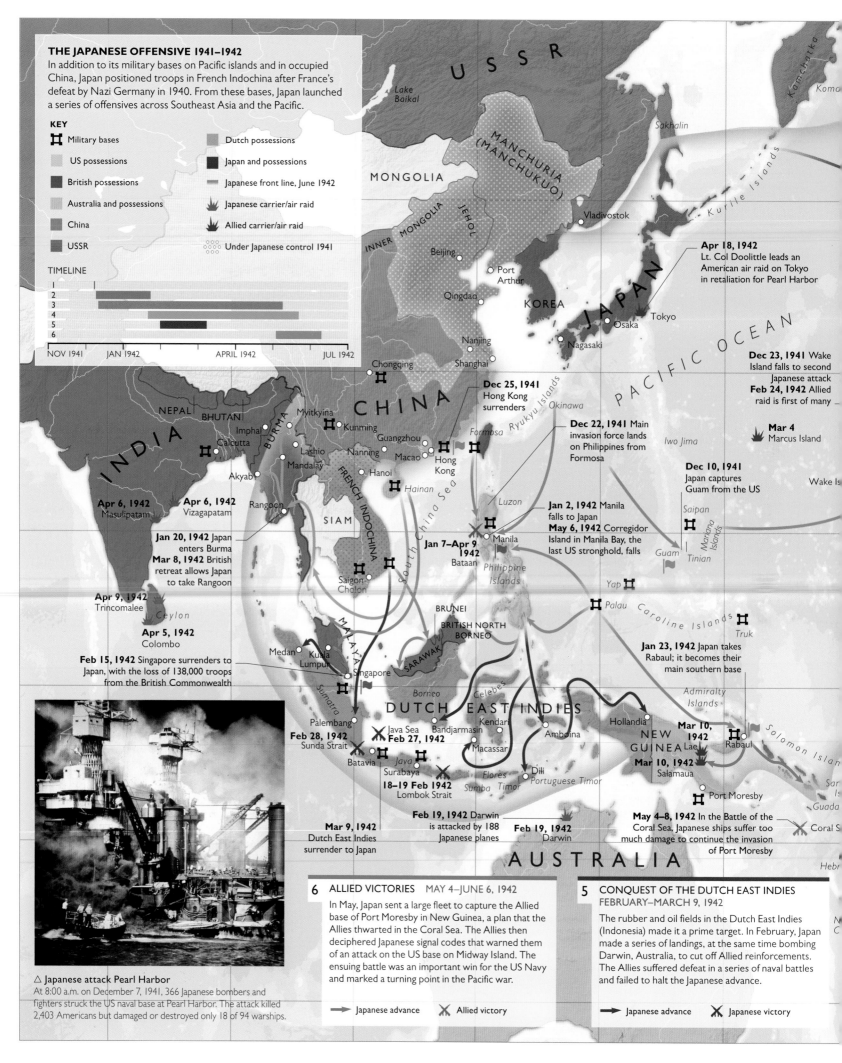

THE JAPANESE OFFENSIVE 1941–1942

In addition to its military bases on Pacific islands and in occupied China, Japan positioned troops in French Indochina after France's defeat by Nazi Germany in 1940. From these bases, Japan launched a series of offensives across Southeast Asia and the Pacific.

KEY

⊞ Military bases

▨ US possessions

■ British possessions

▨ Australia and possessions

▨ China

▨ USSR

▨ Dutch possessions

■ Japan and possessions

▬ Japanese front line, June 1942

✹ Japanese carrier/air raid

✹ Allied carrier/air raid

⊙ Under Japanese control 1941

TIMELINE

1
2
3
4
5
6

NOV 1941   JAN 1942   APRIL 1942   JUL 1942

Apr 18, 1942
Lt. Col Doolittle leads an American air raid on Tokyo in retaliation for Pearl Harbor

Dec 23, 1941 Wake Island falls to second Japanese attack
Feb 24, 1942 Allied raid is first of many

Mar 4
Marcus Island

Dec 25, 1941 Hong Kong surrenders

Dec 22, 1941 Main invasion force lands on Philippines from Formosa

Dec 10, 1941 Japan captures Guam from the US

Jan 2, 1942 Manila falls to Japan
May 6, 1942 Corregidor Island in Manila Bay, the last US stronghold, falls

Apr 6, 1942 Masulipatam

Apr 6, 1942 Vizagapatam

Jan 20, 1942 Japan enters Burma
Mar 8, 1942 British retreat allows Japan to take Rangoon

Apr 9, 1942 Trincomalee

Apr 5, 1942 Colombo

Feb 15, 1942 Singapore surrenders to Japan, with the loss of 138,000 troops from the British Commonwealth

Jan 7–Apr 9 1942 Bataan

Jan 23, 1942 Japan takes Rabaul; it becomes their main southern base

Mar 10, 1942

Mar 10, 1942 Salamaua

Feb 28, 1942 Sunda Strait

Feb 27, 1942 Java Sea

18–19 Feb 1942 Lombok Strait

Mar 9, 1942 Dutch East Indies surrender to Japan

Feb 19, 1942 Darwin is attacked by 188 Japanese planes

Feb 19, 1942 Darwin

May 4–8, 1942 In the Battle of the Coral Sea, Japanese ships suffer too much damage to continue the invasion of Port Moresby

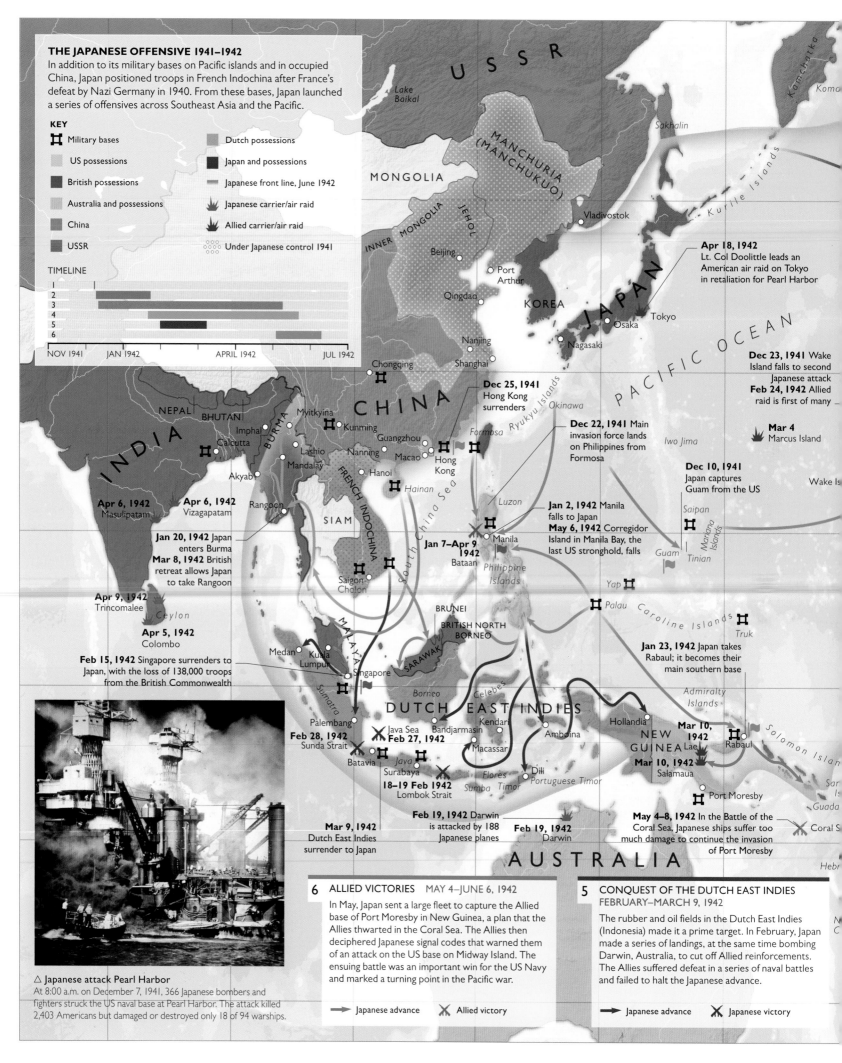

△ **Japanese attack Pearl Harbor**
At 8:00 a.m. on December 7, 1941, 366 Japanese bombers and fighters struck the US naval base at Pearl Harbor. The attack killed 2,403 Americans but damaged or destroyed only 18 of 94 warships.

6 ALLIED VICTORIES MAY 4–JUNE 6, 1942

In May, Japan sent a large fleet to capture the Allied base of Port Moresby in New Guinea, a plan that the Allies thwarted in the Coral Sea. The Allies then deciphered Japanese signal codes that warned them of an attack on the US base on Midway Island. The ensuing battle was an important win for the US Navy and marked a turning point in the Pacific war.

→ Japanese advance   ✗ Allied victory

5 CONQUEST OF THE DUTCH EAST INDIES FEBRUARY–MARCH 9, 1942

The rubber and oil fields in the Dutch East Indies (Indonesia) made it a prime target. In February, Japan made a series of landings, at the same time bombing Darwin, Australia, to cut off Allied reinforcements. The Allies suffered defeat in a series of naval battles and failed to halt the Japanese advance.

→ Japanese advance   ✗ Japanese victory

THE WAR IN THE PACIFIC

In 1931, Japan began a project to establish an extensive empire in Asia by occupying northeast China, then launching a full-scale invasion of the country in 1937. This brought Japan into conflict with the United States and the European colonial powers in the region and, in 1941, the war extended to Southeast Asia and the Pacific.

Throughout 1941, the United States tried to force Japan to abandon its invasion of China (see pp.288–289) using a policy of economic blockade. The Japanese responded with a risky plan for a wider war. Their attack on the American naval base at Pearl Harbor, Hawaii, was designed to cripple the US Pacific Fleet, leaving the Japanese Imperial Navy in command of the ocean while the Japanese army conquered Southeast Asia, the source of raw materials such as rubber and oil. Initially, the plan worked brilliantly, but the "sneak attack" on Pearl Harbor created such outrage in the US that any future compromise or peace based on acceptance of Japanese domination of Asia became inconceivable. The US entered World War II as a result.

Although Nazi Germany declared war on the United States in support of Japan, the conflicts in the Pacific and Europe remained essentially separate. Japan's defeat of the European colonial powers in Southeast Asia, especially the fall of British Singapore, was a fatal blow to white racial prestige in Asia. But the Japanese proved exploitative rulers and won little support from other Asian peoples in their "Co-Prosperity Sphere." American victory in the naval battle of Midway in June 1942 marked the end of the period of rapid Japanese expansion.

> *"Before we're through with them, the Japanese language will be spoken only in hell."*
>

GENERAL DOUGLAS MACARTHUR
1880–1964

When he was appointed US Army Commander in Southeast Asia in 1941, Douglas MacArthur already had a distinguished military career behind him, including service in World War I and a spell as US Chief of Staff. Forced to evacuate the Philippines in 1942, he famously promised "I shall return," a promise he kept in 1944. As Allied supreme commander, he received the Japanese surrender in 1945 (see pp.302–303) and played a leading role in Japan's postwar political reconstruction. Commanding UN forces in the Korean War (see pp.316–317) from 1950, MacArthur quarreled with US government policy and President Truman relieved him of his duties in 1951.

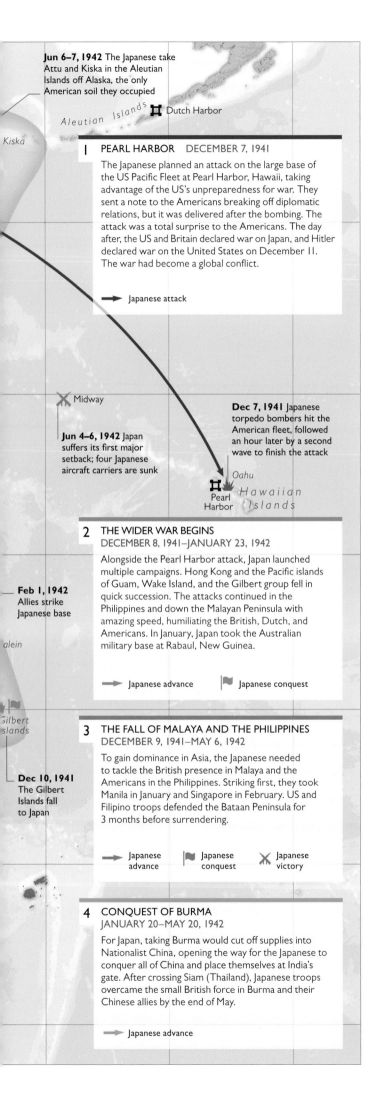

Jun 6–7, 1942 The Japanese take Attu and Kiska in the Aleutian Islands off Alaska, the only American soil they occupied

Aleutian Islands — Dutch Harbor

Kiska

1 PEARL HARBOR DECEMBER 7, 1941

The Japanese planned an attack on the large base of the US Pacific Fleet at Pearl Harbor, Hawaii, taking advantage of the US's unpreparedness for war. They sent a note to the Americans breaking off diplomatic relations, but it was delivered after the bombing. The attack was a total surprise to the Americans. The day after, the US and Britain declared war on Japan, and Hitler declared war on the United States on December 11. The war had become a global conflict.

→ Japanese attack

Midway

Jun 4–6, 1942 Japan suffers its first major setback; four Japanese aircraft carriers are sunk

Dec 7, 1941 Japanese torpedo bombers hit the American fleet, followed an hour later by a second wave to finish the attack

Oahu
Pearl Harbor *Hawaiian Islands*

2 THE WIDER WAR BEGINS
DECEMBER 8, 1941–JANUARY 23, 1942

Alongside the Pearl Harbor attack, Japan launched multiple campaigns. Hong Kong and the Pacific islands of Guam, Wake Island, and the Gilbert group fell in quick succession. The attacks continued in the Philippines and down the Malayan Peninsula with amazing speed, humiliating the British, Dutch, and Americans. In January, Japan took the Australian military base at Rabaul, New Guinea.

Feb 1, 1942 Allies strike Japanese base

alein

→ Japanese advance   ⚑ Japanese conquest

Gilbert Islands

Dec 10, 1941 The Gilbert Islands fall to Japan

3 THE FALL OF MALAYA AND THE PHILIPPINES
DECEMBER 9, 1941–MAY 6, 1942

To gain dominance in Asia, the Japanese needed to tackle the British presence in Malaya and the Americans in the Philippines. Striking first, they took Manila in January and Singapore in February. US and Filipino troops defended the Bataan Peninsula for 3 months before surrendering.

→ Japanese advance   ⚑ Japanese conquest   ✕ Japanese victory

4 CONQUEST OF BURMA
JANUARY 20–MAY 20, 1942

For Japan, taking Burma would cut off supplies into Nationalist China, opening the way for the Japanese to conquer all of China and place themselves at India's gate. After crossing Siam (Thailand), Japanese troops overcame the small British force in Burma and their Chinese allies by the end of May.

→ Japanese advance

GERMANY DEFEATED

Confronted by the combined strength of the US, the Soviet Union, and Britain, Germany was overwhelmed in the later stages of World War II. The scale of destruction mounted through the war, leaving Europe a continent of ruins and refugees.

The tide of war turned decisively against Nazi Germany and its Axis allies in the course of 1943. On the Eastern Front, Soviet armies, victorious at Stalingrad (see pp.296–297), began an unstoppable advance westward that would eventually carry them all the way to Berlin. In the Atlantic, the menace of German U-boats was overcome after years of heavy losses of shipping. US troops entered the war against Germany by landing in North Africa. Meeting up with the British in Tunisia, they crossed the Mediterranean to invade Sicily and Italy, bringing about the downfall of Germany's ally Benito Mussolini. But Nazi leader Adolf Hitler remained defiant even after the Western Allies invaded Normandy, France, in summer 1944. Surviving an attempted assassination, Hitler led a fight to the finish. The alliance between the Western powers and the Soviet Union held firm in pursuit of unconditional surrender. After a hard-fought struggle for command of the air, the US and British air forces devastated German cities. In spring 1945, Allied troops, invading Germany from east and west, took possession of a ruined country as Hitler committed suicide in his Berlin bunker.

"We have a new experience. We have victory—a remarkable and definite victory."

WINSTON CHURCHILL, ON EL ALAMEIN VICTORY, 1942

WINSTON CHURCHILL
1874–1965

In May 1940, maverick Conservative politician Winston Churchill took power in Britain at the head of a coalition government. His rousing speeches and fighting spirit sustained morale in Britain, and he worked tirelessly to maintain good relations with his fellow Allied powers, the US and the Soviet Union, during World War II. He was voted out of office in an election 2 months after victory in Europe in 1945.

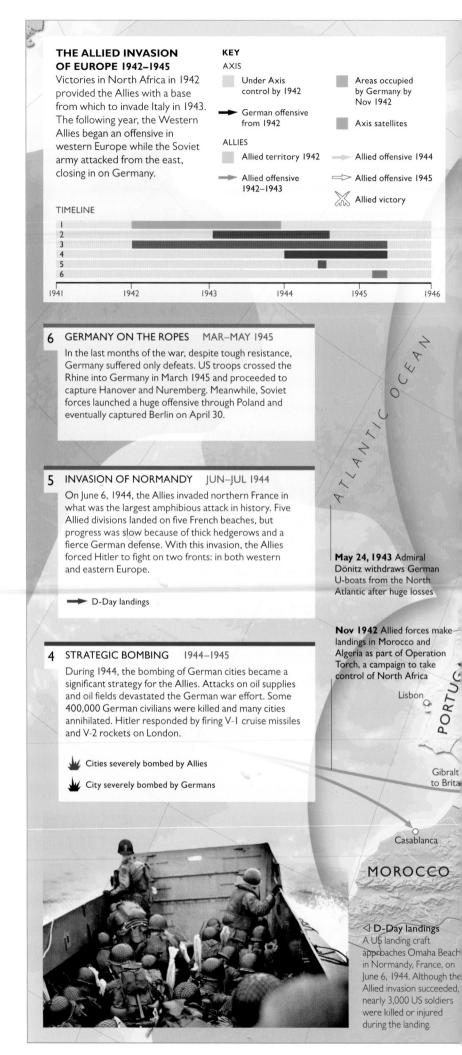

THE ALLIED INVASION OF EUROPE 1942–1945

Victories in North Africa in 1942 provided the Allies with a base from which to invade Italy in 1943. The following year, the Western Allies began an offensive in western Europe while the Soviet army attacked from the east, closing in on Germany.

KEY

AXIS
- Under Axis control by 1942
- German offensive from 1942
- Areas occupied by Germany by Nov 1942
- Axis satellites

ALLIES
- Allied territory 1942
- Allied offensive 1942–1943
- Allied offensive 1944
- Allied offensive 1945
- Allied victory

TIMELINE

1 | 2 | 3 | 4 | 5 | 6

1941 | 1942 | 1943 | 1944 | 1945 | 1946

6 GERMANY ON THE ROPES   MAR–MAY 1945

In the last months of the war, despite tough resistance, Germany suffered only defeats. US troops crossed the Rhine into Germany in March 1945 and proceeded to capture Hanover and Nuremberg. Meanwhile, Soviet forces launched a huge offensive through Poland and eventually captured Berlin on April 30.

5 INVASION OF NORMANDY   JUN–JUL 1944

On June 6, 1944, the Allies invaded northern France in what was the largest amphibious attack in history. Five Allied divisions landed on five French beaches, but progress was slow because of thick hedgerows and a fierce German defense. With this invasion, the Allies forced Hitler to fight on two fronts: in both western and eastern Europe.

→ D-Day landings

4 STRATEGIC BOMBING   1944–1945

During 1944, the bombing of German cities became a significant strategy for the Allies. Attacks on oil supplies and oil fields devastated the German war effort. Some 400,000 German civilians were killed and many cities annihilated. Hitler responded by firing V-1 cruise missiles and V-2 rockets on London.

- Cities severely bombed by Allies
- City severely bombed by Germans

May 24, 1943 Admiral Dönitz withdraws German U-boats from the North Atlantic after huge losses

Nov 1942 Allied forces make landings in Morocco and Algeria as part of Operation Torch, a campaign to take control of North Africa

ATLANTIC OCEAN

PORTUGAL

Lisbon

Gibraltar to Britain

Casablanca

MOROCCO

◁ **D-Day landings**
A US landing craft approaches Omaha Beach in Normandy, France, on June 6, 1944. Although the Allied invasion succeeded, nearly 3,000 US soldiers were killed or injured during the landing.

1 BATTLE FOR THE ATLANTIC 1942–1943

Between 1942 and 1943, millions of tons of Allied shipping was sunk by the German submarine force, or U-boats. Germany concentrated its attacks in the mid-Atlantic, out of range of Allied aircraft, but from 1943, Allied aircraft could fly long range and find the U-boats with radar; Germany was forced to withdraw.

— Allied air cover 1940   — Allied air cover 1943

Area of U-boat success 1942   Area of U-boat success 1943

2 THE NAZI–SOVIET CONFLICT 1943–1944

After the defeat at Stalingrad in 1943 (see pp.296–297), Hitler gambled on a huge tank battle to decimate the Russians at Kursk. The gamble failed; the Soviet army had a better command structure than the various Axis forces. The Soviet counter-advance into Romania and Hungary brought about the surrender of Hitler's allies.

⚑ Axis surrender 1944

3 THE MEDITERRANEAN 1942–1945

In 1942, the defeat of the Axis armies, under Erwin Rommel, at El Alamein in Egypt was a turning point for the Western Allies. They went on to invade Italian Libya and Sicily, then Italy itself in 1943. When the Italians surrendered, the Germans occupied Italy and continued the fight without their main ally until May 1945.

Nov 1943–Apr 1945 One-third of Berlin's houses are destroyed in a long bombing campaign by the Allies

Feb 13–14, 1945 The Allies firebomb Dresden, devastating the city and killing thousands of civilians in one of the most controversial acts of World War II

Apr 25, 1945 Soviet and US troops meet at the River Elbe. Both allies fight on until unconditional surrender from Germany

Jan 1944 Soviet Army crosses the old Polish border

Jul 1944 Soviet Army reaches the Vistula River opposite Warsaw; the Germans suffer 850,000 casualties
Jan 17, 1945 Soviet troops liberate the Polish city of Warsaw

Jun 22, 1944 Stalin orders Operation Bagration, a massive offensive into the Baltic states and western Poland

August 25, 1944 Paris is liberated after the German garrison there finally surrenders

Jul 5–Aug 23, 1943 Axis assault on Kursk is met with 1.3 million soldiers and 3,400 tanks from the Soviet Union; Axis forces are defeated

Sep 8, 1943 Italy surrenders to Allied forces
Oct 13, 1943 Italy declares war on Germany

Jul 1943 The Allies capture Sicily and prepare for the invasion of Italy

Nov 1942 The Allies win a clear victory over German–Italian troops at El Alamein

May 13, 1943 240,000 Axis forces surrender in Tunisia

Nov 1942 The Siege of Malta is finally lifted. Malta is strategically important for control of the Mediterranean

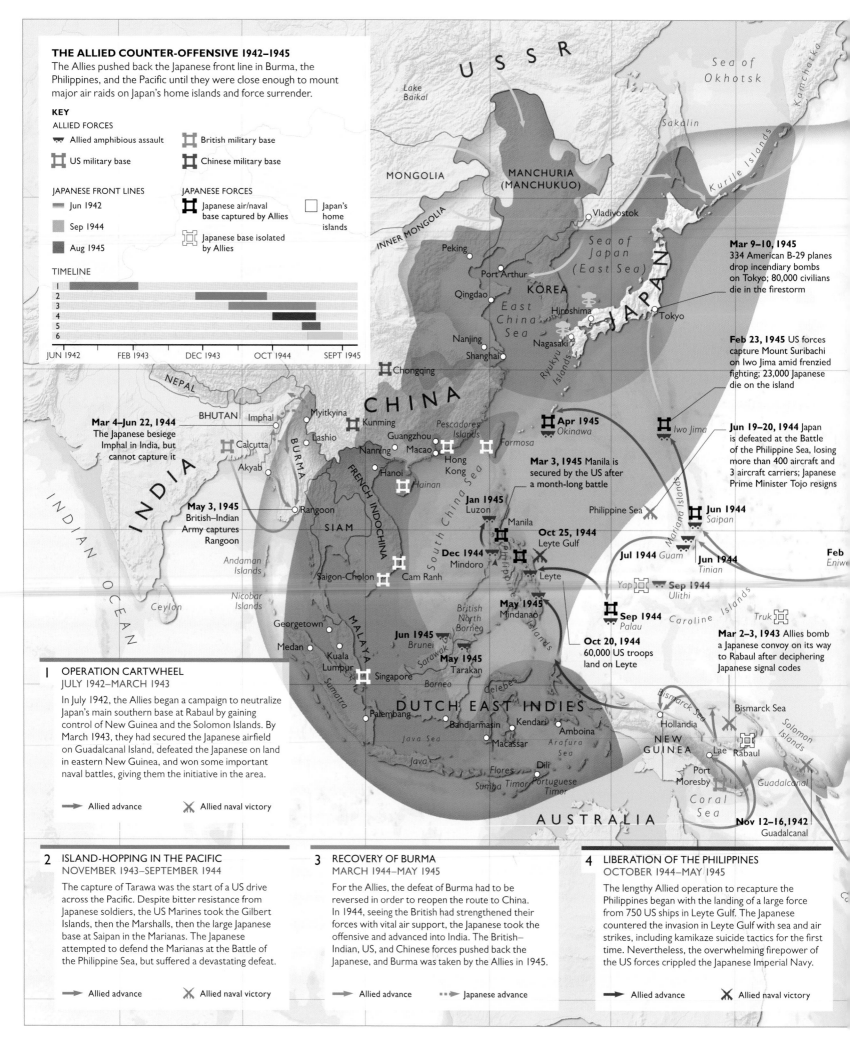

THE ALLIED COUNTER-OFFENSIVE 1942–1945

The Allies pushed back the Japanese front line in Burma, the Philippines, and the Pacific until they were close enough to mount major air raids on Japan's home islands and force surrender.

KEY

ALLIED FORCES

⊟ Allied amphibious assault

⊞ US military base

⊞ British military base

⊞ Chinese military base

JAPANESE FRONT LINES

▬ Jun 1942

▬ Sep 1944

▬ Aug 1945

JAPANESE FORCES

⊞ Japanese air/naval base captured by Allies

⊞ Japanese base isolated by Allies

☐ Japan's home islands

TIMELINE

1
2
3
4
5
6

JUN 1942 — FEB 1943 — DEC 1943 — OCT 1944 — SEPT 1945

Mar 9–10, 1945 334 American B-29 planes drop incendiary bombs on Tokyo; 80,000 civilians die in the firestorm

Feb 23, 1945 US forces capture Mount Suribachi on Iwo Jima amid frenzied fighting; 23,000 Japanese die on the island

Jun 19–20, 1944 Japan is defeated at the Battle of the Philippine Sea, losing more than 400 aircraft and 3 aircraft carriers; Japanese Prime Minister Tojo resigns

Mar 4–Jun 22, 1944 The Japanese besiege Imphal in India, but cannot capture it

May 3, 1945 British–Indian Army captures Rangoon

Mar 3, 1945 Manila is secured by the US after a month-long battle

Jan 1945 Luzon

Dec 1944 Mindoro

Oct 25, 1944 Leyte Gulf

Oct 20, 1944 60,000 US troops land on Leyte

May 1945 Mindanao

Jun 1945 Brunei

May 1945 Tarakan

Jun 1944 Saipan

Jul 1944 Guam

Jun 1944 Tinian

Feb Eniwe

Sep 1944 Ulithi

Sep 1944 Palau

Apr 1945 Okinawa

Jun 1944 Saipan

Mar 2–3, 1943 Allies bomb a Japanese convoy on its way to Rabaul after deciphering Japanese signal codes

Nov 12–16, 1942 Guadalcanal

1 OPERATION CARTWHEEL
JULY 1942–MARCH 1943

In July 1942, the Allies began a campaign to neutralize Japan's main southern base at Rabaul by gaining control of New Guinea and the Solomon Islands. By March 1943, they had secured the Japanese airfield on Guadalcanal Island, defeated the Japanese on land in eastern New Guinea, and won some important naval battles, giving them the initiative in the area.

→ Allied advance   ✕ Allied naval victory

2 ISLAND-HOPPING IN THE PACIFIC
NOVEMBER 1943–SEPTEMBER 1944

The capture of Tarawa was the start of a US drive across the Pacific. Despite bitter resistance from Japanese soldiers, the US Marines took the Gilbert Islands, then the Marshalls, then the large Japanese base at Saipan in the Marianas. The Japanese attempted to defend the Marianas at the Battle of the Philippine Sea, but suffered a devastating defeat.

→ Allied advance   ✕ Allied naval victory

3 RECOVERY OF BURMA
MARCH 1944–MAY 1945

For the Allies, the defeat of Burma had to be reversed in order to reopen the route to China. In 1944, seeing the British had strengthened their forces with vital air support, the Japanese took the offensive and advanced into India. The British–Indian, US, and Chinese forces pushed back the Japanese, and Burma was taken by the Allies in 1945.

→ Allied advance   ┄► Japanese advance

4 LIBERATION OF THE PHILIPPINES
OCTOBER 1944–MAY 1945

The lengthy Allied operation to recapture the Philippines began with the landing of a large force from 750 US ships in Leyte Gulf. The Japanese countered the invasion in Leyte Gulf with sea and air strikes, including kamikaze suicide tactics for the first time. Nevertheless, the overwhelming firepower of the US forces crippled the Japanese Imperial Navy.

→ Allied advance   ✕ Allied naval victory

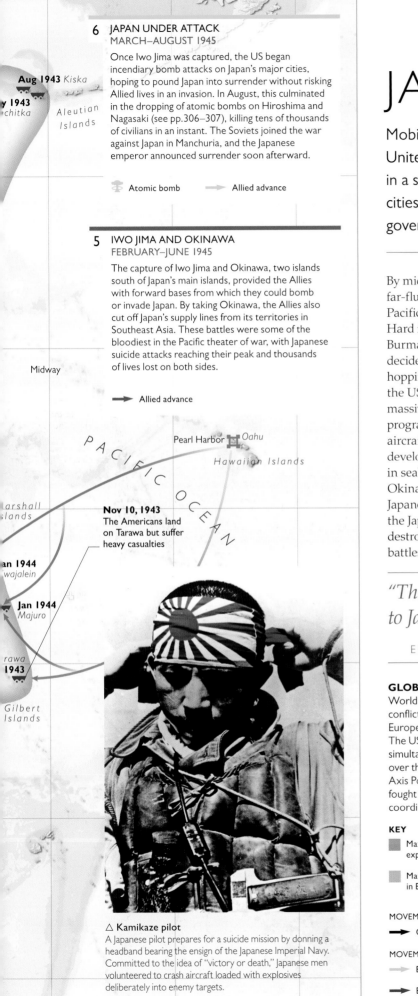

6 JAPAN UNDER ATTACK
MARCH–AUGUST 1945

Once Iwo Jima was captured, the US began incendiary bomb attacks on Japan's major cities, hoping to pound Japan into surrender without risking Allied lives in an invasion. In August, this culminated in the dropping of atomic bombs on Hiroshima and Nagasaki (see pp.306–307), killing tens of thousands of civilians in an instant. The Soviets joined the war against Japan in Manchuria, and the Japanese emperor announced surrender soon afterward.

☁ Atomic bomb   → Allied advance

5 IWO JIMA AND OKINAWA
FEBRUARY–JUNE 1945

The capture of Iwo Jima and Okinawa, two islands south of Japan's main islands, provided the Allies with forward bases from which they could bomb or invade Japan. By taking Okinawa, the Allies also cut off Japan's supply lines from its territories in Southeast Asia. These battles were some of the bloodiest in the Pacific theater of war, with Japanese suicide attacks reaching their peak and thousands of lives lost on both sides.

→ Allied advance

Nov 10, 1943
The Americans land on Tarawa but suffer heavy casualties

△ **Kamikaze pilot**
A Japanese pilot prepares for a suicide mission by donning a headband bearing the ensign of the Japanese Imperial Navy. Committed to the idea of "victory or death," Japanese men volunteered to crash aircraft loaded with explosives deliberately into enemy targets.

JAPAN DEFEATED

Mobilizing its superior industrial resources and manpower, the United States overcame extremely determined Japanese resistance in a series of fierce battles in the Pacific from 1942 to 1945. Japan's cities were laid waste by American bombing, and its imperial government was forced to sign a humiliating surrender.

By mid-1942, Japan had established a far-flung defensive perimeter in the Pacific to protect its conquests in Asia. Hard fighting continued in China and Burma, but the outcome of the war was decided by an American thrust "island-hopping" across the Pacific, bringing the US within reach of Japan itself. A massive American shipbuilding program created a powerful fleet of aircraft carriers, while the US Marines developed an unprecedented expertise in seaborne landings. From Tawara to Okinawa, each island was defended by Japanese soldiers to the last man, but the Japanese Imperial Navy was destroyed in a series of large-scale sea battles. Outclassed Japanese aviators were compelled to use "kamikaze" suicide tactics to attack the American fleet, but with limited effect.

By the summer of 1945, it was clear that Japan had lost the war. The Japanese government was split between those who wanted to fight to the death and those who wished to seek a peace deal that might preserve some element of independence. The Americans, however, demanded unconditional surrender. In August, the United States destroyed the cities of Hiroshima and Nagasaki with atom bombs, and the Soviet Union, previously neutral, attacked Japanese forces in Manchuria. The Japanese government finally bowed to the inevitable and surrendered.

"The war situation has developed not necessarily to Japan's advantage."

EMPEROR HIROHITO, SURRENDER BROADCAST, AUGUST 15, 1945

GLOBAL WARFARE
World War II was a truly global conflict, with theaters of war in Europe, Africa, Asia, and the Pacific. The US fought all the Axis Powers simultaneously, sending troops all over the globe. Japan and the other Axis Powers, although allies, fought separate wars, failing to coordinate their strategy.

KEY
■ Maximum extent of Japanese expansion in Asia/Pacific
■ Maximum extent of Axis Powers in Europe/USSR

MOVEMENT OF AXIS TROOPS
→ German   → Japanese

MOVEMENT OF ALLIED TROOPS
→ British   → American
→ British Commonwealth   → Soviet

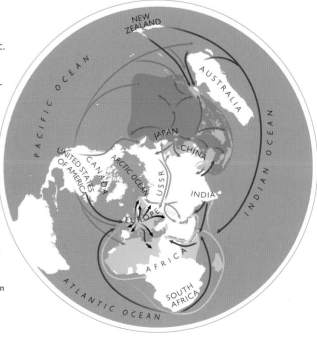

Hiroshima destroyed
Within seconds of detonation of the first atomic bomb, the city of Hiroshima lay in ruins. Nearly 70,000 people are believed to have died immediately. Here, the shattered Nagarekawa Methodist Church stands out.

HIROSHIMA AND NAGASAKI

In August 1945, the US dropped the world's first atomic bombs on the Japanese cities of Hiroshima and Nagasaki in a bid to end World War II. It led the world to a new, and controversial, nuclear age. For Japan, its impact was cataclysmic.

On May 10, 1945, 3 days after Germany had surrendered to the Allies and ended the war in Europe, a group of US scientists and military personnel met in Los Alamos, New Mexico. The top minds within the Manhattan Project—the American effort to build an atomic bomb—focused on how to end Japanese resistance in the Pacific. The island-hopping strategy adopted by the US Navy had brought B-29 bombers within range of the Japanese archipelago, and they carried out massive aerial bombing

attacks. Yet Japan refused to surrender. US president Harry Truman authorized the use of two atomic weapons against Japan, believing it would be a less bloody way to secure surrender than an invasion.

The final attack
At the meeting at Los Alamos in May, the experts had deliberated on which Japanese cities to attack. The targets needed to have some military significance. Four cities,

△ **Human shadow**
The intense heat of the detonation in Hiroshima left "shadows" of people and objects exactly as they were at 8:15 a.m. on August 6, 1945.

including Hiroshima and Nagasaki, were chosen. Over the summer of 1945, Japanese attempts to negotiate a formula for surrender were rebuffed by the Allies. Then, on July 28, 1945, a demand from the Allies to surrender unconditionally or face destruction was rejected by the Japanese high command.

On August 6, 1945, the crew of the *Enola Gay*, the B-29 bomber assigned to drop the first bomb on Hiroshima, took off. At 8:15 a.m., "Little Boy" was dropped. Three days later, the US dropped "Fat Man" on Nagasaki. Estimates of people killed in the two bombings range as high as

246,000. On August 15, 1945, Japan surrendered. More atomic bombs were planned, although Japan's emperor was also influenced by the Soviet invasion of Manchuria and the starvation that was already widespread. The surrender was formalized on board the USS *Missouri* on September 2, 1945.

The bombings had helped to hasten the end of WWII but launched a nuclear arms race between the US and the Soviet Union that lasted until the 1990s.

▽ **"Fat Man"**
Nicknamed Fat Man, the atomic bomb dropped on Nagasaki on August 9, 1945, created winds of 620mph (1,000km/h) and temperatures of 12,700°F (7,050°C).

"I realize the tragic significance of the atomic bomb … We thank God that it has come to us, instead of to our enemies."

HARRY S TRUMAN, US PRESIDENT, AUGUST 9, 1945

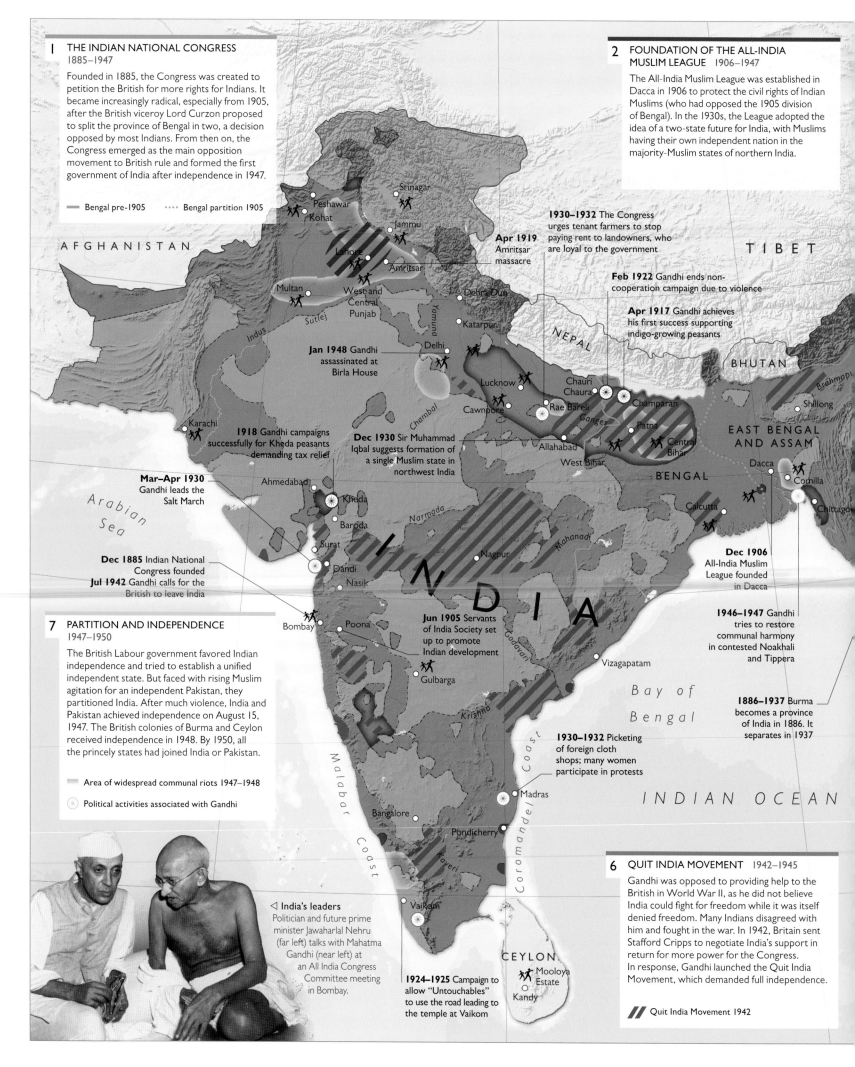

1 THE INDIAN NATIONAL CONGRESS
1885–1947

Founded in 1885, the Congress was created to petition the British for more rights for Indians. It became increasingly radical, especially from 1905, after the British viceroy Lord Curzon proposed to split the province of Bengal in two, a decision opposed by most Indians. From then on, the Congress emerged as the main opposition movement to British rule and formed the first government of India after independence in 1947.

—— Bengal pre-1905   ···· Bengal partition 1905

2 FOUNDATION OF THE ALL-INDIA MUSLIM LEAGUE 1906–1947

The All-India Muslim League was established in Dacca in 1906 to protect the civil rights of Indian Muslims (who had opposed the 1905 division of Bengal). In the 1930s, the League adopted the idea of a two-state future for India, with Muslims having their own independent nation in the majority-Muslim states of northern India.

1930–1932 The Congress urges tenant farmers to stop paying rent to landowners, who are loyal to the government

Apr 1919 Amritsar massacre

Feb 1922 Gandhi ends non-cooperation campaign due to violence

Apr 1917 Gandhi achieves his first success supporting indigo-growing peasants

Jan 1948 Gandhi assassinated at Birla House

Dec 1930 Sir Muhammad Iqbal suggests formation of a single Muslim state in northwest India

1918 Gandhi campaigns successfully for Kheda peasants demanding tax relief

Dec 1906 All-India Muslim League founded in Dacca

Mar–Apr 1930 Gandhi leads the Salt March

Dec 1885 Indian National Congress founded
Jul 1942 Gandhi calls for the British to leave India

1946–1947 Gandhi tries to restore communal harmony in contested Noakhali and Tippera

Jun 1905 Servants of India Society set up to promote Indian development

1886–1937 Burma becomes a province of India in 1886. It separates in 1937

7 PARTITION AND INDEPENDENCE
1947–1950

The British Labour government favored Indian independence and tried to establish a unified independent state. But faced with rising Muslim agitation for an independent Pakistan, they partitioned India. After much violence, India and Pakistan achieved independence on August 15, 1947. The British colonies of Burma and Ceylon received independence in 1948. By 1950, all the princely states had joined India or Pakistan.

▬▬ Area of widespread communal riots 1947–1948

⊛ Political activities associated with Gandhi

1930–1932 Picketing of foreign cloth shops; many women participate in protests

◁ **India's leaders**
Politician and future prime minister Jawaharlal Nehru (far left) talks with Mahatma Gandhi (near left) at an All India Congress Committee meeting in Bombay.

1924–1925 Campaign to allow "Untouchables" to use the road leading to the temple at Vaikom

6 QUIT INDIA MOVEMENT 1942–1945

Gandhi was opposed to providing help to the British in World War II, as he did not believe India could fight for freedom while it was itself denied freedom. Many Indians disagreed with him and fought in the war. In 1942, Britain sent Stafford Cripps to negotiate India's support in return for more power for the Congress. In response, Gandhi launched the Quit India Movement, which demanded full independence.

⫽⫽ Quit India Movement 1942

AFGHANISTAN · TIBET · NEPAL · BHUTAN · INDIA · CEYLON

Srinagar · Peshawar · Kohat · Jammu · Lahore · Amritsar · Multan · West and Central Punjab · Dehra Dun · Katarpur · Delhi · Lucknow · Chauri Chaura · Champaran · Shillong · Karachi · Rae Bareli · Patna · EAST BENGAL AND ASSAM · Cawnpore · Central Bihar · Dacca · Comilla · Allahabad · West Bihar · BENGAL · Calcutta · Chittagong · Ahmedabad · Kheda · Baroda · Narmada · Surat · Mahanadi · Dandi · Nasik · Nagpur · Bombay · Poona · Godavari · Gulbarga · Vizagapatam · Krishna · Bangalore · Madras · Pondicherry · Vaikom · Mooloya Estate · Kandy

Indus · Sutlej · Yamuna · Chambal · Ganges · Brahmaputra · Arabian Sea · Bay of Bengal · Indian Ocean · Malabar Coast · Coromandel Coast · Kaveri

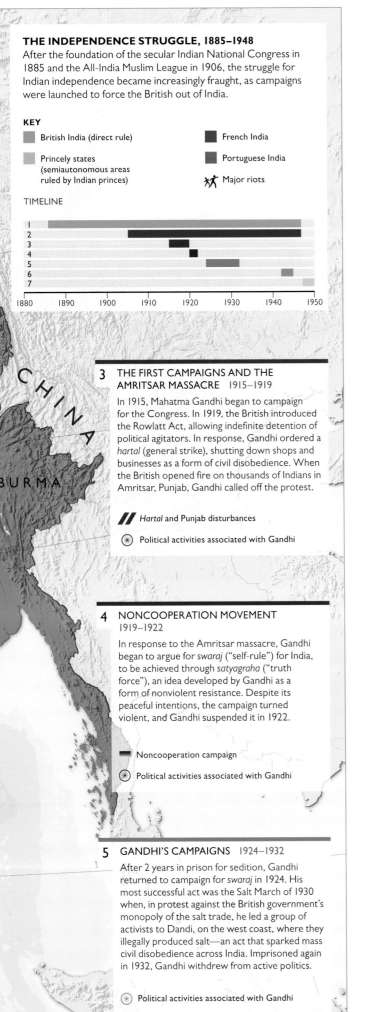

THE INDEPENDENCE STRUGGLE, 1885–1948
After the foundation of the secular Indian National Congress in 1885 and the All-India Muslim League in 1906, the struggle for Indian independence became increasingly fraught, as campaigns were launched to force the British out of India.

KEY

■ British India (direct rule)

■ Princely states (semiautonomous areas ruled by Indian princes)

■ French India

■ Portuguese India

🏃 Major riots

TIMELINE

1 2 3 4 5 6 7

1880   1890   1900   1910   1920   1930   1940   1950

3 THE FIRST CAMPAIGNS AND THE AMRITSAR MASSACRE   1915–1919

In 1915, Mahatma Gandhi began to campaign for the Congress. In 1919, the British introduced the Rowlatt Act, allowing indefinite detention of political agitators. In response, Gandhi ordered a *hartal* (general strike), shutting down shops and businesses as a form of civil disobedience. When the British opened fire on thousands of Indians in Amritsar, Punjab, Gandhi called off the protest.

▓ *Hartal* and Punjab disturbances

✳ Political activities associated with Gandhi

4 NONCOOPERATION MOVEMENT 1919–1922

In response to the Amritsar massacre, Gandhi began to argue for *swaraj* ("self-rule") for India, to be achieved through *satyagraha* ("truth force"), an idea developed by Gandhi as a form of nonviolent resistance. Despite its peaceful intentions, the campaign turned violent, and Gandhi suspended it in 1922.

■ Noncooperation campaign

✳ Political activities associated with Gandhi

5 GANDHI'S CAMPAIGNS   1924–1932

After 2 years in prison for sedition, Gandhi returned to campaign for *swaraj* in 1924. His most successful act was the Salt March of 1930 when, in protest against the British government's monopoly of the salt trade, he led a group of activists to Dandi, on the west coast, where they illegally produced salt—an act that sparked mass civil disobedience across India. Imprisoned again in 1932, Gandhi withdrew from active politics.

✳ Political activities associated with Gandhi

PARTITION OF INDIA

The campaign to end British rule over its Indian empire was one of the most successful such movements in colonial history. Although marked with occasional and often appalling violence, the campaign stressed nonviolent resistance based on the beliefs of one of its most inspirational leaders, politician and activist Mahatma Gandhi.

Britain's efforts to hold on to India were undermined by a massacre of unarmed Indians by British troops in Amritsar, Punjab, in 1919. In response, Gandhi initiated a nonviolent, noncooperation campaign for independence, which was led mainly by the secular Indian National Congress. However, the religious divide within India, between Hindus and Muslims, complicated matters. The All-India Muslim League began to campaign for an independent Muslim state called Pakistan, which would be created through partition.

After Britain declared war on Germany in 1939 on behalf of India—without consulting Indian leaders—the Congress launched the Quit India Movement, calling for civil disobedience to upset the British war effort. By 1945, Britain was economically drained by the war, and the government began to plan for withdrawal from India. It supported partition reluctantly and, amid a crisis that saw millions of Hindu and Muslim refugees cross the new borders, the divided empire finally achieved its independence on August 15, 1947.

"At the stroke of the midnight hour, when the world sleeps, India will awake to life and freedom."

JAWAHARLAL NEHRU, INDIA'S 1ST PRIME MINISTER, AUGUST 14, 1947

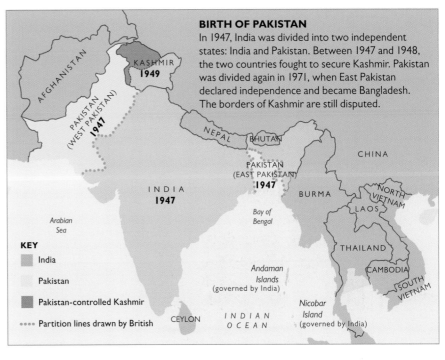

BIRTH OF PAKISTAN
In 1947, India was divided into two independent states: India and Pakistan. Between 1947 and 1948, the two countries fought to secure Kashmir. Pakistan was divided again in 1971, when East Pakistan declared independence and became Bangladesh. The borders of Kashmir are still disputed.

KEY

■ India

■ Pakistan

■ Pakistan-controlled Kashmir

•••• Partition lines drawn by British

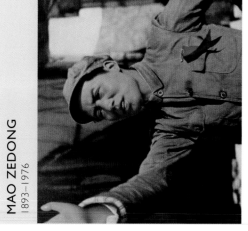

The ruler of communist China from 1949 until his death in 1976, Mao Zedong trained as a teacher in Hunan before traveling to Peking (Beijing). While working as a librarian at Peking University, he became a communist, and he helped to found the Communist Party in 1921. In 1934, Mao guided 86,000 communists on the Long March. He became chairman of the party in 1943. As leader, he modernized China, but his radical policies were ruthless and ambitious and caused huge loss of life.

THE FOUNDING OF COMMUNIST CHINA

Between 1927 and 1949, an ideological divide split China, as Mao Zedong's Communist Party fought China's Nationalist Party for the future of the country. Eventually, after years of civil war, Japanese occupation, and World War II, Mao emerged as ruler of a new communist China.

The Chinese Communist Party (CCP) was set up in Shanghai on July 23, 1921. At first, it collaborated with China's Nationalist Party, the Kuomintang (KMT), but the alliance was severed in 1927, when the KMT, under the rule of a new leader, anti-communist Chiang Kai-shek, turned on their rivals (see pp.288–289). The KMT destroyed the communists in all major cities, and the CCP was forced to retreat to Jiangxi province in southern China, where they established the Soviet Republic of China in 1931. In 1934, they were forced to abandon their base when they were surrounded by KMT forces. Under the guidance of the future Chairman of the Soviet Republic of China, Mao Zedong, the fragments of the Communist Party

undertook the "Long March"—a year-long trek to the northern province of Shaanxi. It was a good strategic base, being both far away from the KMT and close to supply routes from the USSR.

Japanese invasion during World War II briefly forced the CCP and KMT to collaborate again to some extent. After the war, US negotiators tried to reconcile the two parties, but civil war broke out. The KMT had early victories, but the CCP gained the support of the rural peasantry, and their army swelled. They quickly gained ground by splitting the KMT forces into isolated pockets. By 1949, the Kuomintang had collapsed. On October 1, 1949, Mao announced the establishment of the People's Republic of China.

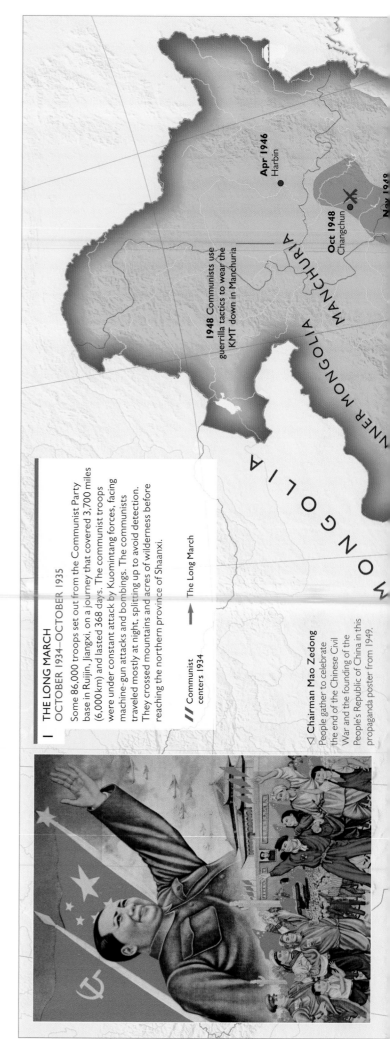

Apr 1946
Harbin

1948 Communists use guerrilla tactics to wear the KMT down in Manchuria

Oct 1948
Changchun

Nov 1949

MANCHURIA

INNER MONGOLIA

MONGOLIA

THE LONG MARCH
OCTOBER 1934–OCTOBER 1935

Some 86,000 troops set out from the Communist Party base in Rujin, Jiangxi, on a journey that covered 3,700 miles (6,000 km) and lasted 368 days. The communist troops were under constant attack by Kuomintang forces, facing machine-gun attacks and bombings. The communists traveled mostly at night, splitting up to avoid detection. They crossed mountains and acres of wilderness before reaching the northern province of Shaanxi.

⏸ Communist centers 1934

➡ The Long March

▽ **Chairman Mao Zedong**
People gather to celebrate the end of the Chinese Civil War and the founding of the People's Republic of China in this propaganda poster from 1949.

Jan 1949 Peking (Beijing)

Oct 11, 1948 Battle of Jinzhou is a turning point in the civil war; leads to CCP control of the northeast

May 1949 Qingdao

Jan 9, 1949 Communist victory at the Battle of Tianjin persuades 500,000 KMT troops to switch sides

Jan 1949 Tianjin

Sep 1948 Jinan

May 1949 Mao has the support of rural China but needs to capture the cities. Shanghai falls with relatively little collateral damage

1949 As cities such as Hangzhou fall to the CCP, Mao swiftly sends in officers to oversee a smooth takeover

May 1949 Shanghai

Oct 10, 1934 The communists set out from Ruijin, Jiangxi, which has been their power base throughout the early 1930s

May 1949 Hangzhou

Aug 1949 Fuzhou

Jan 1949 Xuzhou

Apr 1949 Nanjing

Jun 1948 Kaifeng

Jun 8, 1948 Despite having a larger army, the KMT suffer a quick defeat

May 1949 Wuhan

May 1949 Nanchang

Nov 1931 Ruijin

Oct 1949 Xiamen

FUJIAN

JIANGXI

HONG KONG (governed by UK)

HUBEI

Oct 1, 1949 Mao announces the establishment of the People's Republic of China

Apr 1949 Taiyuan

Apr 1948 Luoyang

Aug 1949 Changsha

Oct 1949 Guangzhou

GUANGDONG

Nov 1949 Gulin

Apr 1950 HAINAN

Oct 1935 Yan'an

SHAANXI

Aug 1949 Xi'an

Nov 1949 Chongqing (Capital of China 1938–1945)

Jan 1935 Zunyi

Nov 1949 Guiyang

Nov 25–Dec 3, 1934 The first major battle, the Battle of Xiangjiang River costs Mao's Red Army roughly half of its troops

Jan 1935 During a meeting of the Communist Party in the captured city of Zunyi, Mao emerges as the dominant communist leader

May 29, 1935 At the Battle for Luding Bridge, 22 communist soldiers capture the bridge—a crucial river crossing—despite heavy fire

Sep 16, 1935 The last major hurdle for Mao's forces, they capture Lazikou Pass after climbers are sent up the steep cliff at night to bypass KMT defenses

Oct 20, 1935 Communists reach Yan'an, which becomes their headquarters

Sep 1949 Xining

Aug 1949 Lanzhou

Yellow River

Yangtze

C H I N A

K O R E A

EAST CHINA SEA

TAIWAN

PHILIPPINES

SOUTH CHINA SEA

BURMA (MYANMAR)

VIETNAM

FRENCH INDOCHINA

Jan 10, 1949 Battle of Beijing is a major defeat for the KMT

2 FIGHTING RESUMES 1945–1948

The communists gained much from the Japanese occupation of China (1937–1945); they developed their guerrilla warfare methods and seized weapons from the Japanese. When the civil war resumed in 1945, the CCP used these advantages to move south and seize territory, including the major cities of Luoyang and Kaifeng. By 1948, they controlled over one-third of China.

- Communist control by 1946
- Area under Japanese control 1944
- → Principal communist campaigns
- • Communist takeover, with date
- ✕ Major battle

3 COMMUNIST VICTORY 1948–1949

As the CCP advanced, the KMT retreated to the south. Many were not prepared to surrender, and the KMT won several battles. However, the CCP split the KMT forces into small groups, weakening them. By January 1949, the Kuomintang were forced to withdraw from Beijing. Mao declared the People's Republic of China in October 1949, and by 1950, the CCP had seized Hainan Island and Tibet.

- Communist control by mid-1949

4 TAIWAN DECEMBER 1949

Guangzhou was the last stronghold of the Kuomintang. After it fell to the Communist Party on October 14, 1949, 1.2 million people fled to the island of Formosa (Taiwan), 100 miles (160km) off the coast of China. Kuomintang leader Chiang Kai-shek left for the island on December 12, 1949, and set up the Republic of China.

- Taiwan

LONG MARCH TO VICTORY

Forced from its base in the province of Jiangxi in 1934, the CCP fled north, gaining support along the way. The war against Japan helped the party greatly, allowing them to take control of Japanese-occupied Manchuria and then move south, seizing KMT territory.

TIMELINE

1930 1935 1940 1945 1950

SUPERPOWERS

By the end of World War II, two of the Allies—the US and USSR—had emerged as the world's dominant powers. Owing to their military might and global political influence, they became known as "superpowers." The ideological gulf that separated them generated regular conflict in the era of the Cold War.

△ **Powerful weapon**
On November 1, 1952, the US detonated the first hydrogen bomb, code named Ivy Mike. It was 1,000 times more powerful than the atomic bombs dropped on Hiroshima and Nagasaki.

The USSR had been an unexpected ally in World War II, and Britain and the US made common cause with Stalin's dictatorship in the overthrow of Hitler's European "New Order." As the Red Army advanced into eastern Europe, it became clear that Stalin wanted to dominate the region politically, an ambition that drove a wedge between the wartime allies and opened the way to what was christened the Cold War. The first major conflict came over the future of Berlin, which was inside the Soviet zone of Germany but was controlled by all four major allies: Britain, the US, France, and the USSR. In 1948, Stalin tried to cut Berlin off from the West in order to incorporate it fully in the Communist bloc, but a Western relief effort that came to be known as the Berlin Airlift brought food and supplies to West Berliners, and after 318 days, Stalin abandoned the blockade. The battle line between the two superpowers was now clear.

Growing tensions

By the time of the Berlin crisis, both the USSR and the US had come to realize that there was now no possibility of peaceful collaboration. Soviet influence rapidly spread, and with the triumph of

△ **Anti-communist propaganda**
The outbreak of war in Korea brought the Cold War to east Asia. Propaganda produced during the period was used to antagonize South Koreans against the communists.

communism in China, North Korea, and North Vietnam, it seemed likely that Soviet power would pose a profound threat to the West. In the US, a wave of anti-communism was unleashed in the early 1950s as the American public came to realize that the Soviet superpower represented a menace to American interests. When communist North Korea invaded the South, the US used its influence in the United Nations to organize an alliance to contain the threat.

The Korean War was only one of a number of proxy wars in which the US and the USSR looked to enhance their global influence as the new superpowers.

At the core of American and Soviet superpower status was the possession of a large arsenal of nuclear weapons. By 1953, both states had tested the hydrogen bomb, whose destructive power eclipsed the atomic bombs dropped on Japan in 1945. As the stockpiles of bombs built up, no other state could match the military potential of the superpowers. Competition between them was symbolized by the Space Race, in which each side sought to outdo the other. The USSR successfully launched the *Sputnik 1* satellite in 1957 and boasted the first man in space, the first woman in space, and the first spacewalk. Only with the American success in sending a manned mission to the Moon in 1969 did the race

DEADLY RIVALRY

In 1945, the emergence of the US and USSR as superpowers was founded on their capacity to build, test, and accumulate nuclear weapons in massive quantities. The Cold War, so called because no direct military action was taken, led to deep divisions and animosity between the two countries and their respective allies. The threat of nuclear annihilation was constant, but after the Cuban Missile Crisis in 1962, the rivalry between the two nations played out in the Space Race.

Aug 1945 The US drops atomic bombs on the Japanese cities of Hiroshima and Nagasaki, starting the nuclear arms race

Aug 29, 1949 The Soviet Union tests its first nuclear bomb, and the arms race escalates

Jun 24, 1950 The Korean War begins: North Korea invades the south, with Stalin's support

Mid-1950s The USSR and its affiliated communist nations in eastern Europe begin talks for forming the Warsaw Pact, ultimately signed in May 1955

NUCLEAR WEAPONS

THE COLD WAR

THE SPACE RACE

1945

1950

Jun 24, 1948–May 12, 1949 The first major crisis of the Cold War occurs—Stalin blockades Berlin; an effort from various countries saves Berliners from starvation

Apr 4, 1949 NATO is formed between the US and other western nations

◁ **Concrete divide**
An East German worker makes repairs to the hastily built Berlin Wall—a 28-mile (45-km) scar that cut through the German capital, dividing east from west.

"Mankind must put an end to war or war will put an end to mankind."

JOHN F. KENNEDY, US PRESIDENT, 1961

become more equal. The nuclear confrontation in the 1950s did not provoke war between the two superpowers because neither side could risk retaliation. But in 1962, to counter the stationing of American missiles in Turkey, Nikita Khrushchev, the Soviet leader, authorized the establishment of Soviet missile sites in Cuba, the site of Castro's pro-Soviet revolution. In the end, the USSR backed down from President Kennedy's ultimatum to end the project, and a more serious crisis was averted.

The coming of détente

From the Cuban crisis onward, the two superpowers looked for ways to reduce the nuclear risks. A so-called "red telephone" line was installed between leaders in Moscow and Washington so that they could communicate directly during a crisis. In August 1963, the first Test Ban Treaty was signed, and in 1972, talks between the two superpowers produced SALT I, the first serious effort to scale back the nuclear arsenals. Although

both superpowers continued to spend heavily on defense and to play out political battles between them in other parts of the world, there emerged a greater willingness to talk and to avoid the open hostility of the 1940s and 1950s. When the Soviet bloc collapsed in 1989–1991, the USSR's status as a superpower disappeared. By the 1990s, the US was, for the time being, the sole superpower.

▽ **The American dream**
This Cadillac convertible epitomizes the growing prosperity of America's middle class, asserting capitalism as superior to communism.

CALIFORNIA
DRM CARS

Feb 17, 1958 The Campaign for Nuclear Disarmament (CND) is formed; its iconic emblem becomes one of the most recognized in the world

May 5, 1961 Alan Shepard, flying on *Freedom 7*, becomes the first American in space

Aug 13, 1961 Barbed wire is put up as the first stage of construction of the Berlin Wall, which splits east Berlin from west

Mar 18, 1965 Soviet cosmonaut Alexei Leonov makes the first spacewalk in history, beating American rival Ed White by almost 3 months

Jul 1, 1968 The Non-Proliferation Treaty is signed to make countries holding nuclear weapons commit to a cautious undertaking to disarm

1960

1965

1970

Oct 4, 1957 The USSR launches the world's first man-made satellite, *Sputnik I*; it takes 98 minutes to orbit Earth

Apr 12, 1961 Soviet cosmonaut Yuri Gagarin becomes the first human to travel in space in his spacecraft, *Vostok I*

May 25, 1961 US president John F. Kennedy pledges to the American public to put the first man on the Moon

Oct 16, 1962 The Cuban Missile Crisis begins—a tense stand-off between the US and USSR in Cuba brings the world to the brink of nuclear war

Jul 20, 1969 American astronaut Neil Armstrong becomes the first man to walk on the Moon; the historic event is watched live on television worldwide

THE COLD WAR

After World War II ended in 1945, bitter rivalry between the US and the USSR dominated international affairs and led to many global crises. Known as the Cold War, this period of extreme political tension, which lasted for almost half a century, was as much a conflict of ideology and influence as military action.

The US and the USSR emerged from World War II as the most powerful victors. Although formerly allies, the two nations had major political and economic disagreements about the world's future, with the US promoting democracy and capitalism and the USSR supporting communism. By 1949, communist regions had emerged throughout eastern Europe, and China had emerged as a communist state, intensifying international division. The Western nations set up the North Atlantic Treaty Organization (NATO) military alliance, and the Soviet bloc responded with the Warsaw Pact. Competition escalated as first the US, then the USSR, acquired and tested nuclear weapons, initially to be delivered by aircraft, later by missiles and submarines (see pp.324–325).

The Cold War never developed into a direct war because the threat of nuclear retaliation was too great. However, armed conflicts between proxy countries across the globe became frequent. The USSR would back smaller, non-nuclear communist regimes, while the US would retaliate by supporting anti-communist forces in the same conflict. Few countries avoided taking sides, although some did remain nonaligned.

This new style of war was not just a military conflict, however; scientific, technological, cultural, and propaganda wars between the two superpowers were intense. Despite the antagonism between the two major powers, the Cold War did keep a kind of peace in place for almost half a century, although at huge cost to those nations where the conflict became "hot."

> *"Whether you like it or not, history is on our side. We will bury you."*
>
> NIKITA KHRUSHCHEV, SOVIET PREMIER, NOVEMBER 18, 1956

GERMANY DIVIDED

After World War II, the four victorious allies divided Germany and its capital, Berlin, between them. In 1949, the US, French, and British merged their sectors to form West Germany, with a new capital in Bonn; East Germany and East Berlin remained under Soviet control. In 1961, the East Germans built a wall to separate the communist East from capitalist West Berlin.

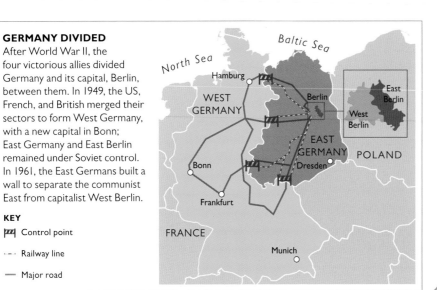

KEY

🚩 Control point

- - - Railway line

— Major road

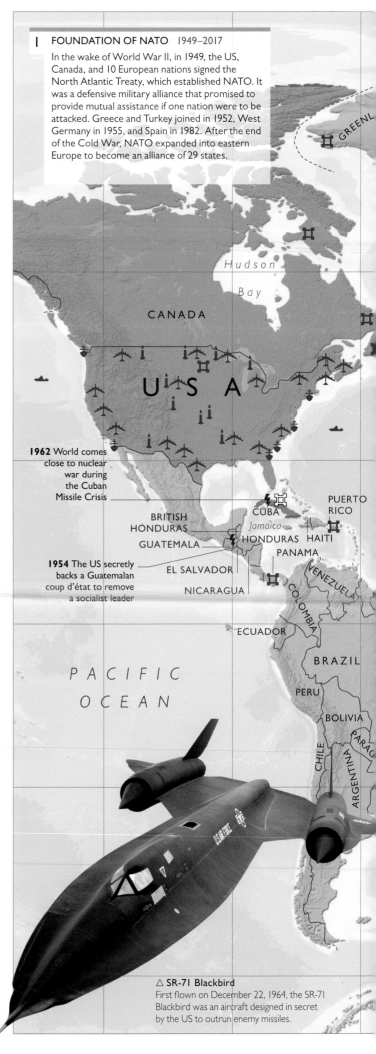

FOUNDATION OF NATO 1949–2017

In the wake of World War II, in 1949, the US, Canada, and 10 European nations signed the North Atlantic Treaty, which established NATO. It was a defensive military alliance that promised to provide mutual assistance if one nation were to be attacked. Greece and Turkey joined in 1952, West Germany in 1955, and Spain in 1982. After the end of the Cold War, NATO expanded into eastern Europe to become an alliance of 29 states.

1962 World comes close to nuclear war during the Cuban Missile Crisis

1954 The US secretly backs a Guatemalan coup d'état to remove a socialist leader

△ **SR-71 Blackbird**
First flown on December 22, 1964, the SR-71 Blackbird was an aircraft designed in secret by the US to outrun enemy missiles.

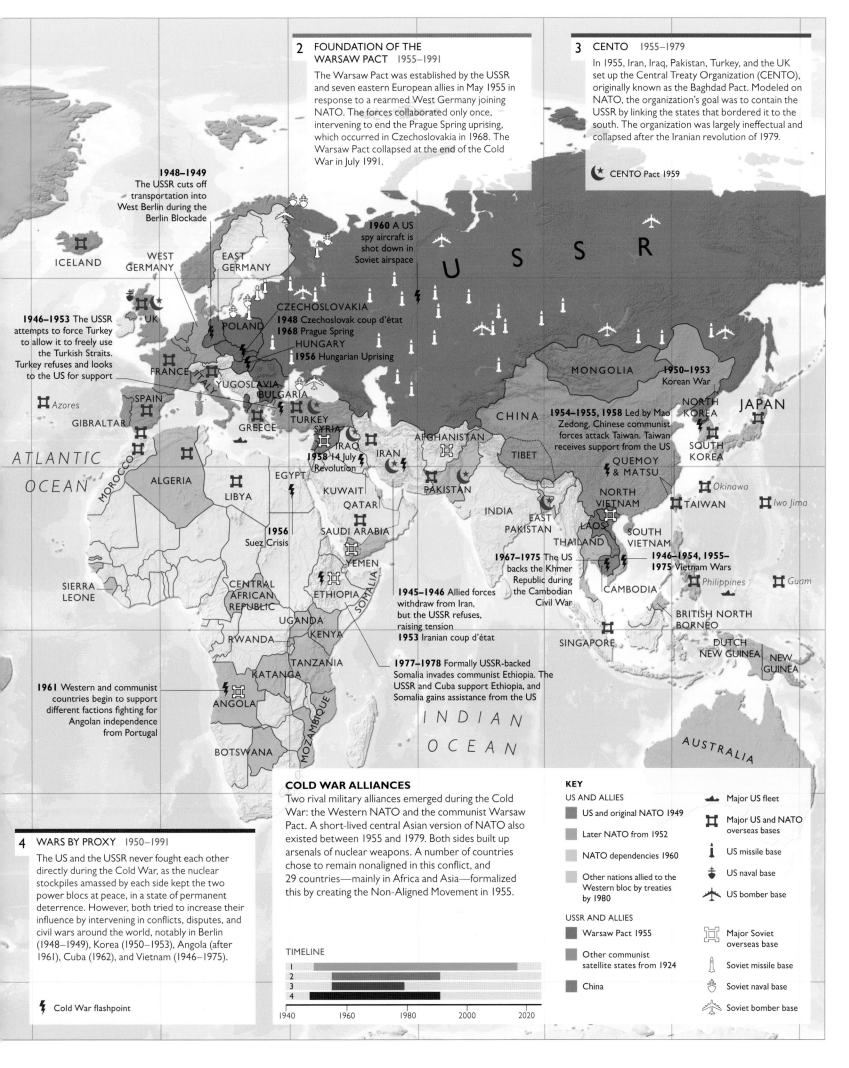

2 FOUNDATION OF THE WARSAW PACT 1955–1991

The Warsaw Pact was established by the USSR and seven eastern European allies in May 1955 in response to a rearmed West Germany joining NATO. The forces collaborated only once, intervening to end the Prague Spring uprising, which occurred in Czechoslovakia in 1968. The Warsaw Pact collapsed at the end of the Cold War in July 1991.

3 CENTO 1955–1979

In 1955, Iran, Iraq, Pakistan, Turkey, and the UK set up the Central Treaty Organization (CENTO), originally known as the Baghdad Pact. Modeled on NATO, the organization's goal was to contain the USSR by linking the states that bordered it to the south. The organization was largely ineffectual and collapsed after the Iranian revolution of 1979.

☪ CENTO Pact 1959

1948–1949 The USSR cuts off transportation into West Berlin during the Berlin Blockade

ICELAND

WEST GERMANY

EAST GERMANY

1960 A US spy aircraft is shot down in Soviet airspace

U S S R

1946–1953 The USSR attempts to force Turkey to allow it to freely use the Turkish Straits. Turkey refuses and looks to the US for support

UK

POLAND

CZECHOSLOVAKIA
1948 Czechoslovak coup d'état
1968 Prague Spring

HUNGARY

1956 Hungarian Uprising

MONGOLIA

1950–1953 Korean War

FRANCE

YUGOSLAVIA
BULGARIA

Azores

SPAIN

GIBRALTAR

TURKEY

GREECE

SYRIA

IRAQ

IRAN

AFGHANISTAN

CHINA

1954–1955, 1958 Led by Mao Zedong, Chinese communist forces attack Taiwan. Taiwan receives support from the US

NORTH KOREA

JAPAN

SOUTH KOREA

TIBET

QUEMOY & MATSU

Okinawa

Iwo Jima

MOROCCO

ALGERIA

LIBYA

EGYPT

1958 14 July Revolution

KUWAIT

QATAR

1956 Suez Crisis

SAUDI ARABIA

INDIA

EAST PAKISTAN

PAKISTAN

NORTH VIETNAM

LAOS

THAILAND

SOUTH VIETNAM

TAIWAN

ATLANTIC OCEAN

SIERRA LEONE

YEMEN

CENTRAL AFRICAN REPUBLIC

ETHIOPIA

SOMALIA

UGANDA

KENYA

RWANDA

1945–1946 Allied forces withdraw from Iran, but the USSR refuses, raising tension
1953 Iranian coup d'état

1967–1975 The US backs the Khmer Republic during the Cambodian Civil War

CAMBODIA

1946–1954, 1955–1975 Vietnam Wars

Philippines

Guam

BRITISH NORTH BORNEO

SINGAPORE

DUTCH NEW GUINEA

NEW GUINEA

1961 Western and communist countries begin to support different factions fighting for Angolan independence from Portugal

TANZANIA

KATANGA

ANGOLA

MOZAMBIQUE

1977–1978 Formally USSR-backed Somalia invades communist Ethiopia. The USSR and Cuba support Ethiopia, and Somalia gains assistance from the US

INDIAN OCEAN

AUSTRALIA

BOTSWANA

4 WARS BY PROXY 1950–1991

The US and the USSR never fought each other directly during the Cold War, as the nuclear stockpiles amassed by each side kept the two power blocs at peace, in a state of permanent deterrence. However, both tried to increase their influence by intervening in conflicts, disputes, and civil wars around the world, notably in Berlin (1948–1949), Korea (1950–1953), Angola (after 1961), Cuba (1962), and Vietnam (1946–1975).

⚡ Cold War flashpoint

COLD WAR ALLIANCES

Two rival military alliances emerged during the Cold War: the Western NATO and the communist Warsaw Pact. A short-lived central Asian version of NATO also existed between 1955 and 1979. Both sides built up arsenals of nuclear weapons. A number of countries chose to remain nonaligned in this conflict, and 29 countries—mainly in Africa and Asia—formalized this by creating the Non-Aligned Movement in 1955.

KEY

US AND ALLIES

■ US and original NATO 1949

■ Later NATO from 1952

NATO dependencies 1960

Other nations allied to the Western bloc by treaties by 1980

USSR AND ALLIES

■ Warsaw Pact 1955

Other communist satellite states from 1924

■ China

⚓ Major US fleet

⊞ Major US and NATO overseas bases

⬆ US missile base

⚓ US naval base

✈ US bomber base

⊞ Major Soviet overseas base

⬆ Soviet missile base

⚓ Soviet naval base

✈ Soviet bomber base

TIMELINE

1
2
3
4

1940   1960   1980   2000   2020

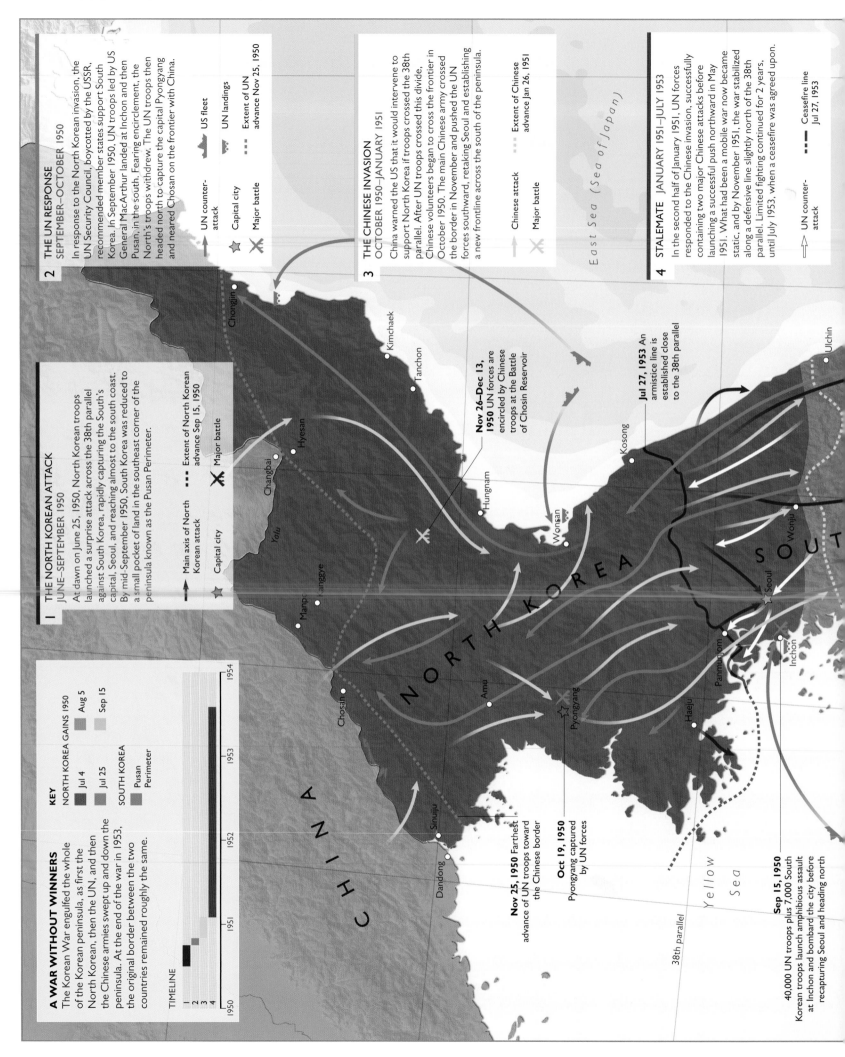

A WAR WITHOUT WINNERS

The Korean War engulfed the whole of the Korean peninsula, as first the North Korean, then the UN, and then the Chinese armies swept up and down the peninsula. At the end of the war in 1953, the original border between the two countries remained roughly the same.

KEY

NORTH KOREA GAINS 1950
- Jul 4
- Aug 5
- Jul 25
- Sep 15

SOUTH KOREA
- Pusan Perimeter

TIMELINE

1 2 3 4

1950 1951 1952 1953 1954

1 | THE NORTH KOREAN ATTACK
JUNE–SEPTEMBER 1950

At dawn on June 25, 1950, North Korean troops launched a surprise attack across the 38th parallel against South Korea, rapidly capturing the South's capital, Seoul, and reaching almost to the south coast. By mid-September 1950, South Korea was reduced to a small pocket of land in the southeast corner of the peninsula known as the Pusan Perimeter.

→ Main axis of North Korean attack

★ Capital city

▬▬▬ Extent of North Korean advance Sep 15, 1950

✕ Major battle

2 | THE UN RESPONSE
SEPTEMBER–OCTOBER 1950

In response to the North Korean invasion, the UN Security Council, boycotted by the USSR, recommended member states support South Korea. In September 1950, UN troops led by US General MacArthur landed at Inchon and then Pusan, in the south. Fearing encirclement, the North's troops withdrew. The UN troops then headed north to capture the capital Pyongyang and neared Chosan on the frontier with China.

→ UN counter-attack

★ Capital city

✕ Major battle

▰▰ US fleet

◣ UN landings

▪▪▪ Extent of UN advance Nov 25, 1950

3 | THE CHINESE INVASION
OCTOBER 1950–JANUARY 1951

China warned the US that it would intervene to support North Korea if troops crossed the 38th parallel. After UN troops crossed this divide, Chinese volunteers began to cross the frontier in October 1950. The main Chinese army crossed the border in November and pushed the UN forces southward, retaking Seoul and establishing a new frontline across the south of the peninsula.

→ Chinese attack

✕ Major battle

▪▪▪ Extent of Chinese advance Jan 26, 1951

4 | STALEMATE
JANUARY 1951–JULY 1953

In the second half of January 1951, UN forces responded to the Chinese invasion, successfully containing two major Chinese attacks before launching a successful push northward in May 1951. What had been a mobile war now became static, and by November 1951, the war stabilized along a defensive line slightly north of the 38th parallel. Limited fighting continued for 2 years, until July 1953, when a ceasefire was agreed upon.

⇨ UN counter-attack

▬▬▬ Ceasefire line Jul 27, 1953

Nov 26–Dec 13, 1950 UN forces are encircled by Chinese troops at the Battle of Chosin Reservoir

Jul 27, 1953 An armistice line is established close to the 38th parallel

Nov 25, 1950 Farthest advance of UN troops toward the Chinese border

Oct 19, 1950 Pyongyang captured by UN forces

Sep 15, 1950 40,000 UN troops plus 7,000 South Korean troops launch amphibious assault at Inchon and bombard the city before recapturing Seoul and heading north

East Sea (Sea of Japan)

Yellow Sea

38th parallel

CHINA

NORTH KOREA

SOUT[H]

Chongjin
Kimchaek
Tanchon
Hyesan
Changbai
Yalu
Kanggye
Manpo
Chosan
Amu
Sinuiju
Dandong
Pyongyang
Hungnam
Wonsan
Kosong
Wonju
Seoul
Panmunjom
Inchon
Haeju
Ulchin

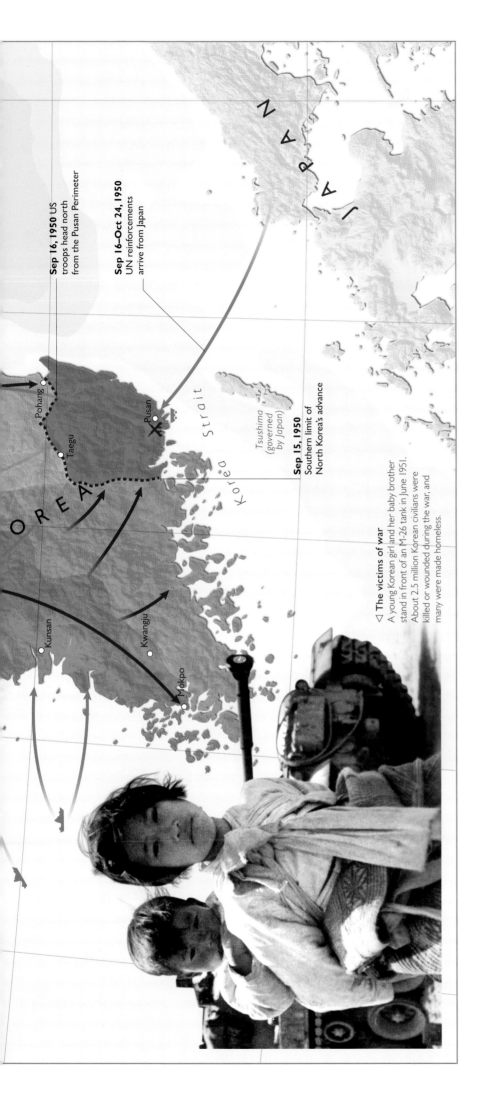

Sep 16, 1950 US
troops head north
from the Pusan Perimeter

Sep 16–Oct 24, 1950
UN reinforcements
arrive from Japan

Pohang

Pusan

Taegu

KOREA

Korea Strait

Tsushima
(governed
by Japan)

Sep 15, 1950
Southern limit of
North Korea's advance

Kunsan

Kwangju

Mokpo

JAPAN

▽ **The victims of war**
A young Korean girl and her baby brother
stand in front of an M-26 tank in June 1951.
About 2.5 million Korean civilians were
killed or wounded during the war, and
many were made homeless.

KIM IL-SUNG
1912–1994

Born near Pyongyang, Kim Il-Sung was the leader
of North Korea from 1948 until his death in 1994.
He became involved in communism as a student
and in the 1930s joined an anti-Japanese guerrilla
group. In 1940, he traveled to the USSR and later
became a major in the Soviet Army. At the end of
World War II, he returned to Korea intent on
creating a unified communist nation.

KOREAN WAR

The Cold War became "hot" in June 1950, when North Korean forces attacked South
Korea in an attempt to unite the Korean peninsula under communist control. The war
continued for 3 years, with the Chinese supporting the North and the US the South;
the expected confrontation between the USSR and the US never happened.

In 1945, at the end of World War II, the US and USSR occupied
the Japanese colony of Korea. They divided the country along the
38th parallel, with Soviet forces taking control of the north and
the US the south. The intention was to rule jointly for 5 years until
Korea became independent, but disagreements between the
two countries about Korea's future solidified the division. Both
North Korea and South Korea held their own separate elections in
1948, and the USSR and US withdrew their troops the following
year. However, North Korea intended to unify the peninsula under
communist rule, and with tacit Soviet support, but no promise

of troops, it attacked South Korea in June 1950. The invasion
was unexpected, enabling the North Korean troops to occupy
almost the entire peninsula. US, South Korean, and Allied
troops, endorsed by the UN, responded from July. The frontline
then changed as UN troops headed north, only to be met in
November by a Chinese invasion. By the middle of 1951, there
was a stalemate, which resulted in an agreed armistice in July
1953 to withdraw forces either side of the 38th parallel. That
armistice remains in force, as no permanent peace treaty
has been signed to end the war.

1 THE PHILIPPINES 1935–1946

The US had acquired the Philippines from Spain after success in the 1898 Spanish–American War. The islands were granted Commonwealth or autonomous status in 1935, but were then occupied by the Japanese between 1941 and 1945. After liberation, the Philippines became an independent republic on July 4, 1946.

2 INDONESIA 1945–1949

The Indonesian National Party proclaimed the country's independence from the Netherlands on August 17, 1945. After much fighting between the two countries, as well as a communist insurrection, independence was achieved on December 27, 1949, although constitutional links remained with the Dutch crown until 1956.

3 FRENCH INDOCHINA 1945–1954

At the end of Japanese occupation in 1945, the Viet Minh nationalist independence coalition, led by Ho Chi Minh, occupied Hanoi and proclaimed a provisional government. The French tried to restore colonial rule, leading to war in 1946. They were defeated, and on July 20, 1954, they granted independence to Cambodia, Laos, and Vietnam.

CHINA

TAIWAN

Macao **1999** Hong Kong **1997**

BURMA **1948**

Dien Bien Phu

LAOS **1954**

Hanoi

Gulf of Tongking

Hainan

Yangon (formerly Rangoon)

Bay of Bengal

THAILAND

1954 French suffer massive defeat at hands of General Giap and the Viet Minh at Dien Bien Phu

1954 Vietnam is divided in two at the Geneva Accords, with both parts being granted independence

Andaman Islands to India

CAMBODIA **1954**   VIETNAM **1954**

Andaman Sea

Nicobar Islands to India

Phnom Penh

Saigon (Ho Chi Minh City)

Gulf of Siam

South China Sea

Manila

PHILIPPINES

1946

Sulu Sea

1984 Brunei gains independence from the UK as an independent sultanate

BRITISH NORTH BORNEO (SABAH) **1963**

BRUNEI **1984**

MALAYSIA

MALAYA **1957**

SARAWAK **1963**

Celebes Sea

1965 Having joined Malaysia in 1963, Singapore then leaves to become an independent island republic in 1965

SINGAPORE **1963**

Borneo

Celebes

Sumatra

INDONESIA **1949**

Java Sea

Banda Sea

Java

EAST TIMOR **2002**

Flores

Sumba   Timor

1975 Indonesia occupies the Portuguese colony of East Timor, which gains its independence in 2002

Timor Sea

PACIFIC OCEAN

Philippine Sea

6 HONG KONG AND MACAO 1997–1999

In 1997, with the end of Britain's 99-year lease on the New Territories, Hong Kong was handed back to China. Portugal then returned Macao to Chinese rule in 1999, abolishing the last remaining European colony in Asia. The age of European colonialism in Asia was now over.

● Hong Kong   ▲ Macao

5 NEW GUINEA 1949–1975

After occupation by Australia in World War I, the northeastern half of New Guinea became an Australian mandate. It remained under Australia's control until 1975, when it became independent as Papua New Guinea. Western New Guinea had been a Dutch colony, but in 1963, it became part of Indonesia under the name of Irian Jaya.

AUSTRALIA

END OF COLONIAL RULE

The imperial powers that had colonies in Southeast Asia slowly granted their former lands independence after the end of World War II, starting with the US in the Philippines in 1946, and ending with Portugal handing over Macao to China in 1999. The transition was often violent, with fighting particularly intense in Indonesia and French Indochina.

KEY

- UK
- France
- Netherlands
- US
- Portugal
- Australia
- Independence from colonial rule

TIMELINE

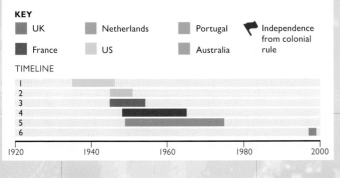

1920   1940   1960   1980   2000

△ **The fight for independence**
Protesters gather in 1975 to support an East Timor independence party. Having gained independence from Portugal in November 1975, East Timor was then occupied by Indonesia 9 days later.

Jayapura

IRIAN JAYA **1963**

TERRITORY OF NEW GUINEA

PAPUA NEW GUINEA **1975**

TERRITORY OF PAPUA

New Guinea

1963
Netherlands ...ds over Irian to Indonesia

Coral Sea

Port Moresby

4   MALAYA 1948–1963

The Japanese occupation of Malaya (1942–1945) stirred up nationalist sentiment, prompting the British to set up the Federation of Malaya in 1948. The federation united the territories and guaranteed the rights of the Malay people. It gained full independence in 1957. In 1963, the new state of Malaysia was formed, including the Federation of Malaya and the British colonies of Sarawak, Sabah, and Singapore.

DECOLONIZATION OF SOUTHEAST ASIA

In 1945, all of Southeast Asia, except Thailand, was nominally under colonial control. However, it was a time of great change; within 30 years, former empires had disappeared, and what had previously been colonies were replaced by independent states. The final colonial relics were handed over at the end of the 20th century.

During World War II, the Japanese invaded Southeast Asia, driving out the colonial powers. In 1945, at the end of the war, the colonial powers returned. However, their right to rule was now seriously challenged, as they were seen to have been weak in the face of Japanese aggression. Nationalist sentiments, stirred up by the Japanese occupation, were on the rise. Indonesian nationalists proclaimed independence even before the Dutch had time to return to Indonesia, and the Viet Minh, a Vietnamese independence group, surprised the French with their own declaration. One by one, the imperial powers started to leave the region.

The US was the first to go, leaving the Philippines peacefully in 1946, followed by the Dutch from Indonesia in 1949, after much fighting. The French left Indochina in 1954, after losing a major battle in Vietnam, then the British left Malaya between 1957 and 1963, their departure complicated by a communist uprising. The merged state of Papua New Guinea gained its independence from Australia in 1975, while Brunei gained its independence from Britain in 1984. After the British departed from Hong Kong in 1997, Macao—the last European colony in Asia—was handed over by the Portuguese to China in 1999. The colonial era was over.

"You can kill ten of my men for every one I kill of yours. But even at those odds, you will lose and I will win."

HO CHI MINH, VIETNAM'S LEADER, TO FRENCH COLONIALISTS, 1946

SUKARNO
1901–1970

Sukarno was a charter member of the Indonesian National Party, which was formed in 1927. He was jailed for political activities in 1929, and then spent 13 of the next 15 years in prison or exile. Politically astute during the Japanese occupation of 1942–1945, he emerged as the de facto president of Indonesia in November 1945. Sukarno steered Indonesia to independence in 1949, and gained great prestige as leader of the nonaligned Bandung Conference in 1955. His increasingly authoritarian tendencies and confrontation with Malaya caused him to lose power to the army leader General Muhammad Suharto in 1967.

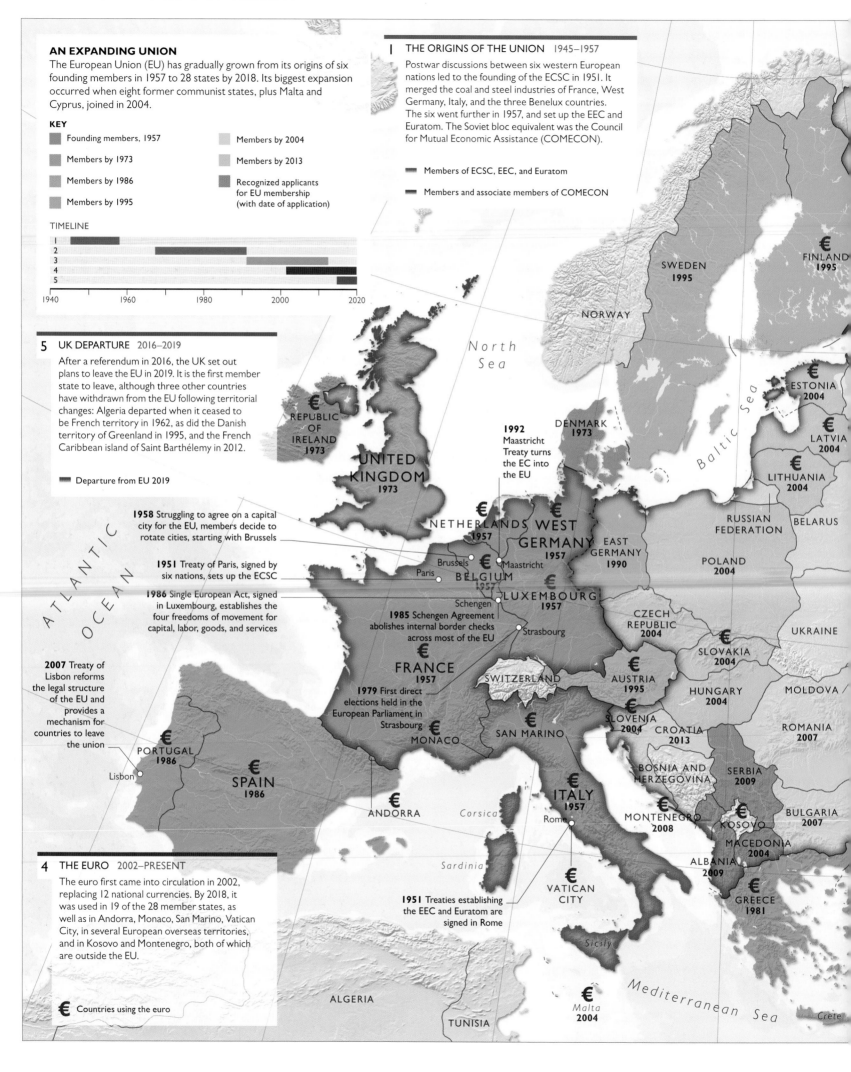

AN EXPANDING UNION

The European Union (EU) has gradually grown from its origins of six founding members in 1957 to 28 states by 2018. Its biggest expansion occurred when eight former communist states, plus Malta and Cyprus, joined in 2004.

KEY

- Founding members, 1957
- Members by 1973
- Members by 1986
- Members by 1995
- Members by 2004
- Members by 2013
- Recognized applicants for EU membership (with date of application)

TIMELINE

1
2
3
4
5

1940   1960   1980   2000   2020

THE ORIGINS OF THE UNION 1945–1957

Postwar discussions between six western European nations led to the founding of the ECSC in 1951. It merged the coal and steel industries of France, West Germany, Italy, and the three Benelux countries. The six went further in 1957, and set up the EEC and Euratom. The Soviet bloc equivalent was the Council for Mutual Economic Assistance (COMECON).

- Members of ECSC, EEC, and Euratom
- Members and associate members of COMECON

5 UK DEPARTURE 2016–2019

After a referendum in 2016, the UK set out plans to leave the EU in 2019. It is the first member state to leave, although three other countries have withdrawn from the EU following territorial changes: Algeria departed when it ceased to be French territory in 1962, as did the Danish territory of Greenland in 1995, and the French Caribbean island of Saint Barthélemy in 2012.

- Departure from EU 2019

1958 Struggling to agree on a capital city for the EU, members decide to rotate cities, starting with Brussels

1951 Treaty of Paris, signed by six nations, sets up the ECSC

1986 Single European Act, signed in Luxembourg, establishes the four freedoms of movement for capital, labor, goods, and services

2007 Treaty of Lisbon reforms the legal structure of the EU and provides a mechanism for countries to leave the union

1992 Maastricht Treaty turns the EC into the EU

1985 Schengen Agreement abolishes internal border checks across most of the EU

1979 First direct elections held in the European Parliament in Strasbourg

1951 Treaties establishing the EEC and Euratom are signed in Rome

4 THE EURO 2002–PRESENT

The euro first came into circulation in 2002, replacing 12 national currencies. By 2018, it was used in 19 of the 28 member states, as well as in Andorra, Monaco, San Marino, Vatican City, in several European overseas territories, and in Kosovo and Montenegro, both of which are outside the EU.

€ Countries using the euro

Map labels

NORWAY

SWEDEN 1995

FINLAND 1995

North Sea

Baltic Sea

ESTONIA 2004

LATVIA 2004

LITHUANIA 2004

RUSSIAN FEDERATION

BELARUS

REPUBLIC OF IRELAND 1973

UNITED KINGDOM 1973

DENMARK 1973

NETHERLANDS 1957

WEST GERMANY 1957

EAST GERMANY 1990

POLAND 2004

Brussels

Maastricht

Paris

BELGIUM 1957

LUXEMBOURG 1957

Schengen

CZECH REPUBLIC 2004

UKRAINE

SLOVAKIA 2004

Strasbourg

FRANCE 1957

SWITZERLAND

AUSTRIA 1995

HUNGARY 2004

MOLDOVA

SLOVENIA 2004

CROATIA 2013

ROMANIA 2007

ATLANTIC OCEAN

PORTUGAL 1986

Lisbon

SPAIN 1986

ANDORRA

Corsica

MONACO

SAN MARINO

ITALY 1957

Rome

VATICAN CITY

BOSNIA AND HERZEGOVINA

MONTENEGRO 2008

SERBIA 2009

KOSOVO

MACEDONIA 2004

BULGARIA 2007

Sardinia

ALBANIA 2009

GREECE 1981

Sicily

Mediterranean Sea

ALGERIA

TUNISIA

Malta 2004

Crete

△ "Europe united"
This poster from the Cold War era encourages European countries to unite as protection from the USSR. A key reason the EU was founded was to prevent another outbreak of world war.

2 EXPANSION OF THE UNION 1967–1992

In 1967, the ECSC, EEC, and Euratom were merged into the European Communities (EC). The UK, Ireland, and Denmark (including Greenland) joined in 1973, Greece in 1981, and Spain and Portugal in 1986—the latter three being former dictatorships. East Germany joined when it merged with West Germany in 1990. In 1986, the Single European Act set up the single market in goods and services.

1987 Turkey applies for EC membership; it enters into a customs union with the EU in 1996

Black Sea

TURKEY
1987

3 GROWTH OF THE EU 1992–2013

The Maastricht Treaty, signed in 1992, took European integration further. It launched its plans for economic and monetary union, leading to a single currency and the euro. It marked the end of the EC and the start of the EU. Austria, Finland, and Sweden joined in 1993, followed by an influx of 10 new states from eastern Europe and the Mediterranean in 2004. Bulgaria and Romania followed in 2007 and Croatia in 2013, bringing EU membership up to 28 states.

€
Cyprus
2004

RUSSIAN FEDERATION

EUROPEAN UNITY

Since the end of the Roman Empire in 476 CE, the dream of a united Europe has existed in some form or other. In 1951, following the mass devastation of World War II, six western European nations began a process that would ultimately lead to a political and economic union of 28 member states.

World War II was the third time in 70 years that France and Germany had been at war with one another. To end this age-old conflict, and to confront the extreme nationalism that had so recently devastated Europe, French and West German politicians began to plan a new future together. In the 1951 Treaty of Paris, they merged their coal and steel industries with those of Italy and the three Benelux countries (the Netherlands, Luxembourg, and Belgium), forming the European Coal and Steel Community (ECSC). This union was a precursor to the European Economic Community (EEC) and the European Atomic Energy Community (Euratom), which were established by the same six countries in the Treaty of Rome in 1957. From then on, the competencies and the membership of the EEC grew. In 1967, it was renamed the European Communities (EC), and in 1992 it became the European Union (EU). Waves of new members joined after 1973, and in 2002 a single currency, the euro, was introduced by 12 member states. All EU member states have been at peace with each other since joining the organization, and membership is coveted by former communist states in the Balkans. Only a few European nations are outside the Union. However, 40 years of expansion were dashed in 2016 when the UK announced plans to leave the EU.

"The coming together of the nations of Europe requires the elimination of the age-old opposition of France and Germany."

ROBERT SCHUMAN, FRENCH FOREIGN MINISTER, MAY 9, 1950

ROBERT SCHUMAN
1886–1963

One of the founding fathers of the EU, Robert Schuman was born a German national in Luxembourg. His mother was from Luxembourg, and his father, who came from Alsace, was French at birth but became German when the region was annexed by Germany in 1871. In 1919, when Alsace was reunited with France after World War I, Robert Schuman became a French national. As French foreign minister, he helped to set up the Council of Europe in 1949, to enhance human rights, and, together with French economist Jean Monnet, he was a guiding light in setting up the European Coal and Steel Community (ECSC) in 1951—the forerunner of the EU.

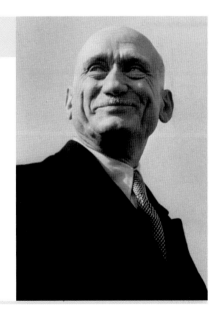

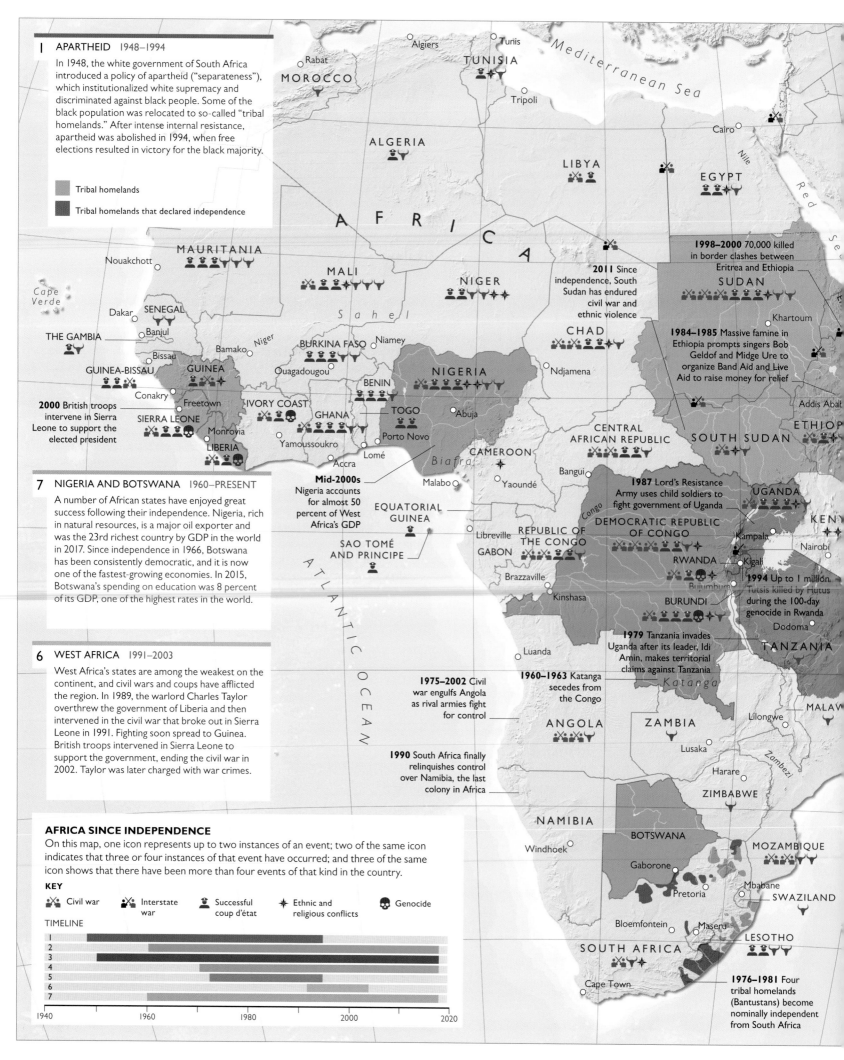

1 APARTHEID 1948–1994

In 1948, the white government of South Africa introduced a policy of apartheid ("separateness"), which institutionalized white supremacy and discriminated against black people. Some of the black population was relocated to so-called "tribal homelands." After intense internal resistance, apartheid was abolished in 1994, when free elections resulted in victory for the black majority.

Tribal homelands

Tribal homelands that declared independence

7 NIGERIA AND BOTSWANA 1960–PRESENT

A number of African states have enjoyed great success following their independence. Nigeria, rich in natural resources, is a major oil exporter and was the 23rd richest country by GDP in the world in 2017. Since independence in 1966, Botswana has been consistently democratic, and it is now one of the fastest-growing economies. In 2015, Botswana's spending on education was 8 percent of its GDP, one of the highest rates in the world.

6 WEST AFRICA 1991–2003

West Africa's states are among the weakest on the continent, and civil wars and coups have afflicted the region. In 1989, the warlord Charles Taylor overthrew the government of Liberia and then intervened in the civil war that broke out in Sierra Leone in 1991. Fighting soon spread to Guinea. British troops intervened in Sierra Leone to support the government, ending the civil war in 2002. Taylor was later charged with war crimes.

AFRICA SINCE INDEPENDENCE

On this map, one icon represents up to two instances of an event; two of the same icon indicates that three or four instances of that event have occurred; and three of the same icon shows that there have been more than four events of that kind in the country.

KEY

Civil war | Interstate war | Successful coup d'état | Ethnic and religious conflicts | Genocide

TIMELINE

1940   1960   1980   2000   2020

Map labels and annotations:

Mediterranean Sea

AFRICA

Sahel

MOROCCO — Rabat
ALGERIA — Algiers
TUNISIA — Tunis
LIBYA — Tripoli
EGYPT — Cairo
Nile
Red Sea

MAURITANIA — Nouakchott
MALI — Bamako
NIGER — Niamey
CHAD — Ndjamena
SUDAN — Khartoum
Cape Verde
SENEGAL — Dakar, Banjul
THE GAMBIA — Banjul
GUINEA-BISSAU — Bissau
GUINEA — Conakry
SIERRA LEONE — Freetown
LIBERIA — Monrovia
BURKINA FASO — Ouagadougou
BENIN — Porto Novo
NIGERIA — Abuja
IVORY COAST — Yamoussoukro
GHANA — Accra
TOGO — Lomé
CAMEROON — Yaoundé
CENTRAL AFRICAN REPUBLIC — Bangui
SOUTH SUDAN
ETHIOPIA — Addis Ababa
Biafra
EQUATORIAL GUINEA — Malabo
SAO TOMÉ AND PRINCIPE
GABON — Libreville
REPUBLIC OF THE CONGO — Brazzaville
DEMOCRATIC REPUBLIC OF CONGO — Kinshasa
Congo
UGANDA — Kampala
KENYA — Nairobi
RWANDA — Kigali
BURUNDI — Bujumbura
TANZANIA — Dodoma
Katanga
ANGOLA — Luanda
ZAMBIA — Lusaka
MALAWI — Lilongwe
ZIMBABWE — Harare
MOZAMBIQUE
Zambezi
NAMIBIA — Windhoek
BOTSWANA — Gaborone
SWAZILAND — Mbabane
LESOTHO — Maseru
SOUTH AFRICA — Pretoria, Bloemfontein, Cape Town

ATLANTIC OCEAN

Niger

1998–2000 70,000 killed in border clashes between Eritrea and Ethiopia

2011 Since independence, South Sudan has endured civil war and ethnic violence

1984–1985 Massive famine in Ethiopia prompts singers Bob Geldof and Midge Ure to organize Band Aid and Live Aid to raise money for relief

2000 British troops intervene in Sierra Leone to support the elected president

Mid-2000s Nigeria accounts for almost 50 percent of West Africa's GDP

1987 Lord's Resistance Army uses child soldiers to fight government of Uganda

1994 Up to 1 million Tutsis killed by Hutus during the 100-day genocide in Rwanda

1979 Tanzania invades Uganda after its leader, Idi Amin, makes territorial claims against Tanzania

1960–1963 Katanga secedes from the Congo

1975–2002 Civil war engulfs Angola as rival armies fight for control

1990 South Africa finally relinquishes control over Namibia, the last colony in Africa

1976–1981 Four tribal homelands (Bantustans) become nominally independent from South Africa

2 DEMOCRATIC REPUBLIC OF CONGO
1960–PRESENT

The DR Congo's independence in 1960 created a series of crises. The mineral-rich province of Katanga, hoping to secede, broke out in violence, and the recently elected Prime Minister Patrice Lumumba called on the USSR for support. Fearing communist influence in Africa, the US encouraged Congolese President Joseph Kasa-Vubu to depose Lumumba. The chief of staff of the army, Joseph-Désiré Mobutu, then launched a coup against both leaders, installing a new government. He assumed power in 1965, ruling the country (which he renamed Zaire in 1971) as a dictator.

3 FAMINE 1950–PRESENT

While famine has affected parts of the continent for centuries, from the 1950s, increasingly severe desertification; the effects of climate change, such as droughts; and problems caused by civil war caused famine to become more frequent across much of Africa. Millions have died, despite the intervention of international aid agencies.

Y Famine

4 EAST AFRICA 1970–PRESENT

From 1970–1993, Eritrea fought a long war to free itself from Ethiopia, which had taken control of it following World War II. It eventually won its independence, becoming a one-party repressive state. South Sudan fought for independence from Sudan from 1989–2005, becoming the world's newest state in 2011, when it peacefully gained independence. Central government in Somalia has collapsed since 1991 as rival warlords and Islamic groups have battled for control.

990s Somaliland
and Puntland both
declare their
independence
from Somalia

5 GREAT LAKES REGION 1972–1994

Conflict has affected much of the Great Lakes region. In 1979, Tanzania invaded Uganda to expel the tyrannical leader Idi Amin, after he tried to annex the Kagera Region in Tanzania. In Rwanda and Burundi, rivalry between two ethnic groups, the Hutu and the Tutsi, has led to ongoing conflict. A genocidal attack by Hutus against Tutsis in Rwanda in 1994 resulted in up to 1 million deaths. Many refugees fled to the DR Congo, where fighting continued.

▽ **A new dawn**
The election of Nelson Mandela as the first black president of South Africa in 1994 marked the end of apartheid, in force since 1948.

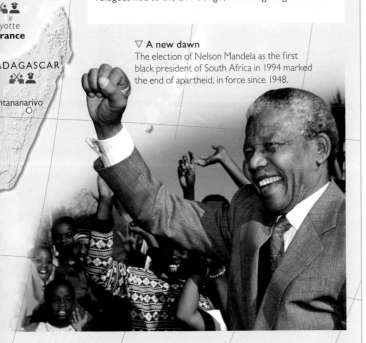

DECOLONIZATION OF AFRICA

The liberation of Africa from European rulers created 54 independent nations, many of them unprepared for the tasks of government and administration. Their recent history has been varied; while some continue to struggle with war and famine, others have been successful politically, socially, and economically.

The move toward decolonization and independence from Europe began in the 1950s, when colonies began to demand self-rule. At that time, only Egypt, Ethiopia, Liberia, and South Africa were independent nations. Libya was the first to gain its independence, in 1951 (from France and the UK), followed by Tunisia and Morocco (from France) and Sudan (from the UK) in 1956. From then on, new African countries appeared almost annually. Most gained independence peacefully, although French resistance to Algerian independence led to a brutal civil war from 1954–1962, and Portugal's refusal to hand over its five African colonies led to wars of revolt until 1974. A white-minority revolt in Rhodesia (which became Zimbabwe) delayed its independence from the UK until 1980.

By 1990, every country in Africa was independent, but many faced problems, including numerous changes of government through civil wars, coups d'état, and military dictatorships, as well as issues such as widespread poverty and famine. However, many countries are now experiencing success, including economic growth, increasing political stability, and social reform.

"The best way of learning to be an independent sovereign state is to be an independent sovereign state."

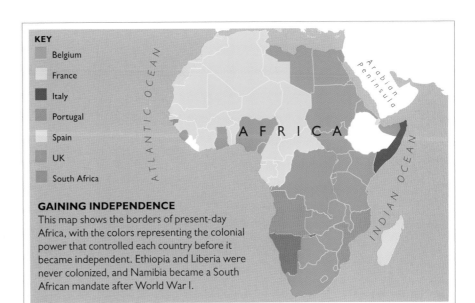

KEY
- Belgium
- France
- Italy
- Portugal
- Spain
- UK
- South Africa

GAINING INDEPENDENCE
This map shows the borders of present-day Africa, with the colors representing the colonial power that controlled each country before it became independent. Ethiopia and Liberia were never colonized, and Namibia became a South African mandate after World War I.

ROCKETS AND THE SPACE RACE

The development of the nuclear bomb and rocket technology during World War II triggered a postwar arms race between the US and the USSR. As the Cold War escalated, this race also headed into space, as each side used its rocket technology to travel to the Moon and beyond.

On September 8, 1944, Germany deployed the world's first long-range ballistic missile, the V-2 rocket. It was a devastating weapon, capable of traveling up to 200 miles (320 km) and reaching a top speed of 3,580 mph (5,760 kph). A few months earlier, it had also accidentally become the first artificial object to reach outer space when a test launch went wrong, and the rocket headed vertically off its launch site. From this military beginning emerged the technology both to carry intercontinental ballistic nuclear warheads to their distant targets and to power spacecraft and satellites into space.

At the end of World War II, and with the Cold War escalating (see pp.314–315), the US and the USSR scrambled to seize as much of this new German technology as possible. Some of the German scientists who had developed the V-2 rocket were recruited by the US to work on its military and space programs, while the Soviets based their missile program on the German rocket technology they had seized when they took over eastern Germany in 1945. The superpowers now began to fight a war on two fronts. A nuclear arms race started, with the US and the USSR each amassing enough weaponry to destroy the Earth many times over. Only the certainty of mutual destruction prevented all-out war. In a war that was as much about propaganda as weaponry, a race to reach space also began, with each country fighting to earn the international honor of having one of their men become the first person on the Moon.

PROPAGANDA
SOVIET POSTER

The US and the USSR used propaganda to promote their political ideology—capitalism or communism—and to criticize the beliefs of their enemy. Both superpowers were eager to send the first person into space because whoever achieved this victory would be able to use it for propaganda purposes and prove the superiority of their technology. This poster celebrates the USSR's victory, which came in 1961, when it sent Yuri Gagarin into space.

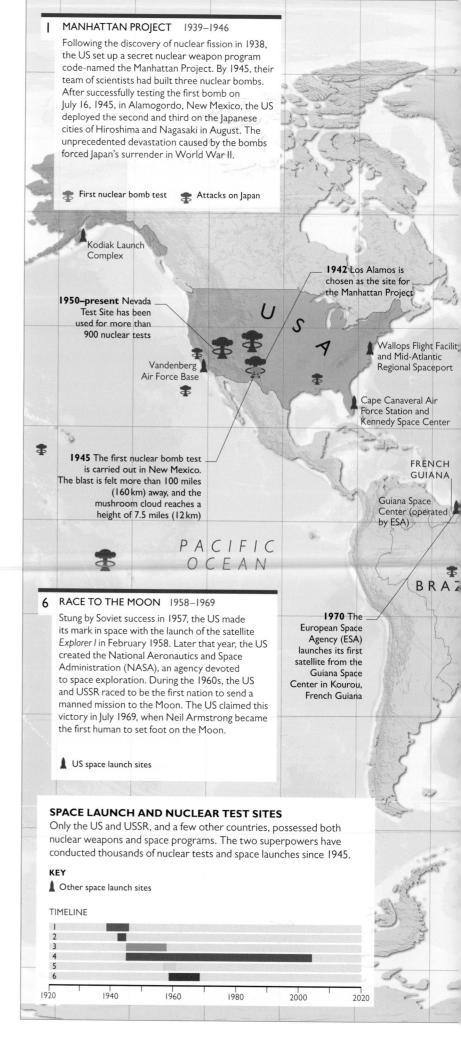

1 MANHATTAN PROJECT 1939–1946

Following the discovery of nuclear fission in 1938, the US set up a secret nuclear weapon program code-named the Manhattan Project. By 1945, their team of scientists had built three nuclear bombs. After successfully testing the first bomb on July 16, 1945, in Alamogordo, New Mexico, the US deployed the second and third on the Japanese cities of Hiroshima and Nagasaki in August. The unprecedented devastation caused by the bombs forced Japan's surrender in World War II.

☁ First nuclear bomb test   ☁ Attacks on Japan

Kodiak Launch Complex

1942 Los Alamos is chosen as the site for the Manhattan Project

1950–present Nevada Test Site has been used for more than 900 nuclear tests

Vandenberg Air Force Base

1945 The first nuclear bomb test is carried out in New Mexico. The blast is felt more than 100 miles (160 km) away, and the mushroom cloud reaches a height of 7.5 miles (12 km)

USA

Wallops Flight Facility and Mid-Atlantic Regional Spaceport

Cape Canaveral Air Force Station and Kennedy Space Center

FRENCH GUIANA

Guiana Space Center (operated by ESA)

PACIFIC OCEAN

BRAZ

6 RACE TO THE MOON 1958–1969

Stung by Soviet success in 1957, the US made its mark in space with the launch of the satellite *Explorer I* in February 1958. Later that year, the US created the National Aeronautics and Space Administration (NASA), an agency devoted to space exploration. During the 1960s, the US and USSR raced to be the first nation to send a manned mission to the Moon. The US claimed this victory in July 1969, when Neil Armstrong became the first human to set foot on the Moon.

1970 The European Space Agency (ESA) launches its first satellite from the Guiana Space Center in Kourou, French Guiana

▲ US space launch sites

SPACE LAUNCH AND NUCLEAR TEST SITES

Only the US and USSR, and a few other countries, possessed both nuclear weapons and space programs. The two superpowers have conducted thousands of nuclear tests and space launches since 1945.

KEY

▲ Other space launch sites

TIMELINE

	1920	1940	1960	1980	2000	2020
1						
2						
3						
4						
5						
6						

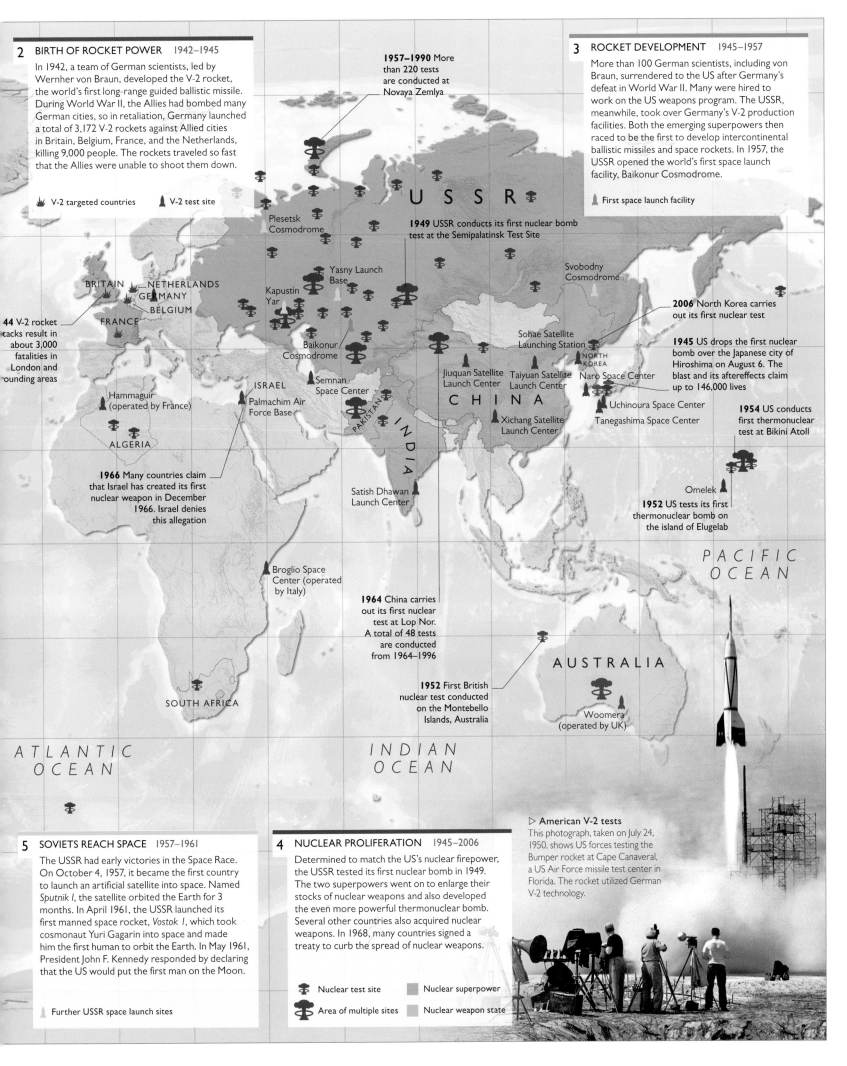

2 BIRTH OF ROCKET POWER 1942–1945

In 1942, a team of German scientists, led by Wernher von Braun, developed the V-2 rocket, the world's first long-range guided ballistic missile. During World War II, the Allies had bombed many German cities, so in retaliation, Germany launched a total of 3,172 V-2 rockets against Allied cities in Britain, Belgium, France, and the Netherlands, killing 9,000 people. The rockets traveled so fast that the Allies were unable to shoot them down.

🏹 V-2 targeted countries   🔺 V-2 test site

1957–1990 More than 220 tests are conducted at Novaya Zemlya

1949 USSR conducts its first nuclear bomb test at the Semipalatinsk Test Site

3 ROCKET DEVELOPMENT 1945–1957

More than 100 German scientists, including von Braun, surrendered to the US after Germany's defeat in World War II. Many were hired to work on the US weapons program. The USSR, meanwhile, took over Germany's V-2 production facilities. Both the emerging superpowers then raced to be the first to develop intercontinental ballistic missiles and space rockets. In 1957, the USSR opened the world's first space launch facility, Baikonur Cosmodrome.

🔺 First space launch facility

2006 North Korea carries out its first nuclear test

1945 US drops the first nuclear bomb over the Japanese city of Hiroshima on August 6. The blast and its aftereffects claim up to 146,000 lives

1954 US conducts first thermonuclear test at Bikini Atoll

1952 US tests its first thermonuclear bomb on the island of Elugelab

44 V-2 rocket attacks result in about 3,000 fatalities in London and surrounding areas

1966 Many countries claim that Israel has created its first nuclear weapon in December 1966. Israel denies this allegation

Plesetsk Cosmodrome

Yasny Launch Base

Kapustin Yar

Baikonur Cosmodrome

Semnan Space Center

Svobodny Cosmodrome

Sohae Satellite Launching Station

NORTH KOREA

Naro Space Center

Uchinoura Space Center

Tanegashima Space Center

Jiuquan Satellite Launch Center

Taiyuan Satellite Launch Center

Xichang Satellite Launch Center

USSR

CHINA

INDIA

PAKISTAN

ISRAEL
Palmachim Air Force Base

Hammaguir (operated by France)

ALGERIA

BRITAIN
NETHERLANDS
GERMANY
BELGIUM
FRANCE

Broglio Space Center (operated by Italy)

Satish Dhawan Launch Center

Omelek

1964 China carries out its first nuclear test at Lop Nor. A total of 48 tests are conducted from 1964–1996

1952 First British nuclear test conducted on the Montebello Islands, Australia

SOUTH AFRICA

AUSTRALIA

Woomera (operated by UK)

PACIFIC OCEAN

ATLANTIC OCEAN

INDIAN OCEAN

▷ **American V-2 tests**
This photograph, taken on July 24, 1950, shows US forces testing the Bumper rocket at Cape Canaveral, a US Air Force missile test center in Florida. The rocket utilized German V-2 technology.

5 SOVIETS REACH SPACE 1957–1961

The USSR had early victories in the Space Race. On October 4, 1957, it became the first country to launch an artificial satellite into space. Named *Sputnik 1*, the satellite orbited the Earth for 3 months. In April 1961, the USSR launched its first manned space rocket, *Vostok 1*, which took cosmonaut Yuri Gagarin into space and made him the first human to orbit the Earth. In May 1961, President John F. Kennedy responded by declaring that the US would put the first man on the Moon.

🔺 Further USSR space launch sites

4 NUCLEAR PROLIFERATION 1945–2006

Determined to match the US's nuclear firepower, the USSR tested its first nuclear bomb in 1949. The two superpowers went on to enlarge their stocks of nuclear weapons and also developed the even more powerful thermonuclear bomb. Several other countries also acquired nuclear weapons. In 1968, many countries signed a treaty to curb the spread of nuclear weapons.

💥 Nuclear test site   Nuclear superpower

💥 Area of multiple sites   Nuclear weapon state

I am a man
Civil rights protesters walk past the US National
Guard, who can be seen with fixed bayonets, on
March 29, 1968, in Tennessee. Dr. Martin Luther
King Jr. was assassinated less than a week later.

CIVIL RIGHTS AND STUDENT REVOLTS

Activists have campaigned for human rights since the turn of the 20th century. In the 1960s, the US and France in particular saw popular pressure for reform.

From the abolition of slavery to voting rights for women, social movements have been an instrument of change across the world. The US in the 1950s was a country riddled with racial inequality. In December 1955, Rosa Parks, a black civil rights activist, refused to give up her seat on a bus to a white passenger in Alabama. Her arrest sparked the modern civil rights movement. In August 1963, Dr. Martin Luther King Jr., a leading proponent of civil rights in the US, gave an inspiring speech to about 250,000 protesters, setting out his vision of a country free of prejudice. Segregation was abolished in 1964; the following year, all black people were given voting rights.

The year 1968 became the year of revolutions. Even as there were massive demonstrations in the US against the Vietnam War, student riots in Paris over poor university campus facilities spread across France. About 8 million workers joined the students and went on strike, calling for change. This was the defining moment of a year that saw young people across the Western world protest against outmoded bureaucracies, oppressive regimes, racial and gender inequality, and prejudice against sexual minorities. Although the protests in France died down, the events of 1968 inspired a generation.

MA168

DEBUT D'UNE LUTTE PROLONGEE

△ **French May**
A poster proclaims the "beginning of a long struggle" during the civil unrest spearheaded by students in May 1968 in France.

DESEGREGATION IN THE AMERICAN SOUTH

In the 1950s, many aspects of life were still racially segregated in the southern states of the US. The states identified on this map all enforced segregation until 1957. By 1964, they had begun to desegregate to varying degrees.

KEY
AFRICAN AMERICANS IN SCHOOLS WITH WHITES, 1964

- 0–1%
- 1.5–6%
- 28–60%

THE VIETNAM WARS

The two major wars in Vietnam after World War II were by far the most violent conflicts in Southeast Asia in the 20th century. Between them, they lasted almost 30 years and involved several major global powers. Although Vietnam had declared its independence in 1945, it was not fully achieved until 1975, once all foreign forces had left and the country was unified.

Fighting in Vietnam began when the Japanese occupied the French-ruled colony during World War II. The Viet Minh, a nationalist organization, led the resistance from 1941. After Japan was defeated in 1945, the French returned to Vietnam, and again the Viet Minh took up arms against the foreign forces. The ensuing and protracted war between Vietnam and France—known as the First Indochina War—began in 1946 and ended in the decisive defeat of the French at Dien Bien Phu in 1954. The now-independent Vietnam was then divided into the communist north and republican south. After a

partial lull, fighting broke out again in 1956, as the North Vietnamese fought to unite the country under their leadership. The war that then erupted—called the Second Indochina War, or the Vietnam War—was in many ways a proxy struggle within the global context of the Cold War, with the US supporting South Vietnam, and the USSR and China on the side of North Vietnam. The war also spread into Laos and Cambodia. Eventually, in the face of defeat, the US negotiated its way out of the war in 1973, paving the way for an eventual North Vietnamese victory and reunification of Vietnam in 1975.

GENERAL GIÁP
1911–2013

Vo Nguyen Giáp is considered to be one of the greatest military strategists of the 20th century, having mastered both conventional and guerrilla war tactics. Leading the Viet Minh resistance against Japanese occupation of Vietnam during World War II, he also led North Vietnamese forces against the French and then the US. His victory at Dien Bien Phu, in March–May 1954, is seen as one of the greatest military victories in modern history.

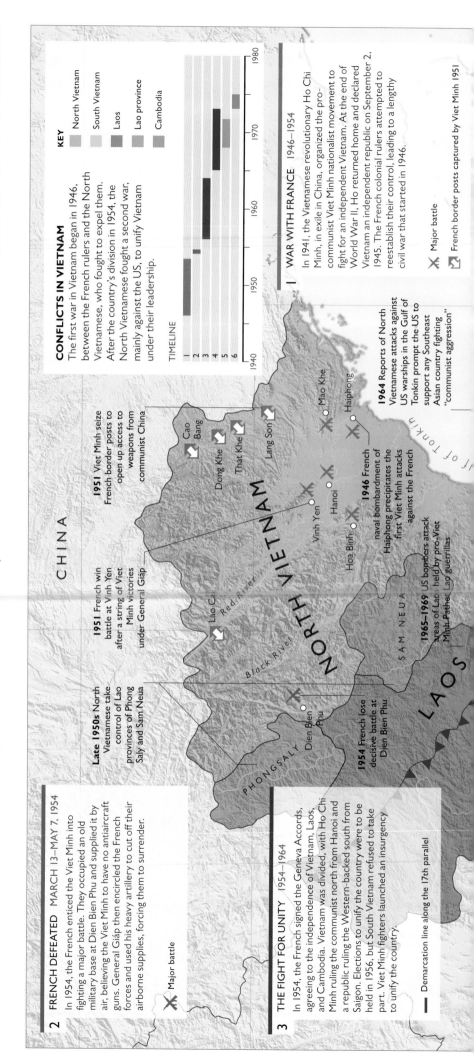

CONFLICTS IN VIETNAM

The first war in Vietnam began in 1946, between the French rulers and the North Vietnamese, who fought to expel them. After the country's division in 1954, the North Vietnamese fought a second war, mainly against the US, to unify Vietnam under their leadership.

TIMELINE

KEY
- North Vietnam
- South Vietnam
- Laos
- Lao province
- Cambodia

1940 | 1950 | 1960 | 1970 | 1980

1 WAR WITH FRANCE 1946–1954

In 1941, the Vietnamese revolutionary Ho Chi Minh, in exile in China, organized the pro-communist Viet Minh nationalist movement to fight for an independent Vietnam. At the end of World War II, Ho returned home and declared Vietnam an independent republic on September 2, 1945. The French colonial rulers attempted to reestablish their control, leading to a lengthy civil war that started in 1946.

✕ Major battle

↩ French border posts captured by Viet Minh 1951

2 FRENCH DEFEATED MARCH 13–MAY 7, 1954

In 1954, the French enticed the Viet Minh into fighting a major battle. They occupied an old military base at Dien Bien Phu and supplied it by air, believing the Viet Minh to have no antiaircraft guns. General Giáp then encircled the French forces and used his heavy artillery to cut off their airborne supplies, forcing them to surrender.

✕ Major battle

3 THE FIGHT FOR UNITY 1954–1964

In 1954, the French signed the Geneva Accords, agreeing to the independence of Vietnam, Laos, and Cambodia. Vietnam was divided, with Ho Chi Minh ruling the communist north from Hanoi and a republic ruling the Western-backed south from Saigon. Elections to unify the country were to be held in 1956, but South Vietnam refused to take part. Viet Minh fighters launched an insurgency to unify the country.

— Demarcation line along the 17th parallel

Map labels

CHINA

Cao Bang
Dong Khe
That Khe
Lang Son
Mao Khe
Haiphong
Vinh Yen
Hanoi
Hoa Binh
Lao Cai
Red River
Black River
NORTH VIETNAM
SAM NEUA
Dien Bien Phu
PHONGSALY
LAOS
Gulf of Tonkin

1951 Viet Minh seize French border posts to open up access to weapons from communist China

1951 French win battle at Vinh Yen after a string of Viet Minh victories under General Giáp

Late 1950s North Vietnamese take control of Lao provinces of Phong Saly and Sam Neua

1946 French naval bombardment of Haiphong precipitates the first Viet Minh attacks against the French

1954 French lose decisive battle at Dien Bien Phu

1964 Reports of North Vietnamese attacks against US warships in the Gulf of Tonkin prompt the US to support any Southeast Asian country fighting "communist aggression"

1965–1969 US bombers attack areas of Laos held by pro-Viet Minh Pathet Lao guerrillas

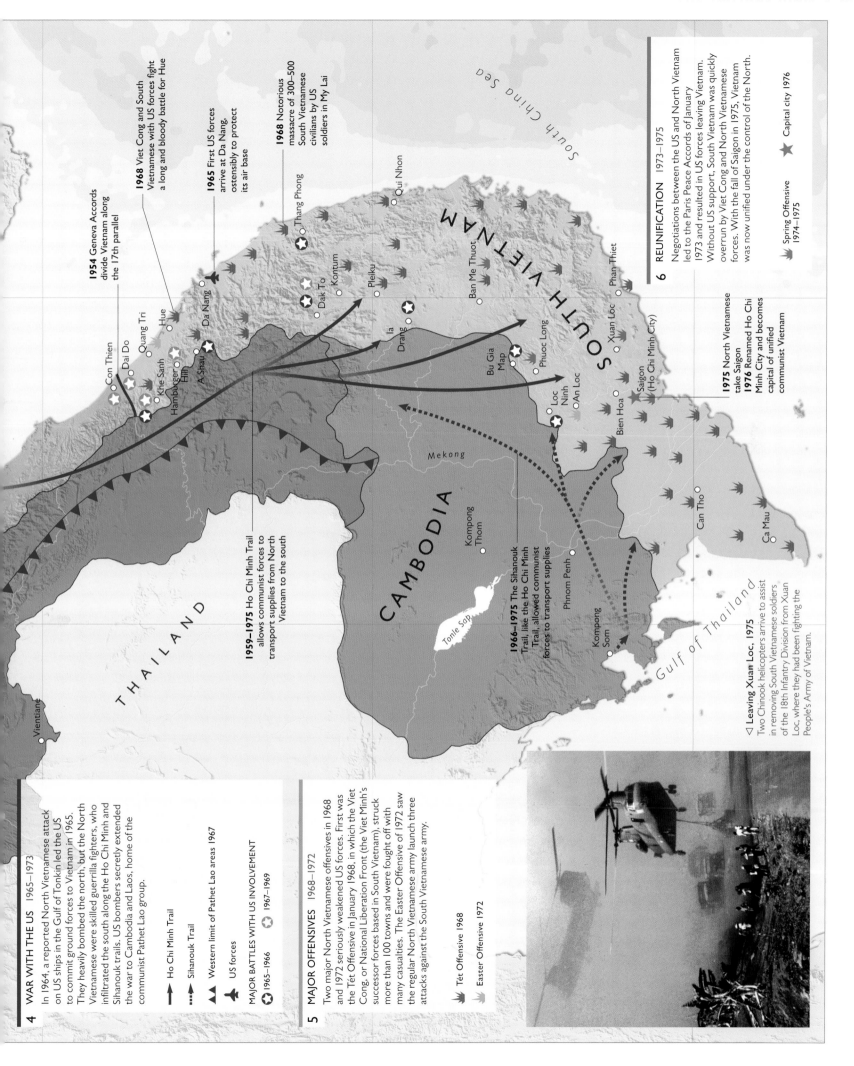

South China Sea

МА ИТЭ ІV НТUОƧ *(SOUTH VIETNAM)*

1954 Geneva Accords divide Vietnam along the 17th parallel

1968 Viet Cong and South Vietnamese with US forces fight a long and bloody battle for Hue

1965 First US forces arrive at Da Nang, ostensibly to protect its air base

1968 Notorious massacre of 300–500 South Vietnamese civilians by US soldiers in My Lai

Thang Phong

Qui Nhon

Kontum

Dak To

Pleiku

Ia Drang

Ban Me Thuot

Phan Thiet

Xuan Loc

Con Thien

Dai Do

Quang Tri

Hue

Khe Sanh

Hamburger Hill

A Shau

Da Nang

Bu Gia Map

Phuoc Long

Loc Ninh

An Loc

Bien Hoa

Saigon (Ho Chi Minh City)

Can Tho

Ca Mau

1959–1975 Ho Chi Minh Trail allows communist forces to transport supplies from North Vietnam to the south

Mekong

CAMBODIA

Kompong Thom

Tonle Sap

Phnom Penh

Kompong Som

1966–1975 The Sihanouk Trail, like the Ho Chi Minh Trail, allowed communist forces to transport supplies

THAILAND

Vientiane

Gulf of Thailand

6 REUNIFICATION 1973–1975

Negotiations between the US and North Vietnam led to the Paris Peace Accords of January 1973 and resulted in US forces leaving Vietnam. Without US support, South Vietnam was quickly overrun by Viet Cong and North Vietnamese forces. With the fall of Saigon in 1975, Vietnam was now unified under the control of the North.

↦ Spring Offensive 1974–1975   ★ Capital city 1976

1975 North Vietnamese take Saigon
1976 Renamed Ho Chi Minh City and becomes capital of unified communist Vietnam

▽ **Leaving Xuan Loc, 1975**
Two Chinook helicopters arrive to assist in removing South Vietnamese soldiers of the 18th Infantry Division from Xuan Loc, where they had been fighting the People's Army of Vietnam.

4 WAR WITH THE US 1965–1973

In 1964, a reported North Vietnamese attack on US ships in the Gulf of Tonkin led the US to commit ground forces to Vietnam in 1965. They heavily bombed the north, but the North Vietnamese were skilled guerrilla fighters, who infiltrated the south along the Ho Chi Minh and Sihanouk trails. US bombers secretly extended the war to Cambodia and Laos, home of the communist Pathet Lao group.

→ Ho Chi Minh Trail
⇢ Sihanouk Trail
▲▲ Western limit of Pathet Lao areas 1967
✈ US forces

MAJOR BATTLES WITH US INVOLVEMENT

⊛ 1965–1966   ⊛ 1967–1969

5 MAJOR OFFENSIVES 1968–1972

Two major North Vietnamese offensives in 1968 and 1972 seriously weakened US forces. First was the Tét Offensive in January 1968, in which the Viet Cong, or National Liberation Front (the Viet Minh's successor forces based in South Vietnam), struck more than 100 towns and were fought off with many casualties. The Easter Offensive of 1972 saw the regular North Vietnamese army launch three attacks against the South Vietnamese army.

↦ Tét Offensive 1968
↦ Easter Offensive 1972

1 GUATEMALA 1954–1996

Following a coup in 1944, Guatemala was led by the first two democratically elected presidents: Juan José Arévalo and Jacobo Árbenz. Both based many of their policies on US President Franklin Roosevelt's New Deal. The US government believed this new Guatemalan government to be pro-communist, and in 1954 the CIA funded an invasion to overthrow it, installing the dictator Carlos Castillo Armas. Guerrilla activity against the military government increased from the 1960s, leading to a civil war that ended in 1996.

⚔ Civil war   🛡 Military coup

☭ Guerrilla activity

1954 CIA-funded force of 480 men invades Guatemala

1960–1996 Civil war breaks out between the Guatemalan government and left-wing groups

2 CUBAN MISSILE CRISIS   OCTOBER 1962

In 1959, Fidel Castro came to power in Cuba. Initially, the US accepted his regime, but Cuba's links with the USSR soon soured relations. In early 1961, the US cut off diplomatic ties with Cuba, and in April 1961, the US attempted to overthrow Castro with the failed Bay of Pigs invasion. In October 1962, aerial images of Soviet nuclear missiles on board ships traveling toward Cuba convinced US President John F. Kennedy to impose a blockade around Cuba. For 13 days, the two superpowers threatened global nuclear destruction. The blockade was eventually lifted after a tacit compromise between the US and the USSR.

▮ Potential range of Soviet missiles   ▮ US naval blockade

✈ Soviet jet and missile bases   ✈ US air base   ⚓ US naval base

1962 The US enforces a naval blockade of Cuba

1961 Cuban exiles supported by the CIA attempt to invade Cuba at the Bay of Pigs

1962 The USSR builds missile bases in Cuba

1962 US Task Force 136 patrols the seas in a blockade of Cuba

1980s The US establishes a military presence in Honduras

1984–1990 Contra rebels, who are largely based in Honduras, attack the Nicaraguan Sandinista government. They are funded by the US

1999 The US returns control of the Panama Canal Zone to the government of Panama

7 HAITI   1994–2004

The lengthy Duvalier family dictatorship was toppled in Haiti in 1986. In 1990, the radical priest Jean-Bertrand Aristide won the presidential election, but he was soon forced out by a military coup. The brutality of the military regime, along with the threat of a US invasion, brought Aristide back to power in 1994. His second term, which began in 2000, was ended by a US-backed coup in 2004, leading to Aristide's exile.

🛡 Military coup   🚁 US troops

6 PANAMA   1977–1999

US relations with Panama had been difficult due to American ownership of the Panama Canal Zone since 1903. A treaty was eventually signed in 1977 to hand over the zone by 1999, but in 1989, American troops invaded Panama to seize leader General Manuel Noriega after he was indicted by federal grand juries on charges of drug trafficking, racketeering, and money laundering.

☭ Guerrilla activity

1983 The US intervenes in Grenada to oust the island's revolutionary government

5 NICARAGUA   1979–1990

Installed with US support in 1927, the Somoza family ruled Nicaragua until it was ousted by the socialist Sandinista National Liberation Front (FSLN) in 1979. At first, the US supported the new government, but it suspended aid in 1980 when it came to light that Nicaragua was arming rebels in El Salvador. Under President Ronald Reagan, the CIA supported the Contra rebels who were fighting the Sandinista government. The FSLN were defeated at the polls in 1990.

✊ Contra rebels   ✊ Revolution

Map labels

ATLANTIC OCEAN

PACIFIC OCEAN

Caribbean Sea

Gulf of Mexico

U S A

MEXICO

Chicago
St. Louis
New York City
Philadelphia
Washington, DC
Jacksonville
Mobile
New Orleans
Tampa
Miami
Key West
Havana
Monterrey
Tampico
Mexico City
Veracruz

CUBA
BAHAMAS
JAMAICA
HAITI
DOMINICAN REPUBLIC
Santo Domingo
PUERTO RICO
San Juan
VIRGIN ISLANDS
ANTIGUA AND BARBUDA
GUADELOUPE
MARTINIQUE
ST. LUCIA
BARBADOS
TRINIDAD AND TOBAGO
GRENADA
NETHERLANDS ANTILLES
Caracas

BRITISH HONDURAS
GUATEMALA
EL SALVADOR
HONDURAS
NICARAGUA
COSTA RICA
Panama Canal
PANAMA
Panama City

VENEZUELA
GUYANA
COLOMBIA
ECUADOR
PERU
BRAZIL

In 1970, Salvador Allende became the President of Chile—the first Marxist to be elected through open elections. Opposition groups soon declared his rule unconstitutional, and he was overthrown by General Augusto Pinochet in a military coup supported by the CIA in 1973. Pinochet's anti-communist dictatorship was marked by numerous human rights violations, but he held on to power until 1989.

🔊 Military coup

US INTERVENTION IN CENTRAL AND SOUTH AMERICA

Since the end of World War II, the US has intervened in numerous Central and South American nations, overthrowing elected governments and supporting right-wing or military alternatives. Its interventions in Cuba almost brought the world to the brink of nuclear war.

TIMELINE

1
2
3
4
5
6
7

1950   1970   1990   2010

◁ **Revolution in Cuba**
Communist rebel leader Fidel Castro and his army celebrate. Castro overthrew the dictatorship of Fulgencio Batistá to come to power in Cuba in 1957. Castro then ruled Cuba as a one-party socialist state for the next 50 years.

3   DOMINICAN REPUBLIC   1961–1965

After the assassination of dictatorial President Rafael Trujillo in 1961, a left-wing democratic government under Juan Bosch led the Dominican Republic. Bosch was overthrown in a military coup in September 1963, but a pro-Bosch revolt soon broke out. Concerned that this situation was similar to events in Cuba, US President Lyndon Johnson sent in troops to crush the uprising and allow a repressive government to take power.

🔊 Military coup   ✈ US troops

BOLIVIA

CHILE

ARGENTINA

○ Santiago

CHE GUEVARA
1928–1967

Born in 1928 to a left-wing, middle-class Argentine family, Ernesto Guevara—later known by the nickname Che, meaning "friend"—was a Marxist revolutionary and the leader of the guerrilla army during the Cuban Revolution. As a student, he took two motorcycle journeys around Latin America; the appalling conditions he saw, which he attributed to the capitalist US exploiting Latin America, consolidated his revolutionary ideas.

US INTERVENTIONS IN LATIN AMERICA

Since the 19th century, the US's foreign policies in Central and South America have been geared toward protecting its business interests in the region. Fearful of communist influence, the US has often become involved—covertly and otherwise—in Latin American politics.

In 1823, US President James Monroe announced a formal doctrine that any efforts by nations to take control of independent states in the American continent would be viewed as "the manifestation of an unfriendly disposition toward the United States." Over a century later, this doctrine enabled the US to exert control over its southern neighbors during the Cold War (see pp.314–315) in order to prevent the spread of communism in the region. As a result, there is barely a country in the region that has remained unaffected in some way by American intervention. Elected governments have been overthrown in Guatemala, Chile, and Haiti; a left-wing government was undermined in Nicaragua; democratic uprisings have been quashed in El Salvador and the Dominican Republic; and authoritarian governments have been supported in Honduras and elsewhere. US military intervention to overthrow the convicted drug trafficker and leader of Panama General Manuel Noriega, as well as to bring a recently deposed government back to power in Haiti, reinforces the picture of the US engaging actively in Latin American politics.

The effect on the countries invaded or influenced by the US has been considerable, with many enduring long periods of military or authoritarian rule. The end of the Cold War in 1991, and the resumption of relations between the US and Cuba in 2015 after 54 years, led to a revival of multiparty democracies. These changes also increased political and economic stability in the region, despite a long-running civil war in Colombia and upheavals in socialist Venezuela.

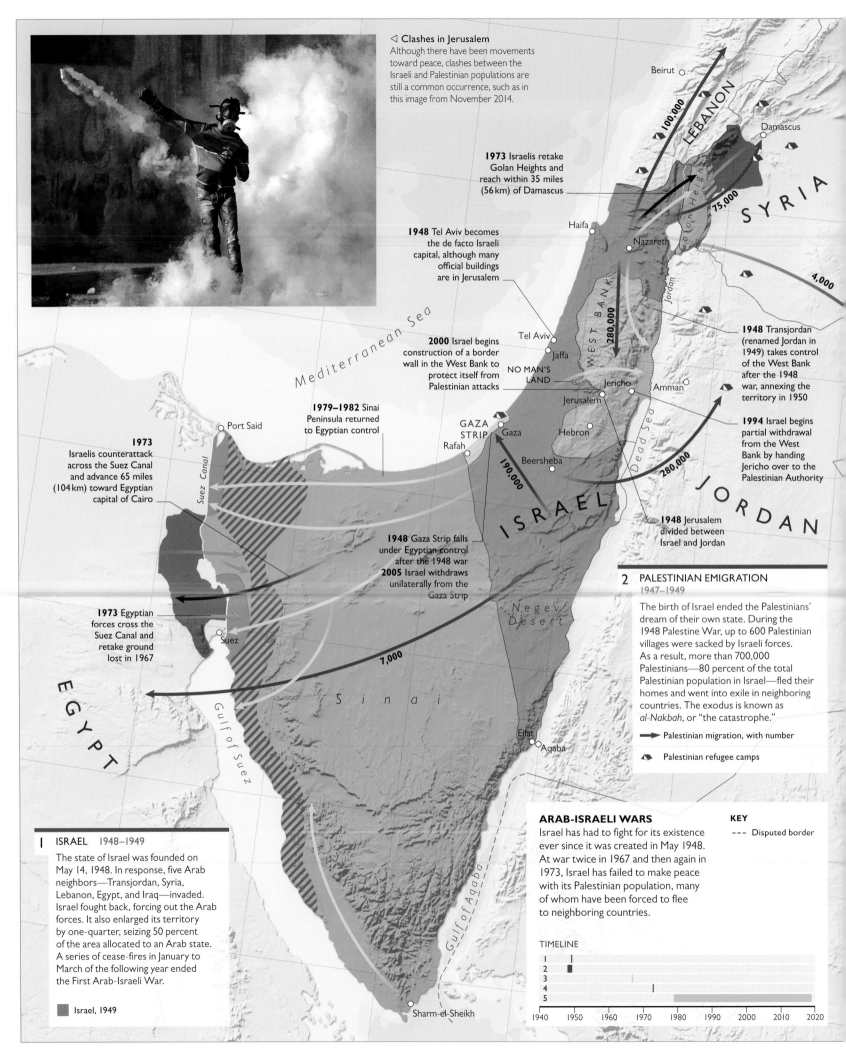

◁ **Clashes in Jerusalem**
Although there have been movements toward peace, clashes between the Israeli and Palestinian populations are still a common occurrence, such as in this image from November 2014.

1973 Israelis retake Golan Heights and reach within 35 miles (56 km) of Damascus

1948 Tel Aviv becomes the de facto Israeli capital, although many official buildings are in Jerusalem

2000 Israel begins construction of a border wall in the West Bank to protect itself from Palestinian attacks

1979–1982 Sinai Peninsula returned to Egyptian control

1973 Israelis counterattack across the Suez Canal and advance 65 miles (104 km) toward Egyptian capital of Cairo

1948 Gaza Strip falls under Egyptian control after the 1948 war
2005 Israel withdraws unilaterally from the Gaza Strip

1973 Egyptian forces cross the Suez Canal and retake ground lost in 1967

1948 Transjordan (renamed Jordan in 1949) takes control of the West Bank after the 1948 war, annexing the territory in 1950

1994 Israel begins partial withdrawal from the West Bank by handing Jericho over to the Palestinian Authority

1948 Jerusalem divided between Israel and Jordan

Beirut

LEBANON

Damascus

SYRIA

Golan Heights

Haifa

Nazareth

WEST BANK

Jordan

Tel Aviv

Jaffa

NO MAN'S LAND

Jericho

Amman

Jerusalem

GAZA STRIP

Gaza

Hebron

Dead Sea

Rafah

Beersheba

JORDAN

ISRAEL

Mediterranean Sea

Port Said

Suez Canal

Negev Desert

Suez

EGYPT

Gulf of Suez

Sinai

Eilat

Aqaba

Gulf of Aqaba

Sharm-el-Sheikh

100,000

75,000

4,000

280,000

190,000

280,000

7,000

2 PALESTINIAN EMIGRATION
1947–1949

The birth of Israel ended the Palestinians' dream of their own state. During the 1948 Palestine War, up to 600 Palestinian villages were sacked by Israeli forces. As a result, more than 700,000 Palestinians—80 percent of the total Palestinian population in Israel—fled their homes and went into exile in neighboring countries. The exodus is known as *al-Nakbah*, or "the catastrophe."

➤ Palestinian migration, with number

◆ Palestinian refugee camps

ARAB-ISRAELI WARS
Israel has had to fight for its existence ever since it was created in May 1948. At war twice in 1967 and then again in 1973, Israel has failed to make peace with its Palestinian population, many of whom have been forced to flee to neighboring countries.

KEY

--- Disputed border

TIMELINE

	1940	1950	1960	1970	1980	1990	2000	2010	2020
1									
2									
3									
4									
5									

1 ISRAEL 1948–1949

The state of Israel was founded on May 14, 1948. In response, five Arab neighbors—Transjordan, Syria, Lebanon, Egypt, and Iraq—invaded. Israel fought back, forcing out the Arab forces. It also enlarged its territory by one-quarter, seizing 50 percent of the area allocated to an Arab state. A series of cease-fires in January to March of the following year ended the First Arab-Israeli War.

■ Israel, 1949

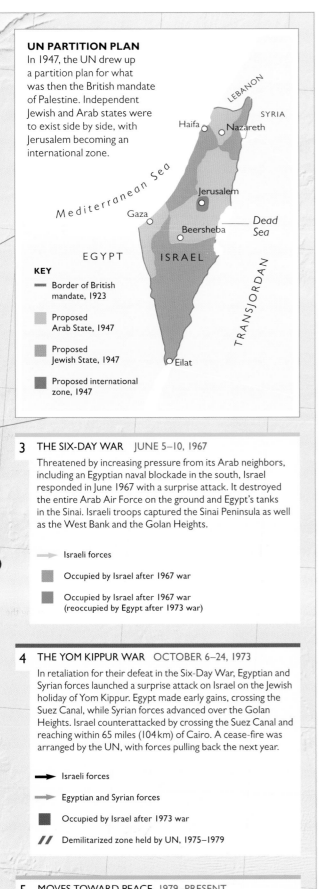

UN PARTITION PLAN
In 1947, the UN drew up a partition plan for what was then the British mandate of Palestine. Independent Jewish and Arab states were to exist side by side, with Jerusalem becoming an international zone.

KEY
- Border of British mandate, 1923
- Proposed Arab State, 1947
- Proposed Jewish State, 1947
- Proposed international zone, 1947

3 THE SIX-DAY WAR JUNE 5–10, 1967
Threatened by increasing pressure from its Arab neighbors, including an Egyptian naval blockade in the south, Israel responded in June 1967 with a surprise attack. It destroyed the entire Arab Air Force on the ground and Egypt's tanks in the Sinai. Israeli troops captured the Sinai Peninsula as well as the West Bank and the Golan Heights.

- Israeli forces
- Occupied by Israel after 1967 war
- Occupied by Israel after 1967 war (reoccupied by Egypt after 1973 war)

4 THE YOM KIPPUR WAR OCTOBER 6–24, 1973
In retaliation for their defeat in the Six-Day War, Egyptian and Syrian forces launched a surprise attack on Israel on the Jewish holiday of Yom Kippur. Egypt made early gains, crossing the Suez Canal, while Syrian forces advanced over the Golan Heights. Israel counterattacked by crossing the Suez Canal and reaching within 65 miles (104 km) of Cairo. A cease-fire was arranged by the UN, with forces pulling back the next year.

- Israeli forces
- Egyptian and Syrian forces
- Occupied by Israel after 1973 war
- Demilitarized zone held by UN, 1975–1979

5 MOVES TOWARD PEACE 1979–PRESENT
In 1979, Israel signed a peace treaty with Egypt and handed back the Sinai Peninsula. The 1993 Oslo I Accord created a Palestinian government, the Palestinian Authority, which was given some jurisdiction in the Gaza Strip and the West Bank. Israel withdrew from Gaza but has been reluctant to relinquish Jerusalem and the West Bank.

- West Bank
- Gaza Strip

ISRAEL AND THE MIDDLE EAST

A Jewish population has existed in Palestine for centuries, but the founding of the Zionist Organization in 1897 marked new efforts to create a Jewish homeland in the region. The state of Israel created such a place but sparked a series of wars.

In November 1947, the United Nations, the overseers of the British mandate over Palestine (see pp.284–285), decided to partition the territory into independent Palestinian and Jewish states, in part as a response to Jewish displacement after the Holocaust. As a result of this declaration, violence broke out between the two sides, and British control broke down. The plan was abandoned, and the British ended their mandate over Palestine on May 14, 1948. The head of the Jewish Agency and future prime minister David Ben-Gurion then immediately declared the foundation of the independent state of Israel. Israeli forces promptly captured swathes of Palestinian territory and drove many of its people into exile in nearby countries. Israel's Arab neighbors became involved in the conflict, while Israel successfully fought back.

After decades of turmoil, both sides began to make steps toward peace. In 1979, Egypt and Israel signed a peace treaty, with Egypt recognizing the state of Israel and Israeli forces withdrawing from occupied Sinai. In 1993, Israel signed an accord with the Palestinian Liberation Organization—which for the first time recognized the existence of Israel—and began to disengage from the Gaza Strip and the West Bank. However, Israel's intention to cede land for peace has proved difficult to put into practice, with the result that relations with Palestinians remain fraught.

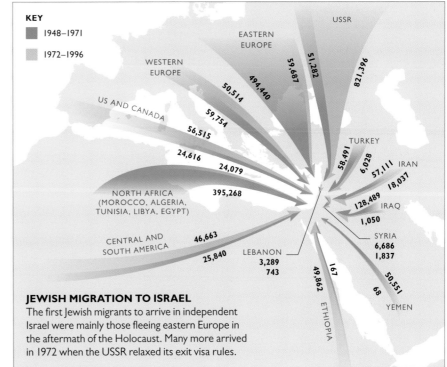

KEY
- 1948–1971
- 1972–1996

USSR — 821,396
EASTERN EUROPE — 59,687
— 51,282
WESTERN EUROPE — 494,440
— 50,514
US AND CANADA — 59,754
— 56,515
— 24,616
— 24,079
NORTH AFRICA (MOROCCO, ALGERIA, TUNISIA, LIBYA, EGYPT) — 395,268
TURKEY — 58,491
— 6,028
IRAN — 57,111
— 18,037
IRAQ — 128,489
— 1,050
SYRIA — 6,686
— 1,837
CENTRAL AND SOUTH AMERICA — 46,663
— 25,840
LEBANON — 3,289
— 743
— 167
— 49,862
— 50,551
— 68
ETHIOPIA
YEMEN

JEWISH MIGRATION TO ISRAEL
The first Jewish migrants to arrive in independent Israel were mainly those fleeing eastern Europe in the aftermath of the Holocaust. Many more arrived in 1972 when the USSR relaxed its exit visa rules.

ECONOMIC BOOM AND ENVIRONMENTAL COST

The world has seen staggering economic growth during the 20th and 21st centuries, leading to unprecedented wealth. The subsequent environmental damage to the planet, however, has led many experts to call for urgent action to prevent an irreversible global crisis.

△ **Fuel crisis**
A sign at a service station informs the public of fuel shortage during the 1973 oil crisis, when oil-producing Arab countries placed an embargo on exports.

In 1944, before World War II had even concluded, delegates from 44 countries met to restructure the world's international finance systems with a focus on introducing a stable system of exchange rates and rebuilding war-damaged economies in Europe. The International Monetary Fund (IMF) was set up to facilitate international currency exchange, and the World Bank was established to make long-term loans to hard-hit nations. In 1947, the US introduced the Marshall Plan, pumping billions of dollars of investment into western Europe. This helped to restore confidence in the world economy and led to extraordinary growth.

Japan in particular benefited from these initiatives, and the country invested in steel and coal, shipbuilding, and car production, turning to high-tech products in the 1960s. Other Asian countries, such as Taiwan, Singapore, Malaysia, and South Korea, copied the Japanese model. This collective success became known as "Asian tiger economics."

Crisis and recovery

In 1973, Egypt and Syria invaded Israel, and the Organization of Arab Petroleum Exporting Countries (OAPEC) stopped oil being exported to any country supporting Israel. Oil prices tripled, and industrial output

◁ **Booming city**
The Hong Kong night is illuminated by its many skyscrapers. The city is just one of the outstanding economic success stories in Southeast Asia.

THE PRICE OF SUCCESS

Changes to the world economy after World War II led to rapid economic growth. Awareness of the environmental cost lagged far behind the boom. Publicity about damaging oil spills, pesticides, and pollution led to the first global climate conference in 1979. By this time, economic growth was bringing lower air quality and industrial waste and depleting natural resources. The continuing rise in population has caused particular concern and intensified efforts to tackle global warming and secure food and water supplies.

1944 The International Monetary Fund (IMF) is founded

1947 The Marshall Plan is rolled out, according to which the US offers financial assistance to postwar economies

1960s Total human population reaches the 3 billion mark

ECONOMIC GROWTH

ENVIRONMENTAL COST

1950

1960

1970

1947 The GATT treaty (General Agreement on Tariffs and Trade) is formed to boost economic recovery

1950s Japan and Germany both experience exceptional economic growth despite the effects of war

1962 Publication of *Silent Spring* by American biologist Rachel Carson leads to a ban of the insecticide DDT after Carson links it with cancer and damage to the environment

◁ **Toxic air**
A coal-fired power plant in England expels pollutants and greenhouse gases. Stricter air-pollution rules in Europe have sounded the death knell for energy production from coal.

in many countries dropped. The embargo lasted until 1974. The oil crisis led to a worldwide global recession, and in response, many countries changed their economic policies.

Control passed from the state to the private sector, and deregulation became the new driving force, allowing free trade to open up. China moved to allow private enterprise and rapidly developed the trappings of capitalism. Over the coming decades, it would become one of the world's largest and most influential economies. India was influenced by the success of the Asian tiger economies, while Brazil and Mexico also embarked on economic reform, drastically improving living standards. The reunification of West and East Germany in 1990 resulted in a new major force in the world economy. Despite a devastating financial crisis in 2008, the world, it seemed, had never been richer.

Environmental cost

This economic success came at a price. On October 31, 2011, the United Nations (UN) announced the birth of the 7 billionth person on Earth, heightening concern about the planet's capacity to support so many people. More crops were needed to feed the growing population, and more resources were needed to support the lifestyle of more affluent citizens. Urbanization and population growth strained the environment, and scientists found evidence that human activity is to blame for recent climate change (global warming).

"Population growth is straining the Earth's resources to the breaking point."

AL GORE, FORMER US VICE PRESIDENT

Developing nations were urged to reduce carbon emissions, thought to affect climate change, yet in 2015, India was opening a coal mine a month to lift its 1.3 billion citizens out of poverty. Developing nations objected to being told by developed nations to curb their ambitions for growth. In the 2000s, the world saw record levels of rainfall, as well as severe drought, melting icecaps, and natural disasters. Scientists warned that humans could pass the threshold beyond which climate change would be irreversible. With 7 billion people on the planet, the drain on natural resources was inevitable. In 2015, world leaders signed the Paris Climate Accord, and 196 nations adopted the first global climate deal, limiting global warming to 3.6°F (2°C).

Today, the UN estimates that by 2050, the global population will reach 9.7 billion. While the last two centuries have brought astonishing opportunities and wealth, challenges from war, pollution, and inequality remain grave.

▽ **Catching the sun**
Around 70,000 solar panels in the Nevada Desert provide 25 percent of the power used at the Nellis Air Force Base. It is the largest solar power plant in the western hemisphere; such projects are held up as models for renewable energy.

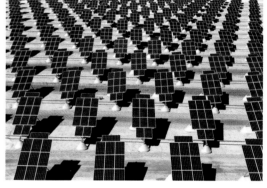

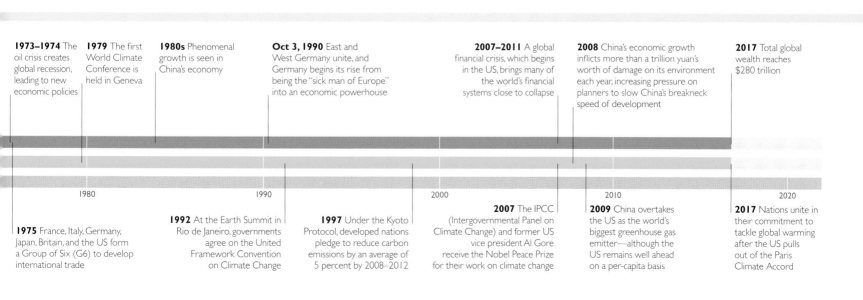

1973–1974 The oil crisis creates global recession, leading to new economic policies

1979 The first World Climate Conference is held in Geneva

1980s Phenomenal growth is seen in China's economy

Oct 3, 1990 East and West Germany unite, and Germany begins its rise from being the "sick man of Europe" into an economic powerhouse

2007–2011 A global financial crisis, which begins in the US, brings many of the world's financial systems close to collapse

2008 China's economic growth inflicts more than a trillion yuan's worth of damage on its environment each year, increasing pressure on planners to slow China's breakneck speed of development

2017 Total global wealth reaches $280 trillion

1980   1990   2000   2010   2020

1975 France, Italy, Germany, Japan, Britain, and the US form a Group of Six (G6) to develop international trade

1992 At the Earth Summit in Rio de Janeiro, governments agree on the United Framework Convention on Climate Change

1997 Under the Kyoto Protocol, developed nations pledge to reduce carbon emissions by an average of 5 percent by 2008–2012

2007 The IPCC (Intergovernmental Panel on Climate Change) and former US vice president Al Gore receive the Nobel Peace Prize for their work on climate change

2009 China overtakes the US as the world's biggest greenhouse gas emitter—although the US remains well ahead on a per-capita basis

2017 Nations unite in their commitment to tackle global warming after the US pulls out of the Paris Climate Accord

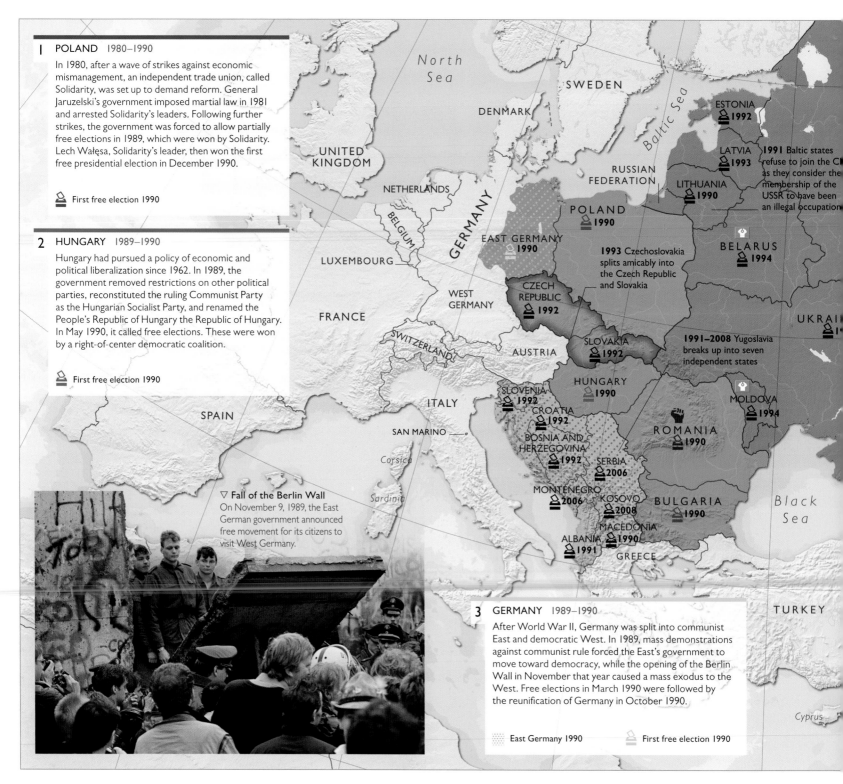

1 POLAND 1980–1990

In 1980, after a wave of strikes against economic mismanagement, an independent trade union, called Solidarity, was set up to demand reform. General Jaruzelski's government imposed martial law in 1981 and arrested Solidarity's leaders. Following further strikes, the government was forced to allow partially free elections in 1989, which were won by Solidarity. Lech Wałęsa, Solidarity's leader, then won the first free presidential election in December 1990.

⚖ First free election 1990

2 HUNGARY 1989–1990

Hungary had pursued a policy of economic and political liberalization since 1962. In 1989, the government removed restrictions on other political parties, reconstituted the ruling Communist Party as the Hungarian Socialist Party, and renamed the People's Republic of Hungary the Republic of Hungary. In May 1990, it called free elections. These were won by a right-of-center democratic coalition.

⚖ First free election 1990

1991 Baltic states refuse to join the CIS as they consider their membership of the USSR to have been an illegal occupation

1993 Czechoslovakia splits amicably into the Czech Republic and Slovakia

1991–2008 Yugoslavia breaks up into seven independent states

▽ **Fall of the Berlin Wall**
On November 9, 1989, the East German government announced free movement for its citizens to visit West Germany.

3 GERMANY 1989–1990

After World War II, Germany was split into communist East and democratic West. In 1989, mass demonstrations against communist rule forced the East's government to move toward democracy, while the opening of the Berlin Wall in November that year caused a mass exodus to the West. Free elections in March 1990 were followed by the reunification of Germany in October 1990.

▦ East Germany 1990   ⚖ First free election 1990

THE COLLAPSE OF COMMUNISM

The fall of communism in Europe and the dissolution of the USSR were among the most momentous events in modern history. Yet they were also among the least predicted, because it was internal weaknesses, rather than external pressures, that brought about their end. Change came quickly, and the effects were long-lasting.

The election of Mikhail Gorbachev as General Secretary of the Soviet Communist Party in March 1985 promised much-needed reforms in the USSR. He began to restructure the state and pledged economic and political change. Dissidents were released from prison, and private enterprise was encouraged. Crucially, in 1988, he declared the abandonment of the Brezhnev Doctrine, formulated in 1968 by Leonid Brezhnev, under which the USSR asserted its right to intervene militarily in the internal affairs of other communist countries in order to maintain strict communist rule. Relinquishing this doctrine gave the green light to eastern European communist nations to begin political reforms, as they now became aware that they could not rely on Soviet help to maintain their oppressive rule if opposition arose. As the eastern European nations, led by Poland and then Hungary, began to liberalize their political structures, the USSR came under pressure from its increasingly rebellious republics.

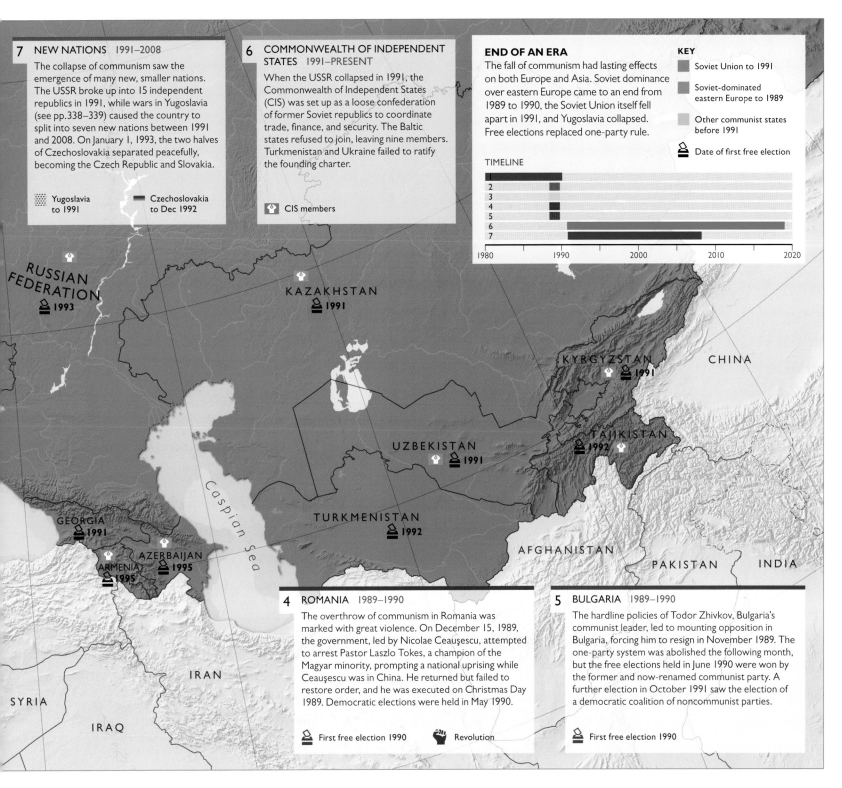

7 NEW NATIONS 1991–2008

The collapse of communism saw the emergence of many new, smaller nations. The USSR broke up into 15 independent republics in 1991, while wars in Yugoslavia (see pp.338–339) caused the country to split into seven new nations between 1991 and 2008. On January 1, 1993, the two halves of Czechoslovakia separated peacefully, becoming the Czech Republic and Slovakia.

- Yugoslavia to 1991
- Czechoslovakia to Dec 1992

6 COMMONWEALTH OF INDEPENDENT STATES 1991–PRESENT

When the USSR collapsed in 1991, the Commonwealth of Independent States (CIS) was set up as a loose confederation of former Soviet republics to coordinate trade, finance, and security. The Baltic states refused to join, leaving nine members. Turkmenistan and Ukraine failed to ratify the founding charter.

- CIS members

END OF AN ERA

The fall of communism had lasting effects on both Europe and Asia. Soviet dominance over eastern Europe came to an end from 1989 to 1990, the Soviet Union itself fell apart in 1991, and Yugoslavia collapsed. Free elections replaced one-party rule.

KEY
- Soviet Union to 1991
- Soviet-dominated eastern Europe to 1989
- Other communist states before 1991
- Date of first free election

TIMELINE

1980 — 1990 — 2000 — 2010 — 2020

4 ROMANIA 1989–1990

The overthrow of communism in Romania was marked with great violence. On December 15, 1989, the government, led by Nicolae Ceauşescu, attempted to arrest Pastor Laszlo Tokes, a champion of the Magyar minority, prompting a national uprising while Ceauşescu was in China. He returned but failed to restore order, and he was executed on Christmas Day 1989. Democratic elections were held in May 1990.

- First free election 1990
- Revolution

5 BULGARIA 1989–1990

The hardline policies of Todor Zhivkov, Bulgaria's communist leader, led to mounting opposition in Bulgaria, forcing him to resign in November 1989. The one-party system was abolished the following month, but the free elections held in June 1990 were won by the former and now-renamed communist party. A further election in October 1991 saw the election of a democratic coalition of noncommunist parties.

- First free election 1990

Gorbachev tried to restructure the Soviet Union as calls grew in the Baltic states and elsewhere for full independence, but he was opposed by demonstrations in Ukraine and by the Russian Federation leader, Boris Yeltsin. Fatally weakened by an attempted communist coup in August 1991 and a decisive vote for Ukrainian independence in December, Gorbachev was forced to resign as president on Christmas Day 1991. The next day, the USSR itself was disbanded, and Soviet communism—founded in 1917—had ended.

"The threat of world war is no more."

MIKHAIL GORBACHEV, SOVIET PRESIDENT, MAKING HIS FAREWELL SPEECH ENDING THE USSR, DECEMBER 1991

PERESTROIKA AND GLASNOST
RUSSIAN POLICIES

Mikhail Gorbachev became General Secretary of the Soviet Communist Party in 1985 and President of the USSR in 1990. Aiming to secure warmer relations with the West, he set out two new policies: *perestroika* (liberal economic restructuring) and *glasnost* (political openness).

West meets East
Mikhail Gorbachev (right) met US President Ronald Reagan (left) several times to improve East–West relations.

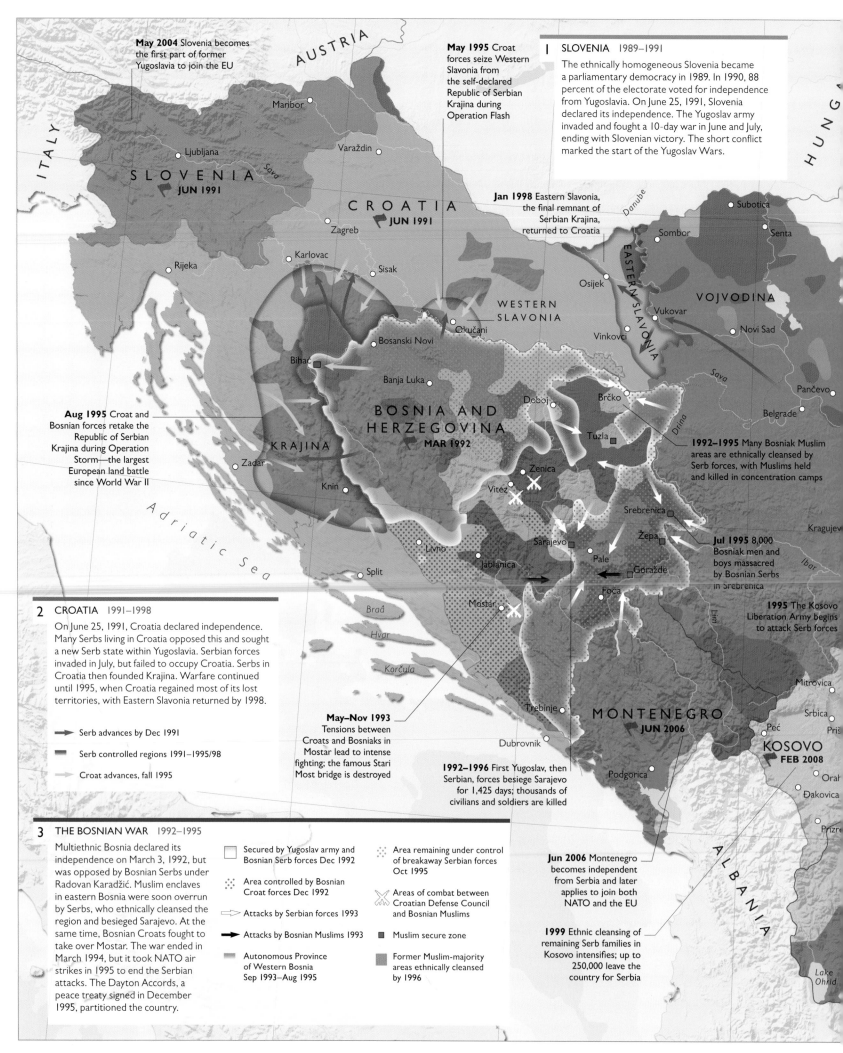

May 2004 Slovenia becomes the first part of former Yugoslavia to join the EU

May 1995 Croat forces seize Western Slavonia from the self-declared Republic of Serbian Krajina during Operation Flash

SLOVENIA 1989–1991

The ethnically homogeneous Slovenia became a parliamentary democracy in 1989. In 1990, 88 percent of the electorate voted for independence from Yugoslavia. On June 25, 1991, Slovenia declared its independence. The Yugoslav army invaded and fought a 10-day war in June and July, ending with Slovenian victory. The short conflict marked the start of the Yugoslav Wars.

AUSTRIA

Maribor

Varaždin

Jan 1998 Eastern Slavonia, the final remnant of Serbian Krajina, returned to Croatia

Ljubljana

Sava

HUNGARY

SLOVENIA
JUN 1991

CROATIA
JUN 1991

Danube

Subotica

Sombor

Senta

Zagreb

Osijek

Vukovar

VOJVODINA

Rijeka

Karlovac

Sisak

WESTERN SLAVONIA

Vinkovci

Novi Sad

EASTERN SLAVONIA

Okučani

Bosanski Novi

Sava

Bihać

Banja Luka

Doboj

Brčko

Pančevo

Belgrade

Aug 1995 Croat and Bosnian forces retake the Republic of Serbian Krajina during Operation Storm—the largest European land battle since World War II

KRAJINA

BOSNIA AND HERZEGOVINA
MAR 1992

Tuzla

Drina

1992–1995 Many Bosniak Muslim areas are ethnically cleansed by Serb forces, with Muslims held and killed in concentration camps

Zadar

Knin

Zenica

Vitez

Srebrenica

Kragujev

Adriatic Sea

Livno

Sarajevo

Žepa

Jul 1995 8,000 Bosniak men and boys massacred by Bosnian Serbs in Srebrenica

Split

Jablanica

Pale

Goražde

Foča

Ibar

1995 The Kosovo Liberation Army begins to attack Serb forces

2 CROATIA 1991–1998

On June 25, 1991, Croatia declared independence. Many Serbs living in Croatia opposed this and sought a new Serb state within Yugoslavia. Serbian forces invaded in July, but failed to occupy Croatia. Serbs in Croatia then founded Krajina. Warfare continued until 1995, when Croatia regained most of its lost territories, with Eastern Slavonia returned by 1998.

→ Serb advances by Dec 1991

■ Serb controlled regions 1991–1995/98

→ Croat advances, fall 1995

Brač

Mostar

Hvar

Korčula

Trebinje

Dubrovnik

Lim

MONTENEGRO
JUN 2006

Podgorica

Mitrovica

Srbica

Peć

Priš

KOSOVO
FEB 2008

Orah

Đakovica

May–Nov 1993 Tensions between Croats and Bosniaks in Mostar lead to intense fighting; the famous Stari Most bridge is destroyed

1992–1996 First Yugoslav, then Serbian, forces besiege Sarajevo for 1,425 days; thousands of civilians and soldiers are killed

Jun 2006 Montenegro becomes independent from Serbia and later applies to join both NATO and the EU

1999 Ethnic cleansing of remaining Serb families in Kosovo intensifies; up to 250,000 leave the country for Serbia

ALBANIA

Prizre

Lake Ohrid

3 THE BOSNIAN WAR 1992–1995

Multiethnic Bosnia declared its independence on March 3, 1992, but was opposed by Bosnian Serbs under Radovan Karadžić. Muslim enclaves in eastern Bosnia were soon overrun by Serbs, who ethnically cleansed the region and besieged Sarajevo. At the same time, Bosnian Croats fought to take over Mostar. The war ended in March 1994, but it took NATO air strikes in 1995 to end the Serbian attacks. The Dayton Accords, a peace treaty signed in December 1995, partitioned the country.

☐ Secured by Yugoslav army and Bosnian Serb forces Dec 1992

▨ Area controlled by Bosnian Croat forces Dec 1992

⇨ Attacks by Serbian forces 1993

➡ Attacks by Bosnian Muslims 1993

▨ Autonomous Province of Western Bosnia Sep 1993–Aug 1995

▨ Area remaining under control of breakaway Serbian forces Oct 1995

✕ Areas of combat between Croatian Defense Council and Bosnian Muslims

■ Muslim secure zone

▨ Former Muslim-majority areas ethnically cleansed by 1996

ETHNIC COMPOSITION OF YUGOSLAVIA

Yugoslavia was a multiethnic nation, comprising five main groups of people—Bosniaks, Croats, Macedonians, Serbs, and Slovenes—as well as substantial minorities of Albanians, Bulgarians, Hungarians, and Romanians. Most groups were mainly Roman Catholic or Orthodox, while the majority of Bosniaks were Muslims.

KEY

- Serb and Montenegrin
- Croat
- Bosniak (after 1996 "ethnic cleansing")
- Slovene
- Albanian
- Macedonian
- Hungarian
- Bulgarian
- Romanian

TIMELINE

	1980	1990	2000	2010
1				
2				
3				
4				
5				

△ **Bosniak refugees**
Millions of Bosniak Muslims were displaced during the Bosnian War (1992–1995) as Serbian forces carried out ethnic cleansing. In this photograph, a man and his two grandchildren rest at a United Nations refugee camp in Kladanj.

5 THE FINAL BREAK-UP 1991–2008

Unlike other former republics, Macedonia achieved its independence peacefully in September 1991, with the Yugoslav army withdrawing 9 months later. Serbia and Montenegro formed the Federal Republic of Yugoslavia in 1992, renamed Serbia and Montenegro in 2003. In June 2006, Montenegro became independent from Serbia. Finally, Kosovo declared itself independent from Serbia in 2008.

🚩 Independence

Sep 1991 Macedonia (known officially as the Former Yugoslav Republic of Macedonia, in recognition of Greece's dispute over its name) declares independence

4 KOSOVO 1990–1999

Majority Albanian Kosovo declared its independence in 1990, but it did not receive international recognition. The Kosovo Liberation Army began to fight the Serbs in 1995, leading to full-scale war in February 1998. More than 1 million Albanian Kosovars fled and thousands more were killed before a NATO bombing campaign in 1999 forced Serbian forces to depart.

▬ Kosovo Liberation Army (KLA) stronghold

➡ Serb forces 1999

WAR IN YUGOSLAVIA

In the 1990s, the multiethnic but unified Socialist Federal Republic of Yugoslavia fell apart in the bloodiest series of wars fought in Europe since World War II.

Under the rule of leader Josip Broz Tito (1892–1980), Yugoslavia was a federation of six socialist republics, with two autonomous provinces inside Serbia. After Tito's death, a Serbian nationalist revival, led by Slobodan Milošević, started the country's disintegration by opposing Slovenian and Croatian independence in June 1991. Yugoslav (Serbian) forces moved in, and over the next decade, the nationalist drive to reorganize the territory along ethnic lines led to mass killings of civilians and other atrocities, giving the world a new phrase: "ethnic cleansing."

The conflict spread to Bosnia in 1992, where Serbs ethnically cleansed large areas of Bosniak Muslims. A fragile peace was eventually reached in 1995 with the signing of the Dayton Accords. The final tragedy was fought out in Kosovo, as Serbs tried to crush an uprising by the Kosovo Liberation Army. NATO stepped in, forcing the Serbs out of Kosovo in 1999. By 2008, seven new states had emerged from the once-unified country. The conflicts cost 140,000 lives and displaced nearly 4 million people.

> *"No country of people's democracy has so many nationalities as this country has."*
>
> JOSIP BROZ TITO, LEADER OF YUGOSLAVIA, 1948

BREAK-UP OF YUGOSLAVIA

In 1946, Yugoslavia became a federation consisting of six socialist republics, with Kosovo and Vojvodina being autonomous provinces of Serbia. By 2008, all six republics and Kosovo were independent states, with Vojvodina remaining an autonomous province of Serbia.

KEY

- Socialist Federal Republic of Yugoslavia
- Autonomous provinces

GLOBALIZATION

Globalization—the free movement of goods, people, money, knowledge, and culture around the world—was once seen as the answer to worldwide poverty, but inequality and political instability have led to a populist backlash.

Globalization is not a recent phenomenon. Countries have traded with each other for thousands of years; yet after World War II, technological advances, together with the lowering of trade barriers and the communication revolution, transformed the way nations interacted.

△ **Taking to the streets**
Following demonstrations in Seattle in 1999, subsequent WTO meetings in cities around the world became a focus for similar protests, sometimes involving confrontations between security forces and demonstrators.

Globalization promoted economic growth in developing countries, yet in practice this often meant that industries would move from rich countries, where labor was expensive, to poor countries, where it was cheaper. Multinational corporations became increasingly global, locating production plants overseas in order to take advantage of lower costs and taxes. The growth of the internet allowed people to conduct business across the globe without leaving their office. International trade in goods, services, and financial capital became more widespread than ever before, further driven by China's decision to open its economy to the world in the late 80s and by the collapse of the Soviet bloc in the early 90s.

Reactions and protests

A backlash against globalization had begun in the early 90s. It intensified in November 1999 as protesters in Seattle, Washington, took to the streets at the World Trade Organization (WTO) conference. Once applauded by economists, globalization was now fiercely contested as widening the gap between the rich and poor. Ordinary people were portrayed as victims of ruthless corporate domination, with large corporations exploiting the poor in search of new profits. The debate continues today, as political parties advancing protectionist and anti-immigration policies, including a return to local economies, have found wide support across much of the Western world.

◁ **Advertising in Asia**
The logos of global corporations have become ubiquitous, even in countries such as China that were until relatively recently closed to foreign trade.

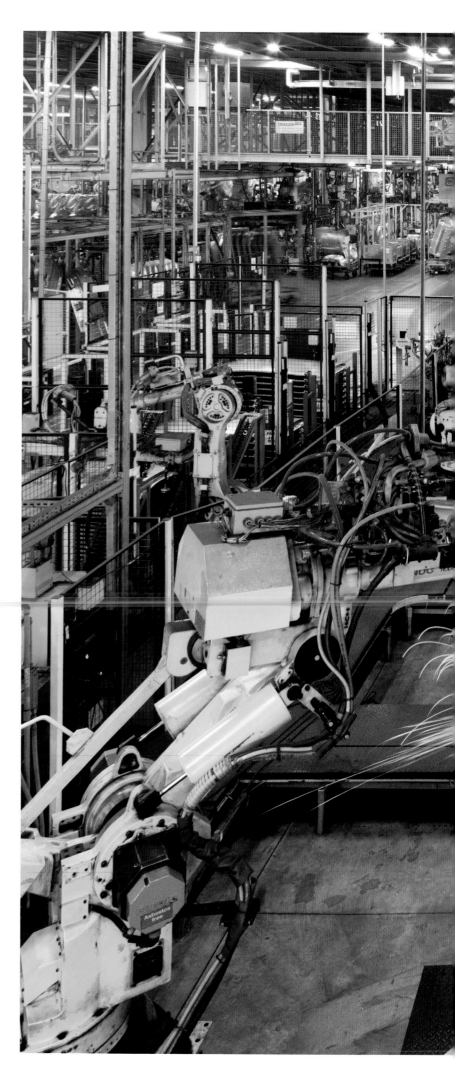

High-productivity industry
With its high-tech production lines, the
Japanese car company Nissan's investment in
the UK has transformed the UK's car industry.
Nissan's factory (seen here) in Sunderland, UK,
is regarded as a success story of globalization.

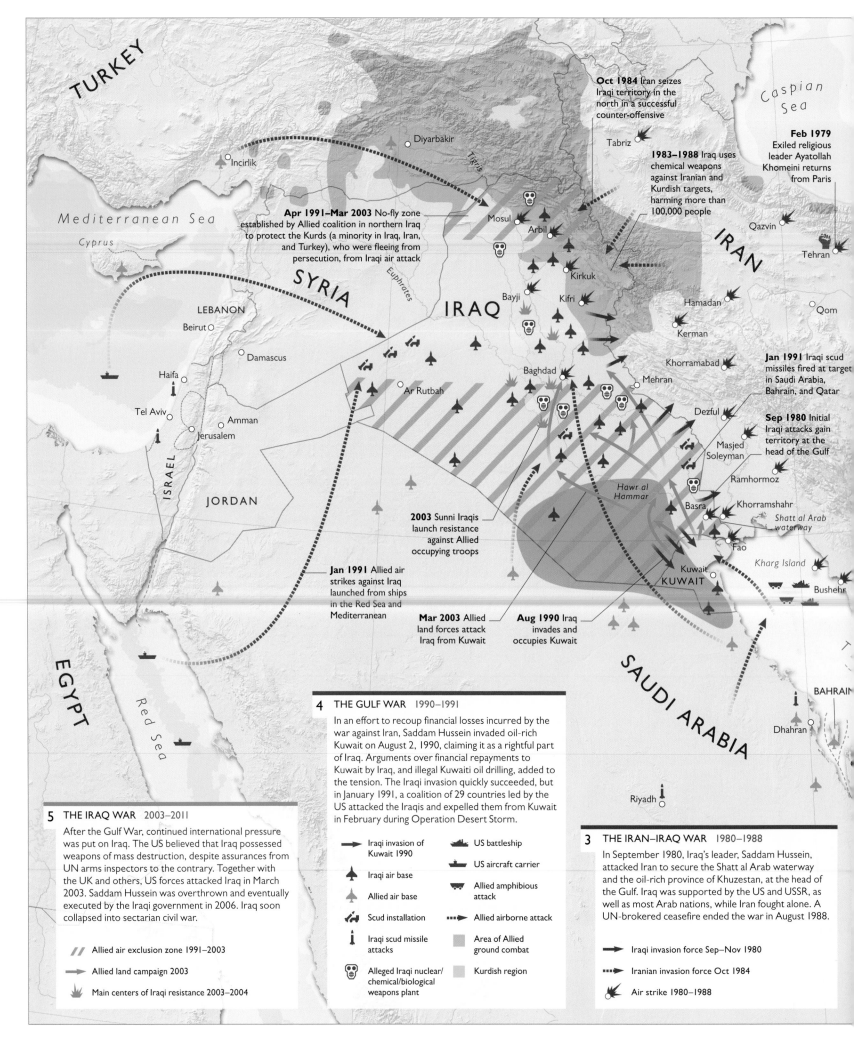

TURKEY

Mediterranean Sea

Cyprus

Incirlik

Diyarbakir

Tigris

Oct 1984 Iran seizes Iraqi territory in the north in a successful counter-offensive

Tabriz

Caspian Sea

Feb 1979 Exiled religious leader Ayatollah Khomeini returns from Paris

Qazvin

1983–1988 Iraq uses chemical weapons against Iranian and Kurdish targets, harming more than 100,000 people

Apr 1991–Mar 2003 No-fly zone established by Allied coalition in northern Iraq to protect the Kurds (a minority in Iraq, Iran, and Turkey), who were fleeing from persecution, from Iraqi air attack

Mosul

Arbil

Kirkuk

Tehran

IRAN

SYRIA

Euphrates

IRAQ

Bayji

Kifri

Hamadan

Qom

Kerman

LEBANON

Beirut

Damascus

Baghdad

Mehran

Khorramabad

Jan 1991 Iraqi scud missiles fired at target in Saudi Arabia, Bahrain, and Qatar

Haifa

Ar Rutbah

Dezful

Sep 1980 Initial Iraqi attacks gain territory at the head of the Gulf

Tel Aviv

Amman

Jerusalem

Masjed Soleyman

Ramhormoz

ISRAEL

JORDAN

Hawr al Hammar

Basra

Khorramshahr

Shatt al Arab waterway

2003 Sunni Iraqis launch resistance against Allied occupying troops

Fao

Kharg Island

Jan 1991 Allied air strikes against Iraq launched from ships in the Red Sea and Mediterranean

Mar 2003 Allied land forces attack Iraq from Kuwait

Aug 1990 Iraq invades and occupies Kuwait

KUWAIT

Kuwait

Bushehr

EGYPT

Red Sea

SAUDI ARABIA

BAHRAIN

Dhahran

Riyadh

4 THE GULF WAR 1990–1991

In an effort to recoup financial losses incurred by the war against Iran, Saddam Hussein invaded oil-rich Kuwait on August 2, 1990, claiming it as a rightful part of Iraq. Arguments over financial repayments to Kuwait by Iraq, and illegal Kuwaiti oil drilling, added to the tension. The Iraqi invasion quickly succeeded, but in January 1991, a coalition of 29 countries led by the US attacked the Iraqis and expelled them from Kuwait in February during Operation Desert Storm.

5 THE IRAQ WAR 2003–2011

After the Gulf War, continued international pressure was put on Iraq. The US believed that Iraq possessed weapons of mass destruction, despite assurances from UN arms inspectors to the contrary. Together with the UK and others, US forces attacked Iraq in March 2003. Saddam Hussein was overthrown and eventually executed by the Iraqi government in 2006. Iraq soon collapsed into sectarian civil war.

▶ Iraqi invasion of Kuwait 1990	◀▬ US battleship
▲ Iraqi air base	▬ US aircraft carrier
▲ Allied air base	▬ Allied amphibious attack
⛢ Scud installation	▸▸▸ Allied airborne attack
⌁ Iraqi scud missile attacks	Area of Allied ground combat
☠ Alleged Iraqi nuclear/ chemical/biological weapons plant	Kurdish region

// Allied air exclusion zone 1991–2003

➔ Allied land campaign 2003

⚑ Main centers of Iraqi resistance 2003–2004

3 THE IRAN–IRAQ WAR 1980–1988

In September 1980, Iraq's leader, Saddam Hussein, attacked Iran to secure the Shatt al Arab waterway and the oil-rich province of Khuzestan, at the head of the Gulf. Iraq was supported by the US and USSR, as well as most Arab nations, while Iran fought alone. A UN-brokered ceasefire ended the war in August 1988.

➔ Iraqi invasion force Sep–Nov 1980

▸▸▸ Iranian invasion force Oct 1984

✺ Air strike 1980–1988

CONFLICT IN THE GULF

Three major wars have been fought in the Gulf since the Iranian Revolution of 1979. The longest, between 1980 and 1988, was prompted by the Iraqi invasion of Iran. The other two, from 1990 to 1991 and in 2003, were centered on Iraq.

KEY

_____ National borders

------ Disputed national borders

TIMELINE

1
2
3
4
5

1970   1980   1990   2000   2010   2020

Apr 1980 A US helicopter, used to rescue 63 hostages held in the US embassy in Tehran, crashes in Tabas

Tabas

Shiraz

△ **On patrol**
During Operation Desert Storm (1991), US and Saudi fighter aircraft patrolled the skies over Kuwait as oil wells set alight by Iraqi forces burned freely below them.

1 THE IRANIAN REVOLUTION 1979

Resistance against the autocratic rule of the Shah of Iran led to demonstrations in the holy city of Qom in 1977 and 1978. Riots soon spread to the capital, Tehran, with demonstrators calling for the return of the exiled Shia religious leader Ayatollah Khomeini. The Shah eventually fled Iran in January 1979; Khomeini set up a religious government, one of only two theocracies in the world alongside the Vatican City.

✊ Revolution in Tehran

Abu Dhabi

J.A.E.

2 IRAN AFTER THE REVOLUTION
1979–PRESENT

The new government of Iran, led by Ayatollah Khomeini, became the world's first Shia government. It adopted strong anti-American and anti-Israeli policies and supported radical Shia groups, such as Hezbollah in Lebanon and, more recently, pro-government forces fighting in the Syrian civil war.

IRAN AND THE GULF WARS

The resurgence of Shia Islam in Iran after the revolution of 1979, and the establishment of a Shia clerical government in Tehran, unsettled the Middle East. Between 1980 and 2003, three major wars took place in the Persian Gulf, all of them involving Iraq.

In 1980, Saddam Hussein, the leader of Iraq (which was dominated by Sunnis, although the majority of Iraqis were Shias), invaded neighboring Iran, still in turmoil after a revolution, to gain land and access to Iranian oil reserves. Thus began a long, bloody, but inconclusive war, which also involved many other countries. This conflict ended when the UN brokered a ceasefire in 1988, which brought to an end the longest conventional war of the 20th century.

Two years later, in what is known as the Gulf War, Saddam invaded Kuwait in order to gain its oil reserves to rebuild his military war machine. A US-led coalition of 29 countries, including many of Iraq's Arab neighbors, evicted the Iraqis from Kuwait in 1991, although Saddam Hussein remained in power. After the war, Iraq was subject to economic and military sanctions. It was also suspected of stockpiling weapons of mass destruction. Despite UN weapons inspectors failing to find such weapons, the US and Britain used their possible existence as justification to attack and invade Iraq in 2003, together with Australia, Poland, Spain, Italy, and Denmark. Unlike the Gulf War, the invasion was not supported by the UN. US forces carried out a search for Saddam, who had fled into hiding, and he was captured in December 2003. The coalition handed him over to Iraqi authorities in June 2004, and in 2006, he was tried and executed by an Iraqi Special Tribunal. Iraq then collapsed into sectarian chaos and civil war, further destabilizing an already unstable region. A civil war in Syria, which broke out in 2011, added to the turmoil in the Middle East, as rival Sunni and Shia forces fought it out.

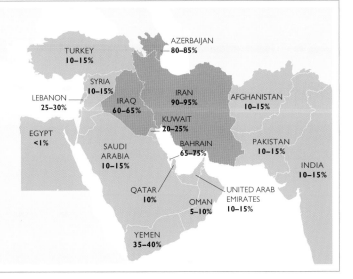

KEY

■ Shia majority

■ Sunni majority

SHIA POPULATIONS
Although most of the world's Muslims are Sunni, about 12 percent are Shias. Shias form a majority in Iran, Iraq, Azerbaijan, and Bahrain, with sizeable minorities elsewhere in the Middle East. This map indicates the percentages of Shia Muslims in each country.

TURKEY 10–15%
AZERBAIJAN 80–85%
SYRIA 10–15%
LEBANON 25–30%
IRAN 90–95%
IRAQ 60–65%
AFGHANISTAN 10–15%
KUWAIT 20–25%
EGYPT <1%
SAUDI ARABIA 10–15%
BAHRAIN 65–75%
PAKISTAN 10–15%
QATAR 10%
UNITED ARAB EMIRATES 10–15%
OMAN 5–10%
INDIA 10–15%
YEMEN 35–40%

THE COMMUNICATION REVOLUTION

Advances in technology have brought about profound changes in the social, economic, and political landscape. Nowhere has the impact been felt more than in the field of communications, which is transforming every aspect of our daily lives.

△ **Space Age communication**
The world's first active communication satellite, Telstar 1 was jointly built by the US, French, and British broadcasting agencies.

Until World War II, communications had been limited to messages sent by mail or by telegraph and telephone. During World War II, a surge in new thinking resulted in the forerunner of digital computers—the Electronic Numerical Integrator and Calculator (ENIAC).

The invention of the transistor in 1947 and the microchip in 1958 led to electronic components becoming smaller. Advances in rocket technology allowed satellites to be sent into orbit. In 1962, the Telstar 1 satellite was launched, sending telephone calls, fax messages, and TV signals flying through space.

During the Cold War, the US Defense Department was concerned about how it might communicate during a nuclear attack. This led to the creation of the Advanced Research Projects Agency Network (ARPANET) in 1969, a system of four computers communicating using standard protocols. By the 1980s, greater and more integrated use of computers, adoption of the ARPANET protocols, and advances in communications methods resulted in a widely available and global network of computers: the Internet. The smartphone made the internet a mobile resource. Social networking had an impact on education, healthcare, and culture. It was also used by protesters during the Arab Spring (2011) and has since become an inherent part of politics.

◁ **A connected world**
Smartphones have become an integral part of people's lives. They are not only used to navigate and send messages, but also to record and share moments on social media platforms.

"The information highway will transform our culture ... as Gutenberg's press did the Middle Ages."

BILL GATES, FROM *THE ROAD AHEAD*, 1995

Booting up
Unveiled on February 14, 1946, ENIAC—the first fully programmable computer—was originally devised to measure the trajectory of a shell. It weighed 27 tons (24 tonnes) and was filled with 20,000 vacuum tubes; 7,200 diodes; and several miles of wiring.

POPULATION AND ENERGY

After 1950, two of the main problems that faced the world were rising population and increasing energy consumption. Although population growth varies across the continents, the world's total population passed 3 billion in 1960 and then 7 billion in 2011.

China has the largest population in the world, and from 1970–2000, the country's population increased by 50 percent—an addition of more than 444 million people, more than the total population of the US in the year 2000 (282 million).

In 1950, poor, preindustrialized countries had high birth and death rates, but as they developed, first the death rate declined (particularly in infancy) due to better health care and nutrition, and then the birth rate declined in response to lower infant mortality. In the developed world, where these processes had already happened during industrialization, the population barely increased in the late 20th century, unless it was affected by immigration or inflows of migrant workers. In Africa, rapidly rising populations placed an ever-increasing strain on the countries' limited resources, including water, grazing land, and energy.

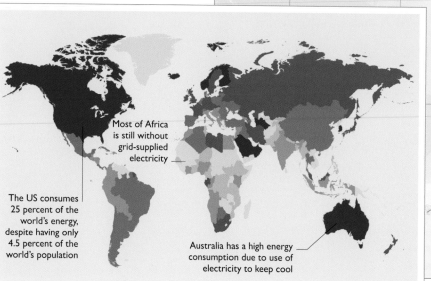

▷ **Abu Dhabi luxury**
The United Arab Emirates is a prosperous, oil-rich country. It has one of the highest levels of energy use, due to the luxury lifestyle led by its people and use of energy to keep cool in the high temperatures.

WORLD ENERGY USE

Energy use varies greatly from country to country. In 2014, wealthy, developed, and oil-rich nations used 50 times more energy per capita than the poorest nations. Latitude was also an important factor, with high-latitude countries, such as Canada, using more energy to keep warm.

ENERGY USE PER CAPITA, 2014

KG of oil equivalent

0	500	1000	2,500	5,000 +
0	4	7	18	36 +

Barrel of oil equivalent

No data

Most of Africa is still without grid-supplied electricity

The US consumes 25 percent of the world's energy, despite having only 4.5 percent of the world's population

Australia has a high energy consumption due to use of electricity to keep cool

THE AMERICAS 1950–2010
In this period, two-thirds of the total population of the Americas lived in just three countries: the US, Mexico, and Brazil. Both the US and Canada supported immigration, increasing their populations, while emigration from the Caribbean islands kept their populations largely static.

1951–2001
Pro-immigration policies more than double Canada's population

1990–2010 Foreign-born population of the US doubles from 20 to 40 million due to immigration

1960 Brazil's rate of population increase begins to decline as rising prosperity causes falls in birth and death rates

1950 Argentina has one of the continent's lowest population growth rates due to its low birth rate

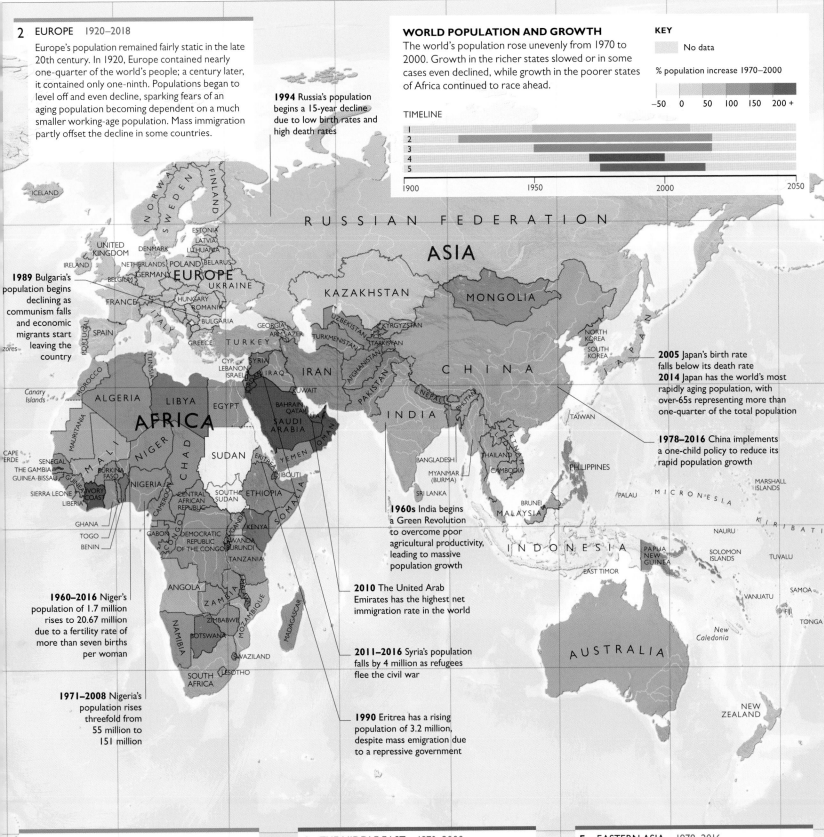

2 EUROPE 1920–2018

Europe's population remained fairly static in the late 20th century. In 1920, Europe contained nearly one-quarter of the world's people; a century later, it contained only one-ninth. Populations began to level off and even decline, sparking fears of an aging population becoming dependent on a much smaller working-age population. Mass immigration partly offset the decline in some countries.

1994 Russia's population begins a 15-year decline due to low birth rates and high death rates

WORLD POPULATION AND GROWTH

The world's population rose unevenly from 1970 to 2000. Growth in the richer states slowed or in some cases even declined, while growth in the poorer states of Africa continued to race ahead.

KEY

No data

% population increase 1970–2000

−50   0   50   100   150   200 +

TIMELINE

1
2
3
4
5

1900   1950   2000   2050

1989 Bulgaria's population begins declining as communism falls and economic migrants start leaving the country

2005 Japan's birth rate falls below its death rate
2014 Japan has the world's most rapidly aging population, with over-65s representing more than one-quarter of the total population

1978–2016 China implements a one-child policy to reduce its rapid population growth

1960s India begins a Green Revolution to overcome poor agricultural productivity, leading to massive population growth

1960–2016 Niger's population of 1.7 million rises to 20.67 million due to a fertility rate of more than seven births per woman

2010 The United Arab Emirates has the highest net immigration rate in the world

2011–2016 Syria's population falls by 4 million as refugees flee the civil war

1971–2008 Nigeria's population rises threefold from 55 million to 151 million

1990 Eritrea has a rising population of 3.2 million, despite mass emigration due to a repressive government

3 AFRICA 1950–2018

Africa's population increased rapidly from 229 million people in 1950 to 630 million in 1990. As it rose, it overtook the combined population of the Americas and, by 2000, Europe. Africa's countries were among the poorest in the world. Where people subsisted from the land, the population could outstrip land productivity and availability of clean water. Since 2000, Africa has experienced the world's fastest urbanization.

4 THE MIDDLE EAST 1970–2000

With small local populations and rapid economic growth, the oil-rich countries of the Middle East, notably the Gulf States, solved their labor shortages by mass immigration. The population of many countries doubled from 1970–2000. The United Arab Emirates' population saw the highest percentage increase in the world, multiplying by more than 12 times from its 1970 level (from just under 250,000 people to over 3 million).

5 EASTERN ASIA 1978–2016

East Asia includes the world's two most populous nations: China and India. While India's growth rate remained high, China reduced its growth with its one-child policy, implemented in 1978–1980, which charged a fee to parents having a second child. It abolished the policy in 2016 as it faced the growing problem of a population with too many men (since the policy led to parents favoring male children) and too many elderly people.

TIMELINE

PREHISTORY 15 MYA–3000 BCE

c. 15 MYA

The first hominids, or great apes, appear—they are ancestors of gorillas, chimpanzees, orangutans, and humans.

c. 7.2 MYA

Sahelanthropus tchadensis arises; this hominid species, known only from vestigial fossil remains found in Chad in 2001–2002, is the earliest known member of the Hominini subfamily, a small group that includes humans but excludes the other living great apes.

c. 3.6 MYA

Footprints found in volcanic ash in east Africa indicate that the hominin *Australopithecus afarensis* is walking upright by this time; it has a brain about one-third the size of a modern human's and thumb-opposed hands, potentially enabling the use of tools. Other findings, including that of the partial female skeleton discovered in Ethiopia in 1974 and nicknamed Lucy (dated c. 3.2 MYA), indicate that the species lived in family groups.

c. 3.3 MYA

The date of stone tools found at the Lomekwi archaeological site in Kenya—the oldest yet discovered; they mark the start of the Paleolithic or Old Stone Age (which ends around 15,000–10,000 years ago). At Dikika in Ethiopia, the remains of a 3-year-old *Australopithecus* female confirm that the species is adapted both for bipedalism

600

million years ago. The time when multicellular life evolved on Earth.

(walking on two feet) and for tree-climbing. This increased mobility facilitates the move from forests to open savanna, opening up new opportunities for hunting and food gathering.

c. 2.8 MYA

A mandible fragment from this time is found in the Afar region of Ethiopia in 2013; it is currently the earliest fossil assigned to the genus *Homo*, to which the modern human species belongs.

2.4–1.4 MYA

Paranthropus boisei, a hominin species distinguished by its large jaws and cheek teeth and powerful jaw muscles, inhabits the Olduvai Gorge region of east Africa. The jaws earn the species its nickname of "Nutcracker Man."

c. 1.9 MYA

The date of remains found in the 1950s at Olduvai Gorge in Tanzania by Louis and Mary Leakey, to which they will give the name *Homo habilis* ("Handy man"); some anthropologists have since queried the attribution, putting the fossils in the *Australopithecus* genus instead.

c. 1.8 MYA

Homo erectus evolves, with a bigger brain than *Homo habilis*. Food remains indicate that the species was omnivorous, but with a higher proportion of meat in its diet than other primates. Fossilized remains

of *Homo erectus*, its Asian variant, indicate that the species spread quickly across Eurasia; specimens discovered at Dmanisi in Georgia and dating from this time are currently considered the earliest hominin remains found outside of Africa.

c. 1.5 MYA–800,000 BCE

Oval and pear-shaped handaxes of the type known as Acheulean spread from Africa to south and west Asia and Europe; the first remains of the axes are identified in St. Acheul, near Amiens, France, in 1859. One of the characteristic tools of Stone Age people, their dispersal is closely associated with the diffusion of *Homo erectus*.

c. 700,000–200,000 BCE

Homo heidelbergensis spreads through Africa, Europe, and western Asia. First described from remains found near Heidelberg in Germany in 1908, the species has a bigger brain than *Homo erectus* and uses more developed tools; it is the first early human species to build shelters. The Neanderthal population is thought to have evolved from this line.

c. 500,000 BCE

Fire and a wide range of stone tools are in use by human ancestors in China, as evidenced by remains found in a cave at Zhoukhoudian, near Beijing, in the 1920s ("Peking Man").

c. 400,000 BCE

Neanderthals appear; remains of the group have been found in Europe and western Asia. Shorter and stockier than other hominins, the Neanderthals will in time interbreed with *Homo* species, contributing to the DNA of modern humans.

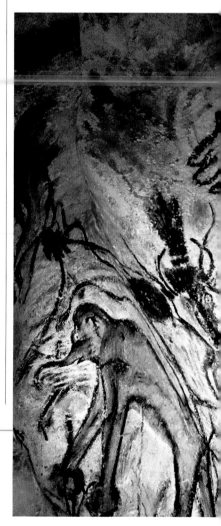

◁ Acheulean handaxe
Dating from around 1.5 MYA–800,000 BCE, this handaxe was made by hammering flakes off a piece of flint.

c. 300,000 BCE

Hominin fossils found at Jebel Irhoud, Morocco, in 2017 that have been dated to this time are the earliest known examples of *Homo sapiens*—anatomically modern humans. The species is distinguished by a high, thin-walled cranium, a steep forehead, and a flat, vertical face with a protruding chin.

c. 180,000–80,000 BCE

The first dispersals of *Homo sapiens* out of Africa are documented by finds in the Levant from 194,000–177,000 BCE and in China from 120,000–80,000 BCE.

c. 170,000 BCE

The estimated date for the existence of "Mitochondrial Eve"—the most recent common ancestor of all living humans as traced back through the matrilineal

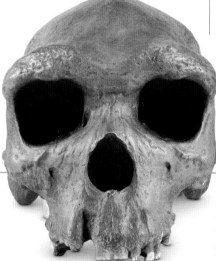

◁ *Homo heidelbergensis* skull
This species prevailed from around 700,000 to 200,000 BCE; its members lived in cooperative groups and hunted large animals using wooden spears set with stone spearheads.

▷ Chauvet Cave art (replica)
Animal images drawn in charcoal on the walls of the Chauvet Cave in southern France date back at least 30,000 years. A replica of the cave has been built to preserve the vulnerable originals.

genetic line (so-called because the DNA used in this analysis is from subcellular mitochondria, which are inherited only from mother to daughter).

c. 80,000–40,000 BCE
Genetic evidence suggests *Homo sapiens* dispersed through the Middle East and along the southern coast of Asia, possibly after the Toba event.

c. 75,000 BCE
The estimated date of the Toba supereruption—a volcanic event centered on what is now Lake Toba in Sumatra, Indonesia; the event may have caused a "global winter" affecting hominin populations across the world.

c. 65,000 BCE
The date of the earliest archaeological sites in Australia—evidence of the ancestors of today's Aboriginal

population; they are thought to have traveled by island-hopping through Indonesia, suggesting that boats were in use by this time.

c. 45,000 BCE
The earliest "European early modern human" remains date back to this time. This population of *Homo sapiens* was named Cro-Magnon when it was discovered in a rock shelter of this name in the Dordogne, France, in 1868.

c. 43,000 BCE
Aurignacian tool-making techniques, characterized by parallel-sided stone blades (rather than the previous flakes) and finely worked bone and antler points, spread across eastern Europe, reaching the west of the continent between 40,000 and 33,000 BCE. The peoples would travel long distances to find suitable tool-making materials.

c. 40,000 BCE
Hand stencils are painted in caves in Sulawesi, Indonesia; they are thought to be the oldest human markings, predating European cave art. At about this time, the Neanderthals are thought to have died out in Europe.

c. 35,000 BCE
The Venus of Hohle Fels, an image carved out of mammoth ivory and found in a cave in southern Germany, is the earliest known of the Venus figurines, which are statuettes of (mostly) female figures thought to have been fertility symbols.

c. 30,000 BCE
The first settlers arrive in Japan and in the Solomon Islands in Oceania. In sites around Europe, the earliest evidence of grindstones being used to mill wild cereal grains dates from this time.

c. 24,500 BCE
The last glaciation (commonly called the Ice Age) of the current Quaternary geological era is at its peak.

c. 24,000–14,000 BCE
Estimated date range for the settling of North America by hunter-gatherers crossing from Siberia over the Beringia land bridge that spanned what is now the Bering Strait; since archaeological evidence is sparsely distributed across North America, the date is speculative.

c. 18,000 BCE
Ceramic fragments found in southern China indicate that pottery is being produced by this time.

c. 15,000 BCE
The estimated date of the cave paintings found at Lascaux in the Dordogne region of France.

c. 14,700 BCE
The first evidence of dog remains buried beside humans (found in a quarry in a suburb of Bonn, Germany) strongly indicates that dogs had been domesticated by this time.

c. 14,000 BCE
The Jomon culture, distinguished by cord-marked pottery, is established in Japan.

c. 13,000 BCE
The Clovis culture, named for the site in New Mexico where it was first identified and characterized by distinctive bone and ivory tools, makes its appearance. Clovis remains have been found from Oregon down to Chile; they are associated with a hunter-gatherer lifestyle that included hunting mammoths, bison, mastodon, sloths, and tapirs. It was once regarded as the first Native American culture, ancestral to developments throughout North and South America, but earlier, non-Clovis sites have now been found.

c. 12,000 BCE
The earliest Saharan rock art depicts rhinos, aurochs (wild cattle), antelopes, and other animals pursued by the region's hunter-gatherers.

c. 11,000 BCE
Rock paintings are created in Pedra Furada, Brazil, seemingly representing a tradition that differs from the Clovis culture.

c. 10,500 BCE
Cattle are first domesticated in Mesopotamia and in what is now Pakistan. DNA evidence suggests that one evolutionary line of living domestic cattle may have arisen from a herd of aurochs near the village of Çayönü Tepesi, in southeastern Turkey, near the modern border with Iraq.

c. 10,200 BCE
The start for the Neolithic, or New Stone Age, according to the ASPRO chronology of the Middle East. The Neolithic will see the birth of farming and the widespread domestication of animals; it ends with the adoption of metal tools, ushering in the Bronze Age.

c. 10,000 BCE
The last glaciation of the present Quaternary Era ends, marking the start of Earth's current warmer interglacial period. By this time, sheep are being domesticated in Mesopotamia. Radio carbon dating of stone tools found near campfire remains indicate that hunter-gatherer communities are by now settled in the Valley of Mexico.

32

The percentage of land covered by ice in the last glaciation.

c. 9500 BCE
Farming is underway in the Fertile Crescent lands of the Levant and Mesopotamia; evidence shows wheat, barley, peas, and lentils all being cultivated. The ensuing Agricultural Revolution will in time lead to a surge in the world's population as food supplies become more reliable and widespread.

c. 9000 BCE
Circles of stone pillars are erected at Göbekli Tepe, a site in eastern Turkey; these are currently the earliest known megaliths. Corn is first domesticated at about this time, in southern Mexico. The land bridge linking Siberia and North America finally disappears beneath the waters of the Bering Strait as sea levels rise following the retreat of the Ice Age glaciers.

c. 8700 BCE
The first copper tools are in use, made from naturally occurring deposits of the metal.

△ **Saharan rock art**
This painting, made in red iron oxide in the Acacus Mountains, Libya, dates back to 12,000 BCE; it shows a hunt in progress.

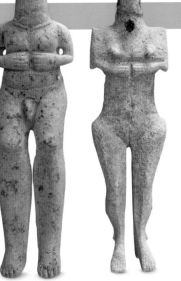

▷ **Cycladic figurines**
The Cycladic islands in the Aegean Sea were settled by people from Anatolia from about 3200 BCE; they shaped the marble they found there into clean-lined anthropomorphic figurines.

c. 8200 BCE
Rice is being cultivated in the Pearl River region of China and spreads to the Yellow and Yangtze valleys; millet is also being grown in China by this time. Some experts estimate that rice was domesticated as early as 13,500 BCE.

c. 8000 BCE
Settled since c. 10,000 BCE by hunter-gatherers attracted by its freshwater spring, Jericho (in modern-day Palestine) has by now become a fortified town of at least 300 inhabitants who support themselves by growing emmer wheat, barley, and pulses; the town is surrounded by a wall (which may have afforded some protection against flooding). A defensive tower 28 ft (8.5 m) in height is built within the walls.

c. 7000 BCE
Çatal Höyük is flourishing in Anatolia as a large settlement with an estimated population of 7,000.

c. 6500 BCE
Lead beads found at Çatal Höyük represent evidence of metal smelting.

c. 5500 BCE
The first known smelted copper objects date from this time; the earliest bronze objects, made of a copper–arsenic alloy, also appear. A painted disk found in Kuwait and assigned to this period has the earliest known depiction of a ship under sail. The Tărtăria tablets, discovered at a Neolithic site in Romania, bear symbols considered by some archeologists to be the world's earliest form of writing.

c. 5050 BCE
The Chinchorro people of northern Chile are the first culture known to mummify their dead.

c. 5000 BCE
Lower Mesopotamia, between the Tigris and Euphrates Rivers, is populated by a west Asian people called the Sumerians; over the next two millennia Sumer will become, along with Egypt, the Indus Valley, and coastal Peru, the seat of one of the world's earliest urban civilizations, developing masonry and pottery and building the towns of Uruk and Eridu.

c. 4500 BCE
Bones and carved images of horses found in graves in the Volga River region of central Russia suggest that horses have been domesticated there by this time. Finds from Serbia show tin-alloy bronze objects making their first appearance. Obsidian, prized by Neolithic tool-makers for its hardness and sharp edges, is being traded by now in Mesopotamia.

c. 4000 BCE
At Carnac in Brittany, northern France, the world's largest accumulation of megaliths is growing; eventually (by about 3300 BCE), it will incorporate more than 3,000 separate standing stones. Austronesians from Taiwan or the Philippines begin their Pacific migration.

c. 3600 BCE
Neolithic farmers in Malta, possibly from Sicily, build the temple complex at Skorba. In Mesopotamia, symbols representing numbers are being impressed on clay tablets as a way of keeping accounts—an early form of writing that will eventually develop into cuneiform.

c. 3500 BCE
Evidence from Mesopotamia, the North Caucasus region, and eastern Europe shows wheeled vehicles coming into use at about this time; the earliest schematic depiction of a four-wheeled wagon is on the Bronocice Pot, dated to around 3400 BCE and found in Southern Poland. In Crete, the Minoan civilization is starting to take shape.

c. 3300 BCE
Approximate start of the Bronze Age in the Middle East, when bronze begins supplementing stone for tool-making and other uses. The Indus Valley civilization starts to develop in the northeast of the Indian subcontinent, as previously scattered populations gather into permanent settlements that will eventually become fortified towns.

c. 3200 BCE
Newgrange, a circular mound 280 ft (85 m) wide and containing tunnels and chambers, is constructed in Ireland; its exact purpose is unclear, but it probably has a ritual function. The Cycladic culture is spreading across the islands of the Aegean Sea; it is known for its flat female statuettes made out of the local white marble.

c. 3150 BCE
The Narmer Palette is produced. It is an inscribed tablet depicting the unification of Upper and Lower Egypt under the ruler of that name (also known as Menes), who will establish the nation's First Dynasty. It bears some of the earliest known hieroglyphic writing.

3114 BCE
In Mesoamerica, the first date in the Mayan Long Count Calendar.

c. 3100 BCE
Europe's most complete Neolithic village, Skara Brae, is built, indicating that settled communities have formed in the Orkney Islands to the north of Scotland. The site is revealed after the islands are battered by a storm in 1850.

12 ft (3.6 m). The height of the defensive wall built around the settlement of Jericho by around 8000 BCE.

▷ **Skara Brae, Orkney**
Skara Brae, occupied around 3100 BCE, is a settlement of circular one-room dwellings made from stone slabs. The houses would have been roofed with straw or turf.

THE ANCIENT WORLD 3000 BCE–500 CE

3000 BCE

c. 3000 BCE

In Sumer (modern Iraq and Kuwait), around a dozen city-states are flourishing, among them Lagash and Uruk (which has a population of more than 50,000 by this time, making it the largest city in the world). The cities trade with Anatolia, Syria, Dilmun (modern Bahrain), and Elam on the eastern coast of the Persian Gulf (now part of modern-day Iran). In southern Siberia, the Afanasevo Culture of cattle-, sheep-, and goat-herders is established. The first phase of the Stonehenge complex in southern England is built—a circular ditch and bank; construction on the site will continue through the next millennium.

c. 2900 BCE

In China, the Longshan Culture, centered on the lower Yellow River valley, is producing sophisticated, thin-walled black pottery; millet is the main crop and pigs the principal source of meat. In South America, the Norte Chico people build monumental centers on the coast of Peru; Aspero, at the mouth of the Supe Valley, boasts platform mounds endowed with plazas, terraces, and ceremonial buildings.

c. 2700 BCE

The legendary Gilgamesh rules Uruk; his exploits, richly mythologized, are the basis of one of the world's first literary works, the *Epic of Gilgamesh* (c. 2100 BCE).

c. 2630 BCE

Djoser, the first pharaoh of Egypt's Old Kingdom, orders the building of the Step Pyramid at Saqqara as his burial place.

c. 2600 BCE

Objects found in the Royal Cemetery of Ur include the Standard of Ur, a wooden box inlaid with shell, limestone, and lapis lazuli mosaics depicting scenes of feasting and of warfare, including war chariots.

c. 2575 BCE

Pharaoh Khufu (known to later Greeks as Cheops) builds the Great Pyramid of Giza, the oldest of the Seven Wonders of the Ancient World.

c. 2500 BCE

The Indus Valley civilization is at its peak, with the cities of Harappa and Mohenjo-Daro supporting populations of 25,000–40,000 and boasting sophisticated civic facilities and urban planning. In Europe, the Bell Beaker Culture, identified by its distinctive pottery, is flourishing at scattered sites in the west and center of the continent.

c. 2450 BCE

A conflict between the Sumerian city-state of Lagash and its neighbor, Umma, is the first to be historically documented, on the Stele of the Vultures, fragments of which are now preserved in the Louvre Museum, Paris.

◁ **Hero overpowering a lion**
This sculpture of a lion-taming spirit, recovered from the throne room of the palace of Assyrian king Sargon II, is believed to depict Gilgamesh (king of Uruk around 2700 BCE).

▽ **Stonehenge, Amesbury, England**
The neolithic monument of Stonehenge was built in several stages, beginning in 3000 BCE. The stones at its center were erected in about 2500 BCE and then rearranged some 300 years later.

2050 BCE

c. 2334–2279 BCE
Sargon of Akkad conquers Sumer, joining it with his own kingdom to create the world's first empire. He will go on to win further territory from the Hurrians and Elamites in what is now eastern Turkey and western Iran.

c. 2300 BCE
The Bronze Age Unetice culture—named for an archaeological site northwest of Prague, where its remains were uncovered—starts to spread across central Europe. Its people live in straw-thatched wooden houses with storage pits used as granaries and produce handsome metal goods that serve as status symbols for the nobility.

c. 2205 BCE
According to Chinese tradition, the Xia Dynasty, is established under Yu the Great. He is known in legend for holding back the floodwaters of the Yellow River.

c. 2193 BCE
Gutians from the Zagros Mountains overrun Akkad and Sumer, putting an end to the Akkadian Empire.

140 miles (225 km). The distance over which 25-ton stones were hauled to Stonehenge.

c. 2180 BCE
Egypt's Old Kingdom comes to an end as central control disintegrates, ushering in the First Intermediate Period, a time of strife when separate power bases emerge in Upper and Lower Egypt.

c. 2100 BCE
Semitic-speaking Amorites from northern Syria begin to infiltrate into Mesopotamia, possibly driven by drought.

c. 2050 BCE
King Ur-Nammu reunites Sumer, establishing the powerful Third Dynasty of Ur (also called the Sumerian Renaissance); ziggurats (stepped monuments) are built during his reign, and the world's oldest surviving legal code bears his name. In Egypt, Pharaoh Mentuhotep reunites a divided land in 2134 BCE, starting the Middle Kingdom period.

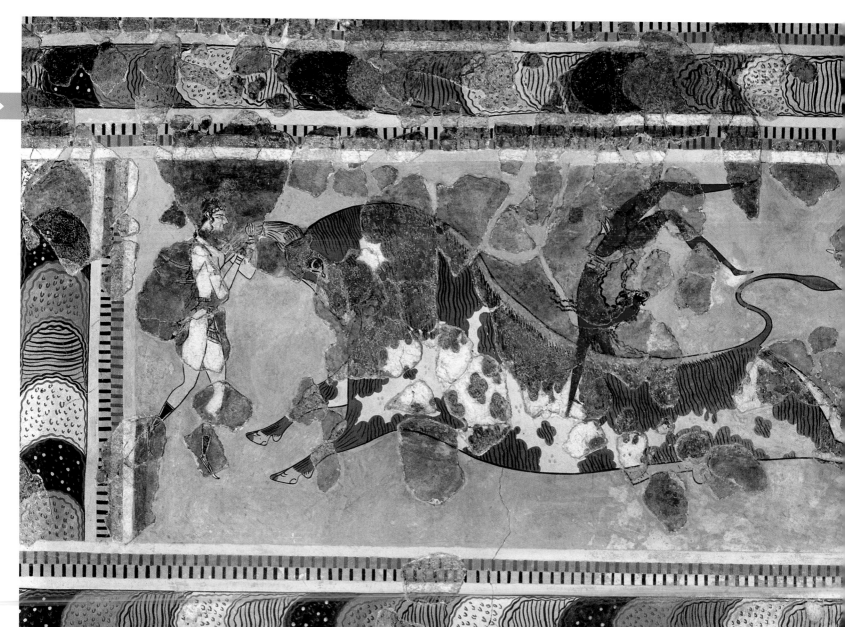

c. 2000 BCE

A rich civilization develops on the island of Crete, centered on the palace complex at Knossos. On the Greek mainland, the Achaeans move into the northern Peloponnese. In Britain, the main stages of construction of Stonehenge are by now complete, while people of the Wessex culture, distinguished by their barrow burials and rich grave goods, have spread widely across central and southern England and are trading extensively with continental Europe.

c. 1960 BCE

Under Pharaoh Amenemhet I, Middle Kingdom Egypt extends its southern frontier as far as the Second Cataract of the River Nile, which is now submerged by Lake Nasser.

c. 1940 BCE

Despite the building of fortifications, the city of Ur falls to Elamites from eastern Iran, who take its last ruler, Ibbi-Sin, into captivity, ending the Third Dynasty; the loss of the city is commemorated in the "Lament for Ur," a 438-line Sumerian poem inscribed on a tablet that is found by archaeologists at Nippur. The defeat marks the end of the golden age of Sumer, whose population has shrunk, as the irrigated lands on which it depended have been affected by salinity.

c. 1900 BCE

Assyria emerges as a major power, with its capital at Assur in the Upper Tigris Valley of northern Mesopotamia. Under the ruler Shamshi-Adad I, the Great Royal Palace is built, and the temple of Assur is enlarged with a ziggurat.

The number of laws enshrined in the Code of Hammurabi, king of Babylon.

◁ **Minoan fresco**
Painted on the east wall of the Minoan palace at Knossos in around 1400 BCE, the fresco depicts bull-leaping, which was possibly a ceremonial practice demonstrating bravery.

◁ **Hittite goddess**
The large pantheon of the Hittites, who created an empire in Anatolia from c.1600–1180 BCE, included many gods appropriated from neighboring cultures.

2000–1450 BCE

Hammurabi transforms his capital, Babylon, from a small city-state into the center of a large state that extends over much of Mesopotamia.

c. 1750 BCE
The Erlitou Culture is flourishing in northern China; it is distinguished by the production of elaborate bronze vessels, including two-handled, legged cauldrons known as dings.

c. 1700 BCE
The Indus Valley civilization collapses, probably because of the gradual drying up of the Saraswati River; the cities of Harappa and Mohenjo Daro are abandoned.

c. 1640 BCE
Speaking a Semitic language and worshipping the storm god Baal, chariot-borne Hyksos move into Egypt. The Middle Kingdom comes to an end and the country enters the Second Intermediate Period, a time of famine and political strife.

c. 1600 BCE
A cataclysmic volcanic eruption on the Greek island of Thera (modern Santorini) has profound effects on the neighboring lands; Knossos and other ceremonial centers on Crete are badly damaged, and though they will later be rebuilt, Minoan civilization will never regain its former glory. The Shang Dynasty under King Tang replaces the Xia, establishing its rule over China's northern plains.

c. 1595 BCE
Hittite invaders from Anatolia sack Babylon, by then a small city-state; Kassites from the Zagros Mountains take advantage of the situation to establish a dynasty that will rule for the next 375 years.

c. 1550 BCE
A Hurrian-speaking people establish the kingdom of Mitanni in northern Syria and southeast Anatolia; in the centuries to come, it will develop into a major regional power.

1532 BCE
Ahmose of Thebes drives the Hyksos out of Lower Egypt, reunifying the country and establishing the New Kingdom. During this period Egyptian power reaches its greatest extent.

c. 1500 BCE
Indo-Iranian Aryans begin to migrate in large numbers into the north of the Indian subcontinent; the Vedas, the oldest Hindu scriptures, will take shape under the auspices of these people over the ensuing Vedic Period (to 600 BCE). In the Pacific Ocean, the Lapita culture is flourishing in Vanuatu, Fiji, Samoa, and Tonga, laying the foundations for subsequent Polynesian and Micronesian cultures.

1470 BCE
Hatshepsut, the best-known of Egypt's female pharaohs and the woman who commissioned the celebrated Deir el-Bahari mortuary temple as her last resting place, sends a major trading expedition to the Land of Punt, somewhere to the south, on the Red Sea.

1456 BCE
Egypt's Pharaoh Thutmose III defeats a coalition of Canaanite states at the Battle of Megiddo, in what is now northern Israel; Tuthmose will go on to restore Egyptian dominance in the area and to expand Egyptian imperial control to its greatest extent.

c. 1450 BCE
Shaushtatar, the ruler of Mittani, invades Assyria and sacks its capital, Assur. By this time, the Karasuk culture, known only from its burials, has replaced the Andronovo culture in southeastern Siberia; its people are farmers and horse riders who practice metalwork on a large scale.

25,000
The population of the Indus Valley city of Harappa at its height in the Bronze Age.

c. 1800 BCE
The truncated defensive towers known as *nuraghi* are built across all of Sardinia.

c. 1754 BCE
Hammurabi, the sixth ruler of the Amorite First Babylonian Dynasty, issues a celebrated law code; which covers subjects ranging from wage rates and the legal liability to inheritance, sexual conduct, and divorce. Over the course of his 42-year reign, from 1792 to 1750 BCE,

▷ **The mortuary temple of Hatshepsut**
Located near the Valley of the Kings on the west bank of the Nile, the colonnaded temple (reconstructed in the 20th century) took 15 years to build during Hatshepsut's reign (1478–1458 BCE).

▷ **Tutankhamun with Ankhesenpaaten**
Tutankhamun, who reigned in 1332–1323 BCE, is pictured with his wife under the rays of Aten (the radiant disk of the Sun) in this detail on the gilded wooden throne found in his tomb.

1400–701 BCE

c. 1400 BCE

The Olmecs, Mesoamerica's first major civilization, flourish in south-central Mexico. Noted for their monumental sculpted heads, the Olmecs practice such enduring innovations as ritual bloodletting and play an often lethal Mesoamerican game, involving a heavy rubber ball. Around this time, Crete is occupied by Mycenaeans from the Greek mainland, who adopt many Minoan customs and adapt the Minoan Linear A script for their own use.

1392 BCE

Assyria breaks free of its subjection to the kingdom of Mitanni, inaugurating the Middle Assyrian state, which endures until 1056 BCE.

1353–1336 BCE

Akhenaten, the "heretic pharaoh," reigns in Egypt. He does away with the worship of the traditional Egyptian gods and instead introduces a short-lived monotheistic cult that is dedicated to Aten, or the radiant disk of the Sun; to further the religious revolution, he eventually moves the nation's capital from Thebes to a new site at el-Amarna called Akhetaten, "Horizon of the Aten."

c. 1332–1323 BCE

Under the boy-king Tutankhamun, Akhenaten's controversial religious reforms are reversed, and Egypt soon returns to the worship of its old gods; the dead pharaoh's name is removed from monuments, and attempts are made to erase his memory from the historical record.

c. 1274 BCE

Hittite forces led by Muwatalli II halt an Egyptian advance under Rameses II at the Battle of Kadesh (fought near the modern Syrian–Lebanese border), ending an attempt by the pharaoh to reassert control over Canaan; it is thought to be one of the largest chariot battles ever fought.

c. 1220 BCE

Assyrian king Tukulti-Ninurta I captures Babylon, putting an end to the Kassite Dynasty that had ruled the city for more than 350 years.

c. 1210 BCE

Under the Shutrukid Dynasty, Elam (a civilization based in present-day Iran) is at the height of its power; its armies raid deep into Mesopotamia to carry back trophies to its capital, Susa.

c. 1200 BCE

By this time, the Phoenician people, based on the eastern coast of the Mediterranean Sea, are using a 22-letter alphabet, made up entirely of consonants. The Middle East enters a period of major change, known as the Bronze Age Collapse, with the Hittite Empire breaking up under attack from Phrygian and Assyrian invaders, while in Greece, the overthrow of the Mycenaean culture ushers in a prolonged dark age; some scholars believe that this time of troubles provided the backdrop for later Homeric legends of the Trojan War. In Mesoamerica, the Olmecs are at their zenith, with major ceremonial centers at San Lorenzo, Tres Zapotes, and La Venta.

c. 1175 BCE

Egyptian forces under Rameses III repel an attempted invasion by a coalition called (in Egyptian sources) the Sea Peoples—possibly the same assailants who had caused the downfall of the Hittite Empire, though their precise identity remains obscure; subsequent to their defeat, some of the Sea Peoples are thought to have settled in the southern Levant.

c. 1100 BCE

Hillfort construction is now well advanced at many sites across western Europe. In India, ironworking has reached the Ganges Plain. In Greece, the Dorian people, distinguished by their Doric dialect, are moving east and

south from their original homeland in the mountains of Epirus (near the modern Greek border with Albania) to settle the Peloponnese.

c. 1056 BCE

The Middle Assyrian state suffers significant reverses on the death of King Ashurbelkala, following an uprising against his rule that allowed Aramean tribes to press in from Syria on its western borders.

c. 1046 BCE

According to Chinese tradition, King Wu defeats Zhou, the last ruler of the Shang Dynasty, at Muye in east-central China, starting the Zhou Dynasty, the longest-lasting in Chinese history.

50 tons. The weight of the largest of the Olmec heads found at the La Cobata archaeological site.

▷ Prisoners of Sennacherib
This relief from the palace of Sennacherib in Nineveh (in modern-day Iraq) records prisoners taken from Lachish, in Judah; by the Assyrians in 701 BCE.

c. 1000 BCE

The Phoenician civilization is at its peak, with major centers at Tyre and Sidon on the Levantine coast and a network of trading stations located around the Mediterranean Sea. In the Biblical lands, tradition holds that David is ruler of the joint kingdoms of Israel and Judah, following the death of King Saul at the Battle of Gilboa. In Mesoamerica, the Mayan people are starting to establish themselves in the Yucatán peninsula.

970–931 BCE

The traditional dates given for the reign of Solomon as king of Israel and Judah, after succeeding his father David, who

c. 900 BCE

By this time, the Vedic Aryans are living as settled farmers, forming kingdoms in northern India—first Kuru, then Panchala and Videha. In Greece, the (perhaps legendary) lawgiver Lycurgus gives Sparta the communistic form of military-minded government for which it would become lastingly famous; his laws promote the values of equality, military fitness, and austerity among all members of society.

814 BCE

Carthage is founded on the North African coast as a colony of the Phoenician city-state of Tyre.

"Let me not then die ingloriously and without a struggle, but let me first do some great thing that shall be told among men hereafter."

HOMER, FROM THE *ILIAD*, c. 750 BCE

dies after reigning for 40 years. Celebrated for his wisdom, Solomon builds Jerusalem's First Temple and hosts a visit from the Queen of Sheba (thought to be Saba, a nation spanning the southern lands of the Red Sea).

c. 800 BCE

Following the end of the Greek dark age, the population expands, smaller settlements come together to form influential city-states, and colonies begin to appear on the Mediterranean and Black Sea coasts. In Italy, the Villanovan culture of the area north of Rome introduces iron to the Italian peninsula; it will develop into the powerful and wealthy Etruscan civilization. To the north, the Hallstatt culture has replaced the earlier Urnfield culture in central and western Europe; supported by farming and skilled in metalworking, its tribal societies are increasingly stratified under an elite of warrior chieftains, but also trade widely, both locally and with the Mediterranean lands.

776 BCE

The traditional date of the first Olympic Games, held at Olympia, Greece's wealthiest religious center.

c. 771 BCE

The capital of the Zhou Dynasty is moved from Zhongzhou to Chengzhou, marking the beginning of the Spring and Autumn period of Chinese history; it takes its name from the *Spring and Autumn Annals*, an ancient chronicle of the official history of the state of Lu over a 250-year period, which is traditionally claimed to have been compiled by Confucius.

753 BCE

The traditional date for the foundation of Rome by Romulus.

c. 750 BCE

In Greece, the *Iliad* and the *Odyssey*, epic poems traditionally attributed to Homer, are written down; these works provide the basis of Greek education and culture throughout the Classical age and become hugely influential in the Renaissance, when they are rediscovered by 14th-century

scholars in Italy. The mound-building Adena Culture spreads from its center in the Ohio Valley across the eastern woodlands of North America.

c. 744 BCE

The crown of Assyria is seized by Pul, who takes the name Tiglath-Pileser III. He introduces extensive political, civil, and military reforms throughout his reign. The Nubian ruler Piye conquers Egypt, establishing the 25th or Kushite Dynasty, which will control the country until it is conquered by the Assyrians in 671 BCE.

733 BCE

Settlers from Corinth found Syracuse as a Greek colony on the Sicilian coast.

c. 720 BCE

Sargon II, ruler of Assyria, conquers the kingdom of Israel, forcing large numbers of Israelites into exile and giving rise to legends of the 10 lost tribes.

c. 701 BCE

Assyrian king Sennacherib invades Judah and besieges Jerusalem to collect a tribute from its ruler Hezekiah.

330

ft (100 m). The diameter of the largest extant earthworks made by the Adena Culture.

◁ Olmec head
The Olmecs, whose civilization began to flourish around 1400 BCE, were accomplished sculptors. They are best known for the colossal male heads that they carved from basalt boulders.

700 BCE

c. 700 BCE
In Assyria, King Sennacherib builds an aqueduct and creates a garden for his palace in Nineveh by cutting irrigation channels from the rock. The screw pump (attributed to Archimedes) is in use for irrigation by this time, as are water clocks. Eastern Europe sees the arrival of nomadic Scythians from Central Asia. In Greece, the first city-states make their appearance. Agricultural villages spread in southeastern North America.

689 BCE
Sennacherib destroys Babylon, razing its temples and walls and diverting canals to flood the site.

671 BCE
Memphis in Egypt falls to the Assyrian king Esarhaddon, the youngest son of Sennacherib.

668 BCE
Assurbanipal, the son of Esarhaddon, comes to the Assyrian throne; the empire reaches its greatest extent during his reign.

663 BCE
Assyrian troops sack Thebes after repelling a Nubian invasion of Egypt. Temple treasures that had been collected over the past 14 centuries are looted.

660 BCE
According to legend, Jimmu, the first emperor of Japan, ascends to the throne. In mythology, he is a descendant of the sun goddess Amaterasu.

c. 660 BCE
Corcyra (on Corfu) defeats Corinth in the earliest recorded naval battle between Greek city-states.

c. 650 BCE
The first coins are minted, in the kingdom of Lydia, in Anatolia. The Age of Tyrants—aristocrats who seize absolute power without legal right—begins in many Greek cities, especially in the Peloponnese.

c. 630 BCE
Sparta wages war against the Messenians, conquering most of the southern Peloponnese by 600 BCE.

43
The number of years that Nebuchadnezzar II survived on the throne of the Neo-Babylonian Empire.

Colonists from the island of Thera found Cyrene in Libya, the first of five Greek cities in the region. The poet Sappho is born on the island of Lesbos. Only one of her poems—"Ode to Aphrodite"—survives in complete form.

626 BCE
Nabopolassar secures Babylon's independence from Assyria and founds the Neo-Babylonian Empire. He makes Babylon his capital and rules over Babylonia for the next 20 years.

c. 624 BCE
Thales of Miletus, a leading philosopher, mathematician, and astronomer, is born. He is among the first great thinkers to use theories and hypotheses to explore the nature of natural phenomena and is celebrated as one of the Seven Sages of Greece.

621 BCE
Draco drafts Athens' first written code of law, replacing the previous reliance on oral law; Draconian law will in later times become legendary for the severity of its punishments.

616 BCE
Tarquinius Priscus (Tarquin the Elder) becomes the first Etruscan king of Rome. Construction begins on the Cloaca Maxima, one of the world's earliest sewage systems, and on the Circus Maximus, Rome's first stadium for chariot racing.

612 BCE
The Assyrian Empire crumbles with the sacking of Nineveh and Nimrud by its former vassals, including the Medes and Babylonians. The city of Nineveh becomes depopulated.

609 BCE
King Josiah is killed in battle against Pharaoh Necho II of Egypt, triggering the fall of the Kingdom of Judah.

c. 605 BCE
Birth of Nebuchadnezzar II, who will become the greatest and most powerful of the Neo-Babylonian emperors.

604 BCE
Traditional date for the birth of Lao Tzu, founder of the Chinese religion Taoism.

c. 600 BCE
With the collapse of the Assyrian Empire, much of the Middle East falls to the Medes, whose homeland lies in northwestern Iran. The Neo-Babylonian

◁ **The Palace of King Sennacherib**
The rooms and courtyards of the Assyrian palace at Nineveh (built around 700 BCE) were decorated with carved stone panels showing hunting and other scenes.

▷ **Warring States dagger**
The Warring States period of Chinese history, which began in 475 BCE, was a time of great cultural richness, producing objects such as this decorated dagger.

479 BCE

Empire retains power in Mesopotamia. The first known map of the world is made in Babylon. Ironworking technology reaches Zhou China. The first Upanishads, central texts of the Hindu religion, are usually assigned to this period. Greek settlers found a colony at Massalia on the Mediterranean coast, which eventually develops into the port of Marseilles.

597 BCE
First conquest of Judah by Nebuchadnezzar II of Babylon.

594 BCE
Solon becomes archon (ruler) of Athens; in reforming its laws, he recasts land ownership, protects the property rights of the poor, and bans debt slavery.

587 BCE
Following a revolt in Judah, Nebuchadnezzar II of Babylon destroys Jerusalem's temple and sends the Israelites into exile, the start of the "Babylonian Captivity."

585 BCE
Death of the Biblical prophet Jeremiah, in exile in Egypt. According to historian Herodotus, the Greek astronomer Thales of Miletus predicts a solar eclipse.

573 BCE
The prosperous Phoenician city of Tyre falls to the army of Nebuchadnezzar II after a 13-year siege.

c. 570 BCE
Pythagoras, the Greek philosopher and mathematician, is born on the island of Samos.

563 BCE
Traditional birthdate for Siddhartha Gautama, the Buddha (though some scholars place it at c. 448 BCE). He is born into a royal family in the village of Lumbini in present-day Nepal.

561 BCE
The mental decline and death of Nebuchadnezzar II signals the end of the period of Babylonian greatness.

c. 560 BCE
Croesus succeeds to the throne of Lydia (in western Anatolia) and begins its expansion. He reigns for the next 14 years.

c. 559 BCE
Cyrus the Great comes to power in Persia. In 550 BCE, he defeats the Medes and founds the Persian Empire—which becomes the largest empire yet created.

551 BCE
Birth of Confucius, whose *Analects* provide the central philosophy of the Chinese way of life. In Persia, Zoroastrianism is the main religion.

547 BCE
Cyrus defeats Croesus, the last king of Lydia. Greek philosopher Anaximander, propounder of an evolutionary theory that life developed from creatures living in the oceans, dies.

539 BCE
Cyrus quashes a rebellion in Babylon; the Babylonian empire is absorbed by Persia. Cyrus allows the Israelites exiled in Babylon to return home.

534 BCE
Tarquinius Superbus becomes Rome's last king; the Etruscans are at their height.

530 BCE
Cyrus the Great dies; his son Cambyses II succeeds him as ruler of Persia.

525 BCE
Cambyses II defeats Pharaoh Psammiticus III at the Battle of Pelusium and annexes Egypt.

522–486 BCE
Darius I (the Great) rules Persia, after succeeding Cambyses; under his sway, the Persian Empire will reach its greatest extent. He is succeeded by Xerxes.

c. 520 BCE
Birth of the Greek poet Pindar, whose odes are known for their rich imagery.

509 BCE
The Romans expel Tarquinius Superbus and set up a republic, with Lucius Junius Brutus and Collatinus as the first two annually elected consuls.

507 BCE
Cleisthenes establishes democratic government in Athens.

c. 500 BCE
Bronze coins appear in China. Ironworking spreads to Southeast Asia and east Africa. India's caste system is in place, and the *Puranas* and parts of the epic *Mahabharata* are composed. Nok Culture flourishes in west Africa (centered in modern Nigeria). In Mesoamerica, the Zapotecs use hieroglyphic writing.

499–491 BCE
Greek cities in Ionia, western Anatolia, revolt against Persian rule; their uprising is suppressed.

496 BCE
Rome defeats the Etruscan-led Latin League at Lake Regillus and signs its first treaty with Carthage.

491 BCE
Death of Bimbisara of Magadha, patron of the Buddha and founder of a northern Indian empire.

490 BCE
Greeks led by the prominent Athenian Miltiades defeat the Persians at the Battle of Marathon, ending the first Persian invasion of Greece.

480 BCE
Xerxes' invasion marks the end of the Archaic Period in Greece. In the Classical Period (480–323 BCE), Greece will be dominated in turn by Athens, Sparta, and Macedonia, and Greek culture will reach its peak.

480–479 BCE
Persian forces, sent by Xerxes, invade Greece, overcome resistance at the pass of Thermopylae, and take Athens. However, the Persian navy is defeated at Salamis (480 BCE) and Mycale (479 BCE), and the Spartan leader Pausanias routs their army at Plataea (479 BCE).

◁ **Persian winter palace**
Darius (ruled 522–486 BCE) initiated many building projects in Persia. His winter palace in Persepolis was one of the few buildings at the site to escape destruction by Alexander the Great.

478 BCE

◁ Monte Albán
One of the oldest of Mesoamerican cities, Monte Albán (built c. 450 BCE) was the center of Zapotec Culture, which then dominated much of the territory of the modern state of Oaxaca, Mexico.

c. 478 BCE
Athens founds the Delian League of city-states to counter Sparta's Peloponnesian League.

475 BCE
China enters the Warring States period (to 221 BCE), in which seven leading states jostle for supremacy.

c. 450 BCE
The Celtic La Tène culture emerges in central Europe, eventually supplanting the Halstatt culture; Celts expand their territory east and south and into the British Isles. Steppe nomads are buried with spectacular grave goods at Pazyryk and Noin-Ula in Siberia. In Mexico, the construction of the Zapotec city of Monte Albán begins.

449 BCE
Greece's Persian Wars come to an end after 41 years when Artaxerxes I, the king of Persia, recognizes the independence of the Greek city-states in the Peace of Callias.

447–432 BCE
The ruler of Athens, Pericles, builds a new Parthenon to replace the temple destroyed by the Persians.

c. 445 BCE
Nehemiah rebuilds the walls of Jerusalem, still under Persian rule.

438 BCE
The Greek sculptor Phidias supervises the completion of sculptures designed to decorate the Acropolis in Athens; they will later become known as the Elgin Marbles.

431–404 BCE
The Peloponnesian War leads to the destruction of the Athenian League by Sparta and its allies.

c. 427 BCE
Birth of the Greek philosopher Plato.

c. 424 BCE
Herodotus, the Greek writer known as the "Father of History," dies. He is best known for his work *The Histories*, a critical examination of the origins of the Greco-Persian Wars.

404 BCE
Egypt emerges from Persian rule under Amyrtaeus, the sole pharaoh of the 28th Dynasty.

399 BCE
In Greece, the philosopher Socrates is sentenced to death for corrupting the minds of Athenian youth.

c. 390 BCE
Celtic Gauls settled in northern Italy defeat the Romans at the Battle of the Allia and capture and sack Rome, holding the city for several months.

c. 385 BCE
In Greece, Plato writes his seminal philosophical text, the *Symposium*.

"Wonder is the feeling of a philosopher, and philosophy begins in wonder."

PLATO, QUOTING SOCRATES IN HIS *THEAETETUS*, c. 369 BCE

---

c. 401–399 BCE
The soldier and philosopher Xenophon of Athens leads an army of 10,000 Greek mercenaries, supporting a Persian rebellion from Babylon to the Black Sea, an exploit chronicled in his *Anabasis*.

c. 400 BCE
Celtic Gauls cross the Alps and settle in northern Italy. Carthage dominates in the western Mediterranean. In Mesoamerica, the Olmec civilization is seriously affected by environmental changes and enters its final phase, while the Zapotecs flourish in Monte Albán. The Moche Culture emerges in Peru. Ironworking develops in Korea.

c. 380 BCE
The Chu become dominant among China's Warring States.

371 BCE
The Theban general Epaminondas wins the Battle of Leuctra against Sparta; Thebes remains the dominant power in Greece until his death in battle in 362 BCE.

c. 370 BCE
Mahapadma Nanda founds the Nanda Dynasty in Magadha, north India.

359–336 BCE
Philip II rules Macedonia and wins control of most of Greece.

356 BCE
Shang Yang, chancellor of the western Chinese state of Qin, makes wide-ranging reforms to create a powerful centralized kingdom.

343–342 BCE
A Persian invasion puts an end to Egypt's independence and dethrones the last native line of pharaohs.

341–338 BCE
Rome defeats and dissolves the Latin League, moving closer to complete dominance of central Italy.

336 BCE
Philip of Macedon is murdered; he is succeeded by his son Alexander III, who forces other Greek states into submission (335), then crosses into Anatolia (334) to confront the Persians.

332 BCE
Alexander III (the Great) conquers Egypt and founds Alexandria, one of many new cities across his empire.

331 BCE
At Gaugamela, Alexander defeats Darius III, and the Persian Empire falls to him; his army burns its capital, Persepolis.

326 BCE
Alexander pushes east into India, extending his realm to the Indus River before his troops force him to turn back.

323 BCE
Alexander the Great dies of a fever in Babylon; his vast empire begins to disintegrate as his generals fight for dominance. Egypt falls to Ptolemy Soter, who founds the Ptolemaic Dynasty.

321–297 BCE
Chandragupta Maurya founds the Mauryan Dynasty, which goes on to create the largest empire in Indian history.

◁ **Lion Capital of Ashoka**
This capital topped one of the many columns erected across the Mauryan Empire by Ashoka (268–232 BCE); its design was adopted in 1950 as the official emblem of India.

160 BCE

312 BCE
Rome's first aqueduct is built by Appius Claudius; he also begins the Appian Way, the first of Rome's network of roads across Italy.

311 BCE
Seleucus establishes control of Babylon, going on to create the Seleucid Empire by conquering the former Median and Persian lands of Alexander's empire.

c. 300 BCE
Alexander's empire is partitioned between the Seleucid, Antigonid, Attalid, and Ptolemaic Dynasties. Rice farming reaches Japan from China. The Greek mathematician Euclid lays out the basic principles of geometry in his treatise, the *Elements*.

298–290 BCE
Rome defeats its Samnite enemies in south-central Italy, extending its territory across Italy to the Adriatic.

c. 287 BCE
China's northern states build frontier defenses to keep out Eurasian nomads.

280–275 BCE
Pyrrhus of Epirus lands in Italy and defeats the forces of Rome. The Romans regroup, and he returns to Greece.

c. 268–232 BCE
Ashoka, the Mauryan emperor of India, greatly expands his territories and promotes the Buddhist concept of *dharma* across his empire.

264–241 BCE
The First Punic War between Rome and Carthage ends after 23 years with Rome in control of almost the entire Italian peninsula and Sicily.

c. 250 BCE
Arsaces founds the kingdom of Parthia in lands southeast of the Caspian Sea.

221–210 BCE
In China, the state of Qin conquers the last of its rivals. Its ruler takes the title of Qin Shi Huang, "First Emperor" of a united China; after his death, he is buried in a vast mausoleum with an army of 8,000 terracotta soldiers.

1,200

ft (366 m). The length of the largest geoglyph motifs made by the Nazca.

218–203 BCE
In the Second Punic War, Carthaginian general Hannibal crosses the Alps and defeats the Romans at Lake Trasimene and Cannae. Roman forces regroup under Quintus Curtius Maximus, and Hannibal is ultimately defeated at Zama.

c. 218 BCE
Qin Shi Huang starts construction of what is to become the Great Wall of China, the purpose of which is to keep out invaders from the north. The wall is extended to a length of 1,400 miles (2,250 km) by later dynasties.

206 BCE
Liu Bang conquers the Qin to establish the Han Dynasty, whose rule (to 220 CE) is seen as the golden age of China.

c. 200 BCE
The Middle Yayoi Period (200–100 BCE) in Japan sees a big increase in population. In Ptolemaic Egypt, Alexandria becomes a major center of Greek trade, culture, and learning. In eastern North America,

Ohio's Adena Culture is developing into the Hopewell Culture. To the south in Mesoamerica, the Mayan civilization emerges as small communities on Mexico's Pacific Coast migrate northward to form larger states. The Nazca in Peru create mysterious geoglyphs—long lines in the desert.

197 BCE
A Roman army defeats Philip V of Macedon at Cynoscephalae in Thessaly, driving him back to his own kingdom.

c. 185 BCE
Pushyamitra, Hindu founder of the Shunga Dynasty, takes power in India, assassinating the last Mauryan ruler and persecuting Buddhists.

183 BCE
To avoid falling into Roman hands, Hannibal commits suicide in the Bithynian town of Libyssa.

171–138 BCE
Mithridates I conquers Greek-ruled kingdoms in Persia, establishing the Parthian Empire.

168 BCE
Macedon is defeated by Roman forces at Pydna and is divided by the conquerors into four separate republics.

167–160 BCE
Judah Maccabee and his brothers rebel against the growing influence of Greek culture (Hellenization) of Judea under Antiochus IV, reestablishing traditional Judaism and rededicating the Temple in Jerusalem before Judah's death in battle.

◁ **Alexander defeats Darius III**
This Roman mosaic, made around 100 BCE in the city of Pompeii, depicts the battle in 331 BCE between the armies of Alexander the Great and Darius III.

▷ **Scene with Emperor Wu**
In this silk painting from a history of Chinese emperors, Wu Ti (Han Emperor, 141–87 BCE) welcomes a man of letters.

150,000

Estimated casualties in the fall of Carthage, which is seen by some historians as the first genocide.

149–146 BCE
The Third Punic War between Rome and Carthaginian forces ends in the total destruction of Carthage.

148–146 BCE
After a series of defeats by Rome, Macedonia is annexed and becomes a Roman province.

142 BCE
Having freed Jerusalem from Seleucid rule, the Maccabees make it the capital of the Hasmonaean kingdom; the dynasty rules Judea until 63 BCE.

121–91 BCE
Under Mithridates II, the Parthian Empire reaches its greatest extent.

107–104 BCE
The Roman general Marius reforms the army, allowing poor citizens to become soldiers.

105 BCE
In Africa, Roman forces defeat Jugurtha, ruler of Numidia. In Gaul, Germanic Cimbri raiders overcome a Roman army at Arausio, causing panic in Rome itself until their ultimate defeat at Vercellae in 101 BCE.

c. 101 BCE
China's Han Empire reaches its largest extent under Emperor Wu; the Silk Road carries trade across central Asia to the Mediterranean world, stretching from the Han capital at Chang'an to Antioch (in modern-day Turkey).

c. 100 BCE
Celtic hill forts in western Europe are developed into fortified settlements. Trade links grow between China, Southeast Asia, and India. The Buddhist complex at Sanchi in India—commissioned by Emperor Ashoka in the 3rd century BCE, and famous for its Great Stupa—nears its present form.

91–89 BCE
The Social War—a conflict between the Roman Republic and several cities in Italy—breaks out, driven by discontent over the failure of Rome to give its allies Roman citizenship; this is finally granted to most Italian communities in 88 BCE.

88–82 BCE
Civil war between patricians and populists in Rome ends with the victorious general and statesman Sulla defeating his rivals and having himself declared dictator.

73–71 BCE
Spartacus, a former Roman slave and gladiator, originally from Thrace, leads a revolt (later known as the Third Servile War) that is brutally put down by Roman troops under Crassus and Pompey; Spartacus himself is killed in the fighting.

64–63 BCE
The Catiline Conspiracy to seize power in Rome ends as the consul, Cicero, has its leader Catilina put to death.

52 BCE
Pompey is declared sole consul in Rome after a vote taken in the Centuriate Assembly of the Roman Republic.

49 BCE
Ordered by the Roman Senate to disband his army, Caesar instead crosses the River Rubicon, starting a civil war in Italy. In a decisive battle at Pharsalus in the following year, Caesar defeats Pompey's larger army. Pompey flees to Egypt, where he is murdered in 48 BCE.

> *"Fortune … can bring about great changes in a situation through very slight forces."*
>
> JULIUS CAESAR, FROM *COMMENTARIES ON THE CIVIL WAR*, 68 BCE

63 BCE
Defeated in the last of three wars he has fought against Rome since 89 BCE, Mithridates IV, king of Pontus (a state on the coast of the Black Sea, founded by a Persian dynasty), kills himself.

60 BCE
Julius Caesar, Pompey, and Crassus form a political alliance, sharing power in Rome as the First Triumvirate. Their union lasts until the death of Crassus in battle against the Parthians in 53 BCE.

58–50 BCE
In a series of brilliant campaigns, Julius Caesar conquers Gaul for Rome.

55–44 BCE
Julius Caesar invades Britain to carry out an armed reconnaissance.

44 BCE
Just 2 months after he is declared "dictator in perpetuity," Caesar is assassinated on March 15 by republican conspirators led by Brutus, Decimus, and Longinus.

43 BCE
Roman politician and general Mark Antony forms the Second Triumvirate with Lepidus and Octavian.

42 BCE
At Philippi in Macedonia, Antony and Octavian defeat the forces of Brutus and Cassius, who both commit suicide.

36 BCE
Mark Antony marries Cleopatra, ruler of Egypt, although he is already married to Octavian's sister.

◁ **Baths of Antoninus, Carthage**
After the destruction of Punic Carthage in 146 BCE, the Romans built their own city there. It becomes extremely wealthy, supporting the construction of the largest baths in north Africa.

70 CE

32–30 BCE
The Roman Senate declares war against Cleopatra. Octavian's navy, commanded by Marcus Vipsanius Agrippa, defeats the combined fleets of Antony and Cleopatra off Actium on the Ionian Sea. The two retreat to Egypt, where both commit suicide in 30 BCE. Egypt becomes a Roman province.

27 BCE
Octavian becomes Rome's first emperor, adopting the title Augustus.

c. 19 BCE
The poet Virgil completes his epic poem the *Aeneid*.

4 BCE
The probable date of the birth of Jesus Christ at Bethlehem.

c. 1 CE
By now, the Roman Empire includes around one-seventh of the world's population. Nabateans allied with Rome control trade in the Red Sea. The Buddhist religion spreads across southeast Asia.

9
An alliance of Germanic tribes defeats a Roman army in the Teutoburg Forest, frustrating Augustus's attempts to extend his empire to the River Elbe. In China, Emperor Wang Mang introduces radical reforms that provoke revolts; he is killed in one of these revolts in 23.

125,000
Size of the Roman legionary forces under Emperor Tiberius.

14
Augustus dies after a 40-year reign as emperor and is succeeded by his stepson, Tiberius.

25
Guangwu seizes power in China, establishing the Later (or Eastern) Han Dynasty, which will rule the country until 220.

c. 30
Jesus Christ is crucified on the orders of Pontius Pilate, procurator of the Roman province of Judea.

37
Caligula succeeds Tiberius as emperor, reigning until his assassination in 41.

43
Emperor Claudius orders the Roman invasion of Britain.

c. 50
The Yuezhi, a formerly nomadic people settled in Bactria, north of the Hindu Kush mountains in present-day Afghanistan, lay the foundations of the Kushan Empire. They will eventually control much of northern India.

54
Nero becomes Rome's emperor on Claudius's death.

64
Much of Rome is destroyed in a great fire that reportedly burns for more than 1 week. Nero blames the disaster on the city's Christians, starting a general persecution.

66–70
A Jewish revolt against Rome culminates in the capture and destruction of Jerusalem in 70.

▷ **Augustus of Prima Porta**
This marble statue, dating from the 1st century CE, shows Augustus, the first Roman Emperor. It was found in the villa occupied by his wife after Augustus's death in 14.

▷ **Villa of the Mysteries, Pompeii**
Though buried by ash in the eruption of Vesuvius in 79, the Villa sustained little damage. This fresco on its wall may depict the ceremony of initiation into the cult of Dionysus.

77

20 ft (6 m).

The depth of the ash that fell on Pompeii after the eruption of Vesuvius.

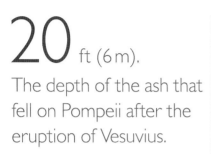

77
The Roman author Pliny the Elder starts work on his *Natural History*, planned as an encyclopedic survey of all areas of knowledge.

79
In southern Italy, Mount Vesuvius erupts, burying the cities of Pompeii and Herculaneum.

91
The Chinese general Ban Chao is given the title Protector of the Western Regions for his work in extending Chinese control over Turkestan and the Tarim Basin; his conquests will later allow increased trade with the West along the Silk Road.

98–116
Under the rule of Emperor Trajan, the Roman Empire

reaches its greatest extent. Following their victorious campaigns in Dacia, north of the Danube, and Parthia, the Romans annexe Armenia, Mesopotamia, and Assyria.

c. 100
Teotihuacan, in the Valley of Mexico, is the largest urban center in Mesoamerica. In Peru, the Moche Culture is rising to prominence.

105
Chinese sources credit Cai Lun with the invention of the paper-making process.

c. 115
Tacitus writes his *Annals*, recounting the history of Rome from the accession of Tiberius to the death of Nero.

117
Hadrian, a cousin of Emperor Trajan, ascends to the imperial throne in Rome.

122–127
Following a visit to Britain by the emperor, Hadrian's Wall is built to protect the Roman Empire's northernmost frontier.

c. 127–150
Kanishka the Great vastly expands the Kushan Empire through north-central India, facilitating the transmission of his Buddhist beliefs into China.

132–135
Simon bar Kokhba leads a Jewish revolt against Roman rule in Judea; after its suppression, Jews are barred from Jerusalem. In China, in 132, Zhang Heng invents a device for registering Earth tremors—the first seismometer.

c. 150
In Alexandria, a Roman province in Egypt, Ptolemy writes the work that will become known as the *Almagest*. This

astronomical compendium dominates thinking about the structure of the universe for more than a millennium. Ptolemy's other great work, *Geography*, similarly sums up the geographical knowledge of his time.

161–180
Marcus Aurelius reigns as the last of the five "Good Emperors" of late 1st- and 2nd-century Rome. A philosopher as well as a military leader, his *Meditations* reflect his Stoic view of life.

180
Commodus succeeds his father Marcus Aurelius, with whom he had co-reigned since 177. His reign is marked by conspiracies and an increasingly dictatorial approach, culminating in his assassination in 192.

184
The rebellion of the Yellow Turbans—peasants so called for their distinctive headbands—breaks out in China in reaction to famine in the countryside and the corrupt rule of court eunuchs. The rising is largely contained by 185, although pockets of resistance continue to flare up for a further 20 years.

c. 200
Jewish scholars assemble the Mishnah, a collection of Rabbinic oral traditions that will become the first of the two components of the Talmud.

c. 210
Death of Galen, physician to several Roman emperors, whose collected writings will dominate Western medical thinking for the next 1,300 years.

◁ **Moche vessel**
The Moche Culture, which became prominent in Peru from around 100, is known for its portrait vessels, which feature detailed, expressive human heads or figures.

212
Roman Emperor Caracalla issues the Antonine Constitution, granting citizenship to all freemen throughout the Empire.

c. 220
The Han Dynasty comes to an end in China, which then enters the Three Kingdoms period (220–280), in which power is divided between the Wei in the north, the Shu in the west, and the Wu in the south of the country. The Three Kingdoms period is among the bloodiest in Chinese history.

224
Ardashir defeats and kills the last king of Parthia, going on to establish the Sassanid Dynasty in Persia.

c. 225
On the death of Pulumavi IV, the territory of the Andhra (or Satavahana) Dynasty, based in the Deccan region of west-central India, fragments into five separate smaller kingdoms.

235
The murder of Emperor Alexander Severus at the hands of mutinous troops inaugurates a period of decline in Rome, which will see more than 20 emperors over the next 50 years; Germanic tribes threaten Rome's frontiers along the Danube and Rhine, invading Italy itself in 259.

238
The port of Histria near the mouth of the River Danube is ravaged by Goth invaders—their first recorded incursion into the lands of the Roman Empire.

c. 245
Chinese sources report a flourishing state (or collection of city-states) at Funan in the Mekong Delta region of what is now Vietnam.

c. 250
Established in Mesoamerica for at least two millennia, the Maya civilization enters its Classic period (to 900), in which city-states and trade flourish. The lodestone compass comes into use in China.

251
The Roman Emperor Decius is defeated and killed by Goth forces under Cniva at Abritus, south of the Danube (in what is now Bulgaria).

268
A Roman army under Emperor Gallienus (also known as Claudius II) defeats a Goth coalition at the Battle of Naissus (near Nis in present-day Serbia), temporarily removing the threat to the empire from the nomadic tribes.

2,000,000 Population of the Maya civilization
in its Classic period, which begins around 250.

270
Zenobia, queen of Palmyra (a wealthy Syrian city that is a tributary to the Roman Empire), conquers Roman Arabia and annexes Egypt. She adds part of Anatolia to her empire and declares independence from Rome.

272
Emperor Aurelian crushes the Palmyran revolt, capturing Zenobia, who lives out the rest of her life in exile in Rome. After a further rebellion in 273, the city of Palmyra is destroyed.

274
Mani, the founder of the Manichaean sect (which preaches a philosophy of dualism, a belief in the forces of light and darkness), dies in prison in Persia; his followers later maintain that he was crucified.

280
Sima Yan of the kingdom of Wei defeats Eastern Wu forces. He reunites China under the Western Jin Dynasty, which itself soon falls into a crisis of succession.

284
After rising through the ranks of the army, Diocletian becomes Roman emperor. His 21-year reign brings stability to a realm that has experienced a century of relative decline.

286
Diocletian appoints Maximian as co-emperor, with responsibility for the west, while Diocletian himself concentrates his efforts on the empire's troubled eastern frontier.

c. 300
Chinese records mention a kingdom called Yamatai, ruled by a priest-queen named Himiko (meaning "sun-child"), in Japan; the location of the kingdom is unknown. Buddhism continues to spread across southeast Asia. The first Polynesian settlers reach the Hawaiian archipelago.

301
Tiridates III makes Christianity the state religion of Armenia—the first country to accept it as such.

◁ **Zenobia and her maid**
This relief from Palmyra depicts Queen Zenobia (who invaded Rome's territories in the east in 270) together with her maid, in the guises of the goddesses Ishtar and Tyche.

303

303–313
Diocletian unleashes a wave of persecution against Christians in the Roman Empire.

311
Xiongnu nomads capture Luoyang, capital of China's Jin Dynasty, and take the Chinese emperor prisoner. In the ensuing years, invaders set up 16 separate kingdoms in northern China, confining imperial power to the south.

312
Constantine defeats his imperial rival Maxentius at the Battle of the Milvian Bridge, winning undisputed power in Rome. In the following year (313), he issues the Edict of Milan, which orders toleration of the Christian faith and permits the establishment of churches across the empire.

"We make a ladder of our vices, if we trample those same vices underfoot."

ST AUGUSTINE OF HIPPO, c.420

c. 320–335
Chandragupta I expands his small kingdom by annexing neighboring states and marrying strategically. He creates the Gupta Empire, stretching across northern and western India.

324
Emperor Constantine orders the construction of Constantinople on the Bosphorus strait between Europe and Asia, taking over the site of the Greek city of Byzantium. In 330, the city is consecrated as the new capital of the Empire, replacing Rome.

325
The Council of Nicaea—the first ecumenical council of the Christian Church—is convened by Emperor Constantine. It codifies Christian beliefs and establishes the Nicene Creed as the hallmark of orthodoxy.

c. 350
In Africa, the city of Meroë—capital of Kush, a long-lasting and powerful kingdom in the Sudan—disappears from the historical record. In Ethiopia, Aksum becomes the first African kingdom to officially adopt Christianity.

361–363
Emperor Julian seeks to reestablish traditional pagan beliefs in place of Christianity as the Roman Empire's official religion. On his death in battle against the Persian Sassanians, the empire is divided into eastern and western portions, the east under Valens and the west under Valentinian I.

c. 370
Hun nomads arrive in Europe in large numbers, migrating from lands north of the Black Sea.

376
Driven south by the invading Huns, Visigothic tribes cross the River Danube into the Roman Empire. Initially accepted, they rebel against harsh treatment and defeat and kill the eastern emperor Valens at the Battle of Adrianople in 378.

◁ **Tikal sculpture**
This vase, embellished with jadeite, is in the form of a man wearing a Mayan feather headdress. It dates from around 450 in the Classic period of Mayan civilization.

496

380–415
In India, Chandragupta II conquers the Saka rulers of the Gujarat region of eastern India, expanding the Gupta Empire to its greatest extent. His reign is notable for a flowering of art, literature, and science.

386
The Tuoba people establish the Northern Wei Dynasty in north China, around the Yellow River delta.

389–392
Theodosius I—the last emperor to rule over both the eastern and western halves of the Roman Empire— proscribes the last elements of paganism and bans the rituals of the Olympics in Ancient Greece, making Christianity (as defined by the Nicene Creed) the official religion of the empire.

399–412
The Buddhist monk Faxian travels on foot from China to India, collecting texts and writing an account of his journey.

c. 400
Christianity is introduced to Ireland. Hinduism continues its spread through southeast Asia. India's two great epics, the *Ramayana* and the *Mahabharata,* are taking on their final form.

402
Emperor Honorius transfers the capital of the western Roman Empire from Milan to Ravenna, which is considered easier to defend.

406
Germanic Vandals cross the River Rhine into Gaul, under pressure from Huns invading from the east. In 409, they move on into Spain.

407
Most Roman legions are withdrawn from Britain to participate in Rome's civil wars. Emperor Honorius subsequently tells Britons to look to their own defenses.

410
Vandal forces under Alaric sack Rome for 3 days, a pivotal event in the fall of the Roman Empire.

421–422
Theodosius II goes to war with the Sassanid emperor over the persecution of Christians in Persia.

426
St Augustine of Hippo publishes his philosophical work *The City of God.*

429
The Vandals cross from their adopted homeland in Spain to north Africa, where they establish a kingdom that will last for a century, until it succumbs to forces of the Byzantine Empire.

435
Under pressure from the Huns, the eastern Roman emperor signs the Treaty of Margus, in which the Romans agree to pay a higher annual tribute to the Huns. There is sporadic warfare for the next 8 years as the Romans fail to keep to its terms.

439
The Northern Wei Dynasty succeeds in unifying northern China. During their rule, Buddhism becomes firmly established in the region, and the Yungang Grottoes are constructed.

c. 450
Angles and Saxons have started to settle in eastern England following the withdrawal of the Roman legions. Slav peoples are raiding and settling in the Balkans. In Mesoamerica, Tikal (in modern Guatemala) is the dominant Mayan city-state. The mausoleum of Galla Placidia is the earliest example of Christian mosaic in Ravenna (in Italy).

451
The Roman general Aetius—in a coalition with the Visigothic forces of Theoderic I—turns back a Hun invasion of Gaul led by Attila at the Battle of the Catalaunian Fields, fought in what is now northern France.

453
Constantinople wins ecclesiastical supremacy over its rival Alexandria at the Council of Chalcedon (now within the city of Istanbul), establishing itself as second only to Rome in the hierarchy of the Christian Church.

455
Vandal forces sack Rome for a second time, destroying its aqueducts and looting treasures from the city. Anglo-Saxon encroachment sends the Celtic Britons westward into Wales, to Ireland, and across the English Channel into what is today called Brittany.

c. 470
After the death of Attila in 453, the Hun empire begins to disintegrate. In India, the Gupta Empire is in decline following the death of Skandagupta in 467.

476
The last Roman emperor, Romulus Augustulus, is deposed. Odoacer, a German commander of Rome's army, replaces him as King of Italy.

484
Peroz I, ruler of Sassanian Persia, is killed in battle against the Hephthalite Huns (a Central Asian people based around Bactria), who force the empire to pay them tribute.

486
Clovis, founder of the Frankish kingdom, defeats the last Roman ruler in Gaul at Soissons.

488–493
An Ostrogothic army invades Italy, taking Ravenna in 493. At a banquet arranged to celebrate the subsequent peace treaty, the Ostrogoth leader Theodoric kills Odoacer, replacing him as King of Italy.

496
The Franks extend their rule into northeastern Gaul. Their leader, Clovis, converts to Christianity.

◁ *The Battle of Milvian Bridge* (detail)
Painted in 1517–1524 by Giulio Romano, this work depicts the battle in 312 between the Roman Emperors Constantine I and Maxentius.

THE MIDDLE AGES 500–1450

c. 500
In the Americas, the Huari state is on the rise in the Andean highlands, and the city of Teotihuacan is at the peak of its influence in Mesoamerica; the Moche state is in decline following catastrophic floods. In Africa, ironworking is spreading across the southern half of the continent. Hinduism is gaining adherents in Indonesia.

507
The Frankish leader Clovis defeats Visigoth forces at Campus Vogladensis (near modern Tours), driving the invaders south into the Iberian Peninsula.

511
On the death of Clovis, the Frankish kingdom is divided into four parts among his sons.

517
Emperor Wu of the Liang Dynasty converts to Buddhism, introducing the religion to central China.

527
Justinian becomes emperor in Constantinople. In his 38-year reign (which ends in 565), the Byzantine Empire will reach its greatest extent.

528
The Byzantine emperor Justinian orders a revision of existing Roman law, which is set out in the *Codex Justinianus*, published in 534.

c. 530
A coalition of princes succeeds in driving the Ephthalites, or White Huns (tribes originating from the region around Bactria), out of India.

531
Khusrow I ascends the Persian throne. In his 48-year reign (to 579), the Sassanian Empire will reach its peak.

533–534
Justinian's general Belisarius defeats the Vandals, winning back North Africa for the Byzantine Empire.

534
The Northern Wei kingdom in the north of China splits into eastern and western halves, neither of which survives beyond the year 557.

c. 535
Benedict of Nursia draws up his guidance for monastic life, *The Rule of St. Benedict*, which will influence Western monasticism to the present day. Extreme weather, probably triggered by a volcanic eruption in the tropics, affects large areas of the Northern Hemisphere, causing drought in Mesoamerica and perhaps triggering the decline of the city of Teotihuacan.

535
Sent by Justinian, Byzantine general Belisarius invades the Ostrogoth kingdom of Italy, capturing their capital of Ravenna in 540; however, resistance continues until 553.

c. 552
Monks smuggle silkworms out of China to Byzantine lands, enabling the beginning of silk production in the West. Buddhism is introduced to Japan by Korean monks.

◁ **Emperor Justinian**
This 6th-century relief panel is believed to show a triumphant Justinian. The woman holding his foot symbolizes nature submitting to the great emperor, who reigned from 528.

553
Silla, one of the three ancient kingdoms of Korea, defeats a neighboring realm to become the dominant power in the Korean peninsula.

554
Forces dispatched by Justinian establish a Byzantine presence in southern Spain.

562
The Avars, a Mongol people who have migrated westward into Europe, establish a kingdom in the lower Danube Basin region. In Mesoamerica, the city-state of Tikal is defeated by forces from Caracol (now in Belize).

568
Germanic Lombards under their ruler Alboin invade and conquer northern Italy, establishing their own kingdom there by 572.

c. 570
Birth of the Prophet Muhammad at Mecca in Arabia.

"The principal division of the law of persons is as follows, namely, that all men are either free or slaves."

EMPEROR JUSTINIAN, FROM *CODEX JUSTINIANUS*, 534

581
General Yang Jian seizes power over the Northern Zhou lands, governing as Emperor Wen of the new Sui Dynasty; he goes on to restore Chinese rule over the northern part of the country after 400 years of division.

592–602
Maurice (Byzantine emperor in 582–602) launches a series of campaigns against the Avars and Slavs, aiming to

1,104 miles
(1,776 km). The length of China's Grand Canal; it is the world's longest artificial waterway.

retain a Byzantine presence in the Balkans. He succeeds, but Roman rule over the Balkans collapses soon after his overthrow in 602.

593
Appointed as regent by his aunt, the Empress Suiko, the ardently Buddhist Prince Shotoku sets out to establish centralized government in Japan.

597
Dispatched from Rome by Pope Gregory the Great, the monk Augustine reaches England, taking on the task of converting the Anglo-Saxon settlers in the south. He is received by King Ethelbert of Kent and establishes an archbishopric at Canterbury.

c. 600
Tibet emerges as a unified state under the rule of Songtsen Gampo, who is traditionally credited with introducing Buddhism to his kingdom. In America, the Plains hunters are adopting the bow and arrow.

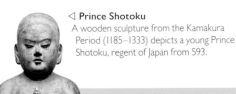

◁ **Prince Shotoku**
A wooden sculpture from the Kamakura Period (1185–1333) depicts a young Prince Shotoku, regent of Japan from 593.

656 ▷

601–609
China's Grand Canal, begun in the previous century, is greatly extended, reaching Beijing in the north and Huangzhou in the south.

602
China's Emperor Wen takes advantage of civil war to crush the native Early Lý Dynasty and restore Chinese rule.

606–647
Harsha of the Pushyabhuti Dynasty builds an empire in northern India, uniting the states of the Gangetic Plain from his capital, Kanauj.

607–627
Hostilities break out again between the Byzantine Empire and Sassanian Persia, which extends its territory in Syria, Mesopotamia, Palestine, and Egypt. The prolonged campaigns will weaken both powers, reducing their ability to resist the coming Arab onslaught.

610
Heraclius accedes to the Byzantine throne and sets about rebuilding its administration; Greek replaces Latin as the language of the empire.

616
The Vandals expel the Byzantines from southern Spain.

618
Following the murder of its last emperor, the Sui Dynasty in China is replaced by the Tang, who will rule the country for the next three centuries.

622
Muhammad and his followers leave his hometown of Mecca for Medina. Known as the Hegira, the migration marks the start of the Muslim calendar.

624
Muhammad defeats the Meccans at the Battle of Badr, a turning point in the establishment of the Muslim faith.

626
A combined attack by Avars, Slavs, and Sassanian Persians fails to take Constantinople, the Byzantine capital.

628
The Indian mathematician Brahmagupta introduces the concept of zero as a number in its own right.

630
The city of Mecca surrenders to the forces of Muhammad.

632
On the death of Muhammad, the new Muslim caliphate starts under Abu Bakr.

633
The Chalukya rulers of an empire in south-central India defeat Harsha's forces at the Narmada River, frustrating his attempts to annex the Deccan.

634
Umar, a senior companion of the Prophet Muhammad, succeeds Abu Bakr as Muslim caliph.

635
Nestorian missionaries (those following the doctrine of the patriarch Nestorius) bring Christianity to China.

636
Fired up by their new Islamic faith, Arab forces erupt out of Arabia into Byzantine Syria, taking Damascus. They also confront the Sassanian Empire, defeating a Persian army at the Battle of al-Qadisiya and winning control of all Mesopotamia (modern Iraq).

639
The Frankish kingdom fractures, with power increasingly passing—in the following decades—from short-lived kings to the mayors of the palace.

642
Alexandria falls to the Arabs, completing their conquest of Byzantine Egypt. That year, they also decisively defeat the Sassanian emperor at the Battle of Nehavend in southern Iran.

651
Yazdegerd III, the deposed last Sassanian emperor, is killed, ending the dynasty.

656–661
The Caliphate of Ali is marked by civil war in the Muslim community; Ali is defeated and assassinated in 661. The split between Ali's followers and opponents lives on to the present day in the division between Shia and Sunni.

▷ **The Death of King Dagobert I**
A manuscript illustration presents a deathbed scene in which the Frankish king, Dagobert, divides his empire between his sons Sigeburt and Clovis in 639.

▷ **The Lindisfarne Gospels**
The title page of St. John's Gospel displays the meticulous design of the Lindisfarne Gospels, which are believed to be the work of just one artist-monk, Eadfrith, in the period around 715.

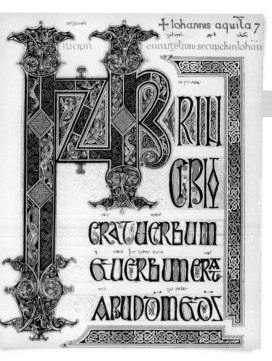

661

661
On the death of Ali, Muawiyah—the victor of the Muslim civil war—establishes the Umayyad Caliphate. The dynasty, based in Damascus, will rule the Muslim world until 750 and become one of the largest empires in history.

664
British churches accept the Roman, rather than the Celtic, form of Christianity at the Synod of Whitby.

668
The kingdom of Silla establishes control over the entire Korean peninsula after Chinese forces are expelled.

679
Bulgars conquer territory around the mouth of the River Danube from the Byzantines, establishing the first Bulgarian Empire.

687
Pepin II unites the Frankish lands under his rule, going on to expand their control into Germanic territories to the north and east.

695
In the Mayan lands of Mesoamerica, Tikal reestablishes its preeminence with a decisive victory over the rival city-state of Calakmul.

698
Islamic forces take Carthage, the last Byzantine stronghold in Africa.

700
In Mesoamerica, Monte Alban is in decline, while Teotihuacan has by now been sacked and abandoned. In Peru, the Moche state is also on the wane. In west Africa, the kingdom of Ghana is established about this time.

702
A Berber uprising against the new Arab rulers of North Africa is put down savagely; the Berbers accept Islam.

708
Empress Genmei of Japan establishes Japan's first official currency; 2 years later, she moves her official residence to Nara, which becomes the new capital of Japan.

711
Under a Berber commander, Arab forces invade southern Spain; within 2 years, the lands of the former Visigothic kingdom are almost entirely under Muslim control.

713
Xuanzong becomes emperor of China, starting a 43-year reign that will start as a golden age but eventually deteriorate into corruption and civil war.

714
In India, Arab forces complete the conquest of Sindh and the lower Indus Valley, pushing the expansion of Islam almost to its furthest extent.

c. 715
The Lindisfarne Gospels are created in Anglo-Saxon Northumbria, part of a cultural flourishing of the northern kingdom.

716–717
Byzantine Emperor Leo III the Isaurian (so-called for his Syrian birth) repels a third Arab siege of Constantinople with the help of the recently developed incendiary weapon known as Greek fire.

718
Christian forces defeat a Muslim army at Covadonga in the Asturias region of northern Spain—a victory cited in Spanish sources as the start of the 700-year struggle to reconquer the peninsula for the Christian faith.

724–749
The reign of Emperor Shomu, a devout Buddhist, marks the high point of Japan's Nara period (710–794).

726
Emperor Leo III issues the first of a series of edicts against the veneration of images, launching the Iconoclastic ("image-breaking") movement that will divide the Byzantine Empire for the next 117 years.

732
The Franks under Charles Martel defeat Arab forces at the Battle of Tours, halting their northward expansion into Europe.

740
Leo III defeats Arab forces besieging Akroinon, halting further Islamic expansion into Anatolia. He renames Akroinon Nikopolis ("City of Victory").

750
After their victory at the Battle of the Zab (in present-day Iraq), the Abbasids displace the Umayyads as rulers of the greater part of the Arab world. Lombard forces capture Ravenna, ending the Byzantine presence in northern Italy.

c. 750
On the American continent, the Toltecs begin to move into the Valley of Mexico, while the power of the city-state of Tiwanaku (in what is now Bolivia) is at its peak. In Africa, trade across the Sahara Desert is on the rise.

751
Arab forces halt Chinese expansion westward with a victory at the Battle of the Talas River, near Samarkand.

755
A rebellion breaks out against Tang rule in China; it is led by An Lushan, a general who declares himself Emperor of a new Yan Dynasty. An Lushan is assassinated by his own son in 757, and the Yan state is finally extinguished in 763.

29 Percentage of the world's population under the Umayyad Caliphate at its height—a total of 62 million people.

◁ **Emperor Xuanzong**
This 13th-century painting shows Xuanzong, the ninth ruler of the Tang Dynasty, who reigned from 713 to 756.

756
Abd al-Rahman establishes the Caliphate of Córdoba in southern Spain; as a member of the deposed Umayyad Dynasty, he refuses to acknowledge the suzerainty of the Abbasids in Syria, creating an independent, breakaway state on the Iberian Peninsula.

757
Krishna I of the rising Rashtrakuta Dynasty wins control of much of west-central India from the declining Chalukyas. In England, Offa becomes king of the central kingdom of Mercia, ruling until 796; during his reign, he gives his name to Offa's Dyke, a defensive earthwork protecting his western border against the Welsh.

762
The Abbasid ruler al-Mansur orders the construction of Baghdad on the banks of the River Tigris as the new capital of the Caliphate.

771
Charlemagne becomes sole ruler of the Frankish kingdom.

774
Charlemagne conquers the Lombard kingdom in north Italy.

780
Hyegong, king of Silla, is assassinated at the end of a lengthy civil war, plunging the Korean kingdom into a period of prolonged upheaval.

782
Charlemagne imposes a law code on the Germanic West Saxons, prescribing death for anyone refusing to abandon paganism. Despite frequent rebellions, Frankish rule will subsequently be confirmed.

786–809
Harun al-Rashid reigns as Abbasid Caliph. He brings the Abbasid Caliphate to its peak of power and influence.

789
The Idrisids establish an Arab-Berber dynasty in the lands that will become Morocco. They embrace the Shia branch of Islam.

c. 790
The Tibetan Empire reaches its greatest extent, ruling a realm stretching from modern Afghanistan to western China.

793
Scandinavian Vikings launch their first shipborne raids, crossing the North Sea to sack the monastery of Lindisfarne off the Northumbrian coast of England.

794
In Japan, Emperor Kanmu moves his capital to Kyoto, starting the Heian Period that will see the imperial court at its peak.

c. 800
In Mesoamerica, the Mayan city-states of the southern lowlands are in decline. The cultivation of corn is widespread in North America, and the first farming cultures are developing in the southwest; the mound-building Mississippian Culture is in a formative stage. In Africa, Kilwa Kisiwani is becoming a significant trading center on an archipelago off the Somali coast.

800
On Christmas Day, Charlemagne is crowned Holy Roman Emperor by Pope Leo III in Rome, in recognition of his services in spreading the Christian faith. His reign is marked by a flourishing of culture—the Carolingian Renaissance.

802
In Cambodia, Jayavarman II stages a consecration ceremony to celebrate the independence of his kingdom of Kambuja from Java—an event traditionally seen as marking the birth of the Khmer Empire.

813
Baghdad is besieged and sacked in the course of an Abbasid civil war.

814
Death of Charlemagne; he is succeeded by his son Louis the Pious.

150 miles (240 km). The length of Offa's Dyke on the English–Welsh border.

817
Louis the Pious divides his empire between his three sons, who are expected to serve as co-rulers with him during his lifetime. The lion's share of the empire goes to his eldest, Lothair.

c. 820
The Buddhist temple complex at Borobodur in Java is completed.

827
An Arab army invades Sicily from North Africa, setting in train the Islamic conquest of the island.

831
Louis the Pious charges the monk Ansgar, Archbishop of Hamburg, with the mission of bringing Christianity to the Scandinavian lands.

836
The Abbasid ruler al-Mutasim orders the construction of a new capital for the Caliphate at Samarra, north of Baghdad.

840
The Uighur Khanate, which has ruled over a large part of eastern Asia for almost a century, falls apart in famine and civil war. The Kirghiz, another Turkic people, take control of its lands.

841
A Viking fleet sails up the River Liffey in Ireland, establishing a settlement where the city of Dublin will eventually grow.

◁ **Bust of Emperor Charlemagne**
This 14th-century gilt and silver bust is a reliquary that includes part of the skull of Charlemagne, who was crowned Emperor in 800.

▷ **The ruins of Chichen Itza**
Chichen Itza, in the eastern portion of the Yucatán state in Mexico, was an important Mayan city. The site was developed from around 750, and it became a regional capital in the 10th century.

841

842
In China, the Tang Emperor Wuzong launches a wave of religious persecutions, closing many Buddhist temples and monasteries and proscribing the Manichaean faith, condemning its priests to death.

843
The Treaty of Verdun ends 3 years of warfare in the Carolingian lands following the death of Louis the Pious (in 840); it confirms the division of the empire into three separate kingdoms: east, central, and west, ruled by the dead ruler's three sons.

845
Viking raiders led by the chieftain Ragnar Lodbrok sail up the River Seine to Paris; they are prevented from besieging the city by the payment of a tribute.

846
Saracen raiders attack Rome, sacking Old St. Peter's Basilica but failing to penetrate the city walls.

c. 850
In India, the future Chola kingdom is beginning to take shape in the south, while in Burma, Pagan starts to develop into as a small city-state that will grow over the next two centuries into the capital of the Pagan Empire. In the Mayan lands of Mesoamerica, Chichen Itza has become a major regional capital, while farther south, in what is now Peru, the Chimú people found Chan Chan, which will in time become the largest city in pre-Columbian South America.

858
Kenneth I MacAlpin, who is traditionally held to be the first king of the Scots, dies from a tumor.

859
A chronicle reports the presence of Varangians (Vikings) in northern Russia; they demand tribute from the local Slavic and Finnish tribes. To the west, other Viking groups attack major cities, including Cologne, Paris, and the Carolingian capital of Aachen. Meanwhile in the Mediterranean, shipborne raiders attack ports as far east as Anatolia.

862
Rurik emerges as the leader of the Varangians, establishing a dynasty that will rule over much of western Russia.

865–866
Danish invaders occupy the kingdom of Northumbria in northern England, establishing their capital at York.

867
Basil I usurps the Byzantine throne, establishing the Macedonian Dynasty that will rule until 1056; he will expand the empire to its greatest extent since the Muslim conquests.

868
Sent as Abbasid governor to Egypt, Ahmad ibn Tulun sets up his own independent Tulunid Dynasty, which will govern Egypt and the Levant until the Abbasids reassert control in 905.

869
A Danish force conquers the English kingdom of East Anglia, killing its ruler Edmund the Martyr (who is later venerated as St. Edmund).

873
Norse settlers arrive in Iceland, establishing a base at Reykjavik. In China, Huang Chao leads a rebellion that will severely weaken the ruling Tang Dynasty; before his eventual defeat and death in 884, the rebel leader's forces will temporarily control the southern port of Guangzhou and the imperial capital Chang'an (modern Xi'an).

◁ **Viking ship**
This model of the Oseberg Ship (which was recovered from a Viking burial mound in Norway) shows the type of vessel used in Viking raids. This oak ship would have been rowed by 30 men, reaching speeds of up to 10 knots (18.5 kph).

954

907

The last emperor of the declining Tang Dynasty is deposed and China splits into the interregnum of the Five Dynasties and Ten Kingdoms period.

909

Taking advantage of Berber discontent with Abbasid rule, the Shia Fatimids establish control over a kingdom on the central North African coast.

910

The abbey of Cluny is founded in the Burgundy region of eastern France. Following a strict interpretation of Benedictine rule, it becomes the focus of a monastic reform movement.

911

Charles the Simple cedes land in Normandy to the Vikings, who have settled there, in exchange for their

930

The Althing, the world's first parliament, is established in Iceland; it begins as an outdoor assembly where the country's leaders meet to decide on new laws and to dispense justice.

934

The Shia Buwayhids capture Shiraz, which will become the capital of an empire stretching across Iran and Iraq.

937

Athelstan defeats a combined force of Ireland-based Vikings, Welsh, and Scots at the Battle of Brunanburh, fought in northern England; his victory is sometimes seen as marking the birth of a united English nation.

938

The Vietnamese win independence from Chinese control.

878

At the Battle of Edington, Alfred, ruler of the southern kingdom of Wessex, defeats the Danish army ravaging southern England; in the ensuing peace negotiations, the Danish leader Guthrum agrees to convert to Christianity. Danish power in England will subsequently be restricted to the Danelaw, a swathe of land stretching southeast from the Scottish border to the Thames estuary.

882

Rurik's successor, Oleg, founds the Rus' state in the lands along the Dnieper River, establishing Kiev as its capital.

885–886

Paris resists a prolonged siege by tens of thousands of Vikings.

887

Charles the Fat, who had briefly brought the three parts of Charlemagne's empire back together under his control, is deposed; the Frankish Empire will never again be reunited.

895

Under their leader Arpad, Magyar (Hungarian) tribes cross the Carpathian Mountains to settle in the lands of present-day Hungary.

897

The last king of the Pallava Dynasty dies in battle against the Cholas, who will rule a kingdom in southern India for the next four centuries.

899

The Qarmatians, a religious group with Shia affiliations, establish a republic in eastern Arabia, breaking away from Abbasid control. Death of Alfred the Great, king of Wessex; he is succeeded by his son, Edward, who repels a challenge from his cousin Æthelwold.

c. 900

In Korea, the kingdom of Silla is in steep decline. In North America, farming villages are beginning to appear in the Great Plains region, while in the southwest the Hohokam Culture farmers are digging irrigation channels for their crops. In Mesoamerica, in the wake of the collapse of Teotihuacan, the Toltec people found a state with its capital at Tula in the Valley of Mexico. In South America, the Sican state, centered on the Lambayeque Valley, comes to dominate northern Peru; it maintains its position until its conquest by the Chimú people in the 14th century.

"Remember what punishments befell us … when we did not cherish learning …"

ALFRED THE GREAT, KING OF WESSEX, c. 890

promise to accept the Christian faith and to protect France from further Norse raids. Their leader Rollo becomes the first Duke of Normandy.

918

Taejo founds the Goryeo Dynasty, which will unify Korea by 936 and rule the country for the next four centuries.

919

Henry the Fowler, previously Duke of Saxony, becomes King of East Francia, uniting the two realms and replacing the previous Frankish line of rulers with his own Ottonian Dynasty; his accession is generally held to mark the start of the medieval German state.

939–967

Reign of Krishna III, the last great ruler of the Rashtrakuta Dynasty, who will preside over a realm covering much of India and patronize poetry.

945

The Buwayhids take Baghdad, making the Abbasid caliphs their vassals.

c. 950

In Mesoamerica, the Mixtecs sack the Zapotec capital of Monte Albán.

954

Eric Bloodaxe, the last Viking king of York, is driven out of the city by the Anglo-Saxon King Eadred.

◁ **Charles III (the Fat)**
This 13th-century statue in Aachen shows Charles, the great-great-grandson of Charlemagne. He was crowned Holy Roman Emperor in 881; his fall in 887 marked the end of Charlemagne's empire.

◁ **Emperor Taizu**
This silk hanging scroll depicts Zhao Kuangyin, who around 960 became the first ruler of the Song Dynasty.

955–1056

955
Otto I of East Francia defeats the Magyars at Lechfeld, halting their westward expansion.

c. 960
Following an army mutiny, general Zhao Kuangyin becomes ruler of the Later Zhou territories in China. In the course of a 19-year reign, he will win control of the whole of China, ending the Five Dynasties and Ten Kingdoms period and uniting the whole nation under his Song Dynasty.

962
Otto I, "The Great," is crowned Holy Roman Emperor by the pope in Rome, reviving the empire in the west.

963
In Greece, the monk Athanasios founds the monastery of Great Lavra on Mount Athos; it remains the largest of several communities on the holy mountain.

c. 965
Harald Bluetooth, king of Denmark, becomes the first Scandinavian ruler to convert to Christianity.

966
King Mieszko I of Poland is baptized as a Christian. During his long reign (960–992), he greatly expands Poland's frontiers, both through diplomacy and through his many military successes. His reign is generally considered to mark the start of the Polish state.

969
The Fatimids of central North Africa conquer Egypt and found the city of Cairo as their new capital. In the same year, Byzantine forces recapture the city of Antioch from its Muslim rulers.

973
Birth of al-Biruni in the Khwarezm region of central Asia; of Iranian descent, he will prove to be one of the great scholars and polymaths of the age, doing important work in astronomy, mathematics, physics, geography, and history before his death in 1048.

980
Birth of the scholar Avicenna (ibn-Sina) in the Bukhara region of central Asia; he is best remembered for his medical works, the *Book of Healing* and the *Canon of Medicine*.

986
Norse settlers led by Erik the Red arrive in Greenland, founding two colonies on its southwest coast.

987
Hugues Capet is elected King of the Franks, starting the Capetian line of French kings.

66,000 lb (30,000 kg). The amount of silver paid by King Cnut as Danegeld to ward off further Viking raids.

988
Vladimir, ruler of Kiev, accepts Eastern Orthodox Christianity as the religion of his people. Following his baptism, he will marry the sister of the Byzantine Emperor Basil II, sealing an alliance between the two realms.

993
Rajaraja I, ruler of the Chola kingdom in southern India, invades Sri Lanka, capturing the northern part of the island from a native dynasty; he builds a giant Hindu Temple in Thanjavur.

> *"Such is the passing that you must leave, All men must die, and it is vain to grieve."*
>
> FERDOWSI, FROM *SHANAMA*, 1010

999
Bukhara, capital of the Samanid Dynasty (which had ruled Iran and much of central Asia for more than a century), falls to the Turkic Qarakhanids. Mahmud of Ghazni, newly crowned emir of that Afghan city, takes advantage of the Samanid collapse to start building an empire of his own.

c. 1000
In Africa, Islamic influence is spreading in the northwest of the continent and also around Kilwa Kisiwani on the east coast. In South America, the cities of Tiwanaku and Huari are abandoned by this time. In North America, Norse colonists from Greenland establish a settlement on the coast of Newfoundland that will survive for only about 20 years.

1001
Stephen I, later canonized as St. Stephen, becomes the first committedly Christian king of Hungary, doing much to establish the faith in the course of his 38-year reign. In Poland, Griezno has become the seat of the country's first archbishopric. In India, Mahmud of Ghazni wins a victory over a Hindu army at the Battle of Peshawar, opening up northern India to Muslim expansion.

1010
The Persian poet Ferdowsi completes the *Shanama* (*Book of Kings*), a work that will become Iran's national epic.

1011
The Cathedral of St. Sophia is founded in Kiev.

▷ **Brihadishwara Temple, Thanjavur**
This huge temple in Tamil Nadu was built under king Rajaraja I of the Chola Empire. It was classified as a UNESCO World Heritage Site in 2016.

▷ King Cnut
A 15th-century stained-glass panel at Canterbury Cathedral shows Cnut, the Danish warrior-king who ruled England in 1016–1035; he became a generous patron of the church.

1013
Sveyn Forkbeard, king of Denmark, conquers England.

1014
Byzantine Emperor Basil II completes his subjugation of the Bulgarian people on the empire's western frontier; he will become known as "the Bulgar-slayer" for the brutality of the conquest.

1016
Sveyn's son, Cnut, becomes king of England. He will also come to rule Denmark and Norway, creating a short-lived North Sea Empire.

1017
Rajaraja's son Rajendra I sacks Sri Lanka's capital Anuradhapura, extending Chola control over the island.

c. 1020
In Japan, Lady Murasaki Shikibu completes *The Tale of Genji*, sometimes described as the world's first novel.

1025
The Chola ruler Rajendra I launches naval raids on Srivijaya, on the island of Sumatra, and on Pegu in Burma.

1028
Empress Zoe ascends the Byzantine throne, starting a reign that will last for 22 years.

1031
After years of infighting and civil strife, the Umayyad Caliphate of Córdoba disintegrates into a number of separate states when its last ruler is overthrown.

1032–1034
The Holy Roman Emperor Conrad II annexes Provence and the kingdom of Burgundy. He founds the Salian Dynasty that rules over the empire for the next century.

1033–1044
Korea builds the "Thousand Li Wall" to defend the kingdom's northern frontier against the Khitans.

1038
Tibetan-speaking Tanguts launch an attack on northwest China, establishing their own Western Xia kingdom, which will survive until 1227.

1040
The Seljuk Turks defeat a Ghaznavid army at the Battle of Dandanaqan, establishing an independent central Asian empire under their leader Tughril Beg.

1044
Anawrahta becomes ruler of Pagan in what is now Myanmar. In the course of his 32-year reign, he will lay the foundations of the Pagan Empire and come to be considered the founder of the Burmese nation.

1045
The Byzantines take control of Armenia.

1046
Holy Roman Emperor Henry III summons a church council at Sutri in Italy to end faction-fighting in the Catholic Church.

1048
Birth of Omar Khayyam, Persian mathematician, astronomer, and poet.

c. 1050
In North America, the Mound Builder Mississippian Culture is now firmly entrenched in the lands around the central Mississippi River valley. In the southwest, the Ancestral Puebloans are creating complex settlements at sites including Mesa Verde and Chaco Canyon, featuring ceremonial sites known as *kivas*.

1053
Having entered southern Italy as mercenaries over the preceding decades, the Normans defeat the combined forces of the papacy and the Holy Roman Emperor at Civitate, taking Pope Leo IX prisoner. At the Treaty of Melfi 6 years later, the papacy finally recognizes Norman rule in the region.

1054
The schism between the Roman Catholic and Eastern Orthodox branches of Christianity becomes permanent after the Pope and the Patriarch of Constantinople mutually excommunicate each other.

Yaroslav the Wise, the Grand Prince of Rus', dies, leading to a division of the Kievan kingdom.

1055
The Seljuks conquer Baghdad, driving out the Buwayhid rulers; their leader Tughril Beg is made Sultan by the Caliph.

1056
Abu Bakr ibn Umar becomes leader of the Almoravids, creating a Berber Muslim dynasty based in Morocco that will rule much of western North Africa and southern Spain for the next 90 years from its capital of Marrakech, which is founded in 1062.

◁ **Anawrahta, King of Burma**
A statue at Mandalay Fort shows Anawrahta, who founded an empire centered on Pagan, an ancient settlement in the Mandalay Region of modern Myanmar. The empire lasted until 1287.

1057

1057
Anawrahta conquers the Mon people of what is now Myanmar, absorbing them into the Pagan Empire.

c. 1063
Construction starts on St. Mark's Basilica, Venice; the church is consecrated in 1093.

1064
The Seljuk ruler Alp Arslan invades Byzantine Armenia, sacking its capital Ani and massacring the inhabitants.

1066
William the Conqueror invades England, defeating and killing the English leader Harold Godwinson at the Battle of Hastings. Harold, England's last Anglo-Saxon king, had defeated a Norwegian invasion force at Stamford Bridge just 19 days before.

1069
Wang Anshi becomes chancellor of Song China, initiating a program of reforms that will divide the nation. His New Policies will be largely abandoned after the death of his patron, Emperor Shenzong, in 1086.

c. 1070
The influence of Islam spreads in sub-Saharan Africa, carried by traders from the Maghreb; the Kanem rulers of Chad convert to the Islamic faith at about this time.

1071
The Seljuks defeat the Byzantines at Manzikert, and their victory gives them control over much of Anatolia; in 1077, Sultan Suleyman will establish the Sultanate of Rum (so-called because the territory was originally "Roman") in the conquered lands.

1075–1122
The Investiture Controversy sets the papacy and the Holy Roman Emperor at odds over who should have the right to appoint bishops.

c. 1076
The Almoravids of Morocco secure control of the Empire of Ghana.

1077
Excommunicated by Pope Gregory VII in the bitter opening years of the Investiture Controversy, Holy Roman Emperor Henry IV goes to the castle of Canossa in northern Italy to do penance, standing in the snow in a hair shirt for 3 days before Gregory finally agrees to lift the excommunication.

1081
Robert Guiscard, ruler of Norman southern Italy and Sicily, invades the Balkans, defeating the Byzantine Emperor Alexius I outside Durazzo.

1086
William the Conqueror commissions the Domesday Book, a detailed survey of landholdings across much of England and Wales that will be used to assess tax liabilities.

1088–1094
The Chinese inventor Su Song creates a celebrated 40 ft (12 m) astronomical clock in Kaifeng, north-central China.

1091
The Normans complete the conquest of Sicily, first attempted 30 years earlier.

230 ft (70 m).

The length of the Bayeaux tapestry—a record of events leading up to the Norman conquest of England.

c. 1094
Hassan-i-Sabbah founds the Assassins sect of Shia extremists, known for their violent, stealthy tactics; with a number of hilltop strongholds, adherents of the martial sect later become feared by Christian Crusaders, who name Hassan-i-Sabbah "Old Man of the Mountains."

1095
At the Council of Clermont, Pope Urban II launches the First Crusade to retake the Holy Land from Islamic control.

1098
Crusader forces take Antioch in Syria, which the Sicilian Norman Bohemond I later claims as his own principality.

1150

▷ **Southern Song ceramics**
The Song tradition of producing exquisite ceramics continued under the Southern Song (1127). Some items were so valued that they were used to pay taxes to the imperial court.

1099
The Crusaders capture Jerusalem, establishing a Christian presence in the lands of the Levant.

c. 1100
In Europe, towns are expanding and guilds of artisans and craftsmen are springing up to represent the interests of their members. In France, the *Song of Roland* is taking final shape as the first major work of French literature and one of the earliest epics of chivalry.

1115
Abbot (later Saint) Bernard founds the monastery of Citeaux in northeastern France, which will become the mother-house of the Cistercian Order. In northern China, the Jurchen chieftain Aguda proclaims the Jin Dynasty, declaring war against the neighboring Khitan-led Liao state.

1119
Crusaders in Jerusalem found the military Order of the Knights Templar.

condemns simony (the sale of church offices) and promotes clerical celibacy.

1126–1127
Jurchen forces capture the Song capital Kaifeng, and with it the Northern Song emperor; Song rule continues in the south from the Southern Song capital of Hangzhou. In Syria, Imad ad-Din Zengi becomes *atabeg* (governor) of Mosul, launching conquests that will bring him into conflict with the crusader states.

1135
On the death of Henry I, civil war breaks out in England between rival claimants to the throne, Henry's nephew Stephen of Blois and the king's daughter Matilda.

c. 1136
Geoffrey of Monmouth writes his *History of the Kings of Britain*, which will do much to popularize the legend of King Arthur.

1139
Afonso I wrests Portugal from fealty to the kingdom of León, establishing it as an independent kingdom.

c. 1140
Anna Comnena writes the *Alexiad*, a history of the life and reign of her father, the Byzantine Emperor Alexius I Comnenus (who reigned 1081–1118 BCE).

1144
Zengi conquers the Crusader state of Edessa, triggering the Second Crusade. In France, the Basilica of St. Denis, near Paris, is the first to be built in the Gothic style of architecture.

1147
Afonso I takes Lisbon from Muslim control with the help of a Christian fleet en route for the Second Crusade. Another Crusade is proclaimed in north Germany against the pagan Wends, a Slavic people. In Morocco, the Almohads overthrow the Almoravids, taking their capital of Marrakech; over the next 12 years, they will extend their rule over most of North Africa.

1150
Forces of the eastern Iranian Ghurid Dynasty sack Ghazni, capital of the Ghaznavid Empire. In Mesoamerica, the Toltec city of Tula, long in decline, is destroyed. In Europe, universities are developing in Oxford and Paris. Magnetic compasses are being used for navigation in Song China.

> *"My father's deeds … do not deserve to be consigned to Forgetfulness …"*
>
> ANNA COMNENA, FROM THE *ALEXIAD*, c.1140

1113
A papal bull (decree) recognizes the foundation of the crusading Order of the Hospital of St. John in Jerusalem, known as the Hospitallers; the order is charged with the care and defense of the Holy Land. In Cambodia, Suryavarman II ascends the Khmer throne; in his long reign (to 1150), he will oversee the construction of the Hindu temple complex of Angkor Wat.

1122
The Investiture Controversy ends at the Concordat of Worms in a compromise that divides the right to appoint bishops and high ecclesiastical functionaries between the Church and lay rulers.

1123
Pope Callixtus II convokes the First Lateran Council to counter lay influence in ecclesiastical matters; the Council

37

The number of years it took 300,000 workers and 6,000 elephants to build Angkor Wat.

◁ **Angkor Wat**
The construction of this monumental moated temple in northern Cambodia was initiated by Suryavarman II, Khmer king from 1113 to 1150.

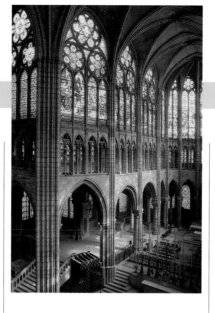

◁ **Basilica of St. Denis**
Completed in 1144, this church in the city of St. Denis (now a suburb of Paris) was the resting place of Louis VII – who died in 1180 – and all but three French kings.

1152

1152
Frederick Barbarossa is elected King of Germany at Aachen. Three years later, in 1155, he will become King of Italy and Holy Roman Emperor.

1154
The son of Geoffrey of Anjou and Matilda (daughter of Henry I of England)—and already one of the greatest landholders in France—Henry II becomes the first Angevin king of England, sparking centuries of strife between the English and French crowns. In the Middle East, Nur ad-Din, son of the *atabeg* Zengi, annexes Damascus, uniting all Syria north of the crusader states under his control.

1156
Frederick Barbarossa creates the Duchy of Austria as a counterweight to its neighbor Bavaria.

> *"The Law teaches that the universe was invented and created by God, and that it did not come into being by chance or by itself."*
>
> IBN RUSHD, FROM *THE DECISIVE TREATISE*, c.1190

1156–1159
The Hogen (1156) and Heiji (1159) rebellions over issues of succession and the transfer of political power shake imperial Japan; they boost the influence of the samurai (warrior) class and set the rival military clans—the Minamoto and the Taira—against one another. The result is the downfall of the Taira and the establishment of a Minamoto shogunate in 1192.

1162
Frederick Barbarossa destroys Milan after subduing it in successive campaigns stretching over two decades.

1167
Sixteen cities in the Lombardy region of north Italy form the Lombard League to resist attempts by Frederick Barbarossa to restrict their freedoms.

1170
In England, Thomas Becket, the Archbishop of Canterbury, is murdered in his cathedral following a drawn-out dispute with King Henry II over ecclesiastical independence.

1171
Saladin, vizir of Egypt, seizes power on the death of the last Fatimid sultan, renouncing its former Shia allegiance; he will later realign Egypt with the Abbasid caliphs in Baghdad.

1173
Muhammad of Ghur captures the former Ghaznavid capital of Ghazni; he will use it as a base from which to build a central Asian empire.

1176
The Lombard League's forces defeat Frederick Barbarossa at Legnano.

1180
The death of Louis VII of France, who oversaw the foundation of the University of Paris and the Second Crusade.

1181
Jayavarman VII becomes Khmer king, rallying his people against the Cham (Vietnamese) and founding the new capital of Angkor Thom.

1185
The Minamoto fleet defeats Taira forces in the naval Battle of Dannoura, fought off the southern tip of Honshu in Japan; in the wake of the battle, the Minamoto leader Yoritomo will establish the shogun system of military rule.

1186
Muhammad of Ghur's forces take Lahore, the last remaining stronghold of the former Ghaznavid Empire, executing its ruler and so ending the Ghaznavid Dynasty.

1187
Saladin routs a crusader army at Hattin, going on to recapture Jerusalem from the Christians.

1189–1192
The forces of the Third Crusade attempt to win back Jerusalem. One of its leaders, Frederick Barbarossa, drowns in Turkey on his way to the Holy Land (1190). The other, England's Richard the Lionheart, takes Cyprus and Acre and wins the Battle of Arsuf (1191) before signing a peace treaty with Saladin that leaves Jerusalem in Muslim hands but guarantees Christians access to the city.

1190
Jayavarman VII's Khmers conquer the Vietnamese kingdom of Champa.

1191
A Japanese monk introduces Zen Buddhism (derived from Chan, a Chinese variant of Mahayana Buddhism) to Japan. The intuitive, fearless path of Zen appeals to the powerful Japanese samurai class.

1192
The Ghurid general Qutb al-Din conquers Delhi and starts the construction of the Qutb Minar minaret.

1194
The Holy Roman Emperor Henry VI conquers Norman-ruled Sicily.

1198
Ibn Rushd (often westernized to Averroes) dies in Marrakesh. He was an Andalusian Muslim philosopher and polymath who did much to preserve the heritage of Plato and Aristotle.

c. 1200
The Chimú people establish themselves in the northern coastal valleys of Peru, while farther inland the Inca, under Manco Capac, are a growing presence around Cuzco, which will become their capital. The Icelandic sagas—stories exploring history, genealogy, and conflict—inspired by the history of Norse settlers in Iceland, are taking shape. Great Zimbabwe is a powerful presence in southern Africa. The Buddhist faith is dying out in northern India, its original heartland.

30,000 The number of soldiers in Saladin's victorious army at the Battle of Hattin on July 4, 1187.

◁ Coin of Henry VI
This 12th-century German coin is struck with an image of Henry VI, the son of Emperor Frederick Barbarossa. Henry became Holy Roman Emperor in 1191, and King of Sicily in 1194.

1204
The army of the Fourth Crusade diverts from its original target of Jerusalem to besiege and sack Christian Constantinople, replacing the emperor with the crusaders' own Latin dynasty.

1206
Having united the Mongol tribes, Temujin is acknowledged as their leader, assuming the title of Genghis Khan. In India, the former slave Qutb ud-Din Aibak founds the Delhi Sultanate; his dynasty (the Mamluk Dynasty) will rule until 1290, while the Sultanate itself will last until 1526. Under the Mamluks, the Quwwat-ul-Islam mosque in Delhi is built.

1208
Pope Innocent III proclaims the Albigensian Crusade against Cathar heretics in southern France.

1209
Founded by St. Francis of Assisi, the Franciscan Order of mendicant monks receives papal approval.

1210
Military victories give the Turkic rulers of the Khwarazm Dynasty a short-lived empire that stretches from the Persian Gulf deep into central Asia; it will fall to Genghis Khan's Mongols by 1220.

1211–1234
Mongol forces conquer the Jin Empire of northern China, capturing their capital Zhongdu (Beijing) in 1215.

1212
Christian forces under Alfonso VIII of Castile defeat the Almohad Muslims at Las Navas de Tolosa, a major step in the Christian Reconquista (reconquest) of Spain.

1215
In England, King John signs the Magna Carta to appease rebellious barons, accepting limitations on royal power.

1217–1221
The Fifth Crusade targets Muslim Egypt but fails to make lasting gains.

1220
Frederick II is Holy Roman Emperor.

1226
Frederick II commissions the Teutonic Knights to forcibly convert the pagan Prussians to Christianity.

780
The length in years of the Reconquista—the recapture of Iberia from Moorish occupation.

1227
Genghis Khan dies while campaigning against rebel Tanguts in China.

1228–1229
Leading the Sixth Crusade, Frederick II regains Jerusalem for the crusader states by peaceful diplomacy.

1232
The papacy sets up the Inquisition as a tool to combat heresy.

1237
Frederick II defeats forces of the Lombard League at Cortenuova in northern Italy.

1240
Alexander Nevsky's victory at the Battle of the River Neva halts Swedish expansion eastward into Russia. Two years later, he will defeat the Teutonic Knights at Lake Peipus.

1241
The north German ports of Hamburg and Lübeck form an alliance, presaging the development of the Hanseatic League, which will dominate Baltic trade for the next three centuries. Mongol forces strike deep into Europe, annexing Russian principalities, winning decisive victories in Poland and Hungary, and only turning back on news of the death of the Great Khan Ögedei, Genghis Khan's son and successor.

◁ The capture of Jerusalem by Saladin
A 15th-century miniature shows the surrender of Jerusalem to Saladin after a short siege in 1187. The loss of the city triggered the launch of the Third Crusade in 1189.

◁ **The Battle of the Neva**
This illustration from a 16th-century chronicle of Russian history shows a scene from The Battle of the Neva in 1240, which occurred during the invasion of Russia by Swedish forces.

1243

24 The number of years spent by Marco Polo traveling to and around Asia, where he befriended Kublai Khan.

1243
The Seljuk sultanate of Rum in Anatolia becomes a Mongol vassal state.

1248–1254
In the Seventh Crusade, King Louis IX (later canonized as St. Louis) of France invades Egypt but is defeated, captured, and ransomed.

1250
On the death of Egypt's last Ayubbid ruler, the sultan's Mamluk slave-soldiers seize power in their own name, founding the Mamluk Sultanate.

1256
Hostilities break out between the Italian trading ports of Venice and Genoa, signaling the start of a struggle for commercial dominance that will last for more than a century. Hulegu founds the Mongol Ilkhanate Empire in Persia.

1257
Mongol forces under Möngke invade the Song lands of southern China.

1258
Hulegu's Ilkhans sack Baghdad and put an end to the Abbasid Caliphate, executing the last caliph.

1259
On the death of the Great Khan Möngke, the Mongol domains across Europe and Asia start to divide into four separate khanates: the Ilkhans in Persia and adjoining lands; the Golden Horde in Russia; the Chaghatai Khanate in central Asia; and the Chinese lands where, in 1271, Kublai Khan will establish the Yuan Dynasty.

1260
The Mamluks defeat a Mongol army at Ain Jalut in Palestine.

1261
The Byzantines reconquer Constantinople from the Latin Dynasty that had ruled it since the time of the Fourth Crusade. In Egypt, the Mamluk Sultan Baybars reestablishes the Caliphate, now based in Cairo.

1265–1274
The philosopher Thomas Aquinas writes his *Summa Theologiae*, attempting to reconcile Christian belief with Aristotelian philosophy.

1266
Norway gives up the Outer Hebrides and the Isle of Man to the kingdom of Scotland in the Treaty of Perth.

1269
Italian Marco Polo, just 6 years old, embarks on an epic expedition to Asia with his father and uncle. He later records his adventures in *The Travels of Marco Polo* (c.1300).

1270
Yekuno Amlak establishes the Solomonic Dynasty, which will rule Ethiopia until the deposition of Emperor Haile Selassie in 1974. In Egypt, Louis IX dies of dysentery while besieging Tunis on the Eighth Crusade.

1272
Kublai Khan moves the capital of his newly established Yuan Empire to Beijing, which he calls Dadu.

1278–1279
Kublai Khan completes the conquest of the Song realm, becoming the first non-native ruler of a united China. In India, the Chola kingdom finally comes to an end following a string of military defeats.

1281
The second of two attempted invasions of Japan by Kublai Khan (the first was in 1274) is thwarted in part by a typhoon, known to later Japanese as the kamikaze or "divine wind."

1287
Mongol forces invade Myanmar, putting an end to the Pagan Empire.

1290
The Teutonic Knights finally subjugate the last southern Baltic pagan tribes.

1291
Acre, the only remaining Christian stronghold in the Holy Land, falls to the Mamluks, extinguishing the Crusader presence in the Levant.

1295
The Ilkhans convert to Islam, aligning with the faith of most of their subjects.

c. 1300
Introduced by traders from the Middle East, Islam spreads through the Indonesian islands and the Malay peninsula, replacing Buddhism and Hinduism.

▷ **Kublai Khan**
This 13th-century portrait depicts the leader of the Mongol Empire and founder of Yuan Dynasty that governed China from 1261 to 1368.

c. 1308
Italian poet Dante Alighieri begins work on the *Divine Comedy*, completing it a year before his death in 1321. It is considered one of the most significant literary works of the Middle Ages.

1309
After his election in 1305, French Pope Clement V moves the seat of the papacy to Avignon in France, where it will remain until 1377.

1312
The Knights Templar are brutally suppressed by Philip IV of France; following the loss of the Holy Land, their fellow military order the Hospitallers have, 2 years earlier, established a new base on the Greek island of Rhodes. In Africa, Mansa Musa ascends to the throne of Mali; he becomes legendarily rich in gold and uses this wealth to strengthen the country's cultural centers, particularly Timbuktu, which he annexes in 1324. Egyptian Mamluks occupy the Christian kingdom of Makuria in Nubia and try to impose Islam, inaugurating a period of civil strife.

1313
Ozbeg Khan ascends to the throne of the Golden Horde (a Mongol Khanate) and accepts Islam as the state religion, banning shamanism and other non-Islamic religious practices.

67

The number of years that the papacy was based in the French city of Avignon.

1314
A Scots army led by Robert the Bruce defeats a much larger English force led by Edward II at Bannockburn, guaranteeing Scotland's status as an independent nation.

1324
Osman I, ruler of a small enclave in Anatolia, dies. His realm will be the first home of the Ottoman Dynasty, named for him.

1325
The Aztecs found their capital city, Tenochtitlán, on an island in Lake Texcoco, where modern Mexico City now stands. In India, Muhammad bin Tughluq becomes ruler of the Delhi Sultanate; during his 26-year reign, he suppresses multiple rebellions and the sultanate reaches its greatest extent.

1326
The Ottomans, under Osman I's son, Orhan, capture Bursa in Anatolia from the Byzantines.

1331
Stephen Dushan becomes King of Serbia; before his death in 1355, he will build an empire in southeastern Europe.

1333
In the Kemmu Restoration, Emperor Go-Daigo of Japan overthrows the Kamakura shogunate, temporarily restoring imperial power

1336
Harihara I establishes the Hindu Vijayanagara Empire, which will dominate the Deccan Plateau region in southern India for the next two centuries.

1337
The Hundred Years' War breaks out when Edward III of England refuses to do feudal homage for his continental

possessions to Philip VI of France; sporadic fighting between the two nations will continue until 1453.

1347
First recorded in Asia in 1331, the plague known as the Black Death reaches Europe.

1348–1353
In Italy, Boccaccio writes the *Decameron*, which frames 100 tales told by a group of people escaping the Black Death.

1350
Hayam Wuruk becomes raja of Majapahit, based on the Indonesian island of Java; in his 39-year reign, the empire will reach its greatest extent, stretching from the Malay Peninsula through the Philippines.

"I came into a place void of all light, which bellows like the sea in tempest, when it is combated by warring winds."

DANTE ALIGHIERI, FROM THE *DIVINE COMEDY*, c.1308

1351
The Red Turban revolt breaks out in the Yangtze River region of China, directed against the Mongol Yuan Dynasty. The Ayutthaya kingdom is founded; the Thai nation will eventually develop from this kingdom.

1354
Ottoman forces capture the Gallipoli peninsula in Thrace from the Byzantine Empire, giving the Turkish dynasty its first foothold in Europe.

1356
A decree called the Golden Bull fixes the procedure for the election of Holy Roman Emperors, omitting any mention of a papal role—a significant step in the centuries-old power struggle between Church and State.

▷ **Mamluk cavalry**
An illustration from the 14th-century *Complete Instructions in the Practices of Military Art* shows the cavalry of the Mamluks—the dynasty that ruled over Egypt and Syria from 1250 to 1517.

Der Tod zum Papst. · Der Tod zum Kaiser. · Der Tod zum Kaiserin. · Der Tod zum König.

Der Tod zum Grafen. · Der Tod zum Abt. · Der Tod zum Ritter. · Der Tod zum Juristen.

Der Tod zum Kaufmann. · Der Tod zur Aebtissin. · Der Tod zum Krüppel. · Der Tod zum Waldbruder.

Der Tod zum Schultheiss. · Der Tod zum Blutvogt. · Der Tod zum Narren. · Der Tod zum Krämer.

Der Tod zum Bauer. · Der Spiegel aller Welt. · Der Tod zum Maler.

1368

1368

The Black Death has, by now, killed more than one-third of Europe's population. In China, rebel leader Zhu Yuanzhang captures Beijing from the collapsing Mongol Yuan Dynasty, forcing them to retreat to the central Asian steppe; he takes power as Hongwu, first emperor of the new Ming Dynasty.

1370

Timur the Lame (Tamberlane) wins control of the Chagatai Khanate; in the 35 years until his death in 1405, he will defeat forces of the Mamluk Dynasty in Egypt, the Delhi Sultanate in India, and the emergent Ottoman Empire, building a short-lived central Asian empire from his capital of Samarkand; the empire splits into warring factions after his death. Construction of the Bastille, a fortress in Paris, is begun; its function is to defend Paris from the approach of English forces during the Hundred Years' War.

1371

An Ottoman army under the Sultan Murad I defeats Byzantine forces at the Battle of Maritsa and conquers most of the Balkans.

1375

The Chimú take control of the Lambayeque Valley of northern Peru from their Late Sican neighbors.

1378

The Catholic Church's Western Schism gets underway, with rival popes established in Rome and Avignon; it will not be healed until 1417.

1380

Russia's Prince Dmitri defeats the forces of the Golden Horde at Kulikovo; although not decisive (Moscow will be sacked 2 years later), the battle marks a turning point in the struggle to free the country from Mongol rule.

◁ **The Basel Dance of Death**
This 19th-century watercolor is a copy of a fresco in a Basel church that records death dancing with victims of the Black Death, the plague that ravaged Europe in the mid-14th century.

▷ **Aztec vase**
This polychrome ceramic vase depicting Tlaloc, god of rain, is from the Main Temple of Tenochtitlán—a settlement that grew into the largest and most powerful city in Mesoamerica in the 15th century.

1440

1381
In England, the Peasants' Revolt against serfdom and high taxes is suppressed. Theologian John Wycliffe translates the Bible into English.

1382
In Egypt, the ruling Bahri Mamluks are succeeded by the Burji Dynasty, another group of Mamluks.

1386
Foundation of the University of Heidelberg, the oldest such institution in Germany. Construction begins on Milan's cathedral; it is not completed for another 500 years.

1386–1400
Geoffrey Chaucer writes the *Canterbury Tales*, a long poem in Middle English that follows the journey of a group of pilgrims from London to St. Thomas Becket's shrine at Canterbury Cathedral. The story becomes very popular in its time.

1387
After resisting attempts at forcible conversion for more than a century, Lithuania, Europe's last pagan realm, voluntarily accepts Christianity.

1389
Invading Ottoman forces defeat a Serbian army at Kosovo, reducing Serbia to vassal status in the following years.

1396
The Ottomans defeat a crusader army raised from across Europe at Nicopolis in Bulgaria, putting an end to the Second Bulgarian Empire.

1397
The Kalmar Union unites the Swedish, Norwegian, and Danish crowns in an attempt to counter the growing power of the Germanic Hanseatic League. In Italy, the Medici Bank is founded in Florence; over the next century, it will become the largest financial institution in all of Europe.

1398
Timur defeats the army of the Delhi Sultanate and sacks Delhi, leaving it in ruins.

c. 1400
On the Malay Peninsula, Malacca is founded by Parameswara, the last Raja of Temasek (Singapore); over the ensuing century, it becomes a major port for east–west trade.

1402
Timur takes Ankara, capturing the Ottoman Sultan Bayezid I, who dies in captivity the following year.

1405
The Ming Yongle Emperor dispatches the first of seven "treasure voyages" launched over the next 28 years; these maritime expeditions extend Chinese influence as far as east Africa and the Persian Gulf.

1407–1424
Chinese forces occupy Dai Ngu (modern-day Vietnam) and attempt to integrate it into their empire, but they are eventually beaten back by Le Loi, founder of the Le Dynasty.

1415
King John I captures Ceuta on the North African coast, making it Portugal's first African possession. In central Europe, the religious reformer Jan Hus is burned at the stake as a heretic, sparking the rebel Hussite movement. In France, English forces under Henry V win the Battle of Agincourt, gaining the initiative in the Hundred Years' War.

1417
The Council of Constance ends the Western Schism, in which two men simultaneously claimed to be pope.

1419
In the Defenestration of Prague, Hussite demonstrators throw seven city council members to their death out of a window of the city's New Town Hall, sparking the Hussite Wars.

c. 1425
Under the rule of Philip the Good, Duke of Burgundy from 1419 to 1467, the Low Countries in general, and Bruges in particular, become centers of the arts; Bruges is home to Jan van Eyck, who paints the *Arnolfini Portrait* in 1434.

1428
In the Valley of Mexico, the Aztecs enter the Triple Alliance with the city-states of Texcoco and Tlacopan; they will come to dominate the coalition, which in time will form the basis of the Aztec Empire.

1429
In France, Joan of Arc, aged just 19, relieves the siege of Orleans; even though she is captured and burned at the stake in 1431, her intervention proves a turning point for the French forces in the Hundred Years' War.

1431
Long in decline, Angkor is sacked by Ayutthaya raiders; by the end of the century, the former Khmer capital will be largely abandoned.

1434
Gil Eanes sails past Cape Bojador, opening up the coast of west Africa to exploration by Portuguese sailors; they benefit from the development of three-masted ships, as well as from the patronage of Prince Henry the Navigator.

1436
Completion of the dome of Florence Cathedral, engineered by Filippo Brunelleschi, concludes 140 years of construction.

1438
Pachacuti becomes ruler of the Incas; in his 34-year reign, he transforms a small kingdom in the valley of Cuzco into a major regional presence.

1440
Frederick III is the first Habsburg to be crowned Holy Roman Emperor; the title remains in the family thereafter until its abolition in 1806.

50,000,000
The estimated number of people killed by the Black Death in the 14th century.

▷ **Joan of Arc**
This illustration shows the "Maid of Orléans," sword in hand. A hero to the French, she was canonized in 1920 by Pope Benedict XV.

THE EARLY MODERN WORLD 1450–1700

1450

c. 1450–1629
The Mwene Mutapa Empire dominates southeast Africa from its capital in Zimbabwe. Rich in gold, copper, and ivory, it controls the lucrative trade routes from the interior to the Arab kingdoms on the east coast, attracting Portuguese traders who settle in Mozambique from 1505.

1453
The Byzantine Empire falls when the Ottoman Turks capture Constantinople and expand their territory into the Balkans and Greece. The Hundred Years' War (1337–1453) ends when France recaptures Bordeaux, leaving Calais as England's only possession in France; the French retake it in 1558.

1454–1455
The Gutenberg Bible is printed in Mainz, Germany; it is the world's first mass-produced book and the first major book to be produced on a printing press with movable metal type.

1455–1485
The Wars of the Roses: civil war ensues as the rival Plantagenet houses of Lancaster and York (symbolized respectively by a red and a white rose) vie for the English throne; the dynastic struggle ends when Henry Tudor seizes the throne as Henry VII, founding the Tudor Dynasty.

1462–1505
Ivan III (the Great), Grand Prince of Muscovy, consolidates and triples the extent of his domain; he breaks the power of the Golden Horde, which had dominated eastern Europe for 200 years.

1467–1477
The Onin War leads to a century of civil strife—the Warring States period—as Japan's regional magnates (daimyo) seek to destroy their rivals.

1468
The Songhai Empire under Sonni Ali annexes the city of Timbuktu and the remnants of the Mali Empire, creating a vast empire and becoming the leading power in west Africa.

1469
Isabella of Castile marries Ferdinand of Aragon, creating a Christian Spain that dominates 16th-century Europe. Birth of Niccolò Machiavelli, Italian diplomat and philosopher, who argues in *The Prince* (1532) that the state should promote the common good, irrespective of any moral evaluation of its acts.

c. 1470
The Chimor kingdom of Peru's Chimú people, famous for its metalwork, textiles, and pottery, is conquered by the Inca king Pachacuti; the Inca Empire extends about 2,500 miles (c. 4,000 km).

▷ **Chimor ceremonial knife**
This gold knife is adorned with an image of Naymlap, legendary founder of the Sican civilization that preceded the Chimor kingdom in coastal Peru; the Chimor fell to the Inca from around 1470.

180
The print run of the Gutenberg Bible. Only 21 complete copies are known to exist today.

1473
The Aztec emperor Axayacatl conquers the city-state of Tlatelolco; he expands and consolidates the Aztec Empire.

1477
Charles the Bold, Duke of Burgundy, dies; his territories are split between the Austrian Habsburg Empire and the Kingdom of France, but disputes over them continue for centuries.

1482
Portugal builds São Jorge da Mina (Elmina Castle) on the Gold Coast, giving Europe its first settlement in sub-Saharan Africa and allowing Portugal to monopolize west Africa's gold trade. Sandro Botticelli paints *Primavera* (*Spring*), a masterpiece of the Italian Renaissance.

1487
The Aztec Great Temple in Tenochtitlán is rebuilt for the sixth time; it opens with the ritual sacrifice of up to 5,000 people.

1488
Portuguese navigator Bartolomeu Dias becomes the first European to round the Cape of Good Hope at the tip of southern Africa; his expedition opens the sea route to India via the Atlantic and Indian Oceans.

1492
The Reconquista of Spain is completed by the capture of Granada, the last Moorish territory in Spain; Muslims and Jews are expelled from Spain. Supported by the Spanish crown, Genoese explorer Christopher Columbus crosses the Atlantic, believing he can reach China and the East Indies; instead, he lands in the West Indies and "discovers" the New World. Martin of Bohemia creates the oldest surviving globe, the *Erdapfel* ("Earth apple"); the Americas are not shown.

1494
The Treaty of Tordesillas settles a dispute between Spain and Portugal over New World discoveries. Charles VIII of France claims Naples, sparking the Italian Wars (1494–1559) between France and Spain over control of Italy.

1497
Under the commission of Henry VII of England, Venetian navigator John Cabot sails from Bristol in search of Asia; instead, he discovers the mainland of North America, paving the way for the English exploration and settlement of the continent.

1497–1498
Portugal's Vasco da Gama is the first European to reach India via the Cape of Good Hope; his route transforms trade between Europe and Asia.

1498
Columbus reaches South America on his third voyage to the New World, thereby discovering a new continent.

1500
Leading a fleet of 13 ships into the western Atlantic Ocean, Pedro Alvares Cabral sights Brazil and claims it for Portugal. Spanish navigator Vicente Yáñez Pinzón discovers the mouth of

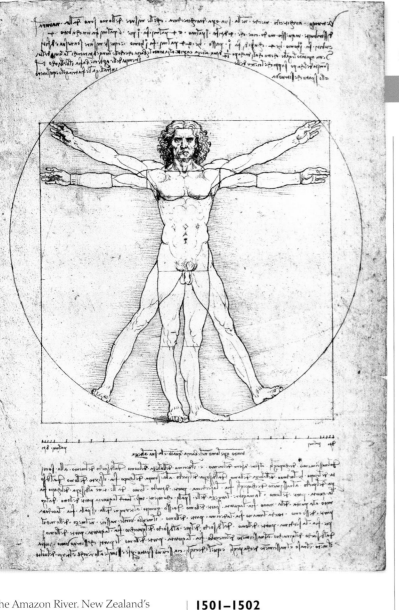

◁ *Vitruvian Man*
This ink drawing was made around 1490 by Leonardo da Vinci to illustrate the perfect geometry of human proportions. The artist went on to create the *Mona Lisa* in 1503–1506.

1529

the Amazon River. New Zealand's Maori Culture enters its classic period, characterized by finely made bone tools and weapons, elaborate wood carvings, textiles, tattoos, some of the biggest war canoes ever built, and a move away from nomadism toward settlement in large hilltop forts and earthworks; this society is only disrupted by the introduction of metal technologies by Europeans arriving in 1642.

1501

Ismail I becomes Shah of Persia and founds the Safavid Dynasty, which rules Iran for over 200 years; he seizes Baghdad, makes Isfahan his capital, and extends the eastern frontier of the empire to Afghanistan and the edge of the Mughal Empire.

1501–1502

Florentine explorer Amerigo Vespucci reaches the coast of Brazil and continues southward to discover that Columbus had not reached the eastern edge of Asia, but a separate continent. In 1507, cartographer Martin Waldseemüller names it America, after Vespucci.

1502

The slave trade between Europe, west Africa, and the Americas begins with a shipment of African slaves sent to Cuba to work in the Spanish settlements.

1503–1506

Leonardo da Vinci paints the *Mona Lisa*, one of the most famous works of the Renaissance; Michelangelo finishes his statue of David.

1510–1511

Afonso de Albuquerque conquers Goa and captures Malacca, laying the foundations of Portuguese hegemony in maritime Southeast Asia.

1513

Spain makes first contact with mainland North America when Juan Ponce de León reaches Florida. He is the first to encounter and describe the Gulf Stream, a powerful current important for ships navigating the Atlantic.

1514

Ottoman forces crush the Safavid Persians at the Battle of Chaldiran, northwest Iran; Sultan Selim I then annexes eastern Anatolia and northern Mesopotamia and conquers large territories in Syria and Egypt, securing almost all the Muslim holy places in southwest Asia.

1517

The Reformation begins when the German monk and theologian Martin Luther publishes his *Ninety-five Theses* in Wittenberg. These challenge the authority of the pope, sparking a revolt that leads to a permanent split between Catholics and Protestants.

1519

Spanish explorer Hernán Cortés lands in Mexico; he captures the Aztec capital Tenochtitlán with the help of Indian allies in 1521; Spain begins its domination of Central America. Charles I, the Habsburg king of Spain, is elected Holy Roman Emperor as Charles V.

1520

Aztec populations crash when Europeans bring smallpox to the Americas; in the next 100 years, around 20 million people, or 90 percent of the population of the New World, are killed by diseases from Europe.

1522

Financed by King Charles I of Spain to find a navigable route around the tip of South America to the Spice Islands (Maluku Islands), Portuguese explorer Ferdinand Magellan completes the first circumnavigation of the globe, though he dies during the voyage.

1526

Babur, a descendent of Mongol warlord Timur, founds the Mughal Empire in northern India; he defeats the Afghan sultan of Delhi, Ibrahim Lodi, and ushers in a new era of order, prosperity, and artistic achievement.

1527

Charles V's imperial troops sack Rome, crushing the papal Holy League and bringing Italy under Spanish rule. In South America, a smallpox epidemic devastates the Inca people of Cuzco.

1529

The Peace of Cambrai provides a break in the Italian Wars; France relinquishes its rights in Italy, Flanders, and Artois; the Holy Roman Emperor, Charles V, renounces his claims to Burgundy. In the Adal Sultanate (present-day Somalia), the imam and general Ahmad ibn Ghazi leads a rebellion against the Ethiopian Christian Empire.

▷ **Emperor Babur**
This detail from an illustration in *Baburnama* (the autobiography of Babur) shows the great Mughal emperor in his camp on his way to conquer Kabul around 1526.

1529–1593

1529–1566

The failed siege of Vienna by the Ottoman sultan Suleiman the Magnificent in 1529 stops the advance of the Ottoman Empire in central Europe. The reign of the sultan is marked by an artistic and cultural revival, advances in the law, and the expansion of Ottoman sovereignty in the Middle East and North Africa.

1531–1533

Spanish conquistador Francisco Pizarro sails from Panama to conquer Peru; in 1533, he captures, ransoms, and executes the Inca emperor Atahualpa, then conquers the Inca capital, Cuzco.

1534

Ignatius Loyola founds the Jesuits, a Catholic missionary order. Henry VIII of England puts himself at the head of the Church of England, after the pope refuses to allow him to divorce his first wife, Katherine of Aragon. Jacques Cartier explores Newfoundland and the Gulf of St. Lawrence, preparing the way for the French colonization of Canada.

1536

The Act of Union formally unites Wales and England. Henry VIII executes his second wife, Anne Boleyn; he starts the dissolution of the monasteries in order to seize their wealth and suppress opposition to the Church of England.

60

The percentage of world silver production coming from Potosí, Bolivia, in the late 16th century.

1537

Jane Seymour gives birth to Henry VIII's long-awaited male heir (the future Edward VI).

1541

Francis Xavier leads a Jesuit mission to Southeast Asia that reaches Goa, the Spice Islands, China, and Japan. The Protestant reformer John Calvin settles in Geneva and steers the city toward a strict Christian rule.

1543

Polish astronomer Nicolaus Copernicus publishes *On the Revolutions of the Heavenly Spheres*, outlining his theory that Earth revolves around the Sun. Andreas Vesalius's *On the Fabric of the Human Body* provides the foundation of modern medicine through its use of evidence provided by human dissection.

1545–1563

The Council of Trent instigates the Counter-Reformation in response to the threat from Protestantism, agreeing to reform and remodel the Catholic Church. The Spanish discover huge silver deposits in Potosí, Bolivia, much of which is minted into coins known as "pieces of eight."

1547

Ivan IV, Grand Prince of Moscow, is proclaimed czar of Russia in. Under his rule, Russia expands east into Siberia and south and takes control of the trade routes to Central Asia; he destroys the Russian *boyars* (hereditary nobility) in his attempt to centralize Russia, earning himself the epithet "the Terrible."

1550

Jesuits reach Brazil and go on to create a network of mission villages, known as *reducciones*, which act as a buffer between Spanish and Portuguese territories in South America.

1552–1555

The Holy Roman Emperor, Charles V, is driven out of Germany by Henri II of France and Maurice of Saxony; he only just evades capture, but is forced to agree to the Peace of Augsburg, which allows German princes to adopt either Lutheranism or Catholicism as the official faith of their state.

1556

Akbar succeeds his father Humayun as Mughal emperor in India at age 14; he rules for nearly 50 years, expanding Mughal power and presiding over a time of cordial Hindu–Muslim relations.

1558

Elizabeth I, the daughter of Henry VIII and Anne Boleyn, becomes Queen of England; she rules until 1603.

1561

St. Basil's Cathedral in Moscow's Red Square is consecrated. It is the city's tallest building.

1565

Spain founds its first colony in the Philippines on Cebu Island.

1568–1648

In the Dutch Revolt, seven northern, predominantly Protestant provinces of the Low Countries rebel against the rule of the Catholic King Philip II of Spain. The United Provinces assert their independence, becoming the Dutch Republic in 1588; the southern provinces remain under Spanish rule.

▷ St. Basil's Cathedral, Moscow
This iconic church in Red Square was consecrated in 1561. It was confiscated by the Soviet State in 1923 and converted into a museum.

▷ **Toyotomi Hideyoshi**
Hideyoshi, pictured here around 1600, rose through the ranks of the army and eventually took control of the military, unifying Japan in 1591 after centuries of civil strife.

1569
Flemish cartographer Gerardus Mercator creates the first world map to reflect the true compass bearing of every landmass; his projection remains widely used.

1570
The Vijayanagar Empire in southern India goes into decline after the Battle of Talikota; it finally collapses in 1646.

1571
Fought in the waters off southwestern Greece, the naval Battle of Lepanto is the last major battle between galley ships; it gives the forces of the Christian Holy League their first victory against the Ottoman Turks, halting Ottoman expansion in the Mediterranean.

1572
More than 3,000 Protestant Huguenots are massacred in Paris on August 24, and up to 20,000 are killed across France

1580
A Spanish force claims the Portuguese crown for Philip II of Spain following the death of the young king Sebastian of Portugal in battle against Morocco; Spain becomes a formidable power.

1585
Spain receives the first commercial shipment of cacao beans from the New World; Europe soon acquires a taste for chocolate. England's first colony in North America is founded by Sir Walter Raleigh on Roanoke Island; colonists arrive in 1587 but it is abandoned in 1590. It is known as the Lost Colony.

1587
Elizabeth I sends Francis Drake to raid Portuguese and Spanish ships and ports; his fleet enters Cadiz harbor, southern Spain, and destroys 30 Spanish ships and thousands of tons of supplies.

"The advantage of time and place in all practical actions is half a victory …"

SIR FRANCIS DRAKE, 1588

---

in the following weeks. It is the worst atrocity in the French Wars of Religion, a 36-year-long conflict between Roman Catholics and Huguenots, which claims an estimated 3 million lives.

1573
Oda Nobunaga overthrows the Ashikaga shogunate (1338–1573) and unites half of Japan under his rule.

1576
At the Battle of Rajmahal, Mughal forces defeat the Sultanate of Bengal in north India and annex the region. The last Sultan of Bengal, Daud Khan Karrani, is captured and executed.

1588
The Spanish Armada, under the command of the Duke of Medina Sidonia, sets out to conquer England for Philip II and the Roman church. It is defeated by terrible weather and the superior tactics and technology of the English fleet, led by Lord Charles Howard and Sir Francis Drake.

1588–1629
Shah Abbas I ("the Great") rules Safavid Persia. The kingdom he inherits is riven by internal disputes and beset by foreign enemies. Abbas, however, restores Persia to formidable power; regains territory from the Ottomans,

Portuguese, and Mughals; creates a beautiful new capital in Isfahan; and encourages trade with Dutch and English merchants, while carpet weaving becomes a national industry.

1589
The world's first industrial machine is designed and built by English clergyman William Lee; its function is to knit stockings.

1590
The Treaty of Constantinople ends the Ottoman-Safavid War; Persia accepts the Ottoman frontiers, which extend to the Caucasus and the Caspian Sea.

c. 1590
Dutch eyewear-maker Zacharias Janssen creates the first compound optical microscope.

1591
The Songhai Empire in the western Sahel enters a period of decline after the death of Askia Daud. Toyotomi Hideyoshi unifies all of Japan under his authority; he moves his power base to Edo (Tokyo) and bans Christianity.

1592
Japan invades Korea but is kept at bay by the Korean fleet and intervention by China; Japan makes several more attempts over the following years.

1593–1606
Habsburgs and Ottomans clash in Hungary and the Balkans. A 13-year-long conflict is fought over territories in Transylvania, Moldavia, and Wallachia; the war—often called The Long Turkish War—costs numerous lives but is ultimately indecisive.

130

The number of ships in the Spanish Armada. They carried more than 30,000 men.

▷ **Japanese gold koban**
Oval coins made from gold and silver were
used under the Tokugawa shogunate, which
began around 1603 and lasted until the
Boshin War of 1868–1888.

1597–1631

c. 1597

The first edition of Shakespeare's tragic
romance *Romeo and Juliet* is published
in two quarto editions. It is likely that
the play was written in 1590–1595.

1598

The Edict of Nantes marks the end
of the French Wars of Religion (1562–
1598); it allows the Calvinist Protestants
(Huguenots) to practice their religion
freely and awards them substantial
rights. Henri IV seeks to heal the
religious divisions in France by uniting
the country in a war against Spain.

1600

Tokugawa Ieyasu wins the Battle of
Sekigahara to gain control of Japan; the
Tokugawa shogunate rules Japan in the
Edo Period (1603–1868), an isolationist
era in which European missions are
violently suppressed. The English East
India Company is granted a Royal
Charter for trade in the East Indies; it
goes on to gain control of substantial
areas in India and China and becomes
a formidable force in the British Empire.
The Yoruba kingdom of Oyo in southern
Nigeria develops into one of the most
powerful empires in the region.

1602

The Dutch East India
Company is founded
and granted a tax-free
monopoly of Asian
trade; it forces the
Portuguese out of the Spice
Islands in 1605 and creates a powerful
trading empire that dominates world
trade for the next two centuries.

1603

James VI of Scotland succeeds
Elizabeth I as James I, uniting the
crowns of England and Scotland.

1604

James VI of Scotland (also James I of
England) commissions the Authorized
Version of the Bible, which remains one
of the world's most used translations of
the work. Italian scientist Galileo Galilei
observes a supernova and concludes
that the universe is able to change.

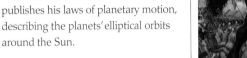

▷ **King Gustavus Adolphus**
This 17th-century painting by Strasbourg-born painter Johann Walter shows Gustavus Adolphus of Sweden at the battle of Breitenfeld in 1631. The king died in battle the following year.

1606
Portuguese (or Galician) navigator Luís Vaez de Torres is the first European to sight Australia. While searching for new trading islands in the east (particularly for the "great land of New Guinea") the Dutch navigator Willem Janszoon lands on the north Australian coast, near what is now the town of Weipa.

1607
The Virginia Company of London establishes the first permanent English settlement in North America in Jamestown, Virginia.

1608
Dutch eyewear-makers invent the telescope, which is used by Galileo Galilei in systematic observations of the night sky; he observes the Milky Way, the Moon, and Jupiter's moons orbiting the planet—findings that later challenge the model of the Universe. Quebec is founded in New France, Canada, by French explorer and cartographer Samuel de Champlain; European demand for beaver and other exotic animal pelts drives French, Dutch, and British expeditions across North America.

1609–1619
German astronomer Johannes Kepler publishes his laws of planetary motion, describing the planets' elliptical orbits around the Sun.

1612
Russia repulses Polish invaders in the Battle of Moscow. The first Romanov czar, Mikhail, is elected in 1613, ending the 15-year interregnum known as the Time of Troubles.

1616
Prominent Manchu chieftain Nurhaci claims the title Great Jin (Khan) of China and declares war on Ming rule in 1618; his descendants found the Qing Dynasty in 1644.

1618
Bohemia's Protestants revolt against Habsburg rule, igniting the Thirty Years' War, which develops from a religious war into a destructive conflict between the major powers of Europe and claims the lives of 8 million people. Jamestown in Virginia receives its first shipment of African slaves.

1620
The Pilgrim Fathers—a group of Puritan colonists—sail from Plymouth, England, aboard the *Mayflower*. They arrive near Boston in November; after Native Americans help them survive the winter, they found the Plymouth Colony.

1621
The settlers from the *Mayflower* celebrate their first harvest in America by eating turkey with the local natives.

1622
Algonquian-speaking Native Americans of the Powhatan Confederacy attack the English colony at Jamestown; more than 300 settlers die.

1624
Cardinal Richelieu becomes King Louis XIII of France's chief minister; he is set on destroying the Huguenots, the power of the French nobles, and the military might of the Habsburgs.

1625
The Dutch found the colony of New Amsterdam (modern New York); they pay the Lenape tribe just 60 guilders (around $1,000) for Manhattan Island.

1628–1629
The English parliament's Petition of Right gives English citizens the right to be protected from overreaches in royal authority; it is one of several measures designed to curb royal power. King Charles dismisses the English parliament in 1629 and rules without it for 11 years.

1631
Sweden's king, Gustavus Adolphus, enters the Thirty Years' War and crushes the army of the Holy Roman Emperor.

102
The number of passengers aboard the *Mayflower* on its voyage across the Atlantic.

◁ **Return to Amsterdam**
This 1599 painting by Hendrick Cornelisz Vroom depicts the second of several Dutch voyages made to the east in search of trade before the formation of the Dutch East India Company in 1602.

◁ **English Civil War helmet**
Lobster-tailed helmets were worn by soldiers on both sides during the English Civil War (1642–1651).

1632

19

The number of years taken to complete the construction of the Taj Mahal in Agra.

1632

Two of the 17th century's greatest thinkers are born: the Dutch philosopher Baruch Spinoza (1632–1677), whose rationalist approach lays the foundations for the Enlightenment; and Englishman John Locke (1632–1704), whose political liberalism influences both the Enlightenment and the Constitution of the United States.

1633

In Japan, the Shogun Tokugawa Iemitsu pursues isolationist policies. He forbids all travel abroad, except for highly restricted voyages by ships to China and Korea; books from abroad are banned; and overseas traders are expelled from the country (except for the Dutch, who are allowed to retain a base near Nagasaki). This period of Japanese isolation will last until 1853. In the Mughal Empire, Shah Jahan ends the tradition of religious tolerance by ordering the destruction of all recently built Hindu temples.

1633–1637

Tulip mania in Holland provides the first example of an economic bubble; prices for tulip bulbs rise dramatically before collapsing, bankrupting many investors.

1634

Work begins on the Taj Mahal, a huge marble mausoleum on the bank of the river Yamuna in Agra. It is commissioned by Shah Jahan in memory of his wife Mumtaz Mahal and is completed in 1653.

1635

France enters the Thirty Years' War against Habsburg Spain in 1635 and the Holy Roman Empire in 1636.

1636

The first institute for advanced learning in North America is founded in Cambridge, Massachusetts. Two years later it is given the name Harvard College in honor of the Reverend John Harvard, a prominent benefactor.

1638

The Ottomans under sultan Murad IV retake Baghdad from the Safavids and are granted Mesopotamia by the Treaty of Qasr-i-Shirin in 1639, ending the Ottoman-Safavid conflict. Galileo formulates the law of falling bodies, which states that bodies of the same material falling through the same medium go at the same speed, regardless of mass.

1642

Dutchman Abel Tasman claims Tasmania for the Dutch, but Maori warriors prevent him from claiming New Zealand. Dutch artist Rembrandt van Rijn paints *The Night Watch*.

1644–1651

Charles I of England's insistence on the "Divine Right" of kings to rule without consulting Parliament triggers the British Civil Wars; Parliamentarians (Roundheads) are set against Royalists (Cavaliers); Charles is convicted of treason for fighting a war against Parliament and beheaded in 1649; Oliver Cromwell heads the new English Commonwealth, and in 1651 his New Model Army defeats Charles's son (Charles II) at Worcester, ending the wars.

1644

China's Ming Dynasty falls to the Manchus, who install the first Qing emperor in Beijing and gain control of all China by 1681.

▷ **Louis XIV**
This 1701 painting shows France's "Sun King," who was crowned in 1654 and took direct rule over France in 1661 after the death of his Chief Minister.

▷ **Emperor Aurangzeb**
This 17th-century painting depicts the Mughal Emperor Aurangzeb, who ruled from 1658, being carried on a palanquin, accompanied by a royal hunting party.

1673

1644–1647
Witchfinder General Matthew Hopkins zealously examines, tortures, and executes hundreds of people accused of witchcraft in the east of England.

1647–1648
The French physicist Blaise Pascal demonstrates the existence of atmospheric pressure and shows that it decreases at higher altitudes.

1648
The Peace of Westphalia brings an end to the Thirty Years' War—a turbulent period of European history—but fatally undermines the authority of the Holy Roman Emperor.

1648–1653
Civil war (the Fronde rebellion) breaks out in France after years of war and peasant uprisings; the monarchy survives, but the protests against royal power are a sign of things to come.

1652
The Dutch East India Company founds Cape Town, South Africa, as a resupply port for company ships trading with Asia. The first of three Anglo-Dutch naval wars (1652–1654, 1665–1667, and 1672–1674) breaks out over control of the seas and shipborne trade.

1656
Oliver Cromwell petitions for Jews to be allowed to return to England; they had been expelled more than 350 years earlier under King Edward I following their demonization as anti-Christian murderers and moneylenders.

1658
Cromwell's reconquest of Ireland and the subsequent "Plantation" (the confiscation of territory and its granting to "Planters") sees two-thirds of Irish land in English or Scottish hands; it creates a long-lasting hatred of the English in Ireland.

1658–1707
The Mughal Empire reaches its greatest extent during the reign of Aurangzeb; he rules over approximately 160 million subjects and controls all but the tip of India's subcontinent.

1659
The Franco-Spanish War ends with the Peace of the Pyrenees; France takes Spain's place as Europe's major power, a position embodied by Louis XIV ("the Sun King") and his lavish court.

1660
The English Restoration returns Charles II to the throne following the collapse of the Commonwealth. The Royal Society is founded in London by royal charter in 1662; dedicated to advancing the understanding of science, it is the oldest scientific society in the world still in existence.

1661
Louis XIV assumes personal rule of France on the death of Cardinal Mazarin, declaring he will rule without a chief minister. Italian physician Marcello Malpighi's rese into the tissues of the human body provides the foundation for the science of microscopic anatomy, paving the way for advances in physiology, embryology, and practical medicine.

1664
The Second Anglo-Dutch War begins; the following year, the Dutch director-general of New Amsterdam peacefully yields the colony to the British.

1668
Spain finally recognizes Portuguese independence. The War of Devolution (1667–1668) ends with the Treaty of Aix-la-Chapelle; a triple alliance of England, Sweden, and the Dutch forces France to abandon its claims to the Spanish Netherlands. Charles II receives Bombay from his Portuguese bride and leases it to the English East India Company. The Bank of Sweden is founded; it is the world's oldest central bank.

c. 1670
The Empire of Mali collapses, after dominating west Africa for 400 years.

1672
English physicist Isaac Newton publishes the results of his experiments into the nature of light.

1672–1678
The Franco-Dutch War begins as Louis XIV invades the Dutch Republic with the support of England and Sweden;

"The State, in choosing men to serve it, takes no notice of their opinions. If they be willing faithfully to serve it, that satisfies."

OLIVER CROMWELL, 1644

1665
The Kingdom of Kongo in central Africa is plunged into 40 years of civil war. English physicist Robert Hooke provides a name for the smallest units of life that he observes through his compound microscope, calling them "cells."

1666
The Great Fire of London ravages the city for 4 days, destroying more than 13,000 houses and 87 churches.

the war ends with the Dutch losing New Amsterdam (New York) to England (for a second time) and France gaining territories in the Spanish Netherlands.

1673
Louis Joliet and Jacques Marquette confirm that the Mississippi reaches the Gulf of Mexico, not the Pacific. Gabriel Arthur crosses the Appalachians via the Cumberland Gap—the main route west in the 18th century.

72
The number of years that Louis XIV occupied the French throne—the longest reign of any European monarch.

1674–1699

6'8" (200 cm). The exceptional height of Peter I (the Great), Czar of All Russia.

c. 1674
Dutch scientist and businessman Antonie van Leeuwenhoek is the first to observe and describe microbes—including protists and bacteria—through a microscope. He calls these tiny organisms "animalcules."

1675–1676
In North America, Metacomet ("King Philip"), chief of the Wampanoag, together with Mohawks of the Iroquois Confederacy, attacks English settlements in New England; the Treaty of Casco agrees to provide tribes with an annual measure of corn for each family settled on Native American lands.

1675–1711
St. Paul's Cathedral in London is rebuilt to a design by architect Christopher Wren, following the Great Fire of 1666.

1678
John Bunyan writes his Christian allegory, *The Pilgrim's Progress*.

1680
The Pueblo people in the colony of New Mexico rebel against the Spanish after the colonizers attempt to crush local religious practices and force Catholism on them. The Spanish retreat but, led by Pedro de Vargas, return to reconquer the Pueblos in 1692.

1682
English Quaker and philosopher William Penn founds Philadelphia, Pennsylvania. Robert de La Salle reaches the mouth of the Mississippi River and claims Louisiana for France. Louis XIV moves the French court from Paris to the palace at Versailles, which he enlarges into one of the largest residences in the world, as a symbol of his absolute power as French monarch. Peter I ("the Great") becomes Czar of All Russia; determined to modernize and reshape Russia as a western European power, he builds a new capital at St. Petersburg, abolishes the titles of *boyars* (nobles), centralizes government, reforms Russian society, restructures the army, builds a navy, and vastly expands the empire.

1683
The Polish king Jan III Sobieski lifts the Ottoman siege of Vienna at the Battle of Kahlenberg; Ottoman power in the Balkans collapses, and Sobieski is hailed as the savior of Christendom. The Qing Empire conquers Taiwan, bringing it under Chinese rule.

1685
After almost a century of tolerance, the Edict of Fontainebleau—issued by Louis XIV—makes Protestantism illegal in France; thousands of Huguenots flee to England, the Dutch Republic, and Prussia.

1686
The League of Augsburg (or Grand Alliance) is formed by England, the United Provinces of the Netherlands, and the Austrian Habsburgs to block Louis XIV's expansion plans in the Nine Years' War (1688–1697).

1687
English physicist Isaac Newton publishes his three-volume work *Philosophiæ Naturalis Principia Mathematica*, a cornerstone of scientific thought. In it, he states his universal law of gravity and his three laws of motion.

Boyne in 1690. Aphra Behn, one of England's first professional writers, makes an early protest against slavery in her novel, *Oroonoko*. Explorer and navigator William Dampier is the first Englishman to visit Australia.

1689
The Treaty of Nerchinsk settles the border between China and Russia.

> "To explain all nature is too difficult a task for any one man or even for any one age. 'Tis much better to do a little with certainty … "
>
> ISAAC NEWTON, 1704

1688
In the Glorious Revolution, James II, the last Catholic king of England, Scotland, and Ireland, is overthrown by a union of English Parliamentarians and his own son-in-law, the Dutch prince William of Orange; William is then crowned William III and rules as joint monarch with his wife, Mary; James flees to France, lands in Ireland in 1689, and is defeated at the Battle of the

1690
The Qing Dynasty begins its conquest of Outer Mongolia (modern Mongolia); by the end of the 18th century, the Chinese empire has almost doubled in size.

1692
The city of Salem, Massachusetts is gripped by witchfinding hysteria; 20 people are convicted and executed for witchcraft.

◁ Newton's telescope
This is a replica of the first reflecting telescope made by Sir Isaac Newton and shown to the Royal Society in 1668. It uses a concave mirror, rather than a lens, to gather light.

1693

A massive earthquake devastates Sicily, southern Italy, and Malta; as many as 60,000 people are killed. The first women's magazine in English, "The Ladies' Mercury," is published in London; it runs for only 4 weeks.

1694

The Bank of England is established; it becomes the central banker for England's private banks, transforming the country's ability to finance wars and imperial expansion.

1696

Having moved its main Bengal trading station to Calcutta in 1690, the English East India Company starts building a large base, Fort William, on the bank of the River Hooghly.

1698

English engineer Thomas Savery patents the first steam-powered engine, which he designs to pump water from mine workings and to towns and cities. He demonstrates the machine to the Royal Society in London the following year.

1699

In response to religious repression under the Mughals, Guru Gobind Singh introduces the five Ks, the five outward signs of Sikhism, and charges his followers with the mission to secure Sikh rule in the Punjab.

60,000

The number of people killed in the 1693 earthquake in southern Italy.

▷ **Emperor Kangxi**
Painted on silk, this portrait shows the Qing leader Kangxi, who greatly enlarged the empire from 1600 and encouraged the spread of Western education in China.

REVOLUTION AND INDUSTRY 1700–1850

1700–1721

A coalition led by Russia and including Poland and Denmark launches an attack on Sweden (the dominant power in the Baltic), beginning the Great Northern War; after 21 years of conflict, Sweden cedes the Baltic ports to Russia in the Treaty of Nystad and Russia emerges as a major power in the region.

> "Generally speaking, the errors in religion are dangerous; those in philosophy only ridiculous."
>
> DAVID HUME, FROM *A TREATISE OF HUMAN NATURE*, 1738–1740

1700

The Spanish king, Charles II, bequeaths his territories to Philip of Anjou, grandson of Louis XIV, the reigning French king; the rest of Europe is alarmed by the increase in French power.

1701

Jethro Tull invents the horse-drawn seed drill, an innovation in the Agricultural Revolution that raises British agricultural productivity in the 17th–19th centuries. Osei Tutu, ruler of Kumasi (in modern Ghana) leads the Asante confederation in west Africa to independence from the Denkyira nation; he takes the name Asantehene and uses his people's military prowess and the Atlantic coastal trade to triple the new state's territories and build a powerful empire.

1701

The English and Dutch ally to support Austria's claim to the Spanish throne and prevent unification of the French and Spanish thrones under the Bourbons Louis XIV and Philip of Anjou; Louis XIV sends an army to the Spanish Netherlands to defend them from the English and Dutch and recognizes James Francis Edward Stuart (the "Old Pretender"), son of the exiled James II,

as king of England, Scotland, and Ireland in place of William III and his wife Mary. This leads to the War of the Spanish Succession (1701–1714).

1704

The first edition of *The Boston News-Letter*, North America's oldest continuously published newspaper, is published; it is subsidized and approved by the British governor. Boston emerges as the principal port for the Atlantic slave trade in the New World.

1705

British astronomer Edmond Halley is the first to predict a comet's return; when the comet returns exactly when he said it would, in 1758, it is named after him. The Husaynid Dynasty comes to power in Tunis, north Africa; it rules until 1957.

1707

Mughal India begins to decline following the death of the emperor Aurangzeb. The Acts of Union unite Scotland and England in the United Kingdom of Great Britain.

1709

Shipwrecked sailor Alexander Selkirk is discovered after 5 years alone on an island in the south Pacific; his story is probably one of the inspirations for Daniel Defoe's novel, *Robinson Crusoe*.

1712

British inventor Thomas Newcomen's improved version of Savery's steam engine is installed in a tin mine; Newcomen's engine was only bettered in 1775 by Thomas Watt's steam engine. Japan publishes its first encyclopedia, *Waka Sansai Zue*.

1713–1714

The Treaties of Utrecht (1713) and Rastatt (1714) end the War of the Spanish Succession and seek to balance power in Europe by separating the French and Spanish crowns; the Spanish Netherlands are ceded to Austria, and Britain receives Newfoundland, Nova Scotia, and Gibraltar.

1714

The Dutch-Polish scientific instrument maker Daniel Gabriel Fahrenheit invents the mercury thermometer; he sets the interval between the freezing and boiling points of water as 180 degrees, with 0 degrees being the temperature of a mixture of ice, water, and ammonium chloride.

1715

Following the death of Queen Anne (r. 1702–1714), the British crown passes to the elector of Hannover, George I. The Jacobite Rebellion, a Scottish Catholic attempt to restore the Stuarts to the throne, fails; Prince James Francis Edward Stuart flees to France. Louis XIV dies after ruling France for 72 years.

1715–1717

The Spanish in Texas encourage the Yamasee and other tribes of Native Americans to attack the British colonists in South Carolina.

1717

Handel's *Water Music*, a masterpiece of the Baroque period, is performed for the first time, on the River Thames in London. English pirate Edward Teach, known as Blackbeard, begins plundering ships in the Caribbean; in 1718, his alliance of pirates blockades Charleston, South Carolina, and takes the crew and passengers of the *Crowley* hostage, demanding the payment of a ransom.

1720

The War of the Quadruple Alliance ends. Austria, Britain, the Dutch Republic (United Provinces), and France succeed in forcing Philip V of Spain to abandon his claim to Sicily and Sardinia; however, Spain regains territory in Pensacola, Florida, and in the north of Spain (from France), and Texas is confirmed as a Spanish possession. It becomes fashionable among young English noblemen to visit Italy on the Grand Tour. In Venice, the artist Canaletto finds customers for his views of the canals among the English tourists.

1720–1721

Qing warriors oust the Zunghar Mongols from Tibet; they install Kelzang Gyatso as the 7th Dalai Lama, and Tibet remains under Chinese protection until 1912.

1721

The Russian Senate and Synod proclaim Peter the Great Emperor of All the Russias; many of Europe's rulers fear he will assert his authority over them.

200,000

The number of slaves carried by British ships in the 1710s and 1720s.

▷ Fahrenheit's thermometer
This 18th-century mercury thermometer is engraved with the Fahrenheit scale. On the reverse side is the signature of its inventor.

1740

Dutch explorer Jakob Roggeveen discovers Easter Island and explores some of the Samoan islands.

1722

Ghilzai Afghans rout Persian forces outside Isfahan, take the city, and assume control of the Persian Empire; in 1729, the Safavid Shah Tahmasp II recovers Isfahan with the help of the Afsharid Persians led by Nader Shah.

1724

The Kingdom of Dahomey in west Africa (now southern Benin) becomes the main supplier of slaves to European traders. Louis XIV's Code Noir, created for France's Caribbean territories, is introduced in Louisiana: it stipulates basic rights for slaves, but also legitimizes cruel punishments.

1725

Italian composer Antonio Vivaldi publishes *The Four Seasons*. In China, the *Imperial Encyclopedia*—10,000 volumes in length—is completed.

1727

Coffee begins to be cultivated in the Caribbean and South America. The Portuguese create the first coffee plantation in Brazil.

1728

Hindu Marathas defeat the Nizam of Hyderabad in the Palkhed Campaign; the campaign establishes Maratha supremacy over the Deccan plateau in southern India. Russia commissions the Danish-born cartographer Vitus Bering to explore the Siberian coast; he navigates the strait (now called the Bering Strait) that separates Siberia from Alaska.

1729

A rise in opium addiction prompts China to ban the sale and smoking of opium, which Britain is bringing from India to trade for Chinese goods; opium smugglers continue to cause problems for China into the 19th century.

1730

The Arabian state of Oman drives the Portuguese from the Kenyan and Tanzanian coasts and expands its dominions in east Africa by gaining control of Zanzibar.

1733

The last of the Thirteen Colonies established by Britain on North America's Atlantic coast is founded and named Georgia. In England, John Kay patents the flying shuttle for looms, which revolutionizes the textile industry. Prussia's army becomes the fourth largest in Europe after King Frederick William I introduces military service.

1735

English carpenter and clockmaker John Harrison creates the marine chronometer, a portable clock capable of keeping time at sea; it enables navigators to work out longitude at sea, considerably improving the safety of long-distance voyages.

1735–1738

Swedish botanist Carl Linnaeus publishes *Systema Naturae* on taxonomy—the science of identifying, naming, and classifying organisms. In 1749, he outlines his system of binomial classification, which uses two Latin names to identify an organism uniquely .

1736

Nader Shah deposes the last Safavid rulers in Persia and takes power himself; he founds the Afsharid Dynasty. French explorer and scientist Charles Marie de La Condamine sends samples of the flexible material, rubber, long-used by the Maya, to Paris.

1737

The Marathas extend their control over northern India at the expense of the Mughal Empire.

1738

David Hume, Scottish economist and empiricist, argues that there can be no knowledge beyond experience in his *Treatise on Human Nature*.

1739

Nader Shah's Persian force occupies Delhi and carries off the riches of the Mughal Empire, including the Koh-i-Noor diamond; Persia now controls all land north and west of the Indus River. The Treaty of Belgrade ends the Austro–Turkish War (1737–1739) and stabilizes the Ottomans' position in the Balkans. French-Canadian brothers Pierre and Paul Mallet open up a route from the Mississippi River to Santa Fe (New Mexico) in the first known crossing by a European of North America's Great Plains. The Viceroyalty of New Granada is created from territory now occupied by Panama, Venezuela, Colombia, and Equador.

1740

The rabbi Baal Shem Tov develops Hasidism in Poland; it is a mystical, revivalist Jewish movement that remains as an influential subgrouping within ultra-orthodox Judaism.

▷ Nader Shah
This contemporary painting depicts Nader Shah, the powerful Persian ruler whose military successes included the capture of Delhi in 1739.

1742

1750
The Treaty of Madrid defines the boundary between Spanish and Portuguese colonies in the New World; it recognizes the extent of Portuguese settlement in Brazil.

1751–1772
French philosopher Denis Diderot publishes his *Encyclopédie*—a catalog of human knowledge, including science, philosophy, politics, and religion—with the intention of helping people to think for themselves; it is a defining work of the Enlightenment.

1752
Diplomat, writer, publisher, and scientist Benjamin Franklin invents the lightning rod; it is one of his many innovations, which also include the Franklin stove, bifocal glasses, swimming fins, and the urinary catheter.

1755
The Great Lisbon Earthquake—and the accompanying tsunami—almost destroy the Portuguese city. The earthquake kills 60,000–100,000 people, making it one of the deadliest in history.

1756–1763
Frederick the Great of Prussia marches into Saxony, beginning the Seven Years' War, in which Hanover, Britain, and Prussia clash with France, Austria, Russia, Saxony, Spain, and Sweden.

1757
Robert Clive ("Clive of India") wins Bengal for the British East India Company at the Battle of Plassey. Prussia wins control of Silesia from Austria at the Battle of Leuthen.

1757–1759
William Pitt (later called "the Elder" to distinguish him from his son, who was also a notable politician) becomes Secretary of State in Britain and is the architect of the conquest of French possessions around the world; Britain

1742
German composer George Frederic Handel's Baroque masterpiece *Messiah* is performed for the first time, in Dublin; it has its London premiere almost a year later. George II personally commands a British army in battle (against the French, in the War of the Austrian Succession); he is the last British monarch ever to do so.

1743
In an attempt to reach the Pacific coast, French brothers Louis Joseph and Francois de La Vérendrye become the first Europeans to see the Rocky Mountains, in Wyoming.

1744
Muslim theologian Muhammad ibn Abd al-Wahhab founds the Salafi movement, a conservative strand of Sunni Islam that advocates a return to fundamentals; he forms an alliance with the family of Muhammad ibn Saud that has lasted over 250 years in Saudi Arabia.

1745–1746
A second Jacobite rebellion again fails in its attempt to return the Stuarts to power in Britain; the Scottish highlanders supporting the "Young Pretender" (Prince Charles Edward Stuart, or "Bonnie Prince Charlie") are massacred by British troops at Culloden.

1747
The murder of Nader Shah, weakens the Persian Empire; Ahmad Shah Durrani breaks with Persia and creates the Durrani Empire, the last Afghan empire, which is the precursor of the modern state of Afghanistan. In west Africa, the kingdom of Dahomey (within present-day Benin) is invaded by the Yoruba of the Oyo Empire and forced to pay tribute.

1748
The Afghans invade Punjab. The Peace of Aix-la-Chapelle ends the War of the Austrian Succession (1740–1748); Maria Theresa, daughter of Holy Roman Emperor Charles VI, is finally confirmed as heir to the Habsburg lands.

1749
The kingdom of Mysore rises to prominence in south India. British Lieutenant General Edward Cornwallis founds the town of Halifax in Nova Scotia.

8.5
Estimated strength of the Great Lisbon Earthquake on the Richter Scale.

▷ **Benjamin Franklin**
An engraving of the American inventor playfully references his 1752 experiments with lightning, suggesting a conductor in an umbrella.

▷ *An Incident in the Rebellion of 1745*
This painting by Anglo-Swiss artist David Morier depicts the charge of the highlanders against the British infantry at the Battle of Culloden.

takes Fort Duquesne in Pennsylvania, Senegal in west Africa, and the French Caribbean island of Guadeloupe from France. In 1759, General Wolfe captures Quebec and much of French Canada for Britain.

1759

The French are defeated by an Anglo–Prussian force at Minden, north Germany; the succession of British victories over the French in the Seven Years' War is described as the *Annus Mirabilis* (year of miracles).

1760

Rebellion spreads after a group of slaves led by Takyi, an enslaved Fante chief from west Africa, overruns plantations in the British colony of Jamaica; it is months before the revolt is suppressed. China's Qing Empire extends into Mongolia after a series of campaigns launched by the Qianlong Emperor.

1761

In India, the Maratha Empire is defeated by Afghans. The British seize Pondicherry, destroying French power in India.

1762

Catherine the Great is proclaimed Empress of Russia; her reign is characterized by wide-ranging reform and territorial expansion. In his book, *The Social Contract*, the French political philosopher Jean-Jacques Rousseau questions the relationship between governments and the governed, attesting that "Man is born free, and everywhere he is in chains"; his writing exerts great influence on the Enlightenment, the French Revolution, and the Romantic movement.

1763

The Seven Years' War ends with British naval supremacy asserted over France and Spain; taxes are raised to pay the national debt incurred in the war, fueling discontent in Britain and in its colonies. Rio de Janeiro becomes the capital of the State of Brazil, part of the Portuguese Empire.

1764

English weaver James Hargreaves invents the "Spinning Jenny," which increases cloth production eightfold.

◁ **Independence Hall**
The Assembly Room in this building in Philadelphia, Pennsylvania, is where the Declaration of Independence was adopted on July 4, 1776.

1768

1768

Russia wins the right to free navigation in the Black Sea in the Russo–Turkish War. English explorer and navigator James Cook sails from Plymouth aboard the vessel HMS *Endeavour* in his first voyage to the Pacific; he reaches New Zealand in 1769 and charts its entire coastline; he reaches mainland Australia in 1770, names Botany Bay, and begins charting the east coast. In Egypt, Ali Bey al-Kabir deposes the Ottoman governor and invades Syria, briefly securing the independence of what had previously been the Mamluk sultanate; the Ottomans regain control by 1773. Spanish Franciscan friars begin building a chain of missions along the Californian coast, founding the main west coast cities in North America, including San Francisco and Los Angeles.

1769–1771

The Industrial Revolution begins when Scottish inventor James Watt patents his version of the steam engine and British industrialist and inventor Richard Arkwright opens the first factory—a water-powered textile mill. The Industrial Revolution transforms the global economy, replacing the rural agricultural economies that exist in many countries with ones based on manufactured goods made in factories clustered in cities.

1772

Austria, Prussia, and Russia partition Poland, taking around one-third of its land and half its population.

1773

Captain Cook, aboard HMS *Resolution*, circumnavigates the continent of Antarctica during his second voyage to the southern hemisphere. In America, merchants dump a valuable cargo of tea into Boston Harbor as a protest against British taxes and governance; the incident becomes known as the Boston Tea Party. Britain responds by issuing the "Intolerable Acts" (1774), authorizing punitive measures against the 13 colonies; the colonies respond by boycotting British goods and trade.

1775–1783

The Revolutionary War (also called the American War of Independence) begins with a skirmish at Lexington between British troops (known as "redcoats") and local militiamen; George Washington is appointed commander-in-chief of the colonial forces. Britain's George III rejects the colonies' Olive Branch Petition and declares that the colonies are in revolt.

1776

The Declaration of Independence of the United States is signed on July 4; drafted by Thomas Jefferson, it asserts that all men are equal and have the right to "life, liberty and the pursuit of happiness," but enslaved Africans are excluded.

> *"The God who gave us life gave us liberty at the same time; the hand of force may destroy, but cannot disjoin them."*

THOMAS JEFFERSON, 1774

1777

In the Treaty of San Ildefonso, Spain retains Uruguay but cedes the Amazon basin to the Portuguese.

1778

France formally recognizes the United States and enters the Revolutionary War against the British, sending a fleet across the Atlantic. Spain and the Dutch Republic support the American cause. Captain Cook is the first European to make contact with the Hawaiian Islands; he is killed there in a dispute over a boat. French chemist Antoine Lavoisier names oxygen and identifies its role in combustion.

1779

Boer (Dutch-speaking) settlers in South Africa clash with Xhosa tribes; it is the start of around 100 years of conflict between settlers and the indigenous peoples of the Eastern Cape.

1780–1782

Tupac Amaru II, a descendent of the last Inca ruler, leads around 75,000 Peruvian Indians and Creoles in an unsuccessful rebellion against Spanish colonial rule.

1780

In the US, Pennsylvania secures the freedom of children born to slaves in the state in the future; the model is slowly adopted in other northern states.

1781

George Washington and his French allies defeat the British at Yorktown, and British General Charles Cornwallis surrenders after this last major battle in the Revolutionary War. German philosopher Immanuel Kant publishes

▷ **Shark-tooth knife**
This ceremonial Maori knife was collected in New Zealand during one of Captain Cook's voyages.

▷ *Dream of the Red Chamber*
This painting presents a scene from *Dream of the Red Chamber* (1791), one of China's Four Great Classical Novels.

17,000
The number of enemies of the French Revolution executed during the Reign of Terror.

his *Critique of Pure Reason*, a hugely influential attempt to answer the question, "What can we know?"

1782
The Treaty of Salbai ends the first of the three wars fought between the British East India Company and the Maratha Empire, ushering in a period of peace.

1783
Crimea is annexed by the Russian Empire under Catherine the Great. The first manned flight of a hot air balloon, designed by the Montgolfier brothers, is made in Paris. Britain recognizes American independence in the Treaty of Paris.

1784
The India Act allows the British East India Company to retain control of trade in India, but political matters are handled by three directors directly responsible to the British government.

1787
Sierra Leone, west Africa, is colonized by settlers who have freed themselves from slavery in America; the Society for the Abolition of the Slave Trade is founded in Britain. The US Constitution is drafted; it is ratified the following year. American inventor John Fitch runs trials of his steamboat on the Delaware River; he goes on to operate the first steamboat service in the US.

1788
The first convicts are transported to the British penal colony in Botany Bay, Australia; nearly 60,000 people settle in Australia over the next 50 years.

1789
George Washington becomes the first president of the United States. The French Revolution begins: the newly formed revolutionary National Assembly vows to produce a constitution; a Parisian mob storms the Bastille prison on July 14. Smallpox brought to Australia by the Europeans decimates the aboriginal population of Port Jackson, Botany Bay, and Broken Bay. Fletcher Christian leads a mutiny on HMS *Bounty*; Captain Bligh is cast adrift.

1790
Pemulwuy and his son Tedbury lead Aboriginal resistance around the Sydney area in Australia in a guerrilla campaign that lasts several years.

1791
Louis XVI attempts to flee Paris but is caught at Varennes; he is returned to the city and imprisoned in Tuileries Palace.

Amendments to the US Constitution included in the Bill of Rights include the freedom of religion. Cao Xueqin publishes his semiautobiographical work, *Dream of the Red Chamber*, which is considered one of China's Four Great Classical Novels (the others being *Romance of the Three Kingdoms*, *Journey to the West*, and *Water Margin*). Austrian composer Wolfgang Amadeus Mozart conducts the orchestra at the premiere of his opera *The Magic Flute* in Vienna.

1792
The French monarchy is abolished and the First French Republic declared. France declares war on Austria, Prussia, and Piedmont; fearful of the spread of revolution, the Netherlands, Spain, Austria, Prussia, Portugal, Sardinia, and Naples, and later Britain, form the First Coalition to fight France in a war that lasts until 1797.

1793
Louis XVI and his wife Marie Antoinette are executed in Paris; the Committee of Public Safety launches a "Reign of Terror" to eliminate enemies of the Revolution. American inventor Eli Whitney patents the cotton gin, which speeds up cotton processing and increases production in the American south. The Fugitive Slave Laws are passed in the United States; they allow southern slave owners to recover escaped slaves from northern states.

1794
France abolishes slavery in its colonies following the Haiti Revolution led by Toussaint Louverture.

1795
Following an unsuccessful uprising against Imperial Russia and the Kingdom of Prussia led by Tadeusz Kościuszko, Poland ceases to exist; its remaining territories are partitioned between Russia, Austria, and Prussia. The British seize the Cape Colony from the Dutch in South Africa.

1796
Edward Jenner pioneers the use of vaccines, inoculating a boy against smallpox by infecting him with the milder cowpox.

1796–1804
The White Lotus Rebellion in central China contributes to the decline of the Qing Dynasty. The White Lotus is a secretive political and religious movement with its roots in ancient Buddhist traditions.

10
The duration in minutes of the first flight ever made in a hot air balloon; it took place on September 19, 1783.

> *The Naked Maja*
Painted by Goya in 1797–1800, *The Naked Maja* (and a clothed companion piece) were commissioned by Manuel Godoy, a royal minister.

1797

200
Years that Jane Austen's *Pride and Prejudice* has remained in print.

1797–1800
Spain's Francisco de Goya paints *The Naked Maja*; he is later brought before the Spanish Inquisition on a charge of moral depravity but escapes prosecution.

1798
In the Wexford uprising, the Society of United Irishmen challenges British rule in Ireland and seeks political reform. An alliance, led by Britain, Austria, and Russia, forms to fight against France; it leads to the War of the Second Coalition (1799–1802). The British navy under Horatio Nelson defeats the French fleet at the Battle of the Nile after a French army commanded by Napoleon Bonaparte invades Egypt.

1799
Napoleon overthrows the French Revolutionary Directory government

and makes himself First Consul. Britain defeats and partitions Mysore in southern India. The Rosetta Stone is discovered by Napoleon's troops in Egypt; it holds the key to understanding Egyptian hieroglyphics.

c. 1800
Romanticism—which emphasizes inspiration, subjectivity, and the individual— emerges in Europe as an artistic, literary, and philosophical form in reaction to the rationalism of the 18th-century Enlightenment; German Romantic composer Ludwig van Beethoven finishes the *Moonlight Sonata* in 1801.

1801
The Act of Union links Britain and Ireland in a United Kingdom.

1801–1804
British mining engineer Richard Trevithick develops the first steam railway locomotive. His engine pulls a train in February 1804.

1803–1805
France sells its territories between the Mississippi River and the Rocky Mountains to the US in the Louisiana Purchase; the territory is extended south to New Orleans in 1804. The Lewis and Clark expedition crosses the western US and reaches the Pacific coast in 1805.

1804
Napoleon assumes the title Emperor of France; the Napoleonic Code declares all men equal and ends hereditary nobility. Uthman dan

Fodio creates the Sokoto Caliphate in west Africa after conquering the Hausa kingdoms; the caliphate is one of the largest states in Africa until defeated by the British in 1903 and abolished.

1805
Admiral Nelson and the British fleet defeat the Franco–Spanish fleet at the Battle of Trafalgar; France is victorious against Russia and Austria at the Battle of Austerlitz.

1805–1807
Britain, Sweden, Russia, Austria, and Prussia counter Napoleon's ambitions in the War of the Third Coalition.

1806
Napoleon abolishes the Holy Roman Empire and defeats Prussia; he attempts to deny the British trade through blockades called the Continental System.

1807
The Third Coalition ends when Russia switches sides and allies with France. The Slave Trade Act abolishes the slave trade in the British Empire.

1808
Napoleon declares his brother, Joseph Bonaparte, the new king of Spain, triggering the Peninsular War (to 1814) with the allied powers of Britain, Spain, and Portugal.

1810
The Mexican War of Independence (to 1821) begins a series of revolts against Spanish rule. Russia withdraws from Napoleon's Continental System and recommences trade with Britain.

1812
Napoleon invades Russia and goes on, after several victories over the Russian army, to occupy Moscow; his troops, however, are forced into a brutal retreat during the winter. Britain and the United States clash in the War of 1812; British troops set fire to the White House in Washington, D. C.

1812–1813
Egyptian forces retake Medina, Jeddah, and Mecca from the Wahhabi; Ottoman rule is reinstated in the area. The English paleontologist Mary Anning discovers the first complete ichthyosaur skeleton in Lyme Regis; her observations of fossils deeply influence scientific understanding of prehistoric life.

1813
In a turning point in the Napoleonic Wars, France is defeated at the Battle of the Nations (Leipzig) by an allied force of Britain, Prussia, and Russia. Simón Bolívar invades Venezuela and captures Caracas; he is proclaimed Libertador (Liberator). English novelist Jane Austen publishes *Pride and Prejudice*.

◁ **The Rosetta Stone**
Originating in Egypt in the 2nd century BCE, the Rosetta Stone was rediscovered in 1799. It is inscribed with Egyptian hieroglyphs, Egyptian demotic script, and Greek (top to bottom).

▷ **Napoleon's retreat**
This contemporary painting records the disastrous retreat of Napoleon's forces from Moscow in 1812, during which the starving troops were relentlessly harried by the Russian army.

1814

Paris is occupied by Anti-French allies who force Napoleon to abdicate and exile him to Elba; Louis XVI's brother, Louis XVIII, is placed on the French throne. After years of war, the balance of power in Europe is settled by the Congress of Vienna (1814–1815).

1815

Napoleon escapes from Elba, gathers an army, and marches to Paris at the start of the "Hundred Days" of his return to power. He is defeated at the Battle of Waterloo by British and Prussian forces under the Duke of Wellington and Gebhard Leberecht von Blücher. Napoleon is exiled to St. Helena, where he dies in 1821; the French monarchy is again restored under Louis XVIII.

1816

The United Provinces of South America (modern-day Argentina) declares its independence from Spain. Shaka becomes chief of the Zulu nation and builds a powerful state in southern Africa.

1818

Spanish rebels defeat Spanish royalists at the Battle of Maipu and secure Chile's independence from Spain.

1819

Spain cedes Florida to the United States and settles the boundary between the Viceroyalty of New Spain and the US; Spain is soon forced to accept the loss of its colonies in Central and South America. Simón Bolívar becomes the first president of the new Republic of Gran Colombia, following independence from Spain. British colonial administrator Stamford Raffles founds the city of Singapore; it gives the British East India Company a base in the Malay peninsula from which to challenge Dutch dominance of the trading routes between China and India.

1820

The Khedive of Egypt, Muhammad Ali, orders an invasion of Sudan; the campaign brings him a vast empire.

1821–1822

Spain acknowledges Mexico's independence. Simón Bolívar secures Venezuela's independence in 1821, and Panama, Colombia, and Ecuador join it to form Gran Colombia, while José de San Martín proclaims an independent Peru. British scientist Michael Faraday creates the first electric motor; 10 years later, he discovers electromagnetic induction and builds the first electric generator.

1822

1822
British mathematician Charles Babbage designs the first programmable computer, a calculator he calls a "difference engine." The Empire of Brazil becomes independent of Portugal.

1823
Joseph Smith starts to record revelations he claims were given to him in a vision by the Angel Moroni, creating what becomes the *Book of Mormon*; he founds the Church of Christ (later the Church of the Latter-Day Saints) in 1831. Costa Rica, Guatemala, El Salvador, Nicaragua, and Honduras declare their independence as a federal republic, the United Provinces of Central America.

1824–1825
José de Sucre wins Bolivia's independence from Spain at the Battle of Ayacucho in 1824. The following year,

George Stephenson and his son Robert open the first railway line to use a steam locomotive to pull passenger trains; it runs between Stockton and Darlington in northeast England.

1825–1832
Alexander Pushkin publishes *Eugene Onegin* in serial form; this novel in verse form becomes a classic of Russian literature.

1826
French inventor Joseph-Nicéphore Niépce makes the earliest surviving photographic prints.

1827
At the Battle of Navarino off the Peloponnese, Britain, France, and Russia sink three-quarters of the Ottoman fleet when the Ottomans refuse to give Greece its independence.

1828
Brazil and Argentina recognize Uruguay's independence. Russia acquires Armenia and declares war on the Ottomans.

1830
The French take control of Algeria. The French Bourbon monarch, Charles X, is replaced with his cousin Louis-Philippe, Duke of Orléans, in the July Revolution in Paris. Belgium demands independence from the Netherlands. Calls for political reform throughout Europe follow amid a wave of rebellion and social unrest. Native Americans are forcibly expelled from the southeast of the US after the Indian Removal Act strips them of rights; they head west along the "Trail of Tears" to Oklahoma. Simón Bolívar dies of tuberculosis.

1830–1832
Japanese artist Katsushika Hokusai produces his masterful woodblock print *Under the Wave off Kanagawa*.

1831
Belgium becomes independent and elects Leopold I as king.

1832
The Great Powers formally recognize Greek independence from the Ottoman Empire; the London Conference creates

> *"Devoured by all crimes and extinguished by ferocity, the Europeans will not deign to conquer us."*
>
> SIMÓN BOLÍVAR, 1830

the Greek monarchy, and in May, Prince Otto of Bavaria becomes the first modern king of Greece as Otto I.

1833
The Slave Emancipation Act bans slavery throughout the British Empire. The British Parliament passes the Factory Act, prohibiting the employment of children under the age of 9. Britain pushes the Argentinians out of the Falkland Islands (Las Malvinas) and begins settling British farmers there.

1835–1840
Around 12,000 Boers from Cape Colony make the "Great Trek" into the South African interior; the majority settle in what becomes Orange Free State, Transvaal, and Natal.

1836
At the Battle of the Alamo, around 200 Texan rebels attempt to hold off a Mexican army of several thousand; they are defeated, but soon Mexico has to recognize the independent Republic of Texas. The first wagon train taking settlers west heads out along the Oregon Trail; in 1841, wagon trains reach California.

1837
Queen Victoria ascends the throne of the United Kingdom, beginning a reign that lasts over 60 years.

2,500
Tons of opium imported into China in the year 1838.

◁ **Simón Bolívar**
This painting puts Bolívar, the "Liberator" of South America, into the famous pose in which Napoleon was pictured by French artist Jacques-Louis David in 1801. Bolívar died in 1830.

◁ *Under the Wave off Kanagawa*
Hokusai's most famous print, made in
1830–1832, is part of a series entitled
Thirty-Six Views of Mount Fuji. The mountain
is visible in the hollow of the wave.

4

The number of words
in the first telegraph
message: "What hath
God wrought?"

leader Abd al-Qadir, bringing an end to
the Algerian war of independence.

1848
Karl Marx and Friedrich Engels publish
The Communist Manifesto. Europe is
wracked by political upheaval in the
"Year of Revolution"; France overthrows
the monarchy to form the Second
Republic with Louis-Napoleon
Bonaparte, as president. The California
Gold Rush (1848–1855) begins when
gold is found at Sutter's Mill.

1850
The Taiping Rebellion begins in China;
it lasts 14 years, claims 20 million lives,
and irrevocably damages the authority
of the Qing Dynasty.

1838
Guatemala, Honduras, and Nicaragua
become independent states. The
slaughter of around 3,000 Zulus at the
Battle of Blood River in southern Africa
allows the Dutch Voortrekkers to
establish the Republic of Natal.

1839
British artist J. M. W. Turner exhibits
The Fighting Téméraire, in which he uses
the scrapping of a ship that fought at the
Battle of Trafalgar as an allegory of the
decline of British naval power.

1839–1840
The First British colonists arrive in
New Zealand.

1839–1842
Britain seeks to curb Russia's growing
influence over Afghanistan in the First
Anglo-Afghan War. China and Britain
clash over trade and the British import
of opium into China; Britain's superior
navy wins this First Opium War; China
opens five "treaty ports" to foreign trade
and cedes Hong Kong.

1840
American artist and inventor Samuel
Morse patents the electric telegraph in
the US; he sends the first message in
1844. The formation of the Magnetic
Telegraph Company in 1845 sees the
technology spread quickly across the
US; the first transatlantic telegraph
cable is laid in 1858.

1841
The first operation using diethyl ether
as an anesthetic is performed; its
efficacy is later publicly demonstrated
by William Morton at the Massachusetts
General Hospital. In 1846, chloroform
is first used as a medical anesthetic.

1842
Disputes surrounding the US–Canadian
border are finally settled by the
Webster–Ashburton Treaty.

1843
The British annex Natal; many Boers do
not recognize British rule and trek over
the mountains into the Orange Free
State and Transvaal provinces.

1845–1854
The Irish potato crop fails due to blight
and poor weather, causing the Great
Famine. More than a million people
die from starvation and associated
diseases, but many more emigrate
over the years that follow, leaving
Ireland severely depopulated.

1846
US commodore James Biddle moors
two warships in Edo Bay in an attempt
to open up trade with Japan; however,
Japan refuses to open its ports to foreign
merchants. The US–Mexican War begins
after the US annexes Texas (1845);
Mexico surrenders in 1847 and cedes
a vast swathe of territory to the United
States. Danish philosopher Søren
Kierkegaard (1813–1855) publishes
*Concluding Unscientific
Postscript to Philosophical
Fragments*, a work that
stresses the individual's
unique position as self-
determining agent and is a
forerunner of existentialism.
The French capture resistance

▷ Queen Victoria's crown
The Imperial State Crown, encrusted
with precious stones, was made for
the coronation of Queen Victoria in
London in 1838.

PROGRESS AND EMPIRE 1850–1914

1851

The Great Exhibition, held in London's Crystal Palace, showcases goods and manufacturers from around the world to over 6 million visitors. Gold is discovered in Australia; in the next 10 years, 500,000 immigrants arrive.

1852

The British recognize the independent Boer republic of Transvaal in South Africa; the Orange Free State is recognized in 1854.

1853–1856

In the Crimean War, Britain, France, and the Ottomans curb Russia's ambitions in the Balkans; Sevastopol is besieged for a year; terrible losses among the French and British prompt Florence Nightingale to organize military nursing services.

1855–1856

Innovations by Britain's Henry Bessemer and Robert Mushet make the mass production of steel possible.

1856–1858

A mutiny by native troops against their British officers develops into an Indian Revolt; it is crushed by the British, who exile the last Mughal emperor and place India under the direct control of the British crown, ushering in the period known as the Raj (to 1947).

1856–1860

In the Second Opium War, Britain and France invade China and force it to open more ports to trade and to legalize opium imports.

1858–1870

The unification of Italy develops out of the Risorgimento movement: France and Piedmont-Sardinia join to end Austrian rule in northern Italy, and Garibaldi secures the south; Victor Emmanuel II is declared king in 1861.

> "All happy families resemble one another, but each unhappy family is unhappy in its own way."
>
> LEO TOLSTOY, FROM ANNA KARENINA, 1877

1859

Charles Darwin publishes *On the Origin of Species by Means of Natural Selection*, outlining his theory of evolution.

1859–1867

France captures Saigon (1859) and establishes protectorates in Cambodia (1863) and Cochin China (1867).

1860–1900

Thousands of Pacific Islanders are coerced or tricked into working as laborers in Peru, Australia, and Fiji.

1861

Russia abolishes serfdom. Abraham Lincoln, an abolitionist, becomes president of the United States; states in the south assert their right to own slaves in defiance of the federal government; seven secede from the Union to form a Confederacy. The Civil War begins with a Confederate attack at Fort Sumter. French chemist Louis Pasteur's experiments demonstrate that airborne microbes cause decay and disease.

1862

In the Civil War, there are Union victories at Shiloh and Antietam and a Confederate victory at the second Battle of Bull Run. Otto von Bismarck becomes prime minister of Prussia; he reforms the army and masterminds the unification of Germany in 1871.

1863

President Lincoln abolishes slavery in the south with the Emancipation Proclamation; the Union takes Vicksburg; Confederate general Robert E. Lee pushes into Pennsylvania, but is defeated at Gettysburg. Having been forced to open Japan to trade with the West, Emperor Komei orders the expulsion of "barbarians" from Japan.

1864

General Ulysses S. Grant becomes commander-in-chief of the Union forces; in the "March to the Sea," Union troops under the command of General William T. Sherman destroy railway lines and towns from Atlanta to Savannah, Georgia. The Paraguayan

president Francisco Solano López starts the War of the Triple Alliance, or Paraguayan War, against Brazil, Argentina, and Uruguay that will kill more than half of Paraguay's population.

1865

The Civil War ends, and General Lee surrenders on 9 April: at the end of the war, 625,000 men are dead and 500,000 are injured. Confederate supporter John Wilkes Booth assassinates President Lincoln on April 14 at Ford's Theatre in Washington, D.C. British surgeon Joseph Lister pioneers modern antiseptics.

1865–1869

Russian novelist Leo Tolstoy publishes *War and Peace*, which draws on his own experiences in the Crimean War (1853–1856).

1866

Prussia crushes Austria in the Seven Weeks War; Austria is excluded from Germany. Austrian monk Gregor Mendel's study of plant hybrids lays the foundations for the science of genetics.

1867

Prussia leads a North German Confederation of 22 states. Franz Josef I is crowned king of Hungary and rules the "dual monarchy" of Austria-Hungary. German social theorist and founder of modern communism Karl Marx publishes *Das Kapital*, outlining his theory of class struggle. The US buys the territory of Alaska from Russia for the sum of $7.2 million.

1868

The Tokugawa shogunate in Japan ends with the restoration of imperial power under Emperor Meiji; his reign (to 1912) sees Japan end its isolationism, implement constitutional government, and modernize.

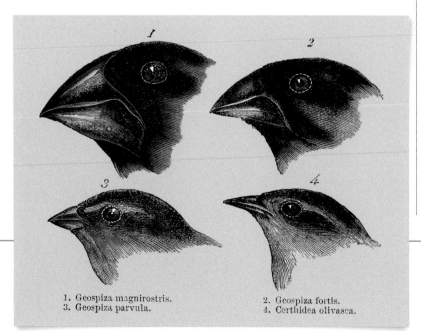

1. Geospiza magnirostris.
2. Geospiza fortis.
3. Geospiza parvula.
4. Certhidea olivasca.

◁ Darwin's finches
Comparative studies of the beak shape and size of different species of finch on the Galápagos Islands contributed to Darwin's theory of evolution, which was set out in his treatise of 1859.

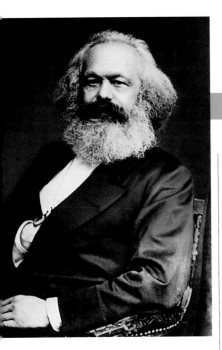

◁ **Karl Marx**
Pictured here in 1875, Marx was a philosopher, economist, and author of *Das Kapital* (1867). He did not live to see his ideas enacted in his lifetime.

1869
In Australia, the Act for "Protection and Management of Aboriginal Natives" gives the government extensive powers over the lives of aboriginals.

1870
Freed slaves in the US are given the right to vote by the Fifteenth Amendment to the Constitution.

1870–1871
The Franco-Prussian War precipitates the collapse of the French monarchy and the creation of the Third Republic; Wilhelm I of Prussia becomes Emperor of Germany, Bismarck its chancellor. The revolutionary Paris Commune demands independence; Paris is blockaded for 6 weeks before government forces violently suppress the commune.

1872
Denmark's Hans Christian Andersen publishes the last installment of his *Fairy Tales*. Cetshwayo succeeds Mpande as Zulu paramount chief; he leads his warriors against the British in 1879, but is captured at Ulundi and exiled to England.

1874
French impressionists, including Claude Monet and Paul Cézanne, hold their first exhibition in Paris. Alexander Graham Bell patents the telephone.

1875–1876
Russian composer Pyotr Ilyich Tchaikovsky writes *Swan Lake*; German composer Richard Wagner's four-opera *Ring Cycle* is first staged in Bayreuth.

1876
Lt. Colonel George Custer and his troops are killed by Sioux and Cheyenne warriors at the Battle of Little Bighorn in the Indian Wars. Britain's Queen Victoria is proclaimed Empress of India.

1877
The British annex Transvaal in South Africa when gold is found there.

1877–1878
The Balkans are reshaped when a Russian-led coalition wins the Russo-Turkish War; Bulgaria, Serbia, Romania, and Montenegro all gain independence from the Ottoman Empire.

1878
Joseph Swan patents the electric bulb in Britain; Thomas Edison soon develops electric lighting for public use.

1880–1881
In the First Anglo-Boer War, Boers in Transvaal rebel against British rule and succeed in establishing the South African Republic.

1881
Mohammed Ahmed proclaims himself the Mahdi in Sudan and begins an 18-year war against the Khedivate of Egypt and later the British in Egypt. The French occupy Tunisia. The "Czar Liberator" Alexander II is assassinated; an anti-Jewish pogrom in Russia follows, forcing many Jews to flee to western Europe, the US, and Palestine.

1882
Germany, Austria-Hungary, and Italy form the Triple Alliance against France. The British occupy Egypt after the Anglo–Egyptian War between Britain and Egyptian and Sudanese forces.

1884
General Gordon begins to evacuate the British from Sudan; he dies when Mahdist forces break their 10-month-

20,000
People killed when the French army suppressed the Paris Commune.

long siege of Khartoum and massacre the Egyptian garrison and 4,000 Sudanese civilians in January 1885.

1884–1885
European powers meet at the Berlin Conference to agree on the rules of colonization in Africa.

1885
German engineers Gottlieb Daimler and Karl Benz independently build the first automobiles powered by an internal combustion engine. The Indian National Congress is the first modern nationalist movement to emerge in the British Empire in Africa and Asia.

▷ **Custer's last stand**
General Custer makes a brave stand, with guns in both hands, as his soldiers go down in defeat, in this romanticized 1889 lithograph of the Battle of the Little Bighorn in Montana, June 25, 1876.

1888

1888–1889
Emperor Pedro II frees Brazil's remaining slaves but refuses to compensate their owners; in 1889, he is overthrown in a coup, and Brazil becomes a republic.

1889
The Eiffel Tower opens in Paris on the centenary of the French Revolution. Dutch artist Vincent van Gogh paints *The Starry Night*, a landmark of the Post-Impressionist movement.

1890
The Battle of Wounded Knee brings an end to the Indian Wars between the Great Plains Native American tribes and the US Army (1854–1890). In West Kimberley, Australia, the aboriginal resistance fighter Jandamarra declares war on European invaders and prevents them settling for 6 years.

1891
German philosopher Friedrich Nietzsche declares "God is dead" in *Thus Spake Zarathustra*. Work begins on the Trans-Siberian Railway connecting Moscow and Vladivostock.

1893
New Zealand is the first country to grant voting rights to women. Sigmund Freud and Joseph Breuer publish *On the Physical Mechanism of Hysterical Phenomena*, a founding work in the emerging field of psychoanalysis.

1894–1895
Japan gains Formosa (Taiwan) and China recognizes Korean independence after the First Sino–Japanese War.

1894–1897
In the Hamidian massacres, around 250,000 are killed in anti-Christian pogroms, directed primarily against Armenians, in the Ottoman Empire.

1895
French brothers Auguste and Nicolas Lumière show the first motion picture, lasting 46 seconds, in Paris. Italian inventor Guglielmo Marconi builds the first wireless, paving the way for the development of radio technology. German physicist Wilhelm Röntgen discovers X-rays.

1896
Emperor Menelik II secures Ethiopia's independence by defeating an invading Italian army at the Battle of Adowa.

1896–1898
The Yukon and Klondike gold rushes fuel a short-lived boom around Dawson City, Canada.

> *"All our scientific and philosophic ideals are altars to unknown gods."*
>
> WILLIAM JAMES, LECTURE AT HARVARD UNIVERSITY, 1884

1898
In the Spanish–American War, Spain cedes Puerto Rico, Guam, and the Philippines to the US and grants Cuba independence; the US annexes Hawaii.

1899
In Colombia, 100,000 die in the War of a Thousand Days.

1899–1902
In the Second Anglo–Boer War, thousands of Boer women and children die in British camps; British "scorched earth" attacks force the Boers to recognize British sovereignty in South Africa.

1900
Waves of immigrants swell the population of the US to around 75 million. Southern Nigeria becomes a British protectorate when French rivals begin to threaten British traders in the Niger Delta. In China, Qing power weakens: Chinese nationalists known as "Boxers" besiege European and US legations in Beijing until an international relief force captures the city in 1901; Russia occupies southern Manchuria. German physicist Max Planck outlines his quantum theory, that radiation comes in discrete packets (quanta) of energy.

1901
Oil is struck at Spindletop in Texas; the US becomes the world's leading oil producer and benefits from the first modern consumer boom. Six colonies in Australian federate to form the Commonwealth of Australia; the Immigration Restriction Act bars people of non-European descent from settling in the country; the policy remains in place until 1950. The death of Britain's Queen Victoria ends a 63-year reign. Italian composer Giuseppe Verdi dies, and thousands line the streets of Milan for his funeral.

1902
US philosopher William James publishes *The Varieties of Religious Experience*, exploring the nature of religion.

1903
In the US, Brothers Wilbur and Orville Wright make the first controlled, sustained flight of a powered aircraft. In Britain, suffragettes Emmeline and Christabel Pankhurst found the Women's Social and Political Union, which advocates the use of civil disobedience to secure the vote for women. Marie Curie wins the Nobel Prize for her work on radioactivity and the discovery of radium.

1904
Britain and France sign a series of agreements, known as the Entente Cordiale; Russia joins them in the Triple Entente in 1907.

1904–1905
Japan and Russia clash over Manchuria in the Russo–Japanese War; Russia is forced to leave Manchuria.

1905
Political and social unrest in the Russian Empire forces Czar Nicholas II to sign the October Manifesto, authorizing the creation of an elected legislature (the Duma). Norway secures independence

◁ **The Starry Night**
In 1889, Vincent van Gogh painted this view from the window of his room at the Saint-Paul asylum in Saint-Rémy. The turbulence in his mind is reflected in the expressive color and form of the work.

1913 ⟩

◁ **English suffragettes**
This 1908 photograph shows the suffragettes Emmeline Pankhurst and her daughter Christabel after leaving Bow Street police station in London, where they had been imprisoned.

1912

The luxury liner RMS *Titanic* sinks on her maiden voyage after hitting an iceberg; 1,513 passengers and crew perish. German geophysicist Alfred Wegener uses fossil evidence and rock formations as the basis for his theory of continental drift, paving the way for the understanding of plate tectonics. Indian polymath Rabindranath Tagore publishes *Gitanjali*; it earns him a Nobel Prize.

1912–1913

The Balkan League, backed by Russia and comprising Serbia, Bulgaria, Greece, and Montenegro, defeats the Ottoman Empire in the First Balkan War; the Ottomans lose their remaining territory in Europe. In the Second Balkan War (1913), Greece and Serbia defeat Bulgaria to gain Macedonia; Serbia's increasing power and alliance with Russia alarm Austria-Hungary and Germany.

1913

Russian composer Igor Stravinsky's avant-garde ballet *The Rite of Spring* causes a sensation and near riot at its premiere in Paris. Danish physicist Niels Bohr describes the structure of the atom. The Ford Motor Company in the US installs the world's first moving assembly line; by 1927, there is one car for every six Americans. British suffragette Emily Davison dies when she throws herself under the king's horse at the Epsom Derby. Unionists in Ulster create the Ulster Volunteer Force to block Ireland gaining more autonomy (Home Rule) from the British; in response, the Irish Volunteers are formed in Dublin.

when the union between the kingdoms of Norway and Sweden (of 1814) is dissolved. The German physicist Albert Einstein describes the relationship between space and time in his special theory of relativity; his general theory of relativity in (1915) explains the effect of gravity on spacetime.

1905–1907

The Maji-Maji rebellion threatens German settlers in East Africa.

1906

Britain launches HMS *Dreadnought*, a new class of battleship and a major development in the arms race with Germany. Mahatma Gandhi develops *satyagraha*, his policy of civil disobedience and passive resistance to be used against British rule in India.

1907

The self-governing colonies of Australia, Canada, and New Zealand are given the status of dominions of the British Empire. Belgian-American Leo Baekeland invents Bakelite, an early plastic. The rebuilt Great Mosque at Djenné in Mali is the world's largest clay building.

1908

The Young Turks—a Turkish nationalist party—demand reform in the Ottoman Empire; Austria-Hungary annexes Bosnia-Herzegovina, and Bulgaria wins recognition of its independence. The first Model T cars are produced at Ford's factory in Michigan.

1909

US Navy engineer Robert Peary claims to have reached the North Pole.

1910

In Portugal, revolutionaries depose King Manuel II and declare a republic. China invades Tibet and deposes the 13th Dalai Lama; it is a short occupation, and Tibet is independent by 1912. Japan annexes Korea. The Union of South Africa is founded as a dominion of the British Empire; it becomes a sovereign republic in 1961. The first Hollywood film is made: D. W. Griffith's *Old California*.

1910–1915

American geneticist Thomas Hunt Morgan's study of *Drosophila melanogaster* fruit flies confirms the link between the inheritance of a specific trait with a particular chromosome.

1910–1920

The Mexican Revolution leads to a new constitution (1917), presidential elections (1920), and agrarian, educational, and political reform.

1911–1912

A revolutionary alliance overthrows the Qing in China; the last emperor Puyi abdicates; Sun Yat-sen becomes the first president of the new Chinese Republic and forms the Kuomintang (Nationalist Party). Italy invades the Turkish province of Libya; it retains control there until 1947. US marines are sent to Honduras to protect American interests. In December, Norwegian explorer Roald Amundsen becomes the first man to reach the South Pole; a month later, British explorer Robert Falcon Scott's expedition reaches the pole, but none of the team survive the return journey. New Zealand-born Ernest Rutherford discovers the atomic nucleus. Later, in 1919, he successfully splits the atom in the world's first artificially created nuclear reaction. US archaeologist Hiram Bingham reaches the lost Inca city of Machu Picchu.

▷ **Model T Ford**
Mass production of Henry Ford's vehicle made driving affordable. More than 15 million of the cars were produced between 1908 and 1927.

THE MODERN WORLD 1914–PRESENT

1914

1914

The Panama Canal opens, connecting the Pacific and Atlantic Oceans. Austrian Archduke Franz Ferdinand is assassinated in Sarajevo on June 28, 1914, by a Bosnian-Serb revolutionary hoping to end Austro-Hungarian rule in Bosnia and Herzegovina; his death ignites World War I. Austria-Hungary declares war on Serbia on July 28; Russia mobilizes in Serbia's defense. Germany declares war on Russia and France on August 1 and implements the Schlieffen Plan, invading France in the hope of swiftly shutting down the war on the Western Front. Britain declares war on Germany and sends the British Expeditionary Force to France; it drives the Germans back in the Battle of the Marne; the Germans begin digging trenches that eventually total 25,000 miles (40,000 km) in length. Russia invades Austria and East Prussia but is defeated at Tannenberg. The Ottoman Empire enters the war in October. British troops invade Turkish-ruled Iraq and German East Africa. Japan joins the war, attacking German holdings in China and the Pacific.

1,197
Number who died in the sinking of the ocean liner RMS *Lusitania* in 1915.

1915

The US occupies Haiti (to 1934) and the Dominican Republic (1916–1924), securing American influence in the region. Germany begins unrestricted submarine warfare, sinking all ships on sight, but temporarily halts the operation after the sinking of the liner RMS *Lusitania* threatens to bring the US into the war. Germany makes the first use of poison gas at the Second Battle of Ypres. Allied troops land at Gallipoli and attempt to end the Turkish blockade in the Dardanelles; they suffer almost 250,000 casualties and begin to evacuate in December. Italy revokes the Triple Alliance, abandons neutrality, and declares war on Austria-Hungary. Countries across Europe abandon the Gold Standard; currency is no longer convertible into gold. The Armenian genocide begins when the Ottoman Empire rounds up Armenians suspected of harboring sympathy for the Russians; by 1923, 1.5 million Armenians have been killed or left to die in concentration camps.

1916

The British crush the nationalist Easter Rising in Ireland. Great Britain introduces conscription for all men aged 18–41. Huge offensives result in mass casualties (400,000 at Verdun, more than a million at the Somme), with little territory gained on the Western Front. The British Grand Fleet and the German High Sea Fleet clash off the coast of Denmark in the Battle of Jutland, the only major naval battle in World War I. Arab nationalists revolt against the Ottoman Empire when Hussein bin Ali, Sharif of Mecca, proclaims himself leader of the Muslim world with the intention of creating a unified Arab state. The Sykes–Picot agreement between Britain and France agrees on how the Middle East will be divided in the event of the Ottoman Empire's defeat. Jeannette Rankin is the first woman elected to the US Congress.

1917

The Russian Revolution erupts in food riots, strikes, and a military mutiny; Czar Nicholas II abdicates, and a provisional government is formed. Bolsheviks under Vladimir Ilyich Lenin and Leon Trotsky seize power; civil war breaks out. In March, the US enters World War I after discovering German foreign minister Arthur Zimmerman's telegram urging Mexico to reclaim Texas, New Mexico, and Arizona. The British

◁ **The last emperor of Russia**
Czar Nicholas II of Russia, pictured here with his family in 1913, was forced to abdicate in 1917. The family was imprisoned and executed on the orders of Bolshevik leader Vladimir Lenin.

1923

Germany becomes a republic. Charles I abdicates, ending the Habsburg monarchy in Austria–Hungary. Female suffrage is granted to British women over 30. Constance Markievicz becomes Britain's first female member of parliament.

"Politics begin where the masses are, not where there are thousands, but where there are millions; that is where serious politics begins."

VLADIMIR ILYICH LENIN, 1918

begin a new push at Ypres; fought in a sea of mud, the campaign ends in slaughter at Passchendaele in Flanders, but at the Battle of Cambrai, the British use of massed tanks provides a way to break the stalemate of trench warfare. The Balfour Declaration, made without consulting Britain's Arab allies, signals Britain's support for a Jewish homeland in Palestine. The first Pulitzer Prizes are awarded in the US.

1918
Czar Nicholas II and his family are shot near Yekaterinburg. Russia exits World War I, losing Poland, Ukraine, Belarus, Finland, and the Baltic states in the Treaty of Brest-Litovsk with the Central Powers. The Allies check Germany's Spring Offensive and launch a counter-offensive, which breaches the defenses of the Hindenburg Line. The war ends as the Ottoman Empire signs an armistice on October 30, Austria on November 3, and Germany on November 11; total casualties number around 37 million, including 15 million dead. Kaiser Wilhelm II abdicates;

585,000
The number of Allied and German troops killed at Passchendaele.

1918–1919
More than 50 million die during the Spanish influenza global pandemic.

1919
The Paris Peace Conference dismantles the German, Austrian, and Ottoman Empires; the Treaty of Versailles imposes war reparations on Germany, set at 132 billion Deutsche Marks in 1921, and restricts its military power. The Weimar Republic is established in Germany. Lenin establishes the Communist International (known as Comintern) to promote communism worldwide. Benito Mussolini founds the Fascist party in Italy to combat socialism. British aviators John Alcock and Arthur Whitten Brown make the first nonstop transatlantic flight. In the Irish War of Independence (to 1922), the Irish Republican Army mounts a campaign against the British government's forces, who are known from the color of their uniforms as "Black and Tans."

1920
The US begins Prohibition (a ban on the production and sale of alcohol). Russia's Red Army is driven back outside Warsaw after its invasion of Poland. The League of Nations is established to prevent conflicts by committing members to collective security and disarmament. Women in the US are enfranchised through the 19th amendment to the Constitution, adopted on August 18.

1921
Six million perish in Russia's famine; victorious in the civil war, Lenin begins to rebuild Russia's economy with the New Economic Policy, allowing a return to private enterprise. The Communist Party of China (CPC) is founded.

1922
The former Russian Empire becomes the Union of Soviet Socialist Republics (USSR). Britain declares Egypt an independent kingdom but retains a military presence to protect the Suez Canal. In Italy, Mussolini and his Blackshirts threaten to march on Rome and seize power; to avoid conflict, King Victor Emmanuel III makes Mussolini prime minister and head of a Fascist government. The British Empire, the largest empire in history, reaches its greatest extent; it covers one-quarter of the world's land. The African National

Congress is formed to combat discrimination against blacks in South Africa. Writer James Joyce publishes his experimental novel *Ulysses* in Paris. British archaeologist Howard Carter uncovers the tomb of Tutankhamun in Egypt. The British Broadcasting Company (BBC) is founded. The Anglo-Irish treaty (signed 1921) ends the Irish War of Independence; it divides Ireland into the Irish Free State and Northern Ireland, with separate parliaments in Dublin and Belfast; William Cosgrave becomes the Irish Free State's first prime minister. Ireland erupts in civil war (to 1923) over the Anglo-Irish Treaty.

1923
After securing Turkish independence in the Turkish War of Liberation (from 1919), President Mustafa Kemal (Ataturk) begins reforming the Turkish republic into a modern secular state. The Treaty of Lausanne settles the long conflict between the Ottoman Empire and France, Britain, Italy, Japan, Greece, and Romania and sets the borders of the Turkish Republic. Germany is crippled by war reparations payments and hyperinflation; the German currency reaches 242 million marks to the dollar; Adolf Hitler, leader of the National Socialist (Nazi) Party, is imprisoned after attempting to grab power in the Munich Beer Hall putsch; while in jail, he writes *Mein Kampf*. Miguel Primo de Rivera leads a military coup in Spain and becomes dictator.

◁ **The Battle of Cambrai**
A British tank is upturned and trapped in an enemy trench in France in 1917. The battle was an early example of tank warfare, although the machines proved unreliable.

◁ **Funerary mask of Tutankhamun**
The discovery by Howard Carter in 1922 of Tutankhamun's intact tomb caused a worldwide sensation. Tutankhamun was an Egyptian pharaoh who ruled from around 1332 to 1323 BCE.

◁ The first televised images
This photograph shows an image on the screen of John Logie Baird's pioneering television system in 1926. The face is that of Baird's business partner, Oliver Hutchinson.

◁ **The first televised images**
This photograph shows an image on the screen of John Logie Baird's pioneering television system in 1926. The face is that of Baird's business partner, Oliver Hutchinson.

1924–1936

1924
Vladimir Lenin dies and Joseph Stalin becomes leader of the Soviet Union after an intense power struggle with Leon Trotsky, Lev Kamenev, and Grigory Zinoviev (who were all members of the first Politburo, founded in 1917). Mahatma ("Great Soul") Gandhi becomes leader of India's National Congress and drives the campaign for an end to the British Raj.

1925
Mussolini becomes dictator in Italy and takes the title *Il Duce* (The Leader). Nationalists in Syria and Lebanon revolt against the French mandate to prepare the countries for self-rule. The Locarno Pact (signed in Switzerland) guarantees peace between Germany, France, Belgium, Britain, and Italy; it restores relations with Germany as a precursor to Germany joining the League of Nations in 1926. The Geneva Protocol prohibits the use of chemical and biological weapons; the US and Japan reject the agreement.

1926
In China, Chiang Kai-shek succeeds Sun Yat-sen as leader of the Chinese Nationalist Party (Kuomintang). Scottish inventor John Logie Baird gives the first public demonstration of television. Reza Khan Pahlavi becomes shah of Iran and begins to modernize the country; his dynasty rules until 1979. Military coups overthrow the governments in Poland and Portugal.

1927
Chiang Kai-shek purges Chinese communists in the Shanghai massacre. In the Soviet Union, Leon Trotsky is expelled from the Communist Party on Stalin's orders and exiled (1929); he is assassinated in Mexico in 1940 by a Spanish-born agent of the NKVD (the organization that what would later become the Soviet Secret Police). American aviator Charles Lindbergh makes the first solo flight across the Atlantic. *The Jazz Singer*, starring Al Jolson and directed by Alan Crosland, is the first talking motion picture. Oil is discovered in Iraq.

1928
Stalin's Five Year Plan (the first of many Soviet plans) aims to transform the Soviet Union through rapid industrialization and the collectivization of farms. Kuomintang forces take Beijing and declare the Nationalist Government of China with Chiang Kai-shek as Chairman; Mao Zedong leads communist resistance in remote rural areas. Penicillin, the first antibiotic, is discovered by Scottish biologist and pharmacologist Alexander Fleming.

1929
Riots in Palestine see Arabs attack Jewish immigrants. The Kenyan politician Jomo Kenyatta travels to London to press the Kikuyu Central Association's demands for equality in Kenya. The Stock Market Crash bursts the American stock market bubble, plunging the world into the Great Depression, which lasts until the late 1930s. American astronomer Edwin Hubble calculates that the Universe is expanding and has more than 100 billion galaxies. Belgian cartoonist Hergé publishes the first Tintin comic strip, *Tintin in the Land of the Soviets*. The BBC runs trials on its first TV broadcasts.

1930
Hundreds of thousands of peasants are sent to gulags (forced labor camps) for resisting the Soviet Union's mass collectivization of farms. The Vietnamese Communist Party is founded by Ho Chi Minh. Thousands join Gandhi's Salt March to protest against government monopolies and British rule in India; Gandhi and around 60,000 others are arrested.

1930
Mass unemployment and political extremism follow the collapse of the world economy: Hitler's Nazi party becomes the second largest political party in Germany; an army revolt brings autocrat Getúlio Vargas to power in Brazil. Ras Tafari becomes Emperor of Ethiopia, taking the name Haile Selassie; in Jamaica, the cult of Rastafarianism views Ras Tafari as the Black Messiah.

1931
In Spain, King Alfonso abdicates after elections return a Republican government. Japan occupies Manchuria; in 1934 it installs Puyi (China's last emperor) as emperor of the new state, which is known as Manchukuo. The

> *"Nonviolence is the first article of my faith. It is the last article of my faith."*
>
> MAHATMA GANDHI, 1922

British Commonwealth is formalized by the Statute of Westminster. Belgian astronomer Georges Lemaître argues that quantum theory supports the idea that the universe came into being from the explosion of a "primeval atom" holding all mass and energy; his ideas are later developed into the Big Bang Theory. The Empire State Building opens in New York.

1932

Britain terminates its mandate in Iraq, and the kingdom becomes independent; Ibn Saʿūd unifies the dual kingdoms of Hejaz and Najd in the new Kingdom of Saudi Arabia. Paraguay and Bolivia go to war over control of the Gran Chaco lowland plain; Paraguay wins, but by 1935, more than 85,000 have died. With more than 12 million people unemployed in the US, newly elected president Franklin D. Roosevelt promises "a new deal" to salvage the economy. In Germany, the Nazis become the largest party in fresh elections to the Reichstag but continue to be excluded from government. American aviator Amelia Earhart becomes the first woman to fly solo across the Atlantic; she disappears over the Pacific in 1937 while attempting to fly around the world.

1932–1933

Soviet collectivization results in the "Great Famine"; 6–8 million peasants die over the winter, including 4–5 million in Ukraine.

2,500,000

The number of people who fled the Great Plains during the years of the US Dust Bowl.

1933

Adolf Hitler is appointed Chancellor of Germany and soon creates a one-party state in which opposition is brutally suppressed by the SS and Gestapo. A nationwide boycott of Jewish shops and businesses begins; the first Nazi concentration camp opens at Dachau; in a crackdown on "un-German" culture, students burn books and Germany's famous school of modern art and architecture, the Bauhaus, is closed. Germany quits the League of Nations. The World Economic Conference fails to agree to global measures to alleviate the Depression. Japan leaves the League of Nations after it declares the occupation of Manchuria illegal.

1934

Hitler authorizes the execution of members of the Nazi Party's paramilitary wing, the Storm Detachment (or Brownshirts), in the Night of the Long Knives; President Hindenburg dies and Hitler becomes *Führer* (leader). The Nazis are banned in Austria by its dictatorial chancellor Engelbert Dollfuss; he is assassinated by Nazis. The Soviet Union joins the League of Nations.

1934–1935

In the Long March, Mao Zedong and his communist forces retreat around 6,000 miles (10,000 km) from the Jiangxi Soviet (a communist base formed in 1931) to Yan'an, evading Chiang Kai-shek's nationalist forces.

1934–1937

Thousands of destitute farmers migrate west to California from the Great Plains after drought, intensive farming, and giant dust storms strip the land of topsoil in the 1932 Dust Bowl disaster.

1935–1939

The US passes several Neutrality Acts that seek to maintain American isolationism and prevent the country from being drawn into foreign conflicts.

1935

Hitler builds Germany's army through conscription (banned by the Treaty of Versailles); the Nuremberg Laws deprive Jews of German citizenship and ban marriage between Jews and non-Jews. Emperor Haile Selassie leads resistance to Italian invasion of Ethiopia; economic sanctions are imposed on Italy.

1936

Germany moves troops unopposed into the demilitarized Rhineland; Britain and France begin expanding their armed forces. Italy annexes Ethiopia; Haile Selassie warns "It is us today; it will be you tomorrow. " With the Anti-Comintern Pact, Germany and Japan declare their hostility to communism and agree that neither country will make any treaties with the USSR; Spain and Italy join the pact in 1937, forming the basis of the Axis Powers. Stalin begins the Great Purge of the Communist party, government officials, army leaders, intellectuals, and peasants with a series of show trials of "Old Bolsheviks;" between 680,000 and 2 million people are killed over the next 2 years. Spain is thrown into Civil War when General Francisco Franco leads a nationalist revolt against the newly elected left-wing Popular Front government. The Nationalists are backed by Germany and Italy, while the Republicans are backed by the Soviet Union and supported by International Brigades of volunteers from Europe and North America; the Nationalists prevail in 1939, and Franco becomes dictator.

1936–1943

1936–1939
Arabs in Palestine revolt against the British administration of the Palestine Mandate; they demand an end to unrestricted Jewish immigration; plans to resolve the crisis by partitioning Palestine between Arabs and Jews have to be abandoned, and the British agree to restrict Jewish immigration.

1937
Japan invades northern China, sparking the Second Sino-Japanese War, which continues throughout World War II; by 1938, Japanese troops have captured Nanjing, Shanghai, Hankou, and Guangzhou, massacring more than 1,000,000 civilians and using rape as an instrument of war in the "Rape of Nanjing"; resistance comes from both the Kuomintang and the communist 8th Route Army. Brazil's President Vargas uses the threat of a communist coup to create a new constitution, the Estado Novo (New State), giving himself dictatorial powers. Pablo Picasso paints the gigantic *Guernica*, a response to the German bombing of the town of Guernica in northern Spain during the Spanish Civil War. The German-built *Hindenburg*, then the world's largest airship, explodes on arrival in the US.

The British engineer Frank Whittle successfully runs trials on his turbojet engine; it is used in Britain's first jet aircraft, tested in 1941.

1938
In the *Anschluss* (unification), German troops march on Vienna and annex Austria in direct contravention of the peace terms of 1919. Hoping to avoid war, Britain and France continue their policy of appeasement and allow Germany to annex Sudetenland from Czechoslovakia. On November 9, *Kristallnacht* (the Night of Broken Glass), the Nazis orchestrate attacks on Jewish homes, businesses, and schools in Germany and Austria.

> *"Never in the field of human conflict was so much owed by so many to so few."*
>
> WINSTON CHURCHILL, 1940

▷ Star of David badge
Following a decree issued by the German Reich in 1941, all Jews over the age of 6 were forced to wear this badge, inscribed with the word "Jude" (German for "Jew").

Japan declares its intention to create a New Order in East Asia, essentially acknowledging its imperial ambitions; the US begins to finance Chiang Kai-shek's resistance to Japan.

1939

World War II begins: Germany invades Czechoslovakia; Britain and France guarantee Polish independence; Hitler and Mussolini sign the Pact of Steel military alliance; the Soviet Union and Germany sign the Molotov-Ribbentrop nonaggression pact (named after the foreign ministers of the two nations); Germany invades Poland on

September 1; Britain and France declare war 2 days later. Poland is partitioned by the Soviet Union and Germany. The Soviet Union attacks Finland. Merchant ships crossing the Atlantic begin to sail in convoy; 114 Allied ships are sunk in the first year of war.

1940

Germany unleashes the *Blitzkrieg* (lightning war) on Europe: Denmark, Norway, the Netherlands, Belgium, Luxembourg, and France are invaded. Britain evacuates 338,000 men from the beaches of Dunkirk, France. France surrenders; the French government

under Marshal Pétain relocates to Vichy; Charles de Gaulle positions himself as the figurehead of the French Resistance. Italy declares war on Britain and France. Britain's Royal Air Force (RAF) blocks the German *Luftwaffe*'s attack in the Battle of Britain, forcing Hitler to abandon plans to invade Britain. Germany begins the mass transportation of prisoners to the Auschwitz concentration camp in southern Poland. The *Luftwaffe* begin mass bombing raids on British cities; the Blitz lasts until 1941; Allied bombers retaliate with raids on Germany. The US restricts sales of iron and oil to Japan in an attempt to curb Japanese aggression; the US Pacific Fleet is moved to Pearl Harbor, Hawaii. The British hold off the Italian invasion of Egypt. Japan, Germany, and Italy form an alliance in the Tripartite Pact.

1941

Germany begins Operation Barbarossa: 3 million troops invade the USSR and advance on Leningrad, besieging the city; by December, the Germans are exhausted and forced to retreat from Moscow. Japan annexes Indochina. Japan bombs the US fleet in Pearl Harbor on December 7 and invades the Philippines and European colonies in Southeast Asia, securing control of the Pacific; the US enters the war.

1942

At the Wannsee Conference in Berlin, senior Nazi officials are briefed on the systematic deportation and extermination of Jews across Europe; by 1945, 6 million Jews have been killed.

A US victory against the Imperial Japanese Navy at the Battle of Midway in the Pacific proves a turning point in the war in the Pacific. Japan begins construction of the Burma–Thailand railway using British, Australian, and Dutch prisoners of war and native laborers; within 3 years, more than 100,000 of them die under appalling conditions. In the Battle of Stalingrad (to 1943), Germans capture the city but are encircled by Soviet troops; few survive the freezing conditions during the siege, and the German defeat is a turning point in the war; more than 1.7 million soldiers are killed, wounded, or captured in the battle. In North Africa, German troops under Erwin Rommel reach the borders of Egypt; defeated by the British at El Alamein, and under pressure from advancing Allied troops, the Axis Powers in Africa surrender (1943). The Quit India campaign sees leaders of the Indian National Congress imprisoned.

1943

Jews in the Warsaw Ghetto resist German efforts to transport them; 13,000 die in the uprising, and most of the remaining 50,000 Jews are shipped to Nazi death camps. At Kursk, the Soviets win the largest tank battle in history. US and British troops invade Sicily; Mussolini is removed from power, and Italy surrenders.

1,000

The number of Jewish synagogues burned on *Kristallnacht*.

◁ *Guernica, 1937*
Pablo Picasso painted this violent, mural-sized masterpiece in response to the deliberate bombing by Nazi aircraft of civilians in the Basque village of Guernica.

1944

1944

The 900-day siege of Leningrad is lifted. Polish troops break the German defensive line in Italy at Monte Cassino; the Allies take Rome. The Allies launch an invasion of occupied France, landing more than 130,000 troops in Normandy on D-Day (June 6); over the coming weeks, more than 3 million Allied troops land in France. Hitler survives an assassination attempt by officers and high officials. General Charles de Gaulle's Free French forces and resistance fighters liberate Paris on August 25. Japanese naval pilots start to mount *kamikaze* suicide attacks on US naval forces in the Pacific. At the Battle of the Bulge in the Ardennes, Hitler launches Germany's final offensive;

German tanks break through the American front line but are defeated in a counterattack; the German troops retreat to Germany.

1945

British Prime Minister Winston Churchill, US president Franklin D. Roosevelt, and Soviet premier Joseph Stalin meet at Yalta to discuss Europe's postwar reorganization. The Red Army takes Poland and marches on Berlin. Hitler commits suicide, and the war in Europe ends when Germany surrenders on May 8. At the Potsdam Conference, Germany, Austria, Berlin, and Vienna are divided into four occupation zones, and parts of Poland, Finland, Romania, Germany, and the Balkans are assigned

to Soviet control. Rather than invade Japan, the US drops the world's first atomic bombs on the Japanese cities of Hiroshima on August 6 and Nagasaki on August 9; Japan surrenders on August 15, ending the war in the Pacific. The Nuremberg trials of leading Nazi war criminals begin. Vietnam is declared an independent republic by Ho Chi Minh ("He Who Enlightens"), leader of the Viet Minh nationalist coalition. The president of the Indian National Congress, Jawaharlal Nehru, demands full independence from Britain. Fifty-one countries sign the newly created United Nations (UN) Charter for the promotion of peace, security, cooperation, and self-determination of nations.

1946

Churchill refers to an "iron curtain" falling across Europe as communist governments are set up in Yugoslavia (1945), Bulgaria and Albania (1946), Poland and Romania (1947), Czechoslovakia (1948), and Hungary (1949). China's communists and nationalists resume civil war. France recognizes Vietnam, Cambodia, and Laos as autonomous states, but resistance to colonial authority soon triggers the First Indochina War (1946–1954).

1947

India becomes independent; to avoid civil war between Hindus and Muslims, a new state (Pakistan) is created in the Muslim-majority areas in the northwest

and northeast of India, 1,000 miles (1,600 km) apart; widespread violence nonetheless follows partition as Muslims flee India and Hindus leave Pakistan. The United States' European Recovery Plan, or Marshall Plan, aims to help Europe's shattered economies recover, thus ensuring a market for American exports and making the spread of communism in western Europe less likely. The UN proposes to divide Palestine into separate Jewish and Arab states. The sound barrier is broken for the first time by American test pilot Chuck Yeager in a Bell X-1 aircraft.

1948

Gandhi is shot and killed by a Hindu fanatic. The South African government begins to increase the amount of legislation that supports its policy of apartheid; the Population Registration Act (1950) makes it compulsory for people to carry a pass identifying their racial group. The state of Israel is proclaimed; soon after, it repulses an invasion by five Arab states (Egypt, Iraq, Lebanon, Syria, and Transjordan) in the First Arab–Israeli War (to 1949). In the first crisis of the Cold War, the Soviet Union blockades Berlin, hoping to force the West to withdraw from West Berlin. Burma and Ceylon become independent. Korea is partitioned into

> *"The seeds of totalitarian regimes are nurtured by misery and want."*
>
> PRESIDENT HARRY S. TRUMAN, 1947

◁ **The bombing of Hiroshima**
On August 6, 1945, an American B-29 bomber dropped an atomic bomb over the city of Hiroshima; approximately 80,000 people were killed in the initial blast alone.

the Republic of Korea in the south and the Democratic People's Republic in the north. Communists in Malaya begin a guerrilla war against British colonial rule; the Malayan Emergency (1948–1960) continues for 3 years after Malaya gains independence (1957). The Universal Declaration of Human Rights is adopted by the United Nations. The World Health Organization (WHO) is set up in Geneva, Switzerland.

1949

Germany is divided into East and West; East Germany is part of the Communist Bloc. Twelve nations join in the North Atlantic Treaty Organization (NATO), a military alliance for mutual defense. Eire becomes the Republic of Ireland. The Soviet Union tests its first atomic bomb. After 4 years of war, the Dutch are forced to accept the independence of the East Indies (Indonesia). The Communists emerge victorious in China's civil war; Mao Zedong declares the People's Republic of China; Chiang Kai-shek and the remnants of the nationalist Republic of China government flee to Taiwan. Following the Arab–Israeli War, the Gaza Strip is controlled by Egypt and the West Bank of the River Jordan by Jordan.

1950

Senator Joseph McCarthy begins his investigation into alleged Communist activity in the US; over the next 4 years, many people—including prominent Hollywood actors and writers—are accused and blacklisted. The Korean War (to 1953) begins when North Korea invades South Korea; in the first major armed confrontation of the Cold War, US and UN troops support the South, while the Soviet Union and China back the North. Tibet is incorporated into the People's Republic of China, but formally remains autonomous under the Dalai Lama.

1951

Mohammad Mosaddegh is appointed prime minister of Iran and nationalizes the oil industry; 2 years later, a US-sponsored coup to replace Mosaddegh fails.

1952

East Germany tightens control of its border with West Germany in an attempt to stop the flow of its citizens to the West. Gamal Abdel Nasser seizes power in a military coup in Egypt. Britain drafts troops into Kenya to deal with the anti-colonial Mau Mau Rebellion (to 1960). At Bikini Atoll in the Pacific, the US tests the first hydrogen bomb.

1953

Stalin dies; under his successor, Nikita Khrushchev, there is a thaw in relations between Russia and the West. The shah returns to Iran after Mosaddegh is ejected in a coup; US and UK support strengthens the shah's position as he reprivatizes the oil industry. In the UK, Francis Crick and

James Watson build on the work of Rosalind Franklin and Maurice Wilkins and discover the double helix structure of DNA (deoxyribonucleic acid), the molecule that governs heredity. New Zealand explorer Edmund Hillary and Sherpa Tenzing Norgay scale Mount Everest, the world's highest mountain.

1954

French rule in Indochina collapses: Vietnam is partitioned into Ho Chi Minh's Democratic Republic of Vietnam in the north and the State of Vietnam in the south; Laos and Cambodia also become independent. The first nuclear-powered submarine, USS *Nautilus*, is

10

megatons of TNT. The yield of the first hydrogen bomb. It is 100 times more powerful than the Hiroshima bomb.

launched. CERN, the European Organization for Nuclear Research, is established in Geneva, Switzerland, to examine the fundamental structure of the universe.

1955

The Eastern Bloc counters NATO with its own military alliance, the Warsaw Pact. Juan Perón is ousted as president in Argentina. Rosa Parks becomes an inspirational figure in the US Civil Rights movement when she breaks Alabama's race laws by refusing to give up her seat on a bus to a white man. The Vietnam War (to 1975) begins: South Vietnam rejects reunification with communist North Vietnam; Viet Minh sympathizers, or "Viet Cong" (Vietnamese Communists), in the South begin an insurgency; the US offers support to Ngo Dinh Diem's government in South Vietnam.

1956

Soviet troops invade Hungary when Prime Minister Imre Nagy withdraws from the Warsaw Pact and asks the UN to recognize Hungary as a neutral state. Egypt's President Nasser nationalizes the Suez Canal; British and French forces occupy the canal but are forced to withdraw, a sign of their declining power. Decolonization continues as France withdraws from Morocco and Tunisia and Britain withdraws from Sudan.

▷ **The conquest of Everest**
Sir Edmund Hillary and Tenzing Norgay are photographed on Mount Everest on May 28, 1953; they reach the summit the next day.

◁ The beginning of the jet age
Entering service with Pan American Airlines in 1958, the Boeing 707 replaced an earlier generation of piston-engined airliners, making international air travel safer and more affordable.

1957

1957

Six countries join the European Economic Community (EEC), created by the Treaty of Rome. The USSR launches the *Sputnik 1* satellite and begins the Space Age. President Sukarno of Indonesia nationalizes Dutch businesses, expels all Dutch nationals, and imposes martial law. Sudan and Ghana are the first British colonies in Africa to gain independence.

1958

Forced industrialization in Mao's "Great Leap Forward" plunges China into one of history's worst famines; over 35 million are worked, starved, or beaten to death. General de Gaulle is elected president of the Fifth Republic in France. NASA (North American Space Agency) is established. The Boeing 707 begins commercial flights across the Atlantic, revolutionizing air travel.

1959

The Cuban Revolution makes Fidel Castro the first communist head of state in the Americas. The Dalai Lama and 80,000 Tibetans flee to India when China takes full control of Tibet. North Vietnamese guerrillas invade South Vietnam; two US soldiers are killed. The US gains its 49th and 50th states: Alaska and Hawaii.

1960

In Africa, 12 French colonies, Congo (Belgian), and Nigeria and Somalia (British) gain independence. The Organization of the Petroleum Exporting Countries (OPEC) is founded to coordinate policy and provide members with economic and technical aid. John F. Kennedy becomes US president.

Civil war (to 1964) breaks out in the Congo; the UN is nearly bankrupted by its attempts to restore order there. The South African government begins the forced resettlement of black South Africans to so-called "black homelands." The US physicist Theodore H. Maiman builds the first laser.

1961

The Soviet rocket *Vostok 1* carries Yuri Gagarin into space. American troops begin to arrive in South Korea. South Africa withdraws from the British Commonwealth and becomes a republic. In the Bay of Pigs invasion, US-trained Cuban exiles invade Cuba, aiming to overthrow Castro's government; they are soon defeated. East German troops build the Berlin Wall; it eventually extends over 100 miles (160 km), dividing the city and encircling West Berlin.

1962

Algeria, Uganda, Jamaica, and Trinidad and Tobago become independent. The first communication satellite, *Telstar I*, relays international telephone calls and transmits its first television signals from Europe to the US. Nuclear war between the US and the Soviet Union is narrowly avoided during the Cuban Missile Crisis.

1963

The Test Ban Treaty, signed by the US, USSR, and UK, ends nuclear testing in the atmosphere. At the March on Washington, civil rights leader Martin Luther King Jr. addresses 250,000 protesters. President Kennedy is assassinated in Dallas; Lee Harvey Oswald is arrested, but is shot soon after. Singapore, Sarawak, and Sabah join the 11 states of the Federation of Malaya to create Malaysia. Jomo Kenyatta becomes prime minister, then president, of a fully independent Kenya.

1964

The UN sends troops to Cyprus (which has been independent from Britain since 1960) after civil war breaks out between the Greek and Turkish populations; Turkish Cypriots are confined to small enclaves of the island. US President Lyndon B. Johnson signs the Civil Rights Act into law, creating equal rights for all, regardless of race, religion, or color. Nelson Mandela, leader of the anti-apartheid Spear of the Nation movement, is sentenced to life imprisonment in South Africa for conspiring to overthrow the state.

> *"Palestine is the cement that holds the Arab world together, or it is the explosive that blows it apart."*
>
> YASSER ARAFAT, 1974

1965

The US begins bombing North Vietnam in the hope that Ho Chi Minh will stop Viet Cong operations in South Vietnam; 500,000 US troops land in South Vietnam. Pakistani troops invade the Indian zone in Kashmir; the UN intervenes to secure a ceasefire.

1966

Mao's Cultural Revolution aims to rid China of "impure elements;" by 1976, much of China's cultural heritage is destroyed in the process.

1967

Indonesia, Malaysia, the Philippines, Singapore, and Thailand form the Association of Southeast Asian Nations (ASEAN). Martial law is imposed in Greece after a military coup. Israel seizes Sinai, the Gaza Strip, West Bank, Golan Heights, and Jerusalem in the Six-Day (or Arab–Israeli) War. One million Igbo people flee Hausa violence for eastern Nigeria, which secedes as Biafra; civil war ensues, and Biafra is reincorporated into Nigeria in 1970. Australian Aborigines are finally given full citizenship rights.

▷ The assassination of JFK
President Kennedy and his wife smile at the crowds lining their motorcade route in Dallas, Texas, on November 22, 1963, just minutes before the president is assassinated.

1975

▷ Moon landings
Apollo 11 Lunar Module pilot Buzz Aldrin walks on the surface of the Moon on July 20, 1969. Aldrin and Armstrong spent less than 22 hours on the lunar surface.

1968
The Viet Cong capture the majority of South Vietnam's towns and villages in the Tet Offensive; the US public is convinced that the Vietnam War is unwinnable. Martin Luther King Jr. is assassinated in Memphis; his death sparks race riots across the US. Warsaw Pact troops invade Czechoslovakia and crush the Prague Spring reform movement. Saddam Hussein plays a prominent role in helping the socialist Ba'ath party seize power in Iraq.

1969
Yasser Arafat becomes leader of the Palestine Liberation Organization (PLO). Mu'ammar al-Gaddafi deposes King Idris and forms the Libyan Arab Republic. Sectarian violence escalates in Northern Ireland; the Troubles continue until 1998. American astronauts Neil Armstrong and Buzz Aldrin are the first men on the Moon.

1970
The Nuclear Non-Proliferation Treaty, ratified by the US, the Soviet Union, Britain, and 40 other countries, aims to prevent the spread of nuclear weapons.

1971
Idi Amin seizes power in Uganda. India supports the Mukti Bahini in the War of Liberation in East Pakistan; East Pakistan becomes the independent state of Bangladesh. Qatar becomes independent from Britain. The People's Republic of China joins the UN.

1972
On Bloody Sunday, British troops open fire on Catholic demonstrators in Londonderry, Northern Ireland; support for the Irish Republican Army grows. Palestinian terrorists kill members of Israel's team at the Munich Olympics. In the Philippines, President Ferdinand Marcos imposes martial law.

1973
US troops finally withdraw from Vietnam. The IRA begins bombing targets in mainland Britain. In the US-backed military coup led by General Augusto Pinochet, Chile's Marxist president Salvador Allende commits suicide (or is murdered) after delivering a farewell speech over the radio. In the Yom Kippur (or October) War, Israel repulses Arab attacks led by Egypt and Syria; OPEC embargoes oil exports to the US and the Netherlands, Israel's main supporters, causing oil shortages and spiraling inflation; oil-importing countries begin to find other sources of oil and invest in coal, gas, and nuclear power. Denmark, Ireland, and the UK join the EEC. Mohammad Daoud Khan seizes power and establishes the Republic of Afghanistan. Companies IBM and Xerox develop prototype personal computers, and the first telephone call from a handheld cellphone is made in the US.

1974
Democracy is restored in Portugal when a bloodless coup brings an end to the dictatorial Estado Novo regime. Portugal's African colonies gain independence: Guinea Bissau in 1974; Cape Verde, Angola, Mozambique, and São Tomé and Príncipe in 1975. Turkish troops occupy northeast Cyprus; Greek Cypriots flee to the south, and the country is partitioned. US President Richard Nixon resigns after being implicated in the Watergate bugging scandal. English scientist Stephen Hawking outlines his theory on black hole radiation, known as "Hawking radiation." Isabel Péron succeeds her husband in Argentina and is Latin America's first female president.

1975
The fall of Saigon to North Vietnamese troops ends the Vietnamese War; North and South Vietnam are reunified in 1976. Civil war breaks out in Lebanon (to 1990). Pol Pot's Khmer Rouge seizes power in Cambodia and begins a reign of terror in which, by 1979, over 1 million people are killed. Civil war (to 2002) erupts in Angola between US-funded guerrillas and South African troops and communist guerrillas funded by the USSR and supported by Cuban troops. Indonesia invades East Timor; decades of guerrilla resistance and brutal suppression follow. The monarchy is restored in Spain when General Franco dies; Juan Carlos I is king.

10
The number of people to have landed on the surface of the Moon since the *Apollo 11* mission of 1969.

◁ Khomeini in Iran
Ayatollah Khomeini waves to supporters after his return to Tehran in February 1979. He declares an Islamic republic and is appointed Iran's political and religious leader for life.

1976

1,000,000 The estimated number of people on both sides killed during the Iran–Iraq War of 1980–1988.

1976
Chairman Mao dies; the Gang of Four (who controlled the government in line with Mao's wishes) are arrested, two are sentenced to death, the others are imprisoned. Syrian peacekeeping troops enter Lebanon. In Soweto, South Africa, 176 people are killed in clashes with the police during anti-apartheid protests.

1977
Prominent black rights activist Steve Biko is tortured to death in prison in South Africa. Pakistan's Prime Minister Zulfikar al Bhutto is overthrown in a military coup; accused of conspiracy, he is executed in 1978. Mengistu Haile Mariam takes control of the Dergue (ruling body) in Ethiopia and begins to build a communist state.

1978
Israeli troops enter Lebanon; the Camp David Accords pave the way for the Egypt–Israel Treaty in 1979. In Afghanistan, Daoud is assassinated and an unstable regime takes over. Vietnamese troops invade Cambodia; in 1979, the Khmer Rouge is overthrown; civil war in Cambodia continues until 1991, when Vietnam withdraws. The first "test-tube baby" is born following conception by *in vitro* fertilization (IVF). Numerous strikes by public sector workers in Britain create the "winter of discontent."

1979
Idi Amin's brutal regime in Uganda is overthrown; he dies in exile in Saudi Arabia in 2003. The US-backed Somoza regime in Nicaragua is overthrown by left-wing Sandinistas; their opponents, backed by the CIA, form a militia known as the Contras. In Iran, an Islamic revolution sees Ayatollah Khomeini return to Iran when the shah is ousted; he leads the Islamic Republic of Iran until his death in 1989; Iranian militants seize 63 hostages from Tehran's US embassy. Soviet troops invade Afghanistan to suppress an Islamist revolt (to 1989) by US-armed guerrilla Mujaheddin forces; 6 million refugees flee to Iran and Pakistan. Panama regains control of the Panama Canal Zone; it gains control of the canal itself in 1999. Saddam Hussein becomes President of Iraq with absolute power.

1980
Rhodesia becomes independent as Zimbabwe; Robert Mugabe becomes Prime Minister. Saddam Hussein's Iraq invades Iran; the Iran–Iraq war (to 1988) results in huge casualties on both sides. The US ends aid to Nicaragua and funds the Contras in Honduras. Polish dockyard strikers form Solidarność, a trade union independent of Communist Party control that swiftly develops, under Lech Wałęsa, into a political movement. The WHO ensures smallpox is the first infectious disease to be eradicated.

1981
President Anwar Sadat of Egypt is assassinated by Muslim terrorists angry at the peace agreement with Israel. Pope John Paul II and US president Ronald Reagan are both shot, but survive. The US hostage crisis in Tehran ends after 444 days, when Iran releases 52 hostages. King Juan Carlos survives a military coup, in which rebels hold members of the Spanish parliament hostage. AIDS (Acquired Immune Deficiency Syndrome) is first identified in the US; scientists identify the HIV virus responsible for AIDS in 1984. The first "keyhole" surgery is performed. Polish government imposes martial law.

1982
Argentinian troops invade the Falkland Islands; a British task force brings the war to an end after 10 weeks; Argentine dictator Leopold Galtieri resigns. Israel invades Lebanon and besieges Beirut, forcing the PLO to move its headquarters to Tunis; militant group Hezbollah emerges in Lebanon and aims to establish an Islamic state there. In Poland, the trade union Solidarność is banned and its leaders arrested.

1983
Tamil Tigers seeking an independent state begin a war in Sri Lanka; they are defeated in 2009. Sudan imposes Sharia law, prompting civil war between the Christian south and Muslim north; South Sudan becomes independent when the war ends in 2005. Terrorists in Lebanon bomb the US embassy in Beirut and the French and US peacekeeping headquarters. The USSR shoots down a Korean airliner it mistakes for a US spy plane. US troops invade Grenada after a Marxist coup raises concerns about the spread of communism; constitutional government is restored in 1984. General Noriega becomes dictator in Panama.

▷ **Polish Solidarity**
Polish police block demonstrators supporting the trade union Solidarność (Solidarity), which has become a national movement of resistance backed by the Roman Catholic Church.

◁ Tamil Tigers
Many young men and boys joined the Tamil Tigers fighting for an independent Tamil homeland in the north of Sri Lanka.

1990

9 billion light-years. The distance of the farthest star detected by the Hubble Space Telescope.

Solidarność is leg alized and Lech Wałęsa becomes Poland's first postcommunist president in 1990; communist regimes fall in Czechoslovakia, Hungary, Bulgaria, Romania, and East Germany; citizens breach the Berlin Wall, symbolically ending the Cold War. Democracy is restored in Chile with the collapse of Pinochet's military regime and election of Patricio Aylwin. British engineer Sir Tim Berners-Lee outlines his concept for a World Wide Web. US troops invade Panama City and capture General Noriega after blasting rock music at the Vatican embassy where he was taking shelter; in the US, he is jailed for drug trafficking and money laundering.

1990
In South Africa, President F. W. de Klerk lifts the ban on the African National Congress (ANC), frees Nelson Mandela, and repeals the remaining apartheid laws (1991). Namibia gains independence from South Africa. UN forces are sent to the Persian Gulf after Iraq invades Kuwait. East and West Germany are reunited as the Federal Republic of Germany. The Hubble Space Telescope (HST) goes into orbit 340 miles (547 km) above Earth's atmosphere. Aung San Suu Kyi's party wins the election in Myanmar, but she is kept under house arrest. The Sandinis tas are defeated in free elections in Nicaragua; Daniel Ortega is replaced by Violeta Barrios de Chamorro.

1984–1985
The Ethiopian famine is one of the 20th century's deadliest disasters, as more than 400,000 people die and millions are left destitute; civil war hampers international relief efforts.

1984
India's prime minister Indira Gandhi orders troops to oust Sikh extremists occupying a complex at Amritsar that includes the Golden Temple (the center of the Sikh religion); she is assassinated by her own Sikh bodyguards soon after. Toxic methyl isocyanate gas leaks from the Union Carbide pesticide plant in Bhopal, India; 500,000 people are exposed and 2,000 die as a result.

1985
In the USSR, Mikhail Gorbachev is elected Executive President; his policies of *glasnost* (openness) and *perestroika* (restructuring) bring Russia closer to the US and Europe. In the UK, a miners' strike ends after 11 months; prime minister Margaret Thatcher succeeds in breaking the power of the industrial unions. A hole in the ozone layer over Antarctica is discovered.

1986
Ferdinand Marcos, dictator of the Philippines, flees after being defeated in the election. The US responds to a terrorist attack on US soldiers in Berlin believed to have been ordered by Libya by bombing Tripoli. Radioactive contamination spreads across Europe after an explosion at the Chernobyl nuclear power plant in Ukraine. The US and Commonwealth impose limited economic sanctions on South Africa in protest against apartheid.

1987
The US and USSR sign the INF (Intermediate-range Nuclear Forces) Treaty. Palestinians fight against Israeli occupation of the West Bank and Gaza in the First Intifada (to 1993). On Black Monday, the US stock market experiences its worst crash since 1929.

1988
A bomb aboard PanAm flight 103 explodes over Lockerbie, Scotland, killing 270 people; Libya accepts responsibility in 2003. Osama bin Laden founds the terrorist organization al-Qaeda. Cuban and South African troops withdraw from Angola and Namibia. Martial law is imposed in Burma, which is renamed Myanmar; opposition leaders, including Aung San Suu Kyi, are imprisoned.

1989
More than 1 million protesters gather in Tiananmen Square, Beijing, to call for economic and political reform; over 3,000 are killed and 10,000 injured when Chinese troops and tanks open fire. Soviet troops withdraw from Afghanistan. A series of revolutions tears down the Iron Curtain: in Poland,

"The essence of perestroika *lies in the fact that it unites socialism with democracy ..."*

MIKHAIL GORBACHEV, FROM *PERESTROIKA*, 1987

◁ **Flag of the European Union**
The Maastricht Treaty, signed in February 1992, laid the foundations for a single European currency and expanded cooperation between countries in a number of areas.

1991–2004

1991
UN forces expel Iraqi troops from Kuwait in the First Gulf War. The Paris Peace Accords end the Cambodian–Vietnamese War. The USSR is dissolved, breaking into 15 countries; Russia, Ukraine, and Belarus form the Commonwealth of Independent States (CIS). Boris Yeltsin is elected first president of the Russian Federation. Yugoslavia disintegrates, and the region descends into a series of civil wars: Slovenia and Croatia declare their independence; Slovenia repels the Serb-dominated Yugoslav People's Army in the Ten-Day War; fighting in Croatia ends in 1995. Mengistu flees Ethiopia when the Ethiopian People's Revolutionary Democratic Front takes control; he is later sentenced to death for crimes against humanity. Civil war (to 2002) breaks out in Algeria between the government and various Islamic militant groups.

1992
The Maastricht Treaty creates the European Union (EU) and commits its 12 signatory states to common citizenship and common economic and defense policies. Bosnia and Herzegovina seek independence from the remnant of Yugoslavia, sparking the Bosnian War (to 1995); Radovan Karadžić's policy of ethnic cleansing results in the systematic destruction of 296 Bosnian Muslim villages and the execution of at least 3,000 Muslims around Srebrenica; in 2016, Karadžić is found guilty of genocide. Mujaheddin rebels oust president Najibullah in Afghanistan; the fundamentalist Muslim Taliban are strengthened. Sectarian violence in India sees Hindus destroy the Babri mosque in Ayodhya; 12 bombs are detonated in Mumbai in response in 1993.

1993
Czechoslovakia splits peacefully into the Czech Republic and Slovakia. Israel and the PLO sign the Oslo Accords; they agree to mutual recognition and set out the principles for Palestinian autonomy. Prince Sihanouk is elected head of state in Cambodia.

1994
In Rwanda, civil war leads to genocide: Hutu extremists massacre 800,000 Tutsis; 2 million Hutus flee to neighboring countries. Nelson Mandela becomes the country's first black president in South Africa's first democratic elections. Russian troops enter the Muslim-dominated region of Chechnya; after a disastrous war, Russia is forced to offer Chechnya almost complete autonomy (1996). The US invades Haiti to restore Jean-Bertrand Aristide to power. In Ireland, a ceasefire is declared by the IRA and Protestant paramilitaries; it is broken in 1995, when the IRA bombs Canary Wharf, London. The Channel Tunnel linking Britain and France opens.

1995
A Gulf War veteran plants a bomb in Oklahoma City that kills 168 people. Israeli prime minister Yitzhak Rabin is assassinated shortly after winning the Nobel Peace Prize with Yasser Arafat and Shimon Perez. UN peacekeepers pull out of Somalia, having failed to secure the end of the civil war. The US Department of Defense completes the first operational satellite-based GPS (Global Positioning System).

> *"Never, never, and never again shall it be that this beautiful land will again experience the oppression of one by another …"*
>
> NELSON MANDELA, 1994

1996
Taliban rebels capture Kabul and declare Afghanistan a fundamentalist Islamic state; Osama bin Laden returns to Afghanistan. Israeli shells kill over 100 civilians in Lebanon; Hezbollah is accused of using civilians as human shields. Created in Scotland, Dolly the sheep is the first mammal to be cloned from an adult cell.

1997
Tutsi rebels attack Hutu refugee camps in Zaire; Laurent Kabila ends dictator Mobutu Sese Seko's 32-year rule, and Zaire is renamed the Democratic Republic of Congo.

1998
The Good Friday agreement ends the Troubles in Northern Ireland and provides the region with devolved government. India and Pakistan begin tests of nuclear weapons. Serbs and ethnic Albanians clash in Kosovo. The financial crisis deepens: Indonesia's economy collapses, and President Suharto resigns; the price of oil drops, contributing to Russia's economic difficulties. In Africa, war breaks out between Eritrea and Ethiopia (to 2000), and the Democratic Republic of Congo descends into civil war again. US missiles hit al-Qaeda targets in Afghanistan and Sudan. US and Britain bomb Iraq after it ceases to cooperate with UN inspectors looking for weapons of mass destruction.

Hong Kong returns to China when Britain's 99-year lease expires. A major financial crisis in Asia leads to an economic slump in many developing countries and the wider world. Industrialized nations agree to cut carbon dioxide and other greenhouse gas emissions to combat global warming in the Kyoto Protocol. Kofi Annan is the first black African to be appointed secretary-general of the UN.

1999
Serbian ethnic cleansing of Kosovan Albanians is halted by NATO bombing; Serbian president Slobodan Milosovic is later charged with

31.4
miles (50.5 km). The length of the Channel Tunnel linking England and France.

▷ **Nelson Mandela victorious**
Mandela became the first nonwhite head of state in South Africa after his party, the African National Congress, won the election of 1994.

▷ **9/11**
Hijacked United Airlines Flight 175 from Boston crashes into the south tower of the World Trade Center and explodes at 9:03 a.m. on September 11, 2001, in New York City.

500mph

(800 kph). The speed of the devastating tsunami in the Indian Ocean in 2004.

war crimes, but dies in prison in 2006. East Timor votes to secede from Indonesia; anti-independence rebels supported by the Indonesian military attack civilians; independence is granted in 2002. General Pervez Musharraf seizes control in Pakistan. Russian forces reassert Russian control over Chechnya after Chechen rebels begin to attack Russian targets. President Yeltsin resigns, leaving former KGB agent Vladimir Putin as acting president. Portugal returns Macau to Chinese control more than 430 years after Portugal first leased the territory (1557).

2000

Vladimir Putin wins the presidential election in Russia. Israel pulls out of South Lebanon after 22 years of occupation. More than 3,000 Israelis and Palestinians are killed in the Second Intifada. Bashar al-Assad becomes president of Syria. The first crew arrives at the International Space Station (ISS).

2001

On September 11, 2,996 people are killed in four al-Qaeda terror attacks in the US. The US declares a "war on terrorism" and, with the UK, attacks targets in Afghanistan thought to be harboring Osama bin Laden; the war in Afghanistan ends in 2014. China has the fastest-growing economy in the world and is admitted to the World Trade Organization.

2002

US President George W. Bush describes the countries of Iraq, Iran, and North Korea as the "axis of evil." The Euro is introduced in 12 European countries. Civil war in Sierra Leone and Angola ends. In the US-led invasion of Afghanistan, the Taliban are swept from power. In Bali, 200 are killed when Islamist terrorists bomb a club. Over 100 die when Chechen militants besiege a Moscow theater. US troops return to the Gulf when Iraq denies that it has weapons of mass destruction.

2003

Civil war erupts in Darfur, west Sudan. The State Union of Serbia and Montenegro emerges as Yugoslavia ceases to exist. The Iraq War begins as a US-led coalition invades Iraq and topples Saddam Hussein's government; it struggles to stabilize the country and contain insurgency. Scientists publish the results of the Human Genome Project, identifying the DNA sequence of a full set of human chromosomes. The SARS virus, a new form of pneumonia, spreads globally.

2004

In Madrid, Islamic terrorists place bombs on commuter trains, killing 191. Ten countries join the EU, most of them former communist states in eastern Europe. An earthquake of magnitude 9.1–9.3 off Sumatra triggers the most destructive tsunami in history; more than 200,000 people in 11 countries across the Indian Ocean and Southeast Asia lose their lives; millions are made homeless. Chechen rebels take a school hostage in Beslan, southern Russia; more than 300 people are killed.

▷ **Obama campaign button**
Democrat Barack Obama was elected as the 44th President of the United States in 2008, winning 59.2 percent of the popular vote.

6.9 trillion dollars. The value wiped off global stock markets in the 2008 crash; it is the largest fall in history.

2005

Mahmoud Abbas becomes president of the Palestinian Authority after the death of Yasser Arafat. Syria withdraws from Lebanon, and Israel withdraws from Gaza. In London, 52 people die when Islamist suicide bombers target public transportation. In Ireland, the Provisional IRA announces that it will cease its armed campaign and pursue its goals through peaceful political means. In the US, the city of New Orleans is devastated by Hurricane Katrina; in Pakistan, an earthquake kills more than 70,000 people in Kashmir.

2006

In Palestine, Hamas—the Sunni-Islamist fundamentalist organization—wins the parliamentary elections. In the month-long Lebanon War, Hezbollah captures two Israeli soldiers; Israel responds with air and rocket strikes on south Lebanon; the UN brokers a ceasefire, and an international force occupies south Lebanon. North Korea begins its testing of nuclear weapons. Serbia and Montenegro split into separate nations. Basque separatist organization ETA announces a ceasefire, ending 40 years of terrorist activity.

2007

In occupied Iran, sectarian violence between Sunni and Shia militias escalates. Political enemies the DUP and Sinn Fein agree to share power in the Northern Ireland Assembly. Pratibha Patil becomes the first female President of India. Russia cuts oil supplies to Poland, Germany, and Ukraine during a dispute with Belarus.

2007–2011

A global recession follows the collapse of the Lehman Brothers investment bank; banks worldwide face insolvency and throttle lending. Bulgaria and Romania join the EU, which now has 27 member states.

2008

Barack Obama becomes the United States' first African-American president. Kosovo declares independence from Serbia. Nepal becomes a republic after abolishing the monarchy. Russia invades the Russian enclaves of South Ossetia and Abkhazia in Georgia. Australia's prime minister apologizes to the "Stolen Generations" of indigenous children removed from their families.

2009

Israel invades Gaza to halt rocket attacks by Hamas; it withdraws 3 weeks later. Russia ends military operations in Chechnya; jihadists remain active in the region. A global pandemic of swine flu kills 17,000.

2010

In Haiti, around 230,000 people die in a devastating earthquake. The International Monetary Fund (IMF) and EU bail out the Greek and Irish economies with huge loans, but insist on the introduction of severe austerity measures. Myanmar's military regime releases pro-democracy leader Aung San Suu Kyi. Argentina's economic crisis sees the country go through five presidents in 1 month. The nonprofit WikiLeaks organization publishes more than 90,000 classified reports about US involvement in the war in Afghanistan. An explosion at the Deepwater Horizon oil rig spills 200 million gallons of oil into the Gulf of Mexico.

▷ **The fall of President Mugabe**
People in Zimbabwe take to the streets in 2017, demanding that Robert Mugabe resign as President—a post he had held for 37 years.

2011
In the Arab Spring, pro-democracy rebellions erupt across North Africa and the Middle East: in Egypt, President Hosni Mubarak hands power to the army after mass protests; in Libya, Mu'ammar al-Gaddafi's regime is toppled, but civil war follows; in Syria, civil war begins with a violent crackdown on civilian dissenters. South Sudan becomes independent of Sudan, but ethnic tensions fuel civil war in 2013. Osama bin Laden is killed by US special forces in Pakistan. The war in Iraq ends, and US troops withdraw. Three fission reactors at Fukushima Nuclear Power Plant in Japan melt down after being damaged by a tsunami that kills 20,000.

2012
Mohammed Morsi of the Muslim Brotherhood wins Egypt's presidential elections. Schoolgirl, blogger, and human rights activist Malala Yousafzai is shot and wounded by the Taliban in Pakistan; she survives and becomes the youngest Nobel laureate in 2014. In Africa, civil war breaks out in the Central African Republic; there are coups in Mali and Guinea-Bissau. Austrian skydiver Felix Baumgartner, diving from a helium balloon 24 miles (39 km) above Earth, is the first person to break the sound barrier without any machine assistance.

2013
French forces intervene against Islamist insurgents fighting the government in northern Mali. Syria's government pledges to hand over its chemical weapons for destruction after denying responsibility for a chemical attack on Ghouta. Violence breaks out in Egypt after President Morsi is ousted in a military coup. A shopping mall in Nairobi, Kenya, is attacked by fundamentalist Islamist militants belonging to the al-Shabaab group.

2014
The Ebola virus kills 11,000 people in west Africa by 2016. In Ukraine, the pro-Russian president is ousted; Russia invades eastern Ukraine and annexes Crimea; the US imposes sanctions on Russia. Israel launches air strikes on Gaza; a ground offensive follows. In Nigeria, Islamic extremist group Boko Haram kidnaps 276 schoolgirls. Civil war resumes in Libya: the democratically elected government in Tobruk faces Islamist factions in Tripoli and Benghazi. The terrorist group Islamic State of Iraq and the Levant (ISIL, also known as ISIS or Daesh) occupies territory in northern Iraq and Syria; more than 3 million refugees flee to neighboring countries.

2015
Egypt begins air strikes targeting ISIL in Libya. A Saudi-led Arab coalition begins military intervention in Yemen, attacking Iranian-backed Houthi rebels in the south. Al-Shabaab shoots 148 people, mainly students, at Garissa University in Kenya. Iran agrees to limit its nuclear program if sanctions are eased. Russia begins air strikes against ISIL and anti-government forces in Syria. ISIL destroys ancient sites in Syria and is responsible for multiple attacks across the world. The Paris Accord commits nearly 200 countries to reducing carbon emissions. The Zika fever epidemic begins in Brazil and rapidly spreads throughout the Americas, causing worldwide alarm. Surgeons in New York perform the first full facial transplant.

> "A girl has the power to go forward in her life. And she's not only a mother, she's not only a sister, she's not only a wife."
>
> MALALA YOUSAFZAI, 2014

2016
The United Kingdom votes to leave the European Union. Barack Obama is the first US president to visit Cuba since 1928. In November, Donald Trump becomes US President; within months, he is embroiled in an investigation into alleged collusion with Russia. Islamist terror continues, with multiple attacks in France, Germany, and Belgium. Fifty-two years of conflict in Colombia ends when the government and the Revolutionary Armed Forces of Colombia–People's Army (FARC) agree a peace deal.

2017
President Trump's decision to pull out of the Paris Accord to combat climate change makes the US the only country in the world not to be part of the agreement. A military coup forces Robert Mugabe to resign after 37 years as President of Zimbabwe. Islamist terror attacks continue in Europe in Manchester, London, Barcelona, Turkey, France, Germany, Russia, and Belgium.

North Korea fires a ballistic missile across Japan and continues its nuclear testing; international condemnation is followed by increased sanctions. More than 20 million people face starvation and famine in Yemen, Somalia, South Sudan, and Nigeria. Reports emerge that the Syrian government has dropped toxic gas on a rebel-held town; the US launches a missile strike on the Syrian air base at Sharyat. The autonomous region of Catalonia declares independence, but Spain refuses to recognize it; Catalan leaders are arrested. Thousands of Rohingya Muslims flee Myanmar after experiencing systematic violence, amounting to ethnic cleansing.

2018
In China, the government brings in a change to the constitution that lifts term limits for its leaders; the sitting president Xi Jinping effectively becomes "President for Life." In Russia, Vladimir Putin is elected as president for a fourth term. North Korean leader Kim Jong-un crosses into South Korea to meet with President Moon Jae-in; he is the first North Korean leader to cross the Demilitarized Zone since its creation in 1953. The United States, together with the UK and France, bombs Syrian military bases in response to a chemical attack launched by Bashar al-Assad on civilians in Ghouta. Social media company Facebook is rocked by scandal relating to its sharing of personal data.

◁ **Tragedy in Japan**
A magnitude-9 earthquake shakes northeastern Japan, unleashing a savage tsunami that destroys 250,000 buildings. It is thought to be the costliest natural disaster in history.

INDEX

Page numbers in **bold** refer to main entries.

ACKNOWLEDGMENTS

Dorling Kindersley would like to thank the following people for their help in the preparation of this book: Ann Baggaley, Carron Brown, Thomas Booth, Chris Hawkes, Cecile Landau, and Justine Willis for editorial assistance; Chrissy Barnard, Amy Child, Phil Gamble, and Renata Latipova for design assistance; Steve Crozier for image retouching; Katie John for proofreading; and Helen Peters for indexing.

DK India would like to thank Arpita Dasgupta, Tina Jindal, Rupa Rao, and Isha Sharma for editorial assistance; Simar Dhamija and Meenal Goel for design assistance; Ashutosh Ranjan Bharti, Deshpal Dabas, Mohammad Hassan, Zafar Ul Islam Khan, and Lokamata Sahu for cartographic assistance; Shanker Prasad and Mohd Rizwan for DTP assistance.

The publisher would like to thank the following for their kind permission to reproduce their photographs: (Key: a-above; b-below/bottom; c-center; f-far; l-left; r-right; t-top)

2 Alamy Stock Photo: Science History Images. **4 Getty Images:** De Agostini Picture Library (tr). **Robert Gunn:** Courtesy of Jawoyn Association (tl). **5 Alamy Stock Photo:** The Granger Collection (tr). **Getty Images:** Photo Josse / Leemage (tl). **6 Alamy Stock Photo:** Paul Fearn (tr). The **Metropolitan Museum of Art:** Gift of John Stewart Kennedy, 1897 (tl). **7 Getty Images:** Galerie Bilderwelt (tl). **8–9 Bridgeman Images:** Pictures from History. **10-11 Robert Gunn:** Courtesy of Jawoyn Association. **12 Alamy Stock Photo:** The Natural History Museum (tl). **Getty Images:** DEA / G. Dagli Orti / De Agostini (c). **13 Bridgeman Images:** Caves of Lascaux, Dordogne, France (c). **Science Photo Library:** ER Degginger (tl). **14 Alamy Stock Photo:** Puwadol Jaturawutthichai (crb). **Dorling Kindersley:** Oxford Museum of Natural History (ca). **15 akg-images:** CDA / Guillemot (cr). **Science Photo Library:** John Reader (tr). **17 Alamy Stock Photo:** Chronicle (br); Paul Fearn (c). **18 Getty Images:** Kerry Lorimer (cl). **18–19 Robert Gunn:**

Courtesy of Jawoyn Association. **21 Alamy Stock Photo:** Phil Degginger (cl). **22 © CNRS Photothèque:** © C. Jarrige (cb). **Dorling Kindersley:** The Museum of London (cla). **23 akg-images:** Bible Land Pictures / Jerusalem Photo by: Z.Radovan (t). **Alamy Stock Photo:** blickwinkel (cr). **24 Getty Images:** DEA / G. Dagli Orti / De Agostini (c). **26 Getty Images:** DEA / A. De Gregorio / De Agostini (bl). **27 Alamy Stock Photo:** www.BibleLandPictures.com (bl). **28–29 Getty Images:** De Agostini Picture Library. **30 Dorling Kindersley:** University of Pennsylvania Museum of Archaeology and Anthropology (cla). **Getty Images:** Kitti Boonnitrod (cra). **31 Alamy Stock Photo:** World History Archive (tc). **Getty Images:** Leemage (crb). **32 Bridgeman Images:** Iraq Museum, Baghdad (br). **33 Dreamstime.com:** Kmiragaya (br). **35 Getty Images:** Art Media / Print Collector (bl). **36 Alamy Stock Photo:** Heritage Image Partnership Ltd (br). **Dorling Kindersley:** The University of Aberdeen (bl). **37 Alamy Stock Photo:** Kylie Ellway (br). **39 Getty Images:** DEA / G. Nimatallah / De Agostini (tc, br). **40 Alamy Stock Photo:** World History Archive (c). **42 Getty Images:** DEA / G. Dagli Orti / De Agostini (cl). **42–43 Getty Images:** De Agostini Picture Library. **44 Getty Images:** Nathan Benn (bl). **45 Getty Images:** Dea / A. Dagli Orti / DeAgostini (cla). **46 Alamy Stock Photo:** imageBROKER (cl). **Bridgeman Images:** Musee des Antiquites Nationales, St. Germain-en-Laye, France (cr). **47 Alamy Stock Photo:** robertharding (crb); The Print Collector (tl). **48 Getty Images:** Dea / G. Dagli Orti / DeAgostini (bl). **49 Alamy Stock Photo:** MuseoPics - Paul Williams (bl). **50 akg-images:** Erich Lessing (bc). **51 Bridgeman Images:** (br). **52 Getty Images:** Ernesto Benavides / AFP (tr). **53 Getty Images:** Werner Forman / Universal Images Group (br). **54–55 Alamy Stock Photo:** Lanmas. **54 Alamy Stock Photo:** Peter Horree (bc); North Wind Picture Archives (cla). **57 Bridgeman Images:** Pictures from History (c). **58 Getty Images:** CM Dixon / Print Collector (cl). **59 Bridgeman Images:** Werner Forman Archive (br). **60 Getty Images:** Leemage (bl). **62 Alamy Stock Photo:** Konstantinos Tsakalidis (cla). **Dorling Kindersley:** The University of Aberdeen (c). **63 Getty Images:** Michael Dunning (tl). **Photo Scala, Florence:** courtesy of the Ministero Beni e Att. Culturali e del Turismo (cr). **64 Alamy**

Stock Photo: ART Collection (bc). **65 Getty Images:** DEA / G. Nimatallah / De Agostini (cr). **66 Getty Images:** DEA / G. Dagli Orti / De Agostini (crb). **68 Getty Images:** Dea / A. Dagli Orti / De Agostini (bc). **69 Getty Images:** Chris Hellier / Corbis (br). **70 Alamy Stock Photo:** Angelo Hornak (cl). **70–71 Alamy Stock Photo:** MCLA Collection. **73 Alamy Stock Photo:** Dinodia Photos (bl); Robert Preston Photography (tr). **74 Getty Images:** UniversalImagesGroup (bl). **76 Alamy Stock Photo:** David Davis Photoproductions (cl); Yong nian Gui (bl). **76–77 Alamy Stock Photo:** Oleksiy Maksymenko Photography. **78 Alamy Stock Photo:** Granger Historical Picture Archive (cl). **81 Getty Images:** DEA Picture Library (ca, br). **82 Bridgeman Images:** Pictures from History (crb). **84 Bridgeman Images:** Pictures from History / David Henley (bl). **86 akg-images:** André Held (bc). **87 123RF.com:** Lefteris Papaulakis (bc).**88–89 Getty Images:** Photo Josse / Leemage. **90 Alamy Stock Photo:** Ian Dagnall (c). **Dreamstime.com:** Sean Pavone / Sepavo (cla). **91 Alamy Stock Photo:** ART Collection (tl). **Bridgeman Images:** Ancient Art and Architecture Collection Ltd. (cr). **93 Getty Images:** Werner Forman / Universal Images Group (bl); Universal History Archive (br). **94 123RF.com:** Mikhail Markovskiy (br). **Bridgeman Images:** Private Collection / Archives Charmet (bl). **96 akg-images:** Pictures From History (bc). **97 The Metropolitan Museum of Art:** Theodore M. Davis Collection, Bequest of Theodore M. Davis, 1915 (tr). **98 Getty Images:** Kristin Piljay (bc). **Michael Czytko, www.finemodelships.com:** (crb). **100 Alamy Stock Photo:** Pere Sanz (cl). **100–101 Getty Images:** DEA Picture Library. **103 Alamy Stock Photo:** Granger Historical Picture Archive (br). **Getty Images:** Photo Josse / Leemage (tl). **105 Alamy Stock Photo:** Kumar Sriskandan (br). **Getty Images:** Leemage (tl). **107 Getty Images:** Photo Josse / Leemage (br). **108 Bridgeman Images:** Basilica di San Giovanni Battista, Monza, Italy / Alinari (cla). **Getty Images:** CM Dixon / Print Collector (cb). **109 Alamy Stock Photo:** Granger Historical Picture Archive (r); Chris Pancewicz (tl). **111 Alamy Stock Photo:** The Picture Art Collection (br). **113 Getty Images:** Ann Ronan Pictures / Print Collector (br). **RMN:** RMN-Grand Palais (Cluny Museum - National Museum of the Middle Ages) / Jean-Gilles Berizzi (c). **115 Alamy Stock Photo:** Pictorial Press Ltd (tl). **116–117 Bridgeman Images:** Musee Conde, Chantilly, France. **117 Bridgeman Images:** Pictures from History (bc). **Getty Images:** Imagno (cr). **119 Alamy Stock Photo:** Everett Collection Inc (tl). **120 akg-images:** (c). **122 Alamy Stock Photo:** MCLA Collection (bc). **123 Alamy Stock Photo:** Jon Bower Spain (crb). **124 Bridgeman Images:** De Agostini Picture Library / G. Dagli Orti (cl, cra). **125 Alamy Stock Photo:** Ariadne Van Zandbergen (tl); ephotocorp (crb). **127 Alamy Stock Photo:** Images & Stories (br). **128 akg-images:** Pansegrau (tl). **129 Getty Images:** DEA Picture Library (br). **130 Getty Images:** Heritage Images (bl). **132 Alamy Stock Photo:** Pictorial Press Ltd (br). **134 Getty Images:** photographer (br); photo by Pam Susemiehl (bl). **136 Getty Images:** Werner Forman / Universal Images Group (bc). **138–139 Getty Images:** Print Collector. **139 Bridgeman Images:** Bibliotheque Nationale, Paris, France (br). **Getty Images:** Werner Forman / Universal Images Group (cra). **141 Alamy Stock Photo:** Regula Heeb-Zweifel (br). **Museum of New Zealand Te Papa Tongarewa:** (c). **142 Alamy Stock Photo:** Science History Images (tr). **Getty Images:** Mladen Antonov (bc). **145 Alamy Stock Photo:** Peter Horree (bl).**146–147 Alamy Stock Photo:** The Granger Collection. **148 Alamy Stock Photo:** Peter Horree (tl). **149 Dorling Kindersley:** Maidstone Museum and Bentliff Art Gallery (tl); Whipple Museum of History of Science, Cambridge (cr). **151 Alamy Stock Photo:** The Granger Collection (br). **153 Alamy Stock Photo:** INTERFOTO (tr). **154 Getty Images:** Fine Art Images / Heritage Images (cl). **154–155 Photo Scala, Florence:** Photo Schalkwijk / Art Resource / © Banco de México Diego Rivera Frida Kahlo Museums Trust, Mexico, D.F. / © DACS 2018. **157 Getty Images:** adoc-photos (br). **158 Bridgeman Images:** Granger (bc). **159 Alamy Stock Photo:** The Granger Collection (bl). **160 Alamy Stock Photo:** World Photo Collection (c). **Bridgeman Images:** British Library, London, UK / © British Library Board. All Rights Reserved (cla). **161 Bridgeman Images:** (cr). **Wellcome Images http://creativecommons.org/licenses/by/4.0/:** (tl). **162 Bridgeman Images:** Pictures from History (bc). **163 Getty Images:** PHAS / UIG (crb). **164–165 Alamy Stock Photo:** Science History Images. **164 Alamy Stock Photo:** Falkensteinfoto (bl). **Bridgeman Images:** British Library, London, UK (cl). **166 Getty Images:** DEA / G. Dagli Orti / De Agostini (bc). **167 Alamy Stock Photo:** FineArt (br). **168–169 Bridgeman Images:** Deutsches Historisches Museum, Berlin, Germany / © DHM. **169 Getty Images:** DEA Picture Library (br). **170 Getty Images:** DEA / G. Nimatallah / De Agostini (cla). **171 Getty Images:** The Print Collector (br). **172 Getty Images:** De Agostini Picture Library (bl). **173 Bridgeman Images:** Private Collection / Archives Charmet (br). **174 Alamy Stock Photo:** Peter Horree (tl). **Bridgeman Images:** Private Collection (c). **175 Alamy Stock Photo:** Heritage Image Partnership Ltd (cr). **Getty Images:** DEA / G. Dagli Orti / Deagostini (tr). **177 akg-images:** (bl). **Alamy Stock Photo:** Dinodia Photos (tr). **178 Bridgeman Images:** (tl). **Getty Images:** DEA / A. C. Cooper (br). **180 Getty Images:** De Agostini Picture Library (tl). **181 Bridgeman Images:** Pictures from History (bl). **182–183 Getty Images:** Fine Art Images / Heritage Images. **183 Alamy Stock Photo:** Pictorial Press Ltd (ca). **Library of Congress, Washington, D.C.:** map55000728 (br). **184 Rijksmuseum, Amsterdam:** Purchased with the support of the Rembrandt Association (bc). **185 Alamy Stock Photo:** Peter Horree (bl).**186–187 The Metropolitan Museum of Art:** Gift of John Stewart Kennedy, 1897. **188 Alamy Stock Photo:** Science History Images (cl). **Boston Tea Pary Ships & Museum, Historic Tours of America, Inc:** (cra). **189 Alamy Stock Photo:** Art Collection 2 (cr); Science History Images (tl). **190 Getty Images:** Edward Gooch (tr). **193 akg-images:** (br). **194 Dorling Kindersley:** Museum of English Rural Life, The University of Reading (clb). **Rijksmuseum, Amsterdam:** (tl). **195 Alamy Stock Photo:** The Protected Art Archive (cr). **Getty Images:** Photo12 / UIG (tl). **196 Getty Images:** Universal History Archive (bl). **197 Alamy Stock Photo:** North Wind Picture Archives (br). **198 Yale University Art Gallery:** (bc). **199 The Metropolitan Museum of Art:** Gift of John Stewart Kennedy, 1897 (br). **201 Getty Images:** De Agostini Picture Library (tc); UniversalImagesGroup (tr). **202 Bridgeman Images:** Museum of Art, Serpukhov, Russia (cl). **202–203 Bridgeman Images:** Musee National du Chateau de Malmaison, Rueil-Malmaison, France. **204 Library of Congress, Washington, D.C.:** LC-DIG-ppmsca-09855 (bc). **205 Getty Images:** Photo Josse / Leemage (tr). **206 Bridgeman Images:** Private Collection (bc). **207 Bridgeman Images:** Galerie Dijol, Paris, France (tr). **209 Getty Images:** John Parrot / Stocktrek Images (br); Peter Willi (clb). **211 Getty Images:** Ann Ronan Pictures / Print Collector (crb); Fine Art Images / Heritage Images (br). **212 Alamy Stock Photo:** North Wind Picture Archives (tl). **Getty Images:** Science & Society Picture Library (clb). **213 Getty Images:** Science & Society Picture Library (tl); ullstein bild Dtl. (cr). **214 Getty Images:** Science & Society Picture Library (tl). **215 Alamy Stock Photo:** Heritage Image Partnership Ltd (tr). **Dorling Kindersley:** National Railway Museum, York / Science Museum Group (crb). **216 Alamy Stock Photo:** AF archive (bl); Granger Historical Picture Archive (cl). **216–217 Getty Images:** Photo Josse / Leemage. **218 Bridgeman Images:** Bibliotheque Nationale, Paris, France / Archives Charmet (tr). **Getty Images:** Fine Art Images / Heritage Images (bc). **220 Getty Images:** Universal History Archive (clb). **222–223 Provenance , Galerie Nader Pétion Ville Haiti:** Collection Of Mr. Jean Walnard Dorneval , Arcahaie Haiti. **222 Rex by Shutterstock:** The Art Archive (cl). **224 Alamy Stock Photo:** Peter Horree (bc). **225 akg-images:** Pictures From History (br). **226 Alamy Stock Photo:** Science History Images (tc). **227 Getty Images:** PHAS / UIG (tr). **228–229 Alamy Stock Photo:** Paul Fearn. **230 Alamy Stock Photo:** Everett Collection Historical (c). **Rex by Shutterstock:** Roger-Viollet (cla). **231 Alamy Stock Photo:** Pictorial Press Ltd (cr). **Getty Images:** W. Brown / Otto Herschan (tl). **233 akg-images:** (c). **234 Alamy Stock Photo:** Granger Historical Picture Archive (bl). **Getty Images:** Schöning / ullstein bild (cl). **234–235 Bridgeman Images:** Musee de la Ville de Paris, Musee Carnavalet, Paris, France. **236 Getty Images:** Stefano Bianchetti (clb). **237 Getty Images:** Stock Montage / Hulton Archive (br). **238 Getty Images:** DEA Picture Library / DeAgostini (cb). **240 Alamy Stock Photo:** Pictorial Press Ltd (cb); The Granger Collection (cla). **241 Alamy Stock Photo:** INTERFOTO (c). **Getty Images:** Sean Sexton (tr). **242 Bridgeman Images:** © Look and Learn (bc). **243 Getty Images:** Hulton Archive (br). **244 Dorling Kindersley:** © The Board of Trustees of the Armouries (cl). **244–245 Getty Images:** Popperfoto. **246 Getty Images:** UniversalImagesGroup (tl). **247 Getty Images:** Sovfoto / UIG (br). **248 akg-images:** Pictures From History (tl). **250 Alamy Stock Photo:** Photo 12 (bl). **Rex by Shutterstock:** Universal History Archive (c). **250–251 Rex by Shutterstock:** Granger. **252 Alamy Stock Photo:** Everett Collection Historical (bc); Paul Fearn (tr). **255 Alamy Stock Photo:** Artokoloro Quint Lox Limited (br). **256 Getty Images:** Buyenlarge (bl). **258–259 Getty Images:** Bettmann. **259 Alamy Stock Photo:** The Granger Collection (c). **Getty Images:** Bettmann (br). **260 Getty Images:** Bettmann (cr). **262 Alamy Stock Photo:** Paul Fearn (tl). **Getty Images:** Leemage (tr). **264 akg-images:** (tl). **267 Alamy Stock Photo:** Chronicle (br); Paul Fearn (bc). **269 Getty Images:** Culture Club (br); ullstein bild Dtl. (bl). **270–271 Getty Images:** Galerie Bilderwelt. **272 Alamy Stock Photo:** Paul Fearn (cla); Pictorial Press Ltd (cl). **273 Alamy Stock Photo:** Science History Images (tl). **Getty Images:** Sovfoto / UIG (cb); Universal History Archive (cr). **274 Alamy Stock Photo:** Universal Art Archive (br). **276 Dorling Kindersley:** Imperial War Museum, London (cla). **Getty Images:** Buyenlarge (bl). **276–277 Getty Images:** UniversalImagesGroup. **278 Alamy Stock Photo:** Granger Historical Picture Archive (bc). **279 Getty Images:** Time Life Pictures (crb). **281 Alamy Stock Photo:** Paul Fearn (br). **282 Getty Images:** Keystone (cl); Universal History Archive (bl). **282–283 Mary Evans Picture Library. 285 Alamy Stock Photo:** Photo 12 (br). **Getty Images:** Keystone-France (cla). **287 Alamy Stock Photo:** Science History Images (bl). **288 Alamy Stock Photo:** Granger Historical Picture Archive (bl). **290 Bridgeman Images:** Pictures from History / Woodbury & Page (bl). **291 Getty Images:** Print Collector (br). **292 Alamy Stock Photo:** Pictorial Press Ltd (bc). **Getty Images:** Keystone-France (br). **294 Bridgeman Images:** Pictures from History (cr). **Getty Images:** Bettmann (cl). **295 Alamy Stock Photo:** dpa picture alliance (crb). **Getty Images:** Bettmann (tl). **297 Alamy Stock Photo:** 502 collection (cl). **Getty Images:** Hulton Archive (br). **299 akg-images:** (br). **Getty Images:** Galerie Bilderwelt (cla). **300 Getty Images:** Universal History Archive / UIG (bl). **301 Getty Images:** Bettmann (br). **302 Alamy Stock Photo:** Prisma by Dukas Presseagentur GmbH (br). **Getty Images:** Central Press (bl). **305 Getty Images:** Apic / Retired (bl). **306–307 Hiroshima Peace Memorial Museum:** Shigeo Hayashi. **306 Getty Images:** Universal History Archive / UIG (br). **307 Getty Images:** Prisma by Dukas (br). **308 Getty Images:** Central Press (bl). **310 Alamy Stock Photo:** age fotostock (br). **Getty Images:** Print Collector (tl). **312 Alamy Stock Photo:** Science History Images (cla). **Bridgeman Images:** Peter Newark Military Pictures (c). **313 akg-images:** (tl). **Dorling Kindersley:** Stewart Howman / Dream Cars (crb). **314 Getty Images:** jondpatton (br). **317 Alamy Stock Photo:** robertharding (tr). **Getty Images:** RV Spencer / Interim Archives (bl). **319 Alamy Stock Photo:** World History Archive (br); Penny Tweedie (cl). **321 Alamy Stock Photo:** Shawshots (tl). **Getty Images:** Jon Feingersh (br). **323 Getty Images:** Louise Gubb (bl). **324 Getty Images:** Science & Society Picture Library (bc). **325 Getty Images:** Science & Society Picture Library (br). **326–327 Getty Images:** Bettmann. **327 Getty Images:** Fototeca Storica Nazionale (cr). **328 Alamy Stock Photo:** World History Archive (tl). **329 Getty Images:** Dirck Halstead (br). **331 Getty Images:** Bettmann (tr, bl). **332 Getty Images:** Muammar Awad / Anadolu Agency (tl). **334 123RF.com:** danielvfung (cl). **Alamy Stock Photo:** ClassicStock (cla). **335 Alamy Stock Photo:** eye35.pix (tc); PJF Military Collection (crb). **336 Getty Images:** Gerard Malie (clb). **337 Getty Images:** Wally McNamee (br). **339 Getty Images:** David Turnley / Corbis / VCG (cl). **340–341 Getty Images:** James Sebright. **340 Getty Images:** Ulrich Baumgarten (bl). **Rex by Shutterstock:** Dennis M. Sabangan / EPA (ca). **343 U.S. Air Force:** (cl). **344 Getty Images:** Science & Society Picture Library (cl); Stefan Wermuth / AFP (bl). **344–345 Getty Images:** Jerry Cooke. **346 Getty Images:** Allan Baxter (cb). **348–349 Alamy Stock Photo:** Science History Images. **350 Dorling Kindersley:** Gary Ombler / Oxford Museum of Natural History (bl). **Getty Images:** Science & Society Picture Library (tr). **350–351 Alamy Stock Photo:** Andia (br). **352 Alamy Stock Photo:** blickwinkel (t). **353 Alamy Stock Photo:** Constantinos Iliopoulos (tl); Florian Neukirchen (br). **354–355 Getty Images:** Frans Sellies (b). **355 Getty Images:** DEA / G. Dagli Orti / De Agostini (tl). **356 Getty Images:** Leemage / UIG (bl). **357 Alamy Stock Photo:** RF Company (tr). **Getty Images:** DEA / Ara Guler / De Agostini (bc). **358 Getty Images:** Apic / Retired / Hulton Archive (tr). **359 Alamy Stock Photo:** Konstantin Kalishko (bl). **Getty Images:** Werner Forman / Universal Images Group (tr). **360 Alamy Stock Photo:** Lanmas (bl). **361 Alamy Stock Photo:** eFesenko (bl). **Bridgeman Images:** Christie's Images (tr). **362 Alamy Stock Photo:** Ariadne Van Zandbergen (tc). **363 123RF.com:** wrangel (tc). **Getty Images:** David Lees / Corbis/VCG (bl). **364 Alamy Stock Photo:** Nataliya Hora (bl). **Bridgeman Images:** Bibliotheque Nationale, Paris, France (tr). **365 Bridgeman Images:** Vatican Museums and Galleries, Vatican City (r). **366 Dorling Kindersley:** Dave Rudkin / Birmingham Museum and Art Galleries (bl). **Getty Images:** DEA / A. Dagli Orti / De Agostini (tr). **367 Getty Images:** DEA / G. Dagli Orti / De Agostini (bc). **368-369 Bridgeman Images:** Vatican Museums, Vatican City / Pictures from History (bl). **369 Getty Images:** Leemage / Corbis (tc). **370 Alamy Stock Photo:** MuseoPics - Paul Williams (bl). **371 Bridgeman Images:** Asian Art Museum, San Francisco / Pictures from History (tl); Brabant School, (15th century) / Bibliotheque de L'Arsenal, Paris, France / Archives Charmet (br). **372 Bridgeman Images:** Pictures from History (bl). **Getty Images:** Bettmann (tr). **373 Getty Images:** DEA / A. Dagli Orti / De Agostini (bl). **374 Alamy Stock Photo:** Heritage Image Partnership Ltd (bl). **374-375 Sam Nixon:** (t). **375 Bridgeman Images:** German School, (13th century) / Aachen Cathedral Treasury, Aachen, Germany / De Agostini Picture Library / A. Dagli Orti (bc). **376 Bridgeman Images:** Pictures from History (tl). **Getty Images:** Frédéric Soltan / Corbis (br). **377 Getty Images:** Print Collector (tr). **378 Bridgeman Images:** Pictures from History / David Henley (tl). **378-379 Alamy Stock Photo:** Peter Sumner (b). **379 Getty Images:** Heritage Images / Museum of East Asian Art (tr). **380 akg-images:** Hervé Champollion (tl). **381 Bridgeman Images:** German School, (12th century) / Germanisches Nationalmuseum, Nuremberg, Germany (tl). **Getty Images:** Photo Josse / Leemage / Corbis (bl). **382 Getty Images:** Heritage Images / Fine Art Images (tl, br). **383 akg-images:** Pictures From History (br). **384 akg-images:** (l). **385 Bridgeman Images:** De Agostini Picture Library / A. De Gregorio (tl). **Getty Images:** Kean Collection / Staff (br). **386 Bridgeman Images:** Museo del Oro, Lima, Peru (bl). **387 akg-images:** Roland and Sabrina Michaud (br). **Bridgeman Images:** The Stapleton Collection (tl). **388 Getty Images:** DEA / W. Buss / De Agostini (br); Leemage / Corbis (tl). **389 Alamy Stock Photo:** Paul Fearn (tr). **390 Bridgeman Images:** Pictures from History (tr). **390-391 Getty Images:** Heritage Images / Fine Art Images (bl). **391 Getty Images:** DEA Picture Library / De Agostini (tr). **392 Dorling Kindersley:** Richard Leeney / Maidstone Museum and Bentliff Art Gallery (tl). **Getty Images:** UniversalImagesGroup / Universal History Archive (br). **393 Alamy Stock Photo:** MCLA Collection (tc). **394 Bridgeman Images:** State Hermitage Museum, St. Petersburg, Russia (tr). **Getty Images:** Science & Society Picture Library (bl). **395 Getty Images:** Fine Art / VCG Wilson / Corbis (r). **396 Bridgeman Images:** Christie's Images (bc). **397 Getty Images:** Heritage Images / Fine Art Images (br); Photo Josse / Leemage / Corbis (tl). **398 Bridgeman Images:** Coram in the care of the Foundling Museum, London (tl). **Getty Images:** Apic / Retired / Hulton Archive (br). **398-399 Alamy Stock Photo:** GL Archive (br). **400 Alamy Stock Photo:** Diego Grandi (tl). **Getty Images:** Werner Forman / UIG (b). **401 Bridgeman Images:** Pictures from History (tc). **402 Alamy Stock Photo:** The Print Collector (tr). **Getty Images:** DEA Picture Library / De Agostini (bl). **403 Alamy Stock Photo:** Falkensteinfoto (b). **404 Alamy Stock Photo:** Granger Historical Picture Archive (bl). **405 Alamy Stock Photo:** World History Archive (br). **Getty Images:** Historical Picture Archive / Corbis (tl). **406 Getty Images:** Print Collector (bl). **407 Getty Images:** Bettmann (tl); Historical / Corbis (br). **408 Getty Images:** Fine Art / VCG Wilson/Corbis (bl). **409 Dorling Kindersley:** Gary Ombler / R. Florio (br). **Getty Images:** Hulton Archive / Stringer (tl). **410 Getty Images:** Universal History Archive / UIG (b). **411 Alamy Stock Photo:** IanDagnall Computing (tl). **Getty Images:** UniversalImagesGroup (br). **412 Getty Images:** Keystone-France / Gamma-Keystone (b); Print Collector / Ann Ronan Pictures (tl). **413 Getty Images:** Universal History Archive / UIG (tr). **414-415 Bridgeman Images:** Museo Nacional Centro de Arte Reina Sofia, Madrid, Spain / © Succession Picasso / © DACS 2018 (bl). **415 Getty Images:** Galerie Bilderwelt (tr). **416 Getty Images:** Bettmann (tr); SuperStock (bl). **417 Alamy Stock Photo:** Granger Historical Picture Archive (b). **418 Getty Images:** Bettmann (bc); Museum of Flight Foundation / Corbis (tl). **419 Alamy Stock Photo:** Science History Images (tr). **420 Getty Images:** Bettmann (tl); Peter Turnley / Corbis/VCG (bl). **421 Getty Images:** Roger Hutchings / Corbis (tl). **422 123RF.com:** paolo77 (tl). **Getty Images:** Per-Anders Pettersson (br). **423 Getty Images:** Spencer Platt / Staff (tr). **424 Alamy Stock Photo:** Granger Historical Picture Archive (tr). **Getty Images:** Mike Clarke / Staff (b). **425 Alamy Stock Photo:** Newscom (tr)

All other images © Dorling Kindersley

For further information see: www.dkimages.com

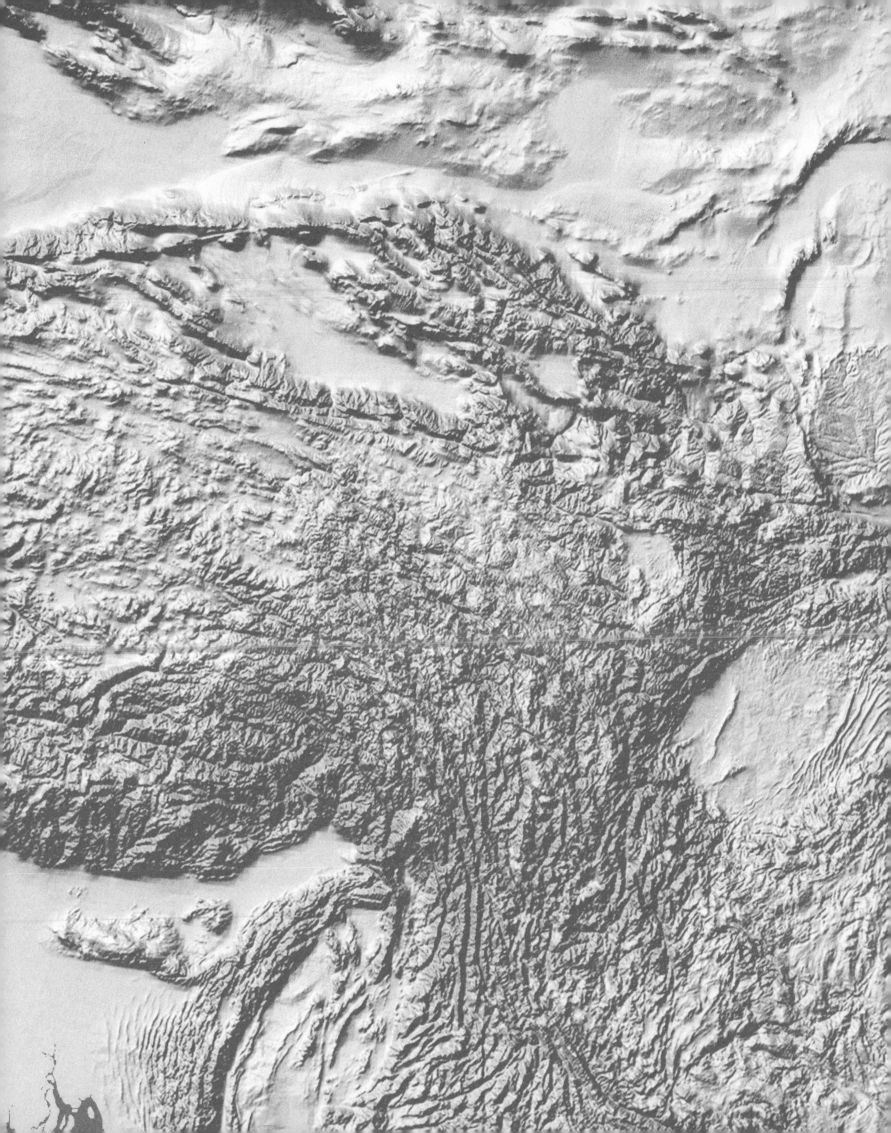